THE TAFT COURT

The Taft Court offers the definitive history of the Supreme Court from 1921 to 1930 when William Howard Taft was chief justice. Using untapped archival material, Robert C. Post engagingly recounts the ambivalent effort to create a modern American administrative state out of the institutional innovations of World War I. He shows how the Court sought to establish authoritative forms of constitutional interpretation despite the culture wars that enveloped prohibition and pervasive labor unrest. He explores in great detail how constitutional law responds to altered circumstances. The work provides comprehensive portraits of seminal figures such as Oliver Wendell Holmes Jr. and Louis Dembitz Brandeis. It describes William Howard Taft's many judicial reforms and his profound alteration of the role of chief justice. A critical and timely contribution, *The Taft Court* sheds light on jurisprudential debates that are just as relevant today as they were a century ago.

Robert C. Post is the Sterling Professor of Law at Yale Law School. He served as the sixteenth Dean of Yale Law School from 2009 to 2017. He specializes in constitutional law, with particular emphasis on the First Amendment. His book *For the Common Good: Principles of American Academic Freedom* (with Matthew W. Finkin) has become the standard reference text for the meaning of academic freedom in the United States.

THE OLIVER WENDELL HOLMES DEVISE HISTORY OF THE SUPREME COURT OF THE UNITED STATES

General Editor: MAEVA MARCUS

VOLUME I, *Antecedents and Beginnings to 1801*, by Julius Goebel, Jr.

VOLUME II, *Foundations of Power: John Marshall, 1801–1815*, by George L. Haskins and Herbert A. Johnson

VOLUMES III–IV, *The Marshall Court and Cultural Change, 1815–1835*, by G. Edward White

VOLUME V, *The Taney Period, 1836–1864*, by Carl B. Swisher

VOLUME VI, *Reconstruction and Reunion, 1864–1888, Part One A*, by Charles Fairman

VOLUME VI, *Reconstruction and Reunion, 1864–1888, Part One B*, by Charles Fairman

VOLUME VII, *Reconstruction and Reunion, 1864–1888, Part Two*, by Charles Fairman

SUPPLEMENT TO VOLUME VII, *Five Justices and the Electoral Commission of 1877*, by Charles Fairman

VOLUME VIII, *Troubled Beginnings of the Modern State, 1888–1910*, by Owen M. Fiss

VOLUME IX, *The Judiciary and Responsible Government, 1910–1921*, by Alexander M. Bickel and Benno C. Schmidt, Jr.

VOLUME X, *The Taft Court: Making Law for a Divided Nation, 1921–1930*, by Robert C. Post

VOLUME XI, *The Hughes Court: From Progressivism to Pluralism, 1930–1941*, by Mark V. Tushnet

VOLUME XII, *The Birth of the Modern Constitution: The United States Supreme Court, 1941–1953*, by William W. Wiecek

THE
Oliver Wendell Holmes
DEVISE

HISTORY OF
THE SUPREME COURT
OF THE UNITED STATES

VOLUME X.1

THE OLIVER WENDELL HOLMES DEVISE

History of the SUPREME COURT of the United States

VOLUME X.I

The Taft Court

Making Law for a Divided Nation,
1921–1930

Robert C. Post
Yale Law School

CAMBRIDGE
UNIVERSITY PRESS

Shaftesbury Road, Cambridge CB2 8EA, United Kingdom

One Liberty Plaza, 20th Floor, New York, NY 10006, USA

477 Williamstown Road, Port Melbourne, VIC 3207, Australia

314–321, 3rd Floor, Plot 3, Splendor Forum, Jasola District Centre,
New Delhi – 110025, India

103 Penang Road, #05–06/07, Visioncrest Commercial, Singapore 238467

Cambridge University Press is part of Cambridge University Press & Assessment,
a department of the University of Cambridge.

We share the University's mission to contribute to society through the pursuit of
education, learning and research at the highest international levels of excellence.

www.cambridge.org
Information on this title: www.cambridge.org/9781009336215
DOI: 10.1017/9781009336246

© The Oliver Wendell Holmes Devise 2024

This publication is in copyright. Subject to statutory exceptionand to the provisions
of relevant collective licensing agreements,no reproduction of any part may take
place without the writtenpermission of Cambridge University Press & Assessment.

First published 2024

Printed in the United Kingdom by TJ Books Limited, Padstow, Cornwall

A catalogue record for this publication is available from the British Library.

*A Cataloging-in-Publication data record for this book is available from the Library of
Congress*

ISBN – 2 Volume Set 978-1-009-33621-5 Hardback
ISBN – Volume X.I 978-1-009-34621-4 Hardback
ISBN – Volume X.II 978-1-009-34617-7 Hardback

Cambridge University Press & Assessment has no responsibility for the persistence
or accuracy ofURLs for external or third-party internet websites referred to in this
publicationand does not guarantee that any content on such websites is, or will
remain,accurate or appropriate.

*That from this noise, this mêlée, there issues
 a grand and crabby music.*
                              Geoffrey Hill
History teaches, but it has no pupils.
                              Antonio Gramsci

To Shiloh and Willa
May they inhabit a future that has learned from its past.

Contents

List of Plates	*page* xii
List of Figures	xiii
List of Tables	xix
Acknowledgments	xx
Note on Sources	xxii
Preface	xxv
List of Cases	xliii
PROLOGUE: MR. TAFT TAKES CHARGE	1

PART I: CONSTRUCTING THE TAFT COURT: APPOINTMENTS — 31

1	JOHN HESSIN CLARKE AND GEORGE SUTHERLAND	35
2	WILLIAM RUFUS DAY AND PIERCE BUTLER	59
3	MAHLON PITNEY AND EDWARD TERRY SANFORD	84
4	JOSEPH MCKENNA AND HARLAN FISKE STONE	117

PART II: THE HOLDOVER JUSTICES — 161

5	OLIVER WENDELL HOLMES	163
6	WILLIS VAN DEVANTER	225
7	JAMES CLARK MCREYNOLDS	259
8	LOUIS DEMBITZ BRANDEIS	295

CONTENTS

PART III: THE INCOMPARABLE CHIEF JUSTICESHIP OF WILLIAM HOWARD TAFT   373

9   TAFT'S HEALTH   377
10   TAFT AS A JUSTICE   387
11   *MYERS V. UNITED STATES*   401
12   THE CONFERENCE OF SENIOR CIRCUIT COURT JUDGES   448
13   RESHAPING THE SUPREME COURT   476
14   THE CHANGING ROLE OF CHIEF JUSTICE   502
15   THE CHIEF JUSTICE AS CHANCELLOR   509
16   LOBBYING FOR JUDICIAL APPOINTMENTS   536
17   CREATING A NEW SUPREME COURT BUILDING   550

PART IV: THE TAFT COURT AS AN INSTITUTION   595

18   JUDICIAL OPINIONS DURING THE TAFT COURT   599
19   DISSENT DURING THE TAFT COURT   610
20   THE AUTHORITY OF THE TAFT COURT   649

PART V: SOCIAL AND ECONOMIC LEGISLATION   681

21   "EVERYTHING IS ON EDGE": WORLD WAR I AND THE AMERICAN STATE   689
22   CABINING THE CONSTITUTIONAL IMPLICATIONS OF THE WAR   720
23   DIMINISHING JUDICIAL DEFERENCE   732
24   *ADKINS V. CHILDREN'S HOSPITAL*   755
25   PRICE FIXING AND PROPERTY AFFECTED WITH A PUBLIC INTEREST   792
26   THE PROTECTED REALM OF FREEDOM   822
27   RATEMAKING AND JUDICIAL LEGITIMACY   879

PART VI: THE POSITIVE LAW OF PROHIBITION   917

28   PROHIBITION, THE TAFT COURT, AND THE AUTHORITY OF LAW   921
29   PROHIBITION AND DUAL SOVEREIGNTY   948
30   PROHIBITION AND NORMATIVE DUALISM   968
31   PROHIBITION AND POSITIVE LAW   993
32   PROHIBITION AND LAW ENFORCEMENT   1024
33   *OLMSTEAD V. UNITED STATES*   1061

CONTENTS

PART VII: FEDERALISM AND THE AMERICAN PEOPLE — 1101

34	Federalism and World War I	1103
35	Dual Sovereignty and Intergovernmental Tax Immunities	1110
36	Normative Dualism and Congressional Power	1121
37	The Dormant Commerce Clause and the National Market	1160
38	National Judicial Power and the American People	1193

PART VIII: LABOR, EQUAL PROTECTION, AND RACE — 1217

39	Labor and the Jurisprudence of Individualism	1227
40	Labor and the Construction of the National Market	1304
41	Government by Injunction	1375
42	*Truax v. Corrigan*	1399
43	The Equal Protection Clause and Race	1430
	Epilogue: Chief Justice Taft Exits the Scene	1494
	Index	1519

Plates

1	William Howard Taft takes the oath of office as chief justice of the United States, July 11, 1921	*page* 369
2	Formal group portrait of the Taft Court on January 11, 1922	369
3	Formal group portrait of the Taft Court on April 10, 1923	370
4	The Taft Court pays a courtesy call on President Coolidge, October 1, 1923	370
5	The Taft Court pays a courtesy call on President Coolidge, October 6, 1924	371
6	Formal group portrait of the Taft Court on May 3, 1926	371
7	The Taft Court inspects a plaster model of the proposed new Supreme Court Building in the Russell Senate Office Building on May 17, 1929	1096
8	The Taft Court pays a courtesy call on President Hoover on October 7, 1929	1096
9	Oliver Wendell Holmes and Louis Dembitz Brandeis arrive at Court on March 8, 1930	1097
10	Cartoon depicting the effect of the *Coronado* decision and injunctions on organized labor	1098
11	Cartoon attacking judicial review after the announcement of *Adkins*	1098
12	Cartoon lampooning Sutherland's opinion in *Adkins*	1099
13	Cartoon praising *Pierce*	1099

Figures

Figure P-1	Percentage of decisions in which a participating justice either authors or joins an opinion for the Court, 1921–1928 terms	*page* 10
Figure I-1	Percentage of decisions in which a participating justice either joins or authors an opinion for the Court, 1921 term	32
Figure I-2	Percentage of decisions in which a participating justice either joins or authors an opinion for the Court, 1916–1921 terms	32
Figure I-3	Percentage of decisions in which Clarke participated and authored or joined an opinion for the Court, by term	36
Figure I-4	Percentage of decisions in which Clarke participated and joined the same opinion as another justice, 1916–1921 terms	37
Figure I-5	Percentage of decisions in which Clarke participated and joined the same opinion as another justice, 1921 term	38
Figure I-6	Percentage of decisions in which Clarke and Brandeis participated and joined the same opinion, by term	38
Figure I-7	Percentage of decisions in which Sutherland participated and joined the same opinion as another justice, 1922–1928 terms	42
Figure I-8	Percentage of decisions in which Sutherland participated and voted with another justice in conference	43
Figure I-9	Percentage of decisions in which a justice participated and was willing to change a conference vote to join a Court opinion or to join a Court opinion despite registering uncertainty in conference	43
Figure I-10	Number of votes recorded at conference that switch to join the opinion of a justice, divided by the number of that justice's opinions in conference cases	44
Figure I-11	Number of opinions authored by Sutherland, by term	44

List of Figures

Figure I-12	Percentage of Court's opinions authored by Sutherland, by term	45
Figure I-13	Percentage of decisions in which Day participated and joined the same opinion as another justice, 1916–1921 terms	60
Figure I-14	Percentage of decisions in which Day participated and joined the same opinion as another justice, 1921 term	60
Figure I-15	Percentage of decisions in which Butler participated and joined the same opinion as another justice, 1922–1928 terms	64
Figure I-16	Percentage of decisions in which Butler participated and voted with another justice in conference	65
Figure I-17	Percentage of Court's opinions authored by Butler, by term	65
Figure I-18	Percentage of a justice's published opinions that were unanimous in conference	66
Figure I-19	Percentage of a justice's unanimous published opinions that had dissenting or uncertain votes in conference	66
Figure I-20	Percentage of decisions in which Pitney participated and joined the same opinion as another justice, 1916–1921 terms	85
Figure I-21	Percentage of decisions in which Pitney participated and joined the same opinion as another justice, 1921 term	86
Figure I-22	Average number of days from argument to the announcement of a unanimous opinion, by justice, 1921–1928 terms	86
Figure I-23	Percentage of decisions in which Sanford participated and joined the same opinion as another justice, 1922–1928 terms	87
Figure I-24	Percentage of decisions in which Sanford participated and voted with another justice in conference	88
Figure I-25	Percentage of Court's opinions authored by Sanford, by term	92
Figure I-26	Percentage of decisions in which McKenna participated and joined the same opinion as another justice, 1921–1924 terms	119
Figure I-27	Percentage of decisions in which McKenna participated and voted with another justice in conference	119
Figure I-28	Percentage of Court's opinions authored by McKenna, by term	121
Figure I-29	Percentage of decisions in which Stone participated and joined the same opinion as another justice, 1924–1928 terms	132
Figure I-30	Percentage of decisions in which Stone participated and voted with another justice in conference	133

List of Figures

Figure I-31	Percentage of decisions in which Stone joins a common opinion with another justice, by term	133
Figure I-32	Average number of pages in a unanimous opinion by Stone, by term	134
Figure I-33	Percentage of Court's opinions authored by Stone, by term	134
Figure II-1	Percentage of Court's opinions authored by Holmes, by term	174
Figure II-2	Average number of pages in a unanimous opinion, by author, 1921–1928 terms	174
Figure II-3	Percentage of decisions in which Holmes participated and joined the same opinion as another justice, 1921–1928 terms	178
Figure II-4	Percentage of decisions in which Holmes participated and voted with another justice in conference	179
Figure II-5	Percentage of Court's opinions authored by Van Devanter, by term	229
Figure II-6	Percentage of decisions in which a justice participates and votes in conference with the justice with whom he is most likely to vote	233
Figure II-7	Percentage of decisions in which Van Devanter participated and voted with another justice in conference	234
Figure II-8	Percentage of decisions in which Van Devanter participated and joined the same opinion as another justice, 1921–1928 terms	234
Figure II-9	Percentage of decisions in which Taft participated and voted with another justice in conference	235
Figure II-10	Percentage of decisions in which Taft participated and joined the same opinion as another justice, 1921–1928 terms	235
Figure II-11	Percentage of Court's opinions authored by McReynolds, by term	267
Figure II-12	Percentage of decisions in which McReynolds participated and joined the same opinion as another justice, 1921–1928 terms	268
Figure II-13	Percentage of decisions in which McReynolds participated and voted with another justice in conference	268
Figure II-14	Percentage of decisions in which a justice participates and chooses to be the only dissenter, 1921–1928 terms	269
Figure II-15	Percentage of decisions in which Brandeis participated and joined the same opinion as another justice, 1921–1928 terms	316
Figure II-16	Percentage of decisions in which Brandeis participated and voted with another justice in conference	316
Figure II-17	Percentage of Court's opinions authored by Brandeis, by term	317

List of Figures

Figure III-1	Percentage of Court's opinions authored by Taft, by term	378
Figure III-2	Average number of pages in a unanimous Taft opinion, by term	379
Figure III-3	Number of decisions in a term that Taft does not author or join the majority opinion	380
Figure III-4	Total federal district court cases by fiscal year, 1915–1930	454
Figure III-5	Criminal prosecutions by the United States in federal district courts by fiscal year, 1915–1930	455
Figure III-6	Bankruptcy cases in federal district courts by fiscal year, 1915–1930	455
Figure III-7	Federal district civil cases to which United States is a party by fiscal year, 1915–1930	456
Figure III-8	Federal district court cases to which the United States is not a party by fiscal year, 1915–1930	456
Figure III-9	Appellate caseload of the Supreme Court, by term, 1888–1930 terms	478
Figure III-10	Appellate caseload of the Supreme Court, by term, 1910–1930 terms	481
Figure IV-1	Percentage of decided cases on the appellate docket disposed of by full Court opinion, by term, 1912–1929 terms	601
Figure IV-2	Number of full opinions by jurisdiction, by term, 1921–1928 terms	602
Figure IV-3	Percentage of full opinions by jurisdiction, by term, 1921–1928 terms	602
Figure IV-4	Number of full opinions, by term, 1912–2017 terms	604
Figure IV-5	Number of full opinions, by term, 1921–1928 terms	605
Figure IV-6	Average number of pages in a full opinion: White, Taft, Rehnquist, and Roberts Courts	605
Figure IV-7	Average number of days from argument to the announcement of a unanimous opinion: White, Taft, Rehnquist, and Roberts Courts	606
Figure IV-8	Percentage of full opinions that are unanimous: White, Taft, and Roberts Courts	606
Figure IV-9	Average number of pages in a full opinion by jurisdiction, by term, 1921–1928 terms	607
Figure IV-10	Average days from argument to the announcement of a full opinion by jurisdiction, by term, 1921–1928 terms	607
Figure IV-11	Percentage of full opinions that are unanimous by jurisdiction, by term, 1921–1928 terms	608
Figure IV-12	Percentage of full opinions that are unanimous, 1912–2017 terms	611
Figure IV-13	Percentage of decisions in which a justice participates and either joins or authors the Court opinion, 1915–1920 terms versus 1921–1928 terms	613

LIST OF FIGURES

Figure IV-14	Percentage of full opinions that are unanimous, 1921–1928 terms	613
Figure IV-15	Percentage of decisions in which a justice participates and either joins or authors the opinion of the Court, by justice, by term, 1921–1928 terms	614
Figure IV-16	Dissenting votes as a percentage of full opinions, by term, 1916–1928 terms	615
Figure IV-17	Percentage of decisions in which Stone participates and either authors or joins the opinion of the Court, by term	618
Figure IV-18	Unanimity and the conference cases	621
Figure IV-19	Percentage of decisions in which a justice participates and switches a vote in conference to join a published Court opinion	622
Figure IV-20	Percentage of dissenting votes in conference that a justice changes in order to join a published Court opinion	622
Figure IV-21	Unanimity of conference cases, by term, 1922–1928 terms	623
Figure IV-22	Percentage of published conference cases that are unanimous as a multiple of the percentage of the conference cases that are unanimous in conference, by term	624
Figure IV-23	Unanimity and the conference cases, by jurisdiction	624
Figure IV-24	Unanimity and the conference cases by jurisdiction, by term, 1922–1928 terms	625
Figure IV-25	Percentage of published conference cases that are unanimous as a multiple of the percentage of the conference cases that are unanimous in conference, by jurisdiction, by term, 1922–1928 terms	625
Figure IV-26	Number of citations to law review articles per Court opinion, 1921–1928 terms, 1997 term, 2011 term	660
Figure IV-27	Number of citations to treatises and to law reviews in Court opinions, by justice, 1921–1928 terms	660
Figure IV-28	Number of citations to treatises and to law reviews in dissents, by justice, 1921–1928 terms	661
Figure IV-29	Number of citations to law reviews in Court opinions and dissents, by justice, 1921–1928 terms	662
Figure IV-30	Number of citations to law reviews and treatises in Court opinions, by term, 1921–1928 terms, 1997 term, 2011 term	663
Figure IV-31	Citations to law reviews and treatises in Court opinions and in dissents, 1921–1928 terms	663
Figure IV-32	Number of citations to law reviews and treatises in Court opinions and in dissents, 1997 and 2011 terms	664
Figure V-1	Percentage of decisions in which a participating justice on the Taft Court joins or authors an opinion for the Court, 1921–1928 terms	682

xvii

List of Figures

Figure VI-1	Percentage of full opinions that are unanimous in prohibition decisions versus in nonprohibition decisions, 1921–1928 terms	927
Figure VI-2	Percentage of decisions in which a justice participates and joins or authors an opinion for the Court, prohibition decisions versus nonprohibition decisions, 1921–1928 terms	927
Figure VI-3	Number of percentage points by which a justice is more likely to join or author an opinion for the Court in a prohibition decision than in a nonprohibition decision	928
Figure VIII-1	Lynchings by year and by race, 1882–1940	1222

Tables

Table P-1 Number of opinions authored by each justice *page* 9
Table I-1 Number of opinions authored by each justice, 1921 term 32

Acknowledgments

I HAVE BEEN LABORING on this volume for more than thirty years. It has benefited from the indispensable work of generations of research assistants, far more than I can name or individually thank. They know who they are, and I hope they know also that I am deeply grateful for their contributions. The volume has also benefited from the critical assessment of many colleagues who have read and improved this manuscript throughout my (too) many years in legal scholarship. The mistakes, of course, are solely mine. But much of what is good and useful in these pages comes from them. I am especially indebted to the critical appraisals of my wife, Reva Siegel. I am also grateful for the patient and careful assistance of my editor, Maeva Marcus, and for the support of the Library of Congress and the Supreme Court itself. I am especially appreciative of Franz Jantzen's kind help in making available a fine selection of illustrations for this volume.

Early versions of various chapters in this book have been previously published. I would like to acknowledge:

Defending the Lifeworld: Substantive Due Process in the Taft Court Era, 78 BOSTON UNIVERSITY LAW REVIEW 1489 (1998).

Judicial Management and Judicial Disinterest: The Achievements and Perils of Chief Justice William Howard Taft, 1998 JOURNAL OF SUPREME COURT HISTORY 50.

The Supreme Court Opinion as Institutional Practice: Dissent, Legal Scholarship, and Decisionmaking in the Taft Court, 85 MINNESOTA LAW REVIEW 1267 (2001).

Federalism in the Taft Court Era: Can It Be "Revived"?, 51 DUKE LAW JOURNAL 1513 (2002).

Federalism, Positive Law, and the Emergence of the American Administrative State: Prohibition in the Taft Court Era, 48 WILLIAM & MARY LAW REVIEW 1 (2006).

Mr. Taft Becomes Chief Justice, 76 UNIVERSITY OF CINCINNATI LAW REVIEW 761 (2008).

ACKNOWLEDGMENTS

Tension in the Unitary Executive: How Taft Constructed the Epochal Opinion of Myers v. United States, 45 JOURNAL OF SUPREME COURT HISTORY 168 (2020).

The Incomparable Chief Justiceship of William Howard Taft, 2020 MICHIGAN STATE LAW REVIEW 1.

Willis Van Devanter: Chancellor of the Taft Court, 45 JOURNAL OF SUPREME COURT HISTORY 287 (2020).

Note on Sources

THIS MANUSCRIPT WAS originally written in the genre of a law review publication, in which text and footnotes are in continual dialogue, one with the other. But I have been asked to move my footnotes to endnotes. Those interested in the major story line can read the text alone, but readers who wish richer narratives or a more serious engagement with primary sources can explore the endnotes, which offer supplemental commentary. In the endnotes I have erred on the side of inclusion to make available to modern readers the immensely rich archival material that exists for students of the Court during the 1920s.

In this volume I have used the Holmes and Brandeis papers that are located at the Harvard Law School. I have used the Clarke papers located at Case Western Reserve. All other references to a person's "papers," unless otherwise explicitly noted, will be to archives located at the Library of Congress.

To minimize repeated citations of common sources, I have used this list of abbreviated citations:

"BRANDEIS FAMILY LETTERS": THE FAMILY LETTERS OF LOUIS D. BRANDEIS (Melvin I. Urofsky & David W. Levy, eds., Norman: University of Oklahoma Press 2002).

"*Brandeis-Frankfurter Conversations*": Melvin I. Urofsky, *The Brandeis-Frankfurter Conversations*, 1985 SUPREME COURT REVIEW 299.

"BRANDEIS-FRANKFURTER CORRESPONDENCE": "HALF-BROTHER, HALF SON": THE LETTERS OF LOUIS D. BRANDEIS TO FELIX FRANKFURTER (Melvin I. Urofsky & David W. Levy, eds., Norman: University of Oklahoma Press 1991).

"2 LETTERS OF LOUIS D. BRANDEIS": 2 LETTERS OF LOUIS D. BRANDEIS (Melvin I. Urofsky & David W. Levy, eds., Albany: State University of New York Press 1972).

NOTE ON SOURCES

"3 LETTERS OF LOUIS D. BRANDEIS": 3 LETTERS OF LOUIS D. BRANDEIS (Melvin I. Urofsky & David W. Levy, eds., Albany: State University of New York Press 1973).

"4 LETTERS OF LOUIS D. BRANDEIS": 4 LETTERS OF LOUIS D. BRANDEIS (Melvin I. Urofsky & David W. Levy, eds., Albany: State University of New York Press 1975).

"5 LETTERS OF LOUIS D. BRANDEIS": 5 LETTERS OF LOUIS D. BRANDEIS (Melvin I. Urofsky & David W. Levy, eds., Albany: State University of New York Press 1978).

"HOLMES-EINSTEIN CORRESPONDENCE": THE HOLMES-EINSTEIN LETTERS: CORRESPONDENCE OF MR. JUSTICE HOLMES AND LEWIS EINSTEIN 1903–1935 (James Bishop Peabody, ed., London: MacMillan & Co. 1964).

"HOLMES-FRANKFURTER CORRESPONDENCE": HOLMES AND FRANKFURTER: THEIR CORRESPONDENCE, 1912–1934 (Robert M. Mennel & Christine L. Compston, eds., Hanover: University Press of New England 1996).

"1 HOLMES-LASKI CORRESPONDENCE": 1 HOLMES-LASKI LETTERS: THE CORRESPONDENCE OF MR. JUSTICE HOLMES AND HAROLD J. LASKI, 1916–1935 (Mark DeWolfe Howe, ed., Cambridge: Harvard University Press 1963).

"2 HOLMES-LASKI CORRESPONDENCE": 2 HOLMES-LASKI LETTERS: THE CORRESPONDENCE OF MR. JUSTICE HOLMES AND HAROLD LASKI 1926–1935 (Mark DeWolfe Howe, ed., Cambridge: Harvard University Press 1953).

"1 HOLMES-POLLOCK CORRESPONDENCE": 1 HOLMES-POLLOCK LETTERS: THE CORRESPONDENCE OF MR. JUSTICE HOLMES AND SIR FREDERICK POLLOCK 1874–1932 (Mark DeWolfe Howe, ed., Cambridge: Harvard University Press 1942).

"2 HOLMES-POLLOCK CORRESPONDENCE": 2 HOLMES-POLLOCK LETTERS: THE CORRESPONDENCE OF MR. JUSTICE HOLMES AND SIR FREDERICK POLLOCK 1874–1932 (Mark DeWolfe Howe, ed., Cambridge: Harvard University Press 1946).

"HOLMES-SHEEHAN CORRESPONDENCE": HOLMES-SHEEHAN CORRESPONDENCE: THE LETTERS OF JUSTICE OLIVER WENDELL HOLMES AND CANON PATRICK AUGUSTINE SHEEHAN (David H. Burton, ed., Port Washington: Kennikat Press 1976).

"VIVIAN": WILLIAM HOWARD TAFT: COLLECTED EDITORIALS, 1917–1921 (James F. Vivian, ed., New York: Praeger 1990).

In denominating correspondence, I have referred to justices by their initials:

ETS: Edward Terry Sanford
GS: George Sutherland
HFS: Harlan Fiske Stone
JCM: James Clark McReynolds
JHC: John Hessin Clarke
JM: Joseph McKenna
LDB: Louis Dembitz Brandeis

Note on Sources

MP: Mahlon Pitney
OWH: Oliver Wendell Holmes
PB: Pierce Butler
WHT: William Howard Taft
WRD: William R. Day
WVD: Willis Van Devanter

Preface

THIS BOOK TELLS the story of the Supreme Court during the period when William Howard Taft was its chief justice, from 1921 through 1930. It is also Volume X of the Oliver Wendell Holmes Devise History of the Supreme Court of the United States. As anyone familiar with the Devise knows, the series has experienced a long, distinguished, and troubled history.[1]

Supported by funds left to the United States government in his will by Oliver Wendell Holmes, supervised by the Librarian of Congress and a Permanent Committee appointed by the president, the Devise History "has an altogether official feel to it."[2] It has produced in its authors a felt obligation to be both comprehensively exhaustive and scrupulously impartial.[3]

The burden of composing a Devise History is amply illustrated by my own long engagement with this volume. I began working on this book in 1988, almost thirty years after its original assignment to Alexander Bickel. Bickel died before beginning to write about the Taft Court,[4] and Robert Cover then assumed responsibilities of authorship. Tragically, Cover also passed away before assaying the volume. By the time this volume descended to me, the Permanent Committee, in the name of then-editor Stanley Katz, encouraged a foreshortened, thematic approach to the material.

Although I have striven to take advantage of that encouragement, I have not been able entirely to escape the foreboding sense that a Holmes Devise volume ought to be a history of record. I have done my best to sublimate that responsibility into the endnotes, which are extensive and detailed. My primary aim, however, has been to compose a text that sets the jurisprudence of the Taft Court within the cultural context of its decade. If there is a single theme that threads its way throughout this volume, it is how the Court's seemingly technical doctrines were fashioned in continuous dialogue with the popular preoccupations of its era. As a form of human action, law cannot be reduced to abstract theory or prescription. It is made in the rich complexity of historical time.

The 1920s was a tumultuous, transitional period in American life. Jazz, flappers, radio, and cars burst onto the scene. Yet so did prohibition, fundamentalism, the KKK, and 100 percent Americanism. It was a time of intense ambivalence.

Preface

Americans sought "tomorrow's technology in the guise of yesterday's virtues."[5] The Taft Court was charged with the thankless task of constructing law for a society that was deeply confused about what it wanted. Like the country, the Court was torn between nostalgia for old certitudes and the aspiration to appropriate the emerging realities of a modern administrative state.

The jurisprudence of the Taft Court cannot be understood without appreciating the massive cultural impact of World War I. The war came suddenly to America, bringing with it an unprecedented profusion of government regulations. Into a country in which every government restriction had been resisted in the name of *laissez-faire*, and in which every federal intervention had been bitterly contested in the name of states' rights, the war instantly spawned a huge national bureaucracy empowered to control virtually every intimate detail of life. Although it was recognized that these new administrative capacities were necessary to survive in the brutal world of the twentieth century, they were nevertheless experienced as repulsive and intolerable.

In 1920, the nation elected Warren G. Harding with a sweeping mandate to return the country to normalcy. The Supreme Court was to be one instrument of that return. Harding appointed four new justices to the Court in less than two years – William Howard Taft (June 1921), George Sutherland (September 1922), Pierce Butler (December 1922), and Edward T. Sanford (January 1923). It was hoped that they would restore the constitutional world that had been devastated by the exigencies of the war. But that task was complicated by the fact that Americans also wanted to apply the innovative administrative techniques they had mastered during the conflict. The genie of modernity could not simply be stuffed back into the fragile bottle of *laissez-faire*.

Forms of economic and statistical analysis pioneered by wartime bureaucracies, for example, were adopted and aggressively deployed by Herbert Hoover in his Department of Commerce. They were also at the heart of the postwar transformation of the Interstate Commerce Commission, which suddenly became a national agency authorized to manage every aspect of the nation's rail system, both intra- and interstate. The Taft Court accurately registered the nation's ambivalence about the revelations of the war. The Court embraced some new kinds of regulation, and it rejected others. It accepted some new expansions of federal power, and it rejected others.

There is no doubt that the Taft Court succeeded in restoring economic liberty to the center of the American constitutional order. Contrary to the claims of some historians, the Taft Court did not seek to use the Fourteenth Amendment to prohibit class legislation.[6] The war had ratified and sanctified the public interest. The constitutional question was not so much whether state regulation was captured for the benefit of particular classes as whether government management was so intrusive that it compromised the necessary independence of Americans. Pervasive wartime regulation sharply focused judicial concern on whether government control left "the citizen... reduced to an automaton – a mere creature of the state."[7] The ambition of the Court was to protect a core realm of economic and moral freedom that it believed lay at the foundation of the American republic.

PREFACE

If the Taft Court is now remembered at all, it is for vigorously reviving constitutional protections for freedom of contract in ways that would lead directly to the great constitutional crises of the New Deal. The Court reaffirmed due process rights that many sophisticated legal thinkers in 1921 believed had long ago been repudiated. Although during World War I the federal government had comprehensively regulated prices, the Taft Court created strict new constitutional rules prohibiting the expansion of price controls beyond antebellum precedents. The Court effectively shifted to government the burden of justifying intrusive social and economic regulations, requiring the state to demonstrate that such legislation bear "a real and substantial relation" to an appropriate end.[8]

The Court's aggressive reassertion of economic rights prompted a lively debate about the nature of constitutional law. Robert Cover has famously written that law exists in a "normative world" in which "every prescription is insistent in its demand . . . to be supplied with history and destiny, beginning and end, explanation and purpose."[9] Law, suggests Cover, acquires authority when embedded in persuasive narratives. As members of the Taft Court confronted an uncertain and divided public, they debated how to explain their constitutional decisions in a manner that would earn the authority of law and not be dismissed as the mere "personal economic predilections" of the justices.[10]

At least four distinct narratives about the nature and purpose of constitutional law are visible within the Taft Court. I sketch these in Part II, which offers portraits of the remarkable justices who were on the Court when Taft arrived in 1921, and who were also on the Court when he departed in 1930: Oliver Wendell Holmes, Willis Van Devanter, James Clark McReynolds, and Louis Dembitz Brandeis. One narrative sought to ground the authority of the Constitution in shared social customs and traditions; a second in a common commitment to material prosperity; a third in the collective political project of perfecting democracy. A fourth asserted that the authority of law, including constitutional law, arose from society's need to establish orderly processes of adjustment among groups engaged in an existential competition for survival.

Perhaps the most important of these narratives, and the one most difficult for moderns to grasp, imagined that law inheres in what Thomas Cooley called "public sentiment . . . crystallized in general custom."[11] Those who held this perspective believed that law was "not a body of commands imposed upon society" by a legislature, but instead "exists at all times as one of the elements of society springing directly from habit and custom."[12] Law was the spontaneous self-ordering of society itself. This was as true of constitutional law as it was of common law. Hence the point of the Fourteenth Amendment was to protect "those privileges long recognized at common law as essential to the orderly pursuit of happiness by free men."[13]

This narrative privileged judge-made law over legislation. The latter was dismissed as "a mere product of sovereignty," "the mere product of popular will or of a legislative majority of the hour,"[14] produced by "the gusty and unthinking passions of temporary majorities."[15] The job of the judge, whether declaring common law or constitutional law, was to distinguish "the false and the temporary"

xxvii

Preface

from "the real and the permanent."[16] Encompassed within the latter were traditional freedoms deemed ethically necessary for adult citizenship in America. These were protected by "fundamental rights,"[17] most especially by rights of property and contract. Legal elites in the late nineteenth and early twentieth centuries gravitated toward this perspective, no doubt in part because its underlying commitment to history and tradition produced a potent skepticism of the emerging administrative state. Of all members of the Taft Court, McReynolds embodied this perspective in its purest form.

Few now understand law as a form of spontaneous social ordering. This is because we have inherited the positivism that Holmes pioneered in the late nineteenth century. Holmes flatly rejected the equation of law with custom and tradition. Influenced by his experience of the Civil War, as well as by his observations of labor unrest, Holmes denied that America was unified by overarching sentiments, mores, or values. Holmes instead imagined American society as an unending struggle among groups competing for power. The function of law was to express the will of the group able to dominate society, and the function of courts was to apply that will. Legislatures were the "mouthpiece"[18] of the state because legislatures were institutions designed to channel social conflict into orderly and peaceful processes of change responsive to society's dominant opinion. Legislation, like law itself, was an alternative to war.

Holmes told a very different story about America than did McReynolds. Although Americans in the 1920s yearned for the moral certitudes of McReynolds's narrative, they also sought to use government to impose new and controversial forms of social and economic order. Paradigmatic is the vastly ambitious experiment of prohibition, which invoked the force of the federal government to control the most intimate details of everyday life. Holmes's perspective was attractive to those who sought to use the nascent administrative state to regulate society to achieve purposive goals. Holmes enjoined courts faithfully to implement the requirements of positive law. In so doing, Holmes inverted priorities prevalent among legal elites. He privileged legislation over judge-made law.

Holmes argued that judges ought to exercise the prerogative of judicial review very sparingly. Legislation should be invalidated as unconstitutional only when absolutely required by "the literal meaning and plain intent of a constitutional text."[19] Prohibitionists and progressives seized upon Holmesian positivism to protect legislative reforms from constitutional mutilation at the hands of conservative courts committed to the defense of traditional common law rights. The debate between these competing narratives of law played itself out during the 1920s in subjects ranging from constitutional interpretation to statutory construction to the application of general federal common law.

A third distinct form of conservative jurisprudence prominent in the 1920s, most especially in the figure of Taft himself, did not derive constitutional rights from custom, but instead from a pragmatic calculation of economic incentives. Taft believed that rights of property and contract were necessary to underwrite the entrepreneurial incentives required for the growth of civilization. Taft believed that these rights made possible the "accumulation of wealth" that was the measure

Preface

of "progress." Property and contract deserved vigorous constitutional protection because they were the very "keystone of our society."[20] Although Taft has sometimes been described as a legal formalist,[21] in fact he most characteristically regarded law as an instrument of policy, very much in the vein of contemporary advocates of law and economics.

Other members of the Taft Court, like Butler and Sutherland, shared Taft's perspective, which was quite widespread in the 1920s. As Butler put it, government regulations of property and contract that weakened "individual initiative and development" would, "more than war, work the ruin of the nation."[22] Those who held this view postulated that beneath the relatively superficial veneer of legislation lay a fundamental and shared American commitment to economic expansion and prosperity. Constitutional decisions would be received as authoritative so long as they protected rights necessary to sustain that deep commitment. Exemplifying this outlook is a decision like *United Railways and Electric Co. v. West*,[23] which held that public utilities were constitutionally entitled to an 8 percent return to attract sufficient capital for maintenance and growth. Foreshadowing the profound changes in the constitutional status of property that would occur in the subsequent decade, the decision provoked a fierce, unexpected backlash during debates over Hughes's nomination to replace Taft.[24]

Finally, there was yet a fourth narrative visible on the Taft Court. Although this narrative was in the 1920s articulated only by Brandeis, it has since been incorporated into the basic fabric of American public law. Brandeis held that the purpose of the American Constitution is to create a successful democracy. Brandeis agreed with Holmes that courts should defer to legislation, but Brandeis did not hold this position merely because statutes expressed the dominant opinion of society. Brandeis advocated judicial deference because legislation represented both the training ground and the outcome of self-government. Legislation was to be respected because democracy was to be respected. Unlike Holmes, therefore, Brandeis believed that courts ought actively to intervene to protect constitutional rights necessary for the maintenance of democracy. The difference between the two justices can be seen in a case like *Meyer v. Nebraska*,[25] in which Brandeis joined a Court opinion striking down a state statute forbidding the teaching of foreign languages, but in which Holmes dissented.[26]

Like Taft, Brandeis was sensitive to the incentive effects of property rights, but, unlike Taft, he believed that the purpose of property was not merely to generate material prosperity. Brandeis thought that the function of property was instead to produce conditions necessary for the full development of democratic citizens. He was therefore far more willing than Taft to condone restrictions on traditional property rights. Like McReynolds, Brandeis viewed constitutional rights through the moral lens of independent human agency, but, unlike McReynolds, Brandeis imagined that persons became moral agents not merely by participating in the market or by exercising customary rights, but primarily by engaging in the political project of perfecting society.

Each of these four narratives offered an analytically distinct story about how the Court might establish the authority of its constitutional decision-making. Members

PREFACE

of the Taft Court would, in practice, frequently slide unself-consciously among these different accounts of constitutional law. Different contexts would trigger different emphases for different justices. Taft, for example, was at times quite aware of the need for the Court to interpret the Constitution in light of a "crystallization of public sentiment" reflecting "the general and dominant opinion of all the people in a community."[27] And he was at other times quite capable of deferring to legislative judgments in a perfectly Holmesian manner.[28] Important Taft Court decisions, like *Adkins v. Children's Hospital of the District of Columbia*,[29] hover indecipherably between an account of property as essential for the construction of independent moral agency and an account of property as necessary to sustain material growth.[30] Still other decisions, like *United Railways and Electric Co. v. West*,[31] are historically and theoretically significant because they unambiguously turn on one narrative or another.

Holmes and Brandeis have become iconic figures in the history of American law because they inhabited their profound jurisprudential principles with consistency and force. Other members of the Taft Court lacked this intellectual discipline and clarity. Taft himself believed that whereas Holmes and Brandeis failed to appreciate proper constitutional limitations, McReynolds was too reactionary to offer a sure guide to constitutional adjudication. Taft, a man filled with practical common sense, led his Court down a sensible middle path. Compromised from the beginning, it was a path that has led chiefly to obscurity. The Taft Court has not survived in our cultural memory as has, for example, the Hughes Court.

The positive law of prohibition placed extreme pressure on the jurisprudential attitudes of Taft Court justices. Prohibition was rooted in the Constitution itself, and yet it was caught in the maws of a culture war so intense that large sectors of the population denied the legitimacy of federal prohibition. There was plainly no crystallized public sentiment with regard to the bone-dry Volstead Act,[32] which had been fastened on the country by white rural protestant churches acting through the relentless single-issue politics of the Anti-Saloon League. Urban elites and ethnic workers openly rebelled against federal prohibition, so that the entire country felt itself caught in the throes of a disorienting epidemic of lawlessness.

The federal government responded by ramping up efforts to use criminal law to enforce prohibition. Contemporary Fourth Amendment jurisprudence largely emerged from the Taft Court's efforts to modernize search and seizure law in the face of twentieth-century innovations like the automobile. Throughout the decade, prohibition came to exemplify the horrors of positive legislation running roughshod over traditional beliefs and values. There were endless calls for the nullification of the Eighteenth Amendment. The question for the Taft Court became how, in such circumstances, to sustain the authority of the Constitution itself.

The issue split conservatives on the Taft Court into two factions. McReynolds, Sutherland, and Butler, convinced that social mores were the ultimate source of legal authority, sought to ameliorate the rigors of prohibition by remaining faithful to custom and tradition. They believed that only through such a strategy could they preserve the legitimacy of the Constitution. But conservatives like Taft, Van Devanter, and Sanford instead concluded that the rule of law could be upheld

Preface

only if the technical legal rigors of prohibition were strictly enforced at all costs. In the discrete context of prohibition, these three justices forged an innovative fusion of conservatism and Holmesian positivism that would not reemerge until the jurisprudence of William Rehnquist half a century later.

Although Holmes experienced no difficulty enforcing the strenuous demands of national prohibition, Brandeis was more torn. On the one hand, prohibition was the outcome of democratic deliberation and so merited deference and respect. On the other hand, prohibition enforcement was so violent and intrusive that it threatened to undercut the democratic project itself. Under the pressure of prohibition, Brandeis began to realize that the very legitimacy of the administrative state required that it be constrained by basic dignitary norms. These norms, however, were rooted in precisely the customs and traditions that conservatives had always prized. As he explored this issue in his influential dissent in *Olmstead v. United States*,[33] Brandeis anticipated the development of a liberal communitarian jurisprudence that would not again arise until the 1960s in cases like *Katz v. United States*[34] and *Griswold v. Connecticut*.[35]

Prohibition raised rather large questions of federalism. Throughout the 1920s the relationship between the federal government and the states provoked pervasive uncertainty and confusion. The Taft Court inherited an account of federalism that centered on the metaphor of "dual sovereignty," which imagined that the powers of federal and state governments were each exercised in separate and distinct spheres. In the context of congressional power, this metaphor morphed easily into a position of "normative dualism," which held that Congress ought to be prohibited from legislating, even within its own proper sphere, in ways that might undermine the reserved powers of the states. The value at stake in questions of federalism was that of self-governance. States were figured as natural units of self-determination, whereas federal regulations were always potentially tainted as the oppressive dictates of a distant and unresponsive bureaucracy.

Traditional understandings of federalism were upended by World War I. During the crusade to make the world safe for democracy, the federal government had reached out to touch every corner of life. The Taft Court, tasked with returning to normalcy, was required to produce a convincing account of the proper relationship between national and state governments. This proved quite beyond the Court's capacity. The Taft Court patched together a confused mélange of contradictory and ambivalent intuitions. Sometimes the Court encouraged congressional control over national markets, and sometimes it asserted a scrupulous normative dualism that prohibited federal legislation. In seeking to understand this pattern, it is clear that the Court interpreted federal structure in light of its commitment to protecting the economic freedom enshrined in ordinary property rights. Although the Constitution theoretically distinguishes questions of rights from questions of structure,[36] this was manifestly not the case during the Taft Court era.

In certain doctrinal areas, like intergovernmental tax immunity or the dormant Commerce Clause, the Taft Court was guided by the metaphor of dual sovereignty. The Court was intent on maintaining a proper separation between the distinct spheres of federal and state power. The highly integrated economy of the 1920s, however, rendered the metaphor of separate spheres hopelessly inadequate. Harlan Fiske Stone, the youngest member of the Taft Court, and the only justice trained in the legal pragmatism of Holmes, sought in vain to push the Court toward more modern jurisprudential premises. Stone argued that federal and state governments should not be conceptualized as occupying separate spheres, but instead as possessing distinct interests that needed to be weighed and balanced, one against the other. Stone's deep insight into the future of constitutional law would have to wait a full decade before coming into general use, perhaps because it required the Court to assert forms of policy-making authority that in the 1920s it was not yet prepared explicitly to acknowledge.[37]

Although the Taft Court would loudly proclaim the values of normative dualism, it was in fact a highly nationalist institution. Protecting national markets from state interference had been a priority of the Supreme Court since the late nineteenth century, and the Taft Court remained faithful to this project. Not only did the Taft Court use dormant Commerce Clause doctrine to accomplish this end, it also interpreted individual Fourteenth Amendment rights to ensure that states did not balkanize the national market. Another weapon in the Taft Court's arsenal was general federal common law, which national Article III courts applied in cases arising within their diversity jurisdiction. The overlap between constitutional and common law rights, between individual rights and structural imperatives, was extensive and deliberate.

Weaned on the positivism of Holmes, we now assume that a court is authorized to speak only for the law of a specific jurisdiction. A court declares the national law of the federal Constitution, for example, or the statutory law of a state. Courts do not enforce, in Holmes's pungent phrase, the law of some "brooding omnipresence in the sky."[38] But when the Taft Court applied general common law, it imagined itself as speaking neither for national law nor for state law. Instead, it conceived itself as expressing the crystallized public sentiment of the entire American people. It is for precisely this reason that throughout the 1920s Holmes waged an unrelenting war on the presumption of federal courts in diversity jurisdiction to declare general common law.

Within the Taft Court there was a good deal of substantive overlap between constitutional law and general common law. It may take a difficult leap of historical imagination, but the unique voice of the Taft Court cannot be understood until it is appreciated that the Court did not interpret the Fourteenth Amendment in light of specifically federal law, as would a modern court, but instead in light of the ideals of the entire American people, as would a common law court. In such contexts, the Taft Court lost all track of the separate spheres of state and federal sovereignty. It articulated the shared vision of a united American people, much as a common law court might articulate the ideals of a single society united by common values and traditions.

This image was often jarringly out of place in postwar America, which was a nation frequently in savage conflict with itself. In 1919 the country experienced vicious labor and racial violence. It was by observing judicial efforts to control industrial struggles that Holmes was struck with the foundational insight of his legal

PREFACE

life, which is that society was not unified but agonistic.[39] Throughout the 1920s, however, the Taft Court would nevertheless insist on speaking for what it claimed were common values. The results were at times catastrophic.

An obvious example of the discrepancy between the Court's aspiration to articulate shared ideals and the messy fact of cultural polarization was the Court's effort to impose law on the struggle between capital and organized labor. This conflict was so bitter that in the 1920s it was commonly characterized in images of "industrial warfare."[40] The Taft Court used labor injunctions to subordinate that war to the rule of law. Taft himself had been instrumental in theorizing labor injunctions when he was an appellate federal judge in the last decade of the nineteenth century. Labor injunctions were far-reaching and brutally effective. They not only evaded basic procedural protections against criminal sanctions, like the jury, but they also imposed general rules of conduct on large masses of people who were effectively strangers to the court.

Federal courts issued labor injunctions to enforce common law protections for property or to implement federal anti-trust legislation prohibiting illegal boycotts and strikes. Federal anti-trust statutes were so vague that they were explicitly interpreted to incorporate common law precedents distinguishing legal from illegal forms of union organizing. In seeking to control the war between capital and organized labor, in other words, federal courts imagined themselves as speaking for the shared ideals of all Americans, as would any common law court.

Organized labor hated federal equity, which it branded "government by injunction." It is no small irony that in seeking to ground the authority of law in the articulation of common ideals, federal courts instead pushed organized labor to allege that courts were not articulating law at all. Organized labor charged that federal courts were instead merely protecting the interests of the large national corporations from which most federal judges were drawn. Matters grew so tense that organized labor repeatedly called for strictly limiting federal equity power, repealing federal anti-trust statutes, and overturning the institution of judicial review.

Like virtually everything else in the decade, the Taft Court's response to industrial strife must be understood in light of World War I, when the nation had explicitly acknowledged the legitimacy of unions, which were deemed necessary to produce the labor stability required for accelerated wartime production. As co-chair of the National War Labor Board, Taft vigorously embraced what he called the "group system" in labor markets.[41] In the urgent push for normalcy after the Armistice, however, American employers sought to displace unions and reclaim lost control over their employees.

Caught between employers and unions, the Taft Court equivocated. It validated the constitutional role of unions and labor picketing, but it awarded employers decisive advantages in the industrial struggle for control of the workplace. Although the Court understood that as a practical matter national labor policy required recognizing unions, it could not bring itself to repudiate the premise that constitutional rights were ultimately individual rights, not group rights. The Court's ambivalence crippled the nation's efforts to develop an effective national labor policy.

The Taft Court allowed unions some power, but not too much. Taft feared that if unions grew too powerful, property rights could no longer perform their constitutional function of facilitating economic growth. In its efforts to protect managerial initiative, the Taft Court overreached. Its misjudgments were so severe that Congress in 1932, under the administration of Herbert Hoover, passed the Norris-LaGuardia Act,[42] which stripped federal courts of their authority to issue injunctions to govern labor disputes. It was a humiliating setback for a Court that imagined itself as creating law in the name of the spontaneous beliefs of the entire American people.

There was no equivalent pushback to decisions of the Taft Court addressing questions of race, where the Court also sought to speak for "the established usages, customs, and traditions of the people" and to lend legal authority to their "racial instincts."[43] Despite its commitment to individualism in other contexts, the Taft Court upheld Southern apartheid. The Court faithfully expressed Northern Republican attitudes toward questions of race, which might be encapsulated in the formula of separate but equal. In practice, the formula meant that Northern Republicans sought to retain the loyalty of Southern Blacks with weak promises of civil and political rights, while simultaneously upholding the constitutionality of segregation to tempt Southern whites to desert the Democratic Party.

It was obvious to all that Southern segregation undermined the realization of rights guaranteed in the Reconstruction Amendments. Taft was perfectly aware that the South was stripping Blacks of constitutional rights given them "years ago."[44] While chief justice, Taft was also chair of the Board of Hampton Institute, a Virginia school founded during Reconstruction for the vocational education of Southern Blacks. In that capacity Taft witnessed firsthand the humiliations of Southern apartheid.

Taft was convinced, however, that the only hope for the improvement of Southern Blacks lay in the appeasement of Southern white elites. Although Taft sought vigorously to enforce the positive law of the Eighteenth Amendment over the objections of urban sophisticates and ethnic workers, he was unwilling to press the positive law of the Fourteenth and Fifteenth Amendments. He argued that any such effort would be counterproductive because courts could not overcome engrained Southern racism. The Taft Court unanimously reaffirmed *Plessy* and explicitly approved segregated schooling in Mississippi in *Gong Lum v. Rice*.[45]

During the Taft Court era, the Equal Protection Clause was a text in search of a purpose. It no longer distinguished legislation serving the public good from legislation serving the interests only of particular classes, as it had in the decades after Reconstruction.[46] The Clause was chiefly used by the Taft Court to pursue goals like protecting the national market or safeguarding the prerogatives of employers. It offered racial minorities little or no real constitutional protection.[47] The Court would not reinterpret the Clause to address questions of Southern apartheid until the Great Migration had produced significant Black voting blocks in Northern and border states. Blacks were not accorded effective constitutional rights until they began to appear in American politics as active and influential political actors. The first such appearance, as powerful as it was unexpected,

Preface

involved the National Association for the Advancement of Colored People's successful effort to block the nomination of John J. Parker to succeed Edward T. Sanford on the Court.

The large themes that preoccupy much of this volume cannot be squeezed precisely into the period between June 30, 1921, and February 3, 1930, when Taft was chief justice of the United States. I have taken the liberty of expanding my discussion somewhat beyond the strict boundaries of Taft's chief justiceship. I have sought to sketch both the history out of which the Taft Court's decisions emerged and the future toward which they pointed. By assigning volumes to periods that largely correspond to the regimes of particular chief justices, however, the founding Permanent Committee of the Holmes Devise implicitly endorsed a view of historical change that emphasized institutional leadership.

I confess that I have been unusually fortunate in this regard. Although Taft is now all but forgotten, in his time he was a commanding figure. As the only man in the history of the country ever to have served as both president and chief justice, Taft's judgments carried formidable weight. This was true not only in the context of cases like *Myers v. United States*,[48] which decided for the first time in the nation's history that a statute was unconstitutional because it infringed the inherent Article II powers of the president, but also in the context of the internal dynamics of the Court itself. As Brandeis once remarked to Frankfurter, members of the Court "will take from Taft [but] wouldn't from us. If good enough for Taft good enough for us – they say, & a natural sentiment."[49]

Taft came to the Court with a dense and powerful political network, unlike anything ever seen before or since. He used his influence to stunning effect. In less than nine years, Taft changed the nature of federal courts, transforming them from a collection of independent judges into a coherent branch of the federal government overseen by the chief justice. He reconfigured the Supreme Court from a final appellate tribunal into what contemporaries called a "ministry of justice,"[50] an institution that could choose its own docket to manage the development of federal law. He reconstituted the position of chief justice, converting it into a role that was closer to an English lord chancellor than to that of any previous American judge. For several years, Taft played an active and important role in vetting nominees for Article III judgeships, and by the end of his life he had performed the almost impossible task of securing a new home for the Supreme Court. It is because of Taft that, for the first time in its history, the Court was able to move out from under Congress's thumb. Taft accomplished all this despite suffering a severe heart attack in 1926 that left him a semi-invalid.

In the end, however, Taft was but one of the thirteen justices who worked together to constitute the Taft Court. It is impossible to reconstruct the personal and institutional dynamics that shaped Taft Court decisions without having a firm sense of the distinct individual personalities and commitments of its members. Where possible, we can recover these biographical facts from published writings and personal archives. But our historical sources for the Taft Court are distributed

Preface

very unequally, and history tends to be written from the perspective of those who leave the most complete and accessible records.

On this account, Taft is fortunate indeed. He not only bequeathed us an extraordinarily large portfolio of published writings, but also an immense (and largely unpublished) archive of personal correspondence and memoranda that runs to more than 600,000 items.[51] At the end of every week, Taft would dictate long, gossipy letters recounting recent events to his family and friends. This invaluable trove of material affords privileged access to Taft's thoughts and feelings. They make it inevitable that much of this history will be told through Taft's eyes. By contrast, other justices on what can be called the "conservative" wing of the Court have left us only thin collections of correspondence and meager libraries of published writings. This is true of Justices Sutherland and Van Devanter.[52] The lived experience of still other justices – like Butler, Clarke, Day, McKenna, McReynolds, Pitney, and Sanford – is difficult or impossible to reconstruct because surviving records are so sparse.

Holmes, Brandeis, and Stone, by contrast, have each left us not only excellent archival records, but also many superb publications. For these three justices, and for these three justices only, we possess relatively comprehensive files that chronicle the drafting and reception of their opinions. These files offer a privileged glimpse into the inner, everyday workings of the Taft Court. But this glimpse is available only from the perspective of what we might now term the "liberal" wing of the Court. The risk of capture, of seeing the Court only through the eyes of those whose case files remain intact, is obvious.

We are therefore especially fortunate also to have available an unusual, unpublished resource that illuminates otherwise invisible aspects of the Taft Court's practices. After oral argument and before distributing opinions, justices of the Court would meet to discuss their cases in private conferences, where they exchanged candid opinions and took preliminary votes. The justices recorded their conference deliberations and votes in docket books. The solemn practice of the justices was to destroy these docket books at the end of each term, so that their discussions could remain forever confidential.[53]

Through a remarkable serendipity, Supreme Court Curator Gail Galloway discovered Justice Butler's docket books for the 1922–1924 terms and Justice Stone's docket books for the 1924–1929 terms. For reasons that are now unknown, they were preserved in a locked trunk at the Supreme Court building, a structure that did not even exist at the time these books were produced.[54] These docket books open a unique and comprehensive window into the day-to-day workings of the Taft Court.

Because it is difficult to know just which cases in the 1929 term should be allocated to the Taft Court and which to the Hughes Court, I have throughout this volume attempted to code the votes of the justices in conference during the 1922–1928 terms.[55] During that period, the Butler and Stone docket books allow us to tally votes in some 1,200 of the 1,381 published full opinions issued by the Court. These 1,200 opinions, which for ease of reference I shall call the "conference cases," appear representative. As published, for example, 86 percent of the

PREFACE

conference cases were unanimous, as were 86 percent of the total set of 1,381 opinions announced by the Court in the 1922–1928 terms.

Comparing the justices' votes at conference with their votes in final published opinions tells us a great deal about the internal dynamics of the Taft Court. It allows us to learn, for example, that Van Devanter, whom scholars have always considered an abject "failure,"[56] was actually, by an impressive margin, the justice who most often persuaded colleagues to change their views in conference and join his published opinions.[57] Similarly, they establish that Butler, whom scholars have also dismissed as a failure, was the second most powerful justice in corralling wayward votes.[58] The docket books also reveal that McKenna and Sanford were the least likely to attract doubting justices to join their published opinions, so that Taft assigned them the easiest cases, with the highest percentage of unanimous votes in conference.[59]

Access to the Court's secret voting in conference also permits us to identify essential Taft Court decision-making practices that might otherwise remain invisible. It would be a serious mistake to imagine the Taft Court as simply the modern Court staffed with different personnel. Members of the Taft Court abided by institutional norms that sharply distinguish it from the contemporary Court. Foremost among these was a norm of acquiescence, by which Taft Court justices felt bound to refrain from dissenting except in extraordinary circumstances. Carefully parsed, the norm tells us a great deal about how members of the Taft Court conceived the nature and purpose of law, how they believed the authority of the Court was best sustained, and how they imagined the relationship between the project of declaring law and the project of knowing law.

We should be careful not to project on to the past our own tacit understandings of such fundamental questions. The Taft Court was probably the last moment in the Court's history when it could authentically inhabit decision-making practices appropriate for a final appellate tribunal whose primary task was to settle disputes between litigants. These practices presupposed an account of the Court's authority quite different from that assumed by the institutional norms of the contemporary Court, particularly with respect to the role of public opinion and the community of legal expertise.[60]

I have written this volume so that it can be read straight through, from the beginning to the end, like any other monographic history. The chapters build on one another. One cannot fully comprehend the norm of acquiescence, for example, unless one first understands how the Judiciary Act of 1925 shifted the audience for Court opinions from litigants to the public at large, which is a question that I take up in Chapter 13. One cannot fully appreciate the intellectual crisis provoked by prohibition without first grasping the role of custom in traditional conservative jurisprudence, which I discuss in Chapter 5. One cannot fully understand the Taft Court's refusal to adopt constitutional tests like balancing unless one first understands how members of the Court understood the sources of their own authority, which I discuss in Chapter 20. And so on.

For the reader who primarily seeks an encyclopedic resource, however, I have also attempted to divide the chapters of this volume into small digestible topics. If a reader wishes to learn about the complexities of intergovernmental tax immunity doctrine, she can refer to Chapter 35. If she wishes to learn about the Court's mysterious, far-reaching decision invalidating a state statute prohibiting labor injunctions, she can consult Chapter 42, which discusses *Truax v. Corrigan*.[61] Cross-references to relevant discussions are liberally provided.

Unlike some prior Holmes Devise volumes, I have not tried comprehensively to cover all topics that might potentially be of interest. Much of importance has been omitted. My ambition has instead been to select themes that illuminate the drama of a serious and gifted Court struggling to adjust American public law to the emergence of the modern American state under conditions of extreme polarization and social unrest. It is a moving and instructive spectacle, one worthy of our closest attention and respect. It reveals a great deal about the implicit premises of pre-New Deal jurisprudence, as well as about the immanent structures of our own constitutional thought. It allows us better to appreciate the mysterious alchemy by which the Court aspires to transmute judicial opinions into law deserving the allegiance of all Americans.

PREFACE

Notes

1. *See* Stanley N. Katz, *Official History: The Holmes Devise History of the Supreme Court*, 141 PROCEEDINGS OF THE AMERICAN PHILOSOPHICAL SOCIETY 297 (1997); Eben Moglen, *Holmes's Legacy and the New Constitutional History*, 108 HARVARD LAW REVIEW 2027 (1995).
2. Katz, *supra* note 1, at 303.
3. Devise histories have posed a special challenge to readers: Should they dip in and out of its volumes, as if they were mere works of encyclopedic reference, or should they instead engage them as they would any ordinary monographic history, knowing that themes on offer might be subject to arbitrary amputation due to the procrustean dates of a particular chief justiceship? *See, e.g.*, Sanford Levinson, *Review of William M. Wiecek, The Birth of the Modern Constitution*, 26 LAW AND HISTORY REVIEW 730 (2008).
4. Bickel had originally been assigned to author a history of the White and Taft Courts. Benno Schmidt ultimately completed Bickel's manuscript about the White Court. *See* ALEXANDER M. BICKEL & BENNO C. SCHMIDT, JR., THE JUDICIARY AND RESPONSIBLE GOVERNMENT 1910–1921 (New York: MacMillan Publishing Co. 1984).
5. ROBERT H. WIEBE, SELF-RULE: A CULTURAL HISTORY OF AMERICAN DEMOCRACY 148–49 (University of Chicago Press 1995).
6. Barry Cushman, *Teaching the Lochner Era*, 62 ST. LOUIS UNIVERSITY LAW JOURNAL 537, 540–41 (2018).
7. Children's Hosp. v. Adkins, 284 F. 613, 623 (App. D.C. 1921), *aff'd*, 261 U.S. 525 (1923).
8. Louis K. Liggett Co. v. Baldridge, 278 U.S. 105, 111 (1928).
9. Robert M. Cover, *Foreword: Nomos and Narrative*, 96 HARVARD LAW REVIEW 4, 5 (1983).
10. Morehead v. New York *ex rel.* Tipaldo, 298 U.S. 587, 633 (1936) (Stone, J., dissenting).
11. T.M. Cooley, *Labor and Capital before the Law*, 139 NORTH AMERICAN REVIEW 504, 504 (1884).
12. James C. Carter, *The Ideal and the Actual in the Law*, in REPORT OF THE THIRTEENTH ANNUAL MEETING OF THE AMERICAN BAR ASSOCIATION 235 (Philadelphia: Dando Printing and Publishing Co. 1890).
13. Meyer v. Nebraska, 262 U.S. 390, 399–400 (1923).
14. John F. Dillon, *Address of the President*, in REPORT OF THE FIFTEENTH ANNUAL MEETING OF THE AMERICAN BAR ASSOCIATION 200 (Philadelphia: Dando Printing & Publishing Co. 1892).
15. William H. Taft, *The Right of Private Property*, 3 MICHIGAN LAW JOURNAL 215, 218 (1894).
16. HARLAN F. STONE, LAW AND ITS ADMINISTRATION 48–49 (New York: Columbia University Press 1915).
17. Meyer v. Nebraska, 262 U.S. 390, 401 (1923).
18. Old Dominion Steamship Co. v. Gilmore, 207 U.S. 398, 404 (1907).
19. Forbes Pioneer Boat Line v. Board of Commissioners of Everglades Drainage District, 258 U.S. 338, 340 (1922).

PREFACE

20. William H. Taft, *Recent Criticism of the Federal Judiciary*, in REPORT OF THE EIGHTEENTH ANNUAL MEETING OF THE AMERICAN BAR ASSOCIATION 251 (Philadelphia: Dando Printing & Publishing Co. 1895).
21. Stanley I. Kutler, *Chief Justice Taft and the Delusion of Judicial Exactness – A Study in Jurisprudence*, 48 VIRGINIA LAW REVIEW 1407 (1962).
22. Pierce Butler, *Educating for Citizenship: Duties the Citizen Owes to the State*, 12 CATHOLIC EDUCATIONAL ASSOCIATION BULLETIN 123, 130–31 (November 1915). Sutherland frankly asserted that "the perfect freedom of the individual, within certain broad limits, to do as he pleases is so vital to the lasting progress of humanity that whoever seeks to interfere with it must assume the burden of demonstrating the necessity." GEORGE SUTHERLAND, SUPERFLUOUS GOVERNMENT: AN ADDRESS BY SENATOR SUTHERLAND OF UTAH 4 (Cleveland: Cleveland Chamber of Commerce 1914).
23. 280 U.S. 234 (1930).
24. *See infra* Chapter 27, at 891–94.
25. 262 U.S. 390 (1923).
26. For a discussion, see *infra* Chapter 26.
27. William Howard Taft, *Is Prohibition a Blow at Personal Liberty?*, 36 LADIES HOME JOURNAL 31, 78 (May 1919). For a good example, see the discussion of Brooks v. United States, 267 U.S. 432 (1925), in *infra* Chapter 36, at 1132–34.
28. *See infra* Chapter 10 at 391–92; Chapter 24, at 765–66.
29. 261 U.S. 525 (1923).
30. *See infra* Chapter 24; Chapter 26, at 834–35. For a good example of indecipherability, see the discussion of Village of Euclid v. Ambler Realty Co., 272 U.S. 365 (1926), in *infra* Chapter 26, at 835–43.
31. 280 U.S. 234 (1930). *See infra* Chapter 27, at 890–91.
32. National Prohibition Act, Pub. L. 66-66, 41 Stat. 305 (October 28, 1919).
33. 277 U.S. 438 (1928).
34. 389 U.S. 347 (1967).
35. 381 U.S. 479, 494 (1965) (Goldberg, J., concurring). For a discussion, see *infra* Chapter 33, at 1067–69.
36. Query whether this is in fact true. *See, e.g.*, National Federation of Independent Business v. Sebelius, 567 U.S. 519 (2012).
37. For a discussion of Stone's unique attraction to the authority of expertise, see *infra* Chapter 20, at 654–62; for a discussion of the relationship between the authority of expertise and the balancing tests proposed by Stone, see *infra* Chapter 37, at 1171–73.
38. S. Pac. Co. v. Jensen, 244 U.S. 205, 222 (1917).
39. Oliver Wendell Holmes, *The Gas-Stokers' Strike*, 7 AMERICAN LAW REVIEW 582 (1873).
40. *Labor and the Public*, NEW YORK TIMES (December 8, 1921), at 17.
41. William Howard Taft, *National War Labor Board* (November 26, 1918), in VIVIAN, at 125–26.
42. Pub. L. 72-65, 47 Stat. 70 (March 23, 1932).
43. Plessy v. Ferguson, 163 U.S. 537, 551 (1896).
44. William Howard Taft, *The Negro Problem in America*, 50 SOUTHERN WORKMAN 10, 13 (1921).
45. 275 U.S. 78 (1927).

Preface

46. V.F. Nourse & Sarah A. Maguire, *The Lost History of Governance and Equal Protection*, 58 DUKE LAW JOURNAL 955 (2009).
47. *But see* Nixon v. Herndon, 273 U.S. 536 (1927); Harmon v. Tyler, 273 U.S. 668 (1927).
48. 272 U.S. 52 (1926).
49. *Brandeis-Frankfurter Conversations*, at 307 (July 1, 1922).
50. Gregory Hankin, *U.S. Supreme Court under New Act*, 12 JOURNAL OF THE AMERICAN JUDICATURE SOCIETY 40, 40 (August 1928).
51. A word should be said about Taft's many letters, which are a rich and irresistible historical resource. *See* Kate MacLean Stewart, *The William Howard Taft Papers*, 15 LIBRARY OF CONGRESS: QUARTERLY JOURNAL OF CURRENT ACQUISITIONS 1 (1957). Taft was a faithful and assiduous correspondent, dictating daily letters to his secretary, Wendell W. Mischler, who then typed them with carbon copies. Taft kept the vast bulk of his correspondence, but as he began to think of arranging them into a memoir, doubts came into his mind:

> The older I grow, the more certain I am that the publication, unedited, of the impression of hasty and intimate opinions on issues and persons does not contribute to the truth of history, because intimate letters are like intimate conversations. What is said in them is often hasty, the result possibly of some temporary resentment or impatience, and can not be taken as the best evidence of a man's considered views. I agree that they are often very interesting, but I think they are often misleading, and that a good many people have suffered in their reputation and a good many inaccurate views have been formed from reading such material.

WHT to J.C. Hemphill (February 24, 1926) (Taft papers). Taft's reputation has no doubt suffered because of the many caustic and intemperate remarks that are scattered throughout his letters.

It should be said at the outset that Taft in his letters sometimes appears far more irascible – more mean-spirited and narrowly partisan – than he actually was. No doubt if Taft had lived long enough, he would have edited his vast correspondence and much valuable if sensational material would have been lost to history. As Taft wrote a friend:

> I have a habit that isn't a particularly good one and often risks a good deal of trouble in making free personal comments on persons whose participation in current matters attracts such comments. I know, from having examined some of the letters I have written in the past, that my literary executors ... will have to exercise the greatest care in cutting out a lot of things that were prompted by the moment's interest and that were really not judicial utterances and doubtless not justified. Intimate correspondence of that sort is not by any means the most reliable source of information as to one's real judgment about others and about events. What is said under such circumstances is said right off the reel, without deliberation and without sense of responsibility, and I have often thought that real injustice has been done in the revelation of private letters from men in whose lives the public takes an interest.

WHT to James R. Sheffield (May 3, 1927) (Taft papers). *See* WHT to Mrs. Frederick J. Manning (November 15, 1925) (Taft papers) ("I presume that it is the strictures that I may have yielded to in dealing with men when active in affairs which the ordinary publisher of sensational tendencies would regard as valuable for exploitation, a subject matter that I would most anxiously wish to suppress.").

I confess that in this volume I have taken the liberty of frequently citing Taft's many pungent and spontaneous observations. Virtually every student of Taft has taken this same liberty. Taft is correct, however, that his off-the-cuff remarks can often be highly misleading. An important caution to keep in mind, therefore, is that although Taft was a man with a quick temper and a ready tongue, he was in life most often deliberate and fair. He rarely acted on his own worst impulses. He used his daily correspondence as a kind of therapy to exorcise the feelings that he would in actual life suppress.

52. Although Van Devanter was a dominating presence on the Taft Court, the precise convictions underlying his jurisprudence are almost impossible to reconstruct. Van Devanter's correspondence is largely personal. He left no records of his judicial work and, in contrast to Taft, Sutherland, and even Butler, refused to publish articles that explained his thinking. We are left primarily with the evidence of Van Devanter's opinions, which are highly doctrinal and opaque. They reveal Van Devanter's conclusions but not his reasons.

53. Justice McReynolds's clerk for the 1936 term, John Knox, recalls that after the justice showed Knox his docket book, he said "rather sharply, 'That book will *not* be preserved after this term of Court! Next June I shall take it downstairs myself and stand before the big furnace in this building and watch it burn up. A book like that must be destroyed at the end of each term!'" THE FORGOTTEN MEMOIR OF JOHN KNOX: A YEAR IN THE LIFE OF A SUPREME COURT CLERK IN FDR'S WASHINGTON 84 (Dennis J. Hutchinson & David J. Garrow, eds., University of Chicago Press 2002). Paul Freund, who clerked for Brandeis in the 1932 term, recalls that "When I was a law clerk ... I had access to the docket book of Justice Brandeis. It was burned with the others at the end of the term, and I hope that custom still obtains." *Remarks of Paul A. Freund, A Colloquy, Proceedings of the Forty-Ninth Judicial Conference of the District of Columbia Circuit* (May 24, 1988), reprinted in 124 F.R.D. 241, 347 (1988).

54. I was lucky to be present at the moment of discovery. I remember that we had to call twice for the services of a locksmith, first to unlock the trunk and then again to open the locked leather docket books. For a discussion of the reliability of docket books, see Forrest Maltzman & Paul J. Wahlbeck, *Inside the U.S. Supreme Court: The Reliability of the Justices' Conference Records*, 58 JOURNAL OF POLITICS 528 (1996). The Taft Court docket books have since been nicely scrutinized in Barry Cushman, *Inside the Taft Court: Lessons from the Docket Books*, 2015 SUPREME COURT REVIEW 345.

55. Because Butler joined the Court in January 1923, his docket book for the 1922 term does not record conference votes for cases before that time.

56. Albert P. Blaustein & Roy M. Mersky, *Rating Supreme Court Justices*, 58 AMERICAN BAR ASSOCIATION JOURNAL 1183, 1186 (1972).

57. *See* Figure I-10.

58. *Compare* Blaustein & Mersky, *supra* note 56, and Figure I-10.

59. *See* Figures I-10, I-18, and I-19.

60. *See infra* Chapter 20.

61. 257 U.S. 312 (1921).

Cases

A.B. Small Co. v. American Sugar Refining Co., 267 U.S. 233 (1925), 726
Abbate v. United States, 359 U.S. 187 (1959), 964
Abilene & Southern Ry. Co.; United States v., 265 U.S. 274 (1924), 218, 352–55
Abrams v. United States, 250 U.S. 616 (1919), 46, 115, 360, 630
Adair v. United States, 208 U.S. 161 (1908), 59, 68, 118, 137, 199, 202, 850, 1230–31, 1233, 1239, 1245, 1257, 1260, 1261, 1265–66, 1301, 1302
Adams v. Tanner, 244 U.S. 590 (1917), 291, 330, 849, 1472–73
Adams; United States v., 281 U.S. 202 (1930), 636
Addyston Pipe & Steel Co.; United States v., 85 F. 271 (6th Cir. 1898), aff'd, 175 U.S. 211 (1899), 387, 395, 1122, 1135, 1358–59
Adkins v. Children's Hosp. of the District of Columbia, 261 U.S. 525 (1923), xxx, xl, 56, 58, 87, 100, 119–20, 127–28, 136, 137, 158–59, 255, 391–92, 397, 674–75, 721, 755–66, 770, 792, 796, 800, 823, 828, 834–35, 837, 838, 839, 849, 856, 872, 879, 891, 895, 899, 1014, 1068, 1200, 1201, 1215
Aetna Ins. Co. v. Hyde, 275 U.S. 440 (1928), 81, 896–97, 903
A.G. Spalding & Bros. v. Edwards, 262 U.S. 66 (1923), 639
Agnello v. United States, 269 U.S. 20 (1925), 82, 966–67, 1023, 1058
A.L. Reed Co. v. Whiteman, 144 N.W. 885 (N.Y. 1924), 1279
Alabama v. King & Boozer, 314 U.S. 1 (1941), 1118
Alabama & Vicksburg Ry. Co. v. Jackson & Eastern Ry. Co., 271 U.S. 244 (1926), 1140–41
Alaska S.S. Co. v. McHugh, 268 U.S. 23 (1925), 1176–77
Albrecht v. United States, 273 U.S. 1 (1927), 251, 350–51
Allgeyer v. Louisiana, 165 U.S. 578 (1897), 849, 1193–94, 1202–5
Allis-Chalmers Co. v. Iron Molders' Union No. 125, 150 F. 155 (E.D. Wisc. 1906), 1279, 1280
Ally Bank v. Lenox Fin. Mortg. Corp., 2017 WL 830391 (D. Minn. March 2, 2017), 363–64
Alpha Portland Cement Co. v. Massachusetts, 268 U.S. 203 (1925), 1182, 1188–89
Alston v. United States, 274 U.S. 289 (1927), 1153–54
Ambler Realty Co. v. Village of Euclid, 297 F. 307 (N.D. Ohio 1924), 866, 875
American Column & Lumber Co. v. United States, 257 U.S. 377 (1921), 46, 49–50, 696, 709–10, 711–12, 713–14, 715
American Furniture Co. v. International Bhd. of Teamsters, Chauffeurs, Warehousemen and Helpers of America, 268 N.W. 250 (Wisc. 1936), 1428–29
American Linseed Oil Co.; United States v., 262 U.S. 371 (1923), 290, 696–97, 700, 712–14, 715
American Mills Co. v. American Surety Co. of New York, 260 U.S. 360 (1922), 521
American Ry. Express Co. v. Levee, 263 U.S. 19 (1923), 640, 1141–43
American Steel Foundries v. Robertson, 269 U.S. 372 (1926), 1011
American Steel Foundries v. Tri-City Cent. Trades Council, 257 U.S. 184 (1921), 78, 610–12, 633, 1025, 1038, 1225, 1233, 1236–37, 1239–48, 1249, 1250, 1251–53, 1258, 1259, 1260, 1275,

List of Cases

1277, 1278, 1283–84, 1285–86, 1290, 1292–93, 1294, 1295, 1308, 1314, 1315, 1356, 1381, 1399, 1401–2, 1403, 1413, 1415
American Tobacco Co.; FTC v., 264 U.S. 298 (1924), 290–91
American Tobacco Co.; United States v., 221 U.S. 106 (1911), 276–77
Andersen v. Shipowners' Ass'n of the Pac. Coast, 31 F.2d 539 (9th Cir. 1929), cert. denied, 279 U.S. 864 (1929), 1358
Anderson; United States v., 269 U.S. 422 (1926), 160
Anderson v. Shipowners Ass'n of the Pac. Coast, 272 U.S. 359 (1926), 1358
Apex Hosiery Co. v. Leader, 310 U.S. 469 (1940), 395, 1355–56
Arizona Copper Co. v. Hammer, 250 U.S. 400 (1919), 275, 290, 292, 294, 358, 1210, 1265–66
Arizona Employers' Liability Cases, 250 U.S. 400 (1919), 118, 137
Arkansas ex rel. Utley v. St. Louis-San Francisco Ry. Co., 269 U.S. 172 (1925), 160
Arkansas Natural Gas Co. v. Arkansas R.R. Comm'n, 261 U.S. 379 (1923), 1462–63
Arkansas Railroad Comm'n v. Chicago, Rock Island, & Pac. R.R. Co., 274 U.S. 597 (1927), 1139
Arthur v. Oakes, 63 F. 310 (7th Cir. 1894), 1368
Asakura v. Seattle, 265 U.S. 332 (1924), 1486
Atchison; In re, 284 F. 604 (S.D. Fla. 1922), 1397
Atchison, Topeka & Santa Fe Ry. Co. v. Gee, 139 F.582 (S.D. Iowa 1905), 1279
Atchison, Topeka & Santa Fe Ry. Co. v. Matthews, 174 U.S. 96 (1899), 771
Atchison, Topeka & Santa Fe Ry. Co. v. United States, 279 U.S. 768 (1929), 352–55
Atchison, Topeka & Santa Fe Ry. Co. v. Wells, 265 U.S. 101 (1924), 363–64, 1141–43, 1183–84
Atlantic Coast Line R.R. Co. v. Daughton, 262 U.S. 413 (1923), 289, 352–55
Atlantic Coast Line R.R. Co. v. Davis, 279 U.S. 34 (1929), 521–22
Atlantic Coast Line R.R. Co. v. Driggers, 279 U.S. 787 (1929), 521–22
Atlantic Coast Line R.R. Co. v. Southwell, 275 U.S. 64 (1927), 362–63, 521–22, 639
Atlantic Coast Line R.R. Co. v. Standard Oil Co., 275 U.S. 257 (1927), 1145
Atz v. Andrews, 84 Fla. 43 (1922), 1075
Austin v. Tennessee, 179 U.S. 343 (1900), 1184
A.W. Duckett & Co. v. United States, 266 U.S. 149 (1924), 208–9

Bailey v. Alabama, 219 U.S. 219 (1911), 1472–73
Bailey v. Drexel Furniture Co., 259 U.S. 20 (1922), 49–50, 78, 397, 671–72, 673, 970, 975, 979, 992, 1103–4, 1107, 1126–28, 1129, 1130–31, 1132, 1134, 1145, 1146–47, 1153, 1154, 1156, 1198, 1203, 1225, 1308, 1313–14, 1339, 1340, 1341, 1345–46, 1351, 1354, 1409, 1415
Bakelite Corp.; Ex parte, 279 U.S. 438 (1929), 258
Baldridge. See Louis K. Liggett Co. v. Baldridge
Balint; United States v., 258 U.S. 250 (1922), 1086–87
Baltic Mining Co. v. Massachusetts, 231 U.S. 68 (1913), 1188–89
Baltimore & Ohio R.R. Co. v. Goodman, 275 U.S. 66 (1927), 173, 206, 207
Baltimore & Ohio R.R. Co. v. Groeger, 266 U.S. 521 (1924), 521–22
Baltimore & Ohio R.R. Co. v. Parkersburg, 268 U.S. 35 (1925), 352–55
Baltimore & Ohio R.R. Co. v. United States, 264 U.S. 258 (1924), 247–48
Baltimore & Ohio Southwestern R.R. Co. v. Burtch, 263 U.S. 540 (1924), 1156–57
Baltimore & Ohio Southwestern R.R. Co. v. Settle, 260 U.S. 166 (1922), 352–55
Balzac v. Porto Rico, 258 U.S. 298 (1922), 97
Bank of America v. Whitney Cent. Nat'l Bank, 261 U.S. 171 (1923), 352–55
Banton v. Belt Line Ry. Corp., 268 U.S. 413 (1925), 81, 896–97
Barber Asphalt Paving Co. v. Standard Asphalt & Rubber Co., 275 U.S. 372 (1928), 258
Barbier v. Connolly, 113 U.S. 27 (1884), 1296, 1404, 1419
Barnette v. Wells Fargo Nevada Nat'l Bank, 270 U.S. 438 (1926), 249–50
Bartkus v. Illinois, 359 U.S. 121 (1959), 964
Bartles v. Iowa, 262 U.S. 404 (1923), 368, 848, 852, 866
Bartles; State v., 181 N.W. 508 (Iowa 1921), 848–49
Bateman; United States v., 278 F. 231 (S.D. Cal. 1922), 1046, 1049, 1053–54
Bedford Cut Stone Co. v. Journeyman Stone Cutters' Ass'n, 9 F.2d 40 (7th Cir. 1925), 1362
Bedford Cut Stone Co. v. Journeyman Stone Cutters' Ass'n, 274 U.S. 37 (1927), 87, 100, 350–51, 787–88, 1324–35, 1355, 1362, 1364–66, 1369–70, 1371, 1381, 1386, 1415, 1505–6
Beech-Nut Packing Co. v. P. Lorillard Co., 273 U.S. 629 (1927), 114, 153, 200–1

List of Cases

Beech-Nut Packing Co.; FTC v., 257 U.S. 441 (1922), 643, 844
Benedict v. Ratner, 268 U.S. 353 (1925), 251
Berger v. United States, 255 U.S. 22 (1921), 854
Berkeness; United States v., 275 U.S. 149 (1927), 966–67
Berwind-White Coal Mining Co.; United States v., 274 U.S. 564 (1927), 291, 352–55, 363
Bethel v. New York City Transit Auth., 92 N.Y.2d 348 (1998), 200
Bhagat Singh Thind; United States v., 261 U.S. 204 (1923), 1226, 1452, 1453–55, 1456, 1457, 1458, 1459, 1467, 1486
Biddle v. Perovich, 274 U.S. 480 (1927), 248–49
Bilokumsky; United States ex rel. v. Tod, 263 U.S. 149 (1923), 352–55
Binderup v. Pathe Exch., Inc., 263 U.S. 291 (1923), 1180
Black & White Taxicab & Transfer Co. v. Brown & Yellow Taxicab & Transfer Co., 276 U.S. 518 (1928), 1199–200, 1211–15
Blake v. McClung, 172 U.S. 239 (1898), 1431, 1463
Block v. Hirsh, 256 U.S. 135 (1921), 137, 358, 723–24, 728–29, 793, 797, 805, 814
Blodgett v. Holden, 275 U.S. 142 (1927), 100
Bluefield Water Works and Improvement Co. v. Public Serv. Comm'n of West Virginia, 262 U.S. 679 (1923), 81, 884, 888, 890, 896–97, 902, 912
Board of Pub. Util. Comm'rs v. New York Tel. Co., 271 U.S. 23 (1926), 81, 896–97
Board of Trade of City of Chicago v. Olsen, 262 U.S. 1 (1923), 58, 397, 1129, 1132, 1133, 1151–52, 1164, 1166, 1180
Board of Trustees of Univ. of Alabama v. Garrett, 531 U.S. 356 (2001), 748–49
Booth & Bro. v. Burgess, 72 N. J. Eq. 181 (Ch. Div. 1906), 1329, 1364
Borderland Coal Corp. v. International Org. of Mine Workers of America, 275 F. 871 (D. Ind. 1921), rev'd sub nom. *Gasaway v. Borderland Coal Corp.*, 278 F. 56 (7th Cir. 1921), 1290, 1354
Bossert v. Dhuy, 221 N.Y. 342 (1917), 1364
Boston v. Jackson, 260 U.S. 309 (1922), 396
Bothwell v. Buckbee, Mears Co., 275 U.S. 274 (1927), 1204–5
Bountiful Brick Co. v. Giles, 276 U.S. 154 (1928), 53
Bowen v. City of Atlanta, 159 Ga. 145 (1924), 875–76
Bowman v. Chicago & Northwestern Ry. Co., 125 U.S. 465 (1888), 1175–76
Bowsher v. Synar, 478 U.S. 714 (1986), 443
Boyd v. United States, 286 F. 930 (4th Cir. 1923), 1053–54
Boy Scouts of America v. Dale, 530 U.S. 640 (2000), 749–50
Brace Bros. v. Evans, 5 Pa. Co. 163 (Pa. Ct. Common Pleas 1888), 1359–60
Brasfield v. United States, 272 U.S. 448 (1926), 639
Brenner v. Manson, 383 U.S. 519 (1966), 528
Brewster v. Lanyon Zinc Co., 140 F. 801 (8th Cir. 1905), 239
Briggs v. Elliott, 132 F. Supp. 776 (E.D.S.C. 1955), 1492
Brims; United States v., 272 U.S. 549 (1926), 1364–65
Brimstone R.R. & Canal Co. v. United States, 276 U.S. 104 (1928), 896–97
Broadrick v. Oklahoma, 413 U.S. 601 (1973), 1422
Bromley v. McCaughn, 280 U.S. 124 (1929), 58, 254, 752
Brooks v. United States, 267 U.S. 432 (1925), xl, 1132–34, 1157–58, 1159
Brooks-Scanlon Corp. v. United States, 265 U.S. 106 (1924), 728
Brown v. Allen, 344 U.S. 443 (1953), 668
Brown v. Board of Educ., 347 U.S. 483 (1954), 651, 653, 668, 1433, 1434
Brown Holding Co. v. Feldman, 256 U.S. 170 (1921), 137
Brush Elec. Co. v. City of Galveston, 262 U.S. 443 (1923), 896–97
Buchanan v. Warley, 245 U.S. 60 (1918), 875, 876–77, 1226, 1440, 1472, 1491
Buck v. Bell, 274 U.S. 200 (1927), 82, 203–4, 1403–4, 1419
Buck v. Kuykendall, 267 U.S. 307 (1925), 1186, 1187, 1190–91
Buckley; State v., 258 P. 1030 (Wash. 1927), 1090–91
Budd v. New York, 143 U.S. 517 (1892), 817–18
Bunch v. Cole, 253 U.S. 250 (1923), 242
Bunting v. Oregon, 243 U.S. 426 (1917), 118, 137, 759, 765–66, 772–73
Burdeau v. McDowell, 256 U.S. 465 (1921), 962–63, 1087–88
Burnet v. Coronado Oil & Gas Co., 285 U.S. 393 (1932), 199, 787–88

xlv

LIST OF CASES

Burnham v. Dowd, 217 Mass. 351 (1914), 1329, 1364
Burns v. United States, 274 U.S. 328 (1927), 81
Burns Baking Co. v. Bryan, 264 U.S. 504 (1924), 81, 246–47, 767
Butchers' Union Co. v. Crescent City Co., 111 U. S. 746 (1884), 849
Butler v. Perry, 240 U.S. 328 (1916), 291, 861
Byars v. United States, 273 U.S. 28 (1927), 966–67, 1023, 1047–49

California v. Thompson, 313 U.S. 109 (1941), 1190
California Co-Operative Canneries; United States v., 279 U.S. 553 (1929), 251, 352–55
Cambridge Loan & Bldg. Co.; United States v., 278 U.S. 55 (1928), 640
Caminetti v. United States, 242 U.S. 470 (1917), 1159
Candelaria; United States v., 271 U.S. 432 (1926), 239
Cantwell v. Connecticut, 310 U.S. 296 (1940), 860
Carolene Products Co., United States v., 304 U.S. 144 (1938), 127, 151, 1068, 1086, 1226, 1433, 1434, 1450, 1460, 1461, 1493
Carroll v. United States, 267 U.S. 132 (1925), 58, 136, 293, 390, 396, 946, 962, 966–67, 1026–30, 1047–52, 1053, 1054–58, 1059–60, 1066, 1071, 1507
Carson Petroleum Co. v. Vial, 279 U.S. 95 (1929), 386, 1179
Carter v. Carter Coal Co., 298 U.S. 238 (1936), 1154–55
Carter v. Virginia, 96 Va. 791 (1899), 1397
Carver; United States v., 260 U.S. 482 (1923), 493–94
Case; People v., 190 N.W. 289 (Mich. 1922), 1049
Casey v. United States, 276 U.S. 413 (1928), 178–79, 221–23
Cedar Rapids Gas Light Co. v. Cedar Rapids, 223 U.S. 655 (1912), 896, 912
Cement Mfrs. Protective Ass'n v. United States, 268 U.S. 588 (1925), 713, 715
Central R.R. Co. v. United States, 257 U.S. 247 (1921), 98, 352–55
Central Union Tel. Co. v. Edwardsville, 269 U.S. 190 (1925), 1210
Chambers v. Baltimore & Ohio R.R. Co., 207 U.S. 142 (1907), 609
Champion v. Ames, 188 U.S. 321 (1903), 137
Champlain Realty Co. v. Brattleboro, 260 U.S. 366 (1922), 1179
Chandler v. Florida, 449 U.S. 560 (1981), 749–50
Chandler v. Neff, 298 F. 515 (W.D. Tex. 1924), 1467
Charles Wolff Packing Co. v. Kansas Ct. of Indus. Relations, 262 U.S. 522 (1923), 56, 793–99, 800, 805–6, 810, 811, 812–13, 814–15, 825, 827, 828, 834, 837, 845–46, 849, 1155, 1250–51, 1299
Charles Wolff Packing Co. v. Kansas Ct. of Indus. Relations, 267 U.S. 552 (1925), 813
Chase Nat'l Bank of the City of New York v. United States, 278 U.S. 327 (1929), 58, 249–50
Chastleton Corp. v. Sinclair, 264 U.S. 543 (1924), 723–25, 728, 730–31, 732, 734, 735, 737
Chemical Foundation, Inc.; United States v., 272 U.S. 1 (1926), 383–84
Chesapeake & Ohio Ry. Co. v. Leitch, 276 U.S. 429 (1928), 521–22
Chesapeake & Ohio Ry. Co. v. Mihas, 280 U.S. 102 (1929), 521–22
Chesapeake & Ohio Ry. Co. v. Nixon, 271 U.S. 218 (1926), 362–63, 521–22
Chesapeake & Ohio Ry. Co. v. Stapleton, 279 U.S. 587 (1929), 1141–43, 1147–48, 1158
Chicago, Burlington & Quincy R.R. Co. v. Iowa, 94 U.S. 155 (1876), 895
Chicago, Burlington & Quincy R.R. Co. v. McGuire, 219 U. S. 549 (1911), 849
Chicago, Burlington & Quincy R.R. Co. v. Osborne, 265 U.S. 14 (1924), 362–63
Chicago, Indianapolis & Louisville Ry. Co. v. United States, 270 U.S. 287 (1926), 352–55
Chicago, Milwaukee & St. Paul Ry. Co. v. Coogan, 271 U.S. 472 (1926), 521–22, 1141–43
Chicago, Milwaukee & St. Paul Ry. Co. v. Pub. Utils. Comm'n, 274 U.S. 344 (1927), 1139
Chicago, Milwaukee & St. Paul Ry. Co. v. Risty, 276 U.S. 567 (1928), 249–50, 254
Chicago, Rock Island & Peoria Ry. Co. v. Perry, 259 U.S. 548 (1922), 1462–63
Chicago & Northwestern Ry. Co. v. Alvin R. Durham Co., 271 U.S. 251 (1924), 1141–43
Chicago & Northwestern Ry. Co. v. Nye Schneider Fowler Co., 260 U.S. 35 (1922), 639
Chicago Great Western R.R. Co. v. Schendel, 267 U.S. 287 (1925), 521–22
Child Labor Tax Case. See Bailey v. Drexel Furniture Co.
Children's Hosp. of the District of Columbia v. Adkins, 284 F. 613 (App. D.C. 1921), aff'd, 261 U.S. 525 (1923), xxxix, 777–78, 846–47
Citizens Nat'l Bank v. Durr, 257 U.S. 99 (1921), 1183
Claire Furniture Co.; FTC v., 274 U.S. 160 (1927), 290–91, 610–12, 633

LIST OF CASES

Clark v. Poor, 274 U.S. 554 (1927), 352–55, 1185
Clark Distilling Co. v. Western Maryland Ry. Co., 242 U.S. 311 (1917), 1178, 1204
Cleveland, Cincinnati, Chicago & St. Louis Ry. Co. v. United States, 275 U.S. 404 (1927), 352–55
Cockrill v. California, 268 U.S. 258 (1925), 1486
Cohen Grocery Co.; United States v., 255 U.S. 81 (1921), 726, 805
Cohn & Roth Elec. Co. v. Bricklayers, 92 Conn. 161 (1917), 1364
Colgate v. United States, 280 U.S. 43 (1929), 396
Collector v. Day, 78 U.S. 113 (1870), 1111, 1116
Collins v. Loisel, 259 U.S. 309 (1922), 97
Colorado v. United States, 271 U.S. 153 (1926), 319–20, 366–67, 1140
Commercial Credit Co. v. United States, 276 U.S. 226 (1928), 966–67
Commissioner v. Coronado Oil & Gas Co., 285 U.S. 393 (1932), 644–45
Commonwealth v. See name of defendant
Compañia General de Tabacos de Filipinas v. Collector of Internal Revenue, 275 U.S. 87 (1927), 396, 1194, 1202–4
Connecticut v. Glidden, 55 Conn. 46 (1887), 1359–60
Connelly v. Union Sewer Pipe Co., 184 U.S. 540 (1902), 1406, 1421
Connolly v. General Constr. Co., 269 U.S. 385 (1926), 154, 774, 845–46
Connolly v. Union Sewer Pipe Co., 184 U.S. 540 (1902), 771
Continental Ins. Co. v. United States, 259 U.S. 156 (1922), 639
Cook; People v., 188 N.Y.S. 291 (N.Y. App. Div. 1921), 960–61
Cooley v. Board of Wardens, 53 U.S. 299 (1851), 1169–70, 1185
Coppage v. Kansas, 236 U.S. 1 (1915), 59, 68, 85, 96, 118, 137, 769–70, 846, 1231–33, 1234, 1236, 1239, 1245, 1257, 1258, 1260, 1261, 1265–66, 1285, 1401
Corneli v. Moore, 257 U.S. 491 (1922), 946, 966–67
Corona Cord Tire Co. v. Donovan Chemical Corp., 276 U.S. 358 (1928), 434
Coronado Coal Co. v. United Mine Workers of America, 268 U.S. 295 (1925) (*Coronado II*), 1315–17, 1319, 1330, 1332, 1355–56, 1358
Coronado I. See United Mine Workers of America v. Coronado Coal Co.
Corrigan v. Buckley, 271 U.S. 323 (1926), 877, 1418
Craig v. Hecht, 263 U.S. 255 (1923), 10
Crowe; State v., 130 Ark. 272 (1917), 767
Crump v. Virginia, 84 Va. 927 (1888), 1359–60
Cudahy Packing Co. v. Hinkle, 278 U.S. 460 (1929), 639, 1182, 1188–89
Cudahy Packing Co. v. Parramore, 263 U.S. 418 (1923), 53, 255, 273–74, 294, 776–77, 779
Cumming v. Richmond County Bd. of Educ., 175 U.S. 528 (1899), 1438, 1471
Cunard Steamship Co. v. Mellon, 262 U.S. 100 (1923), 58, 946, 966–67
Curran; State v., 220 Ala. 4 (1929), 747–48
Curtis Publishing Co.; FTC v., 260 U.S. 568 (1923), 10, 290–91, 396, 641, 844–45

Dagenhart. See Hammer v. Dagenhart
Dahnke-Walker Milling Co. v. Bondurant, 257 U.S. 282 (1921), 224, 257–58, 1168, 1182
Darby; United States v., 312 U.S. 100 (1941), 986, 989
Daugherty; United States v., 269 U.S. 360 (1926), 282, 1153
Davis v. Corona Coal Co., 265 U.S. 219 (1924), 1210
Davis v. Farmers' Co-Operative Equity Co., 262 U.S. 312 (1923), 363–64, 1141–43, 1183–84
Davis v. George B. Newton Coal Co., 267 U.S. 292 (1925), 727, 728
Davis v. L.N. Dantzler Lumber Co., 261 U.S. 280 (1923), 1143
Davis v. Wechsler, 263 U.S. 22 (1923), 1141–43
Davis v. Williford, 271 U.S. 484 (1926), 250–51
Day-Brite Lighting, Inc. v. Missouri, 342 U.S. 421 (1952), 748–49
Dayton-Goose Creek Ry. Co. v. United States, 263 U.S. 456 (1924), 390–91, 397, 693–94, 896, 899–900, 902, 903, 1139, 1143
Debs; In re, 158 U.S. 564 (1895), 1241, 1265, 1280, 1376–77, 1379, 1387
Debs; United States v., 64 F. 724 (Cir. Ct. N.D. Ill. 1894), 1387
Delaware, Lackawanna & Western R.R. Co. v. Koske, 279 U.S. 7 (1929), 521–22
Delaware, Lackawanna & Western R.R. Co. v. Morristown, 276 U.S. 182 (1928), 81
Department of Transportation v. Association of American Railroads, 575 U.S. 43 (2015), 706

xlvii

LIST OF CASES

Desist v. United States, 394 U.S. 244 (1969), 748–49
Des Moines Gas Co. v. Des Moines, 238 U.S. 153 (1915), 896
Diaz v. Gonzalez y Lugo, 261 U.S. 102 (1923), 640
Die Deutsche Bank Filiale Nurnberg v. Humphrey, 272 U.S. 517 (1926), 200–1
Di Re; United States v., 332 U.S. 581 (1927), 1057
Direction Der Disconto-Gesellschaft v. United States Steel Corp., 267 U.S. 22 (1925), 200–1
Director General of Railroads v. Kastenbaum, 263 U.S. 25 (1923), 197–98
Di Santo v. Pennsylvania, 273 U.S. 34 (1927), 156–57, 644–45, 1172, 1182, 1189–91
Dodge v. United States, 272 U.S. 530 (1926), 966–67
Donham v. West-Nelson Co., 273 U.S. 657 (1927), 787–88
Donnelley v. United States, 276 U.S. 505 (1928), 82, 1072–74
Dorchy v. Kansas, 264 U.S. 286 (1924), 805–6, 811–12
Dorchy v. Kansas, 272 U.S. 306 (1926), 805–6, 811–12, 1038, 1248, 1288
Doremus; United States v., 249 U.S. 86 (1919), 59–60, 69, 282
Douglas v. New York, New Haven & Hartford R.R. Co., 279 U.S. 377 (1929), 257–58
Douglas v. Noble, 261 U.S. 165 (1923), 352–55
Downes v. Bidwell, 182 U.S. 244 (1901), 112
Doyle v. Continental Ins. Co., 94 U.S. 535 (1876), 1206
Dred Scott v. Sandford, 60 U.S. 393 (1856), 227, 789, 915–16, 1070–71, 1385, 1422
Druggan v. Anderson, 269 U.S. 36 (1925), 966–67
Dugan v. Ohio, 277 U.S. 61 (1928), 966–67, 1042
Dumbra v. United States, 268 U.S. 435 (1925), 159, 966–67, 1047–49
Duplex Printing Press Co. v. Deering, 254 U.S. 443 (1921), 3, 16, 85, 96, 1242, 1262, 1280, 1283, 1324, 1326, 1327, 1329, 1330, 1331, 1361, 1364, 1366, 1367–68, 1373, 1378, 1400–1
Dysart v. United States, 272 U.S. 655 (1926), 290

Eastman Kodak Co.; FTC v., 274 U.S. 619 (1927), 290–91
E.C. Knight Co.; United States v., 156 U.S. 1 (1895), 395, 1121–22, 1125–26, 1135, 1175–76, 1338, 1357
Edgar A. Levy Leasing Co. v. Siegel, 258 U.S. 242 (1922), 728–29
Educational Film Corp. of America v. Ward, 282 U.S. 379 (1931), 1119
Edward Hines Yellow Pine Trs. v. Martin, 268 U.S. 458 (1925), 1209
Edwards v. Douglas, 269 U.S. 204 (1925), 58, 352–55
Elkins v. United States, 364 U.S. 206 (1960), 962, 1047–49
Emmons Coal Mining Co. v. Norfolk & Western Ry. Co., 272 U.S. 709 (1927), 114
Empire Trust Co. v. Cahan, 274 U.S. 473 (1927), 1211
Employers' Liability Cases, 207 U.S. 463 (1908), 1156–57
Equitable Trust Co. v. First National Bank, 275 U.S. 359 (1927), 114
Erie R.R. Co. v. Tompkins, 304 U.S. 64 (1938), 497–98, 1102, 1199, 1201, 1209–10, 1211, 1216
Euclid. See Village of Euclid v. Ambler Realty Co.
Eureka Pipe Line Co. v. Hallanan, 257 U.S. 265 (1921), 1180
Evans v. Gore, 253 U.S. 245 (1920), 287, 643–44, 670
Everson v. Board of Educ., 330 U.S. 1 (1947), 860
Ewig v. California, 538 U.S. 11 (2003), 748–49
Excess Income of St. Louis & O'Fallon Ry. Co., 124 I.C.C. Reports 3 (Feb. 15, 1927), 905, 906
Exchange Bakery & Restaurant v. Rifkin, 245 N.Y. 260 (1927), 1286
Exxon Corp. v. Governor of Maryland, 437 U.S. 117 (1978), 748–49

Fairchild v. Hughes, 258 U.S. 126 (1922), 97
Fairmont Creamery Co. v. Minnesota, 274 U.S. 1 (1927), 291, 767, 822–23, 825, 844, 845, 973, 1068
Farmers' Loan & Trust Co. v. Minnesota, 280 U.S. 204 (1930), 200–1
Farmers' Loan & Trust Co. v. Northern Pac. R.R. Co., 60 F. 803 (7th Cir. 1894), 1289
Farrington v. Tokushige, 273 U.S. 284 (1927), 851
Fasulo v. United States, 272 U.S. 620 (1926), 82
Federal Baseball Club of Baltimore v. National League of Prof'l Baseball Clubs, 259 U.S. 200 (1922), 362–63, 641, 1156
Fenner v. Boykin, 271 U.S. 240 (1926), 1210

List of Cases

Fenske Bros., Inc. v. Upholsterers' Int'l Union, 358 Ill. 239 (1934), 1428–29
Fenton; United States v., 268 F. 221 (D. Mont. 1920), 1053–54
Ferguson v. Skrupa, 372 U.S. 726 (1963), 748–49
Ferry v. Ramsey, 277 U.S. 88 (1928), 200–1
Fidelity & Deposit Co. v. Tafoya, 270 U.S. 426 (1926), 254, 287–88, 1182, 1194–95, 1204
Fidelity & Deposit Co. v. United States, 259 U.S. 296 (1922), 97, 120, 138, 352–55
Fidelity National Bank & Trust Co. v. Swope, 274 U.S. 123 (1927), 673–74, 675
Finegan; Ex parte, 270 F. 665 (N.D.N.Y. 1921), 960–61
Finley v. United Mine Workers of America, 300 F. 972 (8th Cir. 1924), 1355
First Evangelical Lutheran Church v. County of Los Angeles, 482 U.S. 304 (1987), 866
First Nat'l Bank v. Missouri, 263 U.S. 640 (1924), 255
First Nat'l Bank of Aiken v. J.L. Mott Iron Works, 258 U.S. 240 (1922), 641
Flannery; United States v., 268 U.S. 98 (1925), 58
Flint v. Stone Tracy Co., 220 U.S. 107 (1911), 1113, 1119, 1188–89, 1432, 1464
Forbes Pioneer Boat Line v. Board of Comm'rs of Everglades Drainage Dist., 258 U.S. 338 (1922), xxxix, 200–1
Ford v. United States, 273 U.S. 593 (1927), 253, 966–67
Foster-Fountain Packing Co. v. Haydel, 278 U.S. 1 (1928), 1180, 1187
Fox Film Corp. v. Doyal, 286 U.S. 123 (1932), 1119
Fox River Paper Co. v. Railroad Comm'n, 274 U.S. 651 (1927), 640
France v. French Overseas Corp., 277 U.S. 323 (1928), 638
Frank v. Magnum, 237 U.S. 309 (1915), 1025, 1039–41
Free Enterprise Fund v. Public Company Accounting Oversight Bd., 561 U.S. 477 (2010), 419
Frick v. Webb, 263 U.S. 326 (1923), 1486
Friedlander v. Texas & Pac. R.R. Co., 130 U.S. 416 (1889), 997, 1012–13
Frost v. Corporation Comm'n, 278 U.S. 515 (1929), 255
Frost & Frost Trucking Co. v. Railroad Comm'n, 271 U.S. 583 (1926), 845–46, 1191, 1205, 1206–7
FTC v. See name of defendant
Funk v. United States, 290 U.S. 371 (1933), 1090–91

Gaines v. Washington, 277 U.S. 81 (1928), 486–87
Galveston Elec. Co. v. Galveston, 258 U.S. 388 (1922), 352–55, 896–97
Gambino v. United States, 275 U.S. 310 (1927), 254, 951, 962–63, 966–67
Gamble v. United States, 139 S.Ct. 1960 (2019), 964
Gardner v. Chicago Title & Trust Co., 261 U.S. 453 (1923), 640
General American Tank Car Corp. v. Day, 270 U.S. 367 (1926), 81–82
George M. Bush & Sons Co. v. Maloy, 267 U.S. 317 (1925), 1186
Georgia Ry. & Power Co. v. Decatur, 262 U.S. 432 (1923), 1462–63
Georgia Ry. & Power Co. v. Railroad Comm'n of Georgia, 262 U.S. 625 (1923), 881, 883–84, 896–97, 898, 902, 906
German Alliance Ins. Co. v. Lewis, 233 U.S. 389 (1914), 118, 137, 742, 792–93, 795–96, 799, 804–5, 817–18
Gibbons v. Ogden, 22 U.S. 1 (1824), 1152
Gibbons; State v., 203 P. 390 (Wash. 1922), 1090–91
Gilchrist v. Interborough Rapid Transit Co., 279 U.S. 159 (1929), 896–97
Giles v. Harris, 189 U.S. 475 (1903), 166, 190, 1435, 1467
Gill Engraving Co. v. Doerr, 214 F. 111 (S.D.N.Y. 1914), 1364
Gillespie v. Oklahoma, 257 U.S. 501 (1922), 1111, 1112, 1117–18, 1186
Gitlow v. New York, 268 U.S. 652 (1925), 115, 630, 644, 833, 859, 1038–39
Gleason v. Seaboard Air Line R.R. Co., 278 U.S. 349 (1929), 997, 998, 1012
Glidden Co. v. Zdanok, 370 U.S. 530 (1962), 528
Godcharles v. Wigeman, 113 Pa. 431 (1886), 847
Gold Clause Cases, 272, 292–93, 296
Goldman v. Crowther, 128 A. 50 (Md. 1925), 866
Goltra v. Weeks, 271 U.S. 536 (1926), 270–71, 290
Gong Lum v. Rice, 275 U.S. 78 (1927), xxxiv, xl, 127, 152, 877, 1226, 1433, 1437–38, 1444, 1449–51, 1454, 1459, 1470–71, 1482

xlix

LIST OF CASES

Gooch v. Oregon Short Line R.R. Co., 258 U.S. 22 (1922), 633, 1011, 1012, 1083, 1084
Gorham Mfg. Co. v. Wendell, 261 U.S. 1 (1923), 396
Gorieb v. Fox, 274 U.S. 603 (1927), 870
Graham v. Du Pont, 262 U.S. 234 (1923), 1150
Graham v. Richardson, 403 U.S. 365 (1971), 1421
Grant Constr. Co. v. St. Paul Building Trades, 136 Minn. 167 (1917), 1364
Gratz; FTC v., 253 U.S. 421 (1920), 271–72, 291, 844–45
Graves v. New York ex rel. *O'Keefe*, 306 U.S. 466 (1939), 1120
Great Northern R.R. Co. v. Brosseau, 286 F. 414 (D.N.D. 1923), 1294
Great Northern R.R. Co. v. Merchants Elevator Co., 259 U.S. 285 (1922), 352–55
Great Northern R.R. Co. v. Sutherland, 273 U.S. 182 (1927), 352–55
Green v. County Sch. Bd., 391 U.S. 430 (1968), 1492
Greer v. Connecticut, 161 U.S. 519 (1896), 1175
Greer v. United States, 245 U.S. 559 (1918), 1090–91
Greiner v. Lewellyn, 258 U.S. 384 (1922), 97
Griswold v. Connecticut, 381 U.S. 479 (1965), xxxi, xl, 748–49, 928, 947, 1069, 1088
Grogan v. Hiram Walker & Sons, 259 U.S. 80 (1922), 243, 929–30, 966–67, 1015
Grosfield v. United States, 276 U.S. 494 (1928), 946, 966–67
Grossman; Ex parte, 267 U.S. 87 (1925), 396, 1394–95
Grovey v. Townsend, 294 U.S. 45 (1935), 1469
Gulf, Mobile & Northern R.R. Co. v. Wells, 275 U.S. 455 (1927), 521–22
Gulf Refining Co.; United States v., 268 U.S. 542 (1925), 82
Gundy v. United States, 139 S.Ct. 2116 (2019), 706

Hamilton v. Kentucky Distilleries & Warehouse Co., 251 U.S. 146 (1919), 730–31, 929–30, 932, 1014
Hamilton v. Regents of the Univ. of California, 293 U.S. 245 (1934), 77
Hammer v. Dagenhart, 247 U.S. 251 (1918), 59–60, 69, 137, 969–70, 979, 992, 1103, 1106, 1126,
 1130–31, 1133, 1134, 1135, 1145–46, 1152, 1153, 1154, 1157–58, 1159, 1179, 1199, 1307,
 1313–14, 1338, 1339, 1340–41
Hammond v. Schappi Bus Line, 275 U.S. 164 (1927), 645–46
Hanover Fire Ins. Co. v. Harding, 272 U.S. 494 (1926), 1195, 1204–5, 1207
Harkin v. Brundage, 276 U.S. 36 (1928), 253, 1210
Harmon v. Tyler, 273 U.S. 668 (1927), xli, 876–77, 1226, 1440, 1452, 1454, 1458, 1472, 1491
Harrigan v. Bergdoll, 270 U.S. 560 (1926), 1210
Hawes v. Georgia, 258 U.S. 1 (1922), 966–67
Hawkins v. Bleakly, 243 U.S. 210 (1917), 96
Heath v. Alabama, 474 U.S. 82 (1985), 964
Hebert v. Louisiana, 272 U.S. 312 (1926), 257–58, 963, 964, 966
Heiner v. Donnan, 285 U.S. 312 (1932), 752
Heiner v. Tindle, 276 U.S. 582 (1928), 639
Heisler v. Thomas Collier Co., 260 U.S. 245 (1922), 1163–64, 1165–66, 1167, 1170, 1174,
 1178–80, 1186, 1192, 1356
Heller v. Doe, 509 U.S. 312 (1993), 748–49
Helson v. Kentucky, 279 U.S. 245 (1929), 1171, 1188, 1189
Helvering v Gerhardt, 304 U.S. 405 (1938), 1120
Henderson Water Co. v. Corporation Comm'n, 269 U.S. 278 (1925), 1140
Herbert v. Louisiana, 272 U.S. 312 (1926), 1215
Herkert. See United Leather Workers' Int'l Union v. Herkert & Meisel Trunk Co.
Hester v. United States, 265 U.S. 57 (1924), 966–67, 1062, 1067, 1075–76, 1085, 1086
Heyer v. Duplicator Mfg. Co., 263 U.S. 100 (1923), 218
Hicks v. Poe, 269 U.S. 118 (1925), 352–55
Highland v. Russell Car & Snow Plow Co., 279 U.S. 253 (1929), 247, 720–23, 726–27, 728
Hill v. Wallace, 259 U.S. 44 (1922), 610–12, 633, 1128–29, 1146–47, 1149–51, 1153
Hilsinger; United States v., 284 F. 585 (S.D. Ohio 1922), 1053–54
Hipolite Egg Co. v. United States, 220 U.S. 45 (1911), 137, 1159
Hitchman Coal and Coke Co. v. Mitchell, 245 U.S. 229 (1917), 85, 96, 1217–18, 1228, 1233–34,
 1239, 1242, 1246–47, 1257, 1258, 1260, 1266, 1268, 1283, 1286, 1287, 1315, 1378, 1401,
 1491–92

1

List of Cases

Hodel v. Indiana, 452 U.S. 314 (1981), 748–49
Hoffman v. Missouri ex rel. *Foraker*, 274 U.S. 21 (1927), 363–64, 1141–43, 1183–84
Hoke & Economides v. United States, 227 U.S. 308 (1913), 137, 1134, 1159, 1216
Holden v. Hardy, 169 U.S. 366 (1898), 40, 52, 770, 771, 782, 1232, 1266, 1404, 1419, 1472–73
Holsum Baking Co. v. Green, 45 F.2d 238 (N.D. Ohio 1930), 747–48
Hooper v. California, 155 U.S. 648 (1895), 1202
Hopkins v. Oxley Stave Co., 83 F. 912 (8th Cir. 1897), 1361, 1372
Hopkins; State ex rel. *v. Howat*, 198 P. 686 (Kan. 1921), 805–6, 808, 810, 816
Houston, East & West Texas Ry. Co. v. United States, 234 U.S. 342 (1914), 1136
Howat v. Kansas, 258 U.S. 181 (1922), 805–6, 816
Hubbard; United States v., 266 U.S. 474 (1925), 352–55, 366, 1186
Hudson v. Parker, 156 U.S. 277 (1895), 468
Hudson v. United States, 272 U.S. 451 (1926), 153
Hudson County Water Co. v. McCarter, 209 U.S. 349 (1908), 1175
Hughes v. State, 278 F. 231 (S.D. Cal. 1922), 1053–54
Hughes; United States ex rel. *v. Gault*, 271 U.S. 142 (1926), 223
Hughes Bros. Timber Co. v. Minnesota, 272 U.S. 469 (1926), 1179
Humes v. United States, 276 U.S. 487 (1928), 352–55
Humphrey's Executor v. United States, 295 U.S. 602 (1935), 416, 430, 444
Hunt; Commonwealth v., 45 Mass. 111 (1842), 1242, 1262
Hurtado v. California, 110 U.S. 516 (1884), 53
Hygrade Provision Co. v. Sherman, 266 U.S. 497 (1925), 1187

ICC v. United States ex rel. *Los Angeles*, 280 U.S. 52 (1929), 396
Illinois Cent. R.R. Co.; United States v., 263 U.S. 515 (1924), 640, 844, 1140–41
Indiana v. Bailey, 61 N.E. 730 (Ind. 1901), 850–51
Indian Territory Illuminating Oil Co. v. Oklahoma, 240 U.S. 522 (1916), 1117
Industrial Accident Comm'n v. Davis, 259 U.S. 182 (1922), 1156–57
Industrial Ass'n of San Francisco v. United States, 268 U.S. 64 (1925), 1135, 1187, 1318–19, 1332, 1356–58, 1365, 1370
Ingenohl v. Walter E. Olsen & Co., Inc., 273 U.S. 541 (1927), 200–1, 1213–14
Inman S.S. Co. v. Tinker, 94 U.S. 238 (1876), 1175–76
Interborough Rapid Transit Co. v. Lavin, 247 N.Y. 65 (1928), 1286
International News Serv. v. Associated Press, 248 U.S. 215 (1918), 360
International Ry. Co. v. Davidson, 257 U.S. 506 (1922), 352–55, 641
International Shoe Co. v. FTC, 280 U.S. 291 (1930), 290–91
International Shoe Co. v. Shartel, 279 U.S. 429 (1929), 81–82, 254
International Stevedoring Co. v. Haverty, 272 U.S. 50 (1926), 844, 996–98, 1012
International Textbook Co. v. Pigg, 217 U.S. 91 (1910), 609
Interstate Busses Corp. v. Holyoke St. Ry. Co., 273 U.S. 45 (1927), 1187
Investors' Syndicate v. Porter, 52 F.2d 189 (D. Mont. 1931), rev'd, *Porter v. Investors' Syndicate*, 287 U.S. 346 (1932)., 684–85
Iron Molders' Union No. 125 v. Allis-Chalmers Co., 166 F. 45 (7th Cir. 1908), 1241, 1250–51, 1279, 1286, 1292
Irwin v. Gavit, 268 U.S. 161 (1925), 58
Ives v. South Buffalo Ry. Co., 201 N.Y. 271 (1911), 124, 142, 307

Jackman v. Rosenbaum Co., 260 U.S. 22 (1922), 214–16, 640
Jackson; United States v., 280 U.S. 183 (1930), 396
Jacob Ruppert v. Caffey, 251 U.S. 264 (1920), 929–30, 932, 939–40, 989, 1007
James Everard's Breweries v. Day, 265 U.S. 545 (1924), 966–67, 973–75, 976, 985–87, 988
Jaybird Mining Co. v. Weir, 271 U.S. 609 (1926), 1117
Jay Burns Baking Co. v. Bryan, 264 U.S. 504 (1924), 330, 331, 358, 727, 730, 732–38, 739, 741, 744, 745–46, 747–50, 751, 758, 802, 823, 828, 849, 939–40, 973, 1068
Jin Fuey Moy v. United States, 254 U.S. 189 (1920), 1090–91
John E. Thropp's Sons Co. v. Seiberling, 264 U.S. 320 (1924), 497–98
John P. King Mfg. Co. v. City Council of Augusta, 277 U.S. 100 (1928), 115, 224, 361–62, 491–93
Jonas Glass Co. v. Glass Bottle Blowers Ass'n, 77 N.J. Eq. 219 (1908), 96

List of Cases

Jordan v. Tashio, 278 U.S. 123 (1928), 1464
J.W. Hampton, Jr. & Co. v. United States, 276 U.S. 394 (1928), 397, 401, 419, 436–38, 693, 706

Kansas City Southern Ry. Co. v. Jones, 276 U.S. 303 (1928), 521–22
Karges Furniture Co. v. Amalgamated Woodworkers' Local Union, 75 N.W. 877 (Ind. 1905), 1279
Katz v. United States, 389 U.S. 347 (1967), xxxi, xl, 1068, 1069, 1086
Katz; United States v., 271 U.S. 354 (1926), 249–50, 966–67, 1030–31, 1059
Keith v. Johnson, 271 U.S. 1 (1926), 1209
Keller v. Adams-Campbell Co., 264 U.S. 314 (1924), 497–98
Kendall v. United States, 37 U.S. 524 (1838), 444
Kennedy; United States ex rel. v. Tyler, 269 U.S. 13 (1925), 1210
Kentucky Fin. Corp. v. Paramount Auto Exchange Corp., 262 U.S. 544 (1923), 1431, 1463
Keogh v. Chicago & Nw. Ry. Co., 260 U.S. 156 (1922), 287–88, 352–55, 366
Keokuk & Hamilton Bridge Co. v. Salm, 258 U.S. 122 (1922), 251
Kercheval v. United States, 274 U.S. 220 (1927), 82
Klesner; FTC v., 274 U.S. 145 (1927), 290–91, 396
Kline v. Burke Constr. Co., 260 U.S. 226 (1922), 1207, 1210
Knickerbocker Ice Co. v. Stewart, 253 U.S. 149 (1920), 1014–15, 1176–77
Knights of the Ku Klux Klan v. Strayer, 26 F.2d 727 (W.D. Pa. 1928), 1037–38
Kostka; People v., 4 New York Criminal Reports 429 (1886), 1262

Lacoste v. Department of Conservation, 263 U.S. 545 (1924), 1179
Lafaro; People v., 165 N.E. 518 (N.Y. 1929), 962
Lake Shore & Michigan Southern Ry. Co. v. Ohio ex rel. Lawrence, 173 U.S. 285 (1899), 1186–87
Lambert v. United States, 282 F. 413 (9th Cir. 1922), 1053–54
Lambert v. Yellowley, 272 U.S. 581 (1926), 58, 945–46, 966–67, 974–75, 976, 987–91, 992, 998, 1071
Lanza; United States v., 260 U.S. 377 (1922), 951–53, 963, 964–66, 1071, 1101, 1110, 1116
Lara; United States v., 541 U.S. 193 (2004), 964
Larsen v. Ruce, 100 Wash. 642 (1918), 767
Lawrence v. St. Louis-San Francisco Ry. Co., 274 U.S. 588 (1927), 352–55, 367, 1140
Lawton v. Steele, 152 U.S. 133 (1894), 1472–73
Leach v. Carlile, 258 U.S. 138 (1922), 46
Lee v. Chesapeake & Ohio Ry. Co., 260 U.S. 653 (1923), 1197, 1208–9
Lee; United States v., 274 U.S. 559 (1927), 966–67, 1056–57, 1059–60, 1062, 1075–76, 1078–79
Lehigh Valley R.R. Co. v. Board of Pub. Util. Comm'rs, 278 U.S. 24 (1928), 393, 398, 1139–40
Leisy v. Hardin, 135 U.S. 100 (1890), 1178
Lemke v. Farmers' Grain Co., 258 U.S. 50 (1922), 1174, 1182, 1187, 1191–92
Lewellyn v. Electric Reduction Co., 275 U.S. 243 (1927), 249–50
Liberty Oil Co. v. Condon Nat'l Bank, 260 U.S. 235 (1922), 521, 528
Liberty Warehouse Co. v. Burley Tobacco Growers' Co-Operative Mktg. Ass'n, 276 U.S. 71 (1928), 676, 716, 1405–6, 1421
Liberty Warehouse Co. v. Grannis, 273 U.S. 70 (1927), 657–59, 673–74, 675, 676
Liggett & Myers Tobacco Co. v. United States, 274 U.S. 215 (1927), 726–27
Lincoln v. United States, 197 U.S. 419 (1905), 191–92
Linder v. United States, 268 U.S. 5 (1925), 975–76, 992, 1153
Lindsley v. Natural Carbonic Gas Co., 220 U.S. 61 (1911), 236, 255, 256, 1404, 1406–8, 1409, 1410, 1419, 1430–31, 1457
Lion Bonding & Surety Co. v. Karatz, 262 U.S. 77 (1923), 1210
Lipke v. Lederer, 259 U.S. 557 (1922), 287–88, 1150
Lipoff v. United Food Workers Indus. Union, Local No. 107, 33 Pa. D. & C. 599 (Ct. C.P., Phila. Cnty. 1938), 1428–29
Lochner v. New York, 198 U.S. 45 (1905), 59, 68, 118, 119–20, 137, 298–99, 307, 328–29, 367, 687, 737, 749, 756, 758–59, 765–66, 770, 771–72, 783, 803, 828, 835, 849, 998, 1015, 1414
Loewe v. Lawlor, 208 U.S. 274 (1908), 1361
Logan v. United States, 144 U.S. 263 (1892), 1090–91
London Guarantee & Accident Co. v. Industrial Accident Comm'n of California, 279 U.S. 109 (1929), 386, 1176–77

List of Cases

Lone Wolf v. Hitchcock, 187 U.S. 553 (1903), 227, 239
Long v. Rockwood, 277 U.S. 142 (1928), 1114, 1119
Lopez; United States v., 514 U.S. 549 (1995), 1158
Los Angeles & Salt Lake R.R. Co.; United States v., 273 U.S. 299 (1927), 352–55
Los Angeles Brush Mfg. Co. v. James, 272 U.S. 701 (1927), 468
The Lottery Case, 188 U.S. 321 (1903), 1159
Louis K. Liggett Co. v. Baldridge, 278 U.S. 105 (1928), xxxix, 740–41, 742–43, 753, 755, 758, 767, 849, 973
Louis K. Liggett Co. v. Lee, 288 U.S. 517 (1933), 1464
Louis Pizitz Dry Goods v. Yeldell, 274 U.S. 112 (1927), 659, 676, 844
Louisville & Nashville R.R. Co. v. Barber Asphalt Paving Co., 197 U.S. 430 (1905), 202, 205
Louisville & Nashville R.R. Co. v. Central Iron & Coal Co., 265 U.S. 59 (1924), 640
Louisville & Nashville R.R. Co. v. Sloss-Sheffield Steel & Iron Co., 269 U.S. 217 (1925), 352–55
Louisville & Nashville R.R. Co. v. United States, 258 U.S. 374 (1922), 97, 120, 138
Louisville Gas & Elec. Co. v. Coleman, 277 U.S. 32 (1928), 100, 218
Love v. Griffith, 266 U.S. 32 (1924), 1435, 1467
Lucas v. Alexander, 279 U.S. 573 (1929), 81–82, 155
Lucas v. Forty-Fourth General Assembly of the State of Colorado, 377 U.S. 713 (1964), 749–50
Luckenbach Steamship Co. v. United States, 280 U.S. 173 (1930), 396
Ludey; United States v., 274 U.S. 295 (1927), 640
Lustig v. United States, 338 U.S. 74 (1949), 962

Macallen Co. v. Massachusetts, 279 U.S. 620 (1929), 1113, 1114, 1115, 1118, 1119, 1120, 1188–89
MacKenzie v. A. Engelhard & Sons Co., 266 U.S. 131 (1924), 290
Magnum Import Co. v. Coty, 262 U.S. 159 (1923), 497–98
Mahler v. Eby, 264 U.S. 32 (1924), 397
Ma-King Products Co. v. Blair, 271 U.S. 479 (1926), 966–67
Mammoth Oil Co. v. United States, 275 U.S. 13 (1927), 82
Maple Flooring Mfrs. Ass'n v. United States, 268 U.S. 563 (1925), 697, 700, 701
Marcus Brown Holding Co., Inc. v. Feldman, 256 U.S. 170 (1921), 728
Marion & Rye Valley Ry. Co. v. United States, 270 U.S. 280 (1926), 1143
Marr v. United States, 268 U.S. 536 (1925), 58
Marron v. United States, 275 U.S. 192 (1927), 82, 966–67, 1047–49
Maryland v. Soper, 270 U.S. 9 (1926), 966–67
Mason v. United States, 260 U.S. 545 (1923), 1209
Massachusetts v. Mellon, 262 U.S. 447 (1923), 1123, 1135–36, 1175
Massachusetts State Grange v. Benton, 272 U.S. 525 (1926), 287–88
Matthew Addy Co. v. United States, 264 U.S. 239 (1924), 727
Maul v. United States, 274 U.S. 501 (1927), 361–62, 966–67, 1031, 1057, 1059–60
May v. Henderson, 268 U.S. 108 (1925), 159
Mayor of Vidalia v. McNeely, 274 U.S. 676 (1927), 1186
McCabe v. Atchison, Topeka & Santa Fe R.R. Co., 235 U.S. 151 (1914), 1475
McCardle v. Indianapolis Water Co., 272 U.S. 400 (1926), 81, 884–85, 888, 896–97, 901, 902–4, 906
McCarthy v. Arndstein, 266 U.S. 34 (1924), 361–62
McCaughn v. Ludington, 268 U.S. 106 (1925), 58
McConaughey v. Morrow, 263 U.S. 39 (1923), 396, 401, 419
McConnell v. Pedigo, 18 S.W. 15 (Ky. 1892), 1211–12
McCray v. United States, 195 U.S. 27 (1904), 1126, 1128, 1146
McCulloch v. Maryland, 17 U.S. 316 (1819), 973, 986, 1111, 1116, 1419
McElvain; United States v., 272 U.S. 633 (1926), 82
McGautha v. California, 402 U.S. 183 (1971), 749–50
McGrain v. Daugherty, 273 U.S. 135 (1927), 237, 258, 609
McGuire v. United States, 273 U.S. 95 (1927), 966–67
McKenna v. Anderson, 31 F. 1016 (2d Cir. 1919), cert. denied, 279 U.S. 869 (1929), 157–58
McMillan Contracting Co. v. Abernathy, 263 U.S. 438 (1924), 489–90
Medimmune, Inc. v. Genentech, 549 U.S. 118 (2007), 324–25

liii

List of Cases

Mellon v. Michigan Trust Co., 271 U.S. 236 (1926), 294
Mercantile Trust Co. v. Wilmot Rd. Dist., 275 U.S. 117 (1927), 640
Metcalf v. Mitchell, 269 U.S. 514 (1926), 156, 1114–15, 1119–20, 1171–72
Meyer v. Nebraska, 262 U.S. 390 (1923), xxix, xxxix, 275, 291–92, 320, 367–68, 767, 817, 827–32, 833–34, 835, 845, 848, 849, 850–51, 853–55, 860–61, 891, 1199, 1211, 1472–73
Michaelson v. United States, 266 U.S. 42 (1924), 1381–86, 1393, 1394–95, 1397, 1400
Michigan Cent. R.R. Co. v. Mix, 278 U.S. 492 (1929), 352–55, 1141–43, 1183–84
Michigan Pub. Utils. Comm'n v. Duke, 266 U.S. 570 (1925), 81, 1173–74, 1191
Midland Valley R.R. v. Barkley, 276 U.S. 482 (1928), 366, 1141–43
Milam v. United States, 296 F. 629 (4th Cir. 1924), 1046, 1049, 1053–54
Miles v. Graham, 268 U.S. 501 (1925), 643–44
Milheim v. Moffat Tunnel Improvement Dist., 262 U.S. 710 (1923), 899
Miller v. Board of Pub. Works of the City of Los Angeles, 195 Cal. 477 (1925), 877–78
Miller v. Schoene, 276 U.S. 272 (1928), 249–50
Milwaukee Social Democratic Pub. Co. v. Burleson, 255 U.S. 407 (1921), 46
Minneapolis, St. Paul & Sault Ste. Marie Ry. Co. v. Goneau, 269 U.S. 406 (1926), 521–22
Minneapolis & St. Louis R.R. Co. v. Peoria & Pekin Union Ry. Co., 270 U.S. 580 (1926), 352–55
Minnesota v. Barber, 136 U. S. 313 (1890), 849
The Minnesota Rate Cases, 230 U.S. 352 (1913), 903
Missouri v. Public Serv. Comm'n, 273 U.S. 126 (1927), 673–74
Missouri, Kansas & Texas Ry. Co. v. May, 194 U.S. 267 (1904), 1419
Missouri ex rel. Barrett v. Kansas Natural Gas, 265 U.S. 298 (1924), 1164–66, 1167–68, 1170, 1180, 1187
Missouri ex rel. Burnes Nat'l Bank v. Duncan, 265 U.S. 17 (1924), 58, 1116–17
Missouri ex rel. Missouri Ins. Co. v. Gehner, 281 U.S. 313 (1930), 636
Missouri ex rel. St. Louis, Brownsville & Mexico Ry. Co. v. Taylor, 266 U.S. 200 (1924), 363–64, 645–46, 1141–43, 1183–84
Missouri ex rel. Southwestern Bell Tel. Co. v. Public Serv. Comm'n of Missouri, 262 U.S. 276 (1925), 881, 883–84, 888, 896–97, 898, 900, 901–2
Missouri Pac. R.R. Co. v. Aeby, 275 U.S. 426 (1927), 521–22
Missouri Pac. R.R. Co. v. Boone, 270 U.S. 466 (1926), 352–55, 645–46, 1139–40
Missouri Pac. R.R. Co. v. Porter, 273 U.S. 341 (1927), 844, 1141–43
Missouri Pac. R.R. Co. v. Reynolds Davis Grocery Co., 268 U.S. 366 (1925), 352–55
Mobile v. Bolden, 446 U.S. 55 (1980), 748–49
Mobile v. Kimball, 102 U.S. 691 (1880), 1175–76
Moore v. Dempsey, 261 U.S. 86 (1923), 1025, 1039–41
Moore v. New York Cotton Exch., 270 U.S. 593 (1926), 1156
Moore; In re, 209 U.S. 490 (1908), 1208
Moores & Co. v. Bricklayers' Union, 10 Ohio Dec. Reprint 665 (Cincinnati Supr. Ct. 1889), aff'd, 51 Ohio St. 605 (1889), 1244, 1284–85, 1305, 1320–22, 1323, 1326, 1329, 1359, 1363–64
Moragne v. State Marine Lines, Inc., 398 U.S. 375 (1970), 1011
Morehead v. New York ex rel. Tipaldo, 298 U.S. 587 (1936), xxxix, 159, 667, 787–88, 821
Moreland; United States v., 258 U.S. 433 (1922), 135–36, 388–90, 392, 396, 630, 646
Morris v. Duby, 274 U.S. 135 (1927), 1185
Morrisdale Coal Co. v. United States, 259 U.S. 188 (1922), 118, 135, 726–27
Morrison v. California, 291 U.S. 82 (1934), 1485
Morrison v. Olson, 487 U.S. 654 (1988), 444
Morrison v. Work, 266 U.S. 481 (1925), 247–48, 352–55
Morse Dry Dock & Repair Co. v. The Northern Star, 271 U.S. 552 (1926), 270, 271, 290
Mountain Timber Co. v. Washington, 243 U.S. 219 (1917), 96, 137
Mugler v. Kansas, 123 U.S. 623 (1887), 1014
Muller v. Oregon, 208 U.S. 412 (1908), 298–300, 301, 328, 329, 363–64, 736, 748, 764, 766, 770–71, 792
Municipal Suffrage to Women; In re, 160 Mass. 586 (1894), 202
Munn v. Illinois, 94 U.S. 113 (1876), 732–33, 742, 792, 795–96, 804, 814, 895
Munn v. People, 69 Ill. 80 (1873), 742
Murphy v. Sardell, 269 U.S. 530 (1925), 153–54, 643–44, 787–88
Murphy v. United States, 272 U.S. 630 (1926), 966–67

List of Cases

Murray; United States v., 275 U.S. 347 (1928), 396
Myers v. United States, 58 Ct. Cl. 199 (1923), 420, 1134
Myers v. United States, 264 U.S. 95 (1924), 1397
Myers v. United States, 272 U.S. 52 (1926), xxxv, xli, 293, 350–52, 396, 401–18, 440–47, 451, 452, 657, 1507

Napier v. Atlantic Coast Line R.R. Co., 272 U.S. 605 (1926), 352–55, 366, 640, 1141–43
Nardone v. United States, 302 U.S. 379 (1937), 1084, 1085
Nashville, Chattanooga & St. Louis Ry. Co. v. Tennessee, 262 U.S. 318 (1923), 641, 1139
Nashville, Chattanooga & St. Louis Ry. Co. v. Wallace, 288 U.S. 249 (1933), 324–25
Nashville, Chattanooga & St. Louis Ry. Co. v. White, 278 U.S. 456 (1929), 207, 254, 638–39
National Ass'n of Window Glass Mfrs. v. United States, 263 U.S. 403 (1923), 633
National Federation of Indep. Business v. Sebelius, 567 U.S. 519 (2012), xl
National Life Ins. Co. v. United States, 277 U.S. 508 (1928), 1118
National Prohibition Cases, 253 U.S. 350 (1920), 939–40, 958–59, 970, 971–72, 977, 979–80, 985, 1007
National Woodwork Mfrs. Ass'n v. NLRB, 386 U.S. 612 (1967), 1365
Near v. Minnesota, 283 U.S. 697 (1931), 849
Nebbia v. New York, 291 U.S. 502 (1934), 275, 798–99, 817
Nebraska Dist. Of Evangelical Lutheran Synod of Missouri v. McKelvie, 187 N.W. 927 (Neb. 1922), 849
Nebraska ex rel. Kelley v. Ferguson, 144 N.W. 1039 (Neb. 1914), 850–51
Nebraska ex rel. Sheibley v. Sch. Dist. No. 1 of Dixon County, 49 N.W. 393 (Neb. 1891), 850–51
Nectow v. City of Cambridge, 277 U.S. 183 (1920), 828–29, 839
Newberry v. United States, 256 U.S. 232 (1921), 1467
New England Divisions Case, 261 U.S. 184 (1923), 1140–41
New Jersey Bell Tel. Co. v. State Bd. of Taxes, 280 U.S. 338 (1930), 1189
New Orleans v. Dukes, 427 U.S. 297 (1976), 748–49
New Orleans Land Co. v. Brott, 263 U.S. 98 (1923), 633
New River Co.; United States v., 265 U.S. 533 (1924), 138–39
New River Collieries Co.; United States v., 262 U.S. 341 (1923), 722, 727, 763, 778
New State Ice Co. v. Liebmann, 285 U.S. 262 (1932), 323, 360, 749–50, 819, 1216
New York v. Charles Schweinler Press, 214 N.Y. 395 (1915), 330
New York v. Williams, 189 N.Y. 131 (1907), 330
New York, Philadelphia & Norfolk Tel. Co. v. Dolan, 265 U.S. 96 (1924), 1216
New York Cent. R.R. Co. v. Johnson, 279 U.S. 310 (1929), 640
New York Cent. R.R. Co. v. New York & Pennsylvania Co., 271 U.S. 124 (1926), 1139
New York Cent. R.R. Co. v. White, 243 U.S. 188 (1917), 96
New York Cent. R.R. Co. v. Winfield, 244 U.S. 147 (1917), 323–24
New York Cent. R.R. Co.; United States v., 279 U.S. 73 (1929), 212, 289
New York Coffee & Sugar Exch.; United States v., 263 U.S. 611 (1924), 1156
New York Dock Co. v. The Poznan, 274 U.S. 117 (1927), 155–56
New York ex rel. Bryant v. Zimmerman, 278 U.S. 63 (1928), 858, 1025, 1038–39
New York ex rel. Rosevale Realty Co. v. Kleinhert, 268 U.S. 646 (1925), 868–69
New York ex rel. Woodhaven Gas Light Co. v. Public Serv. Comm'n of New York, 269 U.S. 244 (1925), 81
New York Life Ins. Co. v. Dodge, 246 U.S. 357 (1918), 849
Nichols v. Coolidge, 274 U.S. 531 (1927), 100
Nigro v. United States, 276 U.S. 332 (1928), 58, 254, 282, 1129–30, 1133, 1153–54
Nixon v. Condon, 286 U.S. 73 (1932), 1469
Nixon v. Herndon, 273 U.S. 536 (1927), xli, 1226, 1435–37, 1438, 1440, 1452, 1454, 1458, 1465, 1466–69
NLRB v. Jones & Laughlin Steel Corp., 301 U.S. 1 (1937), 1145, 1246, 1285
Nobles of the Mystic Shrine v. Michaux, 279 U.S. 737 (1929), 247
Noble State Bank v. Haskell, 219 U.S. 110 (1911), 775–76
Nollan v. California Coastal Comm'n, 483 U.S. 825 (1987), 748–49
Norfolk & Western Ry. Co. v. Public Serv. Comm'n of West Virginia, 265 U.S. 70 (1924), 751, 767, 1139–40

LIST OF CASES

Norman v. Baltimore & Ohio R.R. Co., 294 U.S. 249 (1935), 272, 292, 296
Normand; State v., 76 N.H. 541 (1913), 744
North Carolina R.R. Co. v. Lee, 260 U.S. 16 (1922), 1143
Northern Pac. Ry. Co. v. Department of Pub. Works of Washington, 268 U.S. 39 (1925), 896–97
Northern Securities Co. v. United States, 193 U.S. 197 (1904), 166–67, 190–92, 642
Northern Securities Co.; United States v., 120 F. 721 (8th Cir. 1903), 239
North Laramie Land Co. v. Hoffman, 268 U.S. 276 (1925), 160
Northwestern Mut. Life Ins. Co. v. Wisconsin, 275 U.S. 136 (1927), 1118
Nortz v. United States, 294 U.S. 317 (1935), 272, 292, 296

Oakes v. United States, 172 F. 305 (8th Cir. 1909), 239
Obergefell v. Hodges, 576 U.S. 644 (2015), 748–49, 860
Ohio ex rel. Clarke v. Deckebach, 274 U.S. 392 (1927), 1487–88
Ohio Utils. Co. v. Public Utils. Comm'n of Ohio, 267 U.S. 359 (1925), 896–97
Oklahoma Natural Gas Co. v. Oklahoma, 258 U.S. 234 (1922), 118, 135
Old Dominion Steamship Co. v. Gilmore, 207 U.S. 398 (1907), xxxix, 201
Oliver Iron Mining Co. v. Lord, 262 U.S. 172 (1923), 1179–80, 1353
Olmstead v. United States, 277 U.S. 438 (1928), xxxi, xl, 82, 173, 179, 206, 224, 254, 350–51, 358, 390, 396, 434, 657, 671, 928, 947, 966–67, 1061–71, 1072–95
O'Malley v. Woodrough, 307 U.S. 277 (1939), 670
Omnia Commercial Co. v. United States, 261 U.S. 502 (1923), 726–27
One Ford Coupe Automobile; United States v., 272 U.S. 321 (1926), 58, 82, 945–46, 966–67
Opelika v. Opelika Sewer Co., 265 U.S. 215 (1924), 81–82, 610–12, 633
Opinion of the Justices; In re, 166 A. 640 (N.H. 1933), 1428–29
Opinion of the Justices; In re, 275 Mass. 580 (1931), 1428–29
Oregon v. Mitchell, 400 U.S. 112 (1970), 1467
Oregon Lumber Co.; United States v., 260 U.S. 290 (1922), 255, 352–55, 643
Oregon-Washington R.R. & Navigation Co. v. Washington, 270 U.S. 87 (1926), 273, 293, 1187
Oster v. Kansas, 272 U.S. 465 (1926), 249–50
Ottinger v. Consolidated Gas Co. of New York, 272 U.S. 576 (1926), 896–97
Ownbey v. Morgan, 256 U.S. 94 (1921), 147–48
Ozark Pipe Line Corp. v. Monier, 266 U.S. 555 (1925), 1182
Ozawa v. United States, 260 U.S. 178 (1922), 1452–53, 1455, 1456, 1457, 1458, 1467, 1484, 1485, 1489–90

Pacific Gas & Elec. Co. v. City and County of San Francisco, 265 U.S. 403 (1924), 896–97
Pacific Livestock Co. v. Ellison Ranching Co., 46 Nev. 351 (1923), 1397
Pacific States Paper Trade Ass'n; FTC v., 273 U.S. 52 (1927), 290–91, 1157, 1180
Packard v. Banton, 264 U.S. 140 (1924), 1206–7
Paducah v. Paducah R.R. Co., 261 U.S. 267 (1923), 81, 896–97
Palmer Transfer Co. v. Anderson, 115 S.W. 182 (Ky. 1909), 1211–12
Palmetto Fire Ins. Co. v. Connecticut, 272 U.S. 295 (1926), 1204
Panama R.R. Co. v. Johnson, 264 U.S. 375 (1924), 1176–77
Panama R.R. Co. v. Rock, 266 U.S. 209 (1924), 255, 996, 997, 998, 1011, 1012–13
Panhandle Oil Co. v. Mississippi ex rel. Knox, 277 U.S. 218 (1928), 1112–13, 1114, 1117–19, 1171, 1188–89
Paris Adult Theatre I v. Slaton, 413 U.S. 49 (1973), 748–49
Park v. United States, 294 F. 776 (1st Cir. 1924), 1049–52, 1053–54
Patton v. United States, 281 U.S. 276 (1930), 618, 636
Paul v. Virginia, 75 U.S. 168 (1868), 1177–78, 1202, 1206
Peck v. Fink, 2 F.2d 912 (D.C. Cir. 1924), 730
Pennsylvania v. West Virginia, 262 U.S. 553 (1923), 69, 70, 257–58, 287–88, 1160, 1161–63, 1167, 1175, 1178, 1180–81, 1182
Pennsylvania Coal Co. v. Mahon, 260 U.S. 393 (1922), 192, 205, 214–16, 728–29, 837, 866, 867, 872
Pennsylvania Gas Co. v. Public Serv. Comm'n, 252 U.S. 23 (1920), 1187
Pennsylvania R.R. Co. v. United States R.R. Labor Bd., 261 U.S. 72 (1923), 811, 1038, 1140–41, 1258–59, 1301–2

List of Cases

Pennsylvania R.R. Co.; United States v., 266 U.S. 191 (1923), 641
Pennsylvania R.R. System and Allied Lines Federation No. 90 v. Pennsylvania R.R. Co., 267 U.S. 203 (1925), 1259–60, 1302
People v. See name of defendant
Perkins; United States v., 116 U.S. 483 (1886), 407–8, 411, 429
Permian Basin Area Rate Cases; In re, 390 U.S. 747 (1968), 912
Perry v. United States, 294 U.S. 330 (1935), 272, 292–93, 296
Petterson v. Louisville & Nashville R.R. Co., 269 U.S. 1 (1925), 352–55
P.F. Petersen Baking Co. v. Bryan, 290 U.S. 570 (1934), 745, 748
Phelps v. United States, 274 U.S. 341 (1927), 727
Piano & Organ Workers v. P. & O. Supply Co., 124 Ill. App. 353 (1906), 1329
Pierce v. Society of Sisters, 262 U.S. 510 (1925), 817, 827, 830–34, 835, 843, 848, 854–55, 856, 859, 860–61, 1472–73
Pierce v. Society of Sisters, 268 U.S. 510 (1925), 767
Pierce v. Stablemen's Union, 156 Cal. 70 (1909), 1364
Pine Hill Coal Co. v. United States, 259 U.S. 191 (1922), 243
Planned Parenthood of Southeastern Pennsylvania v. Casey, 505 U.S. 833 (1992), 860
Plant v. Woods, 176 Mass. 492 (1900), 203, 1263, 1321–22, 1359
Plessy v. Ferguson, 163 U.S. 537 (1896), xxxiv, xl, 127, 1438, 1442, 1451, 1452, 1454, 1471, 1483, 1486
Plyler v. Doe, 457 U.S. 202 (1982), 748–49
Pocket Veto Case, 279 U.S. 655 (1929), 114–15
Pollock v. Farmers' Loan & Trust Co., 157 U.S. 429 (1895), 642, 667, 854–55
Pope Motor Car Co. v. Keegan, 150 F. 148 (N.D. Ohio 1906), 1279
Porterfield v. Webb, 263 U.S. 225 (1923), 1456–57, 1458, 1486, 1488, 1489
Port Gardner Inv. Co. v. United States, 272 U.S. 564 (1926), 946, 966–67
Power Mfg. Co. v. Saunders, 274 U.S. 490 (1927), 1195, 1205–6, 1463
Price Fire & Water Proofing Co. v. United States, 261 U.S. 179 (1923), 493–94
Printz v. United States, 521 U.S. 898 (1997), 1116–17
Prudential Ins. Co. v. Cheek, 259 U.S. 530 (1922), 1155
Public Utils. Comm'n v. Attleboro Steam & Elec. Co., 273 U.S. 83 (1927), 1167–68, 1180–82, 1187
Purity Extract & Tonic Co. v. Lynch, 226 U.S. 192 (1912), 739, 752, 825, 939–40, 973, 986, 987, 991
Purvis v. United Bhd., 214 Pa. 348 (1906), 1329, 1364
Pusey & Jones Co. v. Hanssen, 261 U.S. 491 (1923), 352–55

Quaker City Cab Co. v. Pennsylvania, 277 U.S. 389 (1928), 218, 247, 1431–33, 1457, 1464
Quercia v. United States, 289 U.S. 466 (1933), 526

Radice v. New York, 264 U.S. 292 (1924), 780–81
Raffel v. United States, 271 U.S. 494 (1926), 640, 670
Railroad Comm'n v. Eastern Texas R.R. Co., 264 U.S. 79 (1924), 1139
Railroad Comm'n of California v. Los Angeles Ry. Corp., 280 U.S. 145 (1929), 81, 896–97
Railroad Comm'n of California v. Southern Pac. Co., 264 U.S. 331 (1924), 250, 311, 355, 361–62, 610–12, 633, 1139–40
Railroad Comm'n of Wisconsin v. Chicago, Burlington & Quincy R.R. Co., 257 U.S. 563 (1922), 366–67, 1123–24, 1128, 1136, 1138, 1143, 1145, 1167, 1168, 1313–14, 1345–46, 1354
Ramsay Co. v. Associated Billposters, 260 U.S. 501 (1923), 1156
Ray Consol. Copper Co. v. United States, 268 U.S. 373 (1925), 58
Raymond Bros.-Clark Co.; FTC v., 263 U.S. 565 (1924), 290–91
Reading Co.; United States v., 270 U.S. 320 (1926), 1143
Real Silk Hosiery Mills v. Portland, 268 U.S. 325 (1925), 1168, 1182
Red Cross Line v. Atlantic Fruit Co., 264 U.S. 109 (1924), 1176–77
Reid; United States v., 53 U.S. 361 (1851), 1090–91
Rembert; United States v., 284 F. 996 (S.D. Tex. 1922), 1053–54
Rhea v. Smith, 274 U.S. 434 (1927), 1210

List of Cases

Ribnik v. McBride, 277 U.S. 350 (1928), 56, 87, 100, 130–31, 158–59, 799, 801–2, 817, 820, 821, 1299
Rice v. Gong, 104 So. 105 (Miss. 1925), 1470, 1482
Richardson v. Kentucky, 141 Ky 497 (1911), 1397
Richmond v. Deans, 37 F.2d 712 (4th Cir. 1930), 1491
Richmond Screw Anchor Co. v. United States, 275 U.S. 331 (1928), 396
Rider; United States v., 261 U.S. 363 (1923), 639
Risty v. Chicago, Rock Island & Pac. Ry. Co., 270 U.S. 378 (1926), 160, 1209, 1213
Ritchie v. People, 155 Ill. 98 (1895), 329
Robbins v. Shelby County Taxing Dist., 120 U.S. 489 (1887), 1175–76
Roberts v. Boston, 59 Mass. 198 (1849), 1438, 1471
Roberts v. United States Jaycees, 468 U.S. 609 (1984), 854
Roberts & Shaefer Co. v. Emmerson, 271 U.S. 50 (1926), 1462–63
Robertson v. Railroad Labor Bd., 268 U.S. 619 (1925), 352–55
Roschen v. Ward, 279 U.S. 337 (1929), 287–88, 754
Rosen v. United States, 245 U.S. 467 (1918), 1090–91
Russell Motor Car Co. v. United States, 261 U.S. 514 (1923), 728

St. Louis, Brownsville, & Mexico Ry. Co. v. United States, 268 U.S. 169 (1925), 352–55, 361–62
St. Louis, Brownsville & Mexico Ry. Co.; Missouri ex rel. *v. Taylor*, 266 U.S. 200 (1924), 352–55
St. Louis, Kennett & Southeastern R.R. Co. v. United States, 267 U.S. 346 (1925), 498
St. Louis & O'Fallon Ry. Co. v. United States, 22 F.2d 980 (E.D. Mo. 1927), 906
St. Louis & O'Fallon Ry. Co. v. United States, 279 U.S. 461 (1929), 81, 885–90, 896–97, 900, 903–4, 906–7, 909–11, 915
St. Louis & Southwestern Ry. Co. v. Nattin, 277 U.S. 157 (1928), 1183
St. Louis Cotton Compress Co. v. Arkansas, 1194, 1202–5
St. Louis-San Francisco Ry. Co. v. Alabama Pub. Serv. Comm'n, 279 U.S. 560 (1929), 352–55, 639, 1140
St. Louis-San Francisco Ry. Co. v. Mills, 271 U.S. 344 (1926), 249–50, 1295
St. Louis-San Francisco Ry. Co. v. Public Serv. Comm'n, 261 U.S. 369 (1923), 1140–41, 1186–87
Salem Trust Co. v. Manufacturers' Fin. Co., 264 U.S. 182 (1924), 1209, 1212
Salinger v. Loisel, 265 U.S. 224 (1924), 258
Samuels v. McCurdy, 267 U.S. 188 (1925), 82, 254, 946, 966–67
San Antonio Indep. Sch. Dist. v. Rodriquez, 411 U.S. 1 (1973), 748–49
Sandoval; United States v., 231 U.S. 28 (1913), 239
Sanford & Brooks Co. v. United States, 267 U.S. 455 (1925), 352–55
Santa Fe Pac. R.R. Co. v. Payne, 259 U.S. 197 (1922), 243
Schlesinger v. Wisconsin, 270 U.S. 230 (1926), 87, 100, 154, 739, 740, 742, 871, 973, 986
Schmidinger v. Chicago, 226 U.S. 578 (1913), 733, 735–36, 737, 738, 742, 792
Schwimmer; United States v., 279 U.S. 644 (1929), 81, 87, 100, 127, 151–52
Seaboard Air Line Ry. Co. v. United States, 261 U.S. 299 (1923), 727
Seattle Trust Co. v. Roberge, 278 U.S. 116 (1928), 849
Second Employers' Liability Cases, 223 U.S. 1 (1912), 236, 255, 1156–57
Second Russian Ins. Co. v. Miller, 268 U.S. 552 (1925), 160
Security Mortg. Co. v. Powers, 278 U.S. 149 (1928), 289
Seeman v. Philadelphia Warehouse Co., 274 U.S. 403 (1927), 639
Selzman v. United States, 268 U.S. 466 (1925), 966–67, 987
Shafer v. Farmers' Grain Co., 268 U.S. 189 (1925), 257–58, 1174, 1182, 1187, 1191–92
Shanks v. Delaware, Lackawanna & Western R.R. Co., 239 U.S. 556 (1916), 1156–57
Shapiro v. Thompson, 394 U.S. 618 (1969), 748–49, 1421
Shaw v. Gibson-Zahniser Oil Corp., 276 U.S. 575 (1928), 826–27, 847
Shea v. Louisiana, 470 U.S. 51 (1985), 748–49
Shurtleff v. United States, 189 U.S. 311 (1903), 422
Silver v. Silver, 280 U.S. 117 (1929), 1462
Silverman v. United States, 365 U.S. 505 (1961), 1084, 1085
Silverthorne Lumber Co. v. United States, 251 U.S. 385 (1920), 962
Sinclair v. United States, 279 U.S. 263 (1929), 82
Sinclair Refining Co.; FTC v., 261 U.S. 463 (1923), 291, 844

List of Cases

Sisal Sales Corp.; United States v., 274 U.S. 268 (1927), 294
Sischo; United States v., 262 U.S. 165 (1923), 640
Slaughterhouse Cases, 83 U.S. 36 (1872), 849, 958–59, 1227, 1262
Small Co. v. American Sugar Refining Co., 267 U.S. 233 (1925), 845–46
Smietanka v. First Trust & Sav. Bank, 257 U.S. 602 (1922), 118, 135
Smith v. Allwright, 321 U.S. 649 (1944), 1469
Smith v. Illinois Bell Tel. Co., 270 U.S. 587 (1926), 896–97
Smith v. Speed, 11 Okla. 95 (1901), 1397
Smyer v. United States, 273 U.S. 333 (1927), 255
Smyth v. Ames, 169 U.S. 466 (1898), 880, 881, 883, 884, 886, 888, 895, 899
Smyth v. Asphalt Belt Ry. Co., 267 U.S. 326 (1925), 247–48, 352–55
Snyder v. United States, 285 F. 1 (4th Cir. 1922), 1053
Sonneborn Bros. v. Cureton, 262 U.S. 506 (1923), 311, 355, 361–62, 633, 1180, 1187
South Carolina v. United States, 199 U.S. 437 (1905), 646, 1116
South-Eastern Underwriters Ass'n; United States v., 322 U.S. 533 (1944), 1202
Southern Pac. Co. v. Arizona ex rel. *Sullivan*, 325 U.S. 761 (1945), 748–49
Southern Pac. Co. v. Jensen, 244 U.S. 205 (1917), xl, 643–44, 1176–77, 1212
Southern Pac. Co.; United States v., 259 U.S. 214 (1922), 69
Southern Ry. Co. v. Clift, 260 U.S. 316 (1922), 812–13
Southern Utils. Co. v. City of Palatka, 268 U.S. 232 (1925), 209–10
Springer v. Government of the Philippine Islands, 277 U.S. 189 (1928), 397, 436–38
Sprout v. City of South Bend, 277 U.S. 163 (1928), 115, 361–62, 1185
Stafford v. Wallace, 258 U.S. 495 (1922), 59–60, 69, 397, 1116, 1125–26, 1128, 1129, 1132, 1133, 1143–44, 1152, 1164, 1166, 1179, 1180, 1313–14, 1354
Standard Oil Co. v. Marysville, 279 U.S. 582 (1929), 81, 639
Standard Oil Co. of New Jersey v. Southern Pac. Co., 268 U.S. 146 (1925), 81, 727
Standard Oil Co. of New Jersey v. United States, 221 U.S. 1 (1911), 1330, 1358, 1366
Standard Oil Co. of New Jersey; United States v., 173 F. 177 (8th Cir. 1909), 239
Starr v. Laundry and Dry Cleaning Workers' Local Union, 155 Or. 634 (1936), 1428–29
State v. See name of defendant
State Indus. Comm'n v. Nordenholt Corp., 259 U.S. 262 (1922), 1176–77
Stebbins v. Riley, 268 U.S. 137 (1925), 1462–63
Steele v. Drummond, 275 U.S. 199 (1927), 81
Steele v. United States, 267 U.D. 498 (1925), 1047–49
Stettler v. O'Hara, 69 Or. 519 (514), aff'd, 243 U.S. 629 (1917), 756, 767–68
Stevens v. Arnold, 262 U.S. 266 (1923), 289, 641
Stone v. Farmers' Loan & Trust Co., 116 U.S. 307 (1886), 895
Stone & Downer Co.; United States v., 274 U.S. 225 (1927), 396, 717
Stromberg v. California, 283 U.S. 359 (1931), 1423
Sturges & Burn Mfg. Co. v. Beauchamp, 231 U.S. 320 (1913), 752, 1155
Sullivan; United States v., 274 U.S. 259 (1927), 1015
Sultan Ry. & Timber Co. v. Department of Labor, 277 U.S. 135 (1928), 224
Sun Ship Building Co. v. United States, 271 U.S. 96 (1926), 498, 636
Sutherland v. Mayer, 271 U.S. 272 (1926), 726
Swendig v. Washington Water Power Co., 265 U.S. 322 (1924), 248
Swift v. Tyson, 41 U.S. 1 (1842), 1197, 1209, 1211, 1212, 1213
Swift & Co. v. United States, 196 U.S. 375 (1905), 1122, 1125, 1135, 1144, 1152
Swiss Nat. Ins. Co. v. Miller, 267 U.S. 42 (1925), 291

Taff Vale v. Amalgamated Soc'y of Ry. Servants, [1901] A.C 426. 1308, 1342
Taft v. Bowers, 278 U.S. 470 (1929), 294
Taubel-Scott-Kitzmiller Co. v. Fox, 264 U.S. 426 (1924), 231, 251, 639
Terminal Taxicab Co. v. Kutz, 241 U.S. 252 (1916), 815
Terrace v. Thompson, 263 U.S. 197 (1923), 1226, 1438, 1455–57, 1458, 1472, 1486
Terrace v. Thompson, 274 F. 841 (W.D. Wash. 1921), 1487
Terral v. Burke Constr. Co., 257 U.S. 529 (1922), 1196, 1197, 1206–7
Terry v. Ohio, 392 U.S. 1 (1968), 1056–57

List of Cases

Texas & New Orleans R.R. Co. v. Brotherhood of Ry. and Steamship Clerks, 281 U.S. 548 (1930), 1260–61, 1303
Texas & Pac. Ry. Co. v. Gulf, Colorado & Santa Fe Ry. Co., 270 U.S. 266 (1926), 365
Texas Transport & Terminal Co. v. New Orleans, 264 U.S. 150 (1924), 1168–69, 1182–83
Thomas v. Cincinnati, New Orleans & Texas Pac. Ry. Co., 62 F. 803 (Cir. Ct. S.D. Ohio 1894), 395, 1137–38, 1263–64, 1307–8, 1322–23, 1326, 1328–29, 1387
Thompson; United States v., 257 U.S. 419 (1922), 200–1
Thompson; United States v., 936 F.2d 1249 (11th Cir. 1991), *cert. denied*, 502 U.S. 1075 (1992), 1091–92
Thornhill v. Alabama, 310 U.S. 88 (1940), 1423
Toledo, Ann Arbor & Northern Michigan Ry. Co. v. Pennsylvania Co., 54 F. 730 (Cir. Ct. N.D. Ohio 1893), 395, 1274, 1329, 1360, 1362, 1365, 1372, 1379, 1393
Toledo, St. Louis & Western R.R. Co. v. Allen, 276 U.S. 165 (1928), 521–22
Topeka Edison Co.; State v., No. 3524 (KCIR, March 29, 1920), 811–12
Toyota v. United States, 268 U.S. 402 (1925), 255, 1485
Trenton v. New Jersey, 262 U.S. 182 (1923), 1175
Trenton Potteries Co.; United States v., 273 U.S. 392 (1927), 713–14
Tri-City Cent. Trades Council v. American Steel Foundries, 238 F. 728 (7th Cir. 1916), 1280
Truax v. Bisbee Local, No. 380, 19 Ariz. 379 (1918), 1361–62, 1416, 1417
Truax v. Corrigan, 20 Ariz. 7 (1918), 1417
Truax v. Corrigan, 257 U.S. 312 (1921), xxxvii–xxxviii, xlii, 59, 69, 78, 85, 96, 119–20, 136, 137, 202, 330, 360, 360, 392, 397, 646, 748–49, 777, 849, 1038, 1225, 1293, 1361–62, 1381, 1386, 1393, 1398, 1399–415, 1416–29, 1430–31, 1453, 1457, 1488–89
Truax v. Raich, 239 U. S. 33 (1915), 849, 1472–73
Trusler v. Crooks, 269 U.S. 475 (1926), 1149
Tucker v. Alexander, 275 U.S. 228 (1927), 249–50
Tumey v. Ohio, 273 U.S. 510 (1927), 966–67, 1025–26, 1041, 1042–43
Turner v. United States, 396 U.S. 398 (1970), 221–23
Tutun v. United States, 270 U.S. 568 (1926), 352–55
Twining v. New Jersey, 211 U.S. 78, 849
Tyson & Bro. v. Banton, 273 U.S. 418 (1927), 56, 87, 100, 129–31, 157–58, 159, 223–24, 799–801, 817, 818, 819–20, 821, 822, 825, 828, 838, 839, 845, 870, 879, 1014–15

Union Pac. R.R. Co. v. Peniston, 85 U.S. 5 (1873), 1117–18
Union Slaughter-House & Live-Stocking Land Co. v. Crescent City Live-Stock Landing & Slaughter-House Co., 111 U.S. 747 (1884), 815
United Fuel Gas Co. v. Railroad Comm'n of Kentucky, 278 U.S. 300 (1929), 155, 254, 636, 812–13
United Leather Workers' Int'l Union v. Herkert & Meisel Trunk Co., 265 U.S. 457 (1924), 254, 1135, 1145, 1187, 1317–18, 1319, 1325–26, 1330, 1356, 1357, 1358
United Leather Workers' Int'l Union v. Herkert & Meisel Trunk Co., 284 F. 446 (8th Cir. 1922), 1356
United Mine Workers of America v. Coronado Coal Co., 258 F. 829 (8th Cir. 1919), 1337
United Mine Workers of America v. Coronado Coal Co., 259 U.S. 344 (1922) *(Coronado I)*, 78, 610–12, 633, 975, 992, 1025, 1038, 1122, 1135, 1145, 1225, 1304–17, 1325–26, 1327, 1330, 1336, 1337, 1339, 1341–44, 1345–49, 1350–51, 1353, 1355, 1356, 1358, 1415
United Mine Workers of America v. Red Jacket Consol. Coal & Coke Co., 18 F.2d 839 (4th Cir.), cert. denied sub nom. *Lewis v. Red Jacket Consol. Coal & Coke Co.*, 275 U.S. 536 (1927), 1287, 1355, 1491–92
United Rys. and Elec. Co. v. West, 280 U.S. 234 (1930), xxix, xxx, xl, 890–94, 896–97, 911–12, 914, 915, 1505–6
United States v. See name of defendant
United States Shipping Bd. Emergency Fleet Corp. v. Western Union Tel. Co., 275 U.S. 415 (1928), 294
United Zinc & Chemical Co. v. Britt, 258 U.S. 268 (1922), 46, 49–50, 98, 173, 206–7
Untermeyer v. Anderson, 276 U.S. 440 (1928), 100, 218, 643

Vaello Madero; United States v., 142 S.Ct. 1539 (2022), 1428
Van Oster v. Kansas, 272 U.S. 465 (1926), 81–82, 966–67

List of Cases

Van Pelt; State v., 136 N.C. 633 (1904), 1364
Vatune; United States v., 292 F. 497 (N.D. Cal. 1923), 1053–54
Vegelahn v. Guntner, 167 Mass. 92 (1896), 1243–44, 1264, 1277–78, 1294
Vigliotti v. Pennsylvania, 258 U.S. 403 (1922), 946, 966–67
Village of Euclid v. Ambler Realty Co., 272 U.S. 365 (1926), xl, 56, 236, 255, 643–44, 835–43, 862–63, 865, 867–68, 869–72, 873–74, 875, 876, 877–78, 879, 1261, 1440, 1491–91
Virginia; Ex parte, 100 U.S. 339 (1879), 1467
Virginian R.R. Co. v. United States, 272 U.S. 658 (1926), 352–55

Wabash Ry. Co. v. Elliott, 261 U.S. 457 (1923), 1143
Walling v. Michigan, 116 U.S. 446 (1886), 1175–76
Walton Lunch Co. v. Kearney, 236 Mass. 310 (1920), 1397
Ward v. Village of Monroeville, 409 U.S. 57 (1972), 1042
Ward & Gow v. Krinsky, 259 U.S. 503 (1922), 96, 772–73
Washington v. W.C. Dawson & Co., 264 U.S. 219 (1924), 643–44, 648, 670, 776–77, 1176–77
Washington ex rel. Stimson Lumber Co. v. Kuykendall, 275 U.S. 207 (1927), 820–21
W.C. Ritchie & Co. v. Wayman, 244 Ill. 509 (1910), 329–30
Weaver v. Palmer Bros. Co., 270 U.S. 402 (1926), 81, 154, 738–40, 741, 751, 752, 758, 767, 849, 871, 939–40
Webb v. O'Brien, 263 U.S. 313 (1923), 1486, 1487–88
Weedin v. Chin Bow, 274 U.S. 657 (1927), 675
Weeks v. United States, 232 U.S. 383 (1913), 962, 1044–45, 1047–49, 1089
Weinberger v. Wiesenfeld, 420 U.S. 636 (1975), 1428
Weller v. New York, 268 U.S. 319 (1925), 800, 818
West. See United Rys. and Elec. Co. v. West
West v. Kansas Natural Gas, 221 U.S. 229 (1911), 1161, 1178
West v. Standard Oil Co., 278 U.S. 200 (1929), 289
West Coast Hotel v. Parrish, 300 U.S. 379 (1937), 767–68, 791, 861
West Virginia State Bd. of Educ. v. Barnette, 319 U.S. 624 (1943), 748–49
Western & Atl. R.R. v. Georgia Pub. Serv. Comm'n, 267 U.S. 493 (1925), 812–13, 1139–40
Western & Atl. R.R. Co. v. Hughes, 278 U.S. 496 (1929), 521–22, 640
Western Meat Co.; FTC v., 272 U.S. 554 (1926), 58, 350–51
Western Paper Makers' Chemical Co. v. United States, 271 U.S. 268 (1926), 352–55
Western Union Tel. Co. v. Georgia, 269 U.S. 67 (1925), 638–39
Western Union Tel. Co. v. Pendleton, 122 U.S. 347 (1887), 1175–76
Whalen v. Roe, 429 U.S. 589 (1977), 749–50
White v. Mechanics Securities Corp., 269 U.S. 283 (1925), 200–1
White River Lumber Co. v. Arkansas, 279 U.S. 692 (1929), 236, 248, 254, 255, 256
Whiting v. Hudson Trust Co., 234 N.Y. 394 (1923), 1211
Whitman v. American Trucking Ass'ns, Inc., 531 U.S. 457 (2001), 706
Whitney v. California, 274 U.S. 357 (1927), 127, 151, 358, 360, 368, 817, 1038–39, 1423
Willcox v. Consolidated Gas Co., 212 U.S. 19 (1909), 896
Williams v. Evans, 139 Minn. 32 (1917), 767
Williams v. Riley, 280 U.S. 78 (1929), 287–88
Williams v. Standard Oil Co., 278 U.S. 235 (1929), 56, 802–3, 821
Williamsport Wire Rope Co. v. United States, 277 U.S. 551 (1928), 352–55
Willing v. Chicago Auditorium Ass'n, 277 U.S. 274 (1928), 324–25, 352–55, 675, 676
Wilson v. Illinois Southern R.R. Co., 263 U.S. 574 (1924), 248–49, 258
Wilson v. New, 243 U.S. 332 (1917), 774, 793–94, 795, 797, 798, 806, 814, 1299
Winsted Hosier Co.; FTC v., 258 U.S. 483 (1922), 97
Wisconsin v. Illinois, 278 U.S. 367 (1929), 612, 633
Wisconsin, Minnesota & Pac. R.R. Co. v. Jacobson, 179 U.S. 287 (1900), 1140–41
Wisconsin Rate Case. See Railroad Comm'n of Wisconsin v. Chicago, Burlington & Quincy R.R. Co.
Wisner; Ex parte, 203 U.S. 449 (1906), 1197, 1208
Wolfe v. United States, 291 U.S. 7 (1934), 1090–91
Wolff Packing Co. See Charles Wolff Packing Co. v. Kansas Ct. of Indus. Relations
Wong Doo v. United States, 265 U.S. 239 (1924), 258

LIST OF CASES

Woodbridge v. United States, 263 U.S. 50 (1923), 396
Woodruff; Commonwealth ex rel. *v. Benn*, 284 Pa. 421 (1925), 408–9, 431
Work v. Braffet, 276 U.S. 560 (1928), 249–50
Work v. United States ex rel. *Lynn*, 266 U.S. 161 (1924), 258
Wyeth v. Cambridge Bd. of Health, 200 Mass. 474 (1909), 849

Yamashita v. Hinkle, 260 U.S. 199 (1922), 1484–85
Yeiser v. Dysart, 267 U.S. 540 (1925), 213
Yick Wo v. Hopkins, 118 U.S. 356 (1886), 849, 1472–73
Young; Ex parte, 209 U.S. 123 (1908), 1210
Youngstown Sheet & Tube Co. v. Sawyer, 343 U.S. 579 (1952), 418, 447
Yu Cong Eng v. Trinidad, 271 U.S. 500 (1926), 849, 1472–73

Zahn v. Board of Pub. Works of City of Los Angeles, 274 U.S. 325 (1927), 643–44, 872
Ziang Sung Wan v. United States, 266 U.S. 1 (1924), 1072–74
Zucht v. King, 260 U.S. 174 (1922), 352–55

Prologue
Mr. Taft Takes Charge

F RANKLIN ROOSEVELT ONCE remarked that America was the "place of the second chance."[1] He could have pointed to the remarkable career of William Howard Taft as proof. Crushingly defeated in his bid for a second term as president in 1912, Taft was resurrected as chief justice of the Supreme Court of the United States on June 30, 1921. It was, as the *New York Times* later remarked, "a 'comeback' unprecedented in American political annals."[2] Taft became the only man in American history to head two different branches of the federal government. The combination proved propitious, for Taft's presidential perspective forever changed both the role of the chief justice and the institution of the Court.

As Taft himself was the first to acknowledge, he was a very fortunate man.[3] The definitive biography is by Henry F. Pringle,[4] and I will not recapitulate it here. Suffice it to say that Taft was born on September 15, 1857, the son of a prominent Cincinnati attorney, Alphonso Taft, who in 1876 had served in President Grant's Cabinet as both secretary of war and attorney general. After his graduation from Yale in 1878, William Howard Taft capitalized on these impeccable Republican connections, as well as on his own manifest talent, to slide easily from position to position.

In 1880, after receiving a degree from the Cincinnati Law School, Taft was appointed assistant prosecuting attorney of Hamilton County in Ohio. Seven years later he was appointed a superior court judge. In 1890 President Harrison made him United States solicitor general, and two years later Harrison elevated him to the Sixth Federal Circuit Court. President McKinley appointed him the first governor of the Philippines in 1901, and in 1904 he became Theodore Roosevelt's secretary of war. Hand-picked by Roosevelt as his successor, Taft virtually inherited the presidency in 1908. "Whenever an office fell," Taft remarked, "my plate was up."[5]

As president, Taft's good fortune temporarily ran out. It would have taken great political skill to bridge the widening gap between the progressive and conservative wings of the Republican Party, but Taft was no such politician. He possessed neither charisma nor raw political talent.[6] His fate was sealed when Theodore Roosevelt, his erstwhile mentor, decided to split the Republican vote by running for president on the ticket of the Progressive Party. Caught between Roosevelt and Wilson, Taft was butchered in the 1912 election. He received only eight electoral votes, representing the states of Vermont and Utah.[7]

It was a near total repudiation, but Taft received it graciously. In a characteristic display of a wit that was simultaneously self-deprecating and also sharply pointed at Roosevelt, Taft told the Lotos Club in New York that a swift dose of chloroform would be the best method of disposing of ex-presidents. It "would secure the country from the troublesome fear that the occupant could ever come back" and "relieve the country from the burden of thinking how he is to support himself and his family, would fix his place in history, and enable the public to pass on to new men and new measures."[8]

After his defeat, Taft considered but rejected the possibility of practicing law in New York. "I felt that as six members of the Supreme Court bore my commission, and as I had appointed 30 per cent of the rest of the Federal judiciary, it was not fair to the Courts for me to go into the practice."[9] Instead Taft retired to Yale Law School as Kent Professor of Constitutional Law. Determined to remain active and publicly visible,[10] he became president of the American Bar Association in 1913–1914, a regular and widely syndicated columnist for the Philadelphia *Public Ledger*,[11] and a frequent and prominent speaker on matters of national interest.[12] He particularly stressed the need to maintain a strong and efficient judicial system.[13] Taft projected an image of such earnest and disinterested goodwill that he quickly became, in the famous phrase of the journalist George Harvey, "our worst licked and best loved President."[14]

Two aspects of Taft's public rehabilitation are particularly significant. The first is his collegial co-chairmanship, with prominent labor attorney Frank P. Walsh,[15] of the National War Labor Board.[16] Created by Woodrow Wilson to mediate labor disputes during World War I, the Board explicitly recognized "the right of workers to organize in trade-unions and to bargain collectively, through chosen representatives," and it affirmed that this "right shall not be denied, abridged, or interfered with by the employers in any manner whatsoever." The Board shocked industrial leaders by declaring official support for the right of employees to receive a "living wage" that would "insure the subsistence of the worker and his family in health and reasonable comfort."[17] In the course of defending these rights, Taft developed a close working relationship with Walsh, voting with him against employer representatives on the Board.[18]

Before his stint on the National War Labor Board, Taft had been implacably opposed by organized labor, which had fiercely objected to his possible nomination to the Supreme Court in 1916 because Taft was "known among labor men everywhere as the father of the offensive injunction rule of procedure in labor disputes" and because Taft's "emphatically pronounced" "opposition to labor organizations

Prologue: Mr. Taft Takes Charge

and the exercise by them of their normal and legitimate functions"[19] rendered him abhorrent. But Taft's co-chairmanship of the National War Labor Board appeared to soften Taft's attitude toward organized labor,[20] which in turn "resulted in a change of heart toward him by many labor leaders."[21]

In March 1921, Samuel Gompers, legendary president of the American Federation of Labor ("AFL"), although angry at Taft's public support of the Supreme Court's recent antilabor interpretation of the Clayton Act in *Duplex Printing Press Co. v. Deering*,[22] nevertheless forthrightly conceded:

> [I]n some important respects, Mr. Taft has made much progress since his occupancy of the White House. He has given much proof of an increasing breadth of vision. He has shown a growing comprehension that has led a great many well-disposed men and women to hope at times that a new and progressive William H. Taft was emerging from the shell of the extremely conservative and easy-going William H. Taft, who once was described as "a very large body completely surrounded by politicians."[23]

The second important aspect of Taft's rehabilitation was his support of Woodrow Wilson's campaign to enter the League of Nations. Taft had always been committed to the cause of substituting legal procedures for war. As president he had negotiated and signed arbitration treaties with Great Britain and France "that were revolutionary when compared with previous agreements for the pacific settlement of disputes" because they required arbitration "in all matters of national interest and honor."[24] The treaties came under fierce attack by, among others, Theodore Roosevelt, who charged that they reflected an "ingrained personal timidity" that was "more afraid of war than of any dishonor, personal or national."[25] The treaties were so mutilated by the Senate that Taft withdrew them.

After his defeat in 1912, Taft continued to press the cause of international arbitration, assuming in 1915 the leadership of the League to Enforce Peace.[26] When Woodrow Wilson subsequently sought to convince the Senate to approve the League of Nations, Taft was one of very few Republicans willing publicly to defend him. Standing side by side with his successor on the stage of Metropolitan Opera House, Taft strongly supported Wilson's commitment to the League in a speech that "carried great and convincing weight with his audience."[27] The following month the *World's Work* reported that "out of the present welter of political antagonisms in this country one figure of statesmanlike size is emerging and giving American public life a tone which it sadly needs":

> That is ex-President Taft. His appearance on the same platform with President Wilson indicates that there is at least one of our public men who recognizes other motives than selfishness and partisanship. It is one of those spectacles which the American spirit admires above all else. The new hold which Mr. Taft is obtaining upon the affections and respect of the American people is becoming a fundamental fact in our national situation and one which is not unlikely to affect profoundly the history of the next two years.[28]

It took real courage for Taft to speak "kind words of President Wilson when speaking anything except defamation and condemnation of the president was considered treason by the old guard in the senate. Taft was for peace when peace was looked upon as a crime by some of the leaders of his party."[29] Although Taft's support of Wilson may have earned him the opposition of "the 'irreconcilables' to the Treaty of Versailles,"[30] it also "won for him a respect and even affection which he had been unable to win for himself during his years as executive and administrator."[31]

The upshot was that just as America veered to the right in the presidential election of 1920, Taft emerged as a national figure of broad, almost nonpartisan appeal, "at the very height of his popularity, a far bigger man, a more valuable citizen, than ever before."[32] To Taft's immense good fortune, the new president, Warren G. Harding, was, like Taft himself, a conservative Ohio politician. Eight years younger than Taft, Harding had longstanding ties to the elder man, whom he affectionately called the "Big Chief."[33] Harding had in fact nominated Taft at the infamous Republican convention of 1912, where Taft's cadre of party-regulars had ruthlessly crushed Roosevelt's attempt to obtain the party's endorsement.[34] Above the protests of the dissidents, Harding had intoned: "Progression is not proclamation or palaver. It is not pretence nor play on prejudice. It is not the perturbation of a people passion-wrought, nor a promise proposed. Progression is everlastingly lifting the standards that marked the end of the world's march yesterday and planting them on new and advanced heights to-day. Tested by such a standard, President Taft is the greatest progressive of the age."[35]

Although Harding equivocated on the League of Nations in 1920, Taft dutifully supported his candidacy. In a remarkably candid article, Taft argued that the greatest "domestic issue" in the election was "the maintenance of the Supreme Court as the bulwark to enforce the guaranty that no man shall be deprived of his property without due process of law":

> Mr. Wilson is in favor of a latitudinarian construction of the Constitution of the United States to weaken the protection it should afford against socialistic raids upon property rights, with the direct and inevitable result of paralyzing the initiative and enterprise of capital necessary to the real progress of all. He has made three appointments to the Supreme Court. He is understood to be greatly disappointed in the attitude of the first of these [James Clark McReynolds] upon such questions. The other two [Louis Dembitz Brandeis and John Hessin Clarke] represent a new school of constitutional construction, which if allowed to prevail will greatly impair our fundamental law. Four of the incumbent Justices are beyond the retiring age of seventy, and the next President will probably be called upon to appoint their successors. . . . Who can be better trusted to do this – Mr. Cox, the party successor of Mr. Wilson, or Mr. Harding the standard bearer of the Republican party?[36]

After the election, Taft received an invitation from Harding to visit at Marion, Ohio. To Taft's "great surprise," Harding "plunged at once" into a discussion of political appointments.[37] Harding confided that "Sutherland wants the Supreme

Prologue: Mr. Taft Takes Charge

Bench and I am going to put him there,"[38] after which Harding added, as Taft recounted to his wife:

> "By the way", he said, "I want to ask you, would you accept a position on the Supreme Bench?" He said "because if you would, I'll put you on that Court". I said it was and always had been the ambition of my life. I had declined it twice for reasons I explained, but I was obliged to say that now under the circumstances of having been President, and having appointed three of the present Bench and three others, and having protested against Brandeis, I could not accept any place but the Chief Justiceship. He said nothing more about it and I could not make out whether he concluded that was satisfactory or whether he did not further wish to commit himself.[39]

Harding's broad hint, subsequently confirmed,[40] set Taft off on a concerted campaign to fulfill his dream of becoming chief justice, a campaign that has been well reported in the literature.[41] Harding's plan to nominate Taft was complicated by what appears to have been Harding's previous commitment to appoint George Sutherland, who had been one of Harding's "principal" advisers during the presidential campaign,[42] to the first available Supreme Court vacancy.[43] As luck would have it, the first vacancy arose when Chief Justice White died on May 19 from an operation to lance an abscess in his prostate.[44] Caught between his commitment to give Sutherland the first available seat and his commitment to appoint Taft chief justice, Harding put Taft's nomination on hold while he struggled to find a way to appoint both Taft and Sutherland.[45]

Speculation concerning Harding's plans ranged from elevating William Day to the chief justiceship on the understanding that he would retire after six months, and in the meantime appointing Sutherland to Day's old position as an associate justice,[46] to inducing Holmes or McKenna to retire by offering them a position in England on the Disarmament Commission.[47] Taft hung fire for about six weeks, frying, as he said, "in the juice of doubt and worry."[48] Taft went so far as to confide to Pierce Butler that, "as a matter of fact, I don't expect to be appointed."[49]

In the end it was Harding's attorney general, Harry Daugherty, who broke the deadlock. Daugherty was an old-school Ohio politician who had close ties to Taft that dated back to Taft's own presidential campaigns.[50] Daugherty had supported Taft in 1912,[51] so that, as Taft later recalled, "Harry and I had been very warm friends, and . . . he had done much for me at a time when friends were needed."[52] In June 1921, Daugherty pushed hard for Taft's appointment,[53] arguing, as Harding candidly acknowledged in his press conference announcing Taft's nomination, that "the Department of Justice was anxious to see a Chief Justice named" so that work could immediately begin to relieve the "congestion" of federal courts caused by "arrests made under the provisions of the Volstead act."[54] Taft's nomination went to the Senate at 4:00 pm on June 30, 1921, and he was confirmed shortly thereafter in a direct floor vote without referral to a committee, by a vote of 61–4.[55]

Fittingly enough, what finally propelled Taft into the chief justiceship was the urgent need to reorganize the administration of federal courts. Some in the popular press, recalling the widespread view that Taft had failed as president because "[h]e had too judicial a mind,"[56] counted this as a strike against Taft's nomination, arguing that because his "tastes" were "judicial rather than executive," he could have only "small predilection" for the task of organizing "the work of the court and infus[ing] into it the efficiency which is more conspicuously recognized in commercial affairs."[57]

This objection radically misunderstood Taft's abilities. Taft was an ineffective president because he was, in William Allen White's lovely phrase, "innocent of politics."[58] But Taft had always been a crackerjack administrator.[59] Henry L. Stimson, who served presidents from Theodore Roosevelt to Harry Truman, regarded Taft as the best organized and "most efficient" president of them all.[60] Judicial administration was in fact what best suited Taft's talents.

Charles Evans Hughes accurately observed that Taft's career "fittingly culminated in his work as Chief Justice," because the "efficient administration of justice was, after all, the dominant interest of his public life."[61] Few presidential candidates indeed would have staked their campaign, as Taft did in 1908, on the ground that "the greatest question now before the American public is the improvement of the administration of justice, civil and criminal, both in the manner of its prompt dispatch and the cheapening of its use."[62]

Once confirmed as chief justice, Taft turned his formidable executive ability toward the rationalization and improvement of the federal judiciary, with the consequence that, as Felix Frankfurter acknowledged, he became a great "law reformer," with "a place in history ... next to Oliver Ellsworth, who originally devised the judicial system."[63] Taft's achievements are legion, ranging from the design and construction of the modern Supreme Court building to the pathbreaking reform of the Supreme Court's jurisdiction in the Judiciary Act of February 13, 1925,[64] which transformed the United States Supreme Court from a tribunal of last resort into something like the supervisor of the system of federal law.

Taft's administrative skills also served him well within the Court itself. He was ruthlessly efficient, moving heaven and earth to diminish the Court's embarrassingly large backlog of cases.[65] Brandeis remarked to Frankfurter that Taft, "like the Steel Corporation, is attaining [all] time production records."[66] In the popular press it was rapidly recognized that "The spirit of speed and efficiency lurking in the corpulent form of an ex-President of the United States has entered the Court and broken up its old lethargy."[67]

Within the Court, however, the dominant image of Taft was not that of a disciplinarian, but rather of a man who could dispose "of executive details ... easily" and "get through them without friction."[68] "The new chief justice makes the work very pleasant," Holmes said. "He is always good natured and carries things along with a smile or a laugh. (It makes a devil of a difference if the C.J.'s temperament diminishes friction.) He is very open to suggestions and appreciates the labors of others. I rather think the other JJ. are as pleased as I am."[69] Brandeis concurred in this positive assessment: "On the personal side the present C.J. has admirable qualities, a great improvement on the late C.J.; he smooths out difficulties instead of making them. It's astonishing he should have been such a horribly bad President, for he has considerable executive ability.

Prologue: Mr. Taft Takes Charge

The fact, probably, is that he cared about law all the time and nothing else. He has an excellent memory, makes quick decisions on questions of administration that arise and if a large output were the chief desideratum, he would be very good."[70]

Taft's genial and prepossessing personality was particularly useful in managing the Court's potentially contentious conferences. Holmes remarked that "The meetings are perhaps pleasanter than I ever have known them – thanks largely to the C.J."[71] Brandeis agreed: "Things go happily in the Conference room with Taft – the judges go home less tired emotionally and less weary physically, than in White's days."[72] The justices also appreciated how "fairly" Taft distributed case assignments.[73] Stone later remarked that "there was never a Chief Justice as generous to his brethren in the assignment of cases."[74]

Taft himself conceived of the chief justice as "the head of the court, and while his vote counts but one in the nine, he is, if he be a man of strong and persuasive personality, abiding convictions, recognized learning, and statesmanlike foresight, expected to promote teamwork by the court, so as to give weight and solidarity to its opinions."[75] Taft maintained within his Court, as Augustus Hand later wrote him, "a certain leadership that is enormously important and I don't believe has ever existed since the times of Marshall himself. Indeed I think Brandeis, in the left wing, greatly appreciates this and knows how much it means to have a C.J. whom the Court will in certain respects follow and at any rate will 'rally around.'"[76]

By the time incapacitating strokes forced Taft to resign on February 3, 1930[a], his energetic revitalization of the Court and his vigorous reformation of the federal judiciary had won over even old and implacable enemies. California Senator Hiram Johnson, for example, had been Theodore Roosevelt's running-mate in 1912, and he had been one of the four unyielding votes against Taft's confirmation in 1921. He had then justified his opposition in very strong terms: "I felt that I would be false to the old Roosevelt fight, false to every principle in which I believed, false to myself, and false to my country, if I voted for Taft's confirmation.... Yesterday, we may have changed the course of our country, we may have altered the history of the world by placing in the position where he was the deciding vote in the most powerful tribunal of the universe, a man devoid of learning, judicial temperament, and of principle."[77] Yet by the time Taft died in March 1930, even Johnson could affirm to the press that "Of recent years I have become very fond of Chief Justice Taft. It was with the utmost regret that I learned of the necessity of his resignation. I feel that he has rendered a great and lasting public service and that his death is a very severe loss to the nation."[78]

In March 1930, Taft was "a widely loved personality."[79] Franklin Roosevelt, then governor of New York, ordered state flags to be hung at half-staff for thirty days to signify the "universal sorrow" and "affectionate esteem" of the people of the state.[80] Taft's standing was never higher than at the moment of his demise.[81] It has since sunk into deep oblivion, which suggests that judicial administration is not the platform on which to erect an enduring judicial reputation.[82] We do not tend to remember great judicial reformers, but instead to honor judges who craft striking

---

[a] Taft ceased participating in the Court's deliberations in the first week of January 1930. When we speak of the "Taft Court," therefore, we are essentially referring to the 1921 through 1928 terms, with a small fraction of the 1929 term.

opinions or who convey deep jurisprudential vision. Taft could do neither. He readily confessed to "great difficulty in the matter" of "judicial style,"[83] so that on his retirement *Time Magazine* could ruthlessly encapsulate his career with the pithy assessment: "Outstanding decisions: none."[84]

It is not that Taft wrote few opinions; indeed, as Table P-1 illustrates, he wrote more opinions than anyone else on the Court during his tenure, a remarkable accomplishment given his extraordinary commitments to judicial administration and reform.[b] It is rather that Taft's opinions were, as Holmes observed, "rather spongy,"[85] so that they seemed indistinct and unmemorable.[86] When Frankfurter complained that Taft's opinions were "loose & mischievous in dicta & language even when *result* is right," Brandeis noted that Taft "can't help it – he can't write and think closely."[87] Taft, said Brandeis, possessed "a first-rate second-rate mind."[88] At the time of his death, even Taft's supporters recognized that "His name will not be ... connected with any outstanding decisions – as are the names, for instance, of Chief Justice Marshall and Chief Justice Taney."[89]

The weakness of Taft's opinions was also their strength. They were so suffused with common sense as to be utterly unremarkable. They expressed with clarity and force the conventional pieties of his time. Taft only rarely permitted ideological principles to override a practical and "political sense of proportion."[90] Thus while Taft vigorously opposed the "radical" views of Brandeis, which he interpreted as "in favor of breaking down the Constitution, or making it a mere scrap of paper," he was equally opposed to the "reactionary" views of McReynolds,[91] which in Taft's view failed to appreciate the many ways in which the Constitution was "a political instrument" that needed to be adapted "to new conditions."[92]

The upshot was a fuzzy and genial conservatism, memorable neither for its intransigence nor for its intellectual perspicuity. Taft's jurisprudence perfectly vindicated "the determination of President Harding to return the country to a condition of 'normalcy.'"[93] As Brandeis cannily observed, Taft's easy and privileged career had produced a judge without "*Weltschemrz*";[94] Taft had "all the defects but also the advantages of the aristocratic order that has done well by him. He accepts it, but doesn't sweat & labor to maintain his position."[95]

There is no doubt but that Taft stood at the dead center of the Court he undertook to lead. As chief justice, Taft participated in some 1,583 decisions;[c] he dissented in only

---

[b] Table P-1 calculates the number of opinions authored by each justice in the full terms during which he participated in the Taft Court, which is defined as the 1921 to 1928 terms, inclusive. In each period, Taft produced by far the greatest number of opinions. As Sanford wrote Van Devanter after Taft suffered a heart attack in the summer of 1926, Taft must become "reconciled to taking things more easily and not doing so large a share of the joint task – unduly large – as he has been." ETS to WVD (August 26, 1926) (Van Devanter papers).

[c] Unless otherwise noted, I shall in this book use the phrase a "decision" of the Court to refer to a case (or cases) decided by a full opinion, as distinct, for example, from a case (or cases) decided by a memorandum opinion or by a denial of *certiorari* or by the bare issuance of a judgment. Used in this way, a single "decision" may dispose of several cases, insofar as the latter are defined by distinct docket numbers.

Table P-1 Number of opinions authored by each justice

Court Terms	Taft	Holmes	Van Devanter	McReynolds	Brandeis	Sutherland	Butler	Sanford	Stone
1921–1928	249	205	94	172	193				
1922–1928	222	176	84	152	170	143			
1923–1928	176	146	70	129	143	113	137	113	
1925–1928	110	86	39	78	87	60	88	69	95

THE TAFT COURT

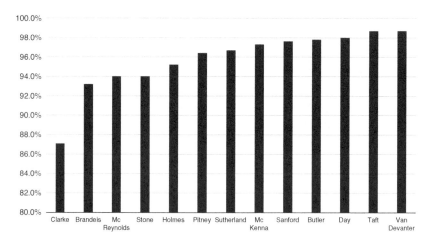

Figure P-1 Percentage of decisions in which a participating justice either authors or joins an opinion for the Court, 1921–1928 terms

nineteen. He authored or joined the opinion for the Court in 98.7 percent of its decisions.[d] Taft's vision of "progressive conservatism"[96] was not merely idiosyncratic; it characterized the Court itself. In part this was because Taft presided over an institution that was infused with the same commitment to "normalcy" that had led to Taft's own nomination.

Taft's centrality reflected the fact that his hesitations and limitations "were probably shared by the dominant people" of his time.[97] Taft took charge of the Court at a moment when the nation was attempting to assimilate the seismic implications of World War I, which had snapped "old certainties like rotten boards."[98] The massive federal intervention unleashed by the Wilson administration to prosecute the war landed squarely athwart fierce constitutional debates about the proper role of national power and government regulation of the economy.

---

[d] Taft issued one opinion "*dubitante*" in FTC v. Curtis Publishing Co., 260 U.S. 568 (1923). He also published one concurring opinion in Craig v. Hecht, 263 U.S. 255 (1923). Taft's record was equaled during the period of his chief justiceship (which included a fragment of the 1929 Term) only by Willis Van Devanter. During Taft's tenure, Van Devanter participated in 1,591 decisions, dissenting in only 21. Van Devanter wrote no separate concurrences, and, like Taft, he either authored or joined the opinion for Court in 98.7% of its decisions. (During the 1915–1920 terms, by contrast, Van Devanter joined or authored only 96.2% of the Court's opinions.) In Figure P-1, I have calculated the percentage of decisions during the 1921–1928 terms in which each participating Justice either authored or joined the Court's opinion. The percentages range from 87.1% (John Hessin Clarke) to 98.8% (Willis Van Devanter). I have in this book generally confined statistical analysis to the 1921–1928 terms, inclusive, in order to avoid having to guess at a date by which to mark the precise end of the Taft Court.

Prologue: Mr. Taft Takes Charge

The war revealed the future of the American state with intolerable clarity, undercutting the entire framework of the preexisting constitutional order. Yet the country's pell-mell retreat to "normalcy" testifies to the nation's unwillingness frankly to face the new realities of the twentieth century. Throughout the 1920s the nation vacillated between attempting to deny the lessons of the war and tentatively exploring the powerful new administrative possibilities suddenly made available by wartime innovations. The country as a whole shared Taft's ambivalences and confusions.

It is clear that the Taft Court was, like Taft himself, caught at the cusp between two eras.[99] Its jurisprudence can be succinctly summarized as a hesitant effort both to conserve prewar pieties and to accommodate the consequences of profound social change.

THE TAFT COURT
Notes

1. "Address on the Occasion of the Fiftieth Anniversary of the Statue of Liberty," October 28, 1936, in 5 THE PUBLIC PAPERS AND ADDRESSES OF FRANKLIN D. ROOSEVELT 542 (New York: Random House 1938).
2. *Taft Gained Peaks in Unusual Career*, NEW YORK TIMES (March 9, 1930), at 27.
3. "Fortune has been so good to me in every way." WHT to Charles P. Taft (April 17, 1923) (Taft papers).
4. HENRY F. PRINGLE, THE LIFE AND TIMES OF WILLIAM HOWARD TAFT: A BIOGRAPHY (New York: Farrar & Rinehart, Inc. 1939).
5. William Howard Taft, *Legal Ethics*, 1 BOSTON UNIVERSITY LAW REVIEW 173, 173 (1921).
6. William Allen White offers an evocative portrait of Taft's political ineptitude:

   [I]n all his long career of office-holding, beginning with 1881 and lasting through his life until he ran for President, he was elected to office only once, and that as Judge of the Superior Court of Ohio, where he had no contact with politics in his campaign and served but a few months. ... It was well said [of] him by O.K. Davis, a reporter who knew him for a dozen years at the height of his political activities, that Taft's bump of political sagacity was a dent. ... Figuratively, he used to come out upon the front stoop of the White House and quarrel petulantly with the American people every day. ... He conceived a statesman's job as an opportunity to do his work honestly, intelligently, courageously .... It was impossible even for his bitterest enemies to cast him for a villain in their hours of curdling hate, because of the easy gurgle of his laugh and the sweet insouciance of his answer which turned away wrath. ... And the American people who chastised him, observing him chuckle as he rubbed the red place where their rage had blistered him, loved him for his merry countenance.

   WILLIAM ALLEN WHITE, MASKS IN A PAGEANT 328–29, 330 (New York: McMillan & Co. 1928). Marveling at Taft's resurrection as chief justice, where "the clamor of the mob and the movements of the democracy are all the same to him and his court," White remarked on how "lightly the clamor and bitterness of the few years in the White House touched this man!" *Id.* at 344. As chief justice, Taft was "a smiling Buddha, placid, wise, gentle, sweet, and as noble as a man may be in this poor worm-eaten earth." *Id.*
7. Wilson received 6,286,214 popular votes; Roosevelt 4,126,020, and the incumbent Taft only 3,483,922. "Mr. Bryan said in the course of the campaign that I had been elected to the Presidency by a large majority and would be relegated to private life by a unanimous vote," Taft reported to the Republican Clubs of Boston and New York two months after the disastrous campaign. "When I read what he said I thought he was as poetic and as unreliable in his prophecies as usual, but in truth nothing but Vermont and Utah prevented a literal fulfillment of his forecast, and he was nearer than ever before in his life to a fact. I think I have separated myself sufficiently from the humiliation of defeat to be able to look upon the history of my administration with calmness and clearness of vision, affected only by the fact that I was one of the principal actors and naturally inclined to give the best color to everything which I did or attempted to do." The Address of President Taft at the Banquet of the Union League Club of New York (January 4, 1913), at 3 (Taft papers).
8. William Howard Taft, *The Presidency*, 73 THE INDEPENDENT 1196, 1200 (1912).

Prologue: Mr. Taft Takes Charge

9. WHT to Thomas W. Shelton (June 24, 1923) (Taft papers).
10. Taft's transformation was widely noticed. Typical is this 1914 poem:

> When Mr. Taft was President, it often was averred
> That, though he talked considerably, he never said a word. ...
> And when you met a Senator who looked plumb dazed and daft.
> You knew he'd had an interview with old Bill Taft.
>
> But when to blest retirement he was prompted to withdraw ....
> And lo! There was a smashing punch in everything he said. ...
>
> And now when we have breakfasted we eagerly peruse
> The glaring headlines which set forth: "TAFT HOLDS DECIDED VIEWS."
> We notice how he swats T.R.; with gaping mouth we read
> Of what he thinks of Mexico, or corporation greed.
> No shifty straddling talk is this, it's Biff! And Bang! And Bing! ...
> He gets his enemies in range and rakes 'em fore and aft;
> He sure is some performer, now he's just Bill Taft.

> James J. Montague, *The Metamorphosis*, ST. LOUIS STAR AND TIMES (December 29, 1914), at 12.

11. Taft's editorials are collected and republished in VIVIAN.
12. As the *New York Times* observed in 1914, Taft may not be "front page" news, but "for a man nominally in retirement he both gets and takes a lot of newspaper space." *Can He Have Meant the Colonel?*, NEW YORK TIMES (October 20, 1914), at 12. *See* Tatler, *Notes from the Capital*, 101 THE NATION 771 (1915) (Taft's "ready response to calls from all over the Union, for occasions which will assure him a large audience on the spot and a yet larger one through the press, enables him to interpret for the American people many of the political and social omens of the day, the full significance of which might otherwise be overlooked or misapprehended."). Muckraking journalist Ray Stannard Baker has left us with a fascinating portrait of one of Taft's speeches:

> While I found myself in rather hearty disagreement with nearly every position he took ... still I was curiously interested both in the man himself and in what he said. He is a really significant figure today in our public life: he represents a definite point of view.
>
> While Mr. Taft was in the White House he never seemed quite real. He was always a little out of focus – subdued by his environment. ... The other night, listening to his address, I felt that here, at last, was the real Mr. Taft – saying with great vigor what he believes – and has always believed. ... [B]ehind his words one feels the full thrust of his sincere and robust personality.
>
> He looks even happier than he did when he was in the White House. He *is* happier, his friends say. He is much in demand as a lecturer. ...
>
> I was interested in what Mr. Taft said. It may set men to thinking more keenly upon the principles of government. It is perhaps as important to have honest men who hold back, as it is to have honest men who go ahead.

> Ray Stannard Baker, *Signs of the Times as Seen by Mr. Taft*, 58 HARPER'S WEEKLY 7–8 (May 9, 1914). In 1915, *The Nation* reported that five federal judges "were unanimous in their opinion of the value of the service [Taft] was doing the country by his temperate public discussion of current history from the point of view of one who had recently had much to do with making it." *Notes from the Capital, supra,* at 770.

13. *See, e.g.*, William H. Taft, *The Attacks on the Courts and Legal Procedure*, 5 KENTUCKY LAW JOURNAL 3 (1916). Taft advocated judicial reforms designed to remedy "the delay in hearing and decision of causes" and "the excessive cost of litigation." *Id.* at 10. Taft was particularly concerned publicly to oppose "the attack upon our judiciary and the proposal, by judicial recall, or recall of judicial decisions, to destroy its independence and thus to take away from the arch of government, the keystone." *Address of President Taft to the General Court of Legislature of Massachusetts*, March 18, 1912, Sen. Doc. No. 451, 62d CONG. 2d SESS., at 6. *See* William Howard Taft, *The Future of the Republican Party*, 186 SATURDAY EVENING POST 3–4, 32–33 (February 14, 1914); William Howard Taft, *The Courts and the Progressive Party*, 186 SATURDAY EVENING POST 9 (March 20, 1914).
14. *President Names Hughes Chief Justice as Taft Resigns because of Ill Health When Trip to Asheville Fails to Aid Him*, NEW YORK TIMES (February 4, 1930), at 2. The observation was a common one. The *New York Times* observed, for example, that Taft "was more widely beloved as an ex-President, even by those who had ostracized him politically, than he was as President, and was welcomed back to the exalted position of Chief Justice not only with the 'highest admiration,' ... but with a popular affection such as few men in the history of the nation have enjoyed." *A Modern Aristides*, NEW YORK TIMES (September 17, 1927), at 16.
15. In his chairmanship of the controversial United States Commission on Industrial Relations, which had been established by Woodrow Wilson in 1913, Walsh "stood out as an undaunted agitator, and became the leader around whom American radicalism has tried to rally." *Industrial Conflict*, 4 NEW REPUBLIC 89, 90 (1915). For a good discussion of Walsh's efforts, see JAMES WEINSTEIN, THE CORPORATE IDEAL IN THE LIBERAL STATE 1900–1918, at 172–213 (Boston: Beacon Press 1968).
16. *See* William Howard Taft, *National War Labor Board* (November 26, 1918), in VIVIAN, at 124.
17. UNITED STATES DEPARTMENT OF LABOR, BUREAU OF LABOR STATISTICS, NATIONAL WAR LABOR BOARD: A HISTORY OF ITS FORMATION AND ACTIVITIES, TOGETHER WITH ITS AWARDS AND THE DOCUMENTS OF IMPORTANCE IN THE RECORD OF ITS DEVELOPMENT 30, 32 (Washington D.C.: Government Printing Office 1922) (Bulletin of the United States Bureau of Labor Statistics No. 287).
18. VALERIE JEAN CONNER, THE NATIONAL WAR LABOR BOARD: STABILITY, SOCIAL JUSTICE, AND THE VOLUNTARY STATE IN WORLD WAR I at 43, 66 (Chapel Hill: University of North Carolina Press 1983).
19. Unanimous Resolution of the United Mine Workers, January 24, 1916, forwarded by letter of January 25, 1916, to Woodrow Wilson from William Green. National Archives, Department of Justice, Taft Folder. From his earliest days as a state court judge, Taft had fully supported the use of judicial injunctions to restrict secondary boycotts. *See* Alpheus T. Mason, *The Labor Decisions of Chief Justice Taft*, 78 UNIVERSITY OF PENNSYLVANIA LAW REVIEW 585, 587–601 (1930). In his inaugural address as president, Taft had staunchly defended "the power of the federal courts to issue injunctions in industrial disputes." William Howard Taft, *Inaugural Address*, 44 CONG. REC. 1, 5 (March 4, 1909). As a result of such attitudes, Samuel

Prologue: Mr. Taft Takes Charge

Gompers had himself written to Woodrow Wilson to express his dismay that Taft might be nominated to the Supreme Court to fill the vacancy created by the death of Justice Joseph Lamar. Samuel Gompers to Woodrow Wilson, January 7, 1916, National Archives, Department of Justice, Taft Folder. Gompers said that Taft "was known as the father of [the] abuse of the writ of injunction." *Id.*

> There is lacking in Mr. Taft's attitude toward fundamental principles of human and industrial justice an indefinable something that we call "heart understanding" – an understanding alone which enables the possessor to project himself into the experiences, the sorrows, the yearnings of others. Without this quality justice becomes cold and impersonal – in fact ceases to be justice and deteriorates into legalism
>
> Mr. Taft's experiences have not given him a knowledge of the affairs of the world of labor, and the bent of his mind has made it impossible for him to secure that knowledge by intuition and human sympathy.

Id.

20. Thus, for example, the *Omaha Bee* observed that "in Omaha last summer [Taft] made the statement that he had almost entirely altered his views on the labor question, a result of his experience on the War Labor Board." *Taft for Chief Justice*, OMAHA BEE (July 2, 1921), at 4. For an example of Taft's altered attitude, see Carl W. Ackerman, *Industrial Security Threatened Only by Bourbons, Taft Says*, PUBLIC LEDGER (October 13, 1919), at 19. Although Taft's "heart understanding" (Gompers to Wilson, *supra* note 19) of the challenges faced by organized labor, and of the intractable unreasonableness of many large employers, appears to have been enhanced by his experiences on the War Labor Board, there is little evidence that his settled convictions were significantly altered. *See* Mason, *supra* note 19.

21. *Taft Is Nominated as Chief Justice of U.S. Supreme Court*, DALLAS MORNING NEWS (July 1, 1921), at 1. *See Taft at Williamstown To-Morrow*, TIMES-UNION (of Albany New York) (July 28, 1921), at 4 ("Taft's work as a member of the War Labor Board, during the war, did much to allay opposition to his supreme bench appointment on the theory that he was ultra-conservative. His decisions on the board were, in the main, more satisfactory to labor than the employers."). Frank Walsh wrote Taft after the latter's appointment: "The great people of our equally great nation will feel sure that the solemn tribunal of Justice will offer a place of refuge for the weak and oppressed as well as the rich and powerful. It is with a feeling of great honor that I pen these poor lines to the one of few Chief Justices that carries into that sacred office a real, generous soul and a great, kind heart." Frank P. Walsh to WHT (August 2, 1921) (Taft papers). Matthew Woll, president of the International Photo-Engravers' Union, wrote, "My association with you as a member of the National War Labor Board has convinced me of your great fitness for this exalted and most responsible position ... and I feel too that your intimate contact with industrial relations has given you a practical vision of our industrial life which will help mould the opinions and the decisions of the greatest judiciary in our modern civilization and in a way which will permit of the great mass of our people – the workers – of expressing their aims, hopes and aspirations in a peaceful, orderly and rational manner and without undue restriction and in full accord with the rights and privileges accorded them under our liberal constitution." Matthew Woll to WHT (August 3, 1921) (Taft papers). Taft answered Woll by acknowledging "the advantage that came to all, I hope, and to me, I think, of a more intimate knowledge of the

attitude of both sides in the relation between labor and capital. It is an experience that I value much." WHT to Matthew Woll (August 10, 1921) (Taft papers).

Gus Karger, Taft's intimate friend, wrote Taft to observe that Samuel Gompers himself was pleased by Taft's appointment:

> I had a very pleasant interview at the White House today with old Sam Gompers. "In the language of the street", he said, "Mr. Taft's appointment tickled me to death. I know of no one who has his legal attainments, coupled with his experience". He testified to the fact that you had "broadened" and paid tribute to your services on the War Labor Board. "You know we have often been on opposite sides", he added. "But no matter how much we may have differed, I always entertained a very warm admiration for him." Coming from an old political adversary, I calls it plumb handsome.

Gus Karger to WHT (September 3, 1921) (Taft papers). *See also Taft Gets the Biggest of Plums*, 13 NONPARTISAN LEADER 4 (July 25, 1921) ("Though his administration as president was a failure and he carried only two of the 48 states when he ran for re-election, he functioned well on the war labor board, where he was associated with men who understood labor's problems and where he had an opportunity to get labor's viewpoint first hand, and see the greed of big business employers.... Taft wants to be fair, we think, and it may be that on the court, where he is compelled to hear both sides of every question, he may turn out better than progressives predict.").

22. 254 U.S. 443 (1921). For Taft's support of the decision, see William Howard Taft, *Gompers and the Law* (January 12, 1921), in VIVIAN, at 525–26.

23. Samuel Gompers, *The Courts and Mr. Taft on Labor*, 28 AMERICAN FEDERATIONIST 220 (1921). See *Our Industrial Victory*, 8 PROCEEDINGS OF THE ACADEMY OF POLITICAL SCIENCE IN THE CITY OF NEW YORK 214–21 (February 1919). Others on the left were less forgiving. *See, e.g., Mr. Chief Justice Taft*, 27 NEW REPUBLIC 230, 231 (1921) ("The press greets Mr. Taft's appointment with almost universal acclaim. ... Whence the change from Taft, the target of the Progressives, to Taft, their acclaimed? Surely it's the same Mr. Taft. True, during the war there was discernible in him a slight interlude, due partly to the general wooing of Labor, and partly to Mr. Taft's genial submissiveness to the constant stimulus of Frank Walsh. But it was only an interlude. The same stand-pat pieties and timidity which led Mr. Taft to denounce Roosevelt for 'laying the axe at the root of the tree' and 'profaning the Ark of the Covenant' have inevitably made him an easy prey to post-war fears and hysteria."); *Harding May Fill Supreme Tribunal with Sutherland*, NEW YORK WORLD (May 23, 1921), at 7 ("William Howard Taft's friends have by no means given up hope of his succession to the Chief Justiceship, though organized labor is objecting to him because of the views he has indicated in recent publications, which have apparently quite neutralized the favor he gained on the War Labor Board.").

24. E. James Hindman, *The General Arbitration Treaties of William Howard Taft*, 36 THE HISTORIAN 52, 56–57 (1973). For a more negative view, see John P. Campbell, *Taft Roosevelt, and the Arbitration Treaties of 1911*, 53 JOURNAL OF AMERICAN HISTORY 279 (1966). At the time, the *New York Times* described the treaties as "perhaps the crowning achievement of Mr. Taft's administration." NEW YORK TIMES (August 4, 1911), at 6.

Prologue: Mr. Taft Takes Charge

25. Theodore Roosevelt, *The Peace of Righteousness*, 99 THE OUTLOOK 66 (September 9, 1911). Taft responded by ridiculing war, the only alternative to arbitration, as the "absurd" modern equivalent of the old "duello."

> Of course you say if your national honor is involved you want to go on to the field of battle and vindicate your honor. That is all right if you have got the heaviest battalions and the most guns and the best disciplined army and you win. Then you parade up and down the battlefield and your leaders become Presidents and you have vindicated your honor, but is it if the nation that has insulted you has a larger number of troops and a better disciplined army and better guns and you are driven off the field of battle, and you have to surrender – that does not satisfy your honor very well. Does it decide anything[?] Does battle decide anything except that men who win have the strongest army? Does it decide anything about honor[?] Does it decide anything of vital interest on any basis of equality or justice[?] So I say there is nothing dishonorable but there is everything moral and there is everything progressive in substituting for war any question of national honor or of vital interest a decision by a board of arbitration of just and impartial men who shall proceed in their decision on principles of law and equity.

Address of President Taft at Pocatello, Idaho (October 6, 1911) (Taft papers).

26. PRINGLE, *supra* note 4, at 928–36. *See* WILLIAM HOWARD TAFT, TAFT PAPERS ON LEAGUE OF NATIONS (Theodore Marburg & Horace E. Flack, eds., New York: MacMillan Co. 1920). In 1912, Taft wrote Elihu Root that his Yale professorship would "enable me to proclaim the evangel of constitutionalism and international peace – the two subjects that I have been anxious to use the rest of my life so that someday we shall secure that advantage which we lost during my administration." WHT to Elihu Root (November 20, 1912) (Taft papers). Taft's leadership of the League prompted the praise even of liberal democratic Justice John H. Clarke. *See* John H. Clarke, *A Call To Service: The Duty of the Bench and Bar to Aid in Securing League of Nations to Enforce the Peace of the World*, 4 AMERICAN BAR ASSOCIATION JOURNAL 567, 574 (1918) ("A group of distinguished American statesmen, lawyers and publicists, with former President Taft as their leader, have rendered a great public service by formulating a constitution or convention for such a league, which may serve as a starting point for discussion now and when the time shall come for settling the terms of the treaty of peace.").

27. *The League Necessary to Peace*, NEW YORK TIMES (March 5, 1919), at 10. The *Times* reported that "the audience showed its appreciation, with the President, of his presence on the same platform with ex-President Taft, when Mr. Wilson called attention to this fact, saying he was happy to associate himself with Mr. Taft and praising him for his 'elevation of view and a devotion to public duty which is beyond praise.'" *Wilson Says He'll Stay till It's Over and Bring Treaty Back*, NEW YORK TIMES (March 5, 1919), at 2. According to the *Times*, "The first applause for Mr. Taft came when he spoke of how he valued the opportunity to be at the meeting and to give it a nonpartisan flavor. He raised a general laugh when he referred to his own administration as one 'the President has long forgotten.' There was more laughter when he told of his attempt to have a recalcitrant Senate approve some arbitration treaties, which came back to him 'crippled and truncated, so that their own father could not recognize them.'" *Id.*

28. *A Great American Statesman*, 37 WORLD'S WORK 612 (April 1919). The liberal editor Norman Hapgood recalls in his autobiographical memoir that "In those days

the Republicans were being divided into those, like Mr. Taft, who were seeking the good of their country and the world, and those who, led by Senator Lodge, were seeking primarily to ruin a President of the opposite party." NORMAN HAPGOOD, THE CHANGING YEARS: REMINISCENCES OF NORMAN HAPGOOD 248 (New York: Farrar & Rinehart 1930). "I shall not forget the impression [Taft's] round and smiling person made when he explained that his work was causing him to be called 'a Bolsheviki,'. ... Shaking all over with amusement, with gestures to emphasize his roundness, he would ask of the audience, '*Do I look* like a Bolsheviki?'" *Id.*

29. *The Fight on Taft*, WICHITA DAILY EAGLE (July 2, 1921), at 4 ("The real reason for the opposition is that Taft favors American participation in the League of Nations. Wichitans will recall that Mr. Taft made one of the most logical pleas for the League that was delivered in the Wichita Forum during the trying times of the fight that was led by Borah, Johnson and Lafollette against the League. These three irreconcilables [who voted against Taft's confirmation as chief justice] are not willing to lay aside their prejudice against the leading figure in their party, merely because Mr. Taft failed to show symptoms of ptomaine poisoning every time the League was mentioned."). Several years later Taft's close friend George D. Seymour wrote him "that no American in [Taft's] generation had shown any one single act of devotion to an ideal and courage in any way comparable to your appearance on the stage in Carnegie Hall with Mr. Wilson in support of the League of Nations, when every other prominent Republican had been besought to appear on the same platform with him and had declined. A few days after this, [Connecticut] Governor Woodruff came into my office and fairly 'wept' over the occurrence, saying that you had made a profound political mistake and had absolutely cut yourself off from any political preferment by appearing on the stage with Wilson, when every other Republican of influence had refused to do so." George D. Seymour to WHT (July 1, 1921) (Taft papers). *See Taft at Williamstown To-Morrow*, *supra* note 21 ("His insistence on following his conscience regardless of political effect, it is said in inside Republican circles, probably prevented his receiving the Republican nomination for president last year. Had he been willing to deal with Republican senators opposed to the League of Nations, he could have had the nomination on a platter, it is stated. But he would not. When he appeared on the same platform with President Wilson in New York, in support of the league, his name was stricken from the roster of presidential eligibles.").

30. *Judge Taft's Appointment*, SAVANNAH PRESS (July 2, 1921), at 6 ("The surprising thing is that there should have been opposition to his confirmation. It is significant that the fight was led by the 'irreconcilables' to the Treaty of Versailles – Senators Borah of Idaho, Johnson of California, La Follette of Wisconsin and Watson of Georgia. These are the men who fought the Treaty and the Peace Pact in and out of the Senate and who doubtless were displeased with the early efforts of Judge Taft, who seemed to favor the work of President Wilson and his associates in Paris. For Judge Taft first spoke upon the same platform as the ex-President and did what he could in the first stages of the contest to make the League of Nations popular with the people."). *See Talk of Taft as a Possible Chief Justice*, POST-STANDARD (Syracuse, New York) (May 20, 1921), at 5 ("He is not so popular in official Washington. The senators have not forgiven him for the service he gave to Mr. Wilson's league of nations. They feel that he is of too tolerant a partisanship. ... [H]e will have the strong opposition of the irreconcilables.");

Prologue: Mr. Taft Takes Charge

Chief Justice Taft, LOS ANGELES TIMES (July 2, 1921), at 4 ("The opposition displayed by the 'bitter-enders' in the Senate will not lessen the confidence which the American people feel both in his ability and his disinterestedness.").

31. *Chief Justice Taft*, GALVESTON DAILY NEWS (July 2, 1921), at 6 ("[T]he large-minded way in which he conducted himself during the war and afterward in support of Mr. Wilson's administration, though of a political complexion different from his own in most particulars, won for him a respect and even affection which he had been unable to win for himself during his years as executive and administrator. America loves a good loser, and there have been few better losers than Mr. Taft."). *See Chief Justice Taft*, DALLAS MORNING NEWS (July 2, 1921), at 12; *Chief Justice Taft: The Appointment Is as Gratifying to the Nation as to Its Recipient*, SAN FRANCISCO CHRONICLE (July 1, 1921), at 24 ("With the lengthening distance from the period when he was the subject of political differences the partisan feeling of that time has given way entirely before universal recognition of his great qualities and character. When he went through the country a few years ago to plead for his league to enforce peace it was a triumphal progress in which Americans, irrespective of whether they had formerly been friends of enemies or whether they favored the cause he was presenting, united everywhere in warm tribute to his personality."); J.M. Dickinson, *Chief Justice William Howard Taft*, 37 AMERICAN BAR ASSOCIATION JOURNAL 331, 331 (1921) ("Perhaps nothing so exalted him in the admiration and established him in the esteem of the people as his courageous and patriotic support of a not too friendly administration throughout the war.").

32. *The New Chief Justice*, HONOLULU STAR-BULLETIN (July 1, 1921), at 6. *See Chief Justice Taft*, PITTSBURGH DISPATCH INDEPENDENT (July 1, 1921), at 6 ("Since his retirement from the Presidency Mr. Taft has gained greatly in popular understanding. He developed a breadth of view in the discussion of affairs that disarmed many who were his most vigorous critics while in the White House."). Writing in 1928, William Allen White articulated an important dimension of Taft's new-found appeal when he observed that as President Taft had been "both a throwback and a forecast, a terrible muddle; a throwback to the eighties of the last century, a forecast of the twenties in this century." WHITE, *supra* note 6, at 327.

33. Gus Karger to WHT (June 14, 1921) (Taft papers); Gus Karger to WHT (June 21, 1921) (Taft papers).

34. For the story of the convention, see PRINGLE, *supra* note 4, at 796–814. For Roosevelt's accusation that Taft's delegates used "every species of fraud and violence," see Theodore Roosevelt, *A Confession of Faith: Address before the National Convention of the Progressive Party in Chicago*, in THEODORE ROOSEVELT, PROGRESSIVE PRINCIPLES: SELECTIONS FROM ADDRESSES MADE DURING THE PRESIDENTIAL CAMPAIGN OF 1912, at 124 (Elmer H. Youngman, ed., New York: Progressive National Service 1913).

35. MILTON W. BLUMENBERG, OFFICIAL REPORT OF THE PROCEEDINGS OF THE FIFTEENTH REPUBLICAN NATIONAL CONVENTION 378–79 (New York: Tenny Press 1912).

36. William Howard Taft, *Mr. Wilson and the Campaign*, 10 YALE REVIEW 1, 19–20 (1920). Felix Frankfurter, writing in the *New Republic*, immediately rose to the bait: "Mr. Taft deserves our gratitude for his candor in recognizing that the Supreme Court involves political issues to be discussed like other political issues. In 1912,

Mr. Taft was shocked that Roosevelt should dare drag the Court into the political arena. But now Mr. Taft warns us that no issue is more important than the views of the candidates as to future Justices. Of course that means we must study past decisions, the line-up of the Justices, their attitude toward economic ('property') questions, the attitude of likely appointees toward such questions. . . . Mr. Taft has now made respectable what was heretofore tabooed. The door to the Holy of Holies has been opened. Others will follow where Mr. Taft's profanation leads." *Taft and the Supreme Court*, 24 NEW REPUBLIC 208, 209 (1920).

37. WHT to Helen Herron Taft (December 26, 1920) (Taft papers). The meeting between Taft and Harding took place on December 24.

38. *Id.* "I said he would make a fine Judge," Taft commented to Harding, adding that Sutherland "was, after Root, the ablest lawyer in the Senate." *Id.*

39. *Id.* The next day was Christmas, and the surprised Taft sent Harding a note:

> I was so much startled by the personal question you asked me that I am afraid that my answer was confused and seemed presumptuous and unappreciative. Ever since I came to the Bar, I have aspired to the Supreme Court as my life's goal. Twice I was obliged to decline the opportunity for reasons I explained. Then I was young and would have been glad to take an associate justiceship and work up from the junior membership toward the head and perhaps to the chief justiceship if fortune favored. But now I am sixty-three and could not expect to serve more than ten years. I have been President. I signed the commissions of six members of the Court, and three are still on the Court. I joined four presidents of the American Bar Association in petitioning the Senate to reject the nomination of Brandeis as not a fit one to be made and have not changed my mind, and I would feel ill at ease to come into the Court after having been President as the junior of my own appointees and of the man I tried to defeat. Were I Chief Justice I would hope, by reason of having been President, to have some little more influence in securing a greater solidarity of opinion among the judges so necessary to maintain the Court's influence with the public. It was for this reason that I ventured to say that I could only accept the Chief Justice's position. The present Chief Justice when I have seen him in the years past has said for me that he was holding on for me and to return the place to a Republican administration. I can't say that he still feels this way though I know he greatly rejoiced at your election. Even if you conclude that some one else ought to be chief justice as well you may, I hope you will believe me when I say that I am deeply grateful for what you said to me yesterday, and that it was one of the great honors of my life and makes this Christmas for me the brightest and happiest of my life.

WHT to Warren G. Harding (December 25, 1920) (Harding Papers in the Ohio History Connection). (I am grateful to Walter Stahr for this letter). The next day Taft wrote his wife that "[I] was non-plussed at the way in which he took me into his confidence and was nearly struck dumb when he asked me if I would go on the Supreme Court and I felt I spoke in a confused way. . . . I don't feel at all confident it will work out as I would like it, but it is more favorable to my hope and life ambition than I thought possible. . . . I did not think I would tell you . . . because I don't want to raise your hopes to have them dashed, but I concluded I owed it to you, Darling." WHT to Helen Herron Taft (December 26, 1920) (Taft papers). Harding responded to Taft's Christmas note with a short letter acknowledging that "I appreciate fully all that you have to say concerning yourself and your ambitions. I have already told you of my abiding esteem and good will and I need not repeat it here." Warren G. Harding to WHT (January 4, 1921) (Taft papers).

Prologue: Mr. Taft Takes Charge

40. *See* Warren G. Harding to WHT (January 4, 1921) (Taft papers); WHT to Horace D. Taft (January 19, 1921) (Taft papers) (Harding's note "seems to me to indicate that he wishes me to understand that his announced purpose to put me on the Bench was abiding and that he sympathized with my desire to be Chief Justice only.").
41. *See, e.g.*, ALPHEUS THOMAS MASON, WILLIAM HOWARD TAFT: CHIEF JUSTICE 66–87 (New York: Simon and Schuster 1965).
42. J. Francis Paschal, *Mr. Justice Sutherland*, in MR. JUSTICE 204 (Allison Dunham & Philip B. Kurland, eds., University of Chicago Press 1964). Sutherland "was one of the Big Three among Harding's advisers at Marion, Colonel Harvey and Richard Washburn Child being the others." *Meaning of the Supreme Court Shift*, 74 LITERARY DIGEST 15 (September 16, 1922). *See* Warren G. Harding to GS (August 6, 1920) (Sutherland papers) ("[H]ow I need you, and I need you greatly, and I wish you would arrange to come to me as soon as you can and stay with me as long as your affairs permit."); Warren G. Harding to GS (November 16, 1920) (Sutherland papers) ("You helped me mightily and I am grateful. We were very happy to have you at Marion for so long a time and thereby fell quite in love with you. . . . You know how grateful I am.").
43. *See* Judson C. Welliver to GS (December 10, 1920) (Sutherland papers) ("I have gathered a pretty definite impression that you are not going to be a member of the Cabinet and that you will be the first appointee to the Supreme Bench."); WHT to Charles P. Taft (May 25, 1921) (Taft papers); WHT to Mabel Boardman (May 31, 1921) (Taft papers) ("The President seems to feel that he is complicated by a promise to Sutherland to put him on the Bench at the first opportunity, although he has made a distinct promise to make me Chief Justice, and I have declined to accept any other place.").
44. On May 15, McReynolds observed that "The Chief Justice is in the hospital & has had some sort of an operation wh. is reported to have been successful. He has been in a bad way for months & I presume will never be very well again. The last utterances from him indicated that he intended to be on the bench again in the Autumn. Possibly Day may conclude to quit – but I doubt that he will. None of the others have any idea of going off." JCM to J.M. Dickinson (May 15, 1921) (Dickinson papers at the Tennessee State Library & Archives). White's death prompted Holmes to write to his friend Harold Laski, "You may wonder if I am thinking of [the Chief Justiceship]. Not in any sense except that all possibilities occur to one and that no doubt a few here and there have named me. They would not appoint so old a man – and although I think I know my place with regard to the higher aspects of the law, I should not expect it of the appointing power. That is not the kind of thing that excites me much. . . . I wonder how many men are pulling wires now. I give you my word of honor that I am not. I don't even know what, if any, wires I could pull." OWH to Harold J. Laski (May 27, 1921), in 1 HOLMES-LASKI CORRESPONDENCE, at 339. Willis Van Devanter, by contrast, was intent on subtly pulling wires. On May 26, a week after White's death, he wrote his close friend, District Judge John C. Pollock:

> Some suggestion has been made that the appointment will go to one of the senior members of the court as now constituted with the idea that it will be more or less temporary, but my impression is that there is nothing in this. Confidentially, Justices McKenna, Day, McReynolds and Clarke have said to me that they would be glad to see me appointed, but I realize that an

expression of their views may not be solicited and cannot with propriety be given unless solicited. Senator Kellogg has volunteered to me the statement that he intends to recommend me and to recommend that ex-Senator George Sutherland be named in my place. Ex-Senator Bailey seems to think I will be the man, and others have volunteered a friendly interest, but I am neither saying nor doing anything nor permitting any of these statements to bring me any sense of elation or to change the current of my mind. Pleasant commendation by intimate friends or by those who in social intercourse prefer to be agreeable rather than otherwise is not to be taken for anything beyond what it really is, so I am not counting on anything but merely attending to my present responsibilities.

WVD to John C. Pollock (May 26, 1921) (Van Devanter papers). The next day Van Devanter wrote Pollock recounting conflicting assessments of Taft's chances:

> The fact that the President is not a lawyer, and the further fact that even a hasty or casual committal seems sacred to him, may be important factors in the ultimate outcome. It is known that he had a rather long conference with Judge Taft about the duties of the President, etc., shortly after the election, and they had a long conference on the same subject very shortly following the inauguration. Something may have been said in a generous and appreciative way on one or both of those occasions without particularly weighing it before it was said.... Another circumstance might appeal rather strongly to President Harding who does not think well of Mr. Wilson. The latter on becoming President sent word, as I happen to know, to Judge Taft that he was going to put him on the Supreme Court as a soon as a vacancy occurred. When a vacancy did occur Mr. Wilson rather promptly appointed McReynolds. When the next vacancy occurred, through the death of Justice Lamar, the President of the American Bar Association and four living ex-presidents of the Association, some of one party and some of the other, asked Mr. Wilson to appoint Judge Taft and suggested that it would be a fitting time for him to step over the party wall as Mr. Taft had done in appointing Justice Lamar. Instead, Mr. Wilson appointed Brandeis. This story, which is quite true, might appeal rather strongly to a fair-minded man like Mr. Harding and might cause him impulsively to say that he was going to do what his predecessor promised and yet failed to do.

WVD to John C. Pollock (May 27, 1921) (Van Devanter papers). When Pollock offered to assist Van Devanter in securing the appointment, John C. Pollock to WVD (June 2, 1921) (Van Devanter papers), Van Devanter played coy:

> Of course, there is nothing which I can do with propriety. No doubt there will be those who think that my opinions represent the only work which I do, and of course it would be quite inadmissible for me or my friends to intimate that I have any responsibility for the opinions of others or have done any work on them. At all events, no one outside of the court itself could speak of this no matter what they surmise. Aside from other elements of impropriety it would give offense in quarters where offense would be harmful. This has been a term in which dissents were quite frequent, and yet there has not been a single dissent from any of my opinions during the term. There are some who merely count the number of opinions regardless of their substance or the direction in which they go. When one does work on that line he can do what superficially seems a volume, and then the other federal courts and the state courts may grope as best they can in an effort to find out what was intended. My ideas and inclinations are not in that direction. It leads to uncertainty and confusion, makes for instability and in the long run results in tremendous waste. The number of petitions for rehearing during the term has been unusually large, but in my cases only one was presented. People outside do not know this and in the nature of things would not be supposed to know. Again, comment on it, save by someone inside, might arouse resentment

Prologue: Mr. Taft Takes Charge

    where a kindly feeling now exists. The only things for me to do is to take my usual vacation and let come what will.

    WVD to John C. Pollock (June 7, 1921) (Van Devanter papers). Van Devanter threw in the towel three days later, conceding the inevitability of Taft's appointment. "My impression is that nothing more should be done by my friends. I fear that under the circumstances it would not be welcome, and this becomes a little more pointed with me when I reflect that Mr. Taft appointed me to my present place and also that I must serve with whomever is appointed for a considerable time." WVD to John C. Pollock (June 10, 1921) (Van Devanter papers).

45. *See* Frank B. Brandegee to WHT (May 23, 1921) (Taft papers) ("My impression is that the President would like to put both you and Sutherland on the Supreme Bench. I think he would like to make these appointments at the same time, but there is only one vacancy at present."); Gus Karger to WHT (May 25, 1921) (Taft papers) (Harding's "desire is . . . to send in your name and Sutherland's at the same time.").

46. Frank B. Brandegee to WHT (May 23, 1921) (Taft papers); Frank B. Brandegee to WHT (May 30, 1921) (Taft papers) ("I cannot be mistaken . . . in thinking that he has got some plan of offering the position to Day for a short period, provided he can induce Day to get off the Court, because he did say that he would like to appoint you and Sutherland at the same time, and in order to do this there must be two vacancies."); WHT to Mabel Boardman (May 31, 1921) (Taft papers) ("He had some thought of appointing Day to hold the office for three or four months and get the title and then retire. This would give him an opportunity to put Sutherland on, and then to appoint me after Day had retired. That is trifling with a great office, and I don't favor any such arrangement. I don't want to be a party to it. . . . At the present time I am a good deal discouraged over the matter, because I had supposed it was so clearly understood that there would not be any hesitation. However, I have had so much that I have no right to become resentful at disappointments."); *Day Calls on Harding; Possibility of His Elevation to Chief Justice Discussed Anew*, NEW YORK TIMES (June 8, 1921), at 4. *See* FRANCIS RUSSELL, THE SHADOW OF BLOOMING GROVE: WARREN G. HARDING IN HIS TIMES 441–42 (New York: McGraw-Hill Book Co. 1968).

47. WHT to Horace D. Taft (June 7, 1921) (Taft papers) ("The Chief Justiceship is in abeyance. . . . Harding can't 'jar loose' either Holmes or McKenna without some inducement. . . . It is possible that Harding has in mind to offer to Holmes or McKenna a place on this Disarmament Commission that Harding is evidently framing in connection with the passage of the Naval Appropriation Bill. . . . Now Holmes loves England. He is the best known of our Judges there. His father had a great [?] in London after he was 75 and the son is jealous of the father. That shows his character. It would be very alluring to him to end his career in such a conspicuous activity in 'our old home.' The Bench would be well rid of him for his influence is not good on the Bench. He is always or generally with Brandeis. Perhaps, however, McKenna is the man and what his predilections are for such a mission I do not know."); Luther A. Brewer to WHT (June 9, 1921) (Taft papers) (Harding has "gone so far as to sound out Holmes and Day on the question of their resigning only to learn that neither one had any intention of so doing."); WHT to Charles P. Taft (June 9, 1921) (Taft papers). *See* George Wickersham to WHT

23

(June 14, 1921) (Taft papers) ("Daugherty told me, in confidence, that the President had had an intimation that there might be another vacancy in the Supreme bench, and that he had withheld action on the Chief Justiceship hoping that he might be able to fill the two places at once, putting George Sutherland into the Associate Justiceship.").

48. WHT to Horace D. Taft (June 11, 1921) (Taft papers). Taft comforted himself with the thought that "the place is so great a one that it should not come in an easy way ... and if it does come, one will be quite willing to have gone through some suspense and some worry before getting it." WHT to Gus Karger (June 21, 1921) (Taft papers).

49. WHT to PB (May 26, 1921) (Taft papers). Taft and Butler had become acquainted during the arbitration proceedings to determine the value of the Grand Trunk railroad system, which was in the process of being acquired by the Canadian government. Butler represented the Canadian government, while Taft had in July 1920 been appointed one of the three arbitrators. *See Acquisition of Grand Trunk and Subsidiary Concerns*, in ANNUAL REPORT OF THE DEPARTMENT OF RAILWAYS AND CANALS FOR THE FISCAL YEAR FROM APRIL 1, 1920 TO MARCH 31, 1921, at 128–204 (1921); A.W. CURRIE, THE GRAND TRUNK RAILWAY OF CANADA 461–68 (University of Toronto Press 1957); LESLIE T. FOURNIER, RAILWAY NATIONALIZATION IN CANADA: THE PROBLEM OF THE CANADIAN NATIONAL RAILWAYS 100–6 (Toronto: Macmillan Company of Canada 1935); John A. Eagle, *Monopoly or Competition: The Nationalization of the Grand Trunk Railway*, 62 CANADIAN HISTORY REVIEW 27 (1981). Taft enjoyed Butler's professional style. When Butler cross-examines a witness, Taft wrote his wife, "we could keep awake." WHT to Helen Herron Taft (February 19, 1921) (Taft papers). *See* WHT to Helen Herron Taft (July 8, 1921) (Taft papers). Butler and Taft evidently struck up a warm association. *See* WHT to Helen Herron Taft (June 24, 1921) (Taft papers). On May 23, Butler wrote to congratulate Taft "upon your prospective (now, as I understand, fully assured) appointment to Chief Justice of the United States." PB to WHT (May 23, 1921) (Taft papers). "But the country is to be congratulated much more than you are," Butler continued. "Now, as much as – even more than – at any time, the quality of the men constituting the court is important. Your fellow citizens, and especially lawyers of the country, heartily approve the President's purpose and, because you will be the chief, will rely with greater confidence upon the Supreme Court. Your friends, and I have long counted myself one, are glad that in the record of illustrious and varied public service . . . you stand first in the history of the country":

> One who was present when [White] took the oath of office as Chief Justice said to me that he saw "a senior associate administer the oath of office of chief justice to a junior associate, a Republican to a Democrat appointed Chief Justice by a Republican President, a Union soldier to a Confederate soldier, a Presbyterian to a Roman Catholic, who took the oath on the King James bible". I answered that he saw a good deal that spoke well for the President and for the United States.

Id.

50. *See* JAMES M. GIGLIO, H.M. DAUGHERTY AND THE POLITICS OF EXPEDIENCY 34 (Kent State University Press 1978).

51. Daugherty was a faithful Taft supporter throughout the ill-fated campaign. *See id.* at 57–83.

Prologue: Mr. Taft Takes Charge

52. WHT to Gus Karger (May 10, 1922) (Taft papers). Taft observed that he was "much impressed with Harry Daugherty's determination to make his Department as effective as possible in the fulfillment of its functions, and I prophesy that he will be one of the successful Attorneys General." WHT to Max Pam (March 28, 1921) (Taft papers).
53. *See* WHT to Horace D. Taft (June 7, 1921) (Taft papers) (Max Pam reported that "Daugherty was going to press for my appointment before July 1st and he asked Max to give me the message that he was on the job and it was all right."); George Wickersham to WHT (June 14, 1921) (Taft papers) (Daugherty "was all for you.").
54. *Harding Appoints Taft Chief Justice*, NEW YORK TRIBUNE (July 1, 1921), at 2. The *Washington Post* reported that "Mr. Harding is understood to have been advised by legal officers of the administration that all the Federal courts were so congested with business that prompt action during the summer recess was necessary in order to expedite litigation as much as possible." *Taft Chief Justice*, WASHINGTON POST (July 1, 1921), at 5. *See Taft Is Nominated as Chief Justice of U.S. Supreme Court*, DALLAS MORNING NEWS (July 1, 1921), at 1 ("Originally it had been Harding's intention to delay naming a successor to the late Chief Justice White until just before the October term. ... Since White's death, however, developments necessitated alteration of this plan. Foremost among these developments has been the jam in the courts of all large cities resulting from a vast number of prosecutions ordered against alleged violators of the Volstead prohibition law. The Department of Justice is trying to work out a plan for special commissions to handle prohibition cases, for extra Judges in seriously affected districts or for some other measures to relieve the congestion and in this reorganization work Attorney General Daugherty stressed the need of having a Chief Justice of the Supreme Court to aid him. The first work, therefore, that the new Chief Justice will take up will probably be that involved in adjusting court facilities, particularly in large cities east of the Mississippi River, to meet the demands of prohibition cases."); Gus Karger to WHT (June 30, 1921) (Taft papers) ("The courts are congested," Harding said at the press conference announcing Taft's nomination, "and the Chief Justice will be a factor in bringing on a better situation. Additional judges will be needed, there may be need of authorization of commissioners; something must be done to relieve the courts of cases of the less criminal type, I mean cases growing out of the Volstead act. The courts are all clogged up. It is the problem of the Department of Justice to work this out and the Attorney General wants the Chief Justice to help work it out.").
55. 61 CONG. REC. 3253 (June 30, 1921); *Harding Appoints Taft Chief Justice; Senate Confirms Him, 61 to 4*, NEW YORK TRIBUNE (July 1, 1921), at 1. Taft wrote his wife, "My darling Nellie – Well that has happened which I have always doubted coming true. I am now Chief Justice of the United States lacking only the qualifying oath." WHT to Helen Herron Taft (June 30, 1921) (Taft papers). Voting against Taft were Senators Borah (Idaho), Johnson (California), La Follette (Wisconsin), and Watson (Georgia). "Senator Borah led the fight against the former president. He declared that Mr. Taft ceased the practice of law thirty years ago, and that since that time he had been in politics. He argued that Mr. Taft, who is 63 years of age, is within seven years of what he termed the age where by law a man is considered to have reached the age of incompetence." *Ex-President Taft Succeeds White as Chief Justice*, NEW YORK

TIMES (July 1, 1921), at 1. The next day, Taft wrote Nellie that "You will observe that Borah attacked my legal qualifications. He did not seem to get very far with it, tho' perhaps there is more of truth in it than you and my friends would be willing to admit. We will see." WHT to Helen Herron Taft (July 2, 1921) (Taft papers).

56. *Notes from the Capital*, *supra* note 12, at 770.
57. *Chief Justice Taft*, NEW YORK EVENING POST (July 1, 1921), at 6:

> Any qualification upon Mr. Taft's fitness for the Chief Justiceship concerns the administrative duties of the position. The Chief Justice ... has responsibility of keeping the court as nearly abreast of its business as possible. This demands the exercise of executive abilities.... He must organize the work of the court and infuse into it the efficiency which is more conspicuously recognized in commercial affairs. For this part of his task, Mr. Taft admittedly has small predilection. But he cannot complain if an occupation which in general he finds highly congenial imposes upon him one uncongenial duty.

See The New Chief Justice, *supra* note 32, at 6 ("The fact is, and it is recognized by his closest and most sympathetic friends, that Mr. Taft has a judicial, not an executive, mind; he is a keen judge and constructive critic of the actions of others but he himself is not a doer, he is lacking in initiative, an indispensable attribute of leadership.").

58. WHITE, *supra* note 6, at 333–34. Taft's nomination was nevertheless attacked by progressive Republican Senator William E. Borah of Idaho on the ground that Taft was merely a politician, not a judge. Borah contrasted Taft with Justice Charles Evans Hughes, who had resigned from the Court to become the Republican candidate for president in 1916: "[H]aving taken an able lawyer from the Supreme Bench four years ago and made a politician of him, it was now proposed to take a politician – a man who has devoted practically his mature life to politics – and put him on the Supreme Bench in the interest of party politics." *Taft Chief Justice of Supreme Court*, NEW YORK HERALD (July 1, 1921), at 1.

59. Alpheus Thomas Mason, *President by Chance, Chief Justice by Choice*, 55 AMERICAN BAR ASSOCIATION JOURNAL 35, 39 (1969). Taft viewed his attempted improvements of the management of the executive branch as among his most important contributions as president. In his address accepting the 1912 Republican nomination for the presidency, for example, Taft proclaimed:

> During this administration we have given special attention to the machinery of government with a view to increasing its efficiency and reducing its cost.... I have secured an appropriation for the appointment of an Economy and Efficiency Commission, consisting of the ablest experts in the country, and they have been working for two years on the question of how the Government departments may be reorganized and what changes can be made with a view to giving them greater effectiveness for governmental purpose on the one hand, and securing this at considerably less cost on the other.

Speech of William Howard Taft Accepting the Republican Nomination for President of the United States, Sen. Doc. No. 902, 62nd CONG. 2d SESS. (1912). *See* William Howard Taft, *National Budget Plan* (July 24, 1919), in VIVIAN, at 244.

60. THEODORE H. WHITE, THE MAKING OF THE PRESIDENT 1960, at 399 (New York: Atheneum Publishers 1961).
61. *Taft's Life Praised as Truly American*, NEW YORK TIMES (March 9, 1930), at 1.

Prologue: Mr. Taft Takes Charge

62. *Taft Wants Quick and Cheap Justice*, NEW YORK TIMES (August 2, 1908), at 1.
63. FELIX FRANKFURTER, FELIX FRANKFURTER ON THE SUPREME COURT 487–88 (Cambridge: Belknap Press 1970). *See* Mason, *supra* note 59, at 39 ("As a judicial architect, Taft is without peer."). Frankfurter credited Taft for adapting the federal judicial system "to the needs of a country that had grown from three million to a hundred and twenty million."
64. Pub. L. 68-415, 43 Stat. 936 (February 13, 1925).
65. Taft's old friend, Charles E. Barker, reports that on his deathbed in January 1930 Taft said to him that "I can report that my one great ambition as Chief Justice has been accomplished. The docket is up to date, so I guess I've earned a few weeks' rest." CHARLES E. BARKER, WITH PRESIDENT TAFT IN THE WHITE HOUSE: MEMORIES OF WILLIAM HOWARD TAFT 71 (Chicago: A. Kroch & Son 1947).
66. LDB to Felix Frankfurter (March 6, 1925), in BRANDEIS-FRANKFURTER CORRESPONDENCE, at 196.
67. Herbert Little, *The Omnipotent Nine*, 15 AMERICAN MERCURY 48 (September 1928).
68. OWH to Frederick Pollock (October 2, 1921), in 2 HOLMES-POLLOCK CORRESPONDENCE, at 79.
69. OWH to Baroness Charlotte Moncheur (June 2, 1922) (Holmes papers).
70. *Brandeis-Frankfurter Conversations*, at 313 (June 28, 1923). Brandeis characterized Taft as "very nice – gentlemanly in dealing with case involving Ballinger. He talks long in Conference but he's a cultivated man & only other except Holmes you can talk to about things other than law without need of diagrams & spelling it out." *Id.* at 302 (April 17, 1922).
71. OWH to Frederick Pollock (February 24, 1923), in 2 HOLMES-POLLOCK CORRESPONDENCE, at 113–14.
72. *Brandeis-Frankfurter Conversations*, at 322 (August 6, 1923).
73. *Id.* at 321 (August 6, 1923).
74. HFS to Thomas Reed Powell (January 30, 1940) (Stone papers). When Frankfurter asked Brandeis about Taft's assignment of cases, Brandeis replied that "Taft tries to distribute fairly, on whole. Many case [sic] C.J. takes for himself because important, others because points are interesting, though cases not important, others because some justices don't like to take a case." *Brandeis-Frankfurter Conversations*, at 321 (August 6, 1923).
75. William Howard Taft, *Chief Justice White* (May 20, 1921), in VIVIAN, at 581.
76. Augustus Hand to WHT (September 18, 1929) (Taft papers). On Taft's ability to rally the Court, see Henry J. Friendly, *Review of the Unpublished Opinions of Mr. Justice Brandeis*, 106 HARVARD LAW REVIEW 766, 768 (1958). Friendly was Brandeis's law clerk during the 1927 term. *See also* David J. Danelski, *The Influence of the Chief Justice in the Decisional Process*, in COURTS, JUDGES, AND POLITICS: AN INTRODUCTION TO THE JUDICIAL PROCESS 695–703 (Walter F. Murphy & C. Herman Pritchett, eds., New York: Random House 1979). Important to Taft's leadership was the goodwill that he cultivated with his colleagues. When Taft generously and spontaneously took the initiative to arrange the details of Mrs. Holmes's funeral, for example, Holmes exclaimed, "How can one help loving a man with such a kind heart?" OWH to Harold Laski (June 15, 1929), in 2 HOLMES-LASKI CORRESPONDENCE, at 1158. After Taft retired, Holmes commented that "We all loved Taft and grieved at his bodily collapse." OWH to Nina

Grey (February 26, 1930) (Holmes papers). Frankfurter, who had reason to know, commented that Taft "always had the love and affection of his colleagues." FRANKFURTER, *supra* note 63, at 490.

77. Hiram Johnson to Raymond Robins (July 1, 1921) (Johnson papers at the University of California at Berkeley). On July 2, 1921, Johnson wrote his sons:

> Day before yesterday Taft's name was sent to the Senate as Chief Justice of the United States Supreme Court. . . . I said he was unfit to be the Chief Justice. . . . It is another instance, where I have been put in a woeful minority. . . . I can't help it, however. I would think myself the most contemptible of men if I did not at least vote against the confirmation of man like Taft. In my opinion he is, first, without the qualifications for a United States Supreme Court Judge, and secondly, he is crooked, both intellectually and otherwise, and thirdly, I think he was a traitor to his country in the League of Nations fight. . . . I think in the press the nomination is with practical unanimity praised. This may be so with the people, too. I do not know. . . . The incident was very depressing to me. . . . Taft deciding the grave problems which will come to us in the next few years is the most sinister thing that has come to us thus far in the administration. I confess that I went home Thursday night as low in spirits as I have ever been here.

Hiram Johnson to his Sons (July 2, 1921), in 3 THE DIARY LETTERS OF HIRAM JOHNSON: 1919–1921 (New York: Garland Publishing Co. 1983). *See* Hiram Johnson to Harold L. Ickes (July 2, 1921) (Johnson papers at the University of California at Berkeley).

78. Quoted in *Taft's Life Praised as Truly American, supra* note 61, at 26.
79. LDB to Felix Frankfurter (May 8, 1930), in BRANDEIS-FRANKFURTER CORRESPONDENCE, at 424.
80. *State Tribute to Taft*, NEW YORK TIMES (March 10, 1930), at 5. On the "universal regret" that greeted Taft's resignation on February 3, 1930, see Richard V. Oulahan, *President Names Hughes Chief Justice as Taft Resigns because of Ill Health when Trip to Asheville Fails to Aid Him*, NEW YORK TIMES (February 4, 1930), at 2.
81. His "lasting monument" was said to be that he "laid the foundation for a reorganization of the judicial administration in this country." *Jurist Here Adds Tribute*, LOS ANGELES TIMES (March 12, 1930), at 2.
82. This despite the eulogy of the *Los Angeles Times*, which predicted that Taft's "name will . . . be . . . connected with . . . the speeding up and modernizing of the Supreme Court and its reorganization to cope fully with its work. Directly and indirectly, Taft exercised a profound influence on court procedure, and if the law's delay, of which complaint has been made from time immemorial, shall ever cease to be a subject of complaint it will be in large part due to him." *William Howard Taft*, LOS ANGELES TIMES (March 10, 1930), at 4.
83. WHT to Clyde B. Aitchison (December 4, 1925) (Taft papers). Taft once wrote plaintively to Holmes in appreciation of the latter's opinions: "When I read them, I marvel. They read so well and so easily and I ask why can't I, but I can't." WHT to OWH (May 6, 1927) (Holmes papers).
84. *Judiciary: Hughes for Taft*, 15 TIME MAGAZINE 11–12 (February 10, 1930).
85. OWH to Harold J. Laski (January 15, 1922), in 1 HOLMES-LASKI CORRESPONDENCE, at 398.
86. It was said at the time of his death that "While as Chief Justice . . . Taft delivered several notable opinions of a pioneering quality, it is certain that his words will not be studied

Prologue: Mr. Taft Takes Charge

and pondered over as, say, the decisions of Marshall, of Taney, or even of Fuller." Stephen Bonsal, *The Man Who Served Us – Taft*, WORLD'S WORK (April 1930), at 79.
87. *Brandeis-Frankfurter Conversations*, at 310 (November 30, 1922). Brandeis noted that Taft "doesn't sufficiently work over materials." *Id.* at 307 (July 1, 1922).
88. *Id.* at 313 (June 28, 1923). The year before Holmes had used almost the exact same formulation to describe Taft, observing that "I doubt if he can go higher than the first rate second rate." OWH to Harold Laski (July 12, 1921), in 1 HOLMES-LASKI CORRESPONDENCE, at 346.
89. *William Howard Taft*, *supra* note 82, at 4.
90. WHT to Robert McDougal (October 13, 1924) (Taft papers).
91. WHT to Elihu Root (December 21, 1922) (Taft papers).
92. WHT to GS (September 10, 1922) (Taft papers).
93. *Chief Justice Taft*, NEW YORK CALL (July 2, 1921), at 8.
94. *Brandeis-Frankfurter Conversations*, at 303 (April 17, 1922). At times Brandeis could more sharply characterize Taft's lack of depth: "As a matter of fact the present Chief, with all his good nature & kindliness & the quality that makes everybody like him, looks like many a benevolent, good-natured distillery drummer I used to see in the days when I was counsel for some distilleries. His face has nothing in it – it's so vapid." *Id.* at 333 (August 3, 1924). Taft himself, in his own characteristically self-deprecating way, remarked to his brother four years later that "the men who are taken for me, and who rejoice in it and tell me of it, are smooth, light-complexioned, men with a mustache and curvilinear outline in front, without any intelligence in their faces and look something like successful bootleggers." WHT to Horace Taft (May 23, 1928) (Taft papers).
95. *Brandeis-Frankfurter Conversations*, at 303 (April 17, 1922). Compare the judgment of Charles A Beard:

> Mr. Taft was a very dogmatic man, given to conservative legalism, easy-going, ... solicitous about getting the "right" kind of men on the bench, ... and from first to last a veritable and monumental embodiment of the American middle class in its upper ranges.

Charles A. Beard, *Review of The Life and Times of William Howard Taft by Henry F. Pringle*, 40 COLUMBIA LAW REVIEW 950, 950 (1940). In Mark DeWolfe Howe's view, the ultimate "explanation of Taft's mediocrity" lay in "the uneasy fear of change which lay behind the cheerful surface." Mark DeWolfe Howe, *Review of The Life and Times of William Howard Taft by Henry F. Pringle*, 53 HARVARD LAW REVIEW 505, 505 (1940).

> The warm heart of Taft, his patient industry, his sympathy for individuals, his thoroughly shrewd intelligence were qualities which should have made his contribution to American life something of permanent importance.... His virtues were so many and so appealing that his failure to achieve greatness is an almost tragic story.... In the last analysis [the explanation of Taft's failure] seems to lie in the crippling fear of change which so warped intelligence and sympathy that understanding and imagination were destroyed.

Id. at 506–7.
96. WHT to Gus Karger (January 31, 1916) (Taft papers). *See* Frank H. Hiscock to WHT (July 6, 1921) (Taft papers) ("We all know that you will bring to the duties of

the office that combination of progressiveness and conservatism which will adjust the law to the new requirements of a constantly changing civilization, but which will not regard passing fantasies, theories and desires of the moment as good substitutes for those fundamental principles which are the basis of our system of jurisprudence.").

97. Howe, *supra* note 95, at 506.
98. ROBERT H. WIEBE, SELF-RULE: A CULTURAL HISTORY OF AMERICAN DEMOCRACY 171 (University of Chicago Press 1995).
99. Taft's own personal ambivalence concerning reform is best illustrated in a letter he wrote his sister-in-law at the end of his life, in which within three sentences he reported both that "I am going to devote myself to lobbying" Congress in order to ensure the passage of important legislation creating a new Supreme Court Building, and that "I really don't feel particularly troubled when legislation is not pressed through because it means that Congress is not doing anything much, which means that it is not doing injurious things." WHT to Mrs. Charles P. Taft (December 8, 1929) (Taft papers).

PART I
CONSTRUCTING THE TAFT COURT: APPOINTMENTS

When Taft assumed the chief justiceship on June 30, 1921, the justices of the Court were, in order of seniority: Joseph McKenna, Oliver Wendell Holmes, William R. Day, Willis Van Devanter, Mahlon Pitney, James C. McReynolds, Louis D. Brandeis, and John H. Clarke. Figure I-1 shows their voting during the 1921 term. Day was plainly a central figure on the Court; Clarke, by contrast, was relatively marginal. Figure I-2 shows that this configuration had been relatively stable since at least the 1916 term. Table I-1 indicates that the most productive justices on the Court during the 1921 term were Holmes and Taft; the least productive were Van Devanter and Pitney.

Many of the Taft Court justices were old and ailing. Even before he became chief justice, Taft believed that the Court was "in a bad plight,"[1] and he confirmed this diagnosis for himself once he took the center chair. "Our Court is not in a strong condition," he wrote his brother:

> Holmes does his work with just as much dispatch as ever, but he is suffering from asthma, and I suspect it is of a cardiac character. His breathing is stertorous at times. ... Pitney ... had a nervous breakdown last year, and he has a good many cases on his hand which he is not getting rid of. Day had the grip, and while he continues work – and they all do in the sense that they attend conference – they are the weak members of the Court, to whom I cannot assign cases. The worst and most embarrassing member, however, is the oldest member, McKenna. I don't know what course to take with respect to him, or what cases to assign to him. In case after case assigned to him he will write an opinion, and bring it into conference, and it will meet objection because he has missed a point.[2]

THE TAFT COURT

Table I-1 Number of opinions authored by each justice, 1921 term

Court Term	Taft	McKenna	Holmes	Day	Van Devanter	Pitney	McReynolds	Brandeis	Clarke
1921	27	18	29	15	10	11	20	23	20

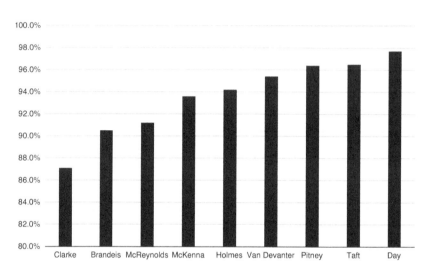

Figure I-1 Percentage of decisions in which a participating justice either joins or authors an opinion for the Court, 1921 term

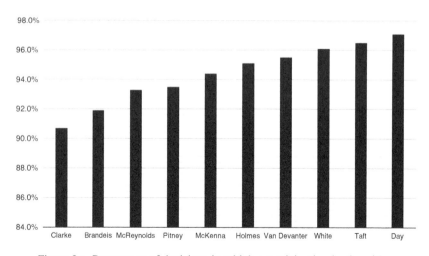

Figure I-2 Percentage of decisions in which a participating justice either joins or authors an opinion for the Court, 1916–1921 terms

32

Constructing the Taft Court: Appointments

As usual, fortune smiled on Taft. By 1923, three associate justices had retired, and Harding was able to transform the Court into a younger and more vigorous institution. With his extensive network of well-placed Washington contacts and effortless administrative authority, Taft played an important (and some would say even outsized) role in influencing the selection of the Court's new members. Within a short period of time, he was able to preside over a Court that largely reflected his outlook and values. Harding appointed George Sutherland to replace John H. Clarke, Pierce Butler to replace William R. Day, and Edward Sanford to replace Mahlon Pitney. These three appointments pushed the Court decisively to the right. For the remainder of the decade, the Taft Court would with accelerating rigor police the constitutionality of social and economic legislation.

The Court experienced one further change during the 1920s – Calvin Coolidge would appoint Harlan Fiske Stone to replace Joseph McKenna. McKenna was a sadly weak justice, but Stone would grow into one of the Court's most important members. Stone began his judicial career as a close companion of Van Devanter and Butler on the dominant conservative wing of the Court, but by the end of the decade he would shift his allegiance and become one of the famous dissenting trio of Holmes, Brandeis, and Stone.[3]

Notes

1. "Holmes is over eighty, McKenna is nearly eighty.... Day looks quite feeble and as you know, he has never been strong. Pitney is not very well and the Court is overwhelmed with cases of tremendous import." WHT to Jacob M. Dickinson (April 23, 1921) (Taft papers). Jacob Dickinson had been secretary of war under Taft. Coincidentally, McReynolds had written Dickinson the preceding February that "Our Court is all to pieces. Old age is doing its work & utter unfitness adds greatly to the difficulties. I almost despair & have been thinking much of giving up the place & going into something or another – where the surroundings will be more agreeable." JCM to J.M. Dickinson (February 28, 1921) (Dickinson papers at the Tennessee State Library & Archives).
2. WHT to Horace D. Taft (April 17, 1922) (Taft papers). *See* WHT to Learned Hand (October 26, 1922) (Taft papers) ("[T]he truth is the Court has been shot to pieces.... Judge Day has been doing no work, and goes off on the 14th. Judge Van Devanter has had trouble with his eyes, and Judge McReynolds has the gout. Judge Pitney is at home ill. Judge Holmes writes opinions most promptly, but can not be asked to do committee work. Nor can Judge McKenna.").
3. *Lauds "Minority" Trio in the Supreme Court*, NEW YORK TIMES (March 17, 1930), at 18.

CHAPTER 1

John Hessin Clarke and George Sutherland

BORN THREE DAYS after Taft, John Hessin Clarke had been on the Court for a scant five years when Taft became chief justice. Clark was appointed by Wilson in July 1916. Clarke had been a successful Ohio newspaper publisher and corporate lawyer.[1] He was campaigning for the Senate as a progressive Democrat when, at McReynolds's urging, Wilson appointed Clarke to the federal district court in July 1914. Although Taft was personally fond of Clarke,[2] he did not much "like" Clarke's "legal politico-economic views."[3] Taft regarded Clarke as representing a "new school" of "latitudinarian construction of the Constitution," "which if allowed to prevail will greatly impair our fundamental law."[4] Taft also deplored Clarke's tendency to dissent from the Court's opinions,[5] which, as Figure I-1 illustrates, was by far the most developed of anyone on the Court.[6]

Clarke was so supportive of state regulation, national power, and the rights of labor, that he was characterized in the popular press "as an ultra-radical,"[7] as a fit companion to Brandeis and Holmes on the left wing of the Court.[8] But Clarke fundamentally differed from Brandeis and Holmes in his attitude toward the law. Whereas Brandeis and Holmes prized legal craft and architecture, Clarke tended to regard law as an overtly political instrument of policy.

In Taft's view, Clarke made up his mind "as if each case was something to vote on as he would vote on it in the Senate or in the House, rather than to decide as a Judge."[9] Clarke "is much more of an orator than he is a lawyer," added Taft. "He has certain set notions against corporations and in favor of labor unions, which make him decide many cases before he hears them. Although he and Clarke often agreed, Holmes often commented to me on that feature of his judicial decisions."[10] Holmes himself regarded Clarke's opinions as "sentiment and rhetoric."[11] "He is a very dear, affectionate creature," Holmes observed, but "I wish his writing was more to my taste than I can pretend."[12]

Although Clarke was well liked on the Court,[13] he grew to detest the "bone labor" of "studying musty records of cases one-half of which are of no consequence

THE TAFT COURT

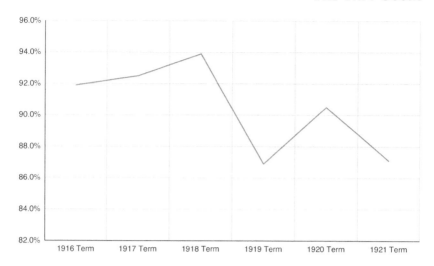

Figure I-3 Percentage of decisions in which Clarke participated and authored or joined an opinion for the Court, by term

in the world to anybody except the parties to them, and which never should have been permitted to go" to the Supreme Court.[14] Lacking an intrinsic concern with the law, Clarke began to find "the uninteresting grind of the Court"[15] "irksome in the extreme."[16] As he wrote Holmes: "What did I care whether a drunken Indian was cheated out of his lands before he died or not, or whether it was *constitutional* to clean out a ditch in Iowa & etc."[17] Clarke even congratulated Taft upon his appointment with the dour observation that "the late Chief Justice – peace to his ashes – did not much overstate the fact when he said that Supreme Court service was a dog's life."[18]

A year later, when Taft sent Clarke a copy of the Court's official letter of regret at Clarke's resignation, Clarke could not resist the opportunity to vent:

> I wonder if you would care to know that the feeling of relief I have from the irritating futility of the certioraris, from the Fourteenth Amendment nonsense, and from the necessity of spelling out reasons for the obvious is very like the sense of freedom that used to come to me a long while ago ... at the end of a school year. The fictitious importance of official place is as dust in the balance to ... the happiness of being able to do and say just what I please.[19]

Amused, Taft wrote back that while he "enjoyed much reading" Clarke's letter, "I gather from its tone that you did not know in writing it that we intend to print our letter to you and yours to us" in the U.S. Reports.[20]

Throughout his service on the Court, Clarke suffered particular humiliation from "the insulting and overbearing and contemptuous attitude of" James Clark McReynolds.[21] As Taft told the story to Elihu Root, "McReynolds has a masterful, domineering, inconsiderate and bitter nature. He had to do with Clarke's selection

36

John Hessin Clarke & George Sutherland

as a District Judge, and felt, therefore, that Clarke, when he came into the Court, should follow him. And when Clarke, yielding to his natural bent, went often with Brandeis, McReynolds almost cut him. McReynolds has been childish in his relations to Clarke, and it has been a very uncomfortable thing for Clarke."[22] Although McReynolds has been much scored for his anti-Semitic intolerance of Brandeis and Cardozo, his brutal harassment of the vulnerable Clarke is certainly one of his blackest moments.[23] The hostility between Clarke and McReynolds is visible in Figures I-4 and I-5.

Throughout his tenure Clarke functioned at the margin of the Court, as Figures P-1 and I-2 suggest.[24] Figure I-3 shows that Clarke's identification with the Court was at a low ebb when Taft entered the Court. Although Figure I-4 evidences Clarke's general alignment with Brandeis, Figure I-6 demonstrates that even that relationship was deteriorating by the 1921 term.

We have evidence that Clarke began to speak of retirement as early as March 1921,[25] but what finally pushed him over the edge was the death of his sister Ida, his closest living relative, on March 3, 1922.[26] Clarke wrote Taft that "I am passing through an experience so crushing that it seems, for me, just now, the end of all earthly interests. My sister was both a sister and a brother to me all through life."[27] Clarke sunk into a deep depression, so that in July he could report that "my situation is quite paralyzing me. I mean I find myself without initiative or desire to go anywhere or to do anything, – all interest in life has so gone out of me."[28] By late August he had reached a decision:

> I have definitely decided to resign my office as of Sept. 18 when I shall be 65 years old. ... [T]he death of my sister has taken all interest out of life for me

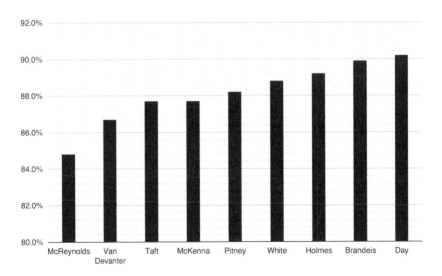

Figure I-4 Percentage of decisions in which Clarke participated and joined the same opinion as another justice, 1916–1921 terms

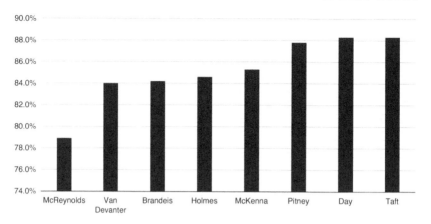

Figure I-5 Percentage of decisions in which Clarke participated and joined the same opinion as another justice, 1921 term

Figure I-6 Percentage of decisions in which Clarke and Brandeis participated and joined the same opinion, by term

and I see no reason for going forward doing work which for the most part has become irksome in the extreme to me. I feel that in my present state of mind I cannot do as good work even as I have been doing & that I owe it to the country as well as to myself not to work on with my enthusiasms quite dead. ... [M]y spirit is broken & while I have the consolation of knowing that I did all in my power to make my sisters [sic] lives comfortable & happy yet my affections were so centered in them & the care of them that I cannot recover a normal outlook on life.[29]

John Hessin Clarke & George Sutherland

"I wish to have time to get acquainted with my own soul before it parts from my body," Clarke said, and "to do what I can to urge our country – in a non-political way – to enter the League of Nations."[30]

On September 1, Clarke wrote Harding announcing his resignation effective on September 18, Clarke's sixty-fifth birthday.[31] Harding promptly issued a handwritten note accepting Clarke's offer, and he made known his intention to "send to the Senate the nomination of George Sutherland of Utah for the vacancy made by Justice Clarke's retirement."[32] On September 5 the Senate unanimously approved Sutherland, waiving the usual referral to the Judiciary Committee.[33] It would prove to be a significant turning point in the history of the Court.

Woodrow Wilson immediately grasped the momentous implications of the substitution. He wrote Clarke saying how "deeply sorry" he was at Clarke's resignation:

> Like thousands of other liberals throughout the country, I have been counting on the influence of you and Justice Brandeis to restrain the Court in some measure from the extreme reactionary course which it seems inclined to follow.
>
> In my few dealings with Mr. Sutherland I have seen no reason to suspect him of either principles or brains, and the substitution is most deplorable.
>
> The most obvious and immediate danger to which we are exposed is that the courts will more and more outrage the common peoples [sic] sense of justice and cause a revulsion against judicial authority which may seriously disturb the equilibrium of our institutions, and I can see nothing which can save us from this danger if the Supreme Court is to repudiate liberal courses of thought and action.[34]

For his part, by contrast, Taft believed that "Sutherland is a safe and good appointment, and the exchange of him for Clarke makes greatly for the strengthening the Court in the direction in which I would have it strengthened."[35] "I am very glad to have Sutherland substituted for Clarke in the Court," Taft wrote his brother. "Sutherland is a much abler man, a much sounder lawyer and not a hidebound conservative, but a reasonable one. He has tempered his views by long political experience – a process which makes him a much more useful Judge than one who, like Holmes, has had no political experience and proceeds as if the American Constitution were as malleable as the British Constitution."[36]

Like Taft, Sutherland came to the bench with a prominent national reputation. Born in 1862 in Buckinghamshire, England, Sutherland was brought to Utah the following year "when it was a thinly settled territory forming part of a vast, inhospitable wilderness identified on the maps of the day as 'The Great American Desert.'"[37] At a time when "nobody worried about child labor,"[38] Sutherland was forced to work at the age of 12,[39] eventually saving enough money to fund two years at what would become Brigham Young University[40] and a year at the University of Michigan Law School, where he studied under Thomas M. Cooley.[41]

Sutherland returned to Utah in 1883 and began a successful law practice. Sutherland became a member of Utah's first state legislature, Utah's representative to Congress, and, from 1905 to 1917, a United States senator from Utah. In the Senate, Sutherland "won a very high reputation as a constitutional lawyer. ... He was regarded as perhaps Elihu Root's weightiest colleague and compeer on constitutional questions."[42] In 1916, just a few weeks before losing his first popular election as senator,[43] Sutherland was elected president of the American Bar Association.[44] He remained "an intimate friend and close adviser" of his former Senatorial colleague Warren Harding, "coming nearer being the 'Colonel House' of the Harding Administration than any other man."[45]

Sutherland's record was not that of a thoughtless reactionary. He was actively involved in matters of legal and judicial reform.[46] He was "an acknowledged leader" of the movement for women's suffrage, having introduced a version of the Nineteenth Amendment in the Senate in 1915.[47] In the Utah legislature, Sutherland prepared and advocated for a statute imposing an eight-hour workday on mines and smelters. The statute was eventually upheld by the Supreme Court in the milestone case of *Holden v. Hardy*.[48] In the United States Senate, Sutherland was a strong supporter of La Follette's Seamen's Act of 1915,[49] so that Andrew Furuseth, the legendary president of the International Seamen's Union, came to regard Sutherland as "a lover of freedom . . . a man who in the protection of freedom to all men regardless of their station in life, may be trusted and relied upon under all possible conditions."[50]

In 1916, Samuel Gompers took "pleasure in saying that Senator Sutherland has been, not only sympathetic, but very helpful in the passage of many measures through the United States Senate which the organizations of Labor have urged for enactment,"

> such as the railroad men's Hours of Service Law; the Employers' Liability Law; the popular election of United States Senators; legislation in behalf of children; the right of petition; the literacy test contained in the Immigration Bills; Eight Hour legislation and Industrial Education and Vocational Trade Training measures.
>
> He has vigorously opposed the speeding up schemes, known as the "Taylor System" in Government establishments, and in behalf of the miners in the notable contests in West Virginia, Colorado, and Michigan, Senator Sutherland vigorously championed Federal investigations during those controversies and was otherwise helpful in obtaining the restoration of civil rights for the oppressed mine workers in the states mentioned. . . .
>
> He is one of the members of the United States Senate whom we always feel free to approach and solicit his assistance on matters proposed that will redound to the welfare of all the people.[51]

Sutherland was the prime intellectual force behind the effort to enact a federal workmen's compensation scheme for employees of common carriers engaged in interstate commerce.[52] Arguing that the displacement of traditional common law "rules and defenses" was constitutional because they were "no longer justly applicable to modern industrial conditions,"[53] Sutherland noted that there was "a growing feeling that the individualist theory has been pushed with too much stress upon the dry logic of its doctrines and too little regard for their practical operation from the humanitarian point of view."[54] John W. Davis recalls that as a member of the House he was initially opposed to the workmen's compensation bill, but that Sutherland's "masterful report" in favor of the legislation's "advanced position" was so persuasive that it "completely converted me to its support."[55] Sutherland argued that the common law could be altered or abrogated, "with the limitation that those '*fundamental rights* which that system of jurisprudence ... has always recognized' shall not be infringed, and that [legislation] must be 'within the limits of those *fundamental principles* of liberty and justice which lie at the base of all our civil and political institutions.'"[56]

Sutherland believed that the possibilities of reform were limited by the fact that "there are certain fundamental social and economic laws which are beyond the power, and certain underlying governmental principles, which are beyond the right of official control, and any attempt to interfere with their operations inevitably ends in confusion, if not disaster."[57] Sutherland was thus willing to require an eight-hour work day for some especially stressful forms of work, but not for all work, and he was utterly unwilling to accept legislation that sought to fix wages or prices.[58] He believed that "too much government carries us in the direction of tyranny and oppression, and, in the language of Wendell Philips, 'kills the self-help and energy of the governed.'"[59] He condemned efforts to exempt labor from the application of anti-trust laws as "utterly indefensible ... class legislation."[60]

Sutherland deeply valued the institution of judicial review. He denounced reforms like the initiative, referendum and recall, because he viewed direct democracy as incompatible with "the preservation of the people's liberties."[61] He opposed the admission of Arizona to the Union because the territory's proposed constitution authorized the recall of judges, which Sutherland regarded as creating "not an 'empire of laws' to be executed with impartiality and exactness, but an empire of men who punish not according to some fixed and definitely prescribed rule, but according to their undefined, unrestrained, and unlimited discretion."[62] Believing in the necessity of constitutional principles endowed with "stability and permanency,"[63] Sutherland was appalled by Theodore Roosevelt's advocacy on behalf of the recall of judicial decisions.[64]

After his service in the Senate, Sutherland grew increasingly concerned over the nation's "mania for regulating people," a "craze for change" that drove "a widespread demand for innovating legislation."[65] He particularly objected to "the tremendous increase during late years in the number and power of administrative boards, bureaus, commissions and similar agencies," because he regarded bureaucracy as a form of "*petty* despotism."[66] He emphasized that government "must not be allowed to wander too far from its normal and traditional functions, nor interfere overmuch with the liberty of the individual to work out his destiny here ... in his own way."[67] Sutherland believed that "the liberty of the individual to control his own conduct is the most precious possession of a democracy and interference with it is seldom justified except where necessary to protect the liberties or rights of other individuals or to safeguard society."[68] He asserted that "doubts should be resolved in favor of the liberty of the individual and his power to freely determine and pursue his own course in his own way."[69]

As Sutherland ascended to the Court, therefore, he was, like Taft, a national figure of a strongly conservative bent, who could nevertheless boast a genuine

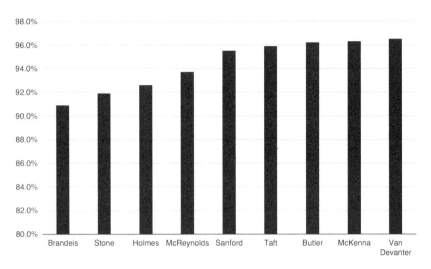

Figure I-7 Percentage of decisions in which Sutherland participated and joined the same opinion as another justice, 1922–1928 terms

record of achievement. He exuded gravitas. Sutherland and Taft had enjoyed a long professional relationship.[70] Taft wrote Sutherland an extended letter of welcome to Court, noting that "you now come into the Court with a general opinion as to the functions of the Court similar to my own."[71] Taft confided to Van Devanter that Sutherland "will be one of our kind I think."[72]

It is apparent from Figure I-7 that Sutherland's voting on the Taft Court was most naturally aligned with its conservative wing. Figure I-8 suggests that this tendency might have been even more pronounced in conference. Yet Sutherland, like Taft, was capable of flexibility and adjustment. While he could lead the conservative charge against price regulation,[73] he could also author a profoundly innovative opinion sanctioning urban zoning.[74] Figure I-10 reveals that Sutherland exercised substantial influence on the voting of his peers; he was comparatively successful in persuading colleagues to shift their votes at conference and join his opinions. Figure I-9 illustrates that as a general matter Sutherland was also quite accommodating to views other than his own. William O. Douglas remembers him as "a tempered and reasonable man who also, as his decisions indicate, was zealous in upholding the rights of individuals before the law."[75] He was, in Brandeis's words, a man of "character & conscience."[76] He was also personally charming and prepossessing.[77]

During his time on the Taft Court, Sutherland suffered recurring bouts of illness, the effects of which are illustrated in Figures I-11 and I-12.[78] But Sutherland's lucid, systematic, and articulate intelligence nevertheless catapulted him into a position of intellectual leadership on the conservative wing of the Court.[79] Because of what even Taft regarded as the "rather ... formal cut" of his "mind,"[80] Sutherland was driven to implement the full range of his "rather

John Hessin Clarke & George Sutherland

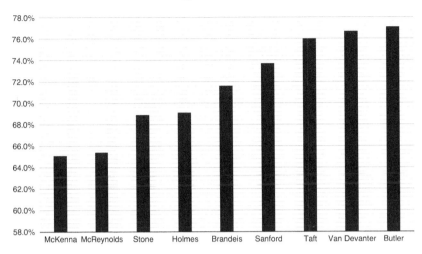

Figure I-8 Percentage of decisions in which Sutherland participated and voted with another justice in conference

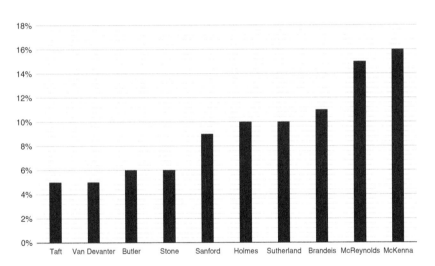

Figure I-9 Percentage of decisions in which a justice participated and was willing to change a conference vote to join a Court opinion or to join a Court opinion despite registering uncertainty in conference

conceptualist notions of the meaning and application of the Fourteenth Amendment."[81] Taft's innate practical good sense led him at first to resist this tendency,[82] but, as his own health deteriorated, Taft ultimately came to rely increasingly on Sutherland's stiffer, more unbending formality.[83]

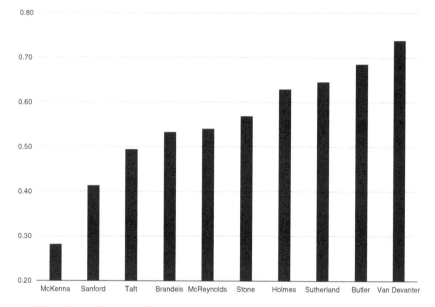

Figure I-10 Number of votes recorded at conference that switch to join the opinion of a justice, divided by the number of that justice's opinions in conference cases

Figure I-11 Number of opinions authored by Sutherland, by term

The abstract and formal clarity of Sutherland's approach earned him the honor in 1964 of having written "more opinions that have been specifically overruled than any other Justice in the history of the Supreme Court. Of those opinions

John Hessin Clarke & George Sutherland

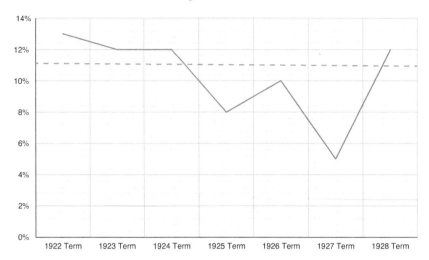

Figure I-12 Percentage of Court's opinions authored by Sutherland, by term. An even distribution of cases would assign 1/9, or 11%, to each justice.

repudiated by name since the reconstruction of the Court in the late 1930s, Sutherland was the author of more than 20 per cent."[84] The substitution of Sutherland for Clarke, in short, steered the Court sharply to the right. It signaled, commented *The Nation*, "a drear outlook indeed."[85]

Notes

1. Clarke receives a full-scale biographical treatment in HOYT LANDON WARNER, THE LIFE OF MR. JUSTICE CLARKE: A TESTAMENT TO THE POWER OF LIBERAL DISSENT IN AMERICA (Cleveland: Western Reserve University Press 1959).
2. "Clarke is a good fellow and I like him. He is a manly, generous, courageous man." WHT to Horace D. Taft (September 7, 1922) (Taft papers). *See* WHT to William R. Stansbury (September 5, 1922) (Taft papers).
3. WHT to Horace D. Taft (September 13, 1922) (Taft papers).
4. William Howard Taft, *Mr. Wilson and the Campaign*, 10 YALE REVIEW 1, 19–20 (1920).
5. "There is a good deal of dissent in the Court, which I deprecate. Three of the nine are pretty radical, and occasionally they get some of the brethren, which is disquieting; but still we must work on and keep the Constitution as strong in its useful operation as we can." WHT to Sir Thomas White (January 8, 1922) (Taft papers).
6. Figure I-3 demonstrates that Clarke manifested a willingness to dissent from the time he first joined the Court.
7. *A New Supreme Court Justice*, 132 THE OUTLOOK 50 (September 13, 1922). For a study of Clarke's jurisprudence, see David M Levitan, *The Jurisprudence of Mr. Justice Clarke*, 7 MIAMI LAW QUARTERLY 44 (1953).
8. Figure I-4 demonstrates that Clarke was indeed close to Brandeis, although somewhat less so to Holmes. Clarke's relationship with Brandeis was definitely cooling as Taft became chief justice, as Figure I-6 demonstrates. Clarke differed from Holmes and Brandeis in his substantive view of civil liberties. *See, e.g.*, Abrams v. United States, 250 U.S. 616 (1919); Milwaukee Social Democratic Pub. Co. v. Burleson, 255 U.S. 407 (1921); Leach v. Carlile, 258 U.S. 138 (1922). He also differed in his understanding of anti-trust law, *see, e.g.*, American Column and Lumber Co. v. United States, 257 U.S. 377 (1921); and in his approach to private tort law, see, e.g., United Zinc & Chemical Co. v. Van Britt, 258 U.S. 268 (1922).
9. WHT to Elihu Root (September 13, 1922) (Taft papers). Taft observed that Clarke's "views are so fixed by his prejudices with respect to certain classes of cases that even Holmes has said to me that he made up his mind in advance of the argument." *Id. See* WHT to Charles D. Hilles (September 9, 1922) (Taft papers). "Clarke," observed Brandeis to Felix Frankfurter, "practically never changes his views." *Brandeis-Frankfurter Conversations*, at 305 (June 18, 1922).
10. WHT to Horace D. Taft (September 7, 1922) (Taft papers). Brandeis remarked to Frankfurter that Clarke "'always "dilated with a wrong emotion," as Rufus Choate said, on the subject, sustaining power of carrier to limit amount of his liability.' And F.F. added: 'or Employers Liability cases.' 'Yes, and Employers Liability cases. Those cases never wearied of calling forth his long and weary dissent.' I [Brandeis] said to him [Clarke] about Employers Liability, 'Don't you see that the worse the law is the more it will stimulate the unions to demand workmen's compensation laws, for the union railroad men are to blame, for having resisted it.' 'No – he would shake his head and go on writing dissents.'" *Brandeis-Frankfurter Conversations*, at 332 (August 3, 1924).
11. OWH to Harold Laski (March 26, 1922), in 1 HOLMES-LASKI CORRESPONDENCE, at 413. Laski believed that Clarke, although "a nice fellow," possessed "an obstinate and pedestrian mind." Harold Laski to OWH (September 6, 1922), *id.* at 446.

John Hessin Clarke & George Sutherland

12. OWH to Harold Laski (March 26, 1922), *id.* at 413. Holmes later wrote Laski that "I didn't admire Clarke's rhetoric, but he believed it – which is something." OWH to Harold Laski (September 10, 1922), *id.* at 445.
13. WARNER, *supra* note 1, at 114. McKenna confided to Taft that "I had affection for Clarke." JM to WHT (October 23, 1922) (Taft papers). Upon Clarke's retirement, Holmes wrote Laski that "I shall miss his affectionate companionship." OWH to Harold Laski (September 10, 1922), in 1 HOLMES-LASKI CORRESPONDENCE, at 445. When Clarke retired, Holmes sent him a sad, warm note: "I shall miss you in every way. . . . I shall miss your tales and the affectionate feelings that you radiate and generate. I shall miss your criticism and I repeat I shall miss you." OWH to JHC (September 6, 1922) (Holmes papers).

    Curiously enough, Clarke's closest attachment on the Court was to his ideological opposite, the conservative Willis Van Devanter. Clarke considered his friendship with Van Devanter "much the pleasantest of my life in Washington and I shall always regret that it did not begin earlier. It is a rare thing in this life to meet a man one can trust without reserve as I know I could trust you." JHC to WVD (September 8, 1922) (Van Devanter papers). The normally staid and reserved Van Devanter responded in kind: "To me our relations have been so comfortable, so very different from almost all others, that I shall miss you as I have never missed any one before. I feel that I have been leaning on you without realizing it – going to you as to a living and ever dependable fountain." WVD to JHC (September 3, 1922) (Clarke papers). Van Devanter regarded Clarke "as the embodiment of courage, gentleness and large vision." *Id. See also* WVD to JHC (October 4, 1922) (Van Devanter papers) ("Personally I have much difficulty in reconciling myself to your absence. I knew my attachment for you was strong, but it was even stronger than I realized.").
14. John Hessin Clarke, *Methods of Work of the United States Supreme Court Judges*, 20 OHIO LAW REPORTER 398, 402, 407 (1922). *See* John Hessin Clarke, *Observations and Reflections on Practice in the Supreme Court*, 8 AMERICAN BAR ASSOCIATION JOURNAL 263 (1922). Clarke wrote that "the most trying fact of it all was the conferences. So futile for the most part and so little like what I had imagined, and what the country imagines they must be." JHC to WVD (July 28, 1924) (Van Devanter papers). Five years later he wrote Van Devanter that "those Saturday conferences" "were the greatest disappointment of my service at Washington." JHC to WVD (April 6, 1929) (Van Devanter papers).
15. JHC to WVD (October 2, 1922) (Van Devanter papers).
16. JHC to WVD (August 23, 1922) (Van Devanter papers). *See* JHC to WHT (August 31, 1922) (Taft papers) ("I may add in the confidence of our friendship that the work has become extremely irksome to me and I feel that I cannot spend the few years that remain to me over cases for the most part such as I would not have accepted during many years of my practice."). After his retirement, Clarke wrote Taft that his "impatience with the trifling and technical character of much of the work I was obliged to do" had "been growing on me for several years so that I couldn't restrain something of expression of it in my New York Address." JHC to WHT (September 12, 1922) (Taft papers). Clarke's New York address is reproduced in the AMERICAN BAR ASSOCIATION JOURNAL, *supra* note 14. Of Clarke's complaint, Brandeis wryly observed to Frankfurter that "I am reminded of: 'Wenn ich ein Künstler wär, ich mahlte traun nur hübsche mädchen interessante Frauen.' [If I were an artist, I would

paint only pretty girls and interesting women.] Holmes, J. would have a different opinion of the 'unimportant cases.'" LDB to Felix Frankfurter (October 2, 1922), in BRANDEIS-FRANKFURTER CORRESPONDENCE, at 121.
17. JHC to OWH (September 12, 1922) (Holmes papers).
18. JHC to WHT (July 1, 1921) (Taft papers). Clarke would later greet his successor, George Sutherland, with a note that apologized for "delay sending my congratulations until you should be safely anchored in what the late Chief Justice, with candor & with what later on seemed to me entire accuracy, described as 'a dogs life.' But most men do not think so ill of it and I am writing to wish you every happiness and the largest measure of success in the discharge of the duties of your great office." JHC to GS (October 4, 1922) (Sutherland papers).
19. JHC to WHT (October 31, 1922) (Taft papers). Clarke added: "I shall watch the work of you all with a critical but friendly eye and shall take occasion in a half-dozen speeches which are scheduled to say a word in your behalf.... The lawyers may damn the Court but nevertheless as yet they trust and all but revere it. There is magic in the long black robe, My Masters, – 'motley's the only wear.'"
20. WHT to JHC (November 2, 1922) (Taft papers). The official exchange of letters appears at 260 U.S. v (1922). Clarke was quite proper in his formal response, sublimating his irritation into "the expression of the hope that the bill pending in Congress to modify the imperative statutory jurisdiction of the Court may soon become a law, so that you may not be so burdened with unimportant cases as you now are, and so have more time and strength for the consideration of the many causes of great public concern constantly coming before you, and the decision of which is so fateful to our Country." *Resignation of Mr. Justice Clarke*, 260 U.S. v, vi–vii (1922).
21. WHT to Horace D. Taft (September 7, 1922) (Taft papers). *See* WHT to Warren G. Harding (September 5, 1922) (Taft papers) ("It seems a curious circumstance, though I could explain it, that [Clarke] and McReynolds were bitter enemies, due largely to McReynolds' overbearing and insulting attitude toward Clarke.").
22. WHT to Elihu Root (September 13, 1922) (Taft papers). Clarke himself termed the situation "deplorable and harassing." JHC to Woodrow Wilson (September 9, 1922) (Wilson papers). When Clarke eventually retired in 1922, McReynolds refused to sign the Court's traditional letter of regret. 260 U.S. v (1922). "We have written a letter of regret to Clarke," Taft wrote his son Robert, "which McReynolds would not sign.... This is a fair sample of McReynold's [sic] personal character and the difficulty of getting along with him. Fortunately no love is lost between him and Clarke." WHT to Robert A. Taft (October 26, 1922) (Taft papers).
23. According to Dean Acheson, Clarke "had the misfortune to offend Justice McReynolds as my boss had, but whereas Justice Brandeis was untouched by the fact that Justice McReynolds never spoke to him, this upset Justice Clarke deeply. Justice Holmes tried for years to patch this up, but you couldn't patch these things up with Justice McReynolds.... Eventually [Clarke] threw in the towel [and] resigned from the Court." Dean Acheson, *Recollections of Service*, 18 ALABAMA LAWYER 355, 363 (1957). It should be noted that when Taft gently questioned Clarke "whether you do not give undue weight in your conclusion to certain phases of your judicial life which were outrageous and exasperating but which in retrospect will not seem important," WHT to JHC (September 5, 1922) (Taft papers), Clarke responded by asking Taft not to "think that I was influenced by the boor. I am of a temperament much too combative when unfairly treated to permit such a thing to

influence me to such a decision as I reached. Rather it would have kept me there to see it through, unpleasant though it was." JHC to WHT (September 12, 1922) (Taft papers).
24. Figure I-3 illustrates by term how likely Clarke was to author or join an opinion for the Court.
25. WARNER, *supra* note 1, at 112.
26. *Id.* at 133 n.3. Clarke's only other sister, Alice, had died on March 28, 1921. *Id.* Clarke was a lifelong bachelor.
27. JHC to WHT (March 7, 1922) (Taft papers). Clarke wrote Van Devanter that "I am passing through waters that are deep & dark & cold. I have always, heretofore, been able to summon resolution sufficient to enable me to meet conditions before me but this is so frustrating that I continue to be overwhelmed by it entirely." JHC to WVD (March 7, 1922) (Van Devanter papers).
28. JHC to WVD (July 7, 1922) (Van Devanter papers).
29. JHC to WVD (August 23, 1922) (Van Devanter papers).
30. JHC to WHT (August 31, 1922) (Taft papers). Taft wrote Van Devanter that "I am greatly surprised to hear of Clarke's determination to retire, for while I knew that he was saying things that indicated his impatience with the burden of his duties of the Court, I did not suspect that it was really serious. . . . Clarke was so contemptuous of McReynolds' statements that he was going to retire that he would hardly make them himself without intending to carry them through." WHT to WVD (August 31, 1922) (Taft papers). On Clarke's career after resignation, see Carl Wittke, *Mr. Justice Clarke – A Supreme Court Judge in Retirement*, 36 MISSISSIPPI VALLEY HISTORICAL REVIEW 27 (1949).
31. JHC to Warren G. Harding (September 1, 1922) (Harding papers). The *New Republic* would term the "retirement of Mr. Justice Clarke from the Supreme Court at the youthful age of sixty-five . . . little short of an affront to our most venerable institution." Walton H. Hamilton, *The Ages of the Justices*, 32 NEW REPUBLIC 168 (1922).
32. *Justice Clarke Out of Supreme Court*, NEW YORK TIMES (September 5, 1922), at 1.
33. 62 CONG. REC. 12169 (September 5, 1922).
34. Woodrow Wilson to JHC (September 5, 1922) (Wilson papers). Wilson's concern was echoed in some press reports. "The public really has a grievance in Justice Clarke's resignation," ran one editorial. "He occupied a strategic place. He is a liberal among conservatives, and he was needed." *Justice Clarke's Resignation*, NEW YORK GLOBE AND COMMERCIAL ADVERTISER (September 5, 1922), at 14. The *Chicago Tribune* remarked that Clarke's replacement by Sutherland "will leave Justice Brandeis the only 'radical' member of the court." *Sutherland to Succeed Clarke on U.S. Bench*, CHICAGO TRIBUNE (September 5, 1922), at 12. *The Nation*, by contrast, took the position that Clarke's resignation "alters the complexion of the Supreme Court not at all, for he has been succeeded by ex-Senator Sutherland, a lawyer of the conventional type but possessed of ability and learning, who can be depended upon to uphold the existing order and defend property against all comers quite as strongly as his predecessor." 115 THE NATION 267 (1922).

Clarke himself took exception to Wilson's suggestion that he and Brandeis were natural allies:

> Judge Brandeis and I were agreeing less & less frequently in the decision of cases involving what we call, for want of a better designation, liberal principles. It is for you to judge which was falling away from the correct standards.

> During the last year in the Hardwood Anti-Trust Case [American Column and Lumber Co. v. United States, 257 U.S. 377 (1921)], which I wrote, B and Holmes dissented, B writing an opinion. It is one of the most important anti-trust cases ever decided by that Court for it involved for the first time "the open competition plan" which was devised with all the cunning astute lawyers & conscienceless businessmen could command to defeat or circumvent the law....
>
> In the last child labor case [Bailey v. Drexel Furniture Co., 259 U.S. 20 (1922)] I alone dissented. Unfortunately the case was considered and decided when one of my sisters was dying and I could not write a dissenting opinion....
>
> In a personal injury case involving the doctrine of attractive nuisance [United Zinc & Chemical Co. v. Van Britt, 258 U.S. 268 (1922)] the Chief Justice & Justice Day joined in an opinion which I wrote dissenting from the rule that contributory negligence of a trespassing child of tender years barred recovery in a case of flagrant poisoning of the water in a pool in an unfenced common in which two children perished when bathing. ... You doubtless noted how we differed with respect to war legislation.
>
> There is much more, but this will suffice to show that in leaving the Court I did not withdraw any support from Judge Brandeis. One or the other of us was shifting or had shifted his standards so that in critical or crucial cases we were seldom in agreement. Our personal relations, of course, continued entirely cordial.

JHC to Woodrow Wilson (September 9, 1922) (Wilson papers). On Clarke's deteriorating voting relationship with Brandeis, see Figure I-6.

35. WHT to George Wickersham (September 18, 1922) (Taft papers).
36. WHT to Horace D. Taft (September 13, 1922) (Taft papers). *See* WHT to Charles D. Hilles (September 9, 1922) (Taft papers) ("I think Sutherland is judicial, and he certainly has ability. His mind is rather of a formal cut, but his wide governmental experience and his really very excellent knowledge of constitutional and other law, together with his knowledge of practical politics (for that helps on the Bench), will make him a great improvement on his predecessor as a Judge.").
37. George Sutherland, *A Message to the 1941 Graduating Class of Brigham Young University*, June 4, 1941, p. 2 (Sutherland papers) ("*Message*"). Harlan Stone believed that Sutherland's "life experiences and his outlook were typically American and typical also of those Justices who came to this Court from beyond the Mississippi River during the period between the outbreak of the Civil War and the first World War." *In Memory of Honorable George Sutherland*, 323 U.S. clxi, clxix (1944).

The standard biography of Sutherland is JOEL FRANCIS PASCHAL, MR. JUSTICE SUTHERLAND: A MAN AGAINST THE STATE (Princeton University Press 1951). Sutherland has also received a book-length treatment in HADLEY ARKES, THE RETURN OF GEORGE SUTHERLAND: RESTORING A JURISPRUDENCE OF NATURAL RIGHTS (Princeton University Press 1994). For shorter studies, see Samuel R. Olken, *The Business of Expression: Economic Liberty, Political Factions and the Forgotten First Amendment Legacy of Justice George Sutherland*, 10 WILLIAM & MARY BILL OF RIGHTS JOURNAL 249 (2002); Samuel R. Olken, *Justice George Sutherland and Economic Liberty: Constitutional Conservatism and the Problem of Factions*, 6 WILLIAM & MARY BILL OF RIGHTS JOURNAL 1 (1997); Sarah H. Cleveland, *The Plenary Power Background of Curtiss-Wright*, 70 UNIVERSITY OF COLORADO LAW REVIEW 1127 (1999); R.A. Maidment, *A Study in Judicial Motivation: Mr. Justice Sutherland and Economic Regulation*, 1973 UTAH LAW REVIEW 156; John Knox, *Justice George Sutherland*, 24 CHICAGO BAR RECORD 16 (1942); R. Perry Sentell, Jr., *The Opinions of Hughes and Sutherland and the*

Rights of the Individual, 15 VANDERBILT LAW REVIEW 559 (1962); Harold M. Stephens, *Mr. Justice Sutherland*, 31 AMERICAN BAR ASSOCIATION JOURNAL 446 (1945); John F. Reinhardt, *Mr. Justice Sutherland*, 12 UNIVERSITY OF KANSAS CITY LAW REVIEW 43 (1943); Alpheus Thomas Mason, *The Conservative World of Mr. Justice Sutherland*, 32 AMERICAN POLITICAL SCIENCE REVIEW 443 (1938).

38. Sutherland, *"Message," supra* note 37, at 4.
39. David Burner, *George Sutherland*, in 3 THE JUSTICES OF THE UNITED STATES SUPREME COURT 1789–1969: THEIR LIVES AND MAJOR OPINIONS 2133 (Leon Friedman & Fred L. Israel, eds., New York: Chelsea House Publishers 1969).
40. PASCHAL, *supra* note 37, at 5–15. At the time the institution was known as the Brigham Young Academy. Sutherland's favorite teacher at the Academy was Karl G. Maeser. Sutherland, *Message, supra* note 37, at 8–13. Paschal reports that Maeser was a firm believer in the philosophy of Herbert Spencer. PASCHAL, *supra* note 37, at 9. Sutherland was not himself a Mormon, although he maintained close ties to the Mormon community. In 1921, he reported that "I don't agree with the Mormon theology, but I do have the utmost respect for the Mormon people. They are law-abiding, industrious, home-loving, debt paying, honest and conscientious people and I am glad to number among them some of my very warmest friends. Years ago I objected very seriously, of course, to the practice and teaching of polygamy, but that has been abandoned for many years and is today as dead as slavery.... I have no affiliation with any church, and I have no favorites among them. I think the churches on a whole do an immense amount of good and I should not like to see them established. The Mormon Church today, so far as my observation goes, measures up to the others in this respect." GS to W.W. Baldwin (January 15, 1921) (Sutherland papers).
41. PASCHAL, *supra* note 37, at 9, 15–20.
42. *Justice Clarke's Retirement*, NEW YORK TIMES (September 6, 1922), at 14. "Chief Justice Taft has been quoted as saying that Mr. Sutherland was the greatest constitutional lawyer in the Senate, and numerous other eminent members of the bar have expressed the same opinion. ... [T]he opinion expressed ... is that Mr. Sutherland was the ablest lawyer in Congress. That opinion was expressed by John W. Davis." *The New Supreme Court Justice*, NEW YORK TIMES (September 10, 1922), § 7, at 3. In February 1921, Sutherland received an honorary Doctor of Laws Degree from George Washington University. The citation read: "Foremost amongst the modern expounders of Constitutional Law; consistent advocate of strict adherence to the American system of Government as absolutely essential to individual liberty, national security and international harmony." William Miller Collier to GS (February 23, 1921) (Sutherland papers).
43. GS to George M. Hanson (December 31, 1916) (Sutherland papers). Sutherland had previously been elected senator by the Utah state legislature.
44. Sutherland said of his election as American Bar Association president that "it really was a greater honor than being elected to the Senate, because nothing influences" the American Bar Association "except the belief that they are doing the right thing." GS to George M. Hanson (December 31, 1916) (Sutherland papers).
45. *The New Supreme Court Justice, supra* note 42, at 3.
46. "In matters of judicial administration, Sutherland was always one of the most enlightened and progressive men in the Senate." PASCHAL, *supra* note 37, at 55. In the Senate, Sutherland was a leader in the movement to revise and recodify provisions

of the federal criminal and judicial codes. *Id.* at 53–54. *See* George Sutherland, *The Nation's First Penal Code*, 189 NORTH AMERICAN REVIEW 107 (1909).

47. 53 CONG. REC. 75 (December 7, 1915). *See* PASCHAL, *supra* note 37, at 92 (Sutherland "lost no opportunity to further the cause. He spoke at memorial services for a militant suffragist. He received delegations from various women's organizations, counseling them as to their tactics and providing them good copy. The women, for their part, acknowledged that he was their 'powerful ally' and praised him for his 'generous help and support.'"); ARKES, *supra* note 37, at 3–12; David E. Bernstein, *Revisiting Justice George Sutherland, the Nineteenth Amendment, and Equal Rights for Women*, 20 GEORGETOWN JOURNAL OF LAW & PUBLIC POLICY 143 (2022). Sutherland's speech in support of what would eventually become the Nineteenth Amendment, which was reproduced and distributed in pamphlet form, may be found at 53 CONG. REC. 11318–19 (July 20, 1916) ("Any argument which I may use to justify my own right to vote justifies ... the right of my wife, sister, mother, and daughter to exercise the same right. ... [O]ther superstitions which in the past have denied women equal opportunities for education, equality of legal status – including the right of contract and to hold property – and all the other unjust and intolerant denials of equality have disappeared, or are disappearing, from our laws and customs.").

48. 169 U.S. 366 (1898). On Sutherland's role, see 48 CONG. REC. 6797 (May 20, 1912) ("I believe very thoroughly in the 8-hour day. I have been an advocate of it for many years. As a member of the legislature of my own State in 1896 I had the honor of assisting in the preparation and enactment of the 8-hour law ... applying to mines and smelters. ... I would make this line of division – it is not a very accurate line; not a line that could probably be laid down in exact words in legislation; but, roughly speaking, I would make this line of division – wherever a man is engaged in mechanical work or in manual work which requires the use of the same muscles, hour after hour, I would make the 8-hour day compulsory. ... I would not apply that to the farm, because on the farm the man is engaged in the open air; he is engaged in a multitude of tasks. ... But in the mechanical pursuits I believe thoroughly that the 8-hour day in the end will be better for both the employer and the employee. ... We cannot make such a law that will be effective unless it is compulsory; we can not very well leave to an arrangement between the employer and the employee, because in a contest of that kind I think the employee would usually be at a disadvantage as compared with the employer.").

49. Pub. L. 63-302, 38 Stat. 1164 (March 4, 1915). In the words of Andrew Furuseth, Sutherland "became an earnest champion of legislation which would restore to us our rights as men. ... There was nothing that he could do that he did not gladly do. There was no time that he was not ready with encouragement and advice and any action that would advance the legislation." Andrew Furuseth to D.O. Jacobs (July 5, 1916) (Sutherland papers).

50. *Id*. Furuseth urged labor in Utah to support Sutherland in the 1916 election. "I would think it a great national loss, a real national misfortune, to lose Senator Sutherland from the United States Senate." *Id*.

51. Samuel Gompers to O.E. Asbridge (June 30, 1916) (Sutherland papers).

52. *Message of the President of the United States Transmitting the Report of the Employers' Liability and Workmen's Compensation Commission*, Sen. Doc. No. 338, 62nd CONG. 2nd SESS. (February 21, 1912) ("*Report*"). As president,

John Hessin Clarke & George Sutherland

Taft praised the "very able and satisfactory" report of the Commission, which had been chaired by Sutherland. Taft noted that "the discussion of the constitutional questions which have arisen in respect to the validity of the bill is of the highest merit." *Id.* at 6. Taft "sincerely" hoped that Sutherland's "carefully drawn bill" would be expeditiously passed. *Id.* at 5, 8. *See* William H. Taft, *The Attacks on the Courts and Legal Procedure*, 5 KENTUCKY LAW JOURNAL 3, 18–19 (1916) (questioning why the federal Workman's Compensation Act, "which has been prepared with great care by Senator Sutherland to meet constitutional and other objections" has not yet passed Congress). Although a federal workmen's compensation bill was not adopted until 1916, Taft in the interim created a compensation scheme for Canal Zone employees that was based upon Sutherland's bill. For a discussion, see PASCHAL, *supra* note 37, at 65–69.

53. *Report, supra* note 52, at 14.
54. George Sutherland, *The Economic Value and Social Justice of a Compulsory and Exclusive Workmen's Compensation Law*, reprinted in Sen. Doc. 131, 63rd CONG. 1st SESS. (1913), at 11. Sutherland would as a justice remain firm in his support of workmen's compensation statutes. *See, e.g.*, Cudahy Packing Co. v. Parramore, 263 U.S. 418 (1923); Bountiful Brick Co. v. Giles, 276 U.S. 154 (1928).
55. *The New Supreme Court Justice, supra* note 42, at 3.
56. *Report, supra* note 52, at 34 (citing Hurtado v. California, 110 U.S. 516, 535–36 (1884)). Sutherland viewed "fundamental" rights and liberties in a decidedly nonpositivistic way. Explaining why Congress could not violate fundamental rights and liberties when legislating for the territories, for example, Sutherland observed that although congressional power over federal territories was otherwise plenary, "such of these individual and civil rights as are beyond the interfering power of Congress, are guaranteed by the fundamental principles of free government rather than by the direct force of the Constitution in which they are formulated. They cannot be denied to the inhabitants of any territory subject to the control of the United States, because they are inherently inviolable; and the Constitution is resorted to not as supreme law for their enforcement but as high proof of their existence and incontrovertible nature." GEORGE SUTHERLAND, CONSTITUTIONAL POWER AND WORLD AFFAIRS 69 (New York: Columbia University Press 1919). Although to modern ears Sutherland's conclusions seem to sound in natural law, Sutherland more probably saw the source of fundamental law to lie in historical experience. *See* George Sutherland, *The Courts and the Constitution*, Sen. Doc. No. 970, 62nd CONG. 3rd SESS. (1912), at 5 ("We learn to distinguish what is wise and righteous from what is wrong and foolish by experience which compels our assent rather than by precept, which only advises our understanding."). Often when Sutherland spoke about natural laws that legislation could not alter, see, e.g., *infra* note 57, he seemed to be referring to the inevitable consequences of failing to take adequate account of the power of individual incentives.
57. George Sutherland, *Principle or Expedient?*, in PROCEEDINGS OF THE 44TH ANNUAL MEETING OF THE NEW YORK STATE BAR ASSOCIATION 265 (Baltimore: Lord Baltimore Press 1921). Sutherland continued: "These laws and principles may be compared with the forces of nature whose movements are entirely outside the scope of human power." *Id.* at 265–66. *Compare* WILLIAM HOWARD TAFT, LIBERTY UNDER LAW: AN INTERPRETATION OF THE PRINCIPLES OF OUR CONSTITUTIONAL GOVERNMENT 42 (New Haven: Yale University Press 1922) ("The lesson must be learned ... that there is only a limited zone within which legislation and governments

can accomplish good. We cannot regulate beyond that zone with success or benefit....
If we do not conform to human nature in legislation we shall fail.").

58. In 1916, Samuel Gompers asked Sutherland his opinion on legislation that would impose an eight-hour workday on all workers. Samuel Gompers to GS (January 7, 1916) (Sutherland papers). Sutherland's reply is worth quoting at length:

> Just how far the statute law should go in dealing with private industrial relations is a difficult and sometimes delicate question. I have always favored laws which had for their object the substantive betterment of workers, such as those which enforce proper sanitary conditions, safety appliances and machinery, adequate, and as far as possible automatic compensation for injuries, and so on. I have also favored, and still favor, by legislation the eight-hour day in industries such as mining, smelting and other industries where long employment is injurious to health. In addition to this, I am in favor of an eight-hour day in all mechanical industries and in all work where the same set of muscles are continuously employed, or where the same strain and attention is continuously required about the work. But whether [an eight-hour day for all workers] should be compelled by legislation, or brought about by the efforts of the employees, aided by public sentiment, is a matter about which I am in serious doubt.
>
> The State is justified in stepping in wherever its police activities are involved, as they are involved in the cases that I have mentioned. If the State undertakes to go further and interfere in the relations of employer and employee, while in many instances and perhaps for a time that interference might result in the betterment of conditions from the point of view of the workmen, there is grave danger that it may be utilized in other instances and in the course of time, to his positive detriment.
>
> Whenever you concede the power to the State to interfere in such matters, you have effectually conceded it whether the results be good or evil. For example, if we once undertook by legislation to fix wages, they may be a first fixed at a high sum, but under this concession they may sometimes be fixed at a very inadequate sum....
>
> My own impression is that the matter of hours of labor, except as stated above, and except in Government work, like the matter of wages can be more safely left to private arrangement in view of the fact that the numerical strength of the labor unions today constitutes a set-off for the money strength of the employer....
>
> P.S. We must be careful not to overdo our legislation and take from the individual the strengthening effect which comes from the struggle to help himself.

GS to Samuel Gompers (January 15, 1916) (Sutherland papers). Sutherland resolutely opposed "the economic folly of attempting to control the movement of prices of ordinary commodities by legislation."

> Not only is any such attempt futile from a practical view point, but it constitutes a distinct departure from ... great political principle.... The power to fix prices by law or administrative order has been uniformly denied by the courts save in those exceptional cases where the business or the service is clothed with a public interest. In all other cases the owner has an inherent, constitutional right to the market price, fixed by what is called the "higgling of the market," irrespective of the extent of his profits. Such a right is, indeed, itself essential property which stands upon an equality with life and liberty, under the guaranties of the Fifth and Fourteenth Amendments.

Sutherland, *Principle or Expedient?*, supra note 57, at 277.

59. GEORGE SUTHERLAND, SUPERFLUOUS GOVERNMENT: AN ADDRESS BY SENATOR SUTHERLAND OF UTAH 2 (Cleveland: Cleveland Chamber of Commerce 1914).

60. 51 CONG. REC. 11804 (July 8, 1914) (discussion of 38 Stat. 609, 652 (1914), prohibiting expenditure of Department of Justice funds for enforcing anti-trust

laws against labor). On Taft's view of such efforts, see *Gompers and the Law* (January 12, 1921), in VIVIAN, at 525 ("a vicious abuse in seeking to array a class against the whole body, politic and social.").
61. Sutherland, *The Courts and the Constitution*, supra note 56, at 11. Sutherland addressed the question at length in a famous speech, 47 CONG. REC. 2793–803 (July 11, 1911), which was republished in pamphlet form as *Government by Ballot*. Taft's views on the initiative, referendum and recall were essentially similar. See WILLIAM HOWARD TAFT, POPULAR GOVERNMENT: ITS ESSENCE, ITS PERMANENCE AND ITS PERILS 42–95 (New Haven: Yale University Press 1913). *See id.* at 64 ("The strongest objection to these instruments of direct government ... is the effect of their constant use in eliminating all distinction between a constitution as fundamental law, and statutes enacted for the disposition of current matters. ... It minimizes the sacredness of those fundamental provisions securing the personal rights of the individual against the unjust aggression of the majority of the electorate.").
62. 47 CONG. REC. 2800 (July 11, 1911). *See id.* at 2802 ("The moment a provision for the recall of the judges of the Supreme Court shall be written into the Federal Constitution, that moment will mark the beginning of the downfall of the Republic and the destruction of the free institutions of the American people."). As president, Taft took a similar position, vetoing the congressional resolution admitting Arizona to the Union. *See Special Message of the President of the United States Returning without Approval House Joint Resolution No. 14*, H. Doc. No. 106, 62nd CONG. 1st SESS. (August 5, 1911), at 2 ("This provision of the Arizona constitution, in its application to county and State judges, seems to me so pernicious in its effect, so destructive of independence in the judiciary, so likely to subject the rights of the individual to the possible tyranny of a popular majority, and, therefore, to be so injurious to the cause of free government that I must disapprove a constitution containing it."). Sutherland's first published address in favor of a strong and independent judiciary was in 1895. *See* George Sutherland, *The Selection, Tenure and Compensation of the Judiciary*, in REPORT OF THE SECOND ANNUAL MEETING OF THE TERRITORIAL BAR ASSOCIATION OF UTAH 47–60 (Grocer Printing Co. 1895) ("Without an honest, capable and independent judiciary, no State can long maintain its dignity nor respectability among the people of the earth." The judiciary "stands as a shield to prevent the exercise of oppressive and arbitrary power on the part of the government itself, whose creature it is, against the citizen, though never so humble and insignificant.").
63. 47 CONG. REC. 2794 (July 11, 1911).
64. George Sutherland, *The Law and the People*, 2 CONSTITUTIONAL REVIEW 90, 93–94 (1918) (reprinting an address delivered on December 13, 1913) ("The demand for the recall of judicial decisions proceeds upon a theory which completely disregards the nature of the judicial function, which is not to register the changing opinions of the majority as to what the Constitution and law ought to be, but to interpret and declare the Constitution and law as they are, whether such interpretation satisfies the desires of many or none at all. ... The effect of the plebiscite will not be to enact a rule for future guidance, binding the majority as well as the minority, but will be simply to give passing expression to the fleeting opinion of the temporary majority, having no binding force upon the less instructed or the more instructed majority of another day. Like idle words written upon the sands the construction of today will disappear tomorrow, only to reappear at a later date, as the sentiment of the majority ebbs and flows."). Taft held quite similar views.

65. George Sutherland, *Private Rights and Government Control*, in REPORT OF THE FORTIETH ANNUAL MEETING OF THE AMERICAN BAR ASSOCIATION 201 (Baltimore: Lord Baltimore Press 1917). Taft also complained of the "disease of excessive legislation." TAFT, POPULAR GOVERNMENT, *supra* note 61, at 41. "The amount of useless legislation in the states of this country is appalling," he said, "and is one of the most distressing signs of the times." *Id.* at 42.
66. Sutherland, *Private Rights and Government Control*, *supra* note 65, at 204. "[T]he things which organized society exacts from its members must be particularized as far as practicable by definite and uniform rules. Liberty consists at last in the right to do whatever the law does not forbid, and this presupposes law made in advance ... and interpreted and applied after the act by disinterested authority. ... It is, therefore, of the utmost importance that the authority which interprets and executes the law should not also be the authority which makes it.... The danger ... which is threatened by the multiplication of bureaus and commissions consists in the commingling of these powers." *Id.* at 204–5. Sutherland especially objected to the establishment of the Federal Trade Commission. *Id.* at 206–8.
67. Sutherland, *Principle or Expedient*, *supra* note 57, at 281.
68. Sutherland, *Private Rights and Government Control*, *supra* note 65, at 202.
69. *Id.* Sutherland would subsequently transform this view into constitutional law in his opinion for the Court in Adkins v. Children's Hospital, 261 U.S. 525, 545–46 (1923): "Freedom of contract is, nevertheless, the general rule and restraint the exception; and the exercise of legislative authority to abridge it can be justified only by the existence of exceptional circumstances."
70. Sutherland had strongly supported Taft in the 1912 election. PASCHAL, *supra* note 37, at 78–81. Sutherland's efforts were credited as an important factor in holding Utah as one of the two states to give their electoral votes to Taft. *Id.* at 81. Sutherland had also supported Taft when Louis Brandeis attacked Taft's secretary of the interior, Richard Ballinger. *Id.* at 61–62. Sutherland had also, like Taft, opposed Brandeis's appointment to the Supreme Court. *Id.* at 116–17; A.L. TODD, JUSTICE ON TRIAL: THE CASE OF LOUIS D. BRANDEIS 157–59, 204–6 (New York: McGraw Hill 1964).
71. WHT to GS (September 10, 1922) (Sutherland papers). Sutherland replied, "I am looking forward with real pleasure to working by your side, and our outlook on things in general is so much the same that I am sure it will be not only a work of pleasure but of cooperation as well." GS to WHT (September 19, 1922) (Taft papers).
72. WHT to WVD (August 19, 1922) (Van Devanter papers).
73. *See* Adkins v. Children's Hospital, 261 U.S. 525 (1923); Tyson & Brother v. Banton, 273 U.S. 418 (1927); Ribnik v. McBride, 277 U.S. 350 (1928); Williams v. Standard Oil Co., 278 U.S. 235 (1929).
74. Euclid v. Ambler Realty Co., 272 U.S. 365 (1926).
75. WILLIAM O. DOUGLAS, THE AUTOBIOGRAPHY OF WILLIAM O. DOUGLAS: THE COURT YEARS 1937–1975, at 12 (New York: Random House 1980).
76. *Brandeis-Frankfurter Conversations*, at 330 (July 6, 1924).
77. Sutherland was personally well liked by all members of the Court. Stone said of him that "his relations with all of his associates were characterized by a personal regard and esteem which found their source in mutual respect." 323 U.S. clxx (1944). Although Brandeis's initial reaction was to be "much disappointed in Sutherland," because "he is a mediocre Taft, has all the latter's weaknesses," *Brandeis-*

John Hessin Clarke & George Sutherland

Frankfurter Conversations, at 310 (November 30, 1922), Brandeis eventually established a "cordial friendship" with Sutherland. PASCHAL, *supra* note 37, at 117; ALPHEUS THOMAS MASON, BRANDEIS: A FREE MAN'S LIFE 537 (New York: The Viking Press 1956). Brandeis commented when Sutherland decided to leave the bench that "his resignation will be regretted by all the Court despite the views on which we have disagreed. He is a man of unusually high character & of true patriotism, as he considers the public welfare." LDB to Jacob H. Gilbert (January 5, 1938), in BRANDEIS FAMILY LETTERS, at 551. "Justice Roberts relates that it was a regular thing for Holmes, on his entry into the conference room, to make for Sutherland, and bending over so low that their heads were almost touching, longingly plead, 'Sutherland, J., tell me a story.' Justice Roberts adds that this entreaty was unfailingly honored to the accompaniment of roars of judicial laughter." PASCHAL, *supra* note 37, at 116.

78. *See, e.g., infra* Chapter 26, at note 150; *infra* Chapter 33, at notes 40–41. Sutherland remained in frail health throughout his service on the Taft Court. At the end of the 1924 term, for example, he was "very tired and far from well." GS to Henry M. Bates (May 16, 1925) (Sutherland papers). His blood pressure soared "to over two hundred" and he "had to drop out for a time." WVD to JHC (June 12, 1925) (Van Devanter papers). He spent three weeks vacationing that summer with Van Devanter in Canada. WHT to GS (July 7, 1925) (Sutherland papers). Taft resolved "to be more careful in the distribution of work to Sutherland." WHT to LDB (July 6, 1925) (Taft papers). Sutherland's blood pressure caused him to miss three weeks of the 1925 term. WHT to Mrs. Frederick J. Manning (January 10, 1926) (Taft papers). Taft was forced to continue "letting up on Sutherland." WHT to Charles P. Taft (June 5, 1927) (Taft papers).

Sutherland was absent from Court from October 3, 1927, to January 3, 1928, 275 U.S. v, seeking medical help in Baltimore for a bad case of "chronic colitis." Thomas R. Brown to WHT (December 22, 1927) (Taft papers). Taft encouraged Sutherland's medical leave. WHT to GS (October 3, 1927) (Sutherland papers) ("I infer that your chief trouble is the worry that you have over being absent from the Court. I told you then, as I tell you now, that that ought not to worry you in the slightest, that we are all ready and can do the work, and that what we are most anxious to do is to get you well again so that you can enjoy and do the work you are capable of doing in the Court.... We all love you, George, and we would all regard it as the greatest loss to the country to have you become discouraged over your work, and we realize what great importance it is to the country that you should be restored to your working capacity. That can not be done without your giving up work and separating yourself from it."). Taft promised Sutherland's doctor that Taft would "save" Sutherland "from some of the usual work, and I shall do it conscientiously." WHT to Thomas R. Browne (December 26, 1927) (Taft papers). *See* WHT to Robert A. Taft (January 1, 1928) (Taft papers) ("Sutherland is coming back to us, but with the injunction from his physician that he shall not work the full speed, and we are going to cut out his passing on certioraris, and I shall not give him any heavy cases.").

The effects of illness on Sutherland's productivity during the 1925 and 1927 terms may be seen in Figures I-11 and I-12.

79. Ted White has observed that of the Four Horsemen "only Sutherland escaped the crisis of 1934–36 with his reputation intact. He had so eloquently articulated the theoretical underpinnings of Fieldian jurisprudence that his opposition to the New

57

Deal seemed on a higher level." G. EDWARD WHITE, THE AMERICAN JUDICIAL TRADITION: PROFILES OF LEADING AMERICAN JUDGES 194 (New York: Oxford University Press 1976). *See* Albert P. Blaustein & Roy M. Mersky, *Rating Supreme Court Justices*, 58 AMERICAN BAR ASSOCIATION JOURNAL 1183, 1185–86 (November 1972) ("It is particularly significant to see Sutherland chosen as near-great by so many 'liberal' professors.").

80. WHT to Charles D. Hilles (September 9, 1922) (Taft papers). In conversation with Frankfurter, Brandeis described Sutherland as "Far-Western Bourgoisie [sic]. More cultured than Butler but mechanical & his law is collected but not digested. But fine character." *Brandeis-Frankfurter Conversations*, at 338 (n.d.). At one point Brandeis commented to Frankfurter that "Sutherland's branch bank opinion almost makes me excuse his minimum wage doings." LDB to Felix Frankfurter (January 31, 1924), in BRANDEIS-FRANKFURTER CORRESPONDENCE, at 155. *See* First National Bank in St. Louis v. Missouri, 263 U.S. 640 (1924).

81. HFS to Learned Hand (January 29, 1945) (Stone papers). Stone added, "I nevertheless was very fond of him, and am well aware of great contributions which he made to the work of the Court during the years I sat on the Bench with him." *Id.*

82. *See, e.g.*, Adkins v. Children's Hospital, 261 U.S. 525, 564 (1923) (Taft, C.J., dissenting) ("I have always supposed that the Lochner Case was ... overruled *sub silentio*.").

83. *See infra* Chapter 25. Taft nevertheless continued to differ from Sutherland in a number of important respects. So, for example, Taft was a far greater supporter of national power than Sutherland, who believed "in the rigid exclusion of the national government from those powers which have been actually reserved to the states." Sutherland, *Private Rights and Government Control*, *supra* note 65, at 212. *See, e.g.*, Board of Trade v. Olsen, 262 U.S. 1 (1923); Missouri *ex rel.* Burnes National Bank v. Duncan, 265 U.S. 17 (1924); Lambert v. Yellowley, 272 U.S. 581 (1926); Nigro v. United States, 276 U.S. 332 (1928). Taft was a more consistent supporter of administrative regulation than was Sutherland, who was opposed to government agencies like the FTC. *See supra* note 66 and accompanying text. *See, e.g.*, FTC v. Curtis Publishing Co., 260 U.S. 569 (1923); FTC v. Western Meat Co., 272 U.S. 554 (1926). Taft was a greater supporter of tough enforcement measures for prohibition than was Sutherland. *See, e.g.*, Cunard Steamship Co. v. Mellon, 262 U.S. 100 (1923); Carroll v. United States, 267 U.S. 132 (1925); United States v. One Ford Coupe Automobile, 272 U.S. 321 (1926); WHT to Horace D. Taft (December 12, 1926) (Taft papers). Taft was also a far more consistent supporter of federal taxation than was Sutherland. United States v. Flannery, 268 U.S. 98 (1925); McCaughn v. Ludington, 268 U.S. 106 (1925); Irwin v. Gavit, 268 U.S. 161 (1925); Ray Consolidated Copper Co. v. United States, 268 U.S. 373 (1925); Marr v. United States, 268 U.S. 536 (1925); Edwards v. Douglas, 269 U.S. 204 (1925); Chase National Bank of the City of New York v. United States, 278 U.S. 327 (1929); Bromley v. McCaughn, 280 U.S. 124 (1929).

84. J. Francis Paschal, *Mr. Justice Sutherland*, in MR. JUSTICE 204 (Allison Dunham & Philip B. Kurland, eds., University of Chicago Press 1964).

85. "It now looks as if Mr. Harding would have the making over of the Supreme Court, which is a drear outlook indeed.... There is plainly nothing to be hoped for from the court until there is a spirit of greater liberalism in the country." 115 THE NATION 267 (1922).

CHAPTER 2

William Rufus Day and Pierce Butler

THE SHIFT IN the Court's orientation was consolidated by a second change in personnel that occurred two months later. William Rufus Day, who had been appointed in 1903 by Theodore Roosevelt, retired on November 14, 1922.[1] Born in 1849, Day was a successful Ohio lawyer who had become the close friend and confidant of William McKinley. McKinley brought Day to Washington D.C. in 1897 to serve as first assistant secretary of state, then as secretary of state, and finally as chair of the American delegation to the Paris Peace Conference that ended the Spanish American War.

In 1899, McKinley appointed Day to the Sixth Federal Circuit Court, where he served with William Howard Taft and Horace Lurton. When Taft twice declined Roosevelt's offer of an appointment to the Supreme Court, believing it his duty instead to remain in Manila as the governor of the Philippines, Roosevelt turned to Day to replace the retiring George Shiras.[2]

A slight,[3] taciturn,[4] modest man, Day was noted for his sound counsel and balanced judgment.[5] On the Court he followed "a middle course" that exerted a moderating influence on both conservatives and liberals.[6] His central role is evident in Figure I-2, which indicates that he was at the dead center of the Court from the 1916 through the 1921 terms[a]. Figure I-1 suggests that he maintained that role after Taft became chief justice. In truth, however, it was difficult to anticipate just where Day would stand on any given question. Dissenting in both *Lochner v. New York*[7] and *Coppage v. Kansas*,[8] Day also joined the Court's opinions in *Adair v. United States*[9] and *Truax v. Corrigan*.[10] Although he authored *Hammer v. Dagenhart*,[11] he also spoke for the Court in *United States v. Doremus*,[12] and he joined the

---

[a] *See* also Figures I-13 and I-14, which well illustrate that for Day "the middle" had a decidedly conservative slant.

THE TAFT COURT

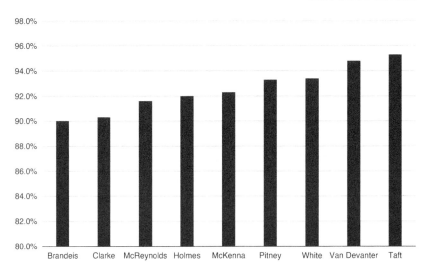

Figure I-13 Percentage of decisions in which Day participated and joined the same opinion as another justice, 1916–1921 terms

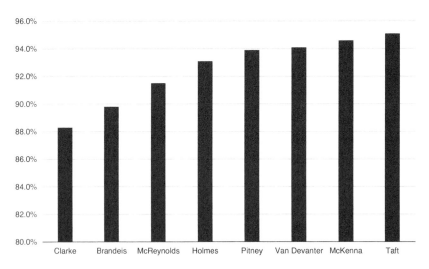

Figure I-14 Percentage of decisions in which Day participated and joined the same opinion as another justice, 1921 term

Court's opinion in *Stafford v. Wallace*.[13] Day seemed to adopt consistently inconsistent positions on the most controversial issues of his time.[14]

Day suffered ill-health throughout his life.[15] For reasons that are not exactly clear, he decided to retire after the 1921 term.[16] On August 10, 1922, Day wrote Taft, explaining:

William Rufus Day & Pierce Butler

> As you well know the unexpected is always happening. On my return to Ohio I received a letter from the President, followed by one from Hughes, asking me to take the place of "Umpire" on a mixed Commission to settle the claims of American citizens against Germany. I should have preferred to await a conference with you before answering, but a prompt reply was deemed necessary. I wrote an acceptance to the President. ... [M]y appointment will require my retirement from the Court. In my opinion I should stay until say Oct 10 in order that I may participate in some matters carried over from last term.[17]

Likely Harding's unexpected and urgent offer was connected with the president's ongoing campaign to create a vacancy to which he could appoint Sutherland.[18]

At least Taft immediately made this connection, writing Harding: "I assume – and am glad to assume – that you will appoint Sutherland to be his successor."[19] The following week, however, news of Clarke's impetuous resignation overtook Day's plans, so that Day's potential resignation did not become public until Sutherland had already been appointed.[20] Day did not officially announce his resignation until October 24.[21] His debt to Sutherland safely paid, Harding was by that time willing to entertain a broad array of potential candidates to fill the vacancy.[22]

Eventually Harding would select Pierce Butler as Day's replacement.[23] The story behind the nomination is fascinating and complex, but it has been well told and I will not repeat its details here.[24] Suffice it to say that both Taft and Van Devanter, who by this time had become Taft's "mainstay in the Court,"[25] were essential in securing Butler's eventual appointment.[26] They believed that maintaining the bipartisan appearance of the Supreme Court required choosing a Democrat to replace Day.[27] Functioning as a close advisor to Harding and Daugherty on the matter of the appointment,[28] Taft considered other candidates, including John W. Davis, but, after Davis privately said he would decline,[29] Taft and Van Devanter concluded that Pierce Butler was "our man."[30]

What counted most to Taft was that Butler was "not enough of a Democrat to hurt."[31] Taft saw quite clearly that "things in our Court are quite uncertain and open a possibility of great opportunity for Harding to make the Court staunch and strong."[32] He supported Butler because Butler was "a broad-minded, courageous, hard-hitting, upstanding man,"[33] by which Taft meant that Butler was a fierce defender of "sound ... constitutional views."[34]

Brandeis later recalled that Butler's nomination had occasioned the "only near heated" argument he had ever had with Taft on the Court. Taft had asked Brandeis

> about possible Democratic names for vacancies on Ct. ... I told him I didn't believe in appointing men as Dem & Rep. Those are not the lines of cleavage on Ct & it's wrong to encourage such belief on part of people. Real line of difference is on progressive, so-called, views as to property. "I don't agree with you, at all," [Taft] said, "and we can't go around looking for men with certain creeds on property." "As a matter of fact, of course, they do" ... "[Taft] referred to what he had done as President, in appointing Dems to Ct. Don't you think I did a good thing?" To which [Brandeis replied], "Times were different then." (Of course the real answer is – he didn't do a good thing and men he appointed *did* have certain views on property. White, Lamar and Lurton.).[35]

Brandeis was accurate in assuming that Taft would evaluate potential candidates based upon their views about property rights. Taft had himself objected to Brandeis's nomination on the ground that Wilson was "seeking to break down the guarantees of the Constitution by selecting men who are radical in their views, who have no idea of preserving the rights of property or maintaining the protection of the Constitution, which has enabled us to live and be strong."[36] Taft was determined to use his influence with Harding to repair the damage inflicted by Wilson in appointing justices like Brandeis.[37] Taft could not have found a better candidate for this purpose than Pierce Butler.[38]

"In the history of the Supreme Court," opined the *New Republic*, "there have been few judges more biased in favor of property than Justice Butler."[39] A bare three years after his appointment *Time Magazine* could summarize Butler: "[R]uthless, intolerant, forceful, impatient with all forms of progressive thought."[40] In 1939, upon joining the Court, William O. Douglas recorded in his diary that Butler was "as able hard-hitting & keen a lawyer as I have ever met. He is a powerful advocate of all vested interests & of laissez faire. When you cross swords with him you have a worthy opponent."[41] Brandeis regarded Butler as "one of the most powerful on [the] Bench."[42] He was, in Holmes's sharp observation, "a monolith. There are no seams that the frost can get through. He is of one piece."[43]

The monolith was forged in "the rigorous demands of pioneer life in the northwest."[44] He was born in a log cabin on March 17, 1866, to poor Irish immigrants who had settled on a dirt-poor farm in Dakota County, Minnesota, 35 miles south of St. Paul.[45] A devout Catholic throughout his life, Butler was ambitious and disciplined. He attended a one-room school house and then Carlton College, from which he graduated in 1887. He studied law at night while he supported himself during the day "in a dairy wrestling milk cans early in the morning."[46] A "dominating figure" of "Viking proportions,"[47] Butler became the county attorney of Ramsay County, a position in which he acquired a reputation as an outstanding trial lawyer with a steel-trap memory, a talent for assimilating and presenting complex patterns of facts, and a gift for aggressive and effective tactics of cross-examination. He subsequently founded his own firm. Although it had a widely varied practice, Butler rapidly became known as the most prominent railroad attorney in the northwest, especially famous for his vigorous advocacy of the position that it would be unconstitutional to set railroad fares below a level that would "permit the earning of a full and fair rate of return upon the value" of a railroad enterprise,[48] as measured by "the cost of reproduction under present conditions."[49]

Butler believed that "the highest function of the State is to see to it that while none shall be wronged, all shall ever be free in the pursuit of happiness and the highest good."[50] He was convinced that "the rising generation must be taught to cherish and defend 'the right of the individual to enjoy those privileges long recognized at common law as essential to the orderly pursuit of happiness by free men.'"[51] To Butler, the contemporary "passion for new enactments,"[52] the tendency to "dwell too much upon the inadequacy of present law and seek to remedy existing evils by a multitude of legislative experiments,"[53] exemplified "a kind of state socialism"[54] that posed the "danger of grave error."[55] "Too much paternalism, too much wet-nursing by the state, is destructive of individual initiative and development. An athlete should not be fed on pre-digested food, nor should the citizens of tomorrow be so trained that they will expect sustenance from the public 'pap.'"[56] America required instead "self-government by self-control."[57]

These principles, in the gentle characterization of Attorney General William D. Mitchell, Butler's longtime law partner, bespoke the "deep conviction that ... a system which allowed him, a simple farmer's boy, to rise to the heights, was worth clinging to."[58] Notwithstanding their pioneer provenance, Butler's principles embraced a strong streak of authoritarianism. Butler believed that a "powerful, well-ordered and alert" government was necessary to contain the unleashed energy of individual initiative and to tutor citizens in the requirements of self-discipline.[59] "The citizen owes allegiance in full measure to the government,"[60] he wrote, and this includes "full and faithful loyalty"[61] as well as "submission to the will of ... lawful authority."[62]

The intolerant implications of these attitudes were fully on display during World War I, when five of Butler's children were in military service. Butler used his position as a regent of the University of Minnesota to purge the faculty of professors he deemed insufficiently loyal or zealous in support of the war. The most notorious case involved William A. Schaper, the respected chair of the Political Science Department, whom Butler accused of being "the Kaiser's man," and whom Butler induced the Board of Regents peremptorily to discharge.[63] Butler afterwards told the *St. Paul Pioneer Press* that Schaper's removal "is in harmony with the present tendency to silence disloyal communities, institutions, publications, officials, and individuals. We must see that sincere loyal Americans are made the instructors of our youth, and not blatherskites such as this man."[64]

It was unlikely that harshly conservative sentiments like these would go unnoticed at any time, but, as Taft remarked to Butler, he had "the misfortune of being appointed to the Bench at a time when there is a radical flare-back, and a movement to attack the Supreme Court and to attack Harding."[65] A quartet of labor cases decided during Taft's first term as chief justice[66] had aroused a hornet's nest of opposition. In the summer of 1922, Senator Robert La Follette had prominently urged a constitutional amendment to eliminate the power of judicial review,[67] a cause which the American Federation of Labor endorsed by "an overwhelming vote."[68] Taft believed that the Court was "facing now another attack of the half a dozen attacks in its history which have been made on the Supreme Court and its powers under the Constitution."[69]

Butler's nomination landed in this inflammatory context as would a torch in oil.[70] Although Taft and Sutherland had both been seen as conservative, they were each also recognized as men of substance, whose careers were tempered by complex and impressive records of national achievement.[71] Butler was by contrast a relative unknown,[72] who appeared to be primarily "the type of reactionary who fights his battles in the open and makes no bones about it."[73] Butler's relative lack of "subtlety"[74] spurred opponents to characterize him as "a bigoted partisan, the nature of whose opinions on all issues which involve the value of corporate property and freedom of speech could be predicted in advance."[75]

Butler's appointment was condemned in the progressive press as "a piece of crass stupidity," because he "is the kind of man who would assuredly use a warped or

THE TAFT COURT

doubtful interpretation of a phrase in the Constitution to prevent needed experiments in economics and government" and thus jeopardize "in the minds of a large and increasing body of his fellow countryman the good faith of an institution which is for many reasons peculiarly dependent for its sufficient functioning upon general popular confidence."[76] "It is certain," commented *The Nation*, that Butler's nomination "will greatly increase the growing sentiment that the tribunal's political powers – that is, its asserted right to declare legislation unconstitutional – be taken from it."[77] It was evident to all that Butler's confirmation would reinforce Harding's (and Taft's) effort to reshape the Court to become a more conservative institution. "The appointment of Pierce Butler to be an associate justice of the United States Supreme Court," wrote Samuel Gompers, "is one of the longest steps yet taken by president Harding back to what he calls 'normalcy.'"[78]

Butler was eventually confirmed on December 21, 1922, with only eight negative votes.[79] He immediately formed an intimate coalition with Taft and Van Devanter, creating a firm conservative axis that decisively cemented the rightward tilt initiated by Sutherland's appointment. Butler's alliance with Taft and Van Devanter is visible in Figure I-15, which illustrates the justices with whom Butler joined in published opinions, but it is far more striking in Figure I-16, which details Butler's spontaneous and confidential voting in conference.

Butler contributed more than his fair share to the Court's work, as can be seen in Figure I-17. He also became a formidable presence, as can be seen in Figure I-10, which measures a justice's capacity to win over reluctant or dissenting votes. Only Van Devanter was more successful in attracting recalcitrant votes for circulated opinions. We can infer from Figure I-18, which summarizes the percentage of a justice's published opinions that were unanimous in conference, that Taft recognized Butler's talents by proportionally assigning to him more than to any other justice difficult cases that had been divisive in conference. Only 47 percent of Butler's published opinions

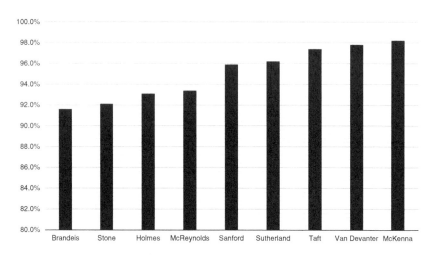

Figure I-15 Percentage of decisions in which Butler participated and joined the same opinion as another justice, 1922–1928 terms

William Rufus Day & Pierce Butler

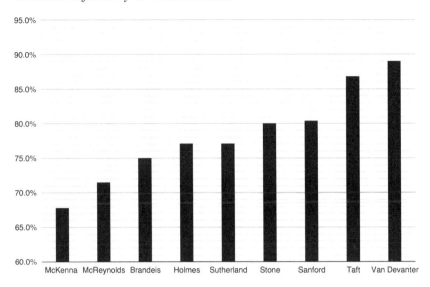

Figure I-16 Percentage of decisions in which Butler participated and voted with another justice in conference

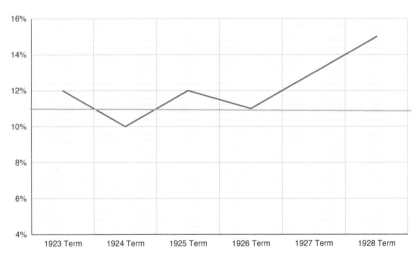

Figure I-17 Percentage of Court's opinions authored by Butler, by term. An even distribution of cases would assign 1/9, or 11%, to each justice.

had been unanimous in conference; by contrast, 76 percent of McKenna's published opinions had been unanimous in conference. Figure I-19 suggests that Butler was quite successful in creating unanimous opinions out of fractured conferences.

On substantive matters, Butler was relentless[80] in pressing theories of rate regulation that he had advanced as an advocate for the railroads,[81] in attacking

THE TAFT COURT

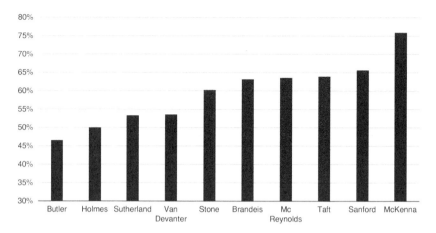

Figure I-18 Percentage of a justice's published opinions that were unanimous in conference

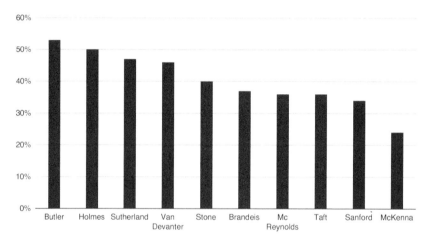

Figure I-19 Percentage of a justice's unanimous published opinions that had dissenting or uncertain votes in conference

meddlesome government regulations of business,[82] and in upholding the demands of public loyalty.[83] Although he hated to dissent,[84] he vigilantly reviewed circulated opinions to ensure their ideological purity.[85]

Perhaps reflecting his Catholic background, Butler was temperamentally opposed to prohibition.[86] He possessed a surprisingly lively sense of "the right of privacy."[87] Somewhat unexpectedly for a former prosecutor, he was also quite protective of the rights of criminal defendants.[88] He was also "a most congenial, pleasant person with great warmth."[89]

William Rufus Day & Pierce Butler
Notes

1. Although the United States Reports notes the day of Day's retirement as November 13. 1922, 260 U.S. iii n.2, Day's official letter of resignation states: "I beg ... to present my letter of resignation of the office of Associate Justice of the Supreme Court of the United States, the same to take effect as of November 14, 1922." WRD to Warren G. Harding (October 24, 1922) (Department of Justice Files, National Archives). *See* Warren G. Harding to WRD (October 24, 1922) (Harding papers) ("Your resignation is hereby accepted, effective, as you suggest, as of November 14. 1922."). The only full-scale study of Day is JOSEPH E. MCLEAN, WILLIAM RUFUS DAY: SUPREME COURT JUSTICE FROM OHIO (Baltimore: John Hopkins Press 1946). For a biographical sketch, see James F. Watts, Jr., *William R. Day*, in THE JUSTICES OF THE UNITED STATES SUPREME COURT 1789–1969: THEIR LIVES AND MAJOR OPINIONS 1773–1789 (Leon Friedman & Fred L. Israel, eds., New York: Chelsea House Publishers 1969). For a study of Day's jurisprudence, see Vernon W. Roelofs, *Justice R. Day and Federal Regulation*, 37 MISSISSIPPI VALLEY HISTORICAL REVIEW 39 (1950). Day received an undergraduate degree from the University of Michigan. He attended one year at the Michigan Law School where he "lived in the home of Thomas M. Cooley." *Id.*, at 42.
2. *See* HENRY F. PRINGLE, I THE LIFE AND TIMES OF WILLIAM HOWARD TAFT: A BIOGRAPHY 238–47 (New York: Farrar & Rinehart, Inc. 1939). Roosevelt wrote Taft at the time, "If only there were three of you! Then I would have put one of you on the Supreme Court, as the Ohio member, in place of good Day; one of you in Root's place as secretary of war, when he goes out; and one of you permanently governor of the Philippines." Theodore Roosevelt to WHT (February 14, 1903), quoted in PRINGLE, *supra*, at 252.
3. Day "stood perhaps five and one-half feet tall" and his weight "surely never approached 150 pounds." Watts, *supra* note 1, at 1776. It was said that when Day's son, William L. Day, who was a strapping six foot tall, appeared before the Court, Holmes dashed off a penciled note that passed among the justices: "He's a block off the old chip." MCLEAN, *supra* note 1, at 62.
4. Day's laconic character was the subject of a famous witticism. McKinley had placed Day as first assistant secretary of state so that he could run the department. The secretary of state, John Sherman, was effectively senile; McKinley had appointed him to secure the election of Mark Hanna to the United States Senate. Day's assistant, Alvee A. Adee, was stone deaf. It was thus said by diplomats at the time: "The head of the Department knows nothing; the First Assistant says nothing; the Second Assistant hears nothing." ARTHUR W. DUNN, I FROM HARRISON TO HARDING 204–5 (New York: G.P. Putnam's Sons, 1922).
5. Clarke said of Day: "Blessed with tact and a rich humor he was a harmonizing influence in conference and his disagreeing on occasion with the liberal or conservative group, into which the court of his day was divided, was so candid and considerate that he was distinctly a favorite with all the members of the court and was constantly looked to for important suggestions." JHC to Joseph E. McLean (April 1, 1942), in MCLEAN, *supra* note 1, at 66. Taft's account is essentially similar to Clarke's: Day's "common sense and his judicial mind are most exceptional. We shall miss his companionship. His wit and humor and equanimity have greatly added to the pleasure of our conferences and our

association." WHT to Warren Harding (August 19, 1922) (Taft papers). Van Devanter recounts "an incident which occurred soon after I came on the Court. Justice Harlan, whose years were advancing, came in shortly before the Court assembled and remarked, with a shrug of the shoulders, 'This is a damp, ugly day. I do not like it'. Nobody responded, and he repeated his observation, looking directly at Justice Day. The latter replied: 'It is all we have, so we cannot well dispense with it.'" WVD to Robert H. Kelley (December 30, 1932) (Van Devanter papers).

Upon Day's retirement, Taft wrote him:

> I am sorry you are to leave the Court for the Court's sake. You are one of its solid pillars which the people of the United States have relied on for two decades. You are one of the members to whom the rest of us have looked for aid and comfort in solution of difficult questions. I don't know what we shall do without your vast experience and wise counsel.
>
> I shall miss you personally more than I can tell. I don't know how I can get on without those helpful "conferences of two" that I was wont to seek when there seemed no way out.
>
> I reciprocate your feeling in regard to our union in judicial work after so many years since the old Sixth Circuit days. It has been full of joy to me to resume those sweet relations; and note it is too bad to break them off again.

WHT to WRD (August 18, 1922) (Taft papers). The next day Taft wrote Van Devanter that "We shall miss dear old Day much. His experience, wise counsel and real wit have made him a fine colleague." WHT to WVD (August 19, 1922) (Taft papers). John W. Davis regarded Day as "one of the wisest men he ever knew." WILLIAM H. HARBAUGH, THE LAWYER'S LAWYER: THE LIFE OF JOHN W. DAVIS 107 (New York: Oxford University Press 1973). "If I were in trouble myself and wanted advice from anybody, I would go to Day, yet nobody knows much about Day." *Id.*

It is striking that both Brandeis and Holmes characterized Day very differently. Brandeis said of Day that he was a "hot little gent." *Brandeis-Frankfurter Conversations*, at 306 (July 1922). Day "couldn't be persuaded by anybody but himself. He does change his own views; he is a fighter, a regular game cock." *Id.* at 305 (June 18, 1922). It is likely that Holmes was referring to Day when he remarked to Pollock, "The meetings are perhaps pleasanter than I ever have known them – thanks largely to the C.J. but also to the disappearance of men with the habit of some of our older generation, that regarded a difference of opinion as a cockfight and often left a good deal to be desired in point of manners." OWH to Frederick Pollock (February 24, 1923), in 2 HOLMES-POLLOCK CORRESPONDENCE, at 113–14.

6. MCLEAN, *supra* note 1, at 65–66.
7. 198 U.S. 45 (1905). *Lochner* struck down a state law setting a maximum number of hours that bakers could be employed to work in any given day or week.
8. 236 U.S. 1 (1915). *Coppage* struck down a state law forbidding yellow-dog contracts.
9. 208 U.S. 161 (1908). *Adair* struck down a federal law making it a crime to discriminate against employees of interstate carriers because of membership in a labor union.

10. 257 U.S. 312 (1921). *Truax* struck down a state statute prohibiting courts from issuing injunctions in labor disputes.
11. 247 U.S. 251 (1918). *Dagenhart* struck down a federal law prohibiting the products of child labor from being transported in interstate commerce.
12. 249 U.S. 86 (1919). *Doremus* upheld a federal law imposing punitive taxation on the sale of narcotics.
13. 258 U.S. 495 (1922). *Stafford* upheld a federal statute regulating the business practices of meat packers.
14. About Day it was said that "there is little to indicate just why he sides with the conservative members in some cases and why in others he is found with the liberals." Joseph D. Sullivan, *Supreme Court and Social Legislation*, 10 GEORGETOWN LAW JOURNAL 1, 3 (1921).
15. *Ex-Justice W.R. Day Dies at MacKinac*, NEW YORK TIMES (July 10, 1923), at 19; *Former Justice Day*, 134 THE OUTLOOK 399 (July 18, 1923).
16. In August 1922, Taft wrote Harding: "Last year, after he had suffered from the grip and had 10 days of very high fever, he told me that his physician had told him that he would probably have to retire in a year or two at any rate, and that he intended to do so." WHT to Warren G. Harding (August 27, 1922) (Taft papers). David Danelski reports (without attribution) that in June "Harding had a conference with Justice Day's son in which he intimated that if the Justice would retire in the next few months he would be appointed chairman of the German-American Mixed Claims Commission then being created. When Day heard this, he wrote the President that if the matter could be worked out along the lines suggested, he would submit his resignation, to take effect in October." DAVID J. DANELSKI, A SUPREME COURT JUSTICE IS APPOINTED 41 (New York: Random House 1964).
17. WRD to WHT (August 10, 1922) (Taft papers). Day continued, "To end an association such as I have enjoyed with the Court for many years will be a severe test of such fortitude as I possess. It grows harder to do as I approach the reality of it. The renewal of intimate association with you has given me untold comfort and pleasure. Your consideration of me in all our relations has been one of the joys of my life." *Id*. Day's appointment, although not his retirement, was announced the following day in the *New York Times*. *Germany Signs Agreement with US to Adjust Claims*, NEW YORK TIMES (August 11, 1922), at 1. The operation of the Claims Commission is discussed in WILHELM KIESSELBACH, PROBLEMS OF THE GERMAN-AMERICAN CLAIMS COMMISSION (Edwin H. Zeydel, trans., New York: Carnegie Endowment for International Peace 1930). Day's function as "Umpire" would be to decide cases in the event of a disagreement between the German and American members of the Commission. Taft wrote Day a sorrowful letter of regret. *See supra* note 5. Taft agreed that Day should postpone the effective date of retirement, in part to wait until the petition for rehearing in United States v. Southern Pacific, 259 U.S. 214 (1922), could be decided. WHT to WRD (August 18, 1922) (Taft papers) ("I agree with you that you ought not to leave us until the 10th of October. There is a petition for rehearing in the Southern Pacific case. They are getting up much ado about nothing in that case and we ought to sit on it promptly. We can't decide cases on the vote of town meetings or chambers of commerce, especially when they are all stirred by the Southern Pacific people by a misleading statement as to the effect of our judgment."). Taft also believed that "We ought to decide the West Virginia gas case [Pennsylvania v. West Virginia,

262 U.S. 553 (1923)] before [Day] goes off because we need his vote and we ought not to have the case reargued a second time." WHT to WVD (August 19, 1922) (Van Devanter papers). Van Devanter had also tried (unsuccessfully) to have Clarke delay his retirement until the West Virginia case could be decided. WVD to WHT (August 27, 1922) (Taft papers). For a discussion of *Pennsylvania v. West Virginia*, see *infra* Chapter 37, at 1160–63.
18. *See supra* Prologue, at 5; *supra* note 16.
19. WHT to Warren G. Harding (August 19, 1922) (Taft papers). Taft continued, "If this be the case, then it will save delays and make a smooth working for the Court to have Justice Day give you his resignation, to take effect say on the 10th or 15th of October, and to have you accept that resignation, and then send in Sutherland's name, the nomination to take effect on the 10th or 15th of October, in accord with the terms of the resignation. Of course as Sutherland was a Senator, his name will be approved without reference to a committee, so that it could be done in the last days of Congress. I hope you will not think I am obtruding in this matter, but the inconvenience of being without a Justice from October until December would be considerable." *Id.* Day, however, had not explicitly said to Harding that he would resign. Warren G. Harding to WHT (August 24, 1922) (Taft papers) ("I should be exceedingly reluctant to write him a request to tender his resignation."); Warren G. Harding to WHT (August 30, 1922) (Taft papers) ("I have felt a great reluctance to do anything that might wound his feelings or to suggest an impatience to fill the vacancy on the Supreme Bench which his retirement would call for.").
20. News of Day's possible retirement broke on September 6. *See Judge Day May Quit High Court Bench*, NEW YORK TIMES (September 6, 1922), at 19 ("It became known today in official circles in connection with the resignation of Justice John H. Clarke, announced yesterday, that Justice Day intended to determine whether his new duties as umpire in the adjudication of German-American claims growing out of the World War would take so much of his time as to make it desirable for him to give up active service on the Supreme Bench."); *May Quit Bench*, CHICAGO DAILY TRIBUNE (September 6, 1922), at 7; *Two Supreme Court Justices Are Expected to Retire*, WALL ST. JOURNAL (September 7, 1922), at 2.
21. WRD to Warren G. Harding (October 24, 1922) (Department of Justice Files, National Archives). *See* Warren G. Harding to WRD (October 24, 1922) (Harding papers); *Justice Day Resigns Supreme Court Seat*, NEW YORK TIMES (October 25, 1922), at 21. Day made his resignation effective as of November 14, 1922. *See supra* note 1. Taft wrote his son that he had "induced" Day "to postpone action until then, because we are now in recess writing opinions in cases in which he voted, and there are some of them in which it will be necessary to have his vote to carry the case." WHT to Robert A. Taft (October 26, 1922) (Taft papers). It is not clear what cases Taft might have had in mind.
22. "The fight is on now for his successor," Taft wrote his brother, "though I don't think it will grow very heated until after the election." WHT to Horace D. Taft (October 26, 1922) (Taft papers).
23. Harding communicated Butler's nomination to the Senate on November 23, 1922. *Democrat Named to Supreme Court*, WASHINGTON POST (November 24, 1922), at 5.
24. *See* DANELSKI, *supra* note 16.

25. WHT to Mrs. Frederick J. Manning (June 11, 1923) (Taft papers) ("My mainstay in the Court is Van Devanter").
26. Taft had come to know Butler well during the Canadian Trunk arbitration. *See supra* Prologue, at note 49. Van Devanter had been close to Butler since Van Devanter's days as a judge on the 8th Circuit. DANELSKI, *supra* note 16, at 35.
27. WHT to Charles D. Hilles (September 9, 1922) (Taft papers) ("There are now on the Bench seven Republicans and two Democrats. Harding has appointed two Republicans. Were he to appoint a Democrat . . . it would please the country very much and would help the Court."); WVD to WHT (September 10, 1922) (Taft papers) ("A Democrat would be very acceptable."); WHT to WVD (September 16, 1922) (Taft papers) ("I fear that Harding can not be induced to appoint a Democrat, though I think it would be a good thing both for the Court and politically."); WVD to Walter H. Sanborn (October 11, 1922) (Van Devanter papers) ("Chief Justice White, a southern democrat, has been succeeded by Chief Justice Taft, a northern republican. Justice Clarke, a northern democrat, has been succeeded by Justice Sutherland, a western republican. Justice Day, a northern republican, may retire within two months. . . . It no doubt would be moving along right lines to select from among men otherwise fitted a democrat, or southern democrat"); WHT to PB (October 25, 1922) (Taft papers) ("The President realizes that it will aid the Court to increase the number of Democrats on the Bench, there now being only two."); WVD to Walter H. Sanborn (October 31, 1922) (Van Devanter papers) ("The President is solely desirous of making the best appointment possible, but he has never had judicial service, is not a lawyer and must put much dependence in others. In referring to President Taft's appointments of democrats to the bench he said, a few days since, 'But, Mr. Chief Justice, I haven't seen any evidence of any marked approval by the country of what you did in that regard.' So you will see that while we judges and lawyers assume a particular ability to weigh judicial appointments, others are disposed to the opinions of men in general to obtain true standards.").

There is evidence that by the middle of October Harding was specifically looking to appoint a Catholic to the bench. *See* Max Pam to Warren G. Harding (October 11, 1922) (Harding papers) (offering "a list" of Catholic candidates that includes Pierce Butler as well as Republican potential nominees, "occurring to me as available in the connection discussed with you Monday."). By the end of the month, it was also clear that Harding had decided to appoint a Democrat. *See* Frank B. Kellogg to Warren G. Harding (October 30, 1922) (Harding papers) ("I have heard . . . that you wish to appoint a Democrat. I consider it wise, of course, to keep the Bench entirely out of partisan politics and have a reasonable number of Democrats on it."). *See* James A. Fowler, *Mr. Justice Edward Terry Sanford*, 17 AMERICAN BAR ASSOCIATION JOURNAL 229, 231 (April 1931) ("It is generally recognized that the political party not in power should have at least three members of the Court, and in filling the vacancy created by the retirement of Justice Day, the President gave but little, if any, consideration to a Republican.").

After Butler's confirmation, it was observed in the press that Butler's appointment would "aid in balancing the political complexion of the Court." *Another Supreme Court Shift*, 76 LITERARY DIGEST 15 (December 9, 1922). Although "there is no politics about the Supreme Court," the *New York Times* noted that "it pleases the public sense of fair play to see a Republican put a Democrat on the bench." *For Associate Justice*, NEW YORK TIMES (November 25, 1922), at 9.

28. *See* Henry W. Taft to WHT, October 26, 1922 (Taft papers) ("The Attorney General was very emphatic in repeating what you had already told me, that he would not approve of anybody for appointment who was not approved by you. I think he also said that the President felt very much that way himself.").

29. Davis was in fact Taft's first choice. WHT to Charles D. Hilles (September 9, 1922) (Taft papers) ("If I were making the appointment, I would appoint John Davis to the Bench from West Virginia."); WHT to George Wickersham (September 18, 1922) (Taft papers) ("If the Administration could be induced to look to Democrats, I think John Davis would be the best man. It would strengthen the Court to have it thought that men were selected for it without regard to political affiliation."). *See* WVD to WHT (September 10, 1922) (Taft papers) ("John W. Davis probably would make a good man. His service as Solicitor Gen'l would be helpful and he is a good lawyer and level headed. He does not run from work and he enjoys a good reputation all over the country."). Pleading poverty, however, Davis ultimately declined to be considered. *See* WVD to John W. Davis (October 28, 1922) (Van Devanter papers) ("Several who are rightly interested in the selection of splendidly equipped men to fill approaching vacancies in our court are thinking of you in that connection. The Chief Justice and I are among them. . . . The question has been raised whether you would accept. Some who enjoy your acquaintance . . . have declared that they know you would not accept. . . . The Chief Justice and I are among those who are loathe to accept the statement as reflecting your attitude. While recognizing that you are not seeking the preferment, we conceive you would deem it a patriotic duty to accept, if the place were tendered."); John W. Davis to WVD (October 31, 1922) (Van Devanter papers) ("[I]f the tender were made at this particular moment, I feel that I could not do otherwise than decline."); WHT to WVD (November 2, 1922) (Taft papers) ("This settles what we had already known. . . . Perhaps I ought not to say that he will live to regret the day, but I think he will.").

30. WHT to WVD (October 27, 1922) (Taft papers) ("I think Pierce Butler is our man."). *See* WHT to Max Pam (October 28, 1922) (Taft papers) ("I consider [Pierce Butler], next to Davis, the best qualified man for our Bench. . . . He is a man who could pull his weight in the boat. He is young, strong, clear-headed, courageous, and he has come up from the bottom by his own exertions, and he is entitled to recognition."); WVD to Walter H. Sanborn (October 31, 1922) (Van Devanter papers) ("[T]here is still much which can be done to show that Butler would be a highly acceptable appointee. . . . I am writing this letter after a talk with the Chief Justice, who takes the same interest in the mention of Butler's name that I do. We are quite agreed that nature cast Butler in a large mold, and that his appointment would be a particularly good one for the country and for the Court.").

Taft formally indicated to Harding his support of Butler on October 30. WHT to Warren G. Harding (October 30, 1922) (Taft papers):

> In your consideration of candidates for the Supreme Bench, I think I spoke to you of Pierce Butler of Minnesota. I have known him for a number of years very well indeed. He was counsel for the Government of Canada in

William Rufus Day & Pierce Butler

> the arbitration of the Grand Trunk valuation, in which I was one of the arbitrators, and heard him in trial and argument for months together. He builded himself up from the bottom. ... He is a Catholic and was a great friend of Archbishop Ireland. Justice Van Devanter knows him well. He has heard him argue one hundred cases in the Circuit Court of Appeals of the Eighth Circuit. ... He is a Democrat of the Cleveland type, but really one I think who would make a great Justice of our Court, such a man of rugged character and force as Justice Miller was. ... As between him and John Davis, it would be hard to chance as to ability, qualifications and judicial temperament.

From Taft's point of view, one of Butler's chief advantages was his devout and well-connected Catholicism. Taft was most afraid that the New York Catholic hierarchy would push Harding into appointing Martin T. Manton, a Catholic judge on the Second Circuit. As Taft wrote Butler, with remarkable candor:

> [T]here has been a conspiracy, which includes some of the Hierarchy of the Catholic Church in New York, to induce the President to appoint an utterly unfit man for our Court who has so many political and other associations that he has been able to mass a formidable amount of influence to be brought to bear upon a President who is not a lawyer, to induce him to make an appointment which I think would be deplorable, not only for the country but for the Catholic Church, some of whose representatives are active in promoting it. The candidate is Manton. He was a damage lawyer and an ambulance chaser in New York for a good many years. ... Manton is now a politician on the Bench. His consultation room is always full of men of that kind. He owns eight or nine laundries in New York, and is rich. He is shrewd and quick, and can be taught to be a competent judge, except that he is lacking in those moral qualities that are indispensable in a useful Judge. He has brought to bear upon the President the intervention of Archbishop Hayes, and the pressure of Burke Cockran and other Catholics from New York. ... In view of this, and to neutralize that influence, it is fortunate that it is possible to secure, as a candidate, you, who are so eminently qualified for the place, and who are a Catholic, so that the Church may do itself credit in recommending you and avoid the condemnation it ought to have were it to be successful in procuring the appointment of a man like Manton. That is the reason why, when I wrote you, I suggested that you should secure a letter directly to the President from Archbishop Dowling and such others of the Hierarchy as can be properly approached and shown the danger the Church is in.

WHT to PB (November 7, 1922) (Taft papers). *See* WHT to Elihu Root (November 19, 1922) (Taft papers) ("There has been a conspiracy on the part of Will Hays and a life insurance agent named Rosen, a Jew, McCooey of Brooklyn, and Archbishop Hayes of New York, to bring all possible influence to bear upon the President to appoint Manton, of the Circuit Court of Appeals .... In order to get a good man, and to prevent such influence from being formidable, we had to start a barrage in favor of Pierce Butler, who is in every way worthy of our Court. I hope we have got the thing into a situation where Butler will be appointed."); WHT to Henry W. Taft (October 27, 1922) (Taft papers) (In order to counter "the pressure for Manton," "the Catholic Hierarchy of the West, and especially of the Northwest, ought to be stimulated to note the qualifications and chance of having Butler appointed, but I don't know how that can be done."); Elihu Root to WHT (November 21, 1922) (Taft papers) ("Manton was one of Wilson's worst appointments. ... During the six years that he has been on the bench he has failed to win the confidence or respect of the bar or of the community. ... He is purely

THE TAFT COURT

a product of intrigue, and if the people get that idea of the Supreme Court they will smash the whole outfit. I think the general judgment would favor having a democrat and a Roman Catholic appointed in order to have a Court with an understanding of all points of view; but the appointment would have to be based primarily on the high character, ability, and standing of the man. If he has no substantial qualification except Church favor, the appointment would be regarded as surrender and there would be the devil to pay.").

When Harding eventually nominated Butler, George Wickersham, Taft's intimate friend who had been his attorney general, wrote to "congratulate" Taft, most especially because "a certain other candidacy, which you wot [sic] of, has been thus defeated." George Wickersham to WHT (November 23, 1922) (Taft papers). Charles Burlingham wrote Taft that "We New Yorkers are all much pleased with the appointment of Butler and the elimination of 'M'." Charles C. Burlingham to WHT (December 4, 1922) (Taft papers). Years later Thomas Reed Powell speculated to Harlan Stone that "the selection of Supreme Court Justices is pretty much a matter of chance," offering many examples, including the fact "that Butler was known to Taft in the Canadian Railways Valuation work and was a Catholic who could be substituted for Manton without having to turn down a Catholic." Thomas Reed Powell to HFS (October 9, 1928) (Stone papers).

Taft's suspicions of Manton were to prove accurate. In 1939 Manton was convicted of accepting bribes. DANELSKI, *supra* note 16, at 195–97. The story is told in JOSEPH BORKIN, CORRUPT JUDGE 23–93 (New York: Clarkson N. Potter, Inc. 1962).

31. WHT to Charles P. Taft 2nd (February 14, 1926) (Taft papers).
32. WHT to Charles D. Hilles (September 9, 1922) (Taft papers).
33. WHT to Mrs. E.B. McCagg (December 30, 1922) (Taft papers). Van Devanter regarded Butler as "a fine lawyer, a broad-gauged, red-blooded man and in every way well fitted for the place." WVD to John C. Pollock (November 22, 1922) (Van Devanter papers).
34. WHT to Warren G. Harding (December 14, 1922) (Taft papers). Although Taft used the phrase in the context of another potential nominee to the Supreme Court, Marshall Bullitt, who had been Taft's solicitor general, he also meant it to apply to Butler. *See infra* note 77.
35. *Brandeis-Frankfurter Conversations*, at 318 (July 3, 1923). Taft had specifically "mentioned Manton of New York." In protesting Butler's nomination, *The Nation* observed that "so long as the Supreme Court continues to exercise political functions by making and unmaking legislation it ought to be representative of the various political views in the country – that it ought to contain not merely Republicans and Democrats but also liberals as well as conservatives." *No Longer Supreme*, 115 THE NATION 653, 653 (1922).
36. WHT to James Markham (October 21, 1916) (Taft papers).
37. "It was a great blessing that in the eight years succeeding my term, Wilson had only three places to fill, and was greatly disappointed and defeated in his purpose in the attitude of McReynolds, and now that one of his appointees retires, so that his purpose in his appointments is now only served by the continuance of Brandeis." WHT to Charles D. Hilles (September 9, 1922) (Taft papers). *See* WHT to Horace D. Taft (September 17, 1922) (Taft papers) ("The Lord seems to have favored the

Court in withholding from Wilson very much opportunity to injure that tribunal, which he has really held in such slight esteem.").
38. Taft's answer to Brandeis is especially striking because in late 1922 Taft was also explicitly seeking candidates who held proper "conservative" attitudes toward property to replace the ailing Mahlon Pitney. *See infra* Chapter 3, at 89.
39. *Four New Dissenters*, 68 NEW REPUBLIC 61, 62 (1931).
40. *Grey Wigs*, 8 TIME MAGAZINE 8, 8 (October 11, 1926).
41. *The Court Diary of Justice William O. Douglas*, 1995 JOURNAL OF SUPREME COURT HISTORY 77, 84. Butler "knows what he wants & how to get it. He has thought through your side from the major premise on and knows its every weakness." *Id.* Five months later, Douglas noted that "Butler's death marked the passing of a doughty warrior who knew how to fight for his principles & on what side his principles lay." *Id.* at 86.
42. *Brandeis-Frankfurter Conversations*, at 336 (June 15–16, 1926).
43. Quoted in 34 TIME MAGAZINE 14 (November 27, 1939). The official Minute submitted to the Court in memory of Butler struck a similar note, stressing that Butler's character "was a unit without internal stress. ... A skillful legal tactician, his sole strategy was to drive forward unswervingly in the direction which he regarded as the right one." *In Memory of Mr. Justice Butler*, 310 U.S. vii, ix (1939) (*"In Memory of Mr. Justice Butler"*). Arthur E. Sutherland, Holmes's law clerk during the 1927 term, recalled the prosecution of a corrupt prohibition official in which the Court had originally "voted for reversal and acquittal. But Butler at conference argued 'em round. Holmes spoke admiringly to me of Butler's force. He said you could see what a prosecuting officer he had made." David M. O'Brien, *Sutherland's Recollections of Justice Holmes*, 1988 SUPREME COURT YEARBOOK 18, 25. The case was Donnelley v. United States, 276 U.S. 505 (1928).
44. Charles Evan Hughes, *Mr. Justice Butler*, 310 U.S. xiii, xvi. Minnesota was "in the main ... still of the frontier when [Butler] began his law practice. To that practice, he brought all of the frontier's best qualities of heart and mind. They were born in him. They inhered throughout his life." *Remarks of Mr. George I. Haight*, PROCEEDINGS OF THE BAR AND OFFICERS OF SUPREME COURT OF THE UNITED STATES IN MEMORY OF PIERCE BUTLER, JANUARY 27, 1940, in I MEMORIALS OF THE JUSTICES OF SUPREME COURT OF THE UNITED STATES 348 (Roger F. Jacobs, ed., Littleton: F.B. Rothman 1981) ("PROCEEDINGS"). DANELSKI, *supra* note 16, contains the best biographical sketch of Butler. *See also* Richard J. Purcell, *Mr. Justice Pierce Butler*, 42 CATHOLIC EDUCATIONAL REVIEW 193 (1944). For a discussion of Butler's philosophy, see FRANCIS JOSEPH BROWN, THE SOCIAL AND ECONOMIC PHILOSOPHY OF PIERCE BUTLER (Washington D.C.: Catholic University Press 1945); David Schroeder, More Than a Fraction: The Life and Work of Pierce Butler (Ph.D. Dissertation, Marquette University 2009).
45. The first Minnesota home of Butler's parents had been burned down by Native Americans. *Remarks of Mr. George I. Haight* in PROCEEDINGS, *supra* note 44, at 347.
46. *Remarks of Robert A. Taft*, in PROCEEDINGS, *supra* note 44, at 352.
47. *From Log Cabin of West to Supreme Court Bench*, NEW YORK TIMES (December 3, 1922), § 9, at 3. "Standing well over six feet, with broad shoulders and of

commanding mien, he is a dominating figure in any gathering." *Id.* According to William Mitchell, Butler "was big, physically and mentally, – a leonine figure. In his years at the bar, whenever he entered a trial court he became instantly the dominating figure, the cynosure of all eyes. He was always a dreaded antagonist at the bar." *Remarks of William D. Mitchell*, in PROCEEDINGS, *supra* note 44, at 363–64.

48. Pierce Butler, *Valuation of Railway Property for Purposes of Rate Regulation*, 23 JOURNAL OF POLITICAL ECONOMY 17, 29 (January 1915). "It is difficult to think of a calamity so great as that which is certain to follow a valuation based upon the theory that the federal Constitution does not protect the full present value of railroad property in rate regulation, and that individual conceptions of right and wrong may be substituted for fundamental principles of organic law." *Id.* at 31. Such a catastrophe would use "legislative authority" to transfer to others "all the rewards which are due to the foresight, wisdom, and enterprise of the men who conceived and constructed wisely." *Id.* at 24.

49. Pierce Butler *et al.*, *In re* Certain Questions Arising under the Act of Congress of March 1, 1913, Providing for the Federal Valuation of All the Property Owned or Used by Common Carriers Subject to the Act to Regulate Commerce, Brief before the Interstate Commerce Commission Filed on Behalf of the Railroad Companies Represented by the Presidents' Conference Committee (September 1, 1915). In times of rising prices, like the 1920s, the "reproduction theory of value" espoused by Butler would constitutionally require government commissions to raise railroad rates, which made the theory controversial during the decade.

50. Pierce Butler, *Educating for Citizenship: Duties the Citizen Owes to the State*, 12 CATHOLIC EDUCATIONAL ASSOCIATION BULLETIN 123, 126 (November 1915).

51. Pierce Butler, *Some Opportunities and Duties of Lawyers*, 9 AMERICAN BAR ASSOCIATION JOURNAL 583, 585 (1923).

52. Butler, *supra* note 51, at 586. "The enormous number of bills introduced in the legislatures shows the extent to which it is thought that welfare can be promoted by lawmaking." *Id.* Butler was convinced that "[d]ignity of law and respect for authority are impaired by too many enactments and regulations. The proper and legitimate scope of government should be carefully regarded. ... That lawmaking may be *overworked* will be admitted by any intelligent observer who does not believe that general welfare will be promoted by transferring all the responsibilities of life from individuals to agencies of the State." *Id.*

53. Pierce Butler, *There Is Important Work of Lawyers as Citizens*, 1916 PROCEEDINGS OF THE MINNESOTA BAR ASSOCIATION 106, at 113.

54. *Id.* at 112.

55. Pierce Butler, Speech at Eucharistic Congress, quoted in *325,000 Attend Open-Air Services in Chicago Stadium*, NEW YORK TIMES (June 23, 1926), at 18. ("There is danger of grave error. Many appear to believe that legislation can take away all the trials and burdens of life, including those that are purely personal; that laws can be devised to furnish employment, prescribe the amount of work and provide for all the needs of life. Notwithstanding that all experience shows the contrary, many seem to think it possible to transfer the responsibilities of life from individuals, to whom they belong, to agencies of the State created to bear them.").

William Rufus Day & Pierce Butler

56. *Id.* "There has been in this country a good deal of teaching which is calculated to impair initiative and to destroy the prime motives for morality, industry, thrift and independence, and which is liable to foster the belief, or hope, that the state, transgressing the limits of its true functions, will undertake to stand in the place of father and mother, husband and wife, brother and sister, and become one vast machine to provide employment and to furnish supplies to meet the needs of the people." *Id.* In Butler's view, to undermine the incentives for "individual initiative and development," to undercut the protections of "private property," "would, more than war, work the ruin of the nation. . . . It would weaken character and leave the individual man and woman without the motive or hope or inspiration necessary to freedom and morality. The hold which individualism has ever had upon democracy should not be loosened." Butler, *supra* note 50, at 130–31.

57. *Id.* at 128. It should also be pointed out that Butler was an early and strong defender of workmen's compensation statutes. *See* Pierce Butler, *Employees' Compensation for Injuries*, 1908 PROCEEDINGS OF THE MINNESOTA BAR ASSOCIATION 32–45.

58. William D. Mitchell, in PROCEEDINGS, *supra* note 44, at 365. In Robert Jackson's more fulsome description: "His character was shaped by the hard way of life that left lasting convictions and attitudes in men who experienced existence in a pioneer country . . . [which] presents the choice between courage and self-discipline – or extinction. It offers a simple and rugged society in which place is won and held only by will and work and worth. It develops intense love of liberty and hatred of restraint and a self-reliance that does not know how to dodge, and never fears to stand firmly and, if need be, alone. These were the primary characteristics of Mr. Justice Butler." Robert Jackson, *Mr. Justice Butler*, 310 U.S. xiv.

59. Butler, *supra* note 50, at 126 ("[T]he State must be powerful, well-ordered and alert, that those to whom it owes protection, each for himself in his own sphere, may have free and well-guarded right and opportunity to seek truth, to enlighten and freely to follow his own conception of right and wrong, and, so long as no injury comes through him to others, to pursue his own course, to be master of his own affairs and to live his own life."). *See, e.g.*, Hamilton v. Regents of the University of California, 293 U.S. 245, 262–63 (1934) ("Government, federal and state, each in its own sphere owes a duty to the people within its jurisdiction to preserve itself in adequate strength to maintain peace and order and to assure the just enforcement of law. And every citizen owes the reciprocal duty, according to his capacity, to support and defend government against all enemies.").

60. Butler, *supra* note 50, at 123. "Full allegiance in this country involves the obligation to support and defend the Federal and State constitutions. These are the instruments declaring safeguards for the freedom and safety of person and the security of private property, and which lay down the fundamental rules of government." *Id.* at 124.

61. Butler, *supra* note 53, at 109.

62. Butler, *supra* note 55, at 18. *See* Butler, *supra* note 51, at 585: "All the forces of society should be called to aid in the development of the proper respect for law. . . . The spirit of lawlessness that threatens now is not confined to cases where horrible crime has been committed, or to those growing out of race or other class troubles."

> The Committee on Citizenship of [the American Bar Association] finds that it is necessary "to re-establish the Constitution of the United States and the principles and ideals of our government in the minds and hearts of the people."

Many things have contributed to lessen devotion to country. Undoubtedly imperfect education in fundamentals on which moral qualities and sound character depend has been one of the most potent causes of this evil. Toleration of efforts to discredit certain laws by showing that they cannot be enforced, lack of effective law enforcement, attempts by numerous organizations to usurp power and ignore authority, and many like things have engendered a dangerous lack of respect for law. The ... destruction of confidence in the established order have impaired patriotic standards everywhere. The ideals of earlier days in the life of the Republic which saved and advanced the interests of country must be restored.

Id. at 587.

63. The story is told in William E. Matsen, *Professor William S. Schaper, War Hysteria and the Price of Academic Freedom*, 51 MINNESOTA HISTORY 131 (Winter 1988); John T. Hubell, *A Question of Academic Freedom: The William A. Schaper Case*, 17 MID-WEST QUARTERLY 111 (January 1976).
64. Quoted in Hubell, *supra* note 63, at 115. In 1938 the University of Minnesota Regents rescinded its precipitous action and reinstated Schaper to the faculty with the rank of emeritus professor. *Id.* at 120.
65. WHT to PB (December 12, 1922) (Taft papers).
66. Child Labor Tax Case, 259 U.S. 20 (1922) (Striking down the Child Labor Tax Law); United Mine Workers v. Coronado Coal Co., 259 U.S. 344 (1922) (holding unincorporated labor unions subject to suit under federal anti-trust statutes); Truax v. Corrigan, 257 U.S. 312 (1921) (striking down an Arizona statute restricting the issuance of injunctions in labor disputes); American Steel Foundries v. Tri-City Central Trades Council, 257 U.S. 184 (1921) (restricting labor picketing).
67. *La Follette Lashes Federal Judiciary*, NEW YORK TIMES (June 15, 1922), at 1; 62 CONG. REC. 9071–82 (June 21, 1922); *Is the Supreme Court Too Supreme?*, 74 LITERARY DIGEST 21 (July 1, 1922); *Coolidge Defends High Court; Opposes an All-Powerful Congress*, NEW YORK TIMES (August 11, 1922), at 17.
68. *Labor Would Curb the Supreme Court*, NEW YORK TIMES (June 23, 1922), at 17; *Labor Gives Wide Publicity to Usurped Power of Courts*, AMERICAN FEDERATION OF LABOR WEEKLY NEWS SERVICE (July 1, 1922), at 1; John P. Frey, *Shall the People or the Supreme Court Be the Final Voice in Legislation?*, 29 AMERICAN FEDERATIONIST 629 (1922); W.B. Rubin, *The Constitution and the Supreme Court*, 29 AMERICAN FEDERATIONIST 675 (1922); Noel Sargent, *The La Follette Veto*, 68 THE FORUM 775 (1922); *Supreme Court Curb Is Planned by Labor*, AMERICAN FEDERATION OF LABOR WEEKLY NEWS SERVICE (September 22, 1922), at 1.
69. WHT to Clarence H. Kelsey (September 12, 1922) (Taft papers).
70. The situation was made worse by the triumph of progressive forces in recently held elections in the Northwest. "Even as little as six or eight weeks ago, it seems unlikely that the appointment would have created much active protest. November 7, however, exercised a profound influence in the Northwest. ... The victory of La Follette in Wisconsin, the triumph of the once repudiated Frazier in North Dakota, and, above all, the defeat of Kellogg by Shipstead in Minnesota – these things have sharply intensified the zeal of all the elements in the Northwest opposed to conservatism." H.A. Bellows, *Pierce Butler, Nominee for the United States Supreme Court*, 132 THE OUTLOOK 652 (December 13, 1922). The situation was so volatile that Day referred to it in his letter of acknowledgment to the Court: "I can not forego an expression of satisfaction that at no time has any serious inroad

been made upon the great and necessary functions of the Court in adjudicating fundamental rights under our system of Government, although such power has been the subject of attack during the entire life of the Republic. If our institutions are to endure ... these powers must be lodged in an impartial and independent tribunal." *Retirement of Mr. Justice Day*, 260 U.S. ix, xi (1922).

71. "There was this to be said of Senator Sutherland, however – he had a reputation as a many-sided lawyer. As much cannot be said of Pierce Butler, for he is not known nationally and his practice has been chiefly in the service of railroads and other corporations in the Northwest. ... There seems to be no excuse for Mr. Butler's nomination unless, as some charge, Mr. Harding's trying to pack the supreme court with friends of the railroads in view of the vital questions in regard to them which are expected to come before the tribunal in the next few years." *No Longer Supreme*, 65 THE NATION 653, 653 (1922).

72. "No man has probably ever been appointed to the United States Supreme Court about whom the general public knew less than it does about Pierce Butler of Minnesota. His nomination ... came as a complete surprise." *Mr. Harding's Supreme Court Appointment*, NEW YORK WORLD (November 25, 1922), at 8. "All that the public yet knows of Pierce Butler," said the *San Francisco Examiner*, "is that he represented the railroads before the Interstate Commerce Commission in the effort to increase the so-called book value of the railroads as a basis for future rate making. It is entirely honorable for a lawyer to have a railroad among his clients; but no lawyer selected and recommended by the railroads or by other public service corporations should ever be made justice of the United States Supreme Court." *Butler's Nomination to U.S. Supreme Court*, SAN FRANCISCO EXAMINER (December 20, 1922), at 32.

73. *A Reactionary for the Supreme Bench*, 33 NEW REPUBLIC 65, 66 (1922).

74. Butler, said Robert Jackson, was "a man of no subtlety or sham, he pronounced his judgments without finesse, indirection, or obscurity. ... His judicial attitude was not one of frosty neutrality, but one of intensity and certitude of conviction on basic philosophies of life and society and law and government." Jackson, *supra* note 58, at xv. William D. Mitchell concurred that "such words as 'subtlety' or 'finesse' have no place in any vocabulary needed to describe him. His directness and candor left no room for mistake as to where he stood. ... Courage and power were personified in him." *Remarks of William D. Mitchell*, in PROCEEDINGS, *supra* note 44, at 363. Charles Evans Hughes also remarked that although Butler "had a passion for exactness," he "was not addicted to subtlety." Hughes, *supra* note 44, at xvi.

75. *The Week*, 33 NEW REPUBLIC 53, 54 (1922).

76. *Pierce Butler and the Rule of Reason*, 33 NEW REPUBLIC 81, 82 (1922). Harding "does not understand how essential a moderate and statesmanlike Supreme Court is to prevent the redistribution of economic and social power from becoming an occasion for violence or a provocation of it. If the President, his associates and successors, continue to commit such serious mistakes, they will in the end provide an excuse, on the part of sections and classes, which are suffering from the existing distribution of economic power and are denied the legal method of changing it, for the very appeal to force which all sensible and humane people are most anxious to avoid." *Id.* at 81–82. *See* 65 THE NATION 594 (1922) (The "appointment is deplorable from every point of view. It degrades the court, strikes a blow at its spiritual

integrity and its independence, and further tarnishes its reputation by making it the abiding-place of intolerant reactionaries.").

77. *No Longer Supreme*, supra note 71, at 653. *See The New Supreme Court Justice*, 133 THE OUTLOOK 163 (January 24, 1923) ("Seldom in the history of our country has an appointment to the Supreme bench encountered opposition so bitter. In Minnesota, the State of his residence, popular feeling against Mr. Butler has been widespread and intense. ... It is because great numbers of people in Minnesota believe that Mr. Butler ... represented [a] reactionary tendency that they opposed him as a nominee for the bench. ... The appointment of Mr. Butler has tended to strengthen the argument of those who hold that the Supreme Court itself is reactionary and that its power to declare laws unconstitutional should be taken from it."); *Pierce Butler and the Rule of Reason*, supra note 76, at 83 ("We trust [the American people] will not have to adopt the revolutionary expedient of putting congressional in the place of judicial interpretation of the Constitution, but adopt it they will, if the Supreme Court is to be packed with Pierce Butlers.").

The attack on Butler seemed to bring out the worst in Taft. He wrote Harding: "I observe that La Follette and Norris are about to attack Butler's nomination. This is not that they can prevent his confirmation, but it is part of the program they are deliberately setting out upon to attack you and the Court and the Constitution. The more blatant they make it, the better I think it will be to unite the conservative elements of the country to resist their plotting against our present social order, and I hope you will feel that the best way to deal with them is to hit them between the eyes by the appointment of staunch friends of the Constitution who will do nothing to sap the pillars of our Government as they have weathered the storm of many assaults and vindicated the wisdom of our ancestors. But I did not intend to get into a discussion of this sort." WHT to Warren G. Harding (December 4, 1922) (Taft papers).

When Butler wrote Taft to complain of the "combination of radical elements" that were opposing his nomination, including "the New Republic," PB to WHT (December 9, 1922) (Taft papers), Taft replied that "I haven't seen what the New Republic has said, because I don't read that paper, but I have no doubt it said everything that it ought not to say. Frankfurter is one of its contributors. It was one of the few papers in the country that attacked my nomination, and really a man whom it does not attack is of questionable reputation as to his loyalty and his sound constitutional view." WHT to PB (December 12, 1922) (Taft papers). He advised Butler "to have the President of the University come down here to rebut these attacks that are prompted by those disloyal traitors whom you assisted in kicking out of the University." WHT to PB (December 5, 1922) (Taft papers). "As I anticipated, La Follette and Norris propose to make use of your nomination as a means of attacking Harding and the Supreme Court, and arousing radical and Non-Partisan League enthusiasm in their present organization and radical bloc in Congress and in the country. Of course it will not defeat your confirmation, but it will, I fear, give you some unpleasant hours by reason of the delays that can be caused in bringing you to us, and by the lies that the vermin whom you have stepped on in the discharge of your duties will be delighted to tell to the Judiciary Committee." *Id.*

78. Samuel Gompers, *Why Pierce Butler?*, 30 AMERICAN FEDERATIONIST 76 (1923).
79. 64 CONG. REC. 813 (December 21, 1922).

William Rufus Day & Pierce Butler

80. Butler, said Brandeis, has his "eye on [the] ball. Great will & shows much self-mastery to control. Hates to be corrected – hangs on a word but hates dissents from him so will yield." *Brandeis-Frankfurter Conversations*, at 338 (n.d.).
81. Brandeis remarked to Frankfurter that "P. Butler is about what people said he was. He is gunning after valuation of land grants in land grant roads." *Brandeis-Frankfurter Conversations*, at 312 (June 12, 1923). At the time of Butler's confirmation, it was asked whether, because of his strong and provocative views, he would disqualify himself from cases involving railroad rate regulation. Butler apparently agreed, subsequently disqualifying himself in St. Louis & O'Fallon Ry. Co. v. United States, 279 U.S. 461 (1929), which determined the methodology to be used to implement the Valuation Act of 1913, Pub. L. 62-400, 37 Stat. 701 (March 1, 1913). *See infra* Chapter 27, at 887 and notes 65–66. The Act required the Interstate Commerce Commission to evaluate the fair value of the nation's railroads as a preliminary to setting rates. Butler's disqualification was in fact merely symbolic, however, because he had already written the reproduction theory of value into the Court's case law in prior decisions addressing the evaluation of utilities other than railroads. *See, e.g.*, Bluefield Water Works and Improvement Co. v. Public Service Commission of West Virginia, 262 U.S. 679 (1923); Board of Public Utility Commissioners v. New York Telephone Co., 271 U.S. 23 (1926); McCardle v. Indianapolis Water Co., 272 U.S. 400, 408–9 (1926). Butler's effectiveness in constitutionalizing the "cost of reproduction" as a baseline for ratemaking produced bitterness among those in the Senate who had originally opposed Butler's nomination. *See* 77 CONG. REC. 4411–13 (May 27, 1933). In 1930, the *New Republic*, in commenting on the controversy caused by Hughes's nomination as chief justice, could remember the example of "Mr. Justice Butler, whose chief eminence as a lawyer was derived from the representation of public utilities and railroads in valuation cases, and who as a judge has helped to write into law many of the very same contentions which he previously urged in behalf of his powerful clients." *The Week*, 62 NEW REPUBLIC 30, 31 (1930).
82. *See, e.g.*, Jay Burns Baking Co. v. Bryan, 264 U.S. 504 (1924); Michigan Pub. Utilities Comm'n v. Duke, 266 U.S. 570 (1925); Weaver v. Palmer Bros. Co., 270 U.S. 402 (1926); Delaware, Lackawanna & Western Railroad Co. v. Morristown, 276 U.S. 182 (1928); Black and White Taxicab and Transfer Co. v. Brown and Yellow Taxicab and Transfer Co., 276 U.S. 518 (1928); Steele v. Drummond, 275 U.S. 199 (1927).
83. United States v. Schwimmer, 279 U.S. 644 (1929); Burns v. United States, 274 U.S. 328 (1927).
84. In the papers of the justices, it is not uncommon to find a draft opinion returned by Butler with a comment like: "I voted the other way and am still inclined that way, but acquiesce for the sake of harmony & the Court." Standard Oil Co. v. Marysville, 279 U.S. 582 (1929) (Stone papers).
85. So, for example, in his draft opinion in Van Oster v. Kansas, 272 U.S. 465 (1926), Stone had originally included a paragraph stating:

> Such a law as we are now considering may be regarded as harsh and unwise, but we are concerned not with its wisdom but with the power of the legislature to enact it. Where as here the challenged statute is within the sphere of legislative power and the particular legal device chosen to make effective the

exercise of the power is consonant with recognized principles, the objection that it is harsh and oppressive must be addressed to the legislative and not to the judicial branch of the government.

(Stone papers). Stone eliminated the paragraph when he received a note from Butler stating: "Is this really necessary? The statements are very general. Can it not be omitted? ... I agree to the result and to the opinion subject to the elimination of the paragraph." For similar examples, see General American Tank Car Corp v. Day, 270 U.S. 367 (1926) (Stone papers); Opelika v. Opelika Sewer Co., 265 U.S. 215 (1924) (Holmes papers); Lucas v. Alexander, 279 U.S. 573 (1929) (Stone papers); International Shoe Co. v. Shartel, 279 U.S. 429 (1929) (Stone papers).

86. *See, e.g.*, Marron v. United States, 275 U.S. 192 (1927); United States v. One Ford Coupe Automobile, 272 U.S. 321, 335 (1926) (Butler, J., dissenting); Samuels v. McCurdy, 267 U.S. 188, 200 (1925). *See infra* Figures VI-2 and VI-3.

87. Sinclair v. United States, 279 U.S. 263, 292 (1929). *See, e.g.*, Agnello v. United States, 269 U.S. 20 (1925); Olmstead v. United States, 277 U.S. 438, 485 (1928) (Butler, J., dissenting). Butler was the only member of the Court to dissent in Buck v. Bell, 274 U.S. 200 (1927), the Holmes decision upholding a law imposing compulsory sterilization on the mentally disabled. The *New Republic* observed that although Butler "may have forgotten his humble origin," he "remembers his Catholic upbringing – he cast the lone dissenting vote in the case which upheld the Virginia statute providing for the sterilization of imbeciles." *Four New Dissenters*, *supra* note 39, at 62.

88. David R. Stras, *Pierce Butler: A Supreme Technician*, 62 VANDERBILT LAW REVIEW 695, 720–25 (2009). Brandeis observed that Butler was "alert to protect [the] accused." *Brandeis-Frankfurter Conversations*, at 338 (n.d.). Harold Leventhal recalls that Stone remarked how "Butler is usually good on search and seizure questions." Harold Leventhal, *Harlan Fiske Stone: Some Reflections*, 49 NEW YORK STATE BAR JOURNAL 24, 55 (1977). *See* Olmstead v. United States, 277 U.S. 438, 485 (1928) (Butler, J., dissenting); United States v. McElvain, 272 U.S. 633 (1926); Kercheval v. United States, 274 U.S. 220 (1927); Fasulo v. United States, 272 U.S. 620 (1926); United States v. Gulf Refining Co., 268 U.S. 542 (1925). In his first term on the Court, Stone authored an opinion upholding a search warrant for intoxicating liquors that had been issued on the basis of an affidavit that failed to disclose the defendant's possession of a permit authorizing the manufacture and sale of wine for nonbeverage purposes. Dumbra v. United States, 268 U.S. 435 (1925). Stone circulated a draft opinion stating that the affidavit was otherwise sufficient, and that "under such circumstances search and seizure are not unauthorized or unconstitutional and under the law, holders of Government permits must rely for protection from the harsh and unreasonable resort to that procedure, on the self-restraint and sense of moral responsibility of law enforcement officers rather than on constitutional limitations." (Stone papers). Butler responded by suggesting that all the words after "unconstitutional" be omitted: "Does not this tend to assure such officers that their own self-restraint is the limit? Can't we avoid that? Disingenuousness in some circumstances might evidence malice, want of probable cause, and the like." (Stone papers). Stone excised the offending language in his published opinion. In appropriate circumstances, however, Butler could be strongly

William Rufus Day & Pierce Butler

in favor of the prosecution of those who betrayed the public trust. *See, e.g.*, Mammoth Oil Co. v. United States, 275 U.S. 13 (1927); Donnelley v. United States, 276 U.S. 505 (1928); *supra* note 43.

89. *The Court Diary of Justice William O. Douglas, supra* note 41, at 86 (November 6, 1939). Holmes remarked to Harold Laski that "Butler has shown none of the difficult qualities that were attributed to him." OWH to Harold Laski (October 19, 1923), in 1 HOLMES-LASKI CORRESPONDENCE, at 555. Brandeis observed to Frankfurter that "Pierce Butler makes a good impression." LDB to Felix Frankfurter (January 3, 1923), in BRANDEIS-FRANKFURTER CORRESPONDENCE, at 132.

CHAPTER 3

Mahlon Pitney and Edward Terry Sanford

Harding's first three appointments to the Taft Court pushed it in a decisively conservative direction. But Harding was not yet finished reshaping the Court. A remarkable fourth vacancy was in the offing during the very months when the Butler nomination was pending.

Justice Mahlon Pitney, who had been appointed by Taft in 1912, was not well. In August 1922, Taft received an ominous message from Florence Pitney, Pitney's wife, that Pitney had undergone surgery for the removal of a cyst in his jaw, and that "he hopes he will be able to resume work on October first."[1] Thereafter Taft began to "get disquieting reports about the condition of Pitney,"[2] culminating in the news in September that Pitney was so "very ill," probably due to strokes, that there was "no prospect that [Pitney] will be able to resume his duties at the opening of the Court," and that retirement had to be considered as a possible option.[3]

After conversations with Florence, Taft offered to secure the passage of a statute entitling Pitney to retire with a full salary, even though Pitney had not yet reached the minimum age of seventy as required by existing legislation.[4] On October 3, Florence reported that Pitney had authorized Taft "to go ahead with the plan" to pass a statute allowing Pitney to retire with a full pension.[5] Taft was as good as his word.[6] The proposed bill became law on December 11,[7] and Pitney retired on December 16, 1922.[8] The upshot of these events is that throughout the fall of 1922 Harding (and Taft) were searching to replace not only Day, but also Pitney.

Like Day, Pitney had been something of a "swing" figure on the Court.[9] His background was that of a tepidly progressive, good-government Republican.[10] He was twice elected as a New Jersey Representative to Congress, became the leader of the New Jersey State Senate, served as an Associate Justice of the New Jersey Supreme Court, and eventually became Chancellor of New Jersey. His nomination to the Supreme Court by Taft had been controversial because of Pitney's support for injunctions to suppress strikes.[11]

Mahlon Pitney & Edward Terry Sanford

As a justice, Pitney was notable for his ongoing hostility to union organizing, authoring such passionate defenses of freedom of contract as *Coppage v. Kansas*,[12] *Hitchman Coal and Coke Co. v. Mitchell*,[13] and *Duplex Printing Co. v. Deering*.[14] Yet Pitney also dissented in *Truax v. Corrigan*,[15] the controversial case in which the Court, speaking through Taft, struck down an Arizona statute prohibiting labor injunctions. Pitney was also the decisive vote to sustain the constitutionality of workman's compensation statutes,[16] so that Brandeis could later remark to Frankfurter that "Pitney has real conscience & steady growth. But for him we would have had no Workmen's Compensation laws – he came around, upon study, though he had been the other way."[17]

Pitney was an honorable,[18] conscientious,[19] garrulous,[20] but basically pedestrian judge. As Holmes put it, "He had not wings and was not a thunderbolt, but he was a very honest, hard working Judge and a useful critic."[21] In Brandeis's view, Pitney "had a great sense of justice affected by Presbyterianism but no imagination whatever. And then he was much influenced by his experience & he had had mighty little."[22] Pitney "could not touch the superlative," noted Holmes, "but he took his work seriously, and was untiring in industry, . . . and, I came to think, truly had intellectual honesty that sometimes brought him out of his prejudices and first judgment."[23] Brandeis contrasted Pitney to Day, whom "no one could . . . change." Pitney "was different," because he had "real character. He welcomed correction and discussion."[24] Figures I-20 and I-21 illustrate Pitney's relatively eclectic alliances on the Court.[25]

If Harding had replaced Pitney with someone of Butler's ideological commitments and longevity, the history of the New Deal would have been entirely altered. But as it happened Harding selected Edward Terry Sanford to fill Pitney's vacancy, and Sanford would suddenly and unexpectedly collapse and die on

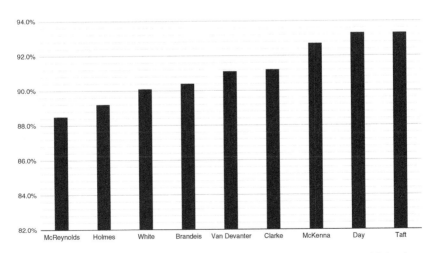

Figure I-20 Percentage of decisions in which Pitney participated and joined the same opinion as another justice, 1916–1921 terms

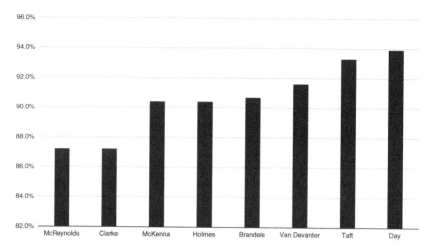

Figure I-21 Percentage of decisions in which Pitney participated and joined the same opinion as another justice, 1921 term

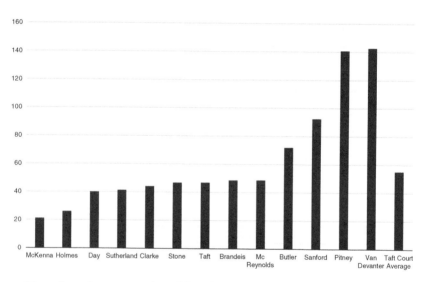

Figure I-22 Average number of days from argument to the announcement of a unanimous opinion, by justice, 1921–1928 terms

March 8, 1930.[26] While he was on the Court, Sanford would cut a judicial profile that was strikingly similar to Pitney's.

Like Pitney, Sanford came to the Court from the bench. He had since 1908 been a respected federal district judge for the Eastern and Middle Districts of Tennessee. Like Pitney, "he was a painstaking and faithful worker" whose

Mahlon Pitney & Edward Terry Sanford

"opinions, generally, were not distinguished in quality."[27] Like Pitney, Sanford was "nice – but [had] no spark of greatness"; he was "thoroughly bourgeois."[28] Like Pitney, Sanford struggled earnestly to keep abreast of his work on the Court, and, like Pitney, he was only sporadically successful. Figure I-22 illustrates that Sanford, like Pitney, took an inordinately long time to draft his opinions.[29] Although Sanford was, in Taft's view, "opinion shy,"[30] he was, like Pitney, intensely conscientious.[31] Like Pitney, Sanford was an essentially conservative justice[32] who nevertheless sought to negotiate something of a middle way between the left and right wings of the Court. "Far from being a Butler or a Sutherland,"[33] Sanford was in person "neither a reactionary nor a radical,"[34] but "a conservative with progressive tendencies."[35]

As a professional matter, these tendencies were visible but scarcely consequential. Figure I-23 illustrates that Sanford mostly voted with the conservative wing of the Court, an inclination that was also evident in conference, as indicated by Figure I-24.[36] Yet Sanford also displayed an independent streak that led him to dissent in such important decisions as *Adkins v. Children's Hospital*,[37] *Tyson & Bros v. Banton*,[38] and *United States v. Schwimmer*,[39] and that prompted him to refuse to join the Court's opinions in such significant cases as *Bedford Cut Stone Co. v. Journeyman S.C. Assn.*,[40] *Schlesinger v. Wisconsin*,[41] and *Ribnik v. McBride*.[42]

How Sanford came to be nominated is the subject of some controversy.[43] In the press it was reported that Sanford's appointment "was the result of the recommendation of William H. Taft,"[44] but this does not appear to be entirely accurate.[45] In fact, as Taft readily acknowledged, "Sanford is not my candidate. He is really the candidate of the Attorney General, who suggested him to me, and took him up vigorously at the instance of Fowler, who used to be the Assistant Attorney General."[46] James A. Fowler, who had been Sanford's close friend and law partner

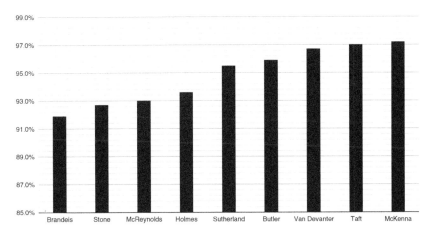

Figure I-23 Percentage of decisions in which Sanford participated and joined the same opinion as another justice, 1922–1928 terms

THE TAFT COURT

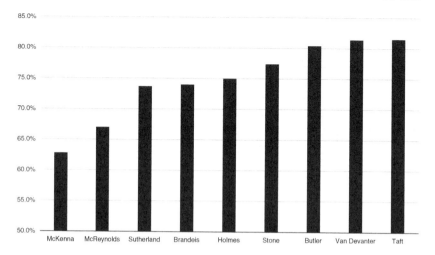

Figure I-24 Percentage of decisions in which Sanford participated and voted with another justice in conference

in Knoxville from 1899 to 1907,[47] had been "the official 'trust buster' of the Government" during the Roosevelt and Taft administrations.[48] He was so successful that Attorney General Daugherty hired him in 1921 as his "first selection" to help reorganize the Justice Department[49] and supervise anti-trust litigation.[50]

On October 25, 1922, the day after Day announced his retirement, Fowler wrote Daugherty to urge the appointment of Tennessee Senator John Knight Shields "if it is the purpose of the President to appoint a Democrat," but "if the President intends to appoint a Republican the bar of this state will unanimously endorse Judge Sanford for the position."[51] Fowler stressed that "The Republican party in the South has never been represented upon the Supreme Bench.... In view of the fact that the solid South has now been broken, and that the Republican party is rapidly growing in many parts of the south, and of the further fact that we can present a man who has no superior elsewhere in the United States, I think it is time that a recognition of this kind be given it."[52]

A month later Fowler pressed Sanford's cause directly with Harding,[53] accompanied by a seemingly coordinated barrage of favorable southern newspaper endorsements[54] that mounted in intensity after the bill to facilitate Pitney's retirement was introduced[55] and Butler's nomination was announced,[56] which signaled that Harding would be making a fourth appointment to the Court that would likely be a Republican.[57] Daugherty was eventually "convinced by Fowler that" Sanford was "the best man."[58] Until the very moment that Harding decided to nominate Sanford, Fowler continued, to the grudging admiration of Sanford's rivals, to accomplish "some effective practical work in behalf of his candidate."[59]

By the end of November, however, "very little [had] been done in the way of anticipating" Pitney's replacement.[60] Harding could not then conceive the possibility of appointing a "second judge from Tennessee when there are so many other states without a member for the Supreme Bench."[61] The claims of large states like New York and Pennsylvania seemed particularly pressing. Spurred by a rumor that Harding had consulted Republican New York Governor Nathan Miller,[62] who had recommended the liberal New York Court of Appeals Judge Cuthbert Pound,[63] Taft prepared a dossier on potential candidates from New York and Pennsylvania,[64] which he sent to Harding on December 4.[65] It is a long, detailed letter, plainly influenced by the fierce political controversy then engulfing Butler in the Senate.[66]

Taft deemed Pound unacceptable because "He is a great dissenter. . . . [H]e evidently thinks it is more important that he should ventilate his individual views than that the Court should be consistent and by team work should give solidarity and punch to what it decides. We have one dissenter on the Bench, and often two. It would not be well, it seems to me, to introduce a third."[67] Taft's focus on Pound's tendency to dissent was a thinly veiled reference to Pound's questionable politics, because on Taft's court dissent was associated with the progressivism of Brandeis. "It would be too bad," Taft said, "if we had another on the Bench who would herd with Brandeis in opinions in that kind of cases, as Brandeis is usually against the Court."[68] Taft was concerned to eliminate from contention candidates who were "on the off side and taken radical views in respect to the police power and other things."[69]

Although the senior senator from New York, James W. Wadsworth, Jr., supported Pound, William M. Calder, New York's junior senator, supported a different judge on the New York Court of Appeals, Frederick E. Crane.[70] Taft regarded Crane as a "light weight,"[71] but Taft nevertheless advised Harding that Crane would be "preferable" to the liberal Pound, even though Taft also believed that Crane ought not to be nominated because "the judgment of the Bar" does not give him "the greatest ability."[72] Taft's advice in this matter faithfully reflected the judgment of his brother and confidante Henry, one of the named partners in the Wall Street firm of Cadwalader, Wickersham & Taft. Henry acknowledged that Crane was not "up to the desired standard," but regarded him as "far" more desirable than Pound, "for he thinks straight, has some regard for the opinion of others, and is conservative."[73]

Taft also advised Harding against choosing another potential New York candidate, Learned Hand, because Hand was a "wild Roosevelt man and a Progressive, and . . . if promoted to our Bench, he would almost certainly herd with Brandeis and be a dissenter. I think it would be risking too much to appoint him." Taft opposed the major potential candidate from Pennsylvania, Robert von Moschzisker, chief justice of the Pennsylvania Supreme Court, because he "is a politician more than he is a judge, and I don't think that his appointment would be a strong one."[74] The charge of being a politician, coming from ex-President Taft, chiefly meant that von Moschzisker was not "a sound constitutional lawyer" who could be trusted to protect property.[75]

Having disqualified, for ideological and other reasons, major candidates from New York and Pennsylvania, Taft urged Harding to appoint Charles M. Hough, a federal judge sitting in New York on the Second Circuit. Hough, Taft reported, "is sound constitutionally"[76] and "a burly, hardhitting, industrious, independent and very able and learned lawyer whom the Bar and the community greatly respect."[77] "Another advantage of the appointment," Taft argued, "would be that it is a promotion. I think appointments to our Court ought not to be limited to judges in the inferior Federal Courts, but I do think there ought to be some promotion to spur those judges to care and effort."[78] Hough, however, was 64 years old, and Harding "had made up his mind not to appoint anybody over sixty."[79] The upshot of Taft's letter, therefore, was to eliminate the most plausible candidates from New York and Pennsylvania.[80]

Harding replied to Taft that he felt no "special obligation to appoint from New York" and that he wished "to name Justice Pitney's successor in a very short time."[81] Taft's forceful intervention had evidently directed Harding's search away from large Northeastern states. Taft's striking success "in keeping out men who he thought would misinterpret the Constitution or increase dissention within the Court"[82] played directly into Fowler's arguments for a southern appointment.[83]

Fowler's efforts to convince Daugherty[84] paid off when Taft reported to Harding in mid-December that he had just "had a long talk" with Daugherty, who "suggested to me a name which had not occurred to me before, but which does commend itself to me as that of a man whose appointment to the Supreme Bench would be on the whole a very satisfactory one. The man is Judge Sanford of the Eastern and Middle Districts of Tennessee."

> He is a conscientious man and a hard worker. . . . He is a man of high culture . . . and most highly respected at the Bar and in the whole community where he is known. His opinions are much regarded through the Southern States where they are better known. . . . His long experience on the District Bench would make him most valuable to us in our Court. He is a staunch Republican, and comes from the only Republican part of the South, to wit, East Tennessee. The objection to him perhaps would be that he comes from the State to which McReynolds is charged, though McReynolds had left Tennessee when he was appointed and had begun practice in New York City.[85]

Between Daugherty's enthusiastic endorsement[86] and Taft's consent, however qualified,[87] Sanford was pushed to the front of the pack.[88] His nomination would for obscure reasons be delayed for several weeks,[89] in part perhaps because of political objections,[90] in part because of the emergence of new candidates,[91] and in part because "there was an attack on Sanford of some sort, perhaps charging him with a lack of decisiveness, and a slowness in disposing of business."[92] Although the charge that Sanford was a "vacillating and fussy" judge who "would be overwhelmed on the Supreme Bench"[93] would, much to Taft's subsequent consternation, ultimately prove true, it was at the time countered by the testimonials of influential litigants[94] and powerful appellate judges on the Sixth Circuit who were responsible for reviewing Sanford's work.[95] Harding nominated Sanford on January 24, 1923,[96] and Sanford was unanimously confirmed on January 29.[97]

The appointment was well received in the progressive press. *The Nation*, for example, applauded "President Harding's choice of Judge Sanford" as "by all odds the best of his several judicial appointments. We greet it with corresponding thankfulness."[98] In truth, however, the press knew virtually nothing of Sanford's constitutional opinions; he was held in high esteem chiefly because of the manifest compassion, fairness, and rectitude with which he had conducted himself as a district judge.

In stark contrast to Butler, who had had to claw his way from obscure poverty to prominence and riches, Sanford had been born on July 23, 1865, into "a home of culture and wealth."[99] Sanford's father had emigrated to Knoxville from Connecticut in the early 1850s. Although "materially destitute,"[100] he soon became one of the richest and most influential businessmen in the area.[101] Sanford was raised to practice the graces of a gentleman. He received a degree from the University of Tennessee in 1883, and then entered Harvard as a junior to earn a second degree in political science in 1885. He took an obligatory year to tour Europe and then returned to Harvard for a law degree, which he received in 1889.[102] Thereafter Sanford practiced law in Knoxville until 1907, actively participating in civic and bar activities.[103] Throughout he was motivated by the values appropriate, as he announced in his class day oration upon graduating from Harvard, to that "class of men . . . whose education fits them to rightly understand their true relations to society and the duty born of their advantages. Noblesse oblige."[104]

At the suggestion of James Clark McReynolds, a fellow Tennessean,[105] Sanford was retained in 1905 as a special Assistant to the United States attorney general in order to help prosecute the so-called Fertilizer Trust. When McReynolds resigned his position in the Justice Department, Sanford replaced him in 1907 as assistant attorney general. In 1908, Roosevelt appointed Sanford a federal district judge for the Middle and Eastern Districts of Tennessee.[106]

Sanford apparently conducted a model courtroom; he was "conscientious, kindly, precise, and open-minded," creating an "impressive dignity" that was full of "the natural courtesy and gentility of one to the manor born."[107] A story that came to exemplify Sanford's rectitude was that "a notorious distiller" on trial for violating prohibition was heard to remark that "I had rather get a year in Judge Sanford's court than go free in any other. . . . I always know that I'm getting a square deal here, and I don't in the other places."[108]

Holmes, who knew a gentleman of breeding when he saw one, characterized Sanford as "born . . . to charm."[109] The culture that made Sanford appear to his contemporaries as charming, courteous, genteel, and stylish,[110] frequently seems to modern eyes cloying and antique.[111] But this same culture also impressed upon Sanford's character an openness that made him the temperamental antipode of Butler. It endowed Sanford with a certain independence of mind that could never quite blind itself to basic human decencies.[112] Sanford's independence was so cabined by natural timidity and caution, however, that, in contrast to Butler, it is difficult to discern any distinct impact made by Sanford on the direction or decisions of the Court. In Stone's estimation, Sanford's "amiability tended to make him a conformist."[113] It has accurately been said of Sanford that his "sweet and compliant personality made him a satellite of the affable Chief Justice Taft."[114]

Figure I-10, which is a measure of a justice's ability to persuade his colleagues to change their conference votes to join his opinions, illustrates Sanford's

THE TAFT COURT

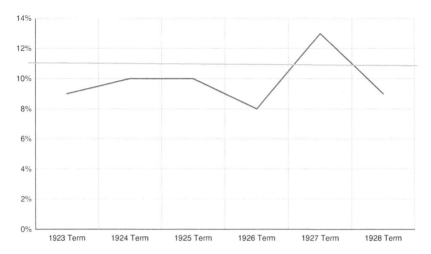

Figure I-25 Percentage of Court's opinions authored by Sanford, by term. An even distribution of cases would assign 1/9, or 11%, to each justice.

weakness within the Taft Court. It is clear that he carried little weight with peers.[115] Figure I-19 illustrates that Sanford, in contrast to justices like Butler and Holmes, had relatively little success persuading colleagues to join opinions that had been controversial in conference. Figure I-18 suggests that Taft, aware of this incapacity, tended to assign Sanford relatively easy cases that had been unanimous in conference. Figure I-25 also suggests that Sanford was largely unable to author his fair share of the Court's cases.

Throughout his tenure on the Court, Sanford performed as a competent craftsman.[116] But in a Court fated to wrestle with the most basic principles of the American constitutional polity, mere professional competence was not enough. Sanford lacked the resources to translate his civility, which in face-to-face dealings so struck his contemporaries, into principles of law. Buffeted between such powerful and determined personalities as Butler, Taft, Van Devanter, Brandeis, Holmes, and Stone, he became, in effect, a mere fellow traveler. During Sanford's memorial proceedings before the Court, a time of ritually exaggerated praise, the best accolade that the initial speaker could offer was: "A member of the Court, when requested by the writer to indicate Justice Sanford's outstanding characteristics as a Judge, emphasized his conscientiousness, his industry, and his fidelity to the Court's decisions."[117]

Sanford's appointment nevertheless marked a remarkable milestone for Harding. In little under two years, he had appointed four members of the Supreme Court. By the end of the decade, Harding's efforts would result in the emergence of a reliable and increasingly unyielding conservative jurisprudence, which would set the stage for the titanic confrontations of the New Deal. By the end of the 1920s, the conservative cast of the Court resulted in its popular denomination as "a 'Harding' Court."[118]

The last appointment to the Taft Court, however, was of an entirely different character, and it was made by President Calvin Coolidge.

Mahlon Pitney & Edward Terry Sanford
Notes

1. Florence S. Pitney to WHT (August 4, 1922) (Taft papers) ("We are devoting the entire summer to an earnest effort to restore his health, and working efficiency to the former standard. He had a surgical operation upon the jaw for removal of a source of local infection, in the form of a cyst, followed by a rest cure, and special diet. After about a month of this we brought him to Morristown, where we have a home for the summer.").

    In truth, Pitney's health had been failing for some time. Before ever being appointed as chief justice, Taft had received a report that "Pitney is not very well." J.M. Dickinson to WHT (April 23, 1921) (Taft papers). Pitney left for a European vacation in summer 1921, *Justice Pitney Goes to Europe*, NEW YORK TIMES (June 26, 1921), at 4, and Taft sent him hopes "that your European trip will do you good. I had heard that you were somewhat under the weather, due to your incessant work. The rest of traveling is something that often proves most efficacious. I hope it may be so in this instance." WHT to MP (July 31, 1921) (Taft papers). In January 1922, Pitney fell ill once again, reporting "the doctor's rather urgent recommendation ... for a period of entire abstention from work." MP to WHT (January 21, 1922) (Taft papers). Pitney wrote Taft that he felt "like an outrageous 'slacker,' lying in bed so long, while you and other brethren toil in the grind. But ... I fear some days of February will have passed before I can get back to my study, and then only on limited hours, at first." MP to WHT (January 27, 1922) (Taft papers). Pitney worried about opinions that needed to be reassigned. Taft wrote back graciously insisting that "you shall forget the Court and your brethren and get well, and not worry about us. ... [U]nderstand that the whole matter is in my hands, and not in yours, and that I shall look after the public interest in a general way if you will look after the public interest in respect to your health." WHT to MP (January 27, 1922) (Taft papers). Taft told his daughter that Pitney was suffering from "a nervous breakdown." WHT to Mrs. Frederick J. Manning (January 28, 1922) (Taft papers). *See* WHT to Horace D. Taft (April 17, 1922) (Taft papers) ("Pitney ... had a nervous breakdown last year, and he has a good many cases on his hands which he is not getting rid of."). *See* WHT to J. Hampton Moore (April 18, 1922) (Taft papers).

2. WHT to Horace D. Taft (September 17, 1922) (Taft papers). The letter continues: "[Pitney] was not well when he left us – he had suffered a nervous breakdown. If he were to give way, it would make three vacancies this year, with McKenna and Holmes, one seventy-nine and the other eighty-two, still on the Bench." *Id.* Among the ominous reports was a letter from Van Devanter:

    > A letter from Asst Atty Genl Riles and one from an attorney for some Okla-Texas oil claimants speak of a visit to Morristown N.J. very recently to get a direction to the receiver from Justice Pitney and say it was not possible even to see the Justice because of his illness. This was given as a reason for coming to me. It is a disquieting statement, particularly as the Justice was glad to attend to such matters last summer. I fear it does not mean that he is recovering, and yet it may only refer to a temporary indisposition. Against the latter view is the fact that they have sent me all their papers etc. here to me. I hope Pitney will come back to Court in good condition.

WVD to WHT (September 10, 1922) (Taft papers). Taft replied, "What you say about Pitney does not surprise me, though it troubles me. I wrote you that Mrs. Pitney wrote me but did not give me any personal assurance of his getting well at Morristown." WHT to WVD (September 16, 1922) (Taft papers). *See* WHT to Charles D. Hillis (September 17, 1922) (Taft papers) ("I am sorry to say, however, that Pitney's health is by no means assured. He has had an operation this summer, and, more than that, last year he broke down nervously. How far he has recovered himself is a serious question.").

3. Florence S. Pitney to WHT (September 18, 1922) (Taft papers):

> I feel that I ought to let you know that my husband has been very ill for several weeks, with a return of the illness from which he suffered during the winter. He is confined to his bed in the care of nurses. Absolute rest and quiet are strictly enjoyed and he is not allowed to be troubled by any business or official matters, and he sees no one but members of his immediate family. He is courageous and hopeful but the doctors do not encourage us to plan to return to Washington for several weeks and there is no prospect that he will be able to resume his duties at the opening of the Court. If his illness should be prolonged, I am quite sure he would not wish to have the Court's work, and particularly your responsibilities, in any way embarrassed by his prolonged absence, and so if you feel that under the circumstances it is his duty to consider resigning, I will talk to him about it if the Doctor thinks consideration of it would not retard his recovery by discouraging him.

News of Pitney's illness became public on September 22, see *Justice Mahlon Pitney Ill*, NEW YORK TIMES (September 22, 1922), at 12, although the press reported that "his condition was not serious."

4. Taft proposed to model the bill on one passed to facilitate the retirement of Justice Moody, 218 U.S. iv n.5 (1909). WHT to Florence S. Pitney (September 27, 1922) (Taft papers).

> Should you and Justice Pitney conclude ... that his present physical condition is such that were he to return to the duties of the Bench, the trouble which he had last year, and the trouble from which he is now suffering, would be constantly recurring, and that in order to live he should have rest from his judicial labors, I will bring the situation to the attention of the members of the Judiciary of both Houses, and I have no doubt that the act will be passed in accordance with your wishes. ... It pains me greatly ... to write this letter or to know that Mr. Justice Pitney's condition is such as to make the suggestion of this letter appropriate; but after my conversation with you yesterday ... I feel it my duty to give you the information it contains. Mr. Justice Pitney's record on the Bench has been excelled by that of none of his contemporaries. He has served the country faithfully for a full ten years, and his present condition and the sacrifice of his health are due to his intense devotion to his work. ...
>
> I cherish the warmest affection and the highest regard for Mahlon Pitney. I am proud of having appointed him to the Supreme Bench, and proud of the work that he has done on it, but if his present condition indicates what I fear, it would be greatly better for him and for his judicial reputation that the course above suggested be taken.

Id. The situation at the end of September was perhaps best summarized by Van Devanter in a letter to his wife:

Mahlon Pitney & Edward Terry Sanford

> The substance of it all is that Justice Pitney has not recovered, but has a pronounced tendency to go back to his troubles of last winter and spring. The doctors think he had a partial stroke at that time, and that he cannot return to work without endangering his life. He was not well enough for the Chief Justice to see him when the latter was in Morristown. A part of the time he has to be assisted in and out of his bed. Just now they are seriously considering whether it is not better for him to retire, and the Chief Justice, in answer to Mrs. Pitney's direct question, advised retirement if his condition was as she and the doctors reported it. The Justice has served 10 years now but is not 70. Of course he can resign any time, but to enable him to retire and continue to receive the salary will require a special act of Congress, such as was passed in the instance of Justice Moody. They are thinking of making an effort very soon to get such an act passed. The Justice will not try to return to the court now, and it is probable that he never will.

WVD to Mrs. Willis Van Devanter (September 29, 1922) (Van Devanter papers). According to Van Devanter, Pitney needed a special act of Congress because, although he had "some means, ... his income without the salary is not sufficient to cover ... reasonable expenses." WVD to JHC (October 4, 1922) (Van Devanter papers). Van Devanter expressed "great regret" at Pitney's potential retirement. "He has been a very earnest, hard-working and efficient member of the Court, and is an unusually high type of man. ... I have the greatest sympathy for him and am inexpressibly sorry that he is not with us again." *Id.*

5. Florence S. Pitney to WHT (October 3, 1922) (Taft papers). "Pitney," Florence wrote, "was very much touched by your friendly interest, and what you said of him, and the way you expressed yourself made it very simple to broach the subject to him. It is so much easier for a person to feel that it is up to him to decide whether he is strong enough to go on with the work, than to be told he is no longer fit for the task":

> He authorizes you to go ahead with the plan and I will get certificates from the Doctors as to his condition and send them to you. He feels perfectly resigned and I think rather relieved now that he knows you are to ask Congress to permit his retirement on pay.
>
> Never can we tell you how much we are indebted to you, and especially for the very considerate way in which you have spoken to me upon the subject. My heart is full of gratitude, and this only half expresses what I feel.

Id. By the opening day of Court on October 2, it had become clear to the public that Pitney was "seriously ill." *Sutherland Takes Office as Justice*, WASHINGTON POST (October 3, 1922), at 5.

6. Taft wrote Florence Pitney on October 8 that "The whole Court is in sorrow at the thought of losing the assistance and comradeship of Justice Pitney. I took them into my confidence yesterday, and we agreed that we would quietly proceed at once, upon the meeting of Congress, to secure the enactment of the bill with promptness. Mr. Justice Sutherland, who has been so long a member of the Senate and a member of the Judiciary Committee, and was in that Committee when the bill for Justice Moody was passed, has said that he would at once begin, in a quiet way, with the members of the Judiciary Committee." WHT to Florence S. Pitney (October 8, 1922) (Taft papers). Taft met with Harding on October 9, and secured the president's commitment personally to recommend "to the Chairmen of the two Judiciary Committees that the bill be promptly passed." WHT to Florence S. Pitney (October 9, 1922) (Taft papers). *See* WHT to Warren G. Harding (October 9, 1922) (Taft papers) (Harding papers).

7. *See* Pub. L. 67-367; 42 Stat. 1063 (December 11, 1922); H.R. Rep. No. 1262, 67th CONG. 3rd SESS. (1922), at 1; *Harding Signs Bill to Retire Pitney*, NEW YORK TIMES (December 13, 1922), at 12. The letters of Pitney's physicians were made public, and they indicated that the justice had suffered disabling strokes, Bright's disease, and "advanced and a widespread arteriosclerosis." *See* 63 CONG. REC. 272-73 (November 27, 1922). There was some debate on the bill, see 64 CONG. REC. 18-19 (December 4, 1922), news of which became public as early as October 31. *May Ask Congress to Retire Pitney*, NEW YORK TIMES (October 31, 1922), at 10. *See Pitney Bill Passes House*, NEW YORK TIMES (December 5, 1922), at 2.
8. *Justice Pitney Resigns*, NEW YORK TIMES (December 17, 1922), at 3. The effective date of the resignation was January 1.
9. Robert David Stenzel, An Approach to Individuality, Liberty, and Equality: The Jurisprudence of Mr. Justice Pitney 139, 547 n.172 (Ph.D. Dissertation, New School for Social Research 1975); Thomas Reed Powell, *Decisions of the Supreme Court of the United States on Constitutional Questions, II, 1914–1917*, 12 AMERICAN POLITICAL SCIENCE REVIEW 427, 427 (1918); Thomas Reed Powell, *The Supreme Court's Review of Legislation in 1921–1922*, 37 POLITICAL SCIENCE QUARTERLY 486, 513 (1922).
10. Biographical work on Pitney is scarce. *See* Fred L. Israel, *Mahlon Pitney*, in 3 THE JUSTICES OF THE UNITED STATES SUPREME COURT 1789–1969: THEIR LIVES AND MAJOR OPINIONS 2001–9 (Leon Friedman & Fred L. Israel, eds., New York: Chelsea House Publishers 1969); Michael R. Belknap, *Mr. Justice Pitney and Progressivism*, 16 SETON HALL LAW REVIEW 381, 400–5 (1986); David M. Levitan, *Mahlon Pitney – Labor Judge*, 40 VIRGINIA LAW REVIEW 733 (1954). The most comprehensive discussion of Pitney is by Stenzel, *supra* note 9.
11. *See* Jonas Glass Co. v. Glass Bottle Blowers Ass'n., 77 N.J. Eq. 219 (1908). The story of his appointment to the Supreme Court is told in ALEXANDER BICKEL & BENNO SCHMIDT, Jr., HISTORY OF THE SUPREME COURT OF THE UNITED STATES: THE JUDICIARY AND RESPONSIBLE GOVERNMENT, 1910–21, at 318–34 (New York: MacMillan Co. 1984).
12. 236 U.S. 1 (1915). *Coppage* held that a Kansas statute forbidding yellow-dog contracts was unconstitutional.
13. 245 U.S. 229 (1917). *Hitchman* held that federal courts could enjoin union efforts to organize employees who had signed yellow-dog contracts.
14. 254 U.S. 443 (1921). *Duplex Printing* held that the Clayton Act did not prevent federal courts from enjoining union organizing efforts otherwise forbidden by federal anti-trust law. David Levitan argues that Pitney's labor injunction cases must be understood in light of his firm support for anti-trust policy and the importance he attached to a competitive marketplace. Levitan, *supra* note 10, at 760–63. "It would appear that this fear of bigness and distrust of combinations and of remote control of men or machines was a crucial factor in his labor decisions." *Id.* at 762.
15. 257 U.S. 312 (1921).
16. New York Central R.R. v. White, 243 U.S. 188 (1917); Hawkins v. Bleakly, 243 U.S. 210 (1917); Mountain Timber Co. v. Washington, 243 U.S. 219 (1917). *See also* Ward v. Krinsky, 259 U.S. 503 (1922).
17. *Brandeis-Frankfurter Conversations*, at 328–29 (July 3, 1924). T.R. Powell commented that "Mr. Justice Pitney's opinion on the constitutionality of the Workmen's

Compensation legislation sets an example of judicial reasoning for judges everywhere to emulate." Thomas Reed Powell, *The Workmen's Compensation Cases*, 32 POLITICAL SCIENCE QUARTERLY 542, 569 (1917).

18. In Van Devanter's words, Pitney was "a good man, a good Judge and a splendid member of the Court." WVD TO JHC (October 9, 1922) (Van Devanter papers).
19. The Court, in its farewell letter to Pitney, gave special emphasis to his "unremitting labor ... the consideration of cases, the preparation of your own opinions, and the most careful examination and criticism of the opinions of your colleagues.... We can not but think that you have sacrificed your health in the earnest effort to do everything possible to further the work of the Court." *Retirement of Mr. Justice Pitney*, 261 U.S. v, vi (1923). It is evident from surviving manuscripts just how active a role Pitney played in reviewing proposed opinions and offering constructive suggestions for change. He proposed helpful changes to Taft's opinion in Balzac v. Porto Rico, 258 U.S. 298 (1922), for example, to which Taft responded, "Thank you ... for your suggestions, all of which I have adopted. I can not say what comfort it is to me to have you and brother Van Devanter go over my work. The old men of the Court, like brother McKenna and me, need it – the young men of the Court, like brother Holmes, do not." WHT to MP (March 31, 1922) (Taft papers). *See* MP to WHT (March 30, 1922) (Taft papers). For examples of changes in Brandeis opinions that were responsive to Pitney's suggestions, see Fairchild v. Hughes, 258 U.S. 126 (1922) (Brandeis papers); Louisville and Nashville Rd. v. United States, 258 U.S. 374 (1922) (Brandeis papers); Greiner v. Lewellyn, 258 U.S. 384 (1922) (Brandeis papers); FTC v. Winsted Hosier Co., 258 U.S. 483 (1922) (Brandeis papers); Fidelity & Deposit Co. v. United States, 259 U.S. 296 (1922) (Brandeis papers); Collins v. Loisel, 259 U.S. 309 (1922) (Brandeis papers).
20. Pitney "talked a good deal," *Brandeis-Frankfurter Conversations*, at 317 (July 3, 1923), which apparently caused some tension on the Court. McReynolds "didn't like" Pitney's "voice & otherwise [Pitney] got on McR's nerves & [McReynolds] treated [Pitney] like a dog," saying "the cruelest things to him." *Id*. Clarke recalled to Van Devanter that Pitney took comfort from "what you & I said to reassure him when the 'boor' [McReynolds] so outrageously insulted him in conference. Of course, his opinion was better than his critic ever wrote & I told him so." JHC to WVD (October 2, 1922) (Van Devanter papers).

Like McReynolds, Holmes was also put off by Pitney's irresistible urge to talk. "At first," Holmes said, Pitney "riled me by excessive discourse." OWH to Frederick Pollock (December 12, 1924), in 2 HOLMES-POLLOCK CORRESPONDENCE, at 150. "When he first came on the bench he used to get on my nerves, as he talked too much from the bench and in conference." OWH to Frederick Pollock (February 24, 1923), *id*. at 113. John W. Davis recalls that while he was solicitor general "Pitney was always eager to get at the argument and always started questioning the lawyer almost as soon as he got underway. In one case he started ... questioning the lawyer almost as soon as the lawyer had said the opening sentences. White turned to Holmes and said, 'I want to hear the argument.' Holmes said, 'So do I, damn him!' That was heard across the bench." WILLIAM H. HARBAUGH, LAWYER'S LAWYER: THE LIFE OF JOHN W. DAVIS 107 (New York: Oxford University Press 1973). Holmes wrote Frankfurter that "as time went on I learned to appreciate more and more [Pitney's] faithful, serious devotion to his job, his great industry and, helped in this as in other things by Brandeis, his intellectual honesty. It is hard to get a man as good as he was, whatever reserves one may make in superlatives." OWH to Felix Frankfurter (December 9, 1924), in HOLMES-FRANKFURTER CORRESPONDENCE, at 177.

21. OWH to Frederick Pollock (February 24, 1923), in 2 HOLMES-POLLOCK CORRESPONDENCE, at 113. In November, Holmes wrote Frankfurter that "Pitney will be a real loss – but I don't expect to see him again." OWH to Felix Frankfurter (November 2, 1922), in HOLMES-FRANKFURTER CORRESPONDENCE, at 147.

22. *Brandeis-Frankfurter Conversations*, at 316 (July 3, 1923). "It was like White," Brandeis continued, "who had been a bank director some 20 years ago & that experience constantly led him astray." *Id.* Brandeis attributed many of Pitney's decisions to his "Presbyterian doctrine of freedom of will. 'These individuals having free choice of right & wrong, choose wrong.' He – Pitney – personally is very kindly, tho in many ways naïve & wholly without knowledge but still can't shake his Presbyterianism or doesn't realize he is in its grip." *Id.* at 308 (July 9, 1922).

23. OWH to Frederick Pollock (December 12, 1924), in 2 HOLMES-POLLOCK CORRESPONDENCE, at 150. An example of Pitney's open-mindedness might be his response to Holmes's proposed opinion in United Zinc & Chemical Co. v. Britt, 258 U.S. 268 (1922): "Thank you for taking pains to make it so clear that it is a pleasure to change my vote, which was given reluctantly under the impression that previous cases in this Court had settled the rule contrary to right reason." (Holmes papers). To Brandeis's proposed opinion in Central Railroad Co. v. United States, 257 U.S. 247 (1921), Pitney responded: "You persuade me that my vote was wrong." (Brandeis papers).

24. *Brandeis-Frankfurter Conversations*, at 322 (August 7, 1923).

25. Figures I-20 and I-21 also illustrate Pitney's temperamental differences with both McReynolds and Holmes. *See supra* notes 20–21.

26. Sanford died on the same day as did Taft himself. *Ex President Taft Dies at Capital*, NEW YORK TIMES (March 9, 1930), at 1. Sanford was replaced by Owen Roberts. Sanford has recently been the subject of a comprehensive and sympathetic biography. *See* STEPHANIE L. SLATER, EDWARD TERRY SANFORD: A TENNESSEAN ON THE US SUPREME COURT (Knoxville: University of Tennessee Press 2018).

27. HFS to A.D. Noyes (November 19, 1930) (Stone papers). "A notable exception," Stone added, "was his opinion in The Pocket Veto Case, 279 U.S. 655, where, in the discussion of the historical and practical considerations affecting the constitutionality of the pocket veto, he set a very high standard both in form and in substance." *Id.*

28. *Brandeis-Frankfurter Conversations*, at 312 (June 12, 1923). Brandeis had little patience for Sanford. "Sanford's mind gives one blurs; it does not clearly register." *Id.* at 316 (July 3, 1923). "Sanford ought never to have been above D[istrict] J[udge] – a dull bourgeois mind – terribly tiresome." *Id.* at 336 (June 15–16, 1926).

29. Figure I-22 measures the average time between argument and publication for unanimous opinions for each justice. During the 1921 term, Pitney's opinions appeared an average of 140.8 days after oral argument. In the period between his appointment and the end of the 1928 term, Sanford's unanimous opinions appeared an average of 92.5 days after oral argument. This was the worst showing for any justice except for Pitney and Van Devanter. Because Pitney was disabled throughout the winter of the 1922, see *supra* note 1, the 1921 term is not a fair example of Pitney's work. If one examines the 1915 through the 1920 terms, however, Pitney

took an average of 89.9 days to produce a unanimous opinion, a showing that is virtually equivalent to Sanford's poor performance.
30. Taft confided to Holmes that both Sanford and Van Devanter "are nervous, they are both opinion shy, and they really need encouragement." WHT to OWH (May 3, 1927) (Holmes papers). At the end of the 1926 term, Taft was forced to take opinions away from Sanford and to assign them to other justices. *See, e.g.*, WHT to ETS (May 3, 1927) (Taft papers); WHT to LDB (May 3, 1927) (Taft papers). When Taft fell ill in the summer of 1929, however, he felt comfortable asking Sanford to take over a patent case that Taft had originally assigned to himself. *See* WHT to ETS (July 4, 1929) (Taft papers); ETS to WHT (July 1929) (Taft papers); ETS to WHT (July 1929) (Taft papers).
31. Like Pitney, Sanford's conscientiousness was legendary. Like Pitney, Sanford had the habit of working himself "into a nervous condition that isn't good for him." WHT to Robert A. Taft (May 29, 1927) (Taft papers) ("He ought to have a rest."). Taft reported to his wife a story that Van Devanter had told him:

> He said Sanford came home to dinner very much down in the mouth and his wife insisted on knowing why he did not eat his dinner and why he omitted meat. After a cross examination, she dragged out of him that he had been frightened by McReynolds' view of the Court and his warning that he Sanford might go the way of Pitney if he did not look out and that he should be careful of what he ate. He said that Taft would not last a year and the whole Court would be in a bad way. McReynolds may be right – No one can tell what a year will bring forth, but I'll do the best I can not to qualify him as a prophet.

WHT to Helen Herron Taft (April 19, 1924) (Taft papers).

Sanford was forever promising Taft that he would soon "do my full share of the labor – I believe I have gotten into better methods of work and can successfully lay aside some of my besetting meticulosity. But verily the writing of an opinion worthy of perpetual type is a task of the highest difficulty that takes every ounce of the best that one may have." ETS to WHT (September 8, 1925) (Taft papers). *See* ETS to WHT (June 9, 1927) (Taft papers) (I "hope to be able to pull my full weight next year."); ETS to WHT (August 10, 1929) (Taft papers) ("I am feeling fit and strong and able, I trust, to carry my full share of the next year's work."). And Taft was forever assuring Sanford, as he had assured Pitney, that "you need a real rest this summer and must have a chance to get your nerves into better condition. You are jaded and you are making too much of difficulties that grow in your imagination." WHT to ETS (May 3, 1927) (Taft papers). *See* WHT to ETS (September 11, 1925) (Taft papers).
32. *See* WHT to PB (September 14, 1929) (Taft papers). "In his public career Justice Sanford was classed as a conservative, particularly on economic issues." *Sanford Collapsed in Dentist's Office*, NEW YORK TIMES (March 9, 1930), at 28.
33. George F. Milton, Jr., Letter, *Our Newest Supreme Court Judge*, 116 THE NATION 150 (1923). "He is a man of great sympathy with man, in the mass and in the individual. ... His intense sympathies for humanity would prevent his enacting a reactionary role."
34. James A. Fowler, *Mr. Justice Edward Terry Sanford*, 17 AMERICAN BAR ASSOCIATION JOURNAL 229, 233 (April 1931). *See* George F. Milton Jr., *Sanford – Neither Radical Nor Reactionary*, 133 THE OUTLOOK 298 (1923).

35. Allen E. Ragan, *Mr. Justice Sanford*, 15 EAST TENNESSEE HISTORICAL SOCIETY'S PUBLICATIONS 74, 77 (1943). *See* George F. Milton, Jr., *The New Justice from Tennessee*, 110 THE INDEPENDENT 117 (February 17, 1923) ("a liberal conservative."); SLATER, *supra* note 26.
36. Given his strong prior association with McReynolds, it is interesting that Sanford was not particularly likely to vote with McReynolds either in published opinions or in conference. It is also interesting that this does not seem to have led to any noticeable tension with McReynolds.
37. 261 U.S. 525 (1923). *See infra* Chapter 24.
38. 273 U.S. 418 (1927). *See infra* Chapter 25, at 799–801.
39. 279 U.S. 644 (1929). *See also* Blodgett v. Holden, 275 U.S. 142 (1927); Louisville Gas & Electric Co. v. Coleman, 277 U.S. 32 (1928).
40. 274 U.S. 37 (1927). *See infra* Chapter 40, at 1324–35.
41. 270 U.S. 230 (1926). *See infra* Chapter 23, at 739–40.
42. 277 U.S. 350 (1928). *See infra* Chapter 25, at 801–2. *See also* Untermeyer v. Anderson, 276 U.S. 440 (1928); Nichols v. Coolidge, 274 U.S. 531 (1927).
43. Excellent accounts of the appointment may be found in Walter F. Murphy, *In His Own Image: Mr. Chief Justice Taft and Supreme Court Appointments*, 1961 SUPREME COURT REVIEW 159, 176–83, and in Stanley A. Cook, Path to the High Bench: The Pre-Supreme Court Career of Justice Edward Terry Sanford 122–74 (Ph.D. Dissertation, University of Tennessee at Knoxville 1977). *See also* SLATER, *supra* note 26.
44. *Much Interested in Education*, NEW YORK TIMES (March 9, 1930), at 28. *See A New Way to Pick Judges*, 76 LITERARY DIGEST 16 (February 10, 1923) ("To let the Chief Justice have some 'say' in the selection of his associates on the Supreme Court has not been usual in our history, and yet, now that it has happened, we find very little criticism."); *Tennessee Man Named to U.S. Supreme Bench*, NEW YORK TRIBUNE (January 25, 1923), at 3 ("Chief Justice William Howard Taft, in the opinion of Senators opposing the appointment, was largely responsible both for this and the naming of Pierce Butler."); Robert Barry, *Judgeship Will Go to Taft's Man*, LOS ANGELES TIMES (January 25, 1923), at 11 ("It was indicated ... that criticism would be registered against the part Chief Justice Taft played in the appointment. One Senator was known to be preparing to charge Mr. Taft with political activity unbecoming his office."); David Lawrence, *Sanford Owes Boost to Taft*, DETROIT NEWS (January 25, 1923), at 28; *Justice Taft Chooses an Associate*, NEW YORK WORLD (January 26, 1925), at 12; *Able Nominee for Supreme Court*, PITTSBURGH POST (January 26, 1923), at 6; *The Supreme Court Vacancy*, NEW YORK TIMES (January 16, 1923), at 20; *Politics Holds Up Pitney's Successor*, NEW YORK TIMES (January 15, 1923), at 7; *Taft Supports Sanford*, NEW YORK TIMES (January 6, 1923), at 3; *A Fitting Appointment*, NEW YORK TIMES (January 7, 1923), at E4; *Sanford Succumbs to Sudden Attack*, WASHINGTON POST (March 9, 1930), at 4 (Sanford's "selection as an Associate Justice of the Supreme Court has been attributed largely to Mr. Taft's influence.").
45. The press reports in fact caused Taft some embarrassment. He apparently wrote Harding a note of apology, to which Harding replied: "I have your note of [yesterday] morning. I had understood that there was some criticism of your activity in discussing the availability of candidates for judicial appointment. My impression was that the criticism grew out of an interview with Senator Spencer relating to the

qualifications of a candidate for appointment in St. Louis. The matter can be of no embarrassment to me. I am always happy to welcome suggestions especially from those who are in a position to know something concerning the matter." Warren G. Harding to WHT (January 15, 1923) (Taft papers).

Taft's note to Harding was sparked by a letter that Taft had received from Charles D. Hilles, who had been Taft's secretary when he was president and who was at the time serving as the chair of the Finance Committee of the Republican National Committee (RNC). Hilles wrote that John Adams and Fred Upham, respectively the chair and treasurer of the RNC, "were here to-day ... and said that Senator Pepper had complained to them that you were interfering in the matter of the selection of a Justice of the Supreme Court and that Sanford was your candidate. ... I speak of it only because I think it would be better if the impression were not given in certain official sources in Washington that you were responsible for the defeat of all candidates who fail of appointment." Charles D. Hilles to WHT (January 12, 1923) (Taft papers). Taft's communication to Harding apparently referred to Pepper, Adams, and Upham. WHT to Charles D. Hilles (January 17, 1923) (Taft papers). Harding's note to Taft, however, referred instead to the titanic struggle then taking place between Taft and Senator Selden P. Spencer, a Republican from Missouri, over the appointment of Spencer's former partner, Vital Garesche, to a district judgeship in St. Louis. The outline of that story is sketched in Walter F. Murphy, *Chief Justice Taft and the Lower Court Bureaucracy: A Study in Judicial Administration*, 24 JOURNAL OF POLITICS 453, 462–65 (1962). *See infra* Chapter 16, at 537 and note 18.

46. WHT to Charles D. Hilles (January 14, 1923) (Taft papers).
47. The firm was Lucky, Sanford and Fowler. Cook, *supra* note 43, at 20.
48. *Merit Guides Wilson in Filling Offices*, NEW YORK TIMES (March 11, 1913), at 3. Fowler was an assistant attorney general from 1908 to 1912, and an assistant to the attorney general from 1911 to 1913. He was so valuable that he was asked to stay on by McReynolds during the beginning of the Wilson administration, when for a period he served as acting solicitor general. *High Place for Davis*, WASHINGTON POST (July 27, 1913), at 8. *See 81 Antitrust Suits; Wickersham Sets Record for Actions under Sherman Law*, WASHINGTON POST (February 17, 1913), at 6; *Monopoly Is Opposed*, WASHINGTON POST (November 2, 1912), at 3. In 1898, Fowler had been the Republican candidate for governor of Tennessee. *See James A. Fowler, Ex-U.S. Attorney; Anti-Trust Specialist Is Dead at 92*, NEW YORK TIMES (November 19, 1955), at 19.
49. *Secretary of Labor Starts Work Early*, NEW YORK TIMES (March 10, 1921), at 3.
50. *To Act in Cement Cases; James A. Fowler Appointed Special Assistant to Daugherty*, NEW YORK TIMES (April 7, 1921), at 18.
51. J.A. Fowler to H.M. Daugherty (October 25, 1922) (Department of Justice Files, File 349, "John Knight Shields," National Archives). Fowler emphasized that he wished "to repeat in writing what I have said to you personally on two or three occasions." *Id.*
52. *Id.* Tennessee had voted for Harding in the 1920 presidential election.
53. J.A. Fowler to Warren G. Harding (November 15, 1922) (Department of Justice Files, File 348, "Edward T. Sanford," National Archives ("DOJ File 348")).
54. *Want Sanford for High Court*, CHATTANOOGA TIMES (November 20, 1922) (DOJ File 348); *Judge Sanford Is Being Considered*, BIRMINGHAM NEWS (November 20 1922) (DOJ File 348); *Judge E.T. Sanford*, NASHVILLE BANNER (November 20,

1922) (DOJ File 348); *Judge Edward T. Sanford*, CHATTANOOGA NEWS (November 20, 1922) (DOJ File 348); *Judge E.T. Sanford*, CHATTANOOGA TIMES (November 21, 1922) (DOJ File 348); J.N. Heiskell to Warren G. Harding (November 21, 1922) (DOJ File 348).

55. *Bill to Retire Justice Pitney*, NEW YORK TIMES (November 22, 1922), at 21.
56. Daugherty had transmitted Butler's nomination to Harding for his signature on November 21, 1922, H.M. Daugherty to Warren G. Harding (November 21, 1922) (Harding papers), and it was announced on November 23. Public discussion of Butler's nomination generally assumed that "the continued illness of Justice Pitney" meant "that the President will, in the near future, make his fourth appointment to the Supreme bench." *Pierce Butler Nominated for Supreme Bench*, CHICAGO DAILY TRIBUNE (November 24, 1922), at 4. See *Democrat Named to Supreme Court*, WASHINGTON POST (November 24, 1922), at 5; *Minnesotan Named for Supreme Bench*, NEW YORK TIMES (November 24, 1922), at 4. Taft wrote Harding a handwritten note on November 25, simultaneously expressing delight "at Butler's appointment" and urging the president to meet with Senator Nelson and Representative Volstead "in respect to the bill to allow Pitney to retire. I have furnished [them] with conclusive professional certificates that mentally and physically he is so weakened that it will be impossible for him ever to return to the Bench. ... We greatly need a full complement of our Justices to tackle some difficult questions we have and are much embarrassed sitting as seven." WHT to Warren G. Harding (November 25, 1922) (Harding papers). As of November 26, Taft was still speaking of Pitney's retirement in the conditional mode. WHT to Mrs. Frederick Johnson Manning (November 26, 1922) (Taft papers) ("Bills have been introduced in the House and Senate to retire [Pitney] with his pension, so that if the bills pass, as I hope they may, his resignation will call for another appointment.").
57. The logic of a Republican appointment was explained by Taft to his brother: "[T]here is a chance – and in many quarters a hope – that places now filled by Holmes and McKenna will become vacant before the end of this Administration, by retirement or in some other way, and that if they are vacant, it will be quite necessary for the President, in order to secure a confirmation of either, to unite the Democrats and Republicans, who are conservative, in confirmation of anyone whom he might wish to appoint. To do this he would have to name a Democrat as one of these two. There are now three Democrats on the Bench. To name [a Democrat] now would make four. ... This would require the President, therefore, in carrying out the purpose I have indicated to leave the Bench with five Democrats and four Republicans. That would not disturb me in the slightest, but to the orthodox party man that would seem like treachery." WHT to Horace D. Taft (January 17, 1923) (Taft papers). On Sanford's endorsements, see *New Supreme Justice*, CHATTANOOGA TIMES (November 25, 1922), at 4:

> President Harding cut several "Gordian knots," as it were, when he appointed the Hon. Pierce Butler of St. Paul Minn. ... It opens the way for the possible appointment of Judge E.T. Sanford, a Tennessean, to the Court when Judge Pitney, of New Jersey, shall have resigned. ... The administration has done practically nothing by way of recognizing the south, although it is known that he entertains a very kindly sentiment toward this section, and especially Tennessee,

the first of the southern states to give its electoral vote voluntarily to a republican candidate for president.

See also A Southern Man for Judge, CHATTANOOGA NEWS (November 27, 1922) (DOJ File 348) ("We believe that the president will appoint a southern man to the vacancy. The south has not now any representative on the supreme bench unless Justice McReynolds is so termed. When he was appointed he had been a resident of New York for fifteen years and is not really to be considered as from the south. If the president should be impelled with the desire to appoint a southerner there is no question but that the appointment will go to Judge Sanford. No other southern republican measures up at all in the class with the brilliant and scholarly Tennessee judge, who has so honored the bench during his service for many years, and whose opinions are so respected all over the country."). DOJ File 348 contains numerous editorials from southern papers to similar effect.

58. WHT to Charles D. Hilles (December 19, 1922) (Taft papers).
59. Charles D. Hilles to WHT (January 18, 1923) (Taft papers): "Fowler of Tennessee has done some effective practical work in behalf of his candidate. The New York Times has supported it editorially, and I attribute this to the fact that Mr. Ochs, who owns the Times, is a Tennessean. Jimmie Williams has followed suit in the Boston Transcript. We must not forget that Jimmie Williams was born in North Carolina and has always had a soft spot for the promising men from that section. Munsey has had an editorial in the Herald in support of the idea of going to the southland for the appointee." At the time Hilles was pushing Harding to appoint a candidate from New York or Pennsylvania. *See* Charles D. Hilles to WHT (December 29, 1922) (Taft papers). When last-minute objections were raised to Sanford's candidacy, Fowler was quick to write long and informative letters to Daugherty answering the charges. *See* J.A. Fowler to H.M. Daugherty, The Qualification of Appointment to Office of Chief Justice (January 18, 1923) (Department of Justice Files, File # 349, National Archives ("DOJ File 349")); J.A. Fowler to H.M. Daugherty (January 20, 1923) (DOJ File 349).
60. WVD to John C. Pollock (November 22, 1922) (Van Devanter papers).
61. Warren G. Harding to W.O. Mims (November 24, 1922) (Harding papers). Mims, a Tennessee attorney, had written Harding to endorse Sanford. Harding replied, "I think I ought to say to you, in all fairness, that unless there were especially compelling reasons it is not likely that I would appoint the second judge from Tennessee when there are so many other states without a member of the Supreme Bench, which are insistingly calling for recognition." The sitting justice from Tennessee was James R. McReynolds.
62. Miller was in fact Taft's own first choice to fill the Pitney vacancy. *See* WHT to Elihu Root (November 16, 1922) (Taft papers):

> What would you think of Nathan Miller for the vacancy which Pitney's resignation would make? I hear from other New York lawyers that Miller was a very excellent Judge, having served as a Supreme Court Judge, as a Judge of the Appellate Division, and also as a Judge of the Court of Appeals. He is certainly a man of affairs, a man familiar with government methods, with that kind of preparation I think is of great advantage to a member of our Bench. Holmes would have made a good deal better Judge, profound as his knowledge of the law is, and

accurate and happy as his power of judicial expression is, if he had had some dealing with affairs in ... executive capacity.

See Elihu Root to WHT (November 17, 1922) (Taft papers) ("I think Miller far and away ahead of anybody else that occurs to me who would be available for the place."). Miller was a determined conservative, who later became a founding member of the anti-New Deal American Liberty League. He was so taciturn that it was said that "as compared with Governor Miller, Calvin Coolidge is a flirt." Charles D. Hilles to WHT (December 29, 1922) (Taft papers). Miller eventually refused to be considered on the ground of financial poverty. "He has these six unmarried daughters, and he has very little money." Charles D. Hilles to WHT (December 2, 1922) (Taft papers). Having just heard John W. Davis decline a potential nomination for the same reason, see *supra* Chapter 2, at note 29, Taft exploded to Wall Street lawyer Charles Burlingham, who was continuing to insist upon an appointment from New York: "If you people in New York were not so eager for money and would be content to live on a reasonable salary (and the same thing is true of Pennsylvania), you might have some representatives on the Bench, but you are all after the almighty dollar. Now put that in your pipe and smoke it." WHT to Charles C. Burlingham (January 16, 1923) (Taft papers).

63. WHT to Charles D. Hilles (December 1, 1922) (Taft papers) ("I have heard ... that Miller had recommended Pound of the Court of Appeals, for the vacancy."). Taft heard this from his brother Henry W. Taft. *See* Henry W. Taft to WHT (December ?, 1922) (Taft papers) ("I heard something about the next vacancy on the Supreme Court today that I want to advise you of at once.... The President telegraphed to Gov. Miller asking him to suggest a judge of this State suitable for appointment to the Supreme Court. Judge Miller in response recommended Judge Cuthbert W. Pound of our Court of Appeals. I do not know enough about Pound's qualities to be of use – I will try to advise myself. But Col. Dykman says (and he, no doubt, reflects the views of Pound's associates on the bench), that Pound is an extremely troublesome member of the court – that he is a 'liberal' and a rather loose-thinker, although with some brains and that the court have [sic] to take a good deal of trouble in bringing him to a sensible view of a situation. Personally he is much liked as he is a gentleman of culture, urbane and full of kindly feelings and in manner genial and attractive.... I do not understand why Miller recommends such a man – he is the antithesis of Miller himself.... I am not sure whether Pound is related to the Harvard Professor, but I think he is – and that would not be a fact particularly favorable to him."). Taft later came to believe that the rumor was false. *See* WHT to Henry W. Taft (December 1, 1922) (Taft papers) ("Harry [Daugherty] tells me that there is nothing in the statement that the President telegraphed to Miller asking Miller to recommend somebody for the Court.... I doubt if the President would make an appointment of that sort without giving me some chance to express an opinion. Harry Daugherty is going to let me know what he hears at the Cabinet meeting to-day."). Charles Hilles explained to Taft what had actually occurred:

> I saw President Harding about it and advocated the appointment of former Governor Miller. The President commissioned me to tender the place to the ex-Governor, and I did so in his quarters at the Gotham Hotel. He declined it. He, however, recommended Cuthbert Pound. [Senator] Wadsworth fell in behind Pound. ... Governor Miller complained that the corporation lawyers were

determined to have only a hard-boiled conservative, and that the President would make a mistake if he should shut the door to a liberalized judge.

Charles D. Hilles to WHT (December 5, 1924) (Taft papers). *See* Charles D. Hilles to WHT (January 18, 1923) (Taft papers).

64. Taft considered it "quite essential that the President should be advised as to the kind of a man Pound is. . . . I am afraid that if we get him into the Court, he may be a bit erratic, and that isn't the kind of a man we want." Taft instructed his brother that "I wish you would pursue your inquiries further among the members of the Bar, and advise me what their verdict is. Among other men with whom you could talk is Nicholas Murray Butler. Let him find out about Pound and let him write a letter directly to the President on the subject, if it turns out that Pound is not the kind of a man that ought to be appointed." WHT to Henry W. Taft (November 29, 1922) (Taft papers). *See* WHT to Henry W. Taft (December 1, 1922) (Taft papers) ("You or somebody in your office ought to know something of [Pound's] opinions, whether he writes good ones and whether he has been on the off side and taken radical views in respect to the police power and other things. . . . I think the President would be inclined to go to New York, and perhaps to go to the Court of Appeals, if he could find the proper man, assuming always that Miller will not take it.").
65. WHT to Warren G. Harding (December 4, 1922) (Taft papers).
66. For the portions of Taft's letter that address Butler's nomination, see *supra* Chapter 2, at note 77.
67. WHT to Warren G. Harding (December 4, 1922) (Taft papers).
68. WHT to Charles D. Hilles (December 1, 1922) (Taft papers). Root advised Taft that Pound is "a good deal of a doctrinaire, liable to go off at half-cock and to be captivated by novelty without thinking it out. I am afraid he would not do at all and that his impressionable quality would make him an easy prey for clever and ingenious propaganda." Elihu Root to WHT (December 13, 1922) (Taft papers). It is worth noting that Karl Llewellyn regarded Pound as "a judge with a consistent record of craftsmanship, forthrightness, and earthy common sense." KARL N. LLEWELLYN, THE COMMON LAW TRADITION: DECIDING APPEALS 106 (Boston: Little, Brown 1960).
69. WHT to Henry W. Taft (December 1, 1922) (Taft papers).
70. Hilles presciently fretted that "What I fear is that we shall get into a situation where Wadsworth and Calder will pull apart and that the President will go to some other state for a man to fill this vacancy." Charles D. Hilles to WHT (December 2, 1922) (Taft papers).
71. WHT to Charles D. Hilles (December 3, 1922) (Taft papers).
72. WHT to Warren G. Harding (December 4, 1922) (Taft papers).
73. Henry W. Taft to WHT (December 3, 1922) (Taft papers).
74. WHT to Warren G. Harding (December 4, 1922) (Taft papers).
75. WHT to Mrs. Frederick J. Manning (December 13, 1922) (Taft papers). As Taft confided to his brother, von Moschzisker "likes to range through the law, and is proving to be a man like Justice Holmes. . . . His idea of the police power is altogether too broad, and we have had to reverse him by a decision of Holmes. [Pennsylvania Coal Co. v. Mahon, 260 U.S. 393 (1922)]. I knew him and I think he is a light weight, and that the pressure for him is mixed up in some way with Pennsylvania politics. Pepper is especially vigorous about him. It is quite possible

that he may be nominated." WHT to Henry W. Taft (January 16, 1923) (Taft papers). Taft believed that von Moschzisker was responsible for Pepper's appointment to the Senate. WHT to Charles D. Hilles (December 31, 1922) (Taft papers). In Taft's eyes George Wharton Pepper was "running for the Presidency" and "cultivating the labor party ... and that leads him to say some things that are quite disloyal to our Court. I don't resent this on the part of a radical, but on the part of a man like Pepper it is most exasperating." WHT to Mrs. Frederick J. Manning (December 13, 1922) (Taft papers). The exasperation was apparently mutual. Pepper's irritation with Taft's interference with von Moschzisker's candidacy led him to complain to Adams and Upham, as described *supra* note 45. Von Moschzisker, it should be noted, vigorously defended judicial review, as well as the Court's record in exercising it, in his book JUDICIAL REVIEW OF LEGISLATION (Washington D.C.: National Association for Constitutional Government 1923).

76. Here, once again, Taft was adopting the judgment of his brother Henry, who had written that "Hough is a man of unusual ability and the force of his intellect which leads him to strong views is not of the type we see in impracticable progressives. He would not line up for instance with Brandeis in responding to the throb of popular impulse in adopting some cloudy theory of social or industrial justice as a basis for a decision as to the meaning of the Constitution." Henry W. Taft to WHT (December 3, 1922) (Taft papers).

77. WHT to Warren G. Harding (December 4, 1922) (Taft papers). Karl Llewellyn regarded Hough as "among the nine greatest of all English-speaking commercial judges." LLEWELLYN, *supra* note 68, at 318.

78. WHT to Warren G. Harding (December 4, 1922) (Taft papers).

79. WHT to Charles D. Hilles (December 19, 1922) (Taft papers). Taft tried to convince Harding that the age limit ought to be waived "when the candidate was one of mere promotion after long service on the Federal Bench, because ... it [is] hard to deny the mead of merit to one who was amply able to do the work for ten years and do it better than most because of his intimate familiarity with the exact work in hand derived from decades of hardest effort in the very field which is important." WHT to Warren G. Harding (December 4, 1922) (Taft papers). But Taft could not overcome Harding's "objection" to Hough's "age," even though he wrote Harding "two or three times" and spoke with him in person. WHT to Charles D. Hilles (December 31, 1922) (Taft papers).

In his letter to Harding of December 4, Taft acknowledged that Cardozo, "a Jew and a Democrat," was "the best Judge in the State of New York," but he added that "I have assumed that you did not desire to appoint two Democrats – certainly not now, and therefore that he was not on the eligible list." WHT to Warren G. Harding (December 4, 1922) (Taft papers). Even though Taft specifically addressed the possibility of "making an appointment from the South," he never so much as mentioned Sanford. That is because in his letter Taft associated the possibility of a southern appointment with the nomination of a Democrat, which could happen only upon the future retirement of Holmes or McKenna. *See supra* note 57. In that connection, Taft mentioned federal District Judge William I. Grubb of Alabama and Judge Nelson Phillips of Texas.

80. Later in the month Taft also reacted with suspicion to the possibility of another candidate from New York, Henry L. Stimson. Elihu Root had first mentioned the

possibility of Stimson, Elihu Root to WHT (December 19, 1922) (Taft papers), and Taft replied, in a letter worth quoting at length:

> I never liked Frankfurter, and have continued to dislike him more the more I have known him. Indeed the only thing I know against Stimson is his good opinion of Frankfurter. I suppose it does not indicate an unsoundness of view as to the Constitution on Stimson's part, for it would be a great disappointment to have him appointed and then find him herding with Brandeis. I should think this quite unlikely, but I know you can give me assurances on the appointment, and that he is not in favor of breaking down the Constitution or making it a mere scrap of paper. The tendency of the Harvard Law School through Frankfurter and Pound ... is to break down that fundamental instrument and make it go for nothing. That I think was Wilson's purpose in appointing Brandeis and Clark [sic]. On the other hand, I feel as if we ought not to have too many men on the Court who are as reactionary on the subject of the Constitution as McReynolds, and that we need men who are liberal but who still believe that the corner stone of our civilization is in the proper maintenance of the guaranties of the 14th Amendment and the 5th Amendment. I believe that Stimson believes that. Let me hear from you about this before I write to the President or speak to him about it.

WHT to Elihu Root (December 21, 1922) (Taft papers). Later that day Taft wrote Harding to recommend Stimson:

> He was for a considerable period a partner of Elihu Root and later was U.S. district attorney under Mr. Roosevelt and me and then I called him into my cabinet as Secretary of War. He is a lawyer of high standing and ability. He made a fine record in the War, becoming Colonel, of one of the artillery regiments I think it was. Root has suggested his name to me in a letter received this morning. He said he had a note from Felix Frankfurter of the Harvard Law School inviting his attention to the fact that Stimson was Supreme Court timber with which Root agrees. The only thing to be said against Stimson's qualifications is that Frankfurter recommends him, but that is to be explained in part at least by the fact that Frankfurter was his assistant in the U.S. Attorney's office and at Stimson's instance I made Frankfurter legal adviser to the Secretary of War in Insular Affairs, and should not be taken as indicating that Stimson shares Frankfurter's view of the Constitution as an outworn instrument. Stimson is fifty-five years old, and a very hard worker. He is a very conscientious man and a better citizen than he is a politician. He ... is opposed to the bonus but was active in securing from Congress provision for the disabled. I submit his name so that it may be added to the eligible from whom you could safely make a choice.

WHT to Warren G. Harding (December 21, 1922) (Harding Papers in the Ohio History Connection). (I am grateful to Walter Stahr for this letter). On the tension between Taft and Frankfurter that went back almost a decade, see BRAD SNYDER, DEMOCRATIC JUSTICE: FELIX FRANKFURTER, THE SUPREME COURT, AND THE MAKING OF THE LIBERAL ESTABLISHMENT 38–42, 101, 132 (New York: W.W. Norton & Co. 2022). The next day Harding acknowledged that even though he "had not thought of [Stimson] heretofore," "[I] confess him to be an available man." Warren G. Harding to WHT (December 22, 1922) (Taft papers).
81. Warren G. Harding to WHT (December 5, 1922) (Taft papers). Harding wrote, in what may in retrospect suggest a mild ambiguity of tone, that "it is all very interesting and helpful to have your friendly suggestions."
82. Murphy, *supra* note 43, at 188. *See* Cook, *supra* note 43, at 132 (Taft "was completely triumphant in vetoing people to whom he had strong objections.").

83. Taft immediately got the point. The next day he wrote Harding to signify his understanding that the president was willing "to go out of New York and Pennsylvania" and to suggest the appointment of John C. Rose, a distinguished federal judge from Maryland on the Fourth Circuit who was "sound constitutionally." WHT to Warren G. Harding (December 6, 1922) (Harding papers). Taft added a postscript: "In my essay of yesterday, I tried to emphasize the wisdom of promoting a Federal Judge of the lower courts who has won a reputation by hard and distinguished service on that Bench." Rose, however, was 61 years old. *See* Warren G. Harding to WHT (December 8, 1922) ("You are aware that I think very well of Judge Rose.").

The argument for a Southern appointment, and for Sanford in particular, was later shrewdly summarized in an article by David Lawrence, the innovative and prominent reporter who was to found *U.S. News and World Report*:

> The desire of the President has been to name a Southerner to the vacancy and promote a man who already had made a record on the Federal bench. . . . Politically speaking the appointment has an indirect value to the Administration. Judge Sanford himself has never been a politician but has been a consistent Republican. His brother is the editor and publisher of the Knoxville Journal and Tribune, one of the most influential Republican newspapers in the South.
>
> Tennessee went Republican last time and the party organization in the state has felt ever since it should have some reward for breaking the solid South. The argument that it doesn't do any good to carry a Southern state since important patronage is doled out anyhow to Republicans from the North has been made again and again. In fact Republicans from Tennessee felt they should have a man in the Cabinet.
>
> The appointment of Judge Sanford, therefore, while not equalizing the political equation, has nevertheless a distinct value to the Harding administration in encouraging other republicans to hope that they will get recognition, too.

Lawrence, *supra* note 44. A decade later Hoover would pursue a similar southern strategy in nominating John J. Parker from North Carolina to replace Sanford.

84. "Fowler of Tennessee presses Sanford. . . . Harry Daugherty has been convinced by Fowler that he is the best man." WHT to Charles D. Hilles (December 19, 1922) (Taft papers).

85. WHT to Warren G. Harding (December 13, 1922) (Taft papers). Six days later Taft confided to Hilles that Harding is "considering Henry Anderson of Richmond, Edward Sanford, the District Judge of Knoxville, and possibly Rose of Baltimore." WHT to Charles D. Hilles (December 19, 1922) (Taft papers). All three were from the South. Taft suggested to Harding that Anderson "may prove to be a fine selection." WHT to Warren G. Harding (December 16, 1922) (Taft papers). Harding thanked Taft for his comments on Anderson and Sanford, "who really seems very much worthy of consideration." Warren G. Harding to WHT (December 19, 1922) (Taft papers).

A week later, Taft wrote Harding to say:

> With Pierce Butler confirmed and the taking effect of Pitney's resignation on the opening of the year, the election of another member of our court will press on you. The eligible you have under consideration are I believe Anderson, Bullitt, Stimson, practitioners, Hough, Rose, Sanford, judges, and possibly Wm.

Mahlon Pitney & Edward Terry Sanford

Moschisker C.J. of Penn. You have just put on two practitioners. Would it not be well to vary with a judge, preferably a federal judge familiar with the work?

If you take either Anderson, Bullitt or Stimson, you will have to go through the same fight in the judiciary committee against either as a corporation lawyer, especially in the case of Anderson. I don't think it anything against Anderson that his success has been won by acting for corporations, because it indicates his ability and professional prowess, but is it not well to make a variation, promote a judge because he can really help the court and avoid now another such controversy?

If you conclude that Hough's age disqualifies him, then I think Rose is the next best fitted, and then Sanford – Rose is 61, Sanford 57. Sanford comes from Tennessee, McReynolds's state, but it is from its Republican part. I hope you have heard from Judge Day about Sanford. He has sat with him on the Bench and heard him argue many cases before the Supreme Court when Sanford was Asst Atty General under Roosevelt who afterwards made him judge. Sanford's would be a southern appointment and so too in a sense would be Rose's. Rose is a patent and admiralty expert as is Hough. Sanford is not. We have not anyone on our Bench who is especially qualified in those fields. As to Wm. Moschisker of Penn. I have been making further inquiries and am convinced that his appointment would be a mistake. He is not of Supreme Court timber. He is a political quantity who helped Pepper to the senatorship and his proposed appointment seethes with Pennsylvania politics. Wire pulling with tact and brightness and ambition have put him where he is and so far as legal preparation and ability, he is out beyond his depth now. He would not add other weight or dignity to the Court.

The Lord give you good deliverance.

WHT to Warren G. Harding (December 27, 1922) (Harding Papers in the Ohio History Connection). (I am grateful to Walter Stahr for this letter). According to Taft, "The President in making his selection to succeed Pitney is not confronted by many candidates who meet his wishes as to age, party, residence and preeminent ability and sound views." WHT to Horace D. Taft (December 28, 1922) (Taft papers).

86. "Harry is strongly for Sanford, and I am bound to say that I think Sanford would be a very good accession to our Bench. He has possibly a defect in the failure promptly to dispose of business in a trial court, which would not manifest in a Court of Appeals." WHT to Charles D. Hilles (December 31, 1922) (Taft papers). In a letter to Fowler two years after Sanford's death, Daugherty recalled his role in the Sanford appointment:

I suppose you know that I had more to do with the appointment of Judge Sanford than anybody else. . . . I knew Sanford's capabilities; I wanted to please Tennessee, and I was always glad to please you and other men like you who would not allow me on their advice to make a mistake. Taft had little to do with the appointment of Sanford and had not considered him when he came to me in a special conference about the appointment of judges. I told him that I was friendly to Sanford of Knoxville, that I knew all about him, but had never talked to him on the subject and was not committed. Taft said, "Let's look him up", and I said it was not necessary as I knew all about him and if he wanted to pick him to pieces to do it in my presence and I would discuss it with him. At the conclusion he said he thought Sanford's appointment would be a fine one, adding "You are lucky and you strike some good ones." I talked to the President about it the day I went to the White House on my return from the hospital where I had been examined and told that I must go to bed and stay there and do nothing for some time because I was sick from exhaustion and overwork. . . . I said to the President "I want to see this vacancy filled before I leave the White House." He asked me who I was going to recommend and I said I wanted to recommend Sanford. He said "All right." I said "Well, let's send for a blank, the vacancy should be filled and I would like to send Sanford's name in immediately." He had his secretary bring in a blank which we prepared and sent in promptly.... Afterwards Taft saw fit to write me a letter in which he said, "Of course, you are the one person responsible for Sanford's appointment which is an excellent one." Taft often "stuck in" unduly, tho not much with me.

H.M. Daugherty to J.A. Fowler (June 18, 1932) (Sanford Papers at the University of Tennessee at Knoxville).

87. "I don't think Sanford is the strongest man, and he isn't my original suggestion, but I so much prefer him to Pound or Crane or the Chief Justice of Pennsylvania that I would now be glad to have him appointed.... One real advantage in the appointment of Sanford or Rose or Hough would be the recognition of the inferior federal judiciary, and that I think is very important." WHT to Henry W. Taft (January 16, 1923) (Taft papers). "While if I were left alone I would not select Sanford, I much prefer him to the Chief Justice of Pennsylvania, to Pound or to Crane." WHT to Charles C. Burlingham (January 16, 1923) (Taft papers). Ironically, Taft had himself highly praised Sanford in 1921. Addressing the Judicial Section of the American Bar Association in Cincinnati on August 30, and speaking in favor of a pending bill to enlarge the size of the federal judiciary, Taft referred to the impossible situation faced by Sanford in having to staff both the Eastern and Middle Districts of Tennessee. "The amount of business there is overwhelming for one man. One able judge died before his time under the strain, and although the incumbent judge is one of the ablest district judges in the United States, and willing and anxious to devote all his time to the avoidance of arrears, the cases are piling up on him from year to year until his future is utterly hopeless, so far as the disposition of business before him is concerned. A Judge for the Middle District has not been furnished. Why? Because for years there was a fear that if the bill went through, one faction or one party would be successful in securing the appointment of its candidate." William Howard Taft, *Adequate Machinery for Judicial Business*, 7 AMERICAN BAR ASSOCIATION JOURNAL 453, 453 (1921). *See* Wynne F. Clouse to WHT (February 15, 1922) (Taft papers); WHT to Wynne F. Clouse (February 17, 1922) (Taft papers); Arthur C. Denison to WHT (April 8, 1922) (Taft papers); WHT to Arthur C. Denison (April 10, 1922) (Taft papers).

88. WHT to Elihu Root (December 21, 1922) (Taft papers) ("My impression is that his disposition will be toward a Judge on the Bench, and that that is likely to be Sanford."); WHT to Charles C. Burlingham (December 25, 1922) (Taft papers) ("I think it likely that the President will take some man who has been on the Bench for some time. He is thinking of Judge Sanford of East Tennessee."); WVD to Walter J. Sanborn (January 6, 1923) (Van Devanter papers) ("The Pitney vacancy is still unfilled. My belief is that District Judge Sanford, of Tennessee, is likely to be the successor.... His opinions show study and learning and seem to point to well-balanced judgment.... Aside from Governor Miller ... I regard Sanford as superior to any of those who are being suggested."); WHT to Charles D. Hilles (January 7, 1923) (Taft papers) ("I don't know what the President is going to do about the appointment, but the report is that he is going to appoint Sanford. If he does so, we shall have a good Judge and colleague.").

Mahlon Pitney & Edward Terry Sanford

89. H.M. Daugherty to WHT (January 16, 1923) (Taft papers) ("I do not know just what is holding up the Associate Justiceship of the Supreme Court. I thought [it was] determined when I left there.").
90. *Politics Holds up Pitney's Successor,* NEW YORK TIMES (January 15, 1923), at 17.
91. In January, Guy D. Goff of West Virginia and Ohio federal District Judge John M. Killits both emerged as candidates for the nomination. *See Two Men Leading for Supreme Court,* NEW YORK TIMES (January 12, 1923), at 10; WHT to Horace D. Taft (January 17, 1923) (Taft papers) ("I don't know exactly what the situation is in respect to Pitney's vacancy. I judged from the newspapers that the President had about made up his mind to appoint Sanford of Tennessee, but there came a delegation from Ohio in favor of a District Judge named Killits, who by no means is fitted for the place, and there came in a delegation for Guy Goff of West Virginia, who also is by no means fitted for the place; and then the Pennsylvania Senators made a drive on the President for Von Moschzisker ... pleading that Pennsylvania had not been represented for twenty odd years, ... so that the President postponed the action which I am inclined to think he had determined on."); J.A. Fowler to H.M. Daugherty (January 18, 1923) (DOJ File 349) ("I have been unable to find out the specific reason why the President has withheld the appointment, but I am rather assuming that it is because Colonel Goff was pressed upon him by some senators after your departure."); Charles Curtis to Warren G. Harding (January 16, 1923) (Harding papers) ("I take great pleasure in joining with the friends of Judge Goff in recommending his appointment."); White House Minute (January 23, 1923) (Harding papers) ("Senator Curtis telephoned today to ask that his letter recommending the appt of Judge Goff to the Supreme Court be withdrawn.").
92. WHT to Horace D. Taft (January 17, 1923) (Taft papers). *See* Charles N. Burch to Warren G. Harding (January 16, 1923) (DOJ File 348) (defending Sanford from criticisms "relative to delay in Tennessee Central Receivership."); A.W. Akers & Walter Stokes to Warren G. Harding (January 17, 1923) (DOJ File 348) (Same); J. A. Fowler to H.M. Daugherty (January 20, 1923) (DOJ File 349) ("It must be kept in mind that Judge Sanford has been a very much overworked man, and necessarily some delays have occurred in disposing of matters which have involved complicated questions of fact and law. He is a Judge who will not decide a case until he has reached a mature judgment; he is exceedingly anxious to reach a correct conclusion, both upon the facts and the law, and is not willing that important matters be disposed of by guess.").
93. Charles C. Burlingham to WHT (January 15, 1923) (Taft papers) ("He won't be the tower of strength you need."). *See* Henry W. Taft to WHT (January 15, 1923) (Taft papers) (Augustus Hand "expressed himself with considerable emphasis that [Sanford] was not a man who would be a helpful member of the Supreme Court. He thought that his inclination was toward a habit of indecision, and that courage in deciding important questions was not his strong point. I inferred that [Hand] thought [Sanford] lacked dignity or weight of character – something of a dilettante."); LDB to Felix Frankfurter (January 29, 1923) in BRANDEIS-FRANKFURTER CORRESPONDENCE, at 135 ("I am told A.N. Hand is strong in condemnation of the Sanford appointment.").
94. *See supra* note 92.

95. *See* WHT to Charles D. Hilles (December 31, 1922) (Taft papers) (Sanford "has possibly a defect in the failure promptly to dispose of business in a trial court, which would not manifest in a Court of Appeals. Judge Knappen, who is the Senior Circuit Judge of that Circuit, has been here ... and he says that [Sanford] would be an admirable selection; that it always has been a great pleasure to have him a member of the Court of Appeals."); Loyal E. Knappen to Harry M. Daugherty (January 2, 1923) (DOJ File 348) ("I have been impressed with [Sanford's] legal learning, his industry, his judicial and scholarly habit of mind, his general culture and engaging personality. His judicial opinions are ably and painstakingly written, and I am impressed that he enjoys work of that kind.... I regard him not only as one of the very best of our district judges, but as unusually adapted to appellate work."); Arthur C. Denison to WHT (January 11, 1923) (Taft papers) ("There is some complaint of delay and some basis for the theory that he has a tendency to be hesitant, but I think they are rather negligible as to justification.... [H]e is not a driver of business. As to hesitancy of opinion: It is not a dominating characteristic ... and I should say it did not go beyond the reasonable limits of caution. Within such limits it is better than too much speed at a conclusion, which is my tendency. I think he would not be happy as a baseball umpire, nor yet in the position of Mr. Justice Brown in the Insular Cases, [Downes v. Bidwell, 182 U.S. 244 (1901)], but few would."); WHT to Charles C. Burlingham (January 16, 1923) (Taft papers) ("I have letters from Denison and Knappen strongly favoring [Sanford]. Denison's letter is exceedingly frank and considers all the adverse suggestions which your letter contains.").
96. 64 CONG. REC. 2326 (January 24, 1923).
97. 64 CONG. REC. 2677 (January 29, 1923). Taft wrote Sanford a warm letter of welcome. "We shall all be delighted to welcome you. We need in the court one fresh from the practice in the court of first instance to represent the cause of the hard pressed District Judges which I fear some of our Court and especially the older members are prone to forget in disposing of cases." WHT to ETS (January 26, 1923) (Sanford papers at the University of Tennessee at Knoxville).
98. 116 THE NATION 137 (1923) ("It is to be hoped that [Sanford] is diametrically opposed in temperament and point of view to Mr. Butler ... who should never have been considered, much less confirmed, for our highest court."). The *New Republic* concurred: "President Harding's appointment of Judge Sanford ... is very much the best which he has made.... [H]e is about as excellent a selection as is likely to come from a man of Mr. Harding's prejudices." 34 NEW REPUBLIC 262 (1923). With some prescience, the *New Republic* warned: "The chief question about him is whether or not he will be able to stand the severe strain of the work. If a Justice of the Supreme Court cannot deal with the cases assigned to him at once rapidly and well, he has to spend excessively long hours at his desk and unless he is young or robust, he often goes to pieces." *Id.*
99. *Alfred E. Sanford Dies in Fall from Hospital Window*, KNOXVILLE JOURNAL (May 23, 1946), at 1. *See Remarks of William L. Frierson*, 285 U.S. xliii, xliv (1930) ("He was well born and accustomed all his life to the society of cultured people.... [H]is lot was one of ... comparative luxury and he was given the best of educational advantages.").

100. Cook, *supra* note 43, at 6.
101. Sanford's father made his fortune in the pharmaceutical industry, as well as in the lumber business. John M. Scheb II, *Edward T. Sanford – Knoxville's Justice*, 41 JOURNAL OF SUPREME COURT HISTORY 176, 177 (2016); *He Aimed for the Senate, But Landed in the Supreme Court*, CURRENT OPINION (April 1, 1923), at 411. He was a Director of the East Tennessee, Virginia and Georgia Railroad, see *The New Directory*, ATLANTA CONSTITUTION (November 21, 1889), at 1, and the publisher of the *Knoxville Journal and Tribune*. See *Oldest Editor Keeps His 85th Birthday*, NEW YORK TIMES (May 11, 1924), at E1.
102. Sanford was involved in the founding of the *Harvard Law Review*. The first issue of the *Review* is dated April 15, 1887. Sanford is first listed as an editor in the issue of November 15, 1887, along with Samuel Williston and George R. Nutter (later to become Brandeis's law partner), both of whom in 1922 wrote Harding in support of Sanford's nomination. *See* Samuel Williston to Warren G. Harding (November 22, 1922) (DOJ File 348) ("I have known Judge Sanford for many years, and have had occasion to become assured of his high character, professional accomplishments and courteous, as well as distinguished, manners."); George R. Nutter to Warren G. Harding (December 6, 1922) (DOJ File 348) (Sanford "was in my college class at Harvard, and graduated with me from the Harvard Law School. He is a man of great ability, well read in the law, of highest professional standing, and I believe would be a credit to the Bench of the Supreme Court.").
103. Sanford was president of the Tennessee Bar Association and a trustee of the University of Tennessee, where he taught law. He was chair of the Board of Trustees of the George Peabody College for Teachers, and president of the Harvard Alumni Association. In 1904 Sanford was the unsuccessful Republican candidate for Tennessee governor. Scheb, *supra* note 101, at 177.
104. ETS, Harvard University Class Day Oration, June 19, 1885, reproduced in Cook, *supra* note 43, at 203. The oration was plainly an occasion for a certain degree of soul baring. Sanford, for example, proclaimed: "The spirit of our college life ... is essentially liberal. The essence of the spirit of liberal investigation is an unprejudiced mind which compels every opinion to appear before the bar of reason and stand the test of an impartial investigation. As an inevitable result, he who can see fairly both sides of the questions often remains for a time entangled in a maze of doubt. ... [I]n all earnest, liberal inquiry temporary indecision is the fruit of earnestness." *Id.* at 199–200.
105. Fowler reports that Sanford and McReynolds were "rather particular friends." Statement of James A. Fowler (Sanford papers at the University of Tennessee at Knoxville).
106. Sanford's longtime friend and former partner J.A. Fowler succeeded him as assistant attorney general.
107. Milton, *supra* note 34, at 299. Milton was the managing editor of *The Chattanooga News*.
108. *Id. See Grey Wigs*, 8 TIME MAGAZINE 8, 8 (October 11, 1926).
109. 281 U.S. v (1930). "Charm" is in fact the characterization that seems repeatedly to have been applied to Sanford. *See, e.g.*, WHT to Horace D. Taft (February 9, 1923) (Taft papers) ("Sanford is a most charming personality. I am quite sure he will make a good member of the Court."); James M. Beck to WHT (February 7, 1923) (Taft papers) ("What a charming personality [Sanford] has!"); *Resolution in*

Proceedings in Memory of Mr. Justice Sanford, 285 U.S. xxxvii, xxxviii (1930) ("He had a personality of unusual charm, and was a most gifted speaker."); *Remarks of William D. Mitchell*, 285 U.S. liii (1931) ("He was in every sense a man of the highest culture. His mastery of the English language and his training in the field of advocacy combined to make him a speaker of unusual ability and charm. But above all his dominant traits of character were kindliness and affection for his fellow men."); William Rule, *The New Supreme Court Justice*, NEW YORK TIMES (February 4, 1923), § 8, at 4 ("He is one of the most charming men imaginable and a delightful companion."). The importance of class to contemporary perceptions of Sanford is summed up in the title of Charles A. Noone's early appreciation: *Edward Terry Sanford: Gentleman, Scholar, Lawyer, Jurist*, 43 COMMERCIAL LAW JOURNAL 34 (1938).

110. "Especially prominent in every activity was [Sanford's] unfailing courtesy and grace. Never lacking in this quality himself, he looked for it in others." *Remarks of Charles Evans Hughes*, 285 U.S. liv (1931). Sanford "is a fine lawyer and a first-class gentleman, a man of the highest honor and character, and of real culture." WHT to Charles D. Hilles (January 7, 1923) (Taft papers).

111. Although contemporaries apparently regarded Sanford as an outstanding orator, see, e.g., Noone, *supra* note 109, at 34, the surviving manuscripts of his speeches, which are located in his papers at the University of Tennessee at Knoxville, now make his addresses seem merely artificial and decorative. So, for example, the opening of Sanford's address at the Harvard Alumni Association Meeting of 1924 reads:

> Again we have come in annual pilgrimage to Mecca. We have assembled in this Springtide of the year, when the beauty of leaf and bud are eloquently prophetic of the flowers of Summer and the fruitage of Autumn, to celebrate in festival rites, the two-hundred and eighty-third Commencement of Harvard; to pledge anew to her the devotion and service of grateful hearts; to gain renewed inspiration from our Mother's voice, bidding us, as of old, to know the truth that shall make us free and to be valiant and firm of faith; and to cherish, in this goodly and gladsome fellowship, the enduring ties of long-time friendships.

Harvard Alumni Association Address (June 19, 1924) (Sanford papers at the University of Tennessee at Knoxville).

Within the Court, Sanford was given to writing notes like: "Yes, O learned senior. The winged arrow of your thought hits the mark precisely." (Return to Holmes's draft opinion in Equitable Trust Co. v. First National Bank, 275 U.S. 359 (1927) (Holmes papers)). For similar remarks, see his returns to Holmes in Emmons Coal Mining Co. v. Norfolk & Western Railway Co., 272 U.S. 709 (1927) ("Yes, honored senior. Deftly Done.") (Holmes papers) and Beech-Nut Packing Co. v. P. Lorillard Co., 273 U.S. 629 (1927) ("Yes, honored Senior. This has the incomparable touch.") (Holmes papers).

112. For a fine sketch of Sanford, see Stephanie L. Slater, *Edward T. Sanford's Tenure on the Supreme Court*, 41 JOURNAL OF SUPREME COURT HISTORY 186 (2016).

113. Stone's summary of Sanford rings true:

> In appearance and demeanor, [Sanford] was always the cultivated gentleman, attracting people to him instantly by his charm of manner and holding them

> by the charm of an intellectual quality difficult to define, which colored his conversation and all his relationships with his fellows. ...
>
> I think it must be said that his opinions, generally, were not distinguished in quality, but this was not always the case. A notable exception was his opinion in the Pocket Veto Case, 279 U.S. 655. ... His amiability tended to make him a conformist. He rarely dissented from the opinions of the majority, or wrote concurring opinions.

HFS to A.D. Noyes (November 19, 1930) (Stone papers).

114. SIDNEY H. ASCH, THE SUPREME COURT AND ITS GREAT JUSTICES 86 (New York: Arco Pub. Co. 1971).
115. HFS to A.D. Noyes (November 19, 1930) (Stone papers). A good example of why Sanford was viewed as a lightweight may be found in court correspondence in the case of Sprout v. City of South Bend, 277 U.S. 163 (1928), in which Brandeis contended in a draft opinion circulated to the Court that under the Act of February 13, 1925, Pub. L. 68-415, 43 Stat. 936, unsuccessful challenges to the constitutionality of city ordinances, as distinguished from unsuccessful challenges to the constitutionality of state statutes, should be required to come to the Supreme Court by discretionary writs of *certiorari* rather than by mandatory writs of error (Brandeis papers). Sanford responded to Brandeis's draft with an unreservedly enthusiastic note: "My hearty congratulations. This is a monumental piece of work, exceedingly well done. I think I shall ... regard the argumentation on the jurisdictional question as a demonstration based on profound and tireless investigation, clear and unanswerable distinctions, and most convincing reasoning. You have, it seems to me, completely set this long perplexing & confusing question at rest in a most satisfactory manner for which we are greatly indebted."

Van Devanter, however, circulated a memorandum taking issue with Brandeis and arguing that such cases ought to be brought to the Court through mandatory writs of error (Brandeis papers). The question came to a head and was decided in Van Devanter's favor in John P. King Mfg. Co. v. City Council of Augusta, 277 U.S. 100 (1928), with only Brandeis and Holmes dissenting. Despite his previously enthusiastic and unreserved endorsement, Sanford, caught between the contending positions, meekly and silently joined Van Devanter's majority opinion.

Milton Handler, Stone's former law clerk, later wrote Stone that "The King case, it seemed to me, was a battle of the gods between the two men who know more about federal jurisdiction than any living person. ... The majority opinion gives too little heed to the important problems of expediency and seems content with a rather formalistic summary of the previous decisions and dicta. I do not think that the door was absolutely shut to a decision based upon expediency. If the question were open, I think that the Brandeis view should have prevailed. A careful examination of the cases relied upon by the majority convinces me that the question was not so closed as to have prevented such a decision." Milton Handler to HFS (May 26, 1928) (Stone papers).
116. Sanford's opinion for the Court in Gitlow v. New York, 268 U.S. 652 (1925), for example, is far more proficient and capable than Clarke's opinion six years before in Abrams v. United States, 250 U.S. 616 (1919). For a discussion of the two opinions, see Robert Post, *Reconciling Theory and Doctrine in First Amendment Jurisprudence*, 88 CALIFORNIA LAW REVIEW 2355 (2000).

117. Remarks of Chauncey G. Parker, *Proceedings in Memory of Mr. Justice Sanford*, 285 U.S. xxxvii, xlii (1931).
118. Herbert Little, *Supreme Court Liberals Keep Things Lively*, HONOLULU ADVERTISER (July 15, 1929), at 10. *See Chief Justice Taft Attacked for Conservative Decision*, WOODWARD OKLAHOMA DAILY PRESS (June 15, 1929), at 1 ("The right wing is predominantly a 'Harding' court.").

CHAPTER 4

Joseph McKenna and Harlan Fiske Stone

After the conclusion of the 1922 term, there remained only a single associate justice whom Taft longed to see retire. "Sutherland is a very able man," he wrote his daughter in June 1923. "So, too, is Butler; and while Sanford has not won his spurs yet, he is developing. If McKenna would only retire and another able man appointed in his place, the Court would be full of strong men." McKenna, Taft complained, "ought to lay down his office. I think he knows it, but he does not want to do it. ... [H]e has got to a point where his mind does not function well. ... He can not see things right, and he makes up his mind now on impressionist principles. He is a Cubist on the Bench, and Cubists are not safe on the Bench."[1]

Although Taft had been anticipating McKenna's departure since 1914,[2] his firsthand experience of McKenna's declining capacities came as a shock. As the senior justice on the Court, having been appointed by President McKinley on January 1, 1898, McKenna was responsible for swearing in Taft as chief justice. Although "McKenna was a modest and loveable man," he was, as Van Devanter remarked to a friend, "underneath ... vain and had unlimited confidence in himself."

> Before Mr. Taft was sworn in as Chief Justice we anticipated that McKenna might become confused in administering the oath; so the Clerk was directed to put it on a slip of paper in capitals so that it might be easily read and McKenna was urged to use the paper. He thought it would be more impressive if he committed the oath to memory and was able to recite it without referring to the paper. The outcome was that he became confused in giving the early part of the oath, reached in his pocket for the paper, could not find it and went ahead as best he could. Some things not in the oath were given and some things in the oath were omitted. The confusion was obvious to every one. McKenna never mentioned it afterwards to any of us and we never mentioned it to him.[3]

Within months Taft grew appalled at McKenna's manifest incompetence. Assigned the opinion in *Morrisdale Coal Co. v. United States*,[4] McKenna circulated such a vague and unacceptable draft that the opinion had to be taken away and given to Holmes.[5] Later that month, in *Smietanka v. First Trust & Savings Bank*,[6] McKenna "wrote an opinion deciding the case one way when there had been a unanimous vote the other, including his own."[7] In *Oklahoma Natural Gas Co. v. Oklahoma*,[8] McKenna authored an opinion for the Court "that we let get through ... which brought a petition for rehearing that is most humiliating to the Court."[9]

Awareness of his own failing capacity made McKenna "sensitive" and liable to lose "his temper at criticism."[10] "He is most humble and deprecatory in manner at first, and then blazes out in something that is very denunciatory and personal. He and Holmes had a controversy the other day in conference, in which Holmes kept his temper, and McKenna lost his."[11] By spring 1922, Taft had become genuinely alarmed. "I don't know what course to take with respect to him, or what cases to assign to him.... The difficulty is of course that McKenna's vote may change the judgment of the Court on important issues, and it is too bad to have a mind like that decide when it is not able to grasp the point, or give a wise and deliberate consideration of it."[12]

McKenna had in fact never been an especially strong justice.[13] The son of an immigrant Irish baker, he was born in Philadelphia on August 10, 1843,[14] during a period of violent anti-Catholic riots.[15] In 1855, his family moved to the northern California town of Benecia. McKenna became a Republican stalwart. He supported high tariffs, sound money, and railroads, eventually representing California in the House of Representatives from 1885 to 1892. Heeding the advice of McKenna's patron, Senator Leland Stanford, Jr., Benjamin Harrison appointed McKenna to the Ninth Circuit,[16] where he served from 1892 until 1897, when his close friend William McKinley drafted him to become attorney general. McKinley's nomination of McKenna to the Court to replace Stephen Field was approved by the Senate without enthusiasm, largely because senators feared that McKenna was incompetent to fill the position.[17]

"In his early years on the bench," McKenna "was frequently irritable, nervous and rather unhappy because he was not familiar with the law nor able to construct an opinion that would adequately express the convictions of his colleagues."[18] His judgment was erratic and unpredictable.[19] He joined the Court's decision in *Lochner v. New York*,[20] but wrote the opinion in *Bunting v. Oregon*,[21] which at the time many believed overruled *Lochner*.[22] He vigorously dissented from *Adair v. United States*,[23] but joined the Court's opinion in *Coppage v. Kansas*.[24] His opinion in *German Alliance Ins. Co. v. Lewis*[25] was perhaps the most expansive account of the police power in the years before the New Deal, yet he obstreperously dissented in the *Arizona Employers' Liability Cases*.[26]

After the First World War, McKenna's instinct seemed to turn more insistently conservative. Holmes, commenting on McKenna's dissents from the Court's decisions upholding rent control during times of emergency[27] noted that the "best defense" of judicial review was "that constitutional restrictions enable a man to sleep at night and know that he won't be robbed before morning – which, in days of legislative activity and general scheming, otherwise he scarcely would feel sure

Joseph McKenna & Harlan Fiske Stone

about. I am afraid McKenna thinks that security at an end."[28] Figures I-26 and I-27 suggest that during the Taft Court era McKenna tended to vote largely with the conservative wing of the Court. Thus, McKenna would cast a decisive vote in *Adkins v. Children's Hospital of the District of Columbia*,[29] which sparked the contentious revival of *Lochnerism* during the 1920s, and he would

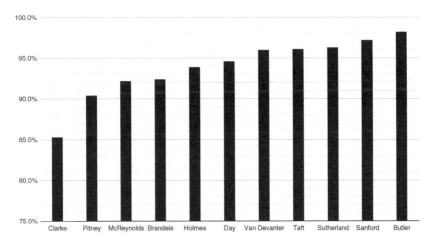

Figure I-26 Percentage of decisions in which McKenna participated and joined the same opinion as another justice, 1921–1924 terms

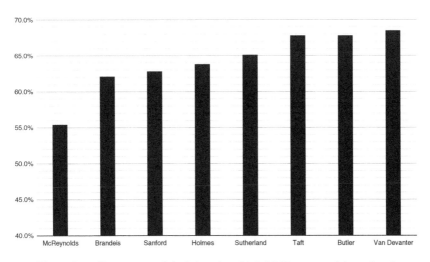

Figure I-27 Percentage of decisions in which McKenna participated and voted with another justice in conference

cast the fifth vote for Taft's controversial opinion in *Truax v. Corrigan*,[30] which struck down a state law restricting the issuance of labor injunctions.

Mostly, however, McKenna was during the 1920s uncertain and confused.[31] Figure I-9 indicates that McKenna was far more likely than any other justice to alter his views in conference to join an opinion for the Court. During the 1922–1924 terms, McKenna joined a Court opinion after dissenting or expressing uncertainty in conference in 16 percent of the cases in which he participated. Often his reasons for doing so were bizarre. In *Fidelity & Deposit Co. v. United States*,[32] for example, he explained his change of vote to Brandeis: "I dared to have an opinion in this case and expressed it by voting. I am not so presumptuous this morning."[33] In *Louisville & Nashville Railroad Co. v. United States*,[34] he wrote Brandeis: "Let's pass the hat around and in that way dispose of the case."[35] The "only way of dealing with him," Brandeis concluded, "is to appoint guardians."[36] "The Chief & Van D. are his guardians – McReynolds tries to handle him but does it badly. He [McKenna] knows he (McK) doesn't count, his suggestions are [not] taken, so every once in a while he sends up a balloon just to show that he is there. . . . Every once in a while McK really does mischief – more often than appears. His opinions are often suppressed – they are held up & held up & gets mad & throws up the opinion and it's given to someone else."[37]

Taken together, Figures I-10 and I-19 demonstrate that McKenna was by far the least likely of any member of the Taft Court to persuade a colleague to change his conference vote to join an opinion. Figure I-18 shows that Taft assigned McKenna disproportionately easy and simple cases that had been unanimous in conference. Yet McKenna remained "thirsting for work and without the slightest intention of retiring,"[38] and Taft considered him "the least likely to wish to go off. He says that when a man retires, he disappears and nobody cares for him, and he stays on the Bench merely to secure a deference to him which he thinks will be gone as soon as he lays down office."[39]

By the start of the 1923 term, Taft noted that McKenna's "inability to hold up his end" was "growing more and more painful and may have to result in some action by the rest of us." "If he doesn't show some intention of withdrawing, we may before the end of the year have to adopt some united action in bringing to bear influence upon him. Of course that will fall on me as the spokesman, and is not a pleasant duty to look forward to, because I shall never be forgiven."[40] In spring 1924, Taft wrote his wife that "Six of us were willing to have me say to McKenna that it was time for him to get off the Court because the work was too much for him to give proper consideration to the cases."[41] But Taft could not unite the Court to speak to McKenna, "because Holmes dislikes to agree, tho' he agrees it ought to be done, and Brandeis does not want it done because I think he would like to have a Democratic President appoint."[42] Figure I-28, however, shows that during the 1923 term Taft on his own sharply curtailed McKenna's allocation of opinions.

At the end of the 1923 term, "McKenna spoke as if we might expect some changes in the Court before we met again," but Taft did not credit him. "If there are to be any changes," Taft said, "I don't think they will be with the old men. Vacation usually gets them ready to come back with a certain determination to stay."[43] The summer of 1924, however, proved "a very bad time" for McKenna, because his wife

Joseph McKenna & Harlan Fiske Stone

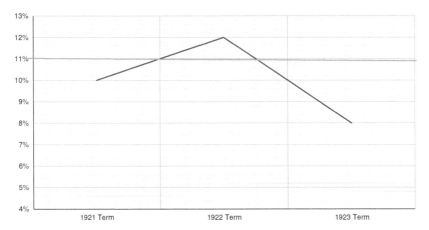

Figure I-28 Percentage of Court's opinions authored by McKenna, by term. An even distribution of cases would assign 1/9, or 11%, to each justice.

was "at the point of death."[44] When she died in early October, McKenna's "family" became "very anxious to have him retire" and were "rather disposed to use the members of the Court to bring this about."[45] This, together with Coolidge's sweeping reelection in November, entirely changed the complexion of the issue. When Taft convened a special meeting of the Court at his home on November 9, it was readily and unanimously agreed that the Court would not "decide any case in which there were four on one side and four on the other, with Mr. Justice McKenna's casting the deciding vote," and also that Taft was "authorized ... to deal with" McKenna "as seemed best."[46]

That night Taft and Van Devanter met with McKenna's son and explained to him the Court's decision, and their intention to attempt to persuade his father to retire. Although the son was asked not to speak to the justice, he apparently did so, for, on the morning of November 10, McKenna telephoned Taft and requested an interview. Taft recorded the event in a memorandum deeply moving for its unflinching simplicity:

> When he first came I told him that we had reached the conclusion that through a lack of physical strength he was not able to command his mental energies in such a way that he could do the work on the Court. ... He was then disposed to argue the questions, and to say that he was up with his work, that he had decided every case that had been assigned him, and that he considered that there was no basis for the conclusion. I told him that I did not wish to go into the argument of such an issue. He said he hoped I would. I told him then I had not assigned anything but the simplest cases to him and that even the opinions in those cases when returned by him had either to be reassigned or else had to be so changed, in order the meet the opinion of the Court, that it was quite evident he could not do the work. ... He said he assumed that we had no authority to end his term, and I said "Of course not", but that we felt it our duty to communicate to him

our views. He did intimate that he thought it was a hard time to have it come to him just after his bereavement. I concluded it was wiser not to enter into that discussion and did not say to him, what of course is the fact, that for two years the situation has been such that we have felt it a violation of our duty not to speak earlier. The Justice then recounted the services that he had rendered to the country, and went back over a long and honorable career, in which of course I was able to join with emphasis.... He then said that he would like to make the resignation take effect as of the first of January, and that he would like to sit with the Court until then, and for me to assign two or three cases in which he might render opinions. ... I acquiesced readily. ... I want to say that while the attitude of the Justice was in some respects that of questioning the soundness of our judgment and the opinion that we had of his work, he was very manly and just as knightly in his way of doing things as one might expect, and I told him so, and thanked him most cordially for making the Conference as little painful as such a Conference could be. ...

After the details were agreed on, we went over the record and our personal associations and his experiences with the various Presidents and with Tom Reed, and with the Circuit Justices in the 9th Circuit, with his Congressional campaigns, especially the one in which he came back as a gold Congressman against the opposition of the silver man, and his record as a whole. I was able to do this because with the exception of Justice McKenna and Senator Warren, and possibly Congressman Burton, I am the oldest in office in public life to-day in Washington, I think.[47]

On January 5, 1925, McKenna announced his last opinion from the bench. Taft declared McKenna's intention to resign and read a letter of appreciation from the Court, to which McKenna responded with prepared remarks.[48] As McKenna concluded, the Marshal of the court laid a basket of red roses in front of him. All rose. "Justice McKenna shook hands with Chief Justice Taft, bowed to his judicial associates, right and left, and then descended from the bench, and made his way out of the courtroom through the public entrance, escorted by the Marshal."[49] On that same day, and without the delay that typically fuels speculation and lobbying, President Coolidge nominated Attorney General Harlan Fiske Stone to fill the vacancy left by McKenna.[50]

Destined to become "one of the great jurists of the entire history of the Supreme Court,"[51] Stone was born in 1872 in the small New Hampshire village of Chesterfield.[52] He came from a rock-ribbed, Yankee, Republican household, with roots going back to 1635. He was broad-shouldered, vigorous, with a sharp mind and a capacious memory. He was a star student and athlete at Amherst College, where Calvin Coolidge was a quiet member of the class just behind him. Stone attended Columbia Law School, where he was so successful that he was called back first as a lecturer, and then in 1910 as the Kent Professor of Law and dean, a position that he occupied until 1923.

It is no exaggeration to say that Stone sparked the revitalization of Columbia Law School, although his "basically conservative instincts" also somewhat dampened the renaissance of legal scholarship that he himself had orchestrated.[53] Stone firmly believed that the "systematic study of legal doctrine as a science," in contrast to "the trade guild tradition of legal study of the past," would produce "a better organization and systematization of our legal knowledge and enable us to penetrate the dogma and fiction and illusions which obscure its realities to the essential principles which underlie formal legal rules."[54] Stone was certain that at its core the common law formed "a remarkably logical and consistent body of rules and principles," which made its study "by the scientific method so attractive and so necessary if one is adequately to understand and apply it."[55]

Stone's field of scholarly expertise was commercial law and equity,[56] and his scholarly contributions importantly influenced the development of New York law.[57] He was also a legendary instructor. No less a student than William O. Douglas described him "as one of the very best, if not the best, law teacher" he ever had. "He instilled skepticism of absolutes, inquisitiveness as to the origins of principles, respect for precision and intolerance for the lack of it, disrespect for dogma, habits of close analysis, and belief in the sturdiness and vitality and adaptability of law."[58] During his time at Columbia, Stone also maintained a lively New York practice in the firm that in 1913 became known as Satterlee, Canfield & Stone.[59] His clients included the likes of the Duchess de Talleyrand (the daughter of Jay Gould) and the Royal Card & Paper Co.[60]

By 1923, when Stone resigned his deanship to become head of litigation at Sullivan and Cromwell,[61] he had become a leader of both American legal academia and the New York Bar. He held views that were mostly conventional among elite New York lawyers. Because he was convinced of the scientific foundations of law, he advocated for raising the standards and professionalism of the Bar, in ways that he knew would adversely affect the opportunities of poor immigrants who were seeking to use the practice of law as a ladder to assimilation and professional success.[62] He warned that "there is far greater danger to our profession and to this Republic by the reverence we do to the cult of incompetency masquerading in the guise of democracy than there will ever be by our adherence to the principle that even a democracy is entitled to have its functions performed by the competent and the well trained."[63]

Stone believed deeply in the expertise and authority of judges. In his 1915 book, *Law and Its Administration*, he defended the common law as "the accumulated wisdom and experience of our whole civilization, not lightly to be trifled with or overturned." He characterized the common law as "justly and properly" a "conservative force in the community," protecting "the rights of those whose rights may be overlooked or temporarily obscured by popular clamor or in times of political excitement."[64] The content of the common law could be ascertained only by judges appointed on the basis of "expert knowledge, experience, and integrity to apply an existing system of law to the settlement of controversies as they arise."[65]

Stone contrasted common law principles to legislation, which he distrusted because it represented "the radical force in the community" that "responds to the popular will."[66] Like Taft, Sutherland, and Butler, Stone decried the "child-like and implicit faith in the efficacy of legislation to bring about the social Utopia." It led to "over-much legislation" that controlled "the minutiae of conduct" and consequently undermined "individual self-control."[67] Stone perceived the structure of the common law as continuously vulnerable to "the dangers which are incurred by legislation which ... is not the product of observed experience rather than of propaganda and emotionalism."[68]

Stone believed that the risks of legislation were especially acute because of the profound social changes that had transformed the nation since the 1880s:[69]

> Disregarding the tendency of society to cure its own ills through the restorative action of time and through its moral resistance to social fault, and impatient of immediate results, we seek a remedy in law before we know the nature of the disease. It is then that we are exposed to all the dangers of attempted social adjustment by legislation whose real applicability and successful operation are rendered doubtful from the outset because it does not rest on the solid foundation of observed and appraised experience.[70]

Insofar as he thought about constitutional law at all, Stone was inclined to regard constitutional limitations on popular legislation applied by the "conservative" legal experience of expert judges as necessary to check emotional and undigested laws.[71] Stone excoriated "the popular criticism of law and courts," which he believed exhibited "an intemperateness and lack of sense of propriety which can be wholly accounted for only by lack of popular faith in legal justice and by a willingness to substitute for it the notions of social and political quacks."[72]

In 1915 Stone even went out of his way to defend the decision of the New York Court of Appeals in the notorious case of *Ives v. South Buffalo Ry. Co.*,[73] which had struck down under the New York Constitution a legislative scheme for workmen's compensation.[74] The controversy that subsequently engulfed the New York court was so intense that it prompted Theodore Roosevelt to propose the recall of state judicial constitutional decisions.[75] Stone considered "the outburst of criticism of the Court of Appeals ... so loud, so ill-tempered, and so misguided, as to startle those who have respect for and faith in our institutions. ... The spirit which ... dictated virulent attacks upon the court ... is ... essentially lawless and subversive of all orderly judicial procedure."[76]

By contrast to his conventionally conservative perspective on matters involving social and economic legislation, Stone held distinctly "liberal views"[77] about questions of civil liberties. These were very much in evidence in a 1921 letter he sent the Senate Judiciary Committee investigating A. Mitchell Palmer's notorious red raids. Stone charged that the Department of Justice had blatantly violated the constitutional rights of noncitizens.[78] Stone's commitment to individual liberties was also visible in his full-throated defense of academic freedom against the intolerance of Columbia President Nicholas Murray Butler, who had prohibited university professors from expressing opposition to World War I.[79] From his experience on a World War I Board of Inquiry constituted to determine whether conscientious objectors to the military draft were entitled to exemptions,[80] Stone distilled the conclusion that "liberty of conscience" was so necessary "to the integrity of man's moral and spiritual nature that nothing short of the self-preservation of the state should warrant its violation; and it may well be questioned whether the state which preserves its life by a settled policy of violation of the conscience of the individual will not in fact ultimately lose it by the process."[81]

Joseph McKenna & Harlan Fiske Stone

Stone's untouchable integrity and reputation was exactly what Calvin Coolidge was looking for when Coolidge concluded that the dogged controversies hanging over Attorney General Harry M. Daugherty required that Daugherty be pushed out of the Cabinet. Daugherty had been crucial in Harding's successful senatorial campaign in 1914, and he had been Harding's campaign manager in the presidential election of 1920. Despite widespread opposition, Harding had brought Daugherty to Washington as attorney general.[82]

Yet Daugherty, "a man totally unprepared for such an office,"[83] soon became swamped in scandal, epitomized by his appointment of the notorious detective William J. Burns to run the FBI.[84] Burns harassed prominent congressmen and public officials who opposed Daugherty, even to the extent of having Herbert Hoover followed. When Senator Burton Wheeler from Montana launched a freewheeling investigation into the abuses of Daugherty's Department of Justice, which included selling official favors by close associates like Jesse Smith and Howard Mannington, Burns responded by ransacking Wheeler's Senate offices.[85] In a crude effort at intimidation, Daugherty had Wheeler indicted in Montana for illegally receiving payments as a United States senator.

Seeking to cleanse the party of the stench of Harding era-scandals before the upcoming presidential election of 1924,[86] Republican leaders concluded that Daugherty had to go.[87] To preserve his incorruptible image, Coolidge needed to appoint a spotless attorney general. An Amherst classmate of both Stone and Coolidge, New York Congressman Bertrand H. Snell, recommended Stone as "a man of unblemished character, not a flaw in his work, one of the outstanding lawyers in the country."[88] Daugherty resigned on March 28, 1924; Stone was confirmed as his replacement on April 7. Taft wrote his wife, "The new A.G. ... is a fine man and will make an excellent A.G. ... I think if all goes well he may come on to our Court."[89]

Stone promptly set to work energetically reforming the Department of Justice. He fired Burns and replaced him with J. Edgar Hoover, who had been the architect of the infamous 1919 Palmer raids. He professionalized personnel at the Department, cleaned up Daugherty-era scandals, and so on.[90] His work was highly regarded,[91] and when Coolidge learned of McKenna's impending retirement, Stone was a natural choice.[92]

"We have got a very fine man, and therefore we rejoice," wrote Taft on January 9.[93] "It is a great pleasure for me to know that I rather forced the President into [Stone's] appointment," Taft later wrote his son. "The President was loath to let him go, because he knew his worth as Attorney General, but I told him that I did not think it was fair to him not to give him the opportunity to accept the Bench if he desired it, and that he was the strongest man we could secure in New York that was entitled to the place, and so he submitted the matter to Stone, and in that way we got him."[94]

Stone expected his confirmation to go through within the week,[95] but unexpectedly Colonel James A. Ownbey, a "veteran Indian hunter and Buffalo Bill's successor as a Western guide,"[96] came forward to complain that Stone had used legal skullduggery on behalf of the estate of J.P. Morgan to cheat Ownbey out of his savings.[97] The charges came down to nothing more than that Stone had represented the Morgan estate before the Supreme Court and had successfully defended the constitutionality of an obscure and manifestly unjust Delaware foreign-attachment statute.[98] The chief effect of Ownbey's complaint was to paint Stone in the colors of Wall Street and J.P. Morgan, which was insufficient to prevent the Senate Judiciary Committee from unanimously recommending his confirmation.[99] "By another week," Stone wrote a friend on January 20, "I shall be 'Mr. Justice.'"[100]

But then a bombshell exploded. Commentators had been puzzled at Stone's refusal to terminate the prosecution of Senator Wheeler in Montana, which Daugherty had instigated to intimidate the Democratic senator who had been investigating the Department of Justice.[101] But Stone in fact had quietly decided in December to expand the prosecution of Wheeler by convening a second grand jury investigation in the District of Columbia, which he disclosed to Wheeler on January 16, 1925.[102] When Stone refused to back down on this decision, the Senate detonated.[103]

Stone's nomination was recommitted to the Judiciary Committee, and for the first time in history a Supreme Court nominee gave public testimony before Congress. On January 28, Stone ably defended his decision to initiate a second investigation;[104] he produced "a complete and convincing demonstration of [his] high purpose and good faith in dealing with the Wheeler case and ... won the esteem and respect of virtually all the members of the committee. He made one of the best witnesses seen at the Capitol in many a day."[105] By presenting the "plain picture of an honest public official doing his duty," Stone maneuvered the Senate into a position where it "could not reject his nomination without indicting itself."[106] Opposition to Stone "dissolved almost literally into very thin air."[107]

Paradoxically, "the best evidence" of Stone's bona fides was his "supreme political stupidity": "No politician, certainly no corrupt politician, about to be elevated to the Supreme Court could conceivably have approved another attempt to indict Senator Wheeler.... The Attorney General has acted so blindly against his own interest that he must have acted in good faith."[108]

The oddest thing about Stone's pursuit of Wheeler in Washington D.C., however, was not its political naïvety, but rather that, as the Department of Justice later admitted in open court, the government's second indictment did not actually allege a violation of "existing law."[109] Federal law capped the number of acres for which a person could obtain leases on federal land for oil and gas, but the government had charged Wheeler only with seeking to obtain too many prospecting permits, which federal statutes did not make illegal. Wheeler's indictment was accordingly dismissed for failure to charge any crime.[110] In retrospect, it is difficult to understand how Stone could have allowed such a facially flawed indictment to proceed, especially at such a sensitive moment.[111]

The Senate Judiciary Committee, knowing nothing of these future events, reported Stone out positively on February 2, with abstentions but without dissent.[112] On February 5, after an "open" executive session featuring a six-hour-long debate, the Senate voted 71–6 to confirm Stone.[113] The irascible southerner James Clark McReynolds wrote Stone offering "best wishes upon your appointment to the bench. I like to hope that you will find the work and association in harmony with your tastes. The slavery of it is sometimes depressing, but there are compensations."[114] Stone took his seat in a simple ceremony on March 2.[115]

Joseph McKenna & Harlan Fiske Stone

Contemporary observers are likely to imagine Harlan Fiske Stone as the far-seeing author of footnote four of *United States v. Carolene Products*, which crystallized the modern framework of judicial review. That framework requires courts to defer to legislative judgments in the context of social and economic legislation, but to carefully scrutinize legislation whenever fundamental civil liberties or civil rights, like freedom of speech or equal protection for "discrete and insular minorities," are at stake.[116]

The Harlan Fiske Stone who joined the Taft Court was not yet this jurist, certainly not with respect to civil liberties or civil rights. As his second law clerk, Milton C. Handler, observed, "Stone was very conservative in those days."[117] Despite his previous defense of freedom of conscience and academic freedom, Stone showed little inclination in the 1920s to assist Holmes and Brandeis in creation of the modern First Amendment. He joined the Court's repressive opinion in *Whitney v. California*,[118] passing up the opportunity to affirm (with Holmes) Brandeis's transformative essay about the meaning of freedom of speech in American democracy.[119] He signed on to the Court's chauvinistic opinion in *United States v. Schwimmer*,[120] thus passing up the opportunity to support (with Brandeis) Holmes's magnificent dissent about freedom of speech and conscience.[121] He also joined the Court's opinion in *Gong Lum v. Rice*,[122] which reaffirmed *Plessy v. Ferguson* and explicitly upheld racial segregation in education.[123]

By contrast, Stone did markedly evolve during the 1920s in his attitude toward social and economic legislation. In 1915, Stone had argued that because "rights of property . . . are essentially personal rights, . . . there is, in many cases, no clear line of demarcation between acts which are unconstitutional because they deprive of personal liberty and those which deprive of property."[124] His staunch defense of controversial decisions like *Ives* led most to anticipate that Stone would join the Taft Court with views that were "entirely 'regular' . . . toward law and politics."[125] Taft certainly shared this expectation. He initially characterized Stone as "a strong addition to our Bench,"[126] "a real Judge, a real lawyer and a hard worker"[127] who "strengthened the Court not only in the brain power and learning but also in solidity of judgment and capacity for labor."[128]

Stone's first clerk, Alfred McCormack, recalls that when Stone took his seat on the bench "he liked the solid virtues. . . . He was drawn to judges in whom he found them – Justice Butler especially, whose wit also attracted Stone, and Van Devanter, who appealed to Stone by reason of his craftsmanship."[129] Stone disliked Brandeis, who advocated the kind of sociological jurisprudence to which as an academic Stone had been hostile.[130] Stone found the "elaborately annotated opinions of Brandeis . . . pretentious," and he believed that Brandeis lacked a sense of "team play" and was too cavalier with established common law doctrines.[131] Although he was drawn to Holmes's deep scholarship[132] and literary flair,[133] as well as to Holmes's "robust wit and flashes of brilliance,"[134] Stone was also "suspicious of Holmes' facility and his sometimes cavalier attitude toward opinions."[135]

The progressive press was in turn suspicious of Stone. It fretted when in October 1925 Stone failed to speak up as the Court struck down Arizona minimum wage legislation despite a Brandeis dissent and a separate Holmes concurrence based "solely" on the precedential authority of *Adkins v. Children's Hospital*.[136] When Stone spurned subtle limiting opinions by Holmes and Brandeis, and instead joined a blunt Court decision striking down an Oklahoma statute requiring employers to pay a "prevailing wage,"[137] the *New Republic* noted archly, "Apparently Mr. Justice Stone does not find it congenial to shiver with Holmes and Brandeis. He prefers the warmth of a solid majority."[138] Stone himself wrote Taft in December 1925 to reassure the chief justice that "I am a team player" and that "I have only been longing to be helpful in the way which I believe we should all be in carrying on the difficult work of the Court – without pride of opinion or over insistence on anything."[139]

As late as June 1926, Brandeis complained to Frankfurter that Stone couldn't make up his mind: "'I think it's wrong. *but*. I think it's right, *but*,' Doesn't know & doesn't take trouble to find out. Van D. (says) if he would only take time enough to think. 'Hasn't written one really good opinion' Van D. thinks. I agree – least valuable member at present."[140] Stone's constant refrain, according to Brandeis, was "had I been on Court I would, or wouldn't have done. ... If he'd only think."[141]

In fact, however, the tide had begun to turn in March 1926, when Stone joined with Holmes and Brandeis to dissent from opinions invoking the Fourteenth Amendment to strike down what would now be characterized as ordinary economic regulation.[142] By 1928 his connection to Holmes and Brandeis had become so solid that Stone could write Holmes that "I think it is good for the dissenters to stand together when they can,"[143] simultaneously telling Frankfurter that "It is a great comfort that when one starts out to 'proclaim the truth' he can usually count on such staunch supporters as Justice Holmes and Justice Brandeis."[144] Reflecting backwards in 1941, Stone recalled: "When I came to the Court from a Wall Street environment, I had no adequate understanding of [Brandeis] but close association with him soon made me realize his great qualities. I count myself particularly fortunate in having had such intimate associations with him and Justice Holmes – two of the great figures of our times."[145]

By 1929, when Stone's former law clerk Milton Handler asked Stone about rumors that President Hoover had invited Stone to join the Cabinet, Stone could reply that "tackling any new job, whether it be the State Department or the Department of Justice, is interesting and engaging, but you know the battle of the ideas that is going on in the Court and consequently know how difficult it would be for me to abandon the fight for anything else."[146] When he first joined the Court, Stone would not have understood himself as engaged in a battle of ideas. By the end of the decade, however, he had become bitterly opposed to the majority of his colleagues on the degree of deference that ought to be accorded to legislative judgments in matters involving social and economic legislation.[147] One of the great puzzles of American constitutional law is why Stone's jurisprudence evolved in this way.[148]

Stone came to the Court as a scholar of private law who had learned from Holmes "that law is not an end, but a means to an end – the adequate control and protection of those interests, social and economic, which are the special concern of government and hence of law."[149] As Stone put it in 1927, "We ought to remember that law is distinctly utilitarian in its object, and the ultimate goal of everything we do with respect to it is to make it more useful."[150] In Stone's eyes, the obligation of courts was to fashion legal doctrine that facilitated the achievement of legal aims. When interpreting the Constitution, therefore, Stone inquired first and foremost into the nature of constitutional ends.[151] Stone's early and justly famous doctrinal innovations in such technical and difficult areas as intergovernmental tax immunity[152] and state "burdens" on interstate commerce[153] flowed directly from this pragmatic and instrumental orientation. But when Stone sought to pursue this same approach in the context of social and economic legislation, he was shut down by his conservative colleagues.

The point can be illustrated by the Court's 1927 decision in *Tyson & Brother v. Banton*, which invalidated New York legislation limiting the resale price of theater tickets. Speaking through Justice Sutherland, the Court ruled that price regulation was inconsistent with the Due Process Clause of the Fourteenth Amendment unless applied to property "affected with a public interest." Although the sale of theater tickets was highly regulated, it did not constitute property affected with a public interest. The power to fix prices, said Sutherland, "is not only a more definite and serious invasion of the rights of property and the freedom of contract, but its exercise cannot always be justified by circumstances which have been held to justify legislative regulation of the manner in which a business shall be carried on."[154]

Holmes, joined by Brandeis, dissented in *Tyson*, on the clean and decisive ground "that a state Legislature can do whatever it sees fit to do unless it is restrained by some express prohibition in the Constitution of the United States or of the State, and that Courts should be careful not to extend such prohibitions beyond their obvious meaning by reading into them conceptions of public policy that the particular Court may happen to entertain." Holmes and Brandeis regarded "the notion that a business is clothed with a public interest and has been devoted to the public use" as "little more than a fiction intended to beautify what is disagreeable to the sufferers."[155]

Stone was not yet ready to join such a radical opinion. Instead he sought to identify and apply the constitutional values that the doctrine of "property affected with a public interest" was designed to protect.[156] Stone reasoned that the "constitutional theory that prices normally may not be regulated rests upon the assumption that the public interest and private right are both adequately protected when there is 'free' competition among buyers and sellers, and that in such a state of economic society, the interference with so important an incident of the ownership of private property as price fixing is not justified and hence is a taking of property without due process of law." He concluded that the doctrinal category of property "affected with a public interest" must therefore refer to "circumstances materially restricting the regulative force of competition, so that buyers or sellers are placed at such a disadvantage in the bargaining struggle that serious economic consequences result to a very large number of members of the community."[157]

Stone thought that without a disciplined and functional account of this kind, the doctrine of "property affected with a public interest" would become merely a free-floating device for judicial nullification. "The phrase 'business affected with a public interest' seems to me to be too vague and illusory to carry us very far on the way to a solution. It tends in use to become only a convenient expression for describing those businesses, regulation of which has been permitted in the past. ... It is difficult to use the phrase free of its connotation of legal consequences and hence when used as a basis of judicial decision, to avoid begging the question to be decided."[158] Stone dissented in *Tyson* because his review of the relevant facts led him to conclude that the market for the resale of tickets was failing in a manner that justified state price regulation.[159]

What is striking about *Tyson* is that the majority simply refused to engage with Stone's efforts to attribute a functional purpose to the doctrine of property affected with a public interest. The majority even refused to discuss Stone's analysis of the relevant market. Sutherland was content in *Tyson* simply to invoke the abstract doctrinal category of property affected with a public interest and then to invalidate the New York statute. Stone was appalled.[160] It offended his sense of professional craft, which had been honed by years of scholarly work searching for the purpose of common law doctrines.

The following year the Court held in *Ribnik v. McBride* that New Jersey could not regulate the price of employment agencies because such agencies were not "affected with a public interest." Sutherland authored the opinion for the Court, and he once again refused to offer a purposive analysis of his own constitutional test. Although he acknowledged that the state could license and "regulate the business of an employment agency," he insisted that the state was nevertheless without "power to fix the prices which the employment agent shall charge for his services."[161] Employment agencies, Sutherland bluntly asserted, did not come within the definition of property affected with the public interest. This was too much for Stone. He was now prepared to argue, as he had not been in *Tyson*, that if used in this way the doctrine was arbitrary and indefensible.

Stone dissented on the ground that there was no tenable distinction "between a reasonable regulation of price and a reasonable regulation of the use of the property, which affects its price or economic return. The privilege of contract and the free use of property are as seriously cut down in the one case as the other."[162] Hence,

> [t]o say that there is constitutional power to regulate a business or a particular use of property because of the public interest in the welfare of a class peculiarly affected, and to deny such power to regulate price for the accomplishment of the same end, when that alone appears to be an appropriate and effective remedy, is to make a distinction based on no real economic difference, and for which I can find no warrant in the Constitution itself nor any justification in the opinions of this court.[163]

The consequential but capricious distinctions drawn by Sutherland pushed Stone to reappraise the basic justification for judicial review in the context of social and economic legislation. It forced him to take a step further than he had been prepared to go in *Tyson*:

> Under the decisions of this court not all price regulation, as distinguished from other forms of regulation, is forbidden. As those decisions have been explained, price regulation is within the constitutional power of a state legislature when the business concerned is "affected with a public interest." That phrase is

not to be found in the Constitution. Concededly it is incapable of any precise definition. It has and can have only such meaning as may be given to it by the decisions of this court. As I read those decisions, such regulation is within a state's power whenever any combination of circumstances seriously curtails the regulative force of competition, so that buyers or sellers are placed at such a disadvantage in the bargaining struggle that a legislature might reasonably anticipate serious consequences to the community as a whole. . . .

I cannot say a priori that the business of employment agencies in New Jersey lacks the requisite "public interest." . . .

In dealing with the question of power to require reasonable prices in this particular business, we should remember what was specifically pointed out by the court in *Tyson v. Banton* that whether a business is affected with a "public interest" turns "upon the existence of conditions, peculiar to the business under consideration." . . .

Some presumption should be indulged that the New Jersey legislature had an adequate knowledge of such local conditions as the circumstances of those seeking employment, the number and distribution of employment agencies, the local efficacy of competition, the prevalent practices with respect to fees. On this deserved respect for the judgment of the local lawmaker depends, of course, the presumption in favor of constitutionality, for the validity of a regulation turns "upon the existence of conditions, peculiar to the business under consideration." *Tyson v. Banton*. Moreover, we should not, when the matter is not clear, oppose our notion of the seriousness of the problem or the necessity of the legislation to that of local tribunals. . . .

There may be reasonable differences of opinion as to the wisdom of the solution here attempted. These I would be the first to admit. But a choice between them involves a step from the judicial to the legislative field. That choice should be left where, it seems to me, it was left by the Constitution – to the states and to Congress.[164]

Judicial review of the "reasonableness" of state social and economic regulation requires sober consideration of relevant facts in light of pertinent constitutional purposes. In *Tyson*, Stone attempted to articulate such purposes for the category of property "affected with a public interest." But the Court ignored him, and in *Ribnik* the Court indicated just how far it was willing to go to prevent government price regulation. Stone became convinced that because the conservative wing of the Court refused to articulate the legal purpose of its own doctrine,[165] they were advancing an ideological rather than a legal agenda. Stone was thus led to take an important step beyond his previous analysis in *Tyson* and to ask whether, and in what circumstances, the Court was entitled to second-guess legislative judgments of fact and policy.

Stone concluded in *Ribnik* that if judicial judgments of reasonableness did not express distinct and defensible *legal* principles, courts had no business interfering with ordinary lawmaking. In the context of social and economic legislation, this required a prophylactic rule of deference that would prevent "the unfortunate position in which a court may find itself if it attempts to write into the Constitution the particular social or economic philosophy in which the judges have been trained."[166]

THE TAFT COURT

Starting from a very different place, Stone arrived at conclusions very close to those of Holmes and Brandeis. His five years on the Taft Court fundamentally altered Stone's understanding of judicial review in the context of social and economic legislation. At the outset, he had believed that the responsibility of courts was to decide "what is reasonable and proper." But by 1930 he had concluded that the presumption of constitutionality required courts only to determine "what is not unreasonable or arbitrary."[167] Driving this transformation was Stone's growing conviction that the Taft Court was not using tools of *legal* reasoning to check government police power, but instead deploying empty legal formulae as a facade for the political views of its members.

Stone's change of heart was noticed by the Court's conservative members. By June 1928, Taft could write his brother Horace that "Stone has become entirely subservient to Holmes and Brandeis. I am very much disappointed in him. I urged Coolidge to appoint him but he hungers for the applause of the law school professors and the admirers of Holmes. If Holmes' dissents in constitutional cases had been followed, we should have no Constitution."[168] Ironically, it was Holmes's own past scholarship on the purposive nature of common law rules that had set Stone on the path to changing his views of constitutional adjudication.

The statistical profile of Stone during the Taft Court period paints a blurry picture. He stands out in Figure I-9 for his reluctance to alter his conference votes to join a Court opinion, yet in most other measures he is in the middle of the pack. Figure I-29 captures a snapshot of Stone as loyal to established authorities like Taft and Van Devanter and yet as also drawn to more radical justices like Holmes and Brandeis. Stone's attraction to the Court's conservative wing is far more pronounced in his voting at conference, as shown in Figure I-30. If we track Stone's development over time, as Figure I-31 seeks to do, we can plainly see both Stone's emerging independence and his developing alliance with Holmes and Brandeis.

Stone took some time to find his footing on the Court. His first opinions tended to be long and academic.[169] They received internal critique,[170] especially from

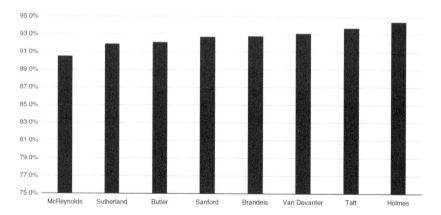

Figure I-29 Percentage of decisions in which Stone participated and joined the same opinion as another justice, 1924–1928 terms

Joseph McKenna & Harlan Fiske Stone

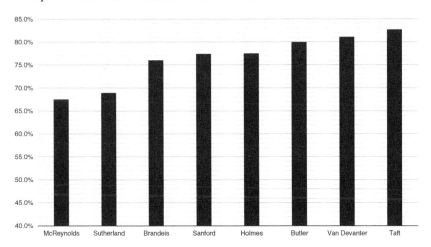

Figure I-30 Percentage of decisions in which Stone participated and voted with another justice in conference

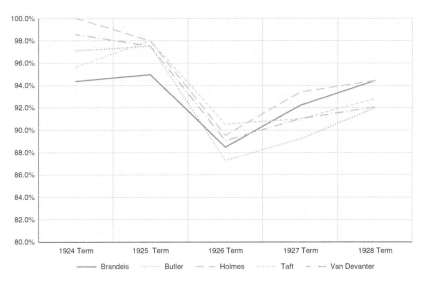

Figure I-31 Percentage of decisions in which Stone joins a common opinion with another justice, by term

McReynolds.[171] At one point, Stone startled his colleagues by inadvertently circulating a draft opinion that concluded with a judgment of *affirmed* rather than the agreed-upon *reversed*.[172] Figure I-32 shows Stone learning from these criticisms and altering his style of opinion-writing. Just as service on the Taft

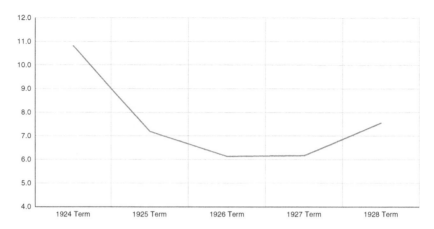

Figure I-32 Average number of pages in a unanimous opinion by Stone, by term

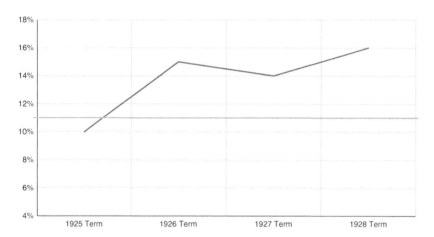

Figure I-33 Percentage of Court's opinions authored by Stone, by term. An even distribution of cases would assign 1/9, or 11%, to each justice.

Court sharpened his understanding of constitutional law, so it trained him in the deployment of judicial craft. Figure I-33 suggests that Stone very quickly became a workhorse on the Court, producing more than his fair share of opinions.

By the conclusion of the Taft Court, Stone was well on his way toward finding his own judicial voice. He was authoring opinions with incisive and original constitutional analysis. He had also become deeply entangled in judicial struggles that would subsequently explode during the New Deal.

Joseph McKenna & Harlan Fiske Stone
Notes

1. WHT to Mrs. Frederick J. Manning (June 11, 1923) (Taft papers).
2. WHT to Charles D. Hilles (July 15, 1914) (Taft papers) ("McKenna is now over seventy and will soon be retiring)."
3. WVD to A.C. Campbell (March 18, 1929) (Van Devanter papers). The tact of the associate justices is evident from Taft's contemporaneous letter to his brother: "Justice McKenna administered the oath. The Clerk who never had officiated in authority as Clerk before, though thirty years an employe of the former Clerks, was considerably more rattled than I was, and forgot to furnish the copy of the oath which the Justice was to administer, and he sent up the Bible instead, so that the Justice trusted to his memory, and it was remarkable. It necessitated a little halt, which was not altogether free from embarrassment, but we got through. It was considerably better than what happened when Chief Justice Fuller swore me in as President. He missed the oath and had me execute the Constitution instead of supporting and defending it." WHT to Horace D. Taft (October 6, 1921) (Taft papers).
4. 259 U.S. 188 (1922).
5. *See* JM to WHT (January 20, 1922) (Taft papers).
6. 257 U.S. 602 (1922).
7. WHT to Horace D. Taft (April 17, 1922) (Taft papers). *See* JM to WHT (February 7, 1922) (Taft papers) ("I must have been absent from the Conference Room when you stated the case and then on my return voted carelessly. I had marked my copy of the transcript with my sign for reversal and, not looking at my docket, I took for granted that the decision was in accordance with my views, and hence the opinion. ... Expressing regrets again at the trouble I have caused and confessing to some shame for my blunder."). Taft eventually wrote the opinion himself. During that same week, McKenna apparently also produced an unacceptable opinion in Hawes v. Georgia, 258 U.S. 1 (1922). *See* JM to WHT (February 6, 1922) (Taft papers).
8. 258 U.S. 234 (1922).
9. WHT to Horace D. Taft (April 17, 1922) (Taft papers). In a cover letter to his petition for rehearing, counsel explained, "I know that it is quite unusual to permit oral argument on petitions for rehearing, but it is so obvious that Mr. Justice McKenna's opinion is based upon a misapprehension of both the facts and the law applicable to the case, that it seems only fair that I should have an opportunity of presenting oral argument on the petition." C.B. Ames to WHT (April 6, 1922) (Taft papers).
10. WHT to Horace D. Taft (April 17, 1922) (Taft papers). In a note written to Van Devanter on February 18, 1922, McKenna apologized for "[m]y bad temper at conference," explaining that it "was a case of bad nerves." JM to WVD (February 18, 1922) (Van Devanter papers).
11. WHT to Horace D. Taft (April 17, 1922) (Taft papers). Taft wrote Holmes a note of appreciation: "I can not refrain from dropping a line to you to say how much I admired your self restraint yesterday under almost intolerable conditions. It was a melancholy situation created by peevish vanity and irritability and a subconsciousness of losing grasp. Your composure and willingness to accommodate, without yielding your expressed opinion commanded the warm praise of the Brethren." WHT to OWH (April 2, 1922) (Holmes papers). Holmes responded: "Of

course your letter gives me very great pleasure, although it does not require much effort to restrain oneself when one perceives the inevitable at work. In addition to what you mention I think he has had domestic affairs to make him nervous, but I have suspected his subconscious to which you refer for some time. I shall add that the Chief Justice makes good humor easier." OWH to WHT (April 2, 1922) (Taft papers).

There was without question some tension between the two octogenarian justices. McKenna was plainly "jealous of Holmes." WHT to Horace D. Taft (April 17, 1922) (Taft papers). And Holmes, in turn, referred to "our sensitive brother." Return on Brandeis's draft dissent in United States v. Moreland, 258 U.S. 433 (1922) (Brandeis papers). Holmes expressed real exasperation at "the oscillations of McKenna." OWH to Frederick Pollock (March 7, 1924), in 2 HOLMES-POLLOCK CORRESPONDENCE, at 129. After McKenna resigned, however, Holmes wrote Frankfurter that "he leaves affectionate memories behind him." OWH to Felix Frankfurter (January 6, 1925), in HOLMES-FRANKFURTER CORRESPONDENCE at 178. "He has a sweet nature and though worn out we shall miss him." OWH to Harold Laski (January 4, 1925), in 1 HOLMES-LASKI CORRESPONDENCE, at 692. Holmes believed that McKenna had "political shrewdness." OWH to Felix Frankfurter (January 6, 1925), in HOLMES-FRANKFURTER CORRESPONDENCE, at 178.

12. WHT to Horace D. Taft (April 17, 1922) (Taft papers). The irony is that Taft had himself just relied on McKenna for his fifth vote in his important opinion for five justices in Truax v. Corrigan, 257 U.S. 312 (1921). David Danelski suggests that Taft also relied on McKenna to obtain his Court in Carroll v. United States, 267 U.S. 132 (1925). *See* David J. Danelski, *A Supreme Court Justice Steps Down*, 54 YALE REVIEW 411, 417–18 (1965). McKenna's mental instability may also have been essential to the decision of the Court in the crucial case of Adkins v. Children's Hospital of the District of Columbia, 261 U.S. 525 (1923). Danelski, *supra*, at 415; David J. Garrow, *Mental Decrepitude on the U.S. Supreme Court: The Historical Case for a* 28th *Amendment*, 67 UNIVERSITY OF CHICAGO LAW REVIEW 995, 1014 (2000).

13. The major published study of McKenna is MATTHEW MCDEVITT, JOSEPH MCKENNA: ASSOCIATE JUSTICE OF THE UNITED STATES (Washington D.C.: The Catholic University of America Press 1946).

14. McKenna was two years younger than Holmes, who had been born on March 8, 1841.

15. MCDEVITT, *supra* note 13, at 1–5.

16. James F. Watts, Jr., *Joseph McKenna*, in 3 THE JUSTICES OF THE UNITED STATES SUPREME COURT 1789–1969: THEIR LIVES AND MAJOR OPINIONS 1724 (Leon Friedman & Fred L. Israel, eds., New York: Chelsea House Publishers 1969).

17. The *New York Times* opined that "No one can envy Attorney General McKenna the certificate of local opinion addressed to the President on his account." "One United States Circuit Court Justice, who sat on the bench with Mr. McKenna in the Ninth Circuit, ... the Judge of the United States District Court of his own district, two Judges of Oregon State Courts, and some half a hundred of lawyers have joined in a protest against the Attorney General's appointment to the Supreme Court. The substance of this objection is that he 'is not, either by natural gifts, acquired learning, or decision of character, qualified for any judicial place of importance, much less for the highest place in the land.'" *A Remarkable Protest*, NEW YORK

Joseph McKenna & Harlan Fiske Stone

TIMES (December 6, 1897), at 6. *See McKenna in the Senate*, NEW YORK TIMES (December 17, 1897), at 3 ("It is apparent there is grave doubt of the duty of the Senate to confirm.... [T]he question in the minds of Senate lawyers will be whether the quality of the court will not be diluted by the addition of Judge McKenna to the bench.... [T]here is a decided lack of enthusiasm about the nomination and some strong criticism of the President's selection. A Republican Senator said this afternoon: 'It is the weakest nomination for the Supreme Court that has been offered to the Senate in many years, certainly the weakest in my recollection.'").

18. MCDEVITT, *supra* note 13, at 202.
19. "McKenna as you say is unpredictable – a few days ago he was saying to me that all in life is a question of circumstances.... He has intimations that perhaps come out oftener in his talk than in his opinions, but he has them." OWH to Felix Frankfurter (April 30, 1921), in HOLMES-FRANKFURTER CORRESPONDENCE, at 112.
20. 198 U.S. 45 (1905).
21. 243 U.S. 426 (1917).
22. *See, e.g.*, Adkins v. Children's Hospital of the District of Columbia, 261 U.S. 525, 563–64 (1923) (Taft, C.J., dissenting).
23. 208 U.S. 161 (1908). *Adair* held unconstitutional a federal statute prohibiting interstate railroads from discriminating against employees on the basis of union membership.
24. 236 U.S. 1 (1915). *Coppage* held that a Kansas statute forbidding yellow-dog contracts was unconstitutional.
25. 233 U.S. 389 (1914). *German Alliance Insurance Co.* held that a state statute regulating fire insurance premiums was constitutional because the business of fire insurance was affected with a public interest.
26. 250 U.S. 400 (1919). *Arizona Copper Co.* upheld the workmen's compensation statute of the State of Arizona. *See* Mountain Timber Co. v. Washington, 343 U.S. 219 (1917). It must be said that throughout his career McKenna displayed a consistent nationalism with regard to questions of federal power. *See, e.g.*, Champion v. Ames, 188 U.S. 321 (1903); Hipolite Egg Co. v. United States, 220 U.S. 45 (1911); Hoke v. United States, 227 U.S. 308 (1913); Hammer v. Dagenhart, 247 U.S. 251 (1918).
27. *See* Block v. Hirsh, 256 U.S. 135, 158 (1921) (McKenna, J., dissenting); Brown Holding Co. v. Feldman, 256 U.S. 170, 199 (1921) (McKenna, J., dissenting).
28. OWH to Felix Frankfurter (April 20, 1921), in HOLMES-FRANKFURTER CORRESPONDENCE, at 110. Holmes continued: "Have you ever noticed his frequent recurrences to where are you going to draw the line? – a mode of argument that to my mind shows a failure to recognize the fundamental fact that, I think I may say, all questions are ultimately questions of degree. But a Catholic perhaps does not look favorably upon so Darwinian a view."
29. 261 U.S. 525 (1923). *Adkins* struck down a congressional statute establishing a minimum wage for women employees in the District of Columbia.
30. 257 U.S. 312 (1921).
31. "He never was a very strong Judge," commented Taft, "but his present lack of grasp is the result of the failure of age. As his lack of grasp makes him sensitive, it makes him obstinate. I don't know exactly what we are going to do." WHT to Mrs. Frederick J. Manning (March 2, 1924) (Taft papers). McKenna, Taft said, "shows most conclusive signs of inability to master any question." *Id.*

The Taft Court

32. 259 U.S. 296 (1922).
33. Brandeis papers.
34. 258 U.S. 374 (1922).
35. Brandeis papers.
36. *Brandeis-Frankfurter Conversations*, at 326 (August 11, 1923). Charles Sumner Hamlin recorded in his diary that while lunching with his friend James C. McReynolds at the Metropolitan Club on August 21, 1924, McReynolds said "that Judge McKenna was in a fairly good physical condition but 'there was nothing here' (touching his head)." (Hamlin papers).
37. *Brandeis-Frankfurter Conversations*, at 326–27 (August 11, 1923).
38. WHT to Helen Herron Taft (September 25, 1923) (Taft papers).
39. WHT to Charles D. Hillis (September 9, 1922) (Taft papers).
40. WHT to Horace D. Taft (November 2, 1923) (Taft papers). "It is too bad," Taft said, because "McKenna is a good fellow and a good man, a man of high principle, somewhat narrow in view, with a mind that has but little logic in it, a Celtic impressionist he is, but his domestic life has saddened him."

> His wife is very delicate and was never laden with brains, though a sweet woman. She is a constant invalid. A daughter is separated from her husband and is flighty and undependable, though living at home. A son married a daughter of Dick Kearns, a rich Missourian, and at Kearn's instance left the Army, where he now would have been a Colonel or a General. They had a child or two. Then the wife died, and although Kearns was amply able to do so, he made no provision in his will for the son, who has returned to the Army as a Captain, with a blighted career. I think McKenna has one daughter who is well married. But he is depressed and not on good terms with the world, though very anxious to maintain his prestige by not retiring. He is exceedingly sensitive and loses his temper and at times creates little scenes in the Conference. On the other hand, he takes no interest in cases except enough to express an opinion, generally professing that he does not understand it, and writing opinions that have to be amended, cut down and criticized, all to his great impatience.

Id.
41. WHT to Helen Herron Taft (April 5, 1924) (Taft papers).
42. *Id.* "More likely," writes Danelski, "Brandeis was thinking of his good friend Holmes. If McKenna was asked to leave, would not the next step be a request that Holmes, who was older, also retire from the Court?" Danelski, *supra* note 12, at 416. It had become clear, however, that by the end of the 1923 term McKenna was deteriorating to the point of publicly undeniable incompetence. His opinions contained language that was like a "fog. He does not know what he means himself. Certainly no one else does." WHT to Helen Herron Taft (May 8, 1924) (Taft papers). Consider, for example, McKenna's dissent in United States v. New River Co., 265 U.S. 533 (1924): "I am unable to assent and yet I hesitate to dissent, – certainly hesitate to do so by unsupported declaration. I am, however, puzzled to go beyond declaration. Exposition seems to be that of demonstrating the certainty and self-evidence of an axiom." *Id.* at 543 (McKenna, J., dissenting). Of this dissent, Taft wrote his wife: "McKenna, just in order to show that there was life left in him, printed a dissenting opinion in which he differed from the entire Court and made a lot of remarks that seemed to me to be quite inapt and almost ridiculous." WHT to Helen Herron Taft (June 10, 1924) (Taft papers). "I try to give him the easiest cases," Taft fretted, "but nothing is too easy for him. He ought to get off but he never

will until he dies and I think he will outlive several of us." WHT to Helen Herron Taft (May 8, 1924) (Taft papers).
43. WHT to Helen Herron Taft (June 10, 1924) (Taft papers).
44. WHT to Charles P. Taft 2nd (October 5, 1924) (Taft papers). "The poor fellow has had a dreary summer," Brandeis told Frankfurter, "with his wife desperately ill, probably dying now." *Brandeis-Frankfurter Conversations*, at 173 (October 3, 1924).
45. WHT to Robert A. Taft (October 12, 1924) (Taft papers). "Mrs. McKenna ... died last week. The Justice is in very frail health and was ordered away from Washington, and he has gone with one of his daughters. His daughters are anxious to have him retire, and so as [sic] his Doctor, but with the pertinacity that grows with age and with weakness, he still hopes to return, because he does not know what else he could do with his time if he were not on the Bench. Undoubtedly he ought to retire, and I am hoping that his family will induce him to do so." WHT to J.M. Dickinson (October 20, 1924) (Taft papers). At about this time, strangely, articles began to appear in the press that McKenna and Holmes wanted to retire. See *Associate Justices McKenna and Holmes Have Told Friends that They Would Retire Some Time after the Election*, NEW YORK TIMES (November 6, 1924), at 21; *Manton and Crane Mentioned for Supreme Court*, BROOKLYN DAILY TIMES (November 6, 1924) (Taft papers) ("The retirement of Associate Justices McKenna and Holmes from the United States Supreme Court is regarded as imminent in Washington."). The articles provoked Clarke to write Van Devanter that "the N. Y. Times has it that H & McK will both resign before the end of the year. You know without my writing it that I think it high time in the one case especially." JHC to WVD (November 9, 1924) (Van Devanter papers).
46. Memorandum, November 10, 1924 (Taft papers). One justice, not identified by Taft, did not attend the meeting. Taft composed a remarkable memorandum describing the meeting and subsequent events, *id*., which is reprinted in WALTER MURPHY & C. HERMAN PRITCHETT, COURTS, JUDGES, AND POLITICS: AN INTRODUCTION TO THE JUDICIAL PROCESS 199–201 (3d ed., New York: Random House 1979). It is a remarkable document, which begins:

> I think it wise to make a confidential memorandum with reference to an interview which I have just had with Mr. Justice McKenna. For some time the members of the Court have been convinced that Mr. Justice McKenna's continuing on the Bench was not making for his reputation as a Judge, and that he was not doing his work as a member of the Court. Mr. Justice Van Devanter and I talked with Dr. Sterling Ruffin, his physician, who concurred with us that his mental grasp was by no means such as it had been, and that he was not able to do hard, sustained mental work. We consulted last summer in respect to it, and he said he would assist us, but that the Justice was quite determined not to give up, that he valued his association with the Court, and did not know what he would do without the Court. It was thought wise to postpone definite action until after the election, so that if Mr. Coolidge was elected, there would be no question of seeking to have a vacancy to be filled by a new Administration. Justice Van Devanter and I consulted Dr. Ruffin again, and found him quite as emphatic in the wisdom of Mr. Justice McKenna's retirement as he ever was. Mr. Justice McKenna's daughters had spoken of their desire that he should go and live in Boston.

47. *Id*.
48. *Retirement of Mr. Justice McKenna*, 266 U.S. iv, vi (1925).

49. *Stone Is Nominated for Supreme Bench as M'Kenna Resigns*, NEW YORK TIMES (January 6, 1925), at 2. "Don't you resign," McKenna reportedly told Holmes during their last encounter. "You have the right to linger superfluous on the scene." Quoted in Danelski, *supra* note 12, at 425. McKenna died on November 21, 1926. Taft helped arrange the funeral. *See* WHT to Robert A. Taft (November 21, 1926) (Taft papers): "He died in a coma and did not suffer a great deal of pain. I have just been down to his apartment to see his daughters and son to make arrangements for the funeral. He is a retired Justice and we are not in the habit of adjourning in such cases, but as we were so close to him, as he has been so recently in the Court and was so long a member, we have concluded to adjourn tomorrow. ... It loses us a day, but, as Judge Holmes said, it would seem a little shocking when he had almost died in our arms for us not to make a note in open court of his passing."

50. 66 CONG. REC. 1227 (January 5, 1925). There had been rumors of McKenna's impending resignation swirling in the press since at least November. *See Will Leave Supreme Court*, NEW YORK TIMES (November 6, 1924), at 21; *Manton and Crane Mentioned for Supreme Court*, *supra* note 45; *McKenna Expects to Quit High Bench*, CHRISTIAN SCIENCE MONITOR (December 24, 1924), at 4; *Vacancy in U.S. Supreme Court Expected Jan. 1*, CHICAGO DAILY TRIBUNE (December 25, 1924), at 32; *Justice McKenna Expected to Retire*, BOSTON DAILY GLOBE (December 25, 1924), at 8. None of this early speculation mentioned Stone as a possible replacement for McKenna. Instead, the conventional wisdom was that "The Pacific Coast is expected to furnish the successor to Associate Justice McKenna." *Wilbur May Get McKenna's Seat*, BOSTON DAILY GLOBE (December 26, 1924), at 13.

51. Charles Fahey, *Mr. Chief Justice Stone*, 59 HARVARD LAW REVIEW 1196, 1196 (1946).

52. The authoritative biography remains ALPHEUS THOMAS MASON, HARLAN FISKE STONE: PILLAR OF THE LAW (New York: Viking 1956). Book-length treatments of Stone are surprisingly rare. *See, e.g.*, SAMUEL J. KONEFSKY, CHIEF JUSTICE STONE AND THE SUPREME COURT (New York: Macmillan Co. 1945); SAMUEL J. KONEFSKY, MR. JUSTICE STONE AND THE COMMERCE CLAUSE (1938); PETER G. RENSTROM, THE STONE COURT: JUSTICES, RULINGS, AND LEGACY (Santa Barbara: ABC-CLIO 2001); MELVIN I. UROFSKY, DIVISION AND DISCORD: The SUPREME COURT UNDER STONE AND VINSON, 1941–1953 (Columbia: University of South Carolina Press, 1997).

53. "Stone was one of the strong forces in legal education in the twentieth century. Assembling a faculty sometimes boisterously imaginative, he brought the Columbia Law School out of the doldrums." John P. Frank, *Harlan Fiske Stone: An Estimate*, 9 STANFORD LAW REVIEW 621, 624–25 (1957). "At the same time, Stone's basically conservative instincts caused him some alarm at the very progress being made under his aegis. That faculty included Walter Wheeler Cook, Herman Oliphant, Underhill Moore and Robert L. Hale. These were men of immensely dynamic minds. As these men began to create what has become modern legal education, Stone drew back, intimidated and aligned himself vigorously with the most conservative elements of his own faculty. It was Stone who insured that the succession to the deanship after he left would not be in educationally 'liberal' hands,

and it was due to Stone that some of the liveliest minds in legal education eventually left Columbia, taking their unsettling imaginations with them." *Id.* at 625.

54. Harlan F. Stone, *Some Aspects of the Problem of Law Simplification*, 23 COLUMBIA LAW REVIEW 319, 331 (1923). Stone was an early and strong proponent of the American Law Institute's efforts to restate the law. *See id.* at 333–37; Harlan F. Stone, *The Significance of a Restatement of the Law*, 10 PROCEEDINGS OF THE ACADEMY OF POLITICAL SCIENCE IN THE CITY OF NEW YORK 3 (July 1923).

55. HARLAN F. STONE, LAW AND ITS ADMINISTRATION 3 (New York: Columbia University Press 1915).

56. *See* ARTICLES BY HARLAN F. STONE, KENT PROFESSOR OF LAW AND DEAN OF THE FACULTY IN THE COLUMBIA LAW SCHOOL (New York 1922).

57. For a summary, see *Tribute to Retiring Justice McKenna; Stone Named to Succeed Him*, 11 AMERICAN BAR ASSOCIATION JOURNAL 24, 25 (1925) ("*Tribute*").

58. William O. Douglas, *Harlan Fiske Stone – Teacher*, 35 CALIFORNIA LAW REVIEW 4, 4–5 (1947).

59. MASON, *supra* note 52, at 87–90; *Tribute, supra* note 57, at 25.

60. *Tribute, supra* note 57, at 25.

61. MASON, *supra* note 52, at 135–40; Charles C. Burlingham, *Harlan Fiske Stone*, 32 AMERICAN BAR ASSOCIATION JOURNAL 322, 323 (1946). At Sullivan and Cromwell, Stone's assignment was to act "in the same role as John W. Davis does for Stetson, Jennings, Russell and Davis and Ex-Gov. Miller of New York for Miller and Otis." *Tribute, supra* note 57, at 25.

62. Stone believed that in "this process of inundating the Bar by the unfit, immigration in the twenty years preceding the last war has played a conspicuous part," bringing to our shores young men "from southern and eastern Europe ... with no acquaintance and often little sympathy with Anglo-American institutions, and sometimes with moral standards differing from those which have prevailed in Anglo-American communities. They find that membership in the Bar, a position of dignity and importance, difficult of attainment in the countries of their origin, may be secured in this country with comparatively little effort by a brief period of study in a part time law school." Harlan F. Stone, *Some Phases of American Legal Education*, 1 CANADIAN BAR REVIEW 646, 659–60 (1923). *See* Harlan F. Stone, *Legal Education and Democratic Principle*, 7 AMERICAN BAR ASSOCIATION JOURNAL 639 (1921). For a good discussion of the context of Stone's attitudes, see JEROLD S. AUERBACH, UNEQUAL JUSTICE: LAWYERS AND SOCIAL CHANGE IN MODERN AMERICA 40–129 (New York: Oxford University Press 1976).

63. Harlan F. Stone, *After a Quarter Century at the Columbia Law School*, 15 COLUMBIA ALUMNI NEWS 219 (No. 13) (January 11, 1924).

64. STONE, *supra* note 55, at 48.

65. *Id.* Common law rights, wrote Stone, "are the bulwark of the minority against the tyranny of temporary majorities; of the weak against the strong. As a conservative force, the common law, if it would preserve its character as law, can only follow with cautious and somewhat tardy steps the sentiment of the community, in order that it may not mistake the false and the temporary for the real and the permanent." *Id.* at 48–49.

66. *Id.* at 49.

67. Harlan F. Stone, *Obedience to Law and Social Change*, 5 PROCEEDINGS OF THE BAR ASSOCIATION OF THE STATE OF NEW HAMPSHIRE 27, 37–38 (No. 3) (1925).

Distrust of legislation was common among legal elites at this time. *See* Roscoe Pound, *Common Law and Legislation*, 21 HARVARD LAW REVIEW 383, 383 (1908); *infra* Chapter 5, at 169.

68. Stone, *supra* note 67, at 34.
69. "In a single generation our conception of the limitations of space and time have been revolutionized and the sources of physical energy and the methods of its employment have been multiplied many fold." *Id.* at 32. Stone observed to his former clerk Milton Handler in 1929 that "the world has never, in its history, changed quite so rapidly as it has in your day and mine." HFS to Milton Handler (December 4, 1929) (Stone papers).
70. Stone, *supra* note 67, at 33. Stone wrote these lines when he was attorney general and responsible for enforcing prohibition, perhaps the most counterproductive and ineffectual legislation in the history of the nation.
71. STONE, *supra* note 55, at 48. Stone believed that judicial assessments of "the constitutionality of state legislation under the Fourteenth Amendment" presupposed "three main propositions": the power of judicial review; the power to enact the relevant legislation; and an evaluation of whether legislation carries out its "purposes ... in a reasonable and proper manner." *Id.* at 153–54. Although the "first two questions are ... questions of law" and "the third ... largely a question of fact," the third question nevertheless posed issues of fact that it was "the sworn duty of the court to determine ... in accordance with its own best judgment, rather than adopt the judgment of the legislature or what it may conceive to be the popular judgment." *Id.* at 154. Stone feared that excessive deference to legislative judgments of reasonableness would in effect transform legal issues of constitutionality into "political" questions. *Id.* at 155. It would obliterate the point of having constitutional restraints, which is to provide protections that "cannot be removed by temporary majorities or without the deliberate and mature consideration which tends to remove popular passion and prejudice from the settlement of political questions." *Id.* at 156. Stone thus directly challenged Felix Frankfurter, who had contended two years before "that constitutional law, in its relation to social legislation, is not at all a science, but applied politics." Felix Frankfurter, *The Zeitgeist and the Judiciary*, 29 THE SURVEY 543 (1913).
72. STONE, *supra* note 55, at 193. In Stone's eyes the progressive era was "more characterized by fantastic political theories and by vague and impractical aspirations for sudden social reform than have characterized any previous period in our political history." *Id.* at 191. In a preface to Herbert Spencer's essay, *The Sins of the Legislators*, Stone in 1916 remarked that "Spencer's vigorous warning furnished food for thought and will perhaps inspire with caution the zealous advocates of such sweeping legislative changes as are involved in the many proposals for the various types of pension law, and minimum wage statutes, and modern legislation of similar character." Harlan F. Stone, *Mr. Stone's Comments*, in HERBERT SPENCER, THE MAN VERSUS THE STATE 241 (Truxtun Beale, ed., New York: Mitchell Kennerley 1916). Strikingly, William Howard Taft in the same volume observed that our "experiments" in "paternalism" have "vindicated many of the arguments of Mr. Spencer against the enlargement of the state duty into minute social regulations and into a field of affirmative state action." William Howard Taft, *Mr. Taft's Comments*, id. at 343.
73. 201 N.Y. 271 (1911).

74. At the very moment that Stone was defending *Ives*, Brandeis was attacking *Ives* as out of touch with "the facts of life." Louis D. Brandeis, *The Living Law*, 10 ILLINOIS LAW REVIEW 461, 466 (1916). In 1913, Stone participated in a successful effort to amend the New York State Constitution to authorize workmen's compensation laws. *See* JOHN FABIAN WITT, THE ACCIDENTAL REPUBLIC 176 (Cambridge: Harvard University Press 2004); JOHN A. FITCH, THE CAUSES OF INDUSTRIAL UNREST 271-72 (New York: Harpers & Brothers 1924).

75. *See A Charter of Democracy: Address of Hon. Theodore Roosevelt before the Ohio Constitutional Convention* (February 21, 1912), Sen. Doc. No. 348, 62nd CONG. 2nd SESS., at 14-18. Stone was appalled by Roosevelt's suggestion, which he regarded as converting "a legal question" into a "political" one. STONE, *supra* note 55, at 154-57. He would later make similar arguments against the proposal of Senator La Follette in the 1924 presidential campaign to allow for congressional override of Supreme Court decisions. *See* William H. Crawford, *La Follette Plan Called a Menace*, NEW YORK TIMES (October 2, 1924), at 4 ("The function of determining these grave questions are essentially judicial in character. . . . They should not be influenced by political clamor or by the passions aroused by political partisanship."). Stone articulated a similar critique of proposals for judicial recall. *See* Harlan F. Stone, *The Issues Involved in the Methods of Selecting and Removing Judges*, 3 PROCEEDINGS OF THE ACADEMY OF POLITICAL SCIENCE IN THE CITY OF NEW YORK ("Efficient Government") 80 (January 1913) (Recall of judges is a great step "not only toward pure democracy, but toward shifting the law, wherever it affects in the same way any considerable number of people, from its semi-scientific basis, as developed by the skill and professional learning of the magistrate and of the legal profession generally, to a political basis.").

76. STONE, *supra* note 55, at 152. Stone's stance was so conservative that the *New Republic* savagely dismissed his book as "devoted to the . . . pious aim of 'contributing to the cause of good citizenship' by strengthening the traditional American faith that God can govern his chosen people only through a constitution, courts, and lawyers." 11 NEW REPUBLIC 127 (1917).

> In recent years shameless skepticism in regard to this faith has raised its head; and this has brought forth a large number of devotional books which, like the one before us, contain just enough information to justify the ways of the Law and the Lawyers to man. . . .
>
> The noble purpose of these books does not call for much original knowledge or novelty; and Dean Stone has in that respect wisely followed the pattern set by ex-President Taft. . . . As the dean of one of our large law schools, however, he has felt peculiarly called upon to rebuke the adherents of sociologic jurisprudence who would make judicial decisions in regard to large public questions depend upon the fallible and sometimes hasty human sciences of sociology and economics, instead of recognizing that a training in the law and elevation to the bench must be sufficient if we are to maintain our system of government. Why need the Supreme Court find out from lay experts the exact hygienic effects of working more than ten hours in a bakery, when it can readily settle the matter by listening to two lawyers? As law embodies only the wisdom of the past, there is an irrefutable presumption against all *modern* theories as to economic or social justice.

Id. William O. Douglas once sought to explain Stone's early constitutional conservatism by his background in private law subjects. "The courses which

Stone taught – personal property, trusts, and mortgages – did not have the reach of public law courses," Douglas said. "They are subjects which lend themselves more readily to conceptualistic treatment." Douglas, *supra* note 58, at 6.

77. *Coolidge Picks New Yorker*, NEW YORK TIMES (April 3, 1924), at 1.
78. *Id. See Charges of Illegal Practices of the Department of Justice*, Hearings before a Subcomm. of the Comm. on the Judiciary of the United States Senate, 66th CONG. 3rd SESS. (February 1, 1921), at 279–80; *Dr. Stone Asks Full Inquiry on Palmer's Raids*, NEW YORK TRIBUNE (February 2, 1921), at 4. In 1919, Stone called upon the bar "to scrutinize critically and jealously those laws whose enactment in principle was doubtless necessary to the prosecution of a great war, which encroach upon the field of individual liberty in placing restrictions upon the free expression of opinion and the free communication of information and the expression of ideas.... [I]n the long run there is greater danger to human progress in the arbitrary repression of truth than in freedom to disseminate falsehood." Harlan F. Stone, *The Lawyer and His Neighbors*, 4 CORNELL LAW QUARTERLY 175, 187 (1919).
79. *See* Harlan F. Stone, *University Influence*, 10 COLUMBIA UNIVERSITY QUARTERLY (October 1918), at 330–39; Harold Leventhal, *Harlan Fiske Stone*, 49 NEW YORK STATE BAR JOURNAL 24, 58 (January 1977). Stone retained a "deep antipathy" toward Butler. Milton C. Handler, *Clerking for Justice Harlan Fiske Stone*, 1995 JOURNAL OF SUPREME COURT HISTORY 113, 115. Stone also objected to a proposal to prohibit socialist law students from receiving diplomas. *See Want Law Schools to Bar Socialists*, NEW YORK TIMES (April 4, 1920), at E1.
80. Stone investigated the reasons behind the conscientious objections of individual draftees. We have one firsthand account of his style of interrogation:

> The little room was filled with men in uniform. Dean Stone sat at a table, with a stenographer next to him....
>
> Dean Stone, sharp-eyed, keen, fired questions at me for twenty minutes. I stood in the center of the floor, hat in hand, and my wet, muddy shoes left a pool on the floor.... What I recall most vividly is ... the swift, sharp questions of the Dean rapped out one after the other with the precision of hammer-blows. But I remember that the chief argument centered about the distinction between force and warfare.
>
> "You are a member of no church?"
>
> "No, sir."
>
> "Socialist?"
>
> "I share many of their beliefs, but I am not a member of the party."
>
> "What would you do if you were attacked, or a burglar entered your house and tried to rape your wife or mother?"
>
> "Resist him. Try to save my wife."
>
> "Then how can you maintain your position in opposition to war? You sanction the use of force."
>
> "I see no analogy whatever in your comparison. I can't concede that this is a defensive war, or that the issue can be stated as simply as your burglar illustration suggests." ...
>
> "I consider you a political objector," he said, "one of those men who believes himself wiser and better informed than any man in the country. That is all."

Joseph McKenna & Harlan Fiske Stone

ERNEST L. MEYER, "HEY! YELLOWBACKS!" THE WAR DIARY OF A CONSCIENTIOUS OBJECTOR 92–95 (New York: John Day Co. 1930).
81. Harlan F. Stone, *The Conscientious Objector*, 21 COLUMBIA UNIVERSITY QUARTERLY 253, 269 (No. 4) (October 1919). *See* Harlan F. Stone, *Remarks*, 1 RECORD OF THE ASSOCIATION OF THE BAR OF THE CITY OF NEW YORK 144, 147 (No. 4) (May 1946) (discussing a 1920 debate about whether five socialist members of the New York State Assembly should be expelled).
82. FRANCIS RUSSELL, THE SHADOW OF A BUDDING GROVE: WARREN G. HARDING IN HIS TIMES 117–22, 245–46, 337 (New York: McGraw-Hill Book Co. 1968).
83. DAVID J. GOLDBERG, DISCONTENTED AMERICA: THE UNITED STATES IN THE 1920S at 49 (Baltimore: Johns Hopkins University Press 1999). In 1922, Frankfurter was moved to observe that "There is probably agreement by informed professional opinion that in the history of this country there never has been a more unlearned and professionally less equipped Attorney General than Harry M. Daugherty." FELIX FRANKFURTER, LAW AND POLITICS: OCCASIONAL PAPERS OF FELIX FRANKFURTER 1913–1938, at 220 (Archibald MacLeish & E. F. Prichard, Jr., eds., New York: Harcourt, Brace and Co. 1939).
84. Burns had developed the case against the McNamara brothers in the famous Los Angeles bombing case. EDWIN E. WITTE, THE GOVERNMENT IN LABOR DISPUTES 162 (New York: McGraw-Hill Book Co. 1932).
85. JAMES N. GIGLIO, H.M. DAUGHERTY AND THE POLITICS OF EXPEDIENCY 130, 171 (Kent State University Press 1978).
86. These scandals included Teapot Dome as well as the many allegations against Charles Forbes's administration of the Veterans' Bureau.
87. GIGLIO, *supra* note 85, at 168–70.
88. MASON, *supra* note 52, at 143. *See* Lauson H. Stone, *My Father the Chief Justice*, 1978 YEARBOOK OF THE SUPREME COURT HISTORICAL SOCIETY 7, 11. Herbert Hoover, by contrast, attributed Stone's selection to the recommendation of Coolidge's close friend and Amherst college classmate Dwight Morrow. HERBERT HOOVER, THE MEMOIRS OF HERBERT HOOVER: THE CABINET AND THE PRESIDENCY: 1920–1933, at 54 (New York: MacMillan Co. 1952). Hoover reported that he had recommended that Coolidge replace Daugherty with former New York Governor Nathan Miller, who declined for financial reasons. *Id.* In his unpublished *Recollections*, Miller confirms this, writing that "In 1924 President Coolidge tendered me an appointment as Attorney General, saying that if I would accept he would consult Senator Borah and other members of the Judiciary Committee of the Senate and see if he could get me confirmed. I replied that if he thought that necessary there did not seem to be any call for me to make the sacrifice required. If he had proposed to send my name to the Senate, I should have consented." (Miller papers at the University of Syracuse). Taft recommended Judge George A. Carpenter for the position. WHT to Calvin Coolidge (March 19, 1924) (Taft papers); WHT to Horace D. Taft (March 6, 1924) (Taft papers). Carpenter had been appointed to the federal judiciary by Taft.
89. WHT to Helen Herron Taft (April 3, 1924) (Taft papers). By contrast, Brandeis wrote Frankfurter, "I am glad you think well of Stone. I am sure some would like to make a vacancy for him on the Court. But, even if one came, it is question[able]

whether he, as a Morgan man, could get the votes before Nov[.], or after if C[alvin] C[oolidge] is beaten." LDB to Felix Frankfurter (April 6, 1924), in BRANDEIS-FRANKFURTER CORRESPONDENCE, at 163.

90. In 1940, Attorney General Robert Jackson remarked that Stone became attorney general "at a time when the country felt actually unsafe because of the misuse that had been made of [the Department of Justice's] powers. . . . He cleansed house and accomplished a quiet regeneration of the Department of Justice. He reorganized the Federal Bureau of Investigation, on a professional basis, and properly confined its activities to investigation of violations of Federal law. He brought into the service of the Government clean, energetic, non-political lawyers, many of whom are with us still." *Address at the 20th Anniversary Dinner of the Federal Bar Association* (January 23, 1940), APPENDIX TO THE CONGRESSIONAL RECORD, 76th CONG. 3rd SESS., at 310. Mabel Willebrandt, who served as an assistant attorney general from 1921 to 1929, noted that "During the short time that Justice Stone was Attorney General he probably won for all time the record for cleaning out more politically evasive Department of Justice officials than anyone else in a similar period. Pop! Pop! Went his guns almost every day. Frequently politicians were hit. . . . He reorganized the prosecuting offices in Massachusetts, New Jersey, Montana, northern Mississippi, southern Alabama, southern Georgia, eastern Louisiana and northern California." MABEL WALKER WILLEBRANDT, THE INSIDE OF PROHIBITION 140 (Indianapolis: Bobbs-Merrill Co. 1929). *See* Eric Shepard, *Why Harlan Fiske Stone (Also) Matters*, 56 HOWARD LAW JOURNAL 85, 97–104 (2012).

91. "In his brief incumbency of the office of less than a year, [Stone] has abolished the most obnoxious abuses where they were operating in full blast under Daugherty and has restored the Department of Justice to its proper, constitutional function. He has done this quietly, as one of his training and academic inclinations would be sure to do." *Mr. Stone's Appointment*, ST. LOUIS POST-DISPATCH (January 7, 1925), at 16. Stone was widely praised as a "fearless administrator." *Stone Is Promoted to Supreme Bench as McKenna Resigns*, NEW YORK HERALD TRIBUNE (January 6, 1925), at 1. *See Stone Is Nominated for McKenna's Seat on Supreme Court*, WASHINGTON POST (January 6, 1925), at 1. Stone later wrote that "I feel in my bones that I have done a good deal to show a lot of people who ought to know, but don't, what can be done for good government in this country." HFS to W.S. Booth (January 20, 1925) (Stone papers). Taft found Stone's work as attorney general to be "very satisfactory." WHT to Charles D. Hilles (December 3, 1924) (Taft papers).

92. Brandeis reports as early as November 20 that Stone was to be tapped as McKenna's replacement. "The Dept. of Justice says the A. G. is slated for the S. C." LDB to Felix Frankfurter (November 20, 1924), in BRANDEIS-FRANKFURTER CORRESPONDENCE, at 182. On December 4, Stone wrote his son Marshall that "Confidentially there is much prospect that I may go on to the Supreme Court by the first of the year. Both the President and Chief Justice have talked about it and I think it is likely to happen if the President can get a new Attorney General to his liking." HFS to Marshall Stone (December 4, 1924), quoted in MASON, *supra* note 52, at 179. Charles Burlingham recounts that Stone had initially recommended Cardozo for the position. Burlingham, *supra* note 61, at 323. Brandeis reports that according to Stone "Coolidge objected to appointing Cardoza [sic] because he didn't want two Jews on the bench." LDB to Felix Frankfurter (January 11, 1930), in

Joseph McKenna & Harlan Fiske Stone

BRANDEIS-FRANKFURTER CORRESPONDENCE, at 406. According to Burlingham, sometime in November Coolidge countered Stone's suggestion of Cardozo with his own intention to nominate Stone. In early January, Van Devanter wrote lumber baron F.L. Finkenstaedt that "The Attorney General has been clearing his desk for two or three weeks preparatory to his selection as a member of our court." WVD to F.L. Finkenstaedt (January 6, 1925) (Van Devanter papers). Decades later, Stone recalled that "it had been agreed with the President a few days before [my nomination] that I was to have the appointment." HFS to Children (November 24, 1939) (Stone papers).

93. WHT to Alfred Holman (January 9, 1925) (Taft papers). "He comes from New York, which has no representative on our Bench. The President was intimately advised of Mr. Stone's qualifications and acted promptly.... I can say to you confidentially that there was a good deal of feeling of fear that the President might think it necessary to take his Secretary of the Navy [Curtis Wilbur, former Chief Justice of the California Supreme Court]." *Id.* On Wilber, see *Stone Nominated for M'Kenna Post in Supreme Court,* NEW YORK WORLD (January 6, 1925), at 1. In the Coolidge papers there is a letter to the president from Nicholas Murray Butler dated December 9, 1924, in which Butler writes: "Ever since my last visit to the White House I have been thinking anxiously over one of the most important questions upon which you touched, namely the sort of man who might be available in this State, if in the not distant future an appointment is to be made to the United States Supreme Court." Butler recommended William D. Guthrie, Benjamin Cardozo, and Harlan Stone. He considered Guthrie too old and intimated that "Cardozo's religious and racial associations" were "an insuperable objection." Nicholas Murray Butler to Calvin Coolidge (December 9, 1924) (Coolidge papers).

94. WHT to Robert A. Taft (July 2, 1925) (Taft papers). Much later, in 1939, Stone confirmed that Taft had indeed informed him "at the time that [Taft] had recommended my appointment to the President." But Stone went on to observe that "I think it can hardly be said that [Taft] 'forced' it. Coolidge had little liking for Taft's well-developed propensity for telling him what he, Taft, thought he should do." HFS to Children (November 24, 1939) (Stone papers). *See* HFS to Thomas Reed Powell (January 30, 1940) (Stone papers). *But see* ROBERT SOBEL, COOLIDGE: AN AMERICAN ENIGMA 266 (Washington D.C.: Regnery Publishing 1998) (Coolidge "had formed a strong relationship" with Taft).

95. HFS to Marshall Stone (January 9, 1925) (Stone papers).

96. *Warren Is Slated for Stone's Place,* NEW YORK WORLD (January 10, 1925), at 1.

97. Herbert L. Satterlee, the senior partner at Stone's firm, was the son-in-law of the elder J.P. Morgan.

98. Ownbey v. Morgan, 256 U.S. 94 (1921). Stone later reminisced that in deciding whether to attend Columbia Law School, a member of the bar had told him if he went to law school, he "would begin by studying law as it was at the time when the Scots came across the border to raid peaceful England, and he added, 'of course, you would never win cases with such stuff.'"

> It gave me some satisfaction in later years to send to the giver of this good advice, a copy of a brief in which I succeeded in persuading the Supreme Court that the attachment laws of Delaware were in accordance with the due process of the Fourteenth Amendment and constitutional for the reason that they were

founded upon the ancient custom of London. This custom, I was able to show as a result of some historical research, was in accordance with the settled principles of English common law procedure going back to the time when the Scots "crossed the border," so that my friend may now be persuaded that the historical aspect of legal doctrine is the "stuff" with which cases may be won on occasion.

Stone, *supra* note 63, at 219.

99. *Committee Approves Stone's Nomination*, NEW YORK TIMES (January 20, 1925), at 2. It did not prevent Senator James Thomas Heflin from declaiming, "No lawyer's duty to his client will warrant him in doing anything that violates the fundamental principles of justice. No lawyer's duty to his client will require him or justify him in invoking technicalities which, if sustained, will deny to the American citizen in the courts of the country his personal and property rights." 66 CONG. REC. 2508 (January 27, 1925).

100. HFS to W.S. Booth (January 20, 1925) (Stone papers).

101. Stone "has done remarkable things in a quiet and unostentatious way in the reorganization of the Attorney General's department. He is honest and able ... The one thing about him which we cannot understand is that he has connived at the indictment of Senator Wheeler; he has refused to insist that this disgusting prostitution of the machinery of justice in Montana, at the instigation of members of the Republican National Committee, be ended." 120 THE NATION 27 (1925). Felix Frankfurter thought that Stone had "continued on lame grounds an indictment which I thought had been most outrageously brought to pass by his corrupt predecessor." FELIX FRANKFURTER REMINISCES: RECORDED IN TALKS WITH DR. HARLAN B. PHILLIPS 190 (New York: Reynal & Co. 1960).

102. *Stone Will Push Action on Wheeler*, NEW YORK TIMES (January 29, 1925), at 2.

103. Albert W. Fox, *Confirmation of Stone Is Jeopardized by Case Here against Wheeler*, WASHINGTON POST (January 24, 1925), at 1.

104. The fullest account of Stone's testimony is in *Stone Will Push Action on Wheeler*, *supra* note 102. Stone's decision to indict Wheeler in the District of Columbia was taken upon the recommendation of Assistant Attorney General William Donovan, Stone's former student, to whom he had given the case for review upon becoming attorney general. *Id*. There is no doubt, however, that Stone endorsed Donovan's conclusions. "Confidentially, you may be interested to know that this inquiry shows that a crime has *undoubtedly* been committed here in an effort to defraud the United States. The evidence of it which would have to be submitted to a grand jury will implicate Senator Wheeler." HFS to Luther E. Smith (January 26, 1925) (Stone papers) (emphasis added). Taft had a low opinion of Donovan, who he said had "fooled Stone." WHT to Robert A. Taft (June 7, 1925) (Taft papers). Brandeis also considered Donovan "a continuing source of danger in many fields." LDB to Felix Frankfurter (January 28, 1930), in BRANDEIS-FRANKFURTER CORRESPONDENCE, at 409. Sutherland thought Donovan "not dependable." GS to WHT (January 25, 1926) (Taft papers). During World War II, Donovan would become the head of the Office of Strategic Services.

105. Albert W. Fox, *Stone Tells Senate Committee He Assumes Full Responsibility for Pressing New Wheeler Case*, WASHINGTON POST (January 29, 1925), at 1. Stone wrote his erstwhile Columbia colleague and law partner that "Of course, I have understood for some time back that this fight was in the offing, but I have been

afraid that it might not come during my term of office. However, the Senators saw to that. I did not, however, foresee that they would deliver themselves into my hands as completely as they did." Stone to G.F. Canfield (January 31, 1925) (Stone papers). Stone's "understanding" of the coming fight should be contrasted to his January 20 letter to W.S. Booth, *supra* note 100; and to his January 9 letter to his son Marshall Stone, *supra* note 95.

106. *Mr. Stone Will Be Confirmed*, DULUTH HERALD (February 2, 1925), at 14. Wheeler's defense counsel in the Department of Justice prosecutions was Senator Thomas J. Walsh, also of Montana. Walsh, a member of the Judiciary Committee, cross-examined Stone during his testimony, which, according to the *Washington Post*, left the public "aghast":

> The Senate has permitted itself to be drawn into a proceeding that constitutes an attack upon the due and orderly administration of justice. This attack cannot be continued and its purpose cannot be consummated without arousing furious and righteous popular resentment against the Senate. . . .
>
> The Senate allowed itself to be drawn into yesterday's astounding proceeding, in which the Attorney General was called to the stand and cross-questioned by the counsel of the man soon to be under grand jury investigation. The cross-questioning was done, not by the counsel in his capacity as counsel, but in his official capacity as a Senator and a member of the Committee on Judiciary, pronouncing upon the qualifications of a Presidential nominee to the highest court in the land.

Thank God for a MAN!, WASHINGTON POST (January 29, 1925), at 6. For an account of the collapse of opposition to Stone's nomination, see Albert W. Fox, *Fight Upon Stone Collapses*, WASHINGTON POST (January 30, 1925), at 1. Stone himself wrote that "The coyotes have been trying to bite me, but I think they have only broken their teeth." HFS to Nathan Abbott (February 3, 1925) (Stone papers). Taft observed to his brother that Walsh's cross-examination of Stone created "an utterly indefensible situation. It caused such a severe criticism in the press that they all abandoned any hope of stopping Stone's confirmation, and that will come in the course of a week, I have no doubt." WHT to Horace D. Taft (February 4, 1925) (Taft papers). *See* HFS to Marshall Stone (February 4, 1925) (Stone papers) ("The papers the country over seem to have taken my part, and the talk now is that the Senate is likely to confirm me this week. I do not know whether they will or not, but I am not worrying about it."). For Walsh's defense of his cross-examination, see 66 CONG. REC. 3033–42 (February 5, 1925).

107. *Mr. Stone's Vindication*, BALTIMORE SUN (February 7, 1925), at 10.

108. *The Flurry over Stone*, NEW YORK WORLD (January 28, 1925), at 12. "A little temporary political flurry produced by ignorance of practical politics should not deprive the country of a man apparently destined to be a great Judge." *Id. See* 41 NEW REPUBLIC 311 (1925): "It is not that anyone doubts either Mr. Stone's rigid personal integrity or his profound legal attainments, but his absence of political flair or instinct is so complete as to be embarrassing to his best friends. The contrast between him and Daugherty is curiously striking. No one with any sense thinks there was anything sinister or dark or political in Mr. Stone's procedure in Washington against Senator Wheeler, just at the time the Senate was considering the confirmation of his appointment to the Supreme

Court. It may or may not have been the right thing to do, but certainly Mr. Stone thought it right and thought it his duty to proceed. There is no question that he made a good impression upon the Senate committee before which he appeared and which subjected him to a right rigid cross-examination. But, politically, it was a silly thing to do. ... 'He may be a great lawyer,' said one friend of the President the other day, 'but he is certainly a damned dummy politically.'"

There persists to this day the hypothesis that Stone might have been "kicked upstairs" because of his innocent and vigorous pursuit of politically explosive anti-trust litigation against Treasury Secretary Andrew Mellon's Aluminum Company of America. JULES ABELS, IN THE TIME OF SILENT CAL 64 (New York: G.P. Putnam's Sons 1969); DONALD R. MCCOY, CALVIN COOLIDGE: THE QUIET PRESIDENT 276 (New York: MacMillan Co. 1967); John W. Johnson, *Harlan Fiske Stone*, in BIOGRAPHICAL ENCYCLOPEDIA OF THE SUPREME COURT: THE LIVES AND LEGAL PHILOSOPHIES OF THE JUSTICES 494 (Melvin I. Urofsky, ed., Washington D.C.: CQ Press 2006). *See, e.g., Mr. Stone and the Aluminum Trust*, BALTIMORE SUN (February 8, 1925), at 8; *Justice Knows No Brother*, THE OUTLOOK (February 18, 1925), at 246; *The Trust Row within the Cabinet*, 84 LITERARY DIGEST 12 (February 28, 1925); but see Stone, *supra* note 88, at 11–12. Stone's successor as attorney general, John Sargent, promptly exonerated the Aluminum Company of guilt. ABELS, *supra*, at 64.

109. *Admits Law Fails to Cover Wheeler*, NEW YORK TIMES (December 1, 1925), at 6.
110. *Court Throws Out Wheeler Charges*, NEW YORK TIMES (December 30, 1925), at 1. See 45 NEW REPUBLIC 200 (1926). The government declined to appeal. Wheeler was also exonerated by a jury on the charges brought against him in Montana. See 42 NEW REPUBLIC 274 (1925); 42 NEW REPUBLIC 57 (1925). The government's case was weak and likely trumped up. For a good account of both criminal proceedings, see Richard T. Ruetten, Burton K. Wheeler, 1905–25: An Independent Liberal under Fire 112–95 (M.A. Thesis, University of Oregon 1957); Ray O. Beezley, The Political Career of Burton K. Wheeler 13–36 (M.A. Thesis, University of Southern California 1951).
111. Wheeler later recalled that Wyoming "Senator Kendrick informed me he had asked Stone point-blank why" Stone had pursued such weak indictments. Stone replied, "They lied to me." Wheeler understood the reply to refer "to Donovan." BURTON K. WHEELER with Paul F. Healy, YANKEE FROM THE WEST: THE CANDID, TURBULENT LIFE STORY OF THE YANKEE-BORN U.S. SENATOR FROM MONTANA 243 (Garden City: Doubleday & Co. 1962); on Donovan, see *supra* note 104. Although it is true that at the Department of Justice Stone was forced to rely on many Daugherty hold-overs who hated Wheeler, see Basil Manly, *Justice Stone and Senator Wheeler*, 42 NEW REPUBLIC 318 (1925), it is nevertheless hard to understand how Stone failed to appreciate the legal inadequacy of the indictment. See HFS to Luther E. Smith (January 26, 1925) (Stone papers); *supra* note 104. The puzzle of "the attitude of Attorney General Stone in the Wheeler case" remained unresolved for many contemporary observers. *See, e.g.*, 120 THE NATION 131 (1925).
112. *Committee Approves Nomination of Stone*, NEW YORK TIMES (February 3, 1925), at 2.

113. 66 CONG. REC. 3057 (February 5, 1925); *Stone Is Confirmed*, LOS ANGELES TIMES (February 6, 1925), at 1. Neither Wheeler nor Walsh recorded a vote. Stone wrote his erstwhile partner William Nelson Cromwell: "I know you would enjoy having me tell you all the details, but the outcome of the matter is that the radical Democratic wing of the Senate which has been riding this Department for some years, have ridden to a fall and the country seems delighted. The editorial notices of the papers of both parties from here to the Pacific Coast are chuckling over it and praising me far beyond my deserts [sic]." HFS to William Nelson Cromwell (February 6, 1925) (Stone papers).
114. JCM to HFS (February 7, 1925) (Stone papers).
115. *Stone Takes Place on Supreme Bench*, NEW YORK TIMES (March 3, 1925), at 1.
116. 304 U.S. 144, 152 n.4 (1938).
117. Handler, *supra* note 79, at 115. At the time of Stone's nomination, Felix Frankfurter observed to Learned Hand, "If Stone is a liberal, so is Sutherland, so is Pierce Butler." Quoted in BRAD SNYDER, DEMOCRATIC JUSTICE: FELIX FRANKFURTER, THE SUPREME COURT, AND THE MAKING OF THE LIBERAL ESTABLISHMENT 156 (New York: W.W. Norton & Co. 2022).
118. 274 U.S. 357 (1927). For a discussion of the case, see PHILIPPA STRUM, SPEAKING FREELY: WHITNEY V. CALIFORNIA AND AMERICAN SPEECH LAW (Lawrence: University Press of Kansas 2015).
119. Stone voted with the majority in conference.
120. 279 U.S. 644 (1929). In *Schwimmer* the Court upheld the government's refusal to naturalize Rozika Schwimmer because she had declined to pledge to take up arms in defense of the United States. Schwimmer, who was 49 at the time, asserted that she was "an uncompromising pacifist." *Id.* at 648. Ironically given Stone's work on the Board of Inquiry during World War I, see *supra* text at note 80, Butler's opinion for the Court stressed the analogy between Schwimmer and the many "pacifists and conscientious objectors" who undermined the war effort. 279 U.S. at 652. Although Stone voted with the majority in conference, he also insisted on certain changes to Butler's draft opinion. Memorandum from HFS to Pierce Butler (May 23, 1929) (Stone papers). Stone's suggestions, which were largely accepted by Butler, chiefly stressed that Schwimmer's refusal to pledge armed support of the United States was dangerous because of its potential effect on others who might be influenced by her views. In the Stone papers there is a delphic letter from Stone to Walter Wheeler Cook (October 9, 1930), stating that "I have ideas of my own [that] I regret that I did not seize the opportunity to express ... in the Schwimmer case." *See* HFS to Walter Wheeler Cook (October 9, 1930) (Stone papers). For a discussion of the case, see Megan Threlkeld, *Citizenship, Gender, and Conscience:* United States v. Schwimmer, 40 JOURNAL OF SUPREME COURT HISTORY 154 (2015). As late as 1931, Thomas Reed Powell could observe that "Mr. Justice Stone is like the former Mr. Justice Clarke in breaking with Justice Holmes and Brandeis on issues of freedom of speech and association, though otherwise they are usually found in the same camp." T.R. Powell, *Supreme Court and State Police Power 1922–1930 – III*, 17 VIRGINIA LAW REVIEW 765, 788–89 (1931).
121. Holmes's dissent became an instant classic: "Some of her answers might excite popular prejudice, but if there is any principle of the Constitution that more imperatively calls for attachment than any other it is the principle of free thought – not free thought for those who agree with us but freedom for the thought that we

hate." 279 U.S. at 654–55 (Holmes, J., dissenting). See *Treason to Conscience*, 128 THE NATION 689 (1929). Holmes himself had nothing but contempt for Schwimmer's pacifism. While the case was still under submission, he wrote Harold Laski, "All 'isms' seem to me silly – but this hyperaethereal respect for human life seems perhaps the silliest of all." OWH to Harold Laski (April 13, 1929), in 2 HOLMES-LASKI CORRESPONDENCE, at 1146. Schwimmer wrote Holmes to thank him for his dissent, to which Holmes somewhat ponderously replied that "you never must thank a judge." "If his decision was of a kind to deserve thanks, he would not be doing his duty. A case is simply a problem to be solved, although the considerations are more complex than those of mathematics. Even when as in your case it was only to interpret a statute, Madam, you appreciate that the opinion of the majority simply meant that they did the sum differently – that duty and reason seemed to them to require a different answer from that which the minority reached. After which protestation, I must add that of course I am gratified by your more than kind expression, and that I thank you." OWH to Rozika Schwimmer (January 30, 1930) (Holmes papers). From Taft's point of view, the "question" in the Schwimmer case was "not what the law of naturalization ought to be, but what it [is] by a statute of Congress, and no matter what it ought to be, we have to stick to the text." WHT to Annie Roelker (July 4, 1929) (Taft papers).
122. 275 U.S. 78 (1927). For a discussion of *Gong Lum,* see *infra* Chapter 43, at 1437–51.
123. In 1915, Stone commented about the Fourteenth Amendment: "Overmuch attention has been given by some writers and critics of the judicial interpretation of the amendment to the fact that the immediate occasion for the passage of the Fourteenth Amendment was the necessity of protecting the slaves lately freed by the Thirteenth Amendment from unjust and discriminatory legislation of the states. Whatever the immediate occasion and purpose of the amendment, it is hardly to be supposed that language so general and unrestricted as that incorporated into our governmental charter should be limited in its interpretation by such considerations, or that the rights and immunities guaranteed to the negro by its provisions could not be availed of by the white man should occasion arise." STONE, *supra* note 55, at 143.
124. *Id.* at 146.
125. A.H. Ulm, *New Supreme Justice Won Spurs as Scholar*, NEW YORK TIMES (January 11, 1925), at XX4. "When Stone was appointed to the U.S. Supreme Court, the intention was that he would buttress the conservative wing. His early years on the Court would indicate that he did not disappoint his sponsors." Frederick J. Hertz, *Review of* HARLAN FISKE STONE: PILLAR OF THE LAW, 38 CHICAGO BAR RECORD 475, 475 (No. 10) (September 1957). Stone was "the man who fooled nearly everyone." *God Save the United States and This Honorable Court,* 13 FORTUNE 82 (May 1936). *See* HFS to WHT (August 4, 1924) (Taft papers).
126. WHT to Robert A. Taft (July 2, 1925) (Taft papers). Taft's judgment was no doubt influenced by the fact that "[w]hen Stone was Attorney General he was anxious to know" Taft's advice with respect to the judicial nominations. WHT to Robert A. Taft (May 3, 1925) (Taft papers).
127. WHT to Charles P. Taft (March 27, 1925) (Taft papers).
128. WHT to Clarence H. Kelsey (June 2, 1925) (Taft papers). The dour McReynolds, by contrast, was not so sure. He wrote Jacob M. Dickinson that "Stone, who is to come on our bench, is rather an unknown quantity. Something of the schoolmaster

seems to cling to him. His constitutional views are matters of doubt." JCM to J.M. Dickinson (February 5, 1925) (Dickinson papers at the Tennessee State Library & Archives). Brandeis shared McReynolds's uncertainties. He wrote Frankfurter that what Stone "will be on the Court 'only the event will teach us in its hour.'" LDB to Felix Frankfurter (January 7, 1925), in BRANDEIS-FRANKFURTER CORRESPONDENCE, at 188.

129. Alfred McCormack, *A Law Clerk's Recollections*, 46 COLUMBIA LAW REVIEW 710, 710 (1946). *See* Stone to Sons (October 19, 1925) (Stone papers). When he first came on the bench, Stone dutifully advocated with Coolidge for the appointment of judicial candidates favored by Van Devanter and Butler. WVD to Walter H. Sanborn (March 16, 1925) (Van Devanter papers).

130. STONE, *supra* note 55, at 41–42; Stone, *Some Aspects of the Problem of Law Simplification*, *supra* note 54, at 327–28; Harlan F. Stone, *Book Review of B. Cardozo, The Nature of the Judicial Process*, 22 COLUMBIA LAW REVIEW 382, 384–85 (1922).

131. McCormack, *supra* note 129, at 714–16.

132. On Holmes's scholarship, see the anecdote recounted by Milton Handler in Handler, *supra* note 79, at 117–19, in which Handler recalls how Holmes offered Stone Holmes's own translation of a passage in a fifteenth-century Yearbook that Holmes had in his personal library, a translation which Stone considered essential to his own opinion in Hudson v. United States, 272 U.S. 451 (1926) (holding that a court could impose a prison sentence after accepting a plea of *nolo contendere*). *See* HFS to Wharton Pepper (February 13, 1935) (Stone papers) (Holmes was "I think, just a little disgusted at the thought that anyone in our Court had to have anybody confirm his translation of the Year Books."); Testimony of Stone, J., *Legislative Establishment Appropriation Bill, 1931* (April 4, 1930), Hearings before Subcommittee of House Committee on Appropriations, 71st CONG. 2nd SESS., at 235 (The case "turned on the effect of a plea of nolo contendere in a criminal case in the Federal courts. Of course that turned on what the plea nolo contendere was, as we took it over from the English law. . . . The determination of the question ultimately turned on the translation of a case in the Year Books in the time of Henry VII.").

133. Upon receiving a draft of Holmes's opinion in *Beech-Nut Packing Co. v. P. Lorillard* Co., 273 U.S. 629 (1927), Stone wrote the senior justice, "Yes Sir. You are the despair of me. When I read an opinion like this I feel like taking up ditch-digging or carpentry or a more suitable occupation." (Holmes papers).

134. "'Holmes and Butler had another spat today,' he would say on returning from conference, and then he would tell the story, as of a case that the Court had debated at several sessions, Holmes and Butler carrying the opposing arguments, until finally Butler's position was accepted with only Holmes dissenting. Then Butler turned to Holmes and said with great solemnity, 'I am glad we have finally arrived at a *just* decision.' 'Hell,' snapped back Holmes, 'Hell is paved with *just* decisions.'" McCormack, *supra* note 129, at 713.

135. *Id.* at 714.

136. 261 U.S. 525 (1923). The case, Murphy v. Sardell, 269 U.S. 530 (1925), involved a summary affirmance of a lower court decision. For the reaction of the *New Republic*, see *Tightening the Bonds*, 44 NEW REPUBLIC 271–72 (1925) ("Again Mr. Justice Holmes and Mr. Justice Brandeis plough their lone furrows. . . . This is

the first case involving a show of colors by Mr. Justice Stone on social legislation. He aligns himself with the majority without reservations. It is too early to assign him a durable place on the spectrum of the Court's range of social opinion. But one's expectations of him in this most vital field of constitutional determinations ought not to be pitched high."). Reading the article, Harold Laski wrote Holmes that he was "immensely interested to note that your colleague Harlan Stone has sided with the conservative party of the court. It is a great pity." Harold Laski to OWH (November 10, 1925), in 1 HOLMES-LASKI CORRESPONDENCE, at 798. Holmes replied, "Don't make a mistake about Stone. He is a mighty sound and liberal minded thinker. In the case to which I suppose you refer he thought as I did but also thought that no countenance should be given to the notion that the decisions of the Court were subject to change of personnel and therefore refrained from joining in my declaration." OWH to Harold Laski (November 29, 1925), *id.* at 800. As early as August 11, 1925, Holmes had written Stone: "I can say ... that your presence on the bench has been a great comfort to me and an important reinforcement for which I am very thankful." OWH to HFS (August 11, 1925) (Stone papers).

137. Connally v. General Constructions Co., 269 U.S. 385 (1926). *Connally* was decided on January 4, 1926.
138. 45 NEW REPUBLIC 279, 280 (1926). The comment, which Brandeis attributed to Felix Frankfurter, prompted him to write Frankfurter the poem:

> Du bist Ende was du bist.
> Setz dir Perucken auf von millionen Locken,
> Setz deiner Feuss auf ellen hohen Socken,
> Du bleibst am End was du bist.

Which can be translated to mean:

> You are in the end what you are
> Put on wigs of millions of locks
> Put on your feet very high socks
> You remain in the end what you are.

LDB to Felix Frankfurter (February 1, 1926), in BRANDEIS-FRANKFURTER CORRESPONDENCE, at 229.
139. HFS to WHT (December 7, 1925) (Taft papers). *Time Magazine* summarized Stone at the outset of the 1927 term as "a sort of anchor man near the Court's level centre, like Chief Justice Taft in position if not in texture." *The Judiciary*, 10 TIME 8, 9 (October 10, 1927).
140. *Brandeis-Frankfurter Conversations*, at 336 (June 15–16, 1926). *But see infra* Chapter 21, at note 112. Drew Pearson writes that it was said of Stone "during those early days that he was 'always right the second time.' His first reaction usually was toward the conservatism of his Englewood-Wall Street days." DREW PEARSON & ROBERT S. ALLEN, THE NINE OLD MEN 103 (Garden City: Doubleday, Doran & Co. 1937).
141. *Brandeis-Frankfurter Conversations*, at 337 (June 17, 1926).
142. *See, e.g.*, Schlesinger v. Wisconsin, 270 U.S. 230 (1926); Weaver v. Palmer Brothers Co., 270 U.S. 402 (1926). *See* Heywood Broun, *It Seems to Heywood Broun*, 41 THE NATION 479 (1928) ("Upon numerous occasions the tally reads: 'Justices Holmes, Brandeis, and Stone dissenting.'").

Joseph McKenna & Harlan Fiske Stone

143. HFS to OWH (June 7, 1928) (Holmes papers). The arc of Stone's development is plainly visible in the contrast between his letter of December 14, 1926, to Noel T. Dowling, noting that in a law clerk "I do not object at all to having a man who has some of the so-called progressive ideas about law, provided it is tempered and restrained by a thorough knowledge of its technique," (Stone papers), and his letter of November 23, 1928, to Young B. Smith, stating that he affirmatively would like a law clerk who had "some originality of thought and has kept abreast of the progressive thought in the law." (Stone papers).
144. HFS to Felix Frankfurter (June 8, 1928) (Stone papers). By the end of the 1927 term, Taft could casually and knowingly refer to "the three dissenters." WHT to Henry Stimson (May 18, 1928) (Taft papers).
145. HFS to Irving Dillard (October 13, 1941) (Stone papers).
146. HFS to Milton Handler (February 19, 1929) (Stone papers). Brandeis believed that Stone "likes the joy of combat." LDB to Felix Frankfurter (May 30, 1930), in BRANDEIS-FRANKFURTER CORRESPONDENCE, at 431.
147. As Stone moved into the orbit of Holmes and Brandeis on questions of economic and social legislation, he became increasingly anathema to the conservative wing of the Court. By the end of his time as chief justice, Taft had given up on Stone, who had "ranged himself with Brandeis and with Holmes in a good many of our constitutional differences," and whose judgments Taft did not "altogether consider safe." WHT to Charles P. Taft 2nd (May 12, 1929) (Taft papers). *See* WHT to Robert A. Taft (February 3, 1929) (Taft papers) ("I have not been greatly impressed with Stone's judgment of men or things.") (Taft papers). Taft and the other conservatives on the Court became suspicious that Stone was seeking to smuggle into his draft opinions propositions of law "that have not been thought out by the whole Court." WHT to Charles P. Taft 2nd (May 12, 1929) (Taft papers). For example, in Lucas v. Alexander, 279 U.S. 573 (1929), Stone at Butler's request removed *dicta* about the legal meaning of "value." PB to HFS (May 9, 1929) (Stone papers). In United Fuel Gas Co. v. Railroad Commission, 278 U.S. 300 (1929), Van Devanter heavily edited Stone's draft. Taft wrote Van Devanter saying "I think all the changes excellent especially the limitation of that statement as to rejection as of any evidential weight regulated rates. [sic] He does not seem to be able to get it from our cases except Brandeis' dissenting opinion and wants to get it into an opinion of the Court. 'Heraus mit it.'" WHT to WVD (December 28, 1928) (Van Devanter papers).
148. On this question, see the excellent discussion in Miriam Galston, *Activism and Restraint: The Evolution of Harlan Fiske Stone's Judicial Philosophy*, 70 TULANE LAW REVIEW 137 (1995).
149. Harlan F. Stone, *The Common Law in the United States*, 50 HARVARD LAW REVIEW 4 (1936).
150. HFS to Walter Wheeler Cook (April 13, 1927) (Stone papers). Stone makes this observation in the context of his consideration of New York Dock Co. v. The Poznan, 274 U.S. 117 (1927), which concerned the question of whether a wharf owner could receive preferential payment from the proceeds of a vessel for wharfage furnished the vessel while in the custody of a United States marshal

under a warrant of arrest in admiralty. Stone wrote about the case to Walter Wheeler Cook that:

> We ought to remember that law is distinctly utilitarian in its object, and the ultimate goal of everything we do with respect to it is to make it more useful.... My observation is that justice fails often because the men who prepare cases, briefs and arguments have ... completely lost sight of the ultimate aim of law and the way it is to be related to social organization and function. A very pretty example of that is a case in which I wrote the opinion last week.... Until the case reached our Court the lawyers had labored all the way up in debating whether or not technical doctrine of admiralty liens applied to the case or didn't, completely losing sight of more fundamental things.

HFS to Walter Wheeler Cook (April 13, 1927) (Stone papers). Cook responded by observing that "The average lawyer (and judge) ... still thinks of the legal universe as divided into so many water-tight compartments, pigeon-holes (logical classes), all with names, and if he thinks he can not find a case like the one he is dealing with already in one of the pigeon-holes, he is lost." Walter Wheeler Cook to HFS (April 29, 1927) (Stone papers). Stone replied, "The habit of attempting to place every case in some fixed category and giving no relief if the case is not one falling within a recognized category is much more common that I had supposed before I came here.... Another very interesting example to me was Reading Company v. Moons, Administrator, reported in 171 U.S. at page 58. Literally volumes of judicial opinions have been written in the attempt to find some perfectly logical solution of the question, when a cause of action 'accrues'. But all these difficulties disappear as soon as one looks to the general purposes of the statute and ... takes into account the particular ends which are to be served by the Statute of Limitations in question." HFS to Walter Wheeler Cook (May 2, 1927) (Stone papers).

151. "Mr. Justice Stone's first efforts in constitutional cases represented a carry-over from his days as a law teacher. He was distrustful of formulas and labels, to say nothing of axioms and maxims, as furnishing answers to hard questions." Noel T. Dowling, *The Methods of Mr. Justice Stone in Constitutional Cases*, 41 COLUMBIA LAW REVIEW 1160, 1166 (1941). "Almost from the beginning of his judicial career, Chief Justice Stone has inveighed against the use of legalistic formulas and labels in the disposition of constitutional cases." KONEFSKY, CHIEF JUSTICE STONE AND THE SUPREME COURT, *supra* note 52, at 260. On Stone's introduction of the methodology of "balancing" into Supreme Court constitutional jurisprudence, see T. Alexander Aleinikoff, *Constitutional Law in the Age of Balancing*, 96 YALE LAW JOURNAL 943, 959–61 (1987).

152. *See, e.g.*, Metcalf v. Mitchell, 269 U.S. 514, 523–24 (1926), in which Stone sought to redefine the doctrine of intergovernmental tax immunity by "recourse ... to the reason upon which the [doctrine] rests." Herbert Wechsler noted that in cases like *Metcalf*, Stone "sought to restate the principles [of intergovernmental tax immunity] in terms of a practical purpose." Herbert Wechsler, *Stone and the Constitution*, 46 COLUMBIA LAW REVIEW 764, 790 (1946). *See* Henry M. Bates, *Chief Justice Harlan F. Stone*, 27 AMERICAN BAR ASSOCIATION JOURNAL 469, 473–74 (August 1941); Dowling, *supra* note 151, at 1166–67; *infra* Chapter 35, at 1114–15.

153. *See, e.g.*, Di Santo v. Pennsylvania, 273 U.S. 34, 44 (1927) (Stone, J., dissenting). Herbert Wechsler observed of Stone's *Di Santo* dissent that "as a solid logician he

was offended ... by the vacuity of the labels mouthed in the opinions." Wechsler, *supra* note 152, at 785. *See* Bates, *supra* note 152, at 473; Dowling, *supra* note 151, at 1167; *infra* Chapter 37, at 1171–73.
154. Tyson & Brother v. Banton, 273 U.S. 418, 431 (1927).
155. *Id.* at 446 (Holmes, J., dissenting).
156. Stone later explained his decision to correspondents in terms that do not seem to me entirely candid. To Herman Oliphant, he wrote: "Holmes, as he usually does, went directly to the heart of the matter. In view of what he had written I hesitated to write at all, but it seemed to me that his opinion might not be understood or at any rate not adequately understood by many lawyers, and therefore I thought it advisable to meet the majority a little more on their own ground. Both he and Brandeis cordially agreed to this, so I wrote what I had to say. A little too much, perhaps, but nevertheless it may be useful later on." HFS to Herman Oliphant (March 3, 1927) (Stone papers). To Walter Wheeler Cook, Stone said, "Of course, nothing better or more complete philosophically could be said than what Holmes said in the Ticket Scalper case, but it was only because I felt that its real significance would not be appreciated by one judge out of one hundred that I wrote mine." HFS to Walter Wheeler Cook (March 17, 1927) (Stone papers). And to Young B. Smith he observed: "it is time we stopped talking nonsense in such phrases as 'affected with a public interest' and 'grant of a business to a public use'. Of course, Holmes comes to the heart of the matter in his dissenting opinion, but it seemed to me it would not be understood by many lawyers and would be considered too radical by others and that therefore it would be useful for me to meet the majority on their own ground." HFS to Young B. Smith (March 3, 1927) (Stone papers).

This correspondence suggests that for Stone the phrase "affected with a public interest" had literally *no* discernible legal meaning, which was Holmes's position. Contrary to what Stone says, however, Holmes's position is relatively simple, and certainly lawyers could easily understand it. If Stone actually accepted Holmes's position, his published dissent was a mere sham; he was making matters more difficult for lawyers to understand, not easier. For some reason, therefore, Stone was concerned in his correspondence to efface the importance of the directly functional account of the phrase that he had constructed in his published opinion. We know that the need for functional doctrine was directly on Stone's mind because of his nearly contemporaneous correspondence with Cook. *See supra* note 150.
157. *Tyson*, 273 U.S. at 451–52 (Stone, J., dissenting).
158. *Id.* Upon receiving the draft of Sutherland's opinion, Stone wrote Holmes that "I am sorry to see any case decided upon the basis of such a paraphrase as 'affected with the public use'." Stone to OWH (February 5, 1927) (Stone papers).
159. Brandeis responded to Stone's dissent with the comment, "This is admirable. Mark me as joining with you." (Stone papers). Stone's effort to transform the category of "property affected with a public interest" into one that had discernible content was well appreciated by commentators. *See, e.g.,* Note, *Constitutional Law – Regulation of Resale of Tickets of Admission to Places of Entertainment*, 25 MICHIGAN LAW REVIEW 880, 884 (1927) ("Its merit lies in the fact that it shifts the emphasis from fugitive classifications and *a priori* definitions to a consideration of the economic environment in which the industry operates.").

The accuracy of Stone's economic analysis can be judged from the fact that the federal government itself later sought to reinstate the effect of the New York law by imposing a tax on tickets sold by scalpers. *See* Pub. L. 70-562, 45 Stat. 791 (May 29, 1928). The tax was upheld in McKenna v. Anderson, 31 F. 1016 (2d Cir.), *cert. denied*, 279 U.S. 869 (1929), even though "it was maintained that Congress undertook to do what the Supreme Court held the State of New York could not do when it passed the 'ticket-scalpers law.'" GREGORY HANKIN & CHARLOTTE A. HANKIN, UNITED STATES SUPREME COURT 1928–1929: A REVIEW OF THE WORK OF THE SUPREME COURT OF THE UNITED STATES FOR OCTOBER TERM, 1928, at 108–9 (Washington D.C.: Library Research Service 1929). On continuing disruptions in the New York market for theater tickets, see Ted Goldsmith, *There's Nothing New in Ticket Speculation: An Inquiry into Past and Present Activities of the Ticket Merchants*, 53 THEATRE MAGAZINE 21 (February 1931).

160. As Stone observed to his old friend John Bassett Moore, "I don't feel so badly about the result in the ticket scalping case as I do about the reasoning which was used to support it. I am anxious to see this Court, of all others, deal with realities rather than meaningless phrases." HFS to John Bassett Moore (May 4, 1927) (Stone papers). Moore had previously written Stone that "There is now rampant in the U.S. a type of conservatism that is appalling by reason of its narrowness, its bigotry and its timidity. Like Carlyle's ostrich, it buries its head in the sand and reasons only 'a posteriori.' When it feels even a gentle zephyr on its exposure, its blinded eyes 'see red' and its addled brain become frantic over the supposed tornado of radicalism. Occasionally, however, it lifts its terrified head long enough to cry aloud for the protection of the Constitution." John Bassett Moore to HFS (March 4, 1927) (Stone papers).

161. Ribnik v. McBride, 277 U.S. 350, 355 (1928).

162. *Id.* at 374 (Stone, J., dissenting). As Stone wrote Herman Oliphant, the work of his dissent was to point "out a little more effectively than has hitherto been done that there is no essential difference between rate regulations and other forms and that to say, as the majority did, that other forms of regulation are permissible is, in effect, to deny the only form of regulation which is appropriate or effective." HFS to Herman Oliphant (June 14, 1928) (Stone papers).

It is noteworthy that four years earlier both Taft and Holmes had made essentially this same point in dissent in Adkins v. Children's Hospital, 261 U.S. 525 (1923). *See id.* at 564–65 (Taft, C.J., dissenting.); *id.* at 569 (Holmes, J., dissenting). In 1915 in his argument to the Court in Stettler v. O'Hara, 243 U.S. 629 (1917), Brandeis had also made this same point:

> Opposing counsel has argued that when you prohibit employment at less than a living-wage you do something which is entirely different from the prohibitions as to hours or conditions of employment. He admits that the legislature may prohibit work in a place which is not sanitary, that it may protect against hazards peculiar to a particular occupation; but he insists that the legislature cannot protect against a deficiency in wages because in some way, which I do not understand, the wage is detached from the occupation. But if there is some distinction which keener minds may be able to follow, it seems to me the court has shown that as a rule of law it cannot regard such a distinction as of any importance.

Joseph McKenna & Harlan Fiske Stone

LOUIS D. BRANDEIS, THE CURSE OF BIGNESS 67 (New York: Viking Press 1934).

163. *Ribnik*, 277 U.S. at 374 (Stone, J., dissenting).

164. *Id*. at 359–75 (Stone, J., dissenting). Holmes returned Stone's draft dissent with the observation that "this is admirable & sockological – my only difficulty in marking my agreement is that I go farther." (Stone papers). Stone responded, "[W]hy not say that you would go further than I and refer to your dissent in the Tyson case? But that you think I go far enough to demolish the majority, or words to that effect? Of course, with respect to your views in the Tyson case, I agree with them, but I think it desirable to meet the majority on their own ground." HFS to OWH (May 24, 1928) (Stone papers). Holmes eventually joined Stone's dissent without reservation.

165. Writing in the *New Republic*, R.G. Tugwell observed that "the majority makes no attempt to meet the theoretical objections to its position; its statement is pure and unreasoned dogma, its use of 'public interest' an obvious statement of prejudice and dislike for bureaucratic meddling." R.G. Tugwell, *That Living Constitution*, 55 NEW REPUBLIC 120, 121 (1928). *See* HFS to Milton Handler (June 19, 1928) (Stone papers).

166. HFS to D.O. McGovney (December 3, 1934) (Stone papers). In this letter Stone explicitly invokes *Tyson* and *Ribnik* as "horrible examples" of the Court's failure to apply principled legal reasoning and instead imposing the socio-economic philosophy of particular judges. Eighteen months later, Stone would make this indictment public and explicit in his dissent in Morehead v. New York *ex rel*. Tipaldo, 298 U.S. 587 (1936), which struck down a New York law requiring minimum wages for women employees. Stone wrote in dissent: "It is difficult to imagine any grounds, other than our own personal economic predilections, for saying that the contract of employment is any less an appropriate subject of legislation than are scores of others, in dealing with which this Court has held that legislature may curtail individual freedom in the public interest." *Id*. at 633 (Stone, J., dissenting). Holmes had reached this same insight decades before, see *Law and the Court* (February 15, 1913), in OLIVER WENDELL HOLMES, COLLECTED LEGAL PAPERS 294–95 (New York: Harcourt, Brace and Co. 1920), as had Brandeis, who in 1911 had publicly announced that "Some judges have decided a law unconstitutional simply because they considered the law unwise. These judges should be made to feel that they have no such right, that their business is not to decide whether the view taken by the Legislature is a wise view, but whether a body of men could reasonably hold such a view." Ernest Poole, *Brandeis: A Remarkable Record of Unselfish Work Done in the Public Interest*, 71 AMERICAN MAGAZINE 481, 493 (1911).

167. Galston, *supra* note 148, at 162. To get some measure of how profoundly Stone changed during his first three years on the Taft Court, *compare supra* note 71.

168. WHT to Horace D. Taft (June 8, 1928) (Taft papers). Taft's lament was apropos of the dissents of Holmes, Brandeis and Stone in Olmstead v. United States, 277 U.S. 438 (1928).

169. *See, e.g.*, May v. Henderson, 268 U.S. 108 (1925).

170. *See* the discussion of Dumbra v. United States, 268 U.S. 435 (1925), in *supra* Chapter 2, at note 88.

171. McReynolds returned Stone's draft in Second Russian Insurance Co. v. Miller, 268 U.S. 552 (1925), with the comment: "I think your conclusions are good. But I think you confuse the opinion by too much detail. It would be easier to understand and to me more satisfactory if you stated the substantive finding of fact below and approved this. Then discuss the *essential* law point and no others. My observation has been that unnecessary discussion returns to plague." (Stone papers). He returned Stone's draft opinion in Arkansas *ex rel.* Utley v. St. Louis-San Francisco Ry. Co., 269 U.S. 172 (1925), with the comment: "This is a writ of error strictly limited by the Act of 1916. I should point out that there was no real question concerning the validity of any authority exercised under the US & dismiss the writ on that ground. Some of the things you have said may lead to trouble. We have enough arising out of too free talk in the past!" (Stone papers). He returned Stone's draft opinion in North Laramie Land Co. v. Hoffman, 268 U.S. 276 (1925), with the observation, "I agree. But I think your opinion would be much better if only half as long. There is really nothing new in the cause and simple statement of the issues with short reply to the points I think would better serve posterity. Think of the 12,000 who should read what you say here." (Stone papers). He returned Stone's draft opinion in Risty v. Chicago, Rock Island & Pacific Ry. Co., 270 U.S. 378 (1926), with the comment, "I think you come out at a proper place. But I cannot understand your statement of the issues. I assume the trouble is with my head." (Stone papers).

Stone's law clerk during the 1926 term reports that "McReynolds, generally, would send a spiteful and malicious comment. For example, in one case he wrote 'Not one lawyer in a thousand would agree with your reasoning, but it's not important enough for me to dissent.' Stone, at the last conference of the recess, would apprise the Justices of the opinions that were ready for announcement the following Monday, indicating that he had a full Court and reading such comments as had been made, including the one from McReynolds. This embarrassed the Tennessean and after a while these hateful endorsements ceased." Handler, *supra* note 79, at 119.

172. United States v. Anderson, 269 U.S. 422 (1926) (Stone papers).

PART II
THE HOLDOVER JUSTICES

Four justices who were members of the Court when Taft became chief justice were still on the Court after Taft's resignation on February 3, 1930. In order of seniority, they were Oliver Wendell Holmes, Willis Van Devanter, James Clark McReynolds, and Louis Dembitz Brandeis. The first and last justices on this list have profoundly shaped our own understanding of law and scholarship, whereas the remaining two are merely names from a long-forgotten past. If we remember them at all, it is as avatars of legal philosophies that we believe have long since passed away. We acknowledge Holmes and Brandeis as among the greatest justices ever to grace the Court, but we dismiss Van Devanter and McReynolds as epic failures.

These categorizations would scarcely have been recognizable in the 1920s. America had then yet to select winners and losers among competing candidates for jurisprudential dominance. Within the Taft Court, all four of these justices were powerful and influential figures, and each struggled to shape the Court to his own distinctive vision of the nature and purpose of law. To compare the outlooks of these four remarkable justices is to reveal explosive and ongoing tensions between conceiving law as the positive will of the state, or instead as the expression of pervasive and customary norms; between emphasizing the need for law to preserve accepted truths or instead to facilitate orderly change; between regarding law as a correction for democracy's pathologies or instead as the foundation of democratic self-governance.

To imagine these four justices arguing at a common conference table is to appreciate the high drama of the Taft Court. The interpersonal and professional dynamics must have been titanic and volatile, as were the intellectual stakes. In the distinct biographies and perspectives of these four larger-than-life figures, we can begin to identify some of the essential jurisprudential battles that characterized the Taft Court's ongoing struggle to make sense of the rapidly changing American legal landscape.

CHAPTER 5

Oliver Wendell Holmes

IN JUNE 1921, Oliver Wendell Holmes, Jr. was the oldest member of the Court, though only the second most senior Justice. "[B]y reason of his rare combination of qualities – his intellectual power and literary skill, his freshness of view and inimitable way of expressing it, his enthusiasm and cheerful skepticism, his abundant vitality and gaiety of spirit – he radiated a constant charm."[1]

Holmes was born on March 8, 1841, the son and namesake of a nationally renowned father.[2] Oliver Wendell Holmes Sr. had authored wildly popular essays like *The Autocrat at the Breakfast-Table*, as well as widely anthologized poems like *Old Ironsides*. He had been a prominent medical reformer as both professor and dean at the Harvard Medical School, championing new and effective techniques for preventing the spread of puerperal fever among women. He had been a founding member of the *Atlantic Monthly*. He had even coined common words and phrases like "Boston Brahmin" and "anesthesia."[3]

Holmes Jr. attended Harvard College,[4] barely finishing[5] before volunteering in 1861 as an officer in the Twentieth Regiment of the Massachusetts Volunteers, the so-called Harvard Regiment. Holmes was something of an abolitionist as a young man,[6] helping to defend Wendell Phillips at an Anti-Slavery Society meeting from the threats of a Boston mob.[7] The Massachusetts Twentieth saw bitter service throughout the Civil War, ranking among the very highest of all Union regiments in casualties. Holmes was famously wounded three times: At Ball's Bluff on October 21, 1861, with a bullet through the chest; at Antietam on September 17, 1862, with a shot through the neck; and finally at Chancellorsville in early May 1863, with a severe wound to the heel.[8]

The suffering, the illness, what he called the "immense ... butcher's bill"[9] of the war, left Holmes exhausted, unnerved, and disillusioned.[10] In Holmes's eyes, he had "started in this thing as a boy. I am now a man and I have been coming to the conclusion for the last six months that my duty has changed."[11] He quit the army at the end of his enlistment in the summer of 1864 for "the ostensible and sufficient reason ... that I cannot now endure the labors and hardships of the line."[12] He began the war as an idealist "in a burst of enthusiasm."[13] He remained in the trenches because of his duty.[14] He chose to leave the army in the summer of 1864 because he felt that compunctions of duty could no longer sustain him in the face of intolerable strain.[15]

The trauma of the war remained forever imprinted on Holmes.[16] When his estate was inventoried after his death in 1935, a small paper parcel was found that contained two musket balls. On the paper Holmes had written, "These were taken from my body in the Civil War."[17] Although in later years Holmes would tend to idealize the war,[18] memorably transforming its grinding, spirit-crushing reality into a flame that through "great good fortune" had "touched with fire" the "hearts" of his generation,[19] the grim presence of the conflict is palpable in Holmes's detached fatalism,[20] his skepticism (which was the other side of his tolerance),[21] and his continuous tendency to see social life in terms of existential struggle.[22]

On returning to Boston, Holmes was forced to decide what to make of his life. In July 1861, before leaving for the army, he had casually observed to his college classmates that "If I survive the war I expect to study law as my profession."[23] Holmes's grandfather on his mother's side, Charles Jackson, had been a prominent and influential justice of the Supreme Judicial Court of Massachusetts from 1813 to 1823. Upon becoming a civilian, Holmes turned to mastering the law with all the "vast and driving ambition"[24] that characterized him throughout his life.[25] Wasting no time, he enrolled in fall 1864 in Harvard Law School,[26] which at the time had three full-time faculty.[27] Holmes later wrote that the law school was then "almost a disgrace to the Commonwealth of Massachusetts" because it "undertook to confer degrees without any preliminary examination whatever."[28] He received his degree in June 1866, and in that year noted in his diary his resolution "to immerse myself in the law completely."[29]

Holmes attached himself to the law firm of Chandler, Shattuck, and Thayer,[30] the last being the same James Bradley Thayer who would eventually become the influential Royall Professor of Law at the Harvard Law School.[31] Although Holmes practiced the craft of appellate and trial litigation, he could not bring himself to abandon his penchant for speculative thinking. He began contributing to (and eventually in 1870 editing) the *American Law Review*. In 1873, he produced a massive new twelfth edition of James Kent's *Commentaries on American Law*. In 1881, at the age of 39, he published *The Common Law*,[32] characterized by some as "the most important book on law ever written by an American."[33]

His accomplishments earned him a professorship at the Harvard Law School in 1882, which he left within the year to accept an appointment as an associate justice on the Supreme Judicial Court of Massachusetts,[34] the same Court on which his grandfather had served. He became chief justice in 1899. While serving on the Massachusetts Court he continued to produce outstanding and original scholarship. His extraordinary articles, like the 1897 lecture *The Path of the Law*,[35] "pushed American legal thought into the twentieth century."[36] Holmes became the first American scholar to articulate a positivist vision of law, insisting "on a sharp distinction between law and morals."[37] He was the first to provide "the intellectual ammunition for the subversion" of the "late-nineteenth-century system of legal formalism"[38] by demonstrating the many circumstances in which judges were "called upon to exercise the sovereign prerogative of choice."[39]

Oliver Wendell Holmes

Holmes "anticipated much of Legal Realism,"[40] eloquently arguing:

> Behind the logical form lies a judgment as to the relative worth and importance of competing legislative grounds, often an inarticulate and unconscious judgment, it is true, and yet the very root and nerve of the whole proceeding. You can give any conclusion a logical form. You always can imply a condition in a contract. But why do you imply it? It is because of some belief as to the practice of the community or of a class, or because of some opinion as to policy. ... Such matters really are battle-grounds.[41]

The implications of this perspective structured Holmes's understanding of the proper role of the judge in the context of public law.

> I think that the judges themselves have failed adequately to recognize their duty of weighing considerations of social advantage. The duty is inevitable, and the result of the often proclaimed judicial aversion to deal with such considerations is simply to leave the very ground and foundation of judgments inarticulate and often unconscious. ... When socialism first began to be talked about, the comfortable classes of the community were a good deal frightened. I suspect that this fear has influenced judicial action both here and in England, yet it is certain that it is not a conscious factor in the decisions to which I refer. I think that something similar has led people who no longer hope to control the legislatures to look to the courts as expounders of the Constitutions, and that in some courts new principles have been discovered outside the bodies of those instruments, which may be generalized into acceptance of the economic doctrines which prevailed about fifty years ago, and a wholesale prohibition of what a tribunal of lawyers does not think about right. I cannot but believe that if the training of lawyers led them habitually to consider more definitely and explicitly the social advantage on which the rule they lay down must be justified, they sometimes would hesitate where now they are confident, and see that really they were taking sides upon debatable and often burning questions.[42]

Holmes articulated forcefully and persuasively, and with an unequalled mastery of the history and minutia of common law, that "the justification of a law for us cannot be found in the fact that our fathers always have followed it. It must be found in some help which the law brings toward reaching a social end which the governing power of the community has made up its mind that it wants."[43] By stressing that "the real justification of a rule of law, if there be one, is that it helps to bring about a social end which we desire,"[44] Holmes inspired the pragmatic vision of law that profoundly shaped a younger generation of legal scholars, including, as we have seen, Harlan Fiske Stone.[45]

In 1902 Theodore Roosevelt, pressed by Holmes's childhood friend Senator Henry Cabot Lodge, nominated Holmes to replace Horace Gray,[46] a distinguished Boston lawyer (and half-brother of Holmes's close friend John Chipman Gray), who had stepped down from the United States Supreme Court due to a stroke on July 9.[47] Holmes was confirmed on December 4,[48] and he was exhilarated by the change. He was "happier than ever before in my life."[49] For the first time he began to feel "from time to time ... as if I was getting a taste of the kind of recognition that I desired."[50]

He liked "the big stage and big questions."[51] He felt as if he could do "my work easily and the C.J. seems to like it and gives rather more cases in consequence. I would like to write them all if I could."[52]

In the Supreme Court, Holmes faced cases that were different from those he had encountered as a state judge.[53] "The work is hard and absorbing – oh how absorbing," he wrote. "The men here may not be very strong on the philosophy or history of the law, but the abler ones administer it as statesmen governing an empire. The variety of great questions, the diversity, even geographical, the tremendous importance of what we do, everything, makes it seem the beginning of a new life on a different plane."[54] Holmes was now "constantly involved . . . in . . . tremendous things, so that while I used to get the infinite from within – in the thought of working out and gradually embodying a philosophic system, I now am so much impressed by the externally grandiose character of the questions and their immediate visible results, that I am more like a man of affairs, or a statesman if only I had the knowledge and experience of such."[55]

The Supreme Court seemed to require Holmes to alter his practice of judging. Speaking in 1901, he had summarized his own judicial practice in Massachusetts: "My keenest interest is excited, not by what are called great questions and great cases, but by little decisions which the common run of selectors would pass by because they did not deal with the Constitution or a telephone company, yet which have in them the germ of some wider theory, and therefore of some profound interstitial change in the very tissue of the law."[56] The great questions he now confronted at the Supreme Court, however, seemed to alter the stakes of his work.

"At times I find it hard to avoid a sense of responsibility, a mark of weakness that I strive to avoid," he wrote a friend. "To feel responsibility is to think, if not of yourself, at least of something else than the problem and your task – But some of the things we deal with, many indeed, are tremendous in their import."[57] Although Holmes made "a concentrated effort to do one's part as a wheel in a tremendous machine,"[58] it gave him "a rumbling uneasiness" that he strove to suppress "in the ultimate indifference, and the thought that nothing matters unless you choose that it should matter."[59] "The importance of the things we have to deal with makes me shudder from time to time but I don't lie awake over them – and try to think of them merely as problems to be handled in just the same way whether they involve $25. – or the welfare of a state or a people."[60]

Holmes found his capacity for indifference sorely tested. In his first term, for example, he spoke for the Court (over three strong dissents) in *Giles v. Harris*,[61] which notoriously denied equitable relief to African Americans seeking to have their Fifteenth Amendment voting rights restored in Alabama. "I think the decision was inevitable," he wrote his friend Clara Stevens, "but it was one of those terrible questions over which one would lie awake if he had not strong nerves. The only way is to think only of the problem and nothing else – to be neither egotist nor altruist according to my tiresomely repeated formula."[62]

Matters soon came to a head in 1904 in the dramatic case of *Northern Securities Co. v. United States*.[63] It must have been cathartic for Holmes publicly to declare in his famous dissent: "Great cases, like hard cases, make bad law. For great cases are called great, not by reason of their real importance in shaping the law of the future, but because of some accident of immediate overwhelming interest which appeals to the feelings and distorts the judgment. These immediate interests exercise a kind of hydraulic pressure which makes what previously was clear seem doubtful, and before which even well settled principles of law will bend."[64]

Holmes's dissent caused a break with Roosevelt, who had previously been very close to Holmes and his wife.[65] But it also appeared to have restored Holmes's own sense of judicial role. He could write a close friend several years later, "I often think not without sadness of the profound difference in the interest of my friend the Chief Justice [Edward Douglass White] and myself – so profound that I never talk about my half. He is always thinking what will be the practical effect of the decision (which of course is the ultimate justification or condemnation of the principle adopted.) I think of its relation to the theory and philosophy of the law – if that isn't too pretentious a way of putting it."[66] Despite sitting in a Court that was the "center of great forces,"[67] Holmes would eventually recover his "indifference" and refuse the temptation to responsibility and statesmanship.[68]

By 1912, Holmes could forcefully rearticulate earlier judicial aspirations: "The thing I have wanted to do and want to do is to put as many new ideas into the law as I can, to show how particular solutions involve general theory, and to do it with style. I should like to be admitted to be the greatest jurist in the world."[69] He resigned himself to the absence of the kind of popular acclaim that had enveloped his father. "[P]eople, unless ... they address and charm a general public, get their recognition from other specialists. ... I like to have the Bar think well of me, but the only thing I care much for is what a few masters scattered here and there say."[70] "The only thing that charms my fancy is to know a thing as a master and to put into it some fundamental ideas, that the public won't know enough to give you credit for."[71]

In the end this renunciation was psychologically unstable.[72] "My friend and colleague White, pitching into me as usual for under brevity and obscurity, told me the other day that there was no man in the U.S. whose reputation so little corresponded to what he had done. ... I can't bother about the appreciation of people who don't know the difference between the first rate and the inferior. Anyhow I am doing the best I can."[73] It made Holmes "lonely" in his "work," meaning in "two-thirds" of his life.[74] "Although I am in the world and surrounded by able men – none of those whom I meet has the same interests and emphasis that I do. ... So that when I say I am lonely, I feel bound to confess that it is egotism – the feeling thrown back on oneself when one sees little attention given to what one thinks most important."[75] Holmes was "well aware" of his own "elements of personal ambition to excel – to do better than others,"[76] but, after his first few terms on the Court, he strove to reconcile himself to his judicial vocation of "preparing small diamonds for people of limited intellectual means."[77]

As the first decade of the twentieth century closed, Holmes was known among legal scholars – especially in England (having received an honorary D.C. L. degree from Oxford in 1909)[78] – but his popular reputation in this country was quite limited. Holmes remained to the general public but one justice among nine.[79] "Nearly thirty years after publication of *The Common Law* and after his first judicial appointment, the public hardly knew him. What it thought it knew was that he was aloof, a Massachusetts intellectual and scholar, the son of his famous father, and an old soldier with a cavalry mustache."[80]

And then Holmes met the young Felix Frankfurter. Frankfurter, an Austrian émigré, had finished first in the Harvard Law School class of 1906 and come to Washington in fall 1911 to work in the Bureau of Insular Affairs of the War Department under his mentor Henry Stimson. He bore a letter of introduction to Holmes from John Chipman Gray. Holmes and Frankfurter became fast friends, and Frankfurter, who had idolized Holmes since his "freshman [year] in the Law School" as "the only sure canon of truth,"[81] in turn introduced Holmes to the remarkable "House of Truth," the most lively and influential political salon in Washington.[82] The house, at 1727 Nineteenth Street, was the gathering place for stalwarts of the *New Republic* like Walter Lippmann and Herbert Croly, as well as for figures like Louis Brandeis, Harold Laski, and of course Frankfurter himself.

"Of all the great talkers in Washington, none compared to Holmes."[83] According to a contemporary witness, Holmes possessed "a grandeur and beauty rarely met among men. ... [H]is presence entered a room with him as a pervading force; and left with him, too, like a strong light put out. Handsome, and aware of it, with thick white hair, intense eyes under heavy brows, and a sweeping white mustache, he had style and dash."[84] Holmes quickly became the star and patron saint of the brightest young American intellectuals.[85] It was largely "because of his friendship with this younger crowd" that "Holmes saw his reputation evolve from a relatively obscure member of the Supreme Court into a judicial icon."[86]

The upshot was that by the time Taft took charge of the Court, Holmes had at last achieved the national reputation for which he had longed.[87] He had become, in the words of Yale Law School Dean Charles E. Clark, "an American institution,"[88] a living embodiment of American government and history.[89] "By 1930, Holmes was probably the only man or woman alive who could remember having had conversations with John Quincy Adams."[90] He not only bore the scars of the Civil War, but he could recall his grandmother describing the move "out of Boston when the British troops came in, before the Revolution."[91]

On June 2, 1924, he received from President Coolidge the Roosevelt Memorial Association medal for distinguished service.[92] "During your long service" in the Supreme Court, Coolidge said, "you have, I think, almost unerringly interpreted the institutions and aspirations of your country. ... In the great body of your contributions to the judicial authority of the nation you have reared a monument, imperishable and unforgettable. This medal will be to you as a testimony to the universal recognition of your great public contributions."[93] In 1931, on his ninetieth birthday, Holmes, "soldier, lawyer, leader of public opinion, associate justice of the Supreme Court of the United States, was greeted ... with a series of tributes such as have rarely been paid to any man in his own lifetime,"[94] and he responded with a short, eloquent, nationwide radio broadcast. Even Taft, at the dedication of Alphonso Taft Hall at Cincinnati University, acknowledged in October 1925 that "Mr. Justice Oliver Wendell Holmes ... continues to honor the Supreme Court as its most brilliant and learned member."[95]

The young progressives of the House of Truth championed Holmes because they saw him as a vehicle for removing "the Court as an obstacle to socioeconomic legislation."[96] The *New Republic*, speaking in 1923, feared that "the Court, as now constituted," would "interpret certain vague clauses of the Constitution too narrowly"

Oliver Wendell Holmes

and hence erect "the Constitution into a barrier against orderly social readjustment."[97] Holmes's pathbreaking jurisprudence was tailor-made for dismantling this barrier.

Conservative legal thought in the first decades of the twentieth century elevated judge-made law over mere legislation,[98] which was dismissed as little more than the "despotism of the mob."[99] There were roughly two distinct kinds of arguments for judicial supremacy. The most sophisticated and thoughtful, exemplified by the titanic figure of James Coolidge Carter, characterized law not as "a body of commands imposed upon society from without, either by an individual sovereign or superior, or by a sovereign body constituted by representatives of society itself," but instead as "one of the elements of society springing directly from habit and custom" whose explication requires "the work of experts who can qualify themselves only by the devotion of their lives."[100] Judges were experts in this task;[101] their job was to articulate the fundamental habits and customs of American society.[102] In 1928, Cardozo would theorize this view by observing that "Law accepts as the pattern of its justice the morality of the community whose conduct it assumes to regulate."[103] Courts were required to discern this morality whenever they had to decide whether social legislation was or was not "reasonable" under the Fourteenth Amendment.[104] Ascertaining whether legislation was constitutionally reasonable was analogous to determining the standard of "reasonable care in negligence cases,"[105] because each required the application of "a community standard."[106]

From his very earliest writings Holmes attacked this analytic framework at its roots. In 1873, in an essay pondering the social and legal implications of a labor union strike, Holmes denied that there was "an identity of interests between the different parts of a community." "The tacit assumption of the solidarity of the interests of society is very common, but seems to us to be false." Drawing on his wartime experiences, Holmes brilliantly tied together a Darwinian perspective on society, legal positivism, and the priority of legislation:

> In the last resort a man rightly prefers his own interest to that of his neighbors. And this is as true in legislation as in any other form of corporate action. All that can be expected from modern improvements is that legislation should easily and quickly, yet not too quickly, modify itself in accordance with the will of the *de facto* supreme power in the community. . . . [W]hatever body may possess the supreme power for the moment is certain to have interests inconsistent with others which have competed unsuccessfully. The more powerful interests must be more or less reflected in legislation; which, like every other device of man or beast, must tend in the long run to aid the survival of the fittest. . . . [I]t is no sufficient condemnation of legislation that it favors one class at the expense of another; for much or all legislation does that; and none the less when the *bonâ fide* object is the greatest good of the greatest number. . . . The fact is that legislation in this country, as well as elsewhere, is empirical. It is necessarily made a means by which a body, having the power, put burdens which are disagreeable to them on the shoulders of somebody else.[107]

The kernel of Holmes's entire jurisprudence may be found in this passage. In modern, heterogeneous societies, legislatures are fora in which competing forces contend for control over the production of law. The source of law is not the spontaneous orderings of custom, but a self-conscious struggle for the "supreme power" of legislation. Courts have no business limiting that power in the name of overarching habits and customs that do not in fact exist. Judicial interference with legislation interrupts the indispensable mechanism by which modern societies use "the orderly change of law"[108] to adjust competing interests that might otherwise become potentially explosive. With respect to legislation, therefore, a court should aim to be, as Holmes once jokingly said should be carved into his epitaph, a "supple tool of power."[109]

A second prominent strand of conservative legal thought conceptualized judges as much-needed disciplinarians. Courts were institutions designed to ensure "that popular action does not trespass upon right and justice as it exists in written constitutions and natural law."[110] Those who held this view, like Justice David Brewer, feared that, with "universal suffrage and a population as heterogeneous as the different races of the world will permit," "an unrestricted and absolute legislative freedom" would authorize "temporary and shifting minorities" to unleash a "tempestuous democratic flood" that would "sweep onward, bearing all things to certain destruction."[111] Legislation did not merit deference because it could be "foisted upon us by any crowd that may happen to gather at the street corner."[112] Legislation was simply a "movement of 'coercion,'" through which, "by the mere force of numbers," a majority could "diminish protection to private property."[113] Courts owed their primary loyalty instead to "the long thought of the people, as deliberately put into the organic instrument, which is to control, and not the short thought that under the pressure of temporary feeling or momentary passion may find expression in legislative action."[114]

This way of thinking was not above invoking custom; it sometimes gestured toward "the eager and earnest protest and cry of the Anglo-Saxon ... for individual freedom and absolute protection of all his rights of person and property."[115] But it laid greatest emphasis on the strict demands of constitutional text[116] or on the imperatives of that natural justice "which is the silver sheen and the golden band in the jeweled diadem of Him to whom all Nations bow and all worlds owe allegiance."[117] Holmes's profound positivism was simply devastating with respect to such soft appeals to natural law.[118] And Holmes's elegant demonstration that general legal principles were indeterminate in deciding particular cases was equally lethal to earnest and sanctimonious assertions that courts were merely applying the literal requirements of the Fourteenth Amendment.

Holmes's work was radical because it inverted the dominant jurisprudential thinking of his time, which awarded priority to judicial decision-making over legislation.[119] Holmes considered legislatures, not courts, to be the "mouthpiece" of the state.[120] The primary duty of a court was to speak for the "sovereign power" that directed the state,[121] which meant "the will of the dominant forces of the community."[122] That will expressed itself in legislation. "The time has gone by," Holmes memorably wrote, "when law is only an unconscious embodiment of the common will. It has become a conscious reaction upon itself of organized society knowingly seeking to determine its own destinies."[123] It was through legislatures, rather than courts, that divided and embattled societies expressed their conscious intentions.

Oliver Wendell Holmes

The abstract and indefinite terms of the Fourteenth Amendment were in the main insufficiently specific to override the express commands of legislation.[124] "What I regard as one of the greatest dangers to our system of giving the last word to the judges," Holmes remarked, "is the tendency to read into the fundamental instrument one's own economic and social views, when the words don't require it."[125] Judicial modesty of a high order was appropriate in the face of demands to use "the Fourteenth Amendment beyond the absolute compulsion of its words to prevent the making of social experiments that an important part of the community desires, in the insulated chambers afforded by the several states, even though the experiments may seem futile or even noxious to me and to those whose judgment I most respect."[126]

Holmes believed that legislation was the medium through which society adjusted its competing social interests. In a passage that was unstable in its use of the word "law" and yet that transparently displayed the essential elements of Holmes's own distinctive jurisprudence, he wrote:

> As law embodies beliefs that have triumphed in the battle of ideas and then have translated themselves into action, while there still is doubt, while opposite convictions still keep a battle front against each other, the time for law has not come; the notion destined to prevail is not yet entitled to the field. It is a misfortune if a judge reads his conscious or unconscious sympathy with one side or the other prematurely into the law, and forgets that what seem to him to be first principles are believed by half his fellow men to be wrong.... We ... need education in the obvious – to learn to transcend our own convictions and to leave room for much that we hold dear to be done away with short of revolution by the orderly change of law.[127]

The Civil War had taught Holmes that society is a battle among contending forces. Judges who lacked warrant apart from their own unconscious sympathies had no business intervening in that battle. The judicial task was instead to channel contenders through orderly processes of legal change, which in modern society meant the enactment of legislation that embodied dominant opinion. Only the clear and explicit words of the Constitution could warrant limiting the expression of that opinion. "I don't disguise that I am disposed to be very cautious and slow in reading my own economic views or anybody else's into the general words of a Constitution.... I think that the tendency to do so is one of the great dangers of the American plan of giving the judges the last word."[128]

Holmes's perspective prominently featured what has now become the common trope of the self-denying judge, "whose first business is to see that the game is played according to the rules whether I like them or not."[129] Insofar as it emphasized the distinction between law and community values, Holmes's positivism brought the trope to the very center of the modern notion of judging.[130] And in Holmes's case the fact of personal self-denial was notoriously and unnervingly accurate.[131] Holmes frequently proclaimed that he loathed "most of the things that I decided in favor of."[132] "I always say, as you know, that if my fellow citizens want to go to Hell I will help them. It's my job."[133]

Holmes personally opposed most of the social reforms that his constitutional jurisprudence required him to approve.[134] He believed "that legislation can't cure things, that the crowd now has substantially all there is, that the sooner they make up their mind to it the better."[135] He believed that "all the strange currents that I see in legislation etc. are wrong to the point of being ridiculous": "The thing I see most plainly is a vast amount of more or less real social discontent based on economic superstition and ignorance of what is possible."[136]

> The social reformers of today seem to me so far to forget that we no more can get something for nothing by legislation than we can by mechanics.... I hold to a few articles of a creed that I do not expect to see popular in my day. I believe that the wholesale social regeneration which so many now seem to expect, if it can be helped by conscious, coördinated human effort, cannot be affected appreciably by tinkering with the institution of property, but only by taking in hand life and trying to build a race. That would be my starting point for an ideal for the law. The notion that with socialized property we should have women free and a piano for everybody seems to me an empty humbug.[137]

If the ideal of the self-denying judge requires an almost inhuman indifference, it is no less than Holmes eloquently expressed in his correspondence. "I look at men through Malthus's glasses – as like flies – here swept away by a pestilence – there multiplying unduly and paying for it."[138] The patriotic gore of the Civil War is palpable in Holmes's attitude: the emotional displacement,[139] the savagery, the fatalism, the skepticism. But no doubt behind the detachment lay also, as Edmund Wilson so keenly discerned, "the impregnable security of belonging to the Boston 'Brahmin' caste," which endowed Holmes with "his unshakable self-confidence, his carapace of impenetrable indifference to current pressures and public opinion."[140]

Paradoxically that security also endowed Holmes with a remarkable openness to ideas. He was not threatened by disagreement.[141] Holmes could conclude his forceful attack on "humbug" with an unexpected and attractive expression of "pleasure to see more faith and enthusiasm in the young men; and I thought that one of them made a good answer to some of my skeptical talk when he said, 'You would base legislation upon regrets rather than upon hopes.'"[142]

In the end, Holmes's personal views about the institution of property were not all that different from those of Taft or Sutherland or Butler.[143] But Holmes believed that in a society fractured about the value of property his own beliefs ought not affect his constitutional interpretation of the "very general language of the Fourteenth Amendment."[144] And, unlike his conservative colleagues, Holmes took pleasure, amounting almost to empathy, at the fighting faiths of those with whom he philosophically differed.[145]

This rendered Holmes, from the perspective of his conservative colleagues, constitutionally suspect. They might respect him on matters involving the common law, but they regarded his constitutional jurisprudence as an abdication of judicial responsibility. Taft wrote his son in 1926 that Holmes "is, in my judgment, a very poor constitutional lawyer, but he is a most learned lawyer, especially in the common law, and he is brilliant, but he lacks the experience of affairs in government that would keep him straight on constitutional questions."[146] "If Holmes' dissents in constitutional cases had been followed," Taft grumbled to his brother,

Oliver Wendell Holmes

"we should have had no Constitution. Holmes has no respect for Marshall, he exaggerates the powers of Congress and thinks they can do anything. ... Holmes has very little knowledge of governmental principles."[147]

Occasionally Holmes's high disdain for ordinary moral sentiments irritated his conservative colleagues.[148] Holmes's dissent in *Olmstead v. United States*, which concerned the question of whether evidence obtained by illegal federal wiretapping was admissible in federal criminal prosecutions, argued that because there was "no body of precedents by which we are bound, and which confines us to logical deduction from established rules," the Court must "choose, and for my part I think it a less evil that some criminals should escape than that the government should play an ignoble part."[149] Van Devanter, passing a newspaper clipping about the case to Taft, snidely noted: "It seems strange to see one who believes and often says that the Constitution does not stand in the way of experiments which have the approval of a dominant sentiment, and who has no abiding moral principles, characterized as a protector of the imperiled minority and as unalterably adhering to high moral principles."[150]

Holmes's conservative colleagues on the Taft Court tended to belittle his iconic status. They dismissed his fame as a product of "the applause of the law school professors"[151] and the hopes of "the younger crowd of college professors."[152] Yet they willingly followed Holmes's lead on common law cases. Most notable are decisions like *Baltimore & O.R. Co. v. Goodman*[153] and *United Zinc and Chemical Co. v. Britt*,[154] in which Holmes exercised what Brandeis called his "incorrigible" appetite to curb "the power & province of a jury."[155] Holmes's opinion in *Britt* was especially memorable because the case was in federal court by virtue of diversity jurisdiction, and yet Holmes seized the occasion to impose a federal rule of common law liability different from that of the jurisdiction in which the case arose.[156] As G. Edward White has perceptively noted,[157] this was quite inconsistent with Holmes's own seminal dissent in *Black & White Taxicab & Transfer Co. v. Brown & Yellow Taxicab & Transfer Co.*,[158] in which Holmes had brilliantly argued that it was "an unconstitutional assumption of powers by the Courts of the United States" to presume to impose in diversity cases a federal common law inconsistent with applicable state common law.[159]

Although Holmes was 80 at the outset of the Taft Court, he remained a workhorse throughout Taft's chief justiceship. He retained his zest for life and for work.[160] As Table P-1 indicates, Holmes authored some 205 opinions from the outset of the 1921 term to the conclusion of the 1928 term. By contrast, Taft authored 249 opinions, Brandeis 193, McReynolds 172, and Van Devanter only 94.[a] We can also see from Figures I-10 and I-19 that Holmes exercised real influence on the Taft Court, if not, perhaps, on matters of constitutional law.[161] As Brandeis remarked, Holmes "is very powerful when he changes his mind, with others."[162]

---

[a] If we take the period between the opening of the 1923 term and the conclusion of the 1928 term, when Sutherland, Butler, and Sanford were also fully participating members of the Court, Taft authored 176 opinions, Holmes 146, Brandeis 143, Butler 137, McReynolds 129, Sutherland 113, Sanford 113, and Van Devanter only 70. Figure II-1, which shows Holmes's yearly productivity as a percentage of the Court's output, illustrates that in most terms Holmes produced more than his fair share of court opinions.

The Taft Court

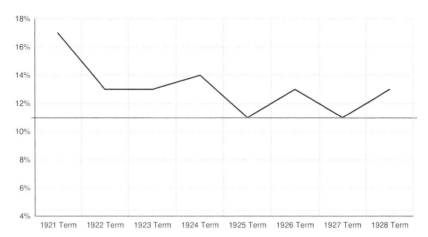

Figure II-1 Percentage of Court's opinions authored by Holmes, by term. An even distribution of cases would assign 1/9, or 11%, to each justice.

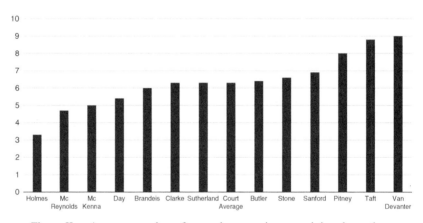

Figure II-2 Average number of pages in a unanimous opinion, by author, 1921–1928 terms

Holmes's opinions were unique. They were short, for one thing.[163] During the Taft Court, the average length of a Holmes opinion was just 3.3 pages. By contrast, as Figure II-2 illustrates, the average Taft Court opinion was almost twice as long, clocking in at 6.3 pages.[b] Virtually alone among his peers, Holmes affirmed the obligation of a judge "to strike the jugular and let the rest go."[164] Upon arriving at the

---

[b] The average opinion by Taft was 8.8 pages, by Van Devanter 9.0 pages, by McReynolds 4.7 pages, by Brandeis 6.0 pages, by Sutherland 6.3 pages, by Sanford 6.9 pages, and by Stone 6.6 pages. By contrast, during the 1993–1998 terms, the average opinion of the Court ballooned to 15.97 pages. During the 2005–2011 terms, the average opinion was 15.99 pages. *See* Figure IV-6.

Oliver Wendell Holmes

Supreme Court, he wrote a close friend that "I don't believe in the long opinions which have been almost the rule here. I think that to state the case shortly and the ground of decision as concisely and delicately as you can is the real way. That is the English fashion and I think it civilized."[165] He worried that "my habit of writing short opinions will . . . make me seem less weighty" with the general public, because "they think that a great opinion indicates itself by padded breast and shoulders. But inherent vitality is the only thing that lasts – and I hope for the best in the long run."[166]

"Cases are like the other problems of life," wrote Holmes. "At first they loom vast, black, immeasurable, but presently they shrink to infinitesimal luminous points."[167] His object in writing an opinion was to capture the precise burning essence of each case. He aspired to avoid "consecrated phrases, which in their day were a revelation, but which in time from their very felicity tend to stop the endless necessary process of further analysis and advance."[168] He worked hard to "throw down his naked thought, unswaddled in pompous commonplaces, to take its chance for life."[169] The powerful influence of Ralph Waldo Emerson[170] is apparent in Holmes's credo that "Every living sentence which shows a mind at work for itself is to be welcomed."[171] "In my fool's paradise," Holmes wrote Lewis Einstein, "I see a philosophy of law and some little touch of a philosophy of life gradually unrolling itself as I write."[172] "When you have put something better than it has been put before, or that is new and penetrating, it makes you walk on clouds."[173]

Because Holmes aspired to have his opinions express the "exuberance"[174] of "personality,"[175] he found it a "slightly exasperating discipline" to "have put my heart into" the composition of an opinion, only to submit it to the review of colleagues.[176] "Somebody is likely to light on a characteristic phrase or a generalization that expresses in a sentence the result of years of reflection and want it struck out."[177] Holmes's conciseness, combined with his effort to display "subtlety in expressing delicate matters,"[178] tended to inspire charges of obscurity.[179] In 1925 Taft wrote Interstate Commerce Commission Commissioner Clyde Aitchison that "Our Court used to write very long opinions – too long. But I am convinced that some of our members in their zeal to shorten what they say are not as helpful as they should be to the Bar and the Public. Our chief function in our Court is not to get rid of cases, it is to clarify the law and to be helpful in other cases. It is not a discharge of that function to be cryptical and leave the reader still guessing."[180]

The "truth of the matter," said Brandeis, is that Holmes "takes joy in the trick of working out what he calls 'a form of words' in which to express desired result. He occasionally says, 'I think I can find a form of words' to which I reply, 'of course you can, you can find a form of words for anything.'"[181] Although Holmes had the "best intellectual machine,"[182] and although he "is more often quoted by lawyers,"[183] Brandeis astutely noted that he "also leaves more loopholes for rehearing petitions than anyone else."[184]

> [Holmes] doesn't realize that others haven't his precipitate of knowledge, they don't know as he knows, and secondly he doesn't sufficiently consider the need of others to understand or sufficiently regard the difficulties or arguments of others. So that he has a surprisingly large [number of] petitions for rehearing in his cases, because he does not seem to have considered arguments of counsel that

are very weighty with them and often he hasn't. Philosophically he would admit difference between truth and consent of others to truth, but he does not regard difference in practice.[185]

Holmes's opinions were not only plentiful, compact, and beautifully written,[186] but they were also produced with remarkable speed,[187] as Figure I-22 illustrates. Taft judged Holmes "the promptest man in his opinions we have on the Bench."[188] When at the age of 86 Holmes suffered from "apprehensions from time to time whether I am showing age in some way that I don't detect," he comforted himself with the thought that "[c]ertainly I don't delay the work as I think every case assigned to me Saturday evening after our conferences, as always happens, has been written and distributed to the Judges on the following Tuesday, or at latest Wednesday morning."[189] Taft characterized Holmes as "thirsting for more cases and he is willing to take them from other Judges to help them out. His quickness is remarkable."[190] "The only thing" that upsets Holmes, Taft wrote his son Robert, "is not to be able to announce the opinion assigned to him on one Saturday night on a week from the following Monday. He is quite impatient if he cannot do that. Of course I don't give him the cases that have very heavy records and that require a great deal of work in reading them, but I give him important cases and try to give him cases that he likes."[191] To hold up the announcement of a Holmes opinion, said Brandeis, "is like sending an executioner after him."[192]

From his first moments on the Court, Holmes would go into "a kind of holy frenzy"[193] or "delirium"[194] when he received a case assignment, typically on the Saturday night after a conference, and he felt impelled to finish the work within two or three days.[195] He then waited impatiently for the assent of his colleagues, striving to announce the opinion by the following Monday.[196] Brandeis thought that Holmes's "desire for speed" had originally been "a point of pride," but that it had become "a vice. ... Holmes can't bear not to have case done the same day it's given to him."[197]

Holmes, acknowledging his own compulsions, expressed his "eternal misgiving whether I have not been too speedy."[198] "I console myself by thinking of the immediate decisions common in England, but they are pretty certain that the case has been adequately argued, and are not bothered by masses of irrelevancies as we are."[199] In 1929, Brandeis wrote Frankfurter that Holmes "has had quite a number of unimportant cases, but I think it also an element that he minimizes the importance of those he gets. Of course, his determination to finish the job on the Sunday following the assignment leads to this."[200] In 1928, in a personal letter to Clarke, Van Devanter authored a darker assessment: "Justice Holmes is breaking some. This is chiefly noticeable in conference and in the fact that many of his opinions do not give an adequate portrayal of the case in hand or of the grounds of the decision. ... The thing which I particularly notice in Justice Holmes is that he is becoming increasingly unable to get at the salient features in a case and to give them the weight and consideration to which they are entitled. But he remains the same attractive man he always has been."[201]

Holmes formed a close alliance with Brandeis during the Taft Court. He had known Brandeis since 1879.[202] At the time of Brandeis's controversial nomination in 1916, Holmes had written a friend:

Oliver Wendell Holmes

> All that I can say is that I have known him ever since Sam Warren got him to come to Boston – and that he always has left me when he has called feeling encouraged about the world and that I have met a good man, as well as a suggestive one – but long before the more public exertions of his I was made aware of an adversely critical attitude on the part of some whose opinions I respected while at the same time I never have understood the justification for it. There have been things that I should criticize. I didn't like his mode of conducting the Ballinger case, and formerly he seemed to me to wish to sink the few. But we all have foibles – and the total impression that I have received, as I say, has been that of a man whom I respected and admired subject to the inquiry why it was that other good men were down on him.[203]

Holmes thought Brandeis's nomination "a misfortune for the Court because whichever way it went half the world would think the less of the Court thereafter – but I expect he will make a good Judge, with 2 Catholics and the opinions on spiritual matters will be mixed."[204] He believed that "Brandeis will be a great gain though . . . I think he has hobbies that sometimes deflect his judgment a little."[205]

Holmes became exceedingly close to Brandeis during the 1920s. Brandeis was "a great solace"[206] and "my great comfort," saying "wise things I couldn't have said."[207] In his "old one horse coupé," Holmes "generally" drove home with Brandeis after work.[208] Holmes commented to Pollock that Brandeis "has done great work and I believe with high motives."[209] "If anything should happen to you," Holmes wrote Brandeis, "the Court and I both would lose an eye."[210] In 1932, Holmes was explicit and remarkably demonstrative for one so characteristically careful in his public words: "Whenever he left my house I was likely to say to my wife, 'There goes a really good man.' I think that the world now would agree with me in adding what the years have proved 'and a great judge.' . . . In the moments of discouragement that we all pass through, he always has had the happy word that lifts up one's heart. It came from knowledge, experience, courage, and the high way in which he always has taken life."[211]

On the surface, Holmes and Brandeis were an unlikely pair. Holmes believed in the growth of large business organizations;[212] Brandeis believed in cutting corporations down to human size. Holmes wrote short opinions polished to aesthetic perfection; Brandeis wrote opinions filled with footnotes and documentation.[213] Holmes once told Brandeis "that I don't think an opinion should be like an essay with footnotes, but rather should be *quasi* an oral utterance."[214] For his part, Brandeis believed that Holmes "highly approved of the inquiry into & reference to facts as the basis of my opinions, tho he does not wholly reconcile himself to my footnotes."[215] If Holmes aimed in his opinions for "inherent vitality,"[216] Brandeis "wrote to educate."[217]

In Holmes's eyes, Brandeis was "not only very able but . . . the most thorough of men. If I wanted to be epigrammatic I should say that he always desires to know all that can be known about a case whereas I am afraid that I wish to know as little as I can safely go on. He loves facts and I hate them except as the necessary peg to hang generalizations on."[218] Holmes was "conscious of shrinking from facts – which Brandeis devours." Holmes loved instead the theoretical "kernel of interest" that he could extract from the heart of cases.[219] Early in their judicial relationship, Brandeis

THE TAFT COURT

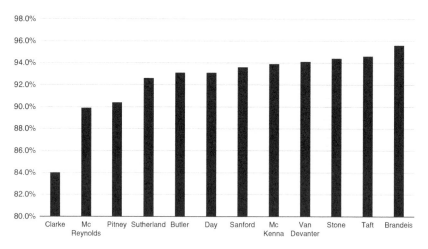

Figure II-3 Percentage of decisions in which Holmes participated and joined the same opinion as another justice, 1921–1928 terms

challenged Holmes to learn the facts of the textile manufacturing industry in Massachusetts, but the effort came to nothing.[220]

If Holmes was himself personally conservative and approved progressive legislation only because he believed that a judge should defer to legislative judgments, Brandeis was himself a passionate advocate for justice and reform. Holmes recalled returning home with Brandeis from a Saturday conference when the latter

> grew really eloquent on the evils of the present organization of society. When I repeated my oft repeated views as to the economic elements he told me they were superficial and didn't deal with the real evil, which was not a question of luxuries or victuals but of power. He was fierce and fine as [to] the men he knew who didn't dare say what they thought because of the power to which they were subject. He compared the Scotsmen who eat oatmeal, but stood up – men. Then said that I hadn't seen and knew nothing about the evils that one who had been much in affairs had seen and known. He bullies me a little on that from time to time. I didn't say more than that I thought that there might be an answer and that every society rested on the death of men – meaning that I surmised that the repressions and extinctions are the inevitable results of the situation.[221]

Yet these two justices, among the greatest ever to serve on the Court, formed a perfectly amazing alliance,[222] as if "by a sort of preestablished harmony."[223] Holmes's closeness to Brandeis can be seen in Figure II-3; Holmes was more likely to join in an opinion by Brandeis than he was in that of any other member of the Taft Court.[c] Holmes was thus actually "glad"[224] when Brandeis dissented from

---

[c] It is fascinating to note, however, that, as Figure II-4 illustrates, Holmes was in the privacy of the conference room more likely to vote with Taft and Van Devanter than with Brandeis.

Oliver Wendell Holmes

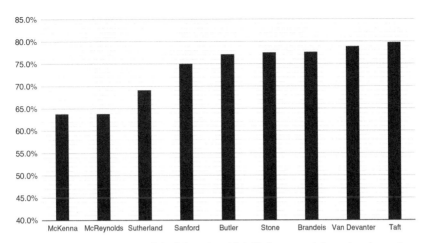

Figure II-4 Percentage of decisions in which Holmes participated and voted with another justice in conference

Holmes's own opinion in *Casey v. United States*,[225] because "it will indicate that there is no preestablished harmony between us."[226]

The conservative members of the Taft Court, however, were suspicious of the bond between Holmes and Brandeis. In 1923, Taft wrote his daughter that Holmes's "age makes him a little more subordinate or yielding to Brandeis, who is his constant companion, than he would have been in his prime."[227] Three years later Taft had come to believe that Holmes's defective constitutional jurisprudence "is not due to his age – it is due to his training and point of view and to the influence which Brandeis has had on him."[228] By 1928, Taft had become exasperated with the relationship between Holmes and Brandeis. "I am very fond of the old gentleman, but he is so completely under the control of brother Brandeis that it gives to Brandeis two votes instead of one."[229]

Holmes himself frequently acknowledged cases in which Brandeis "has perhaps turned the scale on the question whether I should write."[230] But it is far less clear whether Brandeis actually altered Holmes's judgments in particular cases.[d] There are circumstances where it is plausible to conjecture that Brandeis induced Holmes to dissent,[231] and we can identify at least one important decision, *Olmstead v. United States*,[232] in which "Holmes voted the other way till Brandeis got after him and induced him to change on the ground that a state law in Washington forbade wiretapping."[233]

If at the outset of the Taft Court Holmes was much aligned in the public mind with Brandeis because both were viewed as dissenters, by the end of the decade the public was noticing the emerging "tally" of "Justices Holmes, Brandeis, and Stone

---

[d] The contrast between Figure II-3 and Figure II-4 is suggestive in this regard. The difference between the pattern of Holmes's allegiance in published opinions, and his allegiance in the privacy of the conference room, is most striking.

dissenting."[234] This tally also figured prominently in the perception of the Court's conservatives. Only a month before his resignation, Taft could write his brother that "We have a dissenting minority of three in the Court. I think we can hold our six to steady the Court. Brandeis is of course hopeless, as Holmes is, and as Stone is. . . . The truth is that Hoover is a Progressive, just as Stone is, and just as Brandeis is, and just as Holmes is."[235]

In point of fact, however, Holmes was in his personal, political views a lifelong Republican who would have voted for Taft in 1912 and Coolidge in 1924.[236] Holmes was no more a progressive than was Taft himself. That Taft could so fundamentally blur the distinction between political and legal spheres tells us much about the lines of division that would afflict the Taft Court and that would, as we shall see, harden by 1930 into unbridgeable chasms.

Oliver Wendell Holmes

Notes

1. CHARLES EVANS HUGHES, THE AUTOBIOGRAPHICAL NOTES OF CHARLES EVANS HUGHES 171–72 (David J. Danelski & Joseph S. Tulchin, eds., Cambridge: Harvard University Press 1973).
2. Throughout his life Holmes struggled to emerge from the shadow of his father. *See, e.g., Justice Holmes Sighed, He Has Been Taken for His Distinguished Parent Before*, WASHINGTON POST (January 31, 1904), at B3:

    > The latest addition to the Supreme Court circle went to an afternoon tea the other day. He was introduced to the wife of a Western member of Congress. "Ah," said the lady in question, "I am indeed glad to meet you, Mr. Justice. I have read most of your splendid books. That 'Elsie Vedder' of yours is simply fine. I do assure you," archly, "the name of Oliver Wendell Holmes is a household word in our family."
    >
    > Once more the justice attempted to explain that he was only the son of his father, but the lady from the West waived him off with an assurance that he was entirely too modest, and should not hide his literary light under a bushel. Justice Holmes sighed and resumed the supping of his punch.

    When *Time* magazine celebrated Holmes's eighty-fifth birthday in 1926, it featured a flattering portrait of Holmes on its cover. The caption read: "Oliver Wendell Holmes – as venerable as his father." 8 TIME (March 15, 1926). *See Supreme Court, id.* at 8.
3. Even in the 1920s, popular appreciation of Holmes Jr. was frequently entangled with the reputation of his father. *See, e.g., Recipients of the Roosevelt Medals*, PHILADELPHIA INQUIRER (June 4, 1924), at 12; Carson C. Hathaway, *Mr. Justice Holmes Reaches 85*, NEW YORK TIMES (March 7, 1926), at SM1; *Looking Ahead*, 7 TIME 10 (March 15, 1926); *A Sage with the Bearing of a Cavalier*, 88 LITERARY DIGEST 38 (March 27, 1926); *The Judiciary: Supreme Convention*, 10 TIME 8 (October 10, 1927) ("Son and namesake of the poet, wounded in chest and foot as a Civil War volunteer, Mr. Associate Justice Holmes represents all that is spirited, liberal and scholarly in New England."); *Eighty-Eight Years Old and Still Active*, 15 AMERICAN BAR ASSOCIATION JOURNAL 211 (1929).
4. Like his father, Holmes was a member of the Porcellian Club while a Harvard undergraduate. Holmes was also Secretary and the Poet of the Hasty Pudding Society. Saul Touster, *In Search of Holmes from Within*, 18 VANDERBILT LAW REVIEW 437, 445 (1965); CATALOGUE OF THE OFFICERS AND MEMBERS OF THE HASTY-PUDDING CLUB IN HARVARD UNIVERSITY 17, 27 (Cambridge: Metcalf and Co. 1846); CATALOGUE OF THE HONORARY AND IMMEDIATE MEMBERS AND OF THE LIBRARY OF THE PORCELLIAN CLUB OF HARVARD UNIVERSITY 47 (Cambridge: Allen and Farnham 1857). Interestingly, Taft, while attending Yale, was, like his prominent father Alphonso Taft, a member of Skull and Bones, which his father had helped to found. *See* DAVID ALAN RICHARDS, SKULLS AND KEYS: THE HIDDEN HISTORY OF YALE'S SECRET SOCIETIES 63, 280 (New York: Pegasus Books 2017).
5. Fort Sumter was fired upon on April 12, 1861, and Holmes enlisted a few days later, risking the possibility that he would fail to receive his degree. Touster, *supra* note 4, at 445–46. Chance circumstances allowed him to return at the end of the semester to

graduate. EDWARD WHITE, JUSTICE OLIVER WENDELL HOLMES: LAW AND THE INNER SELF 44–46 (New York: Oxford University Press 1993).

6. Holmes later wrote his friend Harold Laski about an "emotional state not unlike that of the abolitionists in former days which then I shared and now much dislike." OWH to Harold Laski (September 18, 1918), in I HOLMES-LASKI CORRESPONDENCE, at 164. *See* OWH to Harold Laski (December 28, 1924), *id.* at 689 ("I had my belly full of isms when young."); OWH to Harold Laski (August 7, 1925), *id.* at 772 ("The only thing I am competent to say from the experience of my youth is that I fear your getting into the frame of mind that I saw in the Abolitionists (and shared) – the martyr spirit.").

7. Touster, *supra* note 4, at 447; MARK DEWOLFE HOWE, I JUSTICE OLIVER WENDELL HOLMES: THE SHAPING YEARS 66–68 (Cambridge: Harvard University Press 1957). Holmes later recalled "the time before the Civil War when I was deeply moved by the Abolition cause – so deeply that a Negro minstrel show shocked me." OWH to Arthur Garfield Hays (April 20, 1928) (Holmes papers).

8. OWH to Mother (May 3, 1863), in TOUCHED WITH FIRE: CIVIL WAR LETTERS AND DIARY OF OLIVER WENDELL HOLMES, JR., 1861–1864, at 92 (Mark DeWolfe Howe, ed., Cambridge: Harvard University Press 1946). Holmes would later characterize his Chancellorsville incapacitation as "an inglorious wound ... were it not for the precedent of Achilles." DEAN ACHESON, MORNING AND NOON 62 (Boston: Houghton Mifflin Co. 1965).

9. OWH to Parents (May 16, 1864), in TOUCHED WITH FIRE, *supra* note 8, at 122 ("nearly every Regimental off[icer] I knew or cared for is dead or wounded.").

10. Holmes wrote his parents, "I am convinced from my late experience that if I can stand the wear & tear (body & mind) of regimental duty that it is a greater strain on both than I am called on to endure. ... I am not the same man (may not have quite the same ideas) & certainly am not so elastic as I was and *I will not acknowledge the same claims upon me under those circumstances* that existed formerly." OWH to Parents (May 30, 1864), in TOUCHED WITH FIRE, *supra* note 8, at 135.

11. OWH to Mother (June 7, 1864), in TOUCHED WITH FIRE, *supra* note 8, at 142–43. There is a famous story about Holmes's evolution from boy to man. It involves his father's long search for his wounded son after Antietam. Oliver Wendell Holmes, Sr., *My Hunt after the Captain*, 10 ATLANTIC MONTHLY 738 (1862). At the story's climax, Holmes Sr. finally locates Holmes Jr. Their resulting conversation is meant to distill Brahmin reserve: "'How are you, Boy?' 'How are you, Dad?'" *Id.* at 760. Later it was said by Alexander Woollcott that Holmes repudiated this version of the conversation: "What [Oliver Wendell Holmes Jr.] had really answered – or so I've heard – was, 'Boy nothing.'" Alexander Woollcott, *"Get Down, You Fool!"*, 161 ATLANTIC MONTHLY 169, 173 (1938).

12. OWH to Mother (June 7, 1864), in TOUCHED WITH FIRE, *supra* note 8, at 143.

13. WHITE, *supra* note 5, at 65.

14. *See* OWH to Oliver Wendell Holmes, Sr. (December 20, 1862), in TOUCHED WITH FIRE, *supra* note 8, at 80 ("I believe I am as ready as ever to do my duty."). Saul Touster observes that after witnessing the pointless massacre at Fredericksburg, "Holmes's disassociation between mind and feeling begins to blossom and take its form. Whatever sympathetic feelings went into his belief in the cause are to be purged, and the cause will be supported, if at all, by 'abstract conviction.' ... But a cause without sympathetic feelings is an empty shell, and is soon transformed into

Oliver Wendell Holmes

'duty' divorced from cause and 'heroism' divorced from meaning." Touster *supra* note 4, at 464. Touster is convincing when he characterizes the famous peroration of *The Soldier's Faith* as the ultimate expression of this "disassociation":

> I do not know what is true. I do not know the meaning of the universe. But in the midst of doubt, in the collapse of creeds, there is one thing I do not doubt . . . and that is that the faith is true and adorable which leads a soldier to throw away his life in obedience to a blindly accepted duty, in a cause he little understands, in a plan of campaign of which he has no notion, under tactics of which he does not see the use.

The Soldier's Faith (May 30, 1895), in THE OCCASIONAL SPEECHES OF JUSTICE OLIVE WENDELL HOLMES 76 (Mark DeWolfe Howe, ed., Cambridge: Harvard University Press 1962) ("OCCASIONAL SPEECHES"). Holmes himself later described the peroration as designed "to bring home by example that men are eternally idealists – (a speech that fools took as advice to young men to wade in gore)." OWH to Clara Stevens (September 3, 1909) (Holmes papers).

15. *See* OWH to Mother (June 7, 1864), in TOUCHED WITH FIRE, *supra* note 8, at 143 ("I can do a disagreeable thing or face a great danger coolly enough when I *know* it is my duty – but a doubt demoralizes me as it does any nervous man – and now I honestly think the duty of fighting has ceased for me – ceased because I have laboriously and with much suffering of mind and body *earned* the right . . . to decide for myself how I can best do my duty to myself to the country and, if you choose, to God – ").

16. In later years, Holmes would frequently recall the story that when his cousin John T. Morse, Jr., who had remained a civilian during the war, asked Holmes why Holmes's "wartime effort to grow a moustache was so much more successful than his own," Holmes replied, "Mine was nourished in blood." HOWE, *supra* note 7, at 8.

17. WHITE, *supra* note 5, at 488. Also found were two Civil War uniforms pinned with a paper that read: "These uniforms were worn by me in the Civil War and the stains upon them are my blood." *Id*.

18. "War, when you are at it, is horrible and dull. It is only when time has passed that you see that its message was divine." *The Soldier's Faith*, *supra* note 14, at 80.

19. *Memorial Day* (May 30, 1884), in OCCASIONAL SPEECHES, *supra* note 14, at 15 ("The generation that carried on the war has been set apart by its experience. Through our great good fortune, in our youth our hearts were touched with fire. It was given to us to learn at the outset that life is a profound and passionate thing.").

20. *See* note 14 *supra*. "The first thing is to recognize the inevitable and to try to put what rationality one can into the semirational prejudices that govern the world." OWH to Felix Frankfurter (March 24, 1914) in HOLMES-FRANKFURTER CORRESPONDENCE, at 20. "Why should we employ the energy that is furnished to us by the cosmos to defy it and shake our fist at the sky? It seems to me silly." *Natural Law*, in OLIVER WENDELL HOLMES, COLLECTED LEGAL PAPERS 315 (New York: Harcourt, Brace and Co. 1920) ("COLLECTED LEGAL PAPERS"). "People damned Rockefeller when he embodied the inevitables. They didn't say, damn order of the universe or the Great Panjandrum yet it was the order of the universe that they disliked." OWH to Felix Frankfurter (November 30, 1919) in HOLMES-FRANKFURTER CORRESPONDENCE, at 77. "The order of things is a peremptory datum – One can like it or lump it, but one has no fulcrum to attack it." OWH to Mrs. Gray (March 28, 1920) (Holmes papers).

21. "Real skepticism," Holmes remarked, "builds all its arrogance on humility and I think with only a seeming paradox might be said to be the most religious of attitudes." OWH to Alice Stopford Green (February 7, 1909) (Holmes papers). Holmes affirmed that "I detest a man who knows that he knows." OWH to Harold Laski (October 24, 1930), in 2 HOLMES-LASKI CORRESPONDENCE, at 1291. "The abolitionists had a stock phrase that a man was either a knave or a fool who did not act as they (the abolitionists) *knew* to be right. So Calvin thought of the Catholics and the Catholics of Calvin. So I don't doubt do the more convinced prohibitionists think of their opponents today. When you know that you know persecution comes easy. It is as well that some of us don't know that we know anything." OWH to Frederick Pollock (August 30, 1929), in 2 HOLMES-POLLOCK CORRESPONDENCE, at 252. *See also* OWH to Harold Laski (May 12, 1927), in 2 HOLMES-LASKI CORRESPONDENCE, at 942 ("The abolitionists as I remember used to say that their antagonists must be either knaves or fools. I am glad that I encountered that sort of thing early as it taught me a lesson."); *Natural Law, supra* note 20, at 311–12 ("[W]hile one's experience thus makes certain preferences dogmatic for oneself, recognition of how they came to be so leaves one able to see that others, poor souls, may be equally dogmatic about something else. And this again means skepticism. Not that one's belief or love does not remain. Not that we would not fight and die for it if important – we all, whether we know it or not, are fighting to make the kind of a world that we should like – but that we have learned to recognize that others will fight and die to make a different world, with equal sincerity or belief. Deep-seated preferences can not be argued about – you can not argue a man into liking a glass of beer – and therefore, when differences are sufficiently far reaching, we try to kill the other man rather than let him have his way. But that is perfectly consistent with admitting that, so far as appears, his grounds are just as good as ours.").

During the war Holmes had come to respect the "unity and determination of the South," OWH to Oliver Wendell Holmes, Sr. (December 20, 1862), in TOUCHED WITH FIRE, *supra* note 8, at 80, and he later praised our "noble enemies in Virginia or Georgia or on the Mississippi." *The Soldier's Faith, supra* note 14, at 81. In 1917 he wrote his friend Harold Laski: "The Confederate gathering here was not without its emotional value – amusing, touching, recalling my youth – and perhaps also a shrewd indication to other countries concerned that we are united. I was more pleased than you would have been at one broad sign displayed: Damn a man who ain't for his country right or wrong." OWH to Harold Laski (June 9, 1917), in 1 HOLMES-LASKI CORRESPONDENCE, at 89–90.

22. *See supra* note 21. "When two crowds determinately wish to make different kinds of a world, if they come in contact I don't see what there is to do but to fight." OWH to Harold Laski (October 24, 1930), in 2 HOLMES-LASKI CORRESPONDENCE, at 1291–92. "When a man is satisfied with himself it means that he has ceased to struggle and therefore has ceased to achieve. He is dead, and may be allowed the thin delight of reading his own obituary." *Address: Dinner of the Chicago Bar Association* (October 21, 1902), in 3 THE COLLECTED WORKS OF JUSTICE HOLMES 532 (Sheldon M. Novick, ed., University of Chicago Press 1995) ("3 COLLECTED WORKS"). "I always have said that the rights of a given crowd are what they will fight for." OWH to Harold Laski (July 23, 1925), in 1 HOLMES-LASKI CORRESPONDENCE, at 762. *See Memorial Day, supra* note 19, at 6–7 ("I think the feeling was right – in the South as in the North. I think that, as life is action and

passion, it is required of a man that he should share the passion and action of his time at peril of being judged not to have lived."); OWH to Frederick Pollock (February 1, 1920), in 1 HOLMES-POLLOCK CORRESPONDENCE, at 36 ("I loathe war – which I described when at home with a wound in our Civil War as an organized bore – to the scandal of the young women of the day who thought that Captain Holmes was wanting in patriotism. But I do think that man at present is a predatory animal. I think that the sacredness of human life is a purely municipal ideal of no validity outside the jurisdiction. I believe that force, mitigated so far as may be by good manners, is the *ultima ratio*, and between groups that want to make inconsistent kinds of world I see no remedy except force. I may add what I no doubt have said often enough, that it seems to me that every society rests on the death of men"); *Natural Law, supra* note 20, at 310, 313, 315–16:

> I used to say, when I was young, that truth was the majority vote of that nation that could lick all others. Certainly we may expect that the received opinion about the present war will depend a good deal upon which side wins (I hope with all my soul it will be mine) ... [O]ur test of truth is a reference to either a present or an imagined future majority in favor of our view. ...
>
> [F]or legal purposes a right is only the hypostasis of a prophecy – the imagination of a substance supporting the fact that public force will be brought to bear upon those who do things said to contravene it. ...
>
> That the universe has in it more than we understand, that the private soldiers have not been told the plan of campaign, or even that there is one, rather than some vaster unthinkable to which every predicate is an impertinence, has no bearing upon our conduct. We shall fight – all of us because we want to live, some, at least, because we want to realize our spontaneity and prove our powers, for the joy of it, and we may leave to the unknown the supposed final valuation of that which in any event has value to us.

Holmes used paradox to reconcile his fatalism and his commitment to action. "[T]he mode in which the inevitable comes to pass is through effort. Consciously or unconsciously we all strive to make the kind of a world that we like." *Ideals and Doubts*, in COLLECTED LEGAL PAPERS, *supra* note 20, at 305. *See* OWH to Lewis Einstein (May 10, 1903) in HOLMES-EINSTEIN CORRESPONDENCE, at 5. Holmes expressed the inverse of the paradox in this way: "Civilization means transcending our own dogmas, and I stick to my paradox that the best man is he who dies for a cause he does not believe in. My respect for ideals is only because of my respect for the function that they express. The function of idealizing is fundamental in human nature." OWH to Ethel Scott (November 28, 1908) (Holmes papers). The function of idealizing was to make men fight. *Id.* Holmes believed that "a paradox takes the scum off your mind." OWH to Felix Frankfurter (December 23, 1921) in HOLMES-FRANKFURTER CORRESPONDENCE, at 119.

23. Quoted in WHITE, *supra* note 5, at 8.
24. WHITE, *supra* note 5, at 476. In 1876, William James characterized his friend Oliver as "a powerful battery, formed like a planning machine to gouge a deep self-beneficial groove through life." William James to Henry James (July 5, 1876), quoted in Ralph Barton Perry, 1 THE THOUGHT AND CHARACTER OF WILLIAM JAMES 371 (Boston: Little, Brown & Co. 1935).
25. Many years later, when Holmes observed his childhood friend Henry James saying "'poor Wendell' and 'poor William' have chosen success," he responded sharply, "Hum. As I observed on reading Amiel years ago, it is not always disgraceful to

succeed. I never knew anyone to elect against it for the sake of avoiding it." OWH to Mrs. Gray (April 30, 1905) (Holmes papers).
26. WHITE, *supra* note 5, at 91.
27. HOWE, *supra* note 7, at 184.
28. *Harvard University, Law School*, 5 AMERICAN LAW REVIEW 177, 177 (1871). The identification of Holmes as the author of this article is by WHITE, *supra* note 5, at 91.
29. Quoted in WHITE, *supra* note 5, at 94.
30. HOWE, *supra* note 7, at 245.
31. Howe believes that Holmes and Thayer each independently reached the conclusion that courts ought to exercise restraint in the context of judicial review; the latter, although ten years older than Holmes, did not instruct the former. HOWE, *supra* note 7, at 246–48.
32. When he received the first copy of the book, Holmes and his wife Fanny "opened a bottle of champagne; he saved the cork for the rest of his life." WHITE, *supra* note 5, at 196.
33. Yosal Rogat, *The Judge as Spectator*, 31 UNIVERSITY OF CHICAGO LAW REVIEW 213, 214 (1964).
34. James Bradley Thayer, who (with the indispensable assistance of Harvard alumnus Louis Brandeis) had been essential in obtaining the funding for Holmes's professorship at Harvard (and who had also secured Holmes's commission to revise Kent's *Commentaries*), was shocked by Holmes's abandonment of his Harvard position without notice or discussion: "He lost his head perhaps? But my experience in editing Kent, which I had been willing to forget, comes all back again and assures me that this conduct is characteristic – that he is, with all his attractive qualities and his solid merits, wanting sadly in the noblest region of human character – selfish, vain, thoughtless of others." Quoted in WHITE, *supra* note 5, at 205.
35. Oliver Wendell Holmes, *The Path of the Law*, 1 BOSTON LAW SCHOOL MAGAZINE 1 (February 1897).
36. Morton J. Horwitz, *The Place of Justice Holmes in American Legal Thought*, in THE LEGACY OF OLIVER WENDELL HOLMES, JR. 69 (Robert W. Gordon, ed., Stanford University Press 1992). "There has been only one great American legal thinker and it was Holmes." *Id.* at 31.
37. *Id.* at 67–68. Hence the famous story told by Learned Hand about Holmes: "I remember once I was with [Justice Holmes]; it was a Saturday when the Court was to confer. It was before we had a motor car, and we jogged along in an old coupé. When we got down to the Capitol, I wanted to provoke a response, so as he walked off, I said to him: 'Well, sir, goodbye. Do justice!' He turned quite sharply and he said: 'Come here. Come here.' I answered: 'Oh, I know, I know.' He replied: ' That is not my job. My job is to play the game according to the rules.'" Learned Hand, THE SPIRIT OF LIBERTY 306–7 (Irving Dilliard, ed., 3rd ed., University of Chicago Press 1960). For an account of this story, see Michael Hertz, *"Do Justice!" Variations of a Thrice-Told Tale*, 82 VIRGINIA LAW REVIEW 111 (1996). Charles Evans Hughes recalls that "when he thought that a case was clear according to his conception of the law, Justice Holmes scorned any suggestion at the conference table of deviating from the result the law required because it would be 'unjust.' He said that it was 'the stinking sense of justice' that bedeviled the proper administration of the law." HUGHES, *supra* note 1, at 176. It should not be forgotten, however,

that Holmes was also quite willing to concede the existence of cases "of imaginable laws which the statute-making power would not dare to enact, even in the absence of written constitutional prohibitions, because the community would rise in rebellion and fight; and this gives some plausibility to the proposition that the law, if not a part of morality, is limited by it. But this limit of power is not coextensive with any system of morals." *Path of the Law, supra* note 35, at 3.

38. Horwitz, *supra* note 36, at 57.
39. Oliver Wendell Holmes, *Law in Science and Science in Law*, 12 HARVARD LAW REVIEW 443, 461 (1899).
40. Horwitz, *supra* note 36, at 51. Holmes "has done more than lead American juristic thought of the present generation. Above all others he has shaped the methods and ideas that are characteristic of the present as distinguished from the immediate past." Roscoe Pound, *Judge Holmes's Contributions to the Science of Law*, 34 HARVARD LAW REVIEW 448, 448 (1921). "Holmes, almost alone, has cracked open the law of these United States." Karl N. Llewellyn, *Holmes*, 35 COLUMBIA LAW REVIEW 485, 487 (1935).
41. *Path of the Law, supra* note 35, at 8.
42. *Id.* at 9–10.
43. *Law in Science and Science in Law, supra* note 39, at 452.
44. *Id.* at 460. *See Holdsworth's English Law*, in COLLECTED LEGAL PAPERS, *supra* note 20, at 290 ("mankind yet may take its own destiny consciously and intelligently in hand."); Pound, *supra* note 40, at 450 (among Holmes's many contributions was "a functional point of view in contrast with the purely anatomical or morphological standpoint of the last century.").
45. *See supra* Chapter 4, at 128. There is no doubt but that Stone knew and had assimilated his Holmes. *See, e.g.*, HFS to Herbert Wechsler (December 1, 1930) (Stone papers) ("I am a great admirer of the Justice and think that his work has had a profound influence on the law."); Harlan F. Stone, *Book Review of The Nature of the Judicial Process*, 22 COLUMBIA LAW REVIEW 382, 383, 386 (1922); Harlan F. Stone, *The Common Law in the United States*, 50 HARVARD LAW REVIEW 4, 7, 20 (1936).
46. Louis Brandeis had clerked for Gray between 1879 and 1881 when Gray was a justice on the Supreme Judicial Court of Massachusetts. TODD C. PEPPERS, COURTIERS OF THE MARBLE PALACE: THE RISE AND INFLUENCE OF THE SUPREME COURT LAW CLERK 45 (Stanford University Press 2006).
47. The story is well told in WHITE, *supra* note 5, at 298–306. Roosevelt had been impressed by the militarism of Holmes's oration *The Soldier's Faith, supra* note 14, but Roosevelt had also needed assurances from Lodge that Holmes would be sound on the insular cases so that the United States could continue to govern its newly acquired colonies without cumbersome constitutional restraints. SHELDON M. NOVICK, HONORABLE JUSTICE: THE LIFE OF OLIVER WENDELL HOLMES 234–36 (Boston: Little, Brown & Co. 1989). "Now I should like to know that Judge Holmes was in entire sympathy with our views, that is with your views and mine and Judge Gray's," Roosevelt wrote Lodge. Theodore Roosevelt to Henry Cabot Lodge (July 10, 1902), in 1 SELECTIONS FROM THE CORRESPONDENCE OF THEODORE ROOSEVELT AND HENRY CABOT LODGE 518–19 (New York: Charles Scribner's Sons 1925). Lodge queried Holmes and vouched for his ideological reliability. "'I told the President you had always been a Republican and never a Mugwump,' said Lodge. 'A Mugwump!' Holmes replied stoutly, 'I should

THE TAFT COURT

think not. Why they are mere elements of dissolution.'" Henry Cabot Lodge to Theodore Roosevelt (July 19 and 26, 1902), quoted in John A. Garraty, *Holmes's Appointment to the U.S. Supreme Court*, 22 NEW ENGLAND QUARTERLY 291, 296 (1949).

Holmes in fact remained a loyal Republican throughout his life. He supported Taft in 1912. OWH to Canon Patrick Augustine Sheehan (November 23, 1912), in HOLMES-SHEEHAN CORRESPONDENCE, at 52 ("I was sorry for Taft in the recent election.... I think that probably Taft was the best man.... I said of the Roosevelt movement that it seemed characterized by a strenuous vagueness that made an atmospheric disturbance but transmitted no message. To prick the sensitive points of the social consciousness when one ought to know that the suggestion of cures is humbug, I think wicked."). He supported Coolidge in 1924, in part because he did not want a Democrat to name his replacement to the Court. *See* OWH to Harold Laski (November 13, 1924), in 1 HOLMES-LASKI CORRESPONDENCE, at 671 ("If I had a vote I should have voted for Coolidge – quite apart from the fact that his election relieves my conscience from the doubt whether I ought to resign so as to give the appointment to him. I think your judgment of Coolidge is prejudiced – and while I don't expect anything very astonishing from him I don't want anything very astonishing."). *See* Harold Laski to OWH (November 26, 1924), *id.* at 678.

48. Holmes's appointment to the Court received largely favorable reviews in the press, although there were endless comparisons to his father. Holmes expressed "rage" to Frederick Pollock over the lack of appreciation of his real contributions to the theory and shaping of law. "It makes one sick when he has broken his heart in trying to make every word living and real to see a lot of duffers ... talking with the sanctity of print in a way that at once discloses to the knowing eye that literally they don't know anything about it." OWH to Frederick Pollock (September 23, 1902) in 1 HOLMES-POLLOCK CORRESPONDENCE, at 106. Holmes had long before acknowledged his own tendency to "grind my teeth in secret rage at the public ignorance of the difference between the first rate and the second rate." OWH to Claire Castletown (May 28, 1897) (Holmes papers). Holmes did receive, however, a knowing appreciation from his longtime acquaintance Louis Brandeis, who presciently wrote that "I trust that years enough may be given you to make the deep impression which you can upon Federal jurisprudence." LDB to OWH (September 3, 1902) quoted in NOVICK, *supra* note 47, at 237. To which Holmes replied, "For many years you have, from time to time, at critical moments, said things that have given me courage, which probably I remember better than you do. You do it again now, with the same effect and always with the same pleasure to me." OWH to LDB (September 4, 1902), quoted in NOVICK, *supra* note 47, at 237.

49. OWH to Mrs. Codman (December 30, 1902) (Holmes papers). *See* OWH to Mrs. Curtis (November 12, 1904) (Holmes papers) ("I am happier on the whole than I ever was in my life."); OWH to Mrs. Curtis (April 21, 1903) (Holmes papers) ("At bottom I am profoundly happy – because – the task I have undertaken is so great and so different. I would not give it up for anything.").

50. OWH to Mrs. Codman (December 30, 1902) (Holmes papers).

51. OWH to Mrs. Curtis (February 7, 1903) (Holmes papers) ("I do like having the last word and knowing that there isn't any incompetent idiot who can reverse you or do anything but swallow what you say."). *See* OWH to Mrs. Codman (February 15,

1903) (Holmes papers) ("I can't put too strongly the feeling of being in a bigger place as far as my business is concerned. The questions are bigger and the advantage of position not to be despised. What one says here is attended to just because it is said here."); OWH to Mrs. Gray (March 2, 1903) (Holmes papers) ("I can't say how much I still like the work – It is much bigger than a state court – and when you do it you know that there is the end. There can't come in some snob and reverse you – which is a comfort. I rather enjoy the element of diplomacy in trying to state things in such a way as to get them swallowed by hesitating throats. Fundamentally it is the same as anywhere else – but also it is very different."). Looking back at his position on the Supreme Judicial Court of Massachusetts, Holmes wrote that "the wonder is whether anyone appreciated or cared for my work. What I have done heretofore is a finished volume. A new one opens and it demands all one's powers." OWH to Mrs. Gray (January 4, 1903) (Holmes papers).

52. OWH to Mrs. Curtis (February 24, 1903) (Holmes papers). "I like to write as many cases as I can," Holmes wrote a friend. OWH to Alice Stopford Green (July 11, 1905) (Holmes papers). He even felt as if his intellectual energy and precision "should count for more than merely one vote." OWH to Mrs. Gray (January 4, 1903) (Holmes papers). "I am a law machine," Holmes said, "drop a case into the hopper and I grind out an answer pretty soon." OWH to Alice Stopford Green (February 8, 1910) (Holmes papers).

53. "The novelty solemnity and augustness of the work has made my past labors seem a closed volume locked up in a distant safe." OWH to John G. Palfrey (December 27, 1902) (Holmes papers).

54. OWH to Clara Stevens (January 10, 1903) (Holmes papers).

55. OWH to Clara Stevens (May 12, 1903) (Holmes papers). *See* OWH to Mrs. Curtis (April 21, 1903) (Holmes papers) ("For the first time in my life I am up against a greatness that comes from outside. Hitherto I have constructed from within what seemed lines of the infinite. Now it is the simple grandiose – the external fact of feeling a vast world vibrate to one's determinations."); OWH to Mrs. Curtis (January 12, 1903) (Holmes papers) ("My chief familiarity is with the Judges. There are some very powerful men amongst them. Indeed they all are men of power and wide experience. It is a pleasure to wrestle with them and to note their ways.").

56. *John Marshall*, in COLLECTED LEGAL PAPERS, *supra* note 20, at 269.

57. OWH to Mrs. Gray (April 12, 1903) (Holmes papers). *See* OWH to Mrs. Curtis (December 21, 1902) (Holmes papers) ("For the first time in my life I have had flashes of a sense of responsibility. You know that I always have said one should not have. ... [T]o feel responsibility is steam out of the boiler – egotism in disguise – but things here are so solemn and tremendous that the thought will break in at times."); OWH to Canon Patrick Augustine Sheehan (March 21, 1908) in HOLMES-SHEEHAN CORRESPONDENCE, at 22 ("A sense of responsibility is a confession of weakness. If I put all my powers into deciding the case and writing my decision, I neither feel responsibility nor egotism, nor yet altruism – I am just all in the problem and doing my best.").

58. OWH to John G. Palfrey (December 27, 1902) (Holmes papers). "At first I felt as if I were among demigods with huge heads and big faces who understood everything with diabolic swiftness. But I begin to hope that I can hold up my end." *Id.*

59. OWH to Mrs. Curtis (May 3, 1903) (Holmes papers). The full passage reads: "My spirit is too flashy and too depressed by a vague feeling of many things, I know not what, to be ... very hopeful. Do you know those vague 'vital feelings of (un)delight' such as to make one aware that a shoelacing is untied or a suspender given way – I do not venture to name feminine counterparts? There are similar uneasinesses about graver affairs – which may point to something specific forgotten or not. I take refuge at such moments in the ultimate indifference, and the thought that nothing matters unless you choose that it should matter. However, this sounds more gloomy than I am. I am not gloomy, only sluggish with a rumbling uneasiness."
60. OWH to Mrs. Gray (May 3, 1903) (Holmes papers).
61. 189 U.S. 475 (1903).
62. OWH to Clara Stevens (May 12, 1903) (Holmes papers). Although Holmes frequently claimed that "I don't read the papers or otherwise feel the pulse of the machine," OWH to Frederick Pollock (May 25, 1906), 1 HOLMES-POLLOCK CORRESPONDENCE, at 124, his letter to Stevens complained that "some papers, only obscure ones so far as I know, have been representing me as a second Taney in respect of probing another Dred Scott decision." OWH to Clara Stevens (May 12, 1903) (Holmes papers). *See* OWH to Canon Patrick Augustine Sheehan (April 16, 1913), in HOLMES-SHEEHAN CORRESPONDENCE, at 64 ("I read no newspapers."); Robert W. Wales, *Some Aspects of Life with Mr. Justice Holmes in His 90th Year*, 28 UNIVERSITY OF FLORIDA LAW REVIEW 395, 397–98 (1976) ("It was well known that [Holmes] never read newspapers, believing that knowledge of matters of any real importance would reach him through other means.").
63. 193 U.S. 197 (1904). Holmes later wrote a close friend of his dissent in *Northern Securities*: "The last term of the Court was interesting. I wrote some judgments which I was glad to have a chance to write and I think I am succeeding in my new place. The most exciting one in a popular sense was the Northern Securities Case, which caused me some pain at the moment, as I was compelled to express an opinion contrary to what the President ardently desired. The newspapers were full of stories of his wrath, etc., but he is all right and the incident is closed. I say it caused me some pain in the sense that it is always painful when you run against what a personal friend is hoping for and perhaps expecting. Of course such considerations have no effect on the mind of one who is accustomed to weigh questions impersonally or who is fit for his business." OWH to Canon Patrick Augustine Sheehan (September 6, 1904) in HOLMES-SHEEHAN CORRESPONDENCE, at 14–15.
64. 193 U.S. at 400 (Holmes, J., dissenting). *Northern Securities* involved the application of the Sherman Anti-trust Act to the merger of two railroads. Holmes had long believed, as he had articulated in a famous dissent from the bench of the Supreme Judicial Court of Massachusetts, that "It is plain from the slightest consideration of practical affairs, or the most superficial reading of industrial history, that free competition means combination, and that the organization of the world, now going on so fast, means an ever-increasing might and scope of combination. It seems to me futile to set our faces against this tendency." Vegelahn v. Gunner, 167 Mass. 92, 108 (1896) (Holmes, J., dissenting). This premise is why Holmes was willing to fight the prejudices of his class to uphold the efforts of labor unions to organize, but it is also why he was unsympathetic to federal anti-trust enforcement. He regarded "the anti-trust legislation that I help to enforce [as] idiotic," OWH to

Oliver Wendell Holmes

Canon Patrick Augustine Sheehan (April 16, 1913), in HOLMES-SHEEHAN CORRESPONDENCE, at 64, and as "an imbecile performance." OWH to Nina Gray (July 28, 1915) (Holmes papers). On Holmes's negative attitude toward anti-trust legislation, see Alfred S. Neely, *"A Humbug Based on Economic Ignorance and Incompetence" – Antitrust in the Eyes of Justice Holmes*, 1993 UTAH LAW REVIEW 1. Holmes later wrote a friend that "I was told that Taft said that my dissent in the Northern Securities case could have been predicted from my opinions in the labor cases. It is not true, so far as my consciousness goes, as I really thought I was interpreting the Sherman Anti-Trust Act without regard to prejudices." OWH to Franklin Ford (May 3, 1907), in PROGRESSIVE MASKS: LETTERS OF OLIVER WENDELL HOLMES, JR. AND FRANKLIN FORD 43–44 (David H. Burton, ed., Newark: University of Delaware Press 1982).

65. "The case was not without its painful side," Holmes wrote John Palfrey, "as it involved going against one's natural crowd." OWH to John G. Palfrey (April 1, 1904) (Holmes papers). Holmes and his wife "were enveloped in the Roosevelts' affection, and Holmes was amused and flattered by the President's attention." NOVICK, *supra* note 47, at 261. But Roosevelt was furious at Holmes's dissent, reportedly saying that "he could carve a justice with more backbone out of a banana." Alger Hiss, RECOLLECTIONS OF A LIFE 49 (New York: Henry Holt & Co. 1988). *See* OWEN M. FISS, TROUBLED BEGINNINGS OF THE MODERN STATE, 1888–1910, at 138 n.94 (New York: MacMillan Co. 1993). Roosevelt wrote Lodge, "From his antecedents, Holmes should have been an ideal man on the bench. As a matter of fact, he has been a bitter disappointment, not because of any one decision but because of his general attitude." Theodore Roosevelt to Henry Cabot Lodge (September 4, 1906) (Lodge papers at the Massachusetts Historical Society). For his part, Holmes wrote Frederick Pollock that "'What the boys like about Roosevelt is that he doesn't care a damn for the law.' It broke up our incipient friendship, however, as he looked on my dissent to the *Northern Securities case* as a political departure.... We talked freely later but it never was the same after that, and if he had not been restrained by his friends, I am told that he would have made a fool of himself and would have excluded me from the White House – and as in his case about the law, so in mine about that, I never cared a damn whether I went there or not. He was very likeable, a big figure, a rather ordinary intellect, with extraordinary gifts, a shrewd and I think pretty unscrupulous politician. He played all his cards – if not more. *R.i.p.*" OWH to Frederick Pollock (February 9, 1921), in 2 HOLMES-POLLOCK CORRESPONDENCE, at 63–64. *See* OWH to J.B. Moore (April 2, 1932) (Holmes papers).

In 1928, Holmes wrote his friend Lewis Einstein that he had "no doubt that" Roosevelt "heartily repented" over his nomination of Holmes "when I didn't do what he wanted in the Northern Securities Case.... Long afterwards, at a dinner at the White House to some labor leaders, I said to one of them who had been spouting about the Judges: What you want is favor – not justice. But when I am on my job I don't care a damn what you want or what Mr. Roosevelt wants – and then repeated my remark to him. You may think that a trifle crude – but I didn't like to say it behind his back and not to his face, and the fact had justified it – I thought and think." OWH to Lewis Einstein (April 1, 1928), in HOLMES-EINSTEIN CORRESPONDENCE, at 279. *See* OWH to Alice Stopford Green (February 7, 1909)

THE TAFT COURT

(Holmes papers) (Roosevelt "would chuck me in a minute, if he could, when I ran against his wishes.").

Holmes faced down another highly political confrontation with Roosevelt over the question of whether William Howard Taft as governor of the Philippines could impose tariffs. The story is told in NOVICK, *supra* note 47, at 278–80. In a short, three-page, unanimous opinion, Holmes invalidated the tariffs because they were imposed without congressional ratification. Lincoln v. United States, 197 U.S. 419 (1905), *aff'd on reargument*, 202 U.S. 484 (1906). Taft was furious. He wrote Elihu Root, if the opinion did "not start you into that profanity which at times is as relieving as a safety valve, I shall miss my guess. ... If there ever was a fool decision, this is it, and turned off as flippantly, though it involves $7,000,000 and the legality of transactions of the government extending over two years, as if it involved a bill at the corner grocer's. ... I think the rest of the Court have merely passed it off without fully examining the foolishness of Holmes." WHT to Elihu Root (April 7, 1905) (Taft papers). Taft later sought with some success to achieve *post hoc* congressional ratification of the tariffs, a story that he proudly recounted in WILLIAM HOWARD TAFT, OUR CHIEF MAGISTRATE AND HIS POWERS 99–103 (New York: Columbia University Press 1916). *See* United States v. Heinszen, 206 U.S. 370 (1907).

66. OWH to Canon Patrick Augustine Sheehan (January 31, 1913), in HOLMES-SHEEHAN CORRESPONDENCE, at 58. *See* OWH to Frederick Pollock (September 24, 1910) in 1 HOLMES-POLLOCK CORRESPONDENCE, at 170 ("I know of no first rate man except White. His writing leaves much to be desired, but his thinking is profound, especially in the legislative direction which we don't recognize as a judicial requirement but which is so, especially in our Court, nevertheless."). As he became used to the Supreme Court, however, Holmes became more comfortable declining the demands of judicial statesmanship: "In general I hate important cases, because they mean public attention not legal significance, and, as I once said, bring a kind of hydraulic pressure to bear that disputes the obvious with a solemnity that when I was younger would have imposed." OWH to Mrs. Gray (January 18, 1921) (Holmes papers).
67. OWH to Mrs. Gray (January 4, 1903) (Holmes papers).
68. Holmes would later write Laski in the context of dismissing Dean Acheson's praise of Justice Brandeis's dissent from Holmes's opinion in Pennsylvania Coal Co. v. Mahon, 260 U.S. 393 (1922), that "statesmanship" might be "an effective word," but that one "needs caution in using it." OWH to Laski (January 13, 1923), in 1 HOLMES-LASKI CORRESPONDENCE, at 474.
69. OWH to Canon Patrick Augustine Sheehan (December 15, 1912), in HOLMES-SHEEHAN CORRESPONDENCE, at 56. *See* OWH to Canon Patrick Augustine Sheehan (August 14, 1910), *id.* at 32 ("My only ambition, I can say without a hint of the least mental reserve, is to do the best work that can be done.").
70. OWH to Canon Patrick Augustine Sheehan (January 31, 1913), in HOLMES-SHEEHAN CORRESPONDENCE, at 58.
71. OWH to Canon Patrick Augustine Sheehan (October 27, 1912), in HOLMES-SHEEHAN CORRESPONDENCE, at 51.
72. As Holmes wrote his close friend John Chipman Gray, "[O]f course for purposes of action and courage one goes ahead on his own will, whatever may be said. But for purposes of joy one needs recognition – intelligent and to the point. One is always so

near to despair that it does not take much to bring in the black humor." OWH to John Chipman Gray (August 17, 1902) (Holmes papers).

73. OWH to Clara Stevens (January 6, 1909) (Holmes papers). "I have not had as much recognition as I should like – but I have had a good deal more than I expected and some from adequate and satisfactory sources and of satisfactory degree – That is much – as much as one can expect in the fighting occupations where there always is someone against you and where it doesn't rain superlatives. Few men in baggy trousers and bad hats are recognized as great by those who see them. They have to wait as Lincoln did for their myth to grow." OWH to Clara Stevens (March 6, 1909) (Holmes papers). In 1904 Holmes complained to John Palfrey, "I have been feeling rather lonely at moments in a legal way – although I always get great comfort from my brother White and the Chief. . . . [W]hen the newspapers begin to drivel, while they say nothing worth hearing they reduce one to confusion so far as to make him wonder whether everything he ever did was done in vain and whether some other kind of man is wanted. However I still have a fighting faith." OWH to John G. Palfrey (April 1, 1904) (Holmes papers). *See* OWH to Alice Stopford Green (May 16, 1909) (Holmes papers) ("Perhaps I told you that some time ago White said to me that he didn't know any man in the country who had so little reputation in proportion to what he had done – I was half pleased, if half sad. It didn't make me change my ways as it was intended to, I suppose. How solemnly we all take ourselves.").

74. OWH to Canon Patrick Augustine Sheehan (April 1, 1911), in HOLMES-SHEEHAN CORRESPONDENCE, at 41.

75. *Id.* Holmes was "ashamed of my outburst," which was uncharacteristically personal, but resolved to "send my letter as I have written it." *Id.* He did add that "we are apt to see our merits as physiological but our failures as sins." *Id.*

76. OWH to Canon Patrick Augustine Sheehan (August 14, 1910), in HOLMES-SHEEHAN CORRESPONDENCE, at 33. In a remarkable passage, bursting with vitality and ambition, Holmes wrote:

> Sadness comes with age – or ought to, I suppose. I sometimes try to force myself to feel worse than I do remembering that my next birthday will make me 70. When you speak of infirmities and my friends here die, I really do feel gloomy, but my interest in life is still so keen, I still want to do so much more work, that in the main I feel pretty cheerful. Especially candor compels me to admit when I am led to think that my work is valued as I should like it to be – and here you will discern the [vanity] I am afraid – but as I believe I said I meet him [death] with a grin and cut under him by recognizing that vanity is only a way to get any work out of me, and that my only significance is that which I have in common with the rest of things, that of being part of it.

OWH to Canon Patrick Augustine Sheehan (September 3, 1910), in HOLMES-SHEEHAN CORRESPONDENCE, at 36–37.

77. OWH to Frederick Pollock (December 1, 1925), in 2 HOLMES-POLLOCK CORRESPONDENCE, at 173. Holmes never did have a very great appreciation of the intellectual capacities of ordinary persons. During the Civil War, for example, he had written his sister that "While I am living *en aristocrat* I'm an out-and-outer of a democrat in theory, but for contact, except at the polls, I loathe the thick-fingered

clowns we call the people – especially as the beasts are represented at political centres – vulgar, selfish & base." OWH to Amelia (November 16, 1862), in TOUCHED WITH FIRE, *supra* note 8, at 71.
78. Holmes wrote a friend, "I am pleased because I have not been in academic circles for a quarter of a century and so this implies a certain recognition – but I don't care *very* much." OWH to Clara Stevens (May 29, 1909) (Holmes papers). The following year Holmes "got an encouragement out of the blue that really pleased me" when he received "an honorary degree from Berlin." OWH to Lewis Einstein (December 19, 1910), in HOLMES-EINSTEIN CORRESPONDENCE, at 58. *See* OWH to Alice Stopford Green (March 25, 1911) (Holmes papers). Although Holmes noted the "somewhat increased indications that my work is appreciated as I should like to have it," OWH to Alice Stopford Green (September 4, 1910) (Holmes papers), he nevertheless found himself battling "a despairing sense that popularity or popular appreciation is to be had only by the sacrifice of ideals." OWH to Lewis Einstein (December 19, 1910), in HOLMES-EINSTEIN CORRESPONDENCE, at 58.
79. Holmes did receive a letter from Taft in 1913, assuring Holmes that he was "essential to the Court and there is no one to fill the place you fill as admirably. You seem younger in feeling and intellectual acuteness and vigor than men of sixty and your dispatch of business is itself an argument that is conclusive on the subject. I beg of you in the interest of everything that you and I think worthy of preservation in what our Fathers handed down to us, don't think of giving up when you are doing such great work and when you can not know what manner of man your successor would be." WHT to OWH (December 30, 1913) (Holmes papers). But this praise was plainly an effort to prevent Democratic President Wilson from filling a slot on the Supreme Court. As if the point were not obvious, Taft explained, "If Wilson were to make as many poor selections for the Bench as he has for the diplomatic corps, we would be in a bad way." *Id.* Taft's real attitude was revealed when, in 1912, he was trying to determine if his son Robert, who would finish first in the 1913 class at Harvard Law School and who was president of the *Harvard Law Review*, should clerk for Holmes. Professor John Chipman Gray, one of Holmes's oldest friends, wrote Taft that "As you know, Judge Holmes' opinions seem sometimes to lack lucidity, but I have known him intimately since boyhood, and I know of no one whose talk on the law is so illuminating." John Chipman Gray to WHT (November 9, 1912), quoted in ALEXANDER M. BICKEL & BENNO C. SCHMIDT, JR., THE JUDICIARY AND RESPONSIBLE GOVERNMENT 1910–1921, at 70 (New York: MacMillan Publishing Co. 1984). "Robert and the President concurred in a decision that it was better 'to get started permanently at once in Cincinnati.' The experience with Holmes, the President thought, would not add much to what Robert had acquired at Harvard." *Id.*
80. BICKEL & SCHMIDT, *supra* note 79, at 69–70.
81. Felix Frankfurter to OWH (February 10, 1912), in HOLMES-FRANKFURTER CORRESPONDENCE, at 4.
82. The name of the house "was inspired by debates between Holmes and its residents about the search for truth." BRAD SNYDER, THE HOUSE OF TRUTH: A WASHINGTON POLITICAL SALON AND THE FOUNDATIONS OF AMERICAN LIBERALISM 1, 37 (New York: Oxford University Press 2017).
83. *Id.* at 24.

Oliver Wendell Holmes

84. ACHESON, *supra* note 8, at 62.
85. *See, e.g.*, Walter Lippmann, *To Justice Holmes*, 6 NEW REPUBLIC 156 (1916) ("He wears wisdom like a gorgeous plume, and likes to stick the sanctities between the ribs."). Harold Laski would eventually persuade Holmes to publish his *Collected Legal Papers* in 1920, and in his preface Holmes gave "a clear nod to the House of Truth": "A later generation has carried on the work that I began nearly half a century ago, and it is a great pleasure to an old warrior who cannot expect to bear arms much longer, that the brilliant young soldiers still give him a place in their councils of war." COLLECTED LEGAL PAPERS, *supra* note 20, at v; Brad Snyder, *The House that Built Holmes*, 30 LAW AND HISTORY REVIEW 661, 701 (2012). The publication of Holmes's *Collected Legal Papers* triggered a widespread scholarly reappraisal of Holmes's importance. *Id.* at 703. For the ongoing efforts of the *New Republic* to proselytize for Holmes, see Morris R. Cohen, *Justice Holmes*, 25 NEW REPUBLIC 294 (1921) (praising Holmes's "rich insight into the ever-recurrent issues of life ... clothed in rare nobility of language"); Viscount Haldane, *Mr. Justice Holmes*, 26 NEW REPUBLIC 34 (1921) (Holmes "is a product of the modern spirit in its Anglo-Saxon aspect, and it is in this aspect that he stands out, as I think, beyond his contemporaries."); *Mr. Justice Holmes*, 33 NEW REPUBLIC 84 (1922) (the *New Republic* "wishes to mark the anniversary of forty years of judicial service, and twenty years of Mr. Justice Holmes with rejoicing and with gratitude. ... The judicial work of Mr. Justice Holmes is the symbol at once of the promise and fulfillment of the American judiciary."); *Judges as Statesmen*, 36 NEW REPUBLIC 62 (1923) (Holmes's opinions "express in flashes of lucid and vivid phrasing a theory of the function of the Supreme Court in relation to legislation which demands far more consideration and acceptance than it usually gets."); *Mr. Justice Holmes*, 46 NEW REPUBLIC 88 (1926) ("The fruit of his wisdom has become part of the common stock of civilization. Wherever law is known, he is known."); Elizabeth Shepley Sergeant, *Oliver Wendell Holmes*, 49 NEW REPUBLIC 59 (1926) ("Here is a Yankee, strayed from Olympus."); Philip Littell, *A Judge's Prose*, 53 NEW REPUBLIC 194 (1928) ("His mind has wings, his skepticism has always criticized itself, a habit that is one sign more of the imaginative power which gives his conciseness so many dimensions."); John Dewey, *Justice Holmes and the Liberal Mind*, 53 NEW REPUBLIC 210 (1928) ("the most distinguished of the legal thinkers of our country"); *Mr. Justice Holmes at Ninety*, 66 NEW REPUBLIC 87 (1931) ("Mr. Justice Holmes' ninetieth birthday ... is an event which belongs not to him but to the nation. It has been his supreme achievement to make the qualities of his mind the symbol of what we value most highly in the national life."). In 1930, Harold Laski published an article in praise of Holmes that was so over the top that even Frederick Pollock was moved to write Holmes:

> The March number of Harper's has come to me by Laski's request. What he says about your judgments is well written and quite true, but I wonder if it does not make you feel a little like one of the actors in that poem of many meanings "The Walrus & the Carpenter":
>
>> "The Carpenter said nothing but
>> 'The butter's spread too thick.'"

Frederick Pollock to OWH (March 24, 1930), in 2 HOLMES-POLLOCK CORRESPONDENCE, at 260. *See* Harold Laski, *Mr. Justice Holmes: For His Eighty-Ninth Birthday*, 160 HARPERS MAGAZINE 415 (March 1930).

We might ask why the members of the House of Truth did not take up Louis Brandeis with the same enthusiasm as they displayed toward Holmes. Brad Snyder observes that "Brandeis's humorlessness was one of the reasons why, despite his ideological affinity with Frankfurter ... the People's Lawyer's was not the hero of the House." SNYDER, *supra* note 82, at 69. Brandeis did indeed complain about Frankfurter's "excessive sociability," LDB to Alice Goldmark Brandeis (November 24, 1913), in BRANDEIS FAMILY LETTERS, at 224, and for his part Frankfurter observed that "Brandeis has depth and an intellectual sweep that are tonical. He has great force; he has Lincoln's fundamental sympathies. I wish he had his patience, his magnanimity, his humor." Quoted in SNYDER, *supra* note 82, at 69, 22. White adds that Holmes was especially attractive to Jewish immigrants like Frankfurter because of Holmes's perfect Brahmin pedigree. WHITE, *supra* note 5, at 359. *See The House that Built Holmes*, *supra*, at 715–16. Another important factor was likely that members of the House of Truth had wholeheartedly supported Roosevelt in 1912, whereas Brandeis had been a major advocate for Wilson and had vigorously attacked the Bull Moose party. *See* LDB to Felix Frankfurter (July 12, 1912), in BRANDEIS-FRANKFURTER CORRESPONDENCE, at 20 (It seems "to me that the duty of Progressives was clearly to support Wilson and practically to capture the Democratic party. The insistence upon a Roosevelt-Republican party seems to me to postpone the real alignment on national, social and economic lines."). The members of the House of Truth did not seem to mind that Holmes's personal politics were deeply conservative.

86. SNYDER, *supra* note 82, at 3. "At Harvard Law School and in the pages of the *New Republic* and the *Harvard Law Review*, Frankfurter made it his mission for the rest of the country to recognize the greatness of ... Justice Holmes." *Id.* at 113. Frankfurter persuaded the editors of the *Harvard Law Review* to devote its April 1916 issue to the Justice in honor of his seventy-fifth birthday. Snyder, *supra* note 85, at 699; 29 HARVARD LAW REVIEW 703 (1916). The issue featured articles on Holmes by John Henry Wigmore, Morris Cohen, and Felix Frankfurter. *See also* Felix Frankfurter, *Twenty Years of Mr. Justice Holmes' Constitutional Opinions*, 36 HARVARD LAW REVIEW 909 (1923); Felix Frankfurter, *Mr. Justice Holmes and the Constitution: A Review of His Twenty-Five Years on the Supreme Court*, 41 HARVARD LAW REVIEW 121 (1927); FELIX FRANKFURTER, MR. JUSTICE HOLMES AND THE CONSTITUTION: A REVIEW OF HIS TWENTY-FIVE YEARS ON THE SUPREME COURT (Cambridge: Dunster House Bookshop 1927).

87. Despite the subsequent ups and downs of Holmes's reputation, see G. Edward White, *The Rise and Fall of Justice Holmes*, 39 UNIVERSITY OF CHICAGO LAW REVIEW 51 (1971), Alexander Bickel's 1957 assessment remains essentially true: Holmes is "one of the towering figures of his time, a many-colored Renaissance Man not to be enclosed within the conventional boundaries of the legal profession or of any other discipline he might have chosen. It has been remarked that no other man of comparable intellect and spirit has been a judge in the United States, or for that matter among English-speaking peoples." ALEXANDER M. BICKEL, THE

Oliver Wendell Holmes

UNPUBLISHED OPINIONS OF MR. JUSTICE BRANDEIS: THE SUPREME COURT AT WORK 241 (Cambridge: Harvard University Press 1957).

88. Charles E. Clark, *Case Study of a Liberal*, 6 SATURDAY REVIEW OF LITERATURE 581 (December 21, 1929).
89. In 1925, Holmes wrote John Henry Wigmore, thanking him for his birthday wishes: "You make it a pleasure to grow old. . . . I hope you will have my experience which has been, I think, that the last fourteen years have been the happiest of my life. . . . I am sure that you must feel the ever growing appreciation of your works, which assures you that your efforts have not been in vain." OWH to John Henry Wigmore (March 9, 1925) (Holmes papers). In 1926, after the considerable publicity that attended his eighty-fifth birthday, Holmes wrote a "dear friend": "I am hard to please but the week has satisfied me so far as the public is concerned. Ultimately only comparatively few count – but public success and recognition has a certain value as one wouldn't have got it in my line unless some competent people had started it. But this public business is like getting rich. After reaching a certain point you can't well help getting richer. And after a certain number of influential superlatives the papers go down like a row of bricks. The time was when the least of the things that have been sent me this week would have given me a new stock of courage. Luckily my head doesn't swell easily. Besides the papers I have had what I should have prayed for from some of the elect. In short I have been more or else in the clouds – striking earth each day 12 N. when I had to listen to arguments." OWH to "My dear friend" (March 14, 1926) (Holmes papers). At about that time Brandeis observed to Frankfurter that "I have never seen O.W.H. so joyously playful as now. He said yesterday at luncheon that the last 15 years – 'his old age' – had been unquestionably the happiest period of his life." LDB to Felix Frankfurter (March 21, 1926), in BRANDEIS-FRANKFURTER CORRESPONDENCE, at 238. Holmes did complain, however, that "They look after me as if I were porcelain and should chip at a touch." OWH to Lady Leslie Scott (December 26, 1929) (Holmes papers).
90. David A. Hollinger, *The "Tough-Minded" Justice Holmes, Jewish Intellectuals, and the Making of an American Icon*, in THE LEGACY OF OLIVER WENDELL HOLMES, JR., *supra* note 36, at 225.
91. *Remarks at a Dinner of the Alpha Delta Phi Club* (September 27, 1912), in 3 COLLECTED WORKS, *supra* note 22, at 539.
92. The two other medal winners that year were Elihu Root and Charles W. Eliot.
93. *Coolidge Lauds Three Roosevelt Medal Winners*, NEW YORK HERALD (June 3, 1924), at 8. According to Brandeis, Holmes "had the joy of a child" in receiving the award. LDB to Felix Frankfurter (June 3, 1924), in BRANDEIS-FRANKFURTER CORRESPONDENCE, at 170. Holmes wrote Ethel Scott, "I was pleased (momentarily) by the recognition, as one doesn't expect it from anyone but a few experts. I said in reply to the President's little speech that for five minutes he made the dreams of a life seem true." OWH to Ethel Scott (June 9, 1924) (Holmes papers).
94. *Holmes, 90, Greets Nation over Radio*, NEW YORK TIMES (March 9, 1931), at 1.
95. WILLIAM HOWARD TAFT, DEDICATION, ALPHONSO TAFT HALL: ADDRESS BY WILLIAM HOWARD TAFT (October 28, 1925) 6 (University of Cincinnati Press 1925). In 1914, Taft had called Holmes's *The Common Law* a "great" book. WILLIAM HOWARD TAFT, THE ANTI-TRUST ACT AND THE SUPREME COURT 29

(New York: Harper & Bros. 1914). After joining the Court, Taft proudly wrote his daughter that "I felt very much pleased Saturday because Judge Holmes after his long experience, said to me that it was the pleasantest Court year he had passed, and that he attributed it to the Chief Justice. That is a compliment worth having." WHT to Mrs. Frederick J. Manning (June 11, 1923) (Taft papers). Taft even took the unusual step of citing Holmes's *The Common Law* in an opinion. Director General of Railroads v. Kastenbaum, 263 U.S. 25, 28 (1923).

96. SNYDER, *supra* note 82, at 114.
97. *Judges as Statesmen, supra* note 85, at 63. "In that event," the *New Republic* darkly warned, "American democracy will eventually deprive the Supreme Court of its supreme function and our conservatives will condemn the progressives for their overthrow of an institution which set up a supposedly rational arbiter of ultimate American political and social controversies. Yet ... the real offender ... will be the Supreme Court itself and not the American democracy. It will have earned its own downfall by attempting to read the personal and professional sympathies and antipathies of its members into the law of the land." *Id.*
98. *See* Horwitz, *supra* note 36, at 42–44.
99. David J. Brewer, *The Nation's Anchor*, 57 ALBANY LAW JOURNAL 166, 167 (1898).
100. James C. Carter, *The Ideal and the Actual in the Law*, in REPORT OF THE THIRTEENTH ANNUAL MEETING OF THE AMERICAN BAR ASSOCIATION 235, 242 (Philadelphia: Dando Printing and Publishing Co. 1890). It followed that "The office of the legislator ... comes in *after* the institution of judicial tribunals and is properly supplemental to their work." *Id.* at 231–32. "Legislation should never attempt to do for society that which society can do, and is constantly doing, for itself. As custom is the true origin of law, the legislature cannot *ex vi termini*, absolutely create it. ... The passage of a law commanding things which have no foundation in existing custom would be only an endeavor to create custom, and would necessarily be futile." *Id.* at 242. *See* Roscoe Pound, *Courts and Legislation*, 7 AMERICAN POLITICAL SCIENCE REVIEW 361, 369, 373–75 (1913). On Carter, see Lewis A. Grossman, *James Coolidge Carter and Mugwump Jurisprudence*, 20 LAW & HISTORY REVIEW 577 (2002); Robert Gordon, *The Ideal and the Actual in Law: Fantasies and Practices of New York City Lawyers, 1870–1910*, in THE NEW HIGH PRIESTS: LAWYERS IN POST-CIVIL WAR AMERICA (Gerard W. Gewalt, ed., Westport: Greenwood Press 1984).

In his early years, Stone admired Carter's historicist view of law. Stone regarded Carter as "philosophical and profound," one of those "outstanding ... Olympians" who "seemed to represent all those qualities which have made the law a great profession, and which most entitles it to public influence and respect." Harlan Fiske Stone, *Remarks of Chief Justice Harlan F. Stone on the Occasion of the Celebration of the Seventy-Fifth Anniversary of the Association of the Bar of the City of New York*, 1 RECORD OF THE BAR ASSOCIATION OF THE CITY OF NEW YORK 144, 152 (March 16, 1946). Before coming to Washington, Stone decried the excess of legislation and believed that "moral standards must become generally settled and accepted by society before they can find expression in law as an established rule of conduct. The moral rule must be a settled principle of social conduct before the law can or should attempt to make that principle mandatory upon all members of the community." HARLAN F. STONE, LAW AND ITS ADMINISTRATION 34 (New York: Columbia University Press 1915). It is only after his experience on the Court that Stone came to conclude that legislation "is not an alien intruder in the house of the common law, but a guest to be welcomed and made at home there as a new and powerful aid in the accomplishment of its appointed task of accommodating the law to social needs." Harlan Fiske Stone, *The Common Law in the United States*, 50 HARVARD LAW REVIEW 4, 15 (1936).

101. "In those cases where customs are doubtful, or conflicting, the expert is needed to ascertain or reconcile them, and hence the origin of the judicial establishment." Carter, *supra* note 100, at 235. *See* JAMES C. CARTER, THE PROVINCES OF THE WRITTEN AND THE UNWRITTEN LAW 11–12 (New York: Banks & Bros. 1889).

102. Taft adopted this view almost in terms when he wrote that "The majority of questions before our courts ... are neither statutory nor constitutional, but are dependent for decision upon the common or customary law handed down from one generation to another, adjusted to new conditions of society, and declared from time to time by courts as cases arise. Thorough study is required to enable a judge to know and understand the whole range of legal principles that have thus to be discriminatingly adapted and applied. Work of this kind requires professional experts of the highest proficiency, who have mastered the law as a science and in practice." William H. Taft, *The Selection and Tenure of Judges*, 7 MAINE LAW REVIEW 203, 205 (1914). On Taft's appreciation of Carter, see William H. Taft, *The Delays of the Law*, 18 YALE LAW JOURNAL 28, 31 (1908).

103. SELECTED WRITINGS OF BENJAMIN NATHAN CARDOZO 274 (Margaret E. Hall, ed., New York: Fallon Publications 1947).

104. *See, e.g.*, Adair v. United States, 209 U.S. 161, 173–74 (1908) ("In every case that comes before this court, therefore, where legislation of this character is concerned, and where the protection of the Federal Constitution is sought, the question necessarily arises: Is this a fair, reasonable, and appropriate exercise of the police power of the state, or is it an unreasonable, unnecessary, and arbitrary interference with the right of the individual to his personal liberty or to enter into those contracts in relation to labor which may seem to him appropriate or necessary for the support of himself and his family?"). As Justice Sutherland would make explicit in 1937, a "reasonable" regulation of contractual liberty in the context of employment relationships is one that respects the "*moral* requirement implicit in every contract of employment, viz. that the amount to be paid and the service to be rendered shall bear to each other some relation of *just* equivalence." West Coast Hotel Co. v. Parrish, 300 U.S. 379, 408 (1937) (Sutherland, J., dissenting) (emphasis added).

105. Burnet v. Coronado Oil & Gas Co., 285 U.S. 393, 410 (1932) (Brandeis, J., dissenting). "Substantive due process is analogous to extratextual, customary constitutionalism, except that it allows constitutional interpreters to pretend that they are adjudicating the meaning of two words of the text rather than applying long-standing customary principles that exist outside the text, which is what they are truly doing." WILLIAM E. NELSON, THE COMMON LAW IN COLONIAL AMERICA: LAW AND THE CONSTITUTION ON THE EVE OF INDEPENDENCE, 1735–76, at 57 (New York: Oxford University Press 2018).

106. Bethel v. New York City Transit Authority, 92 N.Y.2d 348, 353 (1998). The moral underpinnings that underlie constitutional norms of reasonableness, like those that underlie common law norms of reasonableness, are essentially judgments of community customs and mores. *See* Robert Post, *The Social Foundations of Privacy: Community and Self in the Common Law Tort*, 77 CALIFORNIA LAW REVIEW 957 (1989).
107. Oliver Wendell Holmes, *The Gas-Stokers' Strike*, 7 AMERICAN LAW REVIEW 582, 583–84 (1873). The passage also contains a radical critique of longstanding judicial doctrine prohibiting "class legislation."
108. *Law and the Court* (February 15, 1913), in COLLECTED LEGAL PAPERS, *supra* note 20, at 294–95.
109. HUGHES, *supra* note 1, at 175.
110. David J. Brewer, *The Movement of Coercion*, ADDRESS TO NEW YORK STATE BAR ASSOCIATION 19 (January 1893), available at www.minnesotalegalhistoryproject.org/assets/Brewer%20-%20Coercion%20(1893)-CC.pdf.
111. Brewer, *supra* note 99, at 167–70.
112. *Id.* at 167.
113. David J. Brewer, *The Nation's Safeguard*, in PROCEEDINGS OF THE SIXTEENTH ANNUAL MEETING OF THE NEW YORK STATE BAR ASSOCIATION 39 (New York: Stumpf & Steurer 1893).
114. David J. Brewer, *The Federal Judiciary*, in PROCEEDINGS OF THE TWELFTH ANNUAL MEETING OF THE BAR ASSOCIATION OF THE STATE OF KANSAS 83–84 (Topeka: Crane & Co. 1895). The judge "more than any other helps to preserve government of and by the people, and prevents it from degenerating into a mere government of and by a mob. Thus it is all-important in this Republic of ours that there should be a firm and stable judiciary to stand between the temporary wave of public feeling and the permanent and thoughtful purpose of the Nation as expressed in those grand instruments which contain the measure of all rights and the abiding guarantees of justice and equity." *Id.* at 84.
115. Brewer, *supra* note 110, at 21.
116. Brewer, *supra* note 113, at 45–46.
117. Brewer, *supra* note 110, at 21. "[S]ome truths are self-evident, existing before and superior to constitutions, and, therefore, unnecessary of mention therein. Life, liberty, and the pursuit of happiness are lifted beyond the touch of any statute or organic instrument. ... When, among the affirmations of the Declaration of Independence, it is asserted that the pursuit of happiness is one of the unalienable rights, it is meant that the acquisition, possession, and enjoyment of property are matters which human government cannot forbid, and which it cannot destroy." DAVID J. BREWER, PROTECTION TO PRIVATE PROPERTY FROM PUBLIC ATTACK 5 (New Haven: Hoggson & Robinson 1891).
118. "The jurists who believe in natural law seem to me to be in that naïve state of mind that accepts what has been familiar and accepted by them and their neighbors as something that must be accepted by all men everywhere." Oliver Wendell Holmes, *Natural Law*, 32 HARVARD LAW REVIEW 40, 41 (1918). Examples of Holmes's positivism abound during the Taft Court. *See, e.g.*, United States v. Thompson, 257 U.S. 419 (1922); Direction Der Disconto-Gesellschaft v. United States Steel Corp., 267 U.S. 22 (1925); White v. Mechanics Securities Corp., 269 U.S. 283 (1925); Die Deutsche Bank

Filiale Nurnberg v. Humphrey, 272 U.S. 517 (1926); Ingenohl v. Walter E. Olsen & Co., 273 U.S. 541 (1927); Beech-Nut Packing Co. v. P. Lorillard Co., 273 U.S. 629 (1927); Ferry v. Ramsey, 277 U.S. 88 (1928); Farmers' Loan & Trust Co. v. Minnesota, 280 U.S. 204 (1930). Holmes's positivism was so well recognized that when in an opinion he passingly adverted to courts allowing rights that were asserted "contrary to some strongly prevailing view of justice" to be "defeated by subsequent legislation," Forbes Pioneer Boat Line v. Board of Commissioners of Everglades Drainage District, 258 U.S. 338, 339–40 (1922), Taft returned on his draft the teasing comment, "I marvel at your bringing in a 'sense of justice.'" (Holmes papers). In point of fact Holmes's opinion actually turned on the premise that "Courts can not go very far against the literal meaning and plain intent of a constitutional text." 258 U.S. at 340.

119. To get some sense of the radical implications of Holmes's position, consider that in 1892 the eminent John F. Dillon devoted his American Bar Association presidential address to explicating the difference between "legislation" and "law." The former was "a mere product of sovereignty," "the mere product of popular will or of a legislative majority of the hour." John F. Dillon, *Address of the President*, in REPORT OF THE FIFTEENTH ANNUAL MEETING OF THE AMERICAN BAR ASSOCIATION 200 (Philadelphia: Dando Printing & Publishing Co. 1892). The latter, which it was the particular obligation of lawyers to serve, especially in light of contemporary attacks on "the institution of private property" guaranteed in "our written Constitution," was "the enlightened permanent justice of the State," the "eternal and indestructible sense of justice and of right, written by God on the living tablets of the human heart, and revealed in His Holy Word." *Id*. at 201, 203, 206. "Considerations of justice and right ... make up the web and woof and form the staple of a lawyer's life and vocation. ... [T]he lawyer makes a sad mistake who supposes law to be the mere equivalent of written enactments or judicial decisions." *Id*. at 201. Addresses like these should be kept in mind when evaluating the many anecdotes in which Holmes is recorded as declaring his antipathy toward "justice." *See, e.g., supra* note 37.

120. Old Dominion Steamship Co. v. Gilmore, 207 U.S. 398, 404 (1907). In Missouri, K. & T. Ry. Co. v. May, 194 U.S. 267 (1904), Holmes held for the Court that "it must be remembered that legislatures are ultimate guardians of the liberties and welfare of the people in quite as great a degree as the courts." *Id*. at 270. In a dissent joined by White and McKenna, Brown objected that "While fully conceding that the legislature is the only judge of the policy of a proposed discrimination, it is not the only judge of its legality." *Id*. at 270 (Brown, J., dissenting).

121. OWH to Harold Laski (March 4, 1920), in 1 HOLMES-LASKI CORRESPONDENCE, at 248 ("as if a court means anything but a voice of the sovereign power.").

122. OWH to Felix Frankfurter (March 24, 1914), in HOLMES-FRANKFURTER CORRESPONDENCE, at 19. "What proximate test of excellence can be found except correspondence to the actual equilibrium of force in the community," Holmes asked, "that is, conformity to the wishes of the dominant power? ... [T]he proximate test of a good government is that the dominant power has its way." *Montesquieu*, in COLLECTED LEGAL PAPERS, *supra* note 20, at 258. The only excellence of law," Holmes wrote a friend, "is that it expresses the beliefs and wishes of the dominant force of the community." OWH to Alice Stopford Green (July 11, 1905) (Holmes papers).

THE TAFT COURT

123. Oliver Wendell Holmes, *Privilege, Malice and Intent*, 8 HARVARD LAW REVIEW 1, 9 (1894).
124. "It is dangerous to tie down legislatures too closely by judicial constructions not necessarily arising from the words of the Constitution. Particularly, ... it is important for this court to avoid extraction from the very general language of the 14th Amendment a system of delusive exactness." Louisville & N. R. Co. v. Barber Asphalt Pav. Co., 197 U.S. 430, 434 (1905) (Holmes, J.). "I confess that I think that the right to make contracts at will that has been derived from the word 'liberty' in the Amendments has been stretched to its extreme by the decisions." Adair v. United States, 208 U.S. 161, 191 (1908) (Holmes, J., dissenting). In 1894, speaking as a justice of the Massachusetts Supreme Judicial Court, Holmes had opined: "In my opinion, the legislature has the whole law-making power, except so far as the words of the constitution, expressly or impliedly withhold it; and I think that, in construing the constitution, we should remember that it is a frame of government for men of opposite opinions, and for the future, and therefore not hastily import into it our own views, or unexpressed limitations derived merely from the practice of the past." *In re* Municipal Suffrage to Women, 160 Mass. 586, 594 (1894).
125. OWH to Alice Stopford Green (July 11, 1905) (Holmes papers). Holmes saw "great danger in the pedagogical turn natural to judges that interesting experiments will be thwarted by an impression that what doesn't seem about right to the judges must be forbidden by the constitution. There have been decisions by some courts ... that I think idiotical, based on the judicial notion of freedom of contract supposed to be guaranteed by the word liberty. They say that liberty of contract is interfered with by such acts or forbidding turning men off for belonging to a union. Some of the young men that I delight in have written some able books that indicate a new turn of mind. I think most of the experiments and the prevailing economic notions humbug, but that is quite a different matter from saying that they can't be tried." OWH to Alice Stopford Green (December 19, 1914) (Holmes papers).
126. Truax v. Corrigan, 257 U.S. 312, 344 (1921) (Holmes, J., dissenting).
127. *Law and the Court* (February 15, 1913), in COLLECTED LEGAL PAPERS, *supra* note 20, at 294–95. Holmes's use of the word "law" in this passage seems to echo that described in *supra* note 119.
128. OWH to Franklin Ford (January 13, 1911), in PROGRESSIVE MASKS, *supra* note 64, at 83.
129. *Ideals and Doubts* (1915), in COLLECTED LEGAL PAPERS, *supra* note 20, at 307.
130. The distinction between a judge's personal views and the law was of course of ancient and venerable provenance. In Holmes's lifetime the distinction had been profoundly explored in Herman Melville's *Billy Budd.* But by sharply separating law from natural inclinations and common values, Holmes's positivism virtually defined the judge as self-denying in ways that a jurisprudence of custom and tradition did not.
131. "One of the queer aspects of duty is when one is called on to sustain or enforce laws that one believes to be economically wrong and do more harm than good. ... [A]s there is no even inarticulate agreement as to the ideal to be striven for, and no adequate scientific evidence that this rather than that will tend to bring it about, if we did agree as to what we want, I settle down to simple tests. I look at it like going to the theatre – if you can pay for your ticket and are sure you want to go, I have nothing to say. But I think the crowd would not want what they now do, if they saw

further into the facts." OWH to Canon Patrick Augustine Sheehan (November 23, 1912) in HOLMES-SHEEHAN CORRESPONDENCE, at 52–53.
132. OWH to Felix Frankfurter (December 23, 1921) in HOLMES-FRANKFURTER CORRESPONDENCE, at 119.
133. OWH to Harold Laski (March 4, 1920), in 1 HOLMES-LASKI CORRESPONDENCE, at 249. Holmes did not "share the views of the promoters of the statutes which he so readily sustained. He held them valid not because he believed in them but because he believed in the right of the legislature to experiment." HUGHES, *supra* note 1, at 175.
134. "I think one of the most subtle dangers of giving the last word to the Court is that judges read into the Constitution their notions of what is desirable instead of coldly interpreting the document. It has given me pleasure to sustain the constitutionality of law that I believe to be as bad as possible, because I thereby helped to mark the difference between what I would forbid and what the Constitution permits." OWH to John T. Morse (November 8, 1926) (Holmes papers).
135. OWH to Lewis Einstein (October 28, 1912), in HOLMES-EINSTEIN CORRESPONDENCE, at 74. *See* Plant v. Woods, 176 Mass. 492, 505 (1900) (Holmes, C.J., dissenting); OWH to Harold Laski (January 8, 1917), in 1 HOLMES-LASKI CORRESPONDENCE, at 51–52 ("On the economic side I am mighty skeptical of hours of labor and minimum wages regulation, but it may be that a somewhat monotonous standardized mode of life is coming. Of course it only means shifting the burden to a different point of incidence, if I be right, as I think I be, that every community rests on the death of men. If the people who can't get the minimum are to be supported you take out of one pocket to put into the other. I think the courageous thing to say to the crowd, though perhaps the Brandeis school don't believe it, is, you now have all there is – and you'd better face it instead of trying to lift yourselves by the slack of your own breeches. But all our present teaching is hate and envy for those who have any luxury, as social wrongdoers.").
136. OWH to Lewis Einstein (November 24, 1912), in HOLMES-EINSTEIN CORRESPONDENCE, at 75–76. *See Law and the Court*, *supra* note 127, at 293–94.
137. *Ideals and Doubts*, *supra* note 129, at 305–6. Holmes essentially repeated this thought in 1923: "The notion that we can secure an economic paradise by changes in property alone seems to me twaddle. I can understand better legislation that aims rather to improve the quality than to increase the quantity of the population. I can understand saying, whatever the cost, so far as may be, we will keep certain strains out of our blood." Oliver Wendell Holmes, *Introduction*, in RATIONAL BASIS OF LEGAL INSTITUTIONS xxxi (New York: MacMillan Co. 1923). Holmes's persistent invocation of eugenics is no accident. *See, e.g.*, OWH to Elihu Root (March 8, 1907) (Holmes papers) ("It seemed to me formerly that there was another consideration (naturally not be mentioned to them) for the exclusion of some races, namely that, you are determining the future composition of our own."); OWH to Harold Laski (July 17, 1925) in 1 HOLMES-LASKI CORRESPONDENCE, at 761 ("One can change institutions by a fiat but populations only by slow degrees and as I don't believe in millennia and still less in the possibility of attaining one by tinkering with property while propagation is free and we do all we can to keep the products, however bad, alive, I listen with some skepticism to plans for fundamental amelioration. I should expect more from systematic prevention of the survival of the unfit."). His attraction to eugenics no doubt energized Holmes's

harsh rhetoric in Buck v. Bell, 274 U.S. 200 (1927), which authorized the compulsory sterilization of the mentally disabled. In *Buck*, Holmes infamously proclaimed that "Three generations of imbeciles are enough." *Id.* at 207. *Buck* is without question Holmes's "most notorious opinion." NOVICK, *supra* note 47, at 477–78. *See* ADAM COHEN, IMBECILES: THE SUPREME COURT, AMERICAN EUGENICS, AND THE STERILIZATION OF CARRIE BUCK (New York: Penguin Press 2016). After *Buck*, Holmes wrote Harold Laski that he "felt that I was getting near to the first principle of real reform." OWH to Harold Laski (May 12, 1927), in 2 HOLMES-LASKI CORRESPONDENCE, at 942. He wrote his friend the Baroness Moncheur that he had written the case "with some gusto of approval," OWH to Baroness Moncheur (June 18, 1927) (Holmes papers), and to Lewis Einstein that it "gave me pleasure" to establish "the constitutionality of a law permitting the sterilization of imbeciles." OWH to Lewis Einstein (May 19, 1927), in HOLMES-EINSTEIN CORRESPONDENCE, at 267. To get a quick sense of the public controversy surrounding *Buck*, see *To Halt the Imbecile's Perilous Line*, 93 LITERARY DIGEST 11 (May 21, 1927).

138. OWH to Harold Laski (July 23, 1925), in 1 HOLMES-LASKI CORRESPONDENCE, at 762. Holmes's clerk during the 1927 term, Arthur Sutherland, recalls that "I asked him once how he felt toward people generally. 'Oh,' he said with the greatest tolerance and good humor, 'I dare say the generality of mankind is made up of swine and fools.' He accepted the fact without rancor as one accepts the facts of bad weather or old age or evil." David M. O'Brien, *Sutherland's Recollections of Justice Holmes*, 1988 YEARBOOK OF THE SUPREME COURT HISTORICAL SOCIETY 18, 21.

139. Consider, in this light, what Holmes wrote his parents in the midst of the Civil War: "It is singular with what indifference one gets to look on the dead bodies in gray clothes wh. lie all around. ... As you go through the woods you stumble constantly, and, if after dark, as last night on picket, perhaps tread on the swollen bodies already fly blown and decaying, of men shot in the head back or bowels – Many of the wounds terrible to look at." OWH to Parents (June 2, 1862), in TOUCHED WITH FIRE, *supra* note 8, at 51. Or again, speaking now of Union wounded and dead at a hospital where he was being treated for dysentery: "It's odd how indifferent one gets to the sight of death – perhaps, because one gets aristocratic and don't value much a common life – Then they are apt to be so dirty it seems natural – 'Dust to Dust' – I would do anything that lay in my power but it doesn't much affect my feelings." OWH to Mother (December 12, 1862), *id.* at 78. On the origins of Holmes's emotional disassociation, see *supra* note 14.

140. EDMUND WILSON, PATRIOTIC GORE: STUDIES IN THE LITERATURE OF THE AMERICAN CIVIL WAR 782–83 (New York: W.W. Norton 1994). Although White may be correct to note that "beneath Holmes' self-confidence lay a degree of insecurity," WHITE, *supra* note 5, at 370, it was an insecurity that almost always centered on Holmes's persistent doubts about whether his theoretical insights would be deemed to have "touched the superlative" by those he regarded as "competent" to judge. OWH to Baroness Moncheur (May 2, 1921) (Holmes papers). Although Holmes was anxious about the esteem in which he was held by others, he was never insecure about the quality of his own sensibility.

141. "Holmes, in his personal politics, was a conservative. Almost by instinct ... he tended to mistrust Democrats, and he brushed aside socialist talk and writing as

'drool.' Yet his passionate respect for the right of others to think differently than he did – that respect on which all of democracy is ultimately based – led him always to question even his fondest preferences and made him, in the truest sense, an *intellectual* liberal." FRED RODELL, NINE MEN: A POLITICAL HISTORY OF THE SUPREME COURT FROM 1790 TO 1955, at 180 (New York: Random House 1955).

142. *Ideals and Doubts, supra* note 129, at 307. At age 84, Holmes remarked that "If I didn't have a certain number of younger people to freshen me up I should be like a blasted pine tree upon a burnt hillside." OWH to Lady Leslie Scott (July 11, 1925) (Holmes papers).

143. "The function of private ownership is to divine in advance the equilibrium of social desires – which socialism equally would have to divine, but which, under the illusion of self-seeking, is more poignantly and shrewdly foreseen." *Law and the Court, supra* note 127, at 294. When Frankfurter asked Brandeis to explain Holmes's opinion in Pennsylvania Coal Co. v. Mahon, 260 U.S. 393 (1922), in which Holmes had held for the Court that the property of a coal company had been taken, Brandeis remarked, "I account for it by what one would think Holmes is last man to yield to – class bias. He came back to views not of his manhood but childhood.... Heightened respect for property has been part of Holmes' growing old.... He is deeply worried about exhaustion of resources. I said to him, old sentiment N[ew]. E[ngland]. when there wasn't much. 'Aren't you aware that men's apprehensions turn towards over-production & not under-production.' Of course, he wasn't aware & intellectually he can't & it comes hard." *Brandeis-Frankfurter Conversations*, at 320–21 (July 19, 1923; n.d.).

144. Louisville & N. R. Co. v. Barber Asphalt Pav. Co., 197 U.S. 430, 434 (1905) (Holmes, J.).

145. Holmes's empathy for other points of view is very much of a piece with his fondness for the work of Walt Whitman. "I came to" Whitman late, "but I came all right." OWH to Canon Patrick Augustine Sheehan (January 31, 1913) in HOLMES-SHEEHAN CORRESPONDENCE, at 58.

146. WHT to Charles P. Taft 2nd (March 7, 1926) (Taft papers). *See* WHT to Robert A. Taft (March 4, 1928) (Taft papers) ("Had the Court followed him I don't think we would have had much of a Constitution to deal with."); WHT to Learned Hand (March 3, 1923) (Taft papers) ("Association with Justice Holmes is a delight. He is feebler physically, but I cannot see that the acuteness of his mind has been affected at all.... In many ways he is the life of the Court, and it is a great comfort to have such a well of pure common law undefiled immediately next [to] one so that one can drink and be sure one is getting the pure article.").

147. WHT to Horace D. Taft (June 8, 1928) (Taft papers). Taft regarded Marshall as "the greatest Judge that America or the World has produced." WILLIAM HOWARD TAFT, POPULAR GOVERNMENT: ITS ESSENCE, ITSPERMANENCE, AND ITS PERILS 131 (New Haven: Yale University Press 1913). Taft was convinced that Holmes "does not believe in the Constitution at all ... where it imposes any limitation upon legislative authority." WHT to Henry L. Stimson (May 18, 1928) (Taft papers).

148. "I should be glad if we could get rid of the whole moral phraseology which I think has tended to distort the law. In fact even in the domain of morals I think that it would be a gain, at least for the educated, to get rid of the word and notion Sin." OWH to Frederick Pollock (May 30, 1927), in 2 HOLMES-POLLOCK CORRESPONDENCE, at 200. "I am so skeptical as to our knowledge about the

goodness or badness of laws that I have no practical criticism except what the crowd wants. Personally I bet that the crowd if it knew more wouldn't want what it does – but that is immaterial." OWH to FREDERICK POLLOCK (April 23, 1910), in 1 HOLMES-POLLOCK CORRESPONDENCE, at 163. "I think that values like truth are largely personal. There is enough community for us to talk not enough for anyone to command." OWH to Alice Stopford Green (August 20, 1909) (Holmes papers).

149. 277 U.S. 438, 470 (1928) (Holmes, J., dissenting).
150. WVD to WHT (June 20, 1928) (Taft papers).
151. WHT to Horace D. Taft (June 8, 1928) (Taft papers).
152. WHT to Horace D. Taft (December 8, 1929) (Taft papers) ("I have no doubt there is persistent hope, especially by the younger crowd of college professors, that in some way or other Holmes will be continued on the Court while the rest of us die off.").
153. 275 U.S. 66 (1927). The *Goodman* case, which arose out of the Court's diversity jurisdiction, concerned the standard of care that should be applied to the driver of a car at a railroad crossing. Speaking for the Court, Holmes laid down a harsh rule of law reversing a jury's verdict in favor of the plaintiff. The rule was so intolerable that it was overturned only seven years later in Pokora v. Wabash Ry. Co., 292 U.S. 98 (1934). In conference, Brandeis alone voted to affirm the jury's verdict (Stone Docket Book). Brandeis did not dissent from Holmes's opinion for the Court. A bill was introduced in the House to overturn *Goodman*, see H.R. 7901, 70th CONG. 1ST SESS. (December 19, 1927), which provided that "in all causes of action arising from accidents occurring at or on any grade crossing over a street, road or highway . . . no rule shall be adopted . . . by the Federal court of the United States contrary to the law of the State, Territory, or place where such accident occurred." An Ohio attorney, G. Jay Clark, wrote George Norris, then chair of the Senate Judiciary Committee, that the law ought to overturn *Goodman*, an opinion "rendered by Justice Holmes a venerable gentleman" who "does not ride in an automobile but is driven around in a horse drawn conveyance. Since we are living in the twentieth century and for the further reason particularly all of our people either own or ride in an automobile, it seems to the writer that the U.S. Supreme Court has adopted a very harsh rule." G. Jay Clark to George W. Norris (December 27, 1927) (Norris papers). Norris replied that he was actively seeking to strip federal courts of jurisdiction "in all such cases." George W. Norris to G. Jay Clark (January 2, 1928) (Norris papers). State courts generally refused to follow Holmes's extreme rule in *Goodman*. *Aftermath of the Supreme Court's Stop, Look, and Listen Rule*, 43 HARVARD LAW REVIEW 926 (1930). As a result, Holmes's effort to establish a federal common law of tort liability produced "the spectacle of a jurisprudence which varies the duty of care required of a motorist according as the railroad that kills him is incorporated in one state or another." *Id*. at 932.
154. 258 U.S. 268 (1922). In *Britt*, the Court overturned a jury verdict in favor of the family of a child trespasser who had been poisoned by swimming in what appeared to be a pool of clear water, but was actually a toxic brew of sulfuric acid and zinc sulfate. Holmes turned his opinion on the legal duty of care that a landowner owed to a child trespasser. Taft and Day joined a dissent by Clarke which Holmes characterized as "larmoyant . . . more sentiment and rhetoric than reasoning." WHT to Frederick Pollock (March 29, 1922), in 2 HOLMES-POLLOCK

CORRESPONDENCE, at 92. The Court granted *certiorari* in the case, said Brandeis, because "Holmes wanted it." *Brandeis-Frankfurter Conversations*, at 303 (April 17, 1922). Pollock later wrote Holmes that the Court's judgment in *Britt* "seems clearly right. A mere apprehension of possible trespass will not make a license." Frederick Pollock to OWH (May 8, 1922), in 2 HOLMES-POLLOCK CORRESPONDENCE, at 94.

155. *Brandeis-Frankfurter Conversations*, at 310 (November 13, 1927). Holmes disliked juries because he viewed them as inconsistent with a "major" thesis of *The Common Law*, which is "that liability should be fixed by an objective, external standard." Robert W. Gordon, *Holmes' Common Law as Legal and Social Science*, 10 HOFSTRA LAW REVIEW 719, 725 (1982). Holmes believed that subjectivity in law was to be "suppressed and replaced by a description of observable, outward facts." *Id.* In tort law, therefore, judge-made rules were to be preferred over the unpredictable verdicts of juries. Hence the concluding lines of Holmes's opinion in *Goodman*: "It is true ... that the question of due care very generally is left to the jury. But we are dealing with a standard of conduct, and when the standard is clear it should be laid down once for all by the Courts." 275 U.S. at 70. For Holmes's opinion of juries, see *Law in Science and Science in Law*, *supra* note 39, at 457–59.

156. "Holmes saw a chance to decide one of his pet theories & so certiorari was granted. I voted vs. cert. There was no earthly reason for granting it. I voted against the majority opinion, but I couldn't go Clarke's stuff, I was rushed with other work & so would have had to hold up Holmes if I was going to write a dissent & to hold him up from firing off is like sending an executioner after him." *Brandeis-Frankfurter Conversations*, at 327 (September 1, 1923).

157. WHITE, *supra* note 5, at 381–88.

158. 276 U.S. 518 (1928). Thomas Reed Powell once cited to *Black & White Taxicab* as an example of "belated criticism" of the concept of general federal common law "by one who has in his time applied it not infrequently." See Thomas Reed Powell, *The Supreme Court's Control over the Issue of Injunctions in Labor Disputes*, 13 PROCEEDINGS OF THE AMERICAN ACADEMY OF POLITICAL SCIENCE 37, 74 n.64 (1928).

159. "The common law so far as it is enforced in a State, whether called common law or not, is not the common law generally but the law of that State existing by the authority of that State without regard to what it may have been in England or anywhere else." *Black & White Taxicab*, 276 U.S. at 533–34 (Holmes, J., dissenting). Holmes was quite willing to give precedence to state legislation over the common law tort rules that he struggled to establish. In Nashville, C. & St. L. Ry. V. White, 278 U.S. 456 (1929), for example, he upheld a verdict for a plaintiff even though the plaintiff had been grossly negligent under the rule of *Goodman*, because the defendant railroad company had failed to comply with a statutory requirement that it keep a flagman constantly on duty at all street crossings. "When a railroad is built experience teaches that it is pretty certain to kill some people before it has lasted long. But a Court cannot condemn a legislature that refuses to allow the toll to be taken even if it thinks that the gain by the change would compensate for any such loss." *Id.* at 459–60.

160. In 1920, Holmes wrote a friend that "I still cling" to the work, "not, as I fear some or one may, because they don't know what else to do ... but because I like it right down

THE TAFT COURT

to the ground." OWH to Baroness Moncheur (October 18, 1920) (Holmes papers). Holmes wrote John H. Clarke in 1928 that "unlike you, I vitally enjoy" my work and "making little additions to the home we live in – every intellectual effort to add a distinction or to develop a rule gives me an inward joy and I must e'er stick [to] both as long as strength last." OWH to JHC (March 28, 1928) (Holmes papers). In 1925, Taft reported to his brother that "Holmes continues active. He celebrates his eighty-fourth birthday this month and seems to be as acute and as determined to write opinions and get through his work as he ever was. It is a pleasure to be with him." *See* WHT to Charles P. Taft (March 27, 1925) (Taft papers). The following year he wrote his son Robert that Holmes "is a very excellent member of the Court. He is full of good nature and comradeship, has the keenest sense of humor, and we should miss him greatly as a member. It is quite possible he may live to bury several of us. He could not live without the Court. His interest in the progress of the business is just as great as it ever was." WHT to Robert A. Taft (March 7, 1926) (Taft papers). In 1927, Taft sought to relieve Sanford's burden by transferring three cases to Holmes. Taft wrote his wife, "Holmes is wonderful. I gave him three cases this week transferred from Sanford and today he sends three good opinions. His quickness and his power of ... stating the point succinctly are marvelous. His brilliance does not seem to me to abate at all." WHT to Helen Herron Taft (May 6, 1927) (Taft papers). Later that year Taft wrote his wife mourning the "departures of old friends," which "make me sad. Then I turn to Justice Holmes who overtook me on the Conn. Ave. bridge and got out looking like a four year old and showing no changes whatever from last year. In March or April he will be eighty-seven. So some defy the old gentleman with the scythe." WHT to Helen Herron Taft (September 30, 1927) (Taft papers). *See* WHT to Charles P. Taft (March 10, 1928) (Taft papers) ("Judge Holmes had his birthday on Thursday. He was 87 years old, and he is really just as bright as ever."); WHT to Robert A. Taft (March 10, 1928) (Taft papers) (Holmes "will die in harness, if he ever dies.").

161. Holmes was realistic about the potential influence of his account of constitutional adjudication. He wrote Frankfurter, "As to due process of law, I never supposed that I had any particular influence on the Court or that any change was likely with the present membership." OWH to Felix Frankfurter (August 30, 1921), in HOLMES-FRANKFURTER CORRESPONDENCE, at 122–23.
162. *Brandeis-Frankfurter Conversations*, at 320 (July 19, 1923).
163. Taft wrote in response to the draft of one Holmes opinion: "I regard your power in these taking cases to concentrate on the point in few words with admiration and awe." A.W. Duckett & Co. v. United States, 266 U.S. 149 (1924) (Holmes papers). Stone's law clerk during the 1926 term tells a most revealing story about the length of Holmes's opinions:

> I noticed that Holmes' opinions had an uncanny tendency to fill exactly two printed pages. [Holmes's law clerk Thomas Corcoran] explained this conundrum easily enough. Holmes penned each paragraph on a separate sheet of paper and counted the words. That way, if possible, the opinion would end on the last line of the printed page.
>
> Corcoran told a little story to illustrate this predilection. One Monday morning, after studying a new opinion by Holmes, "Tommy the Cork" went into the Justice's chambers and suggested the inclusion of an additional point. Holmes listened and shook his head sadly. "Is the idea no good?" Corcoran asked. "No,

it's a very good idea," Holmes said, "but I can't use it. It would take another paragraph."

Milton C. Handler, *Clerking for Justice Harlan Fiske Stone*, 1995 JOURNAL OF SUPREME COURT HISTORY 113, 120.

164. OLIVER WENDELL HOLMES, *Walbridge Abner Field: Answer to Resolutions of the Bar* (November 25, 1899), in 3 COLLECTED WORKS, *supra* note 22, at 495.
165. OWH to Nina Gray (March 2, 1903) (Holmes papers). *See* OWH to Nina Gray (January 16, 1903) (Holmes papers) ("I hope my opinions will not be despised on account of their brevity, but this far I have been pretty short as compared with the average. Such are the short and simple scandals of the poor as Mr. Dooley says."); OWH to Nina Gray (February 15, 1903) (Holmes papers) ("I shudder when I contrast my short little opinions with the voluminous discourses that are but I hope I am right."); OWH to Nina Gray (November 9, 1906) (Holmes papers) ("I also try to be short – I fear to my momentary detriment at times – The vulgar hardly will believe an opinion important unless it is padded like a militia brigadier general. . . . The little snakes are the poisonous ones.").
166. OWH to Nina Gray (May 3, 1903) (Holmes papers). In 1925, Holmes wrote Frankfurter that although he was pleased with "my share in the term's work," he was nevertheless "apprehensive a few times that my opinions were shorter than Brandeis inwardly approved though he didn't say so but if as I meant to I hit the nail on the head I am content." OWH to Felix Frankfurter (May 30, 1925), in HOLMES-FRANKFURTER CORRESPONDENCE, at 184. Taft wrote his son that "Judge Holmes and Judge McReynolds are very, very short, and while Judge Holmes has a genius for giving a certain degree of piquancy and character to his opinion by sententious phrases, I think often his opinions lost strength and value by his disposition to cut down. And this is also true of McReynolds. The chief duty in a court of last resort is not to dispose of the case, but it is sufficiently to elaborate the principles, the importance of which justify the bringing of the case here at all, to make the discussion of those principles and the conclusion reached useful to the country and to the Bar in clarifying doubtful questions of constitutional and fundamental law. In the old days, this Court, especially in the days of Harlan, Peckham and others, wrote too long opinions and engaged much in quoting from other opinions, so that the Bar grew tired. On the other hand, I think the Bar is not particularly well pleased with too short opinions, for the good reason that I have referred to above." WHT to Charles P. Taft 2nd (November 1, 1925) (Taft papers).
167. OWH to Baroness Moncheur (June 18, 1927) (Holmes papers). Collecting material for his biography of Holmes, Mark DeWolfe Howe received a letter from a Florida attorney:

> Some years ago a little Holmes incident was related to me by the late Pat Odom, a splendid old Jacksonville lawyer of great native ability.
>
> Pat represented the respondent in Southern Utilities Co. v. City of Palatka, 268 U.S. 232 (1925), and he said that when he rose to reply to the petitioner's argument he was prepared to deliver the finest speech of his life, this being his first appearance before the United States Supreme Court. However, he says, that before he had time to say a word Holmes looked straight at him and put one short question which concisely stated the gist of Pat's position. Whereupon Pat simply replied, "yes sir", and sat down. You will note from the report that Holmes delivered the Court's opinion adopting Pat's contention.

Paul Ritter to Mark DeWolfe Howe (January 28, 1952) (Holmes papers). (Howe's notes and correspondence are interspersed throughout the Holmes papers at Harvard.)

168. *Address: Dinner of the Chicago Bar Association, supra* note 22, at 533.
169. *Id.* Holmes strove "to realize the paradox that it is not necessary to be heavy in order to have weight." *Id.* He deplored "the average taste of this country" which he regarded as preferring "what I call half boiled dough – a kind of voluminous flabby writing that I loathe." OWH to Alice Stopford Green (May 16, 1909) (Holmes papers).
170. Holmes regarded Emerson as "one of those who set one on fire – to impart a [thought] was the gift of genius." OWH to Canon Patrick Augustine Sheehan (October 27, 1912) in HOLMES-SHEEHAN CORRESPONDENCE, at 51. *See* OWH to John T. Morse (November 8, 1926) (Holmes papers) (Emerson "set me on fire. He could impart a ferment."). He regarded Emerson as a poet, "whose function is not to discern but to make us realize truth" through "imaginative power." OWH to Canon Patrick Augustine Sheehan (October 27, 1912) in HOLMES-SHEEHAN CORRESPONDENCE, at 51. In crafting his opinions and essays, Holmes clearly strove for this power, most especially in his epigrammatic sentences. Holmes's focus on the vitality of individual sentences reflects Emerson's enormous influence. "A sentence gets its force from short words and that is all," Holmes wrote his friend Lewis Einstein. "Style ... is the personal equation of the writer. ... When the Style is fully formed if it has a sweet undersong we call it beautiful, and the writer may do what he likes in words, or syntax; the material is plastic in his hand to image himself – which is all that anyone can give." OWH to Lewis Einstein (May 10, 1903), in HOLMES-EINSTEIN CORRESPONDENCE, at 5–6.
171. *Law in Science and Science in Law, supra* note 39, at 455. The passage continues: "It is not the first use but the tiresome repetition of inadequate catch words upon which I am observing, – phrases which originally were contributions, but which, by their very felicity, delay further analysis for fifty years. That comes from the same source as dislike of novelty, – intellectual indolence or weakness, – a slackening in the eternal pursuit of the more exact." *Id.* Later in the same article, Holmes writes, "My object is not so much to point out what seems to me to be fallacies in particular cases as to enforce by various examples and in various applications the need of scrutinizing the reasons for the rules which we follow, and of not being contented with hollow forms of words merely because they have been used very often and have been repeated from one end of the union to the other. We must think things not words, or at least we must constantly translate our words into the facts for which they stand, if we are to keep to the real and the true." *Id.* at 460.
172. OWH to Lewis Einstein (June 17, 1908), in HOLMES-EINSTEIN CORRESPONDENCE, at 35. Holmes derived "real intellectual pleasure" from writing up cases "shortly and compactly with a hint at general theory when possible." OWH to Harold Laski (December 17, 1925), in 1 HOLMES-LASKI CORRESPONDENCE, at 806.
173. OWH to Ethel Scott (April 24, 1909) (Holmes papers). Holmes wrote his friend Nina Gray that "The things I most dislike are words intrinsically good that having been happily used by some one with open eyes – are laid hold of by alert semi-

Oliver Wendell Holmes

intelligence and made banal by repetition – such as 'constructive' or 'intensive.' Harmless phrases also are made displeasing by common use – like 'in touch with.' It is a devil of a job to write a language decently." OWH to Nina Gray (July 22, 1924) (Holmes papers).

174. OWH to Frederick Pollock (February 6, 1926), in 2 HOLMES-POLLOCK CORRESPONDENCE, at 175.

175. OWH to Harold Laski (March 1, 1923), in 1 HOLMES-LASKI CORRESPONDENCE, at 486 ("The general function of committees is to take the personality out of discourse. I dare say it has been just as well to have McKenna, Day and others cut out some of my exuberances from opinions of the Court.").

176. OWH to Ethel Scott (April 24, 1909) (Holmes papers). Holmes once wrote about an opinion that "[a]s originally written it had a tiny pair of testicles – but the scruples of my brethren have caused their removal and it sings in a very soft voice now." OWH to Felix Frankfurter (October 24, 1920), in HOLMES-FRANKFURTER CORRESPONDENCE, at 95. *See* OWH to "My Dear Friend" (December 24, 1920) (Holmes papers) ("[T]he opinions that would otherwise have gone last Monday were hung up for others to write dissents and those that then fired have been more or less castrated, though not, I hope, quite deprived of their powers. It is rather an irritation to have pungent phrases cut out, but that makes for safety no doubt, and what one cares for sooner or later one gets a chance to say.") One of the reasons Holmes avowed a "pleasure in writing" dissents was "that you can say just what you think, and don't have to cut out phrases to suit the squeams of your brethren." OWH to Mrs. John Chipman Gray (May 5, 1928) (Holmes papers). "Personally I like to shoot off my mouth without having to secure some one else's agreement." OWH to Mrs. John Chipman Gray (April 21, 1923) (Holmes papers).

177. OWH to Ethel Scott (April 24, 1909) (Holmes papers). *See* OWH to Nina Gray (March 18, 1911) (Holmes papers) (The "brethren pulled all the plums out of my pudding and left it rather a sodden mess. Tis ever thus. I get in a biting phrase and of course someone doesn't like it and out it goes."); OWH to Ethel Scott (November 28, 1908) (Holmes papers) ("[M]y colleague White came in and pitched into an opinion ... and intimated that I must do something different if I wanted to carry the crowd, so instead of belles lettres I sat down and wrote it over again with disgust and distributed copies last night. It is a little brown bird now that can offend no one."); OWH to Harold Laski (December 11, 1930) (Holmes papers) ("Regularly I have told you how I would bring down what I thought was a plum pudding and Day would say that plum is dangerous. And McKenna would remove a raisin and so on until I was left with a mass of sodden dough that I was still supposed to call a plum pudding. Once or twice ... I have even consented to give up what I thought – and I still believe rightly – was the essence of the whole and put a word that I thought empty or wrong. I never have ceased to be troubled with my weak compliance. Never again. But I am pretty easy going about striking out what I merely think good.").

178. OWH to Learned Hand (May 8, 1924) (Holmes papers).

179. At the time Hughes first joined the Court, he reports that "Holmes was not as popular with the bar as he became later. Lawyers complained that he did not adequately set forth the case and that his language was frequently obscure." HUGHES, *supra* note 1, at 173. *See* OWH to Nina Gray (December 25, 1928)

(Holmes papers) ("I sit in my library and scribble away when I am not in Court, and as of old my brethren pitch into me for being obscure and when I go nasty I say that I write for educated men – of course, as if referring to some others than my interlocutor.").

180. WHT to Clyde B. Aitchison (December 4, 1925) (Taft papers). A surviving example of the internal discomfort caused by Holmes's insistence on short opinions is a memorandum by Pierce Butler in United States v. New York Central R. Co., 279 U.S. 73 (1929), which concerned the compensation due railroads during the pendency of proceedings before the Interstate Commerce Commission to increase rates for carrying the mail. Butler wrote Van Devanter about Holmes's draft opinion: "The failure of the opinion to give the language of the act on which it rests is quite remarkable. The principle of just compensation is made the foundation without much by way of showing the change of base giving rise to its application. The importance of the question, the parties & the great sums involved combine to make fuller treatment desirable. But, under the circumstances, it seems to me best to let it be circulated as it is. G.S. & E.T.S. will not decline, I suspect. If vigorous dissent comes, it may be necessary to have the opinion properly expanded. For what it is worth, if anything." Memorandum from PB to WVD (Van Devanter papers). Returns to Holmes's opinion in the case include Taft's earnest "I shall concur in this conclusion because the result is just though I could not find that the language of the act justified it. I am glad it will prevail"; McReynolds's tart "If you did not have the votes this would be wrong"; and Brandeis's deliciously ironic reference to Holmes's positivism, see *supra* note 37, "I am glad you found it possible to yield to your desire to do justice – & I acquiesce." (Holmes papers).

181. *Brandeis-Frankfurter Conversations*, at 334 (August 4, 1924). Holmes avowed that in composing opinions he did not "search for epigrams," because "I write too rapidly to stop for phrases." OWH to Felix Frankfurter (March 21, 1924), in HOLMES-FRANKFURTER CORRESPONDENCE, at 171. But Holmes also stressed the power of "phrases – they put water under the boat and float over dangerous obstacles." OWH to Felix Frankfurter (May 26, 1928), *id.* at 228.

182. *Brandeis-Frankfurter Conversations*, at 304 (June 18, 1922).

183. *Id.* at 307 (July 1, 1922).

184. *Id.* Brandeis himself was particularly perturbed whenever a petition for rehearing was filed in one of his own cases, because he "seemed to believe that the opinion should be powerful enough to convince even the losing party, and when a rehearing was sought he felt a sense of failure." Paul A. Freund, *Justice Brandeis: A Law Clerk's Remembrance*, 68 AMERICAN JEWISH HISTORY 11 (September 1978).

185. *Brandeis-Frankfurter Conversations*, at 335–36 (August 4, 1924). For Brandeis, as his former law clerk Dean Acheson once remarked, "truth was less than truth unless it were expounded so that people could understand and believe." Dean Acheson, *Mr. Justice Brandeis*, 55 HARVARD LAW REVIEW 191, 192 (1941). Holmes's ambition, however, was different. Holmes sought to be recognized by great legal minds as a great legal theorist. "I should say generally," Holmes remarked, "that I assume that I am writing for those skilled in the art and that long-winded developments of the obvious seem to me as out of place in an opinion as elsewhere." OWH to Felix Frankfurter (July 2, 1925), in HOLMES-FRANKFURTER

CORRESPONDENCE, at 186. Hence Holmes could explicitly affirm that "Lucidity is not in the first line however, in my mind, because as Harry James said to me when we both were young some things have to be said obscurely before they can be said plainly. I add when you can be lucid the thought has become a commonplace in your mind and the effort is over, but the most interesting moment is the first arrival at a new thought." OWH to Mrs. Curtis (January 26, 1927) (Holmes papers). *See* OWH to Lewis Einstein (November 12, 1905), in HOLMES-EINSTEIN CORRESPONDENCE, at 20–21 ("I am in full blast and fired off one decision which gives me pleasure although it did not quite satisfy me on a point of form. One cannot be perfectly clear until the struggle of thought is over and you have got so far past the idea that it is almost a bore to state it; but decisions can't wait for that, and writers usually *won't*. Therefore I do not regard perfect luminosity as the highest praise. An original mind really at work is hardly likely to attain it. Those who are perfectly clear are apt to be nearer the commonplace.").

186. "Thank you for the dispatch and the admirable quality of the opinions," Taft wrote Holmes in 1927. "They read so well and so easily and I ask why can't I, but I can't." WHT to OWH (May 6, 1927) (Holmes papers).

187. Holmes had possessed the capacity for dispatch since his days on the Massachusetts Supreme Judicial Court ("SJC"). "Holmes had a gift for penetrating to the core of an intellectual argument in a very brief time. . . . That gift, coupled with his equally unusual capacity to express his thoughts rapidly and economically, resulted in his being able to do the work of an SJC justice in far less time than his colleagues." WHITE, *supra* note 5, at 296.

188. WHT to Robert A. Taft (March 7, 1926) (Taft papers). On his return to Holmes's draft opinion in Yeiser v. Dysart, 267 U.S. 540 (1925), Sutherland noted with a twinkle, "Yes. It seems to me you are exceeding the speed limit and violating the union rules in re output." (Holmes papers).

189. OWH to Lady Clifford (April 27, 1927) (Holmes papers). *See Address of Justice Sutherland*, 20 PROCEEDINGS OF THE TWENTIETH ANNUAL SESSION OF THE STATE BAR ASSOCIATION OF UTAH 61 (1924) ("Most of the justices are unable to do the work of writing the opinions while the hearings are going on. . . . Justice Holmes, however, often completes his work before the week is over. He works with great facility, and by the following Wednesday or Thursday we are all disappointed unless we receive a proposed opinion from him; but most of us usually put it off until the recess.").

190. WHT to Robert A. Taft (May 17, 1925) (Taft papers). *See* WHT to Helen Herron Taft (October 4, 1925) (Taft papers).

191. WHT to Robert A. Taft (May 3, 1925) (Taft papers). From all appearances, with the exception of occasional bouts of annoyance that grew more pronounced as the decade ended, Taft and Holmes had a good personal relationship. In 1923, Taft wrote his daughter that "I am very fond of him, and he certainly adds to the interest of the Court. I often don't agree with him, but he has been so long on the Court, and I have had sufficient judicial experience to realize that differences of that kind make no difference in our kindly and fraternal relations." WHT to Mrs. Frederick J. Manning (June 11, 1923) (Taft papers). Two years later Taft reported to his wife that after Saturday conferences he would drive Holmes and Brandeis "home in my car. Holmes has a one horse coupe but apparently Mrs. Holmes uses the coupe Saturday afternoon for some purpose or else the coachman is given freedom that

afternoon, because they are dependent upon him. I am glad to furnish them transportation. Holmes is marvelously well for a man of his years. He is as careful of himself, however, as it is possible to be." WHT to Helen Herron Taft (May 4, 1924) (Taft papers). In 1922 Brandeis said in conversation with Frankfurter, "Holmes ought to have more influence with the Ct – he is so guileless, so affable, so courteous, so gentle.' I [Frankfurter] interrupted, 'but he lives on so different and so elevated a plane compared with the others.' 'Yes,' LDB, 'it's a case of aristocracy against very ordinary bourgeoisie. Taft is the only other man with whom it is a pleasure to talk – you feel you talk with a cultivated man. He knows a lot, he *reads*, he has wide contacts. Taft's relations with Holmes are very loving, a fine banter, he is quick to catch his points and is altogether fine." *Brandeis-Frankfurter Conversations*, at 307 (July 1, 1922). There is a lovely letter from Taft to his wife reporting that "Justice Holmes recommended three books to me, which I have been reading. One of them is 'Leave it to Psmith'. The other is 'Justice of the Peace', and the third is 'The Greek Commonwealth' by Zimmer [sic]. I enjoyed and had great fun reading 'Leave it to Psmith.' I opened and looked into 'Justice of the Peace' and was afraid I might not enjoy it. I have found the 'Greek Commonwealth' really very interesting. It was particularly recommended to me by Brandeis." WHT to Helen Herron Taft (April 28, 1924) (Taft papers). On the immense influence of Alfred Zimmern's *The Greek Commonwealth* on Brandeis, see PHILIPPA STRUM, LOUIS D. BRANDEIS: JUSTICE FOR THE PEOPLE 237–43 (Cambridge: Harvard University Press 1984).

192. *Brandeis-Frankfurter Conversations*, at 327 (September 1, 1923).
193. OWH to Ethel Scott (November 28, 1908) (Holmes papers).
194. OWH to Ethel Scott (April 24, 1909) (Holmes papers).
195. When Court was in session, Holmes's "usual routine," as he wrote his friend Pollock, was "writing opinions on Sundays and sitting in Court during the week." OWH to Frederick Pollock (March 7, 1924), in 2 HOLMES-POLLOCK CORRESPONDENCE, at 129. "I have an intellectual spasm at the beginning of some weeks until the case assigned to me is written and then settle to comparative repose in the latter part." OWH to Lewis Einstein (January 27, 1925), in HOLMES-EINSTEIN CORRESPONDENCE, at 230.
196. "He can't wait after he circulates his opinions, to have them back and 'to shoot them off.'" *Brandeis-Frankfurter Conversations*, at 315 (July 1, 1923). *See also* OWH to Felix Frankfurter (April 21, 1928), in HOLMES-FRANKFURTER CORRESPONDENCE, at 226 ("It gets on one's nerves after a while always to have something waiting to be done and I shant be sorry when the arguments end.").
197. *Brandeis-Frankfurter Conversations*, at 311 (November 30, 1922). *See* WHT to J. M. Dickinson (December 12, 1928) (Taft papers) ("Holmes is remarkable, and seems to me to be as cheerful as possible, and when I give him an opinion to write, he takes it in with avidity and turns up immediately the next week with it all written.").
198. OWH to Harold Laski (June 26, 1925), in 1 HOLMES-LASKI CORRESPONDENCE, at 755.
199. *Id.* Holmes was especially weak at the outset of the 1922 term because he had undergone a serious prostate operation during the preceding summer, from which he took almost a year to recover. Holmes was, as he wrote Taft, in "the pincers of the gods." WHT to WVD (August 19, 1922) (Taft papers). *See* WHITE, *supra* note

5, at 455–57; WHT to WRD (August 10, 1922) (Taft papers) ("I have a letter from Judge Holmes from the hospital promising to be on hand Oct. 1st and saying that he could still swear. I always fear the effect of the operation on the prostate gland at such an age, however, and he will have to be careful."); WHT to Horace D. Taft (October 8, 1922) (Taft papers) ("Holmes is weak. He has lost his jaunty appearance of youth. He is rather gaunt, he is bent with something like lumbago, and his operation has left him unresilient. I think he is beginning to realize himself that his stay on the Bench ought not to be prolonged. He is making a game fight, but I believe he is wise enough to act on what he sees. He has a very sensible wife, and I should not be surprised if she would not soon conclude to influence him to lay down his office."); WVD to JHC (October 9, 1922) (Van Devanter papers) ("Holmes was even less aggressive than usual. Not infrequently he said he had been sparing himself and was not prepared. He looked thinner than usual and had less color. When he leaned his head back there were hollow places under the chin, on the neck and in the sides of the face. It was not an encouraging sign to me. I had noticed during the week that he slept more than heretofore and that when he did sleep he came nearer collapsing in appearance. Also as the week progressed he walked in a stooping way and not erectly. . . . It is too soon yet to form any definite opinion, but what I have observed suggests that he may not be able to go through the work of the term."); WHT to PB (October 25, 1922) ("Holmes had an operation last summer and he is visibly much less strong than last year. He complains of his weakness. He cannot keep up with the certioraris though he writes opinions in cases assigned to him promptly.").

Jackman v. Rosenbaum Co., 260 U.S. 22 (1922), which was argued on October 4, 1922, concerned the question of whether the Fourteenth Amendment limited ancient Pennsylvania law regarding the mutual obligations and prerogatives of owners of party walls. In his weakened condition, Holmes's usual speed seriously impaired the quality of his work. Brandeis told Frankfurter that Holmes had "actually voted & wrote the other way in" *Jackman*. "The great difficulty is his desire for speed." *Brandeis-Frankfurter Conversations*, at 311 (November 30, 1922). Holmes "hadn't read local Ct's opinion to realize party wall regulation older than particular property & as old as property in Pennsylvania. When he had come around he brought Chief (Taft) around (who has open mind usually). H. is very powerful when he changes his mind, with others." *Brandeis-Frankfurter Conversations*, at 320 (July 19, 1923). At the time Brandeis actually "spoke of fear that Holmes will impair his own reputation by continuing – his own aim not sure." *Id. See id.* at 310–11 (November 30, 1922) (Holmes "seems to have weakened his aim. His aim is no longer sure tho his execution is brilliant."). Brandeis accounted for Holmes's opinion in Pennsylvania Coal Co. v. Mahon, 260 U.S. 393 (1922), see *supra* note 143, in part by the fact that "they cut (caught) him when he was weak (after Holmes' prostate operation) & played him to go whole hog." *Brandeis-Frankfurter Conversations*, at 321 (n.d.).

In fall 1922, Frankfurter wrote Brandeis asking for his assessment of Holmes's condition. On October 19, Brandeis replied that "I delayed writing you about Holmes, J. because I wanted to make up my mind. I now think he is in good form & able to carry the load. He looks well, has attended throughout all sessions & conferences and has written opinions with customary speed. He has been often tired physically & at times mentally; but I think this has been due mainly to the unfortunate fact that he has not been able to work as usual in his study because the repairs incident to elevator construction at 1720 [I Street, Holmes's residence] are not yet completed. The annoyance of living at the Powhatan & traveling to & from, necessarily per carriage, has put much strain upon him." LDB to Felix Frankfurter (October 19, 1922), in BRANDEIS-FRANKFURTER CORRESPONDENCE, at 122. In November, Brandeis wrote to say that "OWH is back in 1720 I [Street] & much happier." LDB to Felix Frankfurter (November 14, 1922), *id.* at 125. And in December, Brandeis noted that "the fortnight's recess for Holmes J. – without other work to do than to read Frazer's 'Golden Bough' has had a wonderful restorative effect. He was much fresher at the Conference yesterday than at any time this term – joyous in spirit & active physically as well as mentally." LDB to Felix Frankfurter (December 28, 1922), *id.* at 130. By January 3, Brandeis reported that Holmes was feeling "so perky yesterday that he insisted on getting out of the carriage . . . to walk with me from 12th & H home. And he said today that he felt better for the walk." LDB to Felix Frankfurter (January 3, 1923), *id.*, at 132. At the outset of the 1923 term, Brandeis observed to Taft that "Holmes thinks himself to be in as good condition as before his operation in 1922 and ready for work." WHT to Helen Herron Taft (September 25, 1923) (Taft papers). *But see* LDB to Felix Frankfurter (February 9, 1924), in BRANDEIS-FRANKFURTER CORRESPONDENCE, at 157 (Holmes "talks considerably about adjusting himself to age etc. And there arise questions of judgment something like last year.").

200. LDB to Felix Frankfurter (January 29, 1929), in BRANDEIS-FRANKFURTER CORRESPONDENCE, at 356. In 1922, Taft wrote his brother that Holmes "is marvelous in the quickness of his work, but [his] work is not as good as it used to be because of his disposition to push it through." WHT to Horace D. Taft (April 27, 1922) (Taft papers). For another possible explanation of Holmes's tendency to minimize the importance of opinions he was assigned to write, see *supra* note 163. Holmes's dyspeptic law clerk during the 1924 term, W. Barton Leach, who later became Story Professor at the Harvard Law School, had a far more dour assessment. Holmes, he said, "got all of the Court's junk. I was convinced at that time, and still am convinced, that the C.J. was doing this deliberately with a view to indicating to OWH as painlessly as possible that his usefulness had ceased." W. Barton Leach to Felix Frankfurter (May 31, 1938) (Holmes papers).

201. WVD to JHC (June 9, 1928) (Van Devanter papers).

202. NOVICK, *supra* note 47, at 147; Oliver Wendell Holmes, *Introduction*, in MR. JUSTICE BRANDEIS (Felix Frankfurter, ed., New Haven: Yale University Press 1932).

203. OWH to Clara Stevens (May 13, 1916) (Holmes papers).

204. OWH to Lady Castletown (June 20, 1916) (Holmes papers).

205. OWH to John Henry Wigmore (July 5, 1917) (Holmes papers). Brandeis "probably believes that economic are the only real motives wherein I think him wrong." OWH to Felix Frankfurter (July 16, 1916), in HOLMES-FRANKFURTER CORRESPONDENCE, at 53.

206. OWH to Harold Laski (October 19, 1923), in 1 HOLMES-LASKI CORRESPONDENCE, at 555.

207. OWH to Harold Laski (October 9, 1921), in 1 HOLMES-LASKI CORRESPONDENCE, at 374. *See* OWH to Harold Laski (March 1, 1923), *id.* at 485 (Brandeis "is a great

comfort and help to me – and the way in which that cuss is loaded with facts on all manner of subjects leaves me gawping.").
208. OWH to Harold Laski (November 21, 1924), in 1 HOLMES-LASKI CORRESPONDENCE, at 675. "We get a short talk together almost every day on the way homeward." OWH to Harold Laski (March 1, 1923), in 1 HOLMES-LASKI CORRESPONDENCE, at 485; OWH to Harold Laski (October 28, 1927), in 2 HOLMES-LASKI CORRESPONDENCE, at 988 ("Brandeis generally comes with me as far as my house, driving home, and we go by the Potomac and around the Lincoln Monument, to get the wrinkles out a little. He is as good as ever."). In 1928, Brandeis wrote Frankfurter that "for the last five days [Holmes] has called me spontaneously – propria persona on the telephone. On four days, to talk opinions. In one case, he read me one on the telephone – a whole opinion. Yesterday, the call was solely to tell me that he had beat me to it, & has discovered the first dandelion on the wall of Potomac basin." LDB to Felix Frankfurter (March 29, 1928), in BRANDEIS-FRANKFURTER CORRESPONDENCE, at 328–29.
209. OWH to Frederick Pollock (October 31, 1926), in 2 HOLMES-POLLOCK CORRESPONDENCE, at 191. Holmes continued: "To me it is queer to see the widespread prejudice against the Jews. I never think of the nationality and might even get thick with a man before noticing that he was a Hebrew. You know the poem: 'How odd – of God – to choose – The Jews.'" *Id.* Five years previously Holmes had directly asked Harold Laski, himself Jewish, "whether loveableness is a characteristic of the better class of Jews. When I think how many of the younger men that have warmed my heart have been Jews I cannot but suspect it, and put the question to you. Brandeis, whom many dislike, seems to me to have this quality and always gives me a glow, even though I am not sure that he wouldn't burn me at a slow fire if it were in the interest of some very possibly disinterested aim. I don't for a moment doubt that for daily purposes he feels to me as a friend – as certainly I do to him and without the above reserve. This, of course, *strictissime* between ourselves. I pause to remark that I have a scarf pin that gives me immense pleasure – it looks so like a cockroach hiding in a corner with a gleam of light upon his back. While interrogating you let me ask also whether you think as it sometimes is said that the Jews always have No. 1 at the bottom more than the rest of the world. I put these things to you as one capable of detached opinions." OWH to Harold Laski (January 12, 1921), in 1 HOLMES-LASKI CORRESPONDENCE, at 304–5. So far as I can tell, Laski discreetly ignored Holmes's inquiries.
210. OWH to LDB, quoted in 5 LETTERS OF LOUIS D. BRANDEIS, at 173 n.1. On the occasion of Brandeis's seventieth birthday, Holmes wrote him: "You turn the third corner tomorrow. You have done big things with high motives – have swept over great hedges and across wide ditches, always with the same courage, the same keen eye, the same steady hand. As you take the home stretch the onlookers begin to realize how you have ridden and what you have achieved. I am glad that I am still here to say: Nobly done." Quoted *id.* at 245 n.3.
211. Oliver Wendell Holmes, *Introduction*, in MR. JUSTICE BRANDEIS, *supra* note 202.
212. *See supra* note 64. Holmes once told Taft that "if they left it to me I should put up a bronze statue" of John D. Rockefeller. OWH to Lewis Einstein (October 28, 1912), in HOLMES-EINSTEIN CORRESPONDENCE, at 74. Holmes remarked that he wanted "to write a psalm on the virtues of monopoly – there is such an insane

frenzy against it now. The Tobacco Case is being argued – under the Sherman Act which aims at making everyone fight and forbidding anyone to be victorious – An imbecile statute, I think, which nevertheless I have done my share to enforce, as is my duty." OWH to Alice Stopford Green (January 10, 1911) (Taft papers). Holmes had good company in this view, for "most American political economists in the late nineteenth century opposed the Sherman Act, believing that industrial monopoly was both inevitable and socially beneficial." Herbert Hovenkamp, *Labor Conspiracies in American Law, 1880–1930*, 66 TEXAS LAW REVIEW 919, 939 (1988).

213. For illustrative examples of the contrast between Holmes's and Brandeis's style of opinion-writing, compare their respective dissents in Quaker City Cab Co. v. Pennsylvania, 277 U.S. 389 (1928); Louisville Gas & Electric Co. v. Coleman, 277 U.S. 32 (1928); and Untermyer v. Anderson, 276 U.S. 440 (1928).

214. OWH to Harold Laski (November 21, 1924), in 1 HOLMES-LASKI CORRESPONDENCE, at 675. Holmes added, "If, however, you are to go the other way I greatly respect the knowledge and thoroughness with which [Brandeis] gathers together all manner of reports and documents."

215. *Brandeis-Frankfurter Conversations*, at 335 (August 4, 1924). On returning Brandeis's draft opinion in United States v. Abilene & Southern Ry. Co., 265 U.S. 274 (1924), Holmes wrote, "Another solid piece of work handsomely done. Though I never shall believe in footnotes in an opinion." (Brandeis papers). In the 205 opinions Holmes authored in the 1921 through 1928 terms, he himself used only a single footnote. *See* Heyer v. Duplicator Mfg. Co., 263 U.S. 100, 100 n.1 (1923). By contrast, in the 193 opinions that Brandeis authored during those eight terms, he averaged 2.99 footnotes per opinion. In dissent Holmes never used a footnote; Brandeis averaged 12.54 footnotes per dissent. Taft averaged .11 footnotes per opinion and never used a footnote in a dissent. Van Devanter averaged 1.83 footnotes per opinion; Butler .94; Stone .58; Sutherland .38; McReynolds .37; and Sanford, strangely, 3.41. Stone averaged 1.54 footnotes per dissent; Butler .6; McReynolds .51; and Sutherland .22. Van Devanter and Sanford never used a footnote in a dissent. As a whole, during its eight complete terms, the Taft Court averaged one footnote for every majority opinion and 3.66 footnotes per dissent. By way of contrast, the Court during its 1998 term had increased its use of footnotes almost sevenfold, so that the Court averaged 6.91 footnotes per majority opinion. (It averaged 5.48 footnotes per dissent.) Footnotes in modern opinions tend to be substantive and argumentative; footnotes during the Taft Court era tended to consist of citations to authority.

216. OWH to Nina Gray (May 3, 1903) (Holmes papers). The image of "song" frequently recurs in Holmes's description of his own style. *See* OWH to "My Dear Friend" (March 29, 1926) (Holmes papers) ("As I said before I think style is largely a matter of the ear. The cadences, and with some masters the undersong not always detected at first, get you without much regard to the meaning."); OWH to Harold Laski (December 6, 1921), in 1 HOLMES-LASKI CORRESPONDENCE, at 709 ("I again realize that sound is the half of immortality. The song of Shakespeare's words counts, I think, as much as their meaning to keep them remembered."); *see also* OWH to Harold Laski (January 13,

Oliver Wendell Holmes

1923), *id.* at 474; OWH to Harold Laski (March 1, 1923), *id.* at 486. Sometimes Holmes used the metaphor of the dance to describe his opinion writing process. *See, e.g.*, OWH to Felix Frankfurter (December 6, 1921), in HOLMES-FRANKFURTER CORRESPONDENCE, at 132 ("Pouf – the sword dance is danced and I think I have kept off the blades in a case just sent to the printer.").

217. MELVIN I. UROFSKY, LOUIS D. BRANDEIS: A LIFE 476 (New York: Pantheon Books 2009). One clerk reports that after he and Brandeis had worked hard on an opinion, and after the clerk was led to believe that the opinion was ready to be circulated, Brandeis suddenly and unexpectedly asked, "Now I think the opinion is persuasive, but what can we do to make it more instructive?" Freund, *supra* note 184, at 11.

218. OWH to Felix Frankfurter (December 3, 1925), in HOLMES-FRANKFURTER CORRESPONDENCE, at 194. "Think not," Holmes continued, "that I don't appreciate the power that his knowledge gives him. The perfect critters must eat hay as well as oats." *Id.* Holmes was aware that "Brandeis had an insatiable appetite for facts and that I hate them except as pegs for generalizations, but I admire the gift and wish I had a barn in which I could store them for use at need. I hope they manure my soil but they disappear in specie as soon as taken in." OWH to Harold Laski (December 27, 1925), in 1 HOLMES-LASKI CORRESPONDENCE, at 810. Holmes confessed to Laski that "We are sitting and having cases that I dislike about rates and the Interstate Commerce Commission. I listen with respect but without envy to questions by Brandeis and Butler using the words of railroading and rate-making that I imperfectly understand. To be familiar with business is a great (secondary) advantage. Someone said of Brandeis, He is not afraid of a Balance Sheet. His experience at the bar is an infinite advantage in many cases." OWH to Harold Laski (February 22, 1929), in 2 HOLMES-LASKI CORRESPONDENCE, at 1135. *See* OWH to Felix Frankfurter (October 23, 1921) (Holmes papers) ("I have felt stupid and muddle-headed at the oral arguments. They always bother me, but the dear Brandeis helps me to understand what the question is – when I know that I am capable of an opinion.").

219. OWH to Nina Gray (December 19, 1925) (Holmes papers). As Holmes observed to his friend Ethel Scott, "I adore cases that enable one to lift at least the corner of a flap that covers a theory." OWH to Lady Leslie Scott (November 21, 1925) (Holmes papers).

220 Holmes wrote Lewis Einstein: "The diabolical Brandeis has skewered my heart by speaking thus as to vacation: 'You talk about improving your mind. You only exercise it dealing with the subjects familiar to you. You should do something new – take an excursion into some domain of unfamiliar fact, e.g. the textile industry in Massachusetts, and, after reading the reports etc., go to Lawrence and see with your own eyes what it means.' I hate facts, and I feel as if it might be a solemn call to duty. We shall see. It has made me squirm within anyhow." OWH to Lewis Einstein (May 22, 1919), in HOLMES-EINSTEIN CORRESPONDENCE, at 187. A week later, Holmes wrote Frederick Pollock:

> Brandeis the other day drove a harpoon into my midriff with reference to my summer occupations. He said you talk about improving your

mind, you only exercise it on the subjects with which you are familiar. Why don't you try something new, study some domain of fact. Take up the textile industries in Massachusetts and after reading the reports sufficiently you can go to Lawrence and get a human notion of how it really is. I hate facts. I always say the chief end of man is to form general propositions – adding that no general proposition is worth a damn. Of course a general proposition is simply a string for the facts and I have little doubt that it would be good for my immortal soul to plunge into them, good also for the performance of my duties, but I shrink from the bore – or rather I hate to give up the chance to read this and that, that a gentleman should have read before he dies. I don't remember that I ever read Machiavelli's *Prince* – and I think of the Day of Judgment. There are a good many worse ignorances than that, that ought to be closed up. I don't know how it will come out.

OWH to Frederick Pollock (May 26, 1919), in 2 HOLMES-POLLOCK CORRESPONDENCE, at 13–14. The following week Holmes was already having second thoughts, writing Laski that "If I follow Brandeis's suggestion I shall have little time for other things." OWH to Harold Laski (June 1, 1919), in 1 HOLMES-LASKI CORRESPONDENCE, at 210. By the following summer the project was effectively dead. "I sat with Brandeis in Farragut Square (close to our house) and had a pleasant farewell talk while a catbird played the mocking bird overhead. In consideration of my age and moral infirmities he absolved me from facts for the vacation and allowed me my customary sport with ideas." OWH to Harold Laski (June 11, 1920), in 1 HOLMES-LASKI CORRESPONDENCE, at 268. Two years later Holmes was positively gleeful about his decision to turn away from empirical investigation, writing Laski: "My boy I mean to enjoy myself if I can – to get the unexpurgated Pepys – even read (going on) John Dewey's last ... but if you think that I am going to bother myself again before I die about social improvement or read any of those stinking upward and onwarders – you err. I mean to have some good out of being old. It seems to me very unlikely that even Brandeis will make me learned on the textile workers of New England and I mean to go my own way, read what gives me pleasure and leave the 'undone vast' for others." OWH to Harold Laski (June 1, 1922), in 1 HOLMES-LASKI CORRESPONDENCE, at 430.

Brandeis recollected the incident in a somewhat different manner from Holmes. He explained to Frankfurter that he had once told Holmes

> that if he really wants to "improve his mind" (as he always speaks of it), the way to do it is not to read more philosophic books, he has improved his mind that way as far it can go, but to get some sense of the world of fact. And he asked me to map out some readings, he became much interested & I told him that I'd see – get some books, that books could carry him only so far & that then he should get some exhibits from life. I suggested the textile industry & told him in vacation time he's near Lawrence & Lowell & he should go there & look about. He became much interested although he said he was "too old." I told him he was too old to acquire knowledge in many fields of fact but not too old to realize through one field what the world of fact was and to be more conscious & understanding of it. With his mind as an instrument, there wasn't anything he couldn't acquire. And so he undertook to do the textiles, but very unfortunately it was the time Mrs. Holmes was very sick & he had her on his mind & studying became a duty instead of, as I hoped, a new interest & possibly, therefore, a relaxation. And so he reported to me, very apologetically, in the Fall his inability to pursue the study.

Oliver Wendell Holmes

Brandeis-Frankfurter Conversations, at 335 (July 19, 1923). In the end, their difference on this point became a source of amusement to the two justices. In 1929, Brandeis wrote Frankfurter to report that "O.W.H. is in fine form. I said to him Monday, 'By Wednesday you – true spendthrift as you are – will have your cases written & then nothing to do for nearly four weeks.' He answered, 'I mean to enjoy myself, reading metaphysics.'" LDB to Felix Frankfurter (March 13, 1929), in BRANDEIS-FRANKFURTER CORRESPONDENCE, at 365. Brandeis later told his clerk David Reisman that he "had no time for metaphysics." David Riesman to Felix Frankfurter (May 22, 1936) (Frankfurter papers).

221. OWH to Harold Laski (January 6, 1923), in 1 HOLMES-LASKI CORRESPONDENCE, at 469. There is an extant letter from Brandeis to Holmes: "Let me summarize: You who pried open the legal door to effort should not close it to hope. The advances made in science and the arts should teach us to be skeptical of alleged facts, but not of possibilities. 'They know not what they do' should be supplemented by 'We know not what they may do.'" LDB to OWH (April 23, 1919) (Holmes papers).

222. "It's perfectly amazing that a man who has had no practical experience to speak of, and no experience at statesmanship, should be so frequently right as to matters that have significance only in their application. I have told him so – how amazing it is." *Brandeis-Frankfurter Conversations*, at 334–35 (August 4, 1924).

223. "[T]he Court has rendered some decisions that I deeply regret. Brandeis and I are together as we are so apt to be, by a sort of preestablished harmony." OWH to Harold Laski (June 12, 1928), in 2 HOLMES-LASKI CORRESPONDENCE, at 1060. *See* OWH to Harold Laski (May 12, 1928), *id.* at 1055 ("There seems a preestablished harmony between Brandeis and me. He agrees with all my dissents and I agree with the only one that he will propound.").

224. OWH to Harold Laski (February 18, 1928), in 2 HOLMES-LASKI CORRESPONDENCE, at 1027.

225. 276 U.S. 413 (1928). *Casey* involved the criminal conviction of a lawyer for purchasing morphine in unstamped packages. The government demonstrated the possession of morphine and relied upon a statutory presumption to prove the purchase of the drug from an unstamped package. The defendant challenged the constitutionality of the presumption. Holmes, writing for a Court that included Taft, Van Devanter, Sutherland, and Stone, concluded that "In dealing with a poison not commonly used except upon a doctor's prescription easily proved, or for a debauch only possible by a breach of law, it seems reasonable to call on a person possessing it in a form that warrants suspicion to show that he obtained it in a mode permitted by the law." 276 U.S. at 418. (The Court later retreated from this broad holding in Turner v. United States, 396 U.S. 398, 424 (1970).) In his dissent Brandeis, writing for himself and Butler, did not reach the question of the constitutionality of the presumption, but concluded that the prosecution must be dismissed "because officers of the government instigated the commission of the alleged crime." *Id.* at 421 (Brandeis, J., dissenting). (McReynolds, Butler and Sanford dissented separately on the constitutionality of the presumption.)

THE TAFT COURT

In response to Brandeis's circulated dissent, Holmes sent a separate memorandum to the justices stating that "I have much sympathy with my Brother Brandeis' feeling about this case but I doubt if we are warranted in going farther than to suggest a possibility that the grounds for uneasiness may perhaps be considered by another (i.e., the pardoning) power. A Court rarely can act with advantage of its own motion, and very rarely can be justified in giving judgment upon grounds that the record was not intended to present.... I am not persuaded that conduct of the officials was different from or worse than ordering a drink of a suspected bootlegger." Memorandum by Holmes, J. Opinion and dissent circulated heretofore (Holmes papers).

After reading Holmes's memorandum, Stone wrote Brandeis, "Before conference I read the record in this case with the thought of coming out where you have come, but considerations which Justice Holmes has mentioned in his memorandum lead me to take the opposite view and I am inclined to stick by it, although I hope to go over the matter again before conference." HFS to LDB (February 3, 1928) (Brandeis papers). To Brandeis, Holmes wrote that he couldn't "believe" that Brandeis's characterization "is the legitimate result of the record," although it "does make me feel very uneasy." OWH to LDB (February 1, 1928) (Brandeis papers). Taft concurred in Holmes's opinion, saying "I don't think you need to soften your difference with B in this case. The idea that a full grown man and a lawyer of much practice with addicts could be led into a crime like this without being a criminal all the time is absurd. I wonder that B. elected such a case as this for his violent outburst." (Holmes papers). Butler, on the other hand, wrote Brandeis "I think your description of the situation is excellent & hope that good may come of it." PB to LDB (February 1, 1928) (Brandeis papers). For popular reaction, see *A Borderline Case*, NEW YORK HERALD TRIBUNE (April 11, 1928), at 16.

Casey pressed the case for a pardon based upon his innocence. He sought supportive letters from Taft, Van Devanter, and Stone. Thomas J. Casey to WVD (June 6, 1928) (Van Devanter papers). Van Devanter refused on the ground that "a pardon should not be granted presently or until after Casey has served a third or a half of his sentence. To grant an absolute pardon now would hardly be in keeping with the fact that a jury has pronounced him guilty and three courts have said there was no error of law in his conviction." WVD to WHT (June 27, 1928) (Van Devanter papers). Stone did support the pardon and visited his successor, Attorney General John G. Sargent, to urge it. Thomas J. Casey to WVD (June 6, 1928) (Van Devanter papers); WVD to WHT (June 15, 1928) (Van Devanter papers). Butler was of the view "that the President ought not to pardon Casey or to make an immediate and pronounced commutation, because to do so would reflect unhappily on the judicial action on the case." *Id*. Taft agreed with Butler and Van Devanter: "I have no doubt of his guilt, and while the sentence was doubtless too heavy a one, he ought to obey the order of Court and go to prison and then rely on clemency after the case has been properly considered." WHT to WVD (July 1, 1928) (Taft papers).

On July 3, 1928, the president fully pardoned Casey, Report of Pardon Attorney James E. Finch, Justice Department Report (1929), H. Doc. 187, 71st CONG. 2nd SESS., Serial # 9269, at 298, in part because the Supreme Court "stood 5 to 4, and the majority opinion indicated doubt as to the guilt of

Oliver Wendell Holmes

the applicant. The Attorney General advised that he be granted a full and unconditional pardon." *Id.* In response to Brandeis's dissent, Holmes had modified his opinion to state: "Whatever doubts we may feel as to the truth of the testimony we are not at liberty to consider them on the only question before the Court. The grounds for uneasiness can be considered only by another power." 276 U.S. at 419–20.

226. OWH to Frederick Pollock (February 17, 1928), in 2 HOLMES-POLLOCK CORRESPONDENCE, at 215. For another case where the "preestablished harmony" failed, see United States *ex rel.* Hughes v. Gault, 271 U.S. 142 (1926). When one of Holmes's closest correspondents implied that he was "under the influence of the Hebs," Holmes replied that "I am comfortably confident that I am under no influence except that of thoughts and insights. Sometimes my brother B. seems to me to see deeper than some of the others – and we often agree. There is a case now on which his printed argument convinced me contrary to my first impression – I do not remember any other case in which the agreement was not independent." OWH to Nina Gray (March 5, 1921) (Holmes papers).

227. WHT to Mrs. Frederick J. Manning (June 11, 1923) (Taft papers).

228. WHT to Robert A. Taft (March 7, 1926) (Taft papers). Chief Justice Hughes agreed. "Justice Brandeis was a resourceful colleague. As Justice Holmes became more and more conscious of the limitations of age he was inclined to depend upon the judgment of his close friend." HUGHES, *supra* note 1, at 301.

229. WHT to Henry Stimson (May 18, 1928) (Taft papers). Taft continued, "He has more interest in, and gives more attention to, his dissents than he does to the opinions he writes for the Court, which are very short and not very helpful. The three dissenters act on the principle that a decision of the whole Court by a majority is not a decision at all, and therefore they are not bound by the authority of the decision, which if followed out would leave the dissenters to be the only constitutional law breakers in the country."

230. OWH to Nina Gray (March 5, 1921) (Holmes papers). *See, e.g.,* OWH to Harold Laski (December 3, 1918), in 1 HOLMES-LASKI CORRESPONDENCE, at 176 ("I am catspawed by Brandeis to do another dissent on burning themes"); OWH to Felix Frankfurter (February 19, 1926), in HOLMES-FRANKFURTER CORRESPONDENCE, at 198 ("I have been spurred by the fiend in the shape of Brandeis into two dissents to the printer."); OWH to Learned Hand (March 10, 1927) (Holmes papers) ("I had some doubt whether [my dissent in Tyson & Bros v. Banton, 273 U.S. 418 (1927)] was worth printing but Brandeis and my secretary said fire it off."); OWH to Felix Frankfurter (November 4, 1927), in HOLMES-FRANKFURTER CORRESPONDENCE, at 218 ("I have no duty more pressing than to meditate whether to write a dissent on the difference between a tax and a penalty, which opens a hobby. I shall consult with Brandeis before doing much. We agree in result, but I don't know whether my approach would have his concurrence."); OWH to Nina Gray (May 5, 1928) (Holmes papers) ("A note from Brandeis ... urging me to write" a dissent); OWH to Harold Laski (October 16, 1929), in 2 HOLMES-LASKI CORRESPONDENCE, at 1192 ("Brandeis ... reminded me of a case argued last term in which he said I should have to write a dissent. I looked at it and sure enough it is one rather specially in my line on which I had and have decided views – one of

those cases in which it seems to one that most judges show limited subtlety. There are cases from time to time that strike bottom notions and bottom notions often are very hazily held."). Unfortunately, I have been unable ascertain any published Holmes dissent that plausibly corresponds to this letter.

231. For example, in John P. King Mfg. Co. v. City Council of Augusta, 277 U.S. 100 (1928), and Sultan Ry. & Timber Co. v. Department of Labor, 277 U.S. 135 (1928), Brandeis and Holmes dissented on the ground that those seeking to challenge in the Supreme Court a decision upholding the constitutionality of a municipal ordinance or an administrative ruling, as distinct from a decision upholding the constitutionality of a state statute, should be required to proceed by way of a discretionary petition for *certiorari* rather than by way of a mandatory writ of error. It is extremely unlikely that a technical jurisdictional question of this nature would have inspired Holmes's dissent without the prompting of Brandeis. *See* Dahnke-Walker Milling Co. v. Bondurant, 257 U.S. 282 (1921), in which Brandeis had earlier dissented on analogous grounds, and in which Holmes had expressed "appreciation" but no "change of heart." (Brandeis papers). As Brandeis said of Holmes, "Few of them realize that questions of jurisdiction are really questions of power between States and Nations. Holmes and Taft for different reasons know little about it because they don't care. Taft because he likes to decide questions as a matter of expediency, where controversies arise; Holmes cares nothing about 'expediency' but likes to decide cases where interesting questions are raised. Holmes is beginning to learn; intellectually he is beginning to appreciate our responsibility, tho not emotionally. I tell him 'the most important thing we do is *not* doing.'" *Brandeis-Frankfurter Conversations*, at 313 (June 28, 1923). Brandeis's reference to Taft was likely inspired by Taft's response to Brandeis's dissent in *Bondurant*, in which Taft had written: "I agree with you but in a case like this do not think it useful for me to dissent. I agree with Justice Van Devanter on the merits." (Brandeis papers).

232. 277 U.S. 438 (1928).
233. WHT to Horace D. Taft (June 12, 1928) (Taft papers).
234. HEYWOOD BROUN, *It Seems to Heywood Broun*, 41 THE NATION 479 (1928).
235. WHT to Horace D. Taft (December 1, 1929) (Taft papers).
236. *See supra* note 47; OWH to Lewis Einstein (October 28, 1912), in HOLMES-EINSTEIN CORRESPONDENCE, at 74.

CHAPTER 6

Willis Van Devanter

ALTHOUGH AS PRESIDENT Taft had appointed five justices to the Supreme Court,[1] only two of these remained when he assumed the chief justiceship – Pitney and Van Devanter. Pitney would be gone within eighteen months, but Van Devanter would remain as "one of the most enduring achievements of the Taft Administration, and very possibly its greatest."[2] If Holmes was a disruptive jurisprudential presence within the Taft Court, a portent of things to come, Willis Van Devanter was, by contrast, its pragmatic conservator of past practices and precedents. Van Devanter was an elegant and careful legal craftsman. More than any other justice, he shaped the Court's everyday decision-making processes. Van Devanter also was an intellectual force behind the Court's turn to the right during the 1920s. His immense influence is now all but lost to modern observers.

Van Devanter was born on April 17, 1859, in Marion, Indiana. He was about eighteen months younger than Taft. Van Devanter's father was a successful local lawyer. Although Van Devanter wanted to go into farming, his father prevailed upon him to attend Indiana Asbury University (now DePauw University) and then Cincinnati Law School, where Van Devanter was a year behind and acquainted with Taft himself.[3] Unlike both Taft and Holmes, who followed career paths that could easily be anticipated, Van Devanter elected as a young man to move to the distant and lawless West. In 1884, within a week of President Chester A. Arthur's appointment of Van Devanter's brother-in-law (John W. Lacey) as chief justice of the Territorial Court for Wyoming Territory, Van Devanter relocated to the frontier town of Cheyenne. In 1885, he offered his services to the new territorial governor, the loyal, shrewd, and astute Francis E. Warren, stalwart Republican, wealthy rancher, and Civil War recipient of the Medal of Honor.

Van Devanter's rise in the new territory was "little short of sensational."[4] He became a commissioner tasked with revising the laws and statutes of Wyoming

Territory in 1886;[5] the city attorney of Cheyenne in 1887;[6] a member of the Territorial House of Representatives in 1888; and, in 1889, at the age of 30, the chief justice of the Territorial Supreme Court. When Wyoming became a state in 1890, Van Devanter was elected to its new Supreme Court and became its first chief justice.[7]

Van Devanter unexpectedly resigned four days after becoming chief justice, without giving advance warning or explanation.[8] He returned to the successful law practice that he had established, traveling throughout the state in stagecoaches and on horseback. In 1890, he formed with his brother-in-law the firm of Lacey and Van Devanter, which became "Wyoming's most prominent law firm,"[9] representing the state's most important economic interests, including cattlemen's associations and the area's most significant railroad, the Union Pacific. Most memorably, Van Devanter defended the cattlemen who, along with a contingent of Texas gunman, had traveled to the northern reaches of the state to exterminate the "rustlers" whom they claimed were stealing cattle.[10] After murdering two suspected rustlers, the excursion was itself surrounded by angry residents and survived only after being extracted by federal troops. The invasion was the outgrowth of ongoing disputes between southern Republican cattle interests and northern settlers. Van Devanter conducted a masterful and effective defense of the gunmen in what later became known as the Johnson County War.[11]

From the moment he arrived in the territory, Van Devanter sought to become an important player in Wyoming Republican politics. Largely because of his close connection to Warren, he "served as Chairman of the Republican State Committee from 1892 to 1895, as a delegate to the Republican National Convention in St. Louis in 1896, and as a member of the Republican National Committee from 1896 to 1900."[12] After Warren became a powerful United States senator,[13] Van Devanter became "Senator Warren's man in Wyoming, his confidant, counsel, and political manager."[14] Van Devanter subsidized Republican newspapers; arranged for political torchlight parades and rallies; provided Republican speakers with free Union Pacific passes (essential in such a large, unpopulated state); financed the transportation of Republican voters to the polls; created a statewide network of Republican clubs; waged election campaigns; drafted platforms and legislation; whipped the unruly Wyoming legislature into line; and in general was the first lieutenant of what became known as the "Warren machine."[15]

Van Devanter remained throughout absolutely loyal to Warren.[16] Van Devanter was an "ideal tool" who was content never to threaten Warren's authority:

> Van Devanter was discreet, kept Warrant's confidences, but faithfully relayed political gossip and intelligence to Warren, giving Warren a trustworthy guide to Wyoming's political climate. . . . Van Devanter, as legislative draftsman and political negotiator, could translate Warren's program into speeches and bills and see that the territorial and state legislature responded. Van Devanter, however, never intruded on questions of policy. Warren decided on the ends; Van Devanter took care of the means. . . . In crisis after crisis, other Republicans would falter or whine, but Van Devanter never wavered in his

Willis Van Devanter

willingness to defend Warren and his program. For such devotion, Warren repaid Van Devanter with the highest gifts he could command.[17]

These gifts included, first and foremost, a relentless effort to advance Van Devanter's career, which included the ambition to become a federal judge[18] and ultimately a Supreme Court justice.[19] Warren's first step was to lobby then Attorney General Joseph McKenna to secure Van Devanter's appointment in 1897 as an assistant attorney general assigned to the Department of the Interior.[20] Van Devanter proved an "efficient bureaucrat,"[21] impressively and effectively managing his department, reducing backlogs, and successfully arguing important cases before the Supreme Court.[22]

It is during this period that Van Devanter acquired his famous expertise in Indian, mining, and water law, and in the law of public lands and patents, all of considerable importance to the governance of the West.[23] Van Devanter notably represented the federal government in the infamous case of *Lone Wolf v. Hitchcock*,[24] which "has been called 'the Indians' *Dred Scott* decision"[25] because it held that Congress could unilaterally abrogate treaties with Native American tribes. In *Lone Wolf*, Van Devanter ably defended the American government's fraudulent seizure and sale of millions of acres of Indian land in Oklahoma.[26] Throughout his career Van Devanter would insist that because Indians adhered "to primitive modes of life, largely influenced by superstition and fetichism, and chiefly governed according to the crude customs inherited from their ancestors," they were "essentially a simple, uninformed and inferior people" who were properly "dependent upon the fostering care and protection of the government."[27]

Despite his success in government, Van Devanter never lost his thirst for judicial office. And when Warren – ever loyal, effective, and imaginative – secured the passage of legislation creating an extra position on the Eighth Circuit, Van Devanter was nominated to the seat by Theodore Roosevelt and confirmed in 1903. Van Devanter acted the part of a moderate Roosevelt liberal, voting (unlike Holmes) to apply the Sherman Anti-Trust Act to the Northern Securities Company,[28] as well as to the Standard Oil Company,[29] and taking a strong stand in favor of national power with regard to the control of federal lands[30] and Indians.[31]

Throughout his time on the Eighth Circuit, Van Devanter actively sought promotion to the Supreme Court.[32] Senator Warren was fully supportive, telling Van Devanter that "We must keep our eye on the sight and our thumb on the keyhole, and not miss a single trick, because the thing will not be complete until you become one of the nine."[33] Almost as soon as Taft became president, Warren let him know in no uncertain terms that "Probably I shall desire nothing during your administration so intensely as I desire the promotion of Judge Willis Van Devanter to the Supreme Court when a vacancy occurs."[34] Warren's opportunity came in 1910 with the death of Chief Justice Fuller[35] and the retirement of Justice William Henry Moody.[36] One of the new appointments would almost certainly have to come from the Eighth Circuit.

The story of Van Devanter's nomination is told elsewhere,[37] but for present purposes it is important to emphasize a curious and mysterious memorandum tabulating the efficiency of Circuit Court judges that somehow ended up in President Taft's files as he contemplated the appointment.[38] The memorandum purported to show that Van Devanter was a "shirker" who was unable to keep up his share of the Eighth Circuit's work.[39] Van Devanter heard of the memorandum from Charles Nagel, Taft's secretary of commerce and labor (and Brandeis's brother-in-law), and he responded to the memorandum's allegations with indignation. "It gives me no little pain because it does me an injustice." Van Devanter pointed to the number of original trials that he had conducted, the difficulty of the opinions that he had undertaken, as well as to the fact that "I have proceeded upon the theory that quality and accuracy are more important, particularly in appellate work where binding precedents are made."[40]

Matters came to a head in December 1910 as Taft contemplated his options. Taft angrily complained to Warren that Van Devanter was not working hard enough. "Almost certainly" with Warren's connivance,[41] Van Devanter responded with a public telegram taking his name out of consideration,[42] together with a long impassioned "private" letter undermining the memorandum's statistics, casting personal doubt on its author, and defending Van Devanter's own performance.[43]

Warren presented the telegram to Taft, who found it "very dignified,"[44] and then Warren cleverly induced Taft to himself request to see Van Devanter's "private" justificatory letter.[45] On December 9, Warren, meeting at 7:00 pm with a sleepy Taft to discuss irrigation matters, also suggested to Taft that appointing Van Devanter's chief rival from the Eighth Circuit, Judge William Cather Hook, would encourage insurgent Republicans to believe that they were controlling Supreme Court appointments. "By this time Mr. Taft's sleepiness had entirely disappeared and he was the most thoroughly awake man you ever saw, his eye snapping fire," Warren wrote Van Devanter, "and the way he raked over the insurgents and what he said about them would not look at all well in print."[46] Taft reported to Warren that the Cabinet, including Nagel, had met and recommended Van Devanter.[47]

Three days later Taft announced his selection of Van Devanter, who was confirmed on December 15, 1910.[48] To Judge Walter H. Sanborn, Van Devanter's colleague on the Eighth Circuit (and the possible author of the offending memorandum), Taft wrote, "I took Van Devanter only after a long investigation in which I found that he had been sick and his wife had been ill and after a full letter of explanation from him. I think perhaps the dilatory habit in respect to turning out opinions could be corrected by close association with a court that sits all the time in the same city, and where the comparison between him and the other judges will be constant and when he knows why it is that I seriously hesitated before taking him."[49]

Unfortunately for Taft, Van Devanter never did learn to correct his "dilatory habit in respect to turning out opinions." Table P-1 illustrates how few opinions Van Devanter wrote during the Taft Court period;[a] in any given configuration of the Court he was invariably its least productive member. Not only did Van Devanter write few opinions, but he also took by far the longest time of any justice to produce

---

[a] Figure II-5 graphically illustrates Van Devanter's underperformance.

Willis Van Devanter

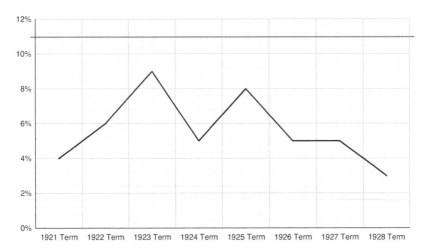

Figure II-5 Percentage of Court's opinions authored by Van Devanter, by term.
An even distribution of cases would assign 1/9, or 11%, to each justice.

those opinions that he did write. Figure I-22 illustrates that the average time from argument to announcement of a unanimous Van Devanter opinion was a whopping 143 days. If one sets aside Pitney's spotty performance during the 1921 term when he was ill,[50] the next most delinquent member of the Taft Court was Sanford, who took only 92.5 days. The average time between argument and announcement of a unanimous opinion during the Taft Court era was 55 days.

Van Devanter was also the most prolix member of the Taft Court. As illustrated by Figure II-2, his opinions were the longest of any justice. His opinions did, however, possess the merit of singular clarity. As John W. Davis observed in his commemorative tribute, pointedly contrasting Van Devanter to Holmes, Van Devanter's "written style ... was Doric rather than Corinthian in its architecture. There was no striving for adornment, no search for novel words, no effort to coin epigrams. At the moment, I do not recall a single sentence of his that might be called epigrammatic. Instead ... he aimed to be a Judge and not a litterateur, and endeavored always to make his meaning so plain that a wayfaring man could not mistake it. And this I take to be the quintessence of merit in a judicial utterance."[51]

Van Devanter's difficulty drafting opinions was a source of pain and concern to Taft. Van Devanter "is very slow in writing his cases," Taft complained to his son. "He is opinion-shy, and he is never content to let an opinion go until he has polished it and worked on it until it is a gem."[52] "It means fine opinions, but very few of them."[53] Given his urgent need to keep the Court current with its docket, Taft occasionally felt impelled "to take most of his cases away from [Van Devanter] and distribute them among the other Justices."[54] At the end of his very first term as chief justice, Taft was forced to reassign three cases from Van Devanter to Holmes.[55]

229

Van Devanter's productivity dropped precipitously during the 1926 term, as can be seen in Figure II-5. At that time Taft was again forced to "redistribute" some of Van Devanter's cases, even though Van Devanter "is very sensitive cross and unreasonable. He does not write and yet he hates to have any comment made or action taken in respect to the matter. I turned over two of his cases to Brandeis but B. thought Van would cherish resentment against him. So I had to take Van's cases myself and turn over some of mine to Br. I told Br. that the experiences of a Ch. Justice were like those of an impresario with his company of artists."[56]

The failure to author opinions is likely why a 1972 study listed Van Devanter as among the eight "failures" in the history of the Court.[57] Yet almost all members of the Court who worked with Van Devanter testified to his powerful and disciplined legal acumen, which commanded "their respect and attention."[58] Charles Evans Hughes praised Van Devanter's "careful and elaborate statements in conference" as "of the greatest value. If these statements had been taken down stenographically they would have served with but little editing as excellent opinions."[59]

Acknowledging "the vigor, sanity, and precision" of Van Devanter's mind, Chief Justice Stone commented that justices of the Court "know well that the public evidences of his judicial activities conceal rather more than they reveal what was his greatest service to the Court and to the public." "At the conference table," Stone said, Van Devanter "was a tower of strength. When his turn came to represent his views of the case in hand, no point was overlooked, no promising possibility left unexplored. His statements were characteristically lucid and complete, the manifest expression of a judgment exercised with unswerving independence. Often his expositions would have served worthily, both in point of form and substance, as the Court's opinion in the case."[60] Van Devanter, observed Brandeis, "both in purpose & abilities can't be compared. He is too much superior to – P[ierce] B[utler]."[61] Van Devanter, Brandeis noted, "can act quickly if there is no decision to write."[62]

For these reasons, Taft came rapidly to view Van Devanter as "the mainstay of the Court,"[63] "the most indispensable man we have in the Court."[64] Successfully urging Yale University to bestow an honorary degree on Van Devanter,[65] Taft wrote Yale President James R. Angell:

> Even members of the Bar who follow the Court's decisions are often not advised of the very great function that one Judge may play in guiding the decisions of the Court, by reason of his experience, his judicial statesmanship, his sense of proportion and his intimate familiarity with the precedents established by the Court of which he is a member, and to which the Court ought to make itself conform as near as may be. The value of a Judge in Conference, especially in such a Court as ours, never becomes known except to the members of the Court. Now I don't hesitate to say that Mr. Justice Van Devanter is far and away the most valuable man in our Court in all these qualities.... Van Devanter exercises more influence ... than any other member of the Court, just because the members of the Court know his qualities.[66]

Whatever Taft might publicly say about Holmes, his private view was that Van Devanter "is, take him all in all, the strongest Judge in this country."[67]

Willis Van Devanter

Taft's view was in part influenced by Van Devanter's intuitive ability to make himself indispensable to those he wished to serve. His long apprenticeship with Warren was the perfect preparation. As early as fall 1922, Brandeis could observe to Frankfurter that "Van D. runs Court now.... He is like a Jesuit general; he is always helpful to everybody, always ready for the C.J. He knows a [great] deal of federal practice & federal specialties, particularly land laws, and then he is 'in' with all the Republican politicians."[68] A year later Brandeis commented that "Van D. was influential with White, as he is with Taft – a very useful man. *Ein treuer Diener seines Herrn.* He would make an ideal Cardinal. He has a mind that can adjust itself to two such different temperaments as Taft and White."[69] Van Devanter "keeps close track of the Chief & of some others – Mc. (who has to be tactfully treated), Sanford, Sutherland. Intimidates some, influence that [comes] from experience."[70]

It seems clear that Van Devanter enjoyed good if not excellent relationships with almost all members of the Court. He was Clarke's closest companion on the bench.[71] He was like a "brother" to Butler.[72] To Sutherland he was "the 'salt of the earth' and no one could be a pleasanter companion."[73] He had, as Stone observed, "a large capacity for friendship.... His relations with his colleagues were marked by his uniform courtesy and helpfulness and by their mutual regard."[74] Taft was correct to conclude that Van Devanter exercised great influence on the Court's deliberations.[75] Figure I-10 shows that Van Devanter was the most likely of all Taft Court justices to persuade others to alter their conference votes to join his opinions. Sutherland once wrote Taft that "if Van Devanter writes the opinion I shall unhesitatingly agree to it. If written by anybody else, I will agree to what you and he accept."[76] Dean Acheson, Brandeis's law clerk during the 1919 and 1920 terms, recalled that:

> Justice Van Devanter was, I think, the most beloved Member of the Court among his colleagues. He was gentle and wise and kind and thoughtful. His colleagues regarded him, so far as Justice Brandeis and Justice Holmes who talked with me were concerned, with the greatest respect in conference. He was the one who made wise and helpful observations. He was the one who in the returns which came from the circulation of draft opinions, made the suggestions or corrections which both Judge Holmes and Judge Brandeis always accepted.[77]

Extant case files contain ample evidence of the great influence exerted by Van Devanter on the work of Brandeis,[78] Butler,[79] Holmes,[80] Stone,[81] McKenna,[82] McReynolds,[83] and Sanford,[84] which at times even extended to the precirculation of draft opinions specifically to Van Devanter for his comments and suggestions. Illustrative is *Taubel-Scott-Kitzmiller Co. v. Fox*,[85] a case raising complicated questions of bankruptcy court jurisdiction, in which Brandeis sent his draft opinion first to Van Devanter because you "have thought so much on kindred questions that I am venturing to ask you to let me have your suggestions before the enclosed opinion goes into general circulation."[86]

It was with Taft, however, that Van Devanter developed an especially close relationship.[87] Taft regarded Van Devanter as "really the closest friend I have on the Court."[88] Taft considered Van Devanter (in contrast to Holmes) "really a fine constitutional lawyer, and he writes most admirable opinions."[89] What Van

Devanter lacked was "what some of our Judges have by reason of their relations to Law Schools – a claque who are continually sounding their praises."[90] Almost as soon as Taft took office, Van Devanter began to insinuate himself into the administration of Court business,[91] and Taft quickly came to trust and rely on Van Devanter's discretion and judgment.[92] He worked closely with Van Devanter in pushing Harding to nominate Pierce Butler to the Supreme Court.[93] When handling the delicate business of McKenna's retirement, Taft turned to Van Devanter to consult with McKenna's doctor and family.[94] He conferred with Van Devanter about the use of Court funds[95] and the administration of Court personnel,[96] as well as about the assignment[97] and composition[98] of opinions. Van Devanter was Taft's proxy in the never-ending process of vetting potential nominees to the lower federal courts.[99] Taft turned to Van Devanter to design and draft the Judiciary Act of 1925[100] as well as the Supreme Court rules necessary to implement the Act.[101] Van Devanter was Taft's loyal assistant during the creation of the new Supreme Court building.[102] When Taft was confined to hospital during his last illness, the doctors barred all visitors except Taft's wife, his longtime secretary Wendell Mischler, and Van Devanter.[103]

Van Devanter was, in short, Taft's intimate confidante in virtually all matters. As Van Devanter wrote a Kentucky lawyer, "the Chief Justice ... and I are not prone to differ."[104] Frankfurter would later capture the essence of their relationship: "Taft ... himself said, and he was very happy to say, with that generosity of his which politicians would do well to, but do not often, imitate, that whatever he did as Chief Justice was made possible by his great reliance on him whom he called his 'lord chancellor,' Mr. Justice Van Devanter."[105]

Taft's reliance on Van Devanter became ever stronger as Taft experienced his own mental acuity diminish over the decade. Once, after Van Devanter returned from a vacation, Taft confided in him that "It is a real comfort to have you back. I am always afraid we may go wrong without you."[106] In 1927, Taft acknowledged to his son:

> I sometimes feel that I do not have time enough in making ready for Conferences to examine with the closeness they deserve the argued and submitted cases, but they are examined by the Court with care. They have more time than I have and sometimes they humiliate me with their pointing out matters that I haven't given time enough to the cases to discover. The familiarity with the practice and the thoroughness of examination in certain cases that Van Devanter is able to give makes him a most valuable member of the Court, and makes me feel quite small, and as if it would be better to have the matter run by him alone, for he is wonderfully familiar with our practice and our authorities. Still I must worry along until I get to the end of my ten years, content to aid in the deliberations when there is a difference of opinion.[107]

Van Devanter and Taft each stood at the dead center of the Taft Court, as Figure P-1 illustrates. In fact, it may perhaps be most accurate to conceive the Taft Court as oriented along an axis that consisted of Taft, Van Devanter, and Butler.[108] Taft regarded Butler as "one of my dearest friends."[109] Although the sparseness of the historical record makes it difficult to reconstruct the exact relationship between Van Devanter and Butler, it is obvious that the two were extremely close.[110] Figure

Willis Van Devanter

II-6, which analyzes the pattern of conference voting, shows that there was a close and distinctive alliance among Taft, Van Devanter, and Butler. Butler voted with Van Devanter more than with any other justice, in 89% of conference cases; his secondary allegiance was with Taft, with whom he voted in 86.8% of conference cases.[111] Van Devanter, in turn, joined with Butler more than with any other justice, in 89% of conference cases, and he aligned himself second-most with Taft, in 88% of conference cases.[112] For his part, Taft voted more with Van Devanter than with any other justice, in 88% of the conference cases, and secondarily with Butler, in 86.8% of conference cases.[113]

Figure II-6 graphically demonstrates the degree of interdependence among Taft, Van Devanter, and Butler.[b] From the time that Butler came on the Court in the 1922 term through the end of the 1928 term, neither Taft nor Butler ever dissented from an opinion by Van Devanter. Van Devanter dissented only once from an opinion by Taft[114] (whereas Butler dissented four times).[115] Van Devanter never dissented from any opinion by Butler, and Taft dissented only once.[116] Throughout the course of the decade, it is fair to say that together Van Devanter and Butler pushed Taft further and further to the right.[117] When Taft was incapacitated in

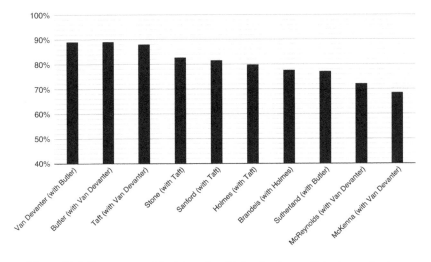

Figure II-6 Percentage of decisions in which a justice participates and votes in conference with the justice with whom he is most likely to vote

---

[b] Figure II-6 also illustrates the influence of Van Devanter, Taft, and Butler on the Court. Of the ten justices with whom Van Devanter served during the period of the conference cases, four voted more with him in conference than with any other justice (Butler, Taft, McKenna, and McReynolds). Three voted most with Taft (Stone, Sanford, and Holmes). Two voted more with Butler than with any other justice (Van Devanter and Sutherland). One Justice (Brandeis) voted most with Holmes.

THE TAFT COURT

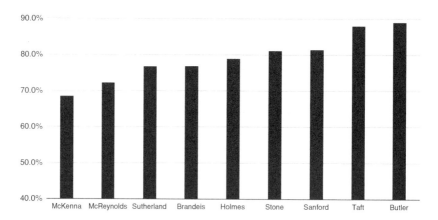

Figure II-7 Percentage of decisions in which Van Devanter participated and voted with another justice in conference

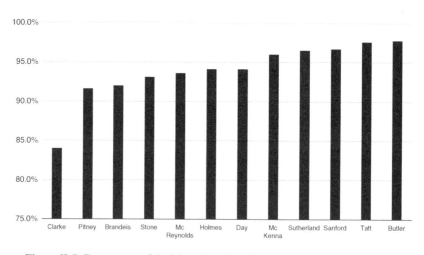

Figure II-8 Percentage of decisions in which Van Devanter participated and joined the same opinion as another justice, 1921–1928 terms

January 1930, it was to Van Devanter and Butler that the Taft family turned to facilitate Taft's resignation and his wishes about who should succeed him.[118]

At the time Taft appointed Van Devanter to the Supreme Court, Van Devanter's ideological commitments were difficult to discern.[119] True, Van Devanter had been berated by William Jennings Bryan for his "known bias toward" railroad interests,[120] but he had also been praised by Senator William Borah as someone who "regards the Constitution as made for man, and not man for the

234

Willis Van Devanter

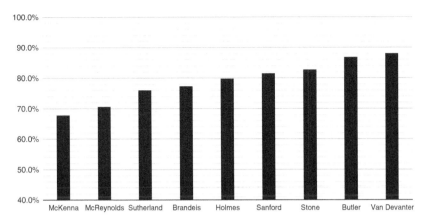

Figure II-9 Percentage of decisions in which Taft participated and voted with another justice in conference

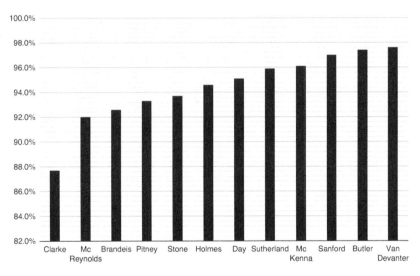

Figure II-10 Percentage of decisions in which Taft participated and joined the same opinion as another justice, 1921–1928 terms

Constitution; accepting neither the theory that the Constitution does not admit of growth or progress nor the more recent faith that it has been outgrown and has become antiquated and out of date, and more or less embarrassing to the fuller realization of the ideals of our civilization."[121] Van Devanter was regarded as "a 'Roosevelt judge,'" and it was "presumed" that his appointment would "be acceptable to the Progressives generally."[122]

In his first years as a justice, Van Devanter authored a masterful and progressive opinion in the Second Employers' Liability Cases,[123] and he articulated a classic formulation of rational basis review under the Equal Protection Clause in *Lindsley v. Natural Carbonic Gas Co.*,[124] affirming that "when the classification" of a statute "is called in question, if any state of facts reasonably can be conceived that would sustain it, the existence of that state of facts at the time the law was enacted must be assumed." "One who assails the classification in such a law must carry the burden of showing that it does not rest upon any reasonable basis, but is essentially arbitrary."[125]

For reasons as yet unexplored, Van Devanter had by the time of the Taft Court become what Holmes could accurately call "in spots ... a very stout conservative."[126] Because Van Devanter neither wrote articles expatiating on his perspective, nor was he given to theoretical explanations in his opinions or his correspondence, it is difficult to attribute a specific jurisprudential perspective to Van Devanter. But we do know from his actions that Van Devanter was highly determined to protect the prerogatives of property. So, for example, Van Devanter (together with Butler and McReynolds) would dissent from Sutherland's seminal opinion in *Village of Euclid v. Ambler Realty Co.*,[127] which authorized local zoning ordinances. Van Devanter was also highly sensitive to discrimination against business corporations. He would, for example, join Sutherland's opinion for the Court striking down under the Equal Protection Clause an Oklahoma statute requiring that permits be awarded to cooperatively owned cotton gins,[128] despite the fact that, as Brandeis made inescapably plain in a crushing dissent, the statute indisputably passed the very *Natural Carbonic Gas* test that Van Devanter had himself authored earlier in his career.[129] Van Devanter would go even further than Sutherland and vote in dissent to strike down the classification at issue in *White River Lumber Co. v. Arkansas*, which involved a statute authorizing the collection of back taxes from corporations but not from natural persons.[130]

In the following decade, Van Devanter would become, in Stone's phrase, "the commander-in-chief of judicial reaction."[131] Stone observed to his children that "I have always felt [that Van Devanter] conceived it his duty to declare unconstitutional any law which he particularly disliked."[132] By the time of his death, Van Devanter would be pilloried in the popular press as "the court's most ardent defender of property rights and ... its most consistently conservative member."[133] As early as 1931, he would be branded by the *New Republic* "as reactionary a judge as ever sat on the Supreme Court," which could be inferred "from his inevitable vote in favor of annulling state welfare acts, against labor unions and against the regulatory findings of state and federal utility commissions."[134]

These characterizations do not capture the subtlety and professional craft of Van Devanter's work during the Taft Court years. It is true that he was squarely at the center of the Taft Court's sharp turn to the right. It is also true that he had strong views about protecting property from government regulations and about the importance of protecting the national marketplace from state regulations.[135] But he often displayed the same kind of institutional pragmatism that characterized Taft himself.[136] His procedural decisions are illustrative,[137] as are his decisions

Willis Van Devanter

concerning inherent institutional authority.[138] In the great case of *McGrain v. Daugherty*,[139] which reversed a lower court decision denying the right of Congress to issue subpoenas for witnesses and documents, the vote of the Court had originally been to affirm, with only Holmes and Brandeis dissenting.[140] Taft assigned the opinion to Van Devanter,[141] who changed his mind and brought the entire Court along with him, thus laying the groundwork for the possibility of independent congressional investigations.

Brandeis himself never lost sight of the formidable, elegant, pragmatic, and far-sighted legal technician that Van Devanter had always been.[142] Brandeis discerned in Van Devanter the "conflict of two deep impulses. Appetite for power & ambition that Court be right. If first is satisfied and not involved, second is strong. ... That's [the] great thing about V. Once having established power he will try to confine his own errors."[143]

Notes

1. Taft appointed Charles Evans Hughes, Joseph Rucker Lamar, Horace H. Lurton, Mahlon Pitney, and Willis Van Devanter. Taft appointed six justices if we count his promotion of Edward Douglass White to chief justice.
2. ALEXANDER M. BICKEL & BENNO C. SCHMIDT, JR., THE JUDICIARY AND RESPONSIBLE GOVERNMENT 1910–1921, at 44 (New York: MacMillan Publishing Co. 1984).
3. WVD to Chauncey R. Hammond (June 21, 1930) (Van Devanter papers); Willis Van Devanter: Associate Justice of the Supreme Court of the United States, in WVD to W.E. Chaplin (April 15, 1929) (Van Devanter papers).
4. James Joseph McArdle, The Political Philosophy of Willis Van Devanter 9 (M.A. Thesis, University of Wyoming 1955).
5. Maurice Paul Holsinger, Willis Van Devanter, The Early Years: 1859–1911, at 67 (Ph.D. Dissertation, University of Denver 1964).
6. M. Paul Holsinger, *Willis Van Devanter: Wyoming Leader, 1884–1897*, 36 ANNALS OF WYOMING 171, 177 (October 1964). Van Devanter resigned the position in 1888. *Id.* at 178.
7. *Id.* at 177, 182–83, 186–88. Advising a friend to try his luck in the Western territories, Van Devanter wrote, "A man grows fourfold more than he would under other conditions." WVD to Melville W. Miller (November 8, 1902) (Van Devanter papers).
8. Holsinger, *supra* note 6, at 188.
9. Holsinger, *supra* note 5, at 109.
10. Lewis L. Gould, *Willis Van Devanter and the Johnson County War*, 17 MONTANA: THE MAGAZINE OF WESTERN HISTORY 18 (Autumn 1967).
11. The best account is in Lewis L. Gould, Willis Van Devanter in Wyoming Politics 103–30 (Ph.D. Dissertation, Yale University 1966). *See also* Holsinger, *supra* note 6, at 190–92.
12. McArdle, *supra* note 4, at 10–11.
13. Warren, the father-in-law of John J. Pershing, served in the Senate from 1890 to 1893, and from 1895 until his death in 1929.
14. BICKEL & SCHMIDT, *supra* note 2, at 46.
15. Daniel A. Nelson, *The Supreme Court Appointment of Willis Van Devanter*, 53 ANNALS OF WYOMING 2, 8 (Fall 1981); Gould, *supra* note 11, at 28–29, 131–221. "A good listener, organizer, and financial manager, Van Devanter could purchase railroad fares, bands, newspapers, and election officials with aplomb and tact, leaving few traces except Republican success in his wake." Gould, *supra* note 11, at 175.
16. "Van Devanter suppressed any budding ideological convictions, and became a political craftsman whose success depended not upon his ability to make decisions, but on his willingness to carry out the decisions of others. Paradoxically, this intellectual repression provided the key to his advancement. Warren admitted Van Devanter to his confidence in the certain knowledge that Van Devanter would never prove a threat to Warren's power." Gould, *supra* note 11, at 28–29.
17. *Id.* at 29. Wallace H. Johnson, *Willis Van Devanter – A Re-examination*, 1 WYOMING LAW REVIEW 403, 409 (2001) ("To Senator Warren's credit, he seemed to really care what happened to Willis Van Devanter. As much as anything, Willis Van Devanter's history is the story of Governor, and then Senator, Warren's loyalty and the good fortune that befell Willis Van Devanter by aligning with Warren when he moved to

Willis Van Devanter

Wyoming."). When Warren, after being defeated in his bid to become a United States senator in 1892, began to mull about not running for reelection, Van Devanter immediately urged him to reconsider. "Personally I want you re-elected to the Senate, and in this I am prompted by a desire to assist the State, to assist the party, to assist you and to assist myself." WVD to Francis E. Warren (April 9, 1892) (Van Devanter papers).

18. Almost immediately upon arriving in Washington in 1891, Warren began to lobby to advance Van Devanter. Asking Van Devanter if he would like a judicial appointment, Van Devanter replied, "Would like position beyond measure." WVD to Francis E. Warren (February 25, 1891) (Van Devanter papers).
19. Francis E. Warren to WVD (February 3, 1897) (Warren papers at the University of Wyoming) ("About the Supreme Bench ... I only mentioned it in passing because I took it for granted every lawyer would like to reach that goal, though knowing full well that but few of the many can reach it. There is no reason why you should not aim as high as that with the many years you still expect to live and thrive.").
20. Describing his interview with McKenna, Warren wrote Van Devanter: "I then told him and I will admit my voice was tremulous and emotional in the conversation at this juncture, that if the President turned us down in this I felt I had no further interest in the patronage of my State, for the gap would be too wide to fill; that we all were intent upon it, and that personally it was the one thing I felt I must have for I should feel disappointed and humiliated beyond measure if it was not granted." Francis E. Warren to WVD (March 10, 1897) (Van Devanter papers).
21. Paul Holsinger, *The Appointment of Supreme Court Justice Van Devanter: A Study of Political Preferment*, 12 AMERICAN JOURNAL OF LEGAL HISTORY 324, 328 (1968).
22. Holsinger, *supra* note 5, at 180–215.
23. For an unflattering biography of Van Devanter that discusses in detail his influence on Western water law, see JAMES H. DAVENPORT, WESTERN WATER RIGHTS AND THE U.S. SUPREME COURT (Jefferson: McFarland & Co. 2020).
24. 187 U.S. 553 (1903).
25. Philip P. Frickey, *Doctrine, Context, Institutional Relationships, and Commentary: The Malaise of Federal Indian Law through the Lens of Lone Wolf*, 38 TULSA LAW REVIEW 5, 5 (2002). The day that *Lone Wolf* was announced "has been called 'one of the blackest days in the history of the American Indian.'" C. Blue Clark, *Lone Wolf v. Hitchcock: Implications for Federal Indian Law at the Start of the Twentieth Century*, 5 WESTERN LEGAL HISTORY 1, 1 (1992).
26. BLUE CLARK, LONE WOLF V. HITCHCOCK: TREATY RIGHTS AND INDIAN LAW AT THE END OF THE NINETEENTH CENTURY (Lincoln: University of Nebraska Press 1994).
27. United States v. Sandoval, 231 U.S. 28, 39, 41 (1913). *See* United States v. Candelaria, 271 U.S. 432 (1926).
28. United States v. Northern Securities Co., 120 F. 721 (8th Cir. 1903).
29. United States v. Standard Oil Co. of New Jersey, 173 F. 177 (8th Cir. 1909).
30. Brewster v. Lanyon Zinc Co., 140 F. 801 (8th Cir. 1905).
31. Oakes v. United States, 172 F. 305 (8th Cir. 1909).
32. Holsinger, *supra* note 21, at 329.
33. Francis E. Warren to WVD (March 12, 1906) (Warren papers at the University of Wyoming). Pushing for Roosevelt to appoint Van Devanter to the vacancy left open by Henry Billings Brown after Taft had refused the position, see Francis E. Warren

to WVD (March 12, 1906) (Warren papers at the University of Wyoming), Warren encouraged Van Devanter: "Things seem to be working rather favorably toward the general end we are seeking. Of course it may be necessary to have lots of time, lots of patience and some close figuring, but we might as well fix our aim directly on the spot we desire to hit, and then bend our energies diplomatically and continuously in that direction." Francis E. Warren to WVD (March 21, 1906) (Warren papers at the University of Wyoming).

34. "I could not, even if I should write countless pages, overstate his character, ability, and desirability from all points, as to age, temperament, resourcefulness, environment, breadth of view and knowledge, etc. I believe that you know Judge Van Devanter quite well. I shall desire at a later date to discuss the matter with you more fully." Francis E. Warren to WHT (March 19, 1909) (Warren papers at the University of Wyoming).
35. Chief Justice Fuller died on July 4, 1910.
36. Justice Moody retired because of illness on November 20, 1910. Crippled by rheumatism, Moody had been ill for a long time and his retirement had been anticipated for many months.
37. *See* BICKEL & SCHMIDT, *supra* note 2, at 44–64; Daniel S. McHargue, *President Taft's Appointments to the Supreme Court*, 12 JOURNAL OF POLITICS 478 (1950); Holsinger, *supra* note 21; Nelson, *supra* note 15.
38. *See* BICKEL & SCHMIDT, *supra* note 2, at 53–57.
39. Alexander Van Orsdel to Francis E. Warren (August 1, 1910), quoted in Nelson, *supra* note 15, at 8.
40. WVD to Charles Nagel (April 19, 1910) (National Archives, DOJ File # 348 ("Willis Van Devanter")).
41. Holsinger, *supra* note 21, at 333.
42. Van Devanter said:

> It is true that I am now behind in Circuit Court of Appeals work but not to extent apparently represented. While this is to be regretted it does not arise from indolence or timidity in reaching conclusions, or hesitancy in giving effect to them. I may have given too much attention to closely contested and important cases, especially where there have been differences of opinion, and may have been too tenacious of my own views, but I have felt justified in my course because it almost always has resulted in unanimity and has tended to produce harmonious rules of decision. I have done much important work in Circuit Courts which, if added to my appellate work, makes my total easily up to average of my associates. I emphatically protest against impressions which seem to have been created, but make no complaint of President's attitude for it is obviously reasonable. I cannot prepare and submit showing in my own behalf now without assuming attitude which would be distasteful to me. For this reason I prefer that further consideration of my name be omitted. Then at some later time when there are no appointments at stake I shall hope the President will permit me personally to make full statement of my work to him and yourself. I will owe this to both because of his consideration of my name and because of your interest in presenting it.

WVD to Francis E. Warren (December 4, 1910) (Van Devanter papers).
43. WVD to Francis E. Warren (December 5, 1910) (Van Devanter papers).
44. Francis E. Warren to WVD (December 7, 1910) (Van Devanter papers).
45. Warren informed Taft of the letter and told him, "Mr. President, I ought not to withhold anything from you, and if you will consider, in reading it, that it was absolutely a confidential, quickly-written, friendly letter such as husband and wife

or brothers might write to each other, I will bring it over and let you see it." Francis E. Warren to WVD (December 9, 1910) (Warren papers at the University of Wyoming). Enticed by the bait, Taft then "said he was very anxious to see [the letter] and would treat it as I desired him to." *Id.*

46. Francis E. Warren to WVD (December 9, 1910) (Warren papers at the University of Wyoming).
47. *Id.* Warren also noted to Van Devanter that Taft had been worried that Senator Knute Nelson of Minnesota, "the high man on the Judiciary," might be "bucking." "Nelson said to-day," Taft commented, that "'I have no candidate, myself, but ask you not to appoint any railroad attorney like Van Devanter and others.'" *Id.*
48. 44 CONG. REC. 335 (December 15, 1910). In one contemporary account, "There certainly can be no doubt that destiny was working overtime when she landed the young Van Devanter at Cheyenne," for his career "proves to all ambitious young men that there are but two things to do if they have the stuff in them. The first is to hook up with destiny; and the second is to let destiny land you in a state where live two men who are going to be tremendous powers in the United States Senate. Simple, is it not?" *Who's Who and Why: The Darling of Destiny*, 183 SATURDAY EVENING POST 25 (March 8, 1911). When "this article was brought to Van Devanter's attention ... he did not like it. He thought it 'not in keeping with the dignity and surroundings of the office which I now hold.'" BICKEL & SCHMIDT, *supra* note 2, at 63 (quoting WVD to W.A. Richards (June 2, 1911) (Van Devanter papers)).
49. WHT to Walter H. Sanborn (December 15, 1910) (Taft papers).
50. *See supra* Chapter 3, at note 1.
51. *Proceedings in Memory of Mr. Justice Van Devanter*, 316 U.S. xxv–xxvi (1942). *See id.* at xx (remarks of William D. Mitchell) ("His style is simple and clear. He was not a phrasemaker and he did not import into his vocabulary words having no settled meaning in the law. His opinions are wholly free from such affectations. No one can fail to understand his reasoning and his conclusions; and, above all, his opinions not only dispose of the cases under consideration, but furnish to the profession a guide and a chart for the future."). Brandeis privately commented to Frankfurter that "Taft wants Ct to guide Bar – indicate direction; doesn't sufficiently work over materials. Van D. does." *Brandeis-Frankfurter Conversations*, at 307 (July 1, 1922).
52. WHT to Robert A. Taft (May 3, 1925) (Taft papers). Chief Justice Hughes agreed. Van Devanter "was slow in getting out his opinions, having what one of his most intimate friends in the Court [Justice Sutherland] described as 'pen paralysis.' This difficulty increased with the years." CHARLES EVANS HUGHES, THE AUTOBIOGRAPHICAL NOTES OF CHARLES EVANS HUGHES 171 (David J. Danelski & Joseph S. Tulchin, eds., Cambridge: Harvard University Press 1973). Describing to Taft Van Devanter's rural summer home in Canada, Sutherland gently mocked Van Devanter's obsessive perfectionism, which no doubt contributed to Van Devanter's writer's block: "Van Devanter is the prince of hearts and best of companions. I have grown to be fonder of him than ever, if that were possible. ... Van Devanter has an excellent garden and keeps a cow, chickens and ducks. He looks after them all conscientiously, and every teat yields milk and every hen lays eggs with logical exactness and strict conformity to the settled precedents and rules of procedures." GS to WHT (July 3, 1925) (Taft papers). *See* WVD to WHT (July 1, 1925) (Taft papers). It is not surprising that Van Devanter's

surviving letters contain intricate remedies for constipation. *See* WVD to William Meyers (October 13, 1924) (Van Devanter papers). It is difficult to imagine that this repressed individual – "as conservative as a Dutch canal, and as calm," *The Judiciary: Supreme Convention*, 10 TIME 8 (October 10, 1927) – had begun life in "the turbulent days of the great Wyoming cattle ranges," *Justice Van Devanter*, NEW YORK TIMES (February 10, 1941), at 16, and that as a young man he had joined hunting parties with the legendary Buffalo Bill Cody. Holsinger, *supra* note 5, at 107 n.1. *See* Attorney General Francis Biddle, *Proceedings in Memory of Mr. Justice Van Devanter*, 316 U.S. at xxv–xxvi (1942). Even during the 1920s, Van Devanter would often go hunting and present his colleagues with a brace or two of ducks. He also enjoyed a good round of golf. On Van Devanter's personal life, see Mark Tushnet, *Willis Van Devanter: The Person*, 45 JOURNAL OF SUPREME COURT HISTORY 308 (2020).

53 WHT to Robert A. Taft (January 16, 1927) (Taft papers). In fall 1927, Van Devanter's wife Dollie suddenly suffered a debilitating stroke. WVD to JHC (December 15, 1927) (Van Devanter papers). "The illness of Van Devanter's wife has made him very slow in his opinions, slower than he ever was, and he was always slow." WHT to Robert A. Taft (March 4, 1928) (Taft papers). "We are not getting along as well in getting rid of opinions as I would like.... Judge Van Devanter is the worst offender in this regard. He is opinion-shy. He writes admirable opinions and he is the man whom we could least spare in the Court, and yet his list of opinions is very small." WHT to Robert A. Taft (March 10, 1929). Van Devanter tended to justify his writer's block by adverting to the special difficulty of the opinions that he had been assigned. *See, e.g.*, WVD to JHC (June 23, 1927) (Van Devanter papers) ("I have not been able to do much of anything in the way of writing opinions. It so happens that those assigned to me call for particular care and do not admit of hasty or rapid disposal."); WVD to JHC (December 15, 1927) (Van Devanter papers) ("Mrs. Van Devanter's illness has disturbed me greatly and has filled me with constant anxiety.... Notwithstanding this, I have kept up my share of the routine work of the Court and have attended to some special matters, the nature of which you will rather readily understand. But I have not been able to do much of anything in the way of writing opinions. It so happens that those assigned to me call for particular care and do not admit of hasty or rapid disposal."). Clarke abetted Van Devanter in these excuses. *See* JHC to WVD (December 12, 1927) (Van Devanter papers) ("I have noted that you are not writing as much as usual & fear that you are not well. And yet it may be that, as heretofore, you have been loaded up with a volume of work which no one else seemed equal to and are buried in it. You have been the 'burden bearer' of the Court ever since I have known you – and it's not fair."). It is not obvious to a contemporary observer, however, that Van Devanter's opinions were especially difficult. A good example is Bunch v. Cole, 253 U.S. 250 (1923), a relatively simple case involving federal preemption of Indian land ownership that nevertheless took Van Devanter some eight months to write. When Taft was occasionally forced to reassign cases away from Van Devanter, the justices to whom Van Devanter's cases were given did not seem to experience any particular difficulty writing them up in a timely fashion. *See, e.g., infra* note 55.

54. WHT to Robert A. Taft (January 23, 1927) (Taft papers). *See* WHT to HFS (January 26, 1927) (Taft papers); WHT to GS (January 27, 1927) (Taft papers); WHT to PB (January 28, 1927) (Taft papers); WHT to Mrs. Frederick J. Manning

Willis Van Devanter

(April 10, 1927) (Taft papers); WVD to OWH (February 13, 1925) (Holmes papers); WHT to Helen Herron Taft (April 28, 1924) (Taft papers):

> I am just through Conference and have assigned the cases. Poor Van Devanter works so slowly with his opinions that he has thirteen cases assigned to him. I didn't give him any to-day. Holmes is so quick that I gave him two.... What disturbs me is the necessity for helping Van Devanter. I am going to talk with Holmes and with Sutherland about it, and then with Van Devanter, to see if we can not relieve him. He has had one case that was assigned to him that has taken a great deal of time. That was the controversy between Texas and Oklahoma over their boundary and a lot of oil which we found to belong to the United States, and out of which our Receiver, Fred Delano, has taken several millions dollars worth of oil. Van Devanter has done very well and it has taken him a good deal of time. Apparently he writes opinions slowly and is not under great pressure to get them disposed of.

See WHT to Helen Herron Taft (May 25, 1924) (Taft papers) ("some are pretty far behind especially Van Devanter"); WHT to Robert A. Taft (April 7, 1929) (Taft papers).

55. WHT to OWH (May 16, 1922) (Holmes papers) ("I am very glad that you have relieved Van Devanter of [Santa Fe Pac. R. Co. v. Payne, 259 U.S. 197 (1922), and Grogan v. Hiram Walker & Sons, 259 U.S. 80 (1922)], and I hope you will be able to get out [Pine Hill Coal Co. v. United States, 259 U.S. 191 (1922)]. It is good of you to take them."). Holmes had in fact already polished off *Grogan* by May 15, and he would announce the other two cases on May 29. On April 12, Van Devanter had written a friend that "The term has been an exceedingly arduous one." WVD to A.C. Campbell (April 12, 1922) (Van Devanter papers).

56. WHT to Helen Herron Taft (May 3, 1927) (Taft papers). *See* Barry Cushman, *Inside the Taft Court: Lessons from the Docket Books*, 2015 SUPREME COURT REVIEW 345, 397–400; Cases Assigned to Justice Van Devanter (Memorandum, February 1927) (Taft papers). Brandeis wrote Taft saying that he was "sorry that it seemed necessary for me to add to your managerial troubles." LDB to WHT (May 3, 1927) (Taft papers). *See* WHT to LDB (May 3, 1927) (Taft papers); WHT to OWH (May 3, 1927) (Taft papers); WHT to HFS (May 3, 1927) (Taft papers) ("I don't think it is necessary for you to speak to [Van Devanter] about it. He is very sensitive on all matters of this kind."); WHT to OWH (May 3, 1927) (Taft papers) ("Brother Brandeis whom I called on to help out with two other of Van Devanter's cases objected because he thought Van rather resisted any one else taking one assigned to him. So he suggested that I transfer to him some of my own cases and take Van's myself. He thinks Van will be less disturbed if the matter is wholly settled between him and me. I am going to do this for B. and perhaps I would better do it for you.... I greatly appreciate your willingness to help out. The brethren are feeling jaded. They grow a little sensitive and the life of a C.J. is not all roses."); WHT to WVD (May 3, 1927) (Taft papers) ("You have too many cases for this recess and [can] not be expected to clean up.... I really assigned you too many."); WVD to WHT (May 4, 1927) (Taft papers) ("I must assent to the change in assignment proposed in your very considerate note of yesterday. It gives me no little pain and embarrassment to have to say this, but I recognize the full propriety of what you propose. The cases must be disposed of."); WHT to Charles P. Taft 2nd (June 5, 1927) (Taft papers).

57. Albert P. Blaustein & Roy M. Mersky, *Rating Supreme Court Justices*, 58 AMERICAN BAR ASSOCIATION JOURNAL 1183, 1186 (1972). Two other "failures" were also members of the Taft Court: James C. McReynolds and Pierce Butler. Twelve justices were rated "Great," of which three were members of the Taft Court: Holmes, Brandeis, and Stone. Fifteen justices were rated "Near Great," of which two were members of the Taft Court: Taft and Sutherland. On Van Devanter's notorious writer's block, see DREW PEARSON & ROBERT S. ALLEN, THE NINE OLD MEN 187 (Garden City: Doubleday 1937) ("Van Devanter's third claim to fame is the fact that during the six years since 1930 he has handed down only twenty-two opinions.").

58. PEARSON & ALLEN, *supra* note 57, at 188. Van Devanter "was not a judge of whom the public generally could gain any very sharply defined impression. He was quiet and unassuming and appeared seldom in public. He made very few speeches, even before gatherings of lawyers, and those were of the conversational and unpretentious sort. He left practically no writings except his opinions. But his comprehensive learning, his industry, his passion for thoroughness and exactness, and his power of clear analysis and forceful exposition marked him, among all those who really knew the work of the Court, as one of its most conspicuously valuable members." Charles Evans Hughes, Jr., *Proceedings in Memory of Mr. Justice Van Devanter*, 316 U.S. at x (1942). Upon Van Devanter's retirement, Brandeis remarked that "no one could fully appreciate his value who has not observed his work in conferences, particularly in the days of White and of Taft, and who has not watched his performance in Court." LDB to Felix Frankfurter (May 26, 1937), in BRANDEIS-FRANKFURTER CORRESPONDENCE, at 597.

59. HUGHES, *supra* note 52, at 171. *See Address of Justice Hughes at Law Institute*, NEW YORK TIMES (May 13, 1938), at 8 ("It was in ... conference that Justice Van Devanter's wide experience, his precise knowledge, his accurate memory and his capacity for clear elucidation of precedents and principle contributed in a remarkable degree to the disposition of the court's business. ... Few judges in our history have rivaled him in fitness by reason of learning, skill and temperament for the judicial office."). As Taft later wrote his son, Van Devanter's "weakness has been that he has been opinion-shy, and while in Conference he can deliver a conclusion that could be put by stenographic announcement right into an opinion. He never gets done looking over the various features that he would like to consider in an opinion, but he is very quick in the preparation of rules and in the organization and formulation of views of the Court into action." WHT to Robert A. Taft (March 17, 1929) (Taft papers).

60. *Proceedings in Memory of Mr. Justice Van Devanter*, 316 U.S. xl–xlii (1942).

61. *Brandeis-Frankfurter Conversations*, at 316 (July 1, 1923).

62. LDB to Felix Frankfurter (August 14, 1929), in BRANDEIS-FRANKFURTER CORRESPONDENCE, at 380. In 1934, Van Devanter wrote his brother-in-law:

> It may be of a little interest to you to know that after the term closed Justice Brandeis particularly asked an opportunity to have a talk with me. In the course of the talk he said that he wished specially to urge that I should not think of retiring; that he did not wish to see any changes in the Court just now, and quite apart from that he wished me to continue on the Court; that the Court specially needed me; that no one could take my place in conference; and that he thought it would be a great misfortune for the Court if I should leave. I thanked him for what he said

Willis Van Devanter

and indicated that I was not prepared to say what I would do. He then renewed his request in even stronger terms and I pleasantly ended the talk. I told Sutherland, and only Sutherland, about it. He said that he believed that Brandeis was sincere in what he said about me and that Brandeis really had more confidence in me than in any other member of the Court. Sutherland then added: "Brandeis probably never talks to you about matters where he knows you and he differ in opinion, but in other matters of general law he usually wishes to know what you think before he comes to a conclusion, and he usually accepts what you say on such questions." It is possible that Justice Brandeis is losing faith in the present administration and its policies. There have been some indications of this, but I have supposed that they would not be carried very far.

WVD to John L. Lacey (June 23, 1934) (Van Devanter papers). William O. Douglas recalls that Van Devanter's "highest credentials were, as Brandeis said, that he was an honest, able, forthright and dependable man who always kept his word. At the end of an argument he could summarize it, state the pros and cons and what the Court should decide. If his words had been recorded, they would have made a perfect opinion. ... We were at opposite poles on many phases of constitutional law, but what drew me to him was our shared love of the outdoors. Van Devanter had been a hunter, fisherman and camper in his early years in Wyoming and I spent many hours listening to his tales. I found him a genuine human being." WILLIAM O. DOUGLAS, THE AUTOBIOGRAPHY OF WILLIAM O. DOUGLAS: THE COURT YEARS 1937–1975, at 11 (New York: Random House 1980).

63. WHT to Mrs. Frederick J. Manning (June 11, 1923) (Taft papers). *See* WHT to Mrs. Frederick J. Manning (January 23, 1927) (Taft papers). Van Devanter "is the mainstay of the Court and if he wrote no opinions at all, we could hardly get along without him." WHT to Robert A. Taft (January 16, 1927) (Taft papers).

64 WHT to Charles P. Taft 2nd (January 23, 1927) (Taft papers). In a remarkably frank letter, Taft wrote his brother Horace that the "trouble" with Van Devanter "is that he insists on writing opinions which involve too great individual investigation and he is not content therefore to get through an opinion within a reasonable time, so that now he has carried opinions for one or two years and he is way behind and this has become a nerve straining situation. ... Van Devanter is our strongest man. He is of the utmost value in the Court, even if he writes no opinions. Indeed, it would be better if he did not write any opinions, because then the others could keep up with the work." WHT to Horace D. Taft (January 17, 1927) (Taft papers).

65. Taft believed that "Van Devanter is a modest man and needs somebody to play his trumpet, and I am delighted to fill that function." WHT to Robert A. Taft (January 16, 1927) (Taft papers). Van Devanter "is one of the most valuable members – the most valuable man we have in the Court, and we can not afford to lose him. I doning [sic] what I can to secure him an LL.D. at Yale, and I think I have got the thing fixed. I have the President's consent and Sam Fisher's, who is at the head of the Committee on Degrees of the Crporation [sic], and Dean Swan. I think these three men can control the Corporation. ... Van is so modest that his merits are not recognized, but I am determined that they shall be." WHT to Charles P. Taft 2nd (January 16, 1927) (Taft papers). Taft was apparently blind to Van Devanter's deep wells of vanity and ambition, as Van Devanter's secretive and abortive campaign to succeed Chief Justice White well illustrates. *See supra* Prologue, at note 44. Van

Devanter's letters at that time illustrate both his intense ambition, highly honed from his days with Warren, and yet his desire to *appear* discreet and modest to those around him. His clever telegram withdrawing his name from consideration as a candidate for the Supreme Court, *supra* note 42, illustrates how self-effacement was a potent weapon in Van Devanter's arsenal for self-advancement. DAVENPORT, *supra* note 23, at 221–27.

66. WHT to James R. Angell (December 2, 1926) (Taft papers). "Sutherland is an excellent man, a man of great experience and a man of force and strength of character," Taft added, "but as compared with Van Devanter, I am sure the friends of both would accord the precedence which the official rank in the Court gives to Van Devanter." To Yale professor William Lyon Phelps, Taft wrote that Van Devanter "is one of the ablest Judges in this country and one of the ablest Judges that we have ever had on the Court, but he is a very modest man and nobody knows the position he occupies on the Court but those who have to do with him in Conference. No one can appreciate his influence except through knowledge gained from the intimacy of the deliberations of the Court over opinions. . . . He is better versed than any member on the Bench in our decisions and keeps us straight. He does not write so many opinions, but they are all admirable when he writes them. I don't know how we could get along without him in Conference. I don't think the Bar realizes generally what a commanding figure he is on the Court. He never advertises and he never seeks publicity. . . . The truth is I think those who refer to the Court who are in the 'know' think when they refer to the Court that they are referring to Van Devanter." WHT to William Lyon Phelps (May 30, 1927) (Taft papers).

67. WHT to Samuel H. Fisher (December 25, 1926) (Taft papers).

68. *Brandeis-Frankfurter Conversations*, at 310 (November 30, 1922). Charles Evans Hughes noted that Van Devanter's "perspicacity and common sense made him a trusted adviser in all sorts of matters. Chief Justice White leaned heavily upon him and so did Chief Justice Taft, especially when the latter began to fail in health." HUGHES, *supra* note 52, at 171. John W. Davis commented in 1941 that "I have heard the statement from Chief Justice White, who leaned on him heavily, that in the conference he was the most helpful member of the Court. More than one of his judicial brethren have expressed the same opinion." *Proceedings in Memory of Mr. Justice Van Devanter*, 316 U.S. at xxvi (1942).

69. *Brandeis-Frankfurter Conversations*, at 322 (August 6, 1923). On Van Devanter's connection to White, see HUGHES, *supra* note 52, at 169 ("[I]t was a familiar scene to see [White] trudging along, generally with Justice Van Devanter in close consultation, and stopping every few blocks to rest his feet."). Brandeis contrasted himself with Van Devanter in his regard: "I could have had much influence with White – I did in beginning, but I made up my mind I couldn't pay the price it would have cost in want of directness & frankness. He required to be managed." *Brandeis-Frankfurter Conversations*, at 322 (August 6, 1923). Brandeis repeated his observation the following year: "Results are . . . achieved not by legal reasoning, but by finesse & subtlety & in the old days, in the middle ages, Van Devanter would have been the best of Cardinals. He is indefatigable, on good terms with everybody, knows exactly what he wants & clouds over difficulties by fine phrases & deft language. He never fools himself, and his credit side is on the whole larger than his debit. But he is on the job all the time." *Id.* at 328 (July 2, 1924). Brandeis's

comments were in the context of Van Devanter's lobbying to suppress dissent in Burns Baking Co. v. Bryan, 264 U.S. 504 (1924). Brandeis told Frankfurter that "Van Devanter 'got busy,' in his personal way, talking & laboring with members of the Court, finally led Sutherland & Sanford to suppress their dissents. Holmes calls that private working with individuals, of which there is a great deal, 'lobbying.'" *Brandeis-Frankfurter Conversations*, at 328 (July 2, 1924). Brandeis once again contrasted his own stance with that of Van Devanter: "One can achieve his results by working for them, but I made up my mind I wouldn't resort to finesse & subtlety and 'lobbying.'" *Id.*

70. *Brandeis-Frankfurter Conversations*, at 336 (June 15–16, 1926).
71. *See supra* Chapter 1, at note 13; WVD to JHC (September 3, 1922) (Clarke papers) (Van Devanter wrote to Clarke that he was was "one of the very few with whom [Mrs. Van Devanter and I] have been proud to maintain really affectionate relations.").
72. *Brandeis-Frankfurter Conversations*, at 330 (July 6, 1924). Butler had been a longtime law partner of William D. Mitchell, *In Memory of Mr. Justice Butler*, 310 U.S. at vii (1939), who was also Van Devanter's personal lawyer. Dollie Van Devanter to William D. Mitchell (April 19, 1924) (Van Devanter papers); Dollie Van Devanter to Messrs. Doherty, Rumble, Bunn & Butler (June 17, 1925) (Van Devanter papers). Butler and Van Devanter together contrived (with Taft's support) to secure Mitchell's appointment as Solicitor General. WVD to William D. Mitchell (February 1, 1925) (Van Devanter papers); William D. Mitchell to WVD (February 18, 1925 (Van Devanter papers); WVD to William D. Mitchell (February 25, 1925) (Van Devanter papers); William D. Mitchell to WVD (June 6, 1925) (Van Devanter papers). Mitchell went on to become attorney general under President Hoover.
73. GS to WHT (June 11, 1925) (Taft papers).
74. Chief Justice Stone, *Proceedings in Memory of Mr. Justice Van Devanter*, 316 U.S. at xliii (1942). Merlo Pusey refers to "the genial and versatile Van Devanter." 2 Merlo J. Pusey, CHARLES EVANS HUGHES 667 (New York: MacMillan 1951).
75. *See, e.g.,* Paul A. Freund, *Justice Brandeis: A Law Clerk's Remembrance*, 68 AMERICAN JEWISH HISTORY 12 (September 1978) (Brandeis was confident that "the opposition will collapse" after receiving Van Devanter assent to a circulated opinion that had been 5–4 in conference, "so great was Van Devanter's standing with his colleagues in matters of procedural law").
76. George Sutherland, Memorandum for the Chief Justice (May 15, 1928) (Sutherland papers) (referring to Quaker City Cab Co. v Pennsylvania, 277 U.S. 389 (1928); Nobles of the Mystic Shrine v. Michaux, 279 U.S. 737 (1929); and Highland v. Russell Car & Snow Plow Co., 279 U.S. 253 (1929)).
77. Dean Acheson, *Recollections of Service with the Federal Supreme Court*, 18 ALABAMA LAWYER 355, 361 (1957). On Brandeis's respect for Van Devanter, see Paul A. Freund, *The Supreme Court: A Tale of Two Terms*, 26 OHIO STATE LAW JOURNAL 225, 226–27 (1965) ("Brandeis had very deep regard for Van Devanter").
78. In Morrison v. Work, 266 U.S. 481 (1925), a case about Indian law, Brandeis circulated his draft to Van Devanter with a note: "My dear Van: This is the opinion of which I spoke. May I trouble you to let me have your suggestions before I circulate it?" (Brandeis papers). In Smyth v. Asphalt Belt Ry. Co., 267 U.S. 326 (1925), a case involving Supreme Court jurisdiction, Brandeis sent Van Devanter a brief request: "My dear Van: This is the case about which Sanford was troubled.

May I trouble you to let me have your suggestions before I circulate this?" (Brandeis papers). In his original draft, Brandeis had authored this paragraph:

> The trial court found, on the evidence and as matter of law, that the railroad which had instituted and brought condemnation proceedings was an independent intrastate carrier, that it was not obliged to conduct an interstate business, and that hence its action in instituting condemnation proceedings, without first obtaining a certificate from the Interstate Commerce Commission, was not in contravention of the federal law. It is this ground, and this only, on which the District Court declared that the bill should be dismissed for lack of jurisdiction, meaning obviously that, upon the facts found, it was not warranted in enjoining the condemnation proceedings.

Van Devanter advised adding to the end of the last sentence the clarifying qualification: "and not that as a federal tribunal it was without power to entertain the suit and inquire into the matters alleged in the bill." Brandeis adopted Van Devanter's suggestion.

The care with which Van Devanter reviewed opinions might be seen from the case file of Baltimore & Ohio Railroad Co. v. United States, 264 U.S. 258 (1924). The plaintiff in error contended that a state court was without jurisdiction to issue a judgment against an out-of-state railroad on the basis of a cause of action arising from negligence based on federal law. In his draft opinion, Brandeis had written that because Congress had "made no provision concerning the remedy, the federal and the state courts have unrestricted concurrent jurisdiction." Van Devanter commented in the margin of Brandeis's draft, "Fed cts not unrestricted. $3,000 must be involved. Enough to say concurrent." In his final draft Brandeis did indeed remove the adjective "unrestricted." Similarly, in West v. Standard Oil, 278 U.S. 200 (1929), a case involving the Teapot Dome scandal and western lands, Brandeis wrote Van Devanter: "Dear V. I am relying upon you to protect from treacherous pitfalls a stranger ranging over rugged country." LBD to WVD (December 15, 1928) (Brandeis papers). In response to Van Devanter's extensive suggestions, Brandeis replied, "Many thanks for your suggestions which I of course adopt." (Van Devanter papers).

79. *See* PB to WVD (May 17, 1924) (Van Devanter papers) ("As to law relating to public lands I am quite 'innocent' – as the Irish say of the 'simple minded.' And I shall be grateful to you for suggestions. . . . Give me the benefit of what occurs to you as you read the draft of opinion enclosed.") This note probably pertains to Swendig v. Washington Water Power Co., 265 U.S. 322 (1924). *See* PB to WVD (May 15, 1929) (Van Devanter papers) (about White River Lumber Co. v. Arkansas, 279 U.S. 692 (1929), discussed in note 130 *infra*); *Brandeis-Frankfurter Conversations*, at 303 (April 17, 1922).

80. "Holmes found [Van Devanter's] careful edits on the returns of his opinions incisive and nearly always accepted them." Stephan Budiansky, OLIVER WENDELL HOLMES: A LIFE IN WAR, LAW, AND IDEAS 336 (New York: W.W. Norton & Co. 2019). In Yeiser v. Dysart, 267 U.S. 540 (1925), for example, which upheld the constitutionality of a Massachusetts statute limiting attorneys' fees for workmen's compensation claims, Van Devanter wrote Holmes that "I quite agree that the statute is valid but think the decision should be put on the ground that the attorney is practicing under a license from the state – is exercising a special privilege by reason of the license – and that the state may see that the privilege is not

Willis Van Devanter

unreasonably used." (Holmes papers). Holmes accordingly added this sentence to the opinion: "When we add the considerations that an attorney practices under a license from the State and that the subject-matter is a right created by statute it is obvious that the State may attach such conditions to the license in respect of such matters as it believes to be necessary in order to make it a public good." 267 U.S. at 541. In Biddle v. Perovich, 274 U.S. 480 (1927), which involved the strange question of whether President Taft had the power to commute the sentence of a prisoner from death to life imprisonment without the prisoner's consent, Holmes had originally written: "A pardon ... is as much a part of the Constitutional scheme as the trial or the Bill of Rights." Van Devanter commented in the margins: "Query: The Bill of Rights says one accused of crime shall be entitled to trial by jury.... In my view this is giving him a privilege which he may waive. And so of other provisions. Some day we must rule on it." (Holmes papers). Holmes responded by modifying his sentence to read: "A pardon ... is a part of the Constitutional scheme." In Wilson v. Illinois Southern R. Co., 263 U.S. 574 (1924), Brandeis worked with Van Devanter to edit the jurisdictional claims in Holmes's circulated opinion: "Van Devanter agrees with me that the passages on pp 2 and 3 – which I have bracketed had better be omitted – If this is done my 'scruples' will be overcome.'" (Holmes papers).

81. Stone's first law clerk, Alfred McCormack, recalls that soon after Stone came on the bench he was assigned the opinion in Barnette v. Wells Fargo Nevada National Bank, 270 U.S. 438 (1926), which had been unanimous in conference. After Stone circulated his opinion, Brandeis unexpectedly and without prior warning produced a dissent arguing that the case should be dismissed for lack of federal jurisdiction, a point that no one on the Court had previously considered. Alfred McCormack, *A Law Clerk's Recollections*, 46 COLUMBIA LAW REVIEW 710, 715 (1946). The case "increased the coolness of Stone" toward Brandeis, which Stone was in any event inclined to feel when he first came on the bench. It did not help matters that Brandeis's dissent turned out to be "virtually impregnable." *Id.* at 714–15. Van Devanter wrote Stone, "The dissent of our Brother Brandeis has just come in. I want to draft a paragraph dealing with the subject discussed in the dissent and to submit it to you for your consideration. I fancy, for the moment at least, I see a way of disposing of the asserted jurisdictional question which may be satisfactory and generally helpful." WVD to HFS (February 25, 1926) (Stone papers). Stone was relieved. "I will be most grateful if you will prepare the paragraph." HFS to WVD (February 25, 1926) (Stone papers). As McCormack put it, "Van Devanter, master of formulas that decided cases without creating precedents, was called in, and with much travail a form of words was devised that asserted jurisdiction without too great risk of future embarrassment." McCormack, *supra*, at 715–16.

Stone's second law clerk reports that Van Devanter "would take a Stone opinion and virtually rewrite it from beginning to end. This, as a brash youngster, infuriated me. When I exploded one day and said to Stone 'I don't know why he doesn't attend to his own assignments, rather than messing up your opinions,' Stone turned to me and said, 'Have you ever read the first line of a Supreme Court opinion?' He then pointed to it and read aloud, 'Mr. Justice Stone delivered the opinion of the Court' (emphasizing the word 'Court'). Thus admonished, I never thereafter expressed any indignation at Van Devanter's practice of rewriting the opinions of others." Milton C. Handler, *Clerking for Justice Harlan Fiske Stone*, 1995 JOURNAL OF SUPREME COURT HISTORY 113, 119.

For an illustrative example of Van Devanter's extensive editing of Stone's draft opinions, see United States v. Katz, 271 U.S. 354 (1926) (Stone papers). In Tucker v. Alexander, 275 U.S. 228 (1927), Stone had concluded his opinion with the judgment "Reversed and Remanded," about which Van Devanter commented: "'And remanded' adds nothing. It follows as a matter of course. Some use it needlessly. But so concise and accurate is this opinion that it should be omitted." (Stone papers). In Work v. Braffet, 276 U.S. 560 (1928), Stone explicitly asked Van Devanter's advice about the accuracy of a sentence about federal land patents in an opinion that had already been released to the public (Stone papers). In Chase National Bank v. United States, 278 U.S. 327 (1929), Stone, in response to Van Devanter's comments, circulated to the entire Court a Memorandum stating that "Justice Van Devanter has called attention to the erroneous assumption involved in the questions propounded by the Court of Claims. I have accordingly added the paragraph at the end of the opinion and, to emphasize the point, made some slight changes in the phraseology of the opinion." (Stone papers). In Chicago, M. St. P. & P.R. Co. v. Risty, 276 U.S. 567 (1928), Stone's initial draft had included the observation: "Several constitutional objections are urged to the state drainage statutes and several preliminary objections are made to the maintenance of this suit. None of the questions presented are free from difficulty." To which Van Devanter objected: "An obvious misfit. The application for interlocutory injunction was denied, not granted. You show the questions are free from difficulty and that we need no aid in solving them. Nothing delicate involved in denying temporary injunction in such a case." (Stone papers). Stone omitted the objectionable language in his final opinion. *See also* St. Louis-San Francisco Ry Co. v. Mills, 271 U.S. 344 (1926) (Stone papers); Lewellyn v. Electric Reduction Co., 275 U.S. 243 (1927) (Stone papers); Miller v. Schoene, 276 U.S. 272 (1928) (Stone papers). To one circulated Stone opinion, Van Devanter responded, "Yes, but you have written discursively and in a vein much like that of a student writing for a law journal." Oster v. Kansas, 272 U.S. 465 (1926) (Stone papers).

82. *See* JM to WVD (February 24, 1921) (Van Devanter papers).
83. Brandeis told Frankfurter that in Railway Commission of California v. Southern Pacific Co., 262 U.S. 331 (1924), "McReynolds first wrote an opinion that I couldn't stand for. I told the Chief that I have [no] love of union stations, was agin' them all, but McR's opinion had too many glaring errors to bother us in the future. Van D. worked with McR & made changes and Chief asked me whether that will remove my sting. I had written a really stinging dissent. They didn't want the Court shown up that way, & corrections weren't adequate & finally the Chief took over the opinion & put out what is now the Ct's opinion & I suppressed my dissent because after all it's merely a question of statuary construction & the worst things were removed by the Chief." *Brandeis-Frankfurter Conversations*, at 329 (July 3, 1924).
84. Memorandum from Edward Sanford to the Court (May 1926), in Davis v. Williford, 271 U.S. 484 (1926) (Taft papers) ("I expressed some doubt in conference whether the judgment of the Supreme Court in this case was final. ... The majority thought otherwise, however, and I have gone over the record very fully with Mr. Justice Van Devanter, who has made it clear to me that, in the light of the whole record, the judgment was to be considered final within the established rule. But he agreed in the view that since to discuss this subject fully would require a rather elaborate setting out of the details of the incidental questions raised in the case and of the stipulations of the parties,

and no question had been raised by the other side as to the finality of the judgment, it was not necessary to mention the remand or refer to this question in any way in the opinion.").
85. 264 U.S. 426 (1924).
86. LDB to WVD (March 26, 1924) (Brandeis papers). Brandeis circulated specially to Van Devanter, for "the benefit of your suggestions before I circulate this," his draft opinion in the bankruptcy case of Benedict v. Ratner, 268 U.S. 353 (1925) (Brandeis papers). In Albrecht v. United States, 273 U.S. 1 (1927), a case raising the controversial question of whether an otherwise valid information could be undermined by an illegal arrest based upon invalid affidavits, Brandeis wrote Van Devanter "Here is the opinion in No. 9 on which I want you and the Chief's suggestions before it is circulated. I found the field covered with doubts and both conflict and dearth of authorities. I hope we can settle and make uniform this matter of practice." LDB to WVD (December 25, 1926) (Brandeis papers). In United States v. California Co-Operative Canneries, 279 U.S. 553 (1929), a case requiring the clarification of the rights of intervenors, Brandeis again asked Van Devanter, "May I have your suggestion before I circulate the opinion?" LDB to WVD (May 14, 1929) (Brandeis papers). Brandeis followed the same procedure in *In re* Buder, 271 U.S. 461 (1926), a case involving appellate Supreme Court jurisdiction. LDB to WVD (May 12, 1926) (Brandeis papers) ("Dear Van: This is the opinion of which I spoke to you Saturday. Please let me have your suggestions before I circulate it."). Van Devanter wrote Brandeis a long memo about the case on May 17 (Brandeis papers), to which Brandeis replied on May 19: "The ground you recommend was the one on which I voted 'no' – But I think that, as a matter of policy, you are clearly right; and I am engaged in redrafting the opinion on that line. May I trouble you to formulate the rule of law which you think should be established – And I should be very glad to hear of any authorities or arguments in support of the construction recommended." (Van Devanter papers). On May 20, Van Devanter responded with a long list of precedents (Brandeis papers). Brandeis ultimately adopted Van Devanter's theory of the case. *See also* WVD to WHT (February 9, 1922) (Taft papers) ("Brandeis just telephoned asking for a talk this afternoon about the Keokuk bridge tax case [Keokuk & Hamilton Bridge Co. v. Salm, 258 U.S. 122 (1922)] and of course I told him to come along, glad to see him, etc. He said he was glad I had written to him; so there may be a good prospect of putting the matter on its right foot.").
87. Van Devanter appears to have genuinely admired Taft. Although Van Devanter's papers are typically full of understatement, as early as 1906 Van Devanter observed to a friend that "nothing better could happen to the Supreme Court" than the appointment of Taft to the bench, and that "I would hope that ere long he would become Chief Justice." WVD to Henry W. Hoyt (March 17, 1906) (Van Devanter papers). In what for him was a burst of enthusiasm, Van Devanter wrote in 1927 that "The Chief Justice, although measurably quieted by the passing years and the weight of great responsibility, is still the big hearted, jovial, and broad gauged man that you knew him to be. He is industrious, judicial, companionable, and always considerate. I think he is a great Chief Justice. I have seen others in the harness whom I greatly respected, but, speaking confidentially, he is easily their superior. It is a fortunate thing for the country and the Court that he was made Chief Justice." WVD to Sylvester G. Williams (December 8, 1927) (Van Devanter papers). Van Devanter counted it "a very distinct personal loss" when Taft resigned in 1930, WVD to Dennis T. Flynn (February 3, 1930) (Van Devanter papers), and he affirmed upon Taft's death that "my effort shall be to

remember the generous and noble nature of the man which was so continuously manifest up to the time of his illness.... I regard it as a great good fortune to have been closely associated with him." WVD to John C. Knox (March 11, 1930) (Van Devanter papers).

88. WHT to Charles P. Taft (June 8, 1927) (Taft papers). *See* WHT to Charles P. Taft 2nd (June 8, 1927) ("Justice Van Devanter and I are the closest friends on the Bench"); WHT to Robert A. Taft (June 8, 1927). Most unusually, Taft would sometimes close his letters to Van Devanter with the salutation "love." WHT to WVD (September 16, 1928) (Taft papers). *See* WHT to WVD (August 1, 1929) (Taft papers).

89. WHT to Charles P. Taft (June 8, 1927) (Taft papers).

90. WHT to William Lyon Phelps (May 30, 1927) (Taft papers).

91. *See, e.g.*, WVD to WHT (February 10, 1922) (Taft papers) (suggesting that steps be taken to instruct the clerk to enforce a new rule requiring the assessment of expenses for the printing of records); WHT to WVD (February 10, 1922) (Van Devanter papers) ("I'll direct the clerk to section 2 Rule X just as you suggest. I'll write him today on the subject."); WHT to William R. Stansbury (February 10, 1922) (Taft papers); William R. Stansbury to WHT (February 16, 1922) (Taft papers).

92. *See, e.g.*, WHT to WVD (December 7, 1921) (Taft papers) ("I am sending you a tentative opinion in the Arizona Truax case. I wish you would look it over and cut and slash as you think wise.... I have not sent this to the whole Court, because I want to have the benefit of your suggestions and corrections before doing so."); WHT to WVD (February 27, 1922) (Van Devanter papers) ("We can't be without you."); WHT to WVD (April 11, 1923) (Van Devanter papers) ("I hope you will consent to help me out by coming to a conference on Sunday afternoon next at three o'clock at my house. I shall not ask such a favor again this year. Can't you take your golf on Saturday instead of Sunday? A critical meeting of the Yale Corporation comes on Saturday. The policy and the right policy of the University may be dependent on my vote. Bear with me."); WHT to WVD (December 26, 1924) (Van Devanter papers) ("Here is a long screed. I sent it to Butler and Sandford [sic] and McKenna. Run it over – It needs some more citations.... [W]hen one wants to convince one's colleagues, he must spread out his authority."); WHT to OWH (June 5, 1926) (Taft papers); WHT to OWH (June 6, 1926) (Taft papers).

93. On Van Devanter's central role in assisting Taft in securing the nomination of Pierce Butler, see DAVID J. DANELSKI, A SUPREME COURT JUSTICE IS APPOINTED (New York: Random House 1964); WVD to George B. Rose (September 23, 1927) (Van Devanter papers).

94. Memorandum, November 10, 1924 (Taft Papers), reprinted in WALTER MURPHY & C. HERMAN PRITCHETT, COURTS, JUDGES, AND POLITICS: AN INTRODUCTION TO THE JUDICIAL PROCESS 199–201 (3d ed., New York: Random House 1979). With regard to McKenna's last opinion, which he insisted on publishing before retiring, Taft wrote Van Devanter, "I enclose McK's opinion. The latter part I had not seen. Run it over – send me your suggestions on a separate paper so that I can incorporate them in my handwriting. The old man is in a hurry to send it out. Let me have your suggestions tonight." WHT to WVD (December 9, 1924) (Van Devanter papers).

95. WHT to LDB (November 11, 1923) (Taft papers).

96. WHT to OWH (June 5, 1926) (Taft papers); Charles Cropley to WHT (June 20, 1928) (Taft papers); WHT to WVD (June 23, 1928) (Van Devanter papers); WVD

to WHT (June 27, 1928) (Van Devanter papers); Horatio Stonier to WHT (June 27, 1928) (Taft papers); WHT to WVD (June 28, 1928) (Van Devanter papers); WHT to WVD (July 1, 1928) (Taft papers).

97. "I am thinking of assigning [Ford v. United States, 273 U.S. 593 (1927)] to Brandeis. It involves the British Treaty over the 12 mile limit and the conspiracy at San Francisco and Vancouver. Holmes and Stone dissented. They may come in. Don't you think we can be safe in that?" WHT to WVD (February 20, 1927) (Van Devanter papers). Eventually Taft took over the opinion himself and wrote for a unanimous court.

98. While drafting his opinion in Harkin v. Brundage, 276 U.S. 36 (1928), Taft wrote Van Devanter, "Brandeis suggests that I say something in the Chicago Receivership case like this. I am entirely willing to do it because I think the use of receiverships in the Federal courts has become too easy and frequent. It is not necessary in the case but it is entirely relevant. What would you think of it?" WHT to WVD (January 31, 1928) (Van Devanter papers). The contents of Brandeis's suggestion have not survived, but may perhaps be inferred from the note that Taft sent Brandeis on January 30, 1928 (Taft papers), to the effect that "I would like to emphasize, even more than I do, the fact that we don't look with favor on these consent receiverships, because they are always at the instance of the corporation itself, and this use of a simple contract creditor is only part of the objectionable features." *See also* WHT to WVD (December 17, 1928) (Taft papers); WHT to WVD (January 25, 1922) (Van Devanter papers); WHT to WVD (December 2, 1922) (Van Devanter papers); WHT to WVD (May 9, 1923) (Taft papers).

99. WHT to Harry M. Daugherty (June 5, 1922) (Taft papers); WHT to WVD (June 1922) (Van Devanter papers).

100. Pub. L. 68-415, 43 Stat. 936 (February 13, 1925).

101. William Howard Taft, *The Jurisdiction of the Supreme Court under the Act of February 13, 1925*, 35 YALE LAW JOURNAL 1, 12 (1925). WHT to WVD (August 15, 1925) (Taft papers); WVD to WHT (September 5, 1925) (Taft papers); WHT to WVD (September 9, 1925) (Taft papers); WHT to PB (September 16, 1925) (Taft papers).

102. *See infra* Chapter 17.

103. WHT to WVD (January 7, 1930) (Taft papers).

104. WVD to Edmund F. Trabue (April 26, 1926) (Van Devanter papers).

105. FELIX FRANKFURTER ON THE SUPREME COURT: EXTRAJUDICIAL ESSAYS ON THE COURT AND THE CONSTITUTION 487 (Philip B. Kurland, ed., Cambridge: Harvard University Press 1970). Frankfurter went on to observe: "Mr. Justice Van Devanter is a man who plays an important role in the history of the Court, though you cannot find it adequately reflected in the opinions written by him because he wrote so few. But Van Devanter was a man of great experience. . . . He had a very clear, lucid mind, the mind, should I say, of a great architect. He was a beautiful draftsman and an inventor of legal techniques who did much to bring about the reforms which were effectively accomplished by Taft as Chief Justice." *Id.*

106. WHT to WVD (March 7, 1927) (Van Devanter papers).

107. WHT to Robert A. Taft (October 23, 1927) (Taft papers).

108. Taft's law clerk during the 1924 term believed that Van Devanter and Butler were the justices who "were closest to him." C. Dickerman Williams, *The 1924*

Term: Recollections of Chief Justice Taft's Law Clerk, 1989 YEARBOOK OF THE SUPREME COURT HISTORICAL SOCIETY 40, 50.

109. WHT to Myron Herrick (June 3, 1928) (Taft papers). *See* David R. Stras, *Pierce Butler: A Supreme Technician*, 62 VANDERBILT LAW REVIEW 695, 708 (2009). To Taft, Butler was "a great big, physically and mentally, broad-minded man." WHT to Horace D. Taft (November 24, 1922) (Taft papers).

110. Van Devanter had been on friendly terms with Butler since Van Devanter's days as an Eighth Circuit judge, DANELSKI, *supra* note 93, at 35, and indeed may have been the person who brought Butler to Taft's attention as a potential nominee for a position on the Supreme Court. *Id.* at 49; Stras, *supra* note 109, at 711; David Schroeder, More Than a Fraction: The Life and Work of Justice Pierce Butler 78 (Ph.D. Dissertation, Marquette University, 2009). In 1922, Van Devanter wrote Butler, "I am glad to be your friend." WVD to PB (November 23, 1922) (Van Devanter papers). Van Devanter treated Butler as a "brother." *Brandeis-Frankfurter Conversations*, at 330 (July 6, 1924). It is apparent from extant case files that Butler and Van Devanter would often team up in responding to circulated opinions. *See, e.g.*, PB to WVD (May 15, 1929) (Van Devanter papers) (re White River Lumber Co. v. Arkansas, 279 U.S. 692 (1929)); Chicago, M. St. P. & P.R. Co. v. Risty, 276 U.S. 567 (1928) (Stone papers); Gambino v. United States, 275 U.S. 310 (1927) (Brandeis papers); United Fuel Gas Co. v. Rd Comm'n of Kentucky, 278 U.S. 300 (1929) (Stone papers); United Fuel Co. v. Pub. Serv. Comm'n of West Virginia, 278 U.S. 322 (1929) (Stone papers); International Shoe Co. v. Shartel, 279 U.S. 429 (1929) (Stone papers); PB to WVD (June 22, 1929) (Van Devanter papers) (re Nashville, C. & St. L. Ry. V. White, 278 U.S. 456 (1929)); Fidelity & Deposit Co. v. Tafoya, 270 U.S. 426 (1926) (Holmes papers).

111. *See* Figure I-16. *Compare* Figure I-15.

112. *See* Figure II-7. *Compare* Figure II-8.

113. *See* Figure II-9. *Compare* Figure II-10.

114. United Leather Workers' International Union v. Herkert & Meisel Trunk Co., 365 U.S. 457 (1924) (holding that in the absence of demonstrated intent to disrupt interstate commerce federal anti-trust law did not apply to a strike against a manufacturer whose goods were shipped in interstate commerce). Such differences as existed between Taft and Van Devanter might be exemplified by Bromley v. McCaughn, 280 U.S. 124 (1929), in which the Court, per Stone, held that the federal gift tax was not an unconstitutional unapportioned direct tax, but instead an indirect excise tax. Van Devanter, Sutherland, and Butler dissented. Butler wrote Stone in response to Stone's circulated opinion: "You have put your best foot forward. 'Excise' is a big word and has been growing for a long time. If you are right, is there a limit to its power of expansion?" PB to HFS (November 15, 1929) (Stone papers). *See* Edwards v. Douglas, 269 U.S. 204 (1925).

115. United Leather Workers' International Union v. Herkert & Meisel Trunk Co., 365 U.S. 457 (1924); Samuels v. McCurdy, 267 U.S. 188 (1925) (holding that the seizure of liquor lawfully acquired before prohibition does not violate the Fourteenth Amendment); Nigro v. United States, 276 U.S. 332 (1928) (upholding a conviction under the Anti-Narcotic Act of December 17, 1914, 38 Stat. 785); Olmstead v. United States, 277 U.S. 438 (1928) (holding that wiretapping without a warrant does not violate the Fourth Amendment).

Willis Van Devanter

116. Toyota v. United States, 268 U.S. 402 (1925) (holding that a Japanese citizen who had served in the United States armed forces during World War I and who had received an honorable discharge could not become a naturalized United States citizen). In contrast, Taft dissented five times from Sutherland opinions during the 1922–1928 terms: Adkins v. Children's Hospital of the District of Columbia, 261 U.S. 525 (1923) (striking down a statute fixing minimum wages for women and children within the District); First National Bank v. Missouri, 263 U.S. 640 (1924) (upholding a state statute prohibiting branch banking as applied to a national bank); United States v. Oregon Lumber Co., 260 U.S. 290 (1922) (ruling against an effort by the United States to recover the value of lands fraudulently obtained on the ground that the United States had previously prosecuted a suit in equity to final judgment of dismissal because of a statute of limitations); Panama R. Co. v. Rock, 266 U.S. 209 (1924) (holding no cause of action for negligent harm in the Canal Zone); Smyer v. United States, 273 U.S. 333 (1927) (refusal to permit recovery on the bond of a postmaster for funds embezzled by an assistant superintendent of mails). Van Devanter dissented twice from Sutherland opinions: Village of Euclid v. Ambler Realty Co., 272 U.S. 365 (1926) (upholding the constitutionality of zoning ordinances); First National Bank v. Missouri, 263 U.S. 640 (1924). Butler dissented three times from Sutherland opinions: Cudahy Packing Co. v. Parramore, 263 U.S. 418 (1923) (upholding the constitutionality of the application of workmen's compensation act as applied to workers who were required to cross railroad tracks on their way to employment); Village of Euclid v. Ambler Realty Co., 272 U.S. 365 (1926); First National Bank v. Missouri, 263 U.S. 640 (1924).
117. *See, e.g.*, White River Lumber Co. v. Arkansas, 279 U.S. 692 (1929).
118. *See infra* Epilogue, at 1502–3.
119. *See* BICKEL & SCHMIDT, *supra* note 2, at 51–52.
120. *Bryan in Attack on Van Devanter*, Detroit Free Press (November 6, 1911), at 9. Van Devanter later returned the favor, writing his sister that "Hitler is the William Jennings Bryan of Germany, and even more of a dreamer and more of an eccentric than Bryan was." WVD to Mrs. John Lacey (March 28, 1932) (Van Devanter papers).
121. William E. Borah, *Justice Willis Van Devanter*, 70 THE INDEPENDENT 457 (1911).
122. *A Review of the World*, 50 CURRENT LITERATURE 18 (January 1911).
123. 223 U.S. 1 (1912).
124. 220 U.S. 61 (1911).
125. *Id.* at 78–79.
126. OWH to Felix Frankfurter (April 20, 1921), in HOLMES-FRANKFURTER CORRESPONDENCE, at 110. DAVENPORT, *supra* note 23, attributes the shift to Van Devanter's unrelenting political opportunism. *Id.* at 221–27. In Davenport's view, Van Devanter was an "ever articulate, ghost writing spinner," who "used exaggeration, self aggrandizement, secrecy, and manipulation to his benefit." Verisimilitude was Van Devanter's "friend, the truth a mere acquaintance. Careful, operative, sly, strategic, master of false impression, he stretched the truth and the justification where it was required." *Id.* at 226–27.
127. 272 U.S. 365 (1926).
128. Frost v. Corporation Commission, 278 U.S. 515 (1929).

129. Holmes commented on Brandeis's dissent, "You have put too much work into this – more than was needed to lay out the opinion. But you certainly have killed it dead." (Brandeis papers).
130. 279 U.S. 692 (1929). Taft, Butler, and Van Devanter dissented in the case. Butler circulated his dissent to Van Devanter in advance, with a note saying: "My study of the case satisfies me – leaves no vestige of doubt – that [the majority] vote was wrong & that the decree should be reversed. I hope you may fully agree. I mentioned the case to George Monday and asked special or careful consideration of my opinion. Of course he promised heartily, but he said he was strongly for affirmance – justifying classification by the suggestion that as to property of the individual the back taxes to be recovered might not 'be worth the candle' – that was all. But Sanford's opinion contains no suggestion of that point. And it seems to me that it cannot not [sic] stand up in reason or authority against the facts brought forward in my dissent. The Chief said he would give the case special attention. Please let me have your suggestions – and do be free with them – so that the thing may go to Sanford & the others. Affectionately." PB to WVD (May 15, 1929) (Van Devanter papers).

By the 1920s, therefore, as Brandeis's clerk shrewdly observed in a memorandum prepared in chambers, Van Devanter had silently in certain kinds of cases come to shift the burden of proof under rational basis review so that the defender of a legislative "classification" actually had to carry the burden of demonstrating the "state of facts" that might justify it. *See* "No. 60," in Frost v. Corporation Commission file (January 30, 1929) (Brandeis papers). For a discussion of how the Taft Court varied the level of scrutiny in equal protection cases when values like protecting the national market or protecting commercial corporations were at stake, see *infra* Chapter 43, at 1430–33.

131. Quoted in M. Paul Holsinger, *Mr. Justice Van Devanter and the New Deal: A Note*, 31 THE HISTORIAN 57, 58 n.3 (November 1, 1968).
132. HFS to Children (February 13, 1941) (Stone papers).
133. *Van Devanter Dies*, NEW YORK TIMES (February 9, 1941), at 47. *See Former Justice Van Devanter*, 27 AMERICAN BAR ASSOCIATION JOURNAL 154 (1941). The portrayal of Van Devanter in the *New York Times* during the Taft Court era is quite different:

> Any one who watches the court in action brings away a picture of him seated at the left of the Chief Justice, his white head erect, his questioning voice aggressive, his gold-rimmed eyeglasses a weapon with which he points and slays a faulty argument. He is a precisionist who has no patience with slovenly presentation. "Why do you say you 'think'?" he demanded of a lawyer whose knowledge of facts seemed to be wobbling. "Aren't you here to present a case to us?" ...
>
> If facial expression is any index, he is a man who dearly loves a contest. In brushes with lawyers who evade the point or are uncertain about references, his eyes sparkle and his jaw sets with a tenacity that looks positively joyous. But in personal conversation he has a delightful old-fashioned courtesy. He is patient in explanation as long as he knows that another mind is trying to follow his.

Mildred Adams, *Three Venerable Justices Who Refuse to Grow Old*, NEW YORK TIMES MAGAZINE (December 8, 1929), at 23.
134. Joseph Percival Pollard, *Four New Dissenters*, 68 NEW REPUBLIC 61, 63 (1931). In 1934, Van Devanter penned an intriguing letter to his sister that illuminates his

Willis Van Devanter

frame of mind. He describes in the letter attending the Spring Gridiron Dinner given by Washington newspaper correspondents. President Roosevelt was in attendance, and he was roasted by Senator David Reed for disregarding the Constitution. FDR rose to affirm that so long as "there are still 9,000,000 of unemployed and so long as this continues to be true we have a state of emergency, the relief of which calls for our best endeavors, and our measures must be fitted to that emergency."

> Then he referred to those who feared that the Constitution would be violated and said: "They do not know what the Constitution is. They think it means today as applied to present conditions what it meant in the beginning, as applied to the conditions of that period. They do not know or realize that the Constitution has changed with the times. Let me illustrate my meaning. In our early maritime history we constructed a great ship and called it 'The Constitution.' We put in it the best timbers which could be found, and we constructed it according to the best plans and experience of that period. We manned it the best we knew how and we sent it forth to do battle. It was crowned with success and achieved wonderful victories. . . . We still have it and we still revere it and have an affection for it because of what it accomplished in its day. But no one would be fool enough now to send it out to fight even a tugboat. . . . So with the Constitution of the United States. We revere it and have an affection for it because of the principles which it reflects, but in its material applications it of necessity has changed in keeping with the changing times and conditions."

Van Devanter was "surprised and worried by the fact that in meeting people who were at the dinner they say nothing about what was said about the Constitution, although rather freely talking about other features and other parts of the speeches. If this means that they regard that part of the speeches as of little or no moment, then we are indeed in an unfortunate situation." Van Devanter commented to his sister that a few nights after the Gridiron dinner he attended a birthday celebration with McReynolds and Judge Covington, who both expressed concern about FDR's speech, but who also reported that they could find few people who seemed disconcerted by it:

> But perhaps this is to be explained by the fact that Moley, Tugwell and various other adherents of the Administration have been saying in various magazine and newspaper articles much the same things about the Constitution that the President said. The President said nothing about the provision in the Constitution permitting changes by way of amendment and none of these other people refer to that provision. They seem to overlook the fact that the Constitution declares that it shall be the supreme law of the land and provides for its own amendment so that if perchance conditions become such that in the sober judgment of most of the people any provision cannot rightly be given effect as written an appropriate change can be made. . . . If the President's position be correct, there is no need for any amendment and the several amendments which have been adopted up until now represent a needless waste of effort and time.

WVD to Mrs. John W. Lacey (April 18, 1934) (Van Devanter papers). In the words of John W. Davis: "Constitutional grants, constitutional limitations and constitutional prohibitions were to [Van Devanter] very real and sacred things." *Proceedings in Memory of Mr. Justice Van Devanter*, 316 U.S. at xxvii (1942).
135. Dahnke-Walker Milling Co. v. Bondurant, 257 U.S. 282 (1921) (striking down a Kentucky statute prescribing conditions under which foreign corporations might purchase Kentucky wheat for interstate delivery); Pennsylvania v. West Virginia,

262 U.S. 553 (1923) (striking down West Virginia limitations on the export of natural gas); Shafer v. Farmers' Grain Co., 268 U.S. 189 (1925) (striking down a North Dakota statute grading wheat). Van Devanter fully believed in the dual sovereignty that was characteristic of the Taft Court's approach to federalism, as can be seen in Hebert v. Louisiana, 272 U.S. 312 (1926), which rejected a challenge to state indictments for manufacturing intoxicating liquor against persons who were already under indictment in federal court for the same acts. Van Devanter wrote, "The due process of law clause in the Fourteenth Amendment does not take up the statutes of the several states and make them the test of what it requires; nor does it enable this court to revise the decisions of the state courts on questions of state law. What it does require is that state action, whether through one agency or another, shall be consistent with the fundamental principles of liberty and justice which lie at the base of all our civil and political institutions and not infrequently are designated as 'law of the land.' Those principles are applicable alike in all the states, and do not depend upon or vary with local legislation." 272 U.S. at 316–17. Van Devanter's strong commitment to a uniform regime of federal law can be seen in his dissent in Douglas v. New York, N.H. & H.R. Co., 279 U.S. 377 (1929), in which, speaking through Holmes, the Court upheld the authority of a New York court to dismiss a suit under the Federal Employers' Liability Act for injury to a Connecticut resident, occurring in Connecticut, by a Connecticut Corporation.

136. *See, e.g.*, Work v. United States *ex rel.* Lynn, 266 U.S. 161 (1924) (pragmatic form of statutory interpretation).
137. Salinger v. Loisel, 265 U.S. 224 (1924) (holding that although res judicata does not apply to prior petitions for habeas corpus, nevertheless courts can use their "sound judicial discretion" to take account of the disposition of past writs); Wong Doo v. United States, 265 U.S. 239 (1924) (same); Barber Asphalt Paving Co. v. Standard Asphalt & Rubber Co., 275 U.S. 372 (1928) (interpreting provisions of equity rules requiring a simple and condensed account of the relevant evidence).
138. *Ex parte* Bakelite Corp., 279 U.S. 438 (1929) (holding that the determination of the Article III status of a court depends upon the power under which the court was created and the jurisdiction conferred).
139. 273 U.S. 135 (1927).
140. Butler Docket Book (1924 term), at 250.
141. Williams, *supra* note 108, at 48–49.
142. For a good example of Brandeis and Van Devanter working in tandem to improve an opinion, see the Brandeis files for Wilson v. Illinois Southern R. Co., 263 U.S. 574 (1924).
143. *Brandeis-Frankfurter Conversations*, at 336 (June 17, 1926). Brandeis observed that "Van Dev. knows as much about jurisdiction as anyone – more than anyone. But when he wants to decide all his jurisdictional scruples go." *Id.* at 313 (June 28, 1923).

CHAPTER 7

James Clark McReynolds

As the cause of free silver began to sweep agrarian America in 1894, Van Devanter and Warren, although staunch Republicans, immediately sensed that strict support of the traditional Republican commitment to the gold standard would prove political suicide in Wyoming. They therefore began a prescient and effective campaign to push the Wyoming Republican Party to advocate coining free silver, while at the same time maintaining support for the fundamental Republican principle of high tariffs.[1] The maneuver demonstrated remarkable political dexterity and flexibility.

Van Devanter's supple response should be contrasted to that of James Clark McReynolds, a moderately successful Nashville lawyer who was "a Democrat by inheritance and education."[2] McReynolds refused to accept the 1896 Democratic platform endorsing bimetallism. He opted to split his party and to run for Congress as a gold Democrat. "I have always adhered to what I conceived to be Democratic principles, and have thought myself a follower of the founders of the Democratic party – but I have never considered it right, honest or patriotic for any citizen to follow an organization when it proclaimed doctrine and advocated principles believed by him to be inimical to the public good."[3] "I believe that the free coinage of silver would be injurious to every man, woman and child in this republic. . . . [W]e have today money as good as the best in the world. If, under free coinage, the dollars are as good as they are now, they will be as hard to get, but if they will not be as good, we do not want them. . . . As an honest man, I must, therefore, oppose it."[4]

McReynolds knew full well that he would lose the election; the regular Tennessee Democratic machine would crush his candidacy. But he believed it a matter of honor to stand up for proper principles. If Van Devanter was insistently "genial,"[5] concerned with how others thought and how they might be swayed in their actions and decisions, McReynolds was the polar opposite. McReynolds was punctilious and abrasive, indifferent to expediency and accommodation. "His code of honor was inflexible and unyielding."⁶ If Van Devanter's easy pragmatism could allow him to accommodate silver coinage, the "salient points" in McReynolds's "character and philosophy were a rigid righteousness, an unyielding determination, and unshakable stability."⁷

On the Taft Court, McReynolds stood most unyieldingly against the positivism of Holmes. McReynolds prized the customs, habits, and mores of the people, "those privileges long recognized at common law as essential to the orderly pursuit of happiness by free men."⁸ He believed that law and morality were indissolubly fused. McReynolds sought to discern and enforce "natural and inherent principles of practical justice."⁹ He thought it essential to protect "the fundamental right which one has to conduct his own affairs honestly and along customary lines."¹⁰

In these attitudes, McReynolds exemplified the traditional view of conservative legal elites that "law" arises from customary practices and that mere "legislation" ought to be strictly disciplined by judicial review. For McReynolds, "a legislative declaration of reasonableness is not conclusive; no more so is popular approval – otherwise constitutional inhibitions would be futile. And plainly, I think, the individual's fundamental rights are not proper subjects for experimentation; they ought not to be sacrificed to questionable theorization." Any other conclusion would be "revolutionary" and lead "straight towards destruction of our well-tried and successful system of government." The proper governance of the nation could not possibly depend upon the "whims or caprices or fanciful ideas of those who happen for the day to constitute the legislative majority."¹¹

McReynolds was born on February 3, 1862, in Elkton Kentucky, in the midst of the Civil War. His father, Dr. John Oliver McReynolds, was "an extremely irascible man, sometimes nicknamed 'The Pope,' because of his firm belief that virtually all his opinions were correct."¹² John McReynolds and his wife were strict Campbellites,¹³ a "fundamentalist" wing of the "Church of the Disciples of Christ" that "viewed the world in absolute terms of good and evil." Their son would remain associated with the Church throughout his adult life.¹⁴

It was said of the elder McReynolds that "critics could not drive him from his beliefs," and that he never compromised "his principles for the sake of popularity."¹⁵ "In a district torn between a divided allegiance to North and South, he was a rampant secessionist,"¹⁶ so much so that he was arrested after the Civil War for adamantly refusing to take the Test Oath. He was saved from imprisonment only by the personal intervention of Grant's Secretary of the Treasury.¹⁷ John McReynolds

> was a strict "States' Rights Democrat". He had no use for Abraham Lincoln or for William Jennings Bryan, the former because of what he had done as President to the hopes and aspirations of the Confederacy and the latter because of his interest in the rise of the common man. Autocratically inclined, he was aware of his position in the community, and there is some indication that he impressed this awareness upon his family. He was not a public-spirited person and had little interest in the affairs of Elkton. ... His individualism, complacency and conservatism are all illustrated by his unyielding attitude toward the establishment of free public school systems. ... The possibility that he would have imposed upon

James Clark McReynolds

his property a tax, the proceeds of which would be used to pay for the schooling of children of unambitious parents, was obnoxious to the elder McReynolds.[18]

Later in life, the future justice would say that his father "had more common sense about more things than any man I ever have known. ... A good doctor, he also was a good business man. If he said a thing was so every one knew that it was so. No person was ever known to question his word."[19] The Civil War, said James C. McReynolds, "gave freedom to our slaves and left us land poor. My father said he would build his fortune over again and he made the promise good in time."[20]

McReynolds was first educated at home, then in a private school run by a cousin, and finally at a private academy.[21] In August 1879, never having "been a hundred miles away from" the tiny village of Elkton,[22] he enrolled in Vanderbilt. He graduated in 1882 as an outstandingly successful undergraduate, spending the next year as a Fellow and Assistant in Natural History and Geology.[23] During the summer of 1883 he enrolled in the law school of the University of Virginia, where he came under the lifelong spell of the most prominent law professor in the South, the lucid and axiomatic John B. Minor.[24]

Graduating in July 1884,[25] McReynolds accepted a two-year position as secretary to Tennessee Senator Howell Edmunds Jackson[26] before establishing a moderately successful but uninspiring legal practice in Nashville,[27] teaching law at Vanderbilt on the side. His unsuccessful congressional bid in 1896 brought him close to J.M. Dickinson, another southern gold Democrat and leader of the Nashville Bar, who moved easily between parties.[28] (Dickinson would later become Taft's secretary of war.) When in 1903 Theodore Roosevelt's attorney general complained to Dickinson about needing a good $30,000-a-year lawyer who would work for $5,000, Dickinson recommended McReynolds, who promptly went to work at the Department of Justice as an assistant attorney general.[29] He resigned after three and a half years of excellent work, briefly accepted a position as a senior associate at Cravath, Henderson and Gersdorff, and then returned to the Department of Justice at the express invitation of Attorney General Charles J. Bonaparte to become a special assistant in charge of the prosecution of the American Tobacco Company under the Sherman Act.[30]

The prosecution made McReynolds's name as a master litigator and anti-trust expert. The case was delicate and complicated, involving questions of both constitutional and statutory interpretation.[31] In crafting his Supreme Court brief, McReynolds adopted a thoroughly pragmatic view of the statute[32] that was carefully designed to appeal to Holmes's narrow view of anti-trust liability.[33] McReynolds was perfectly aware that a litigator's view of a statute should turn "upon the Judge before whom the statute is to be argued and decided. Judges have characteristics, methods and principles, also feelings, just like the rest of us."[34] McReynolds won a smashing victory.[35] "It is scarcely to be conceived that any more comprehensive and effective application of the statute to this vast combination could possibly have been decreed," said Taft's Attorney General George W. Wickersham, McReynolds's superior.[36]

When the time came to negotiate a remedy, however, the defendants put on the table a plan that allowed existing stockholders to retain proportional control over the entities spun-off by the trust's dissolution. McReynolds, who had been charged with negotiating a remedial decree, was contemptuous. "O, yes; it's an old story to me. Speaking, of course, only for myself, I regard it as a plain subterfuge which deserves an expeditious commitment to the scrap heap."[37] But Wickersham disagreed. With the exception of some modifications that failed to challenge the essential structural features of the defendants' plan,[38] he accepted the Tobacco Trust's proffered remedy.[39] "After the close of Mr. Wickersham's remarks, his chief assistant, J.C. McReynolds, made this remark: 'Mr. Wickersham is speaking for the government, not for me.'"[40] Ironically, Louis Brandeis had by then appeared in the case, and he articulated the very objections privately entertained by McReynolds.[41] Brandeis would later publish an editorial defending McReynolds against Wickersham's betrayal.[42]

McReynolds privately asked to be relieved of his "professional connection" with the case,[43] publicly resigning in January 1912 after judicial approval of the plan.[44] It was an electrifying gesture, at least to those committed, in the words of the 1912 Democratic Party Platform, to condemning "the action of the Republican administration in compromising with . . . the tobacco trust."[45] McReynolds's resignation expressed the moral righteousness, the "indomitable belief in the merit of his convictions," that was "the central characteristic" of his personality.[46] It was a characteristic that likely appealed to Woodrow Wilson, who was himself a moralist and an 1896 gold Democrat, and who had also studied law with John Minor at the University of Virginia.

When Wilson was unable to secure his first choices for attorney general,[47] he selected McReynolds at the urging of Colonel Edward M. House, who "considered McReynolds a progressive; in fact, he believed him to be somewhat radical."[48] McReynolds "was made Attorney General solely by reason of his refusal to acquiesce in a surrender by the Taft administration to the tobacco trust after he had won the suit and secured conviction."[49] This was despite the fact that, as Wilson's son-in-law William McAdoo acidly observed, McReynolds "was entirely without prominence in the Democratic Party; he was not widely known; and he had not achieved any outstanding distinction as a lawyer."[50] McReynolds did, however, have the strong support of Louis Brandeis.[51]

McReynolds's tenure as attorney general was made miserable[52] and "stormy"[53] by his moral rigidity and his utter failure "to comprehend the nature of practical political affairs."[54] He quarreled with other members of the Cabinet and government officials. "[T]he President discovered that he did not get along smoothly in harness with others. He appeared to lack the coöperative spirit, and he became unpopular with the leading members of the Senate and the House."[55] "Scornful of office seekers, Attorney General McReynolds offended Congressmen and Senators by being too busy to see them when they came to discuss matters of patronage."[56] He fought "with Senators who charged him with using secret agents to spy on Federal judges and influence their decisions and whom he defied by refusing in the public interest to supply information demanded of him."[57]

James Clark McReynolds

McReynolds threw out of his office a commissioner of the Interstate Commerce Commission in a dispute about whether the Commission should call Charles S. Mellen as a witness in its investigation of the New Haven Railroad system.[58] He wrangled with Nebraska Senator George Norris over a point of honor, spurning Norris's proffer of an apology.[59] He found it arduous and disagreeable "to superintend the publicity of the work of the Administration ... so that the people might know what the Government was doing."[60] He inadvertently sparked a firestorm of controversy when he carelessly authorized a continuance in the trial of the son of a high administration official. The son, who was married, was accused of violating the Mann Act because he had transported a 19-year-old woman across state lines for salacious purposes. The public was outraged. "Mr. McReynolds suddenly found himself accused of using his office to shield from prosecution the son of a prominent Democratic politician in the Government's service."[61]

McReynolds also created controversy by proposing to supplement the inadequate American Tobacco Company decree by imposing a progressive tax on the large remnants of the Tobacco Trust, which still dominated smaller independent tobacco producers.[62] McReynolds's proposal was denounced as "Socialism," as an "assassination of American industrial enterprise" that was "monstrous, oppressive."[63] His "drastic proposition" was attacked as inconsistent with "the Democratic idea of using the taxing power for no other purpose than for raising revenue,"[64] which strikingly was the basis of McReynolds own subsequent opposition as a justice to the use of federal taxing authority to enforce antinarcotic laws.[65] Wilson was described as "much chagrined and disturbed at what he considers the premature publication of the fact that a graduated tax is under consideration. He sent for the Attorney General this morning after reading in the morning papers that the market was panic-stricken by the suggestion that a graduated tax was to be applied on all monopoly products."[66]

All this in a little more than seventeen months in office. It is no wonder that the press labelled McReynolds "the weakling of the Cabinet"[67] and worried that he demonstrated "a capacity for serious mistakes which is alarming in a man occupying his position."[68] His "blazing indiscretion"[69] prompted comparison to the scandals that had engulfed Taft's Secretary of Interior Richard A. Ballinger.[70] There were calls for McReynolds's resignation.[71]

When Justice Horace Harmon Lurton died on July 12, 1914, Colonel House pushed strongly for McReynolds's nomination,[72] as did House's Texas friend Albert S. Burleson.[73] McReynolds's mistakes as attorney general were invariably those of political judgment. His indifference to the thoughts and feelings of others led him into endless miscalculations. Wilson might well have imagined that the political skills required for a Cabinet position were unnecessary for a Supreme Court justice.

There was general agreement that McReynolds had been an effective and dedicated trust-buster who believed that monopoly was "essentially wicked"[74] and who had sought to achieve "prices natural and not unnatural – to see them fixed by the laws of trade and not by combinations among producers."[75] In the weeks following Lurton's death, World War I broke out in Europe. Mrs. Wilson died on August 6 of Bright's disease, virtually incapacitating the president in grief. A distracted Wilson probably had little time to investigate or ponder McReynolds's political beliefs apart from his commitment to "natural" prices.[76]

Wilson took the easy path and nominated McReynolds on August 19.[77] In the famous words of Josephus Daniels, Wilson's secretary of the navy, "Wilson, having confidence in [McReynolds's] ability and integrity 'kicked him up stairs,' by making him Associate Justice of the Supreme Court, where he lived to be the sole exponent of the archaic rule of law."[78] McReynolds was confirmed on August 29, by a vote of 44–6.[79]

Wilson did indeed live to regret his appointment of McReynolds.[80] McReynolds was not a progressive. He held traditional Southern Democratic views. He was suspicious of official power, distrustful of the federal government, jealous of individual rights, and dedicated to traditional State prerogatives. The *New York World* shrewdly observed that "while Mr. McReynolds may not be classed as an extreme reactionary, he has repeatedly exhibited mental traits and inclinations that have given much comfort to reactionaries."[81] As Wilson also ought to have known, political skills are not irrelevant for the Supreme Court bench. This was the thrust of the charge leveled by the *New York Tribune* against Wilson when it argued that the president had made "a serious mistake in selecting for the Supreme Court bench a man of Mr. McReynolds's mental qualities and training. The Attorney General is essentially a partisan and a passionate one. ... The country has been glad to have an aggressive Attorney General, but even in that quasi-judicial post, Mr. McReynolds has displayed a temper for wrangling and a personal bitterness that have much hampered his accomplishments."[82]

By the time of the Taft Court, these deficiencies in McReynolds had become glaringly apparent. His personal idiosyncrasies, sheltered by lifetime tenure, blossomed into full-blown misanthropy. One summer's evening in 1924, McReynolds dined with Charles Sumner Hamlin, the first chair of the Federal Reserve Board, and Hamlin recorded the conversation in his diary:

> He talked in a rambling way attacking everything and everybody. He said that Davis could not be elected; that Judge McKenna was in fairly good physical condition but "there was nothing here" (touching his head); that Judge Holmes was still all right mentally, but extremely narrow and shut out from the world & should have resigned long ago; that he had seriously considered introducing a motion to effect that no case should be referred to a judge, to write an opinion, who was over 75 years of age; that the Court must do something of this kind to preserve itself; that Brandeis, although able in a certain way, had no conception of the spirit of the common law and should never have been appointed; that he distrusted all Jews, as the oriental mind was entirely different from the Anglo-Saxon; that Jewish lawyers looked on law as if handed down from Zion.[83]

The immunity of the bench facilitated McReynolds's rapid descent into overt misogyny[84] and racism.[85] Cultivating "a flauntingly disagreeable character," he was "rude to attorneys, rude to his colleagues, rude to golfers who hurry him on the Chevy Chase links, and positively brutal to anyone who lights a cigarette within twenty feet of his gangling and sinisterly handsome presence."[86]

James Clark McReynolds

Confined within the close quarters of the Court, such behavior was almost intolerable.[87] Brandeis observed that McReynolds had become "The Court's problem. Van D. takes him in hand often – he worries the Ct because of his offensiveness to counsel & in his opinions, & a sensitive temperament like Holmes is positively pained. Holmes now explains him as a 'savage' with all the irrational impulses of a savage. The Chief complains that McR. is everyday becoming more 'meticulous' as to others though his own opinions are simply dreadful."[88]

Taft was deeply offended by McReynolds's "masterful, domineering, inconsiderate and bitter nature."[89] Although Taft was not sorry to see Clarke retire, he disliked the "insulting and overbearing and contemptuous" behavior by which McReynolds had driven Clarke from the bench.[90] He confided to his daughter that "The man on the Court who is least like a colleague is McReynolds. He is a bachelor – selfish to the last degree, an able man, but fuller of prejudice than any man I have known, and one who seems to delight in making others uncomfortable. He has no high sense of duty. He has a continual grouch, and is always offended because the Court is doing something that he regards as undignified, and really seems to have less of a loyal spirit to the Court than anybody."[91]

Before joining the Court, McReynolds had prided himself on his driving work ethic.[92] But the privileges of judicial life rendered McReynolds indolent.[93] "McReynolds is always trying to escape work," observed Taft.[94] Brandeis regarded McReynolds as "very dilatory in his work,"[95] reporting to Frankfurter that McReynolds was "lazy, stays away from Court when he doesn't feel like coming (more rearguments were ordered because McR was absent & didn't listen to arguments & called for a reargument)."[96] William O. Douglas called McReynolds "by nature the laziest person I ever knew."[97] No one denied that McReynolds had "real ability, and great sharpness of intellect."[98] Holmes believed that McReynolds "doesn't do himself justice in his opinions. He often is acute in suggestion and has worked on useful legislation."[99] The point was rather, as Taft complained, "he has been spoiled for usefulness."[100]

McReynolds's notorious anti-Semitism poisoned his relationship with Brandeis[101] and later with Cardozo[102] and Frankfurter.[103] Once in a return to a 1920 dissent circulated by Holmes and joined by Brandeis, in a case holding it unconstitutional to apply a new income tax to the salary of sitting federal judges, McReynolds penned a note saying, "Sorry to see *you* go wrong! Without reference to the present – did you ever think that for 4,000 years the Lord tried to make something out of Hebrews, then gave it up as impossible and turned them out to prey on mankind in general – like fleas on the dog, for example."[104]

The close quarters and ongoing necessities of Court life, however, did moderate somewhat the intensity of McReynolds's intolerance. In 1922, for example, Holmes could observe "a tacit *rapprochement* between McReynolds and Brandeis of which I am glad."[105] In 1923, Holmes remarked that "McReynolds has improved wonderfully and I think is a useful and quite suggestive man. He has some special knowledge and experience and his doubts and difficulties are always worth considering. He controls his impulses much more than at first and now that Clarke has gone, with whom he couldn't get along (queer, for they both are kindly men), and with the present C.J. things go as smoothly as possible."[106] For his part, Brandeis, who had a very tough skin,[107] found McReynolds intriguing, "one of the most interesting men on the present Court."

> He would have given Balzac great joy. I watch his face closely & at times, with his good features, he has a look of manly beauty, of intellectual beauty & at other times he looks like a moron and an infantile moron. I've seen him struggle painfully to think & to express himself & just can't do it coherently. There is the greatest play about his countenance, like the sky on a variable day. It's more than mere temperament, moodiness, however – of course, Holmes says "he isn't civilized – he is a primitive man."[108]

Holmes actually perceived McReynolds as a paradigmatic Southerner. "Poor McReynolds is, I think, a man of feeling and of more secret kindliness than he could get the credit for. But as is so common with Southerners, his own personality governs him without much thought of others when an impulse comes, and I think without sufficient regard for the proprieties of the Court."[109] There is no doubt that Holmes was at times personally exasperated by McReynolds's inconsiderate behavior.[110] But there were also moments when he was touched by McReynolds's kindness. When seriously ill and confined to bed due to his prostate operation in the summer of 1922, for example, Holmes received a surprisingly gracious letter from McReynolds:

> To-night I first learned where you are.
> Of course, I am much distressed by your illness and want you please [to] know that my thoughts and best wishes stand by you every moment. I like to hope that modern surgery will soon restore you to health and happiness where everybody wants to keep you many, many years. There are no more like you and we need you all the time.
> Now and then you will get into the wrong road – but you follow it with such gentle kindness that it is not possible to upbraid you! In fact you almost persuade even me to go with you.
> My affections to you and my admiration of your wonderful qualities is very great.[111]

Even four years later, Holmes could recall that "When I was in hospital [McReynolds] wrote a charming letter to me, which I shall not soon forget."[112] Brandeis was fascinated by McReynolds's strange susceptibility to pain, even as he caused pain to all around him.[113]

If one aspect of "Wilson's mistake"[114] was McReynolds's flagrantly nonjudicial temperament, the other more important dimension of Wilson's folly was McReynolds's rigid and unyielding view of the Constitution. Although himself conservative, Taft nevertheless believed that "we ought not to have too many men on the Court who are as reactionary on the subject of the Constitution as McReynolds."[115] Viewed from the vantage of the titanic constitutional struggles of the New Deal, it is tempting simply to lump McReynolds together with the other three members of what Learned Hand once called "the battalion of death"[116] – Van

James Clark McReynolds

Devanter, Sutherland, and Butler. But close analysis of the Taft Court shows that at least in the 1920s any such classification would be a serious oversimplification.

Figure P-1, for example, indicates that McReynolds was paired with Stone in being less likely to join or author a Taft Court opinion than any justice except Clarke and Brandeis. During the 1921–1928 terms, McReynolds was on board only 94% of the time, as compared to Van Devanter, who was on board in 98.7% of the cases in which he participated; Sutherland, who was on board in 96.7% of cases; and Butler, who was on board in 97.8% of cases. McReynolds clearly presents a different profile than these other three conservative justices. If we look at the justices with whom McReynolds was most likely to be aligned, however, Figure II-12 shows us that in published cases he was most frequently alongside of Sutherland (93.7%), Van Devanter (93.6%), or Butler (93.4%).

Figure II-13 demonstrates that in conference McReynolds was more likely to vote with Van Devanter (72.2%), Butler (71.5%) and Taft (70.6%) than with any other justices[a]. But Figure II-6 shows that, in absolute terms, McReynolds was far more reluctant than his peers (apart from McKenna) to join with *any* other justice in conference. Indeed, while McReynolds voted with Van Devanter in 72% of the conference cases,[117] Van Devanter voted in conference with Butler in 89% of cases, a loyalty that was exactly reciprocated. Perhaps as a consequence, McReynolds was

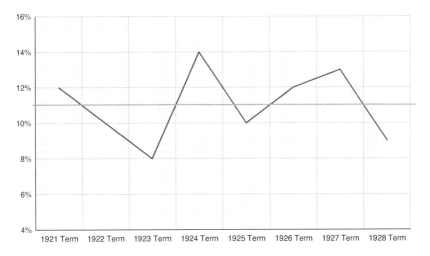

Figure II-11 Percentage of Court's opinions authored by McReynolds, by term. An even distribution of cases would assign 1/9, or 11%, to each justice.

---

[a] Curiously, McReynolds was far less likely to concur with Sutherland in conference than in published decisions. McReynolds joined Sutherland in only 65.4% of decisions in conference, as distinguished with 93.7% of published decisions. *Compare* Figure II-12 and Figure II-13.

THE TAFT COURT

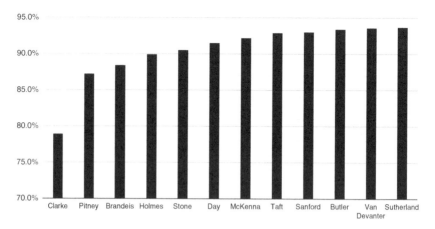

Figure II-12 Percentage of decisions in which McReynolds participated and joined the same opinion as another justice, 1921–1928 terms

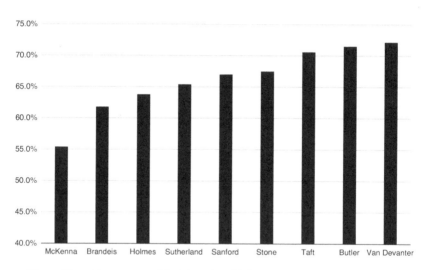

Figure II-13 Percentage of decisions in which McReynolds participated and voted with another justice in conference

more willing than any other justice – apart from McKenna, whose "oscillations" so aggravated Holmes[118] – to switch his vote in conference to join a Court opinion, as is illustrated in Figure I-9.[119] Yet McReynolds was also far more willing than any other justice on the Taft Court to stand out as the sole dissenter in a case, as Figure II-14 demonstrates.[120]

James Clark McReynolds

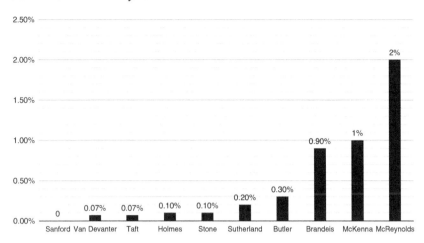

Figure II-14 Percentage of decisions in which a justice participates and chooses to be the only dissenter, 1921–1928 terms

The evidence suggests that during the 1920s McReynolds was largely in coalition with Van Devanter, Butler, Sutherland, and Taft, but also that he was more than willing to stand up for his own distinctive beliefs. The question is thus how McReynolds's beliefs differed from those of his conservative colleagues.

Any answer must begin with McReynolds's distinctively Campbellite heritage,[121] which lent an intense and intolerant moralism to his perception of the world.[122] It is entirely characteristic that in 1935, as the New Deal crisis was gathering steam, McReynolds could open his address to the assembled Bar of Tennessee with prayer – "May we recall the admonition of the great Apostle Paul 'Hold fast to that which is true'" – and close his address with the thought that "The great court where I am now is struggling through a period of intense difficulty. It finds itself confronted day by day with problems which were unknown a little while ago but yet it finds solution from them by resort to those old principles of honor, integrity and justice which have guided the world since the star of Bethlehem first led the wise men to Jerusalem."[123]

The Court, according to McReynolds, could find its path only by resorting to traditional moral truths. These truths were embodied in the common law. For McReynolds, "the moral and legal universes were coincidental."[124] A greater contrast to the positivism of Holmes could not be imagined. McReynolds lived and breathed the fusion of law and morality. McReynolds derived his conception of moral truths from the customary practices of ordinary and normal life, which exemplified "the natural and inherent principles of practical justice which lie at the base of our traditional jurisprudence and inspirit our Constitution."[125] Throughout the 1920s, and especially in the context of prohibition, the Taft Court was torn between the positive law of legislation and the ethical authority of such traditional moral verities. McReynolds differed from his conservative brethren in his unrelenting commitment to the latter.

Take, for example, the otherwise trivial case of *Morse Dry Dock & Repair Co. v. The Northern Star*. The issue in the case was whether, in a contest for access to the assets of a vessel, priority should lie with a lien for repairs or instead with the holder of a mortgage against the ship. Ordinarily the mortgage would take priority, but a recent statute, the Ship Mortgage Act,[126] specifically stated that a mortgage should not be preferred, even if the existence of the mortgage was apparent in the ship's papers, until it had been indorsed by the collector of customs of the port of documentation. The mortgage of *The Northern Star*, although included with the ship's papers, had not been indorsed. Holmes following the clear terms of the statute, conceded that "the statute taken literally may work harshly if by any oversight or otherwise the collector does not do his duty.... But the words of the statute seem to us too clear to be escaped.... We see no room for construction, and there is nothing for the courts to do but to bow their heads and obey."[127]

McReynolds, however, refused to bow his head and obey. It was sufficient for him that the repair company should have possessed constructive knowledge of the mortgage. Resisting the plain words of the statute, McReynolds insisted that "the purpose of this enactment was to protect honest furnishers who exercise diligence, and not to offer a wide-opened door for crooked transactions."[128] The impulse to fuse law with justice was too urgent for McReynolds. But in this instinct he was quite alone. Sutherland, Van Devanter, Butler, and Taft all joined with Holmes to acknowledge the gap between positive law and moral righteousness.[129]

Goltra v. Weeks illustrates a similar point. *Goltra* involved the federal government's repossession of a fleet of towboats and barges that had been leased under stringent conditions, including a right of repossession if, in the judgment of the secretary of war, the lessee had not complied with relevant terms and conditions. Invoking this right, the secretary ordered the fleet repossessed. A military officer promptly removed the vessels across the Mississippi river out of the jurisdiction of the Missouri District Court in which the lessee had brought a suit in equity to challenge the repossession. Taft, interpreting the contract as if it were "between private persons," held it to be "harsh" but "valid and binding," and the repossession therefore proper.[130]

McReynolds, by contrast, could hardly contain himself.

> Theoretically, everybody in this land is subject to the law. But of what value is the theory, if performances like those revealed by this record go unrebuked?
>
> An army officer, having inflated himself into judge and executioner, decided that a fleet of towboats and barges lying in the Mississippi river at St. Louis ought no longer to remain in the custody of a private citizen, who held possession of them under a solemn lease and contract of sale from the United States, and who, in order to make them operative, had expended upon them $40,000 of his own money. Then, waiting until a Sunday arrived, he proceeded to grab the vessels by force and endeavored to run them beyond the jurisdiction of the court.
>
> Action like that is familiar under autocracies, but the prevalent idea has been that we live under a better system.[131]

James Clark McReynolds

Taft's opinion for the Court is constructed along normal, even banal lines of legal reasoning. It uses precedents to articulate legal principles establishing the bounds of permissible contract provisions and remedies. McReynolds's dissent altogether sidesteps this approach. It fashions a simple, striking narrative in which an overweening government officer oppresses an innocent lessee. The moral urgency of the story displaces ordinary legal analysis. Yet McReynolds dissented alone. Taft, Sutherland, Butler, and Van Devanter would not follow him down that path.

The same moralism that suffused McReynolds's opinions in *The Northern Star* and *Goltra* permeated all aspects of his judicial work. He opposed trusts, for example, because they were "essentially wicked."[132] What made them wicked was that they produced "those abnormal contracts and combinations which tend directly to suppress the conflict for advantage called competition – the play of the contending forces ordinarily engendered by an honest desire for gain."[133] Lacking a theory of consumer welfare maximization, McReynolds instead extoled the virtues of *normal* contracts and an *honest* desire for gain.

McReynolds detested the newly constituted Federal Trade Commission ("FTC") precisely because it sought to regulate competition without regard to these common-sense values.[134] Thus in the important case of *FTC v. Gratz*, McReynolds declared for the Court:

> The words "unfair method of competition" are not defined by the statute and their exact meaning is in dispute. It is for the courts, not the commission, ultimately to determine as matter of law what they include. They are clearly inapplicable to practices never heretofore regarded as opposed to good morals because characterized by deception, bad faith, fraud, or oppression, or as against public policy because of their dangerous tendency unduly to hinder competition or create monopoly. The act was certainly not intended to fetter free and fair competition as commonly understood and practiced by honorable opponents in trade.[135]

In vain did Brandeis protest that the Federal Trade Commission Act specifically prohibited "unfair methods of competition," rather than merely acts of "unfair competition," which the Sherman Act already proscribed. Because the public had come to believe that the Sherman Act was "largely ineffective," Brandeis explained that Congress had created the new Commission "in the hope of remedying conditions in business which a great majority of the American people regarded as menacing the general welfare, and which for more than a generation they had vainly attempted to remedy by the ordinary processes of law." Unlike a court, the FTC was meant to serve a "prophylactic" purpose; its mission was "to intervene, before any act should be done or condition arise violative of the Anti-Trust Act."[136] The FTC was created to regulate acts which were not immoral in themselves, but which nevertheless needed to be controlled to prevent threats to competition.

McReynolds would have none of it. He did not believe that government could be "intrusted" with the "management"[137] of ordinary business practices long deemed honorable and acceptable.[138] In his eyes, government was authorized to regulate only dishonorable acts, and courts alone had the capacity to distinguish moral from immoral acts. Only courts could discern "the elements of society springing directly

THE TAFT COURT

from habit and custom" that deserved respect and recognition.[139] Courts acquired this capacity from their long experience articulating common law rights, which in theory directly expressed traditional mores. Because McReynolds regarded the Fourteenth Amendment as "intended to preserve and protect fundamental rights long recognized under the common law system,"[140] he incorporated this affirmation of customary morals directly into his constitutional jurisprudence.

McReynolds believed that the Constitution prohibited state regulation of the "liberty to enter into *normal* contracts, long regarded, not only as essential to the freedom of trade and commerce, but also as beneficial to the public."[141] He thus struck down a Minnesota statute prohibiting price discrimination by milk buyers on the ground that it prevented a dairy corporation "from carrying on its business in the usual way heretofore regarded as both moral and beneficial to the public and not shown now to be accompanied by evil results as ordinary incidents."[142]

The most memorable example of McReynolds's fusion of law, custom, and morality was his dissent in the Gold Clause cases.[143] We know from his 1896 congressional campaign how deeply McReynolds cared about the gold standard. On the day that the Court's opinion in the Gold Clause cases was announced, McReynolds set aside his written text and held a packed courtroom "spellbound," speaking extemporaneously for about half an hour.[144] Although there is no official record of his remarks,[145] and although contemporaneous accounts differ in details,[146] all agree that McReynolds's speech bristled "with scorn and indignation" as he denounced the "repudiation of national obligations" as "abhorrent."[147] Congressional power to regulate currency, he said, is "intended to give Congress the power to meet its honest obligations.... But here we have a monetary system – the intent, I almost said the wickedness of which is almost beyond comprehension.... That never was the law. It never ought to be the law."[148] (In his written dissent, McReynolds also emphasized that "Loss of reputation for honorable dealing will bring us unending humiliation; the impending legal and moral chaos is appalling."[149])

McReynolds's recourse to extemporaneous discourse exemplified a Southern rhetorical tradition that presumed a common moral community between an orator and his audience.[150] Electrifying his audience, McReynolds brought life to that presumption. When he first became a justice in 1914, he invoked his experience as attorney general to urge that judges "take greater pains to explain things to the public so that it may appreciate the situation; and, in some way, I know not how, make all the world *understand* what is really going on in the courts." McReynolds wanted to entrench the judiciary "in the national esteem and confidence."[151] Making the law real to the public meant making it less technical, more comprehensible and responsive to common-sense, intuitive values.

As a justice, McReynolds often strove for those virtues in his own opinions. "I endeavor to confine my opinions to as few words as possible, so that they can be grasped easily at the first reading."[152] McKenna observed that "brevity is a passion with" McReynolds.[153] Figure II-2 illustrates that McReynolds's opinions were indeed brief; next to Holmes, his opinions were the shortest on the Taft Court. It is true that McReynolds's opinions often have a cut-and-paste feel about them,[154] but when they touched on issues that mattered to him, McReynolds would typically include a nugget of earthy prose meant for quotation and designed forcibly to convey the pith of the decision. This is especially true of McReynolds's dissents. If Holmes in his opinions strove for elegance and originality, McReynolds aimed to incite his audience.

In *Oregon-Washington R.R. & Navigation Co. v. Washington*, for example, the Court held that federal legislation preempted Washington's ability to quarantine alfalfa in order to prevent the spread of the alfalfa weevil. McReynolds dissented: "It is a serious thing to paralyze the efforts of a state to protect her people against impending calamity, and leave them to the slow charity of a far-off and perhaps supine federal bureau. No such purpose should be attributed to Congress, unless indicated beyond reasonable doubt."[155] McReynolds's dissent was short – less than 150 words – but it was well calculated to move public opinion. Congress amended the statute within six weeks.[156]

McReynolds's moralism aspired to close the gap between ordinary social understanding and law as a means of social control. McReynolds loathed Brandeis's embrace of the administrative state precisely because it repudiated this aspiration. If Brandeis strove for the warrant of expertise, McReynolds demanded the more immediate authority of ordinary morals. This is probably why McReynolds complained that Brandeis had "no conception of the spirit of the common law,"[157] a spirit that for McReynolds spoke always in the accents of received ethical beliefs.

Carried to an extreme – and McReynolds was in no degree moderate – loyalty to existing beliefs forecloses analytic distance and self-conscious reflection. That is why McReynolds's friend Dean Acheson was accurate to observe that "All of the Justice's thoughts were matters of passionate prejudice. They weren't merely economic prejudices; everything was a prejudice."[158] All the conservative justices on the Taft Court may have agreed that the prerogatives of local state authority should be preserved, but only McReynolds regularly insisted on referring to the "United States" as a plural rather than as a singular noun.[159]

McReynolds's impulse to moralize ordinary market relationships was widely shared by his conservative colleagues on the Court. But other conservative justices on the Court were more willing than McReynolds to accept the need for self-conscious modifications of existing social relationships. A good example of how this question split the conservative wing of the Taft Court is *Cudahy Packing Co. v. Parramore*, which addressed the question of whether it was constitutional to hold an employer liable under a Utah workmen's compensation law for an accident that happened on land not owned by the employer, but rather on a route that was "the only practicable way of ingress and egress for employees." Sutherland's analysis for the Court was incisive and comprehending:

> The modern development and growth of industry, with the consequent changes in the relations of employer and employee, have been so profound in character and degree as to take away, in large measure, the applicability of the doctrines upon which rest the common-law liability of the master for personal injuries to a servant.... Workmen's Compensation legislation rests upon the idea of status, not upon that of implied contract.... The liability is based, not upon any act or omission of the employer, but upon the existence of the relationship which

the employee bears to the employment because of and in the course of which he has been injured. And this is not to impose liability upon one person for an injury sustained by another with which the former has no connection; but it is to say that it is enough if there be a causal connection between the injury and the business in which he employes the latter.... Legislation which imposes liability for an injury thus related to the employment, among other justifying circumstances, has a tendency to promote a more equitable distribution of the economic burdens in cases of personal injury or death resulting from accidents in the course of industrial employment, and is a matter of sufficient public concern to escape condemnation as arbitrary, capricious, or clearly unreasonable.[160]

Sutherland saw that new conditions of large-scale industrial manufacture had rendered irrelevant the traditional moralism of the common law, which was compelling only in a world where personal responsibility was a practical and operative ideal. In the face of giant aggregations of capital that effectively and unilaterally structured conditions of work, the ideal of personal responsibility had become largely fictional with respect to questions of workplace safety. In such contexts, therefore, Sutherland wrote that the operative question ought to be the "equitable distribution of the economic burdens" of inevitable industrial accidents. Pragmatic and worldly, Taft and Van Devanter joined Sutherland in upholding the application of the Utah statute. But McReynolds and Butler dissented. For McReynolds, it was "the duty of courts to uphold the old" way of seeing things.[161]

Throughout his time on the Taft Court, McReynolds stood as an unrelenting avatar of the old way of doing things. McReynolds was committed to the coincidence of law and morality, which he believed was best expressed in traditional common law allocations of rights. He differed from his conservative brethren primarily in the unremitting purity of these commitments. Although colleagues like Taft or Sutherland well recognized and respected the moralism of the market and of the ordinary, normal way of doing things, they also acknowledged the need for modern managerial interventions. This flexibility no doubt stemmed in part from the fact that they viewed the market not merely as set of moral commitments, but also as a structure of incentives designed to increase wealth. This underlying instrumentalism may perhaps have made them more tolerant of legislation that sought to respond to changes in industrial conditions in ways that did not unduly retard what they regarded as necessary incentives.

McReynolds stood apart from his conservative colleagues in his temperamental inclination to de-emphasize the purely instrumental aspects of the market. He was a moralist down to the ground. By the Taft Court era, McReynolds's moral commitments had catapulted him into a full-scale crusade. He had been shocked by wartime regulation and by the Bolshevik revolution – by the passing of "the halcyon days before the great war."[162] By 1923, McReynolds was prepared to go to the mattresses. He lectured his fellow Tennessee lawyers that "the rising tide, if left unchecked, would sweep us to into anarchy.... [I]f we fail, and the men like us fail, Russia presents the future picture. Look ahead, gentlemen, and make your choice. If you believe in the things handed to you by the fathers, gird on your swords and fight for them. If you believe in something else, say so and let us have the end."[163]

James Clark McReynolds
Notes

1. Lewis L. Gould, Willis Van Devanter in Wyoming Politics 185–267 (Ph.D. Dissertation, Yale University 1966).
2. *Mr. McReynolds' Vanity*, NASHVILLE AMERICAN (November 1, 1896), at 2.
3. *McReynolds in the Race*, NASHVILLE AMERICAN (October 23, 1896), at 5.
4. *McReynolds' First Speech*, NASHVILLE BANNER (October 24, 1896), at 1.
5. *See supra* Chapter 6, at note 74.
6. Attorney General Clark, *Proceedings in the Supreme Court of the United States in Memory of Mr. Justice McReynolds*, 334 U.S. xix (1948).
7. *Id.* at xvii. During the 1896 election, McReynolds distributed a circular announcing that "the brief time before the election will not permit me to visit all of the civil districts in the seven counties, and it is necessary for me to ask, by letter the active assistance of gentlemen in whose public spirit and good judgment I have confidence.... *A district like this is entitled to a Representative of whom its people will not be ashamed and I think that my election would insure them at least that much.* If you can aid me in your community and county, I shall greatly appreciate it, and I will especially thank you if you will do what you can in the way of looking after my interests at the polls on the day of election." *Mr. McReynolds' Vanity, supra* note 2 (emphasis added). A supporter of the regular Democratic candidate sent a copy of this leaflet to the local paper, and, stressing the italicized passage, marveled at how one "could embrace more egotism and vanity in so short a sentence." "However," he continued, "it is in keeping with Mr. McReynolds' deportment towards his fellow-man. They should bow to his royalty.... McReynolds! What a jewel!" *Id.*
8. Meyer v. Nebraska, 262 U.S. 390, 399 (1923).
9. Arizona Copper Co. v. Hammer, 250 U.S. 400, 450 (1919) (McReynolds, J., dissenting).
10. Nebbia v. New York, 291 U.S. 505, 554–55 (1934) (McReynolds, J., dissenting).
11. *Arizona Copper Co.*, 250 U.S. at 450–51 (McReynolds, J., dissenting). For the similar views of prominent conservative jurists, see *supra* Chapter 5, at 169 and note 119.
12. Calvin P. Jones, *Kentucky's Irascible Conservative: Supreme Court Justice James Clark McReynolds*, 57 FILSON CLUB HISTORY QUARTERLY 20, 21 (1983).
13. JAMES E. BOND, I DISSENT: THE LEGACY OF CHIEF JUSTICE JAMES CLARK MCREYNOLDS 6 (Fairfax: George Mason University Press 1992); *James C. McReynolds: Last of the Old Guard*, 5 SUPREME COURT HISTORICAL SOCIETY QUARTERLY 4, 5 (Winter 1983).
14. ALEXANDER M. BICKEL & BENNO C. SCHMIDT, Jr., THE JUDICIARY AND RESPONSIBLE GOVERNMENT 1910–1921, at 342 (New York: MacMillan Publishing Co. 1984).
15. Stephen Tyree Early, James Clark McReynolds and the Judicial Process 27 (Ph.D. Dissertation, University of Virginia 1954). It is also said that the "outstanding characteristic" of McReynolds's mother, Ellen Reeves McReynolds, was "a dominance of will which subordinated those around her." *Id.* at 24.
16. Burton J. Hendrick, *James C. McReynolds: Attorney-General and Believer in the Sherman Law*, 27 WORLD'S WORK 27 (November 1913).
17. Early, *supra* note 15, at 26–27.
18. *Id.* at 27–30. Yet it is also said that John McReynolds engaged in many acts of private charity, like the treatment of indigent patients. When his slaves were freed in

the aftermath of the Civil War, John McReynolds bought a farm in Julian, Kentucky, "to provide a home for the freedman." *Id.* at 28–29. *See* BOND, *supra* note 13, at 5. William O. Douglas observed that Justice McReynolds displayed similar tendencies. He "had ... a kind streak. He was extremely charitable to the pages who worked at the Court, and very tender in his relationship toward children." WILLIAM O. DOUGLAS, THE AUTOBIOGRAPHY OF WILLIAM O. DOUGLAS: THE COURT YEARS 1937–1975, at 13 (New York: Random House 1980). *See Remarks of George Wharton Pepper*, in PROCEEDINGS OF THE BAR AND OFFICERS OF THE SUPREME COURT OF THE UNITED STATES IN MEMORY OF JAMES CLARK MCREYNOLDS 25–26 (Washington D.C. 1947) ("PROCEEDINGS").

19. Quoted in James B. Morrow, *No Arbitrary Rule Can Be Made for Breaking Up All the Trusts*, CINCINNATI ENQUIRER (October 19, 1913), at C7. "My father," McReynolds said, "was a model of all that is required to make a man." 22 VANDERBILT ALUMNUS 3 (No. 8) (June 1937). He added that "My mother was a woman lovely in figure, lovely in spirit, superb in her religious belief." *Id. See supra* note 15.

20. Quoted in Morrow, *supra* note 19, at C7. Years later, McReynolds would write his younger brother: "This is father's birthday – 92 years ago. Would that he were back in health and strength. I've missed no other as I have him." JCM to R.O. McReynolds (March 30, 1919) (McReynolds papers at the University of Virginia) ("Virginia McReynolds papers").

21. Early, *supra* note 15, at 36–37. It is well to remember this history as one evaluates McReynolds's opinion in Pierce v. Society of Sisters, 268 U.S. 510 (1925), which struck down an Oregon law prohibiting private schooling between the ages of 8 and 16.

22. James C. McReynolds, 3 VANDERBILT ALUMNUS 237 (No. 8) (June 1918).

23. Doris Ariane Blaisdell, The Constitutional Law of Mr. Justice McReynolds 6–8 (Ph.D. Dissertation, University of Wisconsin 1952).

24. *Id.* at 11–18; Early, *supra* note 15, at 43–48. Throughout his life, McReynolds regarded Minor as "a great man and a remarkable teacher, having as sound and true an influence on the young men of the South as had Theodore W. Dwight on the young men of the North." Quoted in Morrow, *supra* note 19, at C7.

25. BOND, *supra* note 13, at 18.

26. *Id.* at 21.

27. JCM to Jacob M. Dickenson (February 8, 1896) (Dickinson papers at the Tennessee State Library & Archives) ("Things are very dull in the legal line here, and I am almost tempted to look for a job at a dollar per day.").

28. James B. McCraw, Jr., Justice McReynolds and the Supreme Court: 1914–1941, at 23 (Ph.D. Dissertation, University of Texas 1949).

29. *Id.* at 23–27. *See* JCM to Jacob M. Dickenson (April 6, 1903) (Dickinson papers at the Tennessee State Library & Archives).

30. Hendrick, *supra* note 16, at 28–29; BOND, *supra* note 13, at 30–31; McCraw, *supra* note 28, at 27–30.

31. *McReynolds, The Man Who Is Busy Unscrambling Eggs*, 56 CURRENT OPINION 107 (February 1914).

32. In his Brief McReynolds contended:

> The Sherman Act applies when the direct result or necessary tendency of the prohibited thing is the material obstruction, hindrance or restraint of interstate

or foreign commerce. ... Whether such obstruction, hindrance, restraint or tendency exists must be determined by the court in each case presented upon all the facts in evidence; conclusion should depend upon practical, not mere theoretical considerations, and necessarily will be influenced by the status of commerce and the public policy existing at the time. That which did not restrain commerce fifty years ago may do so to-day.

Brief for the United States in United States v. American Tobacco Company (Nos. 118, 119), October Term, 1910, at 49. McReynolds added that "Monopoly is a practical conception, and its existence must be determined by practical considerations, keeping in view the purposes and methods of business." *Id.* at 300.

33. As McReynolds later wrote in a memorandum for a client:

> It seems fairly plain that in [the Standard Oil and American Tobacco Cases] special effort was made to rest the decisions on a basis sufficiently narrow to secure approval by the entire Court. Much said about intent, wrongful purpose, etc., probably was necessary to make them acceptable to Justice Holmes, whose well-known views touching combinations in restraint of trade were announced in his dissent in the Northern Securities Case. ... Upon the facts found by the Court the combination in both cases was within Justice Holmes' definition and *in the Tobacco Cases, at least, the bill was framed and the evidence taken with a special view to satisfying that definition.*

James C. McReynolds, Opinion Prepared for Mr. F.L. Stetson, General Counsel, United States Steel Co. (December 20, 1911) (Virginia McReynolds papers) (emphasis added). *See* Early, *supra* note 15, at 167–68.

34. Quoted in Morrow, *supra* note 19, at C7. Dispositive law, said McReynolds, "is the law as interpreted by the Judges, who are human beings. Every man has grooves in which his thought works. He has a mental policy.... When the man happens to be a Judge, the lawyers who practice in his Court should not alone comprehend the law, but should comprehend the man equally as well. The law of a case, I was cautioned many years since by a very successful trial lawyer ... is sometimes entirely outside the books." *Id.*

35. McCraw, *supra* note 28, at 31–36.

36. *"Our Triumph Is Complete"*, BOSTON DAILY GLOBE (May 30, 1911), at 16.

37. *Tobacco Hearing Set for Oct. 30*, CHICAGO DAILY TRIBUNE (October 17, 1911), at 13. *See Tobacco Plan Fit for Scrap Heap – M'Reynolds*, NEW YORK TRIBUNE (October 17, 1911), at 2. At the time, Wickersham released a mealy statement about ensuring "full and free competition." *Rule for Big Trust*, WASHINGTON POST (October 17, 1911), at 3. McReynolds was forced to declare that "the rumor of a disagreement on the question between Attorney General Wickersham and James C. McReynolds" was "silly." *Talk of Tobacco Fight*, NEW YORK TRIBUNE (October 20, 1911), at 4.

38. *Wickersham Favors Tobacco Plan with His Modifications*, WALL STREET JOURNAL (November 1, 1911), at 1.

39. *Wickersham Amends Tobacco Trust Plan*, NEW YORK TIMES (October 31, 1911), at 14. McReynolds, "who has roundly denounced the Tobacco Trust's plan," refused to sign the government's response. *Id.* Brandeis commented to his wife at the time that he had just had "a long talk with Ass Atty Genl McReynolds who ought to be running the Tobacco Case & is not allowed to. He tried to say little, but I am sure has no more confidence in G[eorge]. W[ickersham]'s doing what 'the people' want than a rampant insurgent." *See*

LDB to Alice Goldmark Brandeis (October 21, 1911), in BRANDEIS FAMILY LETTERS, at 173–74. Brandeis believed that "In Tobacco Wickersham & Taft have behave[d] a la their mode. As Ollie Jame says, 'Left-handed with both hands.'" LDB to Alice Goldmark Brandeis (November 16, 1911), in BRANDEIS FAMILY LETTERS, at 176.

40. *Wickersham Favors Tobacco Plan with His Modifications*, supra note 38, at 6. McReynolds was described as "visibly embarrassed. Independent tobacco interests urged that he attack [the plan] in court, but he told them that he could not attack it without resigning as assistant to Mr. Wickersham, who was supporting it, and that if he did resign he would have no standing in court. He took the position that the Government was his client, and that if the client, through his superior officer, decided to take a certain stand, he could not contest its action any more than a lawyer can go contrary to the decision of a private client." *J.C. M'Reynolds, The New Preceptor for the Trusts*, NEW YORK TIMES (March 9, 1913), at 56. It was said at the time that McReynolds "always prefers an ax to a pruning-knife." 46 LITERARY DIGEST 734 (March 29, 1913).

41. *Wickersham Favors Tobacco Plan with His Modifications*, supra note 38, at 1; *Government Fights Tobacco Trust Plan*, NEW YORK TIMES (October 26, 1911), at 20. The following year, as Attorney General, McReynolds articulated his objections to the Wickersham plan. *J.C. M'Reynolds, The New Preceptor for the Trusts*, supra note 40:

> "What we are trying to do," he said, "is to unwind the ball of yarn you gentlemen have been so busily winding up all these years."
>
> "But," objected the Trust lawyers, "whom can we sell these properties to except the men who built up the business? Who else is there with sufficient capital to buy them?"
>
> "That is your problem," replied Mr. McReynolds. "You bought them in violation of law. Don't ask me to find you a purchaser. I don't care whom you sell them to, so long as you sell them and don't sell them to yourselves. If a court orders a horse sold, it doesn't usually go out and find somebody to buy it."
>
> "But how can we carry out this decree?" persisted the lawyers.
>
> "I don't know how you'll do it," said Mr. McReynolds. "But I can tell you what will happen to you if you don't carry it out. The court will appoint a receiver and sell you out, as the Sherman law provides."
>
> When the lawyers argued that to meet Mr. McReynolds's views would involve a destruction of property rights of the individual defendants, and that this would amount to confiscation, he exclaimed:
>
> "Confiscation? What if it is! Since when has property illegally and criminally acquired come to have any rights?"

42. "These years of ... litigation so ably conducted by the special assistant, Mr. J.C. McReynolds, have been rendered worse than futile by the decree now entered with the approval of the Attorney General." Louis Brandeis, *The Law and the Tobacco Trust: Louis D. Brandeis, Speaks His Opinion of the Outcome of the Government's Case*, NEW YORK TIMES (January 7, 1912), at AFR20. *See Trust's Royal Gift*, WASHINGTON POST (December 16, 1911), at 1 ("The Attorney General came in for a good share of criticism by Mr. Brandeis for his approval of the dissolution decree in the tobacco case."); *Judge Gary Denies the Report*, CINCINNATI ENQUIRER (December 16, 1911), at 1 ("'The trust now is in better shape than it was before

the suit was brought,' replied Mr. Brandeis, smiling, 'for its illegal acts have been legalized.'"); THE CURSE OF BIGNESS: MISCELLANEOUS PAPERS OF LOUIS D. BRANDEIS 101–3 (Osmond K. Fraenkel, ed., New York: Viking Press 1934).
43. JCM to George W. Wickersham (October 30, 1911) (Virginia McReynolds papers). See BOND, *supra* note 13, at 35.
44. *Trust Prosecutor Resigns*, NEW YORK TIMES (January 7, 1912), at 6. "Mr. McReynolds said yesterday that the Tobacco case had been drawn out a couple of years longer than he expected when he first undertook the prosecution, and he had originally expected to retire from the Government service at a considerably earlier date. At the request of Attorney General Wickersham, he continued his work until the plan of disintegration had been decided on by the court." *Id.*
45. 1912 Democratic Party Platform, available at www.presidency,ucsb.edu/docu ments/1912-democratic-party-platform.
46. Early, *supra* note 15, at 176. To his friends, McReynolds "had the temperament, the courage and the persistence of Andrew Jackson whom he much resembled. He had the same fervor for his beliefs, the same antagonism toward his opponents, and the same forcefulness in his determination." LOUIS S. LEVY, YESTERDAYS 98 (New York: Literary Publishers 1954).
47. Wilson's first choice was likely Louis Brandeis. *See* ALPHEUS THOMAS MASON, BRANDEIS: A FREE MAN'S LIFE 385–94 (New York: The Viking Press 1956).
48. WILLIAM G. MCADOO, CROWDED YEARS: THE REMINISCENCES OF WILLIAM G. MCADOO 183 (Boston: Houghton Mifflin Co. 1931). *See* McCraw, *supra* note 28, at 43–47; Blaisdell, *supra* note 23, at 53–59; 1 THE INTIMATE PAPERS OF COLONEL HOUSE: ARRANGED AS A NARRATIVE BY CHARLES SEYMOUR 90–91, 97, 107, 109 (Boston: Houghton Mifflin Co. 1926); JAMES KERNEY, THE POLITICAL EDUCATION OF WOODROW WILSON 296 (New York: The Century 1926) ("Single-handed, House put James Clark McReynolds of Tennessee over as attorney-general. Wilson had never seen him.").
49. JOSEPHUS DANIELS, THE WILSON ERA: YEARS OF PEACE – 1910–1917, at 115 (Chapel Hill: University of North Carolina Press 1944).
50. MCADOO, *supra* note 48, at 184.
51. Brandeis wrote Maurice Leon, "I had the pleasure of meeting Mr. McReynolds in connection with the Tobacco Trust Litigation, and know of his work in that and other connections. I have the highest opinion of his ability and character and should think the country would indeed be fortunate to have him fill the position of Attorney General." LDB to Maurice Leon (February 28, 1913), in 3 LETTERS OF LOUIS D. BRANDEIS, at 35. *See* LDB to Moses Edwin Clapp (March 5, 1913), *id.* at 39 ("McReynolds will make an excellent Attorney General. You may remember what I said of his work when speaking of the tobacco trust prosecution."). After McReynolds's appointment as attorney general, Brandeis wrote to congratulate him: "In deciding upon you for Attorney General President Wilson has made the wisest possible choice. Your record in trust prosecutions will assure the country that the President's trust policy will be carried out promptly and efficiently, and business be freed at last. We are indeed to be congratulated. I intend to call upon you soon, and hope you will have time to talk over our special New England needs." LDB to JCM (March 5, 1913), *id.* at 41. Brandeis evidently struck up enough of a relationship with McReynolds to work for him

for long periods of time, scouting out possible appointments, drafting legislation, and discussing potential cases. *See, e.g.,* LDB to Alfred Brandeis (March 10, 1913), in BRANDEIS FAMILY LETTERS, at 212; LDB to JCM (March 28, 1913), in 3 LETTERS OF LOUIS D. BRANDEIS, at 53; LDB to JCM (August 13, 1913), *id.* at 161; LDB to JCM (September 25, 1913), *id.* at 180; LDB to Alice Goldmark Brandeis (November 22, 1913), in BRANDEIS FAMILY LETTERS, at 221; LDB to Alice Goldmark Brandeis (November 24, 1913), *id.* at 224 ("The interview with the Atty. Genl. lasted 3 hours & only a part of the ground he wanted to cover was exhausted. ... I am to have a further conference with McReynolds later in the week."); LDB to Alice Goldmark Brandeis (December 28, 1913), *id.* at 232 ("1¼ hours with McReynolds"); LDB to JCM (February 22, 1914), in 3 LETTERS OF LOUIS D. BRANDEIS, at 247 ("Have been working as you requested on the so-called 'Trust Bills' and am handing you herewith my suggestions."); LDB to Alice Goldmark Brandeis (March 2, 1914), in BRANDEIS FAMILY LETTERS, at 242 ("McReynolds was very intelligent in his criticisms of the bill & much more helpful than [George Rublee], but he is very conservative. We didn't get very far, despite 3 hrs. conference, partly because he is a great time waster, by the way & largely because he is so tired out that he ought to be off in some vast wilderness."); LDB to Alice Goldmark Brandeis (March 19, 1914), *id.* at 243–44 ("I had an hour & a half with McReynolds on the trust bill & then another hour & a half walking & talking nothings on the Potomac flats. His trust discussion was intelligent but not courageous, & we shall not agree on what should be done re interlocking directors."). Two months before his nomination, McReynolds asked Brandeis "to act as Special Counsel to take charge of his Southern Pacific-Central Pacific dissolution case." LDB to Alice Goldmark Brandeis (June 9, 1914), *id.* at 251.

52. By the end of the year, McReynolds could publicly proclaim in a speech to the Tennessee Society that "I wonder if you know the toil and the sweat and the anxiety that goes with the honor of the place. I can assure that it is no bed of roses, and that the sorrows outweigh the joys." *M'Reynolds Talks of his Burden*, NEW YORK TIMES (December 7, 1913), at 22. After visiting with McReynolds in March 1914, Brandeis reported to his wife that "He is really pretty sick of his job & realizes that the volume of work imposes upon him the impossible." LDB to Alice Goldmark Brandeis (March 2, 1914), in BRANDEIS FAMILY LETTERS, at 242.

53. Dean Acheson, *McReynolds, a Terror in Court, Was a Kindly Man*, WASHINGTON POST (August 25, 1965), at A18.

54. Early, *supra* note 15, at 71, 73. For an account of McReynolds's tenure, see BOND, *supra* note 13, at 38–50. John W. Davis, who served under McReynolds when the latter was attorney general, later said that "No man ever had a more considerate, cooperative or encouraging chief. He was intensely interested in the work and problems of all of his subordinates, prompt with approval where approval was warranted and candid in criticism where criticism was deserved." *Remarks of John W. Davis*, in PROCEEDINGS, *supra* note 18, at 19.

55. MCADOO, *supra* note 48, at 184. McReynolds's relationship with McAdoo deteriorated badly over whether the Department of Justice or the Department of the Treasury should supervise the construction of a new Justice Department building; it is said that by the end the two could communicate with each other only through the president. Ernest Sutherland Bates, *McReynolds, Roberts and Hughes*, 87 NEW

James Clark McReynolds

REPUBLIC 232, 234 (1936); McCraw, *supra* note 28, at 81; KERNEY, *supra* note 48, at 296–97.

56. Bates, *supra* note 55, at 234. Soon after taking office, McReynolds was praised by Colonel House: "I cannot tell you how glad I am that we have a man like you at the helm with the courage and the ability to do the things as they should be done and not as the place hunters desire them." Edward M. House to JCM (March 8, 1913) (House papers at Yale University).
57. Acheson, *supra* note 53.
58. *M'Reynolds in Row Turns Back on Folk*, NEW YORK TIMES (May 14, 1914), at 4 ("Charles C. McChord, a member of the Interstate Commerce Commission, and Joseph W. Folk, ex-Governor of Missouri and the commission's general counsel, were practically ordered out of the office of Attorney General McReynolds to-day by Mr. McReynolds himself. . . . Later Mr. Folk said, with reference to Attorney General McReynolds: 'His conduct was such that we did not care to remain or have anything to say to him.'"). McReynolds appears to have been in the right, because Folk's insistence on examining the head of the notorious New York, New Haven, and Hartford Railroad, Charles S. Mellen, effectively gave the latter "a thorough immunity bath . . . and . . . placed him forever beyond the reach of prosecution for his part in the financial" misdeeds of the railroads. "'Governor Folk played directly into the hands of the railroad lawyers when he summoned Mellen and thereby extended immunity to him,' said a Department of Justice official to-day. 'Nothing has been developed by the examination of Mellen that was not already known to the Attorney General and his assistants. . . . Considerable publicity for Folk and immunity for Mellen are the only results thus far.'" *Mellen Immune, Says M'Reynolds*, NEW YORK TRIBUNE (May 22, 1914), at 2. *See New Haven Suit Ordered by Wilson, and Criminal Aspects to Grand Jury*, NEW YORK TRIBUNE (July 22, 1914), at 1 (quoting McReynolds's letter to Wilson to the effect that "Mellen, and perhaps others, flagrantly culpable, were put on the stand, and any criminal prosecutions hereafter instituted probably will be embarrassed by a claim of immunity interposed in their behalf."). The New York, New Haven, and Hartford Railroad was the longtime object of Brandeis's relentless anti-trust efforts when he was a private Boston attorney. When McReynolds came under attack for his handling of the New Haven railroad anti-trust matter, Brandeis wrote his wife, "The attacks on McR. are fierce, & not justified. Except, of course, that he is a standpatter without a particle of sympathy with insurgent methods." LDB to Alice Goldmark Brandeis (May 23, 1914), in BRANDEIS FAMILY LETTERS, at 249. Brandeis reported that McReynolds was "very much aggrieved over the Folk incident." LDB to Alice Goldmark Brandeis (July 8, 1914), *id.* at 257.
59. 51 CONG. REC. 11175–77 (June 26, 1914). *See Norris Demands Suit in N.H. Case*, NEW YORK TRIBUNE (June 27, 1914), at 13 ("The controversy between Senator Norris and Attorney General McReynolds over the purpose of the Department of Justice with reference to prosecution of the officials of New Haven & Hartford Railroad was carried to the floor of the Senate to-day."); Blaisdell, *supra* note 23, at 62–63.
60. *McReynolds Scores Press*, NEW YORK TIMES (June 13, 1914), at 1 ("'Those not in direct touch with the situation have no idea to what extent certain portions of the press will go to misrepresent the work of the various departments at Washington in order to subserve their own interests,' he said."). It was accurately observed of

McReynolds that "Politics he understands only remotely. McReynolds has not made a single public speech since the fourth of March. It would never occur to him to follow the example of his predecessor, who at one time acted as the political mouthpiece of his Administration." Hendrick, *supra* note 16, at 27.

61. Hendrick, *supra* note 16, at 32. On the so-called Diggs-Caminetti scandal, see Blaisdell, *supra* note 23, at 64–69; McCraw, *supra* note 28, at 62–66; *A Diggs-Caminetti Case in the Cabinet*, 55 CURRENT OPINION 6 (August 1913). It was universally accepted that McReynolds's "granting" of the continuance "was a mistake – a mistake, we may add, none the less serious in its effect because it was one of inadvertence." *The Caminetti Case*, 104 THE OUTLOOK 489 (1913). Yet McReynolds never did seem to understand the political dimensions of the outcry: "'I was simply stunned and amazed at the trouble this act of mine caused,' he says, 'an act purely routine on my part. I did not understand it then; I don't understand it yet. It naturally gave me many days of unhappiness, for to question a man's motives is the thing that hurts his feelings most.'" Quoted in Hendrick, *supra* note 16, at 32.

62. *McReynolds Plans Tobacco Tax to Curb Trust Evil*, ST. LOUIS POST-DISPATCH (June 4, 1913), at 3 ("While such a plan of taxation could not be called a tariff-for-revenue-only measure, McReynolds contends it is an emergency measure devised to meet the pleas of independent tobacco manufacturers that the dissolution of the so-called trust has not relieved them of a situation which, they say, threatens to place them in as much danger as they were from the 'trust' before it was dissolved.").

63. *Taxing to Destroy*, NEW YORK TIMES (June 7, 1913), at 10. See *Danger in Sliding Tax*, NEW YORK TRIBUNE (June 7, 1913), at 18 ("In business circles the measure was generally deprecated, while persons interested in the scientific principles of taxation found it hard to speak a word in its favor."). See *The Attorney-General and Big Business*, 96 THE NATION 588 (1913).

64. *To Hit Tobacco Trust by Taxing*, NEW YORK TIMES (June 4, 1913), at 1. The distinction between a proper tax for revenue and an unconstitutional tax, the enforcement of which is "by its very nature ... a penalty," would later be the premise of McReynolds's opinion for the Court in Lipke v. Lederer, 259 U.S. 557, 561–62 (1922).

65. *See* Anti-Narcotic Act of December 17, 1914, Pub. L. 63-223, 38 Stat. 785, as amended in the Revenue Act of 1918, Pub. L. 65-254 40 Stat. 1057, 1130 (February 24, 1919); Nigro v. United States, 276 U.S. 332, 354 (1928) (McReynolds, J., dissenting); United States v. Daugherty, 269 U.S. 360, 362–63 (1926); Linder v. United States, 268 U.S. 5, 17 (1925) ("The declared object of the Narcotic Law is to provide revenue, and this court has held that whatever additional moral end it may have in view must 'be reached only through a revenue measure and within the limits of a revenue measure.'"); United States v. Doremus, 249 U.S. 84, 95 (1919). McReynolds was described as specifically assuring himself that his own proposal to impose progressive taxes on the large tobacco firms was "constitutional." *Statement on Tobacco Tax*, LOUISVILLE COURIER JOURNAL (June 7, 1913), at 1.

66. *Statement on Tobacco Tax*, *supra* note 65, at 2.

67. *The Attorney-General in Hot Water*, 47 LITERARY DIGEST 39, 41 (July 12, 1913) (quoting the *Boston Journal*).

68. *Id.* at 40 (quoting the *Albany Journal*). "That Attorney General James C. McReynolds is the storm-center of the new Cabinet and that, in all probability,

he will be the first member of the Cabinet to be severed from the government service, are facts that are becoming too patent to be overlooked. There is a good deal of evidence already tending to show that President Wilson is apprehensive that he made a bad bargain when he selected McReynolds as the chief law officer of the incoming administration, for McReynolds is a white elephant of the worst kind." *M'Reynolds Is Poor Selection*, INDIANAPOLIS STAR (July 6, 1913), at 11.
69. *Mr. Bryan Comes to the Rescue*, PHILADELPHIA INQUIRER (July 1, 1913), at 8.
70. *A Cabinet Change Possible*, NEW YORK TIMES (June 30, 1913), at 6 ("It is difficult to see how the precedent established in the case of Secretary Ballinger can be ignored. ... The Attorney General has been a disturbing element from the beginning.").
71. The *Literary Digest* quoted the *New York World*: "The best service James C. McReynolds can now render to the Wilson Administration is to resign the office of Attorney-General of the United States. ... Mr. McReynolds has given to the enemies of the Wilson Administration their first opening. He has proved to be the weak spot in the President's armor. As long as he remains in the office of Attorney-General the Department of Justice will be under suspicion." *The Attorney-General in Hot Water*, *supra* note 67, at 41. *See Say McReynolds May Go*, NEW YORK TIMES (June 11, 1913), at 1 ("A general feeling is manifest among Democratic leaders that this plan is too radical to be taken up at this time of industrial and financial uncertainty."); *Wilson and McReynolds Reported at Odds*, HARTFORD COURANT (June 11, 1913), at 1; *McReynolds Won't Quit*, NEW YORK TIMES (June 14, 1913), at 11; *Wilson May Lose M'Reynolds' Aid*, CHICAGO DAILY TRIBUNE (July 9, 1913), at 4 ("There is no doubt the administration intends to make a record as a 'trust buster.' This is in accordance with the Democratic platform. But Mr. McReynolds unhappily is so constituted that he interprets the platform literally. He does not believe in half way measures, and he has prepared a campaign which would strike terror to the monopolists.").
72. GEORGE CREEL, REBEL AT LARGE: RECOLLECTIONS OF FIFTY CROWDED YEARS 244 (New York: G.P. Putnam's Sons 1947). Two days after his nomination, McReynolds wrote House "You are always generous to me far beyond my merits. Whatever I can do that pleases you – meets in some degree your expectation, I count as doubly worth while. And won't you please know without the shadow of doubt that I never forget, but find a sweet pleasure in remembering the course of my good fortune." JCM to Edward M. House (August 21, 1914) (House papers at Yale University).
73. DANIELS, *supra* note 49, at 541–42:

> About a year before he died, while my wife and I were visiting Mr. and Mrs. Burleson in Austin, the Texan told me, "I was responsible for the appointment of McReynolds," and proceeded to detail the steps he took to influence it. I said:
>
> "Albert, that was one time you gave Wilson bad advice. While I have the same respect for the honesty of McReynolds that you have, history has shown, what I sensed at the time, that McReynolds was congenitally unable to favor the progressive policies Wilson incarnated. He was sound on the tariff, he did a monumental job in convicting the tobacco trust, and is free from influence from any quarter, but on the bench he has shown that the tides of liberalism have never reached him. ... He is the most reactionary justice on the bench."

I am sure that, while always respecting McReynolds' intellectual honesty, Wilson lived to regret he had placed a man on the bench with a mind not open to the need of judicial growth and not willing to uphold humanitarian legislation, as were Holmes and Brandeis.

74. Quoted in Hendrick, *supra* note 16, at 31.
75. Quoted in Morrow, *supra* note 19, at C7.
76. This point is nicely made in BICKEL & SCHMIDT, *supra* note 14, at 349–50.
77. 51 CONG. REC. 13984 (August 19, 1914). Press reports indicate that Wilson had been strongly leaning toward McReynolds since the end of July. *Turns to M'Reynolds*, WASHINGTON POST (July 27, 1914), at 5; *M'Reynolds in Lead for Supreme Court*, NEW YORK TIMES (July 27, 1914), at 1; *Scouts of President Are Busy*, CINCINNATI ENQUIRER (August 1, 1914), at 4. On August 2, McReynolds wrote J.M. Dickinson that "I've not spoken with the President on the subject and do not know what he will finally decide to do. The reports which come to me indicate that he will offer me the place. For some reason it would appeal to me, but there are other things about it which do not suit me. And there is such a fertile field for me back in New York that I would hate to give it all up. If the place is offered my present intention is to accept it as a piece of good fortune and try to be content." JCM to Jacob M. Dickenson (August 2, 1914) (Dickinson papers at the Tennessee State Library & Archives).
78. DANIELS, *supra* note 49, at 115. *See* McCraw, *supra* note 28, at 81. Taft observed at the time that "[i]f Wilson promotes McReynolds, he will put a weak man on the Bench." WHT to Mabel Boardman (July 15, 1914) (Taft papers).
79. 51 CONG. REC. 14421 (August 29, 1914). *See McReynolds Confirmed*, NEW YORK TIMES (August 30, 1914), at 14.
80. "In later years Wilson was credited with the remark that the greatest mistake of his administration was the appointment of McReynolds to the Supreme Court." DREW PEARSON & ROBERT S. ALLEN, THE NINE OLD MEN 224 (Garden City: Doubleday 1937). *See* WHT to Charles D. Hilles (September 9, 1922) (Taft papers) ("It was a great blessing that in the eight years succeeding my term, Wilson had only three places to fill, and was greatly disappointed and defeated in his purpose in the attitude of McReynolds."). Wilson's disappointment is evident in the letter he wrote Clarke upon the latter's retirement: "Like thousands of other liberals throughout the country, I have been counting on the influence of you and Justice Brandeis to restrain the Court in some measure from the extreme reactionary course which it seems inclined to follow." Woodrow Wilson to JHC (September 5, 1922) (Wilson Papers). The omission of McReynolds's name is glaring. Clarke immediately wrote back to Wilson that "McReynolds as you know is the most reactionary judge on the Court." JHC to Woodrow Wilson (September 9, 1922) (Wilson Papers).
81. Quoted in *Mr. McReynolds's Promotion*, 49 LITERARY DIGEST 406 (September 5, 1914).
82. *Mr. McReynolds and the Supreme Court*, NEW YORK TRIBUNE (August 20, 1914), at 6. For the most part, however, press reaction to McReynolds's appointment was tepid. The appointment seemed "to most editors 'respectable but not ideal.'" *Mr. McReynolds's Promotion*, *supra* note 81, at 405. The *Green Bag* noted that because McReynolds had not demonstrated "to the public at least, a judicial temperament, ... his appointment can hardly, in all candor be pronounced one

that visibly and immediately lends strength to the Supreme Court." *The Editor's Bag*, 26 GREEN BAG 499, 499 (1914). Yet the publication conceded that McReynolds "is known to be a man of unquestionable devotion to the public weal, and lofty standards of action. ... Even though the appointment signifies the addition of a somewhat radical factor, this radicalism bids fair to become somewhat mollified, and to become merged to some extent in the personality of the court itself, after the fashion of all judicial self-assertion." *Id.* at 499–500. The *New York Times* comforted itself with the thought that "the discussion of the Justices tends to soften extreme views and reconcile dissent. Mr. McReynolds will come within the radiance of the light of reason." *To the Supreme Bench*, NEW YORK TIMES (August 20, 1914), at 10.

83. Diary of Charles Sumner Hamlin (August 21, 1924) (Library of Congress).
84. BOND, *supra* note 13, at 9–10. "His prejudices extended beyond legal doctrine to women lawyers. Whenever a woman rose to address the Court, he pushed back his chair and left the Bench. Curiously, when the responsibility of presiding at sittings of the Court in the Chief Justice's absence fell to him as senior Associate Justice, he was the soul of courtesy, welcoming woman lawyers graciously; and listening with apparent attention and benevolence to arguments from lawyers of both sexes, which doubtless raised his blood pressure to the bursting point." Acheson, *supra* note 53.
85. Albert Lawrence, *Biased Justice: James C. McReynolds of the Supreme Court of the United States*, 30 JOURNAL OF SUPREME COURT HISTORY 244, 252–53 (2005). As a student at Vanderbilt, McReynolds had published an editorial in the school newspaper arguing that African Americans were "ignorant, superstitious, immoral, and with but small outlook for radical improvement. They are improvident, lazy, and easily imposed upon by designing men. They have a low order of intellect, learn with difficulty, and apparently make small use of what attainment they have acquired. ... To live in terms of social equality with them is entirely out of the question – they are unworthy of it; to treat them as equals in politics, and allow them to hold positions of power and trust to any considerable extent has been shown to be disastrous – they are not fit for such things." VANDERBILT OBSERVER (May 1883), at 2–3, quoted in Blaisdell, *supra* note 23, at 227–28.

McReynolds's law clerk for the 1936 term, John Knox, was required to work out of McReynolds's home apartment, in which two African American servants also worked. One day McReynolds called Knox into his office for a chat:

> "I do feel that this is the time to speak about one thing. I realize you are a Northerner who has never been educated or reared in the South, but I want you to know that you are becoming much too friendly with Harry. You seem to forget that he is a negro and you are a graduate of the Harvard Law School. And yet for days now, it has been obvious to me that you are, well, treating Henry and Mary like equals. Really, a law clerk to a Justice of the Supreme Court of the United States should have some feeling about his position and not wish to associate with colored servants the way you are doing." And with a genuine sigh McReynolds continued, "Of course you are *not* a Southerner, so maybe it's expecting too much of someone from Chicago to act like a Southerner, but I do wish you would think of my wishes in this matter in your future relations with darkies."

THE FORGOTTEN MEMOIR OF JOHN KNOX: A YEAR IN THE LIFE OF A SUPREME COURT CLERK IN FDR'S WASHINGTON 51 (Dennis J. Hutchinson & David J. Garrow, eds., University of Chicago Press 2002).

86. *The Honorable Supreme Court*, FORTUNE (May 1936), at 85.

87. As even McReynolds's close friends testified at his memorial service, "It is not unusual for men of the type of James McReynolds to develop strong and even violent prejudices. The intensity of his conviction that he was right on some constitutional issue often converted his conviction into a point of honor. In such a situation it was as hard for him to respect the man who disagreed with him as it was for him to be tolerant of dishonesty. On such occasions there flared up in him a flame of indignation which he made little effort to quench. ... Men like him are both stimulating and difficult: stimulating because we all need to be reminded of the importance of moral standards; and difficult because at any moment they may convert an argument into a fight." *Remarks of George Wharton Pepper, supra* note 18, at 27. *See Remarks of John W. Davis*, in PROCEEDINGS, *supra* note 18, at 21.
88. *Brandeis-Frankfurter Conversations*, at 329 (July 3, 1924). *See* WHT to Helen Herron Taft (February 1, 1925) (Taft papers) (McReynolds "is most exacting of others in matters in which he is interested and most inconsiderate of the wishes and rights of others.").
89. WHT to Elihu Root (September 13, 1922) (Taft papers).
90. WHT to Horace D. Taft (September 7, 1922) (Taft papers). *See supra* Chapter 1, at 36–37.
91. WHT to Mrs. Frederick J. Manning (June 11, 1923) (Taft papers). Taft complained to his son that McReynolds is "selfish beyond everything, though full of so-called Southern courtesy, but most inconsiderate of his colleagues and others and contemptuous of everybody." WHT to Robert A. Taft (February 1, 1925) (Taft papers).
92. VANDERBILT ALUMNUS, *supra* note 19, at 4 ("Every man (I know nothing of women) ought to learn to do twenty-four hours of consecutive work when it is necessary. If he learns that trick at college, he will find in the great world that he has a vast advantage over men who have been careless."). As a young man, McReynolds was known for his work ethic. BOND, *supra* note 13, at 14–15, 18.
93. As McReynolds wrote his brother, "Increasing laziness retards all my efforts!" JCM to Robert McReynolds (February 24 [1926?]) (Virginia McReynolds papers).
94. WHT to Robert A. Taft (March 4, 1928) (Taft papers). In 1924, Taft wrote his son that "I got through the Conference yesterday all right, and in the absence of McReynolds, everything went smoothly. He is down with lumbago and has gone away for Easter. He is the greatest censor of the Court, takes less responsibility, and is not a demon for work." WHT to Robert A. Taft (April 20, 1924) (Taft papers). Figure II-11 illustrates that McReynolds's production of opinions was erratic, although on the whole it was consistent with what would be required were McReynolds to publish a proportionate share of the Court's opinions.
95. *Brandeis-Frankfurter Conversations*, at 317 (July 3, 1923).
96. *Id.*, at 329 (July 3, 1924). *See, e.g.*, WHT to Robert A. Taft (February 1, 1925) (Taft papers) ("McReynolds tries my patience. Without giving me any word, except after he had gone, he left us this week for a two full days to hunt ducks."); JCM to WHT (November 23, 1929) (Taft papers) ("An imperious voice has called me out of town. I don't think my sudden illness will prove fatal, but strange things some time happen around Thanksgiving.").
97. *The Court Diary of Justice William O. Douglas*, 1995 JOURNAL OF SUPREME COURT HISTORY 77, 86 (Philip E. Urofsky, ed.) (entry for November 16, 1939).

James Clark McReynolds

98. WHT to Robert A. Taft (February 1, 1925) (Taft papers). *See* LDB to Alice Goldmark Brandeis (March 2, 1914), in BRANDEIS FAMILY LETTERS, at 242.
99. OWH to Harold Laski (March 26, 1922), in 1 HOLMES-LASKI CORRESPONDENCE, at 413.
100. WHT to Robert A. Taft (March 4, 1928) (Taft papers).
101. This despite McReynolds's intense working relationship with Brandeis when McReynolds was attorney general. *See supra* note 51.
102. Upon Cardozo's appointment to the Court, Brandeis wrote Frankfurter that "I doubt whether Cardozo would be helped by having him now set wise about McR." LDB to Felix Frankfurter (February 25, 1932), in BRANDEIS-FRANKFURTER CORRESPONDENCE, at 478. For a discussion, see ANDREW L. KAUFMAN, CARDOZO 479–80 (Cambridge: Harvard University Press 1998).
103. Lawrence, *supra* note 85, at 252–53; BOND, *supra* note 13, at 53–55; THE FORGOTTEN MEMOIR OF JOHN KNOX, *supra* note 85, at 36–37, 99–100; PEARSON & ALLEN, *supra* note 80, at 225; 2 MERLO J. PUSEY, CHARLES EVANS HUGHES 670 (New York: MacMillan 1951); FELIX FRANKFURTER REMINISCES: RECORDED IN TALKS WITH DR. HARLAN B. PHILLIPS 101 (New York: Reynal & Co. 1960) ("McReynolds was a hater. . . . He was rude beyond words to that gentle saintlike Cardozo. He had primitive anti-Semitism. A tough-skinned fellow like me could deal with him because I could be just as rude as he could be. . . . I sort of respected him. . . . I respected that he refused to sign a letter when Brandeis left the Court. There was the usual letter of farewell to a colleague, and he wouldn't sign it. I respected that, because he did not remotely feel what the letter expressed, and I despise hypocrites even more than barbarians."). According to Dean Acheson, who was Brandeis's law clerk, although McReynolds was "not on speaking terms" with Brandeis, he nevertheless made clear to Acheson "that this had nothing to do with me. He would treat me with consideration and would expect the same consideration from me." Acheson, *supra* note 53. It does not seem to be the case, however, that McReynolds refused to take a Court photograph because he objected to sitting next to Brandeis. Franz Jantzen, *From the Urban Legend Department: McReynolds, Brandeis, and the Myth of the 1924 Group Photograph*, 40 JOURNAL OF SUPREME COURT HISTORY 326 (November 2015).
104. Evans v. Gore, 253 U.S. 245 (1920) (Holmes papers). McReynolds once wrote his brother: "The other day I ran over to N.Y. The place is dirty – full of Jews & robbers and growing less attractive to me." JCM to Robert McReynolds (December 3 [1920?]) (Virginia McReynolds papers).
105. OWH to Harold Laski (March 26, 1922), in 1 HOLMES-LASKI CORRESPONDENCE, at 413. Four years later, Holmes wrote "Formerly, according to my recollection, [McReynolds] was really insolent to Brandeis, although now there is at least a *modus vivendi*." OWH to Harold Laski (June 6, 1926), in 2 HOLMES-LASKI CORRESPONDENCE, at 842. When Brandeis in fall 1922 circulated his draft opinion in Keogh v. Chicago & Northwestern Rwy. Co., 260 U.S. 156 (1922), McReynolds returned his copy with a rare complement: "I agree & think the result well worked out." (Brandeis papers). In 1923 Brandeis wrote his wife that "My friendly relations with my 'brethren' took a new advance yesterday when I asked McR to write the dissent in a case in which we two are unable to concur with the majority. He seemed greatly pleased at being asked." LDB to Alice Goldmark Brandeis

(May 8, 1923), in 5 LETTERS OF LOUIS D. BRANDEIS, at 93. (The case was possibly Pennsylvania v. West Virginia, 262 U.S. 553 (1923), or Terrace v. Thompson, 263 U.S. 197 (1923), in each of which Brandeis and McReynolds dissented separately on the ground that the Court was without jurisdiction.) Brandeis thought that "McR cares more about jurisdictional restraints than any of them." *Brandeis-Frankfurter Conversations*, at 317 (July 3, 1923). *See, e.g.*, Fidelity & Deposit Co. v. Tafoya, 270 U.S. 426 (1926); Massachusetts State Grange v. Benton, 272 U.S. 525 (1926); Williams v. Riley, 280 U.S. 78 (1929). Commenting on the argument in Roschen v. Ward, 279 U.S. 337 (1929), Brandeis observed with pleasure McReynolds's sharp question to counsel for a plaintiff seeking to enjoin a New York statute. McReynolds asked whether "he would have had a remedy by injunction in State court." Upon receiving an affirmative reply, McReynolds immediately "said, 'I think the decree dismissing bill should be affirmed on that ground. What justification is there for your coming into a federal court to make us construe the state statute[?]'" LDB to Felix Frankfurter (April 11, 1929), in BRANDEIS-FRANKFURTER CORRESPONDENCE, at 369–70. *But see* Lipke v. Lederer, 259 U.S. 557 (1922).
106. OWH to Harold Laski (October 19, 1923) in 1 HOLMES-LASKI CORRESPONDENCE, at 554–55.
107. As Brandeis advised Cardozo, who after joining the Court was suffering "shocks at the treatment received," *see supra* note 102, "dass er sich daruber hinwegsetzen muss," meaning roughly that Cardozo must brush it aside. LDB to Frankfurter (April 10, 1932), in BRANDEIS-FRANKFURTER CORRESPONDENCE, at 484.
108. *Brandeis-Frankfurter Conversations*, at 333 (August 3, 1924).
109. OWH to Harold Laski (June 6, 1926), in 2 HOLMES-LASKI CORRESPONDENCE, at 842.
110. *See, e.g.*, OWH to Harold Laski (February 18, 1928), in 2 HOLMES-LASKI CORRESPONDENCE, at 1027; OWH to Frederick Pollock (April 4, 1928), in 2 HOLMES-POLLOCK CORRESPONDENCE, at 218; OWH to Harold Laski (May 12, 1928), in 2 HOLMES-LASKI CORRESPONDENCE, at 1054–55. Brandeis believed that McReynolds's conduct and comments caused Holmes "pain, much pain." *Brandeis-Frankfurter Conversations*, at 333 (August 3, 1924).
111. JCM to OWH (July 11, 1922) (Holmes papers). McReynolds wrote a similarly gracious letter to Taft when the latter became seriously ill. *See* JCM to WHT (September 6, 1929) (Taft papers). On McReynolds's kindness, see, for example, Acheson, *supra* note 53; Attorney General Clark, *supra* note 6, at xix–xx ("Contrary to public belief, Mr. Justice McReynolds was not a lonely man. He loved the company of those who shared his views and his principles. He had a big heart for the young and for education. While he was in truth unbending in his political and judicial views, he had all of the human qualities that endeared him to all who knew him. ... During his life he followed the practice of giving generously – and anonymously – to charity."). It should be observed, however, that McReynolds died alone and that, quite uniquely, no justice attended his simple funeral in Elkton. *James C. McReynolds: Last of the Old Guard, supra* note 13, at 6; Philippa Strum, *Review of* I DISSENT, 81 JOURNAL OF AMERICAN HISTORY 318 (June 1994) ("so detested by his colleagues that not one of them went to his funeral.").

James Clark McReynolds

112. OWH to Harold Laski (June 6, 1926), in 2 HOLMES-LASKI CORRESPONDENCE, at 842.
113. In contrast to Holmes, Brandeis conceptualized this paradox in the language of German romanticism. McReynolds was to him "a *Naturmensch*": "He has very tender affections & correspondingly hates. He treated Pitney like a dog – used to say the cruelest things to him. Pitney talked a good deal & didn't like his voice & otherwise P got on McR's nerves & he treated him like a dog. But no one feels more P's sufferings now – not as a matter of remorse but merely a sensitiveness to pain. He is a lonely person, has few real friends." *Brandeis-Frankfurter Conversations*, at 317 (July 3, 1923).
114. Lawrence, *supra* note 85, at 253.
115. WHT to Elihu Root (December 21, 1922) (Taft papers). *See* JHC to Woodrow Wilson (September 9, 1922) (Wilson papers).
116. Edward A Purcell, Jr., *Learned Hand: The Jurisprudential Trajectory of an Old Progressive*, 43 BUFFALO LAW REVIEW 873, 914 (1995); James A. Henretta, *Charles Evans Hughes and the Strange Death of Liberal America*, 24 LAW AND HISTORY REVIEW 115, 118 (2006).
117. One study of McReynolds cites the communication of a former clerk for the proposition that "McReynolds was closer to Justices Van Devanter, Sutherland and Butler than to any other justices who sat with him during his tenure, but he felt himself superior to them." Early, *supra* note 15, at 90.
118. OWH to Frederick Pollock (March 7, 1924), in 2 HOLMES-POLLOCK CORRESPONDENCE, at 129.
119. *See* Barry Cushman, *Inside the Taft Court: Lessons from the Docket Books*, 2015 SUPREME COURT REVIEW 345, 404–5. Surviving case files are filled with comments from McReynolds like: "I have my doubts but not the necessary votes. Wherefore I am mum." Jackman v. Rosenbaum Co., 260 U.S. 22 (1922) (Holmes papers). "I shant row with you tho I was inclined to agree with the Dist. Court." Stevens v. Arnold, 262 U.S. 266 (1923) (Holmes papers). "I shan't express any dissent tho I felt there was adequate remedy at law & am disinclined to permit Fed Cts to accept doubtful jurisdiction." Atlantic Coast Line v. Doughton, 262 U.S. 413 (1923) (Brandeis papers). "I voted the other way; but if you get a majority I shall not say anything." Security Mortgage Co. v. Powers, 278 U.S. 149 (1928) (Brandeis papers). "I was inclined to the other view but do not care to say anything if you get a majority." West v. Standard Oil Co., 278 U.S. 200 (1929) (Brandeis papers). "If you did not have the votes this would be wrong." United States v. New York Central Railroad Co., 279 U.S. 73 (1929) (Holmes papers).
120. By contrast, McReynolds's fellow Tennessean, the timid Sanford, never once dissented alone during the 1922 to 1928 terms. Figure II-14 also illustrates why by the end of the decade Taft would sometimes in his mind strangely pair McReynolds with Brandeis. *See, e.g.*, WHT to Horace D. Taft (October 27, 1926) (Taft papers); WHT to Charles P. Taft 2nd (October 31, 1926) (Taft papers) (McReynolds "has no sense of loyalty to the Court and neither has Brandeis."); WHT to GS (April 9, 1927) (Taft papers) (McReynolds "is evidently planning to write a mean opinion against the Court, an indication that brother Brandeis is not the only person who has ambitions in that direction.").

THE TAFT COURT

121. *See supra* text at note 13. "James C. McReynolds was born in a part of the world where men are early taught to fear God and take their own part." *Remarks of John W. Davis*, in PROCEEDINGS, *supra* note 18, at 20.
122. And which, I might add, also lent a decidedly eschatological flavor to McReynolds's thought. In 1915, for example, as he watched the developing European war, McReynolds was beside himself because, as he urgently wrote Colonel House, "Unless I read the signs very badly we are drifting into a terrible state, waiting, waiting is leading towards a wreck.... I cannot help being unhappy over the drift in things diplomatic and ultimately political, if not vital to our very existence. Some miracle may save us, but the victory generally goes to the men who fight for themselves with earnest promptness." JCM to Edward M. House (July 16, 1915) (House papers at Yale University). Three years later McReynolds announced to an audience at Vanderbilt that "There are but two things this day, my fellows, which are worth while, and as truculent as it may sound, let me say the first of these is killing Huns and continuing to kill Huns until those who remain shall be impressed with this idea, that they cannot stamp over the world as conquerors, and that men will not bow their heads to their demands." 3 VANDERBILT ALUMNUS 237 (No. 8) (June 1918).
123. PROCEEDINGS OF THE FIFTY-FOURTH ANNUAL SESSION OF THE BAR ASSOCIATION OF TENNESSEE 65–66 (1935).
124. BOND, *supra* note 13, at 93.
125. Arizona Copper Co. v. Hammer, 250 U.S. 400, 450–53 (1919) (McReynolds, J., dissenting).
126. Pub. L. 66-261, 41 Stat. 988, 1000 (June 5, 1920).
127. 271 U.S. 552, 555–56 (1926). Brandeis, noting his assent to Holmes's opinion, wrote, "I acquiesce with the comforting thought that Congress will help. I note with pleasure this readiness to bow to its will." (Holmes papers).
128. *Id.* at 557 (McReynolds, J., dissenting). For another example of McReynolds's moralism colliding with Holmes's positivism, see MacKenzie v. A. Engelhard & Sons Co., 266 U.S. 131 (1924).
129. Of course, like any lawyer, McReynolds was also at times willing to acknowledge this gap. *See, e.g.*, Dysart v. United States, 272 U.S. 655, 658 (1926) (refusing to uphold a conviction for sending obscene advertisements through the mail "notwithstanding the inexcusable action of petitioner in sending these advertisements to refined women").
130. 271 U.S. 536, 548–49 (1926).
131. *Id.* at 550–51 (McReynolds, J., dissenting).
132. Quoted in Hendrick, *supra* note 16, at 31.
133. United States v. American Linseed Oil, Co., 262 U.S. 371, 388 (1923).
134. McReynolds used every opportunity to undermine the FTC. *See, e.g.*, FTC v. Curtis Publishing Co., 260 U.S. 568 (1923); FTC v. Sinclair Refining Co., 261 U.S. 463 (1923); FTC v. Western Meat Co., 272 U.S. 554 (1926); FTC v. Klesner, 274 U.S. 145 (1927); FTC v. Claire Furnace Co., 274 U.S. 160 (1927); *cf.* FTC v. Raymond Bros.-Clark Co., 263 U.S. 565 (1924); FTC v. Eastman Kodak Co., 274 U.S. 619 (1927); International Shoe Co. v. FTC, 280 U.S. 291 (1930). *But see* FTC v. Pacific States Paper Trade Ass'n, 273 U.S. 52 (1927). In his return to Holmes's draft opinion in FTC v. American Tobacco Co.,

264 U.S. 298 (1924), in which the Court refused to allow enforcement of extremely broad FTC subpoenas on the ground that they were "fishing expeditions into private papers on the possibility that they may disclose evidence of crime," *id.* at 306, McReynolds wrote: "Yes. 'And it is further ordered that the Comm. & all its servants be sent to jail *forever.*'"

135. 253 U.S. 421, 427–28 (1920).
136. *Id.* at 432–35 (Brandeis, J., dissenting). As attorney general, McReynolds had opposed "the enactment of legislation favored by Brandeis that would supplement the Sherman Act." LEWIS J. PAPER, BRANDEIS 189–94 (New Jersey: Prentice-Hall 1983); BOND, *supra* note 13, at 40.
137. United States v. Berwind-White Coal Mining Co., 274 U.S. 564, 587 (1927) (McReynolds, J., dissenting). As McReynolds would write many years later: "Regulation to prevent recognized evils in business has long been upheld as permissible legislative action. But fixation of the price at which A, engaged in an ordinary business, may sell, in order to enable B, a producer, to improve his condition, has not been regarded as within legislative power. This is not regulation, but management, control, dictation – it amounts to the deprivation of the fundamental right which one has to conduct his own affairs honestly and along customary lines." Nebbia v. New York, 291 U.S. 505, 554–55 (1934) (McReynolds, J., dissenting).
138. FTC v. Sinclair Refining Co., 261 U.S. 463, 475 (1923). For this reason, McReynolds consistently interpreted the Trading with the Enemy Act, Pub. L. 65-91, 40 Stat. 411 (October 6, 1917), in the narrowest possible way. He alone dissented in Swiss Nat. Ins. Co. v. Miller, 267 U.S. 42 (1925), which concerned the question of whether the Alien Property Custodian and Treasurer of the United States could retain the assets of a Swiss Corporation owned largely by German stockholders that had been doing business in Germany during the war, in part on the ground that "Confiscation is everywhere disavowed; neutral property may not be used for adjusting claims against belligerents; and ordinary fair dealing requires its release. To seize the effects of a neutral corporation after cessation of hostilities and then hold them solely because of some enemy stockholder, would defeat the lawmakers' honorable intention and give rise to grave suspicion concerning the purpose of our government." *Id.* at 72 (McReynolds, J., dissenting).
139. *See supra* Chapter 5, at 169. Thus in Adams v. Tanner, 244 U.S. 590 (1917), McReynolds authored an opinion for the Court striking down a Washington initiative that effectively prohibited employment agencies from charging fees. McReynolds stated: "We think it plain that there is nothing inherently immoral or dangerous to public welfare in acting as paid representative of another to find a position in which he can earn an honest living. On the contrary, such service is useful, commendable, and in great demand." 244 U.S. at 593.
140. Butler v. Perry, 240 U.S. 328 333 (1916). *See* Meyer v. Nebraska, 262 U.S. 390, 399 (1923) (holding the Fourteenth Amendment protects "those privilege long recognized at common law as essential to the orderly pursuit of happiness by free men."). Butler explicitly endorsed this same view. *See* Pierce Butler, *Some Opportunities and Duties of Lawyers*, 9 AMERICAN BAR ASSOCIATION JOURNAL 583, 585 (1923).
141. Fairmont Creamery Co. v. Minnesota, 274 U.S. 1, 8 (1927) (emphasis added).

142. *Id.* at 9. *See* Arizona Copper Co. v. Hammer, 250 U.S. 400, 450–53 (1919) (McReynolds, J., dissenting).
143. Perry v. United States, 294 U.S. 330, 361 (1935) (McReynolds, J., dissenting).
144. John Snure, *Historic Ruling Read to Tense Crowd in Court*, NEW YORK HERALD TRIBUNE (February 19, 1935), at 12. McReynolds wrote his brother: "The oral statement was wholly extemporaneous – no notes. Whether wise or no may be a question. But I wanted to attract sharp attention to the situation. To that end it seems to have succeeded." JCM to Robert McReynolds (February 23, 1935) (Virginia McReynolds papers). McReynolds continued, "Apparently we have succeeded in getting a good many to think. There is no doubt of the very serious consequences. Constitutional guarantees have been shattered. We would have been much better off if the old standard had been maintained. And it could have been." *Id.*
145. At the request of the *Tennessee Law Review*, McReynolds sent an authorized version of his remarks that was published in 18 TENNESSEE LAW REVIEW 768 (1945). This version was plainly bowdlerized.
146. A few days later the *Wall Street Journal* attempted to compile a complete version of McReynolds's remarks. *Justice McReynolds' Remarks on Gold Case Decision*, WALL STREET JOURNAL (February 23, 1935), at 1.
147. *Constitution Gone, Says McReynolds*, NEW YORK TIMES (February 19, 1935), at 1.
148. *Justice McReynolds' Remarks on Gold Case Decision, supra* note 146, at 2. Brandeis said that "McReynolds' talk was very different from his opinion, was really impressive; better than anything I have ever heard from him." LDB to Felix Frankfurter (February 24, 1935), in BRANDEIS-FRANKFURTER CORRESPONDENCE, at 562.
149. Perry v. United States, 294 U.S. 330, 381 (1935) (McReynolds, J., dissenting). *See id.* at 378. The written dissent is noteworthy for its brash assertion that "Acquiescence in the decisions just announced is impossible." *Id.* at 361–62. Compare this to McReynolds's repeated assertions when he first became a justice that obedience to the judiciary must be maintained to staunch "the tide of opposition [that] ... has risen against judges and courts." *Proceedings of the Judicial Section*, in REPORT OF THE THIRTY-SEVENTH ANNUAL MEETING OF THE AMERICAN BAR ASSOCIATION 968 (Baltimore: Lord Baltimore Press 1914). At that time, McReynolds attempted to inspire the bar to spread "faith and ... trust" in the Court. *Remarks of Mr. Justice James C. McReynolds*, in PROCEEDINGS OF THE FORTY-SECOND ANNUAL SESSION OF THE BAR ASSOCIATION OF TENNESSEE 122 (1923). "Not even the simple things of life, where men's passions and interests conflict, can be conducted without an arbiter; much less these hundred millions of people, with thousands of conflicting interests, continue in security and in prosperity unless the great contests can be settled finally somewhere in a way which the majority is willing to accept. The power of the Supreme Court does not lie in the army, it does not lie in the navy, nor in the militia; it lies in the faith of the people for whom it was created and for whom it toils incessantly." *Id.* "To me the way the people of these United States accept the final determination of their courts is one of the finest indications of their power for self-government, and whenever you hear a demagogue going forth among the people and preaching to them disregard for their courts, and advocating that their decrees be disregarded, you may put him

James Clark McReynolds

down, once for all, as a traitor to the government as you know it, and as it has existed in the past." 7 VANDERBILT ALUMNUS 175 (No. 8) (1922).

150. McReynolds believed strongly in the "tremendous power in the cultured human voice. The very presence of the informed man who speaks with conviction gives his cause peculiar standing. There are some who think that you may put all necessary arguments in print, but to me no brief can take the place of words spoken by a real advocate." *Speech of Mr. Justice J. C. M'Reynolds*, in PROCEEDINGS OF THE FORTY-FIFTH ANNUAL SESSION OF THE BAR ASSOCIATION OF TENNESSEE 133 (1926). *See* 7 VANDERBILT ALUMNUS 174 (No. 8) (1922) ("May I stop here to say to you that it is a lamentable fact that the power of public speaking, the power of advocacy, the power of moving a crowd, seems to be a decaying art.... Why have they forgotten that of all the powers on earth the power of one human being to sway another is one of the most superb and one most to be desired?"). During the Taft Court period, McReynolds delivered an oral dissent in Myers v. United States, 272 U.S. 52 (1926), which deeply offended Taft. WHT to Horace D. Taft (October 27, 1926) (Taft papers). In Carroll v. United States, 267 U.S. 132 (1925), McReynolds also "delivered himself without reference to his written opinion in such a way that Holmes remarked (as Holmes told me) to our new member Stone that there were some people who could be most unmannerly in their dissenting opinion." WHT to Robert A. Taft (March 8, 1925) (Taft papers).

151. REPORT OF THE THIRTY-SEVENTH ANNUAL MEETING OF THE AMERICAN BAR ASSOCIATION, *supra* note 149, at 968.

152. *Snapshots of United States Supreme Court by Mr. Justice McReynolds*, SAN FRANCISCO CHRONICLE (July 22, 1921), at 4. "There are 50,000 lawyers in the United States, of whom 10 per cent read our opinions. I endeavor to confine my opinions to as few words as possible, so that they can be grasped easily at the first reading. If lawyers demanded a decrease in the number of opinions and in the number of volumes, I believe you would see results. Personally, I would like to see the opinions and volumes reduced one-half."

153. JM to WVD (February 24, 1921) (Van Devanter papers). Taft characterized McReynolds's opinions as "very, very short," and as losing "strength and value by his disposition to cut down." WHT to Charles P. Taft 2nd (November 1, 1925) (Taft papers). John W. Davis remarked that "A 'plenitude of words,' to use his own phrase, [McReynolds] abominated." *Remarks of John W. Davis*, in PROCEEDINGS, *supra* note 18, at 22.

154. BOND, *supra* note 13, at 61; FRED RODELL, NINE MEN: A POLITICAL HISTORY OF THE SUPREME COURT FROM 1790 TO 1955, at 219 (New York: Random House 1955).

155. 270 U.S. 87, 103 (1926) (McReynolds, J., dissenting). Sutherland joined McReynolds's dissent.

156. Pub. Res. 69-14, 44 Stat. 250 (April 13, 1926).

157. *See supra* text at note 83. McReynolds's commitment to customary morals may even have been behind his belief that "the oriental [Jewish] mind was entirely different from the Anglo-Saxon." *Id.*

158. Dean Acheson, *Recollections of Service with the Federal Supreme Court*, 18 ALABAMA LAWYER 355, 362 (1957).

159. *See, e.g.*, Mellon v Michigan Trust Co., 271 U.S. 236, 239 (1926) ("In taking over and operating the railroads, the United States acted in their sovereign capacity."); United States v. Sisal Sales Corp., 274 U.S. 268, 276 (1927) ("The United States complain of a violation . . . ."); Taft v. Bowers, 278 U.S. 470, 479 (1929). The first two sentences of Brandeis's opinion in United States Shipping Board Emergency Fleet Corp. v. Western Union Telegraph Co., 275 U.S. 415, 416 (1928), read "By the Post Roads Act, the United States offered privileges of great value to any telegraph company which should elect to accept its provisions. In return, it required . . . ." McReynolds returned the circulated draft of Brandeis's opinion with the suggestion that instead of the word "it" in the second sentence, "*they* is the better word."
160. 263 U.S. 418, 421, 423–24 (1923).
161. Arizona Copper Co. v. Hammer, 250 U.S. 400, 451 (1919) (McReynolds, J., dissenting).
162. 7 VANDERBILT ALUMNUS 175 (No. 8) (June 1922).
163. *Remarks of Mr. Justice James C. McReynolds, supra* note 149, at 121.

CHAPTER 8

Louis Dembitz Brandeis

LIKE McREYNOLDS, LOUIS D. BRANDEIS was "without doubt essentially a moralist."[1] It was not for nothing that Franklin Roosevelt took to calling him "Isaiah."[2] Brandeis's "asceticism and his fundamentally moral outlook gave him, in the eyes of many of his friends, the quality of a saint."[3] "In him the lawyer's genius was dedicated to the prophet's vision, and the fusion produced a magnificent weapon for righteousness. In his hand the sword was fringed with fire."[4] Brandeis believed that democracy demanded "more exigent obedience to the moral law than any other form of government";[5] that the achievement of "social justice" was the most compelling force of his age;[6] that "waste" was "sinful";[7] and that "bigness" was "the greatest curse."[8] The 1919 Palmer raids left him battling a "sense of shame and of sin."[9] Brandeis could "boil ... in indignation" at the "inequity" of federal courts wasting their time on mail fraud cases.[10]

In his memoirs, Dean Acheson, who clerked for Brandeis during the 1919 and 1920 terms, recounts a telling anecdote. During the 1920s, he encountered Manley Hudson, Professor of International Law at Harvard (later a judge on the Permanent Court of International Justice in the Hague). Hudson was holding forth "on Brandeis, the Scientist of the Law, who had brought the methods of the laboratory into the courthouse, who put facts through test tube treatment, and so on." Acheson contrived to have Hudson meet Brandeis in the latter's study, and "to guide the conversation to the growing political issue of prohibition and, in the course of it, to provoke Mr. Hudson into asserting that moral principles were no more than generalizations from the mores or accepted notions of a particular time and place."

> The eruption was even more spectacular than I had anticipated. The Justice wrapped the mantle of Isaiah around himself, dropped his voice a full octave, jutted his eyebrows forward in a most menacing way, and began to prophesy.

Morality was truth; and truth had been revealed to man in an unbroken, continuous, and consistent flow by the great prophets and poets of all time. He quoted Goethe in German and from Euripides via Gilbert Murray. On it went – an impressive, almost frightening, glimpse of an elemental force.

When, at length, we were on the sidewalk in front of Stoneleigh Court, I asked Hudson what he thought now about the Scientist of the Law. He stood there shaking with emotion, making little gestures as though trying to get his cuffs out of his coat sleeves. "Monstrous!" he kept saying. "It's monstrous!"[11]

In contrast to McReynolds, however, Brandeis distinguished his jurisprudence from his morality. This is apparent in the same Gold Clause cases that inspired McReynolds's memorable flight of oratory. No less than McReynolds, Brandeis believed that government's repudiation of its obligations to reimburse in gold was "terrifying in its implications. ... Departures from the moral law are the main causes of our present discontent. Further departures are not 'the way out.'"[12] For Brandeis, the "morals were plain & most important. I don't know whether we shall recover."[13] And yet Brandeis, in contrast to McReynolds, voted for the government's position in the Gold Clause cases, and he did so because, as he had written to the attorney general during his own tumultuous confirmation battle almost twenty years before, "My views in regard to the constitution are ... very much those of Mr. Justice Holmes."[14]

Like Holmes, Brandeis believed that the Court ought to use extreme caution in exercising its power to invalidate "arbitrary, capricious, or unreasonable" social and economic legislation, "lest we erect our prejudices into legal principles."[15] But this stance of self-denial fit far more comfortably with Holmes's cheerful skepticism[16] than it did with Brandeis's passionate moralism.[17] One never knew when Brandeis's zealous commitment to social justice would break through the iron discipline of judicial self-denial.[18] And of course this tension was exacerbated by the fact that Brandeis came to the bench from a history of ardent progressive advocacy that set him distinctly at odds with his brethren on the Taft Court.[19]

Brandeis was born in Louisville, Kentucky, on 13 November 1856, to a family of cultivated and prosperous German-Jewish grain merchants who had escaped from Europe after the failed revolutions of 1848. Brandeis's family was firmly abolitionist. It prospered by selling grain to Northern troops. Brandeis's "earliest memories were of the war. ... I remember helping my mother carry out food and coffee to the men from the North. The streets seemed full of them always. But there were times when the rebels came so near that we could hear the firing. At one such time my father moved us over the river."[20] Brandeis never received a college degree but studied at the Annen Realschule in Dresden during an extended family trip to Europe.

Brandeis's family did not deny their Judaism, but they were unobservant, following "the secular Christianity of the United States, sending each other Christmas greetings and gifts."[21] Brandeis, however, was especially enamored of his abolitionist uncle, Lewis Naphtali Dembitz (after whom Brandeis changed his middle name from David to Dembitz), who was both a practicing Jew and an

Louis Dembitz Brandeis

outstanding attorney. His uncle inspired Brandeis to become a lawyer. Brandeis enrolled at the Harvard Law School in 1875 at the age of 18.

Christopher Columbus Langdell had just begun to establish the radical new case method of Socratic instruction, and nothing could have been more to Brandeis's liking or capacity.[22] He thrived, compiling "the most brilliant record ever made at the Harvard Law School,"[23] an achievement that for decades would inspire hushed reverence.[24] Graduating at the age of 20, Brandeis formed his own law firm two years later with his good friend (and established Boston Brahmin) Sam Warren, who had finished second in Brandeis's Harvard Law School class. Warren's large family paper-mill business was their initial client. To earn income during the firm's early years, Brandeis clerked for Horace Gray, then chief justice of the Massachusetts Supreme Judicial Court (and in 1881 elevated to the United States Supreme Court). Gray considered Brandeis "the most ingenious and most original lawyer I have ever met, and he and his partner are among the most promising law firms we have got."[25]

With his prodigious legal intelligence, Brandeis helped make his firm a commercial success. "While Sam worked the Brahmin side of town, Louis sought business in the German-American and Jewish communities."[26] Brandeis mixed with the Boston elite. He grew friendly with Holmes, even attending the first of the Lowell Lectures that would eventually be published as *The Common Law*. Although it is probable that Brandeis was not invited to Warren's wedding because Warren's bride was virulently anti-Semitic, Brandeis's major contemporary biographer concludes that Brandeis did not at that time view himself as the victim of anti-Semitism.[27]

In his first years in Boston, Brandeis was likely a Republican. He became a Mugwump at about the time of Blaine's nomination in 1884, joining the usual civic societies, advocating the usual causes of good government.[28] During the next twenty years Brandeis gradually evolved from a high-powered business lawyer into a new role that he virtually invented, that of "the 'people's lawyer.'"[29] He came to believe that disagreements could best be resolved by altering the contexts in which they arose, rather than by zealously advocating for one side or another. A famous example involved William H. McElwain, a prominent shoe manufacturer, who hired Brandeis "to help break his workers' resistance to a wage cut."[30] Upon studying the situation, Brandeis proposed that McElwain's firm be reorganized to provide for continuous (rather than episodic) employment, so that both McElwain and his workers would benefit. Brandeis would later famously label this approach being "counsel for the situation."[31] The approach reflected Brandeis's deep need to retain independence from client direction and to follow the dictates of his own judgment.[32]

Brandeis's commitment to good government produced escalating conflicts with entrenched interests in which Brandeis advocated for mobilized constituencies that sought to advance the "public good." So, for example, Brandeis led the fight against Boston Elevated's efforts to run subway lines across the Boston Common, contending that the public should continue to control public land. In the course of these fights, Brandeis conceived and implemented innovative solutions that far outstripped the imagination of his constituencies. In opposing the Boston Consolidated Gas Company, for example, he developed and implemented a sliding scale for gas pricing that incentivized utility efficiency, thus earning the enmity of former allies who had simply sought to impose the lowest possible rates on the gas company.[33]

As Brandeis's reputation grew, so did his practice of inventing new and fresh solutions to complex social issues.[34] He saw these solutions as necessary to avoid catastrophic and destructive battles with vested interests, "with which none in our history save the Revolution and the Civil War can be compared."[35] "The struggle of privilege for privilege is unending and omnipresent,"[36] he warned. "We are sure to have for the next generation an ever-increasing contest between those who have and those who have not. There are vital economic, social and industrial problems to be solved. . . . We need *social inventions*, each of many able men adding his work until the invention is perfected."[37]

The upshot was that although Brandeis came, like Holmes, to view society as the site of ongoing struggle, he simultaneously imagined the possibility of "social inventions" that could somehow transcend that struggle. Holmes never developed any comparable concept of the public good. Holmes sought only to *channel* social contestation by subjecting it to orderly processes of law. By contrast, Brandeis came increasingly to privilege a concept of the public interest that stood outside of social conflict. When acting as a lawyer, Brandeis became ever more uncomfortable with the traditional requirements of zealous representation. When acting as a political reformer, he became ever more determined to free himself from the constraint of having to vocalize the views of his mobilized constituency.[38] He sought in all contexts to express his own perspective about what might serve the best interests of society as a whole. The ambiguity of that position would come back to haunt him when he was nominated to the Supreme Court.[39]

The scope and impact of Brandeis's many public interest activities are staggering. His prodigious legal imagination, his unerring instinct for framing his case in a way that generated positive publicity, his astonishing capacity to master every fact in every obscure and complex controversy, propelled Brandeis to a position of prominence, if not dominance, in the world of progressive legal reform.[40] Accounts of Brandeis's brilliant engagements are contained in his excellent biographies,[41] but for present purposes we shall briefly look at two episodes because of their importance for understanding Brandeis's role within the Taft Court.

First, consider Brandeis's legendary creation of the "Brandeis brief." In 1903, Oregon passed a statute forbidding the employment of women in any "mechanical establishment, or factory, or laundry" for "more than ten hours during any one day."[42] Two years later the Supreme Court struck down under the Fourteenth Amendment a New York statute forbidding the employment of bakers for more than ten hours in a day or sixty hours in a week. In *Lochner v. New York*, the Court interrogated the statute to determine whether it was "an unreasonable, unnecessary, and arbitrary interference with the right of the individual . . . to enter into those contracts in relation to labor which may seem to him appropriate or

Louis Dembitz Brandeis

necessary for the support of himself and his family." The Court held that the New York statute had "no such direct relation to, and no such substantial effect upon, the health of the employee, as to justify us in regarding the section as really a health law. It seems to us that the real object and purpose were simply to regulate the hours of labor between the master and his employees (all being men *sui juris*), in a private business, not dangerous in any degree to morals, or in any real and substantial degree to the health of the employees."[43] The constitutionality of the Oregon legislation was thus thrown into substantial uncertainty. It was challenged just five months after *Lochner* was decided.[44]

The National Consumers' League, which had vigorously supported the Oregon statute and other similar state legislation, was determined to defend the law. The general secretary of the League was Florence Kelley; the chair of its Committee on the Legal Defense of Labor Laws was Josephine Goldmark, Brandeis's sister-in-law.[45] To Kelley's chagrin, but in "what seemed to the men" on the League's Board "a master stroke," an appointment was arranged for Kelley to seek representation from the great New York lawyer Joseph Choate, slayer of the federal income tax and recent ambassador to the Court of Saint James.[46] But Choate could not see the gravamen of the litigation. "'A law *prohibiting* more than ten hours a day in laundry work,' he boomed. 'Big, strong laundry women. Why shouldn't they work longer?'"[47]

So Kelly and Goldmark approached Brandeis, who had all along been their first choice, and who accepted the assignment only a bare two months before oral argument. He insisted that he take no fee and that he be "invited to represent the state of Oregon by the state's attorney in charge of the defense."[48] In a remarkable and daring legal maneuver, Brandeis composed a brief that devoted only two pages to setting forth the legal principles of the case. In the remainder of its 113 pages, the brief recounted American and foreign statutes restricting the hours of women's labor. It quoted extensive excerpts from reports and findings to the effect that "The dangers of long hours for women arise from their special physical organization taken in connection with the strain incident to factory and similar work. ... [P]hysicians are agreed that women are fundamentally weaker than men in all that makes for endurance. ... Overwork, therefore, which strains endurance to the utmost, is more disastrous to the health of women than of men, and entails upon them more lasting injury."[49] None of this material had been introduced during the trial of the case.

Brandeis cited *Lochner* to establish governing legal principles. He quoted the opinion for the proposition that statutes interfering with freedom of contract were constitutional if there was "fair ground, reasonable in and of itself, to say that there is material danger to public health (or safety), or to the health (or safety) of the employees (or to the general welfare)."[50] He audaciously quoted Harlan's dissent for the proposition that "'[W]hen the validity of a statute is questioned, the burden of proof, so to speak, is upon those' who assail it."[51] (The majority opinion in *Lochner* had if anything implied exactly the contrary, asserting that the "fair ground" of inferring "material danger to public health" must be "clearly the case" if constitutional protections for "liberty of contract" are to be overcome.)[52]

Brandeis concluded his brief with a single paragraph asserting that, in light of the massive factual findings quoted in the brief, "it cannot be said that the Legislature of Oregon had no reasonable ground for believing that the public health, safety, or welfare did not require a legal limitation on women's work in manufacturing and mechanical establishments and laundries to ten hours in one day."[53]

The Court swallowed the brief whole, unanimously upholding the Oregon statute. It did not address the question of burden of proof, but it did hold that it was "obvious" that "woman's physical structure and the performance of maternal functions place her at a disadvantage in the struggle for subsistence" and that "as healthy mothers are essential to vigorous offspring, the physical well-being of woman becomes an object of public interest and care in order to preserve the strength and vigor of the race." At the outset of his opinion, no less a defender of the old order than Justice David J. Brewer gave a remarkable tribute to Brandeis: "In patent cases counsel are apt to open the argument with a discussion of the state of the art. It may not be amiss, in the present case, before examining the constitutional question, to notice the course of legislation, as well as expressions of opinion from other than judicial sources. In the brief filed by Mr. Louis D. Brandeis for the defendant is a very copious collection of all these matters, an epitome of which is found in the margin." And then, in a passage that Brandeis must have found especially satisfying, Brewer went on to declare: "Constitutional questions, it is true, are not settled by even a consensus of present public opinion. ... At the same time, when a question of fact is debated and debatable, and the extent to which a special constitutional limitation goes is affected by the truth in respect to that fact, a widespread and long continued belief concerning it is worthy of consideration. We take judicial cognizance of all matters of general knowledge."[54]

The rest, as they say, is history.[55] "To progressive reformers, *Muller v. Oregon* was a momentous triumph."[56] Brandeis's brief was a master stroke that entered legend and catapulted Brandeis into the highest echelon of progressive lawyers. If in 1897 Holmes had opined that "the black-letter man may be the man of the present, but the man of the future is the man of statistics and the master of economics,"[57] Brandeis was the man who represented that future. Laws imposing maximum work hours for women spread throughout the nation, as did the use of what became known as the Brandeis brief.[58]

In 1910, Brandeis used a much expanded version of his brief to persuade the Illinois Supreme Court to reverse its own 1895 precedent[59] holding unconstitutional a statute limiting women's working hours in manufacturing establishments to eight hours a day.[60] To Brandeis, the significance of the change was that in 1895 the Illinois Supreme Court was "reasoning from abstract conception," while in 1910 it was "reasoning from life," taking "notice of those facts of general knowledge embraced in the world's experience with unrestricted working hours."[61]

The difference illustrated a major principle that would come to underpin Brandeis's approach to constitutional law and that would deeply influence his work on the Taft Court: "Whether a measure relating to the public welfare is arbitrary or unreasonable, whether it has no substantial relation to the end proposed, is obviously not to be determined by assumptions or by a priori reasoning. The judgment should be based upon a consideration of relevant facts, actual or possible – *Ex facto jus oritur*. That ancient rule must prevail in order that we may have a system of living law."[62]

At Brandeis's memorial service in 1942, Attorney General Francis Biddle observed that the Brandeis brief, and the principles upon which it was based, "had a profound influence on the method of presenting arguments in cases involving social legislation, and, I suggest, on the outlook of courts to social problems. That judges today are more realistic, less given to the assumption of accepted dogmas, more mature and more curious-minded, is largely due to the influences of Brandeis."[63] Chief Justice Stone equated Brandeis's focus on facts with the common law system itself, which "derived its vitality and capacity for growth – from the very facts which, in every case, frame the issue for decision. And so, as the first step to decision, [Brandeis] sought complete acquaintance with the facts as the generative source of the law."[64]

Behind Brandeis's focus on facts was a characteristic progressive faith that, when presented with sufficient clarity, facts would speak for themselves,[65] that "behind every argument is someone's ignorance, and that disputes generally arise from misunderstanding."[66] "The difficulty in deciding any question that comes up," Brandeis said, "is really the difficulty in getting at the facts. Most men can decide any problem correctly if all of the facts be properly set before them."[67] He thus believed that judges who were hostile to social legislation were "as honest as you can make men,"[68] but that they were ignorant. "What we must do in America is not to attack our judges but to educate them. . . . In the past the courts have reached their conclusions largely deductively from preconceived notions and precedents. The method I have tried to employ in arguing cases before them has been inductive, reasoning from the facts."[69]

It is important to stress that for Brandeis the relevant facts were never confined to those that happened to be put into evidence by the parties in a particular case. Questions of constitutionality were for Brandeis matters of public power that were not to be determined by the hazards of litigation. Courts were to consult, as *Muller* had consulted, "all matters of general knowledge," which included all relevant experience. As Brandeis would later say as a justice, the Court ought to decide issues of constitutionality "in the light of all facts which may enrich our knowledge and enlarge our understanding."[70] Brandeis's colleagues on the Taft Court would sometimes declare a statute unconstitutional based upon the evidentiary record compiled in a particular case, whereas Brandeis would take a much broader view of the universe of relevant facts.[71]

Brandeis's relentless focus on facts gave rise to a style of judging that has become immensely influential. Unlike Holmes's jewel-like pronouncements, which were fundamentally inimitable, Brandeis created a *method* that could be adopted by any diligent jurist and that has in fact become the pattern for modern Supreme Court opinions. It is a method that encourages narrow and discrete judgments; it allows judicial conclusions to change as facts change. It is a method that puts courts in

THE TAFT COURT

dialogue with the purpose and rationale of challenged legislation and thus that potentially stimulates judicial empathy.[72] But, as Brandeis was repeatedly to learn throughout the 1920s, facts do not "argue themselves."[73] Facts alone do not settle genuine differences of principle, which, during the decade of the Taft Court, were to come increasingly to the fore.

The second event in Brandeis's career as a public interest lawyer that bears close examination is the Ballinger-Pinchot episode, which "plagued and doomed the Taft administration."[74] The episode grew out of a personal and policy conflict between Gifford Pinchot, a hold-over Roosevelt appointee who was then head of the U.S. Forest Service and a champion of Roosevelt's conservation policies, and Richard Ballinger, Taft's Secretary of the Interior. The two men had first clashed when Ballinger, as Roosevelt's commissioner of the General Land Office, brought effective and efficient reform to the Land Office and so created a bureaucratic obstacle to Pinchot's aspiration comprehensively to control federal land policies. When Taft appointed Ballinger to be secretary of the interior, Ballinger instituted policies that reflected a Western point of view. As a former mayor of Seattle, he wanted to throw open federal land and resources to the market, which meant making them available to smaller Western entrepreneurs. Pinchot, by contrast, had sought to withdraw federal land and resources from the market, which allowed for planned conservation efforts, but which also advantaged larger Eastern commercial interests.[75]

Louis R. Glavis, a field division chief in the General Land Office, accused Ballinger of improperly allowing federal lands in Alaska containing important coal deposits to fall into the hands of the Guggenheim-Morgan syndicate. With Pinchot's aggressive support, Glavis took his case directly to Taft himself. Taft fired Glavis at Ballinger's insistence, justifying his decision in what seemed to be a well-reasoned report, but in a side letter instructing Ballinger "to be very particular not to involve Mr. Pinchot in this matter."[76] Taft was determined to avoid an open rupture with Roosevelt's personnel and policies.[77] But Pinchot would not be appeased, and Glavis went public with his accusations in a sensational article in *Collier's*. Ballinger was accused of personal corruption, and the Taft administration was accused of selling national lands to special interests. A congressional investigation was authorized.

Collier's learned that the hearings, which would be controlled by Republican stalwarts who supported Taft, would whitewash Ballinger and that *Collier's* would then be sued for libel.[78] The magazine turned to Brandeis for representation. The congressional committee agreed that Brandeis could participate in the hearings to protect Glavis's interests.[79] If the invention of the Brandeis brief illustrates Brandeis's brilliance as an appellate lawyer, the Ballinger-Pinchot hearings illustrate his virtuosity as a trial attorney. Throughout the proceedings he was "savagely aggressive" and "nothing if not effective,"[80] with a preternatural grasp of the relevant facts.[81] He had a litigator's instinct for the jugular.

Through sheer intuitive genius, Brandeis deduced that the memorandum of Attorney General George Wickersham which Taft claimed was the basis for his decision, and which was dated about a month after Glavis's meeting with Taft and just a few days before Taft exonerated Ballinger, could not possibly have been composed in the relevant time period. Brandeis inferred that the memorandum must have been backdated in order to give the impression that Taft's decision to exonerate Ballinger and fire Glavis was based upon careful legal analysis. Brandeis demonstrated that the Wickersham memorandum contained passages refuting charges that had not even been articulated at the time the memorandum was dated.[82]

With this move, Brandeis significantly raised the stakes of the game. He effectively turned the Ballinger-Pinchot hearings into a trial of Taft himself, involving Brandeis in the highest levels of national politics. But, as Brandeis wrote his brother, "there is nothing for us to do but to follow the trail of evil wherever it extends. Fiat Justitia. In the fight against special interest we shall receive no quarter and may as well make up our minds to give none. It is a hard fight. The man with the hatchet is the only one who has a chance of winning in the end."[83]

Remarkably, Brandeis's deduction proved correct, and Wickersham admitted Brandeis's charge in a letter to Congress.[84] But by this point Brandeis was after bigger game. He had learned from a conscience-stricken government stenographer that Assistant Attorney General Oscar Lawler, who had been detailed to the Department of the Interior, had, with Ballinger's own assistance, prepared a secret legal memorandum exonerating Ballinger and had presented it to Taft shortly before the president's decision.

The news was political dynamite. Because the administration had consistently refused to acknowledge the existence of any such Lawler memorandum, Senator George Sutherland, a Republican stalwart and Taft supporter on the Committee, called Brandeis's insinuations "an insult to the President, and I for one, do not propose to be a party to it."[85] The Taft administration flatly stated that there was "absolutely no foundation" for the assertion that Taft's exoneration of Ballinger "was substantially prepared for the president's signature by Assistant Attorney General Lawler." "The President dictated his letter personally as the result of his own investigation of the record in consideration of documents and papers in his possession at the time, and upon the general report to him of the attorney general."[86]

But Brandeis had caught Taft out, and the following day the president sent a fuller clarification to the congressional committee. After hearing Glavis's charges and Ballinger's defense, and knowing that his extensive travel would not permit him adequately to study the record in the case, Taft explained that he had discussed the matter with Lawler and had requested him to "prepare an opinion as if he were President." Taft received Lawler's draft the morning before his decision. He found Lawler's work to be intemperate, containing criticisms "of Mr. Pinchot and Mr. Glavis I did not think it proper or wise to adopt. I only used a few paragraphs from it containing merely general statements." After extensive discussions with Wickersham, Taft redrafted Lawler's opinion and asked the attorney general to create a memorandum, "file it with the record, and date it prior to the date of my opinion, so as to show that my decision was fortified by his summary of the evidence and his conclusions therefrom."[87]

Taft had most likely suppressed the Lawler memorandum in an effort to prevent an overt break with Pinchot.[88] But by sending the congressional committee the Wickersham memorandum, on which he had *not* relied (because it did not exist), and by refusing despite Brandeis's repeated requests to disclose the existence of the Lawler memorandum,[89] which had in fact been materially pertinent to his decision, Taft gave the unmistakable impression of dishonesty, of hiding the true basis for his exoneration of Ballinger. And, of course, this played right into Pinchot's (and soon Roosevelt's) accusations that Taft was secretly defending special interests.

As the editor of *Collier's* observed, "By the time the frightened committee saw the document produced the whole country had decided that there was a conspiracy to shelter Ballinger at any cost. ... As Mr. Brandeis said to me: 'It was the lying that did it. If they had brazenly admitted everything, and justified it on the ground that Ballinger was at least doing what he thought best, we should not have had a chance.'"[90] What Brandeis regarded as "the awfulness of the President-Wickersham-Lawler frauds"[91] became a mortal wound to the Taft administration, which Brandeis exploited with unrelenting and masterful publicity.[92]

The hearings caused a profound change in Brandeis's attitude toward Taft. Brandeis had voted for Taft in 1908.[93] He considered Taft "admirably qualified for the position & doubtless will – if he lives – prove a fine President, rather of the Cleveland type."[94] As the Ballinger-Pinchot hearings began, however, Brandeis became increasingly puzzled by what he regarded as Taft's unthinking rigidity.[95] "The unfitness of Mr. Ballinger is being made more and more apparent, and the folly of the President more and more amazing. We had left him the loop-hole by pointing out how he had been misled; but he insists that he knew and knows it all."[96] Brandeis marveled at Taft's insistence that Ballinger be represented by the Democratic lawyer John J. Vertrees, who in his opening statement launched into a "denunciatory attack on Pinchot" that subverted Taft's larger strategic goal of minimizing his break with Roosevelt.[97] It was a decision that seemed to Brandeis "as unwise as most of the Great Chief Taft's moves."[98]

By the conclusion of the hearings, Brandeis wrote his wife that "I think as ill of WHT's morals now as of his intellect."[99] In 1911, Brandeis would in his private correspondence contemptuously refer to Taft as "the fat man,"[100] as a hopeless "reactionary."[101] On the other side, Taft's loathing for Brandeis, who through almost inhuman ingenuity and persistence had single-handedly undercut the bona fides of Taft's own presidency, would find its full expression when Brandeis was nominated to the Court.

In the meantime, however, the Ballinger-Pinchot episode catapulted Brandeis into national political prominence. He became the indispensable progressive lawyer. Brandeis had little regard for conventional political parties, but he did care passionately about progressive policies. And the policies that most enlisted his commitment were those that freed America from the shackles of what he called "our worship of the false god Bigness."[102] Brandeis relentlessly attacked the large trusts that in preceding decades had come to dominate the American economy. He opposed them not merely because he viewed them as predatory[103] and as inefficient,[104] but, most fundamentally, because he passionately believed that some organizations were "too large to be tolerated among ... people who desire to be free."[105]

Large trusts, in Brandeis's view, were so powerful that they crushed the life out of American workers.[106] Brandeis believed that there was a fundamental incompatibility between "political democracy" and "industrial absolutism."[107] "Men are not free if dependent industrially upon the arbitrary will of another. Industrial liberty on the part of the worker cannot, therefore, exist if there be overweening industrial power. Some curb must be placed upon capitalistic combination."[108] Brandeis argued that it was necessary for the country to limit the size and power of trusts because democracy itself required "free men. It must develop citizens. It cannot develop citizens unless the workingmen possess liberty."[109]

As with much of Brandeis's thought, his approach to the regulation of trusts began with the premise of American democracy. America needed to think hard and carefully about the prerequisites for successful democratic governance. "We Americans ... are committed primarily to democracy. ... And therefore the end for which we must strive is the attainment of rule by the people, and that involves industrial democracy as well as political democracy."[110] "You can not have true American citizenship," Brandeis declared, "unless some degree of industrial liberty accompanies it."[111] This reasoning was to inform many of Brandeis's most blazing dissents while on the Court. He believed that large trusts threatened to strangle not merely the growth of the American economy, but the independence and vigor of American citizens.[112]

As the 1912 presidential election approached, American political parties were divided about how to handle the issue of trusts. Brandeis had become personally close to Republican Senator Robert La Follette from Wisconsin. La Follette shared Brandeis's views about trusts, and indeed Brandeis had supplied La Follette with material for many of his important speeches on the subject.[113] Brandeis fully supported La Follette when the latter sought to lead an insurgent takeover of the Republican Party. But La Follette collapsed with a nervous breakdown in February 1912, which cleared the way for Theodore Roosevelt, who was determined to assume the mantle of progressive change by challenging Taft for the Republican nomination.

Roosevelt was a mesmerizing, charismatic presence, "pretty near irresistible,"[114] who inspired the wholehearted support of progressives like Felix Frankfurter, Learned Hand, and Gifford Pinchot. In what became a suicidal and fratricidal war, Taft secured the official nomination of the Republican Party, while Roosevelt broke away to form the independent Progressive Party. Brandeis could not support "a reactionary Taft administration,"[115] and it became increasingly clear to him that Roosevelt's "so-called Progressive Party"[116] had "practically adopted the Perkins trust policy" that supported large business enterprises.[117] George W. Perkins, a J.P. Morgan banker and board member of the United States Steel Corporation, was the executive secretary of Roosevelt's Progressive Party; he had prominently proclaimed that "the trust has developed naturally. ... It furnishes a more economical and efficient way of doing business.... Would it not be better to preserve the acknowledged good that is in the trusts and eradicate or curb the evil?"[118]

Although he acknowledged that "most of my progressive friends will stand by T.R.,"[119] Brandeis could not stomach "the belief that private monopoly is desirable or permissible, provided it be regulated. That issue seems to me to be a fundamental one – one on which the [Progressive] Party is radically wrong, and so long as it stands for private monopoly and privilege, it cannot be the true means of real progress in this Country."[120] For Brandeis the distinction "between regulation of competition and regulation of monopoly" was "as fundamental as that between Democracy and Absolutism."[121] The Progressive Party's "program of legalizing and perpetuating trusts was a great menace to labor," because it encouraged "the development of new capitalistic combinations, fundamentally hostile to organized labor, and determined by the huge power of combined resources to exterminate unionism from the industries which they would control."[122]

Brandeis therefore opted to support the Democratic candidate,[123] Woodrow Wilson, whose Presbyterian moralism and commitment to competition Brandeis found attractive. Announcing his support, Brandeis declared that Wilson understood "the dangers incident to the control of a few of our industries and finance. He sees that true democracy and social justice are unattainable unless the power of the few be curbed, and our democracy becomes industrial as well as political."[124] The two men met, leaving Brandeis "very favorably impressed with Wilson. He is strong, simple, serious, openminded, eager to learn and deliberate,"[125] with the "qualities of an ideal President."[126]

Brandeis rapidly became, in Arthur Link's words, "the chief architect of Wilson's New Freedom."[127] Brandeis wrote Wilson that

[t]he Democratic Party insists that competition can be and should be maintained in every branch of private industry ... and that, if at any future time monopoly should appear to be desirable in any branch of industry, the monopoly should be a public one – a monopoly owned by the people and not by the capitalists.... The [Progressive] Party, on the other hand, insists that private monopoly may be desirable in some branches of industry, or at all events, inevitable; and that existing trusts should not be dismembered or forcibly dislodged from those branches of industry which they have already acquired a monopoly, but should be made "good" by regulation. ... This difference in the economic policy of the two parties is fundamental and irreconcilable. It is the difference between industrial liberty and industrial absolutism.[128]

Although "in certain important respects he did not go as far as Brandeis had suggested," Wilson nevertheless "became the leading political spokesman of Brandeis's program for the regulation of competition."[129] Brandeis campaigned relentlessly for Wilson,[130] and Wilson in turn came to rely on and value Brandeis's advice. Although Brandeis did not receive a Cabinet appointment with Wilson, to which Brandeis was ambivalently attracted,[131] he nevertheless consulted closely with Wilson about a wide range of subjects and was instrumental in shaping the

Louis Dembitz Brandeis

Wilson administration's stance toward such important legislation as the Federal Reserve Act, the Clayton Anti-Trust Act, and the Federal Trade Commission Act.[132]

Justice Joseph Rucker Lamar, who had been appointed by President Taft, died on January 2, 1916. Almost immediately there were calls for Wilson to fill the vacancy by appointing Taft.[133] But Wilson, who had been elected in 1912 as a minority president, knew that in November he would face a reunited Republican Party in which the rift between insurgents and stalwarts had largely healed. Wilson would be unlikely to win reelection if he could not attract the support of Roosevelt progressives. Although at that time "Brandeis was perhaps the American most hated by big business, financial leaders, and railroad interests,"[134] and although Wilson knew that nominating Brandeis would be enormously controversial, it would nevertheless cement Wilson's position as a champion of progressive causes. It would also earn Wilson the loyalty and support of Jewish voters.[135] It was therefore not merely Wilson's faith in Brandeis's talent and vision that secured the latter's nomination, but also pure, brilliant political calculation.[136] Wilson sent Brandeis's name to the Senate on January 28.

The resulting explosion[137] is legendary and well documented.[138] Brandeis's nomination was referred to the Committee on the Judiciary, which in turn created a subcommittee to hold intense hearings that lasted from February 9 to March 15.[139] The hearings formally focused on allegations that Brandeis's "honesty and integrity" were questionable and that his professional "reputation" among lawyers was "bad."[140] These issues arose in part because of the ambiguous posture Brandeis had often assumed in staking out the radically innovative position of "counsel for the situation."[141]

The focus on Brandeis's character and professional ethics sidestepped the actual objection to Brandeis, which turned on his substantive understanding of law. As it happened, Brandeis had forcefully articulated that understanding in an address called *The Living Law*[142] which he delivered on the day after Lamar's death. Brandeis argued that "recent dissatisfaction with our law" stemmed from the failure of "legal justice" "to conform to contemporary conceptions of social justice." He complained that judges had ignored "newly arisen social needs" by "complacently" applying "18th century conceptions of the liberty of the individual and of the sacredness of private property. ... Where statutes giving expression to the new social spirit were clearly constitutional, judges, imbued with the relentless spirit of individualism, often construed them away." As a consequence, "constitutional limitations were invoked to stop the natural vent of legislation." Citing *Lochner* and *Ives*, Brandeis chided: "Small wonder that there arose a clamor for the recall of judges and of judicial decisions."[143]

The merits of Brandeis's constitutional jurisprudence could not be debated without, as the *Detroit Free Press* clearly saw, recognizing the possibility "that the supreme court of the United States ... was never an impartial body of jurists, but is and has ever been a biased and prejudiced bench, whose unjust decrees must now be checked by injecting into its personnel men who will arrive at their irrevocable decisions by other courses of reasoning than have heretofore influenced the august decisions that have been handed down in Washington. Has the past history of this mighty court been of such a despicable character? The very supposition is monstrous. Yet that is the whole foundation of the demand for Brandeis in most quarters."[144] Those attacking Brandeis's nomination had no intention of creating an official forum in which the class biases of Supreme Court decisions might be debated.

The popular debate over Brandeis nevertheless rapidly assumed overtly political dimensions. Protesting the "indefensible and outrageous" nomination of Brandeis, for example, the *Los Angeles Times* railed: "Brandeis is the radical of radicals, interested in and promoting destructive policies rather than plans for the development and well-being of this great country. A shout of rejoicing over his appointment has gone up from every dynamiter and hell-raiser in the land. His nomination is an obvious appeal by the President for the political support of the Socialists, Gompersites, law-defying labor union bosses, corporation baiters, wreckers of business and all the discontented and dangerous elements of the population."[145] The *Christian Science Monitor*, by contrast, affirmed that

> [t]he antagonism to Mr. Brandeis has ... laid bare the grounds upon which one great element in politics bases its opposition to the policies of another. It has served to show, for the millionth time, that when one undertakes to champion any great reform he must be prepared to encounter the allied and bitter opposition of all those engaged in practices and enterprises in need of reformation. ... It has been difficult, and in some cases seemingly impossible, for certain of the opponents of Mr. Brandeis to credit him with worthy motives in his warfare against social and industrial injustice.[146]

Taft was personally "shocked"[147] at the nomination. His violent reaction was due in part to resentment at Brandeis's role in the Ballinger-Pinchot episode. But it also represented genuine revulsion at Brandeis's jurisprudence. As Taft famously wrote a friend three days after the nomination was announced:

> It is one of the deepest wounds that I have had as an American and a lover of the Constitution and a believer in progressive conservatism, that such a man as Brandeis could be put in the Court. ... He is a muckraker, an emotionalist for his own purposes, a socialist, prompted by jealousy, a hypocrite, a man who has certain high ideals in his imagination, but who is utterly unscrupulous, in method in reaching them, a man of infinite cunning, of marked ability in that direction that hardly rises above the dignity of cunning, of great tenacity of purpose, and, in my judgment, of much power for evil. He is only one of nine on the Court, but one on the Court is often an important consideration; and even if the rest of the Court is against him, he has the opportunity to attack their judgments and weaken their force by insidious demagoguery, and an appeal to the restless element that can do infinite harm. I sincerely hope that he can be defeated in the Senate, but I don't think so. ... When you consider Brandeis' appointment, and think that men were pressing me for the place, *es ist zum lachen*.[148]

Louis Dembitz Brandeis

"The feeling of the members of the court," Taft wrote his brother, "must be intense also on this subject."[149]

Taft clearly understood the challenge posed by Brandeis's understanding of law, as articulated in *The Living Law*. He believed that Brandeis was "an appointment, which if it were repeated a number of times would break down the Supreme Court as a bulwark of the guaranties of civil liberty. He is a Socialist and has an ingenuity and a lack of scruple in method which make him dangerous. As one upon the Bench, he may not be able to do harm, and till he can do harm, he may seem to be more conservative than is expected, but wherever his vote will count to break down the conserving language of the Constitution, it will be cast."[150] Taft accordingly felt duty-bound publicly to oppose the nomination. Assisted by Wickersham,[151] he helped organize a letter that he and six other presidents of the American Bar Association signed. "Taking into view the reputation, character and professional career of Louis D. Brandeis," the letter said, "he is not a fit person to be a member of the Supreme Court."[152] It is striking that not even Taft would explicitly debate the principles that ought to govern the Court's constitutional jurisprudence.[153]

After taking the public testimony of forty-seven witnesses that occupied about 1,500 pages of testimony, the subcommittee on April 3 recommended in a straight party-line vote that Brandeis be confirmed.[154] On May 24, the full Judiciary Committee, also in a straight party-line vote, recommended confirmation. In a searing minority report, signed by, among others, Senator George Sutherland, the Republican members of the Committee opined: "Never before in the history of the country has a man been appointed a Justice of the Supreme Court of the United States whose honesty and integrity were seriously brought in question. It must be evident to any thinking and unbiased mind that this appointment has resulted from something other than the qualifications and fitness of the appointee for the office."[155]

Because Democrats controlled the Senate, and because Wilson demanded and obtained strict party discipline, it was clear that Brandeis would be confirmed. Republican opposition collapsed "as a result of their conclusion that further obstruction will intensify the growing impression that the Republican party is opposed to the elevation of a Jew to the Supreme Court bench."[156] "One of the bitterest contests ever waged against a presidential nominee"[157] ended in an eerie "compromise":[158] There would be no debate on the floor of the Senate, Republicans would not filibuster the appointment, but the majority and minority committee reports, as well as the roll-call vote, would be released to the public.[159] Brandeis was confirmed on June 1, 1916, in a largely party-line vote.[160]

The epic struggle over Brandeis's confirmation set the pattern for many nomination battles that would subsequently mar the history of the Court. The *New Republic* presciently observed that "Mr. Brandeis's enemies have done more to drag the Supreme Court into politics than the most extreme radical. ... For the first time to our knowledge an appointment to the Supreme Court has been dealt with through the ordinary methods of agitation. The precedent has been created by the very men to whom the Court is alleged to be sacrosanct."[161] The coordinated and well-financed campaign against Brandeis meant "that the Supreme Court is to be in politics with a vengeance. It means that a most dangerous precedent has been established, and that the next time a contested appointment is made we may expect press agents, campaign funds, mass meetings, oratory and political jobbery."[162]

Throughout the process Brandeis remained uncharacteristically silent. He directed his defense behind the scenes and refused all public commentary. It was a grueling and humiliating experience, but, as he had written his brother during the Ballinger-Pinchot episode, Brandeis was someone "who would rather fight than eat."[163] Victory was sweet. Brandeis would ascend the bench remarkably free from malice or recrimination, yet he would be steeled in his determination to translate the lessons of his activism into the language of constitutional law. He would find the role of a judge highly compatible with his commitment to personal independence and to advocacy for the public good.

By the commencement of the Taft Court, Brandeis and Taft, despite their fraught personal history, had managed to achieve something of a personal accommodation. The initiative seems to have come from Taft himself. In December 1918, Brandeis wrote his wife:

> Dearest: Had an experience yesterday which I did not expect to encounter in this life. As I was walking toward the Stoneleigh about 1 P.M., Taft & I met. There was a moment's hesitation, & when he'd almost passed, he stopped & said in a charming manner: "Isn't this Justice Brandeis? I don't think we have ever met." I answered: "Yes, we met at Harvard after your return from the Philippines." He at once began to talk about my views on regularity of employment. After a moment I asked him to come in with me. He spent a half hour in 809 [Stoneleigh], talking labor & War Labor Board experiences. Was most confidential – at one point put his hand on my knee. I told him of the great service he had rendered the country by his action on the Labor Board, & we parted with his saying in effect – He hoped we would meet often.[164]

Within days of Taft's confirmation, Brandeis reached out to say that "I am delighted to hear that you have undertaken the task of making more efficient the administration of our law. It is by such intelligent appreciation of existing defects and determined effort to devise remedies that respect for law may be promoted."[165] Taft in turn asked Brandeis to consult on proposals to reform certain practices within the Court, to which Brandeis "most cordially" replied.[166] Taft wrote his brother in October that "Brandeis and I are on the most excellent terms and have some sympathetic views in reference to a change in the relations of the court to the Clerk as to financial matters. He can not be any more cordial to me than I am to him, so that honors are easy."[167] "I've come to like Brandeis very much indeed," Taft wrote his daughter in 1923. "He is a very hard worker. He thinks much of the Court and is anxious to have it consistent and strong, and he pulls his weight in the boat."[168]

Brandeis reported to Frankfurter that Taft was "very nice – gentlemanly in dealing with case involving Ballinger."[169] Frankfurter, who was an intimate of Brandeis, later wrote that although President Taft had "crossed swords very fiercely indeed" with Brandeis, "they became fast friends on the Court."[170] Henry Friendly, who was Brandeis's clerk during the 1927 term, reports that "All feelings of hostility, or even of embarrassment, disappeared once they became colleagues on the Court."[171] We also have good evidence that despite Sutherland's role in the Ballinger-Pinchot episode and Sutherland's signing of the stinging minority report opposing Brandeis's confirmation, Brandeis nevertheless established "cordial relations with Sutherland."[172] Certainly, Sutherland's returns on Brandeis's draft opinions are conspicuously warm and complimentary, even flattering.[173]

These social amenities were important to Brandeis, because they enabled him to participate in the Court's deliberations and to affect its judgments.[174] In his superb study, *The Unpublished Opinions of Mr. Justice Brandeis*,[175] Alexander Bickel has demonstrated that important Taft Court opinions like *Sonneborn Bros. v. Cureton*[176] and *Railroad Commission of California v. Southern Pacific Co.*[177] substantially reflected Brandeis's views as set forth in well-researched independent memoranda to the Court, to which Taft, at least at first, seemed responsive.[178] Brandeis characterized Taft as possessing an "open mind usually."[179]

Taft was not open, however, to Brandeis's constitutional jurisprudence. Brandeis "is certainly a very useful member of the Court," Taft told his son, "save in one field."[180] "Brandeis tries as hard as he can to be a good fellow," Taft remarked to his brother, "and in many respects he is, but when he gets into the field of politics and political economics, his judgment is all awry and his methods are not above criticism."[181] Taft made it his business to ensure that new appointments to the Taft Court would not "herd with Brandeis in opinions in that kind of cases, as Brandeis is usually against the Court."[182] Taft did not want colleagues who would "break down" the Constitution "and make it go for nothing. That I think was Wilson's purpose in appointing Brandeis and Clarke. . . . [W]e need men who are liberal but who still believe that the corner stone of our civilization is in the proper maintenance of the guaranties of the 14th Amendment and the 5th Amendment."[183]

For Taft, the guaranties of the Fourteenth and Fifth Amendments "secured as sacred the right of private property," which underlies the "conservative government we live under" and which protects us "against attacks of anarchy, socialism and communism."[184] Taft and Brandeis differed in many ways in their perspectives on constitutional law, but the most fundamental point of disagreement is that Taft understood the Constitution to establish "the security of private property and free contract" in order to safeguard "the chief agent in the material progress of the human race":

> The certainty that a man could enjoy as his own that which he produced, furnished the strongest motive for industry beyond what was merely necessary to obtain the bare necessities of life. The knowledge that what he saved would enable him to increase and share the result of another's labor was the chief inducement to economy and self control, and this was greatly strengthened as a motive when he came to know that what he saved during his life could be enjoyed after his death by those to whom he was bound by natural affection. In other words, the institution of private property is what has led to the accumulation of capital in the world. Capital represents and measures the difference between the present condition of society and that which prevailed when men lived by what

their hands would produce without implements or other means of increasing the result of their labor, that is, between the utter barbarism of prehistoric ages and modern civilization.[185]

Taft believed that "The very advantage to be derived from the security of private property in our civilization is that it turns the natural selfishness and desire for gain into the strongest motive for doing that without which the upward development of mankind would cease and retrogression would begin. ... With the destruction of private property that motive would disappear and so would the progress of society."[186] "Any change in our social and political system which impairs the right of private property and materially diminishes the motive for the accumulation of capital by the individual," reasoned Taft, "is a blow at our whole civilization."[187] Taft therefore concluded that it was the function of the Supreme Court to protect "sacred" property rights "from the gusty and unthinking passions of temporary majorities" and "to declare void the intermittent attempts of state legislatures and of congress to override them."[188]

Taft was constitutionally committed to the incentives he thought necessary for prosperity and civilization. His jurisprudence was not in any respect formal. It did not primarily rely on the explicit texts of the Constitution, or on natural law, or on *stare decisis*. Taft was not primarily dedicated to custom and tradition, as was McReynolds. He instead held an instrumental view of law, as did Holmes.[189] Taft believed that judicial review and constitutional law were necessary to protect the inducements for the "industry and self-restraint"[190] that created civilization.[191] This was a fundamental imperative that Taft shared with other conservatives on the Taft Court, like Sutherland, who also firmly believed that property rights provided "that great incentive to individual effort which is furnished by the feeling of certainty that one will be allowed to enjoy the fruits of his own industry and genius."[192] Property was constitutionally protected, as McKenna once succinctly put it, for "the purposeful encouragement of individual incentive and energy."[193] This utilitarian defense of property was in fact pervasive and commonplace in the 1920s.[194]

Although Brandeis was personally ascetic, he did not reject property rights; nor did he reject the importance of material growth. But in sharp contrast to Taft and his conservative colleagues, Brandeis believed that "property is only a means"[195] and that its "end" was not economic prosperity, but instead the full development of individual personality. "Property must be subject to that control of property which is essential to the enjoyment by every man of a free individual life. And when property is used to interfere with that fundamental freedom of life for which property is *only a means*, then property must be controlled."[196]

For Brandeis, the constitutional purpose of property rights, and indeed of all constitutional rights,[197] derived from the democratic commitments of the nation. "However much we may desire material improvement and must desire it for the comfort of the individual," Brandeis said, "we must bear in mind all the time ... that the United States is a democracy. ... We Americans are committed ... primarily to democracy."[198] "Our form of government ... compels us to strive for the development of the individual man. Under universal suffrage ... every voter is a part ruler

Louis Dembitz Brandeis

of the state. Unless the rulers have, in the main, education and character, and are free men, our great experiment in democracy must fail. It devolves upon the state, therefore, to fit its rulers for their task."[199] Brandeis believed that "the essentials of American citizenship are not satisfied by supplying merely the material needs or even the wants of the worker."[200] Instead "the development of the individual is ... both a necessary means and the end sought. For our objective is the making of men and women who shall be free, self-respecting members of a democracy."[201]

It was possible, and even likely, that legislation that sought to accord persons "the opportunity of developing their faculties"[202] might intrude on existing common law rights of property and freedom of contract. But Brandeis believed that these rights ought not cabin legislation designed to secure "those higher standards essential to life, health and the performance of the duties of citizenship in a democracy."[203] Courts had no business using existing property rights to second-guess the constitutional efforts of a democracy to perfect the lives of its own citizens. "Our function," Brandeis said, "is to determine, in the light of all facts which may enrich our knowledge and enlarge our understanding, whether the measure, enacted in the exercise of an unquestioned police power and of a character inherently unobjectionable, transcends the bounds of reason; that is, whether the provision as applied is so clearly arbitrary or capricious that legislators acting reasonably could not have believed it to be necessary or appropriate for the public welfare."[204]

Like Holmes, Brandeis believed that courts ought to exercise great deference in evaluating legislation under the Fifth and Fourteenth Amendments. But Brandeis came to this conclusion for entirely different reasons than did Holmes. Holmes thought courts ought to defer to statutes because legislation best reflected the dominant opinion of a community, which was the expression of its sovereignty. By contrast, Brandeis believed that courts ought to defer to legislation because statutes were the result of a democracy that empowered persons to become "free citizens of a free country [who] may perform their duties as citizens."[205] If conservative jurists discounted democracy as a "despotism of the mob,"[206] or as a simple "tyranny of the plurality of the electorate,"[207] Brandeis instead celebrated democracy as the very purpose of the Constitution.

Conservative jurists tended to dismiss legislation as "the mere product of popular will or of a legislative majority of the hour."[208] When exercising judicial review of social and economic legislation they therefore frequently concentrated on only a single constitutional question. They asked whether constitutional rights of property were violated. But Brandeis approached judicial review from a radically different premise. Because he regarded legislation as itself a medium of constitutional self-government, Brandeis believed that courts must always weigh multiple, conflicting constitutional values when exercising the prerogative of judicial review. At a minimum they must balance the harm to democracy caused by judicial invalidation of a statute against whatever other constitutional rights might be at stake. We have now so thoroughly assimilated this basic insight that we can easily miss the profoundly innovative nature of Brandeis's reframing of the question of judicial review.[209] Throughout the Taft Court era, Brandeis alone explored the theoretical implications of imagining democracy as itself a fundamental constitutional commitment.

Brandeis argued that balancing conflicting constitutional principles necessarily involves "a weighing ... of relative social values. Since government is not an exact science, prevailing public opinion concerning the evils and the remedy is among the important facts deserving consideration, particularly when the public conviction is both deep-seated and widespread and has been reached after deliberation. What, at any particular time, is the paramount public need, is necessarily largely a matter of judgment."[210] Because matters of judgment rarely yield clear right or wrong answers, courts ought to respect the popular judgments embodied in legislation, which is both the expression and the training ground of democratic citizenship. If "the end is the development of the people by self-government in the fullest sense,"[211] and if "responsibility is the great developer of men,"[212] judicial deference creates space for citizens to achieve their full civic potential.[213] Courts ought to stay their hand except in those rare cases when legislative judgments are "so clearly arbitrary or capricious that legislators acting reasonably could not have believed it to be necessary or appropriate for the public welfare."

Brandeis observed that the adjustment of competing constitutional interests requires "consideration of the contemporary conditions, social, industrial and political, of the community to be affected thereby. Resort to such facts is necessary, among other things, in order to appreciate the evils sought to be remedied and the possible effects of the remedy proposed."[214] Brandeis argued that courts, in contrast to legislatures, "are ill-equipped to make the investigations which should precede a determination of the limitations which should be set upon" property rights.[215] Because of this institutional limitation, courts should be exceedingly cautious in exercising the prerogative of judicial review.

Brandeis also strongly believed, on the basis of his own experience, that effective solutions to social problems could be attained only through arduous processes of trial and error.[216] It followed that society could not progress unless courts refrained from circumscribing the experimentation necessary for social improvement:

> [A]dvances in the exact sciences and the achievements in invention remind us that the seemingly impossible sometimes happens. There are many men now living who were in the habit of using the age-old expression: "It is as impossible as flying." The discoveries in physical science, the triumphs in invention, attest the value of the process of trial and error. In large measure, these advances have been due to experimentation. In those fields experimentation has, for two centuries, been not only free but encouraged. Some people assert that our present plight is due, in part, to the limitations set by courts upon experimentation in the fields of social and economic science; and to the discouragement to which proposals for betterment there have been subjected otherwise. There must be power in the states and the nation to remould, through experimentation, our economic practices and institutions to meet changing social and economic needs. I cannot believe that the framers of the Fourteenth Amendment, or the states which ratified it, intended to

deprive us of the power to correct the evils of technological unemployment and excess productive capacity which have attended progress in the useful arts.[217]

This chain of reasoning sharply differentiated Brandeis from Holmes. Although both men advocated judicial deference, their jurisprudential premises could not be more different. Holmes was a skeptic who believed that legislation was merely the outcome of social conflict, "the preference of a given body in a given time and place."[218] In the absence of clear constitutional texts, courts had no business interfering in the natural struggles by which societies evolved. Brandeis, by contrast, was a democrat who believed that legislation was intrinsically valuable because it was the vehicle of constitutional self-government. Legislation was the medium through which citizens expressed the promise and responsibilities of self-determination. Unless legislation was entirely arbitrary, courts ought not interfere with how citizens chose to define themselves "in the processes of common living."[219] Deference was justified for Brandeis out of a moral respect for democracy; it was justified for Holmes because legislation was the only mechanism by which modern societies could peacefully accommodate the competing claims of hostile groups.

The difference between Holmes and Brandeis is manifest in their First Amendment jurisprudence. Holmes would protect freedom of speech on the strangely paradoxical and skeptical ground "that the best test of truth is the power of the thought to get itself accepted in the competition of the market, and that truth is the only ground upon which ... wishes safely can be carried out."[220] Brandeis would by contrast protect freedom of speech on the overtly democratic ground "that the greatest menace to freedom is an inert people; that public discussion is a political duty; and that this should be a fundamental principle of the American government."[221]

The conservative Taft Court was not receptive to Brandeis's constitutional views. He was given few if any opportunities to expound his constitutional jurisprudence in Court opinions, so that the decisions he authored for the Court in the 1920s are now largely unknown.[222] Instead his influence resides chiefly in his remarkable dissents, which articulate an influential vision of democratic government as a purposive, value-driven enterprise worthy of respect, as distinct from the site of merely "gusty and unthinking passions."[223] Also influential is Brandeis's view of courts and legislatures as possessing sharply differentiated institutional capacities. Brandeis's vision would ultimately give birth to the legal process school of jurisprudence,[224] which is now all but inescapable for any literate student of American constitutional law. Frankfurter once remarked that quoting from Holmes's decisions "is to string pearls," while quoting from Brandeis's opinions is "to pull threads from a pattern."[225] The pattern woven by Brandeis has now become the basic framework for post-New Deal public law.

Brandeis loathed the 1920s as a "pernicious era of good feeling."[226] With its crass and conspicuous celebration of prosperity, the decade was indeed an inhospitable time for Brandeis's jurisprudential views.[227] Figure P-1 illustrates that within the Taft Court Brandeis was (apart from Clarke) the least likely of any justice to join an opinion for the Court. Figure II-14 shows that, apart from McReynolds and McKenna, he was more than twice as likely as any other justice

THE TAFT COURT

to dissent alone. Figure I-18 suggests that Taft tended to assign Brandeis uncontroversial opinions, probably because, as indicated in Figures I-10 and I-19, Brandeis had at best only a modest ability to attract votes.[228] Figure II-6 shows that he was, like Sutherland and McReynolds, a relatively independent player in conference, but Figure II-15 illustrates that in published opinions he was most likely to join with Holmes.[229] Brandeis was a productive, industrious member of the Court,[230] who wrote opinions of average length[231] in about an average amount of time.[232]

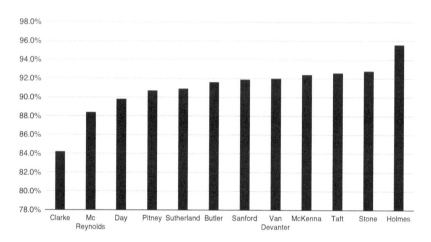

Figure II-15 Percentage of decisions in which Brandeis participated and joined the same opinion as another justice, 1921–1928 terms

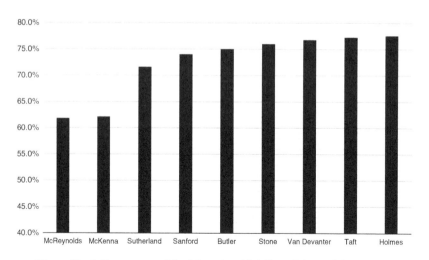

Figure II-16 Percentage of decisions in which Brandeis participated and voted with another justice in conference

316

Louis Dembitz Brandeis

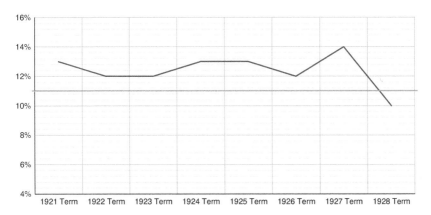

Figure II-17 Percentage of Court's opinions authored by Brandeis, by term. An even distribution of cases would assign 1/9, or 11%, to each justice.

Taft did give Brandeis relatively free rein to lead the Court in the area of transportation, especially in cases involving the Interstate Commerce Commission ("ICC") and the Transportation Act of 1920,[233] which had terminated federal wartime control over railroads and invested the ICC with vast new regulatory powers. At one point Taft jokingly and warmly praised Brandeis as "the pope of interstate commerce regulation."[234] These were difficult cases, involving some of the most complex questions of administrative law of the decade. They exposed an intellectual tension spring-loaded within Brandeis's most basic commitments.

In 1910, appearing before the ICC as an attorney for shippers, Brandeis had opposed a rate increase on the startling ground that railroads could save $1 million a day by adopting principles of scientific management. It was both a brilliant insight and a striking public relations coup.[235] Brandeis had long believed in the necessity of efficient, scientific management; earlier in his career he had seriously tangled with unions about the necessity of introducing scientific management to prevent waste and promote efficiency.[236] As Brandeis explained to the ICC, scientific management left nothing "to chance. All is carefully prepared in advance. Every operation is to be performed according to a predetermined schedule under definite instructions and the execution under this plan is inspected and supervised at every point." The scientific manager "considers a business as an intricate machine," and his goal is to coordinate business processes "so that the machinery of the whole business works with equal smoothness."[237]

The difficulty with this (very progressive) view of efficient management is that it is in serious tension with Brandeis's equally fundamental commitment to industrial liberty, which in his view required division not merely "of profits, but ... also of responsibilities. The employees must have the opportunity of participating in the decisions as to what shall be their condition and how the business shall be run. . . . [T]he right to assist in making the decisions, the right of making their own mistakes, if mistakes there must be, is a privilege which should not be denied

317

to labor. We must insist upon labor sharing the responsibilities for the result of the business."[238] If responsibility was the great developer of men, then labor must have "a vote; not merely a right to be heard, but a position through which labor may participate in management."[239] Only in this way could "the powers of the individual employee ... be developed to the utmost."[240]

Brandeis was caught in toils of a contradiction. On the one hand, he imagined the firm as a well-oiled machine that followed precise plans laid out well in advance by a scientific engineer. But, on the other hand, he also envisioned the firm as the site of political struggle between labor and management, with all the messy compromises entailed in any such democratic political process.[241] The first image of the workplace expresses the need for rational planning to avoid waste; the second expresses the need to foster a responsibility that can arise only from genuine democratic participation.

This double vision runs throughout Brandeis's work. The managerial side of Brandeis would design and advocate for "a comprehensive system which shall extend protection ... to the wage-earners in case of invalidity, superannuation or unemployment";[242] it would diagnose the flaws in a vicious "system" of industrial life insurance and propose instead a well-engineered alternative system of savings bank insurance.[243] The democratic side of Brandeis, by contrast, would proclaim that "progress flows only from struggle."[244] For the man who believed that "fighting, politically & economically, is the price of liberty & life,"[245] it is hard to see how even the best designed system could be anything other than a restraint on individual development and accountability.[246]

The tension between the twin values of efficient management and democratic self-expression is evident in Brandeis's decisions concerning railroad transportation. Brandeis understood full well that the Transportation Act put the ICC into the position of the scientific manager of the nation's vast railroad system. "Congress undertook to develop and maintain, for the people of the United States, an adequate railway system. It recognized that preservation of the earning capacity, and conservation of the financial resources, of individual carriers, is a matter of national concern; that the property employed must be permitted to earn a reasonable return; that the building of unnecessary lines involves waste of resources, and that the burden of this waste may fall upon the public; that the competition between carriers may result in harm to the public, as well as in benefit; and that, when a railroad inflicts injury upon its rival, it may be the public which ultimately bears the loss. The act sought, among other things, to avert such losses."[247]

The ICC was charged with managing the nation's rail system in the interests of the public, which meant in the interests of efficiency. But in this picture what space remained for democratic participation? Throughout his career Brandeis had warmly embraced decentralization and federalism[248] because he viewed states not only as laboratories for experimentation,[249] but also as relatively small communities within which persons could participate in genuine processes of self-governance that might develop them as democratic citizens.[250]

"For a century our growth has come through national expansion and the increase of the functions of Federal Government," Brandeis said. But the "growth of the future ... must be in quality and spiritual value. And that can come only through the concentrated, intensified striving of small groups. The field for special effort should now be the State, the city, the village."[251] The states were for Brandeis fora in which genuine democratic dialogue and struggle could occur. Yet if the ICC were the scientific manager of the nation's entire railroad system, what role would be left for either experimentation or self-governance by states?[252]

In *Colorado v. United States*, for example, the ICC had authorized a railroad to shut down a branch line that was located entirely within the state. Colorado argued that the federal government had no power to regulate intrastate transportation in this way. Brandeis brusquely rejected that claim in the name of efficient management. "This railroad, like most others, was chartered to engage in both intrastate and interstate commerce. The same instrumentality serves both. The two services are inextricably intertwined. The extent and manner in which one is performed, necessarily affects the performance of the other. Efficient performance of either is dependent upon the efficient performance of the transportation system as a whole."[253] Because federal power over interstate commerce was paramount, ICC determinations of the imperatives of interstate commerce were controlling.

Ordinary legal analysis would cease at this point. But because Brandeis was more interested in mediating the tension between democratic self-governance and national management than in the question of abstract legal authority, he continued:

> As every projected abandonment of any part of a railroad engaged in both interstate and intrastate commerce may conceivably involve a conflict between state and national interests, the consent of the Commission must be obtained by the railroad in every case. To ensure due consideration of the local interests, Congress provided that a copy of every application must be promptly filed with the Governor of the state directly affected, that notice of the application must be published in some local newspaper, and that the appropriate state authorities should have "the right to make before the Commission such representations as they may deem just and proper for preserving the rights and interests of their people and the states, respectively, involved in such proceedings." In practice, representatives of state regulatory bodies sit, sometimes, with the representatives of the Commission at hearings upon the application for a certificate. Occasionally, the Commission leaves the preliminary enquiry to the state body; and always consideration is given by the Commission to the representations of the state authorities.
>
> While the constitutional basis of authority to issue the certificate of abandonment is the power of Congress to regulate interstate commerce, ... [t]he sole test prescribed is that abandonment be consistent with public necessity and convenience. In determining whether it is, the Commission must have regard to the needs of both intrastate and interstate commerce; for it was a purpose of Transportation Act 1920 to establish and maintain adequate service for both. The benefit to one of the abandonment must be weighed against the inconvenience and loss to which the other will thereby be subjected. Conversely, the benefits to particular communities and commerce of continued operation must be weighed against the burden thereby imposed upon other commerce. The result of this weighing – the judgment of the Commission – is expressed by its order granting or denying the certificate.[254]

From a strictly legal point of view, Brandeis's disquisition about the relationship between the ICC and state governments was mere *dicta*. But it was characteristic of the sophistication and statesmanship which Brandeis brought to such decisions that he sought to use the moral authority of the Court to encourage political mediation, even as he held, as he was required to do, that ultimate authority lay with the federal government.[255]

Brandeis's extraordinary sensitivity to the need for political solutions that were not reducible to legal rules was the result of a fundamental insight that he brought to American public law.[256] Brandeis believed that legal rights were always to be interpreted so as to sustain the material and political processes constitutive of democratic life. So, for example, Brandeis commented to Frankfurter that insofar as the Due Process Clause was to be extended beyond "procedural regularity," it should be applied "to substantive laws" to protect "things that are fundamental":

Right to speech.
education.
choice of profession.
to locomotion.

These "are such fundamental rights," said Brandeis, that they are "not to be impaired or withdrawn except as judged by 'clear and present danger' test."[257]

This was an approach quite alien to Holmes, who lacked a theory of human flourishing capable of articulating fundamental rights independent of positive law. Holmes sought to protect freedom of speech primarily to facilitate the "clash of conflicting beliefs" so that "the 'natural outcome of a dominant opinion'" might emerge.[258] But Brandeis, by contrast, began with the question of how citizens might adequately be empowered to fulfill their role as "rulers" of a democratic state. Thus when the Taft Court came to decide *Meyer v. Nebraska*,[259] in which it struck down a statute prohibiting the teaching of modern foreign languages before eighth grade, Brandeis joined the Court's opinion, but Holmes dissented. In words that no doubt garnered Brandeis's complete assent, McReynolds proclaimed for the Court:

> In order to submerge the individual and develop ideal citizens, Sparta assembled the males at seven into barracks and intrusted their subsequent education and training to official guardians. Although such measures have been deliberately approved by men of great genius, their ideas touching the relation between individual and state were wholly different from those upon which our institutions rest; and it hardly will be affirmed that any legislature could impose such restrictions upon the people of a state without doing violence to both letter and spirit of the Constitution.[260]

Meyer illustrates that the republican premises of Brandeis's thinking were not unique on the Taft Court. McReynolds also believed that "it is harder and more important to be a good citizen than it is to be a good official."[261] Unlike Brandeis, however, McReynolds was convinced that the independence essential for citizenship required courts constitutionally to protect traditional property rights as well as

Louis Dembitz Brandeis

"those privileges long recognized at common law as essential to the orderly pursuit of happiness by free men."[262] This is because McReynolds imagined that persons became independent only when they were able to exercise traditional common law rights. It is for this reason that McReynolds repudiated as intolerable precisely the regulations of property that Brandeis believed were necessary to underwrite meaningful citizenship under modern industrial conditions.

Seen from this angle, we can begin to appreciate how debates within the Taft Court were at root about diverging visions of the authority of constitutional law. It is apparent that constitutional law for both Brandeis and McReynolds sprang from ethical visions about the nature of the American political community. Brandeis and McReynolds differed in the substance of their visions, but each imagined that the purpose of constitutional law was to define and protect a certain kind of community life. Constitutional law had authority insofar as the public was committed to that form of life. It is striking that the positivism of Holmes contained no such ethical vision. What motivated Holmes instead was the need to establish legal processes capable of peacefully channeling the explosive struggle for "the survival of the fittest"[263] that seethed beneath the seemingly calm surface of society. Holmesian positivism did not purport to offer an account of better or worse forms of American community. It instead conceived constitutional law as rooted in the indispensable but fragile requirements of legality itself.

By contrast, Taft believed that constitutional law ought to protect property rights necessary for "the material progress of the human race."[264] Underlying this belief was the assumption that Americans shared a common commitment to economic growth. Whereas Holmes imagined the nation as caught in the toils of ineradicable social conflict, Taft (and the conservative justices who thought like him) instead envisioned Americans as joined together in dedication to ongoing economic expansion. They imagined that judicial decisions grounded in the need to protect economic development would be authoritative because the country was committed to material growth. They conceived that commitment as deeper and more vital than the public's investment in any statute that might emerge from the superficial give and take of the legislative process. The 1920s were indeed a hospitable time for those who believed in the country's fundamental dedication to prosperity.

Brandeis's distinctive innovation was to construct constitutional law on the premise that Americans were more deeply committed to democratic processes than they were to material growth. Brandeis imagined a constitutional law that privileged democratic engagement over prosperity and hence that categorized the political as lexically prior to the economic. Brandeis's jurisprudence overlapped closely with Holmes's positivism because the latter also emphasized political decision-making over economic growth. But Holmes valued political decision-making as a rule of recognition for law, rather than as an intrinsically valuable way of life. There was little place in Holmes's jurisprudence for a substantive account of the requirements of democratic citizenship, whereas Brandeis built his entire innovative perspective on an explication of those requirements.

Notes

1. Paul A. Freund, *Justice Brandeis: A Law Clerk's Remembrance*, 68 AMERICAN JEWISH HISTORY 7 (September 1978).
2. Henry J. Friendly, *Mr. Justice Brandeis: The Quest for Reason*, 108 UNIVERSITY OF PENNSYLVANIA LAW REVIEW 985, 985 (1960).
3. Attorney General Francis Biddle, *Proceedings in Memory of Mr. Justice Brandeis*, 317 U.S. xxxvii–xxxviii (1942) ("Remarks of Attorney General Francis Biddle"). *See id.* at xii ("Remarks of Learned Hand") ("Others ... must speak of the fiery nature which showed itself when stirred, but which for the most part lay buried beneath an iron control; of that ascesis, which seemed so to increase that towards the end one wondered at times whether, like some Eastern sage, the body's grosser part had not been quite burnt away and mere spirit remained; of those quick flashes of indignation at injustice, pretence, or oppression.").
4. *Id.* at xvii ("Remarks of Paul A. Freund"). *See id.* at xx ("Those who knew him ... would speak finally and above all of his moral intensity, his spiritual greatness. ... His moral judgments were stern, and they probed deep.").
5. LDB to Robert W. Bruere (February 25, 1922), quoted in Donald R. Richberg, *The Industrial Liberalism of Justice Brandeis*, 31 COLUMBIA LAW REVIEW 1094, 1099 (1931). Brandeis's advice in this letter was to "refuse to accept as inevitable any evil in business (*e.g.*, irregularity of employment). Refuse to tolerate an immoral practice (*e.g.*, espionage)." *Id.* at 1098. Brandeis wrote his daughter on her twenty-sixth birthday that she had "been happily born into an age ripe for change; and your own horror of injustice properly beckons you to take an active part in effecting it." LDB to Susan Brandeis (February 24, 1919), in BRANDEIS FAMILY LETTERS, at 328. Brandeis continued: "In laying your plans, bear in mind that time, the indispensable, is a potent factor, and that your own effectiveness is to be measured in terms of a life-time; and that you should have before you half a century of persistent, well directed effort with ever growing power and influence. Be not impatient of time spent in educating yourself for the task, nor at the slowness of that education of others which must precede real progress. Patience is as necessary as persistence and the undeviating aim."
6. Louis D. Brandeis, *The Living Law*, 10 ILLINOIS LAW REVIEW 461, 461 (1916).
7. LOUIS D. BRANDEIS, BUSINESS – A PROFESSION 40 (Boston: Small, Maynard & Co. 1914). *See id.* at 45.
8. LDB to Felix Frankfurter (January 16, 1921), in 4 LETTERS OF LOUIS D. BRANDEIS, at 528. *See* THE CURSE OF BIGNESS: MISCELLANEOUS PAPERS OF LOUIS D. BRANDEIS 107 (Osmond K. Fraenkel, ed., New York: Viking Press 1934).
9. LDB to Susan Goldmark (December 7, 1919), in BRANDEIS FAMILY LETTERS, at 353. *See* DEAN ACHESON, MORNING AND NOON 100 (Boston: Houghton Mifflin Co. 1965) (The 1919 Palmer raids left Brandeis "deeply humiliated and filled with a sense of sense of sin.").
10. LDB to Felix Frankfurter (May 12, 1932), in BRANDEIS-FRANKFURTER CORRESPONDENCE, at 486–87. When Brandeis sought to instigate a campaign to end the system of "tipping" waiters, he stressed above all its "immorality" and "ungentlemanliness." "*It is unAmerican. It is nasty. It is nauseating.*" LDB to Felix Frankfurter (November 26, 1920), *id.* at 48.

Louis Dembitz Brandeis

11. ACHESON, *supra* note 9, at 95–96. At Brandeis's funeral, Acheson quoted virtually the same words of St. Paul that McReynolds had held up to the Tennessee Bar in 1935: "We have heard him say almost in the words of St. Paul, 'Whatsoever things are true, whatsoever things are honest, whatsoever things are just, whatsoever things are pure, whatsoever things are of good report – think on these things.'" Dean Acheson, *Mr. Justice Brandeis*, 55 HARVARD LAW REVIEW 191, 192 (1941). *See supra* Chapter 7, at 269.
12. LDB to Felix Frankfurter (June 13, 1933), in BRANDEIS-FRANKFURTER CORRESPONDENCE, at 523–24. "If the Government wished to extricate itself from the assumed emergency, taxation would have afforded an honorable way out." *Id.* at 523.
13. *Brandeis-Frankfurter Conversations*, at 337 (February 25, 1935).
14. LDB to Thomas Watt Gregory (April 14, 1916), in 4 LETTERS OF LOUIS D. BRANDEIS, at 165.
15. New State Ice Co. v. Liebmann, 285 U.S. 262, 311 (1932) (Brandeis, J., dissenting). It is noteworthy that Brandeis had spent a lifetime opposing precisely the kind of statute he voted to uphold in *Liebmann*.
16. Holmes "often referred to himself" as "Mephistopheles." *See* Brad Snyder, *The House that Built Holmes*, 30 LAW AND HISTORY REVIEW 661, 672 (2012).
17. "Despite his professed devotion to facts, Brandeis was ultimately more interested in using his opinions to articulate and defend American ideals." JEFFREY ROSEN, LOUIS D. BRANDEIS: AMERICAN PROPHET 112 (New Haven: Yale University Press 2016).
18. Soon after Brandeis came on the Court, it decided New York Central v. Winfield, 244 U.S. 147 (1917), in which it invalidated a judgment under a state workmen's compensation statute for an employee of a railroad engaged in interstate commerce, on the ground that Congress had preempted the field. The case "laid me low," Brandeis told Frankfurter. *Brandeis-Frankfurter Conversations*, at 326 (August 10, 1923). Brandeis wrote an impassioned dissent, in which he was joined by Clarke. Holmes recounted to Laski his conversation with Brandeis:

> I thought he was letting partisanship disturb his judicial attitude. I am frank with him because I value him and think he brings many admirable qualifications to his work. In [*Winfield*] when he wrote a long essay on the development of employers' liability I told him that I thought it out of place and irrelevant to the only question: whether Congress had dealt with the matter so far as to exclude state action.

OWH to Harold Laski (January 16, 1918), in 1 HOLMES-LASKI CORRESPONDENCE, at 128. Many years later, Holmes once again observed to Laski that "I am interested ... by your comment on Brandeis. I told him long ago that he really was an advocate rather than a Judge. He is affected by his interest in a cause, and if he feels it he is not detached. I am not surprised that you find him difficult to your business. But his interests are noble, and as you say his insights profound." OWH to Harold Laski (December 11, 1930) (Holmes papers). Holmes was responding to Laski's complaint that in attempting to mediate between Brandeis and the British government over Zionist matters, Laski had found Brandeis "a *very* difficult person."

He is intransigent and dominating and unnecessarily prone to read evil motives into obvious actions. Felix is like clay in his hands, and if it were not for my deep affection for them both, I think I would have told them long ago to go to hell and see what they could accomplish without my intervention. I can't run daily to the Foreign Secretary because Brandeis has doubts about a semicolon – at some point in a negotiation one has to assume that the cabinet really means what it says. I did not realize before how curiously suspicious a nature Brandeis has. He is extraordinarily profound in his insights, but, I should have said, not quite human in his contacts, with the result that he does not always see round a subject.

Harold Laski to OWH (November 30, 1930), in 2 HOLMES-LASKI CORRESPONDENCE, at 1298–99. After receiving Holmes's letter of December 11, Laski replied that "your remark about Brandeis is certainly just."

Since these negotiations with the British government began I cannot remember one telegram of his which has been really helpful. All statesmanship is, after all, the power to compromise on inessentials; he digs himself in on what are really matters of no consequence with the passion of a tiger defending his cubs; and that makes him, in my judgment, much less effective on the big issues where he is really entitled to care. He exercises a strange hold over Felix, for the latter, who can usually be cool and independent, is in these things simply an echo of L.D.B. He gives orders like an omnipotent Sultan and negotiations do not come to a success that way. Moreover he treats his fellow Zionists who differ from him almost as criminals, and, as I think, gravely injures his own prestige by so doing.

Harold Laski to OWH (December 27, 1930), in 2 HOLMES-LASKI CORRESPONDENCE, at 1301–2. It is notable that at about this time Laski published a flattering portrayal of Brandeis which stressed his "deliberate effort to make the Constitution conform to the tasks of an economic statesmanship conceived in the terms of a conscious social philosophy." Harold Laski, *Mr. Justice Brandeis*, 168 HARPER'S MAGAZINE 209, 213 (1934). "It was the importance of Mr. Justice Brandeis' accession to the court that where Holmes was a liberal by negation he was a liberal by positive affirmation. He brought to the court ... an alternative philosophy. ... [W]hereas to most members of the Supreme Court the main purpose of the Constitution was to preserve the rights of private property from invasion by the popular will, to Mr. Justice Brandeis the control of their pathological results by state action was an inherent and desirable function of public power." *Id.* at 212. Although Laski found in Brandeis "a real aloofness of temper, a detachment from the obvious or immediate," he also observed that "No one can see him in action without a new understanding of the Hebraic gift of moral vision. It is not for nothing that he is of the people from whom Isaiah and Maimonides and Spinoza were born." *Id.* at 217.

19. The most notable moment during the Taft Court when Brandeis's own political commitments broke through his stance of judicial self-restraint came in Willing v. Chicago Auditorium Association, 277 U.S. 274 (1928). In that case Brandeis authored an opinion holding that Congress could not authorize federal courts to render declaratory judgments, because any such proceeding was "not a case or controversy within the meaning of Article III of the Constitution." *Id.* at 289. Progressives of Brandeis's generation were politically opposed to the jurisdiction of federal courts because they regarded federal courts as conservative institutions that suppressed necessary social reforms. Brandeis shared this

commitment, seeking assiduously to curtail federal diversity jurisdiction. *See, e.g.*, LDB to Felix Frankfurter (April 2, 1925), in BRANDEIS-FRANKFURTER CORRESPONDENCE, at 200; LDB to Felix Frankfurter (May 11, 1927), *id.* at 292; LDB to Felix Frankfurter (March 16, 1928), *id.* at 327; LDB to Felix Frankfurter (May 10, 1928), *id.* at 331. Although Brandeis believed that "The remedy for prevailing discontent with USSC must be sought in refraining from all constitutional dicta" and "in refusing to consider a constitutional question except in 'cases' or 'controversies' – 'initiated according to the regular course of judicial procedure,'" LDB to Felix Frankfurter (September 19, 1922), in 5 LETTERS OF LOUIS D. BRANDEIS, at 64, he nevertheless seized the occasion in *Willing* to hold declaratory judgments unconstitutional, a judgment so untenable that the Court effectively overturned it five years later in Nashville, C. & St. L. R. Co. v. Wallace, 288 U.S. 249 (1933). *See also* Medimmune, Inc. v. Genentech, 549 U.S. 118 (2007).

Stone wrote separately in *Willing* to stress that Brandeis's constitutional judgment was *dictum* because *Willing* also held that federal jurisdiction had not been conferred by the relevant federal statute. Holmes joined Brandeis's opinion, but warned in his return, "I think it narrow minded ... to hold that Fed courts can't be given power to make declaratory judgments." (Brandeis papers). To Stone, Holmes commented that "I do not care to join in the criticism of this opinion – but I regret the conclusion that we cannot render declaratory judgments." (Stone papers). Brandeis's clerk at the time, Henry Friendly, composed a chambers memorandum to the effect that "I should have thought that a good deal might be said in favor of the constitutionality of the declaratory judgment," (Brandeis papers), and, much later in life, Friendly called *Willing* "surely one of the unhappiest chapters of Brandeis' judicial career." Friendly, *supra* note 2, at 769. Sutherland, by contrast, enthusiastically affirmed Brandeis's opinion: "Yes sir. I do not see how it could be decided otherwise." (Brandeis papers). Taft wrote on his return of Brandeis's opinion that "This makes the matter entirely clear. Borchard will moan but he can not by tears change our jurisdiction." (Brandeis papers). Edwin Borchard, a leading law scholar at Yale, was one of the primary proponents of declaratory judgments. The story of *Willing* is beautifully told in EDWARD A. PURCELL, JR., BRANDEIS AND THE PROGRESSIVE CONSTITUTION 124–32 (New Haven: Yale University Press 2000), which argues that Brandeis reached out in *Willing* to decide the constitutional question in order to kill a pending federal bill that would have authorized federal declaratory judgments.

20. Quoted in Earnest Poole, *Brandeis: A Remarkable Record of Unselfish Work Done in the Public Interest*, 71 AMERICAN MAGAZINE 481 (1911).
21. PHILIPPA STRUM, LOUIS D. BRANDEIS: JUSTICE FOR THE PEOPLE 9 (Cambridge: Harvard University Press 1984).
22. "There could be no stronger proof of the excellence of this system of instruction than the ardor of the students themselves. ... The students live in an atmosphere of legal thought. Their interest is at fever heat, and the impressions made by their studies are as deep and lasting as is compatible with the quality of the individual mind." Louis D. Brandeis, *The Harvard Law School*, 1 GREEN BAG 10, 21 (1889).
23. Henry J. Friendly, *Review of* ALPHEUS THOMAS MASON, A FREE MAN'S LIFE, 56 YALE LAW JOURNAL 423, 426 (1947). Friendly, who became Brandeis's clerk,

received the second highest marks ever recorded at Harvard Law School. *Secretary to Justice Brandeis Nearly Ties His Harvard Rank*, CHRISTIAN SCIENCE MONITOR (September 12, 1927), at 1.
24. James M. Landis, *Mr. Justice Brandeis and The Harvard Law School*, 55 HARVARD LAW REVIEW 184, 184 (1941).
25. Quoted in ALPHEUS THOMAS MASON, BRANDEIS: A FREE MAN'S LIFE 61 (New York: The Viking Press 1956).
26. MELVIN I. UROFSKY, LOUIS D. BRANDEIS: A LIFE 53 (New York: Pantheon Books 2009).
27. *Id.* at 53–54, 76–77, 97. This conclusion seems confirmed by a recently discovered autobiographical account of this period of Brandeis's life. *See* Peter Scott Campbell, *Notes for a Lost Memoir of Louis D. Brandeis*, 43 JOURNAL OF SUPREME COURT HISTORY 27 (2018).
28. MASON, *supra* note 25, at 88–89. "After 1884, Brandeis always referred to himself as a 'democrat with a small "d"' but he was not much interested in party politics and supported from time to time candidates of both parties. . . . In 1884 he was elected to the executive committee of the Civil Service Reform Association of the Fifth Congressional District. In 1887 he joined the Boston American Citizenship Committee." *Id.*
29. Louis D. Brandeis, *The Opportunity in the Law*, 38 AMERICAN LAW REVIEW 555, 559 (1905). This famous article was an address delivered by Brandeis on May 4, 1905, at Phillips Brooks House, before the Harvard Ethical Society. On Brandeis's sobriquet as "the people's attorney," see PHILIPPA STRUM, BRANDEIS: BEYOND PROGRESSIVISM 51 (Lawrence: University Press of Kansas 1993).
30. MASON, *supra* note 25, at 145.
31. UROFSKY, *supra* note 26, at 66–67. Brandeis coined the phrase in the context of his dealings with James T. Lennox, the owner of a tanning company who faced insurmountable debt. Brandeis refused to represent Lennox personally, but instead agreed to become trustee for the company's assets. Lennox, thinking that Brandeis was his lawyer, became furious when Brandeis took the firm into bankruptcy. Lennox retained a second lawyer, Sherman Whipple, who pressed Brandeis about whom Brandeis was actually representing. Whipple later testified at Brandeis's confirmation hearings that Brandeis had told him that Brandeis was never Lennox's lawyer, but rather "counsel for the situation."
32. For a perceptive exploration of both the admirable and troubling aspects of this dimension of Brandeis's character and practice, see Clyde Spillenger, *Elusive Advocate: Reconsidering Brandeis as People's Lawyer*, 105 YALE LAW JOURNAL 1445 (1996).
33. UROFSKY, *supra* note 26, at 131–50.
34. Examples include the creation of savings bank insurance to address the problem of industrial life insurance, *id.* at 155–80; the development of the Protocol in the garment industry with its preferential shop, MASON, *supra* note 25, at 289–315; and the application of scientific management to railroad administration in Interstate Commerce Commission ratemaking proceedings. *Id.* at 315–51. As Brandeis would write: "The need of solving . . . problems is urgent. The inherent difficulties are great. There is insistent demand for political and social invention. The best conceived plans for the amelioration of our conditions will require for success laborious development of details, careful adjustment to local conditions, and great

watchfulness for years after their introduction. We must encourage such social and political invention, though we feel sure that the successes will be few and the failures many." Louis D. Brandeis, *Introduction*, in ALBERT O. BARTON, LAFOLLETTE'S WINNING OF WISCONSIN (1894–1904) (Madison: n.p. 1922). This perspective lay at the foundation of Brandeis's view that federalism was necessary to establish indispensable laboratories for experimentation.

35. THE CURSE OF BIGNESS, *supra* note 8, at 39. "Forward-looking men with statesmanlike progressiveness – which is far-seeing conservatism – have sought to avert a war of classes by removing just causes of discontent." Memorandum, October 19, 1915, quoted in THE BRANDEIS GUIDE TO THE MODERN WORLD 72 (Alfred Lief, ed., Boston: Little, Brown & Co. 1941).

36. Memorandum, August 1912, quoted in THE BRANDEIS GUIDE TO THE MODERN WORLD, *supra* note 35, at 14.

37. Quoted in Poole, *supra* note 20, at 492.

38. For all his faith in inventive expertise, however, there is a side of Brandeis that never lost sight of the fact that "Democracy is in no sense inconsistent with individual leadership; only it must be leadership by consent, and the consent must be actual." LDB to Morris L. Cooke (July 24, 1916), in 4 LETTERS OF LOUIS D. BRANDEIS, at 254. He believed that "In a democratic community men who are to be affected by a proposed change of conditions should be consulted, and the innovators must carry the burden of convincing others at each stage in the process of change that what is being done is right." Address before Society for the Promotion of Business Management (October 23, 1915), quoted in THE BRANDEIS GUIDE TO THE MODERN WORLD, *supra* note 35, at 71. The extraordinary complexity of Brandeis's position is well illustrated in this 1913 letter to Frankfurter:

> To secure social advance we must regard the field of sociology and social legislation as a field for discovery and invention. Research is necessary as in the field of science and invention, as in the field of mechanical and other arts. In the field of mechanical invention, as in other fields of human enterprise, the successes are few and the failures are many. And the successes are rarely one man's work, or the work of a number of men consciously cooperating. The successes come very often by one man building upon another's apparent failure.
>
> I should have little faith, therefore, in a small group of men evolving a social system or important elements of such a system. We must rely upon all America (and the rest of the world) for our social inventions and discoveries; and the value of the inventions and alleged discoveries can best be tested by current public discussion.
>
> On the other hand, it seems to me that a small group of able, disinterested, well-equipped men, who could give their time to criticism and discussion of legislative proposals, discouraging those which appear to be unsound, and aiding those that appear to be sound, would be of great assistance in the forward movement.

LDB to Felix Frankfurter (January 28, 1913), in BRANDEIS-FRANKFURTER CORRESPONDENCE, at 22. Brandeis expressed this same complex perception in his famous letter to his brother about the need to stimulate the development of the University of Louisville. Brandeis observed:

> Growth cannot be imposed upon the University. It must proceed mainly from within. The desire for worthy growth must be deeply felt by the executive

officers and members of the faculty. It must be they who raise the University to standards and extend its usefulness. But the desire may be stimulated by suggestion; and the achievement may be furthered by friendly aid. Thus, there is a large field for the efforts of those outside the University whose capacity, experience and position gives them a wider view and a bolder vision; whose position enables them to secure for the University's projects the approval and support of the community; and whose means enable them to furnish financial aid. From them may come also the encouragement without which few achieve and that informed, friendly supervision, without which few persevere in the most painstaking labors....

[T]he service of money will resemble that of water in agriculture, always indispensable, always beneficent to the point where it becomes excessive, but of little avail unless the soil be rich, naturally or through fertilizers, unless there be appropriate cultivation, and unless the operations be conducted with good judgment.

LDB to Alfred Brandeis (February 18, 1925), in BRANDEIS FAMILY LETTERS, at 402–3.

39. So, for example, Austen G. Fox, who was a lawyer seeking to defeat Brandeis's confirmation, suggested to Amos Pinchot that "[t]he trouble with Mr. Brandeis is that he never loses his judicial attitude toward his clients. He always acts the part of a judge toward his clients instead of being his client's lawyer, which is against the practices of the Bar." Quoted in MASON, *supra* note 25, at 506. The larger point is that "throughout his career, Brandeis remained at the social boundary between insider and outsider. He never conceived of himself as an insider.... At the same time Brandeis was obviously separated from oppressed outsiders by his wealth and status. In this sense, then, he was neither insider nor outsider, but occupied a singular social space between the two." ROBERT A. BURT, TWO JEWISH JUSTICES: OUTCASTS IN THE PROMISED LAND 35 (Berkeley: University of California Press 1988).

40. To this should be added Brandeis's successful assumption of leadership in the American Zionist movement.

41. See especially UROFSKY, *supra* note 26; STRUM, *supra* note 21, at 29; and MASON, *supra* note 25.

42. Muller v. Oregon, 208 U.S. 412, 416 (1908).

43. 198 U.S. 45, 56, 64 (1905). Justice Harlan, joined by Justices White and Day, dissented on the ground that "There are many reasons of a weighty, substantial character, based upon the experience of mankind, in support of the theory that, all things considered, more than ten hours' steady work each day, from week to week, in a bakery or confectionery establishment, may endanger the health and shorten the lives of the workmen, thereby diminishing their physical and mental capacity to serve the state and to provide for those dependent upon them. If such reasons exist that ought to be the end of this case, for the state is not amenable to the judiciary, in respect of its legislative enactments, unless such enactments are plainly, palpably, beyond all question, inconsistent with the Constitution of the United States. We are not to presume that the state of New York has acted in bad faith." *Id.* at 72–73 (Harlan, J., dissenting). Justice Holmes, speaking for himself alone, dissented on the ground that "I think that the word 'liberty,' in the Fourteenth Amendment, is perverted when it is held to prevent the natural outcome of a dominant opinion, unless it can be said that a rational and fair man necessarily would admit that the

statute proposed would infringe fundamental principles as they have been understood by the traditions of our people and our law. It does not need research to show that no such sweeping condemnation can be passed upon the statute before us. A reasonable man might think it a proper measure on the score of health." *Id.* at 76 (Holmes, J., dissenting).
44. NANCY WOLOCH, *MULLER V. OREGON:* A BRIEF HISTORY WITH DOCUMENTS 21 (Boston: Bedford Books of St. Martin's Press 1996).
45. *Id.* at 22–24.
46. JOSEPHINE GOLDMARK, IMPATIENT CRUSADER: FLORENCE KELLEY'S LIFE STORY 151 (Urbana: University of Illinois Press 1953).
47. *Id.* at 154.
48. *Id.* at 155.
49. Brief for Defendant in Error, Muller v. Oregon (No. 107, October Term 1907), at 18.
50. *Id.* at 10, citing 198 U.S. at 61. Brandeis added the words in parentheses to the Court's actual language.
51. *Id.* at 10 (citing 198 U.S. at 68 (Harlan, J., dissenting)).
52. *Lochner*, 198 U.S. at 61.
53. Brief, *supra* note 49, at 113.
54. *Muller*, 208 U.S. at 419–21. Brandeis would later tell Dean Acheson "that when they asked him what title should be put on his Oregon brief, he said 'What Any Fool Knows.' A good part of [Brandeis's] life has been spent in telling stupid people what any idiot ought to have been able to see at a glance." ACHESON, *supra* note 9, at 53. Of course, viewed with modern eyes, "what any fool would know" in the first decade of the twentieth century would today be rejected as unacceptable gender stereotyping.
55. *Muller* "marked an epoch in the argument and decision of constitutional cases, and resulted not only in reversal of prior decisions, but in giving to the courts a wholly new approach." *Brandeis*, 6 NEW REPUBLIC 4, 5–6 (1916). *See* Felix Frankfurter, *Hours of Labor and Realism in Constitutional Law*, 29 HARVARD LAW REVIEW 353, 365 (1916).
56. WOLOCH, *supra* note 44, at 3.
57. Oliver Wendell Holmes, *The Path of the Law*, 1 BOSTON LAW SCHOOL MAGAZINE 1, 11 (February 1897).
58. WOLOCH, *supra* note 44, at 41–42. During the 1920s, for example, Brandeis briefs would be used by those involved in litigation to defend labor unions and restrict the enforcement of yellow-dog contracts. Daniel Ernst, *The Yellow-Dog Contract and Liberal Reform, 1917–1932*, 30 LABOR HISTORY 251, 268, 270 (1989).
59. Ritchie v. People, 155 Ill. 98 (1895). "There is no reasonable ground – at least none which has been made manifest to us in the arguments of counsel – for fixing upon eight hours in one day as the limit within which woman can work without injury to her physique, and beyond which, if she work, injury will necessarily follow. But the police power of the state can only be permitted to limit or abridge such a fundamental right as the right to make contracts when the exercise of such power is necessary to promote the health, comfort, welfare, or safety of society or the public." *Id.* at 114.
60. W.C. Ritchie & Co. v. Wayman, 244 Ill. 509 (1910). In 1909 Illinois had enacted a statute imposing a ten-hour limitation for female work in "any

mechanical establishment or factory or laundry." In 1910, the Illinois Supreme Court held:

> It is known to all men (and what we know as men we cannot profess to be ignorant of as judges) that woman's physical structure and the performance of maternal functions place her at a great disadvantage in the battle of life; that while a man can work for more than ten hours a day without injury to himself, a woman, especially when the burdens of motherhood are upon her, cannot; that while a man can work standing upon his feet for more than ten hours a day, day after day, without injury to himself, a woman cannot, and that to require a woman to stand upon her feet for more than ten hours in any one day and perform severe manual labor while thus standing, day after day, has the effect to impair her health, and that as weakly and sickly women cannot be the mothers of vigorous children, it is of the greatest importance to the public that the state take such measures as may be necessary to protect its women from the consequences induced by long, continuous manual labor in those occupations which tend to break them down physically.

Id. at 520–21.

61. Brandeis, *supra* note 6, at 465. The difference a Brandeis brief could make is well illustrated by the contrast between New York v. Charles Schweinler Press, 214 N.Y. 395 (1915) and New York v. Williams, 189 N.Y. 131 (1907). In the former the New York Court of Appeals upheld legislation barring women from nighttime factory work, legislation which it had struck down eight years earlier in the latter. In 1915, the court noted that in 1907 "the arguments made to us in behalf" of the constitutionality of the statute "were far different than those in the present case," and that the prior court decision had failed "to sustain its constitutionality by reference to proper facts and circumstances." 214 N.Y. at 411.

62. Adams v. Tanner, 244 U.S. 590, 599–600 (1917) (Brandeis, J., dissenting). *See* Truax v. Corrigan, 257 U.S. 312, 356–57 (1921) (Brandeis, J., dissenting); Jay Burns Baking Co. v. Bryan, 264 U.S. 504, 533–34 (1924) (Brandeis, J., dissenting); Brandeis, *supra* note 6, at 467. On Brandeis's "profound belief in the need for facts," see Friendly, *supra* note 2, at 998. Brandeis "was the authentic child of the *Aufklärung;* he had none of today's doubts as to whether the truth could be ascertained. He did not believe with the evangelist that this truth could be found by abiding in the Word or in becoming the disciple of any leader. Neither did he think it came from intuition or from speculation in metaphysics. He thought it could and would come only from the relentless, disinterested and critical study of facts." *Id.* at 999.

63. Remarks of Attorney General Francis Biddle, *supra* note 3, at xxxviii.

64. Remarks of Chief Justice Stone, *Proceedings in Memory of Mr. Justice Brandeis*, *supra* note 3, at xlv.

65. Thus Brandeis advised Frankfurter that the *New Republic* should become "more a journal of fact – than of opinion; which latter is apt to be regarded as mush. That is, it must make its opinions tell through facts, which by their selection & method of presentation argue themselves. And in the end, facts must be presented stripped for action." LDB to Felix Frankfurter (December 1, 1920), in BRANDEIS-FRANKFURTER CORRESPONDENCE, at 51.

66. Remarks of Attorney General Francis Biddle, *supra* note 3, at xxxix.

67. Statement before the Federal Trade Commission, April 30, 1915, quoted in THE BRANDEIS GUIDE TO THE MODERN WORLD, *supra* note 35, at 121. "Nine-tenths of

the serious controversies which arise in life result from misunderstanding, result from one man not knowing the facts which to the other man seem important, or otherwise failing to appreciate his point of view." BRANDEIS, *supra* note 7, at 21.
68. Quoted in Poole, *supra* note 20, at 493.
69. *Id.* Brandeis strongly believed that disagreements would arise less often, and be easier to resolve, if persons concentrated on how to solve particular problems. "[I]n government, as in other spheres of human activity, happiness is usually attained, if at all, as a bi-product [sic]; and ... because of our finite wisdom, and the infinite possibility of error in judgment, we are more likely to be right in turning our thoughts primarily to the simpler problem of means than directly to hoped for ends." LDB to Felix Frankfurter (October 5, 1925), in BRANDEIS-FRANKFURTER CORRESPONDENCE, at 215. Brandeis's views in this regard were similar to those in the virtually contemporary work of John Dewey.
70. Jay Burns Baking Co. v. Bryan, 264 U.S. 504, 534 (1924) (Brandeis, J., dissenting).
71. *See, e.g., id.*; *infra* Chapter 23, at 735-37.
72. Brandeis advocated changes in "the education of our lawyers," which would require that "lawyers should not merely learn rules of law, but their purpose and effect when applied to the affairs of man. In other words, – a study of the facts, human, industrial, social, to which they are to be applied." LDB to Norman Hapgood (July 30, 1912), in 2 LETTERS OF LOUIS D. BRANDEIS, at 656.
73. LDB to Felix Frankfurter (December 1, 1920), in BRANDEIS-FRANKFURTER CORRESPONDENCE, at 51.
74. ALPHEUS THOMAS MASON, BUREAUCRACY CONVICTS ITSELF: THE BALLINGER-PINCHOT CONTROVERSY OF 1910, at 15 (New York: The Viking Press 1941).
75. JAMES PENICK, JR., PROGRESSIVE POLITICS AND CONSERVATION: THE BALLINGER-PINCHOT AFFAIR (University of Chicago Press 1968).
76. WHT to R.A. Ballinger (September 13, 1909) (Taft papers). "I have studiously refrained from mentioning Pinchot's name in the matter because I do not wish to make it impossible for him to remain in the service. I value him highly as a public servant and believe him capable of further great usefulness. ... Should it be necessary, as is not unlikely, to submit all this record and evidence to Congress, I shall be glad to have your authority and that of your subordinates to leave out of your answers any reference to Pinchot or the part he took in bringing Glavis's report to my attention." *Id.*
77. A rupture with Roosevelt "was doubly distasteful to Taft. Politically it was suicidal. Personally it endangered a cherished friendship." PENICK, *supra* note 75, at 134.
78. MASON, *supra* note 25, at 256–57.
79. Subsequently, at his confirmation hearings, Brandeis would be accused of being paid by *Collier's* and actually representing the magazine's interests while purporting to represent Glavis. *Collier's* would not itself have had standing to be represented at the hearings. The hearings took the form of a trial, with Brandeis representing Glavis, George Wharton Pepper representing Pinchot, and John J. Vertrees, a Tennessee lawyer and intimate friend of Taft, representing Ballinger. Vertrees was a Democrat who opposed the ideals of conservation; Vertrees repeatedly emphasized the distinction between Ballinger's and Roosevelt's conservation policies, which was contrary to Taft's strategic interests. PENICK, *supra* note 75, at 152–53.
80. *Id.* at 156.

81. Norman Hapgood, who at the time was the editor of *Collier's*, recalls: "When the hearings began it was expected that Mr. Pepper ... would take the lead, but it required only a few days to prove to everybody that it was necessary for Mr. Brandeis to lead, since he already knew the facts many times better than any of the rest of us. The business of the Land Office ... is very complicated indeed. The only person who was held to understand it in detail was a permanent official named Finney; and he was the most important witness in defense of Ballinger. When Brandeis had finished cross-examining him, Finney came impulsively over to where I was sitting in the committee room, and exclaimed, 'Mr. Hapgood, I have no respect for you. . . . But I want to say that you have a wonderful lawyer. He knows the business of the department today as well as I do.'" NORMAN HAPGOOD, THE CHANGING YEARS: REMINISCENCES OF NORMAN HAPGOOD 186–87 (New York: Farrar & Rinehart 1930).
82. Brandeis wrote his wife, "Yesterday was a terrible day. I felt almost like an executioner & was glad to have Norman Hapgood here to share the responsibility. But it was an awful thing for Wickersham to have done & unfortunately the President (whom we have not mentioned) is as guilty as W. To date back that Attorney General's report so as to make it appear that it was prepared before the President's letter, when in fact it was written after Glavis' Collier Article ... comes pretty near giving false testimony. There was a fearful pall on the assembled company when the point was developed after two hours spent riddling the report for its suppressions and misstatements. But no denial came of my suggestion & none has come since from W. or the White House or any other source." LDB to Alice Goldmark Brandeis (April 23, 1910), in BRANDEIS FAMILY LETTERS, at 147–48.
83. LDB to Alfred Brandeis (May 1, 1910), in BRANDEIS FAMILY LETTERS, at 150. "The chance is none too good," Brandeis continued. "There is a chance – but a chance merely – that the people will now reverse all history and be able to control. The chance is worth taking, because there is nothing left for the self-respecting man to do. But every attempt to deal mercifully with the special interests *during the fight* simply results in their taking advantage of the merciful." *Id*.
84. *See* George Wickersham to Richard Wayne Parker (May 9, 1910), in *Investigation of the Department of the Interior and of the Bureau of Forestry*, Sen. Doc. No. 719 (Vol. 7), 61st CONG. 3rd SESS. (1911), at 4139. Wickersham's admission came in response to a request for documents from the House of Representatives that essentially mirrored Brandeis's repeated requests for documents. Wickersham argued that there was nothing unusual or improper about backdating his report. "The summary and conclusions by the Attorney-General, referred to as appearing in the papers sent by the President to the Senate, is the formal record made up by the President's direction from the document and the rough notes of the Attorney-General, which were before the President when he acted upon the charges made against Secretary Ballinger. This summary was necessarily made up afterwards and properly bore the date of the day when the matter it contained was presented to and considered by the President. There is no mystery about the matter and nothing which may not be freely stated." *Id*. Brandeis believed that "Wickersham and his acts are a fair sample & product of our special interest activities – what Wall St. and high finance make of a finely gifted and no doubt originally honorable man." LDB to Alfred Brandeis (May 1, 1910), in BRANDEIS FAMILY LETTERS, at

150–51. Brandeis considered Wickersham's admission "as to antedating" to be "coupled with lies." It showed "the extent to which men are driven when the path of deceit is entered upon." LDB to Alice Goldmark Brandeis (May 13, 1910), *id.* at 153.

85. *Investigation of the Department of the Interior and of the Bureau of Forestry*, Sen. Doc. No. 719 (Vol. 8), 61st CONG. 3rd SESS. (1911), at 4481. The hearings featured a number of such "peppery exchange[s]" between Sutherland and Brandeis. *See Ballinger in Hot Fight*, NEW YORK TRIBUNE (May 7, 1910), at 7; *Volcano Seems under Them*, CINCINNATI ENQUIRER (May 7, 1910), at 1; *Brandeis Gets Hot in Collar*, LOUISVILLE COURIER-JOURNAL (April 9, 1910), at 2.

86. *Says President Did Not Write Glavis Letter*, CHICAGO DAILY TRIBUNE (May 15, 1910), at 1.

87. WHT to Senator Knute Nelson (May 15, 1910), in *Investigation of the Department of the Interior and of the Bureau of Forestry*, supra note 85, at 4394.

88. PENICK, *supra* note 75, at 161–62.

89. Brandeis was quite aware that he was all along laying "a trap" for the administration. LDB to Alice Goldmark Brandeis (April 26, 1910), in BRANDEIS FAMILY LETTERS, at 149.

90. HAPGOOD, *supra* note 81, at 190. The outright prevarications of the Taft administration were "not especially relevant to proof of the Glavis charges, but neither was the necessity of proving those charges any longer relevant. Ballinger, and with him the administration, were 'convicted' before the public by a document which had been postdated and by the failure to admit frankly the existence of another document. The overall effect was to vindicate both Pinchot and Glavis." PENICK, *supra* note 75, at 162.

91. LDB to Alfred Brandeis (May 13, 1910), in 2 LETTERS OF LOUIS D. BRANDEIS, at 35. As a result of the disclosure of his backdated letter, George Wickersham was denied an honorary degree at the Harvard Law School in 1910. *See, e.g.*, LDB to Abbot Lawrence Lowell (June 16, 1910), *id.* at 352–54 ("you may not be entirely familiar with certain facts affecting the Attorney General developed in the course of the investigation"); LDB to George Rublee (June 29, 1910), *id.* at 362 ("I have just been ... at the Cambridge commencement and from the way people talked to me there I think there is more support for our side than I had supposed; and that there are quite a number of men who are beginning to realize the enormity of the Taft-Wickersham affair. I feel quite sure that it was proposed to give Wickersham a degree, but upon further consideration the proposition was withdrawn."); LDB to Norman Hapgood (March 14, 1916), in 4 LETTERS OF LOUIS D. BRANDEIS, at 118–19 ("I was horrified at Wickersham's making the address for the Law School Association. The inquiry which Lowell made of my office gave me the opportunity of writing him fully. His letter in reply showed how disgruntled he was at getting my letter, but the result of that letter was that Harvard refrained from giving Wickersham the LL.D. which it was expected that he would get, and Wickersham left Cambridge the day before Commencement, after delivering his address. ... I remember very clearly that [Lowell's] letter was a formal one which showed Lowell's disappointment.").

Within a week of Brandeis's demonstration of the backdated document, Senator La Follette launched an attack against the anti-trust policies of the Taft Department of Justice, and in particular against its dropping of charges against the New Haven railroad system, a monopoly that had provoked one of Brandeis's longest and most intense campaigns. *See* BRANDEIS, *supra* note 7, at 255–305; LDB to Alfred Brandeis (April 13, 1910), in 2 LETTERS OF LOUIS D. BRANDEIS, at 329. Wickersham responded to the critique by "practically" reading "the Republican insurgents out of the party." *Wickersham Counts Rebels as Traitors*, NEW YORK TIMES (April 10, 1910), at 2. "'Treason has ever consisted in giving aid and comfort to the enemy. If any one wishes to join the Democratic Party let him do so; but let him not claim to be a Republican and work in and out of season to defeat Republican measures and to subvert the influence of the Republican President.'" *Id*. Brandeis was sure that Wickersham was aware that Brandeis had supplied the facts and figures for La Follette's attack and that it was "some thing he will remember (against me) & which is fully deserved." He observed that Wickersham's "attack on the insurgents ... was quite Taft like, and he is said to be WHT's principal advisor. The Blind leading the Blind." LDB to Alfred Brandeis (April 13, 1910), in 2 LETTERS OF LOUIS D. BRANDEIS, at 329.

Brandeis was quite right about Wickersham's resentment. From this time forward Wickersham held an unwavering hatred for Brandeis, which would become fully mobilized when Brandeis was nominated to the Supreme Court. A.L. TODD, JUSTICE ON TRIAL: THE CASE OF LOUIS D. BRANDEIS 131–32 (New York: McGraw-Hill 1964).

92. *See, e.g.*, LDB to Henry Watterson (May 25, 1910), in 2 LETTERS OF LOUIS D. BRANDEIS, at 335–37; LDB to Mark Sullivan (June 2, 1910), *id*. at 338–39; LDB to Benjamin Bowles Hampton (June 4, 1910), *id*. at 340; LDB to Gifford Pinchot (June 11, 1910), *id*. at 346; LDB to John Foster Bass (June 13, 1910), *id*. at 347 ("I think it clear that the Country has long ago recognized Glavis's merits and Ballinger's demerits, and incidentally has come to a truer appreciation of the President and of the Attorney General"); LDB to Henry Watterson (June 14, 1910), *id*. at 351 (your editorials "will do much towards making the Americans understand the shameful facts. No doubt they will feel sorry for Taft, but unless the truth is proclaimed ninety millions of Americans and their descendants may become subjects for pity."); LDB to Robert Joseph Collier (June 30, 1910), *id*. at 363.

Brandeis stressed three themes in his public relations campaign. The first was that Lawler and Ballinger had "prostituted the law to their purposes." They had "made legal decisions the excuses for reversing policies which did not suit them," and they had used "the law as an excuse instead of as a guide." LDB to Mark Sullivan (June 4, 1910), *id*. at 341.

> That course is as dangerous to the maintenance of respect for law, as is canting hypocrisy to the maintenance of the respect for religion; and is in the present state of public opinion, an extremely dangerous course.
>
> The criticism of Roosevelt, as disregarding the law, is to my mind absolutely unfounded. What Roosevelt did was to recognize that the law was made for the people; that if there is a doubt as to governmental powers, or as to what governmental action should be in a given case, that doubt should be resolved in favor of the people. Ballinger and his like have always resolved doubts against the Government, and in favor of the special interest.

> To my mind the Roosevelt attitude is the only attitude which can preserve in America respect for law, and can overcome the tendency of the people to believe that there is one law for the rich and another for the poor. Ballinger is strict in his construction against the people, loose in his construction in favor of the special interests.

Id. at 341–42. Second, Brandeis sought to conceptualize conservation as a "struggle of the people against privilege, – the struggle of men against property. The whole movement is a movement to develop equality of opportunity."

> This new conservation method of dealing with property recognizes that our old method resulted in the resourseful [sic], able ambitious men acquiring and developing property formerly belonging to the public in a way that made them masters of the large mass of our people; that the new method of dealing with these matters must be such as tends to make Americans financially independent, because without financial independence, there can be no liberty.

Id. at 342. PENICK, *supra* note 75, argues that this framing of the Ballinger-Pinchot quarrel, which is really the only point stressed by Brandeis that involves the underlying structural cause of the congressional hearings, oversimplifies the generic conflict between Ballinger and Pinchot. It was Ballinger who sought to open up federal lands and resources to the smaller "independent" entrepreneurs whose economic opportunity was so dear to Brandeis.

Third, Brandeis sought to portray his defense of Glavis as "a struggle for equal justice; the same equal justice in the public service that the American is entitled to under the law." LDB to Mark Sullivan (June 4, 1910), in 2 LETTERS OF LOUIS D. BRANDEIS, at 342.

> The readiness to sacrifice Glavis was a readiness to sacrifice the small man to the big. Vertrees was constantly calling attention to what he regarded as practically a sacrilege in attacking a man of exalted station. What I endeavored to bring out was that that attitude was entirely un-American: that what we have to do is to protect the small man against the big; that there was no hesitation apparently in Ballinger and his associates going out of their way to destroy Glavis where his destruction appeared to be necessary for the exoneration of Ballinger; that the most extraordinary un-American act of condemning Glavis, not only without a hearing, – without his seeing the evidence produced against him, but without his ever having known that any charge had been preferred against him.

Id. at 342–43.

93. Brandeis had written his brother in June 1908 that "The Taft nomination assures one good candidate." LDB to Alfred Brandeis (June 20, 1908), in 2 LETTERS OF LOUIS D. BRANDEIS, at 191.
94. LDB to Alfred Brandeis (November 4, 1908), in BRANDEIS FAMILY LETTERS, at 123. Brandeis was only "sorry" that Taft had "won by so large a majority. I wish he had had a margin of not over 10. As it is, I am glad the Republicans have the whole administration. There will be no divided responsibility." *Id.*
95. "When he first accepted the assignment to defend Glavis ... Brandeis had no intention of attacking Taft himself. In fact, he was hopeful that the matter could be pursued without involving the president. From the outset Brandeis and his colleagues tried to paint a picture of a leader who had been led astray

by misguided subordinates." LEWIS J. PAPER, BRANDEIS 125 (New Jersey: Prentice-Hall 1983).

96. LDB to Regina Wehle Goldmark (March 2, 1910), in BRANDEIS FAMILY LETTERS, at 325. *See* LDB to Alfred Brandeis (February 28, 1910), *id.* at 324 ("Pinchot's statement has made situation quite hot & profoundly impressed the Com^{te} & hearers. The Pres^t is getting into an ever more uncomfortable position & seems ever more foolish in his actions."). Taft, however, "was a man who stuck by his friends." PAPER, *supra* note 95, at 125. In May 1910, at the conclusion of the hearings, Taft wrote a complaining citizen "If I were to turn Ballinger out, in view of his innocence and in view of the conspiracy against him, I should be a white-livered skunk. I don't care how it affects my administration, and how it affects the administration before the people; if the people are so unjust as this I don't propose to be one of them.... [L]ife is not worth living and office is not worth having if, for the purpose of acquiring public support, we have to either do a cruel injustice or acquiesce in it.'" Quoted *id.* at 125–26. The conclusion of most historians is that "Ballinger's misdeeds, when all was said and done, had really not amounted to much.... Even Brandeis recognized that the charges against Ballinger were not all that serious. Under repeated and close questioning by committee members, the Boston attorney made it clear that he did not accuse the interior secretary of 'corruption' or of violating any particular law (except the one concerning an ex-government employee's involvement in cases that he had handled while on the federal payroll). Nor did Brandeis recommend that Ballinger be impeached. The most he could say was, in effect, that the president had made a bad appointment and that Ballinger was not a trustworthy custodian of the nation's natural resources." *Id.* at 126.
97. LDB to Alice Goldmark Brandeis (March 27, 1910), in BRANDEIS FAMILY LETTERS, at 147. On Vertrees, see *supra* note 79.
98. LDB to Alice Goldmark Brandeis (March 27, 1910), in BRANDEIS FAMILY LETTERS, at 147.
99. LDB to Alice Goldmark Brandeis (May 13, 1910), in BRANDEIS FAMILY LETTERS, at 153. When Gifford Pinchot asked Brandeis to review the manuscript of an article he was about to publish in the *Saturday Evening Post*, Brandeis observed that "I note that you omitted ... any reference to the deceit practiced by Taft in conjunction with Wickersham, which we brought out in the Ballinger Case. Was this a designed omission? I am inclined to think that as the issue is largely a question whether Taft can be trusted, the fact that he undertook to deceive Congress and the country in one of the most deliberate and important affairs, (as to which the evidence was conclusive and facts subsequently admitted by him,) ought to have much weight." LDB to Gifford Pinchot (July 5, 1910), in 2 LETTERS OF LOUIS D. BRANDEIS, at 459.
100. LDB to Alice Goldmark Brandeis (November 25, 1911), in BRANDEIS FAMILY LETTERS, at 181; LDB to Alice Goldmark Brandeis (February 4, 1912), *id.* at 186.
101. LDB to Gifford Pinchot (July 8, 1912), in 2 LETTERS OF LOUIS D. BRANDEIS, at 641.
102. LDB to Harold Laski (September 21, 1921), in 5 LETTERS OF LOUIS D. BRANDEIS, at 17. "Investors of ordinary prudence have learned to insure against accident, error and wrongdoing by not putting all their eggs into one basket. But our unreasoned passion for bigness and for integration has led us to

disregard in social-industrial life that wise warning. Safety lies in diversity, in decentralization, financial and territorial, with protective federations, in maintaining independent supplies of substitutes." LDB to Felix Frankfurter (September 4, 1922), *id.* at 61.

103. BRANDEIS, *supra* note 7, at 200–14.
104. "Private monopoly in business and industry is an exact analogy of political despotism. Liberty, in industry as in politics, leads to best results. When you create a monopoly you remove the stimulus, the incentive, to all business. Monopoly has a deadening effect, because it attempts to substitute a few minds for many minds." *Address before Southern New England Textile Club, Providence* (December 28, 1912), quoted in THE BRANDEIS GUIDE TO THE MODERN WORLD, *supra* note 35, at 179. On a less convincing note, Brandeis also believed that business initiative came from individuals and that there was an absolute limit to the scope of relevant business information that any single individual could comprehend:

> [A] unit in business may be too large to be efficient, and this is no uncommon incident of monopoly. In every business concern there must be a size-limit of greatest efficiency. What that limit is will differ in different businesses and under varying conditions in the same business. But whatever the business or organization there is a point where it would become too large for efficient and economic management.... Man's work often outruns the capacity of the individual man; and, no matter what the organization, the capacity of an individual man usually determines the success or failure of a particular enterprise.... [O]rganization can never supply the combined judgment, initiative, enterprise, and authority which must come from the chief executive officers. Nature sets a limit to their possible accomplishment. As the Germans say, "Care is taken that the trees do not scrape the skies."

THE CURSE OF BIGNESS, *supra* note 8, at 117. *See id.* at 185. "If the Lord had intended things to be big, he would have made man bigger – in brains and character." LDB to Elizabeth Brandeis Rauschenbush (November 19, 1933), in BRANDEIS FAMILY LETTERS, at 533.

105. STAFF OF S. COMM. ON INTERSTATE COMMERCE, 62ND CONG., CONTROL OF CORPORATIONS, PERSONS, AND FIRMS ENGAGED IN INTERSTATE COMMERCE 1174 (Comm. Print 1913). "I have considered and do consider that the proposition that mere bigness can not be an offense against society is false, because I believe that our society, which rests upon democracy, can not endure under such conditions. Something approaching equality is essential. You may have an organization in the community which is so powerful that in a particular branch of the trade it may dominate by mere size. Although its individual practices may be according to rules, it may be, nevertheless, a menace to the community." *Id.* at 1167.

106. *See* THE CURSE OF BIGNESS, *supra* note 8, at 72–73:

> [W]e have the situation of an employer so potent, so well organized, with such concentrated forces and with such extraordinary powers of reserve and the ability to endure against strikes and other efforts of a union, that the relatively loosely organized masses of even strong unions are unable to cope with the situation. We are dealing here with a question, not of motive, but of condition. ... [W]hen a great financial power has developed – when there exists [sic] these powerful organizations, which can successfully summon forces from all parts of the country, which can afford to use tremendous amounts of money in any conflict to carry out what they deem to be their business principle, and can also afford to suffer large losses – you have

necessarily a condition of inequality between the two contending forces. Such contests, though undertaken with the best motive and with strong conviction on the part of the corporate managers that they are seeing what is for the best interests not only of the company but of the community, lead to absolutism.

107. Brandeis, *supra* note 29, at 562. "The people are beginning to doubt whether in the long run democracy and absolutism can co-exist in the same community; beginning to doubt whether there is justification for the great inequalities in the distribution of wealth." *Id. See* Poole, *supra* note 20, at 493.

108. LOUIS D. BRANDEIS, BUSINESS – A PROFESSION 369 (Boston: Hale, Cushman & Flint 1933). "Nor will even this curb be effective unless the workers coöperate, as in trade unions. Control and coöperation are both essential to industrial liberty." *Id.*

109. THE BRANDEIS GUIDE TO THE MODERN WORLD, *supra* note 35, at 53 (Quoting from a *Collier's Weekly* article published on September 14, 1912). Brandeis believed that "industrial liberty is impossible if the right to organize be denied." *Id.* Yet a great trust, like the Steel Trust, "exemplifies the power of combination, and ... has made it its first business to prevent combination among its employees when they sought to procure decent working conditions and living conditions. It stamped out, through its immense powers of endurance, one strike after another. It developed a secret service, a system of espionage among its workingmen, singling out individuals who favor unionism; and anyone fomenting dissatisfaction with existing conditions, as it was called, was quietly discharged. ... Here you have a corporation that has made it its cardinal principle of action that its employees must be absolutely subject to its will. It is treason for an employee to participate with other employees for combination. ... Must not this mean that the American who is brought up with the idea of political liberty must surrender what every citizen deems far more important, his industrial liberty? Can this contradiction – our grand political liberty and this industrial slavery – long coexist? Either political liberty will be extinguished or industrial liberty must be restored." THE CURSE OF BIGNESS, *supra* note 8, at 38–39.

110. THE CURSE OF BIGNESS, *supra* note 8, at 73.

111. CONTROL OF CORPORATIONS, PERSONS, AND FIRMS ENGAGED IN INTERSTATE COMMERCE, *supra* note 105, at 1155. "Universal suffrage necessarily imposes upon the state the obligation of fitting its governors – the voters – for their task; and the freedom of the individual is as much an essential condition of successful democracy as his education. If the Government permits conditions to exist which make large classes of citizens financially dependent, the great evil of dependence should at least be minimized by the State's assuming ... in some form the burden incident to its own shortcomings." BRANDEIS, *supra* note 7, at 53.

112. Addressing the Republican Club of Boston, Brandeis asked, "What would we be worth to our families and to the country if we worked as hard and as long" as U.S. Steel's employees? "Picture to yourselves what a depth of degradation this would bring us. Frick once spoke of these men and described them as being old at the age of forty. ... This big corporation is producing a subject people, a people that are as little free in the [sic] essence as any slave. There is this difference, however, that while a slave is valuable to his owner, this subject race

Louis Dembitz Brandeis

has no value whatever to the men who employ them after they have ceased being able to give the fearful meed of toil demanded of them.... And yet this trust has frequently asserted that it cares for the welfare of its people.... [T]his greatest of all monopolies has made it a special part of its business to see that the labor it employs shall not combine, when combination holds the only hope of the future for these poor people." *Brandeis Assails the Steel Trust,* NEW YORK TIMES (January 14, 1912), at 17. The *Times* reported: "Mr. Brandeis had been frequently interrupted by applause, but at this point of his speech he had to wait for quiet, so long and loud were the marks of approval. He talked with deep sincerity, and came out to the verge of the crowd of men who were listening to him, and seemed to be trying to induce them to get into a movement to better the conditions that he was describing." *Id.*

Once, testifying before Congress, Brandeis elaborately detailed the brutal hours and low wages of the employees of the United States Steel Corporation. He read an article from the day's paper describing the $500,000 pearl necklace that U.S. Steel's CEO and President Elbert Gary had just given to his wife. "Is it not just the same sort of thing which brought on the French Revolution, and which must suggest to everyone in this particular connection the damage which the queen's necklace did in those days? That seems to me to be one of the horrible manifestations, the by-products, of this aggregation of capital. And it is parading before the world the facts in regard to the unearned wealth, unearned by those who are enjoying it and taken out of the lives of the people who are toiling for them." CONTROL OF CORPORATIONS, PERSONS, AND FIRMS ENGAGED IN INTERSTATE COMMERCE, *supra* note 105, at 1225–26. "[W]hatever and however strong our convictions against the extension of governmental functions may be," wrote Brandeis, "we shall inevitably be swept farther along toward socialism unless we can curb the excesses of our financial magnates. The talk of the agitator alone does not advance socialism a step; but the formation of great trusts ... and their frequent corruption of councils and legislatures is hastening us almost irresistibly into socialist measures. The great captains of industry and of finance, who profess the greatest horror of the extension of governmental functions, are the chief makers of socialism. Socialistic thinkers smile approvingly at the operations of Morgan, Perkins and Rockefeller. ... Our great trust-building, trust-abusing capitalists have in their selfish shortsightedness become the makers of socialism, proclaiming by their acts, like the nobles of France, 'After us, the Deluge!'" BRANDEIS, *supra* note 7, at 152–53.

113. *See supra* note 91.
114. LDB to Alfred Brandeis (July 28, 1912), in 2 LETTERS OF LOUIS D. BRANDEIS, at 653.
115. LDB to Gifford Pinchot (July 8, 1912), in 2 LETTERS OF LOUIS D. BRANDEIS, at 641.
116. LDB to Brand Whitlock (September 3, 1912), in 2 LETTERS OF LOUIS D. BRANDEIS, at 662.
117. LDB to Moses Edwin Clapp (September 11, 1912), in 2 LETTERS OF LOUIS D. BRANDEIS, at 670. Brandeis added, "I wish you and Cummins might have had an opportunity of making Roosevelt understand his fallacies." *Id. See* LDB to Norman Hapgood (October 2, 1912), *id.* at 695–96.

118. George W. Perkins, *Wanted – A National Business Court*, 71 THE INDEPENDENT 1173 (1911). Perkins continued: "Congress has ignored every suggestion by Roosevelt, by Taft, by Wickersham, looking toward any method that would preserve any good there is, any benefit or advantage there is to the people in large business undertakings, and has seemed content to let the country drift toward business chaos. What has given us the sweatshop? Competition. What has given us child labor? Competition. What throws labor out of employment? Competition. What causes low wages? Competition. ... And what is our Congress at this moment calling loudly on our Attorney-General to enforce, even to the door of the jail? Competition." *Id.*
119. LDB to Alfred Brandeis (July 10, 1912), in BRANDEIS FAMILY LETTERS, at 192.
120. LDB to Arthur Norman Holcombe (October 3, 1912), in 2 LETTERS OF LOUIS D. BRANDEIS, at 699. "There is no way to safeguard the people from despotism except to prevent despotism," Brandeis wrote. "The objections to despotism and to monopoly are fundamental in human nature. They rest upon the innate and ineradicable selfishness of man. They rest upon the fact that absolute power inevitably leads to abuse. They rest upon the fact that progress flows only from struggle." BRANDEIS, *supra* note 7, at 271.
121. LDB to Arthur Norman Holcombe (September 11, 1912), in 2 LETTERS OF LOUIS D. BRANDEIS, at 670–71. Brandeis would later make similar objections to FDR's National Recovery Administration. "Curb of bigness is indispensable to true Democracy & Liberty. It is the very foundation also of wisdom in things human. ... I hope you can make your progressives see this truth. If they don't, we may get amelioration, but not a working 'New Deal.' And we are apt to get Fascist manifestations. Remember, the inevitable ineffectiveness of regulation, i.e. the limits of efficiency in regulation." LDB to Elizabeth Brandeis Raushenbush (November 19, 1933), in BRANDEIS FAMILY LETTERS, at 533.
122. LDB to the Editor of the *Boston Journal* (September 24, 1912), in 2 LETTERS OF LOUIS D. BRANDEIS, at 678, 682.
123. LDB to Alfred Brandeis (July 10, 1912), in BRANDEIS FAMILY LETTERS, at 192 ("I am coming out for Wilson."). Brandeis had written Pinchot on July 8 that "I have thought over the matter anxiously and have come to the conclusion that we ought to give Wilson the fullest support, not merely to secure his election, but to make it possible for him after the election to carry out really progressive policies." LDB to Gifford Pinchot (July 8, 1912), in 2 LETTERS OF LOUIS D. BRANDEIS, at 641. In what was surely a futile gesture, Brandeis urged Pinchot to use his influence at the forthcoming National Progressive Convention to have the new third party support Wilson, rather than Roosevelt, on the ground that "With Wilson, supported by the Progressive party, we should be sure of a Progressive administration. If the Progressive party fights Wilson, there is not only the chance of a Reactionary Taft administration, but of a Progressive Wilson administration, if he is elected[,] rendered impotent through lack of Progressive support." *Id.*
124. BOSTON AMERICAN (July 10, 1912), quoted in UROFSKY, *supra* note 26, at 341.
125. LDB to Alfred Brandeis (August 29, 1912), in BRANDEIS FAMILY LETTERS, at 194. Wilson "made a great impression upon me. I think he is strong in character and mind, simple, natural and straightforward. I feel confident that he will not yield to improper influences, and that if elected, he will carry forward our policies

unflinchingly, and will succeed if the Progressives of the Country stand behind him." LDB to Moses Edwin Clapp (September 11, 1912), in 2 LETTERS OF LOUIS D. BRANDEIS, at 669-70. "I have no question as to either the character or intelligence of Governor Wilson. He is not only firm and pure-minded, but he is extremely intelligent and open-minded, and he possesses that quality of careful scrutinizing thought which to my mind is more valuable in a statesman than emotionalism, and which is peculiarly needed at the present time." LDB to Arthur Norman Holcombe (September 11, 1912), in 2 LETTERS OF LOUIS D. BRANDEIS, at 671.

126. LDB to Josephus Daniels (September 4, 1912), in 2 LETTERS OF LOUIS D. BRANDEIS, at 663.
127. ARTHUR S. LINK, WILSON: THE ROAD TO THE WHITE HOUSE 489 (Princeton University Press 1968). Link writes that before "Brandeis outlined his program for the regulation of competition to him," Wilson was "dismally ignorant on the subject." "It was, moreover, a happy coincidence that Wilson's and Brandeis's fundamental objectives, the establishment of unhampered competition and the liberation of economic enterprise in the United States, were the same. It is not surprising, therefore, that Wilson time and again went to [Brandeis] for advice with regard to the specific ways of regulating competition. He was an avid student and rapidly absorbed all that Brandeis taught him." *Id.*
128. LDB to Woodrow Wilson (September 30, 1912), in 2 LETTERS OF LOUIS D. BRANDEIS, at 688. After his first long meeting with Wilson at Sea Girt on August 28, Brandeis told reporters that he found Wilson "to be entirely in accord with my own views of what we need to do to accomplish industrial freedom." *Gov. Wilson Agrees with Mr. Brandeis*, NEW YORK TIMES (August 29, 1912), at 3. The Progressive party, Brandeis said, "must fail in all the important things which it seeks to accomplish because it rests upon a fundamental basis of regulated monopoly. ... The important thing to-day, so far as the preservation of our liberty goes, is the industrial relations of man to man. The third party stands out and says that that relation shall be one of absolutism. ... We must undertake to regulate competition instead of monopoly, for our industrial freedom and our civic freedom go hand in hand and there is no such thing as civic freedom in a state of industrial absolutism. Thus the new party in its programme becomes a house divided against itself. There can be no progress for the workingman under an absolutism." *Id.* On his side, the "Governor declared that Mr. Brandeis more than any other man he knew had studied 'corporate business from the efficiency to the political side.' 'I drew him out for my own benefit,' remarked Gov. Wilson." *Id.*
129. LINK, *supra* note 127, at 492.
130. STRUM, *supra* note 21, at 200-1. Brandeis "charged that carrying out the principles of the Progressive platform would destroy the labor unions, the great protection of the workingman against the power of the trusts." *Says Labor's Hope Lies with Wilson*, NEW YORK TIMES (October 11, 1912), at 6.
131. STRUM, *supra* note 21, at 205-6. Wilson backed off appointing Brandeis because of intense opposition from business interests.
132. *Id.* at 208-17; PAPER, *supra* note 95, at 182-96; MASON, *supra* note 25, at 397-408.

133. *See, e.g., Taft for Highest Court*, NEW YORK TRIBUNE (January 6, 1916), at 1 ("Ex-President Taft is suggested by Alton B. Parker as the best equipped man to take the place left vacant on the United States Supreme Court bench."); *Taft Sentiment Grows*, NEW YORK TIMES (January 9, 1916), at 3 ("Members of the Administration are becoming impressed with the widespread demand that has come from practically all sections of the country for the appointment of William Howard Taft .... The desire expressed for Mr. Taft's appointment is particularly marked among Southern Democrats."); *Urge Wilson to Appoint Taft to Supreme Court*, CHICAGO DAILY TRIBUNE (January 12, 1916), at 8 ("President Wilson is urged to appoint former President Taft ... in a letter signed by seven ex-presidents of the American Bar Association." The signers were Elihu Root, Alton B. Parker. J.M. Dickinson, Joseph H. Choate, John T. Richards, Everett P. Wheeler, William P. Bynum, and Peter W. Meldrim); *Taft Urged for Supreme Court by the Democrats of Mississippi; American Bar Leaders Send Plea*, WASHINGTON POST (January 12, 1916), at 4; *Ask Wilson to Put Taft in U.S. Court; Thirty-Two Lawyers of Both Political Faiths Urge Him as Lamar's Successor*, NEW YORK TRIBUNE (January 12, 1916), at 3. Taft was "very proud of the kindly expressions that have come with respect to the mention of my name for the Supreme Court, but of course Wilson won't offer it to me." WHT to Gus Karger (January 16, 1916) (Taft papers). "I am wicked enough to enjoy the assault upon Wilson to force him to offer me an appointment," Taft wrote a friend. "Of course it will fail but he does not like it." WFT to Charles D. Norton (January 16, 1916) (Taft papers). Taft told an old friend that "I haven't the slightest idea that President Wilson will offer me an appointment to the Supreme Bench. ... [W]hile I may do him an injustice, I feel certain that he could not recognize a generous impulse if he met it on the street." WHT to Myron T. Herrick (January 17, 1916) (Taft papers). Three days after the announcement of Brandeis's nomination, Taft wrote a correspondent: "Don't be disappointed at the failure of Wilson to offer me the Supreme Bench. I have been in a state of amusement ever since the suggestion was made, prompted by the view that some people had that he could see either the political wisdom or the fitness of the appointment." WHT to Truman G. Palmer (January 31, 1916) (Taft papers).
134. STRUM, *supra* note 21, at 207.
135. Prior to 1913–14, Brandeis had lived the life of a "completely non-religious, a non-observant Jew," in the words of his daughter, Elizabeth Brandeis Raushenbush. *See* UROFSKY, *supra* note 26, at 407. In 1914, however, Brandeis assumed the leadership of the Zionist movement in the United States and thereby became extremely visible within the Jewish community. *Id.* at 403–29. Taft put it this way: "While Brandeis was a very poor Jew down to the time that he was defeated for Attorney General, he has been a hat-wearing Jew since that time, and has been preaching a return to Zion and Jerusalem. ... [W]hen his name was proposed [for Wilson's cabinet], a committee of the prominent Jews went to the President and told him he was not a Jew. Now he is a Jew all over, and I presume it will arouse jealousy throughout the country if any attempt is made to beat him." WHT to Horace D. Taft (January 31, 1916) (Taft papers). Taft observed that Brandeis's "present superlative and extreme Judaism is a plant of very late growth." Brandeis "was no Jew until he was rejected by Wilson as Attorney-General, because the leading Jews of the country told Wilson that Brandeis was not a representative Jew. Since that time, Brandeis has adopted Zionism, favors the New Jerusalem,

and has metaphorically been re-circumcised. He has gone all over the country making speeches, arousing the Jewish spirit, even wearing a hat in the Synagogue while making a speech .... If it were necessary, I am sure he would have grown a beard to convince them that he was a Jew of Jews. All this has made it politically difficult for not only the Jews but for anybody looking for office where there are Jews, in the constituency, to hesitate about opposing Brandeis." WHT to Gus Karger (January 31, 1916) (Taft papers).

On Taft's public opposition to anti-Semitism, see William Howard Taft, *The Progressive World Struggle of the Jews for Civil Equality*, 36 NATIONAL GEOGRAPHIC MAGAZINE 1 (JULY 1919); *Taft Condemns Ford for Fight against Jews*, CHICAGO DAILY TRIBUNE (December 24, 1920), at 1 ("There is not the slightest ground for anti-Semitism among us. It is a vicious plant. It is a noxious weed that should be cut out. It has no place in free America and the men who seek to introduce it should be condemned by public opinion."). *See also* WHT to Julius Lemkowitz (August 4, 1921) (Taft papers) ("I am glad to have you think that I am a friend of the Jewish race, as I am."). On Brandeis's remarkable conversion to Zionism, which, *contra* Taft, did not in fact seem in any way connected to ambition for higher office, but instead to the discovery of deep personal and familial connections, as well as to his understanding of Zionist ideals as reflecting his own unique vision of democratic self-determination, see UROFSKY, *supra* note 26, at 399–429; STRUM, *supra* note 21, at 224–65; PAPER, *supra* note 95, at 198–208; ROSEN, *supra* note 17, at 146–74; MASON, *supra* note 25, at 441–64; BURT, *supra* note 39, at 117–24.

136. As Taft wrote his friend Gus Karger, "Our worthy President has developed more qualities of Machiavelli than even I, with a full appreciation of the admirable roundness of his character, had suspected. When I think of the devilish ingenuity manifested in the selection of Brandeis, I can not but admire his finesse. ... Wilson has projected a fight, which with master art he will give the color of a contest, on one side of which will be ranged the opposition of corporate wealth and racial prejudice, and on the other side the down-trodden, the oppressed, the uplifters, and labor unions, and all the elements which are supposed to have votes in the election. This will tend to the confirmation because of the white-livered Senators that we have. The Senate has been LaFolletized and Gomperized so that it has ceased to be the conservative body it was." WHT to Gus Karger (January 31, 1916) (Taft papers). In this letter Taft was repeating accepted wisdom among conservative commentators. *See, e.g.*, *U.S. Supreme Court a Political Pawn*, PHILADELPHIA INQUIRER (January 31, 1916), at 1 ("According to those who have been seeking the motive for the appointment of Brandeis, the President has been trying to win a portion of the Progressive Party to the Democratic ranks. He is aware that he was elected by a minority vote; that Colonel Roosevelt and Mr. Taft together had nearly a million and a half more votes than were cast for the Democratic ticket. With the Republican Party reunited, the President is said to realize that he cannot be re-elected unless about three-quarters of a million former Progressives cast their votes for him in 1916."); *Brandeis and Politics*, WASHINGTON POST (January 31, 1916), at 5 ("There is much force in the talk of certain administration politicians that senators 'will not dare' vote against Mr. Brandeis, because if they do they will be open to the charge that they are opposing him because of his race and religion.

In a sense, at least, realization that such a charge would be made handicaps senators of both parties, who would otherwise take an open stand against placing upon the Supreme Court a man whose public career smacked so strongly of extreme radicalism.... [T]his will lead some senators to vote for him who would not vote for one of their own religion with a similar record. Just as no political party in this country would think of taking anti-Semitism into its creed, so no public man would willingly lay himself open to suspicion of entertaining anti-Semitic ideas.").

137. "President Wilson sent a bomb to the United States Senate yesterday in the form of his nomination of Louis D. Brandeis, famous trust buster.... The bomb exploded. With the reading of the nomination senators started for the cloakrooms. To them it was the biggest sensation of the session." *Brandeis Fight Likely*, WASHINGTON POST (January 29, 1916), at 2. *See Brandeis' Name Came as Bomb*, BOSTON DAILY GLOBE (January 29, 1916), at 1 ("Mr. Brandeis had not even figured in the calculations of the politicians of either party. As near as can be learned his name was not included among the 27 men who had been proposed for the position by the leaders of the Democratic party.").

138. *See, e.g.*, TODD, *supra* note 91.

139. *Nomination of Louis D. Brandeis*, 2 Hearings before the Subcommittee of the Committee on the Judiciary of the United States Senate, Sen. Doc. No. 409, 64th CONG. 1st SESS. (1916), at 175.

140. *Id.* at 305. On February 11, A. Lawrence Lowell, the president of Harvard who had long held some unspecified private grudge against Brandeis, led a group of fifty-five eminent Bostonians in urging Massachusetts Senator Henry Cabot Lodge to oppose Brandeis, on the ground that a judicial appointment to the Court "should only be conferred upon a member of the legal profession whose general reputation is as good as his legal attainments are great. We do not believe that Mr. Brandeis has the judicial temperament and capacity which should be required in a judge of the Supreme Court. His reputation as a lawyer is such that he has not the confidence of the people." *Oppose Brandeis*, BOSTON DAILY GLOBE (February 12, 1916), at 1. Perhaps Lowell was still smarting from Brandeis's discrediting of George Wickersham. *See supra* note 91.

141. *See supra* text at notes 31–33. Those making such charges were themselves caught in the toils of contradiction, as the *New Republic* caustically observed: "The theme, the *leitmotif* of the charges, is that Mr. Brandeis has frequently been guilty of double-dealing. He is supposed to be a man who is at once violently partisan for his client, and yet disloyal to him. He is supposed to be without the 'judicial temperament,' and at the same time inclined to be on both sides of a case. Those who attacked him seemed unable to agree on whether he is a ruthless partisan, or a man who is not partisan enough. But they concentrated finally on the belief that he is not the absolute partisan of his client." *The Case against Brandeis*, 6 NEW REPUBLIC 202 (1916). During the hearings Brandeis wrote his brother: "It is rather amusing that one who is not of judicial tenor should be bombarded on the one hand by the financiers for opposing the railroads, and, on the other, by Thorne for favoring the railroads. The hearings seem to be a fit method of clearing the atmosphere. However, it is not my fight." LDB to Alfred Brandeis (February 10, 1916), in BRANDEIS FAMILY LETTERS, at 284.

142. Brandeis, *supra* note 6.

Louis Dembitz Brandeis

143. *Id.* at 463–64.
144. *The Committee Report on Brandeis*, Detroit Free Press (May 25, 1916), at 4.
145. *An Unfit Appointment*, LOS ANGELES TIMES (January 30, 1916), at II4. The *Times* added that "Brandeis is not only a destroyer; he is a hypocrite. After lining his pockets with gold as a result of his work as a crafty lawyer in sheltering from harm great shoe-machinery trusts, he blossomed forth as a special pleader against 'Big Business' and the leader of attacks on railroads and all forms of organized industry and applied wealth."
146. *Mr. Justice Brandeis*, CHRISTIAN SCIENCE MONITOR (June 2, 1916), at 22. See *Mr. Justice Brandeis*, BALTIMORE SUN (June 3, 1916), at 8 ("It is easy to understand why the politicians of the Ballinger class ... should froth at the mouth at the mention of Brandeis' name .... [I]t is evident that the opposition to Mr. Brandeis that did not spring from unworthy motives must have had its origin in temperamental objections to Mr. Brandeis' so-called radicalism."). The *New Republic* argued that if Brandeis's nomination were defeated, the "American people" would conclude "that the agitators are right, that a liberal who has faced the music cannot be appointed to the Court. All those who have believed in the recall of judges would say that here is proof positive of what they have asserted. They would read into it a demonstration that only the tried friend of wealth and power can reach that Court, ... [and] that Mr. Brandeis was beaten because he is the greatest living American engaged in curbing the rich and the powerful." *Saving the Supreme Court*, 7 NEW REPUBLIC 31 (1916). The *New Republic* asserted that if those who opposed Brandeis "had any vision, they would know that the presence of Mr. Brandeis on the Supreme Court ... would give the lie to those who say that the humblest are not represented in the highest tribunal. ... There is deep truth in the statement of one of the most important officials in the government, who said that the Court needs Brandeis now more than he needs it." *Id.* at 31–32. See *Responsibility Accepted*, LOUISVILLE COURIER-JOURNAL (June 3, 1916), at 4 ("Had the nomination been opposed by the Democrats of the Judiciary Committee ... the inference of the public would have been that the Senate was controlled by the interests which fought the nomination, and which failed signally to make a convincing argument and a creditable showing."); Alexander H. Robbins, *Louis D. Brandeis, Associate Justice Supreme Court of the United States*, 82 CENTRAL LAW JOURNAL 403, 404 (1916) ("The country is to be congratulated that after an ordeal that few men could have stood so successfully, the nomination of Mr. Brandeis has at last been confirmed. Any other result would have been a public misfortune, since it would have aroused suspicion, however untrue and unfair ... that big business and ultra-conservatism had succeeded in defeating a man whose only offense seemed to be that he had espoused the public interests too ardently.").
147. WHT to Louis A. Coolidge (March 6, 1916) (Taft papers).
148. WHT to Gus Karger (January 31, 1916) (Taft papers).
149. WHT to Horace D. Taft (January 31, 1916) (Taft papers).
150. WHT to Truman G. Palmer (January 31, 1916) (Taft papers). *See* WHT to James Markham (October 21, 1916) (Taft papers). The *New York Times* took up an analogous theme in opposing Brandeis's nomination. Although the *Times* conceded that "the charges against the professional standing and character of Mr. Brandeis" were unsustainable, *The Brandeis Nomination*, NEW YORK

TIMES (May 25, 1916), at 12, it insisted that "the chief and most serious criticism of the nomination" rested on the proposition that "the court is of prime necessity a conservative body. It must be so, since it is the great regulator of the machinery of Government. It stands between the people and the consequences of their own errors. It is the interpreter of the Constitution, that instrument which is at once the charter of the people's liberties and the measure of their self-denial. A radical upon the bench of the Supreme Court is not easily imaginable." *Mr. Brandeis for the Supreme Court*, NEW YORK TIMES (January 29, 1916), at 8. Advocacy, said the *Times*, belongs "in the legislative hall rather than in the chamber of the court." *Id*. "Theories of social justice" were "questions of purely political nature concerning social welfare" and were thus irrelevant "to questions of law and the constitutional powers of Government." *Id*. "To place upon the Supreme Bench judges who hold a different view of the function of the court, to supplant conservatism by radicalism, would be to undo the work of John Marshall and strip the Constitution of its defenses. It would introduce endless confusion where order has reigned, it would tend to give force and effect to any whim or passion of the hour, to crown with success any transitory agitation engaged in by a part of the people, overriding the matured judgment of all the people as expressed in their fundamental law." *The Brandeis Nomination, supra*.

The jurisprudential work of Holmes, which had been consciously adopted by Brandeis, aimed precisely to demolish the separation of law from social welfare postulated by the *New York Times*. The most sophisticated public commentary, offered in the *New Republic*, fully understood this underlying jurisprudential debate, and it welcomed the discussion prompted by the *Times*. "One public benefit has already accrued from the nomination of Mr. Brandeis. It has started discussion of what the Supreme Court means in American life. From much of the comment since Mr. Brandeis's nomination it would seem that multitudes of Americans seriously believe that the nine Justices embody pure reason, that they are set apart from the concerns of the community, regardless of time, place and circumstances, to become the interpreter of sacred words with meaning fixed forever and ascertainable by a process of ineluctable reasoning. Yet the notion not only runs counter to all we know of human nature; it betrays either ignorance or false knowledge of the actual work of the Supreme Court." *Brandeis*, 6 NEW REPUBLIC 4 (1916).

151. ROSEN, *supra* note 17, at 91; ALEXANDER M. BICKEL & BENNO C. SCHMIDT, JR., THE JUDICIARY AND RESPONSIBLE GOVERNMENT 1910–1921, at 385 (New York: MacMillan Publishing Co. 1984).

152. *Taft and Root Come Out against Brandeis*, WALL STREET JOURNAL (March 15, 1916), at 1; *Taft and Root Oppose Brandeis*, NEW YORK TRIBUNE (March 15, 1916), at 12; *Taft Opposes Brandeis*, NEW YORK TIMES (March 15, 1916), at 4. The other signers were Joseph H. Choate, Simeon Baldwin, Elihu Root, Moorfield Storey, Peter Meldrim, and Francis Rawle. Taft felt so strongly about the letter that shortly before its release he wrote Wickersham, "What has become of the protest that Simeon Baldwin and Elihu Root and I signed as to the Brandeis appointment? I had assumed that it would have been published long ago. Lowell, whom I saw in Boston, was anxious to have it published. I presume we can not defeat the confirmation, but I think we ought to go on record." WHT to George W. Wickersham (March 14, 1916) (Taft papers).

Louis Dembitz Brandeis

The release of the American Bar Association letter made Taft vulnerable to attacks on the ground of the Ballinger-Pinchot affair. "Mr. Taft has reason to remember Mr. Brandeis unpleasantly," the *Baltimore Sun* observed, because of the Ballinger "scandal," and "he would be more than human if his estimate of Mr. Brandeis were not somewhat colored by that recollection." *Why They Protest against Mr. Brandeis*, BALTIMORE SUN (March 16, 1916), at 8. "Of course I knew the muckraking battery would begin," Taft wrote a friend, "and I did what I did in the face of that prospect, because while I did not think it was going to prevent confirmation, I did think it was necessary that the Bar through men that may fairly be called representative should enter a protest." WHT to Charles D. Norton (March 21, 1916) (Taft papers).

For his part, Brandeis was determined to take full advantage of the opportunity offered by Taft. *See* LDB to Norman Hapgood (March 14, 1916), in 4 LETTERS OF LOUIS D. BRANDEIS, at 118 ("I think Taft's injecting himself into this controversy is a fact which, if properly used, will compensate somewhat for the annoyances of the last six weeks; and, if properly used, I think may be of great political importance. It gives opportunity for making clear what we omitted to make clear nearly six years ago – the gravity of Taft's and Wickersham's act in connection with the antedating. I called this to Felix F.'s attention. He will talk with Lippmann; but I think that you, with the aid of Joe Cotton in New York and George [Rublee] in Washington, ought to be able to bring out these matters clearly in the dailies as well as the periodicals."); *Taft Attack on Brandeis a Boomerang*, CHICAGO DAILY TRIBUNE (March 17, 1916), at 7 ("According to administration leaders, Mr. Taft wrote his letter of protest to the senate judiciary committee not because of his regard for the sanctity of the courts but because of the feeling he still entertains for Mr. Brandeis on account of the latter's participation in the Ballinger-Pinchot controversy. . . . Administration leaders insist that Mr. Brandeis proved that Mr. Taft attempted to deceive the Senate when it requested information concerning the charges against Secretary Ballinger."). In its issue of March 23, the *New Republic* wrote: "Of Mr. Taft's irritating characteristics I should put his thick skin first. His self-complacency will always keep him from understanding what happens to him. No man whose skin wasn't thick, and who had done what Mr. Taft did in the Ballinger case, would be dull enough to recall that case by getting into the fight against Mr. Brandeis. Has Mr. Taft no shame? The chair hears none." *Books and Things*, 6 NEW REPUBLIC 219 (1916). The *New Republic* later set Taft's opposition to Brandeis against the fact that Brandeis had uncovered "a conspiracy on the part of President Taft and two members of his cabinet to deceive the American public." *Saving the Supreme Court*, 7 NEW REPUBLIC 31 (1916). Taft was on the verge of filing a libel suit until he was calmed down by the more practical Wickersham, who in a letter said that "nobody but a bunch of Hebrew uplifters of the same stripe as Brandeis would dream of repeating the criticism. Frankly, I should not for one moment seriously think of dignifying them by a libel suit." Wickersham to WHT, quoted in TODD, *supra* note 91, at 179–80.

153. This point was of course not lost on the public. "What the protest of such men as Mr. Taft, Mr. Root, Mr. Choate and former Governor Baldwin represents, it seems to us, is a state of mind, not a knowledge of facts. It is a state of mind which is

347

utterly hostile to what is called modern progress and modern ideas. Real sin, in their view, is that [Brandeis's] state of mind is not their state of mind, that he sees the world with new and not with old-fashioned eyes. Perhaps they may be right and he may be wrong, but they ought to base their protest on that ground and not on his reputation and character." *Why They Protest against Mr. Brandeis*, *supra* note 152. "It is a shameful and cowardly thing," the paper continued, "to blacken a man's character by innuendo." *Id.*

154. While the subcommittee report lay on the table, Holmes wrote his friend Lewis Einstein that "Brandeis's matter hangs along, and I don't know what will happen.... He always left on me the impression of a good man when he called, and I never have fully fathomed the reasons for the strong prejudice against him shown by other good men. Whatever happens it is a misfortune for the Court, for the time being. If he is turned down the proletariat will say only tools of the plutocrats can get in (though the ps. didn't favor me, you may bet). If he gets in many people will think that the character of the Court no longer is above question." OWH to Lewis Einstein (May 14, 1916), in HOLMES-EINSTEIN CORRESPONDENCE, at 128.

155. *Nomination of Louis D. Brandeis*, *supra* note 139, at 305.

156. *Ready to Quit Brandeis Fight*, BOSTON DAILY GLOBE (May 25, 1916), at 1. The Republican National Convention was set to convene on June 7, and Republicans were anxious not to further alienate progressive voters. *See* 86 THE INDEPENDENT 429 (June 12, 1916) ("The Republicans ... by making it a party issue and voting solidly in opposition have committed a serious political blunder. The Democrats will not be slow to make the most of it during the coming campaign. In fact, Mr. Wilson can ask nothing better than to have the Brandeis issue brought before the voters between now and November 4."). Progressive Republican senators like Cummins, Borah, La Follette, and Poindexter argued strongly "that continued opposition to the nomination would not be justified in the public mind." *Id.* It had originally been thought that insurgents like Cummins and Borah would support Brandeis, but evidently the need to heal the divisions of 1912 and present a united Republican front in the 1916 presidential election overrode what otherwise would have been a natural alliance.

157. *Nomination of Louis Brandeis Is Confirmed*, NASHVILLE TENNESSEAN AND THE NASHVILLE AMERICAN (June 2, 1916), at 1. "The gauntlet Mr. Brandeis's nomination has had to run is almost unique in the history of the Supreme Court. He was nominated late in January and since then the fight for and against him has been continuous." *Favors Brandeis Nomination, 10 to 8*, NEW YORK TIMES (May 25, 1916), at 5.

158. *Brandeis Is Confirmed for the U.S. Bench*, ARIZONA REPUBLICAN (June 2, 1916), at 1.

159. *Admit Brandeis Wins*, WASHINGTON POST (May 27, 1916), at 5. The terms of the compromise are officially announced at 53 CONG. REC. 9032 (June 1, 1916), which records that "the injunction of secrecy [is] removed from all matters in relation to said nomination."

160. One Democrat voted against confirmation, and three insurgent Republicans – Robert La Follette, George Norris, and Miles Poindexter – broke ranks to vote for confirmation.

Louis Dembitz Brandeis

161. *The Close of the Brandeis Case*, 7 NEW REPUBLIC 134 (1916). Opposition to Brandeis was organized in part by officers of the United Steel Corporation and the United Shoe Machinery Company. BICKEL & SCHMIDT, *supra* note 151, at 378–79.
162. *The Close of the Brandeis Case, supra* note 161, at 134.
163. LDB to Alfred Brandeis (June 14, 1910), in 2 LETTERS OF LOUIS D. BRANDEIS, at 348. *See* LDB to Alice Goldmark Brandeis (December 9, 1913), in BRANDEIS FAMILY LETTERS, at 230 ("fight – fight – fight is the thing."). During the hearings, Brandeis wrote his brother, "I am leaving the fight to others and we are getting a pretty nice issue built up. . . . I could not afford to decline. . . . It would have been, in effect, deserting the progressive forces. Now my feeling is rather – 'Go it husband, go it Bear' with myself as 'interested spectator.'" LDB to Alfred Brandeis (February 12, 1916), *id.* at 295.
164. LDB to Alice Goldmark Brandeis (December 4, 1918), in 4 LETTERS OF LOUIS D. BRANDEIS, at 370. In 1919, Brandeis would seek to recruit Taft to support the cause of Zionism. LDB to Charles A. Cowen & Alexander Sachs (March 7, 1919), *id.* at 385. Brandeis was not successful. *See* WHT to Henry Morganthau (August 4, 1921) (Taft papers) ("I want to thank you for sending me your article on Zionism. I am bound to say that it is a smashing attack upon the plan presented by the supporters of that project. It is informing and very strong."). Taft would later explicitly affirm to Harding in December 1920 that he had "not changed my mind" that the nomination of Brandeis was "not a fit one to be made." See *supra* Prologue, at note 39.
165. LDB to WHT (July 19, 1921) (Taft papers).
166. *See* LDB to WHT (August 12, 1921) (Taft papers).
167. WHT to Horace D. Taft (October 6, 1921) (Taft papers). Taft's law clerk for the 1924 term, C. Dickerman Williams, reports that in the fall he was in the car with Taft when they were "to pick up Justice Brandeis en route. I was curious about the greeting he would give to Justice Brandeis. ... As we approached Justice Brandeis' apartment house, we saw him standing on the sidewalk in front, waiting. The Chief Justice told me to get out of the car promptly when we reached Justice Brandeis and I did so. He then got out right after me, and going up to Brandeis threw his arms around him with every appearance of affection and said 'My brother.' I concluded that whatever animosity had previously existed between them had ended." C. Dickerman Williams, *The 1924 Term: Recollections of Chief Justice Taft's Law Clerk*, 1989 YEARBOOK OF THE SUPREME COURT HISTORICAL SOCIETY 40, 43.
168. WHT to Mrs. Frederick J. Manning (June 11, 1923) (Taft papers). In this letter, Taft observes that Brandeis "is a Jew and he has some of the characteristics of that race, and in the field of social economics we usually differ. Then it is very hard for him, when he is dissenting in a case, to avoid colored statement of fact and to cut corners." Taft, who was personally not anti-Semitic, nevertheless told George Wickersham, "I wrote to Learned Hand what the President had said about Gus's criticism of his pardons. Learned said that Gus was one of the most restrained persons on the Bench and elsewhere, that he (Learned) was the man who talked too much and not Gus. I did not write to Learned, but his answer reminded me of the story of the old Jew who was selling clothes and got hold of a countryman to sell him a suit. The countryman looked over the suit and tried on the coat and he said

THE TAFT COURT

'They seem to be all right but they smell'. And the Jew said, 'Oh, my friend, it is me you smell, not the clothes'. I told that story to Brandeis, but I left out the racial character of it, though he may have guessed it." WHT to George Wickersham (May 1, 1927) (Taft papers). On Wickersham's latent anti-Semitism, see George Wickersham to WHT (December 4, 1924) (Taft papers).

169. *Brandeis-Frankfurter Conversations*, at 303 (April 17, 1922). This was not because Taft had in any sense forgotten the Ballinger affair. Just before the beginning of the 1921 term, for example, he wrote a correspondent that "My sense of justice was very much shocked by the things which were done in that investigation by people who were gratified to attack me and were willing to sacrifice an innocent man like Ballinger in order to embarrass my Administration. ... No one can tell now what the charges were against Ballinger, and no one can truly say that a single one of them was sustained. The public mind was temporarily afflicted with a diseased sensitiveness created by these men which led the public to suspect everyone. That has passed by and into what the Germans call the 'Eiwigkeit.'" WHT to Mrs. Parsons (August 5, 1921) (Taft papers). In 1924 Taft wrote his former secretary of war, J.M. Dickinson, that he wanted "to talk with you about Ballinger" and about "how utterly unjust the attacks were upon him. It produces a sense of wrong that it is hard for me to repress. Ballinger was an honest man. He never did the slightest thing to justify criticism. . . . And yet they hounded him so that they were able to convince a great many people that he was dishonest. They could not tell anything that he had done, and there is no man among the Democrats who could tell just what he did do. It was due to a conspiracy of Pinchot, Garfield and Brandeis. I don't know whether there is to be any retribution for a thing like that, but if there is they will have to suffer." WHT to J.M. Dickinson (February 20, 1924) (Taft papers).

170. FELIX FRANKFURTER ON THE SUPREME COURT: EXTRAJUDICIAL ESSAYS ON THE COURT AND THE CONSTITUTION 490–91 (Philip B. Kurland, ed., Cambridge: Harvard University Press 1970). *See, e.g.*, WHT to Charles P. Taft (February 26, 1925) (Taft papers): "My brother Brandeis and I sometimes talk over literature. He is very much better read than I am, but occasionally he recommends a book which I am glad to read. The book I have in mind is 'Isabella D'Este', by Julia Cartwright . . . . She was Marchioness of Mantua, born in 1474 and died in 1539. She was a very remarkable woman and has left a most interesting correspondence. I suppose she was the brightest woman of the Renaissance."

Taft's correspondence does show that he occasionally vented outbursts of frustration and anger against Brandeis, especially toward the end of the decade as Taft's declining health rendered him more vulnerable. Brandeis's dissents in Myers v. United States, 272 U.S. 52 (1926), Bedford Cut Stone Co. v. Journeymen S.C. Assoc., 274 U.S. 37 (1927), and Olmstead v. United States, 277 U.S. 438 (1928), seem to have especially rankled Taft. About *Myers*, Taft wrote his brother, "McReynolds and Brandeis belong to a class of people that have no loyalty to the Court and sacrifice almost everything to the gratification of their own publicity and wish to stir up dissatisfaction with the decision of the Court, if they don't happen to agree with it." WHT to Horace D. Taft (October 27, 1926) (Taft papers). *See* WHT to Charles P. Taft 2nd (October 31, 1926) (Taft papers). Less than a month later, however, Taft went out of his way to join Brandeis's dissent in FTC v. Western Meat Co., 272 U.S. 554 (1926). *See* WHT to LDB (November 19, 1926) (Taft papers) ("I think you may add that I concur with you in the dissent. I was at first not inclined to express my differing view, but as you have done so, I shall go with you."). And in December Taft was in the context of Albrecht v. United States, 273 U.S. 1 (1927), praising Brandeis for "a most helpful aid to our brethren and inferior courts," and signing his letter "with best wishes for the New Year which being your 71st is according to the Psalmist more than is your allotment and therefore in one sense is 'all velvet' as I hope it may prove to be." WHT to LDB (December 26, 1926) (Taft papers). About *Bedford Cut Stone*, Taft wrote Sutherland, "I suppose Brandeis has his dissenting opinion already drafted. I never have seen him in such a state of rejoicing after getting Sanford and Stone apparently into his army and into his plan of weakening the Court by boring from within." WHT to GS (January 25, 1927) (Taft papers). (On Brandeis boring from within, see WHT to WVD (June 22, 1927) (Van Devanter papers)). Less than a month after *Bedford Cut Stone* came down, however, Brandeis was cordially accepting extra assignments from Taft in order to relieve Van Devanter's backlog. *See* WHT to LDB (May 3, 1927) (Taft papers); WHT to OWH (May 3, 1927) (Holmes papers); LDB to WHT (May 3, 1927) (Taft papers). About *Olmstead*, which particularly exercised Taft, Taft wrote his brother, "Brandeis was especially severe in his strictures on our lack of dignity and morality and I have no doubt he will find a good many followers. It is trying to have to be held up as amoral by one who is full of tricks all the time. But he can become full of eloquent denunciation without great effort." WHT to Horace D. Taft (June 8, 1928) (Taft papers). For positive Taft correspondence with Brandeis after *Olmstead*, see *infra* note 173.

171. Friendly, *supra* note 2, at 768. Thus when Brandeis, who habitually sent numerous drafts of his opinions to the printer for revisions, privately offered to pay the extra costs entailed by his idiosyncratic style of composition, see LDB to WHT (November 3, 1923) (Taft papers), Taft immediately replied:

> I don't think you need be troubled at all at the cost of your cancellations and changes in your opinions. I have been talking the matter over with Van Devanter, and I agree that of all things in our Court the most important thing is to get our opinions right, and for some of us, especially those of us who go into subjects with some elaboration, it is necessary that we should have our opinions set up before we are able fully to determine the proper form to give them. There is no expenditure in connection with our work which should be freer from limitation than that, and while of course we should have in mind the expense, and try to save it in advance, I think we would make a great mistake if we allowed the fear of expense to interfere with the necessary procedure in making our opinions what we wish them to be. I would not for a minute consider your paying the expense of this out of your purse.

WHT to LDB (November 4, 1923) (Taft papers). Two years later, Taft – apparently in response to the request of one of the justices – circulated to the Court a memorandum that listed the printing costs for each Justice for the past four months:

| Chief Justice | $274.50 |
| Justice Holmes | 5.00 |

Justice Van Devanter	8.00
Justice McReynolds	7.00
Justice Brandeis	337.00
Justice Sutherland	5.00
Justice Butler	–
Justice Sanford	35.00
Justice Stone	12.00

Taft wrote to the Court that, "It has been suggested that the enclosed list is something that we ought to examine with prayer and penance – *mea culpa*." WHT to Brethren (November 27, 1925) (Stone papers). Once again, Brandeis offered to pay for his own printing: "In my court work I obey implicitly Emerson's advice: 'Spend for your expense, and retrench in the expense which is not yours.' Neither a stenographer, nor offices at the Capitol, could help me. But the printer can and does. He helps me think; and he helps me detect errors. I realize that my demands upon him may some time exceed the Court's funds available.... It would not disturb me in the least to pay a few thousand a year from my own funds. And it would disturb me much to curb, in the interest of reduced printers' bills, my efforts to improve my opinions." LDB to WHT (January 3, 1926) (Taft papers).

Once again, although this time with markedly less enthusiasm, Taft supported Brandeis's use of the printer: "I am in favor of economy, but I think we can have too much economy in the matter of perfecting opinions. I am quite willing to try and do better, as I am sure the rest of the members of the Court are, but there is something about the appearance of an opinion in print that neither manuscript nor type-writing prompts, and there isn't anything more important that we do, except in the deciding and composing of opinions, than the perfecting of them for publication. The appropriation for that purpose is large and ought to be, and I have not been advised that we have exceeded it." WHT to LDB (January 4, 1926) (Taft papers). Later that year, in connection with his own long decision in Myers v. United States, 272 U.S. 52 (1926), Taft wrote his brother that he hoped "to get back a proof" of Taft's own "outrageously long" opinion, "so as to see what I can do in cutting it down, for I find that the putting of an opinion in print gives you a better general view of it and furnishes you more opportunity for suggestions of useful changes than if it is typewritten. It is a good method of correcting and revising opinions, although Justice McReynolds complains that most of us do not allow ourselves to be economical in this matter." WHT to Horace D. Taft (September 9, 1926) (Taft papers).

172. MASON, *supra* note 25, at 537. *See* LDB to GS (January 20, 1926) (Sutherland papers) ("We miss you very much."). Sutherland is famously reported to have said about Brandeis, "My God, how I detest that man's ideas, but he is one of the greatest technical lawyers I have ever known." STRUM, *supra* note 21, at 302.

173. *See, e.g.*, Zucht v. King, 260 U.S. 174 (1922) ("An excellent opinion.") (Brandeis papers); United States *ex rel.* Bilokumsky v. Tod, 263 U.S. 149 (1923) ("An exceptionally good piece of work.") (Brandeis papers); United States v. Abilene & Southern Ry. Co., 265 U.S. 274 (1924) ("This is VERY clear and thorough.") (Brandeis papers); Missouri *ex rel.* St. Louis, Brownsville & Mexico ry. Co.

Louis Dembitz Brandeis

v. Taylor, 266 U.S. 200 (1924) ("Put with your usual clearness") (Brandeis papers); Sanford & Brooks Co. v. United States, 267 U.S. 455 (1925) ("I think you will satisfy everybody but appellant.") (Brandeis papers); Baltimore & Ohio Rd. Co. v. Parkersburg, 268 U.S. 35 (1925) ("This seems to be as logical as it is fatal.") (Brandeis papers); Missouri Pacific Railroad v. Reynolds Davis Grocery Co., 268 U.S. 366 (1925) ("I suppose you are right. At any rate I yield with faith in the expert.") (Brandeis papers); Robertson v. Railroad Labor Board, 268 U.S. 619 (1925) ("Clear and thorough as usual.") (Brandeis papers); Petterson v. Louisville & Nashville Rd. Co., 269 U.S. 1 (1925) ("Your well reasoned opinion satisfies my doubts and I agree.") (Brandeis papers); Hicks v. Poe, 269 U.S. 118 (1925) ("No one can deal with the question of substitution better than yourself.") (Brandeis papers); Louisville & Nashville Railroad Co. v. Sloss-Sheffield Steel & Iron Co., 269 U.S. 217 (1925) ("An excellent opinion drawn with your usual painstaking care.") (Brandeis papers); Missouri Pacific Railroad v. Boone, 270 U.S. 466 (1926) ("You put it beyond question.") (Brandeis papers); Chicago, Indianapolis & Louisville Railway Co. v. United States, 270 U.S. 287 (1926) ("I did not hear the oral arguments and was not at the Conference. Your opinion seems right; and, moreover, I have faith in the expert knowledge of the writer.") (Brandeis papers); Minneapolis & St. Louis R.R. Co. v. Peoria & Pekin Union Ry. Co., 270 U.S. 580 (1926) ("As always, clear & to the point.") (Brandeis papers); Western Paper Makers' Chemical Co. v. United States, 271 U.S. 268 (1926) ("Yes sir. With my usual faith in your expert knowledge.") (Brandeis papers); Napier v. Atlantic Coast Line R. Co., 272 U.S. 605 (1926) ("Admirably stated.") (Brandeis papers); Virginian R. Co. v. United States, 272 U.S. 658 (1926) ("Admirably and clearly put") (Brandeis papers); United States v. Los Angeles & Salt Lake Railroad Co., 273 U.S. 299 (1927) ("You have written an exceptionally clear and convincing opinion; and after reading it one wonders how a different view could have been entertained.") (Brandeis papers); Clark v. Poor, 274 U.S. 554 (1927) ("Clear & to the point.") (Brandeis papers); United States v. Berwind-White Coal Mining Co., 274 U.S. 564 (1927) ("A well stated, convincing and useful opinion.") (Brandeis papers); Lawrence v. St. Louis-San Francisco Ry. Co., 274 U.S. 588 (1927) ("Your very clear opinion removes the slight doubt I had, and I fully agree.") (Brandeis papers); Humes v. United States, 276 U.S. 487 (1928) ("You blow learned counsel for petitioners out of the water.") (Brandeis papers); Michigan Central Railroad Co. v. Mix, 278 U.S. 492 (1929) ("Clear and to the point.") (Brandeis papers); Atchison, Topeka & Santa Fe Ry. Co., v. United States, 279 U.S. 768 (1929) ("This reads like what Holmes J. would call 'God's word' and I agree unless some one gives conclusive reason to the contrary.").

Taft also went out of his way to return Brandeis's drafts with flattering comments. *See, e.g.*, Central Railroad Co. v. United States, 257 U.S. 247 (1921) ("This is a good opinion. Clear and informing. I am glad to concur.") (Brandeis papers); International Railway Co. v. Davidson, 257 U.S. 506 (1922) ("I concur in this most satisfactory opinion.") (Brandeis papers); Galveston Electric Co. v. Galveston, 258 U.S. 388 (1922) ("This is a carefully drawn opinion and answers every contention. Much more satisfactory than what Judge Day calls a 'journal entry.'") (Brandeis papers); Great Northern R. Co. v. Merchants Elevator Co., 259 U.S. 285 (1922) ("I am greatly pleased with this opinion and the clear but nice distinction by which you distinguish the cases in which resort to the I.C.C. must be

353

THE TAFT COURT

had from those where it is not necessary. It will inform the courts and the profession and your ignorant colleagues. It will be a leading case showing what this Court is for.") (Brandeis papers); Fidelity & Deposit Co. v. United States, 259 U.S. 296 (1922) ("This is a very satisfactory opinion. I like to have an opinion worked out like this, and not a 'journal entry.'") (Brandeis papers); Baltimore & Ohio Southwestern Rd. Co., v. Settle, 260 U.S. 166 (1922) ("This is a very clear & satisfactory discussion and I am glad you cleared out of the way some of the unnecessary statements of Brewer.") (Brandeis papers); Keogh v. Chicago & Northwestern Ry Co., 260 U.S. 156 (1922) ("It is a well reasoned and convincing opinion which relieves me for while I thought any other conclusion would be unfortunate I did not quite see how it could be clearly justified.") (Brandeis papers); United States v. Oregon Lumber Co., 260 U.S. 290 (1922) (Sutherland wrote the majority opinion in this case, and when Brandeis first circulated his dissent, Taft replied, "Your opinion in the election cases shakes me again. I am studying the cases. I hate to waffle but when we hear such experts in law opposed, we ignoramuses must waffle." Later Taft wrote Brandeis: "I have examined all the Federal authorities. I think you have documented the error in the majority opinion. You can note me as dissenting and concurring in your opinion.") (Brandeis papers); Douglas v. Noble, 261 U.S. 165 (1923) ("This is an admirable opinion.") (Brandeis papers); Bank of America v. Whitney Central National Bank, 261 U.S. 171 (1923) ("Good. You come right up to the bull ring and meet the question.") (Brandeis papers); Pusey & Jones Co. v. Hanssen, 261 U.S. 491 (1923) ("This is very good and will be most useful.") (Brandeis papers); Atlantic Coast Line v. Daughton, 262 U.S. 413 (1923) ("I concur with terror at and respect for your progress through the maze.") (Brandeis papers); United States *ex rel.* Bilokumsky v. Tod, 263 U.S. 149 (1923) ("Certainly Nelles [the appellant's attorney] ought to be satisfied that his shadowy contentions have had close consideration and have been fully and overwhelmingly answered.") (Brandeis papers); United States v. Hubbard 266 U.S. 474 (1925) ("This is very satisfactory to me.") (Brandeis papers); Morrison v. Work, 266 U.S. 481 (1925) ("I concur. You have succeeded in avoiding the merits with masterly strategy.") (Brandeis papers); Smyth v. Asphalt Belt Railway Co., 267 U.S. 326 (1925) ("I concur and am glad that you have explained this so clearly. It is helpful. We have too many per curiams where explanations are needed.") (Brandeis papers); St. Louis, Brownsville, & Mexico Railway Co. v. United States, 268 U.S. 169 (1925) ("This is a most useful opinion and straightens out the law not only for the public but for your colleagues.") (Brandeis papers); Robertson v. Railroad Labor Board, 268 U.S. 619 (1925) ("I knew I found the right man to write this opinion.") (Brandeis papers); Edwards v. Douglas, 269 U.S. 204 (1925) ("I have read this opinion twice. It seems to me masterly and very satisfying. Your knowledge of business terms and corporate bookkeeping stands you in great stead.") (Brandeis papers); Louisville & Nashville Railroad Co. v. Sloss-Sheffield Steel & Iron Co., 269 U.S. 217 (1925) ("This is a most useful opinion. I doubt if anyone else of the Court could have written it.") (Brandeis papers); Tutun v. United States, 270 U.S. 568 (1926) ("This is a very satisfactory discussion.") (Brandeis papers); Great Northern R. Co. v. Sutherland, 273 U.S. 182 (1927) ("This is a most satisfactory opinion. Our friend [Walter] Hines' vague constitutional objections fade into the '*Ewigkeit.*'") (Brandeis papers); United States v. Los Angeles & Salt Lake Railroad Co., 273

U.S. 299 (1927) ("I concur with great pleasure. I think this is an admirable opinion and lays down an authoritative rule for dealing with such valuations that makes it a really leading case. I congratulate you. It is most clarifying and satisfactory.") (Brandeis papers); Cleveland, Cincinnati, Chicago & St. Louis Railway Co. v. United States, 275 U.S. 404 (1927) ("This is a good opinion and I am very glad you hit the judges for not writing at least enough of an opinion to let us know why they acted as they did.") (Brandeis papers); Willing v. Chicago Auditorium Association, 277 U.S. 274 (1928) ("This makes the matter entirely clear.") (Brandeis papers); Williamsport Wire Rope Co. v. United States, 277 U.S. 551 (1928) ("Thank you for straightening this out. It was a work of no easy effort.") (Brandeis papers); United States v. California Co-Operative Canneries, 279 U.S. 553 (1929) ("This clears the deck in a most satisfactory way. I hope the District Ct will think it has heard something drop.") (Brandeis papers); St. Louis-San Francisco Railway Co. v. Alabama Public Service Comm'n., 279 U.S. 560 (1929) ("I concur. I am afraid you don't fully sympathize with Forney Johnston's [appellant's attorney] love to breathe in the atmosphere of the pure air of the Constitution.") (Brandeis papers).

174. The "atmosphere" of the Court, said Brandeis, "is very friendly. When we differ, we agree to differ, without any ill feeling. It's all very friendly." *Brandeis-Frankfurter Conversations*, at 311 (June 12, 1923).

175. ALEXANDER M. BICKEL, THE UNPUBLISHED OPINIONS OF MR. JUSTICE BRANDEIS: THE SUPREME COURT AT WORK (Cambridge: Harvard University Press 1957).

176. 262 U.S. 506 (1923).

177. 264 U.S. 331 (1924).

178. BICKEL, *supra* note 175, at 77–118, 202–9.

179. *Brandeis-Frankfurter Conversations*, at 320 (July 19, 1923). Taft's law clerk during the 1924 term recalls that Taft "once said of an opinion by Brandeis in some case, 'Brandeis has written an opinion that I can only describe as masterly.'" Williams, *supra* note 167, at 50.

180. WHT to Robert A. Taft (November 14, 1926) (Taft papers).

181. WHT to Horace D. Taft (December 26, 1924) (Taft papers).

182. WHT to Charles D. Hilles (December 1, 1922) (Taft papers). *See supra* Chapter 3, at 89.

183. WHT to Elihu Root (December 21, 1922) (Taft papers).

184. William H. Taft, *The Right of Private Property*, 3 MICHIGAN LAW JOURNAL 215, 218, 233 (1894).

185. *Id.* at 232, 220–21. Without capital, Taft continued, "the whole world would still be groping in the darkness of the tribe or commune stage of civilization with alternating periods of starvation and plenty, and no happiness but of gorging unrestrained appetite. Capital increased the amount of production and reduces the cost in labor units of each unit of production. The cheaper the cost of production the less each one had to work to earn the absolute necessities of life and the more time he had to earn its comforts. As the material comforts increase the more possible becomes happiness and the greater the opportunity for the cultivation of the higher instincts of the human mind and soul." *Id.* at 221.

186. *Id.* at 224. The underlying image of society implied in this defense of property is one of sheer individual self-interest and promotion. Because it is difficult (if not

impossible) to construct an attractive image of civilization based upon this premise, Taft, like many in his generation, resorted to religion as a *deus ex machina* to tame the potentially destructive forces of individual selfishness. See Address of William H. Taft at the One Hundredth Anniversary Celebration of All Souls Church, New York (November 16, 1919) (Taft papers) ("Selfishness and worldliness seem more rife than ever. Religion must be the greatest factor in the progress of the World. We must rely on it to soften and ameliorate the other presently indispensable stimulus to progress, the spur of material benefit."). *See Taft Tells Minneapolitans What Constitutes True and Ideal Americanism*, MINNEAPOLIS STAR TRIBUNE (February 12, 1920), at 6 ("How is this natural and indispensable impulse of selfishness in human nature to be moderated so as to prevent our civilization from becoming a more and more material and sordid one? By the influence of religion ... by the perception that happiness does not consist in a mere physical comfort and the accumulation of wealth to furnish it, and that success of this kind without the love of one's fellows, without the love of country, and without the love of God, is a completely unsatisfying thing.").

187. WILLIAM HOWARD TAFT, PRESENT DAY PROBLEMS 218 (New York: Dodd, Mead & Co. 1908).
188. Taft, *supra* note 184, at 218.
189. *See* Max Radin, *The Ancient Grudge*, 7 THE FREEMAN 381, 382 (June 27, 1923). *Compare The Political Function of the Supreme Court*, 29 NEW REPUBLIC 236 (1922) ("Mr. Taft, before his accession to the Supreme Court, had shown impatience ... with those who regard the Constitution as a document of human origin and directed to human ends."); Stanley I. Kutler, *Chief Justice Taft and the Delusion of Judicial Exactness – A Study in Jurisprudence*, 48 VIRGINIA LAW REVIEW 1407, 1408 (1962) ("Taft adhered to the analytical school of jurisprudence," which "contended that judges do not make law; they simply 'receive' what is law and then apply it to the case at hand. The force of stare decisis was an obdurate and resolute command in this procedure. It was believed that such an approach created a logical consistency in law, without which chaos would inexorably ensue. The attitude characterized Taft's nine years on the bench.").
190. Taft, *supra* note 184, at 220. "The right of property," said Taft during the 1912 campaign, is "next to the right of liberty, ... the greatest civilizing institution of history." Socialism, which is the denial of the right of property, means "the taking away of the motive for acquisition, saving, energy, and enterprise. It means stagnation and retrogression. It destroys the mainspring of human action that has carried the world on and upward for two thousand years." Underlying Taft's commitment to property lay the faith that "it is possible in this world that the fruits of energy, courage, enterprise, attention to duty, work, thrift, providence, restraint of appetite and passion will still continue to have their reward; and that laziness, lack of attention, yielding to appetite and passion, dishonesty, and disloyalty will ultimately find their compensation." William Howard Taft, *The Republican Party's Appeal*, 73 THE INDEPENDENT 930 (October 24, 1912).
191. Taft readily conceded that lawyers should "study sociological jurisprudence" and be trained in "economics and ... sociology," so that they could "understand the attitude of the sociological reformer." William H. Taft, *The Social Importance of*

Louis Dembitz Brandeis

Proper Standards for Admission to the Bar, in PROCEEDINGS OF THE THIRTEENTH ANNUAL MEETING OF THE ASSOCIATION OF AMERICAN LAW SCHOOLS 75–76 (1913). He saw that "The social reformers contend that the old legal justice consisted chiefly in securing to each individual his rights in property or contracts, but that the new social justice must consider how it can secure for each individual a standard of living and such a share in the values of civilization as shall make possible a full moral life." *Id.* at 71. But he insisted that judicial protections for common law rights of property were essential to securing "the motive for labor, industry, saving and the sharpening of intellect and skill in the production of wealth and its re-use as capital to increase itself." *Id.* at 66, 70. "Were we to take away the selfish motive involved in private property we would halt, stagnate and then retrograde, the average comfort and happiness in society would be diminished." *Id.* at 71. Taft "insisted upon" the "right of property . . . because it conduces to the expansion of material resources which are plainly essential to the interests of society and progress." *Id.* at 72. Taft's positive attitude toward common law rights of property stemmed primarily from the fact that they correctly calculated the incentives necessary to produce prosperity. But it is clear that Taft also believed in the intrinsic morality of those rights.

192. "[F]or if the hand of power shall ever be permitted to take from 'A' and give to 'B' merely because 'A' has much and 'B' has little, we shall have taken the first step upon that unhappy path which leads from a republic where every man may rise in proportion to his energy and ability, to a commune where energy and sloth, ability and ignorance, occupy in common the same dead level of individual despair. Any attempt to fix a limit to personal acquisition is filled with danger, since, being arbitrary, it is sure to be fluctuating, tending always toward narrower and narrower limits and, in the end, destructive of that great incentive to individual effort which is furnished by the feeling of certainty that one will be allowed to enjoy the fruits of his own industry and genius." George Sutherland, *Principle or Expedient?*, in PROCEEDINGS OF THE 44TH ANNUAL MEETING OF THE NEW YORK STATE BAR ASSOCIATION 278–79 (Baltimore: Lord Baltimore Press 1921).

Butler believed that "[T]here is a tendency toward a kind of State socialism, which is destructive of individual initiative and development. Doctrines which undisguisedly attack private property are advanced by some teachers, who appear not to realize that good morals oppose the unrequited taking of property of one for the use of others, or from a few with the hope or upon the theory that good may come to many. . . . If doctrines such as these . . . are to be adopted, or permitted to gain a substantial foothold, individual initiative will be dangerously impaired. . . . It would weaken character and leave the individual man and woman without the motive or hope or inspiration necessary to freedom and morality. The hold which individualism has ever had upon democracy should not be loosened." Pierce Butler, *Educating for Citizenship: Duties the Citizen Owes to the State*, 12 CATHOLIC EDUCATIONAL ASSOCIATION BULLETIN 123, 130–32 (November 1915). Charles Evans Hughes characterized Butler as "a strong defender of the conception of property rights which he believed to be secured by the accepted construction of the due-process clause. He believed in that conception as an essential stimulus to effort and as holding a better promise of social progress than governmental plans involving restriction of individual initiative." *Mr. Justice Butler*, 310 U.S. xiii, xviii.

Even McReynolds, for all his moralism, could at times observe that laws diminishing property rights "stifle enterprise, produce discontent, strife, idleness, and pauperism." Arizona Copper Co. v. Hammer, 250 U.S. 400, 452 (1919) (McReynolds, J., dissenting).

193. *Block v. Hirsh*, 256 U.S. 135, 162 (1921) (McKenna, J., dissenting).
194. *See, e.g.*, Walter George Smith, *Property Rights under the Constitution*, 10 AMERICAN BAR ASSOCIATION JOURNAL 242, 243 (1924) (Property provides "the greatest incentive to individual effort," and "when the incentive for thrift is taken away, prosperity goes with it.").
195. Quoted in Poole, *supra* note 20, at 493. Brandeis continued: "It has been the frequent error of our courts that they have made the means an end. Once correct that error, put property back into its right place, and the whole social-legal conception becomes at once consistent." *Id.*
196. *Id.*
197. *See, e.g.*, Olmstead v. United States, 277 U.S. 438, 471 (1928) (Brandeis, J., dissenting); Whitney v. California, 274 U.S. 357, 372 (1927) (Brandeis, J., concurring); *infra* notes 205, 220.
198. THE CURSE OF BIGNESS, *supra* note 8, at 73.
199. BRANDEIS, *supra* note 108, at 366. "[W]ith us every man is of the ruling class. Our education and condition of life must be such as become a ruler. Our great beneficent experiment in democracy will fail unless the people, our rulers, are developed in character and intelligence." BRANDEIS, *supra* note 7, at 29.
200. BRANDEIS, *supra* note 108, at 367-68.
201. THE CURSE OF BIGNESS, *supra* note 8, at 270. For Harold Laski, this meant that Brandeis's "criterion for all action is an ethical individualism. I take him to be intellectually, as to ends, a romantic anachronism." Harold Laski to OWH (August 12, 1933), in 2 HOLMES-LASKI CORRESPONDENCE, at 1448. This view of persons, however, was the foundation for Brandeis's more general construction of constitutional rights. It underlay, for example, Brandeis's justly famous and influential dissent in Olmstead v. United States, 277 U.S. 438, 471 (1928) (Brandeis, J., dissenting), in which Brandeis argued that the Fourth Amendment required a warrant before the state could engage in wiretapping. The premise of Brandeis's opinion was that the Fourth Amendment should be interpreted in light of its object, which is "to secure conditions favorable to the pursuit of happiness." *Id.* at 478. Hence "every unjustifiable intrusion by the government upon the privacy of the individual, whatever the means employed, must be deemed a violation of the Fourth Amendment." *Id.* For a full discussion, see *infra* Chapter 33.
202. THE CURSE OF BIGNESS, *supra* note 8, at 51.
203. BRANDEIS, *supra* note 7, at 38.
204. Jay Burns Baking Co. v. Bryan, 264 U.S. 504, 534 (1924) (Brandeis, J., dissenting).
205. THE CURSE OF BIGNESS, *supra* note 8, at 51. *See* BRANDEIS, *supra* note 108, at 366-71:

> Unless the rulers have, in the main, education and character, and are free men, our great experiment in democracy must fail. It devolves upon the state, therefore, to fit its rulers for their task. It must provide not only facilities for development but the opportunity of using them. It must not only provide opportunity, it must stimulate the desire to avail of it. Thus we

> are compelled to insist upon the observance of what we somewhat vaguely term the American standard of living ....
>
> What does this standard imply? In substance, the exercise of those rights which our Constitution guarantees – the right to life, liberty and the pursuit of happiness. Life, in this connection, means living, not existing; liberty, freedom in things industrial as well as political; happiness includes, among other things, that satisfaction which can come only through the full development and utilization of one's faculties. In order that men may live and not merely exist, in order that men may develop their faculties, they must have a reasonable income; they must have health and leisure. ... The essentials of American citizenship are not satisfied by supplying merely the material needs or even the wants of the worker.
>
> Every citizen must have education – broad and continuous. ...
>
> [T]he citizen in a successful democracy must not only have education, he must be free. Men are not free if dependent industrially upon the arbitrary will of another. Industrial liberty on the part of the worker cannot, therefore, exist if there be overweening industrial power. ...
>
> And if the American is to be fitted for his task as ruler, he must have besides education and industrial liberty also some degree of financial independence. ...
>
> Democracy rests upon two pillars: one, the principle that all men are equally entitled to life, liberty and the pursuit of happiness; and the other, the conviction that such equal opportunity will most advance civilization.

With regard to realizing these aspirational and constitutional values, as Brandeis wrote his wife, "only legislation is constructive." LDB to Alice Goldmark Brandeis (June 2, 1911), in BRANDEIS FAMILY LETTERS, at 165.

206. David J. Brewer, *The Nation's Anchor*, 57 ALBANY LAW JOURNAL 166, 167 (1898).
207. William H. Taft, *The Attacks on the Courts and Legal Procedure*, 5 KENTUCKY LAW JOURNAL 3, 4 (1916).
208. John F. Dillon, *Address of the President*, in REPORT OF THE FIFTEENTH ANNUAL MEETING OF THE AMERICAN BAR ASSOCIATION 200 (Philadelphia: Dando Printing & Publishing Co. 1892).
209. There is, for example, no analogous argument in James B. Thayer's seminal essay on *The Origin and Scope of the American Doctrine of Constitutional Law*, 7 HARVARD LAW REVIEW 129 (1893). Thayer ultimately puts the case for judicial deference on the ground that the mission of courts is to determine the bounds of permissible "judgment" that can be exercised by "another department which the constitution has charged with the duty of making it. ... [I]n such cases the constitution does not impose upon the legislature any one specific opinion, but leaves open this range of choice; and that whatever choice is rational is constitutional." *Id.* at 144. Thayer's path-breaking article explains the value of judicial restraint neither in terms of a jurisprudence of positivism, as did Holmes, nor in terms of a jurisprudence of democratic deference, as did Brandeis. *See* ANDREW PORWANCHER, JAKE MAZEITIS, TAYLOR JIPP, & AUSTIN COFFEY, THE PROPHET OF HARVARD LAW: JAMES BRADLEY THAYER AND HIS LEGAL LEGACY 36–40 (Lawrence: University Press of Kansas 2022); but see JAMES BRADLEY THAYER, JOHN MARSHALL: AN ADDRESS 43–47 (Cambridge, MA: The University Press 1901); Samuel Moyn & Rephael Stern, To Save Democracy from Juristocracy: J.B. Thayer and the Tragic Origins of Constitutional Theory, https://papers.ssrn.com/sol3/papers.cfm?abstract_id=4342763.

210. Truax v. Corrigan, 257 U.S. 312, 357 (1921) (Brandeis, J., dissenting).
211. Remarks of Attorney General Francis Biddle, *supra* note 3, at xli.
212. Paul A. Freund, *Mr. Justice Brandeis: A Centennial Memoir*, 70 HARVARD LAW REVIEW 769, 779 (1957). Freund rightly observes that "At the root of [Brandeis's] philosophy ... lay the issue of responsibility – the diffusion of responsibility, the assumption of responsibility, and the identification of responsibility." *Id.* at 776.
213. "The great developer is responsibility." THE CURSE OF BIGNESS, *supra* note 8, at 270. Sometimes Brandeis would say that "Liberty is the greatest developer." LOUIS D. BRANDEIS, OTHER PEOPLE'S MONEY AND HOW THE BANKERS USE IT 208 (New York: Frederick A. Stokes Co. 1914).
214. *Truax*, 257 U.S. at 356–57 (Brandeis, J., dissenting).
215. International News Service v. Associated Press, 248 U.S. 215, 267 (1918) (Brandeis, J., dissenting).
216. *See supra* text at notes 34–37 and note 38; LDB to Felix Frankfurter (January 28, 1913), in BRANDEIS-FRANKFURTER CORRESPONDENCE, at 22.
217. New State Ice Co. v. Liebmann, 285 U.S. 262, 310–11 (1932) (Brandeis, J., dissenting).
218. Holmes, *supra* note 57, at 8.
219. THE CURSE OF BIGNESS, *supra* note 8, at 271.
220. Abrams v. United States, 250 U.S. 616, 630 (1919) (Holmes, J., dissenting). Holmes characteristically spoke about "truth" in an epistemological register that we would now call fallibilism. *See* Vincent Blasi, *Holmes and the Marketplace of Ideas*, 2004 SUPREME COURT REVIEW 1, 19–20. But it is bizarre to say that a proposition is "true" because a majority happens to believe it. And it certainly seems incorrect to say that it is "safe" to act on what most people believe to be true. Matters appear quite otherwise, however, with regard to what Brandeis carefully (but awkwardly) called "political truth." Whitney v. California, 274 U.S. 357, 375 (1927) (Brandeis, J., concurring). The reasons Brandeis gave for respecting freedom of speech sound in the political values of democracy, not in those of epistemology. Although Holmes's defense of freedom of speech seems explicitly to chime with his pragmatism, the most convincing interpretation it can be given lies instead in the necessity Holmes must have perceived for a society to allow its own "dominant opinion" to come to the fore, so that a society could seamlessly adjust to changing circumstances. *See infra* text at note 258. This interpretation would most naturally accord with the foundational rationale for Holmes's own positivism.
221. *Whitney*, 274 U.S. at 375 (1927) (Brandeis, J., concurring). On the contrast between the two justices, see Pnina Lahav, *Holmes and Brandeis: Libertarian and Republican Justifications for Free Speech*, 4 JOURNAL OF LAW & POLITICS 451 (1988).
222. *But see* G. Edward White, *Allocating Power between Agencies and Courts: The Legacy of Justice Brandeis*, 1974 DUKE LAW JOURNAL 195.
223. *See supra* text at note 188.
224. Henry Hart was Brandeis's law clerk during the 1931 term. MASON, *supra* note 25, at 690, contains a complete list of Brandeis's clerks, many of whom would become influential legal scholars of the next generation, including deans of both the Harvard and Yale law schools.
225. Quoted in Freund, *supra* note 212, at 783. "To quote from Mr. Justice Brandeis' opinions is not to pick plums from a pudding but to pull threads

Louis Dembitz Brandeis

from a pattern." Felix Frankfurter, *Mr. Justice Brandeis and the Constitution*, in MR. JUSTICE BRANDEIS 123 (Felix Frankfurter, ed., New Haven: Yale University Press 1932).

226. LDB to Felix Frankfurter (September 28, 1928), in BRANDEIS-FRANKFURTER CORRESPONDENCE, at 342. *See* LDB to Felix Frankfurter (October 15, 1928), *id.* at 348.

227. Paul Freund recounts that when Brandeis "was asked, in the dark days of 1933, whether he believed the worst was over, he would answer almost cheerfully that the worst had happened before 1929." Remarks of Paul A. Freund, *supra* note 4, at xx. As the 1920s began, Brandeis complained to his brother that "We have slipped back badly ... in order – security to life & property; in liberty of speech, action, & assembly; in culture; &, in many respects, morality. Father would have said, 'Pfui.'" LDB to Alfred Brandeis (March 26, 1921), in BRANDEIS FAMILY LETTERS, at 363. In the middle of the decade, Brandeis wrote Frankfurter, "If my history isn't wrong, we are now passing through the first experience in 50 years of actual retreat in social, political, economic progress as evidenced by legislation." LDB to Felix Frankfurter (February 26, 1926), in BRANDEIS-FRANKFURTER CORRESPONDENCE, at 233.

In a moving and revealing letter, Brandeis recounted hearing Calvin Coolidge deliver his Washington birthday address over the radio. It was billed as the "most widely heard speech ever delivered," and Coolidge's theme was that Washington's "ability as a business man was the strong support of his statesmanship." *Text of Most Widely Heard Speech Ever Delivered*, CHRISTIAN SCIENCE MONITOR (February 23, 1927), at 4. Brandeis wrote Frankfurter:

> You cannot conceive how painful, distressful & depressing it was to listen (officially) to Cal's Washington's Birthday address. I think the purpose of those behind (who prepared the address) was to confiscate the whole of G[eorge]. W[ashington]'s good will for Big Business, by showing that we owe everything we value to the qualities of business efficiency, commercial courage & vision & thrift & that these were G.W.'s dominating qualities fitting him for the greatest of the World's achievements.... There is no man in [the] U.S. [who] could have so perfectly – by looks, voice & action – have [sic] deprived G.W. of every idealistic aim or emotion.
>
> When I tried to recall the next most depressing & distressful experience of a lifetime, I had to go back to 1894, when in preparing for the Public Institutions Hearings, I went to Long Island (Boston Harbor) Poor-House hospital & passed through the syphilitic ward. I had a like sense of uncleanness.

LDB to Felix Frankfurter (February 26, 1927), in BRANDEIS-FRANKFURTER CORRESPONDENCE, at 275.

228. We do know that sometimes what were effectively Brandeis opinions appeared under the authorship of another justice. This happened in cases like Sonneborn Bros. v. Cureton, 262 U.S. 506 (1923) and Railroad Commission of California v. Southern Pacific Co., 264 U.S. 331 (1924). *See* BICKEL, *supra* note 175, at 77–118, 202–9. We also know that in a number of cases Brandeis changed his mind after being assigned a case, and that he was then able to carry the Court for his revised views. For example, in St. Louis, B. & M. Ry. Co., v. United States, 268 U.S. 169 (1925), Brandeis's circulation to the Court read "The vote of the conference was to affirm also as to the third claim. Upon closer study of the record I concluded that as to this claim my vote was wrong. With the approval of the Chief

Justice, I have put my views in the form of an opinion." (Brandeis papers). The final opinion conformed to Brandeis's new view. In McCarthy v. Arndstein, 266 U.S. 34 (1924), which held that the privilege against self-incrimination applied to the compelled testimony of a bankrupt, Brandeis circulated to the Court a memorandum that said, "The vote of the conference was to reverse and the case assigned to me for opinion. Upon further study I have concluded that the entry should be judgment reaffirmed and have prepared the annexed memorandum which embodies my views." (Brandeis papers). Brandeis's opinion carried a unanimous Court. Sutherland wrote on his return, "This is in accordance with the view I have entertained all along, and, naturally I cheerfully concur." Taft wrote, "I am inclined to go with you because I don't know where else to go." Van Devanter made several important editing suggestions, which Brandeis accepted (Brandeis papers).

Of course, this process could also work in reverse. In Maul v. United States, 274 U.S. 501 (1927), for example, Brandeis was initially assigned the opinion. Although the judgment was uncontroversial, Brandeis's reasoning departed from the government's theory of the case. WHT to WVD (May 3, 1927) (Taft papers). Van Devanter did not accept Brandeis's new rationale and composed a competing memorandum which ultimately became the opinion of the Court. WHT to LDB (April 5, 1927) (Taft papers); WHT to Brethren (April 22, 1927) (Van Devanter papers). In Sprout v. City of South Bend, 277 U.S. 163 (1928), Brandeis circulated a draft to the Court that reported, "The vote of the conference was to affirm. Further study has led me to the conclusion that the judgment should be reversed." (Brandeis papers). Brandeis also sought to alter the jurisdictional basis of the case. Because it involved the constitutionality of a municipal ordinance, and because Brandeis interpreted the new 1925 Judiciary Act to require mandatory jurisdiction only when the highest court of a state had rejected a constitutional challenge to a state *statute*, as distinct from a constitutional challenge to a municipal *ordinance*, Brandeis changed the judgment to read, "*Writ of error dismissed. Treating the writ of error as an application for certiorari, it is granted. Judgment reversed.*" Van Devanter objected to this interpretation of the Judiciary Act and circulated a competing memorandum in what was originally a consolidated case, but which later became the independent decision of John P. King Manufacturing Co. v. Augusta, 277 U.S. 100 (1928). In *Augusta*, the Court opted for Van Devanter's view of jurisdiction, but in *Sprout* it accepted Brandeis's view of the merits.

229. There are a number of cases in which Brandeis joined Holmes in opinions that seem quite contrary to the basic premises of Brandeis's jurisprudence. In Federal Baseball Club of Baltimore v. National League of Professional Baseball Clubs, 259 U.S. 200 (1922), for example, Holmes held that the Sherman Act did not apply to major league baseball because it did not involve interstate commerce. Brandeis wrote Holmes that "I have grave doubt, but shall acquiesce." (Holmes papers). By contrast McReynolds wrote, "Yes, thanks. You are the very nicest man known to history." (Holmes papers). In Atlantic Coast Line Railroad Co. v. Southwell, 275 U.S. 64 (1927), Holmes reversed a judgment under the Federal Employers' Liability Act of 1908 ("FELA") against a railroad for negligently allowing an employee to be killed. Brandeis wrote Holmes that "I think the question was one for a jury – but the case is of a class in which one may properly 'shut up.'" (Holmes

papers). In Chesapeake & Ohio Railway Co. v. Nixon, 271 U.S. 218 (1926), Holmes overturned a plaintiff's judgment under FELA. Brandeis would have voted the other way, but wrote Holmes, "I acquiesce willingly being contrawise." (Holmes papers). In Chicago, Burlington & Quincy Rd. Co. v. Osborne, 265 U.S. 14 (1924), Holmes upheld equitable jurisdiction, finding that a plaintiff who sought to enjoin the collection of taxes had no adequate remedy at law. This was an important issue to Brandeis, but he wrote Holmes, "I shall acquiesce." (Holmes papers). Reading cases like this, it is difficult to shake the impression that Brandeis was unwilling to differ from Holmes except in unusually important cases.
230. Table P-1; Figure II-17.
231. Figure II-2. *See* WHT to Robert A. Taft (October 24, 1926) (Taft papers) (Brandeis "writes a very concise and satisfactory opinion, but his dissents are of a different character.").
232. Figure I-22.
233. Pub. L. 66-152, 41 Stat. 456 (February 28, 1920).
234. Taft return on the circulated opinion in United States v. Berwind-White Coal Mining Co., 274 U.S. 564 (1927) ("To the pope of interstate commerce regulation. I congratulate you on this opinion. I think it is clearly right, McR J. to the contrary notwithstanding.") (Brandeis papers).
235. *See Will Score Railroads*, BALTIMORE SUN (November 19, 1910), at 15; *Shippers Urge Scientific Management of Railroads*, WALL STREET JOURNAL (November 22, 1910), at 1; *Brandeis, Teacher of Business Economy*, NEW YORK TIMES (December 4, 1910), at SM1; *The Scientific Management of Railways*, 96 THE OUTLOOK 753 (1910); *An Attorney for the People*, 96 THE OUTLOOK 919 (1910); *Higher Efficiency Need of Railroads*, NEW YORK TRIBUNE (January 3, 1911), at 4; *Brandeis Files His Brief*, NEW YORK TIMES (January 3, 1911), at 4. Seeking to call his bluff, the railroads sent Brandeis a telegram care of the Interstate Commerce Commission offering to employ him to discover and root out management waste. He could name his own salary, the railroads said. "This proposition is made to you in the same spirit of sincerity in which you rendered your statement to the commission." *Brandeis Offered Rail Job*, CHICAGO DAILY TRIBUNE (November 24, 1910), at 18. Brandeis quickly turned the tables by accepting the offer ("I am convinced that such a saving is possible through the introduction of scientific management") but declining "any salary or other compensation." *Brandeis Offers to Confer with Railroad Presidents*, WALL STREET JOURNAL (November 30, 1910), at 3.
236. BRANDEIS, *supra* note 7, at 37–50; UROFSKY, *supra* note 26, at 240–43, 294–95. On the Taft Court, Brandeis inspired a line of decisions that turned on the need for managerial efficiency in the administration of the nation's railroads. The cases invalidated under the commerce clause the efforts of states in which the parties did not reside to attract suits against interstate carriers for causes of action that did not arise out of transactions in the forum state. Drawing on the "judicial notice" technique he had pioneered in *Muller*, Brandeis affirmed:

> That the claims against interstate carriers for personal injuries and for loss and damage of freight are numerous; that the amounts demanded are large; that in many cases carriers deem it imperative, or advisable, to leave the determination of their liability to the courts; that litigation in states and jurisdictions remote from that in which the cause of action arose entails absence of employees from their

THE TAFT COURT

customary occupations; and that this impairs efficiency in operation, and causes, directly and indirectly, heavy expense to the carriers – these are matters of common knowledge. Facts, of which we, also, take judicial notice, indicate that the burden upon interstate carriers imposed specifically by the statute here assailed is a heavy one; and that the resulting obstruction to commerce must be serious.

The requirements of orderly, effective administration of justice are paramount. ... The public and the carriers are alike interested in maintaining adequate, uninterrupted transportation service at reasonable cost. This common interest is emphasized by Transportation Act 1920, which authorizes rate increases necessary to ensure to carriers efficiently operated a fair return on property devoted to the public use. Avoidance of waste, in interstate transportation, as well as maintenance of service, have become a direct concern of the public. With these ends the Minnesota statute, as here applied, unduly interferes. By requiring from interstate carriers general submission to suit, it unreasonably obstructs, and unduly burdens, interstate commerce.

Davis v. Farmers' Co-op. Equity Co., 262 U.S. 312, 315–17 (1923). *See* Atchison, T. & S.F. Ry. Co. v. Wells, 265 U.S. 101 (1924); Michigan Cent. R. Co. v. Mix, 278 U.S. 492 (1929); but see Missouri *ex rel.* St. Louis, B. & M. Ry Co. v. Taylor, 266 U.S. 200 (1924); Hoffman v. Missouri, 274 U.S. 21 (1927). Ordinarily a case like *Davis* would turn on the Due Process Clause. But Brandeis was apparently loathe to invoke the Fourteenth Amendment, and instead used as a constitutional hook the dormant Commerce Clause, which allowed him to stress typically progressive arguments resting on efficiency. For a discussion of the way in which Brandeis's decisions were adverse to the interests of the ordinary railroad employees for whom Brandeis was usually so solicitous, see EDWARD A. PURCELL, JR., LITIGATION AND INEQUALITY: FEDERAL DIVERSITY JURISDICTION IN INDUSTRIAL AMERICA, 1870–1958, at 193–95 (Oxford University Press 1992). In his return to the draft opinion in *Davis*, Butler asked it to be noted that he "did not hear or take part in the consideration" of the case, but that he nevertheless thought "it an excellent opinion." (Brandeis papers). Van Devanter thought it "good doctrine convincingly and very clearly stated." (Brandeis papers). And Taft remarked, "You have threaded your way to the end with great success and convincing reasons." (Brandeis papers). Neither the methodology nor the conclusions of *Davis* have subsequently exerted great judicial influence. *See, e.g.*, Ally Bank v. Lenox Financial Mortgage Corp., 2017 WL 830391, at *3 (D. Minn. March 2, 2017) ("*Davis* is limited to its facts.").

237. LOUIS D. BRANDEIS, SCIENTIFIC MANAGEMENT AND RAILROADS: BEING PART OF A BRIEF SUBMITTED TO THE INTERSTATE COMMERCE COMMISSION 8, 17 (New York: The Engineering Magazine 1911). "Planning in advance is of the essence of scientific management. The business engineer makes his plans and specifications covering the process of production before it is entered upon, – extending his directions like the mechanical engineer into minute details in order to secure the perfect product." *Id.* at 11. "[T]he engineer calculates and plans with absolute certainty of the accomplishment of the final result in accordance with his plans which are based ultimately on fundamental truths and natural science. In scientific management, therefore, results are predetermined. Before the work is commenced, it is determined not only as to what shall be done, but how it shall be done, and when it shall be done and what it shall cost." *Id.* at 9.

Louis Dembitz Brandeis

238. THE CURSE OF BIGNESS, *supra* note 8, at 74.
239. *Id.* at 83.
240. BRANDEIS, *supra* note 7, at 17. *See supra* text at notes 211–213. In his discussion of scientific management, Brandeis stressed that "labor unions must participate in fixing ... wages, hours and conditions, and in determining the application to the various businesses of the principles of scientific management." BRANDEIS, *supra* note 7, at 50.
241. When in this frame of mind, Brandeis stressed the "direct adjustment between employer and workmen" that would come from "strong unions." This adjustment could result only from political struggle. "We cannot hope to get on without struggle," Brandeis would say, "In the last resort, labor will fight for its rights. It is the law of life. Must we not fight, all of us, even for the peace that we most crave?" THE CURSE OF BIGNESS, *supra* note 8, at 45.
242. BRANDEIS, *supra* note 7, at 52.
243. *Id.* at 166.
244. *Id.* at 271.
245. LDB to Felix Frankfurter (October 15, 1928), in BRANDEIS-FRANKFURTER CORRESPONDENCE, at 348.
246. Hence Dean Acheson's view of Brandeis, which seems to me true but one-eyed, as someone who never put "the slightest faith in mass salvation through universal Plumb Plans." ACHESON, *supra* note 9, at 52. On the general "ambivalence" in progressive thought as between the inculcation of efficiency and participation in industrial democracy, see Sanford M. Jacoby, *Union-Management Cooperation in the United States: Lessons from the 1920s*, 37 INDUSTRIAL AND LABOR RELATIONS REVIEW 18, 20 (1983).
247. Texas & P. Ry. Co. v. Gulf, C. & S.F. Ry. Co., 270 U.S. 266, 277–78 (1926). The Act provided that the Interstate Commerce Commission must approve the building of track extensions, but that it would have no jurisdiction over the building of industrial tracks "to be located wholly within one state." Brandeis held that extensions were to be distinguished from industrial tracks by reference to the "policy" of the Act. "Where the proposed trackage extends into territory not theretofore served by the carrier ... its purpose and effect are, under the new policy of Congress, of national concern. For invasion through the new construction of territory adequately served by another carrier ... may be inimical to the national interest." *Id.* at 278. Taft commented on his return of Brandeis's draft opinion, "This is very satisfactory and makes clear the needed distinction under Transportation Act 1920 as between extensions and industrial tracks – a real help." Sutherland observed, "This is an exceptionally good opinion and clarifies the rule for the future." Butler replied, "Yes, very good"; Holmes remarked, "Mighty good"; and Van Devanter returned, "Very good." (Brandeis papers).
248. Brandeis "was profoundly attached to the principle of federalism. He lost no opportunity to advise young lawyers that the United States was not Wall Street or even Washington ... that talents and training should be taken back to the home community." *Remarks of Paul A. Freund*, *supra* note 4, at xviii. Brandeis frequently spoke of the need to "make decentralization, devolution locally of governmental functions more attractive." LDB to Felix Frankfurter (December 30, 1920), in 4 LETTERS OF LOUIS D. BRANDEIS, at 520.

THE TAFT COURT

249. "We must encourage ... social and political invention, though we feel sure that the successes will be few and the failures many. Most of these inventions can be applied only with the sanction and aid of the government. It is America's good fortune that her federal system furnishes in the forty-eight states political and social laboratories in which these inventions may be separately worked out and tested, thus multiplying the opportunities for inventors and minimizing the dangers of failure." Louis D. Brandeis, *Introduction*, in BARTON, *supra* note 34.
250. "If we may hope to carry out our ideals in America, it will be by development through the State and local Governments. Centralization will kill – only decentralization of social functions can help." LDB to Susan Brandeis (May 18, 1922), in BRANDEIS FAMILY LETTERS, at 379–80.
251. LDB to Paul Underwood Kellogg (November 7, 1920), in 4 LETTERS OF LOUIS D. BRANDEIS, at 497–98.
252. The unresponsiveness of the New Haven railroad to the local interests of Massachusetts was an important reason why Brandeis was for so long so implacably opposed to its consolidation. BRANDEIS, *supra* note 7, at 285–89; PAPER, *supra* note 95, at 95.
253. 271 U.S. 153, 164 (1926). Brandeis's sense of the managerial scope of Interstate Commerce Commission power was considerable. *See, e.g.*, United States v. Hubbard, 266 U.S. 474 (1925) (holding over McReynolds's dissent that ICC jurisdiction applied to interurban electric railroads); Midland Valley Railroad Co. v. Barkley, 276 U.S. 482 (1928) (holding that ICC jurisdiction preempts common law duties); Keogh v Chicago & Northwestern Rwy. Co., 260 U.S. 156 (1922) (holding that an ICC ruling was conclusive against a suit under the Sherman Act).
254. *Colorado*, 271 U.S. at 167–68. Taft wrote on his return to Brandeis's circulated draft, "This is a good useful and discriminating opinion. I am glad to concur." Sutherland said, "I agree. An exceptionally good job." Butler wrote, "Yes – good," and Sanford opined, "Yes sir – A very fine and light-bearing opinion." (Brandeis papers). Brandeis attempted to tell an analogous story of political negotiation in Napier v. Atlantic Coast Line R. Co., 272 U.S. 605 (1926). In that case Brandeis concluded that the federal Locomotive Boiler Inspection Act preempted Georgia's efforts to require greater safety for engine fireboxes. Brandeis held that the federal legislation "was intended to occupy the field." *Id.* at 613. As in *Colorado*, however, he sought to mitigate the harshness of the holding by appealing to political accommodation. He wrote Frankfurter on the day after the decision came down that he had "endeavored to make clear, as a matter of statutory construction, the 'occupying the field' doctrine. I think the states could be taught, by a similar ABC article that, if they wish to preserve their police power, they should, through the 'state block' in Congress, see to it in every class of Congressional legislation that the state rights which they desire to preserve be expressly provided for in the acts." LDB to Felix Frankfurter (November 30, 1926), in BRANDEIS-FRANKFURTER CORRESPONDENCE, at 263.
255. It is useful to contrast *Colorado* with Taft's decision in Railroad Commission of Wisconsin v. Chicago, B. & Q.R. Co., 257 U.S. 563 (1922), the first of the great Taft Court decisions addressing the authority of the Interstate Commerce Commission under the Transportation Act. In that case, Taft held flatly that

Louis Dembitz Brandeis

"Commerce is a unit and does not regard state lines, and while under the Constitution, interstate and intrastate commerce are ordinarily subject to regulation by different sovereignties, yet when they are so mingled together that the supreme authority, the Nation, cannot exercise complete effective control over interstate commerce without incidental regulation of intrastate commerce, such incidental regulation is not an invasion of state authority or a violation of the proviso. ... The states are seeking to use that same system for intrastate traffic. That entails large duties and expenditures on the interstate commerce system which may burden it unless compensation is received for the intrastate business reasonably proportionate to that for the interstate business. Congress as the dominant controller of interstate commerce may, therefore, restrain undue limitation of the earning power of the interstate commerce system in doing state work. The affirmative power of Congress in developing interstate commerce agencies is clear. In such development, it can impose any reasonable condition on a state's use of interstate carriers for intrastate commerce, it deems necessary or desirable. This is because of the supremacy of the national power in this field." *Id.* at 588–90. Taft's thorough and large-boned opinion addresses *only* questions of ultimate legal authority.

256. Thus Brandeis stressed in Lawrence v. St. Louis-San Francisco Ry. Co., 274 U.S. 588, 594–95 (1927), which concerned potential tension between the Oklahoma Corporation Commission and the ICC in supervising national railroads: "[T]he fact is important that the controversy concerns the respective powers of the nation and of the states over railroads engaged in interstate commerce. Such railroads are subject to regulation by both the state and the United States. The delimitation of the respective powers of the two governments requires often nice adjustments. The federal power is paramount. But public interest demands that, whenever possible, conflict between the two authorities and irritation be avoided. To this end it is important that the federal power be not exerted unnecessarily, hastily, or harshly. It is important, also, that the demands of comity and courtesy, as well as of the law, be deferred to."

257. *Brandeis-Frankfurter Conversations*, at 320 (July 19, 1923). Frankfurter's notes continue: "Holmes says doesn't want to extend XIV. L.D.B. says it means – you are going to cut down freedom through striking down regulation of property but not give protection. Property, it is absurd as Holmes says, to deem fundamental in the sense that you can't curtail its use or its accumulation or power. There may be some aspects of property that are fundamental – but not regard as fundamental specific limitations upon it. Whereas right to your education & to utter speech is fundamental *except* clear and present danger." *Id.*

258. Yosal Rogat & James M. O'Fallon, *Mr. Justice Holmes: A Dissenting Opinion – The Speech Cases*, 36 STANFORD LAW REVIEW 1349, 1368 (1984) (quoting Lochner v. New York, 198 U.S. 45, 76 (1905) (Holmes, J., dissenting)). *See* Gitlow v. New York, 268 U.S. 652, 673 (1925) (Holmes, J., dissenting) ("If in the long run the beliefs expressed in proletarian dictatorship are destined to be accepted by the dominant forces of the community, the only meaning of free speech is that they should be given their chance and have their way.").

259. 262 U.S. 390 (1923).

260. *Id.* at 402. Holmes's dissenting opinion was published in the companion case of Bartels v. Iowa, 262 U.S. 404 (1923).
261. 7 VANDERBILT ALUMNUS 174, 175 (1922). In language that eerily invokes certain themes in Brandeis's *Whitney* concurrence, McReynolds also affirms that "[W]hat a nation is depends upon what its ideals are, and if you are to build up a nation, just as if you are to build up the individual, you must cultivate high ideals; and in addition to that you must inspire that man with sufficient courage to carry those ideals into execution. Somehow, the longer I live the more I think of courage; the more I see of men the more I am amazed at the lack of it; the more I think of national affairs the more I think is the demand for men who believe something, and who are willing to stand by it until the death." *Id.* at 174.
262. *Meyer*, 262 U.S. at 399.
263. Oliver Wendell Holmes, *The Gas-Stokers' Strike*, 7 AMERICAN LAW REVIEW 582, 583 (1873).
264. Taft, *supra* note 184, at 232.

Plate 1 William Howard Taft takes the oath of office as chief justice of the United States, July 11, 1921. Standing beside Taft is Attorney General Harry M. Daugherty. Photograph by Underwood & Underwood, Collection of the Supreme Court of the United States.

Plate 2 Formal group portrait of the Taft Court on January 11, 1922. Photograph by Clinedinst Studio, Collection of the Supreme Court of the United States.

Plate 3 Formal group portrait of the Taft Court on April 10, 1923. Photograph by Harris & Ewing, Collection of the Supreme Court of the United States.

Plate 4 The Taft Court pays a courtesy call on President Coolidge, October 1, 1923. Photograph by William Towles, Collection of the Supreme Court of the United States.

Plate 5 The Taft Court pays a courtesy call on President Coolidge, October 6, 1924. From left to right are Attorney General Harlan Fiske Stone, Pierce Butler, Louis D. Brandeis, Willis Van Devanter, Joseph McKenna, William Howard Taft, Oliver Wendell Holmes, George Sutherland, and Edward T. Sanford. Photograph by Underwood & Underwood, Collection of the Supreme Court of the United States.

Plate 6 Formal group portrait of the Taft Court on May 3, 1926. Photograph by Underwood & Underwood, Collection of the Supreme Court of the United States.

PART III
THE INCOMPARABLE CHIEF JUSTICESHIP OF WILLIAM HOWARD TAFT

The Taft Court included some of the finest jurists ever to grace the Supreme Court bench (Holmes, Brandeis, Stone); some of the weakest (McKenna, Sanford, Clarke); some of the most idiosyncratic (Van Devanter, McReynolds); some of the most forceful (Butler, Sutherland); and some who were merely prosaic (Day, Pitney).

The one justice whom we have not yet considered in detail is Taft himself, who presents a rather large subject of inquiry. Taft was in fact far more than a justice. During his brief tenure on the Supreme Court, Taft inhabited three distinct roles. He was a justice who, like his peers, wrote opinions and voted on the outcome of cases. He was a chief justice, who managed the Court and whose responsibilities expanded to encompass virtually the entire federal judicial system. And he was a judicial reformer, who engaged in political action to promote legislation to improve the operation of federal justice.

Taft exercised each of these three roles with immense capacity and prodigious energy. As a justice, he authored far more opinions than any of his peers, as can be seen in Table P-1. Taft frequently accepted responsibility for drafting the most difficult and important cases facing the Court. He joined or authored opinions for the Court in a staggering 98.7 percent of the cases decided between the beginning of the 1921 term and the conclusion of the 1928 term.[1] As a chief justice, Taft not only steered the Court's deliberations and managed all of its many bureaucratic functions, but also performed such additional tasks as briefing *certiorari* petitions at the Court's conferences,[2] considering *in forma pauperis* petitions, preparing Court orders, and so forth.[3]

As a judicial reformer, Taft fundamentally altered the structure of federal courts, as well as of the Supreme Court itself, through such landmark legislation as the Act of September 14, 1922,[4] and the Judiciary Act of February 13, 1925.[5] As Taft sought aggressively to reform both the Court and the federal judiciary in ways he believed would make them more effective and efficient, he transformed the role of chief justice into something like a chief executive for the federal judiciary. This in turn expanded his administrative responsibilities. The upshot, as Brandeis observed to Frankfurter, was that Taft "does about two men's work – with his added administrative tasks, extra work on certiorari etc. etc."[6] Holmes expressed it well: Taft was man of "unquenchable activity."[7]

It is no exaggeration to say that Taft literally worked himself to death during his years on the Court.[8] He pushed relentlessly on a staggering array of projects until the very end of his tenure. His last great accomplishment, securing funding for the new Supreme Court building that he conceived and helped to design, was consummated on December 20, 1929,[9] barely two weeks before his final collapse.

The Incomparable Chief Justiceship of William Howard Taft
Notes

1. Figure P-1. The pattern of Taft's voting in published opinions and in conference is set out in Figures II-10 and II-9, respectively.
2. *See* WHT to Horace D. Taft (October 6, 1921) (Taft papers) ("At the outset of the term there are a great many applications for what is called 'certiorari'. ... The duty of looking into these cases and of stating them in the conference of the Court for its consideration falls on the Chief Justice. We have about one hundred of these cases, and fifty are for disposition on Saturday in that conference. I am working very hard to get ready to present them to the court for its action."); Statement of Chief Justice William Howard Taft, *Jurisdiction of Circuit Courts of Appeals and of the Supreme Court of the United States* (December 18, 1924), Hearing before the Committee on the Judiciary of the House of Representatives on H.R. 8206, 68th CONG. 2nd SESS., at 27 ("I write out every case that comes up for certiorari and I read it to the court. I think the members of the court are a little impatient sometimes because I give too much detail. Perhaps that is because I am a new member, or was a new member."); C. Dickerman Williams, *The 1924 Term: Recollections of Chief Justice Taft's Law Clerk*, 1989 YEARBOOK OF THE SUPREME COURT HISTORICAL SOCIETY 40, 43; *Address of Justice Sutherland*, 20 PROCEEDINGS OF THE TWENTIETH ANNUAL SESSION OF THE STATE BAR ASSOCIATION OF UTAH 60 (1924).
3. GREGORY HANKIN & CHARLOTTE A. HANKIN, PROGRESS OF THE LAW IN THE U.S. SUPREME COURT 1929–1930, at 5–6 (Washington D.C.: Legal Research Service 1930).
4. Pub. L. 67-298, 42 Stat. 837 (September 14, 1922).
5. Pub. L. 68-415, 43 Stat. 936 (February 13, 1925).
6. *Brandeis-Frankfurter Conversations*, at 321 (August 6, 1923). Taft himself estimated that "I have to do about a third more work than the members of the Court. And it is very continuous and exacting." WHT to Clarence H. Kelsey (May 2, 1923) (Taft papers).
7. OWH to WHT (August 22, 1923) (Taft papers). "Try and curb your disposition to do more than your share of the work of the Court," Clarke once wrote Taft, to which Taft replied, "I love the work, and while I am prepared for anything, I hope that it may continue at least until my ten years have expired." JHC to WHT (September 18, 1927) (Taft papers); WHT to JHC (September 26, 1927) (Taft papers).
8. Early in his career as chief justice, a grueling account of Taft's "typical" workday was published in the press:

    > Mr. Taft is up every morning at 5:30 o'clock. By 6:15 he is at work in his study in his house. (None of the justices has an office. All of them do all of their work at home.) He works until 8:30, when he has breakfast. At 9:00 he is at his desk again and stays there until 10:15, when he starts to walk from his house to the Supreme Court Chamber in the Capitol. That is a little journey of three and seven-tenths miles. When Mr. Taft arrives on Capitol Hill he is in need of a bath and fresh linen. That process requires half an hour. As Chief Justice he then has a certain amount of routine administrative and executive business to dispose. He barely gets through before noon, when the Court opens its session to hear arguments and pleadings. It sits until 4:30 o'clock, with a half hour intermission for lunch.

375

> Mr. Taft drives home every afternoon and is at his desk again at 5:30 o'clock. He works until 6:45, has dinner at 7, goes upstairs to his desk at 8, and gets in two solid hours of labor before going to bed at 10 o'clock.

Edward G. Lowry, Editorial originally appearing in the *Public Ledger* and republished in the *New York Times* (October 28, 1922), at 11.

9. An Act to Provide for the Construction of a Building for the Supreme Court of the United States, Pub. L. 71-26, 46 Stat. 51 (December 20, 1929).

CHAPTER 9

Taft's Health

TAFT JOINED THE Court at the age of 63, an apparently healthy man – obese but living a more or less normal and vigorous life. In 1922, he could joke to a friend who had been committed to a sanitarium because of a weakened heart and rheumatism: "I, too, suffer from a rheumatic knee, though I play golf and do considerable walking. . . . I suppose my heart is pretty weak, too, from having used it too much to pump blood through a great deal of adipose tissue, but still I wear on with the hope that I will last for some little time."[1]

In fact, Taft's blood pressure was far too high, and his heart displayed worrisome indications.[2] A month after writing his friend, he told his son:

> I have had to let up in my regular golf, because I found that with some increase in weight, about ten pounds or more, the walk all the way around the links, especially in warm weather, produced a palpitation of the heart that I did not like, and I am going to confine myself to nine holes from now on. I have got to reduce myself, too. . . . My heart has been all right, so the physicians tell me, but sometimes it is a little tired, and they have discovered a murmur at times. My pulse is very low, but it has always been. It is about 50. My blood pressure sometimes goes up to 180, though it is usually down to 170. All this indicates that I have to be careful if I wish to continue to be active.[3]

Taft suffered his first symptoms of serious cardiac illness in February 1924 when "a sharp digestive" attack brought on disabling heart palpitations.[4] He returned to the Court ten days later feeling "much like myself" and resolving "to try to do less work and possibly to do it better."[5] But in April the palpitations returned.[6] For a month Taft stayed in bed except when in Court, "and then the Doctor thought I ought to take a complete rest and I went to bed for eight days."[7] He was diagnosed with an enlarged heart and cardiac arrhythmia. Treated with digitalis

THE TAFT COURT

and a compound of quinine,[8] he was warned "that I had passed the turn in the road and that I would have to be careful." But he was given "hope that I might live a long time.... It depends upon whether I am sensible and don't overdo and don't overeat and don't over exercise. I don't expect to play golf or to take any other exercise than walking, and not very much uphill."[9]

A slight recurrence on the opening day of the 1924 term frightened Taft.[10] He resolved to mend his ways. "I am able ... to keep up with my work on the Bench," he wrote a friend three months later, "but I do not strain myself to do as much work as I did for the first three years. I have had a warning and I am trying to respect it."[11] But then in June 1926 Taft forgot himself. Along with Van Devanter, Sutherland, Butler, and Sanford, Taft agreed to judge a high school National Oratorical Contest on the subject of "The Constitution," which was designed to "inculcate love of country and good citizenship in the youth of the land."[12] To judge the contest, Taft had to climb "up three or four flights of stairs"[13] to "the top of the theater,"[14] and "that set my heart going."[15]

The palpitations proved "obstinate"[16] and became a turning point in Taft's health. He was forced to miss the closing of Court, and his palpitations persisted throughout his summer vacation in Canada.[17] Taft fretted that his heart condition might "threaten my usefulness on the Bench. I am doing the best I can to abate the trouble, and the three months' vacation that we have helps along.... My general health has been very good, but the work on the Court is persistent and heavy, and it falls especially on the Chief Justice. I love it, and I shall struggle to stay on as long as I can."[18] "The newspapers," he complained to his friend Elihu Root, "are determined to bury me before I am willing to be buried." But "I would like to serve out a full ten" years so as to receive a retirement pension. "If I have strength to fill the decade, I foresee some questions coming before our Court for decision that I should like to take part in deciding."[19]

The start of the 1926 term filled Taft "with a great deal of anxiety."[20] He feared "the change from the lazy life I have been living here to the routine of Court work."[21] He dreaded "the effect upon my heart and me."[22] When he arrived in Washington, Taft reported to his brother that "I am as careful as

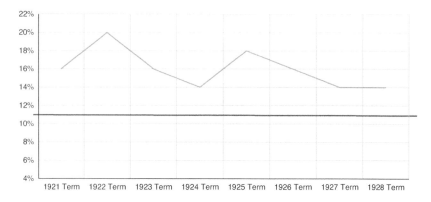

Figure III-1 Percentage of Court's opinions authored by Taft, by term. An even distribution of cases would assign 1/9, or 11%, to each justice.

Taft's Health

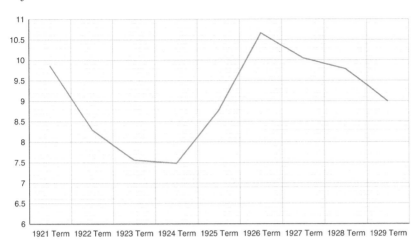

Figure III-2 Average number of pages in a unanimous Taft opinion, by term

I can be. I am trying to see if I cannot hold myself in such [a] way as to continue work. My fibrillation continues but it is not excessive and I am hopeful that by care, I may avoid it being so."[23] He remained relatively stable for a year,[24] but nevertheless for the remainder of his life he judged himself to be a man with a "defective" heart, "so that I have been obliged to lead a life of seclusion and avoid entirely the work of agitation [and] of addresses."[25] He described himself as "really in an invalid state" and required to be "very careful to restrain myself as much as I can."[26] As he wrote the president of the American Philosophical Society, "I am doing the best I can to meet my duties as a partial invalid and under direct medical restraint."[27]

A darker and more frightening disability also began to take hold. In fall 1927, having turned seventy, he wrote his daughter that he feared that "my mental faculties are dulling a bit and that it takes more work for me to get hold of questions and to dispose of them."[28] Taft began to worry about "the elasticity of the arteries, and especially the arteries in the brain."[29] A year later, Taft complained that "I now find that it is much harder for me to concentrate my mind and to bring about the hard application that is necessary to make my work as useful as it used to be when my powers were better."[30] "My mind moves slowly, and I have great difficulty in arranging my opinions as I would like to."[31] "The truth is," Taft wrote a friend, "that my mind does not work as well as it did, and I scatter."[32]

I have recounted Taft's deteriorating health in such detail because it forms an essential backdrop for appreciating Taft's performance of his three roles on the Court. Remarkably, Taft's vigor as a reformer and as an outwardly facing chief justice did not diminish during the decade of his service. He continued energetically to press for useful legislative reform and to expand and innovate the role of chief justice.

But Taft's internal leadership of the Court did noticeably decline. He became less crisp in his grasp and presentation of *certiorari* petitions.[33] He became less proactive in steering the Court to avoid controversial opinions. Taft's previously massive output as a justice declined during the term following his 1924 heart attack, and it began a more protracted and irreversible slide after his 1926 heart attack, as can be seen in Figure III-1. Figure II-2 shows that Taft was always a relatively prolix writer, but Figure III-2 demonstrates that his opinions grew even more lengthy after his 1926 heart attack.[34] In later years, as Taft's cognitive difficulties increased, his opinions grew less cogent.[35] Taft's voting also grew less independent, as Figure III-3 illustrates. Brandeis observed to Frankfurter shortly after Taft's retirement that "the truth is that Taft for some time had really lost his grip and V.D. and Pierce Butler and McReynolds were running him. In addition to his being with them in their desires, they were with him in some of his own independent foolishness."[36]

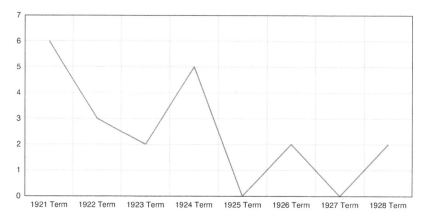

Figure III-3 Number of decisions in a term that Taft does not author or join the majority opinion

Taft's Health

Notes

1. WHT to George Benjamin Edwards (August 23, 1922) (Taft papers).
2. In September 1922, Taft wrote his brother that after eighteen holes of golf and a walk uphill, "I was considerably alarmed at finding that my pulse was going much more rapidly than usual and that that continued for two days. It was a case of palpitation, produced, I doubt not, by over-exertion, and possibly, too, by something I had eaten. ... My pulse has become normal again, and I seem to be all right; but that old heart of mine has had so much to do in times past, and so much to do now, that I have got to treat it gently. I have been told by the physicians that sometimes it sounded like a tired heart, which is only another indication that I am getting on and need to have some sense in what I do. It takes the life out of a game of golf to play only the lower holes, but it is better to take the life out of golf than to take the life out of yourself." WHT to Horace D. Taft (September 7, 1922) (Taft papers).
3. WHT to Charles P. Taft 2nd (September 4, 1922) (Taft papers). Taft's blood pressure continued high throughout his tenure as chief justice. *See, e.g.*, WHT to Horace D. Taft (June 8, 1927) (Taft papers) ("I had the Doctor go over me yesterday and he found that my heart beat was down to 52. He found my blood pressure was 180, but 115 in the diastole, which I think is too high. ... [T]he Doctor seemed to be quite well satisfied.").
4. *See* WHT to Horace D. Taft (February 6, 1924) (Taft papers):

    > I had an attack of palpitation of the heart this morning, brought on I suppose by a sharp digestive attack, and with diarrhea. I sent for the Doctor and he found what I had already found, that my pulse was running fast and irregularly. He said that what I needed was rest, and that I could not go to Woodrow Wilson's funeral this afternoon, where I had intended to go as a pall bearer. I would have given anything to go, not alone to pay a tribute to a deceased President, but also to avoid the circulation against alarming reports as to my illness. I explained that to the Doctor and he seemed to realize the awkwardness of it, but it did not abate his insistence that I should be quiet and run no risk. There is only one living ex-President, and I don't care to reduce that number, so I obey orders. ... I thought I was in fine condition, but I have been gaining some flesh.

5. WHT to Horace D. Taft (February 16, 1924) (Taft papers). *See* WHT to James E. Gregg (February 15, 1924) (Taft papers) ("The truth is I have had a pretty close call to a breakdown. I hope, however, to go back to Court on Monday, with a warning that I can not do all the work there is to do. I was treating myself as I might have treated myself thirty years ago. There is no fool like an old fool. There is some hope, however, if he mends his ways.").
6. WHT to Horace D. Taft (April 25, 1924) (Taft papers) ("I have had a return of that palpitation of the heart. ... I had thought that I was getting along very well indeed ... but I ate something or did something to affect a nerve, and so I am under orders again.").
7. Memorandum of Taft to his Family (June 8, 1924) (Taft papers). "The truth is," Taft wrote the president of Yale, that "I have overdone things in the matter of my work. I have proceeded on the theory that I was younger than I am, and I can not be useful unless I cut out all my activities and devote myself solely to the requirements of the Bench." WHT to James R. Angell (May 31, 1924) (Taft papers).
8. Memorandum, *supra* note 7; WHT to Clarence H. Kelsey (June 7, 1924) (Taft papers). Taft would today likely be diagnosed with paroxysmal atrial fibrillation,

THE TAFT COURT

for which obesity is a known risk factor. Atrial fibrillation is associated with an increased risk of strokes. Quinine is now thought to increase the risk of arrhythmia.

9. WHT to Clarence H. Kelsey (June 7, 1924) (Taft papers). In September, Taft wrote Brandeis that "there has been no recurrence of the heart fibrillation, though at times there has been some thumping that gave me concern, but I hope that it is not a serious symptom. On the whole, I have had a satisfactory summer, although I have had to give up golf and confine such exercise as I have taken to slow walks to the golf course and back again." WHT to LDB (September 9, 1924) (Taft papers). Van Devanter wrote Clarke on October 2 that "The Chief looks well, says he has had a restful summer and is feeling pretty well. His appearance and what he says tend decidedly to refute some alarming reports which I heard when I first arrived, which was before he came." WVD to JHC (October 2, 1924) (Van Devanter papers).

10. *See, e.g.*, WHT to Horace D. Taft (October 10, 1924) (Taft papers):

> The first day of the Court was a pretty exciting one, and I ate some roast pork, something I rarely do, although I love the meat. I had a heavy cold, waked up in a sweat about one o-clock, and found my heart going as it did last January.... Visions of a recurrence of the trouble and of my having to stay home from Court came over me, and I was a good deal alarmed. Indeed it seemed to me as if I might have to give up the office and spend my time trying to live.

Two days later Taft wrote his son, "We had had an unusually heavy docket, and I am afraid I worked too hard on it.... If I find that this is going to recur so as to interfere with my work, I shall have to get out of the Court and devote my attention to living.... It is a serious issue that may present itself. If Coolidge is to be reelected, then there will be no trouble from the standpoint of the friends of the Constitution, but if not, I suppose I shall have to hang on as long as I can, because if there is any chance of Bryan's getting in, it will be difficult to get anybody confirmed in my place.... I must do my work or else cry quits, and I presume this winter will disclose pretty certainly the situation." WHT to Charles P. Taft 2nd (October 12, 1924) (Taft papers). *See* WHT to Mrs. Frederick J. Manning (October 12, 1924) (Taft papers).

11. WHT to Henry E. Coe (January 7, 1925). In February, with his typical bluntness, McReynolds wrote Taft's former secretary of war that "The Chief has at last found out that he must be careful. I fear it is too late. His heart is bad." JCM to J.M. Dickinson (February 5, 1925) (Dickinson papers at the Tennessee State Library & Archives). After a restful summer in 1925, Taft believed that "I have to be very careful, in view of the warnings that I have had, but on the whole I seem to have gotten along so that I am going back to Washington, trusting that with care I may be able to pull my weight into the boat, as I did last year." WHT to S.A. Perkins (September 19, 1925) (Taft papers). *See* WHT to Horace D. Taft (October 5, 1925) (Taft papers). As the term began, Taft wrote a Kansas newspaper editor that "I haven't had a heart attack for more than a year, but it was a severe warning and one that requires me to observe the greatest care, and of course keeps the suggestion before me that when the pump is out of order, or can easily get out of order, no one knows what may happen. However, I have been able to pull my weight in the boat, that is to do my share on the Bench, but I am trying to avoid too intense application in order to pursue the quiet life that is needed." WHT to Charles F. Scott (November 21, 1925) (Taft papers).

Taft's Health

Taft sought to take prudent precautions against the possibility of a forced medical retirement. He had written Coolidge the previous June that "When I visited the White House some days ago, I spoke to you of an amendment to the law which would facilitate my retirement if it seemed wise, after I became seventy. I was born on the 15th of September, 1857, and, if I live, I shall reach the age of seventy on the 15th of September, 1927." WHT to Calvin Coolidge (June 4, 1925) (Taft papers). Taft's proposed amendment would allow judges to accrue noncontinuous retirement credit, so that Taft could count his years as a circuit judge toward his retirement. Coolidge asked Taft to "remind me of this at the time of the opening of Congress." Calvin Coolidge to WHT (June 4, 1925) (Taft papers).

True to his word, Coolidge recommended in his annual message in December that "the terms of years of service of judges of any court of the United States requisite for retirement with pay shall be computed to include not only continuous but aggregate service." *President's Annual Message*, 67 CONG. REC. 463 (December 8, 1925). Coolidge's recommendation was not ultimately enacted into law until 1929. *See* Pub. L. 70-870, 45 Stat. 1422 (March 1, 1929); H. R. Rep. No. 2678, 70th CONG. 2nd SESS. (February 23, 1929); Sen. Rep. No. 1511, 70th CONG. 2nd SESS. (January 26, 1929), at 1.

The significance of Coolidge's proposal was not lost on the sharp-eyed McReynolds, who wrote J.M. Dickinson that "The Ch. Justice has the appearance of being in pretty good health," but "The President's message suggesting the judges be allowed to add all years of service in order to retire was probably intended to help the Ch.J in case of an emergency." JCM to J.M. Dickinson (December 13, 1925) (Dickinson papers at the Tennessee State Library & Archives). When Coolidge's bill became law in March 1929, Taft was asked whether he would take advantage of its provisions. "'I'm not going to retire unless I have to,' he said with a laugh. 'The bill is a fair bill and I appreciate and approve it, but I don't know to whom it is to apply. The President recommended its enactment four years ago. I expect to serve at least until I have been here ten years. That will be in July, 1931.'" *Won't Retire Now, Taft Declares*, NEW YORK TIMES (March 1, 1929), at 3. *See* WHT to R.G. Hepworth (March 5, 1929) (Taft papers).

12. *Los Angeles Boy First in Contest of School Orators*, NEW YORK TIMES (June 5, 1926), at 1. Taft had described a previous version of the contest to his son: "Five of us in the Court are going to sit as judges to determine the best speaker of seven contestants for the best address, twelve minutes in length, on the Constitution. It is a good thing. It has stirred the high school boys and girls all over the country in their interest in the Constitution. It was organized I think by one hundred newspapers of a conservative type, and it has really done much for the educational influence of that fundamental instrument of ours. The President will preside at the contest, and we five will sit in the audience and give our judgment." WHT to Robert A. Taft (May 25, 1924) (Taft papers).
13. WHT to Clarence H. Kelsey (June 9, 1926) (Taft papers). The experience prompted Taft to decide to install an elevator in his home. *Id.*
14. WHT to Horace D. Taft (June 5, 1926) (Taft papers).
15. WHT to Clarence H. Kelsey (June 9, 1926) (Taft papers).
16. WHT to Franklin W. Cram (June 15, 1926) (Taft papers).
17. *See, e.g.*, WVD to PB (June 21, 1926) (Van Devanter papers) ("I saw the Chief Justice Saturday. He was not as much encouraged about his own situation as he would like to be. He had been counting on going away tomorrow, but the doctor was advising

a postponement to Friday. I endeavored to give some reasons for following the doctor's advice and at the same time tried to develop some grounds for encouragement."). On July 7, Taft confessed to his intimate friend Charles Hilles that Stone was correct to advise "that I have to cut down what I have been doing on the Court, and I think he is possibly right that I attempt to do too much." WHT to Charles D. Hilles (July 7, 1926) (Taft papers). Two days later, he wrote Van Devanter after arriving at his summer home in Canada: "I think I have been better here than I was in New Haven. At least the doctor says so. But still the pacemaker of the heart has not got onto its trolley yet. The doctor here, who is a very good doctor, is testing me before he tries another strong dose of digitalis. I haven't done any work, and I have concluded to ask Pierce Butler to take over that long, heavy case of the Chemical Foundation. [United States v. Chemical Foundation, Inc., 272 U.S. 1 (1926)]. I am afraid to undertake it myself, because I must reduce the work this summer as much as I can in order to give full opportunity for a return to normal. Pierce is young and strong, able and willing, and I thought I would trespass on him. He is the only one to whom I can properly give it. He was appointed by Harding and not by Wilson, and I rather think we ought to have somebody other than an appointee of Wilson to consider and decide the case." WHT to WVD (July 9, 1926) (Van Devanter papers).

18. WHT to Alfred L. Ripley (August 5, 1926) (Taft papers). *See* WHT to Mrs. Charles D. Norton (August 10, 1926) (Taft papers):

> I have had, as you know, trouble with my heart for now more than two years. It is recurrent. It is what is called "heart fibrillation." . . . I haven't succeeded as yet this summer in getting back to normal regularity. . . . I don't like it, and I think it may interfere more or less with my work. I have not been five years on the Supreme Bench. If I could be spared for five years more, I could under the law retire on my salary and devote myself to quiet and to an arrangement of my papers for use by my children in such memoirs as they might think it wise to give out if they deem it so. . . .
>
> I love the work in the Supreme Court, but during the term it is hard and pressing, and I don't know whether I shall be able to continue it through the remaining five years, much as I would like to, but whatever comes, I shall never cease to be grateful for what I have had and the opportunities for usefulness which have been presented to me, as well as for the happiness accompanying such a family and such friends.

19. WHT to Elihu Root (August 19, 1926) (Taft papers). "The Doctor tells me that I am getting along well and that I am growing better, and that if I keep myself within the bounds of moderation, and don't attempt too much exertion, my general condition is such as to make it possible for me to live some time." *Id.* Root replied that "The men who have really learned the lesson of taking care of themselves ordinarily have to be taken out and shot by their sorrowing friends in order to get rid of them. I take the same cheerful view of your judicial duties. . . . The best Judge as well as the longest liver is rather unemotional, unimaginative, indifferent, and stodgy. Try being a little stodgy, my dear Porthos, and people will be sending telegrams of congratulation to you on your one hundred and fourth birthday." Elihu Root to WHT (September 8, 1926) (Taft papers). Taft replied, "Your recommendation seems to be that I make myself 'unemotional, unimaginative, indifferent and stodgy'. I don't think that your prescription imposes on me the taking of a very long step. Indeed I think I have already arrived." WHT to Elihu Root (September 17, 1926) (Taft papers).

20. WHT to Charles P. Taft 2nd (September 23, 1926) (Taft papers).

Taft's Health

21. *Id.* Taft wrote Sanford in August that "when I come back I shall not be as well as I was last winter, because my heart beat will probably not be normal, and I must therefore husband my strength and not attempt too much. But I am sure that you brethren will make allowance for my situation and understand me if I favor myself a bit in the distribution of cases." WHT to ETS (August 21, 1926) (Taft papers).
22. WHT to Horace D. Taft (September 23, 1926) (Taft papers).
23. WHT to Henry W. Taft (September 20, 1926) (Taft papers). *See* WHT to Harry C. Coe (October 2, 1926) (Taft papers). Taft reported to his daughter that "I lost some sleep this week, due to nervousness I suppose, and I did think at one time that I was in for a delay, due to my condition, but I got over the symptoms that were disturbing." WHT to Mrs. Frederick J. Manning (October 3, 1926) (Taft papers). "I have a battered old hulk," Taft wrote Second Circuit Judge Charles Hough, "and must rejoice as long as I am able to keep afloat." WHT to Charles M. Hough (December 4, 1926) (Taft papers).
24. The danger posed by his heart condition never left Taft's mind. In a daily memorandum containing his "to-do list" for February 6, 1927, for example, Taft noted that it was "3 yrs ago as I recollect it I had my first attack of fibrillation. It was the day of the funeral of Woodrow Wilson." (Taft papers).
25. WHT to Gordon Edwards (January 28, 1928) (Taft papers).
26. WHT to R. Walton Moore (April 19, 1928) (Taft papers).
27. WHT to Francis X. Dercum (January 7, 1929) (Taft papers).
28. WHT to Mrs. Frederick J. Manning (October 23, 1927) (Taft papers). "However, I have to stay on the Bench until 1931," Taft continued, "in order to earn my pension, and that I must struggle to do, unless I am so weakened that I can not do the work." In this letter, Taft gives a sketch of his day that is worth comparing to the description published in 1922. *See* NEW YORK TIMES (October 28, 1922), at 11, quoted in *supra* Part III, at note 8. Upon the advice of his doctor, Taft had hired a masseur to improve his circulation. The masseur, Taft wrote his daughter,

> comes about six o'clock or a quarter after six, leaves me at a quarter before seven, I rest for twenty-five minutes, and then dress, and I am usually in my study at 8 o'clock, giving me half an hour for work before breakfast. At nine I come back again and have my mail and then work with [my Secretary] until half past eleven, take half an hour to reach the Court, and have lunch at two o'clock – half an hour – and get home at 5 o'clock. Then I take a walk across the bridge for half an hour and rest for half an hour and use the rest of the time for work. I put in about half an hour in the evening, sometimes an hour, reading the newspapers and in reading secular books, and then go to bed at ten, hoping to get to sleep before eleven. If I can only keep this up, I hope I can get through this year as I did last year.

WHT to Mrs. Frederick J. Manning (October 23, 1927) (Taft papers). *See* WHT to Robert A. Taft (October 23, 1927) (Taft papers).
29. WHT to Mrs. Frederick J. Manning (November 20, 1927) (Taft papers). Taft also reported that "My blood pressure has been higher than the doctor likes and higher than I like it, especially in what is called the diastole. My blood pressure is from 170 to 180 in the systole, and about 120 in the diastole. 170 to 180 in the systole is not excessive. It is probably normal for me. It is the diastole that is high." *Id.*
30. WHT to Charles P. Taft 2nd (November 25, 1928) (Taft papers).
31. WHT to Mrs. Frederick J. Manning (December 16, 1928) (Taft papers).
32. WHT to J.M. Dickinson (December 12, 1928) (Taft papers). "The work of the Court not so much in writing opinions as in getting ready for Conferences grows heavier

385

and heavier. I feel tired over it and suffer from a lack of quickness of comprehension, which has not heretofore troubled me much." *Id.*
33. LDB to Felix Frankfurter (May 30, 1930), in BRANDEIS-FRANKFURTER CORRESPONDENCE, at 431; LDB to Felix Frankfurter (October 13, 1929), *id.* at 394.
34. The relative decline in the page length of Taft's opinions in the 1927, 1928, and 1929 terms is likely explained by the fact that, as his health declined, Taft began assigning himself less difficult opinions.
35. *See, e.g.*, Carson Petroleum v. Vial, 279 U.S. 95 (1929); London Guarantee & Accident co. v. Industrial Accident Comm'n of California, 279 U.S. 109 (1929).
36. LDB to Felix Frankfurter (May 30, 1930), in BRANDEIS-FRANKFURTER CORRESPONDENCE, at 431. *See* HFS to John Bassett Moore (May 17, 1943) (Stone papers), quoted in ALPHEUS THOMAS MASON, THE SUPREME COURT FROM TAFT TO BURGER 70 (Baton Rouge: Louisiana State University Press 1979) ("When I first went on the Court in Taft's time, the discussion was very free, although sometimes discursive. During the last of his service there was much more inclination to rush things through especially if he thought he had the support of certain members of the Court."). *See* JONATHAN LURIE, THE CHIEF JUSTICESHIP OF WILLIAM HOWARD TAFT, 1921–1930, at 118 (Columbia: University of South Carolina Press 2019) ("By 1926 Chief Justice Taft was in failing health. Already he had experienced two heart attacks, and ... neither his output of decisions nor his effectiveness as 'the first among equals' matched his earlier years.").

CHAPTER 10

Taft as a Justice

During Taft's first years on the Court, he inhabited the role of justice with a strong independence of mind. From 1892–1900, Taft had been a well-respected and highly influential circuit court judge on the Sixth Circuit.[1] His "classic opinion"[2] in *United States v. Addyston Pipe & Steel Co.*[3] was thought at the time to contain "the most thorough exposition in the American reports of the law relating to restraint of trade."[4] He wrote early and influential opinions setting parameters for federal injunctions to control strikes.[5] Taft knew how to write punchy and effective judicial decisions when he wanted to.

Taft came to the bench with strongly conventional views. Although he acknowledged that the "crystallization of public sentiment" was a fundamental source of law,[6] what in fact moved him most was the thought that the end of government is "the promotion of the happiness of the individual and his progress."[7] Implicit in this view was an outlook that was both materialistic and powerfully individualistic. Taft believed "that government is, of course, for the benefit of society as a whole, but that society is composed of individuals and that the benefit of society as a whole is only consistent with the full opportunity of its members to pursue happiness and their individual liberty. This ... includes freedom from personal restraint, right of free labor, right of property, right of religious worship, right of contract."[8]

Of these freedoms, property rights were for Taft "the keystone of our society,"[9] because "the institution of private property is what has led to the accumulation of capital in the world."[10] "You cannot conceive of a government of individual liberty in which the right of property is not secured," Taft thought, for "the destruction of the right of property is the beginning of the end of individual liberty, because the right of property is that right which secures to the individual the product of his labor and the ownership of his savings, the reward of his industry and self-restraint."[11] Property was prerequisite for civilization itself. "Until human nature becomes far more exalted in moral character and self-sacrifice than it is today, the motive of gain is the only one which will be constant to induce industry, saving, invention and organization, which will effect an increase in production greater than the increase in population."[12]

Taft believed that the Constitution itself protected the incentives necessary to underwrite material progress. He campaigned vigorously for Harding's election, arguing that only Harding could maintain "the Supreme Court as the bulwark to enforce the guaranty that no man shall be deprived of his property without due process of law." "Mr. Wilson is in favor of a latitudinarian construction of the Constitution of the United States," Taft charged, "to weaken the protection it should afford against socialistic raids upon property rights, with the direct and inevitable result of paralyzing the initiative and enterprise of capital necessary to the real progress of all."[13] As Taft confided to his intimate friend Elihu Root, "the corner stone of our civilization is in the proper maintenance of the guaranties of the 14th Amendment and the 5th Amendment."[14]

His view of human nature led Taft to affirm that there was "only a limited zone within which legislation and governments can accomplish good. We cannot regulate beyond that zone with success or benefit. ... If we do not conform to human nature in legislation we shall fail."[15] Religion was important to Taft because it was the only "means of neutralizing the necessarily selfish element in humanity. I say 'necessarily selfish' – I mean ... necessary ... in the progress of the world from an economic standpoint. Religion is the only secure method of neutralizing what is likely to be the bad effect of unrestrained selfishness."[16]

Taft was no libertarian. He believed that law can and should be used effectively to manage society. But Taft was torn between his drive for progressive forms of administrative efficiency and his fear that legislation might unduly constrain necessarily self-interested human behavior. The function of constitutional restrictions was to prevent the latter. An exchange with Brandeis during Taft's first term well captures the complexities of Taft's jurisprudence.

In *United States v. Moreland* the Court was required to decide whether the conviction of a defendant violated the Fifth Amendment because he had been charged in juvenile court by information, rather than by a grand jury, for failing to provide for the maintenance of his minor children. The defendant was sentenced to hard labor at the workhouse for six months. The Fifth Amendment requires that "No persons shall be held to answer for a capital, or otherwise infamous crime, unless on presentment or indictment of a grand jury." In *Moreland*, the Court held that confinement "at *hard labor* inflicted an infamous punishment" and hence required a grand jury indictment.[17]

Joined by Taft and Holmes, Brandeis dissented on the ground that "the dominant purpose" of the District of Columbia workhouse was "not punishment, but rehabilitation"; that the "compulsory labor" at issue was in fact "compulsory education" which occurred "in healthful and attractive surroundings"; that "at the time of the adoption of the Constitution and since," confinement "at hard labor in a work house or house of correction did not imply infamy" but was used for "offenses not deemed serious"; that "hard labor regularly pursued and productively

Taft as a Justice

employed" was an instrument for "reform and rehabilitation" which affirmed "the dignity of labor" and was a "means of restoring and giving self-respect"; and that the meaning of "infamous crimes" in the Fifth Amendment should be interpreted "in harmony with conditions and opinion prevailing from time to time."[18]

In the original draft of his dissent, after referring to the need for a contemporary interpretation of the Fifth Amendment, Brandeis had written, "Our Constitution is not a strait-jacket. It is a living organism. As such it is capable of growth – of expansion and of adaption to new conditions. Growth implies changes political, economic and social. Growth which is significant manifests itself rather in intellectual and moral conceptions than in material things. Because our Constitution possesses this quality of adaption, it has endured as the fundamental law of an ever developing people."[19]

Upon receiving Brandeis's draft, Taft objected to these sentences. Taft advised Brandeis that "they are certain to be used to support views that I could not subscribe to."

> Their importance depends, as old Jack Bunsby used to say, on their application, and I fear that you and I might differ as to their application. I object to them because they are unnecessary here. It seems to me you have sufficiently demonstrated that the expression "hard labor" was used with respect to bridewells and workhouses quite far back, not to mean the hard labor in the penitentiary, which is infamous, but hard labor in a place where such labor is not infamous.... Now it is possible – I have felt that way myself sometimes – that these particular sentences constitute the feature of the opinion that you most like, and therefore that you don't care to eliminate them. If not, I can write a short concurring opinion, avoiding responsibility for those words, and yet availing myself of your demonstration of the innocuous character of the words in question when they occur in respect to punishment not in the penitentiary.[20]

Brandeis replied that "I believe strongly in the view expressed in the last five sentences, but I agree with you that they are not necessary and I am perfectly willing to omit them."[21] Taft then concurred in Brandeis's recirculated opinion, commenting, "Your historical references ought to satisfy any reasonable person that hard labor is not a hard and fast expression but is one the effect of which is to be explained by the context and the circumstances. This is the controlling consideration with me."[22]

The exchange between Taft and Brandeis is noteworthy for several reasons. Its tact and delicacy are striking. This is plainly a conversation between two serious men who fully understand and respect the difference between their views. Brandeis wanted to emphasize the flexibility of constitutional provisions; Taft to stress their relative stability. Yet this difference should not be overstated. Not only did Taft join an opinion arguing that the Fifth Amendment should be interpreted based upon "the context and the circumstances," but he concurred with the basic thrust of Brandeis's dissent, which is that government should be empowered to regulate individual behavior without unduly burdensome or formal constitutional restrictions. This view of the relationship between government and its population appealed to Taft's administrative instincts.

Taft gave firm and lasting expression to these same instincts in the important and enduring opinion of *Carroll v. United States*,[23] which authorized warrantless searches of automobiles (so long as there was probable cause) and which Brandeis joined.[24] *Carroll* swept away centuries of precedent to enable police effectively to control the vehicular traffic that everywhere undermined prohibition during the 1920s. Taft also gave voice to these instincts in *Olmstead v. United States*,[25] which authorized warrantless wiretapping. *Olmstead* gave police far-ranging new tools for identifying and disciplining criminals.

In his years on the Court, Taft as a reformer would constantly seek ways to advance innovations that would be "progressive and helpful,"[26] while Taft as a justice applied a jurisprudence that was explicitly pragmatic and purposeful.[27] He strongly supported executive prerogatives[28] and embraced administrative agencies.[29] He usefully articulated the nature of the delegation power[30] in a manner that acutely distinguished between vagueness in rules addressed to administrative officials and vagueness in rules addressed to the general public.[31]

Nowhere was Taft's practical side more apparent than in his majestic opinions upholding federal commerce power as "fitted" to "the real and practical essence of modern business growth."[32] Taft believed in the necessity of national regulation to sustain the national market. In an opinion upholding the Packers and Stockyards Act of 1921, Taft affirmed Congress's power to regulate the "streams of commerce from one part of the country to another, which are ever flowing," without a "nice and technical inquiry into the noninterstate character of some of its necessary incidents and facilities, when considered alone and without reference to their association with the movement of which they were an essential but subordinate part."[33] In powerful and sweeping language that anticipated later holdings of the New Deal Court, Taft sought to immunize congressional regulation of these streams from nit-picking judicial supervision: "Whatever amounts to a more or less constant practice, and threatens to obstruct or unduly to burden the freedom of interstate commerce is within the regulatory power of Congress under the commerce clause, and it is primarily for Congress to consider and decide the fact of danger and meet it. This court will certainly not substitute its judgment for that of Congress in such a matter unless the relation of the subject to the interstate commerce and its effect upon it are clearly nonexistent."[34]

The same pragmatic, regulatory instinct was fully manifest in Taft's muscular opinion for a unanimous Court in *Dayton-Goose Creek Ry. Co. v. United States*, which upheld the constitutionality of provisions of the Transportation Act of 1920 that required railroads receiving "in excess of a fair return" to remit one half of that excess "to a general railroad revolving fund to be maintained" by the Interstate Commerce Commission to help "the weaker roads more effectively to discharge their public duties." Taft invoked the authority of practical reason brusquely to dismiss the argument that the Act exceeded Congress' commerce power:

> In solving the problem of maintaining the efficiency of an interstate commerce railway system which serves both the states and the nation,

Taft as a Justice

Congress is dealing with a unit in which state and interstate operations are often inextricably commingled. ... The combination of uniform rates with the recapture clauses is necessary to the better development of the country's interstate transportation system as Congress has planned it. The control of the excess profit due to the level of the whole body of rates is the heart of the plan. To divide that excess and attempt to distribute one part to interstate traffic and the other to intrastate traffic would be impracticable and defeat the plan. This renders indispensable the incidental control by Congress of that part of the excess possibly due to intrastate rates which, if present, is indistinguishable.[35]

The practical, progressive side of Taft reached its apogee in his remarkable dissent in *Adkins v. Children's Hospital of the District of Columbia*, in which the Court, speaking through Sutherland, found a minimum wage law for women unconstitutional. In language that sounded distinctly Holmesian in its generous appreciation of the reach of police power, Taft argued:

The boundary of the police power beyond which its exercise becomes an invasion of the guaranty of liberty under the Fifth and Fourteenth Amendments to the Constitution is not easy to mark. Our Court has been laboriously engaged in pricking out a line in successive cases. We must be careful, it seems to me, to follow that line as well as we can, and not to depart from it by suggesting a distinction that is formal rather than real.

Legislatures in limiting freedom of contract between employee and employer by a minimum wage proceed on the assumption that employees, in the class receiving least pay, are not upon a full level of equality of choice with their employer and in their necessitous circumstances are prone to accept pretty much anything that is offered. They are peculiarly subject to the overreaching of the harsh and greedy employer. The evils of the sweating system and of the long hours and low wages which are characteristic of it are well known. Now, I agree that it is a disputable question in the field of political economy how far a statutory requirement of maximum hours or minimum wages may be a useful remedy for these evils, and whether it may not make the case of the oppressed employee worse than it was before. But it is not the function of this Court to hold congressional acts invalid simply because they are passed to carry out economic views which the Court believes to be unwise or unsound.

Legislatures which adopt a requirement of maximum hours or minimum wages may be presumed to believe that when sweating employers are prevented from paying unduly low wages by positive law they will continue their business, abating that part of their profits, which were wrung from the necessities of their employees, and will concede the better terms required by the law; and that while in individual cases, hardship may result, the restriction will inure to the benefit of the general class of employees in whose interest the law is passed, and so to that of the community at large.[36]

This was the side of Taft that could proudly announce in his inaugural address as president that "[t]he scope of a modern government in what it can and ought to accomplish for its people has been widened far beyond the principles laid down by the old 'laissez faire' school of political writers, and this widening has met popular approval."[37]

There was another side to Taft, however, that was suspicious of legislative intrusions on property and contract rights. If Holmes religiously separated his conservative political views from his jurisprudence, Taft let his conservative principles seep deeply into his legal thinking. Taft's break with Roosevelt in 1912 had made him distrustful of excess reformist zeal.[38] He became alarmed when he suspected that the "leviathan, the People" were aroused with "a momentum" that would carry "their earnestness and just indignation beyond the median and wise line."[39] In such moments he called upon the Constitution, which he characterized in a phrase Holmes would never consider using,[40] as "the ark of our covenant."[41]

The sacred function of constitutional rights was to curb democratic enthusiasm and to maintain what Taft regarded as an appropriate respect for fundamental values like property and freedom of contract. It was for this reason that Taft proclaimed in *Truax v. Corrigan*, decided just four months before *Moreland*, that "the Constitution was intended – its very purpose was – to prevent experimentation with the fundamental rights of the individual."[42] The nature of these fundamental rights, the exact location of the line that the democratic leviathan was forbidden to cross, was largely set by Taft's commitment to rights of property and freedom of contract necessary to incentivize the entrepreneurial energy required for economic development.

Truax, which involved an Arizona statute restricting judicial injunctions in labor cases, touched an area where Taft believed that the demos was systematically encroaching on hallowed constitutional rights. The question of the labor injunction had arisen in Taft's 1908 presidential campaign, when there had been an effort to insert a plank in the Republican Party platform limiting equitable remedies in labor contexts. Taft at the time wrote his chief strategist that he "would 'rather cut my hand off' than take from the courts their power to protect property."[43] In his first inaugural address as president, Taft announced that his "convictions are fixed" with regard "to the power of the federal courts to issue injunctions in industrial disputes": "Take away from the courts, if it could be taken away, the power to issue injunctions in labor disputes, and it would create a privileged class among the laborers, and save the lawless among their number from a most needful remedy available to all men for the protection of their business against lawless invasion. The proposition that business is not a property or pecuniary right which can be protected by equitable injunction is utterly without foundation in precedent or reason."[44]

As a politician and as a justice, Taft was concerned to constrain what he regarded as overreaching assaults on property. In one of his last speeches as president, Taft addressed his fellow Republicans about his devastating loss in the 1912 election. He seemed almost reconciled to the victory of "our old-time opponent, the Democratic Party,"[45] but reserved special ire for Theodore Roosevelt and the Progressive Party.[46] Taft condemned "the whole program of the Progressive Party" as "taking from the successful and the conferring on the unsuccessful that which the successful have earned." The price of any such program, Taft declared, was nothing less than the "destruction" of "modern progress." It was the function of

Taft as a Justice

"constitutional limitations," "vindicated through courts," to prevent such a calamity. But "under the system which our progressive friends propose,"

> the limitations themselves are to be subjected to the abolishing power of a referendum, and when they are embodied and enforced in a judgment of a court they may still be lost by a referendum of the judgment to the populace in an election to determine whether the court's decision is right.
>
> Thus it is easily seen that under the progressive program the whole machinery that has been so carefully built up by the older statesmen of this country and of England to save to the individual and the minority freedom, equality before the law, the right of property, and the right to pursue happiness is to be taken apart and thrown into a junk heap and the preservation of such rights or privileges ... is to be left to the charitable impulse of a benevolent administrator.
>
> No one at all familiar with the principles of free government and the tendency of erring and power-loving human nature would be content to have his liberty or his right of property or his right to pursue happiness dependent upon the benevolence of anyone.[47]

As a justice, Taft often struggled to reconcile his attraction to benevolent and effective administration with his suspicion of public restraints on entrepreneurial freedom and property.[48] As Taft himself once put it, it is important to respect "the elasticity of our constitutional restraints and the possibility of squaring them with the change of conditions that calls for greater limitations than have heretofore been deemed necessary. But this does not do away with fundamental principles of our liberties."[49] Taft was "greatly concerned" that popular government "shall continue and be successful in giving to the people at large the best measure of individual liberty on the one hand and the greatest practical efficacy in government on the other."[50]

A good example of this tension is *Lehigh Valley Ry. Co. v. Board of Pub. Util. Comm'rs*, in which a railroad company appealed the order of a state public utility commission requiring it to construct an overhead crossing at the cost of $324,000. The company believed that a satisfactory crossing could be constructed for "at least $100,000 less."[51] Taft's opinion for the Court, over McReynolds's dissent,[52] was almost painfully ambivalent, supporting the necessary discretion of administrators "to avoid danger to the public"[53] while simultaneously signaling that "the protection of the Fourteenth Amendment in such cases is real, and is not to be lightly regarded."[54] Although Taft was prepared to hold that the costs in the case before him were "within reasonable limits,"[55] he nevertheless took pains to "deprecate the impression, apparently entertained by some, that in the safeguarding of railroad crossings by order of state or local authority the exercise of police power escapes the ordinary constitutional limitation of reasonableness of cost. This is apt to give to local boards a sense of freedom which tempts to arbitrariness and extravagance."[56]

The fuzzy line between extravagance and safety was for courts to determine. Opinions like *Lehigh Valley* exposed just how arbitrary that line was. In the end, the

Court could offer only the unadorned judgment of five justices about what was constitutionally "reasonable." The Court could announce such a judgment, but it could not explain it. The authority of the Court's decision was said to lie in its disinterest, in its insulation from the demagogic pressure of politics.[57] When the Great Depression radically undermined public faith in the utility of this insulation, the temporizing constitutional jurisprudence constructed by Taft collapsed.[58]

During the 1920s, however, Taft's jurisprudence was entirely credible. Like Taft himself, the country was caught between the need for efficient government and revulsion at the rapidly expanding prerogatives of the administrative state.[59] As Taft's health deteriorated, his judgment about how to strike a balance between effective administration and rights of property grew increasingly dependent upon the forceful conservative views of colleagues like Van Devanter, Butler, and Sutherland. After his 1926 heart attack, Taft would never again display the independence of mind that he had once demonstrated in his *Adkins* dissent. His instinct about where to limit the overreaching leviathan grew ever more reflexively attached to individual initiative and entrepreneurial freedom. As Taft slipped, the conservative cast of the Taft Court grew more entrenched and unyielding.

Taft as a Justice

Notes

1. As Holmes wrote Laski, Taft "did well as a judge." OWH to Harold Laski (July 12, 1921), in 1 HOLMES-LASKI CORRESPONDENCE, at 346. Holmes was suspicious, however, because, "according to the papers," Taft had said that becoming chief justice was "the ambition of his life. I think I wrote what I thought of that kind of ambition as against the aspiration to touch the superlative in one's work. The last I do not expect (between ourselves) from Taft." *Id. See* WHT to Helen Herron Taft (December 26, 1920) (Taft papers) (Taft told Harding that becoming chief justice "had been the ambition of my life.").
2. Apex Hosiery Co. v. Leader, 310 U.S. 469, 498 (1940).
3. 85 F. 271 (6th Cir. 1898).
4. Remarks of Chief Justice Charles Evans Hughes, *Proceedings in Memory of Chief Justice Taft*, 285 U.S. v. xxix–xxx (1930) ("*Proceedings*"). Taft's opinion in *Addyston Pipe* single-handedly revived the Sherman Act after the Court's devastating opinion in United States v. E.C. Knight Co., 156 U.S. 1 (1895). Taft has been called "the greatest contemporary scholar of the relationship between the Sherman Act and the common law of trade restraints." Herbert Hovenkamp, *Labor Conspiracies in American Law, 1880–1930*, 66 TEXAS LAW REVIEW 919, 951 (1988).
5. *See* Thomas v. Cincinnati, N.O. & T.P. Ry. Co., 62 F. 803 (C.C.S.D. Ohio 1894); Toledo, A.A. & N.M. Ry. Co. v. Pennsylvania Co., 54 F.730 (N.D. Ohio 1893); U. M Rose, *The Law of Trusts and Strikes*, in REPORT OF THE SIXTEENTH ANNUAL MEETING OF THE AMERICAN BAR ASSOCIATION 311–14 (Philadelphia: Dando Printing & Publishing Co. 1893); Samuel Gompers, *Taft, The Injunction Standard Bearer*, 14 AMERICAN FEDERATIONIST 785 (1907); Albert de Silver, *The Injunction – A Weapon of Industrial Power*, 114 THE NATION 89, 90 (1922); JOHN P. FREY, THE LABOR INJUNCTION: AN EXPOSITION OF GOVERNMENT BY JUDICIAL CONSCIENCE AND ITS MENACE 14 (Cincinnati: Equity Pub. Co. 1923[?]); Alpheus T. Mason, *The Labor Decisions of Chief Justice Taft*, 78 UNIVERSITY OF PENNSYLVANIA LAW REVIEW 585 (1930); EDWIN E. WITTE, THE GOVERNMENT IN LABOR DISPUTES 38 (New York: McGraw-Hill Book Co. 1932); Haggai Hurvitz, *American Labor Law and the Doctrine of Entrepreneurial Property Rights: Boycotts, Courts, and the Juridical Reorientation of 1886–1895*, 8 INDUSTRIAL RELATIONS LAW JOURNAL 307, 328–32 (1986).

    During his campaign for president, Taft was branded as "the father of injunctions." *Taft Says He Is Sure of Election*, NEW YORK TIMES (October 2, 1908), at 3. *See Taft and Gompers*, NEW YORK TIMES (October 16, 1908), at 8. Taft responded with "his well known comment: 'To be known as the inventor of government by injunction is not a valuable political asset.'" Comments of Arthur C. Denison, *Proceedings*, supra note 4, at xii. *See* William Howard Taft, *Judicial Decisions as an Issue in Politics*, 33 MCCLURE'S MAGAZINE 201 (June 1909).
6. William Howard Taft, *Is Prohibition a Blow at Personal Liberty?*, 36 LADIES HOME JOURNAL 31, 78 (May 1919).
7. WILLIAM HOWARD TAFT, POPULAR GOVERNMENT: ITS ESSENCE, ITS PERMANENCE AND ITS PERILS 9–10 (New Haven: Yale University Press 1913). *See* WILLIAM HOWARD TAFT, LIBERTY UNDER LAW: AN INTERPRETATION OF THE PRINCIPLES OF OUR CONSTITUTIONAL GOVERNMENT 51 (New Haven: Yale University Press 1922).

THE TAFT COURT

8. WILLIAM HOWARD TAFT, THE ANTI-TRUST ACT AND THE SUPREME COURT 37 (New York: Harper & Brothers 1914).
9. William Howard Taft, *Criticism of the Federal Judiciary*, 29 AMERICAN LAW REVIEW 641, 654 (1895).
10. William Howard Taft, *The Right of Private Property*, 3 MICHIGAN LAW REVIEW 215, 220–21 (1894).
11. William Howard Taft, Speech at Minneapolis, Minnesota, February 11, 1920 (Taft papers).
12. TAFT, LIBERTY UNDER LAW, *supra* note 7, at 25–26.
13. William Howard Taft, *Mr. Wilson and the Campaign*, 10 YALE REVIEW 1, 19–20 (1920).
14. WHT to Elihu Root (December 21, 1922) (Taft papers).
15. TAFT, LIBERTY UNDER LAW, *supra* note 7, at 42.
16. WHT to Emory R. Buckner (November 9, 1922) (Taft papers).
17. 258 U.S. 433, 439 (1922). The result of the decision was to make "it impossible for the Juvenile Court of the District of Columbia to punish for non-support." Charles G. Ross, *Decision of U.S. Supreme Court Holding Sentence at Hard Labor Is an "Infamous Punishment,"* ST. LOUIS POST-DISPATCH (April 20, 1922), at 17.
18. 258 U.S. at 441–51 (Brandeis, J., dissenting). Holmes returned the initial draft of Brandeis's dissent with the comment, "A sockdologer. I am with you with both feet." (Brandeis papers). He later added, "I think you have sockdologized our sensitive brother so fully that I marvel that he is not left alone." (Brandeis papers). The majority opinion was written by McKenna.
19. Brandeis papers.
20. WHT to LDB (March 30, 1922) (Taft papers).
21. LDB to WHT (March 30, 1922) (Taft papers).
22. Brandeis papers.
23. 267 U.S. 132 (1925).
24. For the dramatic story of *Carroll*, see *infra* Chapter 32, at 1026–30. *Carroll* well illustrates Taft's forceful leadership of the Court in the years before his 1926 heart attack.
25. 277 U.S. 438 (1928). For a discussion of *Olmstead*, see *infra* Chapter 33. For a good illustration of Taft's managerial instincts in the context of criminal law, which had been honed by his years as a colonial administrator, see William H. Taft, *The Administration of Criminal Law*, 15 YALE LAW JOURNAL 1 (1905).
26. WHT to Henry W. Taft (May 18, 1926) (Taft papers).
27. *See e.g.*, Gorham Manufacturing Co. v. Wendell, 261 U.S. 1, 4 (1923); Woodbridge v. United States, 263 U.S. 50 (1923); FTC v. Klesner, 274 U.S. 145 (1927); United States v. Stone & D. Co., 274 U.S. 225 (1927); Compania General De Tabacos de Filipinas v. Collector of Internal Revenue, 275 U.S. 87 (1927); Richmond Screw Anchor Co. v. United States, 275 U.S. 331 (1928); United States v. Murray, 275 U.S. 347 (1928); Colgate v. United States, 280 U.S. 43 (1929); ICC v. United States *ex rel.* Los Angeles, 280 U.S. 52 (1929).
28. *See, e.g.*, Luckenbach Steamship Co. v. United States, 280 U.S. 173 (1930); United States v. Jackson, 280 U.S. 183 (1930); Myers v. United States, 272 U.S. 52 (1926); *Ex parte* Grossman, 267 U.S. 87 (1925); McConaughey v. Morrow, 263 U.S. 39 (1923).
29. *See, e.g.*, Boston v. Jackson, 260 U.S. 309 (1922); FTC v. Klesner, 274 U.S. 145 (1927); FTC v. Curtis Publishing Co., 260 U.S. 568, 582 (1923) (Taft, C.J., doubting).

Taft as a Justice

30. J.W. Hampton, Jr. & Co. v. United States, 276 U.S. 394, 409 (1928).
31. "The rule as to a definite standard of action is not so strict in cases of the delegation of legislative power to executive boards and officers." Mahler v. Eby, 264 U.S. 32, 41 (1924).
32. Board of Trade of City of Chicago v. Olsen, 262 U.S. 1, 35 (1923).
33. Stafford v. Wallace, 258 U.S. 495, 519 (1922).
34. *Id.* at 521
35. 263 U.S. 456, 476–77, 484–85 (1924). Taft also ruthlessly dismissed the claim that the redistribution of excess profits was a taking of the railroads' property:

    > We have been greatly pressed with the argument that the cutting down of income actually received by the carrier for its service to a so-called fair return is a plain appropriation of its property without any compensation; that the income it receives for the use of its property is as much protected by the Fifth Amendment as the property itself. The statute declares the carrier to be only a trustee for the excess over a fair return received by it. Though in its possession, the excess never becomes its property, and it accepts custody of the product of all the rates with this understanding. It is clear, therefore, that the carrier never has such a title to the excess as to render the recapture of it by the government a taking without due process.

    Id. at 484.
36. 261 U.S. 525, 562–63 (1923) (Taft, C.J., dissenting).
37. *Inaugural Address of President Taft*, 44 Cong. Rec. 3 (March 4, 1909). As president, Taft conceded that courts "have unduly broadened constitutional restrictions in order to invalidate useful statutes, or have given such statutes a wrong construction. Indeed, I do not hesitate to say that I do not concur in the reasoning of certain courts of last resort as to the constitutional validity of certain social reform statutes, and I am very anxious that the remedies proposed in these statutes should be given effective operation." William H. Taft, *The Judiciary and Progress* (March 8, 1912), Sen. Doc. No. 408, 62nd Cong. 2nd Sess., at 5. *See* Edward Hartnett, *Why Is the Supreme Court of the United States Protecting State Judges from Popular Democracy*, 75 Texas Law Review 907, 949–56 (1997) (arguing that Taft supported the Act of December 23, 1914, Pub. L. 63-224, 38 Stat. 790, which authorized Supreme Court review of state court decisions against the validity of a state statute or authority alleged to be repugnant to the Constitution, in order to "defuse the pressure for radical reform" like the recall of judges and judicial decisions).
38. Doris Kearns Goodwin, The Bully Pulpit: Theodore Roosevelt, William Howard Taft, and the Golden Age of Journalism 704 (New York: Simon & Schuster 2013).
39. Taft, *supra* note 8, at 34.
40. Holmes did use the phrase ironically. *See* Springer v. Government of Philippine Islands, 277 U.S. 189, 211 (1928) (Holmes, J., dissenting).
41. Bailey v. Drexel Furniture Co., 259 U.S. 20, 37 (1922).
42. 257 U.S. 312, 338 (1921).
43. Quoted in Henry F. Pringle, 1 The Life and Times of William Howard Taft: A Biography 350 (New York: Farrar & Rinehart, Inc. 1939).
44. *Inaugural Address of President Taft*, *supra* note 37, at 5. *See* Taft, *supra* note 5, at 201 (discussing Taft's labor decisions).

45. ADDRESS OF PRESIDENT TAFT AT THE BANQUET OF THE UNION LEAGUE CLUB OF NEW YORK (Washington D.C. January 4, 1913) ("UNION LEAGUE ADDRESS"), at 8.
46. "We were beaten in the last election. We ran third in the race. Why is it that we gather here with so much spirit and with so little of the disappointment and humiliation supposed to accompany political disaster? Is it not that in spite of the defeat recorded at the election in November we were still victorious in saving our country from an administration whose policy involved the sapping of the foundations of democratic, constitutional, representative government, whose appeals to the people were calculated to arouse class hatred that has heretofore been the ruin of popular government, and whose contempt for the limitations of constitutional law and the guaranties of civil liberty promised chaos and anarchy in a country that has until this time been the model of individual freedom and effective popular government?" *Id.*
47. *Id.* at 11–12.
48. Taft conceived the tension between using constitutional rights to protect the "individual initiative and enterprise and reward" upon which "our progress" depends and yet liberally construing the Constitution so as to preserve "elasticity of . . . constitutional restraints" to be inherent in government. The trick was to ensure that "where men use their right of liberty or their right of property in such combination as to give them power by duress arbitrarily to control others, the liberty of the individual and his right of property are subject to reasonable governmental control." *Taft Tells Minneapolitans What Constitutes True and Ideal Americanism*, MINNEAPOLIS STAR TRIBUNE (February 12, 1920), at 6.
49. *Id.*
50. UNION LEAGUE ADDRESS, *supra* note 45, at 5.
51. 278 U.S. 24, 31 (1928).
52. "Mr. Justice McReynolds is of opinion that the action of the Board of Public Utility Commissioners was unreasonable and arbitrary, and should be set aside. To permit the commissioners to impose a charge of $100,000 upon the railroad . . . is to uphold what he regards as plain abuse of power." *Id.* at 41.
53. *Lehigh Valley Ry.*, 278 U.S. at 34. "It is not for the court to cut down such expenditures, merely because more economical ways suggest themselves. The board has the discretion to fix the cost. The function of the court is to determine whether the outlay involved in the order of the board is extravagant, in the light of all the circumstances, in view of the importance of the crossing, of the danger to be avoided, of the probable permanence of the improvement and of the prospect of enlarged capacity to be required in the near future and other considerations similarly relevant." *Id.* at 33.
54. *Id.* at 34.
55. *Id.* Taft remarked that "The case before us is one which is near the line of reasonableness, but . . . we think it does not go beyond the line." *Id.* at 35. "This is not to be construed," Taft warned, "as meaning that danger to the public will justify great expenditures, unreasonably burdening the railroad, when less expenditure can reasonably accomplish the object of the improvements and avoid the danger. If the danger is clear, reasonable care must be taken to eliminate it, and the police power may be exerted to that end. But it becomes the duty of the court, where the cost is questioned, to determine whether it is within reasonable limits." *Id.* at 34.
56. *Id.* at 34–35.

Taft as a Justice

57. William H. Taft, *The Selection and Tenure of Judges*, 7 MAINE LAW REVIEW 203, 208–9 (1914):

> It has been my official duty to look into the judiciary of each state, in my search for candidates to be appointed to federal judgeships, and I affirm without hesitation that in states where many of the elected judges in the past have had high rank, the introduction by direct primary has distinctly injured the character of the Bench for learning, courage and ability. . . . The result of the present tendency is seen in the disgraceful exhibitions of men campaigning for the place of state supreme judge and asking votes, on the ground that their decisions will have a particular class flavor. This is the logical development of the view that a popular election is the only basis for determining right and justice; but it is so shocking, and so out of keeping with the fixedness of moral principles which we learned at our mother's knee, and which find recognition in the conscience of every man who has grown up under proper influence, that we ought to condemn without stint a system which can encourage or permit such demagogic methods of securing judicial position. Through the class antagonism unjustly stirred up against the courts, fiery faction is now to be introduced into the popular election of judges. Men are to be made judges not because they are impartial, but because they are advocates; not because they are judicial, but because they are partisan.
>
> It is true that politics have played a part even when judges have been appointed. They have usually been taken from the lawyers of the prevailing party. . . . This has not, however, resulted in political courts, because the control of the government has naturally changed from one party to another in the course of a generation and has normally brought to the Bench judges selected from both parties.

It is notable that Taft's understanding of an apolitical bench was one that was neutral as between political parties, not one that was neutral with regard to disputes about the nature and role of property. *See* Brandeis's comment, *supra* Chapter 3, at 61–62.

58. Taft himself often contrasted the legitimacy he expected to be accorded to judicial decisions with the accountability that he learned (to his dismay) was demanded of politicians. Speaking to Republicans at the end of his disastrous 1912 campaign, Taft observed that "I have been used as a judge to rely upon the publicity of the judgment and opinion to justify the action taken. In executive life, however, it needs great and special effort to secure the publicity that is essential to meet the attacks of misinformed or prejudiced critics. And so it has been that, lacking in this effort, I have had to bear the burden of being thought by the people to be a very different man from that which I think I have been." UNION LEAGUE ADDRESS, *supra* note 45, at 7. *See* William H. Taft, *Personal Aspects of the Presidency*, 186 SATURDAY EVENING POST 6, 32 (February 28, 1914) ("The president should devote close attention to the proper methods of getting to as wide a circle of readers as possible the facts and reasons sustaining his policies and official acts, in order that he may have the support of public opinion in working useful results. I must confess that I was lacking in attention to matters of this kind and was derelict. Both my predecessor and my successor have been far wiser and more careful in this regard. Perhaps it was another result of that judicial training to which I have referred. When the judgment of the court was announced and the opinion was filed it was supposed that all parties in interest would inform themselves as to the reasons for the action taken. Newspaper men and other publishers and writers for the public know, however, that the people do not learn facts and arguments on any subjects by one announcement, and that it needs a constant effort of iteration and reiteration to send the matter home to the people whom it is wished to reach.").

Although Taft was temperamentally inclined to de-emphasize the work of persuasion or explanation in ensuring public uptake of judicial decisions, when Walter Lippmann asked Taft whether it would "not be possible, at the time a decision is handed down to have enough copies available so that correspondents of the interested newspapers could obtain them at once," Walter Lippmann to WHT (January 5, 1925) (Taft papers), Taft promptly replied that "I shall have great pleasure in doing what I can to help you in the matter of getting accurately the statement of what our Court decides in important cases. ... I have felt that your editorial column, like that of many others, has suffered for lack of something like this." WHT to Walter Lippmann (January 8, 1925) (Taft papers). *See* WHT to WVD (July 4, 1925) (Taft papers).

59. For a full discussion, see *infra* Chapter 21.

CHAPTER 11

Myers v. United States

THE SIDE OF Taft that prized government efficiency and managerial authority is perhaps best illustrated by his opinions concerning executive power. In decisions like *J.W. Hampton, Jr. v. United States*[1] or *McConaughey v. Morrow*,[2] Taft sought to expand executive discretion in the service of administrative effectiveness. This inclination is not surprising, given that Taft is the only justice ever to have served as president of the United States. That unique experience is most evident in the "epoch-making"[3] and "landmark"[4] decision of *Myers v. United States*,[5] which Taft considered "one of the most important opinions I have ever written."[6]

The precise question in *Myers* was "whether under the Constitution the President has the exclusive power of removing executive officers of the United States whom he has appointed by and with the advice and consent of the Senate."[7] *Myers* was the first decision in the history of the nation to invalidate on constitutional grounds a congressional statute because it impaired the inherent Article II power of the president. It was as if fate itself had reserved *Myers* until Taft could take his seat at the center of the Court.

Frank Myers, a 37-year-old Democratic activist, was appointed to a four-year term as the first-class postmaster of Portland, Oregon, in April 1913.[8] After an uneventful first term, Myers was reappointed in July 1917. Myers's tenure soon became engulfed in controversy, however, and in January 1920 President Wilson decided to fire him.[9] At the time, the removal of first-class postmasters was governed by an 1876 statute providing that first-class postmasters "shall be appointed and may be removed by the President by and with the advice and consent of the Senate."[10]

Presidents in the past had easily obtained senatorial consent by nominating a successor postmaster. Upon confirming the nomination, the Senate was understood to consent to the removal of the prior incumbent. But for reasons that remain obscure, Wilson refused to nominate a successor or in any other way seek to obtain the consent of the Senate to Myers's removal.[11] Myers therefore sued for the remainder of his salary, some $8,838.72. He lost in the Court of Claims in 1923 on the ground of laches,[12] which was a patent attempt to evade the underlying constitutional issue of whether the president could remove Myers despite contrary congressional legislation.

Myers died in 1924, and his estate continued the litigation.[13] The case was first argued on December 5, 1924.[14] James M. Beck, as solicitor general, appeared for the government, but no one argued Myers's side of the case.[15] Beck effectively conceded that the Court of Claims had incorrectly decided the issue of laches.[16] It appeared that the great constitutional question of presidential removal power could not be avoided.

Knowing that McKenna had agreed to step down from the bench in January,[17] the Court set *Myers* for rehearing. Not only was *Myers* too important a decision to be decided by an incomplete bench, but the Court also believed that the constitutionality of the statute ought to be defended by qualified counsel. Two days after the December 5 argument, Taft wrote Attorney General Harlan Stone that "[t]he Court, after Conference, authorized me to speak to Senator Cummins as the head of the Judiciary Committee, and also incidentally the President of the Senate, to see whether they could not suggest some one to appear at the re-argument as an *amicus curiae*. I hope you will bring this matter to the attention of Beck, and possibly as Attorney General confer with Senator Cummins in respect to what can be done to facilitate a re-argument, with a proper *amicus curiae*."[18] When Cummins concluded that "it was not practicable to ask the Senate to authorize the selection of one or more of its members to appear as an amicus curiae,"[19] the Court itself designated as amicus "to present the views of the legislative branch of the government"[20] the distinguished Republican senator from Pennsylvania, George Wharton Pepper.[21] Reargument of *Myers* was set for April 13–14, 1925, a month after Stone assumed his seat on the bench.[22]

As president, Taft had often encountered the requirements of the statute of 1876. He had sought to remove at least 175 postmasters, always scrupulously adhering to the statute even when the Senate refused to consent to requested removals.[23] He never once challenged the constitutionality of the statute, even though he strongly believed that presidents had the duty and authority constitutionally to interpret the "extent and limitations" of executive power.[24]

Strikingly, Taft had urged Congress to put all postmasters, including first-class postmasters like Myers, "into the classified service" and so remove "the necessity for confirmation by the Senate."[25] "Machine politics and the spoils system," Taft explained, "are as much an enemy of a proper and efficient government system of civil service as the boll weevil is of the cotton crop."[26] Taft had even gone so far as to comply with congressional legislation forbidding removal of members of the Board of General Appraisers in the absence of a showing of "neglect of duty, malfeasance in office, or inefficiency,"[27] commissioning a Board of Inquiry that included Felix Frankfurter to make the necessary statutory findings of malfeasance.[28]

After 1912, Taft was criticized for his legalistic conception of the presidency. Theodore Roosevelt asserted in 1913 that a president ought to adopt a "stewardship" theory of executive leadership:

> My view was that every executive officer, and above all every executive officer in a high position, was a steward of the people bound actively and

affirmatively to do all he could for the people.... I declined to adopt the view that what was imperatively necessary for the Nation could not be done by the President unless he could find some specific authorization to do it. My belief was that it was not only his right but his duty to do anything that the needs of the Nation demanded unless such action was forbidden by the Constitution or by the laws.[29]

Roosevelt contrasted his stewardship theory with the "Buchanan-Taft" school of the "power and duties of the President," which Roosevelt believed converted the chief executive into "the servant of Congress rather than of the people."[30]

Roosevelt rejected the view that the president "can do nothing, no matter how necessary it be to act, unless the Constitution explicitly commands the action." Roosevelt illustrated the contrast between himself and Taft by reference to the removal power. He asserted that the president should form his own judgment of his subordinates without recognizing "the right of Congress to interfere ... excepting by impeachment or in other Constitutional manner." Taft, Roosevelt cruelly alleged, had "permitted and requested Congress to pass judgment on the charges made against Mr. Ballinger as an executive officer."[31]

Taft was stung by Roosevelt's attack, and in 1916 he sought to answer it explicitly and directly.[32] He thought that Roosevelt's "ascribing an undefined residuum of power to the President is an unsafe doctrine and that it might lead under emergencies to results of an arbitrary character."[33] "The true view of the Executive function is, as I conceive it, that the President can exercise no power which cannot be fairly and reasonably traced to some specific grant of power or justly implied and included within such express grant as proper and necessary to its exercise. Such specific grant must be either in the Federal Constitution or in an act of Congress passed in pursuance thereof. There is no undefined residuum of power which he can exercise because it seems to him to be in the public interest."[34] Taft believed that his own view of the constitutional presidency was quite broad enough to "give the President wide discretion and great power, and it ought to. It calls from him activity and energy to see that within his proper sphere he does what his great responsibilities and opportunities require."[35]

Although Taft deeply believed in a "law-governed presidency,"[36] he was also clear that the president was "no figurehead."[37] The president was for Taft clothed with robust authority to carry out the many duties assigned to him by the Constitution.[38] Taft was in fact committed to "a generous interpretation of executive power."[39] He affirmed that when acting within his proper sphere, the president was not at all subordinate to Congress. "The rule seems to be that Congress may not control by legislation the constitutional powers of the President when the legislation in any way limits the discretion which the Constitution plainly confers."[40]

So, for example, President Taft became known as "the father of administrative reorganization and of the executive budget."[41] He believed that the president himself, rather than any department head, ought to be responsible for the federal budget,[42] because he conceived the president as the "general manager of the administration."[43] Congress, fearing loss of authority, resisted Taft's efforts to standardize budgetary practices. In 1912, Congress "put a rider in the appropriation bill directing that in effect no heads of departments, no bureau chiefs and no clerks should be used for the preparation of estimates in any other form than as that directed by the existing statutes."[44] "This was for the purpose," Taft explained, "of preventing my submitting to Congress the estimates for government expenses in the form different from that of the statutes and in accordance with the budget principle."[45] "When the heads of departments applied to me to know what they should do, I directed them to prepare the estimates under the old plan as required by statute and also to prepare the budget as recommended by my Commission [on Economy and Efficiency], and to ignore this restriction, which Congress had attempted to impose."[46]

Taft was quite explicit that he defied the congressional restriction "on the ground that it was my constitutional duty to submit to Congress information and recommendations and Congress could not prevent me from using my subordinates in the discharge of such a duty."[47] As he explained to Congress:

> Under the Constitution, the power to control the purse is given to the Congress. But the same paragraph which makes it the duty of the Congress to determine what expenditures shall be authorized also requires of the administration the submission of "a regular statement and account of the receipts and expenditures" – i.e., an account of stewardship. The Constitution also prescribes that the President shall "from time to time give to the Congress information of the state of the Union and recommend to their consideration such measures as he shall judge necessary and expedient." Pursuant to these constitutional requirements I am submitting for your consideration a concise statement of financial conditions and results as an account of stewardship as well as certain proposals with estimates of revenues and expenditures in the form of a budget.[48]

Taft was similarly adamant about the president's removal power. He affirmed in 1916 that "[i]t was settled, as long ago as the first Congress ... that even where the advice and consent of the Senate was necessary to the appointment of an officer, the President had the absolute power to remove him without consulting the Senate. This was on the principle that the power of removal was incident to the Executive power and must be untrammeled."[49] Taft noted that Congress had attempted to reverse "this principle of long standing by the Tenure of Office Act in Andrew Johnson's time," but that this temporary aberration was caused by "partisan anger against Mr. Johnson. ... It never came before the courts directly in a such a way as to invoke a decision on its validity, but there are plain intimations in the opinion of the Supreme Court that Congress exceeded its legislative discretion in the act."[50]

It is plain, then, that Taft did not approach the *Myers* case as a blank slate. He held definite and strong preconceptions about presidential removal power, which he viewed "through executive-colored glasses."[51] He would bring to *Myers* the entire weight of his presidential experience.

According to Butler's docket book, the Court voted on the case in conference on April 25, 1925. Butler recorded cryptic notes about the position of each justice. Taft spoke first and declared that the case could not be decided on the ground of

Myers v. United States

laches. No one disagreed with him. On the constitutional question, Taft argued that the president's authority to remove was an "ex[ecutive] power" and could not be restrained by the Senate's advice and consent. Holmes thought that the statute should "stand." Van Devanter voted to affirm the "exec[utive] power" of the president. McReynolds was uncertain and passed. Brandeis agreed with Holmes. Sutherland, Butler, and Sanford agreed with Taft. Butler records Stone as voting to affirm the Court of Claims, saying "entitled to look at consequences."[52] Taft assigned the opinion to himself, reporting to his son the next day that because he had a "very important" case to write, he would "be fully occupied" during the subsequent "five weeks."[53]

By mid-May, Taft concluded that he would need to take the entire summer to write the opinion. "Its importance justifies it."[54] In July, Taft reported to Van Devanter that he was "reading Webster and Madison and the speeches of some others on the subject."[55] Yet in August Taft wryly commented to Sutherland from his summer home in Murray Bay, Canada, that "My constitutional post office case I have on my shelves up here with a lot of volumes that I brought, and I see them every day, and have been quite able, without any injury to my conscience, to look at the backs of the volumes and not examine them."[56] "I haven't opened the books on the executive power case," he confessed to Van Devanter four days later, "but must tackle it shortly."[57]

On September 1, Taft wrote his law clerk Hayden Smith asking if Smith could research "the meaning of the words 'Executive power' as contained in Article II, Section I."[58] Two weeks later, he wrote Butler that "the more I think it over, the stronger I am in the necessity for our reaching the conclusion that we have. I agree that in the beginning it might have been decided either way, but it was decided in favor of the view that the Constitution vested the executive power of removal in the president, with only the exceptions that appear in the instrument itself. My experience in the executive office satisfies me that it would be a great mistake to change that view and give to the Senate any greater power of hampering the President and tying him down than they have under the view we voted to recognize as the proper one." Confiding to the Democrat Butler, Taft remarked:

> As I study the injustice that the radical Republicans did to Andrew Johnson, I am humiliated as a Republican. My father was a just man but I thought he sympathized with those who voted to impeach Johnson. I think the feeling against Johnson growing out of the assassination of Lincoln threw into the extremists of the Republican party a power that led to reconstruction and seriously affected to its detriment our country. I think this is usually thought to be the case, and certainly we ought not to allow such a departure from a long established constitutional construction to influence us in a wise interpretation, enforced by a Congress that was almost a part of the Constitutional Convention and whose decision lasted without any real controversy from the first Congress down to the one that was controlled by a militant, triumphant and harsh political group.[59]

Taft drafted a "long opinion" while on vacation at Murray Bay, but after returning to Washington he found that "it does not satisfy me as I read it through, and I have had to do some more reading."[60] By November he was ready to run it by Van Devanter. "I thought that after you had read it, I would ask Stone, Sutherland, Pierce and yourself to have a little conference with me, say Sunday afternoon, to make such suggestions as may occur before I revise it again and circulate it."[61] The next day Taft also invited Sanford to the Sunday conference.[62] Two days after the conference he circulated "a revised copy of the opinion" and asked Van Devanter, Sutherland, Butler, Sanford, and Stone to "read it over and make as many suggestions as you can."[63] Three days later Taft expressed "relief to get the heavy part of [the opinion] out of the way,"[64] and the hope that he would "be able to circulate it early next week."[65]

At this point the documentary record becomes rather more obscure. Stone's law clerk at the time, Alfred McCormack, recalls that Taft named Stone, Butler, and Van Devanter "as a Committee to help with the majority opinion." McCormack remembers that Stone was exasperated by Taft's draft, remarking that "There is nothing left to do with this opinion ... except to rewrite it."

> Accordingly he directed his clerk to go through the opinion and outline the points, arranging them in a logical order. That done, and Stone having revised the outline, the next job was to take the printed proof and a pair of scissors and arrange the material according to the outline, deleting, and where necessary combining and rewriting, to remove duplications, and introducing each point by a topic or transitional sentence.
>
> From that beginning Stone prepared and submitted to Van Devanter and Butler, a new draft of the opinion that was widely different from the original in arrangement and emphasis, with many additions, deletions and revisions of language. The Committee was pleased, and Stone was commissioned to wait upon the Chief and submit the new draft as their joint recommendation. Taft received the document with grace and promised to read it; and later he sent a warm note of thanks, praising Stone's work and adopting the revision as a substitute for his previous draft.[66]

In Stone's papers, there is a November 13 memorandum to Taft, offering numerous editorial recommendations.[67] "I hope you will realize that my suggestions ... are due to the feeling that this is one of the most important opinions of the Court in a generation at least."[68] On November 22, Taft wrote his son that he had circulated a draft of his opinion and was "awaiting the result to see how many will stand by it."[69] There is a second memorandum from Stone to Taft dated November 24, in which Stone appears to have numbered and rearranged the paragraphs in Taft's draft.[70] Apparently after circulation Stone had undertaken to "survey the whole opinion from the point of view of the proper emphasis,"[71] offering basic structural suggestions for reorganization.[72] Four days later Taft wrote his brother to complain that the Court's "youngest member Stone is intensely interested and is a little bit fussy and captious in respect to form of statement, and

Myers v. United States

betrays in some degree a little of the legal school master – a tendency which experience in the Court is likely to moderate."[73]

Taft was in an ungenerous mood because "Brandeis has announced his intention of writing a dissent," and Holmes "is likely to concur with him."[74] Taft did not "know what McReynolds will do. I think he is inclined to go with us, but he objects to long opinions, and he is cantankerous at any rate. He may write a concurring opinion, and he may dissent, although I think not the latter."[75]

Taft was frank to acknowledge that the "opinion has given me a great deal of work and a great deal of anxiety. The rest of the Court have stood by me well and have helped me in going over it and making corrections and suggestions." "The opinion has had to be very long," Taft explained, "because half of it is taken up in an historical review, which is most important in confirming the conclusion. I have been rearranging it some since I circulated it, and have attempted to make the steps in the reasoning more orderly, with a view of enabling the reader to follow the argument more intelligently. I presume it will be the subject of great discussion and doubtless of much criticism."[76] The following day Taft confided to his son that the opinion "has occupied me very intensely, and has been the occasion for my losing some sleep. Those members who agree with me have helped me. When one works on a case all alone and gets very much absorbed, he is not quite sure whether he has lost his sense of proportion as to arguments in the pressure to state them all."[77]

On November 30, Taft received yet a third detailed memorandum from Stone.[78] Stone was worried by *United States v. Perkins,* an 1886 precedent in which the Court had upheld the suit of a naval officer challenging his honorable dismissal by the secretary of the navy on the ground that legislation provided that "no officer in the military or naval service shall in time of peace be dismissed from service except upon and in pursuance of the sentence of a court-martial to that effect." The Court explicitly endorsed the language of the Court of Claims below:

> Whether or not Congress can restrict the power of removal incident to the power of appointment of those officers who are appointed by the President by and with the advice and consent of the Senate, under the authority of the Constitution, (article 2, section 2,) does not arise in this case, and need not be considered. We have no doubt that when Congress, by law, vests the appointment of inferior officers in the heads of Departments, it may limit and restrict the power of removal as it deems best for the public interest. The constitutional authority in Congress to thus vest the appointment implies authority to limit, restrict, and regulate the removal by such laws as Congress may enact in relation to the officers so appointed. The head of a Department has no constitutional prerogative of appointment to offices independently of the legislation of Congress, and by such legislation he must be governed, not only in making appointments, but in all that is incident thereto.[79]

Perkins was the constitutional rock on which the federal civil service was erected, for *Perkins* held that whenever Congress exercised its authority under Article II, Section 2, to vest the appointment of "inferior Officers" in the "Heads of

Departments," it could restrain executive discretion by regulating the terms on which such inferior officers might be removed.

Stone was "somewhat concerned" that under *Perkins* Congress could "vest the appointment of all officers other than those specifically enumerated in Article II, in the heads of departments, but with limitations on the power of removal both by the head of the department and by the President."[80] Stone was "extremely loathe to admit that Congress could set such a limitation on the President's power in the case of purely executive officers on whom he must depend for the execution of the laws." He stressed, therefore, that *Perkins* "said nothing as to the power of the President to remove an inferior officer appointed by the head of a department." He wanted to be sure that in his draft Taft did not inadvertently read *Perkins* to imply that the president lost his "power of removal in the case of purely executive officers," even if the president did not appoint them.[81] The logic of Stone's memorandum threatened to undermine the legal architecture of the civil service.[82]

Taft was apparently irritated that Stone "continues to harp" on his point about *Perkins*. Later that week he wrote Van Devanter, "Stone continues to tinker, but I don't think he helps much." Pondering his response, Taft speculated to Van Devanter, "I might say something like this: 'The Solicitor General has argued that the general grant of executive power to the President gives him the right to remove all Executive officers whether appointed by him or not. We do not find it necessary to consider or discuss this claim. Our conclusions as stated sufficiently dispose of the case.'"[83] No such passage, however, appears in the published version of *Myers*.[84] Nevertheless Taft wrote Stone the following day graciously thanking him for his comments:

> I thank you for the trouble you have taken to help me in the Myers case opinion. I agree with you that we have not had a case in two generations of more importance. It looks now as if we would stand 6 to 3, but if it were 5 to 4, I should be happy for my country that by even so small a margin we could prevent the excesses of congressional action which in view of the McCarl statute[85] we would have to expect. I have adopted your suggestions generally except when Van Devanter anticipated you. There may be one or two instances in which I rather preferred my own phrases when they were equivalent. . . .
>
> As to the President's power to remove all executive officers whether their appointment be vested in the Courts of Law or in the Heads of Departments or not, I do not think we decide it and as it is not necessary for us to decide it, I think we should not mention it. That is Van's judgment about it too.[86]

Taft then settled down to await Brandeis's dissenting opinion.[87] On December 23, Pepper filed with the Court the recently delivered decision of the Pennsylvania Supreme Court in *Commonwealth ex. Rel. Woodruff v. Benn*,[88] which held that the governor could not unilaterally remove a member of the Pennsylvania Public Service Commission whose tenure was protected by legislation prohibiting removal without cause and requiring "the consent of the Senate."[89] The Pennsylvania court reasoned that "Public Service Commissioners must be viewed as deputies of the General Assembly to perform legislative work."[90] Taft wrote Van Devanter that *Benn* "is not important except to suggest that the removal of Interstate

Myers v. United States

Commerce Commissioners doing legislative work may be different from members of purely executive boards and therefore not seemingly included in our decision."[91]

On January 5, 1926, Brandeis finally circulated his dissent. "I thought mine was pretty long," Taft wrote his brother,

> but his is 41 pages with an enormous number of fine print notes, and with citations from statutes without number. So far as I can make it out from a most cursory examination, his chief objection to our opinion is the merit system of the Civil Service. As Congress has complete power to give every inferior office for appointment by the head of a department, and then make provision for the removal, or absence of it, as it chooses, it is a little difficult to see how our conclusion with reference to the power of removal by the President in respect to superior officers has any real application to the question that we have to consider.[92]

Taft then received news that "McReynolds thinks he has to write a dissenting opinion, and wishes to spread himself."[93] McReynolds estimated that his opinion would not be ready until March.[94] "McReynolds," Taft wrote his son, "is always inconsiderate. There is no reason why he should not have written his opinion before, because he knew that Brandeis took the last recess to prepare his."[95]

McReynolds apparently circulated his dissent by March 29, for there is yet another long memorandum on that date from Stone analyzing the opinions of McReynolds and Brandeis.[96] Although Stone had "very little to suggest about" McReynolds's dissent,[97] he devoted six detailed pages to dissecting that of Brandeis.[98] Stone took particular exception to Brandeis's assertion that although "Power to remove, as well as to suspend, a high political officer, might conceivably be deemed indispensable to democratic government and, hence, inherent in the President," the "power to remove an inferior administrative officer appointed for a fixed term cannot conceivably be deemed an essential of government."[99] Stone commented:

> It is difficult to see on what basis this distinction is based unless it be his assumption that the laws can be executed even though incompetent, disloyal, inferior officers be kept in office. Certainly President Lincoln found out differently during the Civil War and the experience of the Government in that time, and especially in the previous administration, points out the fallacy of the assumption that power of removal of inferior officers in the head of departments, either with or without the consent of the Senate, is an adequate provision for the execution of the laws without any reserve power in the President to remove inferior officers regardless of the consent of the Senate.[100]

Stone was also mystified by Brandeis's elaborate invocation of history.

> The opinion appears to be devoted principally to showing that a construction of the Constitution made by Congress in many pieces of legislation is the one which we must adopt because Congress adopted it, and incidentally

because from time to time various presidents did not veto the legislation and sometimes complied with it. Of course inferring presidential acquiescence in a particular construction of the Constitution because presidents did not veto the bills involving that construction or refuse to comply with them is going rather far. Assuming, however, such assent on the part of the executive, I think nevertheless that the whole dissent proceeds on a fallacy.... Congress has no power to change the Constitution. Neither have Congress and the President acting together. Therefore, no more or greater weight can be given to their acquiescence in a particular construction of the Constitution than it is entitled to by its inherent merits.

From this point of view, the value of the early legislative construction of the power of removal lies chiefly in the fact that it occurred soon after the Convention when its events were fresh in mind and the events in Congress, so far as known, developed nothing to indicate that the Congressional construction was a radical departure from the wishes of the Convention.[101]

Taft recognized that the dissents were "very forcibly expressed," and that he would "have to devote my attention to shaping up my opinion and getting it ready for delivery," which he proposed to do "as soon as we get through the hearings" in early May.[102] But in June Taft suffered his heart attack, and he "concluded to take [the opinion] up to Murray Bay and perhaps revamp it, in view of the dissents. I hope I can do this without subjecting myself to intense labors."[103]

At first Taft found it difficult to concentrate. "I am very anxious to revamp my opinion in the Myers case before I go down to Washington, but I can not do anything about it until I feel more at liberty to use my brain in a way that really calls for the proper circulation of the blood."[104] "I have been turning it over in my mind," he wrote Van Devanter. "I think I shall rearrange the opinion by stating first the necessary effect of the Congressional decision of 1789 and the 74 or 75 years of acquiescence in that decision. I am well satisfied with the conclusion reached that evening that we met at my house, that it is well not to make any concession but to take the position that we have already taken – that with that decision and with the obvious abuse of the Tenure of Office Act we can make such a contrast as to make clear the wisdom of our view."[105] By August, however, Taft still had not "yet tackled the job of revamping the opinion."[106]

Taft settled down to serious editing by the end of the month, reporting to Sutherland that "I am working now on a revamping of my opinion ... and shall hope to be able to have it printed and submitted to the five concurring Judges for consideration and criticism before recirculating it. It is likely to be considerably longer, because the discussion in the two dissenting opinions have required some amplification and the consideration of some additional points."[107] Taft finished a first draft of his revisions on September 6,[108] noting that it was "outrageously long."[109] Taft wrote his brother that he hoped "to get back a proof of it before I leave here, so as to see what I can do in cutting it down, for I find that the putting of an opinion in print gives you a better general view of it and furnishes you more opportunity for suggestions of useful changes than if it is typewritten. It is a good method of correcting and revising opinions, although Justice McReynolds

Myers v. United States

complains that most of us do not allow ourselves to be economical in this matter. But these opinions are important, and any means of making them better should not be spared."[110]

Taft sent a second draft of the opinion to the printer on September 20, with instructions to have a revised proof ready for his arrival in Washington on September 25 so that Taft could rapidly revise it and circulate amended copies "to some of my brethren."[111] Taft sent out the revised print on September 28 to Van Devanter, Sutherland, Butler, Sanford, and Stone.[112] "I hope," Taft wrote his brother, that "this is the last stretch."[113] The opinion "has been a very great burden to me, a kind of nightmare, and I shall be greatly relieved when the announcement is made."[114] "I shall feel like a woman who has given birth to a child."[115]

Apparently at the last moment Stone sent yet another long memorandum to Taft on the significance of *Perkins*.[116] Reprising his arguments of the previous year, Stone pleaded with Taft to modify his opinion to disavow the implication of *Perkins* that by legislatively investing the appointment of inferior officers in heads of departments, "the legislature acquired the power to regulate the removal even by the President." In effect, Stone was once again asking Taft to cast constitutional doubt on civil service restrictions. This Taft refused to do.[117]

Taft, who was personally quite committed to the civil service,[118] explained in his opinion that the "evil of the spoils system" concerned "inferior offices," and insofar as appointments with regard to such offices "were vested in the heads of departments to which they belong, they could be entirely removed from politics."[119] Taft appeared to suggest that the power of removal was a function of the executive power of appointment:

> The power to remove inferior executive officers, like that to remove superior executive officers, is an incident of the power to appoint them, and is in its nature an executive power. The authority of Congress given by the excepting clause to vest the appointment of such inferior officers in the heads of departments carries with it authority incidentally to invest the heads of departments with power to remove. It has been the practice of Congress to do so and this court has recognized that power. The court also has recognized in the Perkins Case that Congress, in committing the appointment of such inferior officers to the heads of departments, may prescribe incidental regulations controlling and restricting the latter in the exercise of the power of removal.[120]

Having laid to rest Stone's "logical qualms,"[121] Taft was at last ready to release his great decision. *Myers* was set for announcement on October 25. The night before Taft wrote his son with barely concealed excitement: "Tomorrow I expect to deliver the most important and critical opinion that I have written on the Court."[122]

It would be accurate to say that the *Myers* opinion was constructed through a most unusual process. I know of nothing analogous during the entire Taft Court era.[123] Taft essentially constituted his majority of six into a committee that met twice at his home to discuss the holding, structure, and argument of Taft's opinion.[124] No doubt this was in part because Taft keenly appreciated the enormous importance of the case, which would settle a fundamental question of executive power that had remained open and controversial since the dawn of the Republic but that "now ... has been brought up by the obstinacy of Wilson and Burleson in removing a man and for two years sending no appointment to the Senate for his successor."[125]

Myers's unusual process of composition also signified the great difficulty Taft experienced in summoning adequate forms of constitutional argument. In recent times, the reasoning of *Myers* has been claimed by no less an authority than Antonin Scalia as "a prime example of what, in current scholarly discourse, is known as the 'originalist' approach to constitutional interpretation."[126] Scalia no doubt refers to the fact that Taft, faced with a constitutional text that says nothing at all about the power to remove executive officials, spent a great deal of time and effort explicating what he called the "decision of 1789,"[127] in which the first Congress drafted a statute which presumed that the president was empowered unconditionally to remove the secretary for the Department of Foreign Affairs (the equivalent of the modern secretary of state).[128]

Unlike a modern originalist, however, Taft was unwilling to rest his conclusion entirely on evidence of original meaning. To the contrary, Taft explicitly explained, "We have devoted much space to this discussion and decision of the question of the Presidential power of removal in the First Congress, not because a Congressional conclusion on a constitutional issue is conclusive, but ... because of our agreement with the reasons upon which it was avowedly based."[129] To Taft, *Myers*'s conclusion was supported by "very sound and practical reasons"[130] that he sought elaborately to explicate. Taft invoked a thoroughly purposive and pragmatic interpretation of the Constitution to explain the holding of *Myers*.

"[T]hose in charge of and responsible for administering the functions of government who select their executive subordinates," Taft argued, "need in meeting their responsibility to have the power to remove those whom they appoint." "Made responsible under the Constitution for the effective enforcement of the law, the President needs as an indispensable aid to meet it the disciplinary influence upon those who act under him of a reserve power of removal." It followed that the "imperative reasons requiring an unrestricted power to remove the most important of his subordinates in their most important duties must ... control the interpretation of the Constitution as to all appointed by him." Any other construction of the Constitution, Taft asserted, "would make it impossible for the President, in case of political or other differences with the Senate or Congress, to take care that the laws be faithfully executed."[131]

In a long and furious dissent,[132] McReynolds took sharp issue with Taft's functional logic.[133] He excoriated "the hollowness of the suggestion that a right to remove" inferior officers like postmasters "may be inferred from the President's duty to 'take care that the laws be faithfully executed.'"[134] From 1789 through 1836, the appointment of postmasters was vested in the postmaster general, not in the president.[135] Although Congress could concededly control the terms by which such postmasters might be removed, nevertheless "the President functioned and met his duty to 'take care that the laws be faithfully executed' without the semblance of power to remove any postmaster. So I think the supposed necessity and theory of

Myers v. United States

government are only vapors." "I suppose," McReynolds asserted, that "Congress may enforce its will by empowering the courts or heads of departments to appoint all officers except representatives abroad, certain judges and a few 'superior' officers – members of the cabinet. And in this event the duty to 'take care that the laws be faithfully executed' would remain notwithstanding the President's lack of control."[136]

McReynolds struck at a serious vulnerability in Taft's argument. In his internal memoranda to Taft, Stone had insisted that the functional argument be taken to its logical conclusion and that the president be accorded unrestricted removal power of all executive subordinates, superior and inferior, whether appointed by the president or by the head of a department.[137] But Taft, as a practical politician, refused even to intimate that the Civil Service was constitutionally infirm in this way.[138] Taft's argument was thus left curiously suspended and unsatisfying.

Taft argued that all executive power was lodged in the president by virtue of the "vesting clause" of the Constitution, which provides that "The executive Power shall be vested in a President of the United States of America."[139] He also argued that discretionary authority to remove executive officials was an executive power necessary to ensure that the laws be faithfully executed.[140] It is therefore baffling why *Myers* nevertheless authorized Congress legislatively to regulate the removal power simply by vesting the appointment of inferior executive officers in the heads of departments.[141] Yet Taft was quite explicit on this point:

> The condition upon which the power of Congress to provide for the removal of inferior officers rests is that it shall vest the appointment in some one other than the President with the consent of the Senate. Congress may not obtain the power and provide for the removal of such officer except on that condition. If it does not choose to entrust the appointment of such inferior officers to less authority than the President with the consent of the Senate, it has no power of providing for their removal. . . . It is true that the remedy for the evil of political executive removals of inferior offices is with Congress by a simple expedient but it includes a change of the power of appointment from the President with the consent of the Senate. Congress must determine, first, that the office is inferior; and, second, that it is willing that the office shall be filled by the appointment by some other authority than the President with the consent of the Senate.[142]

Congress's decision to vest the appointment of postmasters in the president meant "that Congress deemed appointment by the President with the consent of the Senate essential to the public welfare, and until it is willing to vest their appointment in the head of the department they will be subject to removal by the President alone, and any legislation to the contrary must fall as in conflict with the Constitution."[143] Taft thus constructed an argument that effectively ceded to Congress constitutional authority to determine when discretionary removal power for inferior executive officers was and was not prerequisite for the president's capacity faithfully to execute the laws. This is surely not an argument that would be embraced by contemporary advocates of a powerful "unitary executive."[144] It was in fact an oddly insecure argument that received scathing reviews in the scholarly literature of the time.[145]

At root, the weakness of Taft's position lies in its failure meaningfully to specify the circumstances that might in fact require unfettered executive control. Presidential appointment is obviously only a proxy, and a rather loose proxy, for the functional necessity of presidential supervision. Whether Congress has chosen to vest the appointment of an inferior executive officer in the head of a department seems only indirectly related to the need for such supervision. The question of necessary executive supervisory authority would instead seem to turn, as Edward Corwin saw immediately, on a functional analysis of "the essential character of the office involved."[146]

In analyzing this question, it is helpful to draw a preliminary distinction. *Myers* importantly distinguished between the creation and design of executive offices, which was a legislative power,[147] and the authority to appoint specific persons to fill those officers or to remove specific persons from those offices, which was an executive power granted by Article II.[148] On the basis of this dichotomy, *Myers* strongly condemned senatorial intrusion into the decision whether to remove specific persons.[149] Any such intrusion was inconsistent with the basic separation of "legislative from the executive functions."[150] This narrow conclusion was sufficient to invalidate the Act of 1876, which required senatorial consent before removing any specific first-class postmaster. Congress cannot "draw to itself, or to either branch of it, the power to remove or the right to participate in the exercise of that power," Taft wrote. "To do this would be to ... infringe the constitutional principle of the separation of governmental powers."[151] The Court has never retreated from this conclusion.[152]

But whether Congress can participate in the removal of specific executive officers is an entirely different question from whether Congress can regulate the procedures and criteria that the President must apply when removing executive officials. At first blush, Congress's legislative authority to fix the obligations of an office, its salary and jurisdiction, would seem also to include authority to determine the grounds on which an officeholder might be removed.[153] This was the point of Holmes's brief dissent. "We have to deal with an office that owes its existence to Congress and that Congress may abolish tomorrow," Holmes said. "Its duration and the pay attached to it while it lasts depend on Congress alone. Congress alone confers on the President the power to appoint to it and at any time may transfer the power to other hands. With such power over its own creation, I have no more trouble in believing that Congress has power to prescribe a term of life for it free from any interference than I have in accepting the undoubted power of Congress to decree its end."[154]

Whether legislative regulations governing the removal of executive officers interfere with the Article II prerogatives of the president would appear to require a functional inquiry into the need for unrestricted executive removal power,[155] which in turn would depend on the kinds of duties that legislation may properly impose on executive officers. In 1926 it had been constitutionally accepted for more than a century that "it would be an alarming doctrine, that congress cannot impose

Myers v. United States

upon any executive officer any duty they may think proper, which is not repugnant to any rights secured and protected by the constitution; and in such cases, the duty and responsibility grow out of and are subject to the control of the law, and not to the direction of the President."[156]

Congress can impose duties on executive officers that are not merely ministerial in nature, and it can seek to insulate the discretion to execute such duties from partisan political control. Sometimes Congress immunizes the discretion of executive officers so that they may exercise apolitical technical expertise, as for example with members of the Federal Reserve Board. Sometimes Congress immunizes the discretion of executive officers so that they may act with disinterested judgment, as for example with judges of the Court of Claims before it became an Article III tribunal. In such instances, Congress limits the authority of presidential removal in order to ensure that the law be executed free from the taint of political oversight.[157]

Taft well understood these issues. In *Myers* he observes:

> Of course there may be duties so peculiarly and specifically committed to the discretion of a particular officer as to raise a question whether the President may overrule or revise the officer's interpretation of his statutory duty in a particular instance. Then there may be duties of a quasi judicial character imposed on executive officers and members of executive tribunals whose decisions after hearing affect interests of individuals, the discharge of which the President cannot in a particular case properly influence or control.[158]

The *Myers* opinion refuses, however, to let these circumstances impair the "unity and co-ordination in executive administration" that Taft deemed "essential to effective action." Taft explicitly concludes that even though legislation may sometimes prevent a president from substituting his judgment for that of an appointed subordinate, the president may nevertheless "consider the decision after its rendition as a reason for removing the officer, on the ground that the discretion regularly entrusted to that officer by statute has not been on the whole intelligently or wisely exercised. Otherwise he does not discharge his own constitutional duty of seeing that the laws be faithfully executed."[159]

In essence, Taft held that presidential supervisory authority categorically overrides any possible legislative determination that presidentially appointed executive officers ought to be insulated from close political supervision. Taft thus created a "paradox that, while the Constitution permitted Congress to vest duties in executive officers in the performance of which they were to exercise their own independent judgment, it at the same time permitted the President to guillotine such officers for exercising the very discretion which Congress had the right to require."[160]

Myers produced a result that can only be described as schizophrenic. Presidential removal power might easily be circumvented by vesting the appointment of inferior executive officers in heads of departments,[161] yet all executive officers appointed by the president were as a matter of constitutional law "removable at the President's will."[162] Neither side of this dichotomy is especially convincing or reasonable. After *Myers*, the Court quietly undermined the first by focusing

415

constitutional attention on the functional question of whether removal restrictions imposed by Congress to protect inferior officers appointed by heads of departments "are of such a nature that they impede the President's ability to perform his constitutional duty."[163] And in *Humphrey's Executor v. United States*,[164] a 1935 decision rightly regarded as severely undercutting *Myers*,[165] a unanimous Court explicitly overturned the second, holding that Congress can regulate the removal of presidentially appointed executive officers, like federal trade commissioners, who act "in part quasi legislatively and in part quasi judicially."[166]

Taft knew full well that not all Article II officials appointed by a president acted in a purely executive capacity. In 1916 Taft had written that "The functions of the President are both legislative and executive. Among the executive functions we shall find a gradual tendency to a division into the purely executive and the quasi-legislative and quasi-judicial duties."[167] It is all the more striking, then, that Taft was so careless in *Myers* in failing to define or limit the "executive officers and members of executive tribunals"[168] to whom the conclusions of *Myers* applied. During the pendency of the case, Taft had toyed with the thought that *Myers* might not apply to interstate commerce commissioners,[169] and several days after the announcement of *Myers* Taft expressed anger at McReynolds's "reference to judicial offices," which in Taft's view had "nothing to do with the case, because we only decide the case as to an executive office and we limit our decision to that. I would be inclined to limit it so at any rate."[170]

Taft's complaint is not entirely candid, for although he explicitly excluded certain Article II judges from the scope of his *Myers* opinion,[171] he nevertheless crafted his opinion in an extraordinarily broad way. We know that Taft specifically meant the opinion to apply to the many so-called independent agencies that McReynolds lists in his dissent, like the "Interstate Commerce Commission, Board of General Appraisers, Federal Reserve Board, Federal Trade Commission, Tariff Commission, Shipping Board, Federal Farm Loan Board, [and] Railroad Labor Board."[172] The officers running these agencies were appointed by the president but nevertheless were accorded fixed statutory terms of office that could be interrupted only for cause.[173]

Taft regarded the proliferation of these agencies as congressional efforts to fragment and undercut the executive power of the president, in much the way that Congress had sought to handicap President Andrew Johnson. Taft wrote his friend Tom Shelton, a southern lawyer,

> I am very strongly convinced that the danger to this country is in the enlargement of the powers of Congress, rather than in the maintenance in full of the executive power. Congress is getting into the habit of forming boards who really exercise executive power, and attempting to make them independent of the President after they have been appointed and confirmed. This merely makes a hydra-headed Executive, and if the terms are lengthened so as to exceed the duration of a particular Executive, a new Executive will find himself stripped of control of important functions, for which as the head of the Government he becomes responsible, but whose action he can not influence in any way. It was exactly this which the two-thirds majority of the Republicans in the Congress

Myers v. United States

after the War attempted to do with the Tenure of Office Act. They attempted to provide that Cabinet officers who had been appointed by Lincoln, and who differed with Johnson as to the policy to be pursued in respect to dealing with reconstruction questions should be retained in office against his will.[174]

Taft was at heart an administrator who deplored "the narrow, factional selfishness of Congress."[175] Several months before the 1924 presidential election, he had complained to his wife that "Congress is unrepresentative. The Senate is at the lowest ebb in its history and the House is not much better."[176] It was precisely Coolidge's "independence of Congress that gives him his strength," and he therefore should "act upon legislation according to his best judgment and the people will approve even though he differs from Congress."[177] Taft expressed an analogous thought in *Myers*: "The President is a representative of the people, just as the members of the Senate and of the House are, and it may be at some times, on some subjects, that the President, elected by all the people, is rather more representative of them all than are the members of either body of the Legislature, whose constituencies are local and not country wide."[178]

The extraordinary reach of *Myers* reflected the priority Taft accorded to the administrative needs of a nationally elected president for control, coherence, and efficiency. Taft regarded these virtues as paramount when compared to the bickering, local, and merely political concerns of Congress. He therefore refused to credit the possibility that laws might in fact be more faithfully executed if specialized, presidentially appointed executive officers were legislatively endowed with some independence from centralized, political control. He regarded the nature of the office, and of the law applied by the office, as irrelevant. What mattered was the impertinence of congressional interference with executive unity and coherence.

In a probing dissent, Brandeis offered a fundamentally different picture of the relationship between the legislative and executive branches. "The doctrine of the separation of powers was adopted by the convention of 1787 not to promote efficiency," he said, "but to preclude the exercise of arbitrary power. The purpose was not to avoid friction, but, by means of the inevitable friction incident to the distribution of the governmental powers among three departments, to save the people from autocracy."[179]

> The President performs his full constitutional duty, if, with the means and instruments provided by Congress and within the limitations prescribed by it, he uses his best endeavors to secure the faithful execution of the laws enacted. ...
>
> Checks and balances were established in order that this should be "a government of laws and not of men." In order to prevent arbitrary executive action, the Constitution provided in terms that presidential appointments be made with the consent of the Senate, unless Congress should otherwise provide .... Nothing in support of the claim of uncontrollable power can be inferred from the silence of the convention of 1787 on the subject of removal. For the outstanding fact remains that every specific proposal to confer such uncontrollable power upon the President was rejected. In America, as in England, the conviction prevailed then that the people must look to representative assemblies for the

protection of their liberties. And protection of the individual, even if he be an official, from the arbitrary or capricious exercise of power was then believed to be an essential of free government.[180]

For Brandeis what mattered was not the independence of the executive from the Congress; what mattered was the interdependence of the two branches. This was because Brandeis regarded unconstrained power as potentially despotic, and he believed that the only realistic constraint on power lay in the checks and balances hardwired into the constitutional scheme. These impediments might well impair administrative efficiency, but this was a feature, not a bug. It was the necessary cost of a Constitution designed to hedge against tyranny. For Brandeis, the ultimate goal of the Constitution was to maximize the subordination of all government actors to general rules of law, which are the antithesis of "arbitrary executive action." Rules of law could legitimately emanate only from the multimember assembly of Congress, notwithstanding its incessant, inefficient, and petty squabbling.

It is ironic that Taft and Brandeis each believed in the value of administrative efficiency and control. In Taft's eyes, this value, combined with the national political accountability of the president, justified creating a powerful chief executive who could at will order the universe of presidentially appointed officials. But Brandeis saw in this combination precisely the danger that Robert Jackson, an attorney general later appointed to the Court to replace Stone, warned against in *Youngstown Sheet & Tube Co. v. Sawyer*. Executive action that "originates in the individual will of the President," said Jackson, is "an exercise of authority without law."[181] Like Brandeis, Jackson believed that "the Constitution diffuses power the better to secure liberty,"[182] and, like Brandeis, Jackson believed that "men have discovered no technique for long preserving free government except that the Executive be under the law, and that the law be made by parliamentary deliberations."[183]

His participation in the Ballinger controversy had impressed upon Brandeis a keen appreciation of the immensity of executive power. The capacious, countrywide political mandate of the president, which Taft believed justified managerial authority, for Brandeis only added to the potential danger of executive power. In *Myers*, Brandeis argued that the Constitution should not be interpreted to facilitate discretionary power. The safety of Republic required that administrative efficiency yield before the discipline of law. Taft, long pilloried as a weak advocate for a "law-governed presidency,"[184] disagreed, carrying the Court with him. He thereby lay the groundwork for a presidency that has more than once been characterized as imperial.[185]

Myers v. United States

Notes

1. 276 U.S. 394 (1928). *Hampton* upheld the constitutionality of the flexible tariff positions of the Fordney-McCumber Tariff Act of 1922. Pub. L. 67-318, 42 Stat. 858, 941 (September 21, 1922). These provisions were attacked as violating "the spirit if not the letter of our theory of constitution. They delegated to the Executive a power of taxation that should normally be exercised by the legislative branch. They gave the President a control over the collection of revenue greater than that possessed by any executive in any other modern democracy. They gave him the power to tax industries out of existence." Thomas H. Gammack, *Taking the Tariff Out of Politics*, 148 THE OUTLOOK 670 (1928).
2. 263 U.S. 39 (1923) (upholding broad executive power over the Canal District).
3. Albert W. Fox, *Senate Fight Seen to Strip President of Removal Power*, WASHINGTON POST (October 27, 1926), at 1. It was contemporaneously observed that "At the beginning of its October term of 1926, the Supreme Court of the United States rendered one of the most important decisions in its entire history, one which, it is declared, 'will undoubtedly rank with the most notable decisions of that court,' because it settled a question as to the division of power between the legislative and executive branches of our government which has been the subject of heated controversy from the foundation of the government to this day." *Presidential Power of Removal from Office*, 11 CONSTITUTIONAL REVIEW 34, 34 (1927).
4. Free Enterprise Fund v. Public Company Accounting Oversight Board, 561 U.S. 477, 493 (2010).
5. 272 U.S. 52 (1926).
6. WHT to Mrs. Frederick J. Manning (October 24, 1926) (Taft papers).
7. *Myers*, 272 U.S. at 106.
8. The story of *Myers* is told in Jonathan L. Entin, *The Curious Case of the Pompous Postmaster: Myers v. United States*, 65 CASE WESTERN RESERVE LAW REVIEW 1059 (2015). *See also* Saikrishna Prakash, *The Story of Myers and its Wayward Successors: Going Postal on the Removal Power*, in PRESIDENTIAL POWER STORIES 165 (Christopher H. Schroeder & Curtis A. Bradly, eds., New York: Foundation Press 2009).
9. The letter demanding Myers's resignation referred to the need "to eliminate the antagonism which existed in the Portland office and bring about needed cooperation." J.C. Koons to F.S. Myers (January 22, 1920), reprinted in *Power of the President to Remove Federal Officers*, Sen. Doc. No. 174, 69th CONG. 2nd SESS. (December 13, 1926), at 6–7. Senate Document 174 contains the entire record of *Myers*, including briefs and a transcript of its oral argument. For a discussion of the possible reasons for Wilson's action, see Entin, *supra* note 8, at 1062–64.
10. 19 Stat. 78, 80 (July 12, 1876). The 1876 statute essentially duplicated the requirements of the Act of June 8, 1872, 17 Stat. 283, 292–93.
11. *See* Entin, *supra* note 8, at 1066–73. Wilson in September 1919 had learned of the disloyalty of Robert Lansing, his secretary of state, whose resignation Wilson demanded and received in February 1920. *Id.* at 1072. In June 1920, Wilson would veto the Budget and Accounting Act of June 1920, which provided that the comptroller general could be dismissed only by a concurrent resolution in Congress. *Id.* Wilson's veto was sustained, but the following year Congress passed an altered version of the statute that allowed the comptroller to be dismissed by a joint

THE TAFT COURT

resolution of Congress presented to the president. Harding subsequently signed the Budget and Accounting Act of 1921 into law. *See* Pub. L. 67-13, 42 Stat. 20 (June 10, 1921); Entin, *supra* note 8, at 1072 n.70.

12. 58 Ct. Cl. 199, 208 (1923).
13. Entin, *supra* note 8, at 1065.
14. In the official United States Reports, the date of the first argument is given as December 5, 1923, but this is an error. *See Journal of the Supreme Court of the United States* (October Term 1924), at 99; Butler's 1924 term docket book, at 249; WHT to Horace D. Taft (December 7, 1924) (Taft papers); WHT to Charles P. Taft 2nd (December 7, 1924) (Taft papers).
15. *Journal of the Supreme Court of the United States* (October Term 1924), at 99. *See* WHT to HFS (December 7, 1924) (Taft papers) (referring to "the case of Myers vs. the United States, argued by Beck, and submitted on brief by the other side"); C. Dickerman Williams, *The 1924 Term: Recollections of Chief Justice Taft's Law Clerk*, 1989 YEARBOOK OF THE SUPREME COURT HISTORICAL SOCIETY 40, 46 ("I happened to be in the courtroom when the *Myers* case was originally reached for argument.... There was no appearance for the estate of the removed officer; he had died before the case reached the Supreme Court. Mr. Beck told the Court that he regretted this non-appearance, because in his opinion the opinion of the District Court [on laches] could not be sustained.").
16. *See supra* note 15. In his brief, Beck had written that he "would be glad to accept" the court's judgment "and thus spare the court the necessity of deciding one of the most important constitutional questions which can arise under our form of Government," but "candor compels me to add ... that the disposition, which the Court of Claims made of the case in this respect, is not entirely convincing to me." Brief for the United States, at 3. Beck added, "I do not mean to confess error, for the action of the very learned and able Court of Claims is entitled to very great respect and the Government should not waive the benefit of this decision in its favor." *Id.* In his second argument of the case, Beck said:

> In this case, I am frank to say, I can find no evidence of any waiver or acquiescence. I do not know what more Mr. Myers could have done in asserting his rights. The pertinacity with which he asserted his title until his commission had expired is worthy of the legendary boy on the burning deck. He stood by his guns in respect to the alleged unlawfulness of his dismissal and awaited an opportunity to serve in an office, of which he consistently asserted he had been unlawfully deprived, until his commission had expired and then within a few weeks thereafter he commenced his suit.

Power of the President to Remove Federal Officers, supra note 9, at 184.

17. *See supra* Chapter 4, at 121–22.
18. WHT to HFS (December 7, 1924) (Taft papers). *See* WHT to HFS (December 23, 1924) (Taft papers); WHT to HFS (December 26, 1924) (Taft papers); HFS to WHT (December 31, 1924) (Taft papers).
19. Albert B. Cummins to James M. Beck (January 29, 1925) (Taft papers).
20. WHT to HFS (December 23, 1924) (Taft papers).
21. *Journal of the Supreme Court of the United States* (October Term 1924), at 182; Albert B. Cummins to James M. Beck (January 29, 1925) (Taft papers); Albert B. Cummins to WHT (January 29, 1925) (Taft papers); James M. Beck to WHT (February 2, 1925) (Taft papers).

Myers v. United States

22. At reargument, Will R. King argued the case for the Myers estate. At the beginning of argument, Taft announced that the Court "should much prefer to have" Stone sit in the case even though "he was Attorney General while the case was in the department." *Power of the President to Remove Federal Officers, supra* note 9, at 153. Taft represented that Stone "took no part in the case and it did not come before him in any official capacity." *Id.* Both King and Beck announced that they would "be very glad to have" Stone sit in the case.
23. Jonathan L. Entin, *The Removal Power and the Federal Deficit: Form, Substance, and Administrative Independence*, 75 KENTUCKY LAW JOURNAL 699, 736 nn.166–67 (1986).
24. WILLIAM HOWARD TAFT, OUR CHIEF MAGISTRATE AND HIS POWERS 2 (New York: Columbia University Press 1916).
25. *Presidential Message on the Financial Condition of the Treasury*, 48 CONG. REC. 591 (December 21, 1911). *See Concerning the Work of the Departments of the Post Office, Interior, Agriculture, and Commerce and Labor and District of Columbia* (December 19, 1912), in 4 THE COLLECTED WORKS OF WILLIAM HOWARD TAFT 340 (David H. Burton, ed., Athens: Ohio University Press 2002). "Annually for four years I recommended that Congress change the method of appointing the postmasters, collectors of internal revenue, and collectors of customs by removing the necessity for confirmation by the Senate, promising that if this were done I would put all these officers under the classified service. But my urgent recommendations fell upon deaf ears." WILLIAM HOWARD TAFT, THE PRESIDENCY: ITS DUTIES, ITS POWERS, ITS OPPORTUNITIES AND ITS LIMITATIONS 59 (New York: Charles Scribner's Sons 1916). *See* William Howard Taft, *Post Office Patronage* (March 16, 1921), in VIVIAN, at 554. "Appointments, except to the more important offices, ought to be in some practical way removed from the presidential duties. The President should not be required to give his time to the selection of any except the judges of the courts, the heads of departments, the political under or assistant secretaries in each department, the ambassadors, public ministers, general officers in the army, and the flag-officers in the navy. This could be done by putting all other offices into the classified service, under the present civil-service law." TAFT, THE PRESIDENCY, *supra*, at 55. The 1924 Platform of the Republican Party proclaimed that "We favor the classification of postmasters in first, second and third class post offices ... within the classified civil service." Platform of the Republican Party, 1924, available at www.presidency.ucsb.edu/documents/republican-party-platform-1924.
26. TAFT, *supra* note 24, at 59. "I cannot exaggerate the waste of the President's time and the consumption of his nervous vitality involved in congressional intercession as to local appointments. Why should the President have his time taken up in a discussion over the question who shall be postmistress at the town of Devil's Lake in North Dakota? How should he be able to know, with confidence, who is best fitted to fill such a place? If we were to follow ordinary business methods in a matter which concerns business only and does not concern general political policies, as we ought to do, would we not leave such appointments to the natural system of promotion for efficiency?" *Id.* at 67. Taft believed "that, if the necessity for confirmation by the Senate of the postmasters, collectors of customs, collectors of internal revenue, land officers, and other local representative of the United States Government in all parts of its jurisdiction were removed, as it might be by act of Congress, and if these officers were covered into the classified service by executive

order, the offices could be run by the present assistants in the classified service; that the places now filled by political appointments could be entirely abolished; that the functions of the Government in these offices would be better performed, and a saving of four million five hundred thousand dollars annually could thus be made. ... Anyone who has had experience with political appointments to local offices knows in his heart that this reform is one of the best that could be adopted. It would greatly help and purify national politics by minimizing the use of Federal patronage for partisan purposes. It would relieve the President of wholly unnecessary worry and strain, and it would help congressmen and senators in the same way." *Id.* at 67. *See* William H. Taft, *Economy and Efficiency in the Federal Government*, 187 SATURDAY EVENING POST 14–15 (February 13, 1915).

27. Pub. L. 60-146, 35 Stat. 406 (May 27, 1908). The statute was meant to overrule the Court's decision in Shurtleff v. United States, 189 U.S. 311 (1903), which had interpreted the previous statute to permit the president to remove members of the Board at will.

28. The story is told in Aditya Bamzai, *Taft, Frankfurter, and the First Presidential For-Cause Removal*, 52 UNIVERSITY OF RICHMOND LAW REVIEW 691 (2018).

29. THEODORE ROOSEVELT, THEODORE ROOSEVELT: AN AUTOBIOGRAPHY 389 (New York: MacMillan Co. 1913).

30. *Id.* at 395.

31. *Id.* at 395–96.

32. For an excellent discussion, see H. Jefferson Powell, *Editor's Introduction* to the republication of WILLIAM HOWARD TAFT, OUR CHIEF MAGISTRATE AND HIS POWERS (Durham: Carolina Academic Press 2002). Powell rightly observes that another target of Taft's work was likely Woodrow Wilson, who in 1908 had written that "Some of our Presidents have deliberately held themselves off from using the full power they might legitimately have used, because of conscientious scruples, because they were more theorists than statesman. They have held the strict literary theory of the Constitution. ... But the makers of the Constitution ... were statesmen, not pedants, and their laws are sufficient to keep us to the paths they set us upon. The President is at liberty, both in law and conscience, to be as big a man as he can. His capacity will set the limit; and if Congress be overborne by him, it will be no fault of the makers of the Constitution." WOODROW WILSON, CONSTITUTIONAL GOVERNMENT IN THE UNITED STATES 70 (New Brunswick: Transaction Publishers 2002). Wilson dismissively noted that "while we were once all constitutional lawyers, we are in these latter days apt to be very impatient of literal and dogmatic interpretations of constitutional principle." *Id.* at 59.

33. TAFT, *supra* note 24, at 144.

34. *Id.* at 139–40. "While the President's powers are broad, the lines of his jurisdiction are as fixed as a written constitution can properly make them." *Id.* at 53. Taft regarded Roosevelt's view as "lawless." TAFT, THE PRESIDENCY, *supra* note 25, at 130.

35. TAFT, THE PRESIDENCY, *supra* note 25, at 141.

36. Powell, *supra* note 32, at xlviii.

37. TAFT, *supra* note 24, at 157.

38. Taft refused to say whether he adopted a departmentalist view of constitutional interpretation. "It is sufficient to say that the court is a permanent body respecting precedent and seeking consistency in its decisions, and that therefore its view of the Constitution, whether binding on the executive and the legislature or not, is likely

ultimately to prevail as accepted law." TAFT, THE PRESIDENCY, *supra* note 25, at 121.
39. LOUIS FISHER, THE CONSTITUTION BETWEEN FRIENDS: CONGRESS, THE PRESIDENT, AND THE LAW 20 (New York: St. Martin's Press 1978). *See* L. Peter Schultz, *William Howard Taft: A Constitutionalist's View of the Presidency*, 9 PRESIDENTIAL STUDIES QUARTERLY 402, 403 (1979); Rene N. Ballard, *The Administrative Theory of William Howard Taft*, 7 WESTERN POLITICAL QUARTERLY 65, 68 (1954).
40. TAFT, THE PRESIDENCY, *supra* note 25, at 106. Taft believed that "[t]here is little danger to the public weal from the tyranny or reckless character of a President who is not sustained by the people. The absence of popular support will certainly, in the course of two years, withdraw from him the sympathetic action of at least one house of Congress, and by the control that that house has over appropriations the executive arm can be paralyzed, unless he resorts to a *coup d'état*, which means impeachment, conviction, and deposition." *Id.* at 139.
41. Ballard, *supra* note 39, at 69. "President Taft was the first chief executive of the nation, or of any American state, who fully grasped and presented the issues of the budget principle in relation to legislation and public administration in any government." Samuel McCune Lindsay, *Editor's Note*, in FREDERICK A. CLEVELAND & ARTHUR EUGENE MCCUNE BUCK, THE BUDGET AND RESPONSIBLE GOVERNMENT vi (New York: MacMillan Co. 1920). "The only serious attempt to formulate a responsible executive budget in our Federal Government, so far as I am aware, took place in 1912. Congress had given to Mr. Taft a Commission on Efficiency and Economy for the purpose of looking into the workings and functions of the executive departments. With its assistance, he undertook, for the first time, to revise and convert the haphazard estimates of the various departments into a responsible programme or budget." Henry L. Stimson, *A National Budget System*, 38 WORLD'S WORK 371, 373 (1919). *See* William Howard Taft, *National Budget Plan* (July 24, 1919), in VIVIAN, at 244; William Howard Taft, *A National Budget System* (September 22, 1919), *id.* at 276–79 ("The most important use of a budget ... is to fix in the minds of the people the definite responsibility of those in power for the cost of government."). Taft created the President's Commission on Economy and Efficiency (known as the "Taft Commission"), which was the country's first systematic effort to assess the potential for administrative and budgetary reorganization of the executive branch. *See* Taft, *Economy and Efficiency in the Federal Government*, *supra* note 26, at 14–15. As Taft affirmed to Congress, "Efficiency and economy in the Government Service have been demanded with increasing insistence for a generation. Real economy is the result of efficient organization." William Howard Taft, *Economy and Efficiency in the Government Service*, 48 CONG. REC. 1026 (January 17, 1912).

In insisting that "proper business methods" be applied to government to increase efficiency, Taft, *Economy and Efficiency in the Federal Government*, *supra* note 26, at 14, Taft was very close in spirit to Brandeis's embrace of scientific management. *See supra* Chapter 8, at 317. Indeed, shortly after Wilson assumed office, Wilson was visited by Brandeis, together with Henry Bruere and F.A. Cleveland, the former head of the Taft Commission, who urged Wilson to continue the work of the Commission. *Wilson for Economy Board*, NEW YORK TIMES (April 5, 1913), at 3. Wilson was unresponsive, "explaining that he had major issues on his agenda and that, while he was interested in its work, it had no place in his administration." PERI E. ARNOLD, MAKING THE MANAGERIAL PRESIDENCY: COMPREHENSIVE REORGANIZATION PLANNING, 1905–1996, at 49 (Lawrence: University of Kansas Press 1998). *See* William Howard Taft, *Economy and Efficiency in the Federal Government, supra* note 26, at 3–4 ("Under the present Administration not a step has been taken in this direction. No advantage has been derived from most valuable work already done and preserved in Government records, and no further work of the same kind has been projected. The New Freedom now being enjoyed under Administration auspices has been described in glowing terms; but real reform in the methods of governmental business, which might materially lighten the growing financial burden of the New Freedom, has not had any serious attention.").

Congress would not prove receptive to the creation of an executive budgeting process until confronted by the deficits created by World War I. "The weight of wartime deficits accomplished what William Howard Taft and Frederick Cleveland could not." ARNOLD, *supra*, at 53. On the Budget and Accounting Act of 1921, see *supra* note 11. Harding strongly supported Taft's pioneering efforts to create an executive budget. Speaking to Congress in 1921, Harding praised the Budget and Accounting Act as "the greatest reformation in government practices since the beginning of the Republic." *Address by the President of the United States*, 62 CONG. REC. 37 (December 6, 1921).

42. William Howard Taft, *Financial Retrenchment and Governmental Reorganization*, 9 PROCEEDINGS OF THE ACADEMY OF POLITICAL SCIENCE IN THE CITY OF NEW YORK 90, 91 (1921). "The President, who is the man that is responsible for the executive departments, ought to have the independent means of finding out through a body of experts whether or not a department is asking more than it ought to have." *Id.* at 93. TAFT, *supra* note 24, at 4–9. Taft's advocacy of budgetary reform reflected his deeper commitment to the importance of a unified and accountable executive branch. As Henry Stimson put it in the context of the need for a national budget prepared by the president: "Only the President can decide upon the broad questions of policy upon which his administration will rest its programme of work for the coming year and put that programme into a shape upon which he is willing to have his administration stand for better or worse before the scrutiny of the national legislature." Stimson, *supra* note 41, at 529–30.

43. Ballard, *supra* note 39, at 73. *See More Powers for President Urged by Taft*, NEW YORK TRIBUNE (May 24, 1921), at 3. Taft's efforts comprehensively to reform the executive branch inspired what by the 1920s became known as the "good government" movement, which consisted of a tripartite commitment to civil service reform, a national budget system, and executive reorganization. *See* JESSE TARBET, WHEN GOOD GOVERNMENT MEANT BIG GOVERNMENT: THE QUEST TO EXPAND FEDERAL POWER, 1913–1933, at 13–16 (New York: Columbia University Press 2022); Jesse Tarbert, *The Quest to Bring "Business Efficiency" to the Federal Executive: Herbert Hoover, Franklin Roosevelt, and the Civil Service Reformers of the Late 1920s*, 31 JOURNAL OF POLICY HISTORY 512 (2019). Herbert Hoover could argue in 1925, for example: "Over many years our people have been striving to better the federal administration. We have succeeded in two major steps; we still have a third equally important and perhaps more difficult one to accomplish. The first was the establishment of government employment based upon merit. The second was the establishment of adequate control of

appropriations through the budget system. There still remains the third and even greater but more obscure waste – that of faulty organization of administrative functions. And the two first steps will never reach the full realization without the third." Herbert Hoover, *200 Bureaus, Boards and Commissions!*, 13 NATION'S BUSINESS 9 (June 5, 1925). Taft remained active and effective in pushing for reform of the federal budget after World War I. TARBET, *supra*, at 42–46.

44. William Howard Taft, *The Boundaries between the Executive, the Legislative and the Judicial Branches of the Government*, 25 YALE LAW JOURNAL 599, 612 (1916). *See* An Act Making Appropriations for the Legislative, Executive, and Judicial Expense of the Government for the Fiscal Year Ending June Thirtieth, Nineteen Thirteen, and for Other Purposes, Pub. L. 62-299, 37 Stat. 360, 415 (August 23, 1912).

45. Taft, *supra* note 44, at 612.

46. *Id. See Message of the President of the United States Submitting for the Consideration of the Congress a Budget*, Sen. Doc. No. 1113, 62nd CONG. 3rd SESS. (February 26, 1913), at 9 ("The head of each department and each independent establishment was directed, in addition to those estimates which are included in the Book of Estimates for appropriations as now required by statute and as sent to Congress, also to make return to the office of the Chief Executive of estimates of the actual expenditures for the same fiscal year, whether derived from old appropriations, proposed appropriations, or deficiency appropriations.").

47. Taft, *supra* note 44, at 612. "I regarded this rider as an unconstitutional attempt to limit my power and duty to submit to Congress from time to time information on the state of the Union, and to recommend to its consideration such measures as I should judge necessary and expedient; and I decided to ignore it." Taft, *Economy and Efficiency in the Federal Government*, *supra* note 26, at 38.

48. *Message of the President of the United States Submitting for the Consideration of the Congress a Budget*, *supra* note 46, at 5. Taft explained:

> The fact that ours is the only great Nation whose Government is doing business without a budget has not been a dominant reason for departure from 123 years of precedent. Such procedure is based on common experience and common sense. It is supported by the best judgment and experience that has obtained in the management of corporate bodies, both public and private. While officers of private corporations are not ordinarily limited by law in such manner as to make it necessary for them to act under formal appropriations, it is the ordinary method of transacting business to have the president of a corporation lay before its board at its annual meeting a report which is also made available to all persons who may be interested; it is common experience for the president, as the responsible head of the executive branch, to set forth what has been done during the past year and what it is proposed that the corporation shall do during the next year; it is common experience for the president as the head of the administration to accompany his proposals with estimates; it is common experience for the president as the head of the executive branch to submit with such estimates recommendations as to how proposed expenditures shall be financed.

Id. Taft made his constitutional case in an open letter to his own secretary of the treasury, Franklin MacVeagh:

> Under the Constitution, the President is entrusted with the executive power, and is responsible for the acts of heads of departments, and their subordinates as his agents.
>
> If Congress is permitted to assume exclusive jurisdiction over what the President may seek to learn about the business transactions by the departments, ...

if heads of departments are to be considered purely as the ministerial agents of Congress in the preparation and submission of estimates, then as far as the business of Government is concerned, the President ... is shorn of most important executive power and duty.

Quoted in *Taft Insistent, Orders a Budget*, NEW YORK TIMES (September 20, 1912), at 7. The story of Taft's confrontation with Congress is told in Ballard, *supra* note 39, at 71–73; ARNOLD, *supra* note 41, at 26–51; STEVEN G. CALABRESI & CHRISTOPHER S. YOO, THE UNITARY EXECUTIVE: PRESIDENTIAL POWER FROM WASHINGTON TO BUSH 250–51 (New Haven: Yale University Press 2008). Control of the budgetary process, of course, represented a major expansion of presidential power. *Id.* at 251.

49. TAFT, *supra* note 24, at 56. Taft was more circumspect in a 1916 law review article, saying simply that "Whether the President has the absolute power of removal without the consent of the Senate in respect to all offices, the tenure of which is not affected by the Constitution, is not definitely settled." Taft, *supra* note 44, at 608. For an early statement of Taft's commitment to the president's removal power, see WILLIAM HOWARD TAFT, FOUR ASPECTS OF CIVIC DUTY 108 (New York: Charles Scribner's Sons 1906).

50. TAFT, THE PRESIDENCY, *supra* note 25, at 54. The "intimation" to which Taft referred was Parsons v. United States, 167 U.S. 324 (1897). *See* Taft, *supra* note 44, at 608.

51. James Hart, *The Bearing of Myers v. United States upon the Independence of Federal Administrative Tribunals*, 23 AMERICAN POLITICAL SCIENCE REVIEW 657, 671 (1929).

52. Stone's law clerk, Alfred McCormack, recalls that "In the *Myers* case Stone felt that the real issue was whether the business of the Executive could be conducted efficiently if every officer confirmed by the Senate were to have a lease on his office until the Senate approved his removal. To Stone it was clear that the position of the Executive under such a restriction would be impossible." Alfred McCormack, *A Law Clerk's Recollections*, 46 COLUMBIA LAW REVIEW 710, 714 (1946).

53. WHT to Charles P. Taft 2nd (April 26, 1925) (Taft papers).

54. WHT to Mrs. Frederick J. Manning (May 17, 1925) (Taft papers).

55. WHT to WVD (July 4, 1925) (Van Devanter papers). "But," Taft continued, "it is remarkable how difficult it is when you have all the time to use any of it for such a purpose."

56. WHT to GS (August 11, 1925) (Sutherland papers). In his letter, Taft advised Sutherland that what he "must not do is to work with the intensity with which you have worked since you have been on the Bench; and if you will only work with me on this subject, we two can control the matter entirely, especially if Mrs. Sutherland is given a voice." *Id.* On Sutherland's illness over that summer, see *supra* Chapter 1, at note 78.

57. WHT to WVD (August 15, 1925) (Van Devanter papers).

58. WHT to Hayden Smith (September 1, 1925) (Taft papers).

> Does the executive power thus stated include the power to appoint and remove executive officers and agents, and would it do so in such a way as to exclude the right of Congress to make appointments and remove appointees, if there were no specific provision in the other sections as to how appointments shall be made? I wish you would consult Montesquieu's "Spirit of the Laws" to see whether he makes any reference to the scope of the executive power as he

Myers v. United States

understood it, and whether it includes the power to appoint and remove executive agents. The framers of the Constitution were very familiar with Montesquieu and it is quite clear that they were well read generally in matters of the structure of government. It is quite possible that you will find nothing. I have here the discussions of the question of the power of removal by Madison in the first Congress, by Webster in subsequent Congresses when the power of removal again came up and the arguments were made in the impeachment trial of Andrew Jackson. [sic] I believe there is a discussion in Pomeroy's "Constitutional Law", and that I have.

Id. Smith replied on September 22 in a letter that cited scattered references and concluded that "I have deduced that executive included in its meaning the power of appointment and that sharing it with the legislative was extraordinary." Hayden Smith to WHT (September 22, 1925) (Taft papers). Smith did not find much about the power of removal – the library was still looking for W.H. Rogers, The Executive Power of Removal – except that Chancellor Kent had in a letter written that although in 1789 "he had leant toward Madison, but now (1830) because of the word 'advice' must have meant more than consent to nomination, he said he had a strong suspicion that Hamilton was right in his remark in the Federalist, no.77, April 4th, 1788: 'No one could fail to perceive the entire safety of the power of removal if it must thus be exercised in conjunction with the senate.'"

59. WHT to PB (September 16, 1925) (Taft papers). On the connection between Taft's repudiation of reconstruction and his assertion of judicial control to protect executive prerogatives, see Nikolas Bowie & Daphna Renan, *The Separation-of-Powers Counterrevolution*, 131 YALE LAW JOURNAL 2020, 2025–31, 2065–82 (2022).
60. WHT to Charles P. Taft 2nd (November 1, 1925) (Taft papers). "I find," Taft added, "that one of the most difficult things in preparing an ... opinion ... is the plan or arrangement of the statement of the facts and the argument to sustain your conclusion. This takes me rather more time than any other feature of a long opinion – I mean an opinion that necessarily has to be long. I have a tendency to length that I try to restrain." *Id.* A month earlier, Taft had complained to his brother that the opinion was "still on the stocks. It is hard for me to compress it and to get it into proper shape. The strategy of framing an opinion is as difficult as anything about the work." WHT to Horace D. Taft (October 5, 1925) (Taft papers).
61. WHT to WVD (November 6, 1925) (Van Devanter papers). The omission of Sanford is telling.
62. *See* WHT to ETS (November 7, 1925) (Taft papers) (Inviting Sanford to the Sunday afternoon conference; "I don't know how the other three will stand, but I want to get [the opinion] into shape so that it will be ready for their careful consideration."). *Compare* WHT to HFS (November 6, 1925) (Stone papers) (Sending Stone "a first draft" of the opinion and inviting him "to confer with Van, Sutherland, Pierce and myself say Sunday afternoon about 3:15") *with* WHT to PB (November 7, 1925) (Taft papers) (Inviting Butler to the Sunday conference; "It is a most important matter and the opinion should be carefully considered.... I am asking the six of them whose votes can be counted on, and I would like to have your suggestions before revising and circulating."). *See* WHT to GS (November 7, 1925) (Taft papers). Taft anticipated that "there will probably be some dissents." WHT to Robert A. Taft (November 8, 1925) (Taft papers). "Brandeis voted no, and I think Holmes did, while McReynolds was doubtful." WHT to Horace D. Taft (November 13, 1925) (Taft papers).
63. WHT to WVD, GS, PB, ETS, and HFS (November 10, 1925) (Taft papers).

64. WHT to Louis More (November 13, 1925) (Taft papers).
65. WHT to Horace D. Taft (November 13, 1925) (Taft papers).
66. McCormack, *supra* note 52, at 711. *See* THOMAS ALPHEUS MASON, HARLAN FISKE STONE: PILLAR OF THE LAW 227 (New York: Viking 1956).
67. HFS to WHT (November 13, 1925) (Stone papers). Stone observed that "To my mind, as a mere matter of exposition of the written document, the fact that the executive power was given in general terms with specific limitations, whereas the legislative powers were specifically enumerated, gives very great importance to the fact that there was no express limit to the power of removal either in the enumerated legislative powers or the enumerated restrictions on executive power." *Id.* at 1. Stone also objected to the possible implication that the President may not have removal power over executive officials "to whom discretion is not delegated." "It is the duty of the President to enforce the laws," Stone wrote, "even though little or no discretion is involved. As Chief Executive he is entitled to faithful and efficient services by subordinates charged only with administrative duties. It is for that reason that the power is conferred and the duty imposed on him to exercise the power of removal, and that, to my mind, is just as *controlling* in the case of officers with little or no discretion as in the case of a cabinet officer." *Id.*
68. *Id.*
69. WHT to Robert A. Taft (November 22, 1925) (Taft papers).
70. HFS to WHT (November 24, 1925) (Van Devanter papers). The memorandum bears the notation in Van Devanter's handwriting, "C.J. sent this to me to work out 'so far as may be advisable.'"
71. *Id.*
72. "I have had the opinion digested paragraph by paragraph. The digest is placed in the form of an outline so that the outline of the opinion as it proceeds from the statement of the question to the final conclusion may be seen in its proper perspective." *Id.* With regard to his proposed revisions, Stone wrote that if "you would like to have me place these suggestions in more concrete form, I should be very glad to attempt it in some detail and submit the result to you, if you will send me three copies of the galley." *Id.*
73. WHT to Horace D. Taft (November 28, 1925) (Taft papers). Roughly a year later Taft noted to Van Devanter that "It is dangerous to manifest too much interest in [Stone's] views because he is apt to wish to write part of the opinion." WHT to WVD (November 11, 1926) (Van Devanter papers).
74. WHT to Horace D. Taft (November 28, 1925) (Taft papers). Brandeis's intention to dissent provoked a stream of angry invective that gradually subsided as Taft dictated a letter to his brother:

> Brandeis puts himself where he naturally belongs. He is in favor evidently of the group system. He is opposed to a strong Executive. He loves the veto of the group upon effective legislation or effective administration. He loves the kicker, and is therefore in sympathy with the power of the Senate to prevent the Executive from removing obnoxious persons, because he always sympathizes with the obnoxious person. His ideals do not include effective and uniform administration unless he is the head. That of course is the attitude of the socialist till he and his fellow socialists of small number acquire absolute power, and then he believes in a unit administration with a vengeance. I suppose we ought not to be impatient with some of our colleagues who do not agree with us, because it is a question which was very earnestly discussed in the First Congress and settled there for three-quarters of a century, but it was agitated again in the time of

Myers v. United States

   Jackson and Webster and Calhoun and Clay, and was of course made the chief
   subject of discussion in Johnson's day and in his impeachment. It is curious that
   the question should have remained undecided by our Court in all that time. ...
   Brandeis is taking time to write his dissent. I don't know when he will finish it, but
   he is a hard worker and I expect to get his dissent in a day or two.

   Id. No doubt Taft had in mind Brandeis's objections to Taft's attempts to fire Glavis.
   See supra Chapter 8, at 302–4.
75. WHT to Horace D. Taft (November 28, 1925) (Taft papers).
76. *Id.* The draft on which Stone commented on November 24 consisted of fifty-eight paragraphs. Although Taft considered this "very long," when Taft's opinion was finally published it had about tripled in size to approximately 170 paragraphs. In the Brandeis papers there is a draft of Taft's opinion dated November 30, 1925, with a covering note announcing, "I am recirculating the opinion in No. 7 – Myers vs. the United States. I have made some change in the arrangement and added some matter." The draft is twenty-eight pages long. Taft's final draft ran to seventy-two pages.
77. WHT to Charles P. Taft 2nd (November 29, 1925) (Taft papers).
78. HFS to WHT (November 30, 1925 (Stone papers).
79. 116 U.S. 483, 484–85 (1886).
80. HFS to WHT (November 30, 1925) (Stone papers).
81. *Id.* Stone was concerned that "we do not foreclose ourselves with respect to the power of removal except as it is actually involved in the present case." *Id.*
82. When the civil service was first created by the Pendleton Act of 1883, 22 Stat. 403 (January 16, 1883), it imposed restrictions on presidential appointments but it regulated removals from office only to the extent of prohibiting removals for giving or refusing to give political contributions. 22 Stat. 407. The thought was apparently that "if civil service restrictions prevented the President from appointing a hand-picked replacement for a person he removed, his incentive to remove for political reasons would disappear." Gerald E. Frug, *Does the Constitution Prevent the Discharge of Civil Service Employees?*, 124 UNIVERSITY OF PENNSYLVANIA LAW REVIEW 942, 955 (1976). Presidents subsequently used executive orders to regulate the procedures and criteria for removal of civil service personnel. *Id.* at 956–57. Eventually Congress enacted the Lloyd-LaFollette Act, Pub. L. 62-336, 37 Stat. 539, 555 (August 24, 1912), which provided that "no person in the classified civil service of the United States shall be removed therefrom except for such cause as will promote the efficiency of said service." The Act codified an executive order issued by Taft himself. *See* Frug, *supra*, at 958. The Act was in force when *Myers* was decided.
83. WHT to WVD (December 5, 1925) (Van Devanter papers). Taft continued: "I am sending you the suggestions of Stone. I'll talk with you about them tomorrow on the 'phone.' I have indicated where I have accepted Stone's emendations and additions." In his brief for the government, Solicitor General Beck had explicitly argued that the "power to delegate the right of appointment to the heads of departments or the courts of law does not affect the constitutional power of the President to see that the laws are faithfully executed, and to this end to remove his subordinates in the executive department who aid him in the discharge of this executive duty." *Brief for the United States on Reargument*, in *Power of the President to Remove Federal Officers, supra* note 9, at 68. *See id.* at 192 (Oral Argument of Solicitor General Beck). By contrast, the amicus brief of George Wharton Pepper argued that "Even the most extreme advocate of the Executive prerogative can scarcely contend that

the President has a vested right to ignore legislative restrictions upon the removal of an officer whose appointment the Congress in the exercise of a constitutional discretion might have vested elsewhere than in the President." *Brief for the Appellant, Filed by George Wharton Pepper, Amicus Curiae*, in *Power of the President to Remove Federal Officers, supra* note 9, at 136.

84. Taft did not adopt Stone's proposed conceptual framework. In his biography of Stone, Mason somehow infers from the memorandum of November 30 that Stone had anticipated the holding of Humphrey's Executor v. United States, 295 U.S. 602 (1935), in which the Court unanimously upheld congressional restrictions on the president's ability to remove FTC commissioners. MASON, *supra* note 66, at 232. At the time of *Humphrey's Executor*, Stone, according to Mason, "had the cold comfort of saying 'I told you so.'" *See* Marquis Childs, *Minority of One*, 214 SATURDAY EVENING POST 14, 15 (September 20, 1941). Although it is true that Stone's memorandum of November 30 emphasized the need for the president to control the performance by Article II officials of "purely executive" functions, rather than of quasi-legislative or quasi-judicial functions, Stone never argued that the president should not have full control over the removal of the latter. If anything, Stone in his 1925 memorandum seems to have been pushing for far wider presidential control over removal powers than that endorsed in *Myers*.

85. Taft is here referring to John Raymond McCarl, the first comptroller general of the United States, who had been appointed pursuant to the Budget and Accounting Act of 1921, *supra* note 11, which prevented unilateral executive removal. McCarl was a progressive Republican, closely associated with Senator George Norris. When announcing his *Myers* dissent from the bench, McReynolds "departed from his text to say that 'we now have a foolish or unwise Comptroller General' and he plainly intimated that in his opinion that officer would not long remain at his present post." George B. Galloway, *The Consequences of the Myers Decision*, 61 AMERICAN LAW REVIEW 481, 499 (1927); *McCarl's Tenure Held at Stake in Supreme Court Decision*, BALTIMORE SUN (October 27, 1926), at 2. McCarl in fact retained his position until 1936.

86. WHT to HFS (December 6, 1925) (Stone papers). Stone replied the next day, "Many thanks for your kind note of last evening. You know I am a team player and I should not have kicked over the traces if you had not accepted any of my views which after all concern only incidental matters of minor importance. I have only been longing to be helpful in the way which I believe we should all be, in carrying on the difficult work of the Court – without, I hope, pride of opinion or over insistence on anything." HFS to WHT (December 7, 1925) (Taft papers).

87. *See* WHT to Robert A. Taft (December 20, 1925) (Taft papers) ("I have heard nothing as yet from the dissenters in my big case. I have been trying to make some changes."); WHT to Horace D. Taft (December 30, 1925) (Taft papers) ("Brandeis tells me that he is going to give me his dissent on Monday next, so that in the course of a week or two the announcement will probably be made. I don't know what McReynolds will do, but I suppose he will dissent also with Holmes."); WHT to Robert A. Taft (January 3, 1926) (Taft papers) ("Brandeis tells me that he will have his dissenting opinion in the Myers case ready to hand me tomorrow. I don't know how much revamping of my opinion his opinion will require, because I don't know what the grounds are he will take. He never has discussed the matter in the Conference, and merely announced his conclusion, so that he may take such an attack as to require further discussion, though I hope it will not be extensive. I haven't heard from

Myers v. United States

McReynolds at all, and while I put him down as dissenting, I don't know just what form his dissent will take, for he has not given any intimation to me of any kind, though he has talked adversely to Sutherland and Van Devanter.").

88. 284 Pa. 421 (1925).
89. *Id.* at 426–27. George Wharton Pepper to WHT (December 23, 1925) (Taft papers).
90. *Benn*, 284 Pa. at 436.
91. WHT to WVD (December 30, 1925) (Van Devanter papers). In 1920, Taft had himself written that "Executive and judicial functions are united in the Interstate Commerce Commission, to the prejudice of each. The executive function in regulating the rightful, useful and safe operation of the railways may easily be separated from the quasi-judicial work of fixing rates, and may be better attended to by a separate board peculiarly qualified." William Howard Taft, *The Cummins Railway Bill* (January 15, 1920), in VIVIAN, at 333.
92. WHT to Horace D. Taft (January 5, 1926) (Taft papers). "However," Taft added, "it may turn out to be a stronger opinion than I indicate in this short reference, and I shall have to take time."
93. WHT to Horace D. Taft (January 7, 1926) (Taft papers).
94. *Id.* "If he is as long as Brandeis, we shall fill a volume.... I have put my opinion away until I hear from McReynolds, because I want to be able to make the changes needed to meet the arguments of the dissent all together."
95. WHT to Robert A. Taft (January 10, 1926) (Taft papers). Taft continued, "But I am old enough to know that the best way to get along with people with whom you have to live always is to restrain your impatience and consider that doubtless you have your own peculiarities that try other people." Taft wrote his daughter that "I have had a great opinion on my hands ever since the summer, and I have gotten it into shape and I was ready to deliver it a month ago, but I have had to wait for two dissenting opinions. One has come in and the other is postponed by the writer until the first of March. I don't suppose it will hurt my opinion to be put in a refrigerator and brought out for furbishing when the others have shot off their guns, but it keeps me in a state of something like suspended animation, as I have not been able to do much else." WHT to Mrs. Frederick J. Manning (January 10, 1926) (Taft papers). *See* WHT to Horace D. Taft (February 22, 1926) (Taft papers); WHT to Horace D. Taft (March 2, 1926) (Taft papers); WHT to Robert A. Taft (March 15, 1926) (Taft papers).
96. HFS to WHT (March 29, 1926) (Stone papers).
97. Stone did observe that "Throughout Mr. Justice McReynold's [sic] opinion he refers to the 'arbitrary' exercise of power of removal by the President as though the whole question is whether an arbitrary power of removal was given to the President or whether a reasonable control of the power of removal was given to Congress. It might be helpful to indicate in a sentence in the prevailing opinion that the fact that this power, wherever it resides, may be used arbitrarily does not determine where it is lodged." *Id.* It is odd that Stone was apparently unable to appreciate the point that for McReynolds, as for Brandeis, "arbitrary" executive action meant discretionary action that was unaccountable to general restrictions of law. *See infra*, text at notes 179–83.
98. So, for example, Stone quoted this sentence in Brandeis's dissent: "It is settled that, in the absence of a provision expressly providing for the consent of the Senate to a removal, the clause fixing the tenure will be construed as a limitation, not as a grant, and that, under such legislation, the President, acting alone, has the power of removal." 272 U.S. at 241 (Brandeis, J., dissenting). Stone commented:

> If this is a constitutional power, it must be acquired under the general grant of executive power and inferred from the President's duty to execute the laws. If this power exists as a constitutional executive power, there is no express limitation of it and the well settled principles of constitutional interpretation referred to in the majority opinion would deny a limitation of it by the legislative branch unless expressly granted.

HFS to WHT (March 29, 1926) (Stone papers). With reference to Brandeis's concession that an implied "constitutional power of suspension" may be attributed to the president, 272 U.S. at 247 (Brandeis, J., dissenting), Stone asked, "how can one infer a constitutional power to suspend from office if one cannot infer a constitutional power to remove from office?" Stone resisted Brandeis's claim, *id.* at 264–65, that an unrestricted executive power of removal was inconsistent with constitutional restrictions on the executive's power of appointment. Stone argued that Brandeis "would, I think, be bound to concede that such statutes [setting criteria for executive appointments] cannot go to the point of eliminating all power of choice on the part of the President in making appointments, and that at some point the legislative power to create offices and define qualifications for them must yield to the Constitutional appointing power. Legislative power to restrict removals must likewise yield to the President's Constitutional power to remove if it exists. Whether or not it exists cannot be established by argument when there is a Constitutional power to create offices and fix qualifications for them which, however, cannot be carried to the point of infringing the President's Constitutional power to nominate and appoint." HFS to WHT (March 29, 1926) (Stone papers).

99. *Myers*, 272 U.S. at 247 (Brandeis, J., dissenting).
100. HFS to WHT (March 29, 1926) (Stone papers). One cannot escape the impression in reading these lines that Stone was still very much in the grip of his recent experience as Attorney General "cleaning house" at the Department of Justice. *See supra*, Chapter 4 at 125 and notes 90–91.
101. *Id.* Stone's objections are strange considering that Taft's opinion for the Court also relied heavily on history and practice after the First Congress.
102. WHT to Robert A. Taft (May 2, 1926) (Taft papers).
103. WHT to Horace D. Taft (June 5, 1926) (Taft papers).
104. WHT to Robert A. Taft (July 16, 1926) (Taft papers).
105. WHT to WVD (July 18, 1926) (Van Devanter papers).
106. WHT to Robert A. Taft (August 2, 1926) (Taft papers).
107. WHT to GS (August 25, 1926) (Sutherland papers). *See* WHT to ETS (August 18, 1926) (Taft papers).
108. WHT to Clarence E. Bright (September 6, 1926) (Taft papers).
109. WHT to Horace D. Taft (September 9, 1926) (Taft papers).
110. *Id.*
111. WHT to Clarence E. Bright (September 20, 1926) (Taft papers).
112. WHT to WVD, GS, PB, ETS & HFS (September 28, 1926) (Taft papers). "I send you for preliminary examination, an opinion revamping the former opinion in the Myers case, made necessary by the extended scope of the dissenting opinions. I hope to be able to compress it some before we shall have discussed it, but I thought it wise to be elaborate in order to invite your consideration of the question. ... I will call you by telephone to fix a time either Friday or Saturday

Myers v. United States

morning at my home for the consideration of this opinion. This will give you time I hope to read it." *Id.* The meeting occurred at 10:00 am on October 13. Taft Daily Task Memorandum (October 12, 1926) (Taft papers).

113. WHT to Horace D. Taft (September 30, 1926) (Taft papers). Taft hoped "to be able to get it to the public before the end of October." WHT to Hayden N. Smith (October 5, 1926) (Taft papers).

114. WHT to Robert A. Taft (October 17, 1926) (Taft papers). "I hope to be able to get rid of an opinion that troubled me last summer and has been troubling me for more than a year, a week from Monday, and when I do that, I shall breathe more freely." WHT to Mrs. Frederick J. Manning (October 17, 1926) (Taft papers).

115. WHT to Horace D. Taft (October 17, 1926) (Taft papers). "The opinion," Taft remarked, "is unmercifully long, but it is made so by the fact that the question has to be treated historically as well as from a purely legal constitutional standpoint." WHT to Mrs. Frederick J. Manning (October 24, 1926) (Taft papers).

116. The memorandum is in Stone's papers and is undated. It is unsigned, but from its logic and composition, and from its typeface, we can infer that the memorandum is almost certainly written by Stone. From the fact that the memorandum refers to *Myers* as having docket number 2, we can infer that the memorandum was written at the beginning of the 1926 term. It is probably to this memorandum that Taft refers in his daily task memo of October 19, 1926, when he states: "Call up Justice Stone about his logical qualms as part of Myers opinion." (Taft papers).

117. Taft read a summary of his *Myers* opinion from the bench on the day that the decision was announced. In his notes for that summary, Taft said that the Civil Service System "applies only to inferior officers not appointed by the President by and with the advice and consent of the Senate, and over the removal of these officers Congress has complete control, and the maintenance or extension of the Merit System is wholly with Congress." Synopsis Delivered at Opinion Announcement, at 13½ (Taft papers). Taft had long been committed to the civil service system. *See supra* notes 25–26, 43.

118. As president, Taft had requested that Congress place within the civil service system "the heads of bureaus in the departments at Washington," arguing that "the extension of the merit system to these officers ... will have important effects in securing greater economy and efficiency." Taft, *Economy and Efficiency in the Government Service*, *supra* note 41, at 1028. "The time has come," Taft had pleaded, "when all these officers should be placed in the classified service." *Id.*

119. *Myers*, 272 U.S. at 173–74.

120. *Id.* at 161–62. A contemporary treatise summarized the impact of *Myers* in this way: "In the Myers case this right of Congress to limit the removing power of executive heads with reference to officers the appointment of whom has been vested in them by Congress was ... fully approved although the point was not involved in the case. It is thus seen that it is established that Congress may vest the removal power in department heads when the appointments are vested in them. There possibly is still unsettled, however, the question whether there remains also in the President a power to remove such officers, derived from the Constitution, of which power Congress cannot deprive him." WESTEL WOODBURY WILLOUGHBY, 3 THE CONSTITUTIONAL LAW OF THE UNITED STATES 1524 (New York: Baker, Voorhis & Co. 1929).

121. *See supra* note 116.

122. WHT to Charles P. Taft 2nd (October 24, 1926) (Taft papers). On the very morning of the announcement, Taft wrote his brother:

> I am announcing an opinion this morning, which is as important a constitution[al] decision as I have ever rendered. ... I have had to write an enormously long opinion, perhaps as long a one as there is in the books. ... As I originally wrote it it was 28 pages, but when Brandeis filed a dissent of 32 pages, with an enormous number of notes in fine print, and McReynolds filed a dissent of 49 pages, I had to double mine in order to cover the points that they insisted on developing. ... It has given me a great deal of work, a great deal of trouble and a great deal of worry, and I expect I shall feel, after I get the thing delivered and into the reports, like a woman who has given birth to a large child.

WHT to Henry W. Taft (October 25, 1926) (Taft papers). Taft's published opinion spreads over seventy-two pages in the United States Reports.

123. We know of other conclaves of concurring colleagues in close cases that Taft summoned to his home for consultation, as for example in Olmstead v. United States, 277 U.S. 438 (1928), see *infra* Chapter 33, at note 46, but nothing approximates the elaborate group writing process that characterized the actual drafting of *Myers*. The process by which Taft constructed his opinion in Corona Cord Tire Co. v. Donovan Chemical Corp., 276 U.S. 358 (1928), is perhaps the polar opposite of *Myers*. *Corona Cord Tire* was a complex patent case in which, as Taft noted to his son, "My colleagues left it to me without themselves voting on the case, and that makes it necessary for me to elaborate a statement of the case and the cases leading me to the conclusion I have. We very rarely do such a thing as this in our Court, but the character of the case is such, with the length of record, that it is difficult to do otherwise. The case was well argued, but nevertheless depends a good deal on the weight of the evidence and an understanding of the issue. It is a very common thing in most Supreme Courts to refer a case to one Judge and let him work it out. We never, or certainly very rarely, do that, and it would be intolerable if we did, but an opinion written under such a delegation is a great time consumer." WHT to Robert A. Taft (March 25, 1928) (Taft papers). *See* ALPHEUS THOMAS MASON, WILLIAM HOWARD TAFT: CHIEF JUSTICE 206 (New York: Simon and Schuster 1965). For what it is worth, Stone's docket book records a unanimous conference vote in *Corona Cord Tire*, with Taft designated as the opinion's author.

124. *See supra* notes 61–62, 112.

125. WHT to Horace D. Taft (November 28, 1925) (Taft papers).

126. Antonin Scalia, *Originalism: The Lesser Evil*, 57 UNIVERSITY OF CINCINNATI LAW REVIEW 849, 851–52 (1989).

127. *Myers*, 272 U.S. at 142.

128. Taft's interpretation of the Decision of 1789 was almost immediately controversial. It was contested in Brandeis's dissent, 272 U.S. at 284–85 (Brandeis, J., dissenting), which argued that the Senate was evenly divided and that the meaning of the House vote was indeterminate due to the complicated sequence of votes initiated by Madison. 272 U.S. at 284–85 (Brandeis, J., dissenting). Brandeis's account was elaborated by Edward Corwin, who concluded that "a mere fraction of a fraction, a minority of a minority, of the House, can be shown to have attributed the removal power to the President on the grounds of executive prerogative." Edward S. Corwin, *Tenure of Office and the Removal Power under the*

Myers v. United States

Constitution, 27 COLUMBIA LAW REVIEW 353, 362 (1927). *See id.* at 369. Corwin argued that *"Myers v. United States* is badly grounded in both history and logic." EDWARD S. CORWIN, THE PRESIDENT'S REMOVAL POWER UNDER THE CONSTITUTION vi (New York: National Municipal League 1927). Corwin's account of the Decision of 1789 was accepted by scholars for more than half a century. *See, e.g.*, CHARLES A. MILLER, THE SUPREME COURT AND THE USES OF HISTORY 52–70, 205–10 (Cambridge: Harvard University Press 1969); DAVID P. CURRIE, THE CONSTITUTION IN CONGRESS: THE FEDERALIST PERIOD 1789–1801, at 49 (University of Chicago Press 1997); Charles S. Collier, *The President's Removal Power under the Constitution*, 77 UNIVERSITY OF PENNSYLVANIA LAW REVIEW 432 (1929); Curtis A. Bradley & Martin S. Flaherty, *Executive Power Essentialism and Foreign Affairs*, 102 MICHIGAN LAW SCHOOL 545, 662–63 (2004). In 2006 Saikrishna Prakash published a new historical study claiming to show "that Chief Justice Taft was right all along." Saikrishna Prakash, *New Light on the Decision of 1789*, 91 CORNELL LAW REVIEW 1021, 1027 (2006). *See* AKHIL REED AMAR, THE WORDS THAT MADE US 353–59 (New York: Basic Books 2021); Aditya Bamzai & Saikrishna Prakash, *The Executive Power of Removal*, 136 HARVARD LAW REVIEW forthcoming (2023) (discussing how the Decision of 1789 came to be understood as a legislative construction that the president had the power to remove all executive officers). Prakash's findings, however, are disputed in Jed Handelsman Shugerman, *The Indecisions of 1789: Strategic Ambiguity and the Imaginary Unitary Executive* (May 8, 2020), available at SSRN: https://papers.ssrn.com/sol3/papers.cfm?abstract_id=3596566. *See* MICHAEL W. MCCONNELL, THE PRESIDENT WHO WOULD NOT BE KING 161–69 (Princeton University Press 2020); J. DAVID ALVIS, JEREMY D. BAILEY, & F. FLAGG TAYLOR IV, THE CONTESTED REMOVAL POWER, 1789–2010, at 16–47 (Lawrence: University of Kansas Press 2013); Jed Handelsman Shugerman, *Presidential Removal: The Marbury Problem and the Madison Solutions*, 89 FORDHAM LAW REVIEW 2085 (2021); Peter L. Strauss, *On the Difficulties of Generalization – PCAOB in the Footsteps of* Myers, Humphrey's Executor, Morrison, *and* Freytag, 32 CARDOZO LAW REVIEW 2255, 2259 (2011).

Whatever the ultimate historical verdict about the precise grounds for the Decision of 1789 in the House of Representatives, it is uncontroverted that, as the political scientist Robert Cushman pointed out in 1928, the "'decision of 1789' concerned the President's power to remove the head of one of the major executive departments," which is a very different question from his power to remove "inferior" officers. "A very sound argument supporting an unrestricted power in the President to remove cabinet officers might be built up on grounds which have little or no bearing upon a similar removal power with reference to minor functionaries." Robert E. Cushman, *Constitutional Law in 1926–1927*, 22 AMERICAN POLITICAL SCIENCE REVIEW 70, 74–75 (1928). "The action of the first Congress, on which Ex-President Taft relies for the most part, is not a precedent for his conclusion, since the first Congress was concerned with a superior officer and since it went no farther than to recognize a presidential power of removal when Congress was silent." Galloway, *supra* note 85, at 491–92. The intrinsic precedential force of the decision of 1789 would thus seem rather limited, although of course scholars continue to argue about

whether the implications of the decision's rationale are more far-reaching than the decision itself. Prakash, *supra*, at 1068–70, 1072–73.
129. *Myers*, 272 U.S. at 136. *See id.* at 176 ("When, on the merits, we find our conclusion strongly favoring the view which prevailed in the First Congress, we have no hesitation in holding that conclusion to be correct."). To Taft, the proximity in time and personnel of the first Congress to the Constitutional Convention was significant but not, as it would be for an originalist, decisive. Taft stressed that the Decision of 1789 "was the decision of the First Congress, on a question of primary importance in the organization of the Government, made within two years after the Constitutional Convention and within a much shorter time after its ratification," and that "Congress numbered among its leaders those who had been members of the Convention. It must necessarily constitute a precedent upon which many future laws supplying the machinery of the new Government would be based, and, if erroneous, it would be likely to evoke dissent and departure in future Congresses.... As, we shall see, it was soon accepted as a final decision of the question by all branches of the Government." *Id.* Taft laid considerable emphasis on the "acquiescence in the legislative decision of 1789 for nearly three-quarters of a century by all branches of the Government." *Id.* at 148. Brandeis's long and detailed opinion vigorously disputed evidence of acquiescence. Brandeis found that legislative restrictions on executive discretion in removals was "a construction given to the Constitution by the concurrent affirmative action of Congress and the President continued throughout a long period without interruption." *Id.* at 291 (Brandeis, J., dissenting).

> The historical data submitted present a legislative practice, established by concurrent affirmative action of Congress and the President, to make consent of the Senate a condition of removal from statutory inferior, civil, executive offices to which the appointment is made for a fixed term by the President with such consent. They show that the practice has existed, without interruption, continuously for the last 58 years; that throughout this period, it has governed a great majority of all such offices; that the legislation applying the removal clause specifically to the office of postmaster was enacted more than half a century ago; and that recently the practice has, with the President's approval, been extended to several newly created offices.

Id. at 283 (Brandeis, J., dissenting).
130. *Id.* at 122.
131. *Myers*, 272 U.S. at 119, 122, 132, 134, 164. "Particular significance," said the *San Francisco Chronicle*, "is attached to the fact that the majority opinion was delivered by Chief Justice Taft, a former President. It may be presumed that his experience in that high office has much to do with the rather practical tone of the argument." *Court Strengthens President's Powers*, SAN FRANCISCO CHRONICLE (October 27, 1926), at 24. The Court's conclusion, added the *Chronicle*, "is in line with modern industrial practice. More power is given to the executive, who from the very nature of his job must make decisions." *Id.* Robert E. Cushman agreed that Taft's argument "rests upon the conviction which Mr. Taft's presidential experience undoubtedly confirmed and emphasized, that the President cannot effectively and responsibly administer his office unless he can control his subordinates through an unrestricted power of removal." Cushman, *supra* note 128, at 74.

Myers v. United States

The deeply pragmatic cast of Taft's sensibility becomes especially visible when the reasoning of *Myers* is contrasted with Sutherland's opinion in Springer v. Government of the Philippine Islands, 277 U.S. 189 (1928), which addressed the question whether the Philippine legislature could appoint directors to certain government corporations. *See A Philippine Decision*, NEW YORK TIMES (May 16, 1928), at 24. Sutherland sought to resolve the question through abstract conceptual pronouncements of this nature: "The Legislature cannot exercise either executive or judicial power; the executive cannot exercise either legislative or judicial power; the judiciary cannot exercise either executive or legislative power. ... Legislative power, as distinguished from executive power, is the authority to make laws, but not to enforce them or appoint the agents charged with the duty of such enforcement. The latter are executive functions." 277 U.S. at 201–2. *Myers* never descends into this kind of formalism.

Holmes, McReynolds, and Brandeis dissented in *Springer*. Holmes seized the occasion to launch an all-out assault on Sutherland's brand of conceptualism, citing, among other decisions, the Court's own recent case of *J.W. Hampton, Jr. v. United States*:

> The great ordinances of the Constitution do not establish and divide fields of black and white. Even the more specific of them are found to terminate in a penumbra shading gradually from one extreme to the other. Property must not be taken without compensation, but with the help of a phrase (the police power), some property may be taken or destroyed for public use without paying for it, if you do not take too much. When we come to the fundamental distinctions it is still more obvious that they must be received with a certain latitude or our government could not go on.
>
> To make a rule of conduct applicable to an individual who but for such action would be free from it is to legislate – yet it is what the judges do whenever they determine which of two competing principles of policy shall prevail. At an early date it was held that Congress could delegate to the courts the power to regulate process, which certainly is lawmaking so far as it goes. With regard to the Executive, Congress has delegated to it or to some branch of it the power to impose penalties; to make conclusive determination of dutiable values; to establish standards for imports; to make regulations as to forest reserves: and other powers not needing to be stated in further detail. Congress has authorized the President to suspend the operation of a statute, even one suspending commercial intercourse with another country, and very recently it has been decided that the President might be given power to change the tariff. It is said that the powers of Congress cannot be delegated, yet Congress has established the Interstate Commerce Commission, which does legislative, judicial and executive acts, only softened by a quasi, makes regulations, issues reparation orders and performs executive functions in connection with Safety Appliance Acts, Boiler Inspection Acts, etc. Congress also has made effective excursions in the other direction. It has withdrawn jurisdiction of a case after it has been argued. It has granted an amnesty, notwithstanding the grant to the President of the power to pardon. A territorial Legislature has granted a divorce. Congress has declared lawful an obstruction to navigation that this court has declared unlawful. Parallel to the case before us Congress long ago established the Smithsonian Institution to question which would be to lay hands on the Ark of the Covenant; not to speak of later similar exercises of power hitherto unquestioned, so far as I know.
>
> It does not seem to need argument to show that however we may disguise it by veiling words we do not and cannot carry out the distinction between legislative and executive action with mathematical precision and divide the

branches into watertight compartments, were it ever so desirable to do so, which I am far from believing that it is, or that the Constitution requires.

Id. at 209–11 (Holmes, J., dissenting). *See* Note, 38 YALE LAW JOURNAL 114 (1928). Brandeis wrote Holmes about this dissent: "A1. I join." (Holmes papers).

Henry Stimson, who at the time was governor-general of the Philippines, wrote Taft after the decision to say that "I am very glad that the Providence which rules over such matters gave us a safe majority of sensible minds on the Board of Control cases. For whatever the justice in Brother Holmes' reasoning and Brother Brandeis' finesse, there is no possible manner of doubt among our crude minds out here, who have to deal with the practical situation, that a decision the other way in this case would have played hob with the cause of progress and good government in these Islands. Now that I have gotten you behind me, I can work out a solution of this matter with my political brethren in the Legislature here." Henry L. Stimson to WHT (June 29, 1928) (Taft papers). Taft explained to Stimson that "So far as [*Springer*] was concerned, we had really decided the principles of it in the Myers case, in that long opinion that I wrote, in which Brandeis and McReynolds and Holmes all thought it necessary to dissent. ... I thought first of taking the opinion myself, and I could have written it so as to bring McReynolds in, but when Sutherland got hold of the case he concluded, and I think probably he was right, that we ought to emphasize the fact that the Myers case really means something and that it has laid down a real constitutional principle. So far as Holmes' dissent is concerned, it is only one of a great number of opinions that he is writing now to indicate that he does not believe in the Constitution at all, as he really does not, where it imposes any limitation upon legislative authority." WHT to Henry L. Stimson (May 18, 1928) (Taft papers). To his brother, Taft remarked: "Holmes has no respect for Marshall, he exaggerates the powers of Congress and thinks they can do anything. He and Brandeis tried to sustain the Philippines Legislature in an effort to take away all executive power from Wood and Stimson but we beat that. Holmes has very little knowledge of governmental principles." WHT to Horace D. Taft (June 8, 1928) (Taft papers).

132. *See Myers*, 272 U.S. at 204 (McReynolds, J., dissenting) ("The President has often removed, and it is admitted that he may remove, with either the express or implied assent of Congress; but the present theory is that he may override the declared will of that body. This goes far beyond any practice heretofore approved or followed; it conflicts with the history of the Constitution, with the ordinary rules of interpretation, and with the construction approved by Congress since the beginning and emphatically sanctioned by this court. To adopt it would be revolutionary.").

133. Taft was disturbed at McReynolds's dissent. "McReynolds and Brandeis, but McReynolds more than Brandeis, have been anxious to call public attention to the opinions and denounce ours as revolutionary." WHT to Mrs. Frederick J. Manning (October 31, 1926) (Taft papers). *See* WHT to George W. Wickersham (October 30, 1926) (Taft papers). McReynolds's explicit charge that *Myers* was "revolutionary," *see supra* note 132, featured prominently in press coverage of the decision. *See, e.g., The Supreme Court as Revolutionary,* 123 THE NATION 468 (November 10, 1926) ("Seldom does a dissenting Supreme Court justice characterize the opinion of the

Myers v. United States

majority of his colleagues as 'revolutionary.' It is the more remarkable when a conservative like Justice McReynolds is moved to such expression."); *The President's "Right to Fire,"* 91 LITERARY DIGEST 5 (November 6, 1926); *Gives President Sweeping Power*, BOSTON DAILY GLOBE (October 26, 1926), at 1; *President Can Get Rid of Appointees*, HARTFORD COURANT (October 26, 1926), at 6; *Right of President to Remove His Own Appointees Upheld*, WASHINGTON POST (October 26, 1926), at 1; *President's Right to Oust Officers Upheld by Court*, BALTIMORE SUN (October 26, 1926), at 15; *President's Ouster Power without Senate Consent Upheld by Supreme Court*, NEW YORK TIMES (October 26, 1926), at 1; *A Great Constitutional Case*, NEW YORK TIMES (October 26, 1926), at 26; *A Revolutionary Decision*, 18 LA FOLLETTE'S MAGAZINE 116 (November 1926).

McReynolds wrote that "A certain repugnance must attend the suggestion that the President may ignore any provision of an act of Congress under which he has proceeded. He should promote and not subvert orderly government." 272 U.S. at 179 (McReynolds, J., dissenting). In a "tense scene" at the oral delivery of *Myers*, McReynolds was apparently even more emphatic than in his written dissent: "'After today,' he said, 'no man can tell what are the powers of the president and congress. Many officeholders are now subject to removal at the caprice of the president. Yesterday we supposed we had a government of specified, limited powers. Today no one knows. It is an amazing proposition.'" Raymond Clapper, *Power to Dismiss Left to President*, ATLANTA CONSTITUTION (October 26, 1926), at 16. *See Give President Power to Oust U.S. Officials*, CHICAGO DAILY TRIBUNE (October 26, 1926), at 3; Thomas Reed Powell, *Spinning Out the Executive Power*, 48 NEW REPUBLIC 369, 370 (1926) ("Once the court ventures to imply limitations on Congress in favor of implied powers of the President, as it did in the Myers case, there is no telling where it will stop. Implication piled on implication may build a tower to heights undreamed of by the Fathers.").

McReynolds's performance at the oral announcement of *Myers* outraged Taft:

> McReynolds of course made himself as objectionable as possible. McReynolds and Brandeis belong to a class of people that have no loyalty to the Court and sacrifice almost everything to the gratification of their own publicity and wish to stir up dissatisfaction with the decision of the Court, if they don't happen to agree with it. McReynolds was so oratorical, so undignified, so untruthful in his statements delivered orally, some of which have gotten into his written opinion, that after he got through, Holmes, who also dissented, spoke to me about it and said that he proposed to change his opinion which had expressed concurrence in the opinions of his fellow dissenters, and merely say that he concurred in the result of their opinions.

WHT to Horace D. Taft (October 27, 1926) (Taft papers). In his dissent, Holmes did indeed merely express his agreement with the "conclusion" of McReynolds's and Brandeis's dissents. 272 U.S. at 177 (Holmes, J., dissenting). Holmes's own dissent was only a page long. "The arguments drawn from the executive power of the President, and from his duty to appoint officers of the United States (when Congress does not vest the appointment elsewhere), to take care that the laws be faithfully executed ... seem to me spider's webs inadequate to control the dominant facts," he said. "The duty of the President to see that the laws be executed is a duty that does not go beyond the laws or require him to achieve

more than Congress sees fit to leave within his power." *Id.* "Holmes' dissent," Taft wrote his son, "is about five lines and hardly seems to indicate that he rises to the question." WHT to Robert A. Taft (October 24, 1926) (Taft papers). Brandeis commented to Holmes about the latter's dissent: "This will help much." (Holmes papers). Two years later Holmes summarized his dissent to his friend Ethel Scott: "[W]hen as here Congress created an office, fixed its compensation, and might abolish it tomorrow, it equally might prescribe a term of duration and require its own consent to a dismissal." OWH to Lady Leslie Scott (March 2, 1928) (Holmes papers).
134. *Myers*, 272 U.S. at 193 (McReynolds, J., dissenting).
135. *Id.* at 192 (McReynolds, J., dissenting).
136. *Id.* at 192, 204 (McReynolds, J., dissenting). "Congress, in the exercise of its unquestioned power, may deprive the President of the right either to appoint or to remove any inferior officer, by vesting the authority to appoint in another. Yet in that event his duty touching enforcement of the laws would remain. He must utilize the force which Congress gives. He cannot, without permission, appoint the humblest clerk or expend a dollar of public funds." *Id.* at 187.
137. *See supra* note 67, and text at notes 78–82, 99–100.
138. *See supra* text at notes 118–120, and note 117.
139. "The vesting of the executive power in the President was essentially a grant of the power to execute the laws." *Myers*, 272 U.S. at 117.
140. "As he is charged specifically to take care that they be faithfully executed, the reasonable implication, even in the absence of express words, was that as part of his executive power he should select those who were to act for him under his direction in the execution of the laws. The further implication must be, in the absence of any express limitation respecting removals, that as his selection of administrative officers is essential to the execution of the laws by him, so must be his power of removing those for whom he cannot continue to be responsible." *Id.* at 117. *See id.* at 134:

> The duties of the heads of departments and bureaus in which the discretion of the President is exercised and which we have described are the most important in the whole field of executive action of the government. There is nothing in the Constitution which permits a distinction between the removal of the head of a department or a bureau, when he discharges a political duty of the President or exercises his discretion, and the removal of executive officers engaged in the discharge of their other normal duties. The imperative reasons requiring an unrestricted power to remove the most important of his subordinates in their most important duties must therefore control the interpretation of the Constitution as to all appointed by him.

141. Art. II, Section 2, Cl. 2 provides that "Congress may by Law vest the Appointment of such inferior Officers, as they think proper, in the President alone, in the Courts of Law, or in the Heads of Departments."
142. *Myers*, 272 U.S. at 162.
143. *Id.* at 163.
144. "Unitary executive theorists read [the Vesting Clause], together with the Take Care Clause, as creating a hierarchical, unified executive department under the direct control of the President. They conclude that the President alone possesses

Myers v. United States

all of the executive power and that he therefore can direct, control, and supervise inferior officers or agencies who seek to exercise discretionary executive power." Steven G. Calabresi & Kevin H. Rhodes, *The Structural Constitution; Unitary Executive, Plural Judiciary*, 105 HARVARD LAW REVIEW 1155, 1165 (1992).

An interpretation of Taft's opinion in *Myers* that would be more consistent with contemporary theories of the unitary executive was offered at the time by Solicitor General James M. Beck, who twice argued the case. *See supra* note 83. Taking a position analogous to that of Stone, Beck wrote in 1926 that "the question still remains whether Congress could create an inferior officer, and, vesting the appointment in some other official, could prevent the President, in the exercise of his constitutional prerogative, from removing such executive officer. Much of the reasoning of the opinion would carry the logical implication that Congress could not thus impair the Presidential prerogative of removal. It is not statutory, but constitutional. The Court has clearly held that the President's power to remove is by virtue of the grant of 'Executive power.' This being so, it seems a logical conclusion that the Congress cannot impair that power simply because it vests the power of appointment in another official. It can change a statutory power, but it cannot change the Constitution by a statute." James M. Beck, *President Gains Power in Old Congress Fight*, NEW YORK TIMES (November 7, 1926), at XX15. *See* Galloway, *supra* note 85, at 505; WILLOUGHBY, *supra* note 120, at 1524.

Taken to its logical conclusion, however, Beck's logic would undermine the Civil Service, which *Myers* strongly intimates is on safe constitutional ground. That is why Beck was forced to concede that Taft's opinion in *Myers* is "not wholly clear" whether the president possesses the constitutional authority to remove at will civil service employees whose appointments are made by Heads of Departments. Beck, *supra*, at XX15. Most who read the opinion were confident that Taft had constitutionally sustained the civil service. *See, e.g.*, Powell, *supra* note 133, at 369 ("Officers not appointed by the President are not covered by the case. The decision, therefore, does not threaten any important civil-service program. ... [I]t leaves unchallenged the earlier case of United States v. Perkins."); Cushman, *supra* note 128, at 77 ("The federal civil service is in no danger, since Congress can place and keep it beyond the reach of direct presidential power of removal."). On the distinction between the president's powers to remove high level officials and inferior officials appointed by heads of departments, see AKHIL REED AMAR, AMERICA'S CONSTITUTION: A BIOGRAPHY 193–94 (New York: Random House 2005).

Needless to say, *Myers* is utterly inconsistent with the view of the unitary executive expressed by former Attorney General Barr, who complains that "the Judiciary has appointed itself the ultimate arbiter of separation of powers disputes between Congress and Executive, thus preempting the political process, which the Framers conceived as the primary check on interbranch rivalry." Attorney General William P. Barr, Nineteenth Annual Barbara K. Olson Memorial Lecture at the Federalist Society's 2019 National Lawyers Convention (November 15, 2019), available at www.justice.gov/opa/speech/attorney-general-william-p-barr-delivers-19th-annual-barbara-k-olson-memorial-lecture.

145. *See, e.g.*, Cushman, *supra* note 128, at 74 ("The dissenting opinions seem clearly to have the better of the argument, both in historical accuracy and in logic.").

THE TAFT COURT

In T.R. Powell's pungent formulation, "The logic is so lame, the language is so inconclusive, the history so far from compelling, that I venture to think that the mainspring of the decision and its only conceivable justification are to be found in the judgment of the majority that the result is one that ought to be reached." Powell, *supra* note 133, at 369. "Congress may vest the appointment of all postmasters in the Postmaster General, as it did up to 1836. It may dictate that these and all other 'inferior officers' shall be appointed by others than the President. In so doing, it may regulate and restrict their removal, notwithstanding the fact that the Constitution invests the President with the executive power and with the duty to see that the laws are faithfully executed. The Chief Justice recognizes this and still insists that this power and this duty carry with them the necessary implication that the President must be free to remove officers whom Congress permits him to appoint." *Id.* at 370–71. As to the decision of 1789, Powell observed: "The first Congress of 1789 went on record in favor of the assumption that it was not necessary for Congress to confer upon the President the power to remove the Secretary of Foreign Affairs, since he would have the power if Congress said nothing about it. It cannot be said that the action of the first Congress goes farther than this. ... The debate in the Senate is not reported." *Id.* at 370.

Powell was equally merciless in his indictment of Taft's explication of subsequent history: "Later Congresses restricted removals by the President, but these, we are told, were later Congresses and were biased by political considerations. Perhaps Vice-President John Adams when he gave that essential casting vote had a political thought that was not wholly impersonal. Since the days of the Tenure of Office Act, Presidents have approved statutes which restricted the President in removing inferior officers. From this, however, we are not to assume that they thought the restriction constitutional. They were coerced into signing by the importance of other elements of the legislation." *Id.* at 370. *See* Galloway, *supra* note 85, at 491–92 ("Does it follow that [the President] has failed since 1876 to see that the laws be faithfully executed? ... The Chief Justice discounts the political motivation behind the action of the first Congress, but emphasizes the partisan bias of later congresses. ... The sharp dichotomy between the Chief Justice's interpretation of the precedent of the first Congress, subsequent executive practice and legislative policy and the actual facts of history as introduced so ably and convincingly by Mr. Justice Brandeis in his margin, leaves the reader dubious of the infallibility of constitutional truths judicially revealed."). "The position of the majority judges is curious," noted *The Nation*:

> They admit that Congress may take from the President the power of appointing inferior officers and, by vesting it in the head of some other department, restrict removals as it will, yet they hold that the moment Congress transfers that appointing power to the President it is deprived of this restrictive power. The decision is, as usual, political rather than legal. The settled habit of the court is so to interpret the Constitution as to prevent legislation which seems to disturb intrenched interests.

The Supreme Court as Revolutionary, *supra* note 133, at 468.
146. Corwin, *supra* note 128, at 366.
147. "To Congress under its legislative power is given the establishment of offices, the determination of their functions and jurisdiction, the prescribing of

Myers v. United States

reasonable and relevant qualifications and rules of eligibility of appointees, and the fixing of the term for which they are to be appointed, and their compensation – all except as otherwise provided by the Constitution." 272 U.S. at 129. In 1918, Taft had strongly condemned Wilson's efforts to have Congress pass legislation authorizing the president "to coordinate and consolidate the executive bureaus, agencies and offices in the interest of economy and more effective administration of the government." William Howard Taft, *The Administration Coordination Bill* (February 14, 1918), in VIVIAN, at 35. Taft considered this legislation an "abdication" of Congress's constitutional obligations, because "The creation of an office is ordinarily regarded as a legislative function." *Id. See also* William Howard Taft, *The Overman Bill* (May 2, 1918), *id.*, at 56–57.

148. *Myers*, 272 U.S. at 117–18, 126, 161. In oral argument Senator Pepper opined that "the act of removing an officer is itself an Executive act, but that prescribing the conditions under which that act may be done is a legislative power, inseparably incident to the legislative power to create the office, to prescribe the duties of the office, to fix the salary, and to specify the term." *Power of the President to Remove Federal Officers*, *supra* note 9, at 172.

149. Taft wrote: "A veto by the Senate – a part of the legislative branch of the Government – upon removals is a much greater limitation upon the executive branch and a much more serious blending of the legislative with the executive than a rejection of a proposed appointment. It is not to be implied. The rejection of a nominee of the President for a particular office does not greatly embarrass him in the conscientious discharge of his high duties in the selection of those who are to aid him, because the President usually has an ample field from which to select for office, according to his preference, competent and capable men." *Myers*, 272 U.S. at 121.

150. *Id.* at 115–16. Taft explained the fact that the Constitution required the advice and consent of the Senate for presidential appointments as an exception that "was to be strictly construed" as a limitation "upon the general grant of the executive power, and, as such," not to "be enlarged beyond the words used." *Id.* at 118.

151. *Id.* at 161. In 1916, Taft had written that "Congress may not exercise any of the powers vested in the President." TAFT, *supra* note 24, at 126.

152. "Congress cannot reserve for itself the power of removal of an officer charged with the execution of the laws except by impeachment." Bowsher v. Synar, 478 U.S. 714, 726 (1986).

153. "Everybody conceded, moreover, that Congress may stipulate the qualifications of appointees, short of designating a specific eligible, although the power of appointment is thereby curtailed. What, then is to prevent Congress from fixing the tenure of an office created by it with resultant curtailment of the removal power? So far as the principle of the separation of powers is concerned the two stand on precisely the same footing." Corwin, *supra* note 128, at 386.

154. *Myers*, 272 U.S. at 295 (Holmes, J., dissenting). Holmes was prepared to take this logic to its ultimate conclusion: "I have equally little trouble in accepting its power to prolong the tenure of an incumbent until Congress or the Senate shall have assented to his removal. The duty of the President to see that the laws be executed is a duty that does not go beyond the laws or require him to achieve more than Congress sees fit to leave within his power." *Id.*

155. Taft had in 1916 laid out the general principle that he believed should control consideration of this question. He wrote that Congress "may not prevent or obstruct the use of means given [the President] by the Constitution for the exercise" of powers "vested in the President." TAFT, *supra* note 24, at 126.
156. Kendall v. United States, 37 U.S. 524, 610 (1838).
157. Pub. L. 63-43, 38 Stat. 260 (December 23, 1913) (setting terms for members of the Federal Reserve Board); Pub. L. 33-122, 10 Stat. 612 (February 24, 1855) (providing that judges of the Court of Claims will "hold their offices during good behavior").
158. *Myers*, 272 U.S. at 135.
159. *Id.* at 134–35.
160. Edward S. Corwin, *The President as Administrator in Chief*, 1 JOURNAL OF POLITICS 17, 50 (1939). Taft had discussed this paradox in 1916. *See* TAFT, *supra* note 24, at 126.
161. Thus Brandeis wrote Frankfurter the day after the decision to advise:

> Senate resentment & plans should take the form:
>
> (1) Of extending classified Civil Service to take in most of the new exempt offices.
> (2) To transfer to heads of Dep. many offices now in President's class.
> There is much else on this & other matters which I hope to write about soon.

LDB to Felix Frankfurter (October 27, 1926), in BRANDEIS-FRANKFURTER CORRESPONDENCE, at 256.
162. Corwin, *supra* note 160, at 46.
163. Morrison v. Olson, 487 U.S. 654, 691 (1988).
164. 295 U.S. 602 (1935).
165. Peter Strauss, *The Place of Agencies in Government: Separation of Powers and the Fourth Branch*, 84 COLUMBIA LAW REVIEW 573 (1984).
166. 295 U.S. at 628. The unanimous Court, per Justice Sutherland, dismissed *Myers* in almost disrespectful terms. "The narrow point actually decided," it said, "was only that the President had power to remove a postmaster of the first class, without the advice and consent of the Senate as required by act of Congress. In the course of the opinion of the court, expressions occur which tend to sustain the government's contention, but these are beyond the point involved and, therefore, do not come within the rule of *stare decisis*. In so far as they are out of harmony with the views here set forth, these expressions are disapproved." 295 U.S. at 626.
167. TAFT, THE PRESIDENCY, *supra* note 25, at 10.
168. *Myers*, 272 U.S. at 135.
169. *See supra* note 91. There is some thought that Taft would "have separated the functions of prosecution and adjudication" within the Interstate Commerce Commission, and subjected the former to presidential control. Ballard, *supra* note 39, at 71 n.35.
170. WHT to Horace D. Taft (November 4, 1926) (Taft papers). "The truth is that McReynolds is quite unprincipled in his method of stating cases," Taft continued. "He does not state them truthfully." McReynolds discusses executive branch judges at 272 U.S. at 181–82, 210–13, 224–25 (McReynolds, J., dissenting).
171. Taft stated in *Myers* that "The questions, first, whether a judge appointed by the President with the consent of the Senate under an act of Congress, not under the

Myers v. United States

authority of Article III of the Constitution, can be removed by the President alone without the consent of the Senate, second, whether the legislative decision of 1789 covers such a case, and third, whether Congress may provide for his removal in some other way, present considerations different from those which apply in the removal of executive officers, and therefore we do not decide them." *Myers*, 272 U.S. at 157–58.

172. *Myers*, 272 U.S. at 181 (McReynolds, J., dissenting). Brandeis's law clerk during the 1925 term, James M. Landis (who subsequently became Dean of the Harvard Law School), later recalled:

> Although the *Myers* case only involved a rather lowly postmaster, Chief Justice Taft in his opinion had a sentence or two to the effect that the same doctrine would apply to members of the so-called independent commissions, such as the Interstate Commerce Commission. Some efforts were made to remove this unnecessary dictum but Taft was adamant. In 1933, when I was with the Federal Trade Commission, President Roosevelt sought to give it some new life. One of the Commissioners appointed by his predecessor was particularly obnoxious to the President. The President sought to get him to resign and after considerable negotiation Commissioner Humphrey promised to do so. But when this was made known by the White House, Humphrey reneged on his promise and the President promptly removed him. During the course of these negotiations the President asked my opinion as to his power to remove Humphrey despite the statutory limitation upon its exercise. I told him that I was probably the greatest authority on that point since I knew that in the *Myers* case Taft had inserted language to cover this exact situation upholding the unlimited power of the President to remove any Presidential appointee including a Federal Trade Commissioner.
>
> After his removal Humphrey sued in the Court of Claims. The case went to the Supreme Court of the United States, a Court to which at that time no Justice had been appointed by President Roosevelt and which was substantially the same as the Court that had decided *Myers*. Surprisingly enough the Court ruled in favor of Humphrey and against the President.

James M. Landis, *Mr. Justice Brandeis: A Law Clerk's View*, 46 PUBLICATIONS OF THE AMERICAN JEWISH HISTORICAL SOCIETY 467, 472 (1957).

173. The fate of the independent agencies was very much on the mind of contemporary commentators on *Myers*. Thus T.R. Powell observed:

> There is no hint that members of administrative commissions are outside the scope of the decision. It is to be assumed, therefore, that the President may henceforth dismiss at will the members of the Interstate Commerce Commission, the Federal Trade Commission, the Board of Tax Appeals, and such a peculiar officer as the Comptroller General. Indeed, the Chief Justice refers to such quasi-judicial officers as ones whom the President must be able to remove if he is to discharge his constitutional duty to see that the laws are faithfully executed. It would seem that the only way in which Congress may possibly protect such officers from Presidential assaults is to deprive the President of power to appoint them.

Powell, *supra* note 133, at 369. *See The Supreme Court as Revolutionary*, *supra* note 133, at 468–69 ("The decision makes it impossible for Congress to give any determined tenure to" "quasi-judicial offices," so that "the fear of removal will henceforth operate to bow hitherto independent officials to the will of the President or of his party speaking through him. The attempts of Congress to set up non-political expert commissions are nullified. An arbitrary Executive has

THE TAFT COURT

free play for his prejudices."); *A Very Serious Decision*, NEW YORK WORLD (October 27, 1926), at 16 ("If it is true, as Justice McReynolds says, that members of the Interstate Commerce Commission, the Federal Reserve, Shipping, Tariff, Trade, Farm Loan, Railroad Labor and similar quasi-judicial, quasi-executive boards can now be removed at 'the President's pleasure or caprice,' then the gravity of the decision is evident."); Galloway, *supra* note 85, at 501 ("The most important officers menaced by the Myers decision are the members" of agencies "such as the Interstate Commerce Commission, the Federal Trade Commission and the Tariff Commission. These agencies need protection because of the semi-judicial nature of their functions; public confidence in their non-partisan character must not be impaired."); *The President's "Right to Fire,"* supra note 133, at 5; *A Revolutionary Decision*, supra note 133, at 164; Hart, *supra* note 51, at 659.

174. WHT to Thomas W. Shelton (November 9, 1926) (Taft papers). *See* WHT to Horace D. Taft (November 1, 1926) (Taft papers); WHT to Casper S. Yost (November 1, 1926) (Taft papers) ("A study of the legislation made under" the inspiration of the Johnson impeachment "will show that not directly but stealthily through the creation of boards who exercised part of the executive power[, it] has been sought to divide that power vested in the President by the Constitution, and it would very much minimize that power if the members of those boards were made free from administrative control through the power of the removal by the President. By making their terms long so as to reach from one term through another or into another, they would strip a new President of much of his capacity to determine and carry out his legitimate policies."); WHT to Horace D. Taft (October 28, 1926) (Taft papers) (*Myers* "curtails the power of the Senate and the power of Congress in erecting executive tribunals and boards that cut down the President's authority, and the members of such boards of course are strongly against the exercise of this Presidential power."); WHT to Oren Britt Brown (November 19, 1926) (Taft papers) (*Myers* "is the greatest constitutional case that I have had to do with, and of course in that respect it was a real opportunity. I think we have come to the right conclusion, in view of the history of the question and its early decision by Congress. I think, too, it is a wise result, in that it secures a proper equilibrium between the legislative and executive branches of the Government. The legislative branch of the Government will never lose its power. It has the whip hand of all the other departments in its law making power and is quite disposed at times to ignore the limitations of the Constitution which set boundaries between the power of Congress and the power of the other branches."); WHT to Clarence H. Kelsey (December 2, 1926) (Taft papers) ("[N]o one can under the current trend fail to observe that Congress pushes its power in every direction by constant legislation, relying on the others affected, especially the other branches of the Government, to enable the legislation that it passes to acquire permanency and constitutional conformity merely by lapse of time. Through the institution of boards whose members have terms that would outlast the Administration, it is possible for Congress to divide up the executive power, take it away from the President and tie his hands in many directions. This can not be done if he has the power of removal which he had uncontested for seventy-three years. I am glad to note that a majority of the press seem to favor the conclusion we reached."); WHT to William M. Hunt (May 5, 1927) (Taft papers)

Myers v. United States

(*Myers* "was the hardest case I have had in the matter of work since I have been on the Bench, but I was convinced we were right and it seemed wisest at a time when it really was not a political issue, to be able to settle the matter. . . . I am hopeful that the question will not be agitated and that the decision may remain as a permanent constitutional feature of constitutional construction.").

175. WHT to Calvin Coolidge (June 4, 1924) (Coolidge papers).
176. WHT to Helen Herron Taft (April 20, 1924) (Taft papers).
177. *Id.* Two months later Taft wrote Coolidge urging him to run for president on a "Coolidge platform" that would "differentiate its candidate from the blind and selfish politicians who have completely misinterpreted the will of the people, and who now find themselves in a situation in which their party can only be rescued by a candidate whose great strength is in the fact that he has been and is for all the people, and opposed to the narrow, factional selfishness of Congress." WHT to Calvin Coolidge (June 4, 1924) (Coolidge papers).
178. *Myers*, 272 U.S. at 123. Taft's insistence as president on executive control of the budget was ultimately rooted in this conception of presidential political accountability. As Taft lectured Congress in 1912:

> The principal governmental objects in which the people of the United States are interested include:
>
> The national defense; the protection of persons and property; the promotion of friendly relations and the protection of American interests abroad; the regulation of commerce and industry; the promotion of agriculture, fisheries, forestry, and mining; the promotion of manufacturing, commerce, and banking; the promotion of transportation and communication; the postal service, including postal savings and parcels post; the care for and utilization of the public domain; the promotion of education, art, science, and recreation; the promotion of the public health; the care and education of the Indians and other wards of the Nation.
>
> These are public-welfare questions in which I assume every citizen has a vital interest. I believe that every Member of Congress, as an official representative of the people, every editor, as a nonofficial representative of public opinion, each citizen, as a beneficiary of the trust imposed on officers of the Government, should be able readily to ascertain how much has been spent for each of these purposes; how much has been appropriated for the current year; how much the administration is asking for each of these purposes for the next fiscal year.

Taft, *Economy and Efficiency in the Government Service*, supra note 41, at 1031.

179. *Myers*, 272 U.S. at 293 (Brandeis, J., dissenting).
180. *Id.* at 292–94 (Brandeis, J., dissenting).
181. Youngstown Sheet & Tube Co. v. Sawyer, 343 U.S. 579, 655 (1952) (Jackson, J., concurring).
182. *Id.* at 635 (Jackson, J., concurring).
183. *Id.* at 655 (Jackson, J., concurring).
184. Powell, *supra* note 32, at xlviii.
185. ARTHUR M. SCHLESINGER, JR., THE IMPERIAL PRESIDENCY (Boston: Houghton Mifflin 1973).

CHAPTER 12

The Conference of Senior Circuit Court Judges

TAFT'S HEART ATTACK at the close of the 1925 term likely diminished his authorial control in *Myers*. But Taft's passionate commitment to administrative effectiveness nevertheless shines through the otherwise baggy sprawl of the opinion. Taft's enthusiasm for managerial efficiency remained undiminished throughout the decade. If after his heart attack Taft's intellectual leadership of the Court diminished along with his failing health, his dedication to improving the effectiveness of judicial administration never flagged. Long concerned with "the storm of abuse heaped upon the Federal Courts,"[1] Taft seized every opportunity to improve them.

Taking a leaf from progressive efforts to subject "institutions ... to close scrutiny" and "to try experiments" to improve them, Taft had from the outset of the twentieth century vigorously proposed "reforms which are in the interest of equalizing the administration of justice as far as possible between the rich and the poor."[2] Taft believed such reforms were urgently necessary to sustain the legitimacy of federal courts. He was convinced that federal justice needed to be made cheaper and more efficient.[3] Taft maintained this focus throughout his presidency,[4] and he redoubled his efforts after leaving office.[5] He urged judges to become "engaged in actual experiment" to improve judicial procedures.[6]

Categorically rejecting reforms calculated to promote "the so-called democratization of the courts," like the "recall of judges and recall of judicial decisions,"[7] Taft sought instead to identify the "grounds upon which the public have a right to complain."[8] "What I am anxious to do," he explained, "is to vindicate courts by remedying the real objections to their administration of justice."[9] "The agitation with reference to the courts, the general attacks upon them, the grotesque remedies proposed of recall of judges and recall of judicial decisions, and the resort of demagogues to the unpopularity of courts as a means of promoting their own political fortunes, all impose upon us, members of the Bar and upon judges of the

The Conference of Senior Circuit Court Judges

courts and legislatures, the duty to remove, as far as possible, grounds for just criticism of our judicial system."[10]

In a major speech at the Cincinnati Law School in 1914, Taft announced that the "chief grounds" for justifiable complaint "are first the delay in hearing and decision of causes; and second the excessive cost of litigation." Taft proposed a six-point platform for congressional reform of federal courts:

> First – The antiquated system of a separation of law and equity should be abolished. ...
>
> Second – The rules of procedure should be completely in control of the Supreme Court or a Council of Judges appointed by the Supreme Court, and they should be rendered as simple as the English rules of procedure are.
>
> Third – The costs should be reduced to a minimum, and that as far as possible they should be imposed upon the Government rather than upon the litigants.
>
> Fourth – Authority and duty should be conferred upon the head of the Federal judicial system, either the Chief Justice, or a council of judges appointed by him, or by the Supreme Court, to consider each year the pending Federal judicial business of the country and to distribute Federal judicial force of the country through the various districts and intermediate appellate courts, so that the existing arrears may be attacked and disposed of.
>
> Fifth – There should be a reduction of the appeals to the Supreme Court, by cutting down to cases of constitutional construction only the review as of right, and by leaving to the discretion of that court, by writ of certiorari, the power to hear such cases from the lower courts as it deems in the public interest.
>
> Sixth – The Federal Workmen's Compensation Act should be passed.[11]

Although Taft would not live to see either the merger of federal law and equity or rule-making authority vested in federal courts,[12] and although Congress would enact the Workmen's Compensation Act before he joined the Court, Taft worked hard and successfully during his time as chief justice to centralize the management of the federal judiciary, to alter the role of the Supreme Court, and to reduce the costs of litigation.

Only three days after being confirmed as chief justice, Taft, in his pajamas before breakfast on a Sunday morning, scratched off some ideas about judicial reform to Attorney General Harry Daugherty.[13] "I have always thought that the existing judicial force of the U.S. might be made doubly efficient in keeping down arrears," he wrote, "if it was applied at points where those arrears have a tendency to accumulate by someone made responsible by law and given authority to direct its use where needed." "I would make the Chief Justice and the Senior Circuit Judges of the nine circuits upon conference with the A.G. and with his initiative a responsible machine for applying the whole judicial force of the U.S. in the inferior Courts of the U.S. to the business to be done." This "would introduce a proper executive principle into the Judicial force of the country." To those who objected "to giving the Chief Justice the powers involved" in such a proposal and who wished instead to lodge responsibility in the whole Supreme Court, Taft answered that it would be "a mistake. In such an executive position, one can act much more effectively and quite as wisely as nine."[14]

Taft appreciated that his proposal presupposed an administrative capacity to determine the comparative state of dockets in different federal districts. He therefore recommended that "it might be well to have a conference each year ... to consider the prospect for the year and to make all possible provision for it. This conference could also make recommendation to the Atty. General as to the need of additional Judicial force and where and of what rank, so that Congress might have the benefit of judgment formed on nothing but the need of service."[15]

Taft well understood that the "fears of labor and western enemies of the Federal Judiciary" would arouse the "real opposition" of those who faced the possibility of "being tried by a Judge not drawn from the vicinage and, therefore, not subject to those ameliorating local influences so dear to a man who is 'up against it.'"[16] But Taft calculated that such resistance could be neutralized by "the strong desire for enforcement" of prohibition. "With Congress in a humor to enforce the Volstead Act, it would seem a good time to secure the right machinery to accelerate business."[17]

Underlying Taft's push for a "proper executive principle" lay a radically new vision of the federal judiciary. As Felix Frankfurter and James Landis observed in their monumental study of federal courts, "the root conceptions of our federal judicial system were independence and localism. ... [N]ot only were the judges rendered independent of the President and Congress; they were rendered independent of each other. ... Mobility of judicial personnel ran counter to all the traditional conceptions of American judicial organization."[18] Because independence and localism were built into the design and practice of federal courts, the federal judicial system as a whole "was without direction and without responsibility. Each judge was left to himself, guided in the administration of his business by his conscience and his temperament. The bases for informed public judgment and self-criticism were wanting, since adequate judicial statistics were unknown."[19] As Taft put it, the federal judiciary was an institution in which "each judge has paddled his own canoe and has done the best he could with his district. He has been subject to little supervision, if any."[20]

Twelve days after his confirmation, Taft journeyed to Washington D.C. from Montreal, where he had been serving as an arbitrator in the Canadian government's effort to acquire the Grand Trunk Pacific Railway. He "had a long talk with the A.G." in which they discussed the "reorganization of the Courts."[21] Taft outlined legislation that could be presented to Congress, and an initial draft of his ideas was prepared for him on July 20.[22] The draft proposed appointing additional district judges in each circuit and authorizing the chief justice to assign those judges "to any and such judicial districts ... as he may in his sound discretion deem advisable ... to the end that the services of said judges may be utilized at those places where the state of the judicial business most requires them." The chief justice was also authorized to summon and preside over a Conference of Senior Circuit Judges empowered to recommend legislation to Congress "adapted to cheapen and expedite litigation in the United States

The Conference of Senior Circuit Court Judges

Courts" and "[t]o make, modify, amend or repeal rules of practice and procedure in all Districts Courts of the United States to the end that pleadings and trials in said courts shall be shortened and simplified, and all causes, civil and criminal, therein, shall be proceeded with and terminated as cheaply and expeditiously as is in any way possible."[23]

It is apparent that Taft, with the eye of a former chief executive, conceptualized the Article III judiciary as a unified branch of national government, tasked with the efficient administration of justice. As Taft had affirmed in his 1914 American Bar Association presidential address, the problem of disposing of litigation must be approached "in the same way that the head of a great industrial establishment approaches the question of the manufacture of the amount that he will need, to meet the demand for the goods which he makes. ... [T]he time has come to introduce into the dispatch of judicial work something of the executive method that great expansion has forced in other fields of human activity."[24]

In the end Taft did not get exactly the bill that he wanted.[25] He got neither judicial rulemaking authority nor a free hand to recommend reform legislation. But the Act of September 14, 1922[26] was nevertheless a major triumph. It marked, as Frankfurter and Landis rightly observed, "the beginning of a new chapter in the administration of federal courts," a chapter that could not have occurred without "the powerful support of the new Chief Justice."[27] The Act authorized the chief justice to summon and preside over a Conference of Senior Circuit Judges.[28] It allowed the chief justice to transfer district judges to where they were most needed so long as there was a certificate of need from the senior circuit judge of the receiving district and a certificate of dispensability from the senior circuit judge of the circuit of origin. The Conference was charged with making "a comprehensive survey of the condition of business in the courts of the United States" and preparing "plans for assignment and transfer of judges," as well as submitting "suggestions to the various courts as may seem in the interest of uniformity and expedition of business."[29] The Act also created twenty-four new district court positions, increasing the number of federal district judgeships by about 20 percent.[30]

Taft lobbied hard for the Act and received the lion's share of the credit for its enactment.[31] It realized the essence of Taft's vision, which he had publicly expressed in an August 1921 address to the Judicial Section of the American Bar Association.[32] It imposed upon Article III courts an "executive principle of using all the judicial force economically and at the point where most needed" by securing "effective teamwork" and an "organized effort to get rid of business."[33] In essence, the Act implied "a functional unification of the United States judiciary."[34]

In *Myers*, Taft imagined the executive branch as an integrated whole, directed to functional ends by the president. The Act of September 14, 1922, conceptualized federal Article III judges as analogously integrated into a single branch of the federal government designed to dispense justice.[35] Previously, as Felix Frankfurter observed, "federal judges throughout the country were entirely autonomous, little independent sovereigns. Every judge had his own little principality. He was the boss within his district, and his district was his only concern."[36] The Act was based on the innovative premise that "the whole judicial force" be "organized as a unit, with authority to send expeditions to spots needing aid."[37]

This premise may seem obvious to us today, but in 1922 it provoked great resistance. No less a judge than Henry D. Clayton (after whom the Clayton Act was named) attacked the Act as manifesting "a dictatorial power over the courts unrecognized in our jurisprudence."[38] Clayton objected to "the war idea of mobilizing judges under a supreme commander as soldiers are massed and ordered." He argued that "judges are not soldiers but servants, and the people only are the masters whom they serve."[39]

To protests like these, Taft responded with the brutal and implacable language of managerial rationality. Although Taft conceded that "in the judicial work a judge does on the bench, he must be independent," he nevertheless insisted that "in the disposition of his time and the cases he is to hear, he should be subject to a judicial council that makes him a cog in the machine and makes him work with all the others to dispose of the business which courts are organized to do."[40] The very idea that judges were "organized" to accomplish a collective purpose transmuted the federal judiciary into a functional branch of government, analogous to the executive branch.

If judges were "cogs in a machine," there must exist some intelligence to direct the machine. Organizations require guidance, and the unification of the judiciary thus implied the "executive management" of "a head charged with the responsibility of the use of the judicial force at places and under conditions where the judicial force is needed."[41] The Act transfigured the federal judiciary from an "entirely headless and decentralized" institution[42] into one that required "executive supervision."[43] Taft defended this transformation as a necessary implication of "introducing into the administration of justice the ordinary business principles in successful executive work."[44]

The Act of September 14, 1922, accordingly altered the role of the chief justice, who, using the Conference of Senior Circuit Judges as a kind of cabinet, became responsible for the management of the judicial branch in the same way that in *Myers* the president was deemed responsible for the management of the entire executive branch.[45] Taft thus expanded the role of chief justice from the administrator of the Supreme Court into something like the administrator of the federal judiciary. It is because of Taft, and because of the innovative vision that gave rise to the Act, that we today so casually refer to the chief justice "[a]s the head of the federal judicial branch."[46] Today chief justices are required by law to "submit to Congress an annual report of the proceedings of the Judicial Conference and its recommendations for legislation,"[47] and chief justices are often expected to deliver an annual "State of the Judiciary Address."[48]

Although the Act did not invest the Conference with the broad mandate to engage in judicial reform that Taft had originally desired,[49] Taft considered "the language of the act" to be "wide" enough to permit him "to make" the Conference into "an instrument for the consideration of many defects in the system and for the recommendation of remedies."[50] During the course of the decade, Taft deftly and effectively forged the Conference into the voice of the organized federal judiciary,

The Conference of Senior Circuit Court Judges

diagnosing problems and offering solutions in the form of both best practices and proposed legislation.

The Conference held its first meeting barely three months after the passage of the Act and promptly set up committees on such subjects as improving the bankruptcy and equity rules, amending appellate procedure, recommending changes in district court procedures to expedite the disposition of pending cases and to purge dead litigation from the docket, and so on.[51] In its second meeting in 1923, the Conference recommended that district judges not allow continuances by agreement of counsel ("except for good cause shown by affidavits"), that the *voir dire* of potential jurors be conducted by judges rather than by counsel, and that legislation be passed simplifying procedure and unifying causes of action. It requested that Congress authorize five additional judgeships.[52] Three months later, in his annual message to Congress, President Coolidge explicitly endorsed this request of what he called the "Judicial Council."[53]

Beginning in 1924, the recommendations of the Conference were officially published in the reports of the attorney general. Over the remainder of the decade, these recommendations included advocating that the "the prohibition unit" be removed from the Treasury Department and "be bodily transferred to the Department of Justice";[54] proposing detailed new bankruptcy rules to the Supreme Court;[55] promulgating precise "suggestions" to district courts about how to eliminate deadwood from their dockets and expedite their proceedings;[56] recommending annual expenditures on judicial libraries and a plan for allocating these funds;[57] cautioning against the abuse of conspiracy charges to convert "a joint misdemeanor into a felony";[58] urging district judges to be careful in granting bail after conviction "to discourage review sought, not with hope of a new trial, but on frivolous grounds merely for delay";[59] advising district courts that "criminal cases should be forced to trial within what the court deems a reasonable time";[60] encouraging circuit courts of appeals to "adopt the plan now followed in the Supreme Court, of advancing, for the earliest hearing possible, all writs of error and habeas corpus cases involving the prosecution of crime, and, so far as the statutes permit, giving them preference over every other class of hearings";[61] suggesting that circuit courts of appeals stay their mandates for not longer than thirty days to provide time for filing petitions for writs of *certiorari*;[62] and recommending that Congress provide a law clerk to each circuit judge.[63]

The Conference also recommended the creation of new judgeships to meet congestion in understaffed districts. It became quickly clear, as Taft wrote Attorney General John G. Sargent, that "while the transfer of Judges from District to District and from Circuit to Circuit is of the utmost benefit, it can not make up for the lack of Judges in Districts where the congestion is hopeless."[64] The Conference accordingly recommended the creation of new federal judgeships each year after 1923. These recommendations proved spectacularly persuasive and successful. By the end of 1930 Congress had adopted all but one of the Conference's many recommendations, creating some nineteen new federal judgeships.[65]

The Conference rapidly became the official voice of the federal judiciary, treated with respect by both Congress and the attorney general.[66] As Taft observed

THE TAFT COURT

as early as 1925, "[t]he truth is I feel as if our Conference was becoming a matter of considerably more importance in Congress and in the press as time goes on, and that we ought to encourage the thought of our importance."[67] The following year, Frankfurter noted that "[t]he actions of the Conference indicate to me the steady growth in its significance and the accumulating influence that it is bound to have with the lower courts and gradually, I am sure, with Congress and the informed thought of the country."[68] By fall 1927, Taft had reason to be gratified at his creation. "A good many people doubted [the Conference's] usefulness," he said, "but all the members of the Conference came to me this time to assure me that their doubts were removed, and it is really accomplishing something."[69]

In 1927, the Conference was able to express official approval of its own work. "The condition of business in the district courts of all the country is much more satisfactory than it was a year ago," it said. "The courts as now organized in the United States are able, we think, to take care of business as it comes in."[70] This was a real achievement. Figure III-4, which charts the total caseload of federal district courts from fiscal 1915 through fiscal 1930, illustrates the rising caseload that in fiscal 1918 had far outpaced the capacity of federal trial courts. The consequent steep rise in judicial backlog, beginning in fiscal 1920 and peaking in fiscal 1923, posed a serious crisis for the federal judiciary. Beginning in fiscal 1925, however, arrears began to decline for the remainder of the decade, as federal district courts were able to terminate more cases than were initiated.[71] Figure III-5 suggests that these changes were largely driven by increased criminal prosecutions (chiefly for prohibition violations), which district judges began to terminate faster than their initiation in fiscal 1924.[72]

Despite Taft's hopes,[73] it is likely that the manifest improvement in the dockets of federal district courts that occurred during the 1920s was not primarily

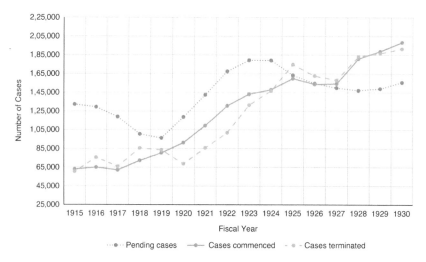

Figure III-4 Total federal district court cases by fiscal year, 1915–1930.
Based on Reports of the Attorney General.

The Conference of Senior Circuit Court Judges

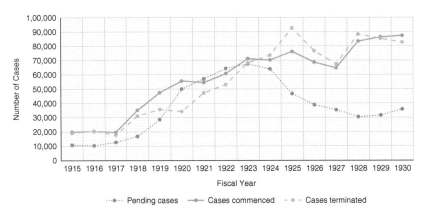

Figure III-5 Criminal prosecutions by the United States in federal district courts by fiscal year, 1915–1930.
Based on Reports of the Attorney General.

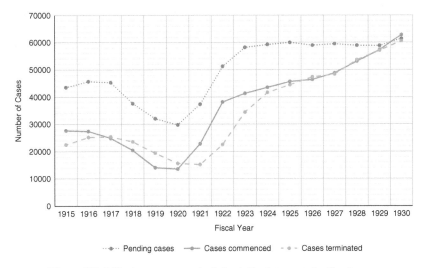

Figure III-6 Bankruptcy cases in federal district courts by fiscal year, 1915–1930.
Based on Reports of the Attorney General.

due to the ability to transfer federal judges created by the 1922 Act. "[T]he assignment of judges from outside circuits turned out to be only an alleviating factor in congested districts, and not a very large one at that."[74] Instead the vast increase in judicial manpower authorized by the Act, as well as the steady augmentations of judicial strength throughout the decade, were probably chiefly responsible for overcoming the congestion crisis of the early 1920s.

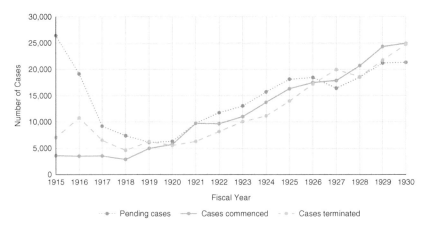

Figure III-7 Federal district civil cases to which the United States is a party by fiscal year, 1915–1930.
Based on Reports of the Attorney General.

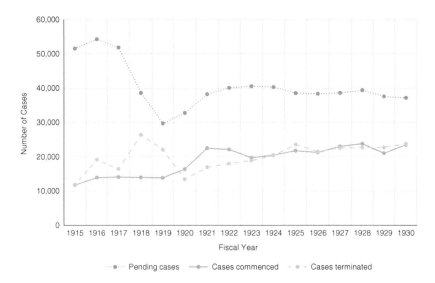

Figure III-8 Federal district court cases to which the United States is not a party by fiscal year, 1915–1930.
Based on Reports of the Attorney General.

One should not lightly disregard, however, the intangible factors created by the Conference, of which Taft was acutely aware. Having district judges report the state of their dockets to senior circuit judges, who in turn met together as a group to discuss the national state of the judiciary, brought district judges for the first time into what Taft called "a mild disciplinary circle" that made "them feel that they are

The Conference of Senior Circuit Court Judges

under real observation by the other judges and the country."[75] On the positive side, it made district judges feel noticed and their work valued, so that the Conference was for Taft "an instrument for creating harmony, coordination and unified action by the hundred or more Judges engaged in the courts of first instance and intermediate appeal."[76] It was a means "to come in touch with the Federal Judges of the country, so that we may feel more allegiance to a team and do more teamwork."[77] Taft believed that forging such "a closer union of the Federal judicial forces" could "not but make for better administration."[78] It produced "teamwork, uniformity in action and an interest by all the judges in the work of each district."[79]

For Taft, this aspiration to unify and inspire the federal judiciary was integral to the institutional responsibilities of the chief justice, on whose shoulders rested the need for achieving "more solidarity of action among the Federal Judges, so that they shall feel that we are all working toward the same end."[80] As Taft wrote one district judge, "We have a tremendous amount of work to carry on, and if we don't coordinate and haven't an esprit, we shall lose opportunity to do the work well. . . . I have been very anxious to have all the members of the Federal Judiciary realize that we are remanded to the top, and that whatever we can to [sic] here in Washington to help, we will do."[81]

Taft was always "glad to keep in touch with District Judges. They are the wheel horses of our system, and I want them to know that they have the deepest sympathy in their efforts in the dispatch of business in the members of the Supreme Court. Don't hesitate to write me whenever you have a suggestion or inquiry to make."[82] Taft liked to write judges to ask them to return "a long gossipy letter so that I may acquire intimate knowledge of the situation"[83] and to lament that "we in the Court here in Washington do not have greater opportunity to meet in the flesh the Judges who are on the firing line in the Federal Judiciary."[84]

In return, district judges throughout the country expressed their appreciation for Taft's attention and concern. As Learned Hand wrote Taft in 1923, "It is a great comfort to know the interest that you take. To be frank, we have never felt it before your incumbency."[85] Hand added a year later that "[a]s I have had occasion to tell you before, I feel I have a vested interest in your being Chief Justice, because you are the first Chief Justice that ever recognized such things as District Courts except when they were officially brought to their attention to reverse."[86]

From this perspective, the Conference was a mechanism through which Taft could fulfill the larger obligations of executive leadership that he understood to be implicit in the role of chief justice. Although Taft deftly deployed the Conference to achieve goals he believed necessary for the improvement of federal courts,[87] he was not willing to confine his personal efforts to those sanctioned by the Conference. So, for example, when Congress in 1927 authorized an additional judgeship for the Northern District of New York,[88] the Conference had not yet recommended any such judgeship. Yet the Senate Report accompanying the legislation quotes a letter from Attorney General John G. Sargent specifically invoking the authority of the chief justice:

> Although the northern district of New York was not included among the districts for which the conference of senior circuit judges has recommended additional district judges, Chief Justice Taft, who presides over the conference, has, since the last meeting of the conference, specially examined the situation in

the northern district of New York and concluded that an additional district judge is needed there. The Chief Justice says:

"I have been examining the statistics of the cases in the northern district of New York and in the western district, and I am bound to concede that the showing is strong for an additional judge in the northern district as well as in the western district."[89]

When specific incidents of egregious judicial delay or abuse were brought to his attention, Taft took it upon himself to take personal action. In 1927, for example, he wrote to prod District Judge John A. Peters into deciding a stale case:

> I write in the interests of the administration of justice, and for the reputation of the Federal Judiciary, that you dispose of the patent case which you now must have had at hand and submitted to you for more than four years. As a fellow member of the Federal judiciary, I urge that you drop everything else and decide this case. ... We none of us can afford to justify the complaints of delays in awarding just rights to litigants. Of course I write this letter with no assumption that I may exercise direct authority over you in the discharge of your duties, but as the head of the Federal Judiciary I feel that I do have the right to appeal to you, in its interest and in the interest of the public whom it is created to serve, to end this indefensible situation.[90]

As "the head of the Federal Judiciary," Taft felt himself responsible for the functioning of the Article III branch of government. This role and this responsibility are among Taft's most enduring legacies.

The Conference of Senior Circuit Court Judges

Notes

1. William H. Taft, *Criticisms of the Federal Judiciary*, 29 AMERICAN LAW REVIEW 641, 673 (1895).
2. William H. Taft, *Delays of the Law*, 18 YALE LAW JOURNAL 28, 30, 39 (1908). Like Brandeis, Taft paired the language of "experiments" with the metaphor of "laboratories." *See Judicial Council Idea Ably Presented*, 9 JOURNAL OF THE AMERICAN JUDICATURE SOCIETY 103, 104 (December 1925); William Howard Taft, *Possible and Needed Reforms in Administration of Justice in Federal Courts*, 8 AMERICAN BAR ASSOCIATION JOURNAL 601, 607 (1922).
3. "'We must make it so,' the President urged, 'that the poor man will have as nearly as possible an opportunity of litigating as the rich man, and under present conditions, ashamed as we may be of it, this is not the fact.'" Quoted in *Our Criminal Trials Disgrace, Says Taft*, NEW YORK TIMES (September 17, 1909), at 2. *See* Kevin J. Burns, *Chief Justice as Chief Executive: Taft's Judicial Statesmanship*, 43 JOURNAL OF SUPREME COURT HISTORY 47, 62 (2018).
4. *See, e.g.*, William Howard Taft, *First Annual Message to Congress*, 45 CONG. REC. 31 (December 7, 1909); *Our Criminal Trials Disgrace, Says Taft*, *supra* note 3.
5. *See* Statement of Hon. William H. Taft, *Reforms in Judicial Procedure: American Bar Association Bills* (February 27, 1914), Hearings before the House Committee on the Judiciary, 63rd CONG. 2nd SESS., at 15, 17 ("There are a great many attacks on our judiciary. There are defects in the administration of justice in this country, undoubtedly ... but the trouble about most of the attacks ... is that they are based on entirely wrong grounds.... I am very much opposed, very much opposed indeed, to the modern suggestions with reference to reforming our courts by the recall of judges and the recall of judicial decisions ... and therefore what I am anxious to do is to vindicate the courts by remedying the real objections to their administration of justice."); William H. Taft, *The Courts and the Progressive Party*, 186 SATURDAY EVENING POST 9, 47 (March 20, 1914) ("The real defects in our present civil system are a failure to dispatch business and a failure to furnish judgment at a small cost.... Mr. Roosevelt has ... seriously injured the administration of justice in this country by his unfounded criticism of the courts.... Still there may come out of the feeling aroused by his unjust attacks and his fantastic remedy, such a popular scrutiny of the real defects in our administration of justice as to enable us to secure a real improvement and thus enable the courts, by a long, hard struggle, to regain the confidence of the public of which Mr. Roosevelt and the Progressive party have unjustly sought to deprive them.").
6. *Remarks of William Howard Taft*, in REPORT OF THE THIRTY-NINTH ANNUAL MEETING OF THE AMERICAN BAR ASSOCIATION 742 (Baltimore: Lord Baltimore Press 1916).
7. William H. Taft, *The Attacks on the Courts and Legal Procedure*, 5 KENTUCKY LAW JOURNAL 3, 4 (1916). Taft believed that these reforms "are destructive of the rights of the individual, take away the protection of the minority against the possible injustice of the majority, and are a mere recurrence to the tyranny of the Stuart Kings in their attempt to subordinate the administration of justice to their arbitrary will, except that the tyranny of the plurality of the electorate is to be substituted for the tyranny of one man. The necessary tendency of such remedies is to destroy the supremacy of the law." *Id.*
8. *Id.* at 10.
9. Statement of Hon. William H. Taft, *supra* note 5, at 17.

10. William Howard Taft, *Address of the President*, in REPORT OF THE THIRTY-SEVENTH ANNUAL MEETING OF THE AMERICAN BAR ASSOCIATION 359, 384–85 (Baltimore: Lord Baltimore Press 1914). "[I]n this day of hysteria and demagoguery and vicious attacks on courts, we must take away any just ground for criticism of our judicial system." William H. Taft, *Legal Ethics*, 2 BOSTON UNIVERSITY LAW REVIEW 161, 170 (1922). Taft's support of procedural reform to undermine radical critiques of judicial power was common among elite lawyers of his time. *See, e.g.*, Walter George Smith, *Civil Liberty in America*, 4 AMERICAN BAR ASSOCIATION JOURNAL 551 (1918).
11. Taft, *supra* note 7, at 10, 14–15.
12. PETER GRAHAM FISH, THE POLITICS OF FEDERAL JUDICIAL ADMINISTRATION 22–23 (Princeton University Press 1973).
13. On the very day of Taft's confirmation, Taft's close friend Gus Karger telegrammed him to say that "Harry [Daugherty] thinks you should come to Washington soon after the fourth to take oath. Desires to put you on committee of judges to determine changes needed in federal judicial organizations." Gus Karger to WHT (June 30, 1921) (Taft papers). Two days later, Taft wrote his wife, "I don't think Daugherty has very definite ideas of what he wants but his general purpose is very important and I am deeply interested in it. He made an excuse for demanding my immediate appointment because he wanted to use me in this matter. This, of itself, requires that I should conform to his purpose at however great inconvenience." WHT to Helen Herron Taft (July 2, 1921) (Taft papers). On Daugherty's concerns about congestion in federal courts, see *Congested Dockets in the Federal Courts Menace to Justice Says Attorney General*, 13 JOURNAL OF THE AMERICAN INSTITUTE OF CRIMINAL LAW AND CRIMINOLOGY 609 (1923).
14. WHT to Harry M. Daugherty (July 3, 1921) (Department of Justice Files, No. 144446, Section 2).
15. *Id.*
16. *Id.* Taft regarded the possibility of visiting judges who represented national rather than local standards as "an advantage, a good bye [sic] product of the proposal." *Id.*
17. *Id.* In his letter, Taft made two brief additional proposals for reform:

> The second change that would help much is to make all offenses in the Federal Jurisdiction except what are real felonies or infamous crimes, punishable by less than a year's imprisonment so that they may be tried on information filed by the District Attorney and shall not require the costly and expensive and delaying attention of a grand jury.
>
> The third change would be new procedure in respect to this "Information" docket as to Jury trials. Here we come close to the Constitution. I should think that a statute might be drawn within the limitations by a provision that when the docket is called, unless a jury be demanded, it shall be deemed to be waived.

Id.
18. Felix Frankfurter & James M. Landis, *The Business of the Supreme Court of the United States – A Study in the Federal Judicial System: VI. The Conference of Senior Circuit Judges*, 40 HARVARD LAW REVIEW 431, 432–33 (1927). In 1921, there did exist two precedents for the power temporarily to transfer district judges to territories other than those to which they had been appointed. The first was the Act of October 3, 1913, Pub. L. 63-18, 38 Stat. 203, which authorized the temporary transfer of judges to the Second Circuit to alleviate congestion in New York City, and the second was the authorization to appoint circuit judges on the Commerce Court for service on any

The Conference of Senior Circuit Court Judges

circuit court. Pub. L. 61-218, 36 Stat. 539, 540 (June 18, 1910). Frankfurter & Landis, *supra*, at 447-48. In December 1921, Taft was asked to certify the transfer of Nebraska Judge Woodrough to New York. Believing that the request might be suspect, Taft wrote Daugherty that "I shall be glad to welcome a time when we can sent [sic] Judges according to the reliable information as to the proportionate needs of the different parts of the country derived from a council of judges who know, rather than make it dependent on the wish of a judge to secure a vacation." WHT to Harry M. Daugherty (December 4, 1921) (Taft papers).

19. Frankfurter & Landis, *supra* note 18, at 434. Roscoe Pound's famous 1906 address on popular dissatisfaction with the administration of justice is conventionally credited with having first "roused the attention of the profession to the relation between our anarchic judicial organization and popular dissatisfaction with the administration of justice." *Id.* at 437. *See* Roscoe Pound, *The Causes of Popular Dissatisfaction with the Administration of Justice*, in REPORT OF THE TWENTY-NINTH ANNUAL MEETING OF THE AMERICAN BAR ASSOCIATION 395 (Philadelphia: Dando Printing & Publishing Co. 1906). Pound had complained of the division of courts into "rigid districts . . . so that business may be congested in one court while judges in another are idle." *Id.* at 412. Pound's paper inspired the creation of an American Bar Association committee, whose 1909 report, according to Frankfurter and Landis, gave "the lead to all contemporary movements for judicial reform. To its principles we owe the momentum for a unified judiciary and a judicial council." Frankfurter & Landis, *supra* note 18, at 437. Frankfurter and Landis observed that "With all the weight of his authority and experience, ex-President Taft directed this general movement for judicial reform into federal channels." *Id.* at 441.

20. William H. Taft, *Adequate Machinery for Judicial Business*, 7 AMERICAN BAR ASSOCIATION JOURNAL 453, 454 (1921).

21. WHT to Helen Herron Taft (July 12, 1921) (Taft papers). Taft wrote his brother, "I suppose I shall take the oath on Monday in the A.G.'s office. Then the A.G. wants me to act as Chairman of a Committee to . . . recommend some means of meeting arrears in the trial courts of the U.S. growing out of this new liquor Amendment and the Volstead Law." WHT to Horace D. Taft (July 8, 1921) (Taft papers).

22. M.C. Herron to WHT (July 20, 1921) (Taft papers).

23. *Id.* The draft act also provided that "the prosecution of all misdemeanors in the United States Courts shall be on information." It also required that each criminal defendant be presented with "two printed forms, one demanding and the other waiving a jury." The Act abolished "all terms of Court in District Courts" and provided that they "shall be held to be constantly in session." It is in this context that Brandeis wrote Taft that he was "delighted to hear that you have undertaken the task of making more efficient the administration of our law. It is by such intelligent appreciation of existing defects and determined effort to devise remedies that respect for law may be promoted." LDB to WHT (July 19, 1921) (Taft papers).

24. Taft, *Address of the President, supra* note 10, at 383-84.

25. *See, e.g.*, WHT to Judge Arthur C. Denison (April 16, 1922) (Taft papers) (noting that the bill "added a limitation that the senior circuit judge of the circuit needing the aid shall certify the need to me, and that the circuit judge of the circuit from which the district judge is to be taken shall certify that it will not interfere with business in his circuit. I do not object to this limitation if it does not result in leaving it largely to the choice of the judge to be assigned whether he shall go or not.").

26. Pub. L. 67-298, 42 Stat. 837 (September 14, 1922).
27. Frankfurter & Landis, *supra* note 18, at 455–56. *See* Note, *Unification of the Judiciary: A Record of Progress*, 2 TEXAS LAW REVIEW 445, 452–53 (1924). The story of the Act is well told in FISH, *supra* note 12, at 24–39.
28. Emphasizing the executive responsibility of the chief justice, the Act provided: "It shall be the duty of every judge thus summoned to attend said conference, and to remain throughout its proceedings, unless excused by the Chief Justice, and to advise as to the needs of his circuit and as to any matters in respect of which the administration of justice in the courts of the United States may be improved."
29. The Conference was not given the power "To make, modify, amend or repeal rules of practice and procedure in all Districts Courts of the United States," as Taft had wished. But Taft's vision has in the end proved highly influential. Currently the Judicial Conference of the United States possesses authority to study "the operation and effect of the general rules of practice and procedure now or hereafter in use as prescribed by the Supreme Court for the other courts of the United States pursuant to law. Such changes in and additions to those rules as the Conference may deem desirable to promote simplicity in procedure, fairness in administration, the just determination of litigation, and the elimination of unjustifiable expense and delay shall be recommended by the Conference from time to time to the Supreme Court for its consideration and adoption, modification or rejection, in accordance with law." 28 U.S.C. § 331.
30. WHT to Charles D. Hilles (February 5, 1923) (Taft papers) ("The passage of the bill to increase the Federal judiciary is one of the most important acts in the history of the judiciary, not only because it adds about 20 per cent to the number of Judges of the courts of first instance, but also because it creates a body of the senior circuit judges of the country from the nine circuits, presided over by the Chief Justice, which is empowered by sending judges from one district and one circuit to another, temporarily to mass the force of the judiciary where the arrears are greatest."); Judith Resnik, *Building the Federal Judiciary (Literally and Legally): The Monuments of Chief Justices Taft, Warren, and Rehnquist,* 87 INDIANA LAW JOURNAL 823, 863 (2012).

Taft had pushed for the appointment of eighteen new district judges, but he wanted them designated as "district judges at large" so that they could be freely moved between districts. WHT to Harry M. Daugherty (August 8, 1921) (Taft papers). The judges were instead appointed to permanent districts. The extra judges were justified by the judicial commission appointed by Daugherty (consisting of judges John E. Sater, W.I. Grubb, John C. Pollock, and district attorneys William Hayward, and Charles F. Clyne) as needed to combat congestion due "not only to our country's normal growth in population and business, but also to the increase of business caused by the War, the subsequent depression and readjustment, the increased activities of the Federal Government as evidenced by statutes enacted under the power of Congress to regulate interstate commerce, the recent internal revenue laws including the income tax and excess profits laws, and especially the national prohibition act." *Report of the Committee Selected by the Attorney General to Suggest Emergency Legislation to Relieve the Federal Courts of Their Congested Condition* (July 21, 1921), in Committee on the Judiciary, H.R. Rep. No. 482, 67th CONG. 1st SESS. (November 17, 1921), at 18. The commission predicted that federal court congestion would decline, so that the new proposed judgeships would not be replaced absent explicit congressional action. *See, e.g.*, Harry M. Daugherty to WHT (July 22, 1921) (Taft papers); Harry M. Daugherty to WHT (August 22, 1921) (Taft papers). In the end, Taft yielded to the sentiment that judges be appointed to fixed and assigned districts. "If we can not get the Judges one way, we must have them the other." WHT to Ralph Peters (November 13, 1921).

Democrats opposed the vast increase in the federal judiciary, suspecting that the increase arose from the efforts of partisan Republicans to pack the courts. WHT to Judge Francis E. Baker (January 22, 1922) (Taft papers); Henry P. Chandler, *Some Major Advances in the Federal Judicial System 1922-1947*, 31 F.R.D. 307, 329 (1962).

31. Taft was recognized as the "author" of the "historical" Act, which realized "the best ideals of judicial organization." *A New Era Opens*, 6 JOURNAL OF THE AMERICAN JUDICATURE SOCIETY 67 (October 1922). "It is not too early now for congratulations over the progress made and the bright prospects, for before long the providential circumstances of Chief Justice Taft's appointment, in view of his broad understanding of the needs of the courts, will be generally recognized. Taking advantage of the need for more judges, which might otherwise have led merely to greater complexity and waste, the Chief Justice has obtained legislation which creates a right foundation for procedural reform." *Id.* "It was singularly fortunate, then, that when the federal trial courts were cracking under undue strain Mr. Taft should have been made administrative head of the entire system. There were, of course, others who appreciated the opportunity for notable legislative advance in respect to the federal courts, but were it not for the great esteem felt for the Chief Justice, and for his tact and persistence, something far inferior to the actual law would have resulted." *New Law Unifies Federal Judiciary*, 6 JOURNAL OF THE AMERICAN JUDICATURE SOCIETY 69 (October 1922). "[I]f any way out of the bogs and quicksands can be found it will be found under the powers established by the new act and through the administration of the Chief Justice, to whose intelligence and unselfish effort its passage is largely due." *Id.* at 70. *See More Federal Judges*, NEW YORK TRIBUNE (April 10, 1922), at 10.

32. Taft, *supra* note 20.

33. *Id.* at 454. For a blow-by-blow of the legislative history and Taft's involvement, see Chandler, *supra* note 30. A glimpse of Taft's version of the negotiations required for passage of the bill may be found in an address he gave to the Chicago Bar Association in December 1921, published as William Howard Taft, *Three Needed Steps of Progress*, 8 AMERICAN BAR ASSOCIATION JOURNAL 34 (1922). Taft stressed that the "most important" feature of the proposed bill (which then had both a Senate and a House version) was its provision "for annual . . . meetings at the call of the Chief Justice, of the senior circuit judges of the nine circuits . . . to take up the question from year to year of the arrears of business, and after conference to agree and recommend a plan, thereafter to be carried out in the discretion of those in authority, for the massing of the extra judicial force at strategic points, and thus overcoming the enemy known as 'arrears in business.'" *Id.* The premise of the bill, Taft explained, was that "Judges should be independent in their judgments, but they should be subject to some executive direction as to the use of their services, and somebody should be made responsible for the whole business of the United States. This council of the Chief Justice and the senior circuit judges of the nine circuits is

as well adapted to do this work as anybody that can be suggested." *Id.* at 35. As Taft later acknowledged, "The Conference means much for producing solidarity and efficiency in the organization of the Federal Judiciary. I got the provision which made it possible into an Act of Congress in 1922, and it is therefore my child." WHT to Mary [Patten?] (October 10, 1927) (Taft papers).

34. *Rally Support for Daugherty Bill: Bar of Entire Country Asked to Lend Assistance in Campaign for Effective Organization of United States Judiciary*, 5 JOURNAL OF THE AMERICAN JUDICATURE SOCIETY 120 (1921).

35. "The judicial system of the United States is unified. [The Act of September 14, 1922] creates a unified system of trial and appellate courts with statistical records, a judicial council, a chief judicial superintendent and the transfer and assignment of judges. It embodies the principle of unification in its entirety." *New Law Unifies Federal Judiciary, supra* note 31, at 69.

36. FELIX FRANKFURTER, FELIX FRANKFURTER ON THE SUPREME COURT 487–88 (Cambridge: Harvard University Press 1970).

37. *The First Conference*, 9 AMERICAN BAR ASSOCIATION JOURNAL 7, 7 (1923).

38. Henry D. Clayton, *Popularizing Administration of Justice*, 8 AMERICAN BAR ASSOCIATION JOURNAL 43, 46 (1922). On the floor of the Senate, Tennessee Senator John K. Shields argued that "I believe there are provisions giving the Chief Justice power over the lower courts which was never contemplated by our system of government.... I consider it a very serious assault upon the independence and dignity of the several judges of the district courts of the United States." 62 CONG. REC. 11669 (August 23, 1922).

39. Clayton, *supra* note 38, at 46. The Act also provoked great resistance on the grounds of localism, because it was said to create "a flying squadron of judges, ... introducing a new practice and new principle in the judiciary of the United States." 62 CONG. REC. 11671 (August 23, 1921) (Remarks of Senator Shields). *See The Proposed "Alien" Judges*, ST. LOUIS POST DISPATCH (April 7, 1922), at 22 ("[I]t is un-American and contrary to our traditions to be subjected to 'alien' Judges.... [T]he right of trial by a jury of the vicinage includes as well a trial before a Judge having some contact with the community in which he serves; ... to send in Judges from distant parts smacks of Jeffreysism."). *See* WHT to Horace D. Taft (April 3, 1922) (Taft papers); WHT to Elihu Root (April 5, 1922) (Taft papers). After the debate on the bill in the Senate, Taft wrote his brother, "Tom Watson of Georgia was in a state of mad fury over the thought of sending a N.Y. Judge down to Georgia to try a patriot for lynching. The shades of Jeffreys ... rose before him and he shuddered to think what a little 'thoroughness' from the North would do to Georgia. It might jail some of their best citizens. Wayne Wheeler of the Anti-Saloon League was working for the bill and helped it. This time he was for law enforcement and of course that was a high crime. The cowards and trimmers are in a bad way between the Anti-Saloon league and the demagogic vote against the Courts." WHT to Horace D. Taft (April 9, 1922) (Taft papers).

Those committed to the values of localism objected not only to Northern judges going South, but also to Southern judges coming North. In 1929, for example, Congressman Fiorello H. La Guardia wrote an outraged letter to Taft because a visiting judge from Arkansas named John Ellis Martineau had berated and humiliated a jury for acquitting a "colored man." "Apparently some Judges cannot understand a white jury acquitting a colored defendant." "It is manifestly unfair to

The Conference of Senior Circuit Court Judges

assign Judges to New York who do not understand local conditions, who are reared in the narrow atmosphere of provincial backwoods and who have strong feelings toward certain races and creeds." Fiorello H. La Guardia to WHT (July 27, 1929) (Taft papers).

40. WHT to Judge Ewing Cockrell (May 5, 1927) (Taft papers). *See, e.g., Power and Responsibility*, 8 AMERICAN BAR ASSOCIATION JOURNAL 625 (1922) ("The principle which the Chief Justice urges in respect to judicial machinery is not one which applies to that branch of governmental administration alone. He is simply attempting to have applied ... the approved ideas which are ... the basis of sound movements of administrative reform throughout the country. Scientific attempts to improve governmental machinery within the last two decades may be generalized as efforts to make the power of officials equal to the responsibility with which they are charged. ... That is the approved formula of efficiency – as far as machinery goes."); *Judicial Efficiency Experts*, 12 AMERICAN BAR ASSOCIATION JOURNAL 32 (1926). In contrast to wild progressive efforts at reform, the Act of September 14 was said to be "based on sound and practical principles and is not merely an illustration of a too common mania for solving problems by the creation of new and multiplied agencies." *The Judicial Council*, 11 AMERICAN BAR ASSOCIATION JOURNAL 508 (1925).

41. Taft, *supra* note 7, at 16–17. *See* WHT to Charles F. Ruggles (November 4, 1924) (Taft papers).

42. Note, *supra* note 27, at 445.

43. Taft, *The Courts and the Progressive Party*, *supra* note 5, at 47. "What is needed," wrote Taft, "is a General Director who shall be able to mass judicial force temporarily at places where the arrears are greatest and thus use what is available to do the whole judicial work. There ought to be more unity in the application of Judges at the strategic points where application is needed." WHT to Angus Wilton McLean (December 1, 1924) (Taft papers).

44. Taft, *supra* note 7, at 16. "One of the reasons why in this country we have got into such great delays in the administration of justice is that Judges have considered themselves independent in the matter of responsibility for the disposition of business, and the method of hearing cases under the old system has become a kind of 'go as you please' method, which does not make for reasonable dispatch in the finishing of cases. Someone, therefore, ought to be made the chief of the body of Judges who cover a certain territory and have the power to assign the business, so that each Judge shall be bound to follow that assignment. There is not the slightest reason why the same strategy ... should not be secured as you find in large business corporations." WHT to Harry A. Hollzer (February 14, 1928) (Taft papers).

45. *See supra* notes 40, 43, 44. Because the judicial conference was an institution that could generate the information necessary to guide executive management, Taft all along considered it "the kernel of the whole progress intended by the bill." Taft, *supra* note 20, at 454. Frankfurter and Landis shared this view: "Hundreds of judges holding court in as many or more districts scattered over a continent must be subjected to oversight and responsibility as parts of an articulated system of courts. The judiciary, like other political institutions, must be directed. An executive committee of the judges, with the Chief Justice of the United States at its head, is a fit and potent instrument for the task." Frankfurter & Landis, *supra* note 18, at 456.

46. Kristin Linsley Myles, Michelle Friedland, Aimee Feinberg, Miriam Seifter, & Michael Mongan, *Hail to the Chief*, 48 TENNESSEE BAR JOURNAL 12, 12 (2012).
47. 28 U.S.C. § 331.
48. *See, e.g.*, John G. Roberts, *2006 Year-End Report on the Federal Judiciary*, 39 THIRD BRANCH 4 (January 2007) ("My second annual report on the Judiciary"); Fred P. Graham, *Burger to Speak on "State of Judiciary"*, NEW YORK TIMES (August 7, 1970), at 29; Warren E. Burger, *The State of the Judiciary Address: The Time Is Now for the Intercircuit Panel*, 71 AMERICAN BAR ASSOCIATION JOURNAL 86 (1985).
49. *Compare supra* texts at notes 23 and 29, and note 29.
50. WHT to Horace D. Taft (December 26, 1922) (Taft papers). "I hope it can be made useful," Taft continued.
51. *The Federal Judicial Council*, 2 TEXAS LAW REVIEW 458, 459 (1924).
52. *Id.* at 461, 463. Echoing Taft's July 3, 1921, letter to Daugherty, *supra* note 17, the Conference also recommended:

> That the chairman of the committee [on Recommendations to District Judges of Changes in Local Procedure to Expedite Disposition of Pending Cases and to Rid Dockets of Dead Litigation] be authorized to prepare a bill, for the approval of the council, upon the subject matter of the following recommendations made by the committee:
> In prohibition and other misdemeanor cases, authorize the United States commissioners, in all cases in which the defendants do not file written demands for jury trial, to take and file written pleas of guilty and to hear the evidence on pleas of not guilty and to file in court their reports of the cases and their recommendations of what judgment should be entered.
> That the conference now express its opinion that such a bill as is referred to in the preceding paragraph would be expedient, provided the machinery proposed is within constitutional limits.

The Federal Judicial Council, supra note 51, at 461. Taft wrote his brother, "The most important suggestions are rules to prevent delay in impaneling a jury which has been a stench in the state courts, and for getting rid of misdemeanor cases in Federal courts when a jury is waived." WHT to Horace D. Taft (September 30, 1923) (Taft papers). The Conference's proposals were later reiterated by the National Commission on Law Observance and Enforcement. *See Proposals to Improve Enforcement of Criminal Laws of the United States*, H.R. Doc. No. 252, 71st CONG. 2nd SESS. (January 13, 1930), at 9–25. Their influence may be seen in the Act of October 9, 1940, Pub. L. 76-817, 54 Stat. 1058. *See also* Act of December 16, 1930, Pub. L. 71-548, 46 Stat. 1029.
53. Calvin Coolidge, *Annual Message to Joint Session of Senate and House of Representatives*, 65 CONG. REC. 98 (December 6, 1923).
54. *Addenda: Recommendations of the Judicial Conference*, in ANNUAL REPORT OF THE ATTORNEY GENERAL OF THE UNITED STATES FOR THE FISCAL YEAR 1924, at iii (Washington D.C.: Government Printing Office 1924). Despite the vigorous opposition of the influential Wayne Wheeler, general counsel of the Anti-Saloon League, see Wayne B. Wheeler, *In re Proposal to Transfer the Prohibition Enforcement Unit to the Department of Justice*, 98 CENTRAL LAW JOURNAL 9 (January 5, 1925), this recommendation was ultimately accepted on May 27, 1930. Prohibition Reorganization Act of 1930, Pub. L. 71-273, 46 Stat. 427 (May 27,

1930). *See* WHT to Horace D. Taft (October 2, 1924) (Taft papers); Wayne B. Wheeler to WHT (November 26, 1924) (Taft papers); WHT to Wayne B. Wheeler (November 27, 1924) (Taft papers).

55. WHT to the Supreme Court (November 25, 1924) (Taft papers) (transmitting detailed proposed amendments to the bankruptcy rules – Recommendations for Amendments to Bankruptcy Rules, Adopted by the Judicial Conference of Senior Circuit Judges (Taft papers)); *Recommendations Adopted by the Judicial Conference of Senior Circuit Judges*, 98 CENTRAL LAW JOURNAL 13, 13–14 (1925). These recommendations were adopted on April 13, 1925. General Orders in Bankruptcy, 267 U.S. 613–16 (1925). For the background of the rules, see *Improving Bankruptcy Practice Conditions*, 10 AMERICAN BAR ASSOCIATION JOURNAL 155 (March 1924).

56. WHT to the District and Circuit Judges of the United States (November 29, 1924) (Taft papers) (enclosing Suggestions of the Judicial Conference to United States District Judges for the Dispatch of Business). In 1927, the Conference reported that "This suggestion has been adopted in a great many districts and has resulted in the removal from the docket of many dead cases, which until their dismissal or removal gave the appearance of a congestion of business which the conditions did not justify and were misleading as to the necessity for additional judges or courts." ANNUAL REPORT OF THE ATTORNEY GENERAL OF THE UNITED STATES FOR THE FISCAL YEAR 1927, at 4–5 (Washington D.C.: Government Printing Office 1927). The 1927 Conference thought it "wise, therefore, to renew and emphasize the suggestion of 1924" that courts dismiss inactive cases. *Id.* at 5. For the effect of the 1924 recommendation, see Figure III-5; *infra* note 72.

57. *Addenda: Recommendations of the Judicial Conference, supra* note 54; *Expenditures of Appropriations for Law Books*, in ANNUAL REPORT OF THE ATTORNEY GENERAL OF THE UNITED STATES FOR THE FISCAL YEAR 1925, at 6–8 (Washington D.C.: Government Printing Office 1925). The Conference's recommendations in this regard were evidently successful. Congress appropriated special funds for court libraries "to be expended under the direction of the Attorney General but subject to the approval of the conference of senior circuit judges established by Section 2 of the Act of September 14, 1922." Pub. L. 68-631, 43 Stat. 1333 (March 4, 1925). "The result is that for the first time in many years the district judges find that they are fairly well supplied with their necessary tools, and the circuit courts of appeals have reasonably satisfactory libraries.... We have no doubt that the efficiency of the Courts has been substantially increased by the aid which this Congressional appropriation has given." ANNUAL REPORT OF THE ATTORNEY GENERAL OF THE UNITED STATES FOR THE FISCAL YEAR 1926, at 9 (Washington D.C.: Government Printing Office 1926).

58. ANNUAL REPORT OF THE ATTORNEY GENERAL OF THE UNITED STATES FOR THE FISCAL YEAR 1925, *supra* note 57, at 5. *See Conspiracy Indictments*, NEW YORK TIMES (June 12, 1925), at 18; *Wheeler Upholds Use of Conspiracy Charge*, BALTIMORE SUN (June 12, 1925), at 2. Brandeis particularly approved of this recommendation. *See* LDB to WHT (July 10, 1925) (Taft papers) ("The recommendation concerning conspiracy should bring an end to an unworthy and dangerous practice."). No immediate law reform followed the Conference's recommendation. *But see Amendment to Section 37 of the Penal Code*, Committee on the Judiciary, Sen. Rep. No. 44, 69th CONG. 1st SESS. (January 16, 1926), at 1–2 (proposing a bill

enacting the recommendation of the Conference). In 1948, Congress amended the penal code substantially to embody the Conference's recommendation. Pub. L. 80-772, 62 Stat. 701 (June 25, 1948).

59. ANNUAL REPORT OF THE ATTORNEY GENERAL OF THE UNITED STATES FOR THE FISCAL YEAR 1925, *supra* note 57, at 6. The report of the conference reads, "The right to bail after conviction by a court or a judge of first instance or an intermediate court or a judge thereof is not a matter of constitutional right." *Id*. *See* WHT to Robert A. Taft (June 7, 1925) (Taft papers) ("Next week if the heat does not melt them, I expect to have here the Senior Circuit Judges of the Country.... [W]e may make some further recommendations as to the District Judges with reference to the granting of bail to people convicted pending appeal. There has been a good deal of misconception about what the rights of a man are who has been convicted by a jury and sentenced. The presumption is he is guilty under those circumstances, but I don't think he ought to be allowed to get out on bail and then delay his appeal, because time always makes for the guilty defendant."). Taft later wrote Brandeis about this recommendation, "I thought it was well, too, that we should advise the District Judges that they were not helpless in responding to a demand for bail after conviction, when the appellate proceedings were evidently taken for delay. There is an opinion by Gray, in the Hudson case I think it is, on this subject, in which I think he goes too far, and which, should we get an opportunity, we can reasonably qualify so as not to prevent District Judges from discrimination in cases of this kind." WHT to LDB (July 6, 1925) (Taft papers). The preceding year, at the Annual Conference of 1924, Taft had made a similar proposal, only to meet an objection from Judge Sanborn "who said in substance: 'Mr. Chief Justice, the Supreme Court ruled in *Hudson v. Parker*, that the accused defendant in criminal cases should not be imprisoned until his conviction had been affirmed by the court of last resort.' Apparently the Chief Justice was not aware of (or had forgotten) *Hudson v. Parker* and could only express his thought that it was unfortunate that a convicted defendant could simply walk out of the courtroom after a verdict of 'guilty.' The Chief Justice did not argue with Judge Sanborn but bided his time." C. Dickerman Williams, *The 1924 Term: Recollections of Chief Justice Taft's Law Clerk*, 1989 YEARBOOK OF THE SUPREME COURT HISTORICAL SOCIETY 40, 42.

60. ANNUAL REPORT OF THE ATTORNEY GENERAL OF THE UNITED STATES FOR THE FISCAL YEAR 1926, *supra* note 57, at 7. *See* Los Angeles Brush Mfg. Co. v. James, 272 U.S. 701 (1927) (discussing, in an opinion by Taft, the tension between unreasonable delay in trying patent cases and the "arguments based on humanity and necessity for the preservation of public order [which] require that criminal cases should be given a reasonable preference," in light of "an emergency due to a lack of judges in some districts which we cannot ignore.").

61. ANNUAL REPORT OF THE ATTORNEY GENERAL OF THE UNITED STATES FOR THE FISCAL YEAR 1927, *supra* note 56, at 6. Brandeis had written Taft on the morning of the first day of the 1927 Conference that "I venture to suggest that you urge upon its members to follow our practice in advancing criminal cases." LDB to WHT (September 27, 1927) (Taft papers). Taft responded, "I have your note of to-day, and I shall bring up to the Conference the matter to which you refer. I think it is a good suggestion, though I am inclined to think that it is probably complied with already by most of the Courts of Appeal." WHT to LDB (September 27, 1927) (Taft

papers). Taft was as good as his word, and the Conference was apparently quite agreeable.

62. ANNUAL REPORT OF THE ATTORNEY GENERAL OF THE UNITED STATES FOR THE FISCAL YEAR 1927, *supra* note 56, at 6. Taft reported to Van Devanter that "I would like to have the Circuit Courts of Appeal know that we are glad to have their cooperation in speeding cases through our Court, and I would not like to give the impression that we don't appreciate their purpose in adopting such a rule. Of course [Judge Walter H.] Sanborn went right back from the Conference and had the rule adopted in his court, and I suppose that has been done pretty well through the country." WHT to WVD (October 31, 1927) (Taft papers).

63. ANNUAL REPORT OF THE ATTORNEY GENERAL OF THE UNITED STATES FOR THE FISCAL YEAR 1927, *supra* note 56, at 6. Citing the recommendation of the Conference, Congress granted this request in 1930. *See* Pub. L. 71-373, 46 Stat. 774 (June 17, 1930); Sen. Rep. No. 830, 71st CONG. 2nd SESS. (May 29, 1930), at 1; H.R. Rep. No. 30, 71st CONG. 2nd SESS. (December 12, 1929), at 1.

64. WHT to John G. Sargent (April 17, 1925) (Taft papers). Taft also noted to the attorney general that Senior Circuit Judge Woods "reports to me that the present District Attorney named Tolbert, in the Western District of South Carolina, is not competent to discharge the duties of District Attorney. I suggest that an agent might be sent to investigate this matter." As an afterthought, Taft added, "I hope you will not think I am trying to intrude in matters that are solely within your jurisdiction; but I am very anxious to make the conference of Circuit Judges as useful as I can and to justify its creation. We need team work to facilitate the agencies available for effective administration of federal justice." Sargent replied, "I assure you that I not only do not think you are intruding in matters in my jurisdiction, but I am very grateful for the assistance received." John G. Sargent to WHT (April 20, 1925) (Taft papers).

65. The story is told in detail in Robert Post, *The Incomparable Chief Justiceship of William Howard Taft*, 2020 MICHIGAN STATE LAW REVIEW 1, 49–50.

66. Indeed, so influential had the Conference become by the end of the decade that Pennsylvania Representative George S. Graham, the powerful chair of the House Judiciary Committee, was moved to declare that "It is true that an act of Congress was passed creating this board of senior judges, but I do not hold, and will never consent to it, so far as I am concerned, that it is necessary to get the imprimatur of that board upon every appointment that Congress chooses to make. We did not surrender our legislative function when we created this board. It was not for the appointment of judges but for getting a full and complete view of the situation so that they might consider these matters from every viewpoint, and make such recommendations to Congress as they might deem proper." Remarks of Representative Graham, 70 CONG. REC. 1743 (January 15, 1929).

67. WHT to A.C. Denison (March 19, 1925) (Taft papers). This was no accident. It was the result of Taft's shrewd bureaucratic infighting. So, for example, that very spring Taft would devise a plan to enable the Conference to seize control of the allocation of extra moneys that Congress, at the Conference's request, had appropriated for judicial libraries. *See supra* note 57. The expenditure of one portion of these funds was explicitly made subject to the approval of the Conference, but the expenditure of a different portion was not. The Conference normally met in the fall, but in 1925 Taft pushed the meeting of the Conference back into June for fear that the latter

portion of the funds "will be gone or apportioned before we get here in September." WHT to A.C. Denison (March 19, 1925) (Taft papers). Taft's ploy was successful, and the Conference produced a detailed plan for the expenditure of all the funds, ANNUAL REPORT OF THE ATTORNEY GENERAL OF THE UNITED STATES FOR THE FISCAL YEAR 1925, *supra* note 57, at 6–8, which was successfully implemented, in effect asserting judicial control over the distribution of Article III budget appropriations. ANNUAL REPORT OF THE ATTORNEY GENERAL OF THE UNITED STATES FOR THE FISCAL YEAR 1926, *supra* note 57, at 9. At its meeting in June 1925, Taft told the Conference that "I have a feeling that the recommendations of this Conference have a good deal of influence. I mean that they are accepted as matters for serious consideration." Report of the Fourth Conference of Senior Judges called by the Chief Justice pursuant to the Act of Congress of September 14, 1922, at 38 (Taft papers).

68. Felix Frankfurter to WHT (October 6, 1926) (Taft papers). *See* WHT to Felix Frankfurter (February 23, 1926) (Taft papers) ("I think on the whole it has been a quite useful body and that it may grow to be more and more useful as we grow more familiar with what can be done by recommendations to the District Judges and by recommendations to Congress. It gives a unity to the Federal judicial force that I think is valuable, and helps the massing of that force at points where the congestion requires more than the regular number of Judges."). *See The Judicial Council, supra* note 40, at 508 ("No one can read the proceedings of this Conference of Circuit Judges, presided over by the Chief Justice of the United States, without reaching the conviction that a new and important agency has been introduced into the administration of federal justice. Its suggestions to district judges, it may safely be assumed, will be followed. They are not merely the expression of a pious hope, but the program of a body with reason for what it does, with a very strong disposition to do something, and with prestige great enough to insure that its proposals will receive careful attention.").

69. WHT to Mary [Patten?] (October 10, 1927) (Taft papers). *See* WHT to Robert A. Taft (October 2, 1927) (Taft papers) ("I am sure [the Conference] is a good thing, that it solidifies the Federal Judiciary, that it brings all the district judges within a mild disciplinary circle, and makes them feel that they are under real observation by the other judges and the country, and it enables the judiciary to express itself in respect of certain subjects in such a way as to be helpful to Congress. A good many of them came to me this time to say that when the Conference was created, they did not think we could do anything, but they admit that they were wrong."). After the 1927 Conference, Judge J. Warren Davis, who had attended representing the Third Circuit, wrote Taft to say, "You have made that conference worth while and its influence will be felt in the speedy disposition of 'dead' cases and cases which ought not be delayed in reaching the Supreme Court. You have the ability to dispatch business with a rare charm and effectiveness." J. Warren Davis to WHT (November 2, 1927) (Taft papers).

Among the early doubters of the Conference was the powerful and cantankerous senior judge of the Eighth Circuit, Walter H. Sanborn. In 1923 he had written his former colleague Van Devanter that "There is more danger of causing delays and wasting time than there is hope of facilitating the administration of justice. The time and labor of the Circuit and District Judges are all needed in the actual work of the courts and it seems to me they are uselessly frittered away by conferences of a few

The Conference of Senior Circuit Court Judges

days of men who do not meet each other constantly and to whom many of the numerous changes that idle men suggest are pressed for adoption. I am personally pretty tired of combating the constant endeavors to change the rules and practices of the courts for I know, as you do, that every change – good or bad – delays the administration of justice because the methods of procedure are known to the Judges and lawyers who do the work now, and every change is new and at first unknown to them all." Walter H. Sanborn to WVD (January 3, 1923) (Van Devanter papers). Sanborn asked Van Devanter to "say nothing about my expressions to the Chief Justice or any other person. I feel about the whole matter as you evidently do, but I do not want to oppose Chief Justice Taft in what he evidently thinks will be of great benefit." *Id*. It is no accident that when Taft authored the Conference's 1927 report, he pointedly quoted Sanborn's assessment that "The condition of the business throughout the circuit is far more satisfactory than it has been at any time within the last five years." ANNUAL REPORT OF THE ATTORNEY GENERAL OF THE UNITED STATES FOR THE FISCAL YEAR 1927, *supra* note 56, at 8.

70. ANNUAL REPORT OF THE ATTORNEY GENERAL OF THE UNITED STATES FOR THE FISCAL YEAR 1927, *supra* note 56, at 7–8. In 1928, the Conference again reported that "it was clear to the conference that the condition of business in all the courts was satisfactory, and showed that there were enough judges to do the business." ANNUAL REPORT OF THE ATTORNEY GENERAL OF THE UNITED STATES FOR THE FISCAL YEAR 1928, at 4 (Washington D.C.: Government Printing Office 1928).

71. In 1926, the Conference declared that it was "gratified at finding that substantial progress had been made during the past year in reducing the delays and congestion of business which recently added judgeships had been created to remove." ANNUAL REPORT OF THE ATTORNEY GENERAL OF THE UNITED STATES FOR THE FISCAL YEAR 1926, *supra* note 57, at 6.

72. In 1926, the Conference reported, "As to the criminal cases, the evidence before the conference, the statistical reports from the Department of Justice, the reports of the district judges, and the knowledge of the members of the conference lead to the conclusion that this result has been due to the increase in the number of judges, to the policy of the Department of Justice in discouraging the prosecution of insignificant and unimportant alleged violations of the law, and to the activity of courts and district attorneys in seeking to remove from the docket the dead cases that can not be tried for lack of evidence." *Id*. Figure III-6 suggests that although the sharp rise in bankruptcy cases that began in fiscal 1921 (as a result of the postwar depression) were an important source of the crisis leading to the 1922 Act, district courts began to catch up with these cases in fiscal 1925 and that the level of arrears did not increase for the remainder of the decade. As Figure III-7 illustrates, civil cases to which the United States was a party constituted in absolute terms a relatively small proportion of the total federal docket; yet the number of such cases also began to rise in fiscal 1918 and continued to climb throughout the decade. In part this reflected the government's shift toward prohibition remedies that involved civil injunctions. In fiscal 1927, there was a sharp rise in terminated cases over initiated cases, which might reflect the impact of the Conference's recommendation to dismiss inactive cases. *See supra* note 56. Figure III-8 demonstrates that although there was a rise in arrears between fiscal 1919 and fiscal 1922, the absolute level of arrears for private litigation remained more or less level for the remainder of the decade.

73. *See, e.g.*, WHT to Warren F. Martin (January 31, 1923) (Taft papers) ("I am exceedingly anxious to organize a campaign in New York City and mass as many Judges as we can, and give them a sample of what can be done."); WHT to Henry Wade Rogers (February 2, 1923) (Taft papers) ("What I wish . . . to do is to come over to New York and have an interview with you and your fellow Judges, especially the District Judges, to see if we can not mass an attack on those discouraging arrears that you have in the Southern District. I shall go over the whole list of Judges in other Circuits with all of you and see if I can not get enough to be formidable in this matter. I would like to give a demonstration of what can be done if Congress will only lend a hand in the matter of disposition of business. . . . I have this matter very much at heart."); WHT to Henry Wade Rogers (February 7, 1923) (Taft papers) ("I mean business about your district."); WHT to Learned Hand (February 25, 1923) (Taft papers) ("I am writing over the country to see where I can get Judges for you, and have had quite a correspondence with Judge Rodgers. . . . I don't know that I can get seven Judges, but I am going to make an effort to get as many as I can."); Learned Hand to WHT (July 2, 1923) (Taft papers) ("As you will see, we are not making great advances on the docket, although there has been continuous work done on it. I may say for your private ear that some of the out of town judges do not work quite so speedily as the local ones. Perhaps they do their work more carefully and better, but when it comes to counting numbers on the docket the results do not appear so good."); Henry Wade Rogers to WHT (July 18, 1923) (Taft papers) ("The progress which has been made in the Southern District of New York during the last year has not availed much and the situation is still bad. A number of Judges have been here from outside districts. . . . They do not seem to have made much of an impression on the congested situation."); WHT to John C. Oldmixon (January 6, 1924) (Taft papers) ("The congestion at New York is a disgrace to the administration of Federal justice. The congestion there is perfectly dreadful. The additional Judges appointed to other partes [sic] of the country are making a real advance, but the mass of business in the city of New York is such that it seems most difficult to make progress. For that reason, the Judicial Council of Circuit Judges which met last September in Washington, and of which I am Chairman, recommended that two additional Judges be created for New York City."); Augustus N. Hand to WHT (January 22, 1925) (Taft papers) ("[O]ur work is seriously behind in this district. . . . [W]e are getting . . . further behind in our work."); WHT to Augustus N. Hand (January 23, 1925) (Taft papers) ("The plan of transferring Judges from one District to another is good but it is not enough, and certainly not for a District that needs additional Judges all the time."); WHT to A.C. Denison (January 23, 1925) (Taft papers) ("Calling in Judges from other Districts is all right for temporary congestion, but nothing will help New York except a substantial addition to the judicial force."); WHT to John G. Sargent (March 20, 1925) (Taft papers) ("The Senior Circuit Judges will be here on the 9th of June, and of course they will bring word with them as to those Judges within their jurisdiction who can be used elsewhere. The truth is that there are very few Judges who can be used. The number of Judges who are furnished by the Omnibus Bill is not enough, and constant inquiry made of the Circuit Judges indicates that it is very difficult for any Senior Circuit Judge to spare a man from his Circuit. I would like to talk with you on this subject."); Augustus N. Hand to WHT (March 3, 1926) (Taft papers) ("I believe we are seeing things move here. . . . I think the Admiralty and Civil Jury dockets will be brought from two years down to one from the date of issue of the summer recess and Equity will I hope be about the same. This will

The Conference of Senior Circuit Court Judges

be a big gain. It is due to your help in getting outside Judges through the winter which we greatly appreciate."); WHT to Augustus N. Hand (May 12, 1926) (Taft papers) ("I am very sorry about the Judges, but I have raked and scraped, and I don't know what more I could do."); Augustus N. Hand to WHT (May 31, 1927) (Taft papers) ("I shall always remember your personal kindness and powerful assistance in helping us here to reduce the terrible arrears of business. We have got the admiralty down from four or five years to one. ... [T]he Civil Jury is, I think, down from two and a half years to fifteen months; the Criminal Docket pretty well clear up – Equity, alone, shows no improvement and is nearly two years behind.").

74. Chandler, *supra* note 30, at 339.
75. WHT to Robert A. Taft (October 2, 1927) (Taft papers).
76. WHT to Felix Frankfurter (August 21, 1925) (Taft papers). So, for example, Judge James Madison Morton, Jr. wrote Taft to say that "I have just received and read the recommendations of the Judicial Conference. I wish you could be a District Judge for a while just to know what excellent work you and the Conference are doing. The recommendation last year about liquor cases, – that the Federal Courts should entertain only the more important ones, – was of the greatest assistance in dealing with the liquor situation. It gave the District Judges solid standing ground from which to urge that course on the United States Attorneys, who are rather inclined to prosecute everybody for everything lest they be accused of favoritism or remissness. The recommendation this year about the use of conspiracy indictments is absolutely sound and much needed." James Madison Morton, Jr. to WHT (June 23, 1925) (Taft papers). Or consider the letter sent to Taft by Judge Frank S. Dietrich: "[T]he administration of justice is deeply indebted to you for your service in bringing about a greater measure of co-ordination in the work of the several courts. I share with others the feeling that what you are doing is of great constructive value. The recommendations of the Conference have given prestige to the efforts of the local judge in expediting trials and eliminating delays incident to practices strongly intrenched [sic] in the traditions of the Bar; already waste of time in impaneling juries has been reduced to a minimum." Frank S. Dietrich to WHT (January 12, 1927) (Taft papers).
77. WHT to Horace D. Taft (December 30, 1921) (Taft papers). The Conference, Judge John F. Sater wrote Taft, "will get us all in touch as never before." John F. Sater to WHT (August 23, 1921) (Taft papers).
78. WHT to Francis E. Baker (October 5, 1922) (Taft papers). *See* WHT to Mrs. Frederick J. Manning (March 25, 1923) (Taft papers).
79. WHT to John F. Sater (August 27, 1921) (Taft papers).
80. WHT to Mrs. Frederick J. Manning (March 25, 1923) (Taft papers). As Taft wrote Augustus Hand, "You need not be grateful to me for anything I can do to help you, for we are in the same boat, and we all have to row, or ought to." WHT to Augustus N. Hand (November 14, 1925) (Taft papers).
81. WHT to Frank S. Dietrich (January 17, 1927) (Taft papers). *See* WHT to Merrill E. Otis (April 9, 1925) (Taft papers) ("I take a warm interest in every District Judge.").
82. WHT to John S. Partridge (January 22, 1925) (Taft papers).
83. WHT to William B. Gilbert (December 15, 1924) (Taft papers).
84. WHT to John M. Cotteral (May 19, 1926) (Taft papers). "I wish you to know that we here at the Nation's Capital," continued Taft, "are fully conscious of the debt that we and the country owe to you District Judges."

473

85. Learned Hand to WHT (March 1, 1923) (Taft papers). Hand added, "I had two chats with Justice Holmes while I was at Washington .... And may I add that your right ear must have been burning at the time he spoke of you, and he has had some experience with Chief Justices?"
86. Learned Hand to WHT (February 8, 1924) (Taft papers).
87. So, for example, when Taft became convinced that the Southern District of New York needed a third extra judge, see *supra* note 73, he wrote Charles Evans Hughes asking him to petition Congress for legislation, adding "I shall do what I can here, and I shall get the Conference of Senior Circuit Judges ... to take action." WHT to Charles Evans Hughes (March 25, 1925) (Taft papers). Sure enough, after its 1925 meeting the Conference recommended a third judgeship for the Southern District.
88. Pub. L. 69-741, 44 Stat. 1374 (March 3, 1927).
89. Sen. Rep. No. 1557, 69th CONG. 2nd SESS. (February 22, 1927), at 2. In its 1927 Report, the Conference retroactively endorsed Taft's recommendation. "Congress at its last session provided for a judge in the northern district of New York which the conference did not recommend, but which it is glad to have had provided." ANNUAL REPORT OF THE ATTORNEY GENERAL OF THE UNITED STATES FOR THE FISCAL YEAR 1927, *supra* note 56, at 7. Other examples of Taft lobbying for judgeships outside the approval of the Conference include Taft's support for an additional judge for the Western District of Michigan to compensate for the incapacitated Clarence Sessions, even though the Conference had not made any such recommendation, see Pub. L. 68-423, 43 Stat. 949 (February 17, 1925); H.R. Rep. No. 1427, 68th CONG. 2nd SESS. (February 10, 1925), at 1 ("This bill has the approval of Chief Justice Taft, who, according to the hearings, has personally investigated the physical condition of Judge Sessions."); Taft's support for an additional judgeship for the Southern District of Florida, see Post *supra* note 65, at 49 n.174; and Taft's support for the appointment of a replacement judgeship for District of Minnesota due to the unexpected suicide of Judge John McGee, who had been appointed to an expiring position under the 1922 Act. See Pub. L. 68-528, 43 Stat. 1098 (March 2, 1925); H.R. Rep. No. 1540, 68th CONG. 2nd SESS. (February 20, 1925), at 1–2 (citing "a communication received from the Chief Justice of the United States which shows the necessity for immediate enactment of this legislation."). See Walter H. Sanborn to WVD (February 19, 1925) (Van Devanter papers); WVD to Walter H. Sanborn (February 27, 1925) (Van Devanter papers) ("The Chief Justice and I just returned from the Capital where we again saw Mr. Graham. ... Mr. Graham was intending to make an effort to get ... the Minnesota district judge bill through"); Walter H. Sanborn to WHT (February 25, 1925) (Taft papers).

Taft disapproved of the efforts of judges other than himself to lobby for additional judgeships outside of the formal procedures of the Conference. So, for example, he wrote Senior Judge Henry Wade Rogers:

> I shall be glad to forward your letter to the Attorney General on the subject of an additional Judge in the Western District of New York. I have no doubt that he is interested, but I very much doubt the wisdom of bringing the matter up in this way, and think that it ought to come through the Council of Judges, just as the other recommendations did. I don't think the Attorney General would recommend it in the absence of such action by the Council, and I am not sure that I would advise him to do so, because we ought not to take action in respect to

which there is no hope of successful issue, or to recommend something which may diminish the effect of that which we have already recommended. I shall delay writing to the Attorney General until I hear from you again.

WHT to Henry Wade Rogers (November 21, 1923) (Taft papers). The following year, in 1924, the Conference recommended an additional judgeship for the Western District of New York, which was authorized in 1927. *See* Post *supra* note 65, at 49 nn.173–74.

90. WHT to John A Peters (October 11, 1927) (Taft papers). Taft wrote a similar letter to Judge William N Runyon: "It has come to me in a semi-official way that you have still undecided a patent case . . . which was argued in November, 1925. . . . I am sure that you are anxious like all of us to justify the existence of the Federal Judiciary, and believe in the useful functions that it performs, and I merely write this not by way of criticism or by way of assuming to exercise any statutory authority I have, but to let you know that the delay in the case to which I refer is made the basis for adverse comment." WHT to William N. Runyon (March 12, 1928) (Taft papers). Runyon was apparently perturbed by Taft's unexpected letter. He wrote back a long, self-justifying letter, expressing "deep concern" at "the semi-official character of your information . . . implying as it did a criticism not born of personal or professional partisanship, but proceeding from impersonal sources, and undertaken in the fulfillment of a duty." William N. Runyon to WHT (March 17, 1928) (Taft papers). Taft replied in a most kind way:

> All I wanted to know was that you were doing the best you could, as I should judge you were doing, and that the matter would work out. . . . [D]on't yield too much to the fear that you may by an early decision reach a wrong result. Courts of Appeal are provided to remedy mistakes in the lower courts. . . . I know a Judge intimately, Judge Hammond, who was an excellent Judge but who thought he was writing for posterity, and almost waited until posterity had come before he got opinions rendered. I don't mean to say that these faults are yours, but I only point out that some very good Judges forget the fact that courts are to decide cases and decide them promptly, in the earnest desire to decide them right.

WHT to William N. Runyon (March 19, 1928) (Taft papers). In such situations, Taft was not above invoking the unique authority of an appointing President. Thus, he wrote Judge Ferdinand A. Geiger:

> A suggestion has come to me with reference to a case . . . which is pending before you. I have no doubt that there are reasons for the delay, which it is said to have been about three years. Of course I have no authority as Chief Justice to make suggestions of this kind to other Judges, but our relations are such, and my pride in you as one of my appointees is so great, that I thought it only a prompting of warmest friendship and admiration for me to call this to your attention.

WHT to Ferdinand A. Geiger (November 17, 1927) (Taft papers).

CHAPTER 13

Reshaping the Supreme Court

TAFT VASTLY EXPANDED the scope of the chief justiceship, whose primary orientation had heretofore been the management of the Supreme Court itself. Taft of course continued to fulfill the obligations of that traditional role. He learned firsthand of its unique demands almost immediately upon assuming office.

Upon returning to Canada after taking the oath of office on July 12, 1921, Taft received an urgent telegram from Senior Associate Justice Joseph McKenna on July 30 informing him that Deputy Clerk Henry McKenney had passed away.[1] This posed a serious difficulty for the Court, because its clerk, James D. Maher, had died the month before. Federal law at the time provided that the clerk could be appointed only by the Court. If the clerk died, the deputy clerk could "perform the duties of the clerk in his name until a clerk is appointed and qualified."[2] The death of Deputy Clerk McKenney, however, left the Clerk's Office, as Assistant Clerk William R. Stansbury telegraphed Taft, "now without an official head and no one authorized to issue official papers."[3] Because the Court was dispersed for its summer vacation, it could not be gathered to appoint a new clerk.

Taft promptly returned to Washington to meet with McKenna. Telegraphic consultation with those associate justices who could be contacted proved unhelpful, which, as Taft wrote his wife, "only shows what McKenna assured me that the other members of the Court expect me to attend to the executive business of the Court and not bother them." McKenna impressed the point on his new chief: "McKenna said I must realize that the Chief Justiceship was an office distinct from that of the Associates in executive control and was intended to be and all of the Associates recognized it, that in judicial decisions all were equal but in management I must act and they would all stand by if ever question was made." Taft boldly and promptly resolved "to do something without statutory authority"[4] and appoint Stansbury "de facto deputy clerk,"[5] exacting "a common law bond from him to protect everybody."[6]

Reshaping the Supreme Court

Throughout his decade on the bench, Taft managed the Court with fluency and ease. "I think Taft is all the better Chief Justice for having been President," Holmes wrote his friend Harold Laski.[7] "He works hard, keeps everything moving, and gets the work done with good temper and humor."[8] Taft placed the vigilant Brandeis on the Committee of Accounts, along with Van Devanter and McReynolds; Brandeis made constant recommendations about improving the Court's finances.[9] Taft continually reformed Court procedures.[10] He conceived and implemented a policy that would expedite all criminal cases.[11] He created a week at the outset of the term in which hearings were suspended while the Court considered *certiorari* petitions "which have collected during the summer."[12] He sought mightily to reduce Court fees.[13] He effectively pushed for legislation regularizing the salary of the Court Reporter, which had heretofore been partially paid out of contracts with private publishers.[14] He rationalized funding for the Marshall's office.[15] He fought hard and constantly for necessary space within the Capitol building where the Supreme Court was then housed.[16]

Taft also struggled to make the Supreme Court a more outwardly facing institution. He had copies of the Court's opinions sent to all state supreme courts[17] because, as he said, "it is of the highest importance that we judges in the courts of last resort, State and National, who are engaged in interpreting the law, should be on close terms with each other and do team-work."[18] He also authorized the distribution of Court opinions to major press organizations.[19]

From the outset, however, Taft realized that the Supreme Court needed legislative reform of its jurisdiction to keep pace with its torrential docket.[20] Taft was therefore forced to step out of the traditional managerial role of a chief justice and into that of an out-and-out judicial reformer. The difficulties facing Taft were not of his own making. The docket of the Supreme Court had a long history of terrible arrears. It had become unmanageable by the end of the 1880s, as is indicated in Figure III-9, when the Court fell a full three years behind in its caseload. In 1891, Congress passed the Evarts Act to remedy the situation.[21] The Act created the United States Circuit Courts of Appeals[22] and for the first time authorized the Court to use the discretionary writ of *certiorari* to determine which cases (within predetermined categories) it would review from these new federal appellate courts.[23]

Although the Evarts Act provided immediate and dramatically effective relief, Figure III-9 shows that by about 1905 the docket and arrears of the Supreme Court began once again to swell. It was during that period that Taft began to articulate an account of the Supreme Court that would justify diminishing its mandatory jurisdiction:

> Generally in every system of courts there are a court of first instance, an intermediate court of appeals and a court of last resort. The court of first instance and the intermediate appellate courts should be for the purpose of finally disposing in a just and prompt way of all controversies between litigants. So far as the litigant is concerned, one appeal is all that he should be entitled to; the community at large is not interested in his having more; for the function of the court of last resort, usually called the Supreme Court, is not primarily for the purpose of securing a second review or appeal to the particular litigant whose case is carried

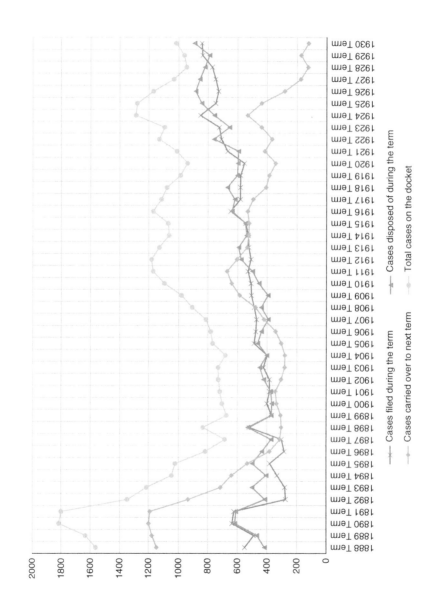

Figure III-9 Appellate caseload of the Supreme Court, by term, 1888–1930 terms. Based on Reports of the Attorney General.

to that court.... [T]he chief reason for granting such a review is to enable the Supreme Court to lay down general principles of law in the interpretation of State or Federal constitutions or statutes, or in the application of the common law, for the benefit and guidance, not of the particular litigant affected, but of the communities at large. Therefore, the appellate jurisdiction of the Supreme Court should generally be limited to those cases which are typical and which give an opportunity to the court to cover the whole field of the law upon the subject involved. The highest function of the Supreme Court of the United States is the interpretation of the Constitution of the United States, so as to guide the other branches of the Government and the people of the United States in their construction of the fundamental compact of the Union.[24]

The Supreme Court, Taft asserted, should not be characterized as a final appellate tribunal, but instead as the supervisor of the system of federal law. The Court did not adjudicate "for the benefit and guidance ... of the particular litigant affected," but instead for "the community at large." At first, Taft advanced this theory primarily to diminish delays and expense in litigation. Reducing the mandatory appellate jurisdiction of the Supreme Court, Taft argued, would decrease the cost of litigation and hence equalize access to justice as between rich and poor.[25]

By 1910, however, the crisis in the Supreme Court's docket had become so pronounced that Taft began to connect his account of the Court to the necessity of reducing its impossibly large workload. In his Annual Message to Congress, President Taft advocated legislation that would reduce the Court's mandatory appellate jurisdiction. "No man ought to have, as a matter of right, a review of his case by the Supreme Court," Taft said. "He should be satisfied by one hearing before a court of first instance and one review by a court of appeals.... The Supreme Court is now carrying an unnecessary burden of appeals of this kind, and I earnestly urge that it be removed."[26]

Taft continued to advocate for this reform after he stepped down from the presidency. In 1914, he argued that it was necessary to strip the Court of mandatory jurisdiction except in cases involving constitutional questions so that the Court could keep up with the ever-expanding business of a growing nation:

> The Supreme Court has great difficulty in keeping up with its docket. The most important function of the court is the construction and application of the constitution of the United States. It has other valuable duties to perform in the construction of statutes and in the shaping and declaration of general law, but if its docket is to increase with the growth of the country, it will be swamped with its burden, the work which it does will, because of haste, not be of the high quality that it ought to have, and the litigants of the Court will suffer injustice because of delay. For these reasons the only jurisdiction that it should be obliged to exercise, and which a litigant may, as a matter of course, bring to the court, should be questions of constitutional construction. By giving an opportunity to litigants in all other cases to apply for a writ of certiorari to bring any case from a lower court to the Supreme Court, so that it

may exercise absolute and arbitrary discretion with respect to all business but constitutional business, will enable the court so to restrict its docket that it can do all its work, and do it well.[27]

Figures III-9 and III-10 demonstrate that just as Taft became chief justice, the docket and arrears of the Court began yet another period of steep increase.[28] The newly installed chief justice told the Chicago Bar Association in December 1921 that the "situation is rendered critical by the accumulating mass of litigation growing out of the war, and especially of claims against the Government which, if allowed to come under the present law to the Supreme Court, will throw us hopelessly behind." Taft argued that "there must be some method adopted by which the cases brought before that Court shall be reduced in number," and yet allow the Court to "retain full jurisdiction to pronounce the last word on every important issue under the Constitution and the statutes of the United States and on all important questions of general law with respect to which there is a lack of uniformity in the intermediate Federal courts of appeal."[29]

In August 1922, Taft reported to the Annual Convention of the American Bar Association that there was then "an interval of 15 months between the filing of a case in the court and its hearing. ... The members of the Supreme Court have become so anxious to avoid another congestion like that of the decade before 1891, that they have deemed it proper themselves to prepare a new bill amending the jurisdiction of the Supreme Court and to urge its passage."[30] Ruling out other methods of reducing congestion in the Supreme Court docket, like imposing "heavy costs" or eliminating diversity or federal question jurisdiction in lower federal courts,[31] Taft contended that the only feasible method for control of the Supreme Court docket was a statute expanding its discretionary jurisdiction.[32]

Taft lobbied hard for the legislation, and the result was his second great judicial reform as chief justice, the Judiciary Act of February 13, 1925,[33] often called the Judges' Bill because it was authored by the Court itself. The origins of the bill remain shrouded in mystery. In 1927, when Felix Frankfurter wrote Taft asking him to clarify the genesis of the Act for Frankfurter's forthcoming article in the *Harvard Law Review*,[34] Taft turned to Van Devanter to assist his memory:

> My recollection is that when I came into the Court, Day was a member of the committee looking to the preparation of further legislation – I mean legislation in addition to the Acts of 1915 and 1916 – to relieve the Court and increase its certiorari jurisdiction and decrease its mandatory jurisdiction, and that I added you to the committee with Day, and later McReynolds, and became myself a member of the committee; that we acted on the suggestion of the Senate Judiciary Committee that we prepare a bill, and my recollection is that I went before the Senate Committee and invited their attention to the matter, and then agreed, with their consent – indeed with their suggestion – that I would induce the three members of the Committee – yourself, McReynolds and Sutherland, to appear before them; that we prepared the bill and took perhaps a year or more to work it out and published two statements in respect to it.[35]

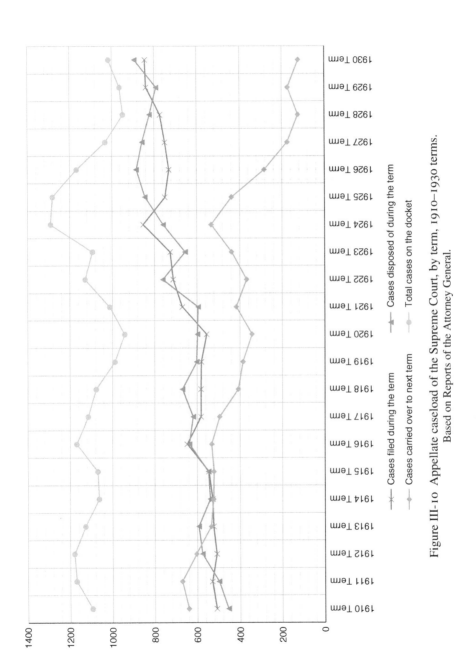

Figure III-10 Appellate caseload of the Supreme Court, by term, 1910–1930 terms. Based on Reports of the Attorney General.

Van Devanter replied with a note challenging Taft's account. Van Devanter sought to correct the record:

> No committee having anything to do with legislation was appointed during Chief Justice White's incumbency. He was unalterably opposed to any action along that line by the Court or even by its members. I drafted the act of 1915 and submitted it to him. He approved it but particularly requested that it be turned over to a legislator who would make it his own and in no way connect the Court or any member of the Court with it. Justice McReynolds drafted the act of 1916 and submitted it to Justice Day and myself, some changes were made, and it was introduced and passed during a summer recess. When Chief Justice White returned in the fall he was much disappointed at what had been done – so much so that he never became reconciled to that act. This is only inside Court history.
>
> It was at the suggestion of Senator Cummins and some others that you appointed a committee to assist in drafting what subsequently became the Act of 1925. You probably would not have appointed the committee but for the request of Senator Cummins who was Chairman of the Senate Judiciary Committee. You designated Justice Day, myself and Justice McReynolds as the committee, but we insisted that you should also be a member and you assented. Justice Day retired from the Court and the remaining members of the committee continued to act until the bill was passed. Justice Sutherland, by reason of his legislative experience, assisted in presenting the matter but was not a member of the committee. I think it well that we should not overlook the fact that it was at the request of Senator Cummins and others that the Court assisted in preparing the last act. According to tradition the Court always has refrained from connecting itself with legislative work.[36]

Van Devanter was crystal clear (and convincing) that the effort to formulate the Judges' Bill began during the tenure of Taft, not that of White. But because Van Devanter was concerned that it might seem improper for the Court to be connected "with legislative work," he repeatedly emphasized that it was essential not to "overlook the fact that it was at the request of Senator Cummins and others that the Court assisted in preparing" the Act.[37] What little documentary evidence we have, however, suggests that Van Devanter's recollection may be inaccurate.

The first surviving written reference to the Judges' Bill occurs in a letter from Taft to Senator Cummins on November 25, 1921. Daugherty had sent Taft for comment and evaluation a pending Senate bill (S. 1831) that would increase the mandatory jurisdiction of the Court in cases involving state enforcement of contracts. Taft wrote Cummins directly to ask what he might "have in mind" in the "proposed" legislation; "Will you give me a concrete case?" Taft asked. In the course of discussing the bill, Taft mentioned that the justices were themselves preparing a bill to reduce the Court's mandatory jurisdiction:

> We are preparing a bill which we hope to bring before your committee, to reduce the obligatory jurisdiction of the Supreme Court in cases from the District of Columbia and in a good many instances where a direct review by the Supreme

Reshaping the Supreme Court

Court is given quite out of keeping with the present system of certiorari, and if this amendment which is proposed in S. 1831 should be adopted, it ought to be incorporated in that bill. I would like to discuss the matter with you. The bill to which I refer is one which has been under consideration by the Supreme Court for some time and which they wish me to go before the committee and present at the request of the Supreme Court.[38]

In discussing the Court's proposed bill, Taft was plainly not responding to a request by Cummins but was instead proposing new legislation to Cummins. This implies that it was the Court itself that had seized the initiative to draft legislation to reduce its own mandatory jurisdiction.[39] Because the proposed legislation had "been under consideration by the Supreme Court for some time," Taft must have begun the effort almost as soon as he joined the Court that summer.

This same timeline appears when the bill is next mentioned in the surviving documentary record, which is in a December 4 letter from Taft to Solicitor General James Beck. Taft wrote Beck to inform him the Court had been considering a jurisdictional bill "for a good many months" and to request Beck's assistance in reviewing it.

> The court has under consideration a bill for the revision of the laws as to proceedings of review in the Supreme Court. A committee consisting of Justice Day and Justice McReynolds have had the matter under advisement for a good many months. We considered it in conference and then made quite a number of changes in the original draft, and then they turned the matter over to me to embody the changes and addition.
>
> I inclose [sic] a copy of a letter which I sent to my colleagues before the conference, for your understanding of the features we have in mind. I wish that you would read the matter over and then submit it to someone in your office who is familiar with the jurisdiction of the Supreme Court. ... The court will take the matter up at the next conference probably, and doubtless will make more changes.[40]

Strikingly, Taft does not refer to any request from Cummins or from the Senate Judiciary Committee. He characterizes the proposed legislation as entirely a matter of the Court's own initiative. Contradicting Van Devanter's 1927 recollection, Taft does not refer to Van Devanter as involved in the bill's initial formulation.[41] Apparently when Taft first joined the Court he had not yet come to depend on Van Devanter, preferring instead to rely on William Day. But, by the end of the month, it seems plain that Van Devanter had come to assume primary responsibility for drafting the bill. On January 7, 1922, Van Devanter wrote his intimate friend Judge Walter Sanborn:

> Here is a printed draft of a proposed bill revising the statutes respecting the jurisdiction of the Supreme Court and the Circuit Courts of Appeals and prescribing the mode of obtaining a review, etc. I drafted it, and it represents the composite opinion of the Chief Justice, Justices Day and McReynolds and

myself, and was today laid before the other members of the Court. It has not been given any other circulation. We are not and do not intend to be engaged in legislative work, but there is a very pressing need for something along this line, and we have been asked to formulate something which others who are engaged in legislative work may take hold of and pass, if they can, without getting things more confused or more complicated than they are now.[42]

It is likely that after the conference mentioned by Taft in his letter to Beck, the Court turned to Van Devanter for either polishing or rewriting. His success in this endeavor may have laid the foundation for Taft's subsequent close and unqualified reliance on his advice and counsel. To Sanborn, Devanter expressed concern that the Court was "engaged in legislative work" and yet simultaneously acknowledged that the Court was in fact so involved. Van Devanter went out of his way to stress, as he would later emphasize to Taft in 1927, that the Court had "been asked" to draft the bill, although his language in this regard is notably vague.[43]

However it came about, what Taft called "our great Supreme Court bill"[44] created an entirely "new dispensation" for the Court by establishing "drastic limitations upon" its mandatory jurisdiction.[45] It was immediately recognized that the Act revolutionized "the appellate jurisdiction of the Supreme Court of the United States"[46] by empowering the Court to use the discretionary writ of *certiorari* to select a large proportion of its own cases.[47] As Taft wrote his son, the Court could now "pick and choose most of the cases that we shall hear."[48] The Act, which was "the most sweeping alteration of the Supreme Court's role ever passed in American history,"[49] directly embodied Taft's vision of the Court as an institution whose function is "not the remedying of a particular litigant's wrong, but the consideration of cases whose decision involves principles, the application of which are of wide public or governmental interest, and which should be authoritatively declared by the final court."[50]

In July 1925, the Court published a new rule to offer guidance about the kind of cases that would possess sufficient national importance to warrant the Court's attention.[51] Although the new rule retained traces of the traditional conception of the Court as a final tribunal designed to correct the errors of subordinate institutions,[52] its major thrust was to recast the Court as an institution committed to supervising the orderly development of federal law.[53] This had been Taft's point all along, and its profound implications were apparent to contemporaries who observed that the Court was now assuming "the function of a ministry of justice":

> The specific rights of particular parties are no longer the essence of the controversies before the Supreme Court. They are mere vehicles whereby the Constitution and the laws of the United States are interpreted, the means whereby the general principles of law are defined, and whereby the rules and conceptions of federal law are made uniform throughout the country. In this respect one might well say that the Supreme Court is abandoning its character as a court of last resort, and assuming the function of a ministry of justice.[54]

Just as the Act of September 14, 1922, had initiated a process that would lead to the creation of a unified federal judicial branch headed by the chief justice, so the

Reshaping the Supreme Court

Judges' Bill established the Supreme Court as the institutional manager of the system of federal law in both state and federal courts. It radically expanded the justices' "options to select the issues they would address, and to manage the appropriate time, case, and factual context in which to break new constitutional ground."[55]

In the long run, the Act would undermine the legitimacy of the Court as a simple dispute settlement mechanism, necessary for the definitive resolution of the many controversies that inevitably arise in any civilized society.[56] The Judges' Bill meant that a Supreme Court decision would henceforth be less like the definitive resolution of a particular case based on preexisting law, than, as Justice Stephen Breyer has written, "an instruction, with respect to law and judicial action, aimed at the future."[57] The Court would spend the next century searching for some way to justify the startling reach and significance of such future-oriented instructions. Along with the Act of September 4, 1922, the Judges' Bill helped reshape Article III courts into a proactive instrument of governance. Within a few short years, Taft had centralized and coordinated judicial power in ways that previously would have been all but inconceivable.[58]

The immediate effect of the Judges' Bill on the Court's docket was nothing short of "marvelous."[59] Figure III-10 demonstrates the precipitous decline in the Court's arrears. At the conclusion of the 1928 term, "the Court . . . caught up with its work. It . . . disposed of all the cases it could have acted upon. . . . In fact, so rapid has been the Court's pace, that its efficiency has become a source of embarrassment to counsel in the preparation of their cases."[60] Addressing the American Law Institute, Taft chuckled, "I can say with respect to the business of the Court that under the beneficent Act of February 13th, 1925, we have made such progress with business that I think members of the Bar are beginning to be a little embarrassed by the proximity of the Court to them."[61] By the end of the 1929 term, Van Devanter could claim that "the Court is now more nearly current with its work than it has been at any time in many years. . . . [C]ases are now reached for argument within about six months after they are docketed. The members of the Court are all agreed that the new system is a great improvement over the old and that it works to the real advantage of litigants."[62]

Although the statute had technically been drafted by Van Devanter,[63] everyone understood that the political impetus for the Act had come from Taft.[64] "His political associations I suppose made it easier to get passed a bill remodeling our jurisdiction . . . that was very important and I think will work well," Holmes wrote his friend Harold Laski.[65] As a former president, Taft was at ease in the political circles of Washington power.[66] He effectively persuaded Coolidge to recommend passage of the Judges' Bill to Congress.[67] He relentlessly and personally lobbied legislators to ensure its passage.[68] He rallied the American Bar Association to throw its weight in support of the bill.[69] Taft in effect stepped outside the traditionally limited role of the chief justice and became an effective and aggressive political actor.

Notes

1. JM to WHT (July 30, 1921) (Taft papers). McKenney was 69 years old and had been an employee of the Court for fifty-two years.
2. Pub. L. 61-465, 36 Stat. 1152–53 (March 3, 1911).
3. William R. Stansbury to WHT (July 30, 1921) (Taft papers).
4. WHT to Helen Herron Taft (August 3, 1921) (Taft papers).
5. WHT to William R. Stansbury (August 3, 1921) (Taft papers).
6. WHT to Helen Herron Taft (August 3, 1921) (Taft papers).
7. OWH to Harold Laski (June 6, 1926), in 2 HOLMES-LASKI CORRESPONDENCE, at 848. Upon Taft's appointment, Holmes had written Laski, "Taft I think will do well as CJ – the executive details, which, as I have said, are the matters upon which the CJ most counts as such, will be turned off with less feeling of friction and more rapidly, I think, than with his predecessor, especially after he had become so infirm. As to opinions we shall see." OWH to Harold Laski (October 9, 1921), in 1 HOLMES-LASKI CORRESPONDENCE, at 373. *See* OWH to Nina Gray (October 12, 1921) (Holmes papers).
8. OWH to Harold Laski (November 13, 1925), in 1 HOLMES-LASKI CORRESPONDENCE, at 797.
9. The financial relationship between the Court and its clerk was especially tricky given that a portion of the clerk's income continued to be taken from fees charged to litigants. WHT to Members of the Court (February 12, 1928) (Van Devanter papers). *See, e.g.*, WHT to LDB (March 12, 1923) (Taft papers); WHT to WVD (March 12, 1923) (Taft papers); WHT to LDB (March 2, 1924) (Taft papers); WHT to JCM (March 6, 1924) (Taft papers); WHT to William R. Stansbury (March 6, 1924) (Taft papers); William R. Stansbury to WHT (March 17, 1924) (Taft papers); WHT to LDB (March 19, 1924) (Taft papers); WHT to William R. Stansbury (March 23, 1924) (Taft papers); LDB to WHT (March 28, 1924) (Taft papers); WHT to LDB (April 8, 1924) (Taft papers); WHT to LDB (December 10, 1924) (Taft papers); LDB to WHT (January 4, 1925) (Taft papers); WHT to LDB (November 30, 1925) (Taft papers); William R. Stansbury to WHT (December 4, 1926) (Taft papers); LDB to WHT (October 13, 1927) (Taft papers); LDB to WHT (December 20, 1928) (Taft papers).
10. *See, e.g.*, WHT to Arthur C. Denison (October 6, 1922) (Taft papers); WHT to William R. Stansbury (October 8, 1922) (Taft papers).
11. 1925 SUPREME COURT JOURNAL 326 (June 1, 1926) ("To expedite the hearing of criminal cases upon the docket of this court, brought here by writ of error directly from State courts or from those courts by appeals from writs of habeas corpus in Federal courts, it is ordered that all cases of this kind upon the docket be advanced for hearing and set during the October sessions of this court at the October, 1926, term. It is further ordered that appeals in Federal criminal cases arising under the laws of the United States and now upon the docket of this court, be also advanced for hearing at the October sessions for the October term of 1926."). *See Supreme Court Stops Delay in Criminal Case Hearings*, NEW YORK TIMES (October 20, 1926), at 1 ("Chief Justice Taft gave notice on the opening of the Supreme Court today that hereafter no unnecessary delays would be permitted in the final disposition of criminal cases appealed to that body. He stated that the Court had decided to do everything possible to expedite hearings and decisions in criminal cases and prevent delays on its

Reshaping the Supreme Court

docket."); WHT to Charles P. Taft 2nd (November 28, 1926) (Taft papers) ("We are pursuing a policy of bringing for immediate hearing every criminal case that is ready, whether State or Federal. We don't propose to have our Court made a refuge for convicted criminals to delay imprisonment, and it is curious to see how many of them fade out as having nothing in them the minute we require them to be set for a hearing."); WHT to Robert A. Taft (November 28, 1926) (Taft papers) ("We find that it has been too often the case that a defendant convicted in a State court would get into our Court by some hook or crook of constitutional suggestion, and then that the case would be forgotten and not pressed to our attention by the State officers. We therefore have adopted the rule of putting these cases out for hearing just as soon as they are ready."); WHT to Newton D. Baker (January 15, 1928) (Taft papers); Gaines v. Washington, 277 U.S. 81, 87 (1928) ("It has not been the practice of the court to write opinions and state its reasons for denying writs of certiorari, and this opinion is not to be regarded as indicating an intention to adopt that practice, but, in view of the fact that the court has deemed it wise to initiate a practice for speedily disposing of criminal cases in which there is no real basis for jurisdiction in this court, it was thought proper to make an exception here, not to be repeated, and write an opinion."); WHT to the Brethren (May 11, 1928) (Taft papers) (stating that the opinion in *Gaines* was designed to "serve notice that we are engaged in expediting our disposition of criminal convictions and not allow a refuge here for delay."); Herbert F. Goodrich, *American Law Institute Adopts Its First Official Draft*, 14 AMERICAN BAR ASSOCIATION JOURNAL 245, 246 (1928) (Remarks of William Howard Taft: "We in our court have determined that those gentlemen who have been unfortunate enough to be convicted in the State courts and in the lower Federal courts are not going to have a period of rest and contemplation before they begin to serve the State in a close relation through us, and we, therefore, are advancing every criminal case that comes into court. When we adjourn for the summer we shall have heard every case on the docket of a criminal character. (Applause.)").

12. LDB to WHT (October 6, 1924) (Taft papers); WHT to GS (August 11, 1925) (Taft papers); WHT to Robert A. Taft (October 20, 1924) (Taft papers); Draft Memorandum (June 7, 1927?) (Taft papers); WHT to George D. Seymour (October 16, 1927) (Taft papers) ("[T]he truth is that I have been overwhelmed by the flow of business in certioraris and in submitted cases that we have had at the beginning of this term. It is the legitimate outcome of our new law, the Act of February 13, 1925, and is an indication that it is working as we wished it to work, but it reveals the necessity of our changing the method we have had at the opening of the term in the disposition of business. We shall have to devote about ten days to certioraris alone, without hearing arguments."); WHT to Robert A. Taft (October 16, 1927) (Taft papers); WHT to Ernest Knaebel (September 18, 1928) (Taft papers); Gregory Hankin, *U.S. Supreme Court under New Act*, 12 JOURNAL OF THE AMERICAN JUDICATURE SOCIETY 40, 43 (August 1928).

13. WHT to Charles Elmore Cropley (January 7, 1929) (Taft papers); WHT to Charles Elmore Cropley (December 22, 1928) (Taft papers); WHT to Members of the Court (February 23, 1928) (Stone papers); WHT to Members of the Court (February 15, 1928) (Stone papers); WHT to Members of the Court (February 13, 1928) (Stone papers); WHT to Members of the Court (February 12, 1928) (Van Devanter papers) ("We ought to take steps at once to reduce substantially the cost to litigants in our Court."); WHT to William R. Stansbury (January 20, 1927) (Taft papers); WHT to

THE TAFT COURT

LDB (December 18, 1926) (Taft papers) (over the objection of Stansbury and Brandeis, Taft "would be glad ... to make the experiment to see whether we could not reduce our printing fee 20 per cent. ... I am itching to reduce expenses to the litigants in our Court."); LDB to WHT (December 18, 1926) (Taft papers); WHT to JCM (December 18, 1926) (Taft papers); William R. Stansbury to WHT (December 16, 1926) (Taft papers); LDB to WHT (December 16, 1926) (Taft papers); WHT to LDB (December 7, 1926) (Taft papers); WHT to JCM (January 4, 1926) (Taft papers); WHT to William R. Stansbury (December 12, 1925) (Taft papers); Statement of Hon. James C. McReynolds in Procedure in Federal Courts (February 2, 1924), Hearings on S. 2060 and S. 2061 before the Subcomm. of the Senate Comm. on the Judiciary, 68th CONG. 1st SESS., at 46 ("During the last year we have materially reduced the cost of the records."); WHT to Loyal E. Knappen (January 15, 1924) (Taft papers); WHT to James M. Beck (September 23, 1923) (Taft papers).

14. Pub. L. 67-272, 42 Stat. 816 (July 1, 1922); H.R. Rep. No. 963, 67th CONG. 2nd SESS. (May 3, 1922), at 3; *Jurisdiction of Circuit Courts of Appeals and United States Supreme Court: Pay of Supreme Court Reporter*, Hearing on H.R. 10479 before the Committee on the Judiciary of the House of Representatives, 67th CONG. 2nd SESS. (March 30, 1922), at 9–12; *Publication of U.S. Supreme Court Reports*, 8 AMERICAN BAR ASSOCIATION JOURNAL 457 (1922); Pub. L. 69-157, 44 Stat. 344 (April 29, 1926); WHT to George Norris (January 4, 1929) (Taft papers). The legislation also gave the chief justice supervision over expenses in the Reporter's Office and provided that the Supreme Court Reports were to be printed at the Government Printing Office.

15. Pub. L. 70-268, 45 Stat. 424 (April 11, 1928); Sen. Rep. No. 436, 70th CONG. 1st SESS. (February 27, 1928); H.R. Rep. No. 300, 70th CONG. 1st SESS. (January 17, 1928); H.R. Rep. No. 1099, 70th CONG. 1st SESS. (April 2, 1928); 69 CONG. REC. 5726 (April 2, 1928); Frank K. Green to WHT (April 13, 1928) (Taft papers) (reform due to "the kindly and untiring efforts of the Chief Justice"); WHT to Frank K. Green (April 15, 1928) (Taft papers).

16. *See, e.g.*, WHT to Charles Curtis (February 26, 1923) (Taft papers) ("I hope you are not going to deny us in the Supreme Court the space which we need for the Clerk's Office. With the very large Senate Office Building you ought to be willing to let the Supreme Court have at least breathing space.... You have taken back all the rooms but three that were assigned to us for the use of the Judges. In our conference room the shelves have to be made so high that it takes an aeroplane to reach them. But two of the justices have rooms in the Capitol.... [Y]ou might be willing to keep your Senate Committees within space which is reasonable in view of the real needs of the judicial branch of government."); Charles Curtis to WHT (February 27, 1923) (Taft papers); WHT to Charles Curtis (February 28, 1923) (Taft papers) ("[W]e will take the room which you have assigned to us, but I shall continue to protest against the fact that you do not allow the Supreme Court to have space enough for its records. The room which the Senate barber shop now occupies in the Capitol should be given to the Court."); Charles Curtis to WHT (March 1, 1923) (Taft papers) ("I know how much the Supreme Court needs additional space and I tried to get them two rooms, but we were unable to make arrangements to get but the one. The Chairman of the subcommittee and myself worked together in this matter and did everything possible. Personally, I am in favor of erecting a new building for the Supreme Court so that they will have all the room the Court needs, not only for the Court, but for all its offices.").

17. *See, e.g.*, WHT to John C. Anderson (October 18, 1921) (Taft papers); Wendell W. Mischler to William R. Stansbury (November 8, 1921) (Taft papers); WHT to James M. Beck (December 23 (1921) (Taft papers). The chief justice of Kentucky wrote Taft to say: "To you, Mr. Chief Justice, I am informed is due the credit of this much needed reform in the method of publishing these opinions. It will be received with gratification by all active members of the legal profession." Flem D. Sampson to WHT (January 13, 1921) (Taft papers).
18. WHT to Flem D. Sampson (January 16, 1921) (Taft papers). Taft declined, however, to send opinions to lower state appellate judges. As he wrote a state judge, "Our appropriation for printing is running rather low, and I am not sure whether I can extend the sending of our opinions to the Judges of your Appellate Court. I took a great interest in bringing them to the Judges of the Supreme Courts of all the States, and have loaded down our printing bills a little beyond what Congress has allowed us." WHT to Julius C. Travis (April 19, 1922) (Taft papers); Robert von Moschziker to WHT (November 13, 1922); WHT to Robert von Moschziker (November 14, 1922) (Taft papers); WHT to William R. Stansbury (November 14, 1922) (Taft papers); William R. Stansbury to WHT (November 15, 1922) (Taft papers).
19. WHT to Herbert Little (December 11, 1928) (Taft papers).
20. "We need legislation to help us." WHT to George Roe Lockwood (January 9, 1923) (Taft papers).
21. Act of March 3, 1891, 26 Stat. 826.
22. Taft was himself among the very first judges appointed to the newly created Court of Appeals for the Sixth Circuit.
23. Edward A. Hartnett, *Questioning Certiorari: Some Reflections Seventy-Five Years after the Judges' Bill*, 100 COLUMBIA LAW REVIEW 1643, 1650–57 (2000); Mason Mazzone & Carl Emery Woock, *Federalism as Docket Control*, 94 NORTH CAROLINA LAW REVIEW 7, 24–26 (2015); William Howard Taft, *The Jurisdiction of the Supreme Court under the Act of February 13, 1925*, 35 YALE LAW JOURNAL 1, 1 (1925). The Evarts Act was badly crafted. *See* McMillan Contracting Co. v. Abernathy, 263 U.S. 438, 441 (1924) ("The act of 1891 was passed to relieve this Court from a discouraging congestion of business. It was evidently intended that the Circuit Court of Appeals should do a large part of the appellate business. The act was not happily drawn, in defining the division of it between those courts and this Court, and many difficulties have arisen."). After studying the record in preparation for circulating an opinion in *McMillan*, Taft wrote a long memorandum to the Court:

> I have wrestled with this Case ... and spent more brain matter, whether gray or not, over it than it deserves.... I am satisfied ... after a full review of the authorities, ... that no ... logical exposition of our decisions can be made, and that the distinctions that I attempted can not be reconciled with a number of them. This was the view which Brother McReynolds took in the beginning, and he was right. I don't know whether it is wise for us to speak as frankly as I do of the lack of logic in our decisions.... The difficulty of harmonizing the language of the statute with our decision reminds me of the story which John Vertrees of Tennessee told me, to express his view of the white and negro social question in the South. He said there was a creek in the neighborhood of his old birthplace called Saskatchequarle Creek, and that a stranger coming to visit Dr. Robinson, an old-timer of that vicinity, asked the Doctor how he spelled the name of the creek. The Doctor's reply was, "Some spell it one way and some do spell it another, but in my judgment there air no correct way of spellin' it." ... All I can say about the matter is that I know more on the subject than I did before, and that

knowledge adds to the fervency of my prayer that the whole field of our appellate jurisdiction and of the Circuit Court of Appeals shall be reformed, so that a wayfaring man, though a fool, may follow the lines of each division.

WHT to Colleagues (December 31, 1923) (Taft papers).
24. William H. Taft, *Delays and Defects in the Enforcement of Law in This Country*, 187 NORTH AMERICAN REVIEW 851, 851–52 (1908).
25. Taft explained:

> Many people who give the subject hasty consideration regard as the noblest product of human wisdom a system of appeals, by which a suit can be brought before a justice of the peace, and carried through the several intermediate courts of appeal to the Supreme Court of the State. How many legislative halls have rung with the eloquence of defenders of the oppressed and the poor, in opposing laws which were designed to limit the appeals to the Supreme Court to cases involving large sums of money or questions of constitutional or other important law? Shall the poor man be denied the opportunity to have his case re-examined in the highest tribunal of the land? Never! And generally the argument has been successful. In truth, there is nothing which is so detrimental to the interests of the poor man as the right which, if given to him, must also be given to the other and wealthier party. It means two, three, and four, and in some cases even five and six years of litigation. Could any greater opportunity be put in the hands of wealthy persons or corporations to fight off just claims and to defeat, injure or modify the legal rights of poor litigants, than to delay them in securing their just due for several years. I think not.

Id. at 855.
26. *President's Annual Message*, 46 CONG. REC. 25 (December 6, 1910).
27. William H. Taft, *The Attacks on the Courts and Legal Procedure*, 5 KENTUCKY LAW JOURNAL 3, 18 (1916). (This article republishes Taft's 1914 Commencement address to the Cincinnati Law School.) *See also* William Howard Taft, *Address of the President*, in REPORT OF THE THIRTY-SEVENTH ANNUAL MEETING OF THE AMERICAN BAR ASSOCIATION 359, 384 (Baltimore: Lord Baltimore Press 1914).
28. The Court's docket and arrears began to climb beginning in the 1920 term. The short-lived increase in the Court's docket after 1914 may have been caused by the Act of December 23, 1914, Pub. L. 63-224, 38 Stat. 790, see Edward Hartnett, *Why Is the Supreme Court of the United States Protecting State Judges from Popular Democracy*, 75 TEXAS LAW REVIEW 907 (1997), which expanded the scope of the Court's jurisdiction, although it did so entirely by expanding the availability of discretionary *certiorari* review. That is likely why the increase in the number of cases filed during the 1915 and 1916 terms was almost entirely matched by the number of cases terminated. The decrease in the Court's total docket and arrears between the 1916 and 1920 terms was probably caused by the Act of September 6, 1916, Pub. L. 64-258, 39 Stat. 726, which made discretionary some of the Court's heretofore mandatory jurisdiction, in part by removing a large number of small Federal Employers' Liability Act cases from its mandatory jurisdiction. *See* Hartnett, *supra* note 23, at 1658–60. The 1916 Act, as Taft later wrote Frankfurter, "was brought about through the active recommendation of Mr. Justice McReynolds, who had been Attorney General, and whose acquaintance with the Judiciary Committee of both the House and Senate enabled him to secure its passage. It was a step toward the reduction of the obligatory jurisdiction of the Court and the enlargement of its jurisdiction by certiorari." WHT to Felix Frankfurter (May 11, 1926) (Taft papers).

29. *The Chief Justice*, 5 CHICAGO BAR ASSOCIATION RECORD 11–12 (December 1921). Taft reported that "[s]ome of us are working on a proposed bill to simplify the statement of the jurisdiction of the Supreme Court and have it embraced in one statute." *Id.* at 11. Taft's address is reproduced as William Howard Taft, *Three Needed Steps of Progress*, 8 AMERICAN BAR ASSOCIATION JOURNAL 34 (1922). It is noteworthy that in January 1922, Taft actually authored a letter in support of a bill increasing (to a minor extent) the jurisdiction of the Supreme Court. *See* Pub. L. 67-144, 42 Stat. 366 (February 17, 1922); 62 CONG. REC. 1227–28 (January 16, 1922) (Remarks of Representative Boies) ("We took the precaution to submit this matter to the Supreme Court of the United States, knowing they were a little jealous of their jurisdiction, and I have copies of the letters here from the Chief Justice of the Supreme Court of the United States and also the Attorney General showing approval of the amendment.").
30. William Howard Taft, *Possible and Needed Reforms in Administration of Justice in Federal Courts*, 8 AMERICAN BAR ASSOCIATION JOURNAL 601, 602 (1922).
31. *Id.* at 603–4. Taft no doubt had in mind a long speech delivered in Virginia by Senator Thomas J. Walsh of Montana on June 8, 1922, in which Walsh argued that proposed legislation to increase the Court's discretionary jurisdiction would create a tidal wave of *certiorari* petitions that would swamp the Court and actually increase the congestion of its docket. He contended that there should be no writs of *certiorari* at all allowed in cases from the Circuit Courts of Appeals, but instead that the Court should have to hear mandatory appeals coming from those courts, appeals that would be limited to the determination of federal questions. 62 CONG. REC. 8549 (June 12, 1922). Walsh argued that diversity jurisdiction, as well as federal question jurisdiction, be removed from lower federal courts.

Taft wrote Brandeis, "I have a commencement address delivered by Senator Walsh against our jurisdiction bill .... Senator Walsh belongs to that character of lawyer who is obstructive and not constructive. He gives an appearance of constructive views by suggesting changes that there is no possibility of having, but when there is anything practical, he is always against it, and that is because he is against the federal courts. That is the real reason why he is not for improving them." WHT to LDB (July 25, 1922) (Taft papers). Taft also wrote Day that "we must look for determined opposition to the bill by Walsh and Shields and the Democrats. They hate the Federal courts and are obstructionists in respect to every proposed reform. Walsh sent me an address made to the Bar Association of Virginia directed chiefly against our Bill and against the Federal Courts' jurisdiction and asked my comment." WHT to WRD (August 18, 1922) (Taft papers).

Justices McReynolds and Day immediately wrote Walsh objecting to his conclusions. *See* JCM to Thomas J. Walsh (June 30, 1922) (Walsh papers) ("If a hearing must be given & oral argument offered in every Federal question involved in every suit important things must be neglected or delayed beyond reason. ... The general theory of the pending bill I think is good. After a litigant has had a hearing in all the State courts or in two Federal Courts the matter may properly end unless there is something about the cause which the court can see is of general importance. The use of certiorari is the only practical way of which I am aware by wh. this end can be reached. And personally I incline to think it will be necessary at some time to confine the jurisdiction of the court almost wholly to causes taken up on certiorari2. ... The great fundamental purpose of the Supreme Court, as I understand, is to settle the law for guidance of courts & counsel and this I think makes it necessary to relieve the court from a multitude of unimportant things wh. consumes time & strength which should [be] devoted elsewhere. The suggestions you make concerning the limitation of the jurisdiction of the lower Federal Courts have much in their favor. But as a practical matter, are they possibilities? I incline to think not."); WRD to Thomas J. Walsh (July 10, 1922) (Walsh papers) ("I have thought for some time that it would be wise to increase the certiorari power of the Court along the line embodied in the bill now before Congress. That course will enable the Court to winnow the wheat from the chaff and to give its attention more fully to the great questions of constitutional law and kindred matters which constitute the great purposes for which the Court was created.").

It may have been because of his close alliance with Walsh that Brandeis refused to endorse Taft's efforts to expand the discretionary jurisdiction of the Court. When Taft asked Brandeis for his support, Brandeis replied:

> *Re* your suggestion of a letter of approval of the pending Jurisdiction Bill.
>
> A clear majority of the Court approve of it wholly. I think it has many admirable features. But a study of our experience during the last eight years has raised in my mind grave doubt whether the simple expedient of expanding our discretionary jurisdiction is the most effective or the safest method of securing the needed relief. For this reason, it cannot be stated that I individually approve the bill.
>
> I am willing that you should say that the Court approves the bill – without stating whether or not individual members approve it. For, in relation to proposed legislation directly affecting the Court, the Chief Justice, when supported by a clear majority, should be permitted to speak for it as a unit; and differences of view among its members should not be made a matter of public discussion.

LDB to WHT (November 30, 1924) (Taft papers). *See* Statement of Chief Justice William Howard Taft (December 18, 1924), *Jurisdiction of Circuit Courts of Appeals and of the Supreme Court of the United States*, Hearing before the Committee on the Judiciary of the House of Representatives on H.R. 8206, 68th CONG. 2nd SESS., at 29 ("I am told by all the members that I can say that the court is for the bill. There may be one member – I do not think there are more – who is doubtful about it, or, I should say, doubtful as to its efficacy; but he said to me that I could say the whole court were in favor of the bill.").

Taft immediately forwarded Brandeis's note to Van Devanter, saying: "Because Walsh is opposed to it, as he told me, because he talked with Walsh, and because he always wishes to appear on the off side and a champion of the offsiders, he declines to help us. This at least seems to me to be the situation." WHT to WVD (December 1, 1924) (Van Devanter papers). *See* WHT to Robert A. Taft (December 14, 1924) (Taft papers) ("I tried to enlist Brandeis in this business, but I smoked him out and found that while he was willing to have the court reported as favoring the bill, he would not himself do anything and intimated doubts about it. That is because Walsh of Montana is against the bill. He tries hard to be a good fellow but he misses it every little while."); WHT to Charles P. Taft 2nd (February 8, 1925) (Taft papers) ("Brandeis was reluctant, but we ran over him. He evidently sympathized with Walsh.").

The day after the bill was signed, Brandeis wrote Frankfurter that "I still think that (except as to Ct of Claims), the bill doesn't touch the most serious unnecessary burdens incident to the prior jurisdictional acts as construed." LDB to Felix Frankfurter (February 14, 1925), in BRANDEIS-FRANKFURTER CORRESPONDENCE, at 193. The exact nature of Brandeis's objections cannot now be determined, but he might have had in mind the distinction between "facial" challenges to the constitutionality of state statutes, and "as applied" challenges to such statutes. *See* Dahnke-Walker Milling Co. v Bondurant, 257 U.S. 282 (1921). Brandeis might also have had in mind the construction of the word "statute" in the new bill. *See* John P. King Mfg. Co. v. City Council of Augusta, 277 U.S. 100 (1928).

Walsh's opposition to Taft's efforts to reform the Court's jurisdiction eventually collapsed, possibly because the proposed statute came to a vote in February 1925, at precisely the moment when Walsh was being bested in his struggle to prevent Stone's confirmation to the Court. *See supra* Chapter 4, at notes 106, 113. At least Taft thought that this was the cause of Walsh's retreat: "Walsh got worsted in his fight with A.G. Stone so he pulled in his horns and the bill passed the House one day and the Senate the next with Walsh helping and coming into conference with us." WHT to Horace D. Taft (March 1, 1925) (Taft papers). Walsh did insist on an amendment to the bill that retained mandatory jurisdiction in some cases coming to the Court from the Circuit Courts of Appeals, but in Taft's view the amendment "did not amount to much." WHT to Robert A. Taft (February 8, 1925) (Taft papers). *See* LDB to Felix Frankfurter (February 14, 1925), in BRANDEIS-FRANKFURTER CORRESPONDENCE, at 193 (The Bill "got through by making some changes insisted upon by T.J. Walsh, the C.J. tells me. I have not seen what these changes are, but I think from what he remembered & particularly from the fact that VanD approved, that they should be satisfactory.").

32. The great advantage of discretionary jurisdiction, as distinct from deciding cases through summary appeals, see Hartnett, *supra* note 23, at 1705, 1715, is that denials of *certiorari* imply nothing about the substantive merits of a case. *See* United States v. Carver, 260 U.S. 482, 490 (1923) ("The denial of a writ of certiorari imports no expression of opinion upon the merits of the case, as the bar has been told many times."). In Price Fire & Water Proofing Co. v. United States, 261 U.S. 179 (1923), for example, Van Devanter requested that Brandeis remove from his circulated draft a citation to "certiorari denied," commenting: "Fear this may convey to some an impression that denial of certiorari may be taken as a precedent of some weight. Merely call it to your attention. Am not insistent." Brandeis removed the reference (Brandeis papers). *But see* James Craig Peacock, *Purpose of Certiorari in Supreme Court Practice and Effect of Denial or Allowance*, 11 AMERICAN BAR ASSOCIATION JOURNAL 681, 683 (1929) (referring to "the impression that the denial of certiorari by the Supreme Court has somehow added to the sanction or authority of the decision cited. But one who has ever chanced to be present in the Supreme Court when some hapless counsel has referred to such a case as a decision of the Supreme Court or as having gained in that way even the slightest additional weight as an authority will never again labor under such an illusion. Such an impression is, however, a natural one, and ... more or less generally prevalent even among otherwise well informed lawyers.").

From the perspective of justices under a *certiorari* regime, cases must be examined "not of course so thoroughly as to decide them in our minds, but fully enough to decide whether they ought to be brought before us – and of course, I should say, in most cases incidentally to have an opinion whether the judgment below is right or wrong." OWH to Lewis Einstein (May 19, 1927) in HOLMES-EINSTEIN CORRESPONDENCE, at 267. The time advantage created by the reform of the

Court's jurisdiction may thus be theorized as the marginal difference between these two different levels of scrutiny, added to the effort it would have taken to craft and publish opinions in cases not accepted by *certiorari.*

33. Pub. L. 68-415, 43 Stat. 936 (February 13, 1925). The legislative history of the statute is well told in Hartnett, *supra* note 23.
34. Felix Frankfurter to WHT (February 15, 1927) (Taft papers).
35. WHT to WVD (February 21, 1927) (Van Devanter papers). (The 1915 Act to which Taft refers is Pub. L. 63-241, 38 Stat. 803 (January 28, 1915), which involved technical amendments to the Court's mandatory and discretionary jurisdiction that among other things prescribed that all bankruptcy cases coming from federal courts of appeal would have to proceed through writs of *certiorari.*) Taft's memory is consistent with his 1922 testimony to Congress:

> The bill has been the subject of very long discussion in the court itself. Before I came into the court a committee had been appointed for its preparation, consisting of Justice Day, Justice McReynolds, and, I suppose, ex officio, the Chief Justice. It was taken up again and a very careful and very much extended examination of it made by the committee, to which Justice Van Devanter was added. I suppose we have spent two or three months in its preparation.

Statement of Hon. William Howard Taft (March 30, 1922), *Jurisdiction of Circuit Courts of Appeals and United States Supreme Court,* Hearing before the Committee on the Judiciary of the House of Representatives on H.R. 10479, 67th CONG. 2nd SESS., at 1. *See* Statement of Chief Justice William Howard Taft, *supra* note 31, at 28 ("When I came into the court, I found Mr. Justice Day at the head of a committee looking to the framing of a bill which looks to the betterment of conditions with respect to the jurisdiction of the courts."). It is also consistent with a letter that Taft sent to the chair of the Senate Judiciary Committee in 1924: "I think it ought to be emphasized, too, that this matter of legislation to enable the Supreme Court to reduce the business before it, by eliminating unimportant cases, had been referred to a committee, and was under consideration, before I came on the Court." WHT to Albert B. Cummins (January 31, 1924) (Taft papers). In 1924, Taft sought to deemphasize his connection to the bill because "there are a number who object to any activity on my part in matters of legislation." *Id.*

36. WVD to WHT (May 11, 1927) (Van Devanter papers).
37. Van Devanter's discomfort with the Court's role is evident in a letter that he wrote a friend. "It is known and is recognized in the hearings and in Congress that the bill was prepared in the court," said Van Devanter. "But I believe it better that this should not be dwelt on." WVD to Charles W. Bunn (February 27, 1925) (Van Devanter papers).
38. WHT to Albert B. Cummins (November 25, 1921) (Taft papers). The next week Taft wrote Cummins to report that the Court regarded S. 1831 as "unnecessary." WHT to Albert B. Cummins (December 1, 1921) (Taft papers). The bill would nevertheless eventually be enacted as Pub. L. 67-144, 42 Stat. 366 (February 17, 1922). *See supra* note 29.
39. About a year later, in 1923, Taft wrote his brother, referring to an early version of the 1925 Act: "I don't think the present Congress will do anything with the bills *I had introduced.* The lethargy and inert opposition to change are most discouraging, but I mean to keep it up, because that is the way to get things through Congress." WHT to Horace D. Taft (February 1, 1923) (Taft papers) (emphasis added).

Reshaping the Supreme Court

40. WHT to James M. Beck (December 4, 1921) (Taft papers).
41. Van Devanter's delayed participation in the drafting of the bill is confirmed by contemporary evidence. *See, e.g.,* WVD to Charles W. Bunn (February 27, 1925) (Van Devanter papers) ("The preparation of the bill was pretty well under way before I got particularly interested.").
42. WVD to Walter H. Sanborn (January 7, 1922) (Van Devanter papers). Van Devanter apparently took over the responsibility of drafting the bill after the Court initially reviewed it in December. *See supra* text at note 40. In March, Taft wrote Senator Cummins: "I enclose herewith a resume of the jurisdiction bill which I sent you some time ago. Shortly afterwards I sent you a very long detailed explanation of each section, with citations and references. This is for use as a report, if you approve it. I have prepared it with the assistance and criticism of my fellow members of the Committee of the Court, Mr. Justice Day, Mr. Justice Van Devanter and Mr. Justice McReynolds." WHT to Albert B. Cummins (March 11, 1922) (Taft papers).
43. At about this time, the American Bar Association ("ABA") Committee on Jurisprudence and Law Reform, chaired by Taft's brother Henry, was advocating that the crisis in the Court's docket be cured by increasing the number of justices on the Court. *See* Hartnett, *supra* note 23, at 1668–69; Henry W. Taft to WHT (April 6, 1922) (Taft papers); WHT to Henry W. Taft (April 6, 1922) (Taft papers) ("The Court are all of them very much opposed to increasing the number of the Court. It would greatly inconvenience us. It would impair the uniformity of decision to have less than the whole Court sit for every case. I hope nothing will be done to give us a town meeting. Consider the danger of setting a precedent to a Demagouge [sic] Democratic Administration."); Henry W. Taft to WHT (April 10, 1922) (Taft papers). Solicitor General Beck evidently agreed with the ABA approach. *See* James M. Beck to WHT (December 16, 1921) (Taft papers). Taft did his best to squelch the idea, writing Beck, "I have your letter of December 16th, but as we have talked over the matter since, it perhaps is not necessary for me to answer it. I hope you will examine with some care the bill that we are taking a good deal of time to prepare in the court, with a view of helping us when the time comes for its introduction. We are all convinced that the only way to help the situation is to enable us to reduce our jurisdiction by cutting off more writs of error and the exercise of the writ of certiorari." WHT to James M. Beck (December 18, 1921) (Taft papers).

Although Beck evidently refused to give up the idea of increasing the number of justices, see James M. Beck to WVD (February 9, 1922) (Van Devanter papers); WHT to WVD (February 4, 1922) (Taft papers), he did eventually testify in favor of the bill. Statement of Honorable James M. Beck, Solicitor General (April 27, 1922), *Jurisdiction of Circuit Courts of Appeals and United States Supreme Court*, Hearing before the Committee on the Judiciary of the House of Representatives on H.R. 10479, 67th CONG. 2nd SESS., at 17. *See* James M. Beck to WHT (February 3, 1922) (Beck papers at Princeton University) ("The main purpose of the draft bill, – to cut down appeals as of right and increase appeals as matter of grace – commends itself to me."); Hartnett, *supra* note 23, at 1669. At about that time, Holmes wrote Frankfurter that although "I am not the man to give advice as to cutting down the jurisdiction, ... I cannot put too strongly my conviction that the increase of number would be a fatal mistake – and I am so near the end of my work that I believe my judgment is free from personal bias if that should be suspected. ... I should be surprised if all the justices did not agree." OWH to Felix Frankfurter (September 9, 1921), in HOLMES-FRANKFURTER CORRESPONDENCE, at 126. The ABA eventually swung around to provide full support to the Court's bill. *See, e.g.*, R.E.L. Saner, *Governmental Review*, in REPORT OF THE FORTY-SEVENTH ANNUAL MEETING OF THE AMERICAN BAR ASSOCIATION 127, 143–46 (Baltimore: Lord Baltimore Press 1924).

44. WHT to Mrs. Frederick J. Manning (February 15, 1925) (Taft papers). As Taft wrote the editor of the *American Bar Association Journal*, he regarded the Act as "a great step in the history of the Court." WHT to Edgar Bronson Tolman (February 25, 1925) (Taft papers). *See* WHT to Mrs. Frederick J. Manning (February 22, 1925) (Taft papers); *Appellate Procedure of U.S. Supreme Court and Circuit Court of Appeals*, 11 AMERICAN BAR ASSOCIATION JOURNAL 145 (1925) (the Act is "a great step in the history of the United States Supreme Court"). One advantage of the Act that Taft always stressed was that "the jurisdiction of the Supreme Court is defined in a great many statutes and special acts, and it has really become almost a trap to catch the unwary." It was necessary, therefore, "to simplify the statement of the jurisdiction of the Supreme Court and have it embraced in one statute." Taft, *Three Needed Steps of Progress*, *supra* note 29, at 35. *See, e.g.*, WHT to A. Owsley Stanley (December 5, 1924) (Taft papers) ("For two years our Court has been very anxious to secure the passage of a bill to give us greater power of certiorari so as to reduce the number of cases which come to us, to simplify the statutes which now contain the procedure of appeal to us, which are very complicated and form a trap for the lawyers.").

45. Felix Frankfurter & James M. Landis, *The Supreme Court under the Judiciary Act of 1925*, 42 HARVARD LAW REVIEW 1, 1 (1928).

46. Charles W. Bunn, *The New Appellate Jurisdiction in Federal Courts*, 9 MINNESOTA LAW REVIEW 309, 309 (1925).

47. For a good description of the complicated changes created by the Act in the Court's jurisdiction, see Taft, *supra* note 23. The Act retained mandatory jurisdiction for portions of the Court's docket. With respect to federal Courts of Appeals, mandatory jurisdiction attached in what Taft called "a narrow class of cases in which the validity of a state statute is questioned as violating the Constitution or a treaty or statute of the United States, and the decision of the lower court is against its validity." *Id.* at 5. In such cases, a litigant faced the choice of having the Court exercise mandatory jurisdiction by a writ of error or appeal, but the jurisdiction of the Court would be limited to the federal question raised, or instead having the Court consider the whole case by applying for a writ of *certiorari*. *Id. But see* Benjamin B. Johnson, *The Origins of Supreme Court Question Selection*, 122 COLUMBIA LAW REVIEW 793, 837–39 (2022). With respect to state courts, mandatory jurisdiction attached whenever a state court of last resort decided a case involving "the validity under the Federal Constitution of a treaty or statute of the United States ... and the decision is against its validity," or whenever "the validity of a statute of a state under the Federal Constitution, treaty or law is questioned and the decision is in favor of its validity." Taft, *supra* note 23, at 5. Mandatory jurisdiction also attached to certain criminal decisions by federal district courts, as well as to certain decisions by three judge district courts. *Id.* at 5–6.

48. WHT to Robert A. Taft (February 8, 1925) (Taft papers).

49. Jonathan Sternberg, *Deciding Not to Decide: The Judiciary Act of 1925 and the Discretionary Court*, 33 JOURNAL OF SUPREME COURT HISTORY 1, 14 (2008).

50. *Id.* at 2. "The real work which the Supreme Court has to do is for the public at large," Taft told the New York County Bar Association, "as distinguished from the particular litigants before it. ... Its main purpose is to lay down important principles of law and thus to help the public at large to a knowledge of their rights and duties

Reshaping the Supreme Court

and to make the law clearer." William Howard Taft, Address to the New York County Bar Association (February 18, 1922) (Taft papers).

51. Revised Rule 35, 266 U.S. 681 (1925):

> A review on writ of certiorari is not a matter of right, but of sound judicial discretion, and will be granted only where there are special and important reasons therefor. The following, while neither controlling nor fully measuring the court's discretion, indicate the character of reasons which will be considered:
>
> (a) Where a state court has decided a federal question of substance not theretofore determined by this court, or has decided it in a way probably not in accord with applicable decisions of this court.
>
> (b) Where a circuit court of appeals has rendered a decision in conflict with the decision of another circuit court of appeals on the same matter; or has decided an important question of local law in a way probably in conflict with applicable local decisions; or has decided an important question of general law in a way probably untenable or in conflict with the weight of authority; or has decided an important question of federal law which has not been, but should be, settled by this court; or has decided a federal question in a way probably in conflict with applicable decisions of this court; or has so far departed from the accepted and usual course of judicial proceedings, or so far sanctioned such a departure by a lower court, as to call for an exercise of this court's power of supervision.

The revised rule was wholly new. *Compare* Rule 37, *Rules of the Supreme Court of the United States* (1918), at 39, available at www.supremecourt.gov/pdfs/rules/rules_1919.pdf. *But see* Layne & Bowler Corp. v. Western Wells Works, 261 U.S. 387, 392 (1923) (opinion by Taft) ("[I]t is very important that we be consistent in not granting the writ of certiorari except in cases involving principles the settlement of which is of importance to the public, as distinguished from that of the parties, and in cases where there is a real and embarrassing conflict of opinion and authority between the Circuit Courts of Appeals. The present case certainly comes under neither head."); Magnum Import Co. v. Coty, 262 U.S. 159, 163 (1923) (opinion by Taft) ("The jurisdiction to bring up cases by certiorari from the Circuit Courts of Appeals was given for two purposes, first to secure uniformity of decision between those courts in the nine circuits, and second, to bring up cases involving questions of importance which it is in the public interest to have decided by this court of last resort. The jurisdiction was not conferred upon this court merely to give the defeated party in the Circuit Court of Appeals another hearing."); Keller v. Adams-Campbell Co., 264 U.S. 314, 319–20 (1924) (opinion by Taft) ("Such an ordinary patent case, with the usual issues of invention, breadth of claims, and noninfringement, this court will not bring here by certiorari, unless it be necessary to reconcile decisions of Circuit Courts of Appeal on the same patent. We therefore find ourselves mistaken in assuming that an important issue of general patent law ... is here involved. The result is that an order must be entered dismissing the writ of certiorari as improvidently granted."); John E. Thropp's Sons Co. v. Seiberling, 264 U.S. 320 (1924) (opinion by Taft).

The new Rule 35 was composed by Van Devanter. WVD to JHC (June 12, 1925) (Van Devanter papers). Taft wrote Van Devanter in June generously acknowledging that "We are all indebted to you, as the country should be, for clearing away the spider webs which have been permitted to persist in our forms and procedure, not really because they come from Marshall's day but because members of the court have been too lazy or too little interested to make the needed changes." WHT to

WVD (June 19, 1925) (Van Devanter papers). Oddly, Taft had written Van Devanter in 1922 that "I have no sympathy with the proposition that the Court ought to define the rules which shall govern it in the issue of the writs of certiorari." WHT to WVD (February 2, 1922) (Taft papers). It is noteworthy that Taft's original conception was that the writ of *certiorari* involved the exercise of "absolute and arbitrary discretion," Taft, *The Attacks on the Courts and Legal Procedure, supra* note 27, at 18, whereas in Van Devanter's elegant (if mysterious) formulation in Rule 35, the Court promised instead to exercise "sound judicial discretion."

Van Devanter's formulation of the rule has remained remarkably stable over the ensuing many years. *Compare* Supreme Court Rule 10 (2017), available at www.supremecourt.gov/filingandrules/2017RulesoftheCourt.pdf. As a result of Erie R. Co. v. Tompkins, 304 U.S. 64 (1938), the modern Supreme Court rule differs in that it focuses on federal law and removes references to local and "general" law.

52. This conception of the Court was eloquently set forth in testimony opposing the Act by Judge Benjamin I. Salinger: "[T]he great function of the supreme Court is to protect rights given by treaty, the Constitution, or other Federal law. On a proper plea set up, the citizen should be able to obtain the protection of such rights – not as a matter of grace or of discretion, but as of right – as protection due from the court which is specially charged with insisting upon reverence for Federal law.... I can not help thinking that every case of violating Federal rights is important in the sense that injury inflicted by the violation should entitle the sufferer, as a matter of right, to have redress in the Supreme Court." Statement of Hon. Benjamin I. Salinger, of Carroll, Iowa (April 18, 1922), *Jurisdiction of Circuit Courts of Appeals and United States Supreme Court*, Hearing before the Committee on the Judiciary of the House of Representatives on H.R. 10479, 67th CONG. 2nd SESS., at 5. *See Limits on Appeals Viewed as a Peril*, NEW YORK TIMES (April 9, 1922), at 1. Traces of this conception of the Court are apparent in how contemporaries interpreted the meaning of the Court's denial of petitions for *certiorari*. So, for example, in 1925 the Court of Appeals for the Ninth Circuit said: "What effect should be given to the denial of a writ of certiorari by the Supreme Court we are not prepared to say, but it would seem that if the Circuit Court of Appeals misconstrued a federal statute and affirmed the conviction of a person innocent of crime, the Supreme Court would undoubtedly review its decision." Lupipparu v. United States, 5 F.2d 504, 504 (9th Cir. 1925).

53. Taft's anxiety for the Court to adopt this role is apparent in a case like Sun Ship Building Co. v. United States, 271 U.S. 96, 99 (1926) ("Valuable time was taken in hearing these cases. After arguments on behalf of the claimants, we declined to hear the other side because of the correctness of the judgments of the Court of Claims was clear. It is fortunate for all that, under the Act of February 13, 1925, judgments of the Court of Claims entered after May 13, 1925, can only be reviewed here after a showing of merits."). In St. Louis, Kennett & Southeastern R.R. Co. v. United States, 267 U.S. 346 (1925), a case coming from the Court of Claims, Taft wrote on his return to Brandeis's circulated draft, "I concur. The new jurisdiction bill will rid of such cases as this." (Brandeis papers).

54. Gregory Hankin, *U.S. Supreme Court under New Act*, 12 JOURNAL OF THE AMERICAN JUDICATURE SOCIETY 40, 40 (August 1928).

55. Stephen C. Halpern & Kenneth N. Vines, *Institutional Disunity: The Judges' Bill and the Role of the U.S. Supreme Court*, 30 WESTERN POLITICAL QUARTERLY 471, 483 (December 1977).

Reshaping the Supreme Court

56. For a discussion, see *infra* Chapter 20.
57. STEPHEN BREYER, THE AUTHORITY OF THE COURT AND THE PERIL OF POLITICS 86 (Cambridge: Harvard University Press 2021).
58. As Senator Walsh remarked, "The House Committee on the Judiciary was told by the Chief Justice that the bill is the work of the Justices of the Supreme Court. If so, it exemplifies that truism, half legal and half political, that a good court always seeks to extend its jurisdiction, and that other maxim, wholly political, so often asserted by Jefferson, that the appetite for power grows as it is gratified." 62 CONG. REC. 8547 (June 12, 1922).
59. GREGORY HANKIN & CHARLOTTE A. HANKIN, PROGRESS OF THE LAW IN THE U.S. SUPREME COURT 1929–1930, at 2 (Washington D.C.: Legal Research Service 1930). "I have no hesitation in saying that the system of certioraris which obtains under the Act of February 13, 1925, works well." WHT to Judge Harry A. Hollzer (September 14, 1928) (Taft papers). "Thus far the 1925 act has enabled the Court to gain upon its arrears," Frankfurter and Landis wrote in 1928. "Not for a hundred years has the Court reached for argument on the regular calendar cases docketed during the term. Last term it achieved this dispatch in its business." Frankfurter & Landis, *supra* note 45, at 14. Despite Brandeis's initial opposition to the bill, *supra* note 31, his biographer Melvin Urofsky writes that "Within a few years, however, he recognized that Taft had been right, as the Court gained control over its docket and eliminated the backlog of cases." MELVIN I. UROFSKY, LOUIS D. BRANDEIS: A LIFE 585 (New York: Pantheon Books 2009).
60. GREGORY HANKIN & CHARLOTTE A. HANKIN, UNITED STATES SUPREME COURT 1928–1929, at 2–3 (Washington D.C.: Legal Research Service 1929). Holmes wrote that in the absence of the Act "we should have to hear many cases that have no right to our time; as it is we barely keep up with the work. We used to be years behindhand. Now I think all the cases on our docket have been put there within a year." OWH to Frederick Pollock (August 30, 1929), in 2 HOLMES-POLLOCK CORRESPONDENCE, at 251. Holmes praised the Act as "a wise measure that saves much time." OWH to Lewis Einstein (September 20, 1926) in HOLMES-EINSTEIN CORRESPONDENCE, at 261. Holmes did complain, however, about the "steady stream of *certioraris* [that] seems to fill every crevice of promised leisure." OWH to Harold Laski (April 17, 1928), in 2 HOLMES-LASKI CORRESPONDENCE), at 1045. For Brandeis, the "moral" of the Act was:

> U.S.S.C. – venerated throughout the land.
> Despite the growth of population, wealth and
> governmental function, & development particularly
> of federal activities[,] the duties of the Court have,
> by successive acts passed from time to time throughout a generation,
> been kept within such narrow limits that
> the nine men, each with one helper, can do the work as
> well as can be done by men of their caliber, i.e. the
> official coat has been cut according to the human cloth.
> Congress, Executive Depts., Commissions & lower federal
> courts. – All subject to criticism or execration.
> Regardless of human limitations, increasing work has been piled upon
> them at nearly every session. The high incumbents,
> In many cases, perform in name only. They
> are administrators, without time to know what they are
> doing or to think how to do it. They are human machines.

LDB to Felix Frankfurter (February 6, 1925), in BRANDEIS-FRANKFURTER CORRESPONDENCE, at 191–92.
61. *Chief Justice Taft's Address*, 15 AMERICAN BAR ASSOCIATION JOURNAL 332 (1929). At this point the article indicates: "Laughter." In Taft's draft of his remarks, the next sentence reads: "We are stepping on their heels." (Taft papers).
62. Willis Van Devanter, *The Supreme Court of the United States*, 5 INDIANA LAW JOURNAL 553, 560 (1930). By contrast, during the 1924 term immediately prior to the enactment of the bill, the Court was, according to Taft, "a year and three months behind" in its docket. WHT to Marcus Kavanagh (December 14, 1925) (Taft papers). By the conclusion of the 1929 term, the Court had "disposed of all the cases which had been argued. This occurred for the first time in about 35 years." HANKIN & HANKIN, *supra* note 59, at 29. Taft's ambition for the Act, as he stated to Congress, was that "We ought to be able to dispose of every case we have during the term, that is, between October and June." Statement of Chief Justice William Howard Taft, *supra* note 31, at 28. *See Vinson Tells A.B.A. of Supreme Court Work; Opinion on Dissents*, 29 OKLAHOMA STATE BAR J. 1269, 1269 (1949) ("The days before passage of the 1925 Act, when it took eighteen to twenty-four months for the Court to reach a case on its docket, are forgotten, and it is assumed by everyone, as it should be, that the Supreme Court is current in its work. The Court will soon have been operating under its basic jurisdictional statute for a quarter of a century, and experience has eloquently proved the wisdom of its architects.").
63. As Van Devanter explained to the General Counsel of the Northern Pacific Railway:

> I want to say to you personally that the bill was written throughout in the court and every amendment put on it was written in the court. The preparation of the bill was pretty well under way before I got particularly interested. Experience has taught me that the subject was complicated and involved and that whatever was done should be done according to some real plan. Again, while I was reluctant to see the court take the matter up, I thought if it did it should do well whatever it did. This resulted in my being drawn into the work. I gave it a great deal of attention and if there be faults in it they are attributable to me more than to any one else; although the judgment reflected in the bill was the composite judgment of all the members of the court rather than the judgment of any individual member.

WVD to Charles W. Bunn (February 27, 1925) (Van Devanter papers). *See* WVD to George B. Rose (March 9, 1925) (Van Devanter papers) ("[I]t fell to me to do the drafting.... About that time the personnel of the Court underwent some changes. Justices Day, Pitney and Clarke all approved the bill; Justices Sutherland, Butler and Sanford came on the Court after the bill was prepared and approved."). Van Devanter's masterful draftsmanship might have been one reason why Taft came so early and so completely to rely on Van Devanter's judgment.
64. Thus, when Congress failed to pass the bill in 1922, Taft wrote the Dean of Indiana Law School: "I had the bills introduced in the last Congress, but they were so hurried in the short session that I did not get an opportunity to go before either committee, and I don't know how much reason I have to hope that the next Congress will act more favorably; but I mean to keep pressing the matter, because that is the only way of getting anything through Congress. Persistence usually wins." WHT to Charles M. Hepburn (April 10, 1923) (Taft papers).

Reshaping the Supreme Court

65. OWH to Harold Laski (November 13, 1925), in 1 HOLMES-LASKI CORRESPONDENCE, at 797.
66. *See* A.H. Ulm, *Behind Scenes of the Supreme Court*, NEW YORK TIMES (January 18, 1925), at SM5 ("Justice Taft, it is said, does not hesitate to 'talk politics' now, though not publicly. He confers with the President and with Cabinet members frequently, and it is stated that when they call on him he freely gives them the benefit of his political knowledge.").
67. In his 1924 State of the Union, Coolidge recommended "immediate favorable consideration" of the bill on the ground that "The docket of the Supreme Court is becoming congested. . . . Justice long delayed is justice refused. Unless the court be given power by preliminary and summary consideration to determine the importance of cases, and by disposing of those which are not of public moment reserve its time for the more extended consideration of the remainder, the congestion of the docket is likely to increase." *Message from the President*, 66 CONG. REC. 54 (December 3, 1924). Taft had written his son that "We are going to make an effort at this session of Congress to try and get our Supreme Court bill through. I don't know whether we can do it, but the only way is to keep trying and after a while we may induce some action. I asked the President to help us and he told me to write him something, which I did. I am afraid he won't put in all I have written, but I can get him started, it will perhaps attract the support of the party members." WHT to Robert A. Taft (November 30, 1924) (Taft papers). Taft had also induced Coolidge to support the bill in 1923. *See Message from the President*, 65 CONG. REC. 98 (December 6, 1923). *See* WHT to Robert A. Taft (December 2, 1923) (Taft papers) ("I wrote a part of his Message – that is I wrote a passage to be embodied in his Message, which he has cut down some, but in effect he has put in all of my recommendations.").
68. WHT to Frank B. Kellogg (May 10, 1922) (Taft papers); WHT to Joseph Walsh (June 5, 1922) (Taft papers); WHT to Horace D. Taft (February 1, 1923) (Taft papers); WHT to A. Owsley Stanley (December 5, 1924) (Taft papers); WHT to Charles P. Taft 2nd (December 14, 1924) (Taft papers) ("I have been writing letters to a lot of Democrats to interest them in the Supreme Court bill. . . . Unless I can get from the Rules Committee of the House a special order giving us a few hours to consider the bill, I am afraid it will fail, but I am hoping I may be able to do that."); WHT to Robert A. Taft (December 14, 1924) (Taft papers) ("I am pressing the Supreme Court procedure bill in the House and in the Senate."); WHT to Charles P. Taft 2nd (February 3, 1925) (Taft papers) ("I have been spending two days at the Capitol to get through a Supreme Court bill.").
69. Hartnett, *supra* note 23, at 1673–74.

CHAPTER 14

The Changing Role of Chief Justice

T AFT'S ENERGETIC TRANSFORMATION of the role of chief justice caused discomfort among his colleagues. Consider, for example, the testimony in 1924 of Van Devanter, McReynolds, and Sutherland in support of the Judges' Bill before the House Judiciary Committee. When Sutherland was about to speak, Representative Montague of Virginia asked whether "you wish to appear as the authors of this bil [sic]?" Before Sutherland could respond, Van Devanter interrupted:

> May I state and let go into the record what occurred? The matter in some way came to the attention of the Judiciary Committee of the Senate. The chairman of that committee communicated with the Chief Justice and requested that the court, members of the court out of their experience, should prepare a bill which would meet the situation. The court hesitated at first, but as a result of further conferences between the Chief Justice and the chairman of the Judiciary Committee of the Senate, the court appointed a committee which drafted a bill, and submitted it to the full court.... In the sense of volunteering, the court did not prepare the bill, but the bill was prepared in the court as a result of the invitation that came in the way I have indicated.[1]

George Graham of Pennsylvania, the chair of the Committee, observed that he was "glad" that it had been made "clear that the Supreme Court has not prepared the bill, thrusting it upon our attention as to what should be done, but that it has been prepared at the request of the Judiciary Committee of the Senate."[2] Representative Ira Hersey of Maine noted that in the Senate report it was asserted that the bill had been prepared by members of the Supreme Court "at the suggestion of the American Bar Association."[3]

The Changing Role of Chief Justice

In fact, the American Bar Association ("ABA") had not suggested to the Court that the Judges' Bill be drafted. It is clear from the documentary record that in 1922 the ABA had instead sought to reduce the Court's workload by increasing the number of justices. Taft had pushed the ABA to support the Judges' Bill, not the other way round.[4] The confusion is instructive, however, for it illustrates the unease prompted by the perception that members of the Supreme Court might actually initiate legislation. It was to avoid that unease that Van Devanter had so swiftly intervened to emphasize that the impetus for the bill had come from Cummins rather than from Taft. The surviving documentary record suggests that Taft had likely pressed the legislation on Cummins, rather than the reverse.[5] It is surely noteworthy that the Senate Judiciary Committee did not itself acknowledge any role in prompting the legislation, asserting instead that it had been initiated by the ABA.

Taft's bold pursuit of the need for statutory reform exemplified Taft's expanded conception of his role as chief justice. Taft had in fact unabashedly proposed new legislation to the attorney general only three days after being confirmed as chief justice.[6] Throughout his time on the Court, Taft felt entirely comfortable recommending and lobbying for legislation he regarded as helpful and constructive. "I have thought that it was part of my duty, as [the head] of the Federal Judiciary system," he wrote the chief judge of New York, "to suggest needed reforms, and to become rather active in pressing them before the Judiciary Committees."[7] This aggressive advocacy of reform represented a radically new conception of the chief justiceship.

Taft's predecessor, Chief Justice White, had been "unalterably opposed" to "the Court or even ... its members" involving themselves in the legislative process.[8] White represented the traditional view, which Taft fully understood, that a "judge should avoid extra-judicial activities ... because they may put him in an attitude actually or seemingly inconsistent with absolute impartiality in the discharge of his judicial duties."[9] But Taft conceived the chief justiceship as closer in spirit and responsibility to a British lord chancellor, who was an executive official with a portfolio that included the administration of justice, than to any previous American conception of a federal judge.[10] As contemporaries recognized, Taft construed "the duties of the position to include administrative reform affecting the entire federal judicial system and also efforts to obtain needed legislation."[11]

Taft frankly acknowledged from the very beginning that "I don't think the former Chief Justice had so much to do in the matter of legislation as I have. I don't object to it, because I think Chief Justices ought to take part in that, but it consumes time and energy."[12] The difficulty was that Taft's efforts to push reform legislation could rather rapidly bring his office "into a field of heated discussion."[13] After advocating for the Act of September 14, 1922, for example, Taft was the object of a harsh personal attack in the Senate by George Norris:

> When these judges come to Washington at the expense of the taxpayers ... what will they do? They will meet with the Chief Justice. They will be dined every evening somewhere. They will be run to death with social activities. They will be killed with social favoritisms before they get down to business. That is especially true in respect to the genial chief justice we have, who dines out somewhere every night. I would like to pause right here to say ... that I do not

believe there is any man who can stick his legs under the tables of the idle rich every night and be fit the next day to sit in judgment upon those who toil.[14]

Taft sought to shrug off these attacks. "If I can get legislation through, I am willing to subject myself to this personal unpleasantness, though of course I would deprecate its affecting the influence of the Court."[15] "I am determined to push a movement for the betterment of the procedure in the Federal courts. I suppose I weigh down such reform by my advocacy of it, in arousing the opposition of certain elements, especially in the Senate, but I don't know why that should prevent my *initiating* matters when nobody is likely to do so."[16]

We know that despite this brave front, Taft felt the sting of personal political criticisms. As he wrote his brother about a different attack: "And so I suffer. I lose sleep at night worrying over it. I think I have inherited Mother's disposition to worry. So all I can do is to have you pray for me, because the 'prayers of the righteous avail much'. If you see my name scored as a disgrace to the Bench and to me and the family, still hold out an anchor of hope for me."[17]

Taft's reconceptualization of the chief justiceship caught him in the toils of serious role-tensions. Taft well understood that "a man who is on the Bench should consider himself cloistered from politics."[18] Taft gave up his regular newspaper column when he became chief justice, explaining: "Certainly, in this country at least, a judge should keep out of politics and out of any diversion or avocation which may involve him in politics. It is one of those characteristic queer inconsistencies in the British judicial system, which was the forerunner of our own, that the highest judicial officer in Great Britain, the Lord Chancellor, is often very much in politics and has always been."[19] Almost as soon as he took office, however, Taft found that he could no longer contain his "bursting expression"[20] in favor of improving the administration of justice, and this involved him precisely in "politics."

Seeking to reconcile his reform efforts with American norms of judicial disinterest, Taft explained that "there were some things that a judge may speak of and may discuss in public and not use a judicial opinion for the purpose" and that "law reform" was one such subject.[21] Judges ought to feel comfortable, for example, addressing professional bar associations on the subject of legal procedure. "One of the most important extra curriculum things that I have to do as Chief Justice," he said in 1923, is "to organize the Bench and the Bar into a united group in this country dedicated to the cause of the improvement of judicial process."[22] Elihu Root commented to Taft that he was "the first Chief Justice to fully appreciate the dynamics of the Bar as an organization. If a national bar spirit can be created it will have an immense effect upon the administration of justice."[23]

Taft began his program of mobilizing the bar almost immediately upon taking office. On August 30, 1921, he spoke to the Judicial Section of the ABA, seeking support for the Act of September 14, 1922.[24] Two days later, he explicitly defended the participation of judges in seeking legislative reform in matters of judicial administration.[25] Four months later, he spoke to the Chicago Bar

The Changing Role of Chief Justice

Association, seeking support for the Judicial Conference statute, as well as for what would eventually become the Judges' Bill.[26]

These speeches aroused comment. The Washington correspondent of the United News sent Taft a letter inquiring "if perhaps some change in the custom of the supreme court, either evolutionary or by some new order made by you, had not taken place. We would be grateful if you would be good enough to say whether the old custom of justices of the supreme court not entering into discussions ... has been abandoned and, if so, what if any procedure was employed in effecting the change."[27] Taft's remarks were explicitly criticized on the floor of the United States Senate as "different from those made by any other Chief Justice."[28] Senator William J. Harris of Georgia opined that "the judiciary is going to be injured, and the people will not have the same high respect for it if the Chief Justice and associate justices of the Supreme Court of the United States make speeches in public not in their line of duty as has been done recently."[29]

But Taft was defiant. Invoking English precedents, he shot back three days later in an address to the New York County Bar Association:

> I venture to think that there are some things that a judge may speak of and may discuss in public and not use a judicial opinion for the purpose. The subject is that of law reform. From the earliest traditions of the English bench from which we get our customs, the judges of the highest courts of Great Britain have taken an interest in and a part in the formulation of legislation for bettering the administration of justice. They have written and spoken on such subjects with entire freedom and without incurring criticism. You doubtless remember that in Campbell's Lives of the Lord Chancellors and the Chief Justices, a part of the story of each life is work done in law reform. Measures of this sort that are put through in England are usually prepared by the law officers of the government and sometimes by the Lord Chancellor himself. The judges of the Supreme Court have taken an active part in the discussion of the measures as they go through their legislative course. And why should it not be so? With their attention constantly directed toward the workings of the machinery of the administration of justice, they are at a more advantageous point of observation and if they use their opportunities, are better able to make recommendations with respect to law reform than any other class in the community.[30]

If at the outset of his chief justiceship Taft could explicitly contrast the cloistered withdrawal required of American judges to the more politically active role of British judges,[31] he was after barely eight months prepared to point to English precedents to justify his own very public efforts at law reform. Taft cited the example of "the Lord Chancellor himself."

Taft never retreated from a commitment boldly to advocate for the improvement of the administration of justice. For the remainder of his tenure as chief justice, he would continue actively to seek legislative reform of judicial procedure.[32] A distant echo of his extraordinary example can still be heard today when we hear chief justices speak about the need for federal courts and Congress to "work together if feasible solutions are to be found to the practical problems that confront today's federal judiciary."[33]

Notes

1. *Jurisdiction of Circuit Courts of Appeals and of the Supreme Court of the United States*, Hearing before the Committee on the Judiciary of the House of Representatives on H.R. 8206, 68th CONG. 2nd SESS. (December 18, 1924), at 23. For a perceptive discussion, see Edward A. Hartnett, *Questioning Certiorari: Some Reflections Seventy-Five Years after the Judges' Bill*, 100 COLUMBIA LAW REVIEW 1643, 1687–89 (2000).
2. *Jurisdiction of Circuit Courts of Appeals and of the Supreme Court of the United States, supra* note 1, at 23. On Graham's sensitivity to judicial encroachments on the legislative prerogatives, see *supra* Chapter 12, at note 66.
3. *Jurisdiction of Circuit Courts of Appeals and of the Supreme Court of the United States, supra* note 1, at 23. The Senate Report actually packed two inaccuracies into a single sentence: "The bill was prepared by a committee of the members of the Supreme Court after a long and careful study of the subject, at the suggestion of the American Bar Association, and has the approval of every member of that court." Sen. Rep. No. 362, 68th CONG. 1st SESS. (April 7, 1924), at 1.
4. *See supra* Chapter 13, at note 43.
5. *See supra* Chapter 13, at 482–83; Hartnett, *supra* note 1, at 1662–63. Felix Frankfurter and James M. Landis delicately observed in 1927 that Taft, "unlike some of his predecessors, ... deemed it the prerogative and even the duty of his office to take the lead in promoting judicial reform and to wait neither upon legislative initiation in Congress nor upon professional opinion." Felix Frankfurter & James M. Landis, *Business of the Supreme Court of the United States – A Study in the Federal Judicial System, VII: The Judiciary Act of 1925*, 40 HARVARD LAW REVIEW 434, 438–39 (1927).
6. *See supra* Chapter 12, at 449.
7. WHT to Frank H. Hiscock (April 12, 1922) (Taft papers).
8. WVD to WHT (May 11, 1927) (Van Devanter papers); *see supra* Chapter 13, at 482. Chief Justice Fuller, by contrast, had offered opinions about pending legislation concerning the jurisdiction of the Court. *See, e.g.*, Letter from Chief Justice Melville W. Fuller (February 1, 1892), 23 CONG. REC. 3285–86 (April 14, 1892).
9. William Howard Taft, *To the Readers of the Tribune*, MINNEAPOLIS MORNING TRIBUNE (July 18, 1921), at 6.
10. The analogy was quite explicit in Taft's mind. *See infra* note 25 and *infra* text at note 30. Ironically, Taft's conception of the chief justiceship may perhaps have been closer to how the Founders initially conceived the position. *See* Justin W. Aimonetti & Jackson A. Myers, *The Founders' Multi-Purpose Chief Justice: The English Origins of the American Chief Justiceship*, 124 WESTERN VIRGINIA LAW REVIEW 203 (2021).
11. *A Federal Commission on Judicature*, 6 JOURNAL OF AMERICAN JUDICATURE SOCIETY 47 (August 1922). So, for example, Taft took it upon himself to reform naturalization procedures to relieve federal courts from the police court crowds and atmosphere that occurred during the process of swearing in citizens. *See* PATRICK WEIL, THE SOVEREIGN CITIZEN: DENATURALIZATION AND THE ORIGINS OF THE AMERICAN REPUBLIC 41–42 (Philadelphia: University of

Pennsylvania Press 2013); An Act to Amend and Supplement the Naturalization Laws, Pub. L. 69-358, 44 Stat. 709 (June 8, 1926).
12. WHT to Horace D. Taft (March 30, 1922) (Taft papers).
13. *Id.*
14. 62 CONG. REC. 5113–14 (April 6, 1922).
15. WHT to Frank H. Hiscock (April 12, 1922) (Taft papers). "But my impression, from a considerable experience in matters of this sort, is that even with the publicity that the position of a Senator secures, such attacks are ephemeral in their effect, and are only remembered by the comparative few who really sympathize with the Senator in his extreme view. It is wonderful what the inevitable and ever-pressing course of events will efface from public memory. It is too bad, however, that we have such blatherskites ... as Norris." *Id.*
16. WHT to Horace D. Taft (April 17, 1922) (Taft papers) (emphasis added).
17. WHT to Horace D. Taft (December 12, 1926) (Taft papers). The most distressing feature of such attacks, Taft wrote the head of the Carnegie Foundation, is that they are used "to attack the Court, which of course, next to my wife and children, is the nearest thing to my heart in life." WHT to Henry S. Pritchett (April 25, 1923) (Taft papers).
18. WHT to HFS (August 1, 1924) (Taft papers).
19. Taft, *supra* note 9. For a discussion of Taft's career as a columnist, see VIVIAN, at vii–xxv.
20. William Howard Taft, Address to the New York County Bar Association (February 18, 1922) (Taft papers).
21. *Id.*
22. WHT to Clarence Kelsey (August 17, 1923) (Taft papers). *See* WHT to Charles Evans Hughes (April 26, 1926) (Taft papers) ("Bar Associations are formed too often for merely social enjoyment and fraternization, with only a modicum of effort to ... exert a controlling influence upon the legislative bodies for real reform measures in respect to courts and legal procedure."); WHT to R.H. Thompson (September 24, 1923) (Taft papers) ("I am strongly in favor of the maintenance of bar associations and the keeping of them in a virile condition to exercise the legitimate influence that members of the bar should have upon the people in the matter of the preservation of our institutions of civil liberty and the maintenance of the supremacy of law through constitutional means. I have made it my function to attend the annual meeting of the American Bar Association for the purpose of keeping in touch with that representative body of American lawyers.").
23. Elihu Root to WHT (September 9, 1922) (Taft papers).
24. William H. Taft, *Adequate Machinery for Judicial Business*, 7 AMERICAN BAR ASSOCIATION JOURNAL 453, 454 (1921).
25. *After-Dinner Oratory at Cincinnati*, 7 AMERICAN BAR ASSOCIATION JOURNAL 605, 606 (1921). The occasion was Taft's address to the closing dinner of the ABA 1921 annual meeting. Taft said:

> Why should not judges, who have so much to do with the administration of justice, take part in your councils and receive from the deliberations the suggestions so valuable that must come from the consideration of the leading members of the bar? And, on the other hand, why should they not be able to aid you in discussing and recommending measures for improvement of the procedure of the law?

> There was a time, possibly, when judges thought that they should keep apart. Of course, there are limitations upon judicial action, but no one who is at all familiar with what are reasonable limitations upon the action of judges can object to their coming into meetings like these and discussing and advancing their views as to improvement in legislative and administrative measures for the dispatch of legal business.
>
> We in this country do not have the great benefit that Parliament has in Great Britain in the presence of the responsible law officer of the Government in the House of Commons and the great jurists, especially the Lord Chancellor, in the House of Lords. . . . While we cannot have that exact system, it seems to me that the American Bar Association has taken a great step forward when it is summoning to aid in its councils the judges of this country. Therefore, it gives me pleasure to say that whenever I can I am coming to the meetings of the American Bar Association. And . . . I am going to discuss those subjects in which I have an interest, and in which I can make a suggestion.

26. *The Chief Justice*, 5 CHICAGO BAR ASSOCIATION RECORD 11–12 (December 1921).
27. Robert J. Bender to WHT (January 4, 1922) (Taft papers). Taft's copy of the letter is marked: "No ans."
28. 62 CONG. REC 2582–83 (February 15, 1922). *See Taft's Public Speeches Criticized in the Senate*, NEW YORK TRIBUNE (February 16, 1922), at 2.
29. 62 CONG. REC 2582–83 (February 15, 1922). Senator Harris also very much objected to Justice Clarke's speech urging cancellation of the foreign war debt. *See Justice Clarke Urges Prompt Cancellation of War Debt*, CHICAGO JOURNAL OF COMMERCE (February 9, 1922), at l; 62 CONG. REC. 2525–26 (February 14, 1922) ("I have the greatest respect and admiration for Justice Clarke. . . . However, I think that the Justices of the Supreme Court of the United States should keep out of any matters that are political. . . . I do not think it is the part of wisdom for a Supreme Court Justice to publicly discuss matters to be decided by Congress.").
30. Taft, *supra* note 20. Taft left no doubt about the target of his remarks: "It is a source of some embarrassment for me to rise here and not to talk to you as I would like to talk to you, free from the fetters of the office which I hold. . . . I am struggling to be worthy of the bench of which I am a member. I am struggling to fall into the customs and requirements of that position. We have been warned in the Senate of the United States what our narrow function is and with due respect to that warning, I am going to confine myself to a written manuscript." *Id*. at 1–2. For press coverage of Taft's speech, see *Taft Approves Laws to Clear Court Dockets*, NEW YORK TRIBUNE (February 19, 1922), at 13; *Taft Backs Bills to Speed Trials*, NEW YORK TIMES (February 19, 1922), at 18.
31. *See supra* text at note 19.
32. "I am especially interested in the matter of procedure, because procedure stands between the abuse of the principles of law and their use for the benefit of mankind. You can have as high and as sound principles of law as possible, but if you have not the procedure by which you can apply them to the ordinary affairs of men, then it does not make any difference what the principles are or how erroneous they may be." *Chief Justice Taft Urges Adoption of Rule-Making Power*, 7 JOURNAL OF THE AMERICAN JUDICATURE SOCIETY 134 (1923).
33. Chief Justice William H. Rehnquist, *1991 Year-End Report on the Federal Judiciary*, 29 THIRD BRANCH 1, 6 (January 1997).

CHAPTER 15

The Chief Justice as Chancellor

SIX MONTHS AFTER his appointment, Taft announced his program of judicial reform to the Chicago Bar Association. Published as *Three Needed Steps of Progress*,[1] Taft proposed three major legislative initiatives: what would become the Act of September 14, 1922; what would become the Judiciary Act of February 13, 1925; and legislation that would authorize the Supreme Court to promulgate rules of procedure for common law cases, effectively fusing law and equity.[2] By the middle of the decade, Taft had accomplished the first two of these proposals. But the last, for which Taft had been advocating since at least 1914,[3] would prove elusive.

Although Taft persuaded Coolidge to recommend that the Court be endowed with rulemaking authority in common law cases,[4] Senator Thomas J. Walsh of Montana, who had fought for Brandeis's confirmation to the Court and against that of Stone, was dead set against the change.[5] Walsh was a powerful senator, and he was able almost single-handedly to prevent action on the legislation[6] despite the strong support of Taft and the American Bar Association ("ABA").[7] It was not until after Walsh's sudden demise in 1933 (while he was FDR's attorney general designate) that the Rules Enabling Act could finally be enacted.[8] By then Taft had long since passed from the scene.

The defeat of legislation to fuse law and equity rankled Taft, not merely because he thought the fusion necessary to reduce the expense of litigation, but also because he was strongly drawn to an equitable authority that would bypass the reliance on juries characteristic of common law actions. As a justice, Taft did his best to expand equitable jurisdiction.[9] He believed that juries made justice inefficient because they "greatly increase the time and expense involved in the disposition of litigation."[10]

Taft was also hostile to juries because he regarded them as given to "unrestrained impulses" and "local prejudice."[11] Juries were prone to follow community sentiment rather than to submit to judicial instruction. Under the "hypnotic influence" of trial counsel, jurors were more likely to produce a verdict that was "the vote of a town meeting than the sharp, clear decision of the tribunal of justice."[12] Taft despised "the irresponsible action of shrewd and eloquent counsel, able to make the worse appear the better reason, whether engaged for one side or the other. This has the tendency not only to reach emotional, unjust, and wrong results, but it drags out the trial far beyond what is necessary."[13]

Taft viscerally disliked Walsh because the senator "made his money out of damage suits and criminal law and his attitude is always of throwing the reins on the back of the jury and minimizing the power of the Court."[14] Taft resented plaintiffs' lawyers who sued corporations where "the plaintiff relies on the supposed sympathy of twelve laymen with the poor plaintiff against the rich corporation, both to find the facts in favor of the plaintiff and also to swell the damages to a large sum." He believed that "[t]he abolition of the jury in civil cases would relieve the public of a great burden of expense, would facilitate the hearing of all civil suits and would not, I think, with proper appeal deprive any litigant of all he is entitled to, an impartial hearing."[15]

Taft recognized that "[w]e cannot, of course, dispense with the jury system. It is that which makes the people a part of the administration of justice and prevents the possibility of government oppression."[16] Yet this recognition was largely superficial. Taft could convince himself, for example, that the only "real objection" to labor injunctions was "the certainty that disobedience will be promptly punished before a court without a jury."[17] Taft was apparently incapable of putting himself into the shoes of someone who might believe that judges were themselves biased officials.[18] He instead imagined judges as disinterested arbiters who were immune to the "buncombe and mere sentiment" produced by counsel.[19] Taft believed that ordinary folk ought simply to defer to professional legal elites like himself.[20]

Republican jurists in the 1920s sought to use federal courts to underwrite a stable national market, which they believed necessary for the growth of large, efficient corporations. This had been traditional Republican policy since the late nineteenth century. Federal fora were important not merely because the substance of federal law was friendly to large corporations, but also because federal judges were more empowered to control juries than were state judges. Federal judges, said Taft, "have the power which the English judges have. . . . [T]he court exercises the proper authority in the management of the trial and assists the jury in a useful analysis and summing up of the evidence, and an expression of such opinions as will help the jury to reach right conclusions. All this tends to eliminate much of what almost might be called demagogic discussion which counsel are prone to resort to in many of the local state courts."[21]

National corporations believed that they suffered in state courts not only from the prejudice of local juries, but also from class hostility directed against wealthy defendants. National corporations were convinced that they could obtain a fairer trial in federal fora where judges retained firm control over juries. In Taft's eyes, federal courts were the "terror of evil-doers" and the epitome of "law and justice" because "the judge retains his traditional control of the manner of the trial and of the counsel."[22] Taft decried the relative laxity of state courts, where legislatures were

The Chief Justice as Chancellor

prone to make a "fetish" of the "institution of trial by jury."[23] "So jealous have legislatures become of the influence of the court upon the jury that it is now, in most states, made an error of law for the court to express his opinion upon the facts. . . . The opportunity which this gives the counsel to pervert the law, and the wide scope which the system in restricting the judge gives to the jury of following its own sweet will, of course, doubles the opportunity for miscarriages of justice."[24]

One might imagine the horror that overwhelmed Taft, then, when he discovered in spring 1924 not only that Senator Thaddeus Caraway of Arkansas had introduced a bill that would make it reversible error for a federal judge to comment on the credibility of witnesses or the weight of evidence,[25] but also that Caraway's bill had noiselessly passed the Senate and been unanimously approved by the House Judiciary Committee.[26] Conceiving himself as the guardian of the federal judiciary, Taft sprang into action.[27] "I am trying to prevent the passage of a bill aimed at the usefulness of the Federal courts," he wrote his wife,

> which seeks to deny to Federal Judges the power to comment on the evidence as the English Judges do. This has always been done in the Federal Courts and has contributed much to their effectiveness. Now these demagogues and damage lawyers are attempting to put the Federal Courts on the basis of the State courts in this regard. The bill has passed the Senate and the Senators yielded supinely, except Reed of Pennsylvania. It has been reported out of the House Judiciary Committee, but I am hoping to hold it over until the next session, in which case I feel fairly confident that I can induce the President to veto it, and I believe his veto would prevent its passage. There is a serious question as to whether it is constitutional, but I would prefer much to have it beaten through a veto than to throw upon the Court the question of its constitutionality.[28]

Taft attempted to secure a commitment from the George Graham, chair of the House Judiciary Committee, to hold hearings on the bill, which Taft hoped would delay legislative action until after the 1924 election. Taft also sought "to have the various Bar Associations . . . apply to the committee to be heard upon this bill in opposition to it, both on the ground of its doubtful constitutionality and also because of its interference with the efficiency of the Federal courts."[29]

Not content with this political maneuvering and mobilization, Taft composed a remarkable Memorandum in opposition to the bill. The cover sheet to the Memorandum, which Taft apparently drafted for his own records, states:

> I am exceedingly anxious to beat the bill . . . because it will really greatly interfere with the Federal judicial system. I was able to hold the bill off last session through Chairman Graham and Snell of the Rules Committee in the House. I have been to see the Attorney General once or twice about it and I saw the President this morning and asked him to read this memorandum. I am quite sure that he will be inclined to veto the bill, but it ought not to come to him, and I think the Attorney General suggests his sending for Graham and Nick Longworth to see whether it can not be shelved. I submitted the memorandum to Van De Vanter [sic] and he fully approved the statement, but he thought that

511

I put a little too much admiration for the English in it. However, as this is not to be published and is only a confidential memorandum for the President and the Attorney General, and as I have only given out one copy in addition to that given to Van Devanter, there is no occasion for changing my view which is stated herein, or ameliorating it with reference to prejudices against England.[30]

The Memorandum itself is a twelve-page document arguing that the Caraway bill would greatly "weaken the usefulness and efficiency of Federal Courts in the dispatch of business involving jury trials." "This bill, if it passes, is calculated to reduce the condition in the Federal Courts to the ineffectiveness of State Courts." On page six, the Memorandum addresses the "question . . . whether Congress may by law effect this demoralizing assault on the trials in our Federal Courts. Fortunately the right of the Judge to exercise this power of summing up to a jury upon the facts is conferred upon him by the Constitution of the United States, and can not be taken away by legislation." The remainder of the Memorandum constitutes a detailed argument for this constitutional opinion, concluding:

> In view of these authorities, it can not be that Congress may take away the power of a Judge of a United States Court in carrying on a jury trial, to comment on the evidence and even express his opinion on the facts, if he leaves the question of facts clearly to the jury ultimately. It was an essential element of a jury trial in the English courts when the Declaration of Independence was signed and our Constitution was framed and adopted and when the 7th Amendment became part of it. That being true, Congress may not impair the institution by attempting to restrain Federal Judges from the discretion to exercise the power vested in them by the fundamental law.[31]

The Memorandum is a stunning document. It is a fully developed advisory opinion, crafted by Taft for the explicit purpose of affecting the outcome of legislation. Taft must have known that the Memorandum was ethically suspect, because he classified it as "confidential" and in the Court showed it only to his most trusted confidant, Van Devanter. Taft strictly curtailed the Memorandum's dissemination outside the Court, circulating it at first only to President Coolidge and to Attorney General Stone.

Taft grew bolder, however, as Caraway continued to press his legislation. Taft wrote his brother Henry that "We stopped the Caraway bill to take away the power of the Federal Judges in charging a jury, and I am going to take time by the forelock to prime Senator David Reed of Pennsylvania on the probable unconstitutionality of such a law."[32] Taft sent Henry a copy of his Memorandum[33] and suggested that Henry "open a correspondence with the only man who opposed it in the Senate, and that was Senator Reed of Pennsylvania. You might send a copy of it also to Senator Cummins and another one to Senator Gillett. Don't make me the author of it, for reasons that you will understand."[34]

Over the next several years, Taft managed repeatedly to kill the Caraway bill,[35] and his tactics never erupted into scandal, although this seems mostly a matter of luck. Taft's passion for efficient judicial administration betrayed him

The Chief Justice as Chancellor

into actions that could scarcely be defended in public. Of course, on the other side of the coin, it is no doubt due to Taft's vigorous intervention that federal judges enjoy to this day the traditional common law prerogative to comment on the weight of evidence and the credibility of witnesses.[36]

The incident nicely reveals the tension between traditional American conceptions of judicial propriety and Taft's conception of the chief justice as a kind of lord chancellor. In 1922, Taft agreed to chair an ABA committee charged with drafting the first American canons of judicial ethics, which were approved in 1924.[37] Canon 23 explicitly supports Taft's long-held view that "A judge has exceptional opportunity to observe the operation of statutes, especially those relating to practice, and to ascertain whether they tend to impede the just disposition of controversies; and he may well contribute to the public interest by advising those having authority to remedy defects of procedure, of the result of his observation and experience."[38] The contemporary Model Code of Judicial Conduct continues this tradition in Rule 3.2:

> A judge shall not appear voluntarily at a public hearing before, or otherwise consult with, an executive or a legislative body or official, except: (A) in connection with matters concerning the law, the legal system, or the administration of justice; (B) in connection with matters about which the judge acquired knowledge or expertise in the course of the judge's judicial duties.

American judges, in contrast to those of England, must sometimes pass on the constitutionality of legislation implementing procedural reform. Taft's Memorandum was ethically suspect precisely because it passionately prejudged a potential constitutional case. Concern with the appearance of prejudgment when advocating for procedural reform is entirely absent from the 1924 Canons,[39] whereas the contemporary Model Code of Judicial Conduct explicitly states that in "consulting with government officials, judges must be mindful that they remain subject to other provisions of this Code, such as . . . Rule 3.1(C), prohibiting judges from engaging in extrajudicial activities that would appear to a reasonable person to undermine the judge's independence, integrity, or impartiality."[40]

In 1921, two months after his confirmation as chief justice, Taft pledged to the ABA that he would stay continually involved in the cause of judicial reform,[41] casually laughing off the possibility of potential conflicts of interest: "If a judge on an occasion like that advances an opinion on a question of law which might subsequently arise in a case before him, he is a pretty poor judge if he cannot ignore the opinion he has already expressed."[42] But no one who read Taft's Memorandum would regard it as a laughing matter; no one would regard him as free from prejudicial prejudgment. As is plainly apparent in today's Model Code of Judicial Conduct, Taft bequeathed to American judges a deep and intractable tension between, on the one hand, the prerogatives of expertise, and, on the other hand, the need to maintain the appearance of impartiality.[43]

Taft lived the entire span of his chief justiceship in the throes of this tension.[44] The danger of constitutional prejudgment lurked in even the seemingly most technical and innocuous of measures. Consider, for example, Taft's involvement in the passage of a bill that transferred jurisdiction of patent appeals from the Court of Appeals of the District of Columbia to the Court of Customs Appeals. Taft strongly supported the bill, to the extent that Acting Commissioner of Patents William A. Kinnan could in congressional hearings testify that "[t]here has been no objection anywhere. It has been indicated that the Chief Justice of the United States has looked into it and approved it. It seems to me to be an efficiency measure."[45]

Taft wrote Walsh urging approval of the bill on the ground that the District Court of Appeals was "very much burdened with business," while the Court of Customs Appeals did "not have enough to do." Despite his private views of Walsh, Taft was sweetly and nonpartisanly solicitous: "I am sorry to impose on you, my dear Senator, another burden, but as I understand you are on the committee for the consideration of this bill, I venture thus to write to you. It will certainly help the administration of justice in the District." From a contemporary point of view, it is striking that Taft included in his letter a long defense of the bill's constitutionality, which began: "I understand that there are two persons who think that the bill is unconstitutional. I can not for the life of me understand how any such doubt could arise. The Court of Customs Appeals is a purely statutory court, and Congress is not limited in any way in the functions which it gives to it."[46] Walsh replied to Taft that he would "make an effort to have the matter put" in shape for approval,[47] and the bill, seemingly uncontroversial, was enacted into law.[48]

It is remarkable that Taft would submit an advisory opinion about the constitutionality of a bill to a senator who was in many ways his arch-opponent. It indicates how unembarrassed Taft must have felt about the practice.[49] This is probably because he regarded the constitutional issue posed by the statute as uncontroversial and settled. Yet constitutional judgment in the United States is seldom a secure thing. Although Taft premised his argument on the fact that the Court of Customs Appeals was an Article I court, within only thirty years Congress would itself declare the (now renamed) Court of Customs and Patent Appeals an Article III court,[50] a conclusion sustained by the Supreme Court of the United States.[51]

From this perspective, the potential for prejudging a possible constitutional case lay coiled within virtually every recommendation Taft made for judicial reform. Even the institutional voice of the Judicial Conference, which Taft created in part to provide support for initiating such reform, offered no defense to this danger. A good example may be found in Taft's attempt to relieve federal courts of the flood of small criminal cases that prohibition swept into their jurisdiction. Not only did these cases clog the docket, but federal judges found them intensely demoralizing.[52]

Almost from the day he took office, Taft believed that legislation was needed to allow United States commissioners to try such cases.[53] In 1923, at the second meeting of the Conference of Senior Circuit Judges, Taft pushed through a resolution to the effect that "[i]n prohibition and other misdemeanor cases" United States commissioners be authorized "in all cases in which the defendants do not file written demands for jury trial, to take and file written pleas of guilty and

The Chief Justice as Chancellor

to hear the evidence on pleas of not guilty and to file in court their reports of the cases and their recommendations of what judgment should be entered."[54] The Conference cautiously endorsed the resolution "provided the machinery proposed is within constitutional limits."[55] Taft regarded the recommendation as one of the "most important" of the Conference.[56]

The recommendation went nowhere, however, and so at the end of 1925 Taft sought, on his own initiative, to revive the plan. He wrote George Graham, chair of the House Judiciary Committee, and Senator Albert Cummins, chair of the Senate Judiciary Committee, that he was "very much troubled about the conditions that prevail in the District Courts of the United States. They are being demoralized by this police court business." Taft proposed an elaborate legislative scheme to remedy the situation that would use commissioners to "try jury trials" in cases for which the punishment was less than two years.[57]

Six months later, in the course of debate on a bill to authorize the appointment of additional district judges, Graham observed on the floor of the House that he was "in conference with representatives of the Senate Judiciary Committee and some of the judges of the Supreme Court trying to work out some scheme by which the courts of the United States might be relieved of some of the very heavy burdens which they are now obliged to carry." Graham pledged to "strive to create some plan by which a minor judiciary may be created."[58]

Representative Duncan Denison of Illinois rose to inquire into "the wisdom of taking into these conferences, in trying to work out legislation that will relieve the courts of a part of their work, the members of the Supreme Court. Does the gentleman think that is a wise policy?" Thrown on the defensive, Graham quickly backpedaled:

> Mr. GRAHAM. Well, without passing any opinion upon the wisdom of the policy, it came about without our solicitation and we attended simply as conferees.
>
> Mr. DENISON. In the constitutional convention ... that theory was abandoned as being unwise, the theory of having the Supreme Court advise the Congress as to legislation, and I think if we should return to that policy it would be a dangerous one.
>
> Mr. GRAHAM. I may say that this conference arose and was called through the intervention of the Supreme Court judges, upon one of whom, the Chief Justice, there depended the duty of reviewing the work in the district courts all over the United States in the congested districts and trying to provide a remedy. He simply called the chairman and the ranking member of each Judiciary Committee in to ask them to take up the subject and see if there could not be some plan devised. That is all.
>
> Mr. DENISON. What I have in mind is this. Suppose the Congress should enact legislation that is intended to create some sort of subordinate courts to relieve the other courts of some of their duties, and afterwards the constitutionality of the legislation should be raised in the courts, if the Supreme Court had been consulted and advised in the preparation of the law, it seems to me it would be embarrassing, and I do not believe the committee of the House ought to do that.

Mr. GRAHAM. I think, perhaps, ethically the gentleman is correct, and I am not going to dispute that proposition, but I do say it was perfectly competent for those who had charge of the court business throughout the country to call our attention to it and ask us to take it up independently; and that is all that was done.

Mr. DENISON. I see no objection to that.

Mr. GRAHAM. That is all that was done. They would not be taken into consideration in framing the legislation for the legislative duty would rest upon the House and the Senate.[59]

Graham deftly defused Denison's challenge by asserting that Taft (and, he might have added, the Judicial Conference) had merely called the attention of Congress to a problem in need of solution, without proposing any particular legislative response. But Graham was playing fast and loose with the facts as we know them from Taft's correspondence and from the recommendations of the Conference. Had the truth been known, Taft might have been acutely embarrassed.

Taft took the point. When Federal District Judge Frances Caffey subsequently wrote him to inquire about the status of the 1923 recommendation of the Conference of Senior Circuit Judges so that he could more effectively lobby for bills expanding the jurisdiction of United States commissioners then pending before Congress,[60] Taft responded with uncharacteristic caution: "I have to be careful in taking part myself in the preparation of such a bill, because any bill is likely to come before our Court for interpretation and inquiry into its validity."[61]

Taft's conception of the chief justiceship led to even deeper contradictions than the possibility of prejudicially prejudging specific legislation. Taft was well aware that "propriety" required an American judge to "keep out of politics and out of any diversion or avocation which may involve him in politics."[62] But it was not possible for a chief justice who regarded himself as the guardian of the federal judiciary to maintain any such separation. A telling example is Taft's opposition to S. 3151, a bill sponsored by Progressive Republican Senator George Norris of Nebraska and strongly supported by Democratic Senator Thomas Walsh.[63] The bill stripped federal district courts of both federal question jurisdiction and diversity jurisdiction.[64] By an ironic stroke of fate, Norris, who thoroughly disliked federal courts – he had once actually proposed abolishing all federal courts except the Supreme Court[65] – was chair of the Senate Judiciary Committee. S. 3151 was reported favorably by the Senate Judiciary Committee without even a hearing.[66]

Taft was appalled by what he regarded as "the remarkable effort made in the Senate by Norris and Walsh to emasculate the jurisdiction of the Federal trial courts ... and to sneak it through without the country's being advised about it."[67] He saw the bill as "a great attack on the administration of justice in this country,"[68] the "most radical bill affecting the usefulness and efficacy of the Federal Judiciary that I remember ever to have heard suggested."[69] Taft threw himself into the task of "trying to save the life of the Federal Judiciary."[70]

It quickly became apparent, however, that Taft's opposition to S. 3151 could not be confined to anodyne expressions of nonpartisan expertise. Thus when Taft wrote "to sound an alarm on the subject" to his friend Casper Yost, editor of the influential *St. Louis Globe-Democrat*, Taft cautioned that "I am so situated that

The Chief Justice as Chancellor

I can not take a political part, but ... I invoke your influence in maintaining the protective power which citizens may secure from the Federal Judiciary in defense of their rights."[71] Yost responded by publishing a lively editorial that made plain the political stakes.[72]

That Taft thoroughly understood and was willing to exploit the explosive politics of S. 3151 is evident from a letter he sent his brother, Henry W. Taft, an influential member of the New York Bar,[73] urging him to begin a public campaign against the bill:

> Now my own judgment about this bill is that if Norris tries to get it through, and is supported by the Democrats, it will prove to be dynamite in the next campaign. It will rouse every negro in the United States, and they cast a great many votes now in the large cities since they have moved north, and when it becomes known to them that they can not resort to the local Federal courts, they will certainly be convinced, as they ought to be, that they are suffering a practical deprivation of their Federal rights and protection. I think you ought to go to the New York Times and to the Tribune and explain the effect of the bill and have editorials printed on the subject. Reference to the negroes will find an echo, and I am quite sure that the Times will feel like warning the Democratic party against any such radical measure. I think you ought to bring it to Hilles' attention and that the opposition to it ought to be made a plank in the National Republican Platform.[74]

When Henry, paralyzed by Charles Evans Hughes's fear that anything "coming from New York" would be dismissed as reflecting "Wall Street interests,"[75] proved inept at generating publicity in opposition to the bill, Taft lost patience.[76] "What I was anxious to do," he explained to his brother, "was to head the movement by an announcement in the New York Times, for there are a great many people who look to the Times as a kind of Bible."[77] Henry accepted the "rebuke" and promptly contacted Rollo Ogden, editor of the *New York Times*.[78] The *Times* subsequently published an editorial strongly opposing the bill.[79]

As Taft well appreciated, the fierce controversy surrounding S. 3151 simultaneously involved politics and the administration of justice; the two were inseparably combined.[80] Taft knew that he could not risk overt involvement, yet his name and views figured prominently in the debate. On the floor of the Senate, for example, Senator Royal Copeland of New York, seeking to have the bill remanded to the Committee for hearings, observed that "I am advised by the attorneys who have spoken to me that the Chief Justice of the Supreme Court feels that the bill is not a good bill in some respects."[81]

In its editorial, the *New York Times* specifically referred to Copeland's comment. It remarked that "[i]t is no secret, since the fact was stated in the Senate by Mr. Copeland of New York, that the Chief Justice of the Supreme Court regards some of the features of this bill as most undesirable and harmful."[82] Two weeks later, Senator Duncan Fletcher of Florida reprinted in the *Congressional Record* an editorial in the *American Bar Association Journal* strongly opposing S. 3151, which relied heavily on arguments attributed to

Taft,[83] as well as an editorial from the *Florida Times Union* that opposed the bill in part on the ground that "the Chief Justice of the United States Supreme Court ... is reported to have said that this bill has features that can be regarded only as most undesirable and harmful."[84]

As a result of the accumulating pressure, Norris was forced to amend his bill to restore federal question jurisdiction.[85] Taft wrote Henry, "I think Norris has heard a good deal about his proposed changes, and ... he does not find them so easy to push through as he thought he would, in view of the agitation you have all stirred up on the subject."[86] Norris's revised bill eventually stalled in the Senate.[87] Yet Taft's intense struggle to defeat it illustrated the uneasy line between disinterested law reform and unabashedly political mobilization. Questions of federal jurisdiction were not merely technical matters that could be delegated to experts; behind them lay large disputes about the regional balance of power within the country.[88] Overtly addressing these disputes in a legislative context may have been appropriate for a lord chancellor, but for an American judge it could only undermine claims of judicial independence and disinterest.

This is not to say, however, that all of Taft's many interventions to improve the administration of justice – and they are far too numerous to detail here – were equally fraught. Taft was remarkably earnest and responsive in his efforts to reform federal courts. A small but telling example may be found in the history of Public Law No. 69–563, which ended the practice in federal courts of charging defendants a fee to receive copies of their own indictments.[89]

In November 1925, Taft received a letter from Joseph Coursey, an unknown lawyer from South Dakota, complaining of "the failure of Federal law ... to provide a copy of the charge to the defendant. ... It seems to me it should be almost fundamental that a defendant be given as a matter of right a copy of the accusation against him."[90] Taft asked Coursey whether the charge for the indictment was imposed "by law, or whether it rests in a local rule of practice."[91] Coursey did "not know whether the rule is one of law or practice," but he did "know positively that in this District we can not obtain such a copy without paying for it except in two cases: namely – if the defendant is charged with homicide or will make a pauper showing."[92]

Taft then wrote Solicitor General William D. Mitchell, asking him to find out "whether it is the practice to furnish defendants with copies of the indictment." He enclosed Coursey's letter, adding "I am rather inclined to think that he has a good case, and that the defendant should be given a copy, at the expense of the Government."[93] Mitchell sent back a detailed, six-page letter, explaining that federal statutes currently required clerks "to charge the accused for copies of the indictments, except in cases involving capital offenses," and that courts deemed the requirements of the Sixth Amendment satisfied "by the formality of reading the indictment to [the defendant] when he is arraigned." Mitchell went on to caution that "if clerks are directed generally to furnish copies of the indictments without charge to the accused, it would greatly increase the volume of work to be performed in the clerk's office, particularly on account of the large number of cases under the National Prohibition Act, and

The Chief Justice as Chancellor

that the clerks' offices are now shorthanded as the result of lack of adequate appropriation."[94]

Not deterred by Mitchell's warning, Taft wrote Albert Cummins, chair of the Senate Judiciary Committee, explaining the situation and commenting that "I should think ... that the Government ought to furnish, at its own expense, indictments to defendants."[95] Taft viewed the question as one of justice, rather than of constitutional compulsion, and he dismissed the potential bureaucratic burden with the observation that clerks could easily type indictments in triplicate. Cummins agreed with Taft's assessment, and he asked Taft to "prepare a Bill relating to furnishing copies of indictments to defendants and send it to me. I will be glad to introduce it."[96]

Taft asked Mitchell to draft a bill, which the solicitor general did, noting that "those in charge of the appropriations for the Department of Justice have estimated that" the bill would "substantially increase the expenses of operating the offices of the clerks of the courts. ... I have explained, however, that this Bill is not being furnished you as a Department measure, but merely as the result of a personal request for a document to supply Senator Cummins' wants."[97] Taft forwarded Mitchell's draft to Cummins, who agreed to "introduce the bill and have it referred to the Committee."[98] The result was Public Law No. 69–563, which was enacted in January 1927.[99]

The Act was not politically controversial. It exemplified the kind of technical improvement in the administration of justice that Taft sought vigorously to bring within the special province of the chief justice. Taft unabashedly initiated the legislation. And in this small but exemplary instance of statutory reform we can glimpse the profundity of the transformation worked by Taft in the position of chief justice. That Taft would take the time to evaluate the unsolicited complaint of an unknown, unsophisticated, provincial lawyer; that he would summon the will and perseverance to remedy that complaint despite bureaucratic opposition; that he could command the personal respect and material assistance of leaders in the executive and legislative branches in this task; all reveal the extent of Taft's staggering success in reconstructing the role of chief justice.

Notes

1. William Howard Taft, *Three Needed Steps of Progress*, 8 AMERICAN BAR ASSOCIATION JOURNAL 34 (1922).
2. On Taft's support for giving the Supreme Court rule-making authority in common law cases, see William Howard Taft, *Possible and Needed Reforms in Administration of Justice in Federal Courts*, 8 AMERICAN BAR ASSOCIATION JOURNAL 601, 604–7 (1922). Taft explicitly invoked English precedents to justify the reform. *See Chief Justice Taft Urges Adoption of Rule-Making Power*, 7 JOURNAL OF THE AMERICAN JUDICATURE SOCIETY 134 (1923).
3. *See supra* Chapter 12, at 449.
4. *Message from the President*, 66 CONG. REC. 54 (December 3, 1924) ("It is also desirable that the Supreme Court should have power to improve and reform procedure in suits at law in the Federal courts through the adoption of appropriate rules.").
5. Thomas J. Walsh, *Reform of Federal Procedure*, Sen. Doc. No. 105, 69th CONG. 1st SESS. (April 23, 1926); Thomas J. Walsh, *The Law's Delays and the Remedy*, NEW YORK TIMES (January 12, 1925), at 14; *Senator Walsh Replies*, 12 AMERICAN BAR ASSOCIATION JOURNAL 651 (1926); Thomas J. Walsh, *Rule-Making Power on the Law Side of Federal Practice*, 13 AMERICAN BAR ASSOCIATION JOURNAL 87 (1927). Taft believed that there would "be no difficulty" in passing the bill "but that Walsh of Montana and Shields of Tennessee are opposed." WHT to Horace D. Taft (December 7, 1924) (Taft papers). He fumed that "Walsh is one of the most narrow-minded men I know, not a useful legislator, because he never looks for progress. He is always looking for criticism." *Id.* Walsh was aided in his opposition by the fact that both Brandeis and McReynolds disapproved the legislation. *See* WHT to Thomas W. Shelton (March 5, 1928) (Taft papers); Thomas W. Shelton to WHT (March 3, 1928) (Taft papers); *Authority for Publication of Rules in Common-Law Actions*, Sen. Rep. No. 440 on S. 759, 70th CONG. 1st SESS. (February 28, 1928), at 1. Taft had discouraged Holmes from also publicly expressing disapproval of the legislation:

> Judge Holmes wrote that he was against the whole business because he thinks that procedure would not help when we have such a poor Bar and such a poor Bench. . . . I rather differed with him in the view that because we are behind England in this regard we ought not to do what we can to better the facilities for proper progress. By my remarks to him, I succeeded in holding back his letter to Walsh, which I was afraid Walsh might use to the disadvantage of the bill.

WHT to HFS (May 18, 1926) (Stone papers). *See* WHT to Henry W. Taft (May 18, 1926) (Taft papers) (describing phone conversation with Holmes and Taft's argument that "if we were to wait until the leopard changed his spots, and the American people and lawyers and judges became better men, we should never do anything that was progressive and helpful," and also condemning the "very poor" Senate judiciary committee "consisting mostly of radicals and progressives.").
6. *See, e.g., Report of the Special Committee on Uniform Judicial Procedure*, in REPORT OF THE FORTY-SEVENTH ANNUAL MEETING OF THE AMERICAN BAR ASSOCIATION 483, 486 (Baltimore: Lord Baltimore Press 1924) ("The jurisdiction bill was very promptly reported out of the full Judiciary Committee of the Senate . . . but there was personal influence enough on the part of one or two Senators to prevent

a report upon the procedure bill (S. 2061), although a majority favored it.... *There ought to be some way of overcoming a personal legislative influence of a character that can defeat a majority, the public will and the administration of justice by smothering bills in committee.*").

7. EDWARD A. PURCELL, JR., BRANDEIS AND THE PROGRESSIVE CONSTITUTION 28–33 (New Haven: Yale University Press 2000). Taft attributed Walsh's opposition to the fact that he was "a very great enemy of the Federal Courts," WHT to Henry W. Taft (July 4, 1924) (Taft papers), a mere plaintiff's lawyer who "lost cases in the Federal trial courts in seeking to impose verdicts on railroads and other corporations with thin cases." WHT to Charles P. Taft 2nd (April 1, 1928) (Taft papers). George Graham of Pennsylvania, the chair of the House Judiciary Committee from 1923 until the end of the decade, also opposed the legislation. *See, e.g.*, Thomas W. Shelton to WHT (January 24, 1925) (Taft papers).

8. Pub. L. 73-415, 48 Stat. 1064 (June 19, 1934). For a nice summary of the history of the statute, including Taft's role in shaping it, see Stephen N. Subrin, *How Equity Conquered Common Law: The Federal Rules of Civil Procedure in Historical Perspective*, 135 UNIVERSITY OF PENNSYLVANIA LAW REVIEW 909 (1987).

9. *See, e.g.*, Liberty Oil Co. v. Condon National Bank, 260 U.S. 235 (1922), which became a major building block in the argument that the Supreme Court could constitutionally create rules of procedure that combined law and equity. *See* Charles T. McCormick, *The Fusion of Law and Equity in United States Courts*, 6 NORTH CAROLINA LAW REVIEW 283, 294–95 (1928); *infra* note 49. *But see* American Mills Co. v. American Surety Co. of New York, 260 U.S. 360 (1922).

10. William H. Taft, *Delays and Defects in the Enforcement of Law in This Country*, 187 NORTH AMERICAN REVIEW 851, 853 (1908). *See* WHT to Henry S. Pritchett (January 17, 1922) (Taft papers) ("The real delay, especially in criminal cases, is due to the jury system ... and the unwillingness to give to judges the opportunity to guide the jury, which they have in both the English courts and the Federal courts, so that a judge can facilitate the trial, and does, and we have no such scandalously lengthy trial[s] as they do in state courts.").

11. William H. Taft, *Criticisms of the Federal Judiciary*, 29 AMERICAN LAW REVIEW 641, 651–52 (1895).

12. William H. Taft, *The Administration of Criminal Law*, 15 YALE LAW JOURNAL 1, 13 (1905).

13. William H. Taft, *The Attacks on the Courts and Legal Procedure*, 5 KENTUCKY LAW JOURNAL 3, 20 (1916). Holmes shared Taft's distaste for juries. *See supra* Chapter 5, at note 155. In Chesapeake & O. Ry. Co. v. Leitch, 276 U.S. 429 (1928), for example, Holmes authored a unanimous opinion overturning a jury verdict for an engineer who was injured "through contact with a mail crane or mail sack hanging from it as he looked from the window of his engine upon the petitioner's road." *Id.* at 430. Holmes expressed his penchant for establishing clear *ex ante* rules of liability: "If there is to be a standard in these cases, and if, as decided, the general rule is that the engineer takes the risk, the railroad should not be made liable for this class of injury except where some unquestionable disregard of obvious precautions is shown." *Id.* at 431. The Court was initially split 4–4, with Sutherland not participating and McReynolds, Brandeis, Sanford, and Stone voting to affirm. When the Court met again Sutherland voted to reverse. When Holmes circulated his opinion, Sanford wrote that in cases "involving mainly an appreciation of the

particular facts the decision of the State Circuit should not be disturbed unless 'error is palpable' – but unless some one else audibly dissents I shall probably silently acquiesce." (Holmes papers). Stone wrote Holmes that his opinion omitted material facts, like "the fact that on this particular occasion the hangar spring of the engine was broken, causing it to lean toward the crane." But, Stone added, "I don't think I care to note a dissent unless others do, but I will wait and see." (Holmes papers). Three weeks after the decision, Clarke wrote Van Devanter: "I had a very cordial and interesting letter from Judge Holmes. ... He referred incidentally to his writing some railroad opinions in which he thought I probably would not have concurred, had I been a member of the Court. He is making no mistake in this, as I think one or two dissenting opinions of mine clearly show. I cannot help but think that the Mail Crane decision is a very unfortunate one." JHC to WVD (April 28, 1928) (Van Devanter papers). Van Devanter replied, "Justice Holmes is breaking some. This is chiefly noticeable in conference and in the fact that many of his opinions do not give an adequate portrayal of the case in hand or of the grounds of the decision. This was particularly true in the Mail Crane case. I thought and said at the time that the opinion was so far inadequate that the decision justly would be subject to criticism. My belief is that if the case were accurately portrayed you would think the outcome right." WVD to JHC (June 9, 1928) (Van Devanter papers). In Atlantic Coast Line R. Co. v. Southwell, 275 U.S. 64 (1927), in which Holmes once again reversed a jury finding of negligence, Brandeis commented to Holmes, "I think the question was one for a jury – but the case is of a class in which one may properly 'shut up.'" (Holmes papers). In Chesapeake & O. Ry. Co. v. Nixon, 271 U.S. 218 (1926), when Holmes reversed a jury verdict, Sanford commented: "I regret that I am not 'converted,' but shall not note any dissent." Brandeis wrote "I acquiesce willingly being contrawise." (Holmes papers).

In truth, it could be said that the Taft Court as a whole displayed a marked hostility to jury verdicts, particularly in cases involving negligence liability under the Federal Employers' Liability Act, Pub. L. 60-100, 35 Stat. 65 (April 22, 1908). For example, in Baltimore & O.R. Co. v. Groeger, 266 U.S. 521, 530–32 (1924), Butler bluntly proclaimed for a unanimous bench that "It is not for the courts to lay down rules which will operate to restrict the carriers in their choice of mechanical means by which their locomotives, boilers, engine tenders and appurtenances are to be kept in proper condition. Nor are such matters to be left to the varying and uncertain opinions and verdicts of juries." *See, e.g.,* Chicago, M. & St. P. Ry. Co. v. Coogan, 271 U.S. 472 (1926); Missouri Pac. R. Co. v. Aeby, 275 U.S. 426 (1927); Gulf, M. & N. R. Co. v. Wells, 275 U.S. 455 (1927); Toledo, St. L. & W.R. Co. v. Allen, 276 U.S. 165 (1928); Kansas City Southern Ry. Co. v. Jones, 276 U.S. 303 (1928); Delaware, L. & W.R. Co. v. Koske, 279 U.S. 7 (1929); Atlantic Coast Line R. Co. v. Davis, 279 U.S. 34 (1929); Atlantic Coast Line R. Co. v. Driggers, 279 U.S. 787 (1929); Chesapeake & O. Ry. Co. v. Mihas, 280 U.S. 102 (1929); but see Chicago Great Western R. Co. v. Schendel, 267 U.S. 287 (1925); Minneapolis, St. P. & S.S. M. Ry. Co. v. Goneau, 269 U.S. 406 (1926); Western & Atlantic R. R. v. Hughes, 278 U.S. 496 (1929).

14. WHT to Elihu Root (January 4, 1926) (Taft papers). *See supra* note 7.
15. Taft, *supra* note 12, at 6. Even in a criminal context, Taft believed that "the jury is the great source of expense and delay, and where it can within constitutional privilege be dispensed with or persuasive opportunity be offered for a waiver of

The Chief Justice as Chancellor

it, it will make for justice by increasing the dispatch of business." WHT to Francis B. James (August 25, 1921) (Taft papers).

16. William H. Taft, *Delays of the Law*, 18 YALE LAW JOURNAL 28, 38 (1908). "But," Taft continued, "every means by which in civil cases litigants may be induced voluntarily to avoid the expense, delay and burden of jury trials ought to be encouraged, because in this way the general administration of justice can be greatly facilitated and the expense incident to delay in litigation can be greatly reduced." *Id.* See WHT to P.W. Moir (November 20, 1925) (Taft papers).

17. Taft, *supra* note 11, at 672. "It is hardly necessary to defend the necessity for such means of enforcing orders of court. If the court must wait upon the slow course of a jury trial before it can compel a compliance with its order then the sanctions of its process would be seriously impaired." *Id.* See William Howard Taft, *Judicial Decisions as an Issue in Politics*, 33 MCCLURE'S MAGAZINE 201, 209 (June 1909).

18. On the widespread distrust of federal judges because they were believed to be biased in favor of large corporations, see *infra* Chapter 41, at 1378–80.

19. William H. Taft, *The Selection and Tenure of Judges*, 7 MAINE LAW REVIEW 203, 214 (1914).

20. On traditional English views of the proper relationship between courts and juries, see JOHN LANGBEIN, RENÉE LETTOW LERNER, & BRUCE SMITH, HISTORY OF THE COMMON LAW: THE DEVELOPMENT OF ANGLO-AMERICAN LEGAL INSTITUTIONS 431–33 (New York: Aspen Publishers 2009); Conor Hanly, *The Decline of Civil Jury Trial in Nineteenth-Century England*, 26 JOURNAL OF LEGAL HISTORY 253, 258–62 (2005). On the American departure from traditional English practice, see LANGBEIN, LERNER, & SMITH, *supra*, at 520–22; Kenneth A. Krasity, *The Role of the Judge in Jury Trials: The Elimination of Judicial Evaluation of Fact in American State Courts from 1795 to 1913*, 62 UNIVERSITY OF DETROIT LAW REVIEW 595 (1985); Renée Lettow Lerner, *The Transformation of the American Civil Trial: The Silent Judge*, 42 WILLIAM & MARY LAW REVIEW 195 (2000). Both John Wigmore and James Thayer agreed with Taft's views on the proper relationship between judge and jury. *See* 1 JOHN H. WIGMORE, A TREATISE ON THE ANGLO-AMERICAN SYSTEM OF EVIDENCE IN TRIALS AT COMMON LAW § 21, at 209–10 (2nd ed., Boston: Little, Brown 1923); JAMES B. THAYER, A PRELIMINARY TREATISE ON EVIDENCE AT THE COMMON LAW 188 (Boston: Little, Brown 1898).

21. William H. Taft, *supra* note 19, at 213–14. In state courts, "opportunity is too frequently given to the jury to ignore the charge of the court, to yield to the histrionic eloquence of counsel, and to give a verdict according to their emotions instead of their reason and their oaths." *Id.* at 214. *See* William H. Taft, *The Courts and the Progressive Party*, 186 SATURDAY EVENING POST 9, 47 (March 20, 1914):

> [S]tate legislatures have cut down the power of the judge so that now in many states he has little more power to exercise than the moderator in a religious conference. In some states he is required to deliver a written charge before argument of counsel, and in others he is permitted only to accept or reject the statements of the law as given by counsel. His opportunity for usefulness is curtailed, his impartiality made the subject of suspicion by most unwise restrictions, and the trial is turned over largely to the control of the lawyers and the little restrained discretion of the jury. The result has been the perversion of justice in jury trials, the infusion into them of much maudlin sentiment and irrelevant considerations, and a dragging out of the trial to such a length that if it be a civil case the cost of litigation is greatly increased, and if it be a criminal case

the public come to treat it as a game of wits and eloquence of counsel rather than the settlement of a serious controversy in a court of justice. Neither the dignity nor the effectiveness of judicial administration under these conditions impresses itself upon the public.

"The creation of an atmosphere of fog and error and confusion," said Taft, "is only possible under a system in which the power of the court to control its own proceedings and to guide the jury to some extent in the way in which it should go, is so limited by rules of judicial procedure laid down by legislative enactment that the judge becomes nothing but a moderator of the proceedings and helpless in the hands of an acute and eloquent counsel for the defense." Taft, *supra* note 10, at 857.

22. Taft, *supra* note 19, at 214.
23. Taft, *supra* note 12, at 12.
24. *Id.* at 13.
25. S. 624, 68th CONG. 1st SESS. (December 10, 1923); 65 CONG. REC. 144 (December 10, 1923). Caraway had been attempting to promote this reform for many years. *See, e.g.*, Ashley Cockrill, *Trial by Jury*, 52 AMERICAN LAW REVIEW 823 (1918).
26. H.R. Rep. No. 816, 68th CONG. 1st SESS. (May 22, 1924); S. 624, Calendar No. 252, 68th CONG. 1st SESS. (March 11, 1924). Taft was in shock. He wrote his friend Tom Shelton, who was a judicial reformer working for the ABA, that "It is inconceivable that men of the supposed professional standing of Brandegee, Cummins and others could have consented, or allowed to pass, without protest, the adoption of this bill. . . . I never supposed that men, in whose conservatism I had great confidence, would lie down as they have done in this case." WHT to Thomas W. Shelton (April 6, 1924) (Taft papers). Taft confided to his son:

> I am very much disgusted to hear that the Judiciary Committee of the Senate has been supine to allow to be slipped through the Committee and the Senate, provisions by which a Judge of the Federal Court shall be forbidden to express his opinion as to the credibility of witnesses of the weight and value of the evidence – that he shall deliver his charge in writing, and before argument of counsel, except in those States in which the law permits the trial judge to deliver his charge after the argument of counsel. It's an evidence of the supineness, lack of real interest and patriotism of the entire body of the Republican party as represented in both Houses of Congress, that such a bill should be put through. . . . Having been buffaloed, they are afraid to do anything, and they allowed these yahoos of the West and crafty damage lawyers like Walsh of Montana and Wheeler of that same State and Dill of Washington to accomplish what they choose apparently in the matter of kind of legislation that is sought for.

"I don't know whether we can induce the new Attorney General [Harlan Stone] to advise the President to veto the bill," Taft continued, "but at least we can try. And then of course the question still arises whether such a provision is in accord with the 7th Amendment." WHT to Robert A. Taft (April 5, 1924) (Taft papers).
27. "The jury bill which passed the Senate was on the Speaker's table and might have been taken up and put right through without reference to the Judiciary Committee of the House, because that committee had reported a similar bill. Graham, however, interfered and secured a reference of the Senate Bill to the committee, and I believe he proposes to have hearings. . . . I haven't had a chance to see Graham, but I have put myself in touch with the Attorney General, who said that he would see him." WHT to Thomas W. Shelton (April 13, 1924) (Taft papers).

The Chief Justice as Chancellor

28. WHT to Helen Herron Taft (April 30, 1924) (Taft papers). Taft continued: "Congressman Snell, who is the Chairman of the Committee on Rules in the House, promised me that he could postpone the bill. I saw the Chairman of the Judiciary Committee, Mr. Graham, and he thinks he can. I think I shall try and see Nick Longworth, the leader of the House, tomorrow, and with those agreed, I hope the plan of delay can be carried out. It will be a good deal easier to induce the President to veto the bill after the election than before."

29. WHT to Thomas W. Shelton (April 13, 1924) (Taft papers). Taft noted that "I am not in a position to appear before the committee myself, because were I to oppose it, it would only sharpen the eagerness of many to put it through." WHT to Gardiner Lathrop (April 27, 1924) (Taft papers). Taft believed that support for the bill arose from the fact "that many of the lawyers in the Senate and the House are damage lawyers and do not welcome the mode of procedure in the Federal Courts. The only thing that can be done is to have the Bar Associations of the various States and cities, who can be roused to the necessity of it, apply for an opportunity to be heard by the Judiciary Committee of the House, where the bill now is, in order to present objections to the bill. I am informed that Mr. Graham is opposed to the bill and is making an effort to carry it over to the next session, so that it may be considered after, rather than before, the Presidential election." *Id.*

On the opposition of the ABA to the measure, see *The Effort to Limit Power of Federal Judges*, 10 AMERICAN BAR ASSOCIATION JOURNAL 303 (1924) ("The bill is part and parcel of a vicious plan to destroy the powers and independence of the Federal Judiciary, and to invade its constitutional prerogatives."); *An Unwise Measure*, 10 AMERICAN BAR ASSOCIATION JOURNAL 332 (1924) ("[T]he proposal is wholly indefensible.... The indisputably greater efficiency of the federal courts as compared with the vast majority of state courts, of English criminal courts as compared with our own, rests on the power which the presiding judge has to control the proceedings."). Yet within the bar there were also dissenting voices. *See Letters of Interest to the Profession*, 10 AMERICAN BAR ASSOCIATION JOURNAL 443 (1924) (Letter of C. Floyd Huff) ("[A] jury trial is a mockery far more so under a system which permits a Judge to make the last argument to the jury."); *id.* at 443–44 (Letter of Alvah J. Rucker). *Compare* Harry Eugene Kelly, *An Impending Calamity*, 11 AMERICAN BAR ASSOCIATION JOURNAL 65 (1925) with *Curbing Federal Judges*, 28 LAW NOTES 182 (1925).

Shelton cleverly planted a story in the *Louisville Times* to the effect that the adoption of the bill would have an "immediate" effect "upon the enforcement of the Volstead Law ... and we can but believe that the enemies of the liquor laws are the ones most active in pushing it." LOUISVILLE TIMES (April 28, 1924). Shelton sent the clipping to Taft with a note: "Don't answer, but just watch the effect of this on the prohibitionists." (Taft papers).

30. Memorandum (December 2, 1924) (Taft papers).
31. *Id.* at 1, 5, 6, 12. "Should there be a progressive majority in the House and Senate," Taft wrote a friend, "it is quite probable that they would attempt to cut down the jurisdiction of the Federal Courts, as they may do by a mere act of Congress, but when it comes to interfering with our powers under the Constitution, they need two-thirds of each House and three-fourths of the states." WHT to Clarence H. Kelsey (September 12, 1922) (Taft papers). Taft was thus prepared to emphasize the very distinction between judicial power and jurisdiction against which he was

525

simultaneously cautioning Sutherland in the context of Michaelson v. United States, 266 U.S. 42 (1924). *See infra* Chapter 41, at 1383.
32. WHT to Henry W. Taft (March 27, 1925) (Taft papers).
33. Henry W. Taft to WHT (March 28, 1925) (Taft papers).
34. WHT to Henry W. Taft (May 28, 1925) (Taft papers). Henry responded by sending Taft a "copy of the proposed report of the [ABA] Committee on Jurisprudence and Law Reform, which I prepared some weeks ago. . . . You will see from the report that I used your memorandum on the Caraway bill freely, adding something of my own." Henry W. Taft to WHT (May 29, 1925) (Taft papers). Taft approved Henry's report, adding: "The point is that the parties are entitled to have the benefit of the discretion of the Judge in aiding the jury . . . and there are many cases where it is absolutely necessary in order that the jury may understand what the issues are and in order to clear the atmosphere of the court room from the utterly irrelevant appeals of counsel. We must have a jury system in order to reconcile the people with the administration of justice, and the only way by which it has been made possible in England is by the power of the Judge to prevent injustice by explaining to the jury the situation, the relevancy of the facts and his judgment on the weight of them, in order to enable them to exercise their exclusive function of ultimately weighing the facts." WHT to Henry W. Taft (May 31, 1925) (Taft papers).
35. When Caraway continued to press his bill, Taft wrote his brother, "[T]he bill has heretofore been beaten through the Judiciary Committee of the House by the active resistance of Chairman Graham. I hope he may do the same thing again if the bill gets through the Senate this session. I enlisted the assistance of the President in suppressing the bill, because he is very much opposed to it, and I think I could induce him to veto it. The last time he urged Gillett and Longworth and Graham to shelve the bill, and they did it. I hope that may be done this year." WHT to Henry W. Taft (May 18, 1926) (Taft papers). *See* WHT to Robert A. Taft (February 6, 1927) (Taft papers) ("We have staved off a bill which has been pending in each Congress to take away the right of the Judge to comment on the evidence in Federal trials. . . . I very much doubt whether under our Federal Constitution, Congress could take away the power of the judge."); WHT to Horace D. Taft (March 20, 1928) (Taft papers) ("The Democratic Senate is doing everything that I don't like to have them do, but I suppose that is to be expected. They have just passed a bill taking away from the Federal Courts the power of the Judge to comment on the evidence in submitting a case to the jury. We hope that we can hold it up in the House, but I don't know whether we can or not. I think I could induce the President to veto it, but whether it would pass over the veto I can not say; and after that would come the question whether the bill is constitutional. . . . If Al Smith gets in, and the Democrats have control of both Houses, the next four years will not furnish a rosy bed, even for Justices of the Supreme Court.").
36. *See* CHARLES A. WRIGHT & ARTHUR R. MILLER, 9 FEDERAL PRACTICE AND PROCEDURE CIVIL § 2557 (2nd ed., Eagan, MN: West Pub. 1995); JACK B. WEINSTEIN & MARGARET A. BERGER, EVIDENCE § 107 (New York: Matthew Bender 1994); Quercia v. United States, 289 U.S. 466, 469 (1933) ("In a trial by jury in a federal court, the judge is not a mere moderator, but is the governor of the trial for the purpose of assuring its proper conduct.").
37. Taft's draft of the Canons was presented to the ABA at its 1923 annual meeting. *Final Report of the Committee on Judicial Ethics*, in REPORT OF THE FORTY-SIXTH

The Chief Justice as Chancellor

ANNUAL MEETING OF THE AMERICAN BAR ASSOCIATION 452 (Baltimore: Lord Baltimore Press 1923). *See* Walter P. Armstrong Jr., *The Code of Judicial Conduct*, 26 SOUTHWESTERN LAW JOURNAL 708, 708–10 (1972). A copy of the 1924 Canons may conveniently be found as Appendix D in LISA L. MILORD, THE DEVELOPMENT OF THE ABA JUDICIAL CODE 131–42 (Chicago: Center for Professional Responsibility, American Bar Association 1992).

38. An earlier draft of this Canon was far more explicit:

> Judges have a peculiar opportunity to observe the operation of statutes, especially those relating to practice, and to ascertain whether they tend to impede the reasonable and just disposition of controversies; they should not be indifferent to shocking results; and they may well contribute to the public interest by advising both the people and their representatives of the result of their observations and experience; there is no need of diffidence in this respect, out of a false fear of being considered to be unduly interfering with another department of the Government.
>
> Judges may well direct diligent effort toward securing from proper authority such modification of laws or rules tending, in their experience, to impede or prevent the reasonable and just disposition of litigation, as will rectify the evils discovered by them.

Charles Boston to WHT (June 8, 1922) (Taft papers) (attached draft at 21). Taft's hand is evident throughout the Canons, as for example in their strong emphasis on the need for an efficient, speedy, and effective judiciary. *See, e.g.*, Canons 2, 6, 7, 8, 18.

39. Canon 33 comes closest to expressing this concern. It provides that a judge should "in pending or prospective litigation before him be particularly careful to avoid such action as may reasonably tend to awaken the suspicion that his social or business relations or friendships constitute an element in influencing his judicial conduct."
40. Rule 3.2, Comment [2].
41. *See supra* Chapter 14, at 504–5.
42. *After-Dinner Oratory at Cincinnati*, 7 AMERICAN BAR ASSOCIATION JOURNAL 605, 606 (1921).
43. On the negotiation of this tension in the first decade of the Republic, see Maeva Marcus & Emily Field Van Tassel, *Judges and Legislators in the New Federal System*, in JUDGES AND LEGISLATORS: TOWARD INSTITUTIONAL COMITY 31–53 (Robert A. Katzmann, ed., Washington D.C.: The Brookings Institution 1988).
44. Only three days after being confirmed as chief justice, Taft wrote Daugherty proposing a reform that Taft acknowledged came "close to the Constitution." *See supra* Chapter 12, at note 17. Taft was perfectly aware of the constitutional controversy surrounding the recommendation that he pushed the Judicial Conference to announce in 1925, which was that bail be routinely denied after conviction. *See supra* Chapter 12, at note 59.
45. Hearings before the House Committee on the Judiciary on H.R. 6687, 70th CONG. 1st SESS. (February 1, 1928), at 6.
46. WHT to Thomas J. Walsh (May 8, 1928) (Taft papers).
47. Thomas J. Walsh to WHT (May 10, 1928) (Taft papers). The next day Taft wrote A. C. Paul that "I sincerely hope that [Walsh] will be able to get the bill through. I fear that the Chief Justice of the Court of Customs Appeals will try to prevent it, but I hope not." WHT to A.C. Paul (May 11, 1928) (Taft papers).

48. Pub. L. 70-914, 45 Stat. 1475 (March 2, 1929).
49. Thus Taft wrote his brother about the Uniform Procedure Bill that he was anxious to have passed: "I am especially anxious with reference to the power that it gives the Court to unite equity and law. ... Of course the suggestion that it is not constitutional is perfectly ridiculous. After we have been making rules for admiralty and equity since the beginning of the Government, to say that we can not make rules for common law procedure is something that nobody but an Irishman with a certain keenness of mind and without any sense of humor would solemnly advance." WHT to Henry A. Taft (May 21, 1926) (Taft papers). For Walsh's constitutional arguments to the contrary, see *supra* note 5. Taft actually sent Senate Judiciary Chair Cummins a memorandum arguing in favor of the constitutionality of the uniform procedure bill authorizing the Supreme Court to make rules of procedure for common law actions. *See* WHT to Albert B. Cummins (May 31, 1926) (Taft papers). The argument turned largely on Taft's own opinion in Liberty Oil Co. v. Condon National Bank, 260 U.S. 235 (1922). *See supra* note 9.

The practice of advisory opinions was not confined to Taft. So, for example, the normally reticent Van Devanter wrote Congressman R. Walton Moore:

> I have ... read with much interest the paper you have prepared relating to the proposed relief of the District Courts by providing for the trial of minor criminal proceedings before some subordinate judicial officer, with a right to appeal from a conviction.
>
> The paper ... is thoroughly well grounded in its portrayal of what constitutionally may be done if deemed expedient. ... No criticism occurs to me that would be helpful.

WVD to R. Walton Moore (January 12, 1927) (Van Devanter papers). *Compare infra* text at note 61. For other examples of Van Devanter engaging in constitutional prejudgment, see WVD to Charles W. Bunn (April 2, 1928) (Van Devanter papers) ("There may be doubt of the power to do what is proposed in the bill altering the functions of judges in jury trials."); WVD to R. Walton Moore (May 29, 1929) (Van Devanter papers).
50. Pub. L. 85-755, 62 Stat. 899 (August 25, 1958).
51. Glidden Co. v. Zdanok, 370 U.S. 530 (1962). The story is well told in Brenner v. Manson, 383 U.S. 519, 526 (1966).
52. *See* WHT to Charles Evans Hughes (March 13, 1926) (Taft papers). Augustus Hand wrote Taft: "Our only real relief is to get rid of petty criminal cases. If we do not do this, this court which has been one of the most important and interesting trial courts anywhere is bound, in my opinion, to sink to a very low level." Augustus N. Hand to WHT (December 9, 1925) (Taft papers). Exemplary is Henry Smith's letter to Taft explaining why he was retiring as a federal district judge:

> I am not conscious of any disability, physical or mental, and would dislike to be considered "shirking," but the burden of the immense criminal business of a police character – especially the flood of liquor cases – has become very great. They involve no questions of legal importance. Just one small criminal case after another, depending wholly upon testimony as to the facts. My egotism, I suppose, persuades me that I am a little thrown away on such work, and impels me to think I had better turn it over to a younger, stronger, and less susceptible mind.

Henry A.M. Smith to WHT (May 23, 1923) (Taft papers).

The Chief Justice as Chancellor

53. Harding announced in nominating Taft that he expected Taft to move rapidly to remedy the congestion overtaking federal courts. "Additional judges will be needed," Harding said, and "there may be need of authorization of commissioners; something must be done to relieve the courts of cases of the less criminal type. I mean cases growing out of the Volstead act." Gus Karger to WHT (June 30, 1921) (Taft papers). *See* George F. Authler, *Taft Confirmed by Senate for Post of Chief Justice*, MINNEAPOLIS MORNING TRIBUNE (July 1, 1921), at 1.
54. *The Federal Judicial Council*, 2 TEXAS LAW REVIEW 458, 461 (1924).
55. *Id. See supra* Chapter 12, at note 52. On the question of constitutionality, see Felix Frankfurter & Thomas G. Corcoran, *Petty Federal Offenses and the Constitutional Guaranty of Trial by Jury*, 39 HARVARD LAW REVIEW 917 (1926).
56. WHT to Horace D. Taft (September 30, 1923) (Taft papers).
57. WHT to Albert B. Cummins (December 3, 1925) (Taft papers); WHT to George Graham (December 3, 1925) (Taft papers).

> How would this suggestion strike you? Provide that in every District there should be appointed a Judicial Commissioner to serve during good behavior, that he should have authority to hold court, try jury trials and have jurisdiction to try misdemeanors and felonies, punishment for which shall not exceed two years' imprisonment; that he should be given the power to compel the defendants to elect whether they desire jury trials within ten days after the filing of the information or the indictment; that he should be required to act also as a regular United States Commissioner, and might be called upon by the District Judge to act as a Master in Chancery or a Referee. . . . I don 't think he ought to be appointed by the President, but that as Judicial Commissioner he might be regarded as an inferior officer, and under the Constitution he could be appointed by the District Court. . . . Can not you think this over and frame a bill? Something ought to be done. I just throw out this suggestion, with the hope that it may germinate into something.

Id. Ever tactful, Taft also sent a similar letter to Senator Walsh, the most influential Democrat on the Senate Judiciary Committee. WHT to Thomas Walsh (December 3, 1925) (Taft papers). Walsh replied that "We are so near together in our ideas concerning the measure for the relief of the District Judges that there should be no difficulty in meeting each other's views." Walsh preferred, however, to lodge the appointment power in the president rather than in district judges. Thomas J. Walsh to WHT (December 4, 1925) (Taft papers). Taft responded that he did "not wish to insist on the appointment by the District Judges," and that he would be "glad to talk further with you about it, because something ought to be done." WHT to Thomas J. Walsh (December 5, 1925) (Taft papers). Taft also asked Augustus Hand for comments on the proposed legislation. Hand responded "Of course I am heartily in favor of such a plan though I have not looked up the law and do not know whether the appointment of magistrates for such a tribunal as you propose can be delegated to the courts." Augustus N. Hand to WHT (December 9, 1925) (Taft papers).
58. 67 CONG. REC. 10942 (June 8, 1926). Graham continued: "One of the great difficulties has arisen by reason of the invasion of what belonged heretofore to the States alone through the adoption of the eighteenth amendment. By the adoption of that amendment a great burden of police work was cast upon the Federal Government without furnishing that Government the proper equipment and machinery for carrying on the work created by the adoption of the eighteenth

amendment and the laws intended to carry it into effect. That is one reason why the business of the courts is suffering, why the courts are congested." *Id.*
59. *Id.* at 10942-43.
60. Francis G. Caffey to WHT (March 17, 1927) (Taft papers). *See, e.g.*, Hearings before the House Committee on the Judiciary on H.R. 5608, H.R. 8230, H.R. 8555, and H.R. 8556, 70th CONG. 1st SESS. (January 17, 1928), at 13 (Testimony of Francis G. Caffey referring to the 1923 recommendation of the Conference of Senior Circuit Court Judges).
61. WHT to Francis G. Caffey (March 21, 1927) (Taft papers). "[B]ut my interest in it is deep," continued Taft, "and I am glad to express the hope that united action will be taken to have the next Congress approach the subject and do the best it can." Pushed by Representative Walton Moore of Virginia, debate on expanding the powers of United States commissioners continued sporadically throughout the decade. *See, e.g.*, WHT to Walton Moore (March 21, 1927) (Taft papers); Walton Moore to WHT (March 22, 1927) (Taft papers); WHT to Walton Moore (March 23, 1927) (Taft papers). The Wickersham Commission also endorsed legislation of this kind. *See* George Cochran Doub & Lionel Kestenbaum, *Federal Magistrates for the Trial of Petty Offenses: Need and Constitutionality*, 107 UNIVERSITY OF PENNSYLVANIA LAW REVIEW 443, 452-53 (1959). Taft wrote Hoover to advocate for legislation expanding the role of commissioners. WHT to Herbert Hoover (March 14, 1929) (Taft papers). Hoover, Taft told his brother, "ought to propose a law for the disposition of the police work in the enforcement of the prohibition act by enacting a law which shall enable the Government to try petty cases without a jury and punish by a small fine of $100 or $200, and from ten to sixty days imprisonment. That will require a test of its validity in our Court, but it ought to be done at once, and that would clear up the situation." WHT to Horace D. Taft (March 10, 1929) (Taft papers). "Of course," Taft sheepishly added in a subsequent letter, "I don't want to give you the impression that I am certain that the Constitution can be so construed as to get rid of petty cases without a jury. I only wanted to say to you that there are a number of good lawyers who think it is possible, and that it would be worth while, in view of the practical advantages such a construction would give, to have the question tested. A man often entertains a general view of a possible constitutional construction until he is brought face to face with it in a court room and becomes charged with the responsibility of meeting it in a declaration of our Court." WHT to Horace D. Taft (March 20, 1929) (Taft papers). Evidently Taft had by the end of the decade become a good deal chastened in the freedom with which he was willing publicly to prejudge constitutional questions.
62. William Howard Taft, *To the Readers of The Tribune*, MINNEAPOLIS MORNING TRIBUNE (July 18, 1921), at 6. It is plain, however, that Taft was involved in active legislative horse-trading, even with his nemesis Walsh, in order to secure the passage of legislation increasing the number of judgeships. *See* WHT to Frederick H. Gillett (February 23, 1927) (Taft papers); Frederick H. Gillett to WHT (February 23, 1927) (Taft papers); WHT to Frederick H. Gillett (February 25, 1927) (Taft papers); Charles H. Parkman to WHT (February 26, 1927) (Taft papers). Taft frequently joked about his ineptitude as a politician as a way of certifying that his efforts to achieve judicial reform were merely the bona fide efforts of a professionally disinterested judge. Thus, he told the Chicago Bar Association in December 1921 that "I seem to have heard a suggestion by way of

The Chief Justice as Chancellor

friendly criticism, when my name was up for the Chief Justiceship, that a politician was being put upon the bench. All I have to say is, that that was news to me (renewed and increasing laughter), and I think it was news to the people." *The Chief Justice*, 5 CHICAGO BAR ASSOCIATION RECORD 11–12 (December 1921). Two years later Taft would write to Coolidge, "Nobody ever accused me of being a politician, except Borah when he opposed my confirmation as Chief Justice, and I do not claim to be at all versed in the science of practical politics." WHT to Calvin Coolidge (December 22, 1923) (Taft papers). "I preferred the office of Chief Justice to that of President," said Taft, "because I prefer the study and decision of legal questions to the executive and political duties of the President." WHT to Fred E. Campbell (May 6, 1925) (Taft papers).

63. S. 3151, 70th CONG. 1st SESS. (February 13, 1928).
64. A year earlier, Brandeis had written Frankfurter essentially recommending such a bill. LDB to Felix Frankfurter (May 11, 1927), in BRANDEIS-FRANKFURTER CORRESPONDENCE, at 292.
65. *See* 62 CONG. REC. 5108 (April 6, 1922) ("In my judgment we ought to abolish every United States district court in America; we ought to abolish entirely the United States Court of Appeals, and leave nothing of our United States judicial system except the Supreme Court of the United States. We ought to give to State judges and State courts all the jurisdiction."). *See* George Norris to G. Jay Clark (January 2, 1928) (Norris papers) ("In fact, I have gone so far as to advocate the abolition of all Federal courts except the Supreme Court.").
66. Sen. Rep. No. 626, 70th CONG. 1st SESS. (March 27, 1928). The Report said simply, "The committee can conceive of no reason why the district courts of the United States should have jurisdiction in these cases." *Id.* at 2.
67. WHT to Horace D. Taft (April 16, 1928) (Taft papers).
68. WHT to George W. Wickersham (March 29, 1928) (Taft papers).
69. WHT to Newton Baker (April 5, 1928) (Taft papers). Taft blasted the Senate as "a most Bolshevik body, and the House is the only one that retains any conservatism at all." WHT to George W. Wickersham (March 29, 1928) (Taft papers). Wickersham replied sympathetically that it was "discouraging to lovers of our institutions, but then, after all, we have had a running fight ever since the enactment of the Judiciary Law of 1789, have we not!" George W. Wickersham to WHT (March 30, 1928) (Taft papers). Taft wrote back, "It is too lonely to swear alone, and therefore I thank you for keeping me company." WHT to George W. Wickersham (March 31, 1928) (Taft papers).
70. WHT to Newton Baker (April 19, 1928) (Taft papers). Van Devanter also sought to arouse political opposition. *See* WVD to Walter H. Sanborn (April 2, 1928) (Van Devanter papers) ("There is real occasion for those who think S. 3151 ... is not in the public interest to make their opinions known."). Sanborn replied that he would "do whatever I can to prevent its passage, but that is not very much. I will express my opinion about it to those whom I know and will try to get some of them to take hold and argue the matter with the members of Congress that they know. There seems to be a very great desire on the part of some of the Democrats to get rid of the federal courts. When, however, they have elected Al Smith there will be so many Democrats that will want to be federal judges that the tide will turn." Walter H. Sanborn to WVD (April 5, 1928) (Van Devanter papers).

71. WHT to Casper Yost (April 5, 1928) (Taft papers).
72. *Federal Courts in Peril*, ST. LOUIS DAILY GLOBE-DEMOCRAT (April 10, 1928), at 18: "Apparently a serious movement is on foot to emasculate the federal courts.... It is high time that Congress and the country were awakening to the perils of this movement, arising from radical elements, and taking measures to suppress it." *See* Casper Yost to WHT (April 10, 1928) (Taft papers). Taft thanked Yost for the editorials: "I feel sure that they will attract attention." WHT to Casper Yost (April 16, 1928) (Taft papers).
73. Henry Taft was a named partner in the firm of Cadwalader, Wickersham & Taft.
74. WHT to Henry W. Taft (April 5, 1928) (Taft papers). Two days later Taft wrote his brother: "What we desire is publicity.... You ... might enlarge on the fact that such a bill as this would destroy the jurisdiction in those cases which McReynolds wrote from Oregon and from Nebraska on the right of the Catholics to maintain separate schools and the right of the Germans to maintain separate education in German. If we can stir up the Germans and the Irish and the negroes to an appreciation of the importance to them of maintaining the jurisdiction of the trial courts, we can make the Democrats a bit chary of burning their fingers with such a revolutionary proposal." WHT to Henry W. Taft (April 7, 1928) (Taft papers). Taft added in a postscript that "I am mistaken as to the German language cases. They came from the Supreme Courts of the States. The other came from the U.S. District Court."
75. *See* Henry W. Taft to WHT (April 18, 1928) (Taft papers).
76. *See* WHT to WVD (April 15, 1928) (Van Devanter papers): "They seem to be slow in New York to take up the question. My brother Harry is preparing the argument for his editorial friends in New York, but he takes so long that they might pass the bill in the Senate before he gets his articles ready."
77. WHT to Henry W. Taft (April 21, 1928) (Taft papers).
78. Henry W. Taft to WHT (April 20, 1928) (Taft papers). Henry Taft also drafted a long report on behalf of the ABA Committee on Jurisprudence and Law Reform. He managed to have the ABA Executive Committee go on record against the bill on April 24. Senator Copeland had the Executive Committee resolution, as well as the report of the Committee on Jurisprudence and Law Reform, reprinted in the *Congressional Record*. 69 CONG. REC. 8077–80 (May 8, 1928). *See also An Unwise and Dangerous Measure*, 14 AMERICAN BAR ASSOCIATION JOURNAL 266 (1928).
79. *Senate and Courts*, NEW YORK TIMES (April 22, 1928), § 3, at 4.
80. "It is a bill that grows out of the Progressive and Democratic union in the Senate," Taft wrote his son. "I should think it doubtful whether it could go through the House as at presently constituted, but if we have a Democratic success in the next election, I think we can count on the probability of the passage of such a bill. They are struggling to save the farmer, but if there is anything that will injure the farmer it will be the rate of interest that will be charged by those who control the capital in the East to be collected from farmers, if eastern capital is not given a place where it can be justly treated." WHT to Robert A. Taft (April 1, 1928) (Taft papers). The bill would "make the administration of justice more of a farce than it is now," Taft wrote his daughter, "but that is the spirit of the Senate. I am hoping the bill will be killed in the House, but it indicates what would happen if there was a Democratic success in the next election." WHT to Mrs. Frederick J. Manning (April 1, 1928) (Taft papers).

The Chief Justice as Chancellor

Taft's deep embroilment in the politics of S. 31541 is evident from the notes of one Henry W. Ward, who wrote a long memorandum summarizing his efforts to mobilize opposition to the bill:

> I had a long conference with the Chief Justice. I found him greatly interested in the matter and, needless to say, strongly opposed to the bill. . . . The suggestions of the Chief Justice were as follows:
>
> (a) The bill is of great political importance; so great that if the so-called independent Republicans, notably Senators Borah and Norris, and the Democratic members of the Senate should come out strongly in favor of the bill, it might be advisable to insert a "plank" in the Republican platform at the coming convention putting the party on record as in favor of vesting to the fullest extent in the inferior federal courts the jurisdiction specified in the third Article of the Constitution.
> (b) The organized negro vote in the north, a part of which the Democratic party is endeavoring to obtain, would be solidly against any Senator or member of Congress who might put himself on record in favor of the bill. . . . If they had no recourse to the federal district courts for the assertion of their rights, they would regard themselves as at the mercy of the hostile courts in many of the States, particularly in the South. This political issue appears to be of particular importance with respect to the candidacy of Senator Deneen of Illinois at the present moment.
> (c) The effect of the bill upon the western farmers and others throughout the country who are borrowers of capital, would be disastrous. . . . [T]he great bulk of [Eastern] capital has been loaned out in reliance upon the right to resort to the federal courts for collection under the jurisdiction based on diversity of citizenship. . . . The State courts would naturally be biased, in such instances, in favor of the local borrowers. . . .
> (d) [The Chief Justice] . . . also expressed entire concurrence in the view that there is no question as to the constitutionality of the elimination of the principal classes and the other classes of jurisdiction now granted by paragraph 1 of Section 24 of the Judicial Code.
>
> The Chief Justice also expressed strong regret that his position deprived him from taking an active part in opposition to the bill, but he did not place any restrictions on my making use of the above suggestions, but, as I understood him, left that matter to my discretion.
> On Thursday morning I called again on Senator Wagner told him in a general way the views of the Chief Justice. . . .
> I then called on Senator GOFF, told him of my conference with the Chief Justice.

Henry M. Ward to WHT (April 7, 1928) (Taft papers). Although Taft later sought to distance himself from Ward, see Henry W. Taft to WHT (April 9, 1928) (Taft papers); WHT to Henry W. Taft (April 10, 1928) (Taft papers); WHT to WVD (April 17, 1928) (Van Devanter papers), it is plain that Ward's memo accurately reflects the extent to which Taft was fully engaged in an obviously political struggle without wishing to be overtly identified as such. The astute Charles Burlingham considered Ward "a blow-hard and a fakir." Charles C. Burlingham to HFS (May 27, 1929) (Stone papers). *See* HFS to Charles C. Burlingham (May 28, 1929) (Stone papers).

81. 69 CONG. REC. 6379 (April 13, 1928). Norris refused to hold hearings on the bill, saying that "it is a bill on which I think no particular hearings are necessary. It is entirely a legal proposition. . . . It is purely a question of practice that the lawyers on the Judiciary Committee understand as well as do other attorneys." *Id.* at 6378.

82. *Senate and Courts, supra* note 79.
83. 69 CONG. REC. 7421–22 (April 30, 1928). *See Whittling Away at the Federal Tribunals*, 14 AMERICAN BAR ASSOCIATION JOURNAL 200 (1928) (citing arguments that Taft had made in 1922, the *ABA Journal* editorial objected to the bill's repudiation of diversity jurisdiction). *See* William Howard Taft, *Possible and Needed Reforms, supra* note 2. In his 1922 speech to the ABA, Taft had explicitly conceded that "of course the taking away of fundamental jurisdiction from the federal courts is within the power of Congress, and it is not for me to discuss such a legislative policy." *Id.* at 604. Yet in allowing his views opposing S. 3151 to be publicly known, Taft was exactly discussing legislative policy. Felix Frankfurter later published an article thanking Norris for sponsoring S. 3151 and provoking discussion about the appropriate scope of federal jurisdiction. Frankfurter virtually reiterated (without attribution) the negative comments about diversity jurisdiction that Brandeis had sent Frankfurter on May 10, 1928. LDB to Felix Frankfurter (May 10, 1928), in BRANDEIS-FRANKFURTER CORRESPONDENCE, at 331–32. *See* Felix Frankfurter, *Distribution of Judicial Power* between *United States and State Courts*, 13 CORNELL LAW QUARTERLY 499, 499 n.1, 521–22 (1928).
84. 69 CONG. REC. 7422 (April 30, 1928).
85. S. 3151, 70th CONG. 1st SESS. (May 8, 1928). *See* 69 CONG. REC. 8077 (May 8, 1928). Somehow Taft managed to acquire a copy of a letter sent by Norris to Lewis Gannett of *The Nation* explaining the proposed change in S. 3151. In the letter, Norris writes that the "principal object of this bill ... is to take away the jurisdiction of the Federal Courts in the diversity of citizenship. It is true the bill takes away some other jurisdictions, but the other items we thought were of very little importance. However, there is no objection to amending the bill so as to confine it entirely to diverse citizenship cases." George Norris to Lewis Gannett (April 28, 1928). Taft sent the letter to Van Devanter, dryly commenting: "I send you herewith a copy of a letter written by Norris ... showing how closely he scrutinized the effect of his bill before introducing it." WHT to WVD (May 4, 1928) (Taft papers).
86. WHT to Henry W. Taft (May 16, 1928) (Taft papers).
87. "I haven't a bit of doubt that we could induce Coolidge to veto the Norris bill," Taft wrote his brother, "but I'm not so sure that we could do so with respect to Smith, although I doubt if he would consent to so radical a measure." WHT to Henry W. Taft (July 11, 1928) (Taft papers).
88. On the intense hostility to federal diversity jurisdiction in Southern and Western states, see Tony A. Freyer, *The Federal Courts, Localism, and the National Economy, 1865–1900*, 53 BUSINESS HISTORY REVIEW 343 (1979); Harry N. Scheiber, *Federalism, the Southern Regional Economy, and Public Policy Since 1865*, in AMBIVALENT LEGACY: A LEGAL HISTORY OF THE SOUTH 69–104 (David J. Bodenhamer & James W. Ely, Jr., eds., Jackson: University Press of Mississippi 1984).
89. Pub. L. 69-563, 44 Stat. 1022 (January 22, 1927). At traditional common law, in the words of Blackstone, "it is usual to deny a copy of the indictment, ... for it would be a very great discouragement to the public justice of the kingdom, if prosecutors, who had a tolerable ground of suspicion, were liable to be sued at law whenever their indictments miscarried." 4 BLACKSTONE'S COMMENTARIES 126

The Chief Justice as Chancellor

(St. George Tucker, ed., Philadelphia: W.Y. Birch & A. Small 1803). The rule denying the defendant a copy of the indictment was abrogated in treason cases in the Treason Trials Act of 1696. *See* JOHN LANGBEIN, THE ORIGINS OF ADVERSARY CRIMINAL TRIAL 90–92 (Oxford University Press 2003).

90. Joseph Coursey to WHT (November 23, 1925) (Taft papers).
91. WHT to Joseph Coursey (November 28, 1925) (Taft papers).
92. Joseph Coursey to WHT (December 15, 1925) (Taft papers).
93. WHT to William D. Mitchell (December 20, 1925) (Taft papers).
94. William D. Mitchell to WHT (January 8, 1926) (Taft papers).
95. WHT to Albert B. Cummins (January 11, 1926) (Taft papers).
96. Albert B. Cummins to WHT (January 12, 1926) (Taft papers).
97. William D. Mitchell to WHT (March 3, 1926) (Taft papers).
98. Albert B. Cummins to WHT (March 5, 1926) (Taft papers).
99. Pub. L. 69-563, 44 Stat. 1022 (January 22, 1927).

CHAPTER 16

Lobbying for Judicial Appointments

C ERTAIN ASPECTS OF Taft's success in redefining the role of chief justice were inimitable. Taft's active participation in the matter of judicial appointments, for example, largely depended upon the intimacy of Taft's political contacts. Although American judicial appointments are made by those with political authority, Taft did his best to use his prestige and political network to wrest authority away from the president and Senate. We have already canvassed Taft's interventions into the nominations of Butler and Sanford,[1] but Taft's immense influence reverberated throughout all levels of the federal judiciary in ways that to this day remain virtually unprecedented.[2]

Even before his appointment as chief justice, Taft insistently volunteered "helpful suggestions" about judicial appointments to Attorney General Daugherty, "because the Federal Judiciary are like the apple of my eye."[3] Three weeks after Taft's confirmation, he was pleased to learn that "the Attorney-General assures me that he expects to talk with me all the time about the selection of Judges, and I am very sure, from what he says, that he is determined to make his Administration a memorable one, and one that will be looked upon with approval by the best people."[4]

Senators who saw judicial appointments as mere political patronage were Taft's perennial opponents.[5] Because federal judges supervising receiverships could appoint corporate officers entitled to healthy fees, a compliant judge could direct significant financial resources to a senator's followers.[6] Taft pressed Daugherty to instruct Harding that "Senators and Representatives and political influences generally should be given to understand that they must not expect, as a matter of patronage, to dominate or dictate ... appointments."[7] Matters came to a head when the Act of September 14, 1922, suddenly created twenty-four new district judgeships (and one circuit judgeship).[8]

Lobbying for Judicial Appointments

Taft advised Daugherty, with the presumption and easy familiarity of a former political confederate, to "insist that these judges shall be selected not by agreement between political quantities but on their merits."[9] Taft professed himself satisfied with Daugherty's stalwart loyalty in the matter of judicial appointments.[10] Daugherty's "relations with me have been most cordial and intimate," Taft wrote his nephew, "and he has consulted me a great deal about judicial appointments, which with me are everything now."[11]

At least during the Harding years, Taft received the full support of the executive branch as he fought with senators to control the flow of judicial appointments.[12] Taft sought to apply the same criteria to lower court judges as he did to potential Supreme Court colleagues: they had to be of good character and not display "an unsoundness of view as to the Constitution."[13] They had to be "staunch friends of the Constitution who will do nothing to sap the pillars of our Government as they have weathered the storm of many assaults and vindicated the wisdom of our ancestors."[14] He did not want judges who would be "on the off side and [take] radical views in respect to the police power and other things."[15] Taft strongly believed that a candidate's "attitude toward the Constitution and accepting its present construction and the accepted jurisdiction of the Federal Judiciary should all be considered before" giving "serious thought" to a nomination.[16]

Taft was prepared to go to enormous lengths to insure the purity of the federal judiciary. So, for example, he engaged in a protracted and bitter battle with Senator Selden Palmer Spencer of Missouri over the appointment to the district court of Spencer's former law partner Vital W. Garesche, whom Taft characterized as "a gangster ... who drinks."[17] Taft believed that Spencer was "threatening ... [to] go Bolshevik unless Garesche is appointed, and of course that would make the loss of one vote on critical issues. ... We must uphold the Federal Judiciary – it is our bulwark – and to have such a man fastened on us would be most distressing."[18]

After Harding's death, Taft noted with approval that Coolidge "has manifested a disposition to appoint good men to the Bench, and I hope I can exercise some influence in this way."[19] Within two months, Taft was explaining to Coolidge the situation in the district court of the Eastern District of South Carolina. "I hope you will permit me to write you on questions of this sort," he said, "where I have any means of information, because of my intense interest in securing a good Judiciary, and my earnest desire to help you in your manifold labors where I think I can be of assistance in a field like this one."[20] "I value your interest and friendly suggestions always," Coolidge replied. "Be sure to let me know when anything occurs to you. ... I am glad to have your judgment."[21] After Daugherty stepped down in scandal, Taft continued to recommend judicial candidates to Attorney General Stone, who was "very glad to receive"[22] Taft's advice and "very anxious to help."[23] Taft viewed Stone as "very satisfactory" on the question of judicial appointments.[24]

After Stone left the administration and joined the Court, however, Taft became aware that Coolidge was "rather disposed to consult Stone," so that Taft's ability to continue to shape appointments was diminished by Stone's interventions.[25] Taft appreciated that his own influence was waning.[26] In part this was because in the new Sixty-Ninth Congress, which began work in March 1925, a "union of the Democrats with the radical Republicans"[27] undercut Coolidge's margin in the Senate, which twice defeated Coolidge's nomination of Charles B. Warren to replace Stone as attorney general.[28] As a result, Coolidge became "loath to turn a Senator down."[29] Coolidge was

> very anxious to preserve the good will of Republican Senators, a good many of whom are quite willing and especially anxious to use the judicial patronage of the President to favor their particular local plans. ... I have tried in the past to influence the President with reference to judicial appointments when I thought an opportunity existed to secure good men, but I think the President thinks that I am too insistent on having good men and am not sufficiently sympathetic with his trials with Senators, and I am going to keep out of the judicial selections hereafter. It takes a great deal of time to run around and it takes me from other work that I need to do, and I don't think I could make my voice prevail against a Senator.[30]

Taft resigned himself to the fact that Coolidge was "much less interested than he was at first" in Taft's advice about judicial appointments.[31] Taft complained to his son that the "President has not consulted me nearly so much about Judges as he did. When Stone was Attorney General he was anxious to know what I knew. I warned the President about Charley Warren, and since that time [he] has not been anxious to have my advice, so I don't tender it. He has made a very poor appointment in the Southern District of California."[32] "The President," said Taft, "looks askance at my non-partisan feeling about Judges."[33]

After Warren's rejection, Coolidge nominated his childhood friend John G. Sargent to be attorney general. In Taft's eyes, it was "painful ... how awkward and clumsy he is. He is honest, but that is about all, and I feel at times like going to the President and telling him so. ... The Department of Justice as at present organized can not be trusted at all to make any good selections for Judges or District Attorneys or Marshals."[34] Sargent was "a good man, but he is stupid and slow and utterly lacking in methods which will secure good appointees for the important places that he has to fill upon recommendation to the President."[35]

Even as his public reputation for influence grew,[36] Taft complained that Coolidge "hasn't good judgment" in regard to appointments and "yields too much to Senators and Congressmen in their demands for patronage in respect to positions as to which he should feel independent."[37] "I don't have any influence at all in the selection of Judges. It has passed to political control, largely through the Senators. A man who insists on the real qualifications as a Judge in the candidate is not one who seems to be successful these days in any recommendation."[38] Taft began to receive dismal notes of consolation: "I presume you are sick of trying to get good Judges appointed and having your efforts ignored," wrote Augustus Hand.[39]

Taft would occasionally get the bit between his teeth and push hard for particular candidates, as for example to ensure that Augustus Hand[40] and Yale Law School Dean Thomas Swan[41] were appointed to the Second Circuit. Taft took some comfort from the fact "that we have succeeded in getting some good ones from Calvin after a while."[42] But for the most part, as Taft wrote Senior Circuit

Lobbying for Judicial Appointments

Judge Arthur Carter Denison, "It seems now that we have got to rejoice if we don't have a bad appointment. We can't aspire to good ones."[43] William Allen White cogently summarized the situation: "So the President let the Senators name the judges, the judges let the Senators have a hand in naming federal receivers whose clerks, attorneys and hangers-on were Senatorial claquers, and the President had his way with the more regular and subservient Republicans in Congress. Chief Justice Taft who had returned to earth from the Heaven of judicial isolation had to see his ideal of a hightoned judiciary wither and fade."[44]

Sinking into a fatalism that would come increasingly to dominate the last years of his life, Taft would observe that "even though among the appointees are a number who ought not to have been selected," the federal judiciary nevertheless "becomes better in its personnel the longer the Judges remain on the Bench, by reason of their judicial experience and education. They are independent, and having no ambition except to stand well with the Bar, they are by their experience and the teaching of the Bar rendered pretty good Judges before they get through."[45] "[T]he truth is that the Federal Judiciary is maintained by the system rather than by the excellence of the appointments. Take a man of average intelligence and education, make him independent, and give him a place where there is real competition among his fellow Judges, and the experience that he must have and the work that he can not avoid doing, and you not infrequently get a good Judge."[46]

Although Taft aspired throughout his tenure to shift the appointment process away from political authority and toward those who possessed professional expertise, in the second half of the decade, and especially after his heart attack of 1926, his efforts were derailed by the senatorial politics of the Sixty-Ninth Congress, as well as by his own flagging energy. Given his work on the Court and the Judicial Conference, he no longer possessed the boundless determination of earlier years to control nominations to the lower federal courts. Instead, in the second half of the decade, he chose to concentrate his remarkable energy on a massive new project: creating a new home for the Supreme Court.

THE TAFT COURT

Notes

1. *See supra* Chapter 2 and Chapter 3; Walter F. Murphy, *In His Own Image: Mr. Chief Justice Taft and Supreme Court Appointments*, 1961 SUPREME COURT REVIEW 159.
2. *See* Walter F. Murphy, *Chief Justice Taft and the Lower Court Bureaucracy: A Study in Judicial Administration*, 24 JOURNAL OF POLITICS 453 (1962).
3. WHT to Harry M. Daugherty (April 11, 1921) (Taft papers). *See* WHT to Harry M. Daugherty (May 2, 1921) (Taft papers) ("If you don't mind it, my interests in the Federal Judiciary, where I know something of the situation, makes me anxious to give you the benefit of what I have learned from considerable experience. I am not butting in, but I am only testifying, without any personal slant, and only with a view to helping if I can.").
4. WHT to Clarence H. Kelsey (July 21, 1921) (Taft papers). To the general public, however, Taft freely dissembled, asserting that "I have nothing to do with the appointment of Judges ... and do not take any part in their selection. ... If I were to get into the business of recommending, with all the people whom I know in the United States, I would be swamped and would not have any time for any other work." WHT to J.G. Butler (December 16, 1921) (Taft papers). *See* WHT to Emily Ruty Collins (December 13, 1921) (Taft papers).
5. "Why is it," Taft asked, "that a Judge who is best fitted never strikes the ordinary politician as the man to take?" WHT to Charles D. Hilles (January 20, 1923) (Taft papers).
6. Taft was appalled, for example, to hear a "prominent lawyer from Kansas City" estimate that a "Judge has patronage in Kansas City worth $80,000 a year. Think of estimating the importance of a Federal Judge by the amount of receiverships or other things that he may have to fill." WHT to Robert A. Taft (March 15, 1925) (Taft papers). Taft advocated "removing all patronage from the courts." WILLIAM HOWARD TAFT, OUR CHIEF MAGISTRATE AND HIS POWERS 69 (New York: Columbia University Press 1916). "I would vest the appointment of receivers in equity to take charge of railroads by the Federal courts in the Interstate Commerce Commission." *Id.* at 70.
7. Harry M. Daugherty to Warren G. Harding (April 8, 1922) (Harding papers).
8. In August 1922, Taft wrote Senator Cummins that he was pleased that Harding could "delay appointments until the Senate shall meet again in December, and thus the question of appointments will not be complicated by the election. It is a most critical and delicate duty that the President will have to perform in selecting all at once so many permanent judges. He will need a full three months to decide upon all the judges." WHT to Albert B. Cummins (August 21, 1922) (Taft papers).
9. WHT to Harry M. Daugherty (June 5, 1922) (Van Devanter papers). Taft and Daugherty went back a long way. Daugherty had "managed Taft's last campaign in Ohio and led his cause in the tumultuous convention in 1912 that split the Republican Party." HARRY M. DAUGHERTY (WITH THOMAS DIXON), THE INSIDE STORY OF THE HARDING TRAGEDY 21 (New York: Churchill Co. 1932). Taft's letter to Daugherty was built on the foundation of a long and trusting friendship:

> I presume the bill for additional judges will pass. I am greatly concerned over the personnel of those judges. You and the Administration will be on trial in respect to the men who are selected. It will cost a great deal of effort to resist the rapacious demands of Senators and Congressmen for particular favorites, who are

Lobbying for Judicial Appointments

not fitted, many of them, to be judges. In the district of New York, I understand that Koenig and Ward and somebody else have agreed as to the slate for the vacancy and for the two other judges, and that Siegel is to be included in them. Now there is a typical instance. If the Administration yields to that, it will stamp the whole panel of judges to be selected. I beg of you to follow the advice of the New York Bar Association, who have no motive except that of getting the best judges, and in your own interest and in the interest of the party, and in the interest of the country, I urge that you and the President insist that these judges shall be selected not by agreement between political quantities but on their merits. . . . My dear Harry, you want to refute your enemies, and you are going to do it, but one of the chief opportunities is through the selection of the highest standard of men for these twenty-five additional judges. I hope you will appoint some Democrats, in spite of the partisan bitterness of the attacks on you. . . . I am deeply concerned in your welfare and in your success, and in that of the Administration, and what I have written is out of a full heart and with a fairly competent knowledge and experience in the particular field to which I am referring.

WHT to Harry M. Daugherty (June 5, 1922) (Van Devanter papers). Taft sent a copy of this letter to Van Devanter, remarking that "I hope he will show it to the President. They will make a great mistake if they don't regard this as one of the most important crises in the Administration. I suppose the bill will come out of conference in a week or two." WHT to WVD (n.d.) (Van Devanter papers). To the extent that Democrats shared his own basic constitutional convictions, Taft was always concerned to make the federal judiciary bipartisan. *See* WHT to Hatton W. Sumners (January 15, 1927) (Taft papers).

10. It is for this reason that Taft struggled to stand by Daugherty in 1924 when scandal engulfed the attorney general's office. "He has stood up in the matter of Judges," Taft wrote his son, "which after all is the chief and most responsible thing he had to do, and he has secured on the whole, against the vicious system of Senatorial selection of candidates for political purposes, a good list of Judges. But for him Harding would have made a wreck of it, I fear, because he was not a lawyer and did not appreciate the importance of the selections." WHT to Robert A. Taft (January 27, 1924) (Taft papers). *See* WHT to Horace D. Taft (February 29, 1924) (Taft papers). Taft, however, was well aware of Daugherty's limitations. In May 1922, for example, Taft wrote his wife that "I fear Harry has not been well advised. It was a mistake for him to take the Attorney General's place. He does not seem to rise to it. He has not organized his office well and he has nobody really to advise him and act for him of great strong character and ability." WHT to Helen Herron Taft (May 21, 1922) (Taft papers). *See* WHT to Charles D. Hilles (May 31, 1922) (Taft papers). For his part, Daugherty wrote that "I am particularly proud of the work done in my administration of the office of Attorney-General in the expansion of the judiciary and the filling of its vacancies. More judges were appointed under Harding and Coolidge up to the time I resigned as Attorney-General than during any other like period in the history of our government. And not one man that I recommended to the President for a Federal judgeship was refused confirmation by the Senate. . . . I made those selections with the greatest care." DAUGHERTY, *supra* note 9, at 112.
11. WHT to Hulbert Taft (January 7, 1923) (Taft papers). *See* WHT to A.R. Kimbell (February 8, 1923) (Taft papers) ("I have so much to do in trying to influence the President in respect to judicial appointments that I am afraid I can not do much in the

Civil Service business."). *But see* White House Memorandum (May 1, 1923) (Harding papers) ("The Chief Justice warns against Henry Lincoln Johnson's recommendation for Superintendent" at the Veterans Hospital at Tuskegee).

12. *See, e.g.*, Warren G. Harding to WHT (January 15, 1923) (Taft papers); WHT to Charles D. Hilles (January 17, 1923) (Taft papers); Charles D. Hilles to WHT (January 18, 1923) (Taft papers) ("I don't want to irritate you by seeming to assume to be the guardian of your person, but I think you are working too hard. It seems to me unfortunate that at a time when a vast number of most important questions are before your Court for determination that you should have to go so thoroughly into the details of the qualifications of the horde of men who are seeking appointment as District Judges throughout the United States. I can well understand that the President, feeling a sense of insecurity in the selection of judges because he is not himself a lawyer, and having made the discovery that the so-called leading lights of the profession are not unselfish in putting forward certain candidates, leans heavily upon you because he knows that you have an eye single to the very best results for the Republic."). At the time Hilles was the Finance Committee chair of the Republican National Committee. Taft replied to Hilles: "Don't be troubled about my labors in respect to Judges – it's a labor of love. It isn't true that Harding imposes the burden on me. It isn't true that he has asked me for my judgment in respect to anybody; but I have tendered it and then he has expressed his satisfaction that I had done so. But he has been very careful never to be affirmative in his request for my advice. It has been my sense of duty that has carried me into the matter." WHT to Charles D. Hilles (January 20, 1923) (Taft papers). Taft nevertheless remained concerned that Harding had "grown a little sensitive about the constant reports that the matter is in a way delegated to me." WHT to Edward Colston (February 21, 1923) (Taft papers).

13. WHT to Elihu Root (December 21, 1922) (Taft papers). *See* WHT to Warren G. Harding (December 6, 1922) (Harding papers).

14. WHT to Warren G. Harding (December 4, 1922) (Taft papers).

15. WHT to Henry W. Taft (December 1, 1922) (Taft papers). *See* WHT to Henry W. Taft (January 16, 1923) (Taft papers) (rejecting Von Moschzisker as a candidate because "his idea of the police power is altogether too broad"). A commitment to judicial efficiency apparently led Taft to make a conspicuous exception for Learned Hand. Six months after objecting to Hand's possible appointment to the Supreme Court, Taft wrote a friend that he and Learned Hand had "become warm friends and are greatly interested in working together to render the administration of justice more effective. While he and I differ on some things, he is a very hard worker and a very effective Judge. We are trying to get rid of the enormous mass of arrears that have accumulated in his district." WHT to Gertrude Ely (May 2, 1923) (Taft papers). The following year Taft urged Coolidge to promote Hand to the Second Circuit, writing Attorney General Harlan Stone:

> I note that we have lost Mayer from the Circuit Bench in the Second Circuit. ... It seems to me that where you have good District Judges, the wisest course is to promote one of them. Learned Hand I think would probably be the best man to take. He is the oldest in commission of the District Judges and is a fine lawyer, and in many ways a brilliant Judge. I appointed him District Judge, and I confess that I was greatly disappointed when he lost his head over Roosevelt, to such an extent as to enter into politics while on the Bench, and I think he ran for

Lobbying for Judicial Appointments

> the office of the Court of Appeals on the Progressive ticket. I was very indignant at him for this, because it seems to me that a man who is on the Bench should consider himself cloistered from politics, but I have come to know Hand better since, and while I think he made an ass of himself at that time, I believe that he has worked hard, has done very good work, and would be a very able member of that Court of Appeals.

WHT to HFS (August 1, 1924) (Taft papers). Stone replied:

> I have gradually been coming to the conclusions which you express with reference to Judge Learned Hand. He is somewhat radical and erratic in his political thinking, but has had a long and satisfactory service as a Judge and practically all the letters I get from members of the Bar whose opinions I value indicate a very general desire that he should be promoted.

HFS to WHT (August 4, 1924) (Taft papers).

16. WHT to John G. Sargent (November 19, 1927) (Taft papers). Van Devanter had a similar perspective. See WVD to Robert E. Lewis (March 28, 1929) (Van Devanter papers) ("If I questioned his fitness in any particular it was along the lines of good balance and stability. In the single argument which I heard him make he manifested a little inclination to warp the Constitution and the law to give effect to what he conceived in the particular case would be an onward and upward view. I noticed that several of my associates understood his argument in the same way. Of course a single argument is not an adequate or a fair test. But the one which he made left in my mind a query as to whether his tendency is towards a balanced judgement and stability. I regard these as essential elements to the proper exercise of the judicial function."). On Daugherty's view of the criteria for federal judges, see *Congested Dockets in the Federal Courts Menace to Justice Says Attorney General*, 13 JOURNAL OF THE AMERICAN INSTITUTE OF CRIMINAL LAW AND CRIMINOLOGY 609, 611 (1923): "I want to say here that no man, no matter what his ability may be, will ever be endorsed by the Attorney General unless he is 100 per cent American in every shape and form. For the federal judiciary is the backbone of our government, and in these times of discontent and vicious radicalism, these judges must stand between the Constitution and the blind gropings of those who are swayed by violent and unscrupulous leaders."
17. WHT to Charles D. Hilles (January 17, 1923) (Taft papers).
18. WHT to Festus J. Wade (February 12, 1923) (Taft papers). "That shows the kind of man Spencer is," Taft continued. "I am the more exasperated because he is a Yale man and makes broad his claims on that subject." The press was well aware of Taft's opposition to Garesche. *See, e.g.*, *Spencer Fails to Weaken Opposition to Garesche*, ST. LOUIS POST-DISPATCH (January 4, 1923), at 4; *Babler Takes Hand in Contest for Judgeship*, ST. LOUIS POST-DISPATCH (December 2, 1923), at 8. After Harding's death, Taft continued to battle against Garesche with Coolidge. "I don't know that Coolidge will follow my advice, but I count myself fortunate that I took time by the forelock to speak to Coolidge about the matter. I think that Coolidge will send for the record and examine it, and, if he does, I think he will find some facts there that will shake a man who has Massachusetts or Vermont ideals of what a Judge should be." WHT to Gus Karger (September 14, 1923) (Taft papers). *See* WHT to Calvin Coolidge (October 6, 1923) (Taft papers); Calvin Coolidge to WHT (October 8, 1923) (Taft papers); WHT to Calvin Coolidge (December 23,

THE TAFT COURT

1923) (Taft papers). In November, Taft summarized the struggle over Garesche in this way:

> I have been engaged in fighting [Garesche] tooth and toe nail. Spencer came to me and tried to induce me to withdraw my opposition, and I flatly declined to do so.... Spencer got himself appointed on the committee to attend Harding's funeral by the President of the Senate, in order that he might go out with President Coolidge on his [railroad] car for the purpose of securing Coolidge's promise to appoint Garesche. By good luck I went on the same car, and before I left Washington was able to put the case to Coolidge in such a way that I think he is convinced – indeed he has told me so.... There is a great deal of discussion of the power of the Supreme Court and the way in which it is exercised, but to one who lives in Washington the real objectionable exercise of personal power is that of small-minded Senators over Federal appointments in their States.

WHT to Fred T. Murphy (November 30, 1923) (Taft papers).

The contest over Garesche's appointment lasted until January 1924, when Coolidge at last nominated Charles B. Davis. The difficulty was that Coolidge needed the votes of every regular Republican senator to sustain his policies and so was reluctant to alienate Spencer. "I saw the President the other morning," Taft wrote his brother. "He told me that he has not as yet succeeded in committing enough Senators to sustain his veto of the bonus bill, but he thought everything looked encouraging.... He is in a situation now where he needs Senatorial votes, and I think, from what he said, he has deliberately made up his mind he will not make two or three judicial appointments which he knows he ought not to make. He will not make any appointments at all until after the crisis. He says it is a great deal better to have no Judge than to have a bad Judge. Of course there is still another alternative and that is to appoint a good Judge, but the appointment of anybody but a bad Judge at this time I presume he thinks would alienate the votes which he hopes to get to sustain his policy of anti-bonus and tax reduction. You thus have a problem of political ethics which practical men meet as he is meeting it." WHT to Horace D. Taft (January 12, 1924) (Taft papers).

19. WHT to Horace D. Taft (September 29, 1923) (Taft papers).
20. WHT to Calvin Coolidge (October 17, 1923) (Taft papers).
21. Calvin Coolidge to WHT (October 17, 1923) (Taft papers).
22. HFS to WHT (April 24, 1924) (Taft papers). *See* WHT to HFS (April 22, 1924) (Taft papers). Taft's letter to Stone in part concerned the unfitness of the chief justice of Kentucky for a position on the Sixth Circuit. Taft was not above manipulating the Act of September 14, 1922, in order to further his designs. Thus he wrote his wife: "Dick Ernst came to see me to-day. He is very much troubled because of the earnest candidacy of a very unfit man to become United States Circuit Judge in the Sixth Circuit.... I told Dick to tell the President that if he would keep the matter open until next fall, I would agree to keep a Judge in the Sixth Circuit who could do the work." WHT to Helen Herron Taft (April 25, 1924) (Taft papers). Taft was explicit to Coolidge about Taft's ability to manipulate the assignment of federal judges. *See* WHT to Calvin Coolidge (June 4, 1924) (Taft papers); Calvin Coolidge to WHT (June 4, 1924) (Taft papers).
23. WHT to A.C. Denison (May 8, 1924) (Taft papers). *See* WHT to HFS (June 7, 1924) (Taft papers); WHT to Alex P. Humphrey (May 8, 1924) (Taft papers).

Lobbying for Judicial Appointments

24. WHT to Charles D. Hilles (December 3, 1924) (Taft papers). "I am very much concerned with the appointment of Judges. There are a good many vacancies. The salaries are so low that it much reduces the number of eligible and invites the candidacy of men who are failures in the profession and who never would be thought of but for the lack of real timber. The vicious disposition of the Senators to use appointments to the Bench for their own political purposes is a thing that the President needs the utmost courage to resist, and somebody has to keep him advised. The present Attorney General is all right, and indeed Daugherty was on this point, but the Senators are persistent and gore the President with their unpatriotic attacks." WHT to Mrs. Frederick J. Manning (November 30, 1924) (Taft papers). *See* WHT to Robert A. Taft (December 14, 1924) (Taft papers) ("The life of the Attorney General in trying to help the judiciary is a dreadful one, and he has my utmost sympathy."); WHT to Walter H. Sanborn (February 28, 1925) (Taft papers) (Noting that Taft would talk to Charles B. Warren, the likely new attorney general, about a judicial appointment to the Eighth Circuit, but that "I am not so convinced that he would be as likely to listen to me as would the retiring Attorney General, who comes to us Monday.").
25. WHT to Robert A. Taft (March 15, 1925) (Taft papers). "At least Van Devanter and Butler are invoking [Stone's] aid," Taft reported to his son. *Id. See* WHT to HFS (November 13, 1925) (Taft papers); WHT to Augustus N. Hand (November 14, 1925) (Taft papers) ("I am going to turn the matter over to Justice Stone."). Stone himself affirmed that "While I take no active part in the selection of Judges, I am anxious to see good Judges appointed, and I am often consulted." HFS to Charles C. Burlingham (October 31, 1925) (Stone papers).
26. Many years later Stone wrote his children: "Coolidge had very little liking for Taft's well-developed propensity for telling him what he, Taft, thought he should do. My own judgment is that many of Taft's letters, published in the recent Life of Coolidge conveying the impression that he was very influential with Coolidge, were not quite accurate. I think the fact was very much to the contrary." HFS to his Children (November 24, 1939) (Stone papers).
27. WHT to Robert A. Taft (March 15, 1925) (Taft papers).
28. In the first vote, Warren was defeated by a margin of one vote when Vice President Dawes famously failed to show up to cast the deciding ballot in a 50–50 tie.
29. WHT to Horace D. Taft (March 14, 1925) (Taft papers).
30. WHT to Robert A. Taft (March 15, 1925) (Taft papers). "People don't understand the outrage of the Senatorial inference in judicial appointments and they don't understand how strong the leverage that a Republican Senator has in these days when so much depends, for the comfort of the President, and for his achieving anything of his broad purposes, upon the vote of a twopenny small-minded United States Senate [sic], and I don't think there are many who don't come within that description." *Id.*
31. WHT to W.W. Chapin (April 16, 1925) (Taft papers). "I am not called in now in respect to judicial appointments. I think my constant interest and my attitude of opposition to Senators have tired the appointing power." WHT to Charles D. Hilles (April 24, 1925) (Taft papers). *See* WHT to Henry Lippitt (April 24, 1925) (Taft papers). Taft's perception that Coolidge became more inclined to defer to senatorial courtesy was later confirmed by Coolidge's secretary, Everett Sanders, who

THE TAFT COURT

observed that Coolidge "became convinced that it was useless to send to the Senate a nomination for an appointment to the Bench in any state where the Senators would make real objection." Quoted in WILLIAM ALLEN WHITE, A PURITAN IN BABYLON: THE STORY OF CALVIN COOLIDGE 286–87 n.14 (New York: MacMillan Co. 1938). *See* DONALD R. MCCOY, CALVIN COOLIDGE: THE QUIET PRESIDENT 172–73 (New York: MacMillan Co. 1967).

32. WHT to Robert A. Taft (May 3, 1925) (Taft papers). At about this time, Brandeis wrote Frankfurter that "We are beginning to reap a fine harvest in Federal Judges. Perhaps it may help in the 'back to the states' movement – however illogically." LDB to Felix Frankfurter (June 20, 1925), in BRANDEIS-FRANKFURTER CORRESPONDENCE, at 205. *See* LDB to Felix Frankfurter (December 25, 1927), *id.* at 315 ("C.C. is doing quite as badly as Harding in the gradual process of undermining the Federal Courts. High authorities within my ken are very sad about it.").
33. WHT to Thomas W. Shelton (April 6, 1927) (Taft papers).
34. WHT to Robert A. Taft (February 7, 1926) (Taft papers).
35. WHT to Charles P. Taft 2nd (February 14, 1926) (Taft papers). *See* WHT to Albert S. Ingalls (August 20, 1928) (Taft papers) ("If Coolidge had any independence on the subject of judicial appointments, I would hope to have some influence, but I haven't any. It is discouraging to one interested in maintaining the high personnel of the Federal inferior judges. It may be as much due to the inefficiency of the Attorney General as to any other cause."). Stone was also inclined to blame the poor quality of appointments on his successor as attorney general rather than on President Coolidge. HFS to Charles C. Burlingham (December 30, 1926) (Stone papers).
36. *See, e.g., Alling May Be Chosen U.S. Judge,* HARTFORD COURANT (July 3, 1927), at 1 ("No matter how acceptable a candidate is to State leaders, it is said the candidate must meet the test of whether he is acceptable to Chief Justice Taft. President Coolidge, it is known, is governed largely by the advice of the Chief Justice in making his appointments to the Federal bench."). *Compare* WHT to Horace D. Taft (October 21, 1927) (Taft papers) ("I shall go and see the President and tell him that Alling isn't up to the mark, but I don't know that it will do any good, with a Senator on the other side.").
37. WHT to Charles D. Hilles (July 7, 1926) (Taft papers). The tone of Taft's correspondence is well illustrated by his annoyance that the administration had selected a judge to fill the new district in Georgia that had been engineered by Taft himself through a recommendation of the Judicial Conference. "I haven't been consulted at all about the Federal Judgeship in Georgia. I got the bill through, but this present Administration makes its selections in a very curious way, and I have very little to do with it." WHT to Charles D. Hilles (June 10, 1926) (Taft papers). On Taft's lobbying to create that judgeship, see WHT to Clark Howell (March 25, 1925) (Taft papers) ("Could you not call attention to the deplorable condition of arrears in the Northern District of Georgia and the absolute necessity for added force? Could you not interest your brother and the other leading members of the Bar to organize a movement to insist that such a place should be created? The Senior Circuit Judges, who meet in Conference under my Presidency on the 9th of June, will be certain to readopt a resolution adopted some time ago, urging the new Congress to provide another Judge. These things are accomplished by taking them up in time. I shall help them as much as I can when they come here by personally addressing both committees on the subject."). Howell was the editor of the *Atlanta Constitution.*

Lobbying for Judicial Appointments

38. WHT to John C. Vivian (May 27, 1928) (Taft papers). Taft was excluded from the nomination process even in his home state of Ohio. *See* WHT to David S. Ingalls (August 10, 1928) (Taft papers) ("I don't expect to have anything to do with the appointment. The Republican Senator who is running for nomination, Senator Fess, is quite insistent on controlling the appointments of Judges in the State, with a view of keeping his fences mended. I haven't patience with such a motive for the selecting of Judges. The President hearkens to Senatorial recommendations, and the Attorney General offers no objection of any real substance. I would intervene with recommendations if I thought they would do any good, but I am quite sure they will not."). *See* WHT to Charles P. Taft 2nd (August 11, 1928) (Taft papers) ("They pay no attention to me at the White House, though of course the President gives me a respectable hearing, but I go and make my statement, and nothing happens."); WHT to A.I. Vorys (September 19, 1928) (Taft papers) ("If we could get good judges in Ohio ... I would thank God. But I shall attribute it to Him and neither to Fess nor to the President, because the last thing that either makes as a basis for the selection is the qualification and fitness of the appointee. They come in after the political needs of Fess are satisfied. I find great difficulty in being patient with either of them. I don't think my recommendations amount to anything with either, but such as they are I shall give them.").
39. Augustus N. Hand to WHT (March 23, 1926) (Taft papers). This was apparently also the experience of other justices on the Court. So, for example, Van Devanter wrote his friend Judge John C. Pollock in 1929:

    > Some times the Circuit Justice is consulted respecting the appointments of circuit judges and district judges within his circuit. When I came here that was the general rule. Of late years the rule has not been followed. My associates so say and my experience is the same.
    >
    > The judicial nominations made by President Coolidge near the close of his administration were made without any consultation with any of us. Some of the nominations were very good and others not so good.

    WVD to John C. Pollock (March 21, 1929) (Van Devanter papers). Stone apparently had the same experience, see HFS to Learned Hand (March 5, 1929) (Stone papers), even though he was in 1929 by far the most politically connected justice.
40. *See, e.g.*, WHT to George Zabriskie (September 7, 1926) (Taft papers) ("I expect to do all I can for Augustus Hand to be a Circuit Judge. . . . He has earned it, and, as you know, I have but little patience with the question of a man's political past as a reason for appointment or non-appointment to a place on the bench that he deserves and is able to fill as well as Judge Hand could fill this."); WHT to Elihu Root (September 17, 1926) (Taft papers) ("Hand is a Democrat, but he is a first class Judge. . . . [H]e is not perhaps quite so brilliant as Learned Hand, but I would rather trust his judgment."); WHT to Learned Hand (September 28, 1926) (Taft papers); WHT to Learned Hand (November 11, 1926) (Taft papers); WHT to Augustus N. Hand (January 5, 1926) (Taft papers); WHT to Charles Evans Hughes (April 26, 1927) (Taft papers) ("He is the kind of a safe Judge that is needed on that Bench. Learned Hand is brilliant but sometimes erratic. . . . If we are to make the Bench a place for the best men, the appointing power should recognize the obligation to promote those who have deserved well and have proven their capacity."); WHT to George W. Wickersham (April 26, 1927) (Taft papers) ("He is needed on that bench

to mix his common sense with Learned Hand's brilliancy."); WHT to Learned Hand (April 27, 1927) (Taft papers) ("I have been doing what I could to bring about the selection of Gus Hand as your colleague. I wrote the President. I stirred up Stone and he went to see the President. I wrote George Wickersham, and he has written a letter. I wrote Hughes and asked him to write a letter, and I wrote to Hilles and asked him to write a letter. The latter was for the purpose of taking care of the political end. Stone had an interview with the President yesterday."); WHT to Learned Hand (April 30, 1927) (Taft papers); WHT to Learned Hand (May 3, 1927) (Taft papers) ("If we win for Gus, it will be a great triumph – that is the truth of it."); WHT to Augustus N. Hand (May 6, 1927) (Taft papers) ("I must face the fact that it is more important what Hilles thinks in this matter than what I think."); WHT to Augustus N. Hand (May 22, 1927) (Taft papers) ("I felicitate you on the prospect of a long, useful, judicial life, and I don't think that one can lead any life that can be more satisfactory than it."); Learned Hand to WHT (May 24, 1927) (Taft papers) ("Your interest was I believe a very potent cause of the result."). Stone was also very much involved in Hand's appointment. *See, e.g.,* Learned Hand to HFS (May 24, 1927) (Stone papers) ("Thanks for your share in it, which I suspect was very important."); HFS to Learned Hand (May 25, 1927) (Stone papers) ("I don't suppose I had much to do with it, but I allowed my views on the subject to be known for what they were worth."); HFS to Charles C. Burlingham (November 19, 1926) (Stone papers); HFS to Learned Hand (November 19, 1926) (Stone papers); HFS to Learned Hand (November 16, 1926) (Stone papers).

41. WHT to Learned Hand (November 16, 1926) (Taft papers) ("I am inclined to press Swan for Rogers' place and then have the President put up Gus Hand for the new Circuit Judgeship that I hope we can get."); Calvin Coolidge to WHT (November 30, 1926) (Taft papers) ("I shall bear in mind all of the fine things you say of Dean Swan. It was a genuine pleasure to see you looking so well."); WHT to John G. Sargent (November 30, 1926) (Taft papers); Thomas W. Swan to WHT (November 30, 1926) (Taft papers) ("[T]hat you desire my appointment as a Circuit Judge I deem as great an honor as would be the appointment itself.... Your suggestion of Mr. Justice Van Devanter as an honorary degree candidate fills me with enthusiasm. I shall try to get the Law School Faculty behind the nomination and hope the corporation will confer the degree at the coming commencement."). Stone also supported Swan's appointment. *See* HFS to Thomas W. Swan (January 6, 1927) (Stone papers) ("I am much gratified at your appointment and none the less so because I had a modest part in it.").

42. WHT to Learned Hand (May 25, 1927) (Taft papers). *See* WHT to Robert A. Taft (June 5, 1927) (Taft papers) ("My only criticism of [Coolidge] would be his selection of men, because I don't think he has good judgment in that regard, and he hasn't done as well by us in the selection of Judges as he might, although he has appointed some good ones.").

43. WHT to A.C. Denison (July 21, 1927) (Taft papers). At about this time, Van Devanter wrote his friend, prominent Arkansas attorney George B. Rose, about the proper way to shape an appointment to the federal bench:

> I do not assume to have any power to control or influence the appointment of District Judges in our circuit but I am deeply interested in the maintenance of right standards and when my recommendation is solicited, as it occasionally is, I endeavor to act impartially and for the good of the service. My suggestion is that

Lobbying for Judicial Appointments

you are going about it in the wrong way. The Attorney General will wish to do the right thing but he knows nothing about the Arkansas bar and must depend on recommendations made by others. At times a representative is sent out to make inquiries but the Department has no one to send out who is really fitted for the purpose. At times (not recently) the reports of such investigations have been submitted to me, and while I regarded the reports as well intended they appeared to me quite unsatisfactory. The better way is for leading members of the bar to get together, canvass the situation candidly and impartially and select a committee to present one, two or three names of men fitted for the position. Then get endorsements, if it reasonably can be done, by political representatives in the community, such as party committeemen, and also endorsements by senators and representatives. A bar committee rightly chosen and acting wisely can go far towards accomplishing all that is needed in this line. The committee could come to Washington and could make a presentation of the matter to the Attorney General and if need be to the President. ...

I may or may not be asked about the matter. If asked I must necessarily be informed else I could not be helpful and could not speak. I have some acquaintance with your bar but it is not general and may be inadequate. If there be aspirants who are not fitted you are at liberty to write me to that effect and to tell why in terms that will be plain; and if there are other aspirants who are fitted you are at liberty to tell me this and to give the reasons – character, experience, age, etc. My acquaintance with you justified me in believing that you would act solely in the interest of good service. ... A real embarrassment in the matter of judicial appointments is that the bar frequently lets the matter go by default, takes no concerted action or makes scattering recommendations which conduct to no desirable result.

WVD to George B. Rose (September 23, 1927) (Van Devanter papers). Taft eventually supported Van Devanter in seconding Rose's recommendations, which were later undercut when Rose himself was forced to walk them back as "a bit too strong and enthusiastic to consist with the facts." WHT to John G. Sargent (November 5, 1927) (Taft papers). "I don't think that those gentlemen with whom I came to see you at the Department of Justice," Taft wrote the attorney general, "were entirely frank in their statement to Van Devanter and me or to you." WHT to John G. Sargent (November 19, 1927) (Taft papers). Taft subsequently performed his own investigation into the potential Arkansas judgeship and unearthed what he regarded as an excellent candidate, a former governor of the state named John Ellis Martineau, who was a Democrat and who in the end was appointed. This was the same Judge Martineau whom Fiorello La Guardia would later accuse of racism in a Brooklyn courtroom in New York, where Martineau had been transferred pursuant to the Act of September 14, 1922. *See supra* Chapter 12, at note 39. *See* WHT to WVD (August 1, 1929) (Taft papers); WHT to Fiorello H. La Guardia (August 2, 1929) (Taft papers).

44. WHITE, *supra* note 31, at 414.
45. WHT to M.S. Sherman (October 29, 1927) (Taft papers). "But we ought not to have to depend on those factors to get good men," Taft grouched. "We ought not to have to educate our Judges at the expense of the public." *Id.* "It seems to be our fate," Taft wrote Senior Circuit Judge A.C. Denison, "to have to train Judges and not to get Judges who are fitted at the time." WHT to A.C. Denison (March 8, 1928) (Taft papers).
46. WHT to George D. Seymour (November 25, 1928) (Taft papers).

CHAPTER 17

Creating a New Supreme Court Building

During Taft's chief justiceship, the Court was housed in what had been the old Senate Chamber. The Court had moved there in 1860 when the Senate decamped for larger quarters. The Old Chamber was an intimate, elegant room, furnished with "columns of native Potomac marble, gray painted walls, and mahogany furnishings."[1] It was a room that echoed with the historical grandeur of Webster, Clay, and Sumner. It held great emotional value for members of the Supreme Court bar.[2] Elihu Root, who was far from maudlin, told Taft that "I have always had a strong feeling, largely sentimental doubtless, in favor of the Court staying where it is. The associations of the chamber in which the court now sits are more interesting and impressive to me than those of any other place that I know; and I have no doubt that they tend to restrain the dangerous radicalism of you and Sutherland."[3]

But the space occupied by the Court was entirely impractical from an administrative point of view.[4] It did not contain enough space for the clerk's office, the marshal's office, or the library. The justices lacked chambers. The Court's records were "scattered throughout the Capitol, the Senate Office Building, and the Library of Congress."[5] There were no facilities for the bar or for the solicitor general. There were no common rooms in which justices could receive and confer with guests. "In our conference room," Taft wrote Kansas Senator Charles Curtis, "the shelves have to be made so high that it takes an aeroplane to reach them."[6] The Senate was continually confiscating space from the Court. The Senate was, as Taft said, "of the porcine variety, ... spreading not only through the building where the Senate Chamber is, but clear to the middle of the Capitol, taking up all the old Congressional Library rooms, and giving us no place for the Bar, making it impossible for us to keep our records in any such shape that we can use them easily, and sending out of the Capitol all but three of the Justices."[7] Taft was forced to engage in a constant and unseemly battle for space.[8]

Creating a New Supreme Court Building

The inadequacy of the Court's quarters had long been recognized. Beginning in 1888, Senator Justin Smith Morrill of Vermont sought repeatedly to pass legislation to provide a new building for the Court.[9] "It is clear that the rooms now occupied in the Capitol by the Supreme Court are deplorably inadequate both in size and number for its proper accommodation – being inferior to what our people often offer to their county courts," Morrill argued, "and it is also equally clear that the space so occupied has long been needed and greatly coveted by Congress for its increasing necessities, for its offices and committees."[10] Even President McKinley in 1898 in his State of the Union Address commented on the "inadequate accommodations provided for the Supreme Court in the Capitol" and suggested "the wisdom of making provision for the erection of a separate building for the court and its officers and library upon available ground near the Capitol."[11]

Although Chief Justices Fuller and White opposed the idea of leaving the old Senate Chamber,[12] Taft was made of different stuff. Court management *mattered* to Taft in ways that it had not mattered to his predecessors. Notwithstanding the nostalgic beauty of the old Senate Chamber, Taft was determined to provide for the administrative necessities of the Court. If his predecessors had shied away from the legislative engagement that would necessarily be entailed in a search for suitable new quarters,[13] Taft actually enjoyed the give and take of the political arena.

The Judiciary Act of February 13, 1925, moreover, fundamentally altered the character of the Supreme Court, transforming it from a simple final appellate tribunal into the supervisor of the entire system of federal law. The Court required a new physical infrastructure adequate to its enlarged role. Taft believed that "as the chief body at the head of the judiciary branch of the Government," the Court deserved "to have a building by ourselves and one under our control."[14] Even if many of his colleagues "would not really enjoy the amplitude and comfort" of a new building, the stakes for the future were high. "[T]hose of us who have responsibility ought to look after the welfare of those who come after us."[15]

At first, however, Taft was preoccupied with other matters. Ever since the report of the McMillan Commission in 1902,[16] which established the plan for the development of Washington's major buildings and parks for the first third of the twentieth century,[17] it had been assumed that a new Supreme Court building would be constructed "on the square directly north" of the Library of Congress and east of the Capitol, where the Supreme Court is now located.[18] Soon after he became chief justice, Taft was contacted by the Commission of Fine Arts, which Taft had established in 1910 to carry on the work of the McMillan Commission.[19]

The Commission of Fine Arts had been asked to advise on a building project on the lot north of the Library of Congress, and it wanted to know if Taft might still desire that piece of property.[20] Two months later, the chair of the Commission asked if Taft might be interested instead in a court building located on the south axis of the White House in the Tidal Basin, where the Jefferson Memorial is now located, so as to symbolize more concretely the symmetry and balance among the three branches of government.[21] Taft dismissed the idea. "My impression is that the Court would prefer to be nearer the Capitol."[22] And in any event, as Taft wrote another correspondent in 1922, "I haven't heard that there is to be a new building for

The Taft Court

the Supreme Court in Washington. Some of my brethren are opposed to it – I would like it – but Congress is in no mood to put up new buildings."[23]

There matters lay, as Taft grew increasingly frustrated by the lack of space to support the administrative infrastructure of the Court.[24] What suddenly spurred him into the intense campaign that would last to the end of his life was Stone's accession to the Court. Three months after taking his seat, Stone wrote Taft to complain about the "difficulties" he was suffering "for want of adequate office facilities." Stone had hoped to find "a suitable house in Washington with sufficient space for a library and an office for my law clerk and clerical assistant, but I have not succeeded in doing that, and may not succeed in doing it until I have built a house." Senator Henry Keyes of New Hampshire had kindly loaned Stone "the office of the Committee on Contingent Expense," but the room would have to be returned when the Senate reconvened in the fall.

> What I need, and need very badly, is a room lighted by daylight, with sufficient wall space to hold a complete set of Federal reports and reference books most commonly used, and a room nearby for the use of my clerical assistants.
>
> There are a number of rooms in the dome of the Capitol which are ideal for this purpose and which I understand were originally assigned to Justices of the Court. These rooms, however, have been gradually taken over by Senators so that the only ones now in use by the Court are those rooms occupied by Mr. Justice Sanford and Mr. Justice Sutherland. I very much hope that some way may be found whereby two of these rooms may be set apart for my use. Rooms at a distance, or in another building, would not be of great service, as I find that I am under necessity of sending to the Supreme Court Law Library for additional volumes.[25]

Taft promised to go begging to the Senate.[26] Two days later, Stone wrote to complain that books in the Supreme Court library had been checked out by legislators and given to friends and remained missing "for weeks and perhaps months at a time." Stone asked that there be a rule prohibiting persons other than justices from withdrawing books (in the absence of duplicates).[27] Taft concurred,[28] but then realized that Stone was raising questions that required structural solutions. "The truth is that if we could have a separate building for the Court and for the Law Library, we could probably get money enough to make our Library very much more comprehensive and useful than it now is. I mean at the next Conference to bring up the question whether we can get a majority of our Court to favor the construction of a new building. I am very much in favor of it, and I would like to have the authority of the Court to invite the Congress to frame legislation on the subject to our needs."[29]

Taft later testified that "We took a vote, and it was 5 to 4" to seek to leave the Capitol and to construct a new Supreme Court building.[30] Voting in favor of the new building were Taft, Van Devanter, Butler, Sanford, and Stone.[31] Taft apparently called for a vote as soon as he could muster a majority of five justices to support the move out of the Capitol. Taft then immediately began to implement the project with striking speed and determination.

Creating a New Supreme Court Building

Taft knew that Senator Reed Smoot of Utah was then pushing a bill to authorize approximately $50,000,000 for the construction of new public buildings in Washington. Taft wanted the Supreme Court to be included in that authorization. He wrote Smoot in July 1925 "with the authority of the Court" to ask for a separate building for the sole use of the Court "as the head of the Federal Judiciary, and, in a constitutional sense, the head of the Judiciary of the Nation."[32] Smoot was unimpressed. He had "carefully refrained from making any statement whatever as to what buildings this money will be expended for," and he did not wish to designate particular buildings in advance of the entire authorization for fear of getting "into a fight on the floor."[33]

It may seem odd to authorize $50,000,000 for federal buildings without having a clear idea of the purpose of the funding, particularly in the tight-fisted budgetary atmosphere of a Coolidge administration that stressed the virtues "of industry, of thrift, and of self-control."[34] It is true that the federal workforce had doubled in the preceding twenty years,[35] and it is also true that there was a desperate need for proper accommodations.[36] But Smoot's bill contributed to a spate of federal construction in the 1920s[37] that did not reflect merely a utilitarian desire to avoid the cost of rental space for inflated bureaucracies or to improve manifestly inadequate facilities. It also expressed the growing conviction that Washington D.C. should be rebuilt "to make the national capital as splendid as our new status in the world."[38] It signified "the dawning consciousness that this capital is an equivalent of the Rome of Augustus."[39]

Writing at the end of the decade, one commentator noted that "[t]he proudest boast of the Emperor Augustus was that he found Rome a city of brick and left it a city of marble. All Washingtonians seem bent upon following in his footsteps and making our national capital, if not a marble city, at least a white city."[40] Taft was fortunate that he could push a project for an impressive marble Supreme Court building – and in the end it would be the most magnificent of all the buildings to emerge from the decade – at exactly the moment when America was becoming infatuated with its own grandeur.[41]

This is not to say that the campaign for the Supreme Court building was easy. In fact it was extraordinarily difficult and would consume Taft for the remainder of the decade. It would require all of Taft's boundless tact, persistence, and influence.

Taft sought to circumvent Smoot's rejection by inducing New Hampshire Senator George Moses to offer an amendment on the floor of the Senate specifically authorizing a Supreme Court building,[42] but the amendment was voted down.[43] Undeterred, Taft realized that the Senate and House versions of the bill differed, and so, lobbying hard and effectively with the House conferees and with Moses,[44] Taft engineered a miraculous transformation. In May 1926 a bill emerged from conference specifically providing for a new building for the Supreme Court.[45]

The next step was for the Building Commission, in consultation with the Commission of Fine Arts, to designate a site for the building and to condemn and acquire the property. This phase of the project also proved problematic. The Building Commission was chaired by the unresponsive Smoot.[46] Taft, even though laid up in the hospital with serious heart fibrillation,[47] quickly summoned his five-person Court majority to press for immediate action. "We are anxious that the place be designated, and that the proceedings be taken for the condemnation of the property at once, for the reason that if there is delay, the property will probably appreciate in value, and it would seem to be wise by your action to fix the date of the valuation as soon as possible.... May we ask, therefore, that at your next meeting of the Board this matter be brought up so that action may be taken?"[48] Taft bombarded members of both Commissions with urgent appeals to action.[49]

When the two Commissions met together on June 17, Taft was still incapacitated, and so he "got Van Devanter to go, together with Stone and Sanford, and Van Devanter presented the matter."[50] Van Devanter recounted the meeting to Butler:

> The thing passed off very pleasantly, save that Justice Stone made some suggestions respecting the architectural features and the size of the building which led to a little discussion and to inquiry whether the site was appropriate for a building of the size outlined by him. It seemed to me this was a mistake so I ventured to put an end to it by saying that we had every confidence that the committee would arrange for a building which in architectural features would be of such dignity as would be entirely fitting and would adjust the dimensions so that they would comport both with our needs and the particular site and surroundings; that these were matters of detail which undoubtedly could be worked out in an entirely satisfactory way by architects such as they would employ; and that a mere glance at the suggested site would demonstrate that its area and dimensions would meet every requirement for the next 500 years. This seemed acceptable to the committee and our Brother Stone acquiesced. The committee did not come to a decision about the site at that time but there is some reason for believing that they will choose the site selected. I endeavored to point out that there was great need for choosing a site in close proximity to the capitol building and to the Congressional Library; that the site suggested near the Tidal Basin was not at all appropriate; and that the building should be devoted entirely to the Court.[51]

The authorization bill attracted a great deal of attention in the press, which stressed the importance of the Court as "the balance wheel by which the affairs of the Nation and its relation to the States are kept in working order" and which therefore deserved to occupy "one of the most imposing buildings in the capital, noted as the most beautiful city of the world, and one whose buildings reflect the wealth and power and dignity of the American people and the greatest Government that ever existed."[52] But the Building Commission did not act, forcing Taft to engage in yet another lobbying campaign to "stir" Smoot up.[53]

The Commission finally concluded in November 1926 that the Court building ought to be situated where the McMillan Commission had long ago sited it, and Taft turned his attention to the next task, which was to secure an appropriation sufficient to acquire the designated lots north of the Library of Congress. The assistant secretary of the Treasury thought that $1,500,000 would be sufficient, but Taft believed that $1,700,000 was closer to the mark.[54] There was also the question of whether the appropriation should go into the General Deficiency Bill or the Urgent Deficiency Bill. The latter would mean "an advance of two months for us, so that we

Creating a New Supreme Court Building

can get in our litigation ahead of the great amount of litigation that is necessary in the condemnation of the triangle and other lots contemplated in the general improvement."[55] Against the advice of the director of the Bureau of the Budget[56] and of Van Devanter,[57] Taft went directly to the secretary of the Treasury for assistance.[58]

Coolidge ultimately transmitted a request to include $1,700,000 in the Urgent Deficiency Bill.[59] Due to opposition in the House, and despite Taft's lobbying, the appropriation was cut down in conference to $1,500,000.[60] Taft fretted as the Urgent Deficiency Bill was held up by a disagreement between the Senate and the House.[61] But the funds were finally appropriated by the end of February 1927, and Taft could report to his son that "[w]e have got through our appropriation of $1,500,000 to purchase our Supreme Court lot, so that I think it is fairly certain now that the lot will be purchased in due time by condemnation, and that we can begin with the next Congress to get our appropriations for the building. My prayer is that I may stay long enough on the Court to see that building constructed. If I do, then I shall have the right to claim that it was my work, for without me it certainly would not have been taken up at this time. It is really very necessary."[62]

The condemnation procedure, however, turned out to be "dreadfully slow and most exasperating."[63] Although Taft hoped it could be settled by summer 1927,[64] it was not ultimately concluded until March 1929.[65] The land was valued at $1,768,000, as Taft had predicted,[66] which required the passage of yet another deficiency bill.[67] Delay was also caused by the "fool law" of the District of Columbia "that requires the making of abstracts ... to be let to the lowest bidder. The company awarded the bid has no adequate organization to do the work."[68] To Taft's intense annoyance, this further delayed the valuation proceedings. Solicitor General William D. Mitchell, a former law partner of Butler and close friend of both Van Devanter and Taft, took it upon himself to speed along the process as best he could.[69]

Delay was also caused by the fact that some of designated lots were occupied by the National Woman's Party (NWP), which in 1921 had purchased a building on the lots known as the "Old Brick Capitol." The building has been put into government use in 1814 after the original Capitol had been burned by the British. Justice Stephen Field had lived in the building for some time, and James Monroe had been inaugurated president there.[70] The NWP had acquired the site to "serve as a watch tower guarding women's interests in all national legislation and keeping the women of all States in touch with what Congress is doing."[71]

The NWP insisted on what Taft (and the jury that ultimately decided the property's valuation) considered an extortionate price for their land, due to its "valuable historical interest."[72] The NWP in fact created a small political furor.[73] "Everything," Taft wrote Van Devanter through gritted teeth, "conspires to delay."[74] The NWP even prompted Arkansas Senator Thaddeus Caraway to introduce a Joint Resolution in the Senate to the effect that the great historical importance of the Old Brick Capitol precluded its ever being torn down.[75] The Resolution passed the Senate but died in the House. In the end, lawyers handling the condemnation concluded that "The Woman's Party agitated so much ... that the jury was influenced to the extent of a few thousand dollars."[76]

Apart from the condemnation of the land, there was also the question of the design of the building itself. Taft had been chair of the Lincoln Memorial Commission,[77] which was generally acknowledged to have produced a masterpiece designed by the architect Henry Bacon. We know that Taft was drawn to Bacon's elegant neoclassicism and that at some time Bacon had produced preliminary sketches for a possible Supreme Court building.[78] But Bacon had passed away in 1924.

In August 1926, after passage of the bill authorizing the construction of the new Supreme Court building, Taft sent inquiries to state Supreme Courts to learn about their architectural facilities.[79] Cass Gilbert, who after Bacon was the leading American practitioner of neoclassical architecture,[80] had earlier designed the Arkansas State Capitol, which at the time housed the Arkansas Supreme Court, and he was then overseeing construction of the West Virginia State Capitol, in which the West Virginia Supreme Court of Appeals would be located.[81] Gilbert was informed of Taft's inquiries by both M.O. Litz, the chief justice of West Virginia, and Edgar Allen McCulloch, chief justice of the Arkansas Supreme Court.[82] Gilbert, who had been musing about designing a home for the Supreme Court since 1899,[83] wrote Taft on September 25 to set up a meeting later that month to discuss the design of spaces suitable for courts.[84] Gilbert had known Taft for a long time. In 1910 President Taft had appointed Gilbert to the Commission of Fine Arts, and the two had remained in touch ever since.[85]

Gilbert was ambitious. He was also artistically and politically conservative,[86] and he saw in the potential commission, as the chair of the Commission of Fine Arts later remarked to him, "the greatest opportunity that has come to an architect since the 1850s to do a monumental building in Washington."[87] Gilbert wanted to construct a building that would answer the many advocates "of the so-called modernist movement" to which he was aesthetically and professionally opposed.[88] Taft and Gilbert evidently hit it off, for in the surviving documentary record we see Gilbert writing Van Devanter two months later in November:

> Since our conversations in Washington of several weeks ago regarding the Supreme Court, I have given very thoughtful study to the subject and I am so deeply interested in it that I have made some sketches in which I have expressed certain ideas that I would like to place before you. I am writing to the Chief Justice today telling him about it.... The designs work out very well indeed and I think I can show you something that would make a very distinguished building suitable for the Supreme Court. I am enthusiastic about it myself and I hope that you will like it.[89]

On December 12, 1926, Gilbert sent Taft "the prints of the drawings we spoke of last night.... The plans show only the Main Floor on which is located the Supreme Court Room and Justice's Rooms and the Second Floor on which is located the Library, Court Reporter, and Lawyers Rooms."[90] Planning with Gilbert apparently proceeded very fast and very far.[91]

It seems that Taft had wasted no time pursuing a two-track approach: pushing the condemnation proceedings, while simultaneously initiating the selection of an

Creating a New Supreme Court Building

architect who could begin the actual planning of the building. Taft was prepared to write Gilbert in spring 1927 that he hoped that the condemnation proceedings would have concluded by the end of the year, and that "we shall be ready to apply for a suitable appropriation to begin the work. That will require legislation which will enable the Secretary of the Treasury to designate an architect. Without committing myself or my colleagues finally, I think I may say that the exhibition of your plans is favorable to the selection of yourself as the architect, but of course it will have to await the form of the legislation and the consideration of those who have the ultimate authority in the matter."[92]

The difficulty with Taft's approach was that Gilbert could not be reimbursed for preliminary planning until he had been selected by a government commission with authority to choose an architect and supervise his work. Until Gilbert was officially hired, he would have to work on speculation. Taft encouraged Gilbert to take this risk in the hope that Gilbert's plans would convince those in authority to hire him.[93] The challenge before Taft was to craft legislation establishing a building commission that would enable the Court to control the choice and supervision of the architect,[94] while at the same time to extract enough work from Gilbert to justify Gilbert's eventual selection. The latter meant bolstering Gilbert's confidence in the inevitability of his ultimate commission.

While away in Canada on summer vacation, Taft had Van Devanter meet with Secretary of the Treasury Mellon. Although Mellon stressed the need to "proceed without bias respecting particular plans and particular architects," Van Devanter "with deference and recognition of the need for unbiased action ... pressed for an early and tentative consideration of such suggestions as Mr. Gilbert could make, and indicated that [Gilbert] had given the subject much consideration and was interested in it independently of who shall be ultimately chosen as the architect."[95]

Van Devanter persuaded Mellon to allow Gilbert to confer with Edward H. Bennett, a Chicago architect and Mellon's special advisor in matters relating to the many public building projects then underway in Washington. "When Gilbert sees Bennett it will be the same as seeing me," Mellon said, "and it will be better because Bennett understands the matter well and I do not. I must necessarily be advised by and rely largely on Mr. Bennett."[96] "Without prejudice to the ultimate adoption of plans and the future designation of an architect," Van Devanter advised Gilbert to seek an opportunity in Washington to meet with Bennett and "to lay before him at an early date the suggestions which you have in mind and the tentative drawing which you have made."[97]

It proved difficult to bring Gilbert and Bennett together. Gilbert awkwardly supposed that Bennett wished to meet with him, rather than the reverse.[98] But eventually the two men did confer, and Gilbert reported that Bennett was supportive.[99] Bennett expressed concern that the northern side of the court building, as Gilbert had sketched it, was not parallel to the northern boundary of the lot slated for condemnation, which (then as now) was bounded by the diagonal Maryland Avenue.[100] Bennett's critique set off a flurry of efforts to move the Court to a different location.[101] But in the end these came to nothing, and Taft wrote

Smoot that "[w]e shall have to content ourselves with the block which is now condemned, and I am hoping that in spite of the irregular character of the block as it now is, it can be made a very satisfactory place for the Court." With characteristic persistence, Taft added, "Could you tell me what would be the prospect of our getting an authority to go ahead with the building as soon as the condemnation is completed? It would mean much to us if we could put the thing right through."[102]

Having secured Mellon's agreement to Gilbert's selection and settled the question of the site, Taft turned his attention in spring 1928 to crafting legislation that would create a commission effectively allowing Taft to choose the building's architect and giving "a free hand to the Architect, subject only to the control of the Commission."[103] This would also prove a delicate, protracted, and difficult task. Without consulting the Court, David Lynn, the architect of the Capitol, who possessed a good many friends in Congress, caused a bill to be introduced that interposed his office between the Court and the building.[104]

Lynn's bill created a Supreme Court building Commission consisting of the chief justice, the chair and the ranking minority member of the Senate Committee on Public Buildings and Grounds, the chair and the ranking minority member of the House Committee on Public Buildings and Grounds, and the architect of the Capitol. Lynn's bill made "the Architect of the Capitol virtually Architect of [the] building," because it appointed the architect of the Capitol the executive officer of the commission and invested the executive officer with "power to appoint consulting architects and others."[105] The bill also gave the architect of the Capitol supervision of the building after it was built. The proposed bill essentially disrupted all of Taft's well-laid plans to ensure Gilbert's selection as the building's architect.

Taft was livid. He had Van Devanter redraft the bill to make Lynn merely the Commission's executive officer, to authorize the Commission to hire "an architect of established national reputation" who would then supervise the construction of the building, and to provide that the architect of the Capitol would be the custodian of the completed Supreme Court building only under "the supervision and direction" of the Court.[106] In a letter of white-hot fury, Taft explained the amendments to Senators Edwards, Warren, Gould, and Swanson, who served on the Senate Public Buildings and Grounds Committee. "I understand that the architect of the Capitol declines to be what he calls a handy man for some other architect though of national reputation," Taft wrote. "Well, we don't insist on having him. . . . It is a very serious matter with us, and we feel very deeply about the mistake that may be made unless we follow the course that has vindicated itself in the selection of the architect."[107]

Taft sent similar angry letters to Senators Ashurst and Fess on the Public Buildings and Grounds Committee[108] and to his old friend Nicholas Longworth, Speaker of the House.[109] He also sent urgent pleas for help to Senators Reed, Shipstead, and Gerry.[110] Taft was hoping to obtain agreement "upon a satisfactory bill. It has given me a great deal of concern, and it has taken me a good deal of time in making clear what we would like in the Court. . . . We are very anxious to have Cass Gilbert as the architect. He is an outstanding figure now among the architects of the country and the World, and we want the best man we can get."[111]

Creating a New Supreme Court Building

On May 10, 1928, Taft did succeed in having his version of the legislation introduced into the House,[112] and a week later he and Van Devanter testified in support of the legislation, over the sullen protestations of Lynn.[113] But Congress was not prepared simply to snub its own architect, and action on the bill was long delayed while a compromise was hammered out. Legislation establishing a "United States Supreme Court Building Commission" was not enacted until December 21, 1928.[114] The legislation provided that the building was "to be so situated, and the exterior thereof to be of such type of architecture and material, as to harmonize with the present buildings of the Capitol group." It altogether sidestepped questions involving the actual construction of the building or its custodianship after it was completed. It kept the architect of the Capitol as a member of the Commission and as its executive officer, although it provided that a second justice of the Court would also be a member of the Commission.[115] It authorized $10,000 for the Commission "to procure, by contract or otherwise, preliminary plans and estimates of costs for the construction, and the furnishing and equipping, of a suitable building . . . for the accommodation and exclusive use of the Supreme Court of the United States." The Commission was to report back to Congress by March 1, 1929.[116]

Taft was satisfied with the compromise because "I think we have arranged for legislation that will enable us to secure" Cass Gilbert's appointment as architect.[117] The Commission itself would procure the required plans, and Taft had spent the summer convincing Commission members that Cass Gilbert was the man to draft them. On June 4, 1928, he had written Senator Henry Keyes, chair of the Senate Public Buildings and Grounds Committee, to the effect that Charles Moore, long-time friend of Taft and chair of the Commission of Fine Arts,

> telephoned me on Saturday last, . . . that he had had a conversation with you and with Mr. Lynn, in which you both said that you were quite willing to allow us, Mr. Justice Van Devanter and myself, to go on the hypothesis that when the bill for the Commission passes, you will use your influence with ours to secure the appointment of Mr. Cass Gilbert as the architect to be given the duty and powers substantially like those in the bill already suggested by us, and that it would be wise to have Mr. Gilbert help in the speedy progress of the building to prepare during the summer the needed sketches and plans, with an estimate of the probable cost, to be submitted to Congress for its consideration after the passage of the bill constituting the Commission.
>
> We had a meeting last night. Mr. Cass Gilbert was here on another matter with his son, Mr. Lynn was good enough to come, Justice Van Devanter was here, and Mr. Frederic Delano, and we talked over the whole matter. Mr. Gilbert discussed it at great length, as indeed did Mr. Lynn. Mr. Gilbert said it was something he had never done before, but with the assurances of the Judges and the probable members of the committee he would go ahead with the work for the purpose of speeding it, in the matter of preparation of preliminary plans and an estimate, assuming the risk in the matter, but depending on our earnest assurance that we would do everything we could to work the matter out as we now are planning it. May I ask you to conform [sic] Mr. Moore's statement with reference to your attitude in the matter?[118]

On June 26, Keyes telegrammed back: "I am very glad to confirm Mr. Moore's statement to you relative to Mr. Gilbert in matter of Supreme Court Building."[119] Taft was delighted, for it was "exactly what I wish, in order that I may show to Mr. Gilbert the basis upon which he may rely in making the sketch of the plans which in order to expedite matters he ought to have ready, with his estimates."[120] "With Keyes in our favor," Taft wrote Van Devanter in July, "and with [the chair and the ranking minority member of the House Committee on Public Buildings and Grounds] Elliott and Lanham, I think we can do something as soon as Congress meets."[121]

By fall 1928, Gilbert was able to report "excellent progress,"[122] and Taft was "delighted to know that things are working themselves out in your mind to meet the difficulties that the situation presents in the matter of the lot."[123] In November, Taft hosted a luncheon of Van Devanter, Stone, and Charles Moore to review Gilbert's plans and sketches.[124] He had wanted to include Lynn,[125] but Gilbert demurred: "I am a little doubtful about going beyond that until the Act of Congress authorizing the work has been passed."[126] By the end of the year, Taft was convinced that Cass Gilbert "has really gotten up a very beautiful building."[127] Gilbert "has been working very hard, because he regards it as his monumental work."[128]

After hosting a dinner for future members of the Supreme Court Building Commission,[129] Taft reported that "They have all practically agreed that we shall select Cass Gilbert as the Architect."[130] Taft's strategy had worked to perfection. Once the legislation creating the Commission passed on December 21, the remaining steps seemed to Taft clear and determinate:

> We shall need an appropriation of upwards of $10,000 to pay for the preliminary sketches and estimates. We shall have to meet and organize, appoint an Architect, who will be Cass Gilbert, and then it will be his business to make the estimates and have them ready on or before the first of March. He will be ready with them, if we are, on or before the first of February. Then will come the struggle as to the amount that Congress will be willing to authorize for the Building. We ought to have $9,000,000. It would not be too much to give us $10,000,000, because we shall be building a building for a century certainly.[131]

Ever the optimist, Taft believed that because Gilbert "has been doing a good deal without authority," the Commission could "get in the sketches and plans and estimates in a month or more."[132]

Once again, however, the way forward lay strewn with brambles. Matters started off auspiciously enough. The minutes of the Commission's first meeting on January 4 recount that Taft, who had been elected chair, "related his consultation with the architect Cass Gilbert upon matters wherein it was felt that the Supreme Court needed advice and suggestions. The chairman asked David Lynn the architect of the Capitol in relation to the standing and ability of Mr. Cass Gilbert, and in answer to this inquiry Mr. Lynn replied that he considered Mr. Gilbert one of the outstanding architects of the city of New York." During the ensuing discussion "it was stated by Senator Reed, that the proposed building should be of such a character that it would reflect the majesty of the United States and the dignity of the Supreme

Creating a New Supreme Court Building

Court of the United States, and that to erect such a building should be the first consideration and question of cost a secondary matter."[133]

At the Commission's second meeting on January 9, over dinner at Taft's home, Cass Gilbert presented his sketches. Senator Reed suggested that it was important to illustrate the plans "by models" as well as by drawings.[134] But the Commission held back from requiring its executive officer to negotiate a contract with Gilbert for the preparation of "plans and specifications," because the deficiency appropriation bill, containing the $10,000 fee for the payment of the contracts, had been held up by a dispute in Congress about prohibition funding.[135] It was uncertain whether the Commission could enter a binding contract without the required appropriated funds. "I hope you will go right on with your work without regard to the appropriation," Taft wrote Gilbert, "for when it passes we want to be in a situation to act at once. ... Don't be impatient, for unless something unfortunate [happens], matters will go on as we desire."[136] The models requested by Senator Reed added to the Commission's embarrassment, however, because the models were estimated to cost approximately $10,000 that could not be advanced out of pocket.[137]

The Commission was required by law to produce its report by March 1, but the deadlock stalling the deficiency bill seemed to stretch on interminably. Gilbert fulfilled his side of the bargain, submitting an estimate of $8,992,000 for the building, exclusive of "fixed or movable furniture and furnishings, mural decoration and sculpture." To account for contingencies, Gilbert recommended an appropriation of $10,000,000.[138] But the Commission remained "in a most exasperating situation."[139] Both the House and Senate agreed to raise the budget of the Commission to $25,000 to pay for the models,[140] but the deficiency bill itself remained mired in seemingly endless controversy. In February, Taft wrote his son about the embarrassment of the delay, because "the time between now" and March 1 "hardly gives us an opportunity to make the report in time."[141]

Something had to be done, and so Taft, working with Richard N. Elliott,[142] the powerful chair of the House Public Buildings and Grounds Committee and member of the Supreme Court Building Commission, sought legislation extending the Commission's deadline. It was a race against time, but on February 23, only a week before the report was due, Congress provided that the report could be postponed until "the first day of the first regular session of the Seventy-first Congress,"[143] which would be in December. The relief was palpable. Even though its funding had not yet materialized, the Commission met on March 3, 1929,[144] and authorized Lynn "to prepare a form of contract with Cass Gilbert ... for the preparation of preliminary plans and estimates of cost and models for the Supreme Court Building."[145] The following day the long-awaited Deficiency Bill finally passed, funding the Commission to the tune of $25,000.[146] In triumph, Taft wrote his daughter, "I am glad to say that we are in a situation now to begin the preliminaries of the work of the new Supreme Court Building. We have selected Cass Gilbert to make the plans."[147]

After so much risk and anticipation, it was a triumphant moment for Gilbert. He confided to his diary: "Thus opens a new chapter in my career and at 70 years of age I am now to undertake to carry through the most important and notable work of my life. God grant me strength, courage and intelligence to do it well."[148] He wrote his wife that he had "asked Chief Justice Taft to give me the pen which he and I used in signing – to which request he smilingly assented. It is a mottled brown penholder with a steel pen. We will keep it as a souvenir."[149] Gilbert was determined to make the edifice "the most perfect and complete monumental building possible, and at the same time meet all of the practical requirements. ... [I]t must, so far as possible, have all the beauty, charm and dignity of the Lincoln Memorial, and all the practical qualities of a first-rate office building – a combination rather difficult to achieve, but nevertheless possible."[150]

Of course, such perfection did not come cheap. Taft worried that "[t]he building is going to be very costly, and I don't know how much effort we shall have to make with the two Houses of Congress to get what we really ought to have."[151] "It is a monumental building, to be made of marble, and is very much more expensive than the ordinary department building which is more in its cost like that of the ordinary office building."[152] The remainder of 1929, however, would prove anticlimactic, a virtual victory lap.[153]

On June 1, the Commission approved its report to Congress.[154] It requested an appropriation of $9,740,000, "exclusive of furniture and book stacks."[155] The Commission met a week later at Taft's hospital bed – Taft had just returned from a week in Cincinnati and the exertion of the railroad trip had caused "an attack of cystitis, due to much alkali in my urine"[156] – to finalize "the bill to be introduced authorizing the construction" of the building.[157] A few days later, bills were introduced in both the House (H.R. 3864)[158] and the Senate (S. 1482),[159] each seeking an appropriation of the $9,740,000 requested by the Commission.[160]

And then nothing much happened, because Taft was "not anxious to press the matter so as to make it too conspicuous."[161] The massive building projects begun earlier in the decade were coming to a climax,[162] and Taft was "hoping the matter may come up in regular form and be passed on as part of the building program."[163] Taft accurately perceived that "the temper of the House and of Congress seems to be toward the expenditure of money for good buildings."[164] The stock market crashed in October, and President Hoover attempted to combat the resulting labor dislocations by sending "telegrams to all state governors, urging them to engage in an 'energetic, yet prudent, pursuit of public works' as a means of absorbing unemployment."[165]

When Congress opened in December, Taft pounced. "I am going out on a campaign tomorrow morning," he told his brother.[166] "I must do something about the Supreme Court Building. Congress has been so slow in the meetings of the committees – indeed in organizing the committees, that we are quite behind and this week I am going to devote myself to lobbying. ... I expect to devote a good deal of time to trying to get the Committee on Buildings and Grounds to appropriate the money necessary to build our Supreme Court Building and to approve the plans."[167]

Taft had a strong ally in Richard N. Elliott. Elliott promptly held hearings that paired consideration of H.R. 3864 with a bill authorizing an increase of

Creating a New Supreme Court Building

$115,000,000 for public buildings in the District of Columbia.[168] His object was plainly to push through the former:

> Ladies and gentlemen, we have already committed ourselves to the construction of the new Supreme Court Building. ... We procured the services of Mr. Cass Gilbert, one of the best architects in the United States, and we had the plans and specifications and estimates prepared, the commission has reported those back to Congress with a unanimous report. ...
>
> This building will necessarily be an expensive building because it has to be rather large to take care of the needs of this court. It has to be an ornamental building for two reasons. One is that the highest court in the land is entitled to it. The other is because it is located among a group of ornamental buildings. ...
>
> The estimate of the cost of this building is $9,740,000. ...
>
> I do not know whether any member of the committee wants any further hearings on this matter or not. If they do not, I would be glad if somebody would move to report this bill for passage.[169]

The bill was unanimously reported to the House. With a speed that no doubt sprang from Congress's respect for Taft and the urgency of his quest, as well perhaps from an awareness of the growing fragility of his health, the bill was enacted into law without opposition on December 20.[170]

It was a triumph for Taft, who at every step had played his cards perfectly. "This has been a great week for me," he wrote his son,

> in that we got through the Supreme Court Bill, and now have sitting in the treasury, subject to call by an appropriation bill, $9,600,000 ready to be spent whenever we need it. Everything is done in respect to the matter, and there is nothing to prevent our building the building except the work. It is a good deal more than I expected. ... Considering the circumstances, I think it is a great achievement. Everybody helped us. There was not any sour person to prevent, and really I was deeply gratified to find how much interest there was in pressing the matter. ... What now remains, so far as I am concerned, is to live long enough to get the building dedicated, but I don't know that I can expect that. However, the step we have taken is irretrievable and can not be changed.[171]

Two weeks later Taft was hospitalized. He would never again return to the Court.

After Taft's formal resignation, Cass Gilbert wrote Taft a note of condolence. "I shall always think of you as the real author of the project and the one to whose vision we shall owe a suitable housing for the Supreme Court of the United States. It will, in fact, be a monument to your honored name."[172] Taft's longtime personal secretary thanked Gilbert for his "kind letter." "I wish I could bring it to the Chief Justice's attention," he wrote, "but I am afraid it is too late to do so. He is in a very weakened condition and he hardly recognizes anyone. ... I know with what pride he selected you as the Architect for the new Supreme Court Building, and I am sorry he can not live to see it erected, for it would be a monument to him."[173] A month later a plaster model of the new Supreme Court building was placed near Taft's casket as he lay in state at the Capitol, to bear "witness to one of Mr. Taft's last contributions to the nation."[174]

Laying the cornerstone of the building that Taft had struggled so mightily to create, Chief Justice Hughes was undoubtedly correct to observe in 1932 that "For the enterprise now progressing to completion ... we are indebted to the late Chief Justice William Howard Taft more than to anyone else. ... [T]his building is the result of his intelligent persistence."[175] In countless ways, the new Supreme Court building embodied Taft's vision of the federal judiciary.[176]

The primary justifications for the building were the "imperative requirements" imposed by "the physical needs of administration."[177] One of Taft's great contributions was to effectively and prominently summon a vision of federal courts as requiring continual management and administrative support. Just as the charm of the Old Senate Chamber meant little without a properly functioning clerk's office, so a prestigious Article III judiciary meant little if it could not efficiently deliver justice. Taft understood this, which is why he pushed so hard for the Act of September 14, 1922. For the same reason, he sought at the end of the decade to create a Court building with the facilities required for efficient managerial functionality. With Gilbert, Taft attempted to ensure that "the practical working elements of the building are as simple and modest and as sanitary as a modern office building should be."[178]

Taft believed that the federal judiciary ought to be as independent as possible. He was committed to the professional autonomy of Article III courts as a separate and equal branch of government. He sought to release judicial appointments from the thumb of political patronage. Leading the Court out from under the Capitol dome, where the Court's every necessity was subject to the political whim of Congress, well expressed this same conviction.[179] The legislation creating the Supreme Court building specified that it would be "for the accommodation and exclusive use of the Supreme Court of the United States."[180] It marked the first moment in its history when the Court could fully control its own space.[181]

The building also signified the equality of the judicial branch within the constitutional tripartite division of powers.[182] Sitting atop a terrace carefully elevated so that the baseline of its columns "corresponded with the base line of columns of the Capitol,"[183] the Court addressed the legislature in a manner "fitting its dignity as one of the three great branches of government."[184] It was an eloquent symbol of the Court's new role after the Judiciary Act of February 13, 1925, which "transformed" the Supreme Court "from a forum that primarily corrected errors arising in ordinary private litigation to a constitutional tribunal that resolved public policy issues of national importance."[185] The Supreme Court was now "the head of the Federal judiciary, and, in a constitutional sense, the head of the Judiciary of the Nation."[186]

The restrained classical design of the Court's new building, its pure white marble exterior, invoked the severe and disinterested virtues necessary for a polity that sought to subject itself to the discipline of law.[187] The Old Senate Chamber had exuded a distinctly different flavor. It was infused with an "easy informality."[188] Justices "often strolled through the public halls, and the procession from the robing

Creating a New Supreme Court Building

room to the courtroom proper was a twice-daily spectacle which tourists always tried to see."[189] In the Court's new home, by contrast, Gilbert deliberately screened off from public view the justices' quarters, entries, and exits.[190] The justices became visible to "the public gaze" only when they magically appeared from behind red curtains to take their seats on the bench, fully robed.[191] In the new courthouse, law became spectacle, detached from ordinary human interaction. Gilbert's building symbolized an ideal of judicial office that stressed formality, abstraction, and authority. In such a setting, the pronouncements of a judge are no longer a communal project. They are instead disinterested words from above or beyond.

It is fair to say that Taft wanted it both ways. He loved judicial authority, but he also loved pressing flesh in living institutions. It is because of the latter that Taft was able to garner legislative support for a new Supreme Court building; but in the design of that building Taft gave himself over entirely to the former. He created a "heaven"[192] of perfect justice that expressed the "purity, eternity, and the majesty of law."[193] But law liberated from grounding in political reality is dangerous rather than inspiring. By the time the Court actually occupied the new building in 1935, it had already thrown down the gauntlet to the New Deal, so that the "white marble temple"[194] began to acquire a hard and cold edge.[195] It would become to some "a building symbolic of the Court's intransigence," a "sepulchral temple of justice."[196]

The generous funding of the new Supreme Court building was made possible by the much larger project of beautifying Washington D.C.[197] Like the Supreme Court building itself, this project was driven by the growing administrative needs of an expanding federal government. Congress chose to address these needs through the architectural metaphor of Augustan Rome.[198] The new federal buildings were the material expression of a postwar Pax Americana.

Cass Gilbert strove for analogous symbolism. He wanted to make the actual Supreme Court courtroom "express the serious beauty and quietly refined splendor of a Courtroom of the classic period of Rome."[199] Taft's brother Henry wrote Gilbert that the courtroom "will be very beautiful, and the selection of the Roman feeling particularly appropriate, as the Romans were the first of the ancients who developed a system of law which has lasted down through the centuries."[200]

The authority of Roman law, however, rested on Roman imperial power. As Gilbert well knew, tropes of Roman architecture instilled thoughts "of the impressive power of Rome."[201] The sociologist David Riesman recalls that Brandeis "with all the power of indignation, detested the building. He hated everything 'Roman' about Washington."[202] Whereas Gilbert sought to instill Americans with "national spirit and patriotic pride" at the august strength of the American state,[203] Brandeis sought just the opposite. He wanted a state that would empower citizens to forge their own destiny.

It is plain that the architectural vocabulary of Gilbert's courtroom instructs its audience passively to receive words spoken from the bench with "respect and reverence."[204] The building as a whole perfectly expresses and radiantly magnifies Taft's response to popular criticisms of the judiciary: courts were never to be degraded by "democratization"[205] but instead to be rendered majestic and powerful. The courtroom of the Supreme Court positions its audience deferentially to receive instruction from elite, professional judges. Within two years of the opening of the building, the positionality of that exchange was to be radically challenged in Roosevelt's court packing plan.

Taft had charged Gilbert to design the building "to last for all time."[206] That meant, as the Building Commission's plans were presented to Congress in 1929, explicitly providing for only "nine suites for justices."[207] The number nine was, as it were, fixed in marble. The *New York Times* passingly observed in 1935 that the building "reflects a confident expectation that nine Supreme Court justices are all we are ever going to have."[208] The nine suites of the building did indeed survive unscathed the thunderous cross-currents of the New Deal constitutional crisis.

Taft, whose reclining figure as a young man was carved in the northern corner of the front portico of the building, would no doubt have liked that outcome. He would fully have approved the Court's subsequent creation of forms of judicial supremacy that have more than fulfilled the august symbolism of Gilbert's building.[209] Having literally worked himself to death to produce a marble incarnation of an idealized image of justice beyond time and politics, Taft has had the last laugh.

But that laugh, if we could actually hear it, would undoubtedly acknowledge what Kent Professor of Constitutional Law Taft at Yale Law School once unconsciously communicated to his student Karl Llewellyn – that the heaven of law is always constructed in the very human "arena" of politics.[210] To the consternation of purists, the unlikely union of the two is forever visible in Taft's incomparable but inimitable efforts to redefine the office of chief justice of the United States.

Creating a New Supreme Court Building
Notes

1. *Residences of the Court: Past and Present: Part II: The Capitol Years*, 3 SUPREME COURT HISTORICAL SOCIETY QUARTERLY 2, 4 (Winter 1981).
2. When laying the cornerstone for the modern Supreme Court building, Chief Justice Charles Evans Hughes was moved to remark that "It is no disparagement of this new enterprise to say that we shall leave that historic room with keen regret. In its dignity, in its simplicity, in its priceless memories as the former Senate chambers and for upwards of seventy years the seat of the Court, that room has no rival. It will be long, indeed, before this beautiful building can boast of the spiritual endowment which has blessed the old home." Charles Evans Hughes, *Address*, 18 AMERICAN BAR ASSOCIATION JOURNAL 728 (1932).
3. Elihu Root to WHT (November 20, 1925) (Taft papers). *See* James M. Beck to Cass Gilbert (November 27, 1933) (Beck papers at Princeton Unniversity).
4. Good descriptions of the Court's difficulties in the old Senate Chamber may be found in the testimony of Taft in Hearings on H.R. 13665, S. 4035, H.R. 5952, S.J. Res. 50, and H.R. 12290 before the House Committee on Public Buildings and Grounds, 70th CONG. 1st SESS. (May 16, 1928), at 3–4, and in the testimony of Van Devanter *id.* at 12–15, 18. In the words of Hughes: "The facilities of the essential offices of Clerk and Marshal have become shockingly insufficient. There is lacking decent provision for the vast accumulation of records. The constantly increasing volumes of the working library for bench and Bar require suitable housing. Counsel in attendance at the Court have been without the simplest conveniences for consultation and preparation for argument. ... Everything considered, I doubt if any high court has performed its tasks with so slender a physical equipment." Hughes, *supra* note 2, at 728.
5. GREGORY HANKIN & CHARLOTTE A. HANKIN, PROGRESS OF THE LAW IN THE U.S. SUPREME COURT 1929–1930, at 5 (Washington D.C.: Legal Research Service 1930).
6. WHT to Charles Curtis (February 26, 1923) (Taft papers). Curtis was the Senate majority leader from 1924 to 1929. He subsequently served as vice president under Herbert Hoover.
7. WHT to Elihu Root (November 22, 1925) (Taft papers).
8. *See supra* Chapter 13, at 477.
9. *See, e.g.*, S. 2727, 50th CONG. 1st SESS. (April 18, 1888); S. 697, 51st CONG. 1st SESS. (January 14, 1890); S. 828, 52nd CONG. 1st SESS. (February 26, 1892); S. 1196, 53rd CONG. 2nd SESS. (December 6, 1893); S. 2492, 54th CONG. 1st SESS. (March 12, 1896).
10. 21 CONG. REC. 3538 (April 19, 1890).
11. 32 CONG. REC. 12 (December 5, 1898).
12. Taft testified to Congress: "The truth is it was the attitude of the two Chief Justices that preceded me that delayed the effort." Hearings on H.R. 13665, S. 4035, H.R. 5952, S.J. Res. 50, and H.R. 12290, *supra* note 4, at 18–19. *See* 54 CONG. REC. 1715–16 (January 19, 1917) (Remarks of James R. Mann) (noting that the Court did not want to leave the Capitol despite their "very scant and insufficient" quarters).
13. Expressing the traditional view of a cloistered and apolitical Court, Illinois Congressman James R. Mann noted in 1917: "The members of the Supreme Court of the United States can not go lobbying. They can not permit one of their

employees to go lobbying. It is beneath their dignity, properly so, to even make a representation in reference to the matter" of a new building. 54 CONG. REC. 1716 (January 19, 1917). Nothing could be further from Taft's sensibility.
14. WHT to Charles Curtis (September 4, 1925) (Taft papers).
15. *Id.* "[I]f we perform any duty to those who come after us we ought to make as much effort as we can to have a separate building." Taft, Hearings on H.R. 13665, S. 4035, H.R. 5952, S.J. Res. 50, and H.R. 12290, *supra* note 4, at 2.
16. On the McMillan Commission, see William Howard Taft, *Washington: Its Beginning, Its Growth, and Its Future*, 27 NATIONAL GEOGRAPHIC MAGAZINE 221, 277-79 (March 1915).
17. The Commission boasted an outstanding membership: Daniel H. Burnham, Frederick Law Olmsted, Jr., Augustus Saint Gaudens, and Charles F. McKim.
18. THE IMPROVEMENT OF THE PARK SYSTEM OF THE DISTRICT OF COLUMBIA, Sen. Rep. No. 166, 57th CONG. 1st SESS. (Charles Moore, ed., Washington D.C.: Government Printing Office 1902), at 38.
19. *See* Pub. L. 61-181, 36 Stat. 371 (May 17, 1910). Taft appointed to the Commission Daniel H. Burnham, Frederick Law Olmsted, Jr., Cass Gilbert, Charles Moore (who had been the private secretary to Senator McMillan), Thomas Hastings, Daniel Chester French, and Francis D. Millet, H. PAUL CAEMMERER, THE COMMISSION OF FINE ARTS 1910-1963 (Washington D.C.: U.S. Commission of Fine Arts 1964).
20. "Unofficially the Commission of Fine Arts are advised that you look with favor upon the idea of erecting a building for the Supreme Court of the United States and are well disposed to a location balancing the Congressional Library." Colonel Sherrill to WHT (December 16, 1921) (Taft papers).
21. Charles Moore to WHT (February 2, 1922) (Taft papers). Taft had appointed Moore to the Commission, see *supra* note 19. Taft would later seek to intervene with President Harding to save Moore's job. *See* WHT to Charles Moore (November 5, 1922) (Taft papers); WHT to Warren G. Harding (September 5, 1922) (Taft papers); WHT to Charles Moore (September 5, 1922) (Taft papers); Charles Moore to WHT (March 10, 1922) (Taft papers); WHT to Cass Gilbert (February 15, 1922) (Taft papers); Francis E. Warren to WHT (February 14, 1922) (Taft papers); WHT to Francis E. Warren (February 11, 1922) (Taft papers); WHT to Cass Gilbert (January 31, 1922) (Taft papers); Cass Gilbert to WHT (January 29, 1922) (Taft papers). During the subsequent struggle to create a separate Supreme Court building, Moore would prove a most valuable ally.
22. WHT to Charles Moore (February 3, 1922) (Taft papers). "I appreciate," Taft nevertheless remarked, "the suggestion of the triangular relation between the three departments of the Government." To Taft's annoyance, the idea was later revived by the New York Chapter of the American Institute of Architects. *See* Elihu Root to WHT (November 20, 1926) (Taft papers); WHT to Charles P. Taft 2nd (November 22, 1925) (Taft papers) ("I think of all the places in the World we would not wish to go, that is it."); WHT to Elihu Root (November 22, 1925) (Taft papers) ("I have always thought that the square corresponding to the Congressional library was the place where our Court Building ought to be in a dignified park-like space, and a building that we can control. I am quite sure that no member of the Court would wish to go down to the place these architects insist upon. I believe in system landscaping, but I think you can carry the analogy between the branches of the Government and the geography of Washington too far. Analogies are all right, but

Creating a New Supreme Court Building

they are mostly used in the pulpit where they are usually wrong."). Herbert Hoover also later revived this idea, see Herbert Hoover to HFS (January 13, 1927) (Stone papers); Cass Gilbert to WHT (November 7, 1928) (Taft papers); WHT to Cass Gilbert (November 9, 1928) (Taft papers); as did Frederic A. Delano, chair of the National Capital Park and Planning Commission. WHT to Cass Gilbert (January 23, 1928) (Gilbert papers at the Supreme Court of the United States); *infra* note 101.

23. WHT to Jules Guerin (December 2, 1922) (Taft papers).
24. *See supra* Chapter 13 at note 16. Taft was even forced to decline an offer to donate Chief Justice Jay's robes to the Court: "The truth is that the quarters of the Court are very contracted. We have luncheon in the Robing Room and haven't room enough even for a sofa upon which to lie down. A few of the Justices are given rooms in the Capitol, but far removed from the Court. The Conference Room is so crowded with our law books that there is no room there." WHT to Mrs. Peter Jay (August 5, 1924) (Taft papers).
25. HFS to WHT (May 25, 1925) (Stone papers).
26. WHT to HFS (May 26, 1925) (Taft papers). As fall approached, Stone grew increasingly frantic about the need for office space, fearing that if he didn't find a house "I shall be about like a stray dog." HFS to WHT (August 30, 1925) (Taft papers). *See* HFS to WHT (October 21, 1925) (Taft papers) ("I have ... received a request from Senator Keyes' clerk requesting me to vacate the room I am now occupying, with the intimation that the sooner I leave the better. Do you think it is too much to ask that the rooms originally assigned to Supreme Court Justices be restored to the Court, and if they are occupied by others, it is only at the sufferance of the Justices entitled to occupy them."). Taft lobbied hard but unsuccessfully for Stone. *See* WHT to Charles Curtis (September 4, 1925) (Taft papers); WHT to HFS (October 22, 1925) (Taft papers). Eventually Senator George Moses of New Hampshire found a room for Stone in the Senate Office Building. HFS to George H. Moses (November 17, 1925) (Taft papers). The room was distant from the Supreme Court library and "below street level" and so "not as well lighted as I would like." HFS to Charles Curtis (November 17, 1925) (Taft papers).
27. HFS to WHT (May 27, 1925) (Taft papers).
28. WHT to Herbert Putnam (May 28, 1925) (Taft papers).
29. WHT to HFS (May 28, 1925) (Taft papers). A number of factors probably contributed to Taft's decision to seek a conference vote at that time. Stone likely constituted a fifth vote in favor of the Court leaving the Capitol. *See infra* note 31. And Taft was of course aware of the large capital building projects then underway in Congress.
30. Taft, Hearings on H.R. 13665, S. 4035, H.R. 5952, S.J. Res. 50, and H.R. 12290, *supra* note 4, at 19.
31. The only remaining documentary record of a vote dates to 1926. *See* WHT, WVD, PB, ETS, HFS to Reed Smoot (June 8, 1926) (Stone papers) ("We, constituting a majority of the members of the Supreme Court, respectively request that you bring before the Building Commission the matter of securing a site for a new Supreme Court Building, in accordance with the provision of the Building Act. We, the undersigned, believe that the best place for a Supreme Court building is the square or block immediately north of the present Congressional Library, and across from and opposite the Capitol grounds."). The four justices opposing the move were apparently Holmes, McReynolds, Brandeis, and Sutherland.

32. WHT to Reed Smoot (July 3, 1925) (Taft papers). Taft laid out the case for a new building:

> Plans have been adopted in the past and bills have been introduced for the erection of such a building, but the conservatism of some of the members, especially the Chief Justices, has interfered with the successful passing of the bill. We have now come, however, to a situation where a majority of the Court is strongly in favor of the construction of a separate building for the Court. Most of the Judges are obliged to have their offices and official studies in their own houses or apartments. As Chief Justice, I have no office at the Capitol and must use the Conference Room and Library of the Court to meet any persons who come to see me at the Capitol, either officially or otherwise. Justice Stone is most embarrassed now by the inability to secure a decent room for himself at the Capitol where he can have his Law Clerk and Secretary do his work. I have pleaded with the Committee of the Senate having control of this matter, and have not been able to secure a proper room for him. The records of the Clerk's office are piling up in such a way as to prevent their being housed in an accessible place. The members of the Bar of the Supreme Court have no place to meet or confer except in the crowded offices of the Clerk. The Marshal's office is greatly congested with his employees. The Library for the Court is so crowded that the shelves have to be carried to the ceiling and the books reached upon step-ladders.

33. Reed Smoot to WHT (July 6, 1925) (Taft papers). Smoot wrote, "There should be enough, if I get this full appropriation, to construct a building for the sole use of the Supreme Court, as suggested in your letter. I know the needs of the Supreme Court for office space. I know that it should have a building constructed in the District for the sole use of the Supreme Court. If we get into a fight on the floor, however, either in the Senate or House, as to just how this money will be expended it may defeat the whole bill."
34. *See Address of the President*, 65 CONG. REC. 96, 99 (December 6, 1923).
35. "President Hoover said that there was need for additional building to house the 70,000 Federal employees, whose number was now twice that of a score of years ago." *Hoover Acclaims Beautified Capital*, NEW YORK TIMES (April 26, 1929), at 14.
36. *See* JOHN W. REPS, MONUMENTAL WASHINGTON: THE PLANNING AND DEVELOPMENT OF THE CAPITAL CENTER 169 (Princeton University Press 1967). When Herbert Hoover became Secretary of Commerce, for example, the Department consisted of "congeries of independent bureaus" that "were housed in fifteen different buildings, mostly rented, and some of them condemned by the District of Columbia fire and health departments." HERBERT HOOVER, THE MEMOIRS OF HERBERT HOOVER: THE CABINET AND THE PRESIDENCY: 1920–1933, at 42 (New York: MacMillan Co. 1952). Hoover recalls that "In 1924, when the new building program for the Departments was authorized by Congress, I secured that the first of these building should be for the Commerce Department. The building was not completed during my term as Secretary, so that for eight years I occupied a corner room of a rented apartment building on Nineteenth Street, especially superheated for summer." *Id.* at 44.
37. *See generally* Emmet Dougherty, *$50,000,000 To Add Beauty and Dignity to Capital's Skyline: Stately Edifices of Classic Design to Accommodate an Army of Clerks*, NEW YORK HERALD TRIBUNE (August 15, 1926), § 3, at 3; Charles H. Whitaker, *Building for the Glory of Washington*, NEW YORK TIMES (March 6, 1927), Magazine at 6.

Creating a New Supreme Court Building

38. Anne O'Hare McCormick, *Building the Greater Capital: A New Washington Rises as the Symbol of America's New Status*, NEW YORK TIMES (May 26, 1929), Magazine at 1.

> The real pressure behind the new Washington is the new America. We have heard a good deal during the past few years of the United States as a great world power, perhaps the greatest. But that conception of our place in the international scheme is new to Americans, and in the country at large has been discounted as political hyperbole. Very slowly the legend has acquired the vitality of a fact, predicated not upon a vague political pre-eminence but upon the clear evidence of our mechanistic supremacy. We begin to see ourselves first among the nations by the tangible standards the populace recognizes – wages, motor power, plumbing. Gradually our primacy has impressed ourselves. The capital, says Mr. Hoover, is "the symbol of the nation."

Id. In 1929, the American Institute of Architects issued a report approving the plan to beautify Washington, proclaiming that "The country at large has caught the idea of a great capital truly representative of the genius and power of the nation." *Would Speed Plan to Beautify Capital*, NEW YORK TIMES (April 24, 1929), at 30. President Hoover approved the Institute's report, declaring in a speech "that in design and utility the new structures should be the symbol of America and the lasting inspiration of the present and future generations." *Hoover Acclaims Beautified Capital, supra* note 35, at 14.

Contrasting American preeminence with Roman dominion, which was based upon "military force," Reinhold Niebuhr proclaimed in the popular press: "We are the first empire of the world to establish our sway without legions. Our legions are dollars. Our empire was developed almost overnight. At the beginning of the World War we were still in debt to the world. . . . [But] our economic relationship to the world was completely altered by the war. We wiped out our debt and put the world in our debt by well-nigh thirty billion dollars in little more than a decade." Reinhold Niebuhr, *Awkward Imperialists*, 145 ATLANTIC MONTHLY 670 (1930). During the 1920s, the United States became "the world's biggest lender, and its economy was the largest in the world: by 1929, it produced 42 percent of the world's output (Great Britain, France, and Germany together produced 28 percent)." JILL LEPORE, THESE TRUTHS: A HISTORY OF THE UNITED STATES 406 (New York: W.W. Norton & Co. 2018).

39. McCormick, *supra* note 38, at 1. The focus on Roman architectural themes dated back at least to the McMillan Commission. *See* Sonja Duempelmann, *Creating Order with Nature: Transatlantic Transfer of Ideas in Park System Planning in Twentieth-Century Washington D.C., Chicago, Berlin and Rome*, 24 PLANNING PERSPECTIVES 143 (2009).

40. Fitzhugh L. Minnigerode, *Washington Doffs Its Brick for Marble: White Masterpieces of Architecture Replace Old Red Buildings as Townsmen Join the Government in Beautification Plan*, NEW YORK TIMES (September 21, 1930), Magazine at 18. "The most notable buildings either recently erected or soon to be erected include the Departments of Commerce, Justice, Posts and Labor. Then we shall see arise in majesty a new building for the Supreme Court, another for the Interstate Commerce Commission, the Archives Building, Independent Offices Building, House of Representatives Annex and a number of lesser ones." *Id.*

41. On the general plan to beautify Washington, see Andrew W. Mellon, *The Development of Washington*, 20 AMERICAN MAGAZINE OF ART 1 (January 1929). The normally miserly Mellon stressed the importance of providing "a magnificent setting for the requirements of modern civilization"; he believed that the city of Washington should be clothed in "that beauty and dignity to which it is entitled." *Id.* at 9.
42. WHT to Robert A. Taft (April 18, 1926) (Taft papers).
43. 67 CONG. REC. 8667-73 (May 4, 1926). On the floor, Smoot argued that the Department of Justice needed a new building far more than the Supreme Court. "We have those employees in temporary buildings ... that are liable to fall down at any time. The Supreme Court is not suffering, nor are Senators suffering, as those people are." *Id.* at 8668. Smoot dismissed Moses's point that most of the justices were forced to work at home by observing that "the Senator knows that they would have offices at home, whether they had two or three rooms down here or not," because they "take their work home at night, and would do it no matter what might happen in the way of getting larger quarters." *Id.* at 8668-69.
44. Catherine Hetos Skefos, *Strictly Construction: The Supreme Court Gets a Home*, 1976 YEARBOOK OF THE SUPREME COURT HISTORICAL SOCIETY 25, 30. *See* WHT to HFS (May 11, 1926) (Stone papers); WHT to Richard N. Elliott (May 11, 1926) (Taft papers); WHT to George H. Moses (May 11, 1926) (Taft papers); WHT to Robert A. Taft (June 17, 1926) (Taft papers).
45. Pub. L. 69-281, 44 Stat. 631 (May 25, 1926); Conference Report, H.R. Report No. 1223 on H.R. 6559, 69th CONG. 1st SESS. (May 17, 1926). Brandeis was disappointed. "I hadn't heard that the U.S.S.C. building project has been killed," he wrote Frankfurter. "I hope so." LDB to Felix Frankfurter (May 23, 1926), in BRANDEIS-FRANKFURTER CORRESPONDENCE, at 241. After the passage of the Act, however, the dissenting justices acquiesced to the decision. Taft later testified that "They all agreed to it after the thing was decided. They are all in favor of it now." Hearings on H.R. 13665, S. 4035, H.R. 5952, S.J. Res. 50, and H.R. 12290, *supra* note 4, at 19.

Two months after passage of the Act, Taft wrote his colleagues asking for suggestions about the new building. Brandeis replied, "The matter of the Supreme Court building I leave wholly to you." LDB to WHT (July 20, 1926) (Taft papers). *See* WHT to OWH (July 21, 1926) (Holmes papers); GS to WHT (August 9, 1926) (Taft papers); ETS to WHT (August 8, 1926) (Taft papers) (Sanford consulted with Milton Medary, Jr., president of the American Institute of Architects, who recommended hiring a "great architect" who could then propose the "plan best adapted to house the physical necessities and express in suitable form the dignity and position of the head of a co-ordinate branch of the Government. He knows of no previous effort to do this – the courts of the various countries being generally housed as adjuncts of the legislative branches."); WHT to ETS (August 21, 1926) (Taft papers). Stone apparently returned so many suggestions that Taft was forced to caution him: "I shall forward them to Moore, but of course this is most informal, and when the matter comes up seriously for consideration, we shall have to discuss it very fully in conference." WHT to HFS (July 27, 1926) (Stone papers).

McReynolds made the most constructive and useful suggestion: "Some valuable information might be obtained by inspecting the quarters provided for the courts of the larger States." JCM to WHT (July 27, 1926) (Taft papers). A week later Taft

Creating a New Supreme Court Building

   instructed his secretary "to write to all the chief Justices of the Supreme Courts of the various States ... requesting them to send him a description of their Supreme Court buildings, for use in constructing the new building for the Supreme Court." Wendell W. Mischler to William R. Stansbury (August 7, 1926) (Taft papers). It was as a result of this inquiry that Cass Gilbert eventually came to Taft's attention. *See infra* text at notes 79–84.
46. Taft wrote his son that by altering the authorization bill, Taft had "interfered with Smoot's plans ... and he is not disposed to help us. ... I have written to other members of the committee, and I think they are quite inclined to help, but Smoot is a dominating kind of fellow and he is hard to beat in that kind of thing and is a cheese-pairing, small-minded kind of fellow without any imagination. He would be glad to include us with the Department of Justice or some other court. He has no soul above small matters." WHT to Robert A. Taft (June 17, 1926) (Taft papers).
47. *See supra* Chapter 9, at 378.
48. WHT, WVD, PB, ETS, HFS to Reed Smoot (June 8, 1926) (Stone papers); *see* WHT to WVD (June 8, 1926) (Van Devanter papers) ("I am anxious that this matter be pressed, and therefore I want to take formal action by the majority of the Court, so that we may require the Commission to give attention.").
49. *See, e.g.*, WHT to Senator Claude A. Swanson (June 8, 1926) (Stone papers) ("The majority of the Court have applied to Senator Smoot, as Chairman of the Building Commission, asking your Commission to take steps to authorize the acquisition of the lot just north of the Congressional Library for a Supreme Court building, in accordance with the Act, and I write to ask you to promote the matter as far as you can as a member of the commission. ... After the proceedings are begun, of course nothing can be done in the way of building or adding to the damages to be imposed on the Government. Quick action, therefore, would be in the interest of economy."). Taft sent this same letter to Commission members Representative Fritz G. Lanham, Representative Richard N. Elliott, David Lynn (architect of the Capitol), James A. Vetmore (supervising architect of the Treasury), and Major U.S. Grant (executive officer of the Commission). *See also* WHT to Charles Moore (June 8, 1926) (Stone papers); Richard N. Elliott to WHT (June 9, 1926) (Stone papers) ("I will be glad to do anything I can to assist you get the site for the Supreme Court as you requested."); Claude A. Swanson to WHT (June 9, 1926) (Stone papers); Reed Smoot to WHT (June 9, 1926) (Stone papers); Fritz G. Lanham to WHT (June 10, 1926) (Stone papers); Charles Moore to WHT (June 10, 1926) (Stone papers) ("Smoot has called a meeting of the two Commissions on June 17th, and there is no question that the Commission of Fine Arts will stand by their recommendation" to purchase the lot north of the Library of Congress); David Lynn to WHT (June 10, 1926) (Stone papers) ("I will do everything in my power to bring about the acquisition of this lot as a site for the future home of the Supreme Court."); WHT to Richard N. Elliott (June 10, 1926) (Stone papers); WHT to Claude A. Swanson (June 10, 1926) (Stone papers); WHT to Reed Smoot (June 10, 1926) (Stone papers); WHT to Charles Moore (June 11, 1926) (Taft papers). Taft also lobbied Treasury Secretary Andrew Mellon. WHT to Andrew Mellon (June 11, 1926) (Taft papers).
50. WHT to Robert A. Taft (June 17, 1926) (Taft papers).
51. WVD to PB (June 21, 1926) (Van Devanter papers). Although Taft regarded Van Devanter and Stone as "the committee of the Court to attend to this matter," WHT to

THE TAFT COURT

WVD (June 8, 1927) (Van Devanter papers), the incident related by Van Devanter makes clear why both he and Taft came increasingly to distrust Stone's practical good sense. "The trouble with our dear friend Stone," Taft wrote Van Devanter, "is that he is too full of views and not too full of tact. I can hear him lecturing to Mellon on the mistakes of architecture in all the public buildings of Washington except the Capitol, the White House, the Lincoln Memorial, and the Washington Monument." WHT to WVD (June 29, 1927) (Van Devanter papers).

52. Will P. Kennedy, *New Home Needed by Supreme Court*, WASHINGTON EVENING STAR (July 21, 1926), at 2. *See* Carson C. Hathaway, *At Last a Home for the Supreme Court*, NEW YORK TIMES (September 26, 1926), Magazine at 13.

53. WHT to George H. Moses (October 3, 1926) (Taft papers); WHT to Charles Moore (November 8, 1926) (Taft papers) ("I saw Senator Smoot yesterday, and I gathered the impression, from what he said, that the Building Commission was to meet this week and to put everything through.... While Smoot demurred to having a Supreme Court building at all, and suggested that it might be wise to wait until the Capitol was enlarged and to put the Supreme Court in there, I rather think that he yielded to the suggestion that was provided in the law and that we should have a lot, and that he will be in favor of that lot. He says it will have to be condemned, because the idea of the owners as to the value of the lot is rapidly expanding.").

54. WHT to Charles Moore (November 24, 1926) (Taft papers). *See* WHT to WVD (November 24, 1926) (Taft papers). Taft ultimately turned out to be correct.

55. WHT to Charles Moore (January 1, 1927) (Taft papers).

56. H.M. Lord to WHT (December 22, 1926) (Taft papers) (The assistant secretary of the Treasury "states that it would interfere, to some extent, with their consideration of this matter as a whole if a special estimate for the Supreme Court building site was submitted in advance with a view to its inclusion in the urgent deficiency bill.").

57. "I supposed they were intending to act as expeditiously as possible and am a little disappointed to find it is otherwise. But as there will be need for their cooperation later on I am disposed to believe it better to let the matter take the course they have selected." Handwritten return by WVD on letter from WHT to WVD (December 27, 1926) (Taft papers).

58. WHT to Charles Moore (January 2, 1927) (Taft papers); WHT to Charles P. Taft 2nd (January 2, 1927) (Taft papers); WHT to Charles Moore (December 28, 1927) (Taft papers).

59. *Communication from the President of the United States Transmitting Supplemental Estimate of Appropriation for the Treasury Department for the Fiscal Year Ending June 30, 1927, for the Acquisition of a Site for a Building for the Supreme Court of the United States, $1,700,000*, H.R. Doc. No. 655, 69th CONG. 2nd SESS. (January 18, 1927).

60. Conference Report, H.R. Report No. 1972 for H.R. 16462, Urgent Deficiency Appropriation Bill, 1927, 69th CONG. 2nd SESS. (February 3, 1927); WHT to Claude A. Swanson (January 25, 1927) (Taft papers); WHT to Charles P. Taft 2nd (January 30, 1927) (Taft papers).

61. "Congress is very exasperating. I am afraid I may lose my appropriation for the Supreme Court lot. I got it along famously and I thought I was going to get it through quickly. It was in the Urgent Deficiency Bill. But they have got into a row over that bill between the two Houses ... and I don't know what is going to happen." WHT to

Creating a New Supreme Court Building

Charles P. Taft 2nd (February 20, 1927) (Taft papers). "I got it into the Urgent Deficiency Bill because I thought it would go through more quickly than if it waited for the General Deficiency Bill, and now it looks as if the General Deficiency Bill might go through and that the Urgent Deficiency Bill might fail. I am going to see what I can do about it." WHT to Robert A. Taft (February 20, 1927) (Taft papers).

62. WHT to Charles P. Taft 2nd (February 27, 1927) (Taft papers). Ironically, Congress had "got a filibuster which seems likely to beat the last deficiency bill in which a great many things necessary are provided for.... By great good luck, I got my appropriation for the Supreme Court lot through in the first and urgent deficiency bill. I thought I was going to lose that, but it has gone through and we are now engaged in seeking to negotiate the purchase of the property preliminary to condemnation proceedings." WHT to George D. Seymour (March 3, 1927) (Taft papers). On the filibuster, see *The Filibuster at Its Worst*, 92 LITERARY DIGEST 5 (March 19, 1927).

63. WHT to Robert A. Taft (November 17, 1928) (Taft papers). *See* WHT to Henry H. Glassie (July 19, 1928) (Taft papers) ("excruciatingly exasperating").

64. WHT to William D. Mitchell (May 25, 1927) (Taft papers).

65. The deficiency bill that was necessary to pay for the costs of condemnation over and above the $1.5 million already appropriated ended up mired in controversy and was not passed until March 4, 1929. Pub. L. 70-1034, 45 Stat. 1614 (March 4, 1929). *See* WHT to William R. Wood (February 4, 1929) (Taft papers); WHT to Robert A. Taft (February 3, 1929) (Taft papers); Mrs. Burnita Shelton Matthews to WHT (February 6, 1929) (Taft papers); WHT to Mrs. Burnita Shelton Matthews (February 7, 1929) (Taft papers). After the deficiency bill passed, moreover, the Treasury department still delayed full payment until all claims on the condemned property were conclusively settled. Mrs. Burnita Shelton Matthews to WHT (March 7, 1929) (Taft papers); WHT to Mrs. Burnita Shelton Matthews (March 9, 1929) (Taft papers).

66. *See supra* note 54; WHT to Charles P. Taft 2nd (November 26, 1928) (Taft papers) ("The result vindicates our judgment, and is a reason too for our feeling that the result is about right."); WHT to Henry H. Glassie (November 22, 1928) (Taft papers).

67. WHT to Robert A. Taft (December 2, 1928) (Taft papers); WHT to Cass Gilbert (December 7, 1928) (Taft papers). The passage of that deficiency bill was in turn delayed. *See supra* note 65.

68. WHT to HFS (June 28, 1927) (Stone papers).

69. William D. Mitchell to WHT (May 24, 1927) (Taft papers); WVD to WHT (June 15, 1927) (Van Devanter papers); WHT to WVD (June 22, 1927) (Van Devanter papers); WVD to WHT (June 25, 1927) (Van Devanter papers); WHT to HFS (June 28, 1927) (Stone papers); WHT to William D. Mitchell (August 12, 1927) (Taft papers).

70. *Women to Keep A "Watch Tower" Facing Capitol*, NEW YORK TIMES (May 9, 1921), at 1.

71. Elsie Hill, temporary chair of the party, quoted in *Women Will Ask Equality in Law*, NEW YORK TIMES (March 21, 1921), at 15. On the history of the party, see CHRISTINE A. LUNARDINI, FROM EQUAL SUFFRAGE TO EQUAL RIGHTS: ALICE PAUL AND THE NATIONAL WOMAN'S PARTY, 1910–1928 (New York University Press 1986); Peter Geidel, *National Woman's Party and the Origins of the Equal Rights Amendment, 1920–23*, 42 HISTORIAN 557 (August 1980).

THE TAFT COURT

72. WHT to Robert A. Taft (November 17, 1928) (Taft papers). "It is just a broken down old building that ought to be removed," said Taft, "but they are a lot of women who are most unprincipled and attempting to use every method possible to squeeze up the amount they are to derive from the Government." *Id.* Charles Moore, chair of the Commission of Fine Arts, considered the historical claims entirely frivolous in light of the drastic architectural changes undergone by the building. Charles Moore to WHT (November 22, 1926) (Taft papers); WHT to Charles Moore (November 24, 1926) (Taft papers). The NWP had purchased the building in 1921 for $134,000, and was seeking to receive $1,000,000 for it during the condemnation proceedings seven years later. 69 CONG. REC. 10374–75 (May 28, 1928) (Remarks of Michigan Representative Louis C. Cramton). Eventually the NWP would receive $299,200. *See infra* note 76.
73. In June 1927, Taft wrote Van Devanter:

> Stone was inclined to urge the Treasury Dept to make some purchases of the lots in the land we seek without condemnation from the Woman's Party.... I discouraged him about this. The Woman's Party would never consent to a reasonable price. They want to include as an element the historical associations of that ramshackle house of theirs. The Treasury would never consent, and it ought not to do so until by condemnation some idea of the proper ratio between the tax assessment and the market value is established. I hope we are not going to have trouble about our plans and architect but this is very tender ground. I think we could take the matter over to ourselves if we wished to make a fight but the softer way is the better way and I think we can count on Mellon's reasonableness.

WHT to WVD (June 29, 1927) (Van Devanter papers).
74. WHT to WVD (July 10, 1928) (Van Devanter papers).
75. S.J. Res. 156, 70th CONG. 1st SESS. (May 3, 1928); 69 CONG. REC. 9057–58 (May 18, 1928); WHT to Harold Phelps Stokes (May 31, 1928) (Taft papers); Henry H. Glassie to WHT (July 6, 1928) (Taft papers). *See Protests Removal of Old Capitol*, EQUAL RIGHTS (June 23, 1928), at 157 ("Our country is not so rich in historic landmarks that we can afford to sacrifice even to an object as worthy as a site for the Supreme Court, a structure so identified with our heroic past."); *The Old Capitol*, EQUAL RIGHTS (June 30, 1928), at 163; *The Old Brick Capitol*, EQUAL RIGHTS (August 25, 1928), at 231. Taft noted with cold political calculation that "the claims of the Woman's Party will turn the stomach of a good many who are willing to vote resolutions when it does not cost anything. More than that, the Woman's party will cease to be important after the election." WHT to Van Devanter (July 10, 1928) (Van Devanter papers). *See* WHT to Cass Gilbert (July 31, 1928) (Taft papers).
76. WHT to Charles P. Taft 2nd (November 25, 1928). Taft wrote his son after the jury verdicts in the condemnation proceedings that the NWP was "content with the award, they need the money, and I hope we can get the thing through. I am to see the women tomorrow morning, but 'There is many a slip twixt cup and the lip', especially in anything that depends on Congress, so you must pray for me." WHT to Robert A. Taft (December 2, 1928) (Taft papers). The NWP eventually received $299,200 for its property. *The Old Brick Capitol Goes to Supreme Court*, EQUAL RIGHTS (December 29, 1928), at 371. It promptly purchased a new headquarters at 2nd and B Streets (NW) for $100,000. *Woman's Party Buys New Home at Capital*, NEW YORK TIMES (March 28, 1929), at 24.

Creating a New Supreme Court Building

77. Taft had presented the Lincoln Memorial to the nation on May 30, 1922. *Harding Dedicates Lincoln Memorial: Blue and Gray Join*, NEW YORK TIMES (May 31, 1922), at 1.
78. WHT to Reed Smoot (July 3, 1925) (Taft papers). The drawings are reproduced in Kennedy, *supra* note 52, and in Hathaway, *supra* note 52. Hathaway writes that "Plans for the structure were drawn by Henry Bacon before his death in February 1924." In 1926, *Time Magazine* showed the justices beaming "benignly at the design for the New Supreme Court building by the late Henry Bacon." *Supreme Court: Grey Wigs*, 8 TIME MAGAZINE 8 (October 11, 1926). In 1922, Taft had written a correspondent that "Of course no one would suit me better than Mr. Bacon" as an architect for a new Supreme Court building. WHT to Jules Guerin (December 2, 1922) (Taft papers).
79. The idea for these inquiries came from McReynolds. *See supra* note 45.
80. Gilbert, comments Geoffrey Blodgett, had "acquired in his youth a conventional reverence for the 'eternal truths' of classical civilization." Geoffrey Blodgett, *The Politics of Public Architecture*, in CASS GILBERT, LIFE AND WORK: ARCHITECT OF THE PUBLIC DOMAIN 65 (Barbara S. Christen & Steven Flanders, eds., New York: W.W. Norton & Co. 2001). Upon Gilbert's death in 1934, it was said that "The list of his most important buildings only would be long enough to prove him the most remarkable architect of his generation in America." *Cass Gilbert Dead: Eminent Architect*, NEW YORK TIMES (May 18, 1934), at 23. Gilbert's reputation has suffered somewhat in the intervening years. *See* Geoffrey Blodgett, *Cass Gilbert, Architect: Conservative at Bay*, 72 JOURNAL OF AMERICAN HISTORY 615 (1985).
81. ANN THOMAS WILKINS & DAVID G. WILKINS, CASS GILBERT'S WEST VIRGINIA STATE CAPITOL (Morgantown: West Virginia University Press 2014).
82. Cass Gilbert to WHT (September 25, 1926) (Gilbert papers in the New York Historical Society). I am grateful to Franz Jantzen for this reference.
83. Blodgett, *The Politics of Public Architecture*, *supra* note 80, at 69.
84. Cass Gilbert to WHT (September 25, 1926) (Gilbert papers in the New York Historical Society).
85. *See supra* note 19. Taft had written Gilbert in 1924: "I look back upon my association with you with the utmost pleasure, and have had the utmost satisfaction in noting the great work you have done in your profession, the monuments you have built to yourself and the honor you have brought to American architecture." WHT to Cass Gilbert (November 27, 1924) (Taft papers). *See* Cass Gilbert to WHT (May 18, 1925) (Taft papers); WHT to Cass Gilbert (May 20, 1925) (Taft papers).
86. On Gilbert's political beliefs, see Blodgett, *The Politics of Public Architecture*, *supra* note 80, at 71. Gilbert would later bitterly oppose the New Deal, observing that "We are sick of doctrinaires, grain trusters, communists, socialists, and politicians in and out of office." Gilbert believed that the Court stood "for the preservation of the rights of the minority – for liberty under law." *Id*.
87. Charles Moore to Cass Gilbert (June 12, 1929) (Gilbert papers at the Library of Congress).
88. Cass Gilbert to Maurice Webb (January 10, 1928) (Gilbert papers at the Library of Congress), quoted in Blodgett, *Cass Gilbert, Architect*, *supra* note 80, at 628. As Gilbert would later write, "The Supreme Court Building ... is built of white marble and it is as pure in style as I can make it. I hope it will cause some reaction against

577

the silly modernistic movement that has had such a hold here for the last few years." Cass Gilbert to Sir Reginald Blomfield (April 5, 1933) (Gilbert papers at the Library of Congress).

89. Cass Gilbert to WVD (November 18, 1926) (Van Devanter papers). Although I have not been able to locate Gilbert's letter to Taft, in Taft's Daily "to-do" memorandum of November 20, 1926, is the notation "Answer Cass Gilbert." It is likely that Gilbert met with Taft and Van Devanter in October to discuss the project. Internal evidence suggests that "Bacon's plan" for the building was Gilbert's "starting point." Alan Greenberg & Stephen Kieran, *The United States Supreme Court Building, Washington D.C.*, 128 ANTIQUES 760, 763 (October 1985). *See* Paul Spencer Byard, *Representing American Justice: The United States Supreme Court*, in CASS GILBERT, LIFE AND WORK, *supra* note 80, at 278.

90. Cass Gilbert to WHT (December 12, 1926) (Gilbert papers at the Supreme Court of the United States).

91. Gilbert's letter explains: "The Ground Story would be all above the ground level and provide ample well lighted rooms about 12' high. There would of course be private entrances and service entrances at the ground story level. And in this story there will be large spaces available for the Clerk, the Marshall, for files and other usage. A slight revision of the space in the Main Story provides rooms for the use of the Attorney General and the Solicitor General when they come to the Supreme Court."

92. WHT to Cass Gilbert (March 9, 1927) (Gilbert papers at the Supreme Court of the United States). Taft, ever wily and sophisticated, continued: "I have thought, however, that it might be well if in the course of a month, I could have a Sunday luncheon here in Washington, with the Secretary of the Treasury and his advisory architect, who comes from Chicago, but is now in California, the three Justices who are more directly interested, Justice Van Devanter, Justice Stone and myself, and Senator Moses, and possibly Senator Smoot, so that we can talk over the matter with a view to formulating definite action."

A word should be said about the attitude of Stone. After the completion of the building, Stone was said to be highly disparaging of it, calling it "wholly inappropriate for a quiet group of old boys such as the Supreme Court." Quoted in ELDER WITT, GUIDE TO THE U.S. SUPREME COURT 781 (2nd ed., Washington D.C.: Congressional Quarterly 1990). "I wonder if we look like the nine beetles in the Temple of Karnak," Cardozo remembers him joking. Quoted in Arthur John Keeffe, *The Marble Palace at 50*, 68 AMERICAN BAR ASSOCIATION JOURNAL 1224, 1229 (1982). "Whenever I look at that building," Stone reportedly said, "I feel that the justices should ride to work on elephants." DREW PEARSON & ROBERT S. ALLEN, NINE OLD MEN 9 (Garden City: Doubleday, Doran & Co. 1937). In May 1935, Stone wrote his sons that the building was "almost bombastically pretentious." Quoted in CLARE CUSHMAN, COURTWATCHERS: EYEWITNESS ACCOUNTS IN SUPREME COURT HISTORY 110 (Lanham: Rowan & Littlefield 2011). A few months later Stone wrote Charles Burlingham that "It makes me sad to think" about "Cass Gilbert's Palace of Justice," and "sadder when I see it, especially its interior." HFS to Charles C. Burlingham (October 4, 1935) (Stone papers). *See* Charles C. Burlingham to HFS (October 3, 1935) (Stone papers).

These reactions are hard to reconcile with the fact that throughout the 1920s Stone was intimately involved in Gilbert's planning, as is suggested by Taft's letter to Gilbert of March 9, 1927. In 1927, for example, Stone wrote Gilbert to say that "the Chief Justice had shown to me the sketches which you had prepared for a Supreme Court Building. I took them home with me and went over them with Mrs. Stone. We found them of absorbing interest and an inspiring suggestion of what could be accomplished in the way of a new building. I would like to have the opportunity sometime to go over them with you to make some suggestions which occur to me which might be of interest to you. I would like very much to see you chosen to prepare the plans. If there is anything I can do to accomplish that end, I hope you will let me know." HFS to Cass Gilbert (March 24, 1927) (Stone papers). *See* Cass Gilbert to HFS (March 30, 1927) (Stone papers). Stone wrote New York lawyer William Nelson Cromwell that "Confidentially, I very much hope that Cass Gilbert will be the architect of the new Supreme Court Building." HFS to William Nelson Cromwell (October 22, 1928) (Stone papers). After receiving a photograph of Gilbert's more developed ideas, Cass Gilbert to HFS (January 15, 1929) (Stone papers), Stone replied: "We are on the way to have a most beautiful building. Certainly the photograph you sent is a delight to the eye. I think the classical form which you have given it is the only adequate treatment." HFS to Cass Gilbert (January 17, 1929) (Stone papers). *See* HFS to Cass Gilbert (January 9, 1929) (Stone papers). After receiving a rendering of the final model of the building, Stone exclaimed: "It seems to me that you have designed a building which is, at the same time, unique and dignified, and appropriate to its setting." HFS to Cass Gilbert (October 7, 1929) (Stone papers). *See* Cass Gilbert to HFS (October 4, 1929) (Stone papers). After the completion of the building, "when a guest at one of the Brandeis Sunday teas remarked that Stone was complaining about the building and about the acoustics and lighting in the courtroom, Brandeis, recalled his law clerk Paul Freund, replied hotly, 'Well, he voted for it!'" DAVID M. O'BRIEN, STORM CENTER: THE SUPREME COURT IN AMERICAN POLITICS 156 (3rd ed., New York: W.W. Norton & Co. 1993).

93. "If you are willing to go on with the work, at your own risk, I shall be glad." WHT to Cass Gilbert (January 23, 1928) (Gilbert papers at the Supreme Court of the United States).
94. WHT to HFS (June 28, 1927) (Stone papers).
95. WVD to WHT (June 25, 1927) (Van Devanter papers).
96. *Id.*
97. WVD to Cass Gilbert (June 25, 1927) (Van Devanter papers). With the exquisite care and tact for which he was so well known, Van Devanter added, "My interest in the subject is only that of getting an entirely suitable building for the Court and as the tentative drawings which you have submitted have elicited my admiration I suggest that you take the course indicated by the Secretary of the Treasury."
98. WVD to WHT (June 28, 1927) (Van Devanter papers); WHT to HFS (June 28, 1927) (Stone papers); WHT to WVD (July 1, 1927) (Van Devanter papers); WHT to WVD (July 2, 1927) (Taft papers); WVD to WHT (July 5, 1927) (Taft papers) ("If Gilbert can handle himself well with Bennett the way will be open to get our building substantially under our own control. Congress will wish to do what is right about it. . . . If Secretary Mellon remains at his present post, there probably will be no trouble; his good sense may be depended on."); WVD to WHT (July 7, 1927) (Taft papers) ("If Gilbert does his part well there is little doubt that the building matter will move along nicely."); WVD to WHT (July 19, 1927) (Van Devanter

papers) ("The marked part of Gilbert's letter to me suggests that he does not understand the matter as I do. According to my information Bennett was not desiring to see Gilbert, but we were assuming that Gilbert was wishing to see Bennett and we were endeavoring to bring them together.").

99. Cass Gilbert to WHT (August 3, 1927) (Gilbert papers at the Supreme Court of the United States). *See* WHT to WVD (August 4, 1927) (Van Devanter papers) (Quoting from Gilbert's telegram: "I had a long conference with Mr. Bennett at my office this morning. He is in hearty sympathy and will act in cooperation. He likes the design and is favorable to my appointment."). In November, Taft reported to his daughter that "Secretary Mellon is very anxious to help us and he is in a position to do so, and I am counting on him." WHT to Mrs. Frederick J. Manning (November 13, 1927) (Taft papers).

100. Cass Gilbert to Edward H. Bennett (September 15, 1927) (Gilbert papers at the Supreme Court of the United States). Gilbert initially rejected Bennett's suggestions: "I agree with you that it would be well to have this façade parallel with the street but if I must choose between that and an unsymmetrical building, I feel sure that you will agree with me that in a building of such serious and monumental character symmetry should be preserved even if one of the lesser facades does not align with the street .... [S]ince our conversation I have thought many times of your suggestion of another location. I think however that the problem will have to be solved in the location now selected. The situation then that exists is this, that we have the Library of Congress, which is out of scale with everything around it. It was wrongly placed in the first instance and is out of harmony with the Capitol and with the Senate and House Office Buildings. That being so, it is not clear to me how the Supreme Court Building can be made part of a framework of which the congressional Library is an element; and since the choice must be made between harmonizing with the Library of Congress and harmonizing with the National Capitol, I have no hesitation in accepting the latter alternative, and I believe you will agree with me. The problem would be easier if we could close Maryland Avenue at this point, but I understand that would probably not be recommended by the authorities." *Id.* Taft immediately approved of Gilbert's response to Bennett: "The suggestion that we should change the location because of the difficulty of securing a proper axis to me is not very formidable. If we allow such reasons to prevail, we shall never get the building located or built either. What has constantly to be done in Washington is to reconcile mistakes made in locating buildings already erected. The lot here chosen by the Building Commission is the one which has always been suggested for the Court." WHT to Cass Gilbert (September 30, 1927) (Gilbert papers at the Supreme Court of the United States).

101. On November 5, Gilbert sent Taft a sketch that located the Court in a symmetrical position on East Capitol Street. *See* Sketch by Cass Gilbert (November 5, 1927) (Gilbert papers at the Supreme Court of the United States) ("My new suggestion for location of Supreme Court. Letter of plat sent to E.H. Bennett today. Referred to in letter to Ch. Justice Taft today."). *See* Sketch of Cass Gilbert, *Scheme for Locating Sup Court on Axis of East Capitol Street* (November 9, 1927) (Gilbert papers at the Supreme Court of the United States). After a luncheon with Charles Moore, Van Devanter, and Gilbert on November 13, Taft was apparently convinced that "we need more land than that which we are now attempting to take. There is a triangle on the other side of Maryland Avenue which we need, and upon which is a costly building of the Methodist Church. I don't know whether we can

Creating a New Supreme Court Building

induce Congress to give it to us, but the architects seem to think that it is necessary." WHT to Charles P. Taft 2nd (November 13, 1927) (Taft papers). *See* WHT to Anson Phelps Stokes (November 16, 1927) (Taft papers) ("I went up to the place with Justice Van Devanter and Senator Smoot yesterday, and I am more strongly convinced than ever that we ought to take that sliver or triangle on which the Methodist Building stands, and close up Maryland Avenue and make a complete square.").

In January, Gilbert sent Taft sketches locating the Court on a lot that included the triangle north of Maryland Avenue. Cass Gilbert to WHT (January 17, 1928) (Gilbert papers at the Supreme Court of the United States) ("I still hope the Congressional Committee will grant all you ask for the Supreme Court, for it will be needed. The building ought not to be put on an irregular shaped plot. . . . I had not intended again mentioning my suggestion about the site on East Capitol Street because neither Mr. Mellon nor Justice Van Devanter favored it. I still think it would be the best site and the land is less expensive . . . . It ought to be looked into. However, I do not expect to mention it again. I am afraid to do so."). Gilbert did in fact mention the East Capitol Street location again, due to "the long delay in the condemnation and the opposition of the ladies who own a part of the Maryland Avenue site." Cass Gilbert to WHT (November 13, 1928) (Taft papers).

In the meantime, Frederic A. Delano, chair of the National Capital Park and Planning Commission of Washington, weighed in with the suggestion that the Court be located in the Tidal Basin. WHT to Cass Gilbert (January 13, 1928) (Gilbert papers at the Supreme Court of the United States). *See supra* note 22. But Taft countered that it would be "admirable" if Gilbert could "start your people to making the investigation that is necessary on the lot as it is now planned, with Maryland Avenue remaining open." *Id.* Delano then suggested a site just north of the Capitol that Gilbert thought had "considerable merit." Frederic A. Delano to Cass Gilbert (January 30, 1929) (Taft papers); Cass Gilbert to WHT (February 1, 1928) (Gilbert papers at the Supreme Court of the United States); Cass Gilbert to WHT (February 3, 1928) (Taft papers). David Lynn, the architect of the Capitol, opposed that site because it interfered with existing plans for expansion of gardens to the north of the Capitol. Frederic A. Delano to WHT (February 6, 1928) (Taft papers). Taft nevertheless asked Delano "to prosecute the matter of which you have written me in your letter of February 6th." WHT to Frederic A. Delano (February 7, 1928) (Taft papers).

It turned out that Charles Moore also had objections to that proposed site, as did Senator Smoot. Cass Gilbert to WHT (February 7, 1928) (Taft papers); Reed Smoot to WHT (February 14, 1928) (Taft papers). Lynn proved "pretty obdurate." Frederic A. Delano to WHT (February 9, 1928) (Taft papers). Lynn counterproposed a site bounded by New Jersey Avenue, First Street, and B and C Streets, which Delano considered "altogether a very magnificent location." *Id.* Taft rejected the proposal because it would make the building "so subordinate as to seem a mere side hill concern." WHT to Frederic A. Delano (February 10, 1928) (Taft papers). *See* WHT to Cass Gilbert (February 10, 1928) (Taft papers). In the end Delano backed off his objections to the original site, Frederic A. Delano to Cass Gilbert (February 13, 1928) (Taft papers), as did Gilbert. Cass Gilbert to WHT (February 14, 1928) (Taft papers) ("It looks as though under all the circumstances surrounding the matter that the original site between East Capitol Street

581

THE TAFT COURT

and Maryland Avenue will be adhered to."). *See* WHT to Cass Gilbert (February 16, 1928) (Taft papers) ("I think you ought now to devote yourself to shaping the front of the block as it is, so as to eliminate its narrower front as far as you can from the picture."). On the siting of the building, see Cass Gilbert to James C. Beck (November 28, 1933) (Gilbert papers at the Library of Congress). This letter is also Gilbert's most elaborate explanation of the choices that went into his design.

102. WHT to Reed Smoot (February 15, 1928) (Taft papers). Smoot answered that "after the condemnation proceedings of the proposed land ... there will have to be an estimate of the cost of the building and a direct appropriation made for the same." Reed Smoot to WHT (February 20, 1928) (Taft papers).

103. WHT to Cass Gilbert (April 24, 1928) (Taft papers).

104. WHT to Nicholas Longworth (May 1, 1928) (Taft papers); S. 4151, 70th CONG. 1st SESS. (April 20, 1928).

105. Message Telephoned by Mr. Cass Gilbert, Jr. for his father (April 25, 1928) (Taft papers).

106. Taft's amended version of the bill may be found in H.R. 13665, 70th CONG. 1st SESS. (May 10, 1928). *See* WHT to Richard N. Elliott (April 26, 1928) (Taft papers); WHT to Henry W. Keyes (April 26, 1928) (Taft papers); WHT to Fritz G. Lanham (April 26, 1928) (Taft papers). Taft's amendments also provided that "an Associate Justice to be designated by the Court" be added to the Commission, giving the Court a total of two members, the Senate two, and the House two. Representatives Elliott and Lanham, the ranking members of the House Public Buildings and Grounds Committee, were sympathetic to Taft's revised bill, which they had seen on April 26. Representative Elliott wrote "So far as I am concerned" there "is nothing" in the proposed changes "that I could not agree to." Richard N. Elliott to WHT (April 27, 1929) (Taft papers). *See* Fritz G. Lanham to WHT (April 27, 1928) (Taft papers); WHT to Henry W. Keyes (May 1, 1928) (Taft papers). Without Taft's knowledge, however, Senator Henry Keyes, chair of the Senate Public Buildings and Grounds Committee, had already introduced S. 4151 on April 20, see WHT to Senator James A. Reed (May 3, 1928) (Taft papers); *supra* note 104, and Taft felt blindsided. "The course taken with respect to [S. 4151] indicates," Taft said, that the architect of the Capitol "did not care to have the Court consulted in the matter, although it is a matter in which it seems to me it would have been proper that the Court should be consulted." WHT to Nicholas Longworth (May 1, 1928) (Taft papers). For his part, David Lynn was highly offended by Taft's proposed revisions. *See* WHT to Richard N. Elliott (April 30, 1928) (Taft papers); WHT to Fritz G. Lanham (April 30, 1928) (Taft papers) ("We have no desire to humiliate the architect of the Capitol, but we have a feeling that when the Commission selects an architect of established national reputation, we ought to make him subject to the Commission alone and not interpose another architect between him and the Commission.").

107. WHT to (separately) Edward I. Edwards, Francis Warren, Arthur R. Gould, and Claude A. Swanson (May 1, 1928) (Taft papers). *See* Edward I. Edwards to WHT (May 3, 1928) (Taft papers) ("For the life of me I can not appreciate the attitude of those responsible for the drafting of the Keyes measure in neglecting to consult your Court prior to the introduction of the Keyes and Elliott measures in the Congress."); Arthur R. Gould to WHT (May 3, 1928) (Taft papers); Claude

Creating a New Supreme Court Building

A. Swanson to WHT (May 5, 1928) (Taft papers). Despite the richness of the Taft collection, it is plain from internal evidence – *see, e.g.*, Robert L. Bacon to WHT (Mary 4, 1928) (Taft papers) – that there is much correspondence that is missing, so that we can only partially reconstruct Taft's lobbying campaign.

108. WHT to (separately) Henry F. Ashurst and Simeon Fess (May 1, 1928) (Taft papers). *See* WHT to George H. Moses (April 26, 1928) (Taft papers).
109. WHT to Nicholas Longworth (May 1, 1928) (Taft papers). Taft sent this same letter to Representative Hatton W. Sumners, who was the ranking minority member of the House Judiciary Committee. WHT to Hatton W. Sumners (May 1, 1928) (Taft papers). Longworth agreed "that the Court should have the choice of the architect of the building, and I think the matter can be easily arranged. I have talked to Elliott and he thinks as I do, and I don't see any real reason why, under such circumstances, Mr. Lynn could not effectively cooperate." Nicholas Longworth to WHT (May 4, 1928) (Taft papers).
110. WHT to James A. Reed (May 3, 1928) (Taft papers); WHT to Henrick Shipstead (May 2, 1928) (Taft papers); WHT to Peter G. Gerry (May 2, 1928) (Taft papers). Reed and Shipstead were members of the Senate Public Buildings and Grounds Committee, which had jurisdiction of the bill. Rhode Island Senator Gerry was not a member of the Committee, but he had offered to donate "his father's very large Law Library of 30,000 volumes, with some rare books" to the Court, on the condition that they be "placed together" in the new "Supreme Court Building as a gift from him." WHT to Cass Gilbert (March 9, 1927) (Gilbert papers at the Supreme Court of the United States). After consulting with Gilbert, Taft had accepted the offer. WHT to Peter G. Gerry (February 7, 1928) (Taft papers). Taft's appeal to Gerry prompted the latter to affirm that "I shall be very glad to do what I can to be helpful in the matter." Peter G. Gerry to WHT (May 3, 1928) (Taft papers).
111. WHT to Robert A. Taft (May 6, 1928) (Taft papers).
112. H.R. 13665, 70th Cong. 1st Sess. (May 10, 1928). Taft complained to Gilbert that "I am so busy trying to get through the work that stands between me and adjournment that I can not spend as much time at the Capitol as I would like to." WHT to Cass Gilbert (May 12, 1928) (Taft papers).
113. Hearings on H.R. 13665, S. 4035, H.R. 5952, S.J. Res. 50, and H.R. 12290, *supra* note 4. On Lynn's obduracy, see *id.* at 10–12. Van Devanter was particularly eloquent on the need for the Court to supervise the custodianship of its completed building:

> Who is the Architect of the Capitol – not as a person – but who is he? He is under, of course, the domination of the Congress of the United States, the legislative branch. We are the judicial branch. We have heretofore found that when, through no fault of our own, we come in contact with the legislative branch, if they want a room, they get it. That is the plain fact; it is true. . . .
>
> [T]he custody of that building . . . ought not be with the representative of the legislative branch of the Government; it ought not to be with anybody who could say, to Senator So-and-so, here is a room in the Supreme Court; you go over and occupy it; or he can say to Representative So-and-so, here is a room over there you go over and occupy it.
>
> There ought to be in connection with that building a declaration that that shall be exclusively for the Supreme Court, so that the court can control that. . . . Let us have the divorce, just as it ought to be.

Id. at 17–18.

114. Pub. L. 70-244, 45 Stat. 1066 (December 21, 1928). The bill was opposed by Alabama Senator J. Thomas Heflin. The power of Taft's genial persuasion can be seen in Reed Smoot's defense of the legislation, which was widely quoted in the press:

> Nearly every justice of the Supreme Court ... [has] to do much of their work at home. There is no place but a cubby-hole or two here at the Capitol Building for the Supreme Court of the United States.... I can not think of any necessity that is more pressing upon the Government than providing a proper place for the Supreme Court of the United States....
>
> Of course, I did not agree with some of the ideas as to closing Maryland Avenue and buying the next block to the north and spreading the Supreme Court from the Library to B Street; I thought that was perfectly silly; I thought that there was no necessity for it at all, but in view of the size of the lot which has been purchased, and the character of the building designed, I wish to say to the Senator it will be an honor to America when it shall have been erected....
>
> Every American is proud that there is [a Library of Congress]. When they go there they will see, across the street, the Supreme Court, a most beautiful building, and they will go in there; and every American's heart will be filled with pride to know that the United States Supreme Court – the greatest body in the world for the administration of law – is housed in a building that will do honor to any country in the world, I do not care what country it is.

70 CONG. REC. 931–32 (December 20, 1928). These remarks stand in sharp contrast to Smoot's initial comments in 1926 on the need for a Supreme Court building, *supra* note 43. *See A Supreme Court Building*, NEW YORK TIMES (December 24, 1928), at 12; Lucille A. Roussin, *The Temple of American Justice: The United States Supreme Court Building*, 20 CHAPMAN LAW REVIEW 51 (2017).

115. This was in accordance with Taft's proposed bill. *See supra* note 106.

116. Taft was so focused on the legislation's enactment that Vice President Dawes reports that Taft called him "[l]ess than fifteen minutes" after its passage "expressing his anxiety to have it signed by President Coolidge before he left Washington for the holidays. This I arranged within an hour, to his considerable satisfaction." CHARLES G. DAWES, NOTES AS VICE PRESIDENT 1928–1929, at 194 (Boston: Little, Brown & Co. 1935).

117. WHT to Mrs. Frederick. J. Manning (November 17, 1928) (Taft papers). *See* WHT to Mrs. Frederick. J. Manning (December 9, 1928) (Taft papers); WHT to Mrs. Frederick. J. Manning (December 16, 1928) (Taft papers). On Taft's nimble creation of the compromise legislation, see WHT to WVD (December 7, 1928) (Taft papers); WHT to (separately) Henry Keyes, Henry F. Ashurst, Richard N. Elliott, Fritz Lanham, and David Lynn (December 7, 1928) (Taft papers) ("The condemnation proceedings pending in the Supreme Court of the District to secure for the Government and the Supreme Court Building two lots on the Capitol Square, have proceeded to such a point that they will be completed ... all within six weeks as soon as the first deficiency appropriation bill shall pass appropriating the $268,000 needed to cover the entire award. Such progress would seem to require that legislation be now enacted to provide for the Commission which was fully discussed in the last session of Congress. It seems to me, therefore, as if it would be wise to have a conference among those immediately interested and taking part in the matter within the next day or

two."). Keyes, Elliott, Lanham, Van Devanter, and Lynn were future commissioners of the United States Supreme Court Building Commission. Taft apparently believed that Ashurst would also be on the Commission, see WHT to Charles P. Taft 2nd (December 23, 1928) (Taft papers), but in fact Ashurst was only the second ranking minority member on the Senate Public Buildings and Grounds Committee. Missouri Senator James A. Reed was the ranking minority member and so became the seventh commissioner. *See* Minutes of the Organization Meeting of the Commission Named in Public No. 644 (January 4, 1929) ("Minutes"). Reed was slated to step down from the Senate on March 4, 1929. Nevertheless at Reed's request special legislation was enacted that permitted him to remain a commissioner. Pub. Res. 70-106, 45 Stat. 1698 (March 4, 1929). On the floor of the Senate, Ashurst generously announced that "I am possessed of no talents that can ever bring me into even the most courteous competition when measured and weighed with those talents of the Senator from Missouri [Mr. Reed], and I hereby gladly and cheerfully waive in his favor such privilege of priority as I might have on this commission." 70 CONG. REC. 3743 (February 19, 1929). *See* Richard N. Elliott to WHT (February 15, 1929) (Taft papers); WHT to Richard N. Elliott (February 16, 1929) (Taft papers); WHT to Charles Moore (March 7, 1929) (Taft papers) (Reed "is very much interested in the work."). On Reed, see *Senator "Jim" Reed as Presidential Timber*, 92 LITERARY DIGEST 12 (February 5, 1927).

118. WHT to Henry W. Keyes (June 4, 1928) (Taft papers).
119. WHT to Henry W. Keyes (July 1, 1928) (Taft papers).
120. *Id.* Taft immediately forwarded Keyes's telegram to Gilbert, asking if Gilbert had "been able to do any work" in the last month. WHT to Cass Gilbert (July 1, 1928) (Taft papers).
121. WHT to WVD (July 10, 1928) (Van Devanter papers).
122. Cass Gilbert to WHT (September 7, 1928) (Taft papers).
123. WHT to Cass Gilbert (September 9, 1928) (Taft papers).
124. WHT to Mrs. Frederick J. Manning (November 17, 1928) (Taft papers).
125. WHT to Cass Gilbert (November 9, 1928) (Taft papers).
126. Cass Gilbert to WHT (November 13, 1928) (Taft papers).
127. WHT to Charles P. Taft 2nd (December 9, 1928) (Taft papers).
128. WHT to Robert A. Taft (December 23, 1928) (Taft papers).
129. *See supra* note 117.
130. WHT to Robert A. Taft (December 16, 1928) (Taft papers). *See* WHT to Charles P. Taft 2nd (December 23, 1928) (Taft papers) (The architect "will be Cass Gilbert").
131. WHT to Charles P. Taft 2nd (December 23, 1928) (Taft papers). *See* WHT to Robert A. Taft (December 23, 1928) (Taft papers); WHT to Cass Gilbert (December 21, 1928) (Taft papers) ("I hope that the land will be ours and paid for before the middle of January. . . . There remains nothing now but to secure the appropriation for $10,000, and that we hope for . . . in January.").
132. WHT to Mrs. Frederick J. Manning (December 16, 1928) (Taft papers).
133. Minutes, *supra* note 117.
134. Minutes of Meeting of January 9, 1929.

THE TAFT COURT

135. WHT to Cass Gilbert (January 15, 1929) (Taft papers). The controversy, according to Taft, involved "the obstinacy of some drys in the Senate." WHT to Charles P. Taft 2nd (February 17, 1929) (Taft papers). This was the same deficiency bill that was required to provide added funds to complete the condemnation proceedings for the land for the Supreme Court building. *See supra* note 65.
136. WHT to Cass Gilbert (January 15, 1929) (Taft papers).
137. Lynn had communicated with his model maker, who was "willing to go ahead with his work" even in the absence of immediate compensation. WHT to Cass Gilbert (January 15, 1929) (Taft papers). But Gilbert insisted that the models be constructed in New York. Cass Gilbert to WHT (January 16, 1929) (Taft papers); Cass Gilbert to WHT (January 18, 1929) (Taft papers). "I am anxious to have the work done here under my personal instruction so that I can visit it frequently while under way. If they are made in Washington I would have to prepare very careful and practically final drawings before the models could be begun and here I can do it more rapidly by personal instruction and by more or less fragmentary sketches explanatory of the cross sections." Cass Gilbert to David Lynn (January 18, 1929) (Taft papers). On the costs, see Cass Gilbert to WHT (January 18, 1929) (Taft papers). On the importance of models to Gilbert's architectural practice, see Sharon Irish, *Cass Gilbert in Practice, 1882–1934*, in INVENTING THE SKYLINE: THE ARCHITECTURE OF CASS GILBERT 18–19 (Margaret Heilbrun, ed., New York: Columbia University Press 2000).
138. Cass Gilbert to WHT (January 29, 1929) (Taft papers).
139. WHT to Cass Gilbert (January 31, 1929) (Taft papers).
140. *Id.*; WHT to William R. Wood (February 4, 1929) (Taft papers).
141. WHT to Charles P. Taft 2nd (February 3, 1929) (Taft papers). To compound Taft's worries, Gilbert began to show signs of impatience at the "very disappointing" delay. Cass Gilbert to WHT (February 5, 1929) (Taft papers). At the beginning of February, Gilbert wrote Taft that "It will take a long time after the plans are adopted to make the working drawings and specifications, so that if we are to get under way actually – under construction – this season, we ought to have definite authority to go ahead *now*." *Id.* Gilbert was also growing anxious about how detailed his estimates ought to be to survive congressional scrutiny, for "I'd like to be prepared in advance for such function as I may be expected to perform." *Id.* He reminded Taft that Taft and Van Devanter had advised Gilbert not to include "such items as furniture, mural decoration, sculpture, etc." in his estimates, "as they would probably run the estimate up too high." "An additional appropriation" would be necessary to cover these expenses. *Id.* Taft sought to comfort Gilbert: "The delay, due to the fight over the deficiency bill, is really most exasperating, but there is nothing to do but to swear and swear with moderation, conscious that ultimately we are going to get it through." WHT to Cass Gilbert (February 8, 1929) (Taft papers).
142. WHT to Richard N. Elliott (February 8, 1929) (Taft papers); Richard N. Elliott to WHT (February 9, 1929) (Taft papers); WHT to Richard N. Elliott (February 13, 1929) (Taft papers); Richard N. Elliott to WHT (February 15, 1929) (Taft papers).
143. Pub. Res. No. 70-90, 45 Stat. 1261 (February 23, 1929).
144. Taft scheduled the meeting on March 3 so that the legislative members of the Commission would not "get away" from Washington with the adjournment of Congress on March 4. WHT to Cass Gilbert (March 7, 1929) (Taft papers).

145. Minutes of Supreme Court Building Commission (March 3, 1929). Gilbert's contract was formally signed at the Commission's meeting of April 10, 1929. Gilbert had essentially worked for two and half years, and had produced detailed plans, all in the hope of eventually being selected as the architect. That Taft could have maintained this arrangement is remarkable.

Oddly, on the motion of Taft and Van Devanter, the Commission on March 3 also "resolved that Senator Reed and the Architect of the Capitol, constitute a committee to take into consideration the enlargement of the proposed Supreme Court lot, to include all the property bounded by Maryland Avenue, First Street, B and Second, which includes the property now occupied by the Methodist Building." At its meeting of April 10, letters were read from the Commission of Fine Arts and the National Capital Park and Planning Commission to the effect that they "were not favorable to the acquisition of additional ground and the closing of Maryland Avenue." Minutes of the Meeting of April 10, 1929, United States Supreme Court Building Commission.
146. Pub. L. 70-1034, 45 Stat. 1609 (March 4, 1929).
147. WHT to Mrs. Frederick J. Manning (March 10, 1929) (Taft papers).
148. Quoted in Blodgett, *Cass Gilbert, Architect, supra* note 80, at 632.
149. Cass Gilbert to Mrs. Cass Gilbert (April 10, 1929) (Gilbert papers at the Library of Congress).
150. Cass Gilbert to WHT (January 16, 1929) (Taft papers).
151. WHT to Charles P. Taft 2nd (April 14, 1929) (Taft papers).
152. WHT to Robert A. Taft (April 14, 1929) (Taft papers).
153. It must be "a building of such dignity and such extent as to represent the Judicial Branch of the Government," Taft told the ALI in May, "And I am glad to say that our experience so far with the Committees is that they are filled with enthusiasm – if I may say so – in regard to the construction of such a building." *Chief Justice Taft's Address*, 15 AMERICAN BAR ASSOCIATION JOURNAL 332 (1929).
154. The report may be found in *United States Supreme Court Building*, H.R. Doc. No. 36, 71st CONG. 1st SESS. (June 11, 1929). The report was approved at the Commission's meeting of June 1. Minutes of the Supreme Court Building Commission (June 1, 1929). At that meeting there was an awkward moment when "The question was asked whether the plans and models when executed would result in a building which would be suitable to all of the members of the Supreme Court for a Court house, to which the Chief Justice replied that he had heard no unfavorable comment upon the plans and that some of the Justices had been very enthusiastic regarding the Court building being constructed from the designs submitted."
155. Taft wrote his daughter that "I don't know whether we can get the appropriation needed, but we are going to do the best we can. We haven't as yet had reason to complain of the generous attitude of Congress in respect to the matter. I am hoping that as Congress is to appropriate a very large amount for the various buildings here, they will not be ungenerous to us in respect to the Supreme Court Building. I am very well satisfied with it as planned." WHT to Mrs. Frederick J. Manning (June 2, 1929) (Taft papers).
156. WHT to Robert A. Taft (June 7, 1929) (Taft papers).
157. Minutes of Supreme Court Building Commission (June 8, 1929). The bedside meeting was reported in the press. *Taft Is Improved*, WASHINGTON POST (June 9, 1929), at 6.

The Taft Court

158. H.R. 3864, 71st CONG. 1st SESS. (June 11, 1929).
159. S. 1482, 71st CONG. 1st SESS. (June 4, 1929) (Calendar day June 11).
160. To give this figure a sense of scale, consider that in January Congress had authorized $8,400,000 for the construction of a new annex to the House office building. Pub. L. 70-649, 45 Stat. 1071 (January 11, 1929). In March it had authorized $4,912,414 for the enlargement of the Capitol grounds. Pub. L. 70-1036, 45 Stat. 1694 (March 4, 1929).
161. WHT to Charles P. Taft 2nd (October 13, 1929) (Taft papers).
162. A good capsule summary of the building program may be found in Richard N. Elliott, *Elliott Describes Building Program*, WASHINGTON POST (June 8, 1930), at R9. Suffice it to say that on March 31, 1930, Congress enacted Pub. L. 71-85, 46 Stat. 136, which authorized a $115,000,000 increase in spending for public buildings in Washington D.C., bringing the total of such expenditures to $227,890,000. Elliott, *supra*, at R12. The House approved that bill on the very same day that it would ultimately approve the appropriation for the Supreme Court. *House Passes $230,000,000 Buildings Bill*, HERALD TRIBUNE (December 17, 1929), at 15. Support for public building on this scale dwarfed the $10,000,000 price of the Supreme Court building.
163. WHT to Robert A. Taft (October 13, 1929).
164. WHT to Robert A. Taft (December 1, 1929) (Taft papers). *See supra* notes 162 and 160.
165. *Mind and Momentum*, 4 TIME 13 (December 2, 1929).
166. WHT to Horace D. Taft (December 8, 1929) (Taft papers).
167. WHT to Mrs. Charles P. Taft (December 8, 1929) (Taft papers). *See* WHT to Charles P. Taft 2nd (December 8, 1929) (Taft papers).
168. *See supra* note 162; Hearings before the House Committee on Public Buildings and Grounds on H.R. 3864 and H.R. 6120, 71st CONG. 2nd SESS. (December 13, 1929).
169. Hearings before the House Committee on Public Buildings and Grounds, *supra* note 168, at 12–13. Elliott added, "I wish to say before you vote, that these plans are entirely satisfactory to the Supreme Court, to all of the members of the court." *Id*. at 13.
170. Pub. L. 71-26, 46 Stat. 51 (December 20, 1929).
171. WHT to Robert A. Taft (December 22, 1929) (Taft papers).
172. Cass Gilbert to WHT (February 4, 1930) (Taft papers).
173. Wendell Mischler to Cass Gilbert (February 5, 1930) (Taft papers).
174. *Hundreds File Past Taft Bier in Capitol*, NEW YORK TIMES (March 12, 1930), at 15. *See Nation Turns Today to Capitol Rotunda*, WASHINGTON POST (March 11, 1930), at 1.
175. Hughes, *supra* note 2, at 728.
176. "The Court's architecture and imagery looked back to enlist the authority of lawmakers long gone. Yet, the building's interior also marked the Court's new legal authority to control its own docket, the Chief Justice's ascendancy as the chief executive of the federal judicial system, and the special role the media would come to play in shaping understandings of the judiciary." Judith Resnik & Dennis E. Curtis, *Inventing Democratic Courts: A New and Iconic Supreme Court*, 38 JOURNAL OF SUPREME COURT HISTORY 207, 208 (2013).
177. *Id*.

Creating a New Supreme Court Building

178. Cass Gilbert to James M. Beck (November 28, 1933) (Gilbert papers at the Library of Congress). Interestingly, given the difficulties with the press that Taft experienced as a politician, Taft was firm that the building provide "for the convenience and comfort of the press. Press association correspondents have space, equipped with chairs, tables and a quietly operating pneumatic tube leading directly to a space reserved for the press on the ground floor, directly in front of the bench, while correspondents for individual newspapers have similar accommodations close by." *High Court Holds Opening Session in New Building*, CHRISTIAN SCIENCE MONITOR (October 7, 1935), at 5. *See* Cass Gilbert, Jr., *The United States Supreme Court Building*, 72 ARCHITECTURE 301, 302 (December 1935) ("For the first time, at the insistence of the late Chief Justice Taft, adequate provision for the press is made in the Court Room and below stairs.").

McReynolds had a very different perspective on the practical functionality of the building. He wrote his brother:

> We are in the new building. From an artistic viewpoint it is admired. From a practical standpoint it is a mess. I never was in favor of it: but really did not suppose that in practice it would be such a failure. To maintain it will cost probably $200,000 a year. Seventy five men & women will be required to keep it clean. It will prove a decided detriment to the Court in my humble judgment. Keep all this to yourself however. No use of advertising my feelings on the subject.
>
> In addition to all else the lighting of the courtroom is so bad that I cannot sit there without bad eye strain. I've been off the bench three days this week. The hope is that corrections can be made during the recess wh[ich] commences next Monday.

JCM to Robert McReynolds (October 24, 1935) (McReynolds Virginia papers).
179. On the rhetoric of "divorce," *see supra* note 113.
180. Pub. L. 71-26, 46 Stat. 51 (December 20, 1929).
181. "[T]he tremendous separate Supreme Court building which is to cover two blocks facing the Capitol ... will, for the first time in the court's history, set it apart physically as well as legally from the co-ordinate legislative and executive branches of the government." Herbert Little, *Taft Made Improvements in Supreme Court*, WASHINGTON DAILY NEWS (February 10, 1930), at 11. In the judgment of contemporary commentators, the building "reflected the degree to which the Court had extricated itself from Congress and achieved its ambition to become the hub of federal judicial authority." Resnik & Curtis, *supra* note 176, at 231.
182. It was understood that "a monumental Supreme Court building" would "establish the judiciary as the equal, architecturally at least, of the legislative and executive branches of the government." Herbert Little, *The Omnipotent Nine*, 15 AMERICAN MERCURY 48, 50 (September 1928).
183. Minutes of the Supreme Court Building Commission (May 23, 1929).
184. Will P. Kennedy, *Supreme Court Home to Be Taft Memorial*, BOSTON TRAVELER (January 2, 1929).
185. Peter G. Fish, *Judiciary Act of 1925*, in THE OXFORD COMPANION TO THE SUPREME COURT OF THE UNITED STATES 477 (Kermit L. Hall *et al.*, eds., New York: Oxford University Press 1992).
186. WHT to Reed Smoot (July 3, 1925) (Taft papers). *See* WHT to Charles Curtis (September 4, 1925) (Taft papers). "[T]he American people ... have

erected the new structure of the Supreme Court on a site near the Capitol, as if to fix it there forever as a coordinate branch of their Government. They expect it to remain secure in all its duties and functions so long as the Government itself endures." *Still the Supreme Court*, NEW YORK TIMES (October 8, 1935), at 22.

187. Gilbert strongly believed in the educational value of architectural form:

> The poor man can not fill his home with works of art. The State can, however, satisfy his natural craving for such things in the enjoyment of which all may freely share, by properly embellishing its public buildings.... There the rich and the poor alike may find the history of the state and the ideals of its government set forth in an orderly and appropriate way in noble inscriptions, beautiful mural paintings and sculpture and in the fine proportions and good taste of the whole design.
>
> It is an inspiration toward patriotism and good citizenship, it encourages just pride in the state, and it is an education to on-coming generations to see these things, imponderable elements of life and character, set before the people for their enjoyment and betterment. The educational value alone is worth to the state far more than its cost.... It is a symbol of the civilization, culture and ideals of our country.

Cass Gilbert, *The Greatest Element of Monumental Architecture*, 136 AMERICAN ARCHITECT 141, 143–44 (August 5, 1929).

188. *Supreme Court Convenes in New Marble Temple*, ST. LOUIS POST DISPATCH (October 7, 1935), § 2, at 1.

189. *Id.* In the old courtroom, "as if to emphasize the closeness of the Court to American life, the bench was barely elevated from the chamber floor. The distance between lawyers in the well of the courtroom and the seated justices was close enough to permit an atmosphere of almost conversational intimacy." SEYMOUR I. TOLL, ZONED AMERICAN 234 (New York: Grossman Publishers 1969). Taft told this story of the old Court:

> As members of the Court go from their Robing Room to the Court room through a winding passage, they pass across the hall or aisle that runs from one end of the Capitol to the other. The Court marches in single file across the hall, and in order to prevent their interruption in this marching, cords are strung from one side of the hall to the other during the march. It is rather a dignified march, with the Justice in their robes and silent. This Justice was going in his regular order, and saw at his side a countryman watching with mouth open this solemn procession, and as the Justice went by he heard this bystander say in entire good faith, "Christ, what dignity!"

WHT to Frank L. Bowman (February 6, 1929) (Taft papers).

190. *Supreme Court Takes Old Chairs in Moving*, NEW YORK TIMES (October 3, 1935), at 27 ("The elaborate new Supreme Court Building ... provides new isolation for the justices. Their offices and conference rooms are in a section of the building from which the public is barred by bronze gates."). The isolation of the justices was baked into the plans from the very beginning. *See supra* note 91; Maxwell Bloomfield, *Architecture of the Supreme Court Building*, in THE OXFORD COMPANION TO THE SUPREME COURT OF THE UNITED STATES 52–53 (Kermit L. Hall, *et al.*, eds., Oxford University Press 2005).

191. *Supreme Court Convenes in New Marble Temple*, *supra* note 188.

Creating a New Supreme Court Building

192. As Taft once said: "I love judges and I love courts. They are my ideals, that typify on earth what we shall meet hereafter in heaven under a just God." Quoted in *Taft Hits Back at Big Business*, EVENING STAR (Washington D.C) (October 6, 1911), at 1.
193. Blodgett, *The Politics of Public Architecture, supra* note 80, at 71.
194. *Supreme Court Meets Today Facing Rulings on AAA and Other Laws Vital to the New Deal*, NEW YORK TIMES (October 7, 1935), at 1.
195. *See High Court Meets Amid New Splendor*, NEW YORK TIMES (October 8, 1935), at 2:

> [T]he intimacy of the rich little old room in the Capitol where the court sat for seventy-five years was missing in the new, majestic chamber with its huge Sienna marble columns, ornate ceiling, heavy crimson hangings and bas-reliefs. The scene was magnificent but it was strange to the court attachés, hundreds of attorneys and spectators and probably to the nine justices, although they did not reveal it.
>
> This unfamiliar atmosphere was prevalent throughout the great building, where spaces seemed vast as compared to the distance from the clerk's office to the court chamber in the Capitol. Lawyers and attendants were lost going from one quarter to another. In the white marble entrance hall one whimsical justice is said to have remarked:
>
> "I wonder if we look like nine black beetles in the temple of Karnak."

See High Court Uneasy in Its New Home; Nostalgia Grips Veterans as They Strive to Settle in Their Superb Quarters , NEW YORK TIMES (October 13, 1935), at 11. Only Sutherland and Roberts moved into their chambers in the new building. Even those who had voted for the building, like Van Devanter, Butler, and Stone, continued working at home. It is only when Justice Black moved into his chambers in 1937 that the building began, as it were, to become domesticated into the lives of the justices. It was not until the Vinson Court in 1946 that all nine justices began regularly working in the building. O'BRIEN, *supra* note 92, at 156.

196. PEARSON & ALLEN, *supra* note 92, at 3–4. "In the 1930s the authors of the Federal Writers' Project *Guide to Washington* wrote that 'the building has a cold, abstract, almost anonymous beauty but is lacking in that power which comes from a more direct expression of purpose.'" WITT, *supra* note 92, at 781. It was said in the press:

> The observer in an airplane, running his eye from the White House along Pennsylvania Avenue to the Capitol, then across the Plaza to the gleaming marble quadrangles of the Supreme Court's new home, is vividly reminded that our government has three coordinate branches. The court did not require a new building in order to pluck the Blue Eagle's feathers, but the new building does symbolize the power and prestige behind that inexorable depluming.

R.L. Duffus, *An Epochal Day for the Supreme Court*, NEW YORK TIMES (October 6, 1935), at 118.

197. *See supra* notes 37–41.
198. Minnigerode, *supra* note 40.
199. Cass Gilbert to Benito Mussolini (August 11, 1932) (Gilbert papers at the Library of Congress). Like many Americans of the time, Gilbert admired Mussolini, and he actively sought the dictator's assistance in acquiring the Italian marble that Gilbert

insisted be used in the courtroom. Gilbert met with Mussolini in June 1933 to discuss the situation:

> I said I had thought it would interest him to know of these matters first hand & that I wanted him to know of them from me, as I had the greatest admiration for him & for what he had done & is doing for Italy. I moved to withdraw. He put out his hand across the table & said very simply "Goodbye – Goodbye"! We shook hands & I turned & walked rapidly to the door, reaching which I turned sharply around and raised my hand in the Roman Salute – as he did the same. And I shall always think of him as standing in the somewhat dim light of that great room alone, with his hand up above his head in that most impressive of gestures, the Roman Salute, which is so characteristic of the great organization he has created – The Facisti – and which he has led so successfully for nearly eleven years.

Cass Gilbert Memorandum, "Mussolini" (June 6, 1933) (Gilbert papers at the Library of Congress).
200. Henry W. Taft to Cass Gilbert (February 15, 1932) (Gilbert papers at the Library of Congress). *See* Hugh Hardy, *Introduction*, in INVENTING THE SKYLINE: THE ARCHITECTURE OF CASS GILBERT, *supra* note 137, at xxxvi.
201. CASS GILBERT, REMINISCENCES AND ADDRESSES 67 (New York: Scribner Press 1935).
202. David Riesman to Geoffrey Blodgett (January 31, 1984), quoted in Blodgett, *Cass Gilbert, Architect*, *supra* note 80, at 634 n.44. Reisman was Brandeis's law clerk. In contrast to his attitude toward Roman imperial power, Brandeis loved the polis of the ancient Greeks. *See* Vincent Blasi, *The First Amendment and the Ideal of Civic Courage: The Brandeis Opinion in* Whitney v. California, 29 WILLIAM & MARY LAW REVIEW 653, 686–89 (1988). Another Brandeis law clerk, Paul Freund, observed that Brandeis "opposed the new Supreme Court building on the ground that it might tend to cause the Justices to lose whatever sense of humility they had theretofore possessed." Paul A. Freund, *The Supreme Court: A Tale of Two Terms*, 26 OHIO STATE LAW JOURNAL 225, 229 (1965).
203. GILBERT, *supra* note 201, at 67.
204. Elihu Root to Cass Gilbert (February 25, 1932) (Gilbert papers at the Library of Congress). Root, whose visage is carved on the Court's front pediment, was rapturous about the new Court building. He wrote Gilbert that "the photographs of the new Supreme Court building ... fill me with joy. ... The interior impresses me as especially fine. I am most deeply impressed when I look at that. It is fortunate that this is so, for the men who are to sit in this room will have no physical power. They will control no treasury and no soldiers. They wield only a moral power but that power is in its nature superior to all other forces of government, and the respect and honor in which the Court is held are essential to the preservation of liberty and order. Here, above all other places, art should express respect and reverence." *Id.* Gilbert included in the "Maxims for My Office Organization" the aphorism: "Remember that dignity of bearing commands respect – familiarity breeds contempt." Quoted in Irish, *supra* note 137, at 1.
205. William H. Taft, *The Attacks on the Courts and Legal Procedure*, 5 KENTUCKY LAW JOURNAL 3, 4 (1916).
206. *Supreme Court Home Will Cost $9,740,000*, NEW YORK TIMES (June 7, 1930), at 1.

207. *United States Supreme Court Building*, supra note 154, at 12.
208. R.L. Duffue, *An Epochal Day for the Supreme Court*, NEW YORK TIMES (October 6, 1935), Magazine at 6.
209. *See, e.g.*, Robert C. Post and Reva B. Siegel, *Protecting the Constitution from the People: Juricentric Restrictions on Section Five Power*, 78 INDIANA LAW JOURNAL 1 (2003).
210. Karl Llewellyn was Taft's student at Yale Law School, and he has bequeathed us a striking portrait of Taft the law professor:

> He knew nothing of case teaching. Someone would be asked to state the case. Taft would correct the statement as needed – which closed the "discussion." Then – and he sold the class (including me, may the Lord forgive me) the idea that this was only for interest, for anecdote – there would be five to fifteen minutes from Taft, the man of politics; Taft, the student of governmental history; Taft, the student of life and man; Taft, who both from inside and from out had seen political arena, the bench, and all varieties of executive office. . . . Taft imparted to us by his manner his own clear feeling that it was no part of "the law" or, really of "the course." Thus – almost the only piece which is still with me – "And I said to Holmes: 'But do you think it was right or fair to leave *that* fact out of consideration?' And," continued Taft with the mountainous chuckle, "he said, 'I'm sorry; I didn't read that far in the record.'"
>
> Such phenomena spell a man who *felt* the bearing of all the "background" and "human" and "situation" factors, and felt also deep value in communicating them, but whose conscious and doctrinal thinking saw them nevertheless as "outside". . . .
>
> The matter is clinched by Taft's treatment of doctrine itself. From time to time . . . he would produce an intellectual scalpel and slice the court's phrased ruling down into an almost nothing. You then got, with another half-ton chuckle: "Mr. Justice Zilch sometimes let enthusiasm run away with him!"
>
> Now I had a good brain and no sense, and this scalpel technique was as exciting to the one as it was uninhibited by the other. I started volunteering applications of it to opinions *which Taft had never had professional reason to distinguish*. Such admiring misuse of his technique . . . seemed to him that of a boor and a blasphemer. He complained to the Dean: he did not want to be subjected to half-grown children in the law "*criticizing* the Supreme Court of the United States."

KARL N. LLEWELLYN, THE COMMON LAW TRADITION: DECIDING APPEALS 21–22 (Boston: Little, Brown & Co. 1960).

PART IV
THE TAFT COURT
AS AN INSTITUTION

Although the individual members of the Taft Court each possessed a distinct, personal perspective, they all participated in a common institution governed by shared norms. These norms coordinated, shaped, and channeled the work of the justices. The routines followed by the Taft Court are in many respects strikingly similar to those that still obtain at the Supreme Court. They were succinctly described in a letter by Taft to the chief justice of Canada:

> Our rule, long established by custom, is to sit five days in the week and hear cases for four hours a day, allowing an hour on each side in each case, unless the time is enlarged by the Court, upon motion, allowing less for interlocutory matters. We hold a Conference every Saturday during our hearings. The Chief Justice states the case, and then invites discussion by the Justices in the order of seniority. After the case is as fully discussed as seems sufficient to satisfy all, a vote is taken, and in that vote the junior member of the Court votes first, and the Chief Justice last. All the cases decided at the Conference on Saturday are assigned for opinion to the various members of the Court by the Chief Justice. I send out the allocation Saturday night. The Judge to whom the case is assigned is then expected to write an opinion. After he has written it, he has it printed in proof sheets, and a copy of the proof is sent to each Judge, who expresses his approval or otherwise of the opinion and notes his criticisms, if he has any, by endorsement. He returns the opinion to the Judge writing it, and on the following Saturday inquiry is made by the Chief Justice for opinions that are ready. The criticisms made by endorsement or otherwise are then considered, and the Court, or a majority of it, authorizes the delivery of the opinion as agreed after criticism and suggestion. If there are dissenting Judges, they are given an opportunity to write the dissent. If a Judge wishes to write a concurring opinion, he may do so, but very few concurring opinions are written. ... The opinion thus made ready is handed down at the session of the Court that meets the Monday after

the Saturday on which the printed opinion was agreed upon. Of course reasonable delay is allowed to any Judge who wishes to dissent and announces [sic] his dissent at the time of handing down the opinion of the Court.[1]

It is fair to say that most of these routines would be familiar to members of the present Court. Aficionados of Supreme Court procedure might notice that during the 1920s the chief justice seems to have assigned all opinions, whether or not he was in the majority, whereas today the chief justice assigns opinions only if he is in the majority.[2] They might notice that the Taft Court sat for five days a week, whereas the contemporary Court sits for only three days a week. And they might be struck by the fact that time allotted for oral argument in the 1920s was quite capacious when measured by modern standards, in which each side is typically granted only thirty minutes for oral argument. Perhaps this was because, as reported by Milton Handler, Stone's law clerk during the 1926 term, "The Court was then a 'cold' bench, with the Justices not seeing the briefs or records until a case was called for argument."[3]

Notwithstanding these relatively minor differences, the work patterns and rhythms of the Taft Court seem so similar to those of the contemporary Court that we might be tempted to assume that the Taft Court was simply an early version of the modern Court, except staffed by a different cast of characters. But this assumption would be a serious mistake. The Taft Court understood its own legal authority and mission in ways that are quite different from the contemporary Court, and this difference affected how members of the Taft Court went about the business of deciding cases.

The justices of the Taft Court were very much in the grip of jurisprudential attitudes and practices associated with the Court's traditional pre-1925 role as a final appellate tribunal.[4] These attitudes and practices shaped the justices' sense of what it meant to compose a judicial opinion, when it was appropriate to dissent, and how the institutional authority of the Court could best be maintained. As the Court began to inhabit the new role staked out by the Judges' Bill, as it gradually evolved into the proactive manager of the system of federal law, the Court began to develop quite different jurisprudential attitudes and practices.

After almost a century of juridical development, there is now quite a sharp jurisprudential divide that separates the contemporary Court from the Taft Court. This gulf is almost invisible to the casual observer, but fortunately it is empirically demonstrable. Statistical and other evidence clearly illustrate the chasm that separates the institutional norms of the Taft Court from those of our own contemporary Court.

The Taft Court as an Institution

Notes

1. WHT to Francis A. Anglin (October 3, 1924) (Taft papers).
2. Taft also does not mention any norms for assigning dissenting opinions. This might have been because dissents were so rare.
3. Milton C. Handler, *Clerking for Justice Harlan Fiske Stone*, 1995 JOURNAL OF SUPREME COURT HISTORY 113, 114. Handler adds:

    There were very few blockbuster cases and Stone had little difficulty making up his mind on the basis of the oral argument, confirming his tentative judgment by glancing at the table of contents of the briefs and skimming those pages that dealt with the issues that interested him.

    Returning to chambers upon the conclusion of arguments, the Justice would sign his mail, leaf through some of the briefs and records, and be ready for his afternoon walk at about 5:30. As you can see, the Justice, like his former student and later colleague, Bill Douglas, was not, at this stage of his judicial career, overburdened by the job of judging.

    Id.
4. For a discussion, see *supra* Chapter 13, at 484–85.

CHAPTER 18

Judicial Opinions during the Taft Court

WE CAN BEGIN our consideration of these issues by looking closely at Clarke's 1922 explanation to Woodrow Wilson about why Clarke had prematurely retired:

> Unless you have much more intimate knowledge of the character of work which a Supreme Court judge must do than I had before going to Washington you little realize the amount of grinding, uninteresting, bone labor there is in writing more than half the cases decided by the Supreme Court. Much more than ½ the cases are of no considerable importance whether considered from the point of view of the principles or of the property involved in them, but, nevertheless, a conscientious judge writing them must master their details with the utmost care. My theory of writing opinions has always been that if clearly stated 9 cases out of 10 will decide themselves, – what the decision should be will emerge from the statement of the facts as certainly as the issues will. In this spirit I wrote always . . . . I protested often, but in vain, that too many trifling cases were being written, that our strength should be conserved for better things.[1]

The contrast to the contemporary Court could not be plainer. No one would now characterize "more than half" of the Supreme Court's cases as "of no considerable importance." No one would today assert that "9 cases out of 10" on the Court's docket "will decide themselves." Every opinion published by the contemporary Court is, in one way or another, consequential; every opinion is, in one way or another, difficult. Ultimately these differences between the modern Court and the Taft Court stem from the Judiciary Act of February 13, 1925.

I do not mean to imply that the Taft Court did not confront difficult and consequential decisions. The Court has always faced divisive and contentious issues. My point is rather that decision-making practices will be different in a Court whose docket contains a large proportion of "trifling cases" than in a Court in which almost every opinion is potentially momentous. These practices will shape the environment in which *all* Court opinions are formed and written.

Figure IV-1 offers a good starting point to delineate the decision-making environment of the Taft Court. In its 1912 term, the Court took the time to compose a full opinion that was either individually signed or published *per curiam* in approximately half of all decided cases on its appellate docket. The other half of decided cases on its appellate docket were disposed of primarily by denials of *certiorari* or through short, unsigned "memorandum opinions" (almost all issued *per curiam*).

This pattern continued until the Act of September 6, 1916[2] increased the Court's discretionary docket. At that time the Court began to publish full opinions for only about a third of the decided cases on its appellate docket, a practice that roughly continued until the 1925 Act. During the 1921 term, for example, there were 669 new cases filed on the Court's appellate docket, which, together with the 343 cases that had been carried over from the 1920 term, created a total appellate docket of some 1,012 cases. Of these the Court decided during the term 595 cases. It published full opinions in 173, or about 29 percent, of these cases. It was this institutional environment that Clarke found so intolerable.

What particularly oppressed Clarke was the large number of trivial cases that arrived in the Court's appellate docket by way of appeal or writ of error. These, together with the Court's original docket, comprised the Court's "mandatory" jurisdiction, meaning those cases that the Court was obligated to decide on the merits, either by full or memorandum opinion.[a] Clarke was correct that a great many of these cases were indeed "trifling."[3] In the 1921 term, 76 percent of the Court's full opinions were authored in cases that came to the Court through its mandatory jurisdiction. The effect of the 1925 Act was to "cut ... to the bone"[4] this mandatory jurisdiction and to substitute instead discretionary review by writs of *certiorari*.

The immediate and striking impact of the Act on the Court's jurisdiction can be seen in Figures IV-2 and IV-3. In its 1924 term, 71 percent of the Court's full opinions were issued in cases that came to the Court by way of its mandatory jurisdiction; only 28 percent of the Court's full opinions were written in cases that arrived via the discretionary writ of *certiorari*. By the Court's 1928 term these numbers were almost reversed. Fifty-five percent of the Court's full opinions were the result of cases that the Court had chosen to hear by *certiorari*; only 38 percent were issued in cases that had been lodged at the Court because of its mandatory jurisdiction. A significant but often overlooked effect of the 1925 Act was to strip away the easy decisions from what

---

[a] I have defined the Court's mandatory docket as those cases coming to the Court by way of writ of error, appeal, or original jurisdiction. Of the 1,554 full opinions published by the Taft Court during the 1921–1928 terms, only 33 came from cases that the Court decided by virtue of its original jurisdiction. I have defined the Court's discretionary docket as those cases coming to the Court through the writ of *certiorari*. There was an uncertain residue of cases that came to the Court by way of certification, extraordinary writs or other motions, or through *both* appeal and *certiorari*. On the ambiguity of certification, see Edward A. Hartnett, *Questioning Certiorari: Some Reflections Seventy-Five Years after the Judges' Bill*, 100 COLUMBIA LAW REVIEW 1643, 1710–12 (2000).

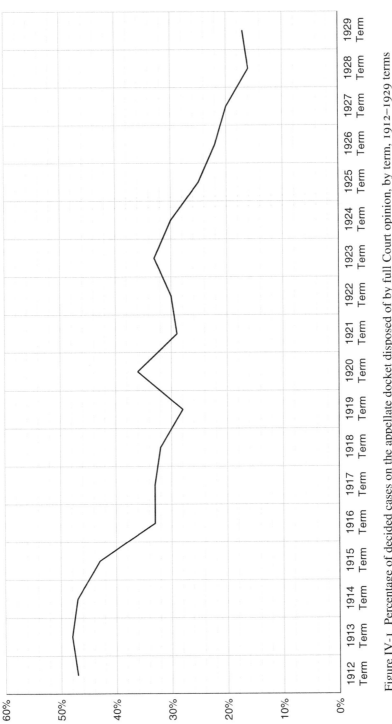

Figure IV-1 Percentage of decided cases on the appellate docket disposed of by full Court opinion, by term, 1912–1929 terms

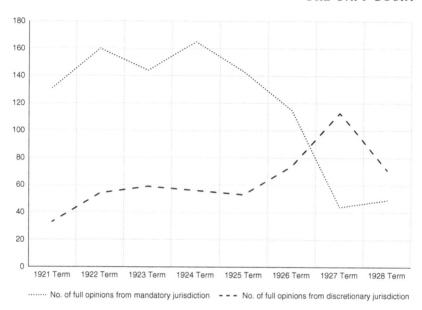

Figure IV-2 Number of full opinions by jurisdiction, by term, 1921–1928 terms

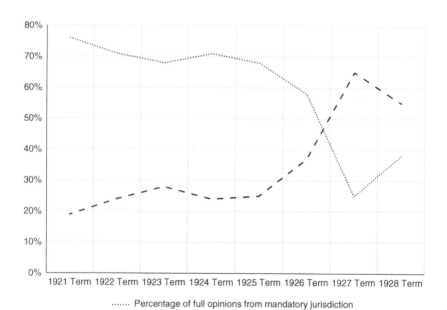

Figure IV-3 Percentage of full opinions by jurisdiction, by term, 1921–1928 terms

Judicial Opinions during the Taft Court

remained of the Court's mandatory jurisdiction, leaving only cases that involved difficult and controversial issues.[b]

The consequence of the shift from mandatory to discretionary jurisdiction, as Figures IV-4 and IV-5 demonstrate, is that the Court was able drastically to reduce the number of full opinions that it would publish each term. In its 1924 term, the Taft Court announced 231 full opinions, which comprised 30 percent of its decided appellate cases. By its 1928 term, the Court issued only 129 full opinions, which comprised only 16 percent of its decided appellate cases. Figure IV-2 demonstrates that this change was due almost entirely to the fact that the Court no longer published so many full opinions in cases in its mandatory docket, which was sharply shrinking. The drop in the number of the Court's published full opinions was a permanent effect of the 1925 Act, as shown in Figure IV-4. The Roberts Court typically issues full opinions in fewer than 90 cases per term, which comprises only an infinitesimal percentage of its total decided appellate docket.

Before 1925, the Court had chiefly been a tribunal of last resort, obligated to decide a great many mundane cases. In such tribunals, opinions serve the principal function of justifying decisions to litigants. Supreme Court opinions were thus numerous, compact, and routine. As Figures IV-6, IV-7, and IV-8 illustrate, the average number of pages for a full opinion during the 1912–1920 terms (roughly the White Court) was 6.9 pages; the average number of days from oral argument to the delivery of a full opinion was sixty-four days. The Court published an average of 229 full opinions per term, and 82 percent of these full opinions were unanimous.[c] The Court's opinions were the product of a work environment primarily responsible for publishing appellate opinions designed to settle disputes, which is to say to terminate strife and avoid extralegal violence.[5]

The 1925 Act "completely overrode" this "obstinate conception that the Court was to be the vindicator of all federal rights."[6] The Act transformed the Court from a tribunal of last resort into the manager of the system of federal law, responsible for supervising the development of national law.[7] The implications of this change for the Court's decision-making processes were profound. As Taft put it, the Court was henceforth required to compose opinions primarily addressed to "the public at large, as distinguished from the particular litigants before it."[8] The upshot of this reorientation is manifest in Figures IV-4, IV-6, IV-7, and IV-8.

The Court, as we now know it, issues far fewer full opinions. Its opinions are longer and more elaborate, swelling to an average of about sixteen pages, more than twice the length of White Court opinions. The modern Court takes almost half again as long to write its full opinions than did the White Court, averaging ninety-five days from argument to delivery in the 2005–2011 terms. And, most strikingly, only

---

[b] After the 1925 Act, cases reaching the Court through its mandatory appellate jurisdiction would consist primarily of those in which a state court had upheld a state statute against claims that it was invalid under federal law, or in which a state court had held invalid a federal statute or treaty, or in which a Circuit Court of Appeals had held a state statute invalid under federal law.

[c] I define a unanimous opinion as one with no separate concurring or dissenting opinions or votes.

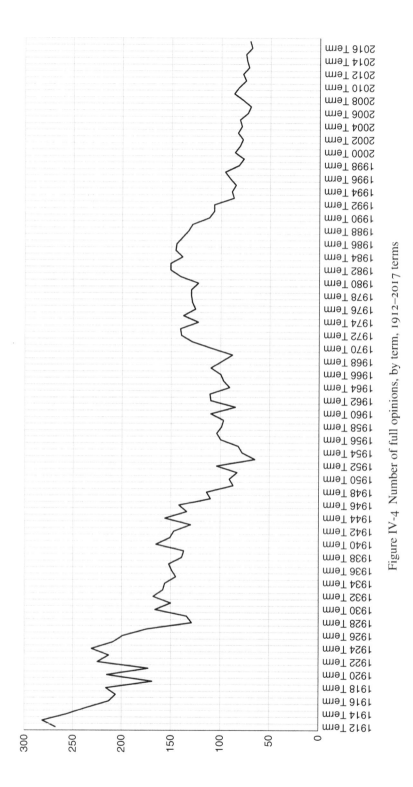

Figure IV-4 Number of full opinions, by term, 1912–2017 terms

Judicial Opinions during the Taft Court

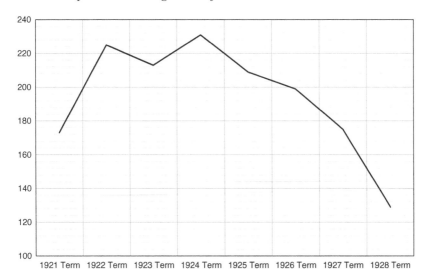

Figure IV-5 Number of full opinions, by term, 1921–1928 terms

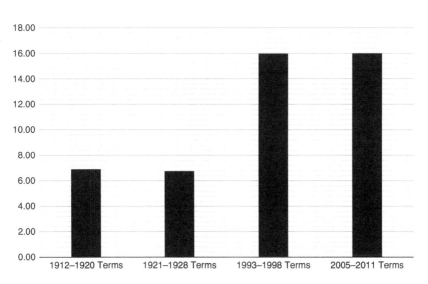

Figure IV-6 Average number of pages in a full opinion: White, Taft, Rehnquist, and Robert Courts

34 percent of the Roberts Court's full opinions in the 2005–2017 terms were unanimous.

Figures IV-6, IV-7, and IV-8 demonstrate that the Taft Court essentially retained the opinion-writing practices of the White Court, even as the 1925 Act

605

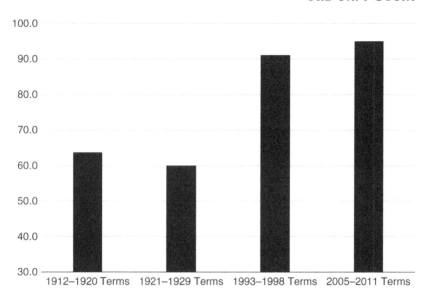

Figure IV-7 Average number of days from argument to the announcement of a unanimous opinion: White, Taft, Rehnquist, and Robert Courts

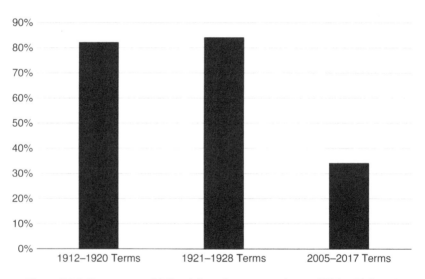

Figure IV-8 Percentage of full opinions that are unanimous: White, Taft, and Robert Courts

Judicial Opinions during the Taft Court

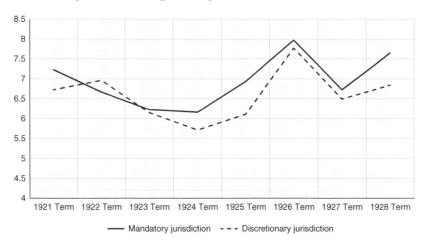

Figure IV-9 Average number of pages in a full opinion by jurisdiction, by term, 1921–1928 terms

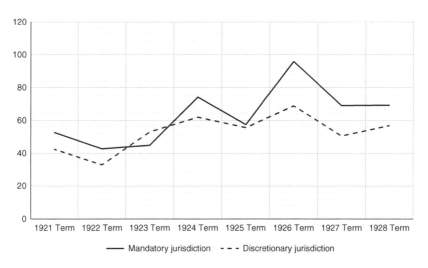

Figure IV-10 Average number of days from argument to the announcement of a full opinion by jurisdiction, by term, 1921–1928 terms

altered the configuration of the Taft Court's docket and transformed the function of its opinions. Although the Taft Court used the tools of the 1925 Act to reduce the number of its full opinions, its opinions were otherwise virtually indistinguishable from those of the White Court in terms of their length, their time of composition,[9] and their rates of unanimity. The dramatic increase in discretionary jurisdiction

607

THE TAFT COURT

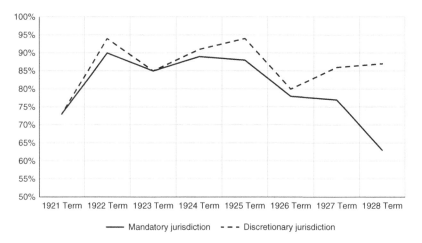

Figure IV-11 Percentage of full opinions that are unanimous by jurisdiction, by term, 1921–1928 terms

established by the 1925 Act failed to affect these dimensions of Taft Court opinion-writing.[d]

If Court opinions must justify themselves to "the public at large" through exposition and persuasion, it is natural to expect them to grow in length and complexity, as well as to become more divisive. This is especially true when opinions are written primarily to resolve controversial and volatile issues specifically selected by the discretionary writ of *certiorari*. It seems plain, then, that Taft Court opinion-writing practices reflected habits and norms that had developed within, and were appropriate for, the judicial ecology of a final appellate tribunal. These habits and norms persisted despite the Taft Court's transition to a new role as supervisor of the system of federal law.

---

[d] Figures IV-9, IV-10, and IV-11 illustrate that these dimensions of Taft Court opinion writing did not appreciably change in the 1925–1928 terms, after the Judges' Bill went into effect, although some incipient trends might perhaps be visible. Strikingly, however, Figure IV-11 demonstrates that the Taft Court became increasingly more likely to issue unanimous opinions in cases coming to the Court through its discretionary jurisdiction than in cases coming to the Court through its mandatory jurisdiction. This is a puzzle that requires explanation. *See infra* Chapter 19, at 623–27.

Judicial Opinions during the Taft Court

Notes

1. JHC to Woodrow Wilson (September 9, 1922) (Wilson papers). *See* John H. Clarke, *Carrying the Case to the United States Supreme Court*, 56 AMERICAN LAW REVIEW 283, 284 (1922).
2. Pub. L. 64-258, 39 Stat. 726 (September 6, 1916). *See supra* Chapter 13, at note 28. The 1916 Act provided, *inter alia*, that the Court's appellate jurisdiction in cases arising under federal bankruptcy proceedings, and in cases arising under the Federal Employers' Liability Act, could be invoked only by way of the discretionary writ of *certiorari*. *See* 39 Stat. 727; FELIX FRANKFURTER & JAMES LANDIS, THE BUSINESS OF THE SUPREME COURT 210–15 (New York: MacMillan Co. 1928).
3. In 1924, Justice Sutherland, testifying before the Senate in support of the Judges' Bill, observed that "a very large proportion of the cases that come" to the Supreme Court "ought never to be there at all." *Procedure in Federal Courts*: Hearings on S. 2060 and S. 2061 before the Subcomm. of the Senate Comm. on the Judiciary, 68th CONG. 1st SESS. (February 2, 1924), at 47; *see also* Statement of Mr. Justice Sutherland, in *Jurisdiction of Circuit Courts of Appeals and of the Supreme Court of the United States*: Hearings on H.R. 8206 before the House Comm. on the Judiciary (December 18, 1924), 68th CONG. 2nd SESS., at 25 (noting that the Court was burdened by "a large number of trifling cases").
4. FRANKFURTER & LANDIS, *supra* note 2, at 299.
5. As the Court itself put it, "The right to sue and defend in the courts is the alternative of force. In an organized society it is the right conservative of all other rights, and lies at the foundation of orderly government." Chambers v. Baltimore & Ohio R. Co., 207 U.S. 142, 148 (1907). *See* Int'l Textbook Co. v. Pigg, 217 U.S. 91, 112 (1910).
6. FRANKFURTER & LANDIS, *supra* note 2, at 260–61.
7. *See supra* Chapter 13, at 484–85; DAVID M. O'BRIEN, STORM CENTER: THE SUPREME COURT IN AMERICAN POLITICS 156–57 (New York: Norton 1993).
8. William Howard Taft, Address to New York County Bar Ass'n (February 18, 1922) (Taft papers). The 1925 Act embodied Taft's theory that the Court's "main purpose is to lay down important principles of law and thus to help the public at large to a knowledge of their rights and duties and to make the law clearer." *Id*.
9. This fact is especially surprising because the Taft Court would regularly hold over cases, not announcing a decision until one or more terms after argument. During the Taft Court a most striking instance of this was McGrain v. Daugherty, 273 U.S. 135 (1927), authored by Van Devanter, which was a case argued on December 5, 1924, but not announced until January 17, 1927. *McGrain* helps to explain the spike in Figure IV-10 in the number of days between argument and decision for cases with mandatory jurisdiction in the 1926 term. It is also important to note that during the 1993–1998 terms the Court decided unanimous opinions almost as quickly as did the Taft Court. The modern Court averaged 61.8 days between oral argument and the announcement of a unanimous opinion, whereas the Taft Court averaged 55.1 days. This strongly suggests that a good deal about the relative delay in the modern Court's announcement of opinions might be explained by the relative absence of unanimous opinions.

CHAPTER 19

Dissent during the Taft Court

I T HAS RIGHTLY been observed that the "increase in the frequency of the issuance of separate opinions is a central event in the history of the Court's opinion-delivery practices."[1] The dramatic collapse of unanimity in the late 1930s is fully evident in Figure IV-12, which tracks the unanimity of full opinions from the 1912 through the 2017 terms.

Although Taft's "absorbing ambition" was, as he put it, "to 'mass' the Court,"[2] and although this ambition has sometimes been adduced as a factor to explain the low rates of dissent during the Taft Court period,[3] Figure IV-12 makes clear that the high rates of unanimity during Taft's tenure cannot primarily be attributed to him personally. They were instead typical of the pre-New Deal Court.[4]

This is not to say that Taft failed to "deprecate"[5] dissents. He in fact hated them.[6] He himself dissented less than any chief justice except John Marshall.[7] Taft remarked to Clarke that "I don't approve of dissents generally, for I think that in many cases, where I differ from the majority, it is more important to stand by the Court and give its judgment weight than merely to record my individual dissent where it is better to have the law certain than to have it settled either way."[8] Taft believed that "[m]ost dissents elaborated, are a form of egotism. They don't do any good, and only weaken the prestige of the Court. It is much more important what the Court thinks than what any one thinks."[9] Hence, as Taft once wrote in response to the circulated draft of a Holmes opinion, "While I make the sign of the scissors to you, I do not intend to do so to the public. I concur."[10]

Nor is it to say that Taft didn't work hard to build consensus and avoid dissents. He believed it an essential task of the chief justice to "be a man of strong and persuasive personality, abiding convictions, recognized learning and statesmanlike foresight, expected to promote team work by the Court so as to give weight and solidarity to its opinions."[11] We know that Taft successfully diminished

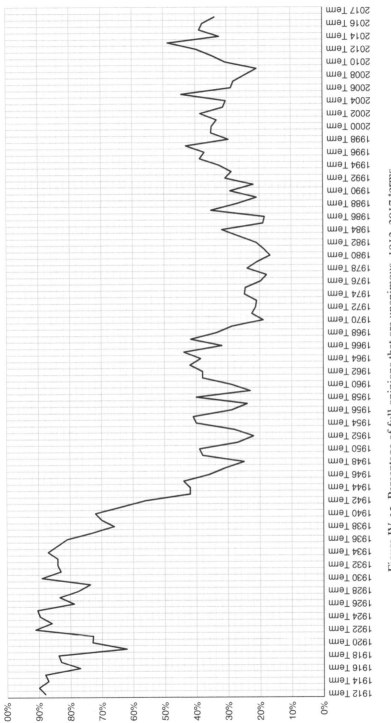

Figure IV-12 Percentage of full opinions that are unanimous, 1912–2017 terms.

Data for the 1930–1957 terms from Karl M. ZoBell, *Division of Opinion in the Supreme Court: A History of Judicial Disintegration*, 44 CORNELL LAW QUARTERLY 186, 205 (1959). Data for subsequent terms from the *Harvard Law Review*.

THE TAFT COURT

dissension in such cases as *United Mine Workers v. Coronado*,[12] *Hill v. Wallace*,[13] *American Steel Foundries v. Tri-City Central Trades Council*,[14] *Railroad Commission of California v. Southern Pacific Co.*,[15] *Opelika v. Opelika Sewer*,[16] and *FTC v. Claire Furnace Co.*[17]

Taft was willing to go to extraordinary lengths to modify his own opinions to accommodate the objections of others. In *Wisconsin v. Illinois*,[18] for example, he worked for an entire summer on an opinion advancing a very broad theory of federal commerce power that he fervently supported. But to attain unanimity he agreed to censor his own views: "I worked all summer on the constitutional part of the opinion, ... and satisfied myself completely by an examination of the briefs and the authorities on the subject, and I parted with it as a child that I was glad to father, if it needed any fathering, and it is a real sacrifice of my personal preference. But it is the duty of us all to control our personal preferences to the main object of the Court."[19]

It is plain from Figure IV-12, however, that Taft's convictions and interventions were responsible for what were at most marginal changes to a practice of unanimity that existed before Taft and that would persist after him. Within the parameters of that practice, many different factors, including Taft's personal efforts, affected the exact degree of the Court's unanimity.[a] Figure IV-14 allows us to look somewhat more closely at the changes in unanimity rates during the Taft Court.

Figure IV-14 indicates that there was a sharp increase in unanimity between the 1921 term (72.8%) and the 1922 term (91.1%). This difference undoubtedly reflects in part Harding's reconstruction of the Court, influenced by Taft's guidance and advice. Each of Harding's appointments was more likely to promote unanimity than his predecessor. Sutherland joined the Court in 96.4% of its full opinions in the 1922 term, whereas Clarke had joined the Court in only 87.1% of its full opinions in the 1921 term. Butler joined the Court in 100% of its full opinions in the 1922 term, and Sanford in 98.9% of its full opinions, whereas Day had joined 97.6% of the full opinions of the Court in the 1921 term, and Pitney 96.3% of its full opinions.

Change in Court personnel is not the entire story, however, for Figure IV-15 shows that Holmes, Van Devanter, McReynolds, and Brandeis were all more likely to join the Court in the 1922 term than they had been in the 1921 term. Figure IV-14 indicates that rates of unanimity remained very high during the 1922–1925 terms, but that they dropped perceptibly during the remainder of the decade. This trend can be seen more clearly in Figure IV-16, which measures dissenting votes as

---

[a] Figure IV-13 offers some rough measure of Taft's ability to create consensus. It examines the voting behavior of the eight justices who both preceded Taft and served with him. Figure IV-13 divides the number of times that a justice joined the opinion of the Court by the total number of decisions in which that justice participated. It then compares the resulting percentage for each justice during the 1915–1920 terms to the percentage for each justice during the 1921–1928 terms. Figure IV-13 indicates that Taft generally had a positive effect, particularly on Justices Van Devanter and McKenna. The seemingly negative effect that Taft had on Clarke is misleading; as Figure I-3 suggests, the 1921 term was for Clarke simply the last straw in a rapidly deteriorating situation as to which Taft was largely irrelevant. It is interesting that Taft seems to have had no effect at all on the willful and independent McReynolds.

Dissent during the Taft Court

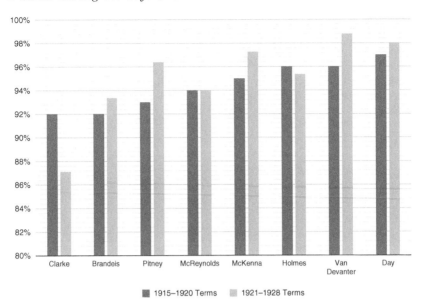

Figure IV-13 Percentage of decisions in which a justice participates and either joins or authors the Court opinion, 1915–1920 terms versus 1921–1928 terms

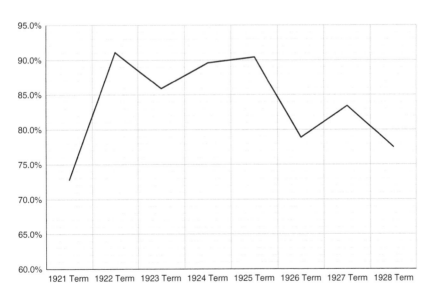

Figure IV-14 Percentage of full opinions that are unanimous, 1921–1928 terms

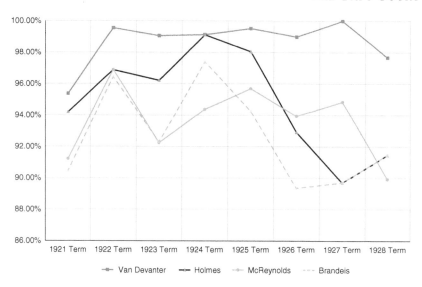

Figure IV-15 Percentage of decisions in which a justice participates and either joins or authors the opinion of the Court, by justice, by term, 1921–1928 terms

a percentage of full Court opinions. Although this pattern might be the result of random fluctuations in the docket, it is possible to identify a number of potential factors that likely contributed to this result.

There is some internal evidence, for example, that during the first half of the 1920s dissent was suppressed within the Court because of the need to fend off external attacks. In 1919 the American Federation of Labor ("AFL") launched an assault on judicial review[20] that unleashed a wave of progressive efforts to restrict the power of the Court to declare federal law unconstitutional.[21] In summer 1922, Brandeis's close friend Robert La Follette advocated for a constitutional amendment that would empower Congress to overturn Supreme Court judgments of unconstitutionality with respect to congressional legislation, a position that the AFL endorsed.[22] We know that Taft was distressed by La Follette's attack.[23] When Sutherland was confirmed to replace Clarke, Taft wrote him a long and very revealing letter:

> I write to congratulate you from the bottom of my heart on your appointment to the Bench, and upon the reception which your nomination and confirmation have had by the American people.... I should judge that the Court is about to enter upon another period of agitation against its powers, such as it had in the period before Marshall came onto the Bench; again after he locked horns with Jefferson and Jackson; again during the period of the Fugitive Slave law; again during the reconstruction days when Thad Stevens and the radical Republicans defied the Court; and again when Bryan and the income tax decision were made

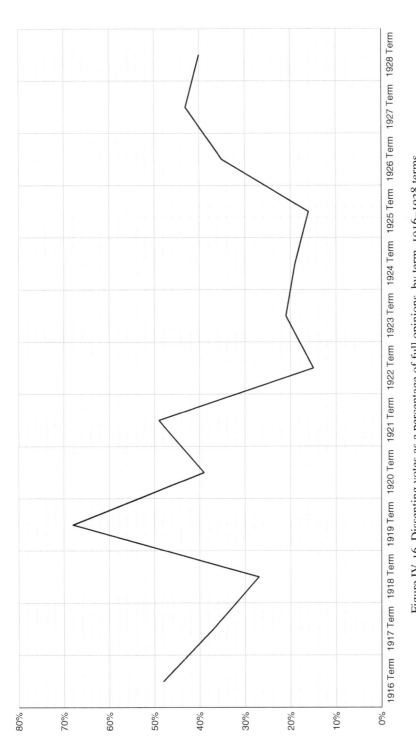

Figure IV-16 Dissenting votes as a percentage of full opinions, by term, 1916–1928 terms.

Data for the 1916–1920 terms from William G. Rice, *How the Supreme Court Mill Is Working*, 56 AMERICAN LAW REVIEW 763, 765 (1922).

THE TAFT COURT

a part of the 1896 campaign. La Follette's overwhelming victory in Wisconsin will put great confidence into the hearts and souls of all who are opposed to property rights and the support which the Constitution gives to them, and who are radically hostile to the existence of the Supreme Court. . . .

While it is unpleasant, I think perhaps it is well to fight out this issue and develop in its clear and unmistakable features what the labor unions and La Follette have in mind with respect to the Government and the change of its constitutional structure. When that issue arises, I can not believe that there is any doubt of the strength of the conservative element in the Republic. It may for the time throw Republicans and Democrats together, as I hope it will. Of course were we to have a radical Congress and a radical Senate, they might take steps either to abolish or to practically destroy much of the useful jurisdiction of the inferior Federal courts. We could be certain that the minute they had power, they would frighten the country into a reaction, which would teach a permanent lesson, but meantime the cause of justice in the country would suffer. Of course we may count on a lot of weak-kneed people who are conservative when conservatism seems to be strong, and are radical when radicalism seems to be sweeping the country; but there are many elements who do not manifest themselves superficially and seem to remain inert until they are startled by a danger that ought to have been long foreseen. And it is upon those elements that the hope and confidence in the preservation of our institutions must be based. Meantime there is nothing for the Court to do but to go on about its business, exercise the jurisdiction it has, and not be frightened because of threats against its existence.

It is most interesting, in view of what we may anticipate, to read the history of the Court just published by Warren. I do not agree with a good many of his statements, nor do I subscribe to some of his conclusions, but he has massed together in historical form the history of the Court to show that, with some periods of quiet, its whole history has been one of threat, attack and defeat of its enemies, and it is a proud record that on the whole the Court never bowed its head for motives of political expediency, to yield its conscientious views and convictions to assaults, of which it has had to meet so many in its life of more than a century and a quarter.

I don't know why I have fallen into this disquisition, except that I note in the press a good deal of excitement over the La Follette election and the attacks of labor organizations upon our Court, and I could not refrain from discussing the situation with you as you now come into the Court with a general opinion as to the functions of the Court similar to my own.[24]

La Follette's assault was far from the only attack that was launched against the Court during the early 1920s. In 1923, for example, Senator William E. Borah proposed legislation that would require the concurrence of at least seven justices before the Court could invalidate any act of Congress.[25] Borah's bill was one of a rash of similar proposed statutes.[26]

Matters came to a head when La Follette included his draft constitutional amendment as a plank in his Progressive Party platform during the 1924 presidential campaign.[27] Contemporary antagonists of the Court, like the prominent labor attorney Jackson Harvey Ralston, seized upon dissents as evidence of the Court's

Dissent during the Taft Court

illegitimate usurpation of power: "To show ... even more clearly the doubtful exercise of power by the Supreme Court ... we need but point to the repeated dissents on the part of a minority continually made against the assumption that the court knew more of the necessities of the times than the legislature. Surely if the majority had based their action upon definitely understood constitutional principles, no differences of moment need have arisen."[28]

The point was not lost in the Court. Taft wrote a friend that La Follette "is probably framing an attack upon the Supreme Court's infamous nullification of valuable laws demanded by the people. He could find a good deal of material in Brandeis's dissenting opinions."[29] By July 1924, Brandeis could explicitly observe to Frankfurter that "the drive against the Court has tended" to reduce dissents.[30]

> The whole policy is to suppress dissents, that is the one positive result of Borah 7 to 2 business, to suppress dissent so as not to make it 7 to 2. Holmes, for instance, is always in doubt whether to express his dissent, once he's "had his say" on a given subject & he's had his say on almost everything. You may look for fewer dissents. That's Van Devanter's particularly strong lobbying with the members individually, to have them suppress their dissents.... [W]hile Butler is not easy to move, the prudential arguments of Van D. as to what is "good – or bad – for the Court" are weighty with him & with all of them.[31]

We can speculate, then, that at least some dissenting votes were repressed during the first half of the 1920s to defend the Court from external assault. After La Follette's resounding defeat in November 1924, however, the Court could breathe a sigh of relief.[32] "The controversy over judicial review subsided for several years after the 1924 election."[33] With external pressure diminished, the justices might have felt freer to express their disagreement during the second half of the decade. The *Christian Science Monitor* could report in 1927 that the Supreme Court was now "the most honored branch of the federal institutions. Qualms as to its impartiality and apprehensions regarding its political prejudice have long since vanished. Attacks upon its decisions are rare, and questions of its integrity do not exist."[34]

Several additional factors no doubt contributed to the slide of unanimity rates during the second half of the decade. The most important of these is the substitution of Harlan Stone for Joseph McKenna. During the 1921–1924 terms, McKenna authored or joined 97.3 percent of the decisions in which he participated; during the 1924–1928 terms, by contrast, Stone joined or authored only 94.0 percent of such decisions. Figure IV-17 shows that Stone entered the Court as the consummate "team player,"[35] but that his willingness to accommodate his conservative brethren sharply diminished in the 1926 term as he began to pull away from the Court's due process jurisprudence.[36]

At about the same time Taft suffered his disastrous 1926 heart attack, which impaired his ability to lead and consolidate the Court. He could no longer energetically and proactively intervene in the Court's deliberations to achieve consensus, as he had done during his early years.[37] The consequent vacuum of leadership allowed factionalism to increase.[38] Tension rose as the conservative members of the

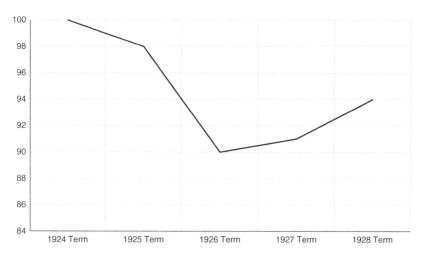

Figure IV-17 Percentage of decisions in which Stone participates and either authors or joins the opinion of the Court, by term

Court became more aggressive in pushing an antiregulatory agenda.[39] The intensity of the struggle is well captured in a memorandum written by Stone to McReynolds just after Taft's resignation. It is worth quoting at length:

> I have your note of yesterday's date. I, of course, do not regard it as presumptuous. On the contrary, I thank you for it, for I hold very strongly that willingness to speak our views and to listen to those of others should guide the actions of all the members of our Court....
>
> I am sure you will give me credit for being sincere in the views which I express. If I did not hold them strongly and believe that very many thoughtful men, trained in the law, would agree with them, I should not take the trouble to write any dissent....
>
> I think you will not misunderstand me when I add that I am profoundly convinced that ... some very serious mistakes have been made by the Court, which would not have been made had it not been for the disposition of the majority to rush to conclusions without taking the trouble to listen to the views of the minority. If the majority overrules the settled decisions of the Court, if it insists on including in opinions, over the protests of the minority, what is not necessary to the decision – see Justice Sutherland's opinion in ... *Patton v. United States*,[40] as the latest example – if it insists on putting out opinions which do not consider or deal with questions raised by the minority, it must, I think, be expected that the minority will give some expression to their views. Otherwise, their function is reduced to registering a vote which is not even published.
>
> What I have written in Nos 281 and 282[41] is, I think you will agree, at least worthy of consideration, but I was not even given an opportunity to state my position at the Conference. If the Court is willing to put out its opinion without meeting that argument or referring to its own decisions ... any consequences for

Dissent during the Taft Court

such ill considered action should not, I think, be attributed to me or what I have written. Very much the same thing might, I think, be said of No. 222.[42] The opinion of the Court is made to rest on propositions that are demonstrably not sound and lead to consequences which, it seems to me, we all ought to be eager to avoid. But if we are not to reach that result, at least the opinion should deal in some plausible manner with the issues raised in my dissent – at least if I am expected to remain silent.[43]

These are very strong words, and yet 74 percent of the Court's opinions in the 1929 term were unanimous.[44] Although the Court was riven with division and tension, it nevertheless decided cases with a degree of unanimity that would be quite unimaginable today, when, as Figure IV-8 illustrates, unanimity rates hover around 34 percent. Fluctuations in the dissent rate during the 1920s, although responsive to many factors – including changes in external circumstances, Court personnel, and Taft's own leadership – nevertheless occurred within channels that mark the Taft Court as committed to forms of institutional solidarity that are genuinely distinct from those of the contemporary Court.

How might we understand the nature of this solidarity? It is sometimes said that the Court's docket during the 1920s was simply less divisive than today. This explanation spotlights the Judiciary Act of 1925, which shifted the Court's docket away from trivial cases previously forced on the Court by its mandatory jurisdiction[45] and toward the more significant and divisive cases selected through discretionary writs of *certiorari*.[46]

Although it is true that full opinions by the Taft Court shifted decisively toward its discretionary jurisdiction, Figure IV-11 illustrates the surprising fact that full opinions written in cases selected through writs of *certiorari* were *more likely* to be unanimous than full opinions stemming from the Court's mandatory jurisdiction. By the 1928 term, 87 percent of full opinions in cases selected by *certiorari* were unanimous, but only 63 percent of full opinions in cases originating in mandatory jurisdiction.[b] As has been repeatedly emphasized in the literature, the Court's rates of unanimity did not begin their free-fall until the late 1930s, as may be seen in Figure IV-12. Thus "changes in the Court's ratio of obligatory to discretionary cases do not coincide with the Justices' patterns of increasing dissent activity."[47] Evidently the centrifugal thrust of discretionary jurisdiction was during the Taft Court contained by more powerful centripetal forces.

We can begin to identify these forces by examining the Butler and Stone docket books described in the Preface.[48] These books create nontrivial issues of

---

[b] Figure IV-11 graphically illustrates the seemingly counterintuitive fact that the 1925 Act actually precipitated a sharp fall in unanimity rates in full opinions in cases coming to the Court by way of its mandatory jurisdiction. Unanimity rates in opinions for cases within the Court's mandatory jurisdiction plunged from 90 percent in the 1922 term to 63 percent in the 1928 term. The decline probably reflects the fact that the cases remaining within the Court's mandatory jurisdiction were likely to be difficult and significant. *See supra* Chapter 18, at footnote b.

THE TAFT COURT

interpretation and classification, but for purposes of analysis I have divided the conference cases into three categories:

1. Cases that were unanimous in conference, which include cases in which the votes of one or more justices were not recorded.
2. Cases in which one or more justices voted in conference against the ultimate resolution of the case.
3. Cases in which one or more justices expressly articulated uncertainty in conference, either by "passing" or "acquiescing" or by otherwise refusing to vote due to indecision.[c]

Of the 1,028 conference cases that were ultimately decided by a published unanimous opinion of the Court, only 58% were also unanimous in conference. Some 30% of these 1,028 cases required a switch in vote to obtain ultimate unanimity, and a further 12% required one or more justices to overcome uncertainty to achieve unanimity. The unanimity rate within the complete set of 1,200 conference cases, as measured by a unanimous vote at conference, was only 50%.[d] But Figure IV–18 shows that the unanimity rate of these same cases as measured by their published opinions was 86%.

It is clear that Taft Court justices routinely changed their votes between conference and the publication of an opinion.[49] In the complete set of 1,200 published conference cases a justice changed his vote to join the Court opinion 680 times.[e] Like Taft, members of the Court were willing to "make the sign of the scissors" in private, but they were reluctant to do so "to the public."[50]

---

[c] I decided that it would be most cautious to assume that if the vote of a justice was not recorded, it was most likely due to immaterial circumstances, like absence or oversight. This assumption possibly *overestimates* consensus within Taft Court conferences.

[d] The unanimity rate was 60% if one counts as unanimous those cases in which Justices express in conference uncertainty, but do not register an explicitly contrary vote. The raw data are these: The set of conference cases consists of 1,200 decisions. Of these 1,028 were ultimately decided unanimously. Of these, 601 were also unanimous in conference; 304 had dissenting votes in conference; and 123 had no dissenting votes but did have justices who registered uncertainty in conference. If one considers the entire set of 1,200 cases, 670 (56%) had the same vote in conference as the ultimately published opinion; in 358 (30%), one or more justices switched his conference vote to join the court opinion; and in 129 (11%), there were no dissenting votes in conference, but one or more justices ultimately resolved an uncertainty expressed in conference in order to join the Court opinion. In eighteen cases (2%), one or more justices who voted with the Court in conference refused to join the published Court opinion; in eleven cases (1%), one or more justices switched their conference vote away from the Court's opinion; in six cases, one or more justices expressed uncertainty in conference but resolved their uncertainty by dissenting from the Court's opinion; in five cases, one or more justices voted against the Court's judgment in conference but ultimately switched their vote to support the Court's judgment while refusing to join the Court's opinion; and in three cases there were switches of votes in both directions, both for and against the Court's ultimate opinion.

[e] Taft changed his vote to join the Court opinion forty-eight times; McKenna, thirty-eight times; Holmes, eighty times; Van Devanter, forty-five times; McReynolds, ninety-nine times; Brandeis, ninety-five times; Sutherland,

Dissent during the Taft Court

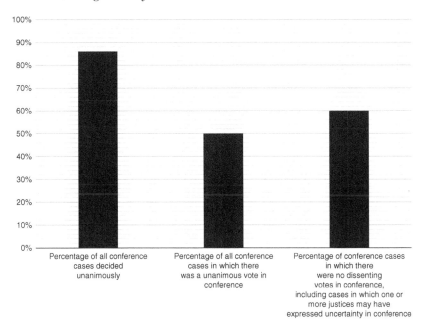

Figure IV-18 Unanimity and the conference cases

The difference between unanimity in published opinions and unanimity in conference voting is summarized in Figure IV-18. It is especially striking that the unanimity rate for the Taft Court in conference was 50 percent, while the average unanimity rate for published full opinions of the Roberts Court is only about 34 percent (Figure IV-8). This might seem to suggest that the Taft Court's spontaneous view of the substantive issues raised by its docket was more cohesive than that

eighty-seven times; Butler, sixty times; Sanford, ninety-three times; and Stone, thirty-five times. Figure IV-19 represents these numbers as a percentage of the total number of cases in which each justice participated. *Compare* Figure I-9. Figure IV-19 shows that McKenna was the justice most likely to switch his conference vote, doing so in 10% of all cases in which he participated. Justice McReynolds was the next most likely, switching his vote in 9% of all cases in which he participated. Justices Van Devanter and Taft, by contrast, switched their conference vote in only 4% of the cases in which they participated. This might be misleading, however, because it seems to suggest that Taft and Van Devanter were stubbornly unwilling to alter their votes. In fact the opposite is true. Figure IV-20 calculates the percentage of a justice's dissenting votes in conference that a justice switched to join a Court opinion. It indicates that Taft and Van Devanter were actually quite willing to change their votes in order to display judicial solidarity, switching (respectively) 80% and 82% of their dissenting votes in order to join an opinion of the Court. By this measure, Justices Stone (54%), Brandeis (60%), and McReynolds (60%) were the least pliable of all the justices.

621

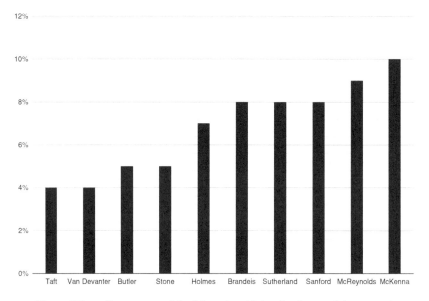

Figure IV-19 Percentage of decisions in which a justice participates and switches a vote in conference to join a published Court opinion

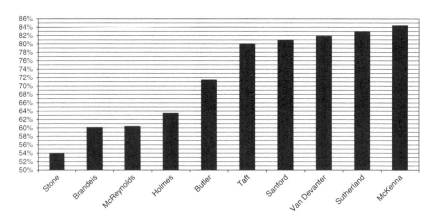

Figure IV-20 Percentage of dissenting votes in conference that a justice changes in order to join a published Court opinion

of the contemporary Court.[51] It has sometimes been said that the high rate of disagreement in the contemporary Court is due to the triumph of legal realism, which is postulated to have "made consensus more difficult" because it validated the legal indeterminacy that Holmes was so concerned to theorize.[52]

Dissent during the Taft Court

A closer inspection of the data, however, requires that this hypothesis be qualified. Figure IV-21 disaggregates the unanimity of the conference cases by term. It indicates that unanimity rates in conference began to drop after the 1925 Act, sinking to 37 percent in the 1928 term. Yet in the 1928 term, 78 percent of the Court's conference cases were published with unanimous full opinions. The percentage of conference cases published with unanimous full opinions can be represented as a multiple of the percentage of such cases that were spontaneously unanimous at conference. The illuminating result is Figure IV-22, which shows that in the 1928 term the Court responded to growing dissensus in conference by sharply increasing its efforts to produce unanimous published opinions.

These effects are even more startling when the conference cases are disaggregated by jurisdiction. Figure IV-23 shows that although the rate of published unanimity was slightly greater for conferences cases selected by discretionary writs of *certiorari* (88%) than for conference cases that came to the Court by way of its mandatory jurisdiction (84%), in fact the former were significantly *less* likely to be unanimous in conference (41%) than the latter (56%). Figure IV-24 disaggregates these numbers by term and shows that the presumably more difficult cases selected by *certiorari* were consistently less unanimous in conference, at least until the 1928 term when the 1925 Act had apparently succeeded in utterly stripping away the trifling cases from the Court's mandatory jurisdiction. The level of disagreement in conference about *certiorari* cases was so great that it approximates the level of dissensus in the published cases of the contemporary Court. If the rate of published unanimous conference cases is represented as a multiple of the rate of unanimity in conference, Figure IV-25 shows that the Court persistently made far greater efforts to publish unanimous opinions in cases selected by *certiorari*.

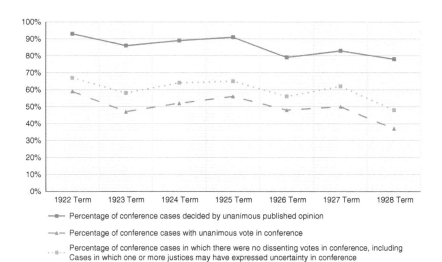

Figure IV-21 Unanimity of conference cases, by term, 1922–1928 terms

The Taft Court

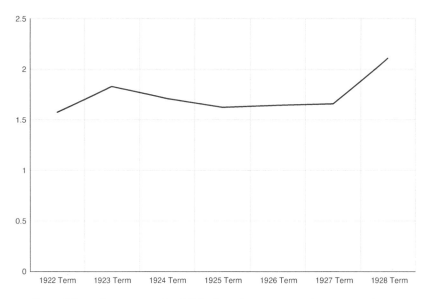

Figure IV-22 Percentage of published conference cases that are unanimous as a multiple of the percentage of the conference cases that are unanimous in conference, by term

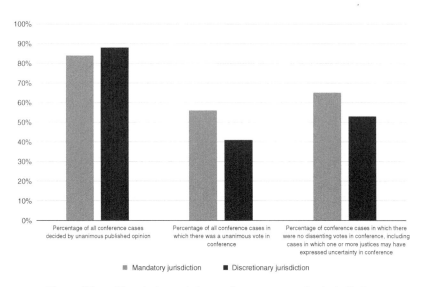

Figure IV-23 Unanimity and the conferences cases, by jurisdiction

Dissent during the Taft Court

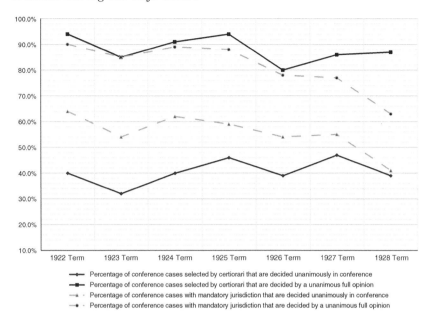

Figure IV-24 Unanimity and the conference cases by jurisdiction, by term, 1922–1928 terms

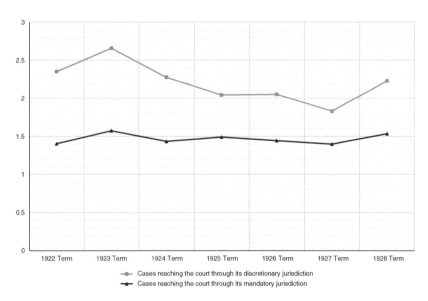

Figure IV-25 Percentage of published conference cases that are unanimous as a multiple of the percentage of the conference cases that are unanimous in conference, by jurisdiction, by term, 1922–1928 terms

Although the unanimity rates of the Taft Court's published full opinions did not precipitously decline as a result of the 1925 Act, the Act nevertheless increased the number of *certiorari* cases, and hence the number of nonunanimous votes in conference. The Act thus put great pressure on the Court's ability to maintain its usual rate of unanimous published full opinions.[53] The high levels of controversy in conference in the 1920s cannot be explained by the subsequent triumph of legal realism.

Although the brute fact of disagreement might be more prominent in the modern Court than in the Taft Court, the major difference between the two Courts appears to lie in the fact that members of the Taft Court went to extraordinary lengths to conceal their conflict from the public by maintaining an outward show of unanimity. That is the lesson of Figures IV-21 and IV-24. Taft Court justices manifestly believed, in the words of Canon 19 of the American Bar Association's 1924 Canons of Judicial Ethics, that a justice should not "yield to pride of opinion or value more highly his individual reputation than that of the court to which he should be loyal. Except in cases of conscientious difference of opinion on fundamental principle, dissenting opinions should be discouraged in courts of last resort."[54]

All members of the Taft Court displayed this commitment to institutional solidarity. Van Devanter put the matter well in 1930: "Unanimity of opinion is very desirable and is always sought, but never at the sacrifice of strong conviction."[55] Butler, for example, regarded dissents as "vanity" and "would rather not have them."[56] He once responded to a Stone opinion with a short disquisition on the subject: "I voted to reverse. While this sustains your conclusion to affirm, I still think a reversal would be better. But I shall in silence acquiesce. Dissents seldom aid us in the right development or statement of the law. They often do harm. For myself I say: 'Lead us not unto Temptation.'"[57] To Holmes, Butler remarked, "I voted the other way & remain unconvinced, but dissenting clamor does not often appeal to me as useful. I shall acquiesce."[58] To another draft opinion Butler responded, "I voted the other way and am still inclined that way, but acquiesce for the sake of harmony & the Court."[59]

Extant returns to circulated draft Taft Court opinions yield numerous analogous examples.[60] Stone, for example, refused to join a proposed Brandeis dissent because Stone had a "general disposition not to dissent unless I feel strongly on the subject."[61] Stone was quite clear that "I always write a dissent with real reluctance, and often acquiesce in opinions with which I do not fully agree."[62] Brandeis was similarly reluctant to dissent. He concurred in an opinion of Stone, noting that "I think this is woefully wrong, but do not expect to dissent."[63] In response to a Holmes opinion, Brandeis remarked, "I think the question was one for a jury – but the case is of a class in which one may properly 'shut up.'"[64]

To an ultimately unanimous Stone opinion, Holmes commented, "I incline the other way. If B[randeis] who I believe voted as I did writes, ... probably I shall concur with him. If he is silent, I probably shall ... shut up."[65] To a Brandeis opinion, Holmes returned, "It does not absolutely convince me, but as you say, I shall acquiesce."[66] Sutherland wrote Brandeis about an opinion published unanimously, "I thought otherwise, but shall probably acquiesce."[67] To an ultimately unanimous Stone opinion, Sutherland replied, "I had a different view, and shall withhold final determination in order to see what the other stubborn members have

Dissent during the Taft Court

to say."[68] Without registering a dissent, Sutherland responded to a Holmes opinion, "Sorry, I cannot agree."[69]

Sanford replied to an ultimately unanimous Holmes opinion with the comment, "I regret that I cannot see my way clear to agree. ... I shall probably not dissent, unless some one else does so."[70] To another opinion, he answered: "I regret that I cannot concur but shall not dissent."[71] To an opinion by Brandeis, McReynolds wrote, "I thought otherwise but do not care to say anything now."[72] To a Holmes opinion, McReynolds commented, "I have my doubts but not the necessary votes. Wherefore I am mum."[73] To another ultimately unanimous Holmes opinion, Van Devanter commented, "I am not satisfied, but if others agree I shall have nothing to say."[74]

McKenna, who, as Figures IV-19 and IV-20 illustrate, was the most inclined of any justice to alter his conference vote, turned concession into a virtual art form of the absurd:

> I voted the other way but my effort is to please so I will accede.[75]

> Plausible if not sound. And being alone there seems no reason for making a fuss.[76]

> I voted the other way but I have resolved on amiability & concession, so submit. I am not sure that I am not convinced.[77]

> You have the art of making the wrong appear the better reason and give me excuse to acquiesce, and as I hail opportunities to be amicable I say yes.[78]

> Narrow treading but there is only one result when one opposes, or tries to oppose, a majority. Besides by yielding one gets the praise of being susceptible to reason.[79]

> Dubitante. There are objections against a plenum and objections against a vacuum but one of them must be true.[80]

In the political science literature, a commitment to institutional solidarity of this kind is sometimes called a "norm of consensus."[81] But if one carefully attends to the language of these exchanges, members of the Taft Court did not so much agree as *acquiesce*. Taft Court justices preserved their differences of opinion but acted on the belief that these disagreements ought not impede published unanimity in the absence of strong conscientious objection. The point was to authorize the Court to present a united front to parties and to the public. Even Holmes consistently proclaimed that "I rather shudder at being held up as the dissenting judge and more or less contrasted with the Court."[82] The norm of acquiescence empowered the Court to produce "the impact of monolithic solidarity on which the authority of a bench of judges so largely depends."[83]

The striking implication of Figures IV-24 and IV-25 is that the Court seems to have striven harder to preserve unanimity as internal rates of dissensus at conference increased. The norm of acquiescence plainly functioned to contain the centrifugal energies unleashed by the 1925 Act. The norm sustained the

THE TAFT COURT

extraordinarily high rates of unanimity that characterized published opinions of the Taft Court, rates that were 30–40 percentage points higher than the rates of unanimity it reached in its conference voting, as can be seen in Figure IV-21.

The question is therefore why the individual justices of the Taft Court were united in their allegiance to a common norm of acquiescence.[84] One hypothesis is that the norm may have been a useful way to diffuse potentially testy relationships among justices. Brandeis once remarked to Frankfurter that "there is a limit to the frequency with which you can [dissent], without exasperating men; ... [Y]ou may have a very important case of your own as to which you do not want to antagonize on a less important case etc. etc."[85] Brandeis noted that the "[g]reat difficulty of all group action ... is when & what concessions to make. Can't always dissent – may have dissented much just then."[86] On one occasion, Brandeis responded to Taft's invitation to join a separate opinion, "I agree with your criticism of the ... opinion. You will recall that I voted the other way; and the opinion has not removed my difficulties ... But I have differed from the Court recently in three expressed dissents and concluded that, in this case, I had better 'shut up,' as in Junior days."[87]

The experience of the contemporary Court, however, rather conclusively demonstrates that a norm of acquiescence is not necessary to sustain amicable working relationships among the justices.[88] We must look for other explanations for the strength of the norm. One plausible possibility is that it was connected to the way in which Taft Court justices experienced their dual obligations to decide cases for the present benefit of litigants and yet also to render decisions that would shape the future substance of the law. These obligations are distinct and can often be in tension with each other. The balance between them might be struck one way when opinions are designed for a tribunal whose chief task is to dispose of numerous routine cases, and it is likely to be struck quite differently when opinions are written for a tribunal whose primary task is to address "the public at large, as distinguished from the particular litigants before it."[89]

Dissent cannot modify the binding and dispositive force of a Court's judgment with respect to the parties before it; at most dissent can mollify a losing party. But if the primary function of a court is instead to shape the future substance of the law, dissent can potentially prove of far greater importance. The trade-off between institutional solidarity and individual conscience is quite different if all that turns on a Supreme Court opinion is the proper adjudication of a dispute between particular parties than if the stakes of a decision also include the subsequent development of the legal system.

These considerations suggest that the concept of the Supreme Court opinion at the core of the Judiciary Act of 1925 was singularly calculated to exert pressure on the norm of acquiescence. As the Court's opinions began to modulate from the relatively routinized dispositions of a court of last resort to strategic interventions designed to shape the ongoing substance of American law, the importance of dissent began to increase. It is not surprising that a norm developed in the former context should begin to falter in the latter. The collapse of unanimity and the changing function of the Supreme Court might thus be intimately connected.

The point requires careful formulation, however, because courts resolve disputes between parties by articulating legal principles, and these principles both

Dissent during the Taft Court

decide specific cases and also become precedents for the resolution of future cases. The audience for all Court opinions, therefore, hovers ambiguously between particular parties and the general legal public. The relationship between these two audiences very much depends upon a jurisprudential account of how law works to accomplish its ends. If judicial opinions are understood to influence the legal system through the enunciation of fixed and stable principles, there is essentially no distinction between opinions addressed to the general legal public and opinions addressed to the parties in a particular case. The purpose of an opinion is to announce permanent legal standards that will simultaneously discharge the Court's obligation to both audiences.

This jurisprudential understanding of law puts potential dissenters into an exceedingly awkward position. Whether a potential dissenter looks to the effect of his dissent on the parties in the case, or to its effect on the future evolution of the law, dissent is impotent[90] and destructive. It undermines the certainty required by law. As Edward Douglass White put it, "The only purpose which an elaborate dissent can accomplish, if any, is to weaken the effect of the opinion of the majority, and thus engender want of confidence in the conclusions of courts of last resort."[91] Even Holmes believed that it was "useless and undesirable, as a rule, to express dissent."[92] If judicial precedent is understood as fixed and certain, a dissenter is relegated to the symbolic position of registering merely personal disagreement with a Court's official judgment.[93] To minimize charges of "egotism,"[94] Canon 19 of the American Bar Association's 1924 Canons of Judicial Ethics strove to limit dissent in "courts of last resort" to "conscientious difference of opinion."[95]

The norm of acquiescence fits comfortably with this jurisprudential perspective. If the institutional justification for dissent is unclear; if dissent carries potentially large deleterious effects for the establishment of law with respect to both litigants and the public; if the benefits to a dissenter are chiefly personal; then a norm of acquiescence offers a face-saving way for a dissenter to mediate between private intellectual disagreement and participation in the common goal of creating official, permanent law.

It should come as no surprise, therefore, that those who sought to suppress judicial dissent in the early 1900s typically appealed to a jurisprudential account of law that stressed fixity and finality.[96] A 1905 article in the *Green Bag* argued that "[t]he fundamental security of all peoples lies, not in the justice, but in the certainty, of their laws," from which it deduced that "the Dissenting Opinion is of all judicial mistakes the most injurious."[97] "There never should be a dissenting opinion in a case decided by a court of last resort," propounded the *Albany Law Journal* in 1898. "No judge, lawyer or layman should be permitted to weaken the force of the court's decision, which all must accept as an unappealable finality."

> It is a maxim of the law that it is to the interest of the public that there should be an end to litigation. It certainly is to the interest of the public that when a question is settled by the highest tribunal, it should remain settled for all time. The result of a dissenting opinion is simply to open up for future discussion, bickering and litigation the question which should then be finally settled by that tribunal. Somebody must settle the question; it must be settled somewhere; that

tribunal has been selected as the final arbiter, and when it once settles it, it should remain settled forever.[98]

One can discern an echo of this position in Holmes's announced reticence "to express his dissent, once he's 'had his say' on a given subject."[99] Holmes believed that "There are obvious limits of propriety to the persistent expression of opinions that do not command the agreement of the Court."[100] If a case or a legal principle were important enough, he was willing to dissent and articulate an understanding of the law different from that announced by the Court.[101] But once his understanding was rejected, Holmes would not continue to insist on his own personal perspective.[102] What mattered was the institutional judgment of the Court. Only in the most consequential circumstances, as for example in the area of freedom of speech, would he candidly repeat a position in the teeth of dispositive contrary judicial resolution. And then he would remark, as he did in his dissent in *Gitlow v. New York*, that "the convictions that I expressed in [*Abrams*] are too deep for it to be possible for me as yet to believe that it and *Schaefer* . . . have settled the law."[103] In the absence of such deep conviction, Holmes implied, acquiescence in settled precedent was necessary to ensure the stability of law.

If Holmes's conception of dissent was compatible with a strong norm of acquiescence, Brandeis by contrast struggled to articulate a conception of dissent that would limit the jurisprudential reach of the norm. Brandeis sought to distinguish circumstances in which judicial finality was a significant jurisprudential virtue from those in which it was not. "In ordinary cases," he said to Frankfurter in 1923, "there is a good deal to be said for not having dissents. You want certainty & definiteness & it doesn't matter terribly how you decide, so long as it is settled. But in these constitutional cases, since what is done is what you call statesmanship, nothing is ever settled – unless statesmanship is settled & at an end."[104]

This is an unusually suggestive passage, because it explicitly ties the norm of acquiescence to an account of how law achieves its purposes, and it offers a discriminating account of the difference between ordinary law, where the value of finality is highly desirable, and constitutional law, where it is not.[105] Brandeis's explanation of the diminished importance of finality in constitutional law does not turn on the primacy of constitutional justice, but rather on the fact that constitutional law is a form of "statesmanship," and statesmanship requires continuous flexibility and growth.[106] It is no act of statesmanship to announce a rule and expect it, in the words of the *Albany Law Journal*, to "remain settled forever."[107]

The point is precisely captured in the exchange between Brandeis and Taft that we discussed in Chapter 10 in the context of *United States v. Moreland*.[108] Brandeis affirmed that the Constitution possessed "the capacity of adaption" because it "is a living organism,"[109] whereas Taft believed that the "very purpose" of the Constitution was "to prevent experimentation with the fundamental rights of the individual."[110] For Taft the object of constitutional law was to "settle" such matters forever.[111] For Brandeis, the object of constitutional law was to facilitate the never-ending process of democratic self-determination.[112]

Dissent during the Taft Court

The jurisprudential difference between Brandeis and Taft implies important consequences for the norm of acquiescence.[113] If law is regarded as continuously and properly evolving, the costs of acquiescence increase, because assent to a mistaken opinion affects the future development of the law. So far from expressing merely conscientious personal disagreement, dissent constitutes, in the famous words of Charles Evans Hughes, "an appeal to the brooding spirit of the law, to the intelligence of a future day, when a later decision may possibly correct the error into which the dissenting judge believes the court to have been betrayed."[114]

If the virtue of law is conceived to lie in its flexibility and adaptability, rather than in its stability and fixity, a potential dissenter must weigh any "dissatisfaction" that a dissent may engender[115] against an obligation to future generations wisely to shape the subsequent development of the law.[116] Once the 1925 Act decisively reoriented the institutional function of the Court toward the management of the law and its reception by the general legal public, and once members of the Court began to regard "growth" as "the life of the law,"[117] the norm of acquiescence was undermined from within. By the end of the 1940s, when, as Figure IV-12 indicates, the norm of acquiescence had utterly collapsed, a justice like William O. Douglas, perhaps the most consummate dissenter in the history of the Court, could affirm that "philosophers of the democratic faith will rejoice in the uncertainty of the law and find strength and glory in it."[118]

THE TAFT COURT
Notes

1. John P. Kelsh, *The Opinion Delivery Practices of the United Supreme Court 1790–1945*, 77 WASHINGTON UNIVERSITY LAW QUARTERLY 137, 178 (1999).
2. ALPHEUS THOMAS MASON, THE SUPREME COURT: FROM TAFT TO WARREN 60 (Baton Rouge: Louisiana State University Press 1968).
3. Thomas G. Walker, Lee Epstein, & William J. Dixon, *On the Mysterious Demise of Consensual Norms in the United States Supreme Court*, 50 JOURNAL OF POLITICS 361, 380–81 (1988); *cf.* Gregory Caldeira & Christopher Zorn, *Of Time and Consensual Norms in the Supreme Court*, 42 AMERICAN JOURNAL OF POLITICAL SCIENCE 874, 878 (1998) ("Of the various explanations [for consensus], none has figured more prominently than the influence of the chief justice"); Stacia L. Haynie, *Leadership and Consensus on the U.S. Supreme Court*, 54 JOURNAL OF POLITICS 1158, 1160 (1992).
4. PAMELA C. CORLEY, AMY STEIGERWALT, & ARTEMUS WARD, THE PUZZLE OF UNANIMITY 19 (Stanford Law Books 2013); Lee Epstein, Jeffrey A. Segal, & Harold J. Spaeth, *The Norm of Consensus on the U.S. Supreme Court*, 45 AMERICAN JOURNAL OF POLITICAL SCIENCE 362, 363 (2001); Walker, Epstein & Dixon, *supra* note 3, at 363; Kelsh, *supra* note 1, at 175–76; Marcus E. Hendershot, Mark S. Hurwitz, Drew Noble Lanier, & Richard L. Pacelle, Jr., *Dissensual Decision Making: Revisiting the Demise of Consensual Norms within the U.S. Supreme Court*, 66 POLITICAL RESEARCH QUARTERLY 467, 472 (2013); Haynie, *supra* note 3, at 1158; *see also* Caldeira & Zorn, *supra* note 3, at 882; David M. O'Brien, *Institutional Norms and Supreme Court Opinions: On Reconsidering the Rise of Individual Opinions*, in SUPREME COURT DECISION-MAKING: NEW INSTITUTIONALIST APPROACHES 91–95 (Cornell W. Clayton & Howard Gillman, eds., University of Chicago Press 1999).
5. WHT to Sir Thomas White (January 8, 1922) (Taft papers).
6. Taft once received an unsolicited letter from one Walter S. Whiton, an unknown attorney in Minneapolis, asking Taft if he did "not think that it would be better all round, if no dissenting opinions of any court were printed or published?" Walter S. Whiton to WHT (April 16, 1923) (Taft papers). Taft replied, "I agree with you about dissenting opinions. I think it would be better to have none, but the custom has grown so now that it can not be eradicated, unless perhaps by act of Congress. But I am quite sure that Congress would not sustain such legislation." WHT to Walter S. Whiton (April 19, 1923) (Taft papers). The Constitution of the State of Louisiana forbade the publication of dissents between 1898 and 1921. Art. 92, Louisiana Constitutions of 1898 and 1913, in BENJAMIN WALL DART, CONSTITUTIONS OF THE STATE OF LOUISIANA 616, 672 (Indianapolis: Bobbs-Merrill 1932). *See* Hunter Smith, *Personal and Official Authority: Turn-of-the-Century Lawyers and the Dissenting Opinion*, 24 YALE JOURNAL OF LAW AND HUMANITIES 507, 513–15 (2012). For a while, Pennsylvania sought to prohibit the printing of dissenting opinions. Alex Simpson Jr., *Dissenting Opinions*, 71 UNIVERSITY OF PENNSYLVANIA LAW REVIEW 205, 206–9 (1923).
7. S. Sidney Ulmer, *Exploring the Dissent Patterns of the Chief Justices: John Marshall to Warren Burger*, in JUDICIAL CONFLICT AND CONSENSUS: BEHAVIORAL STUDIES OF AMERICAN APPELLATE COURTS 53 (Sheldon Goldman & Charles M. Lamb, eds., Lexington: University Press of Kentucky 1986).

Dissent during the Taft Court

8. WHT to JHC (February 10, 1922) (Clarke papers). Ironically enough, Taft's letter to Clarke was in the context of a case, Gooch v. Oregon Short Line R. Co., 258 U.S. 22 (1922), in which Taft joined Clarke's dissent. The opinion for the Court was by Holmes; it held that a railroad's refusal to compensate for personal injuries suffered from a train accident was justified because the plaintiff had failed to comply with a contractual thirty-day notice provision. In the so-called Cummins Amendment of March 4, 1915, Pub. L. 63-325, 38 Stat. 1196, Congress had altered the Interstate Commerce Act of 1887 specifically to ban notice periods of less than ninety days for damage to property caused by railroads. Holmes held for the Court that the policy underlying the Cummins Amendment should not be judicially extended to damage caused by personal injuries. In his letter to Clarke, Taft wrote that "If by joining you in your dissent I would add anything to the implied appeal to Congress to extend the Cummins Amendment to persons, I am inclined to think it my duty to do so." WHT to JHC (February 10, 1922) (Clarke papers). Congress did not amend the Interstate Commerce Act in response to Clarke's dissent.
9. WHT to WVD (December 26, 1921) (Van Devanter papers). Evincing the trust that he had already placed in Van Devanter, as well as his innate and irreducible suspicion of Brandeis, Taft added: "but that sense of proportion is not present in the minds of some of our brethren. As to B[randeis], that sense is not lacking but his ultimate purpose is to break down the prestige of the Court."
10. New Orleans Land Co. v. Brott, 263 U.S. 98 (1923) (Holmes papers). Or, as Taft wrote Holmes with respect to the latter's draft opinion in National Ass'n of Window Glass Manufacturers v. United States, 263 U.S. 403 (1923), "I come in and shut my mouth." (Holmes papers).
11. William Howard Taft, *Chief Justice White* (May 20, 1921), in VIVIAN, at 581.
12. 259 U.S. 344 (1922). *See infra* Chapter 40, at 1304–8. The circumstances are discussed in Stanley I. Kutler, *Chief Justice Taft, Judicial Unanimity, and Labor: The Coronado Case*, 24 THE HISTORIAN 68 (1961), and in ALEXANDER M. BICKEL, THE UNPUBLISHED OPINIONS OF MR. JUSTICE BRANDEIS: THE SUPREME COURT AT WORK 77–99 (Cambridge: Harvard University Press 1957). Bickel also discusses Taft's efforts to "mass the court" in the case of Sonneborn Brothers v. Cureton, 262 U.S. 506 (1923). *See id.* at 100–18.
13. 258 U.S. 44 (1922). The circumstances are discussed in David Joseph Danelski, The Chief Justice and the Supreme Court 188–89 (Ph.D. Dissertation, University of Chicago 1961).
14. *See infra* Chapter 39, at 1239–40. The circumstances are discussed in JONATHAN LURIE, THE CHIEF JUSTICESHIP OF WILLIAM HOWARD TAFT, 1921–1930, at 22–27 (Columbia: University of South Carolina Press 2019), and in Danelski, *supra* note 13, at 180–81.
15. 264 U.S. 331 (1924). The circumstances are discussed in ALPHEUS THOMAS MASON, WILLIAM HOWARD TAFT: CHIEF JUSTICE 211–12 (New York: Simon and Schuster 1965), and in BICKEL, *supra* note 12, at 202–10.
16. 265 U.S. 215 (1924). Taft's efforts are apparent in the case file in the Holmes papers.
17. 274 U.S. 160 (1927). Taft's efforts are apparent in the case file in the Brandeis papers.
18. 278 U.S. 367 (1929).
19. WHT to PB (January 7, 1929) (Taft papers).

THE TAFT COURT

20. For a good summary, see WILLIAM G. ROSS, A MUTED FURY: POPULISTS, PROGRESSIVES, AND LABOR UNIONS CONFRONT THE COURT, 1890–1937, at 170–78 (Princeton University Press 1994).
21. Steven F. Lawson, *Progressives and the Supreme Court: A Case for Judicial Reform in the 1920s*, 42 HISTORIAN 419 (1980).
22. ROSS, *supra* note 20, at 192–217. *See* Earl L. Shaub, *Labor Plans for Slash of Court Power*, SAN FRANCISCO EXAMINER (June 15, 1922), at 11. La Follette's proposal may be found at 62 CONG. REC. 9074–82 (June 21, 1922). For an example of a similar proposed constitutional amendment, see H.R.J. Res. 436, 67th CONG. 4th SESS. (1923); 64 CONG. REC. 2607–15 (1923). For press reactions to La Follette's proposal, see *Is the Supreme Court Too Supreme?*, 74 LITERARY DIGEST 21 (July 1, 1922).
23. Taft believed, however, "that the American people would come to their senses before a proposed amendment could" be passed. WHT to Clarence H. Kelsey (September 12, 1922) (Taft papers). "Nevertheless the friends of our institutions ought to be up and doing to prevent the enemies of society from removing the restraints, without which we would move toward communism, or at least state socialism." *Id*. Taft drew comfort from his "reading three volumes of a work on the Supreme Court of the United States in the history of the country by Charles Warren. . . . He has developed most clearly the fact that the Supreme Court has lived through a great many attacks at every stage of its history; that frequent attempts have been made in Congress to take away its constitutional jurisdiction, but that up to this time they have always failed, showing that on the whole the public opinion of the country insists on the maintenance of the jurisdiction of the Court. I did not realize how massed and strong the attack on the Court had been before Marshall came in, during all of Marshall's life, afterwards during Taney's life, and then during the period immediately after the Civil War." WHT to Charles P. Taft (September 4, 1922) (Taft papers). *See* WHT to Charles Warren (October 28, 1922) (Taft papers) (your book shows how the Court has been "a stormy petrel in the politics of the country," and has been the object of "promoted serious attempts to change and minimize the constitutional function and power of the Court. . . . All of this emphasizes the sound conservatism of the people, in that such menaces and attempts have been defeated in the past, though they seemed more formidable than those of the present day."); Charles Warren to WHT (November 7, 1922) (Taft papers) ("It has been evident, for several years," that the Court "was to pass through another of the recurrent tides of criticism which have occurred at variously recurring periods in American history.").
24. WHT to GS (September 10, 1922) (Sutherland papers). In his letter, Taft refers to CHARLES WARREN, THE SUPREME COURT IN UNITED STATES HISTORY (Boston: Little, Brown & Co. 1922). See *supra* note 23.
25. ROSS, *supra* note 20, at 218–32; S. 4483, 67th CONG. 4th SESS. (1923).
26. *See, e.g.*, H.R. 14209, 67th CONG. 4th SESS. (1923); H.R. 697, 68th CONG. 1st SESS. (1923); H.R. 721, 68th CONG. 1st SESS. (1923).
27. ROSS, *supra* note 20, at 254–84; *see also* KENNETH CAMPBELL MACKAY, THE PROGRESSIVE MOVEMENT OF 1924, at 11, 143 (New York: Columbia University Press 1947).
28 Jackson Harvey Ralston, *Shall We Curb the Supreme Court?*, 71 THE FORUM 561, 565 (1924). *See, e.g.*, John P. Frey, *Shall the People or the Supreme Court be the*

Dissent during the Taft Court

Final Voice in Legislation?, 29 AMERICAN FEDERATIONIST 629, 634 (1922) ("That the members of the Supreme Court hold most opposite views and quite contrary conceptions of constitutional principles, is shown by the large number of dissenting opinions which are handed down, some of which point out that the decision of the majority of the court is not only contrary to American principles, but contrary to the language and intent of the constitution itself."). Charges that dissents undermined the Court's claim to speak with the authority of law were common during the era. John W. Davis, in his presidential address to the American Bar Association, was moved to observe that "much of the current discontent is caused perhaps by the publication of dissenting opinions which serve to fan the flame of public distrust. Certainly, it is not edifying to the lay mind that an opinion representing the considered judgment of the majority of any court should be accompanied at the moment of deliverance by an effort to prove its manifest error." John W. Davis, *Present Day Problems*, 9 AMERICAN BAR ASSOCIATION JOURNAL 553, 557 (1923). *See also* John K. Shields, *Senator Condemns Legislative Efforts to Curb Supreme Court*, NEW YORK TIMES (April 15, 1923), § 8, at 10 ("It will not be improper here to suggest the impropriety of these dissenting opinions for the bad effect they have upon the public mind concerning the wisdom of the court and the certainty of the law. It has been urged, with much force, that when a majority of the court come to a conclusion and solemnly declare the law, its action is as binding upon the minority as upon the parties and the public and the minority by express dissent ought not to challenge the soundness or justice of the judgment but yield to it the obedience and respect that is due the decisions of the court.").

29. WHT to Gus Karger (August 30, 1924) (Taft papers). Ironically, when Samuel Gompers in the pages of the *American Federationist* pressed the case for a constitutional amendment allowing Congress to overturn Supreme Court decisions holding federal statutes unconstitutional, he pointed to Taft's own dissent in Adkins v. Children's Hospital of the District of Columbia, 261 U.S. 525 (1923). Samuel Gompers, *Take Away Its Usurped Power*, 30 AMERICAN FEDERATIONIST 399, 400 (1923).
30. *Brandeis-Frankfurter Conversations*, at 328 (July 2, 1924). Frankfurter himself publicly endorsed La Follette. See Felix Frankfurter, *Why I shall Vote for La Follette*, 40 NEW REPUBLIC 199 (1924).
31. *Brandeis-Frankfurter Conversations*, at 330 (July 6, 1924).
32. *See, e.g.*, WHT to WVD (June 19, 1925) (Van Devanter papers): "As I look back over the Term it seems to me we got through very well. ... We have had no unseemly dissensions among our members. I think the result of the last election does not show that the Court stands any better than it always has with the people but it shows to a great many who were convinced that they could profit by abusing it that they should look for some other field for their demagoguery more profitable. I don't think I am mistaken in thinking that Borah and that ilk are losing interest in efforts to change the Court." Taft wrote his brother Horace that "[t]he greatest failure of La Follette was his attack upon our court. He confessed his failure in his effort to minimize the issue after the campaign was well on." WHT to Horace D. Taft (June 20, 1925) (Taft papers). Brandeis's close friend, Norman Hapgood, wrote in 1926 that "The hard difficulty we encountered in the La Follette campaign was lack of an issue. A definite cure was offered for the too much readiness of the

THE TAFT COURT

Supreme Court to upset certain kinds of legislation, and the cure was probably wrong." *Where Are the Pre-War Radicals?*, 55 THE SURVEY 559 (1926).
33. ROSS, *supra* note 20, at 285.
34. *The Supreme Court's New Term*, CHRISTIAN SCIENCE MONITOR (October 3, 1927), at 16.
35. As Stone remarked to Taft soon after Stone joined the Court: "You know I am a team player." HFS to WHT (December 7, 1925) (Taft papers).
36. *See supra* Chapter 4, at 127–32.
37. *See supra* Chapter 9, at 378–80.
38. A good example of this factionalism may be found in the correspondence surrounding Stone's opinion in United Fuel Gas Co. v. Railroad Commission, 278 U.S. 300 (1929), an "important" case "dealing with the problem of valuation of a natural resource." HFS to Milton Handler (January 22, 1929) (Stone papers). After Stone circulated his opinion, he received the following letter from Van Devanter:

> I looked over your opinion in No 1 and found myself quite reluctant to accept it as written. Accordingly I made various changes which to me seemed desirable. Since then I have shown them to the Chief Justice and Justices Sutherland, Butler and Sanford – these being all that it was convenient to see. They authorize me to say they approve the changes and join me in asking their adoption.

WVD to HFS (n.d.) (Stone papers). In that same note, Van Devanter added that in United Fuel Gas Co. v. Public Service Commission of West Virginia, 278 U.S. 322 (1929), an opinion also circulated by Stone, Van Devanter was proposing changes that were "approved by Sutherland, Butler & Sanford," although Taft had not yet seen them because Van Devanter had "neglected to enclose" them when sending Taft the manuscript.
39. *See infra* Chapter 25.
40. 281 U.S. 276 (1930).
41. United States v. Adams, 281 U.S. 202 (1930).
42. Missouri *ex rel.* Missouri Insurance Co. v. Gehner, 281 U.S. 313 (1930).
43. Memorandum from HFS to JCM (April 3, 1930) (Stone papers). I have been unable to locate the McReynolds memorandum to which Stone is responding.
44. If one looks at the cases cited by Stone in his memorandum, for example, Nos. 281 and 282 were decided unanimously on April 14, 1930, as United States v. Adams, 281 U.S. 202 (1930), in an opinion by Holmes. Patton v. United States, 281 U.S. 276 (1930), which was also decided on April 14, features Holmes, Brandeis, and Stone concurring in the result, but not writing separately. In No. 222, Missouri *ex rel.* Missouri Insurance Co. v. Gehner, 281 U.S. 313 (1930), also decided on April 14, Stone, joined by Holmes and Brandeis, dissented.
45. *See, e.g.*, Sun Ship Bldg. Co. v. United States, 271 U.S. 96, 99 (1926).
46. *See, e.g.*, Stephen C. Halpern & Kenneth N. Vines, *Institutional Disunity*, the *Judges' Bill and the Role of the U.S. Supreme Court*, 30 WESTERN POLITICAL QUARTERLY 471, 480–81 (1977) ("Eliminating the right of appeal in many minor and uncontroversial cases freed the court to concentrate in obligatory appeals on only those cases raising salient national issues. Granting the justices much wider discretion to choose from among the cases appealed to them, the number and nature of those they wished to decide, provided greater opportunity to choose difficult and disputatious cases.

Dissent during the Taft Court

Greater dissent was made more likely not only by the specific reforms of the Act but by the expectation as to how the justices would utilize their new powers. The Act's supporters advanced a conception of the Court as an institution which should reserve its judgments only for the most important national policy questions.").

Chief Justice Vinson made this point in 1949 to explain the decreasing rates of unanimity in Supreme Court opinions:

> [T]he very nature of the Supreme Court's jurisdiction is such that the easy cases, the clear and indisputable cases, very seldom come before the Court. Our discretionary certiorari jurisdiction encompasses, for the most part, only the borderline cases – those in which there is conflict among lower courts or widespread uncertainty regarding problems of national importance. ... Considering, therefore, the importance and difficulty of the cases which the Court must decide, it is not strange that there is some of the same disagreement on the Court as exists among others of the bench and bar concerning the questions decided.

Vinson Tells A.B.A. of Supreme Court Work; Opinion on Dissents, 29 OKLAHOMA STATE BAR JOURNAL 1269, 1273 (1949). *See also* Ben W. Palmer, *Supreme Court of the United States: Analysis of Alleged and Real Causes of Dissents*, 34 AMERICAN BAR ASSOCIATION JOURNAL 677, 679 (1948) ("Under the certiorari system the Court now picks out for adjudication cases involving the most difficult questions of constitutional law and statutory construction; cases of the utmost public or political importance; cases that bring to focus the interests of pressure groups – the claims and contentions of vast social, economic, political, religious and ideological forces that engage the deepest passions and the most aggressive loyalties of minority millions of men and women.").

47. Walker, Epstein, & Dixon, *supra* note 3, at 365. "[T]he discretionary share of the Court's docket rose dramatically immediately following the [1925] Act and remained relatively stable thereafter. ... However, ... significant escalation in both the dissent and concurrence rates did not occur until almost fifteen years later." *Id.*
48. *See supra* Preface, at xxxvi–xxxvii.
49. Political scientists call this voter "fluidity." *See, e.g.*, Forrest Maltzman & Paul J. Wahlbeck, *Strategic Policy Considerations and Voting Fluidity on the Burger Court*, 90 AMERICAN POLITICAL SCIENCE REVIEW 581 (1996). Epstein, Segal & Spaeth, *supra* note 4, report analogous voting fluidity in the Waite Court. They write that 91 percent of their set of 2,863 conference cases were published as unanimous; yet at conference only 60 percent of these cases were unanimous. *Id.* at 366. After studying the Taft Court docket books, Barry Cushman has concluded that the rate of fluidity under Taft was about the same for salient and nonsalient cases. Barry Cushman, *Inside the Taft Court: Lessons from the Docket Books*, 2015 SUPREME COURT REVIEW 345, 407.
50. *See supra* text at note 10.
51. We might, for example, view the certification process as a proxy for difficult cases, because lower federal courts would likely certify only especially significant or especially divisive questions of law. During the 1921–1928 terms the Court published fifty-six full opinions in cases coming to the Court by way of certification from lower federal courts. Of these, 80 percent were unanimous. Of the forty-three of these opinions for which we have conference records, 51 percent were unanimous in conference. For a roughly contemporaneous discussion of certification, see

REYNOLDS ROBERTSON & FRANCIS R. KIRKHAM, JURISDICTION OF THE SUPREME COURT OF THE UNITED STATES §§ 112–19 (St. Paul: West Publishing Co. 1936).

52. O'Brien, *supra* note 4, at 101. *Accord* Pamela C. Corley, Amy Steigerwalt, & Artemus Ward, *Revisiting the Roosevelt Court: The Critical Juncture from Consensus to Dissensus*, 38 JOURNAL OF SUPREME COURT HISTORY 20, 28–29 (2013) ("The Roosevelt Court was populated by the first generation of jurists who came of age under" the influence of legal realism).

53. *See, e.g.*, Hendershot, Hurwitz, Lanier, & Pacelle, *supra* note 4, at 478. In his study of the Taft Court docket books, Barry Cushman sought to identify major salient cases. He concluded that only 55.6 percent of such cases were decided by published unanimous opinion and that only 33.3 percent of those cases were unanimous at conference. Cushman, *supra* note 49, at 407.

54. American Bar Association Canons of Judicial Ethics, Canon 19 (1924), in LISA L. MILORD, THE DEVELOPMENT OF THE ABA JUDICIAL CODE 137 (Chicago: Center for Professional Responsibility, American Bar Association 1992). Taft was chair of the committee that drafted the 1924 Canons. *See supra* Chapter 15, at 513. Before his appointment to the Court, Justice Sutherland was also a member of the committee. Canon 19 was dropped from the ABA's revised Code of Judicial Conduct in 1972. *See* Walter P. Armstrong, Jr., *The Code of Judicial Conduct*, 26 SOUTHWEST LAW JOURNAL 708, 713–14 & n.44 (1972). The Reporter explained that "[t]he Committee rejected the detailed discussion of judicial opinions, philosophy of law, and judicial idiosyncrasies and inconsistencies in old Canons 19, 20, and 21 as being neither helpful nor, for the most part, matters of ethical conduct." E. WAYNE THODE, REPORTER'S NOTES TO CODE OF JUDICIAL CONDUCT 50 (Chicago: American Bar Association 1973).

55. Willis Van Devanter, *The Supreme Court of the United States*, 5 INDIANA LAW JOURNAL 553, 560 (1930). The commitment to solidarity was not meant entirely to suppress dissent. As Van Devanter put it, "Whatever may be the effect upon public opinion at the moment, freedom to dissent is essential, because what must ultimately sustain the court in public confidence is the character and independence of the judges." *Id.*

56. *Brandeis-Frankfurter Conversations*, at 313–14 (June 28, 1923).

57. France v. French Overseas Corp., 277 U.S. 323 (1928) (Stone papers). Butler was so pleased with his disquisition that he sent it under separate cover to Taft. PB to WHT (May 19, 1928) (Taft papers). In that same case, Taft wrote Stone, "I suppose I ought not to dissent. I think we dissent too much especially when a principle has once been decided." (Stone papers).

58. Nashville, Chattanooga & St. Louis Ry. Co. v. White, 278 U.S. 456 (1929) (Holmes papers). In that same case, Butler wrote privately to Van Devanter,

> You and I voted to reverse. The opinion does not change my view of the matter. I still think the ordinance as applied here unreasonable & arbitrary. I also think ... that evidence was erroneously excluded. But it is doubtful whether dissenting opinion or the mere noting of disagreement would do any good; and, unless you incline the other way, I am disposed to acquiesce. What say you?

PB to WVD (January 22, 1929) (Van Devanter papers). Van Devanter wrote Holmes, "I do not agree. But as the matter is open to discussion, I shall not object,

Dissent during the Taft Court

but acquiesce." (Holmes papers). In another Holmes opinion, Butler wrote Holmes, "I voted the other way; but yielding to the weight of reason and votes, I acquiesce." W. Union Tel. Co. v. Georgia, 269 U.S. 67 (1925) (Holmes papers).

59. Standard Oil Co. v. Marysville, 279 U.S. 582 (1929) (Stone papers). To the draft of a Brandeis opinion, Butler replied, "I voted & still prefer to reverse, but I shall acquiesce unless one protests." St. Louis-San Francisco Ry. Co. v. Ala. Pub. Serv. Comm'n, 279 U.S. 560 (1929) (Brandeis papers). In that same case, Sutherland wrote Brandeis, "Not for, but shall not be 'agin.'" *Id.* McReynolds wrote, "I am not wholly in accord with this but do not care to say anything." *Id.*

60. Returns to circulated opinions are preserved primarily in the Holmes, Brandeis, and Stone papers.

61. HFS to LDB (February 16, 1929) (Brandeis papers). The case was Cudahy Packing Co. v. Hinkle, 278 U.S. 460 (1929). For Stone's allegiance to *stare decisis* in the context of minimum wage legislation, see *infra* Chapter 24, at 114.

62. HFS to Felix Frankfurter (June 8, 1928) (Stone papers).

63. Heiner v. Tindle, 276 U.S. 582 (1928) (Stone papers). In that same case, Holmes commented, "My inclination is the other way.... But I don't intend to say anything if you can get a majority." *Id.* In response to the draft of Taft's unanimous opinion in Chicago & Northwestern Ry. Co. v. Nye Schneider Fowler Co., 260 U.S. 35 (1922), Brandeis wrote, "I still think the reasoning as to $100 fee wrong. But the opinion handles the matter so deftly that I think there will be no such lasting harm done as to require dissent. So as our Junior says: 'I'll shut up.'" (Taft papers). Although Holmes acknowledged that Taft's opinion was "plausibly reasoned," he added, "but as I voted the other way and still have some misgivings I retain them to see if any dissent is written. It would not be by me." *Id.*

64. Atl. Coast Line R.R. Co. v. Southwell, 275 U.S. 64 (1927) (Holmes papers). Brandeis joined Holmes's opinion in A.G. Spalding & Bros. v. Edwards, 262 U.S. 66 (1923), even though Brandeis thought that Holmes's "construction of this Constitutional provision is wrong." (Holmes papers). Holmes, in turn, responded to the draft of Brandeis's unanimous opinion in Taubel-Scott-Kitzmiller v. Fox, 264 U.S. 426 (1924), with the observation that "I am unconvinced. I think the other interpretation more reasonable." (Brandeis papers). In that same opinion, McReynolds wrote Brandeis, "I shall not object." *Id.* Butler wrote, "I think you make a strong argument for the result & it is likely you are right. As you know I inclined the other way. I am content – & concur." *Id.* And McKenna answered, "This leaves me no excuse not to be right so I say Yes." *Id.*

65. Seeman v. Phila. Warehouse Co., 274 U.S. 403 (1927) (Stone papers). Brandeis wrote Stone, "I shall probably acquiesce & await Conference before deciding." To the draft of Stone's unanimous opinion reversing a criminal conviction in Brasfield v. United States, 272 U.S. 448 (1926), Holmes wrote, "I shall not dissent.... But I would not reverse for what the Judge did." (Stone papers). In that same case, Sanford wrote Stone, "I regret that I cannot concur except in the result.... But I shall not dissent or express any separate opinion." *Id.* To Taft's draft opinion in Continental Insurance Co. v. United States, 259 U.S. 156 (1922), Holmes responded, "Where reason totters on the throne, Faith takes my hand and leads me on." (Taft papers). In response to Taft's draft opinion in United States v. Rider, 261 U.S. 363 (1923), Holmes wrote, "I defer humbly to the Commander in Chief. What he says goes." (Taft papers).

66. Louisville & N.R. Co. v. Central Iron & Coal Co., 265 U.S. 59 (1924) (Brandeis papers).
67. United States v. Ludey, 274 U.S. 295 (1927) (Brandeis papers). In that same case, Taft wrote, "I concur but these discussions always make my head buzz." *Id.* Sanford wrote, "While I voted to 'reverse' with some doubt, this doubt has been removed by your clear and strong presentation of the case – and I unreservedly concur." *Id.*
68. Fox River Paper Co. v. R.R. Comm'n, 274 U.S. 651 (1927) (Stone papers). Butler commented about Stone's draft, "I voted the other way in this and will withhold further expression until I hear what others say at the Conference." *Id.*
69. United States v. Sischo, 262 U.S. 165 (1923) (Holmes papers).
70. Mercantile Trust Co. v. Wilmot Rd. Dist., 275 U.S. 117 (1927) (Holmes papers). To this same opinion, Brandeis responded, "I do not assent to your interpretation of the statute, but I 'shut up.'" *Id.* To the draft of another ultimately unanimous Holmes opinion, Sanford responded, "I regret that I do not see my way clear to concurring in this view (albeit most persuasively stated), but do not expect to dissent." United States v. Cambridge Loan & Bldg. Co., 278 U.S. 55 (1928) (Holmes papers). To that same opinion, Sutherland wrote, "I give up. You are very persuasive, tho I still 'have my doubts.'" *Id.* Butler wrote, "Doubtfully yes. I shall be glad to consider opposing views if any are expressed." *Id.* And Taft answered, "I concur. I don't like to do so because the result should be different but if Congress wishes it different let it draft the law accordingly." *Id.*
71. Am. Ry. Express Co. v. Levee, 263 U.S. 19 (1923) (Holmes papers). To the draft of an ultimately unanimous Brandeis opinion, Sanford wrote, "I still have great doubt, but shall not dissent." Napier v. Atlantic Coast Line R.R. Co., 272 U.S. 605 (1926) (Brandeis papers). To the draft of an ultimately unanimous Stone opinion, Sanford wrote, "Regret that I cannot agree, but do not expect to dissent." N.Y. Cent. R.R. Co. v. Johnson, 279 U.S. 310 (1929) (Stone papers).
72. W. & Atl. R.R. Co. v. Hughes, 278 U.S. 496 (1929) (Brandeis papers). To that same opinion, Butler responded, "I voted to reverse, but I acquiesce in the views of the majority as attractively put by you." *Id.* Sutherland returned simply, "I yield." *Id.* To another ultimately unanimous Brandeis opinion, McReynolds answered simply, "Sorry but I cannot agree." United States v. Ill. Cent. R.R. Co., 263 U.S. 515 (1924) (Brandeis papers). *See also* Davis v. Cornwell, 264 U.S. 560 (1924) (Brandeis papers), a unanimous Brandeis opinion to the draft of which McReynolds had responded, "Sorry but I cannot agree."
73. Jackman v. Rosenbaum Co., 260 U.S. 22 (1922) (Holmes papers). To another Holmes opinion, McReynolds wrote, "Maybe it should be as it seems destined to be. But yr humble servant has something rather deeper than a doubt." Diaz v. Gonzalez Y Lugo, 261 U.S. 102 (1923) (Holmes papers).
74. Gardner v. Chicago Title & Trust Co., 261 U.S. 453 (1923) (Holmes papers). To the same opinion, Sutherland responded, "I am sorry not to agree with you, at least, for the present." Butler answered, "I still have grave doubt as to the result." *Id.* Brandeis wrote, "I think you are wrong. ... But I ... shall 'shut up' unless others make a stir." *Id.* In another case, Van Devanter wrote Stone, "I do not agree but shall submit." Raffel v. United States, 271 U.S. 494 (1926) (Stone papers). In that same case, Sanford wrote, "This is a strong presentation and while my doubt in the question is not entirely removed, I shall acquiesce in silence unless some one else dissents." *Id.* Butler wrote, "In Silentio." *Id.*

Dissent during the Taft Court

75. Int'l Ry. Co. v. Davidson, 257 U.S. 506 (1922) (Brandeis papers). In that same case, Pitney wrote, "I say nothing." *Id.*
76. First Nat'l Bank of Aiken v. J.L. Mott Iron Works, 258 U.S. 240 (1922) (Holmes papers).
77. Fed. Baseball Club of Baltimore v. Nat'l League of Prof'l Baseball Clubs, 259 U.S. 200 (1922) (Holmes papers). To this draft opinion, Brandeis responded, "I have grave doubt, but shall acquiesce." *Id.*
78. Stevens v. Arnold, 262 U.S. 266 (1923) (Holmes papers). To that same opinion, Brandeis wrote, "I take your word for it." *Id.* McReynolds answered, "I shan't row with you tho I was inclined to agree with the Dist. Court." *Id.* And Taft commented, "I concur, though it is only because of my blind faith in you." *Id.*
79. Nashville, Chattanooga & St. Louis Ry. v. Tennessee, 262 U.S. 318 (1923) (Brandeis papers).
80. United States v. Pa. R.R. Co., 266 U.S. 191 (1924) (Brandeis papers). To the draft of this ultimately unanimous Brandeis opinion, McReynolds responded, "I hold a different view." *Id.* Sutherland commented, "Shall acquiesce." *Id.*
81. Epstein, Segal, & Spaeth, *supra* note 4; O'Brien, *supra* note 4, at 111.
82. OWH to Felix Frankfurter (November 22, 1929), in HOLMES-FRANKFURTER CORRESPONDENCE, at 244–45. "I dislike even the traditional 'Holmes Dissenting.'" OWH to Harold Laski (November 10, 1923), in 1 HOLMES-LASKI CORRESPONDENCE, at 560. *See also* OWH to Miss Little (February 4, 1929) (Holmes papers) ("I rather grieve to be made to appear as chiefly occupied in dissenting. That is not my main business.").
83. LEARNED HAND, THE BILL OF RIGHTS 72–73 (Cambridge: Harvard University Press 1958).
84. An excellent discussion of the collapse of the norm during the chief justiceship of Harlan Stone may be found in Corley, Steigerwalt, & Ward, *supra* note 52.
85. *Brandeis-Frankfurter Conversations*, at 317 (July 3, 1923). Brandeis added that "there may not be time, e.g. Holmes shoots them down so quickly & is disturbed if you hold him up." *Id.*
86. *Brandeis-Frankfurter Conversations*, at 309 (July 20, 1922). A dissenting justice, Brandeis told Frankfurter, doesn't "want to vent feelings or raise rumpus." *Id.* At another point Brandeis observed to Frankfurter that "there are reasons for withholding dissent, so that silence does not mean actual concurrence. (1) All depends on how frequent one's dissents have been when the question of dissenting comes, or (2) how important [the] case, whether it's constitutionality or construction. So that I sometimes endorse an opinion with which I do not agree, 'I acquiesce'; as Holmes puts [it] 'I'll shut up.'" *Id.* at 328 (July 2, 1924).
87. LDB to WHT (December 23, 1922) (Taft papers). The case was FTC v. Curtis Publishing Co., 260 U.S. 568 (1923), and Brandeis ended up joining Taft's opinion, perhaps because the stakes were high enough. Existing documents show Taft negotiating through Van Devanter to effect changes in the McReynolds opinion, even as Taft determined to write separately, "*Dubitante.*"
88. Working relationships among members of the Taft Court should be evaluated in light of Antonin Scalia's description of his Court. *See* Antonin Scalia, *The Dissenting Opinion*, 1994 JOURNAL OF SUPREME COURT HISTORY 33, 40–41 (Dissents "do not, or at least need not, produce animosity and bitterness among the members of the Court. . . . [D]issents are simply the normal course of things.

tion."). *See also* Stanley H. Fuld, *The Voices of Dissent*, 62 COLUMBIA LAW REVIEW 923, 928–29 (1962) ("In conference, each of the judges expresses himself frankly as he believes the law and the facts require and, when it comes time to publish his opinion, whether for majority or for minority, his writing reflects his actual thinking, with no punches pulled, though stated in reasoned and temperate tones. The personal atmosphere of the court is today, as it has ever been, instinct with a feeling of friendliness and good will.").

89. William Howard Taft, Address to New York County Bar Ass'n (February 18, 1922) (Taft papers).
90. Thus the influential legal scholar and lawyer Hampton L. Carson could write in 1894 that "as a general rule, dissenting opinions receive slight attention. The active practitioner is chiefly concerned with the law as it is declared by the majority of a court, and pays little heed to a shrill or feeble shriek as to what it might or ought to be." Hampton L. Carson, *Great Dissenting Opinions*, 22 WASHINGTON LAW REPORTER 585, 585 (1894).
91. Pollock v. Farmers' Loan & Trust Co., 157 U.S. 429, 608 (1895) (White, J., dissenting).
92. Northern Securities Co. v. United States, 193 U.S. 197, 400 (1904) (Holmes, J., dissenting). Holmes once wrote a good friend that "I do not like being made to appear as a dissenting judge, though no doubt I have dissented more than some because I represent a minority on some very fundamental questions upon which both sides should be heard." OWH to Nina Gray (November 22, 1929) (Holmes papers).
93. Stone sometimes represented his practice of dissent in exactly these terms. So, for example, he once wrote T.R. Powell, "One of my colleagues was once greatly surprised when I told him that I did not write a dissent to convince him. He then asked, 'What do you write it for?' I replied: 'So that others will not think that I agree with you, and of course I have to sleep with myself every night and I like to rest well.'" HFS to T.R. Powell (December 16, 1935) (Stone papers).
94. WHT to WVD (December 26, 1921) (Van Devanter papers). *See supra* text at note 9.
95. *See supra* text at note 54.
96. A wide-ranging and vigorous debate about the status of dissent occurred at that time. *See* Smith, *supra* note 6, at 510–26.
97. William A. Bowen, *Dissenting Opinions*, 17 GREEN BAG 690, 693 (1905). "Obviously, if the Dissenting Opinion is injurious at all, it will be most unfortunately so in those cases which are of the greatest public moment. Yet it is the almost unbelievable fact, that it is the uniform justification of dissenting judges that the importance of the case warrants and demands their dissent." *Id.*
98. *Evils of Dissenting Opinions*, 57 ALBANY LAW JOURNAL 74, 75 (1898). The article adds, "The decision should be that of the court, and not of the judges as individuals. The judges should get together and render a decision settling the points in controversy." *Id.* The article goes on to argue:

> Dissenting opinions may be as pleasant to the minority judge as it is for a boy to make faces at a bigger boy across the street, whom he can't whip. They give a judge an opportunity of exhibiting his individual views and opinions. But what good does that do? What cares the public for the judge's individual views,

Dissent during the Taft Court

except in so far as, by reason of his position, they assume the force of law? The only concern of the public is with the decision of the court as a court, so that they may know what it is, and know how to govern themselves.

Id. at 75. From this perspective, dissent was not only useless, it was also destructive of the law itself.

99. *Brandeis-Frankfurter Conversations,* at 330 (July 6, 1924).
100. FTC v. Beech-Nut Packing Co., 257 U.S. 441, 456 (1922) (Holmes, J., dissenting).
101. Holmes was careful, however, to cast his dissent as a disagreement of legal principle rather than as a quarrel with the Court. Just as he frequently regarded opinions as expressions of "pure principle," OWH to Felix Frankfurter (November 6, 1926), in HOLMES-FRANKFURTER CORRESPONDENCE, at 206, so he stressed that in writing dissents "[w]e are giving our views on a question of law, not fighting with another cock," OWH to Harold Laski (November 10, 1923), in 1 HOLMES-LASKI CORRESPONDENCE, at 560. Before agreeing to join a Brandeis dissent, for example, Holmes once insisted that Brandeis remove a sentence to the effect that "[t]he Court gives no reason for declaring [the Federal Gift Tax Act] to be unreasonable." Holmes explained, "I think it better never to criticize the reasoning in opinions of the Court and its members. I feel very strongly about this. Of course it is OK to hit them by indirection as hard as you can." Untermyer v. Anderson, 276 U.S. 440 (1928) (Brandeis papers). Holmes added, "If you will modify these expressions so as to avoid the personal touch I am with you, with delight." *Id.* Holmes edited another Brandeis dissent "to avoid the dogmatic air when one is in a minority." United States v. Or. Lumber Co., 260 U.S. 290 (1922) (Brandeis papers). "Dissenting Judges often say 'This Court' etc.," Holmes observed. "It has an air of horror or contempt and I dislike the phrase extremely. I hope you will change it." *Id.* Although Holmes experienced the "pleasure in writing" dissents as flowing from the power to "say just what you think" without "having to blunt the edges and cut off the corners to suit someone else," it was a pleasure that did not derive from contesting the Court, but rather from the free and independent pursuit of legal principles, the articulation of "some proposition broader than it is wise to attempt except in a dissent." OWH to Nina Gray (May 5, 1928) (Holmes papers). *See also* OWH to Harold Laski (August 16, 1924), in 1 HOLMES-LASKI CORRESPONDENCE, at 646–47; OWH to Baroness Moncheur (January 27, 1928) (Holmes papers).
102. *See, e.g.,* Washington v. Dawson & Co., 264 U.S. 219, 228 (1924) (Separate Opinion of Holmes, J.) ("The reasoning of Southern Pacific Co. v. Jensen, 244 U.S. 205, and cases following it never has satisfied me, and therefore I should have been glad to see a limit set to the principle. But I must leave it to those who think the principle right to say how far it extends."); Miles v. Graham, 268 U.S. 501 (1925) (Holmes had dissented in Evans v. Gore, 253 U.S. 245 (1920), the precedent applied by *Miles*); Murphy v. Sardell, 269 U.S. 530 (1925) ("Justice Holmes requests that it be stated that his concurrence is solely upon the ground that he regards himself bound by the decision in Adkins v. Children's Hospital."); McCardle v. Indianapolis Water Co., 272 U.S. 400, 421 (1926) ("Mr Justice Homes concurs in the result."); Thomas C. Grey, *Holmes on the Logic of the Law,* in THE PATH OF THE LAW AND ITS INFLUENCE 131, 141

(Steven J. Burton ed., Cambridge University Press 2000) (describing Holmes's reluctance to depart from precedent); Thomas C. Grey, *Molecular Motions: The Holmesian Judge in Theory and Practice*, 37 WILLIAM & MARY LAW REVIEW 19, 27–36 (1995) (discussing Holmes's tendency to defer to precedent and legislative judgment). For an example of Justices Van Devanter, McReynolds, and Butler adhering to this same principle, *compare* Village of Euclid v. Ambler Realty Co., 272 U.S. 365 (1926), *with* Zahn v. Board of Public Works of City of Los Angeles, 274 U.S. 325 (1927).

103. 268 U.S. 652, 673 (1925) (Holmes, J., dissenting).
104. *Brandeis-Frankfurter Conversations*, at 314 (July 1, 1923). For contemporary views of constitutional law that build on this insight, see H. JEFFERSON POWELL, A COMMUNITY BUILT ON WORDS: THE CONSTITUTION IN HISTORY AND POLITICS (University of Chicago Press 2002); Robert Post & Reva B. Siegel, *Popular Constitutionalism, Departmentalism, and Judicial Supremacy*, 92 CALIFORNIA LAW REVIEW 1027 (2004); Hanna Fenichel Pitkin, *The Idea of a Constitution*, 37 JOURNAL OF LEGAL EDUCATION 167 (1987); but see Larry Alexander & Frederick Schauer, *On Extrajudicial Constitutional Interpretation*, 110 HARVARD LAW REVIEW (1997).
105. By the 1930s, Brandeis was able to offer a clear line of demarcation. *See, e.g.*, Comm'r v. Coronado Oil & Gas Co., 285 U.S. 393, 406–7 (1932) (Brandeis, J., dissenting):

> Stare decisis is usually the wise policy, because in most matters it is more important that the applicable rule of law be settled than that it be settled right. . . . This is commonly true even where the error is a matter of serious concern, provided correction can be had by legislation. But in cases involving the Federal Constitution, where correction through legislative action is practically impossible, this Court has often overruled its earlier decisions.

Id. Brandeis had been more tentative on this point during the 1920s. *See, e.g.*, Di Santo v. Pennsylvania, 273 U.S. 34, 42–43 (1927) (Brandeis, J., dissenting):

> It is usually more important that a rule of law be settled, than that it be settled right. Even where the error in declaring the rule is a matter of serious concern, it is ordinarily better to seek correction by legislation. Often this is true although the question is a constitutional one. The human experience embodied in the doctrine of stare decisis teaches us, also, that often it is better to follow a precedent, although it does not involve the declaration of a rule. This is usually true so far as concerns a particular statute whether the error was made in construing it or in passing upon its validity. But the doctrine of stare decisis does not command that we err again when we have occasion to pass upon a different statute. In the search for truth through the slow process of inclusion and exclusion, involving trial and error, it behooves us to reject, as guides, the decisions upon such questions which prove to have been mistaken. This course seems to me imperative when, as here, the decision to be made involves the delicate adjustment of conflicting claims of the Federal Government and the States to regulate commerce. The many cases on the Commerce Clause in which this Court has overruled or explained away its earlier decisions show that the wisdom of this course has been heretofore recognized.

Id. (footnotes omitted). For a good discussion of Brandeis's approach to precedent, see Morton J. Horwitz, *Foreword: The Constitution of Change: Legal Fundamentality without Fundamentalism*, 107 HARVARD LAW REVIEW 32, 53 n.99 (1993). For an example of a perspective similar to Brandeis's, see HFS to

Dissent during the Taft Court

John Bassett Moore (April 10, 1929) (Stone papers) ("[O]rdinarily I do not record dissents in matters of statutory interpretation.").

106. Brandeis developed a unique genre of opinion writing to express this function of law. The characteristic rhetoric of a Supreme Court opinion is that of closure; the point is to indicate that a specific resolution of a legal question is both required and decisive. *See* Robert A. Ferguson, *The Judicial Opinion as Literary Genre*, 2 YALE JOURNAL OF LAW AND HUMANITIES 201, 207, 210, 213 (1990). But Brandeis pioneered an idiosyncratic and distinctive style that resisted this framework of closure. Brandeis frequently used his opinions to suggest to legal actors and public officials the myriad possibilities for future legitimate legal action. In Missouri Pacific Railroad v. Boone, 270 U.S. 466 (1926), for example, the concrete legal question for determination was whether state intrastate railway regulations that had been preempted by federal control over railroads during World War I could be enforced without reenactment after cessation of that control on February 29, 1920. Brandeis's opinion stresses the multiple ways that state regulations might acquire legal force after 1920:

> In order to remove doubts as to what tariffs were to be applicable after the termination of federal control, Congress declared that the existing tariffs, largely initiated by the Director General, should be deemed operative, except so far as changed thereafter – that is, after February 29, 1920 – pursuant to law. Such modifications of intrastate tariffs might result from action of the carriers taken on their own initiative. It might result from orders of the Interstate Commerce Commission. It might result from the making either of new state laws or of new orders of a state commission acting under old laws still in force and again becoming operative. Or such modification might result from the mere cessation of the suspension, which had been effected through federal control, of statutes or orders theretofore in force and still unaffected by any action of the authority which made them. In any of these cases, the change would be effected "thereafter;" that is, after the termination of federal control.

Id. at 475–76. The rhetorical structure of this passage, its insistent conjuring of possible methods that "might result" in an effective change of law, serves to negate the closure that ordinary Court opinions strove mightily to make inevitable. Instead, *Boone* unfolds a virtual roadmap for the guidance of public officials attempting to negotiate the complex domain of federal and state railroad regulation. It is hard to imagine a sharper contrast to the typical aesthetic of a Holmes opinion, in which a "shapeless black immensity ... shrinks ... to an infinitesimal luminous point." OWH to Nina Gray (June 5, 1927) (Holmes papers). In opinions like *Boone*, Brandeis's ambition was to open a space for political engagement by illuminating the many paths available for the legal exercise of administrative and legislative discretion. *See, e.g.,* Missouri *ex rel.* St. Louis, Brownsville & Mex. Ry. Co. v. Taylor, 266 U.S. 200, 208 (1924); *supra* Chapter 8, at 319–20.

An important and little noted dimension of Brandeis's focus on facts is that it also served to maintain this open space for potential action. Thus, in Hammond v. Schappi Bus Line, 275 U.S. 164 (1927), Brandeis confronted the question of whether city ordinances regulating buses were consistent with the dormant commerce clause. Instead of laying down a singular rule, he used his opinion to explain how the scope of local competence depended upon contingent facts:

> The contentions made in the briefs and arguments suggest, among other questions, the following: Where there is congestion of city streets sufficient to justify some limitation of the number of motor vehicles to be operated thereon as

645

THE TAFT COURT

> common carriers, or some prohibition of stops to load or unload passengers, may the limitation or prohibition be applied to some vehicles used wholly or partly in interstate commerce while, at the same time, vehicles of like character, including many that are engaged solely in local, or intrastate, commerce are not subjected thereto? Is the right in the premises to which interstate carriers would otherwise be entitled, affected by the fact that, prior to the establishment of the interstate lines, the City had granted to a local carrier, by contract or franchise, the unlimited right to use all the streets of the City, and that elimination of the interstate vehicles would put an end to the congestion experienced? May the City's right to limit the number of vehicles, and to prohibit stops to load or unload passengers, be exercised in such a way as to allocate streets on which motor traffic is more profitable exclusively to the local lines and to allocate streets on which the traffic is less profitable to the lines engaged wholly, or partly, in interstate commerce? Is limitation of the number of vehicles, or prohibition of stops to load or unload passengers, of carriers engaged wholly, or partly, in interstate commerce, justifiable, where the congestion could be obviated by denying to private carriers existing parking privileges or by curtailing those so enjoyed? Are the rights of the interstate carrier in the premises dependent, in any respect, upon the dates of the establishment of its lines, as compared with the dates of the establishment of the lines of the local carrier?
>
> These questions have not, so far as appears, been considered by either of the lower courts. The facts essential to their determination have not been found by either court. And the evidence in the record is not of such a character that findings could now be made with confidence. ... Before any of the questions suggested, which are both novel and of far reaching importance, are passed upon by this Court, the facts essential to their decision should be definitely found by the lower courts upon adequate evidence.

Id. at 170–72.
107. *Evils of Dissenting Opinions*, supra note 98, at 75.
108. *See supra* Chapter 10, at 388–89.
109. Brandeis's draft of dissent in United States v. Moreland, 258 U.S. 433 (1922) (Brandeis papers).
110. Truax v. Corrigan, 257 U.S. 312, 338 (1921).
111. Taft's perspective might be said to reflect the received wisdom of the time. For a good example, see South Carolina v. United States, 199 U.S. 437, 448–49 (1905):

> The Constitution is a written instrument. As such its meaning does not alter. That which it meant when adopted it means now. Being a grant of powers to a government its language is general, and as changes come in social and political life it embraces in its grasp all new conditions which are within the scope of the powers in terms conferred. In other words, while the powers granted do not change, they apply from generation to generation to all things to which they are in their nature applicable. This in no manner abridges the fact of its changeless nature and meaning. Those things which are within its grants of power, as those grants were understood when made, are still within them, and those things not within them remain still excluded.

Id. This same point is today advanced by those who believe in an "originalist" view of the Constitution. *See, e.g.*, Lawrence B. Solum, *The Fixation Thesis: The Role of Historical Fact in Original Meaning*, 91 NOTRE DAME LAW REVIEW 1 (2015).
112. *See supra* Chapter 8, at 320–21.
113. For good discussions of the transition in American jurisprudence to Brandeis's view of constitutional law, see Howard Gillman, *The Collapse of Constitutional Originalism and the Rise of the Notion of the "Living Constitution" in the Course*

of American State-Building, 11 STUDIES IN AMERICAN POLITICAL DEVELOPMENT 191 (1997); Barry Friedman, *The History of the Countermajoritarian Difficulty, Part Four: Law's Politics*, 148 UNIVERSITY OF PENNSYLVANIA LAW REVIEW 971, 1019 (2000); and G. EDWARD WHITE, THE CONSTITUTION AND THE NEW DEAL 198–239 (Cambridge: Harvard University Press 2000). Gillman, Friedman, and White date the demise of the Taft view to about the time when Figure IV-12 suggests that unanimity rates began to collapse.

114. CHARLES EVANS HUGHES, THE SUPREME COURT OF THE UNITED STATES 68 (New York: Columbia University Press 1928).

115. *See Evils of Dissenting Opinions, supra* note 98, at 75: "If a dissenting opinion is well written it impresses not only the particular litigant, but all who read it, with the idea that injustice has been done by the courts; a feeling of dissatisfaction arises, a feeling of great wrong is broadcast. The court has been weakened in popular esteem, for in the opinion of the reader of the dissenting opinion it has lent itself to injustice and inflicted wrong."

116. "Even where the theory of the dissent does not ultimately prevail, its expression is no futile gesture. The law is not a dead or static mechanism. It is a living organism which grows and develops to meet the ever-shifting panorama of life." Joseph M. Proskauer, *Dissenting Opinions*, 160 HARPER'S MONTHLY MAGAZINE 549, 554 (1930). To Frankfurter, Stone commented that Proskauer's article was "good and very instructive to a lot of people who think law, especially in our Court, is a system of mathematics. Sometime, though, I think if it were applied with scientific precision, that we might come out better than we do now." HFS to Felix Frankfurter (April 4, 1930) (Stone papers). On the relationship between Brandeis's view of law to Stone's own practice of dissent, see HFS to Felix Frankfurter (June 8, 1928) (Stone papers):

> I always write a dissent with real reluctance, and often acquiesce in opinions with which I do not fully agree, so you may know how strongly I have really felt in order to participate in so many dissents as I have recently. But where a prevailing view rests upon what appears to me to be false economic notions, or upon reasoning and analogies which will not bear analysis, I think great service is done with respect to the future development of the law, in pointing out the fallacies on which the prevailing view appears to rest, even though the particular ruling made should never be reversed.

Frankfurter answered this letter by affirming, "I also share your conviction as to the 'great service' which is rendered by dissenting opinions for the future development of the law." Felix Frankfurter to HFS (June 11, 1928) (Stone papers).

Stone would soon become entirely comfortable with this position. *See* Harlan F. Stone, *Dissenting Opinions Are Not Without Value*, 26 JOURNAL OF THE AMERICAN JUDICATURE SOCIETY 78, 78 (1942) ("While the dissenting opinion tends to break down a much cherished illusion of certainty in the law and of infallibility of judges, it nevertheless has some useful purposes to serve. . . . Its real influence, if it ever has any, comes later, often in shaping and sometimes in altering the course of the law."); HFS to T.R. Powell (December 16, 1935) (Stone papers) ("Of course I agree with you that no amount of criticism will affect the courts today, but it is likely to have a profound effect on the courts of the next generation.").

The changing jurisprudential understanding of law may be illustrated by an exchange that occurred during the 1930 debate in the Senate over the confirmation of Hoover's unsuccessful nomination of John J. Parker to replace Sanford. New York Senator Robert F. Wagner, opposing Parker, extolled Holmes's dissenting opinions because they "enter into the soil of the judicial process and ... slowly through the years irrigate it and fertilize it until ... in time [they] bring forth a living law which more closely corresponds to ideal justice." Wagner praised dissents precisely because in his view constitutional law did not consist of "a lifeless set of wooden precepts moved about according to the rules of a mechanical logic"; the quality of a Supreme Court Justice must therefore be assessed by the criterion of "statecraft." 72 CONG. REC. 8033–34 (April 30, 1930). Wagner's view was countered by Delaware Senator Daniel O. Hastings, who, defending Parker, observed that "I never agree with the dissenting opinion of any court. I learned long ago that the majority opinion of every court was controlling, and that it is not worth while to bother with what somebody said in a dissenting opinion. I learned that before I got very far in the practice of the law, and it still holds good." *Id.* at 8029.

117. Washington v. W.C. Dawson & Co., 264 U.S. 219, 236 (1924) (Brandeis, J., dissenting).

118. William O. Douglas, *The Dissent: A Safeguard of Democracy*, 32 JOURNAL OF THE AMERICAN JUDICATURE SOCIETY 104, 105 (1948). Douglas, who was Stone's student, continued:

> Certainty and unanimity in the law are possible both under the fascist and communist systems. They are not only possible; they are indispensable; for complete subservience to the political regime is a *sine qua non* to judicial survival under either system. . . .
>
> When we move to constitutional questions, uncertainty necessarily increases. A judge who is asked to construe or interpret the Constitution often rejects the gloss which his predecessors have put on it. . . . And so it should be. For it is the Constitution which we have sworn to defend, not some predecessor's interpretation of it. *Stare decisis* has small place in constitutional law. The Constitution was written for all time and all ages. It would lose its great character and become feeble, if it were allowed to become encrusted with narrow, legalistic notions that dominated the thinking of one generation.
>
> So it is that the law will always teem with uncertainty.

Id. at 105–6. Douglas's celebration of uncertainty should be compared to the anxiety expressed in a roughly contemporaneous prize-winning essay:

> [E]volution rather than revolution should be the rule. If the decisions of a court are consistently accompanied by concurring or dissenting opinions which represent attempts to substitute the impulses of the present for the wisdom of the past, the law suffers, and the only possible prediction is one of chaos. There are those who charge that some of our appellate courts have already reached this chaotic condition.

R. Dean Morehead, *Concurring and Dissenting Opinions*, 38 AMERICAN BAR ASSOCIATION JOURNAL 821, 884 (1952).

CHAPTER 20

The Authority of the Taft Court

THE NORM OF acquiescence allows us to glimpse not only the jurisprudence of the Taft Court – how it conceived the nature of law – but also the Court's understanding of its own authority as an institution. Members of the Taft court experienced the norm of acquiescence as essential for the Court's authority. "Solidarity of opinion" was, as Taft wrote Harding in 1920, "necessary to maintain the Court's influence with the public."[1] Dissents were troublesome because they implied that Court decisions were not compelled by legal necessity, but instead by political calculation. As former Indiana Senator Albert Beveridge put it: "[W]hen five able and learned justices think one way, and four equally able and learned justices, all on the same bench, think the other way and express their dissent in powerful argument, sometimes with warm feeling, is it not obvious that the law in question is not such a plain infraction of the Constitution as to be unconstitutional 'beyond all question'?"[2]

The norm of acquiescence suppressed embarrassing divisions that might provoke suspicion that Court opinions expressed the private views of individual justices rather than the dictates of impersonal law. As Canon 19 of the 1924 Canons of Judicial Ethics put it: "It is of high importance that judges constituting a court of last resort should use effort and self-restraint to promote solidarity of conclusion and the consequent influence of judicial decision."[3] Unanimity sustained the "influence" of judicial decision-making, which Taft identified with "the prestige of the Court,"[4] because it reassured the public that the Court spoke with the warrant of the law.

The authority of the Court derives from its commission to declare law. Dissent threatens that authority by blurring the boundary separating legal from political judgment. As the *Albany Law Journal* made explicit in 1898: "A dissenting opinion is to some extent an appeal by the minority – from the decision of the majority – to the people. But what can the people do? They can't alter it; they can't change it; right or wrong, they must respect and obey it. Why shake the faith of the people in the wisdom and infallibility of the judiciary? Upon the respect of the people for the courts depends the very life of the Republic."[5]

Invoking the same image of the Court as that which Gilbert would later enshrine in the architecture of Taft's new Supreme Court building,[6] the *Albany Law Journal* presupposed that the task of the Court was to declare law that "the people" were bound to "respect and obey." The very "life of the Republic" depended upon passive popular acceptance of judicial decision-making. Dissent disrupted this acceptance by suggesting the wicked possibility that the emperor might have no clothes, that judicial judgments might merely reflect the idiosyncratic views of individual justices. Once the public lost faith that judicial decisions expressed determinate legal principles, the influence and authority of the Court would be put at terrible risk.

By the 1920s, however, elites no longer believed that legal questions yielded determinate answers.[7] Holmes had convincingly demonstrated that judges are often "called upon to exercise the sovereign prerogative of choice."[8] Taft, for example, clearly understood and accepted Holmes's point. Taft keenly appreciated that constitutional adjudication must often turn on practical understandings of American government. As he wrote Sutherland upon the latter's appointment to the bench:

> I do not minimize at all the importance of having Judges of learning in the law on the Supreme Bench, but the functions performed by us are of such a peculiar character that something in addition is much needed to round out a man for service upon that Bench, and that is a sense of proportion derived from a knowledge of how Government is carried on, and how higher politics are conducted in the State. A Supreme Judge must needs keep abreast of the actual situation in the country so as to understand all the phases of important issues which arise, with a view to the proper application of the Constitution, which is a political instrument in a way, to new conditions.[9]

If the Constitution was a "political instrument" whose application to "new conditions" required "a sense of proportion" derived from practical experience, its meaning was plainly not susceptible to singular and definitive interpretation. Legal indeterminacy of this kind raises very fundamental questions about the institutional authority of the Court. If constitutional interpretation does not depend on "learning in the law" but on the "higher politics" of the state, why should "the people" defer to judgments of the Court? Why might they be obliged to respect and obey them?

A possible answer to this question is that law, however indeterminate, is nevertheless distinct from politics; that the Court is charged with declaring law; and that the Court's judgments, like all law, must command respect and obedience. The Court's ability to claim for its decisions the authority of law thus depends upon public trust in the good faith of the Court's decision-making. That is why the norm of acquiescence acquires special significance during times of legal uncertainty. The hope is that the norm will reinforce an otherwise wavering popular confidence that the Court's judgments merit the public reverence and submission claimed by law.[10]

The Authority of the Taft Court

Public trust in the Court came under intense stress during the 1930s, when the Court's decisions were assaulted by the transformative President Franklin Delano Roosevelt. During the turbulent struggle over the New Deal, even the norm of acquiescence could not suppress growing public suspicion that the Court's hostility to the administrative state was based not upon legal principles and but instead upon the "personal economic predilections"[11] of conservative justices. Matters grew so bad that the historian Barry Friedman has asserted that the Court was required to strike a "tacit deal" in which "the American people would grant the justices their power, so long as the Supreme Court's interpretation of the Constitution did not stray too far from what the majority of the people believed it should."[12] What Friedman describes as a deal, however, might perhaps better be conceptualized as a transformation in the Court's authority produced by subtle but profound changes in the *kind* of law for which the Court purported to speak.

The law that the *Albany Law Journal* imagined the Court as imposing had nothing to do with what the public wanted or thought. The *Journal* conceived law as peremptory and autonomous from public opinion. That is why the *Journal* could confidently affirm the categorical obligation of the public to respect and obey judicial decrees. It is surely no accident that this is law seen from the perspective of litigants before a final appellate tribunal. Litigants have no choice but to accept the ultimate judgments of the legal system. The dispute settlement function of courts cannot succeed unless final juridical decisions are acknowledged as dispositive.

The Judges' Bill, however, shifted the primary audience of the Court from litigants to the general public, and the general public is not situated like a litigating party who has no choice but to respect and obey the decisions of final appellate courts.[13] From the public's point of view, Supreme Court decisions do not simply resolve existing controversies. Supreme Court opinions look forwards as well as backwards. They establish, in Stephen Breyer's words, "law and judicial action, aimed at the future."[14] Events in the 1930s would amply demonstrate the many options available to a public that wished to oppose Supreme Court decisions provoking adverse attention and interest.

As Supreme Court decisions came increasingly to be understood from the standpoint of the general public, therefore, they also came to seem less like peremptory and binding decrees and more like enunciations of proposed public policy.[15] In the words of the historian Howard Gillman, the law declared by the Court began to be experienced as "an instrument of evolving social needs and not a fixed instruction from historical legislators."[16] We might reformulate Gillman's point in this way: As Court decisions were experienced less like the resolution of disputes between two parties and more like instructions directed to the public for the future governance of the polity, the authority of these decisions came increasingly to depend upon their perceived desirability.

Although the vast majority of the Court's decisions were (and are) "of low salience,"[17] a Court that selected its cases to manage the future development of federal law ultimately became identified in the public mind with decisions that aroused sustained public attention. *Brown v. Board of Education*[18] is a paradigmatic example. Over the decades, it became apparent that the legitimacy of the Court could be maintained only if it were able to articulate law whose desirability was sufficiently consonant with public opinion to preserve public support for the Court's judgments. The authority of the Court, in other words, came increasingly to depend upon its capacity to perceive and shape public opinion.

Alexander Bickel would later explicitly articulate this point: "Virtually all important decisions of the Supreme Court are the beginnings of conversations between the Court and the people and their representatives. They are never, at the start, conversations between equals. The Court has an edge, because it initiates things with some immediate action, even if limited. But conversations they are, and to say that the Supreme Court lays down the law of the land is to state the ultimate result, following upon a complex series of events, in some cases, and in others it is a form of speech only."[19] "The Court is a leader of opinion, not a mere register of it," Bickel wrote at mid-century. "But it must lead opinion, not merely impose its own; and – the short of it is – it labors under the obligation to succeed."[20]

The upshot is that the institutional authority of the Court came very much to depend upon its success in leading opinion. Members of the Taft Court, who imagined they were deciding a kind of law that was independent of public opinion, would likely have found this reorientation all but incomprehensible. Consider, for example, this telling anecdote about Brandeis's law clerk:

> In November 1944, the *Associated Press* even went so far as to informally ask the Justices to issue off-the-record comments on their opinions. Frankfurter asked Graham Claytor, former clerk to Associate Justice Louis D. Brandeis, what he thought Brandeis' response would have been and then circulated Claytor's reply to the other justices. Claytor wrote: "[Brandeis] would not have expected a responsible news agency so far to forget the Court's judicial function as to ask it to interpret for the papers its own decisions. Such an attitude indicates a state of mind which has come to look upon the Court not as a tribunal but rather as a colorful source of sensational if complex news stories."[21]

In Brandeis's mind, a "tribunal" declared law that the public was obliged to respect and obey, not to discuss and evaluate.

For our purposes, the key point about the altered nature of the Court's authority is that it liberated justices from any necessary allegiance to the collective judgment of the Court. It was no longer obviously true that "it is much more important what the Court thinks than what any one thinks."[22] This was because individual justices could persuade and educate the public just as effectively as could the collective institution of the Court. Thus justices began to argue that democracy itself obligated individual members of the Court to contribute to the development of public opinion. William O. Douglas, for example, explicitly conceptualized dissent as a form of political speech, no different from the political speech of any citizen:

> Disagreement among judges is as true to the character of democracy as freedom of speech itself. . . .

The Authority of the Taft Court

> Democracy, like religion, is full of sects and schisms.... No man or group of men has a monopoly on truth, wisdom or virtue. An idea, once advanced for public acceptance, divides like an amoeba....
>
> The truth is that the law is the highest form of compromise between competing interests; it is a substitute for force and violence.... It is the product of attempted reconciliation between the many diverse groups in a society. The reconciliation is not entirely a legislative function. The judiciary is also inescapably involved. When judges do not agree, it is a sign that they are dealing with problems on which society itself is divided. It is the democratic way to express dissident views. Judges are to be honored rather than criticized for following that tradition, for proclaiming their articles of faith so that all may read.[23]

Because "no ... group of men has a monopoly on truth," Douglas conceived Supreme Court justices as "proclaiming their articles of faith," rather than as participating in the institutional and authoritative pronouncement of a law imposed on the people and radically disconnected from mere public opinion. From this perspective it was only a short step to conceive dissent as, in the words of William J. Brennan, a contribution "to the marketplace of competing ideas."[24]

There is no doubt that some such transformation contributed to the eventual transfiguration of the Taft Court's norm of acquiescence into a contemporary ethic "of individual expression."[25] The norm of acquiescence is now invoked only in truly exceptional cases, like *Brown*, when the Court feels obliged to emphasize that it actually is announcing the kind of impersonal law that ought to command respect and obedience. This transformation has been accompanied in our own time by a full-scale crisis about how to distinguish law from politics.[26]

It is important to keep in mind, however, that this crisis had not yet materialized during the era of the Taft Court. Taft, for one, would have been appalled by the notion that the law declared by the Court required for its authority the supplemental support of public opinion, even though he was prepared to acknowledge that the Court's legal judgments entailed political judgments. And Holmes surely did not believe that the law announced by the Court was merely politics by another name, even though he was prepared to acknowledge that the Court's decisions involved discretion and choice. La Follette's frontal assault on the Court's exercise of judicial review, which sought explicitly to vindicate the Court's constitutional decisions in public opinion, did not strike a responsive chord with any Taft Court justice.[27]

No member of the Taft Court was tempted to ground the authority of the Court's decisions in public opinion, and every Taft Court justice accepted the need to invest the Court with an authority that was more important than that of its individual members. Throughout the 1920s, in short, members of the Court continued to act as though they believed the Court required forms of legitimation appropriate to a tribunal whose function was to declare principles of law that were autonomous from public opinion and that commanded respect and obedience. They continued to imagine that the Court's judgments required the kind of peremptory authority needed definitively to resolve disputes between litigants. This suggests that they had not yet assimilated the profound and disconcerting implications of the Judiciary Act of February 13, 1925.

Although the acknowledgment of legal indeterminacy did not cause members of the Taft Court to challenge the authority of the Court as an institution, it did pose unsettling questions about the Court's epistemological capacity correctly to decide cases. The authority to declare law is inseparable from the authority accurately to ascertain the contents of the law. But if the substance of law is indeterminate, how might members of the Court know whether they had correctly declared the law in any given case? Legal indeterminacy led the Taft Court's liberal members to question whether the epistemological authority of the Court correctly to declare law depended upon its expertise – upon its ability accurately to ascertain the actual content of law – or whether it depended instead upon the finality of the Court's judgments, which is to say upon the need for the Court's decisions to be dispositive. The latter form of authority was most closely associated with the Court's dispute settlement function. Decisions of courts of last resort must be accepted by litigants as correct, whatever their content might be.

Both forms of epistemological authority are visible in a fascinating letter sent by Holmes to John Henry Wigmore at the beginning of the twentieth century. Holmes distinguished what we may call the authority of expertise from what we may call the authority of finality. The Court exercises the authority of expertise when it claims correctly to declare law because of its privileged insight into the substance of law. By contrast, the Court exercises the authority of finality when it claims accurately to declare law because of the need definitively to settle disputes. Holmes characterized the authority of finality as "ultra-academic," meaning "beyond academic considerations" and commanding respect simply "because it is a decision."[28] Robert Jackson would later famously summarize this kind of the authority by observing that "We are not final because we are infallible, but we are infallible only because we are final."[29]

Holmes was uncertain whether the epistemological legitimacy of the Court was best underwritten by the authority of expertise or by the authority of finality:

> I have sometimes criticised the Harvard Law Rev. for the offhand and august way in which it says that a case may be supported or cannot be. After all there is something ultra academic – I do not mean academic in the extreme but beyond academic considerations – in the opinions of an experienced Judge. And the young men of a law school don't realize that. But of course a judicial opinion like a scientific one must stand or fall on its reasons not on dogma, but as the legal premises are not qualified with the accuracy of science, and as the main justification of the law in my opinion is the fact that it has come out this way rather than some other which so far as I can see is equally good, I think the decisions of an important Court must command a certain respect because it is a decision and the opinion of experienced men, whether it seems right academically or not. Of course you won't think that this means I am getting personally into a *noli me tangere* frame of mind. I welcome every criticism from logic to English, and try to learn from it. But if anyone is to dogmatize it must be the man in power not the law student.[30]

On the one hand, Holmes conceived the epistemological authority of a Court to declare law to derive from the need to settle disputes. When presented with a case, a Court must decide one "way rather than some other which so far as I can

The Authority of the Taft Court

see is equally good." Because "legal premises are not qualified with the accuracy of science," the "opinion of experienced men" should command respect simply because the state has invested them with the official power to decide, whether their view of the law "seems right academically or not." The implication of this authority is that the content of the law is nothing more than what appellate courts declare it to be.

Yet, on the other hand, Holmes also acknowledged that the epistemological authority of a court must "stand or fall on its reasons,"[31] which implies that the authority of a court is subject to evaluation by those competent to assess legal reasoning. A judgment of a court must earn respect because it is correct, not merely command respect because it is a decision. On this account, law is not just what courts finally decide that it is. The law instead requires justification, which is to say that it must be conceived as a purposive instrument that can be calibrated in better or worse ways.[32] Hence the Court's claim to an authority of expertise must rest on its ability to convince those qualified to judge that it has correctly ascertained the law in light of the law's purposes.

Holmes could never quite reconcile the conflict between these two different perspectives.[33] His robust commitment to *stare decisis*, and his firm support of the norm of acquiescence, imply a profound commitment to the importance of maintaining the ultra-academic authority of finality. We can infer that although Holmes persuasively argued as a theorist that law should be regarded as an instrument for bringing "about a social end which we desire,"[34] he nevertheless as a judge acted as if the essential function of the Court was to settle conflicts. His judicial practice suggested a paradoxical allegiance to the view that in the end law was whatever the Court decided that it was. The Court was infallible because the Court was final.

Stone, by contrast, was far more attracted to the authority of expertise. In 1942, Stone observed that "a considered and well stated dissent ... can properly [appeal] only to scholarship, history and reason, and if the business of judging is an intellectual process, as we are entitled to believe that it is, it must be capable of withstanding and surviving these critical tests."[35] Unlike Douglas, who postulated the general public as the audience for judicial work, Stone imagined opinions as addressed to those in a position to evaluate the technical, "intellectual" work of judging, which is reducible neither to political will nor to official prerogative. As Stone wrote Frankfurter, in a letter sadly wondering whether "dissenting has any utility beyond enabling the dissenter to live comfortably with himself":[36] "I take some comfort ... to know that there are those who study our work with painstaking care and appreciate its significance."[37]

A nineteenth-century judge attracted to the authority of expertise would have located the relevant audience of competent specialists in the practicing "profession."[38] It is striking, however, that Stone looked instead to the legal academy. This is because legal scholarship by the 1920s had begun to challenge the claims of the bench and the bar to authoritative legal expertise.[39] As early as 1917 Charles Evans Hughes had complained that the "rapid growth" of primary legal material had made "the best judicial work" impossible; the only solution was to "look to the faculties of our law schools." Legal scholars, he said, "bring to the bench and bar the incalculable advantage of the best informed and critical judgment when our need for it is greatest."[40]

A decade later Benjamin Cardozo addressed "the old prejudice" against "law teachers." "For a long time," he remarked, "the practicing lawyers, and the judges, recruited for the most part from the ranks of the practitioners, were suspicious that there would be a loss of practical efficiency if the teachers in the universities were not made to know their place." But, Cardozo noted, "[w]ithin the last ten or fifteen years the conspiracy of silence has been dissolving" due to "a disturbance of the weights of authority and influence": "Judges and advocates may not relish the admission, but the sobering truth is that leadership in the march of legal thought has been passing in our day from the benches of the courts to the chairs of universities. ... [T]he outstanding fact is ... that academic scholarship is charting the line of development and progress in the untrodden regions of the law."[41]

Speaking to an audience of academics, Learned Hand confirmed in 1926 "that you will be recognized in another generation anyway, as the only body which can be relied upon to state a doctrine, with a complete knowledge of its origin, its authority and its meaning."[42] By 1941, Charles Evans Hughes could remember the days "thirty years" before when "Mr. Justice Holmes would refer somewhat scornfully to the 'notes' in law school reviews which ventured, not always with modesty, to criticize pronouncements of the Supreme Court. I recall that at one time he admonished counsel who had the temerity to refer to them in argument that they were merely the 'work of boys.' He thought the limit had been reached when what he had said in his judicial opinions was approved by the students as being 'a correct statement of the law.'"[43] But, Hughes explained, matters are now quite different. "It is not too much to say that, in confronting any serious problem, a wide-awake and careful judge will at once look to see if the subject has been discussed, or the authorities collated and analyzed, in a good law periodical."[44]

Stone's turn to legal academia was thus not the idiosyncratic response of a former Dean of the Columbia Law School. It reflected the fact that law schools had become a "'fourth estate' of the law,"[45] bringing to bear a breadth and depth of comprehension that threatened to strip judges of the mantle of expert authority. Brandeis was especially appreciative of academic expertise. He told Frankfurter that "[m]uch of the best and original legal thinking in America during the last generation is to be found in the law journals."[46] Brandeis believed that "law schools ought not to let Ct get by – country ought to insist on quality,"[47] and in dissent he would explicitly invoke law review articles for the proposition that "helpful discussion by friends of the Court, have made it clear that the rule declared is legally unsound."[48]

Dissents that appealed to the expertise of legal academia posed the delicate question of whether judges or academics were more qualified accurately to ascertain the correct substance of the law. In the 1920s, justices like Stone and Brandeis adopted Hand's view that judges "have little opportunity to go into questions as thoroughly and as scientifically as can those engaged in research in the universities."[49] Insofar as the Court's epistemological authority rested on expert knowledge rather than finality, Stone's and Brandeis's perspective potentially undermined the Court's claim of unique capacity to declare law.

This represented a direct challenge to an important pillar of the Court's epistemological authority, and it did not go unnoticed. Taft was himself a sophisticated former Yale law professor, and he was perfectly capable of writing the secretary of the *Yale Law Journal* (and future dean of the Yale Law School) to congratulate him "on the growing prestige" of the publication and to commend him on the *Journal's* doing "great good in considering carefully and discussing freely and frankly and criticizing the opinions of the Courts."[50] But the implicit threat to the Court's institutional position posed by the law reviews in fact rankled Taft. He dismissed articles attacking the Court's decisions as "the way the academicians . . . get even with us."[51] When the erstwhile Solicitor General James M. Beck sent Taft a scholarly article criticizing Taft's opinion in *Myers v. United States*,[52] Taft dryly noted that "another Commission of University Professors is engaged in reversing the Supreme Court. The continuance of the discussion is not a matter which causes me to sit up nights."[53]

Underlying the irony lay real anger. That members of the Court would undermine the Court's epistemological authority by pandering to academic expertise was almost intolerable. Near the end of his life, Taft dismissed Stone because "he hungers for the applause of the law school professors and the admirers of Holmes."[54] Taft's ire at Brandeis's dissent in *Olmstead v. United States*[55] modulated easily into resentment at the scholars for whom Brandeis wrote: "His claques in the law school contingent will sound his praises and point the finger of scorn at us, but if they think we're going to be frightened in our effort to stand by the law and give the public a chance to punish criminals, they are mistaken, even though we are condemned for lack of high ideals."[56]

Part of this anger was no doubt because legal scholars had become entangled in the Court's own factional divisions. Not only were "the dissenting minority of three"[57] lionized in the law journals,[58] which must have been personally galling,[59] but the progressive cast of American legal academia in the 1920s was quite hostile to the conservative constitutional vision of the majority of the Court.[60] "I have no doubt," Taft wrote his brother, "there is persistent hope, especially by the younger crowd of college professors, that in some way or other Holmes will be continued on the Court while the rest of us die off."[61] Of the unremitting criticisms of legal scholars, Taft remarked that "these gentlemen are so much torn by their anxiety about the Supreme Court that it is a wonder we are able to survive it."[62]

When the occasional academic dared to trespass upon the boundaries of judicial prerogative, the reaction of Taft and other conservative justices could be swift and murderous, as Stone learned to his chagrin in 1927. After the Court decided *Liberty Warehouse Co. v. Grannis*, which held that federal courts had "no jurisdiction" to proceed in a diversity suit according to the terms of "the Declaratory Judgment Law of Kentucky,"[63] Professor Edwin Borchard of the Yale Law School, long a passionate advocate for a federal declaratory judgment statute,[64] wrote Stone to express his concern that the Court "has recently taken what I believe to be a very unfortunate 'sideswipe' at the declaratory judgment as a procedural method for challenging the constitutionality of a statute." He explained to Stone that he was "writing a comment on the case, and on the dangers to the declaratory judgment involved in it, for the Yale Law Journal," and he asked if it would be "proper" for him to send it "to each member of the Court."[65]

Stone replied that "I would say that I think it would be quite in order for you to send your article in the Law Journal to all the members of the Court."[66] Borchard accordingly sent a copy of his comment to each justice,[67] with an accompanying letter that referred to the inadequacy of the reasoning in *Grannis* and suggested that occasion be taken, "if you find it consistent, to prevent the unfortunate result to which the Court's opinion ... may easily lead."[68] Borchard sent a copy of his letter to Stone, together with a note explaining what he had done and observing that "It would be too bad if, through an inadvertence, such a useful procedure as the declaratory action should be strangled. I trust you will be convinced that this is so, and will use your influence in the Court to obtain some reconsideration of the procedure in question."[69]

Three days later, Stone wrote Taft to express his concern about *Grannis*:

> I think we will have in increasing measure statutes like those involved in ... the Grannis case ... and that we ought to be extremely cautious about limiting the utility of such statutes.
>
> I have been troubled about the decision in the Grannis case for that reason and my sense of discomfort has not been allayed by reading in the April number of the Yale Law Review, at page 845, a comment on the Grannis case which expresses my own doubts about it.
>
> I don't know how you or any of the other members of the Court would feel about reopening the question in the Grannis case, but I think that there is some ground for giving the question some thought.[70]

To Stone's evident surprise, Taft responded in a white fury:[71]

> Replying to your letter of April 18th and the question of declaratory judgments raised by Borchard in his general assault upon the Court by letter, I am inclined to think that I had better allow the thing to proceed just as it is until somebody raises the question again. Borchard has aroused the indignation of the members of the Court at his method of attempting to induce the Court to reconsider or rehear the issue in which he is so much interested. Our brother Butler was particularly incensed. I haven't answered Borchard's letter, and I am rather inclined not to do so. If I did, I might have to write him a disciplinary letter. It is burdensome to do so.[72]

Flustered, Stone retreated, writing Taft a letter agreeing that "there is nothing to be done further at present upon the subject matter of the Liberty Warehouse case."[73] Stone repeated "what I said to you orally – that my writing to you on this subject was entirely on my own initiative," adding that "It was not inspired by Borchard's letter, as I did not receive it until the day after I had sent my letter to you." Stone acknowledged that Borchard's letter "shows a lack of a sense of

The Authority of the Taft Court

propriety which perhaps merits a positive rebuke, although I shall content myself by not answering it." Stone concluded his letter by returning to what was for him the central point: "I am more concerned with the thoroughness and scientific quality of our decisions and opinions than I am with the lack of propriety of others for whom we are not responsible, even though they ought to know better."[74]

Borchard incensed the Court because he inadvertently crossed the boundary between academic and judicial authority. He impertinently implied that the Court ought to act on the force of superior reasoning, even though that reasoning was advanced by a mere scholar. Borchard failed to defer to the Court's ultra-academic authority to declare law. The indignation aroused by Borchard's letter demonstrates that justices of the Taft Court were keen to defend its institutional prerogatives. Stone was oblivious to the incendiary potential of Borchard's letter because, like Borchard, he believed that the Court's epistemological authority in part depended upon the "scientific quality" of its opinions. That is why Stone could so casually refer Taft to the reasoning of a legal academic as a guide for Court policy, without seeming to realize just how potentially explosive such a reference could be.[75]

Other members of the Court, however, were determined to put scholarly expertise in its place. When Stone circulated a draft opinion in *Louis Pizitz Dry Goods Co. v. Yeldell*,[76] which concerned the constitutionality of an Alabama statute authorizing recovery of punitive damages against an employer for wrongful deaths caused by the negligent acts of employees, he cited in support of his argument an article by his former Columbia colleague (and eventual successor as dean) Young B. Smith.[77]

Butler immediately pounced. "I have hastily examined this article. You cite it generally, I think it is not helpful – certainly it is not necessary. Some having axes to grind write for Law Reviews in the attitude of advocates or propagandists. I do not suggest anything of the sort as to Mr. Scott [sic], but the fact that others do make it at least doubtful whether this Court ought to cite such writings – At least so it seems to me."[78] Van Devanter agreed. "To me it seems quite inappropriate to cite law journals."[79] Taft also piled on. "I doubt the wisdom of reference to a Law Review."[80] Outnumbered and opposed by the Taft-Van Devanter-Butler axis of the Court, Stone withdrew from the field, omitting the reference and writing Smith: "Confidentially, I cited your article ... in the Pizitz case, but some of the brethren are so opposed to citing Law Review articles that I finally took it out."[81]

Today, of course, the Court routinely cites law review literature.[82] Figure IV-26 compares the rate of citations to law review articles in Court opinions during the Taft Court era with the rate of such citations in opinions by the contemporary Court.[83] Figure IV-26 shows that the rate of citations to law reviews has increased more than twenty-five-fold, from .026 citations per majority opinion to .68 in the 2011 term.[84] Brandeis is sometimes identified as the justice who broke the barrier against citing law reviews in Supreme Court opinions.[85] Figure IV-27 indicates that of all Taft Court justices, only Brandeis and Stone were likely to cite law reviews in their opinions.

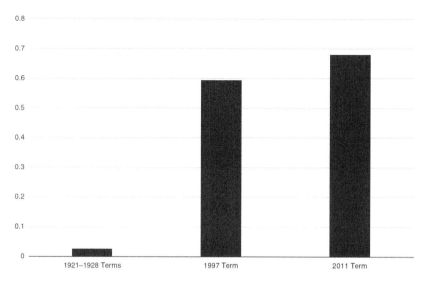

Figure IV-26 Number of citations to law review articles per Court opinion, 1921–1928 terms, 1997 term, 2011 term

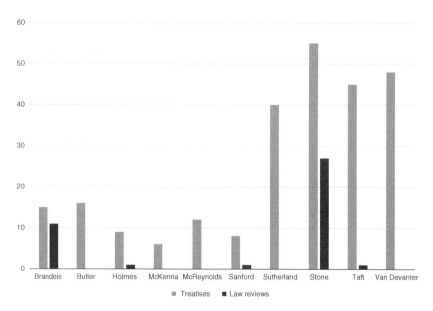

Figure IV-27 Number of citations to treatises and to law reviews in Court opinions, by justice, 1921–1928 terms

The Authority of the Taft Court

A close inspection of Figures IV-28 and IV-29, however, suggests that Brandeis primarily referred to law reviews in his dissents,[86] and that it was Stone who most systematically began to incorporate references to law review articles in his opinions for the Court. Whereas Brandeis was content to invoke the prestige of legal academia primarily to cast doubt on Court decisions, it was Stone who sensed that the Court's institutional authority to declare law required the supplementation of expertise, even as the Court was in the act of adjudicating a case. It was Stone who began to craft opinions appealing to the authority of expertise as well as to the authority of finality, and so undermining the assumption that law was simply whatever the Court might declare it to be.

Cardozo very quickly recognized the profound implications of this transformation. Not only did it signal a "change of leadership" from "the benches of the courts to the chairs of universities,"[87] but it also expressed "a recognition of the truth that an opinion derives its authority, just as law derives its existence, from all the facts of life. The judge is free to draw upon these facts wherever he can find them, if only they are helpful. No longer is his material confined to precedents in sheepskin."[88] Cardozo saw, in other words, that the struggle to open up court opinions to legal scholarship was not merely a competition for status between judges and scholars, but that it also indicated a change in how judges understood the nature of law.

As courts came gradually to internalize Holmes's theoretical insight that law was an instrument for the satisfaction of social needs, it became increasingly clear that it was an instrument that could be wielded in better or worse ways. Distinguishing one from the other required expertise. It required an understanding of "all the facts of life" and not merely familiarity with "precedents in sheepskin." Not coincidentally, it was Stone, and Stone alone, who during the Taft Court era

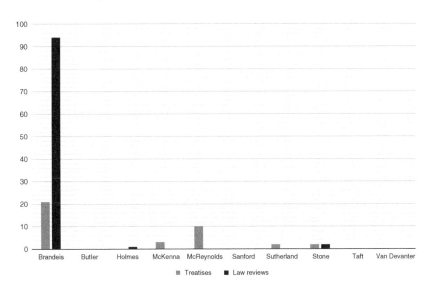

Figure IV-28 Number of citations to treatises and to law reviews in dissents, by justice, 1921–1928 terms

THE TAFT COURT

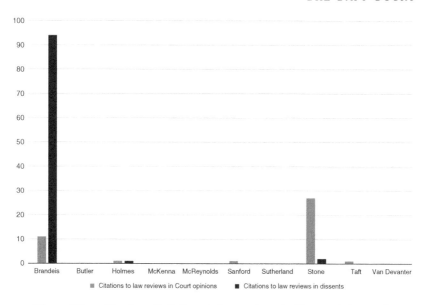

Figure IV-29 Number of citations to law reviews in Court opinions and dissents, by justice, 1921–1928 terms

began to propose innovative doctrinal tests like balancing, whose application required the Court explicitly to invoke the authority of this kind of expertise. Other members of the Taft Court, including Brandeis, were cautious about formulating doctrine that so bluntly involved the Court in case-by-case efforts to satisfy relevant social needs.[89]

We can perhaps sharpen our perception of this shift in authority by noting that, as Figure IV-30 indicates, justices in the Taft Court era were far more willing to cite legal treatises and encyclopedias in their opinions than they were to cite law review articles. Figure IV-29 shows that Taft Court justices were barely willing to cite law review articles at all.[a] If legal treatises were long associated with practitioners and judges like Story, Kent, and Cooley,[90] law review articles were instead the preferred domain of "the academic scholar."[91]

---

[a] During the 1921–1928 terms, the Taft Court cited treatises and encyclopedias at the rate of .16 citations per majority opinion, as compared to a rate of .03 citations per majority opinion for law review articles. *See, e.g.*, Max Radin, *Sources of Law – New and Old*, 1 SOUTHERN CALIFORNIA LAW REVIEW 411, 416 (1928) ("If we place the authorities cited in the order of apparent importance, we should find the following series: first, reported cases of the same jurisdiction; second, reported cases of outside jurisdictions; third, cyclopedias and repertories; fourth recent treatises; fifth, old treatises; and sixth and last, articles in legal periodicals. Citations of the last class are very few indeed, although they are increasing slightly."). Figure IV-31 illustrates that, during the Taft Court era, law review articles were more than twice as likely to be cited in dissents than in court opinions, while legal treatises and encyclopedias were about six times more likely to be cited in court opinions than in dissents. Figure IV-32 indicates that although law review articles seem to have lost their distinctive association with dissent in the 1997 term, this association was nevertheless very much in evidence during the 2011 term.

The Authority of the Taft Court

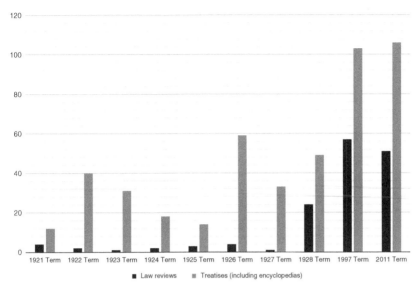

Figure IV-30 Number of citations to law reviews and treatises in Court opinions, by term, 1921–1928 terms, 1997 term, 2011 term

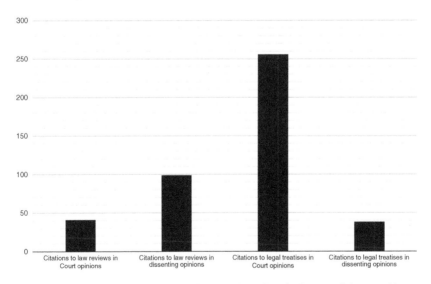

Figure IV-31 Citations to law reviews and treatises in Court opinions and in dissents, 1921–1928 terms

The ambition of treatises and encyclopedias was to present "an accurate account of the law"[92] as judges had constructed the law.[93] By contrast the ambition of law review articles was to present an account of what the law should be. Law

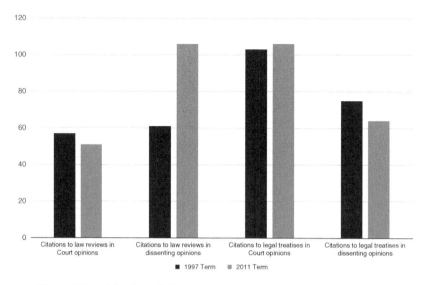

Figure IV-32 Number of citations to law reviews and treatises in Court opinions and in dissents, 1997 and 2011 terms

review articles assessed judicial opinions on the assumption that law was "an instrument of social engineering,"[94] so that the success of any given judicial opinion could be ascertained by the application of "a scientific apprehension of the relations of law to society and of the needs and interests and opinions of society of to-day."[95] Law reviews, in short, imagined law as a policy-oriented instrument whose proper exercise could be vindicated only by the authority of expertise.[96]

This suggests that the contemporary Court's routine citation of law review articles expresses and sustains the premise that law is a purposive enterprise for the governance of society. It would follow that the authority of contemporary courts to declare law rests in some nontrivial measure on their claim competently to know how to design law to fulfill its objectives. The struggle in the Taft Court over the citation of legal scholarship illuminates the beginning of this significant conceptual shift.

Taken to its logical conclusion, the authority of expertise carries important implications for the norm of acquiescence. A federal Court of Appeals judge conducted an informal poll about the desirability of dissents in the late 1930s. He found that "lawyers and judges" were "100% against dissenting opinions," but that "law school professors . . . love dissenting opinions."[97] If legal professionals understood courts to declare an "ultra-academic" law that demanded passive obedience and respect, law professors instead preferred courts to declare the kind of law that requires vindication in the same kind of debate that characterizes scholarly disciplines.

In our own time, Antonin Scalia, who celebrated dissents, has emphasized the analogy between academic and judicial disagreement. He writes that separate opinions, by enabling, indeed compelling, the Justices of the Court, through their personally signed majority, dissenting and concurring opinions, to set forth clear and consistent positions on both sides of the major legal issues of the day, ... ha[ve] kept the Court in the forefront of the intellectual development of the law. In our system, it is not left to the academicians to stimulate and conduct discussion concerning the validity of the Court's latest ruling. The Court itself is not just the central organ of legal *judgment*; it is center stage of significant legal *debate*.[98]

The point of the norm of acquiescence is to shut down debate in the service of cultivating deference to judicial judgments. The norm is a natural expression of the authority of finality, because it emphasizes the importance of legitimating peremptory juridical decision-making. The norm of acquiescence was thought to promote public trust that courts authoritatively settle disputes according to impersonal law. But law in this context is whatever courts declare it to be. Judicial authority to declare such law can be maintained only if judicial institutions are otherwise trusted, which is a lesson the Court learned to its chagrin during the New Deal era.

By contrast, the authority of expertise cannot be achieved by suppressing debate. It can be vindicated only by public acceptance that courts have correctly declared law. The legitimacy of court decisions is earned through the kind of open dialogue that characterizes the formation of public or scholarly judgment. It is no coincidence, therefore, that the most sophisticated account of the ultimate disintegration of the norm of acquiescence emphasizes that justices during the Roosevelt Court "reshaped the Court from one in which institutional opinions were the norm into a body of law professors who saw their job as constructing individual law review articles."[99] As Justice Frankfurter, who "pushed the hardest" against the norm of acquiescence, would later write Stone: "We ought to deal with one another's opinions as though they were writings in a law review."[100]

The "academic atmosphere"[101] that came to pervade the Court by the late 1930s would have been alien to justices of the Taft Court. During the 1920s, all members of the Court, including even Stone, sharply constrained the expression of their own personal perspectives because they believed that indiscriminate dissent threatened the necessary authority of the Court. One can see this clearly in the Court's response to the Judges' Bill. Figures IV-24 and IV-25 show that the Court redoubled its efforts to present a unanimous face to the public as private disagreements increased in the wake of the 1925 Act. By their actions, members of the Taft Court signaled their belief that the legitimacy of the Court, both epistemological and otherwise, ultimately depended upon what Taft called its "weight and solidarity"[102] rather than upon the persuasiveness of its reasons.

Buried within the dry statistics of unanimity and citation, then, lies an invisible but significant story about the evolving institutional authority of the Court. Insofar as the Court was a simple final appellate tribunal, its authority could rest securely on the widely acknowledged importance of peaceably settling disputes. Although the 1925 Act transformed the Court into the proactive supervisor of federal law, members of the Taft Court nevertheless remained firmly committed to the ultra-academic authority characteristic of final appellate tribunals. The modern Court, having thoroughly assimilated the implications of the Judges'

Bill, plainly looks to quite different sources of authority to sustain a legitimacy that must justify much more than resolving disputes between particular parties.

In subsequent chapters of this history, we shall begin to consider the substantive jurisprudence advanced by the Taft Court. The nation had undergone a seismic transformation during World War I, and the pressing question that infiltrated virtually all aspects of American public law during the subsequent decade was whether the profound alterations wrought by the war should be embraced or repudiated. Today the Taft Court is chiefly remembered as strenuously seeking to cabin the epic forces unleashed by the war. In the process, the Court became increasingly vulnerable to the charge that it was speaking from political rather than legal principles. The Taft Court responded by seeking to suppress dissents to shore up public trust that it was in fact declaring law.[103] But this response proved a mere momentary stay against the oncoming confusion.

As skepticism of the Court began to spread, the Court's authority of finality began correspondingly to weaken, preparing the ground for the now familiar jurisprudential controversies we associate with the New Deal. At its root, the looming crisis stemmed from the dwindling commitment of the public to "respect and obey" the Court's version of law simply because the Court had declared it. The Taft Court sought to bolster that commitment by doubling down on the norm of acquiescence. But the 1920s may have been the last moment in the Court's history when the Court could authentically imagine itself as speaking with the authority of a simple final appellate tribunal whose judgments were primarily addressed to litigants. Within a decade the Court would begin to adopt decision-making practices that would supplement the Court's authority by reaching out to public opinion and to the community of legal expertise.

Notes

1. WHT to Warren G. Harding (December 25, 1920) (Harding Papers in the Ohio History Connection). *See, e.g.*, WHT to Horace D. Taft (February 28, 1922) (Taft papers) ("We had a unanimous judgment in that case, which gives it a good deal of weight.") (referring to the Wisconsin Rate Case, 257 U.S. 503 (1922)).
2. Albert J. Beveridge, *Common Sense and the Constitution*, 196 SATURDAY POST 25, 119 (December 15, 1923). *See* Jackson Harvey Ralston, *Shall We Curb the Supreme Court?*, 71 THE FORUM 561, 565 (1924).
3. American Bar Association Canons of Judicial Ethics, Canon 19 (1924), in LISA L. MILORD, THE DEVELOPMENT OF THE ABA JUDICIAL CODE 137 (Chicago: Center for Professional Responsibility, American Bar Association 1992).
4. WHT to WVD (December 26, 1921) (Van Devanter papers).
5. *Evils of Dissenting Opinions*, 57 ALBANY LAW JOURNAL 74, 75 (1898). The article reproduced a lecture delivered by Henry Wollman on Pollock v. Farmers' Loan & Trust Co., 157 U.S. 429 (1895).
6. *See supra* Chapter 17, at 565–66.
7. As Cardozo famously put the point in 1921: "As the years have gone by, and as I have reflected more and more upon the nature of the judicial process, I have become reconciled to the uncertainty, because I have grown to see it as inevitable. I have grown to see that the process in its highest reaches is not discovery, but creation." BENJAMIN N. CARDOZO, THE NATURE OF THE JUDICIAL PROCESS 166 (New Haven: Yale University Press 1921).
8. Oliver Wendell Holmes, *Law in Science and Science in Law*, 12 HARVARD LAW REVIEW 443, 461 (1899).
9. WHT to GS (September 10, 1922) (Sutherland papers).
10. For a good expression of that reverence, see Elihu Root to Cass Gilbert (February 25, 1932) (Gilbert papers at the Library of Congress); *supra* Chapter 17, at note 204.
11. Morehead v. New York *ex rel.* Tipaldo, 298 U.S. 587, 633 (1936) (Stone, J., dissenting).
12. BARRY FRIEDMAN, THE WILL OF THE PEOPLE: HOW PUBLIC OPINION HAS INFLUENCED THE SUPREME COURT AND SHAPED THE MEANING OF THE CONSTITUTION 4 (New York: Farrar, Status & Giroux 2009). *See, e.g.*, Or Bassok, *The Supreme Court's New Source of Legitimacy*, 16 UNIVERSITY OF PENNSYLVANIA JOURNAL OF CONSTITUTIONAL LAW 153 (2013).
13. For a discussion of the dialectical relationship between the Court and the public, see Robert C. Post and Reva B. Siegel, *Democratic Constitutionalism*, in THE CONSTITUTION IN 2020 (Jack M. Balkin & Reva B. Siegel, eds., New York: Oxford University Press 2009); Robert C. Post & Reva B. Siegel, *Roe Rage: Democratic Constitutionalism and Backlash*, 42 HARVARD CIVIL RIGHTS-CIVIL LIBERTIES LAW REVIEW 373 (2007).
14. STEPHEN BREYER, THE AUTHORITY OF THE COURT AND THE PERIL OF POLITICS 86 (Cambridge: Harvard University Press 2021).
15. On the tension between these two understandings of law, see Robert C. Post and Reva B. Siegel, *Popular Constitutionalism, Departmentalism, and Judicial Supremacy*, 92 CALIFORNIA LAW REVIEW 1027 (2004).
16. Howard Gillman, *The Collapse of Constitutional Originalism and the Rise of the Notion of the "Living Constitution" in the Course of American State-Building*, 11

STUDIES IN AMERICAN POLITICAL DEVELOPMENT 191, 220 (1997). This kind of law has been usefully theorized as "responsive law" in PHILIPPE NONET & PHILIP SELZNICK, LAW AND SOCIETY IN TRANSITION: TOWARD RESPONSIVE LAW (New York: Harper & Row 1978).
17. Frederick Schauer, *Foreword: The Court's Agenda – and the Nation's*, 120 HARVARD LAW REVIEW 4, 35 (2006). Most low salience decisions are even now received by the public as declaring law that must be respected and obeyed. But low salience decisions are by definition cases in which the public is uninterested.
18. *Brown v. Board of Education*, 347 U.S. 483 (1954).
19. ALEXANDER M. BICKEL, THE SUPREME COURT AND THE IDEA OF PROGRESS 91 (New Haven: Yale University Press 1978).
20. ALEXANDER M. BICKEL, THE LEAST DANGEROUS BRANCH: THE SUPREME COURT AT THE BAR OF POLITICS 239 (2nd ed., New Haven: Yale University Press 1986).
21. Pamela C. Corley, Amy Steigerwalt, & Artemus Ward, *Revisiting the Roosevelt Court: The Critical Juncture from Consensus to Dissensus*, 38 JOURNAL OF SUPREME COURT HISTORY 20, 47 (2013).
22. WHT to WVD (December 26, 1921) (Van Devanter papers).
23. William O. Douglas, *The Dissent: A Safeguard of Democracy*, 32 JOURNAL OF THE AMERICAN JUDICATURE SOCIETY 104, 105–6 (1948).
24. William J. Brennan, Jr., *In Defense of Dissents*, 37 HASTINGS LAW JOURNAL 427, 435 (1986). *See, e.g.*, Jesse W. Carter, *Dissenting Opinions*, 4 HASTINGS LAW JOURNAL 118, 118 (1953) ("The right to dissent is the essence of democracy."); *id.* at 123 ("Freedom of speech is one of the greatest rights guaranteed to the individual by the Bill of Rights and is an essential ingredient of any democracy. It applies no less to the dissenting judge than it does to the average citizen.... [T]he same right to freedom of expression should be accorded judges as is accorded legislators or the executive in their respective fields."); Richard B. Stephens, *The Function of Concurring and Dissenting Opinions in Courts of Last Resort*, 5 UNIVERSITY OF FLORIDA LAW REVIEW 394, 400 (1952) ("Freedom of expression for the appellate judge is closely related to the constitutional guarantee of freedom of speech.").
25. David M. O'Brien, *Institutional Norms and Supreme Court Opinions: On Reconsidering the Rise of Individual Opinions*, in SUPREME COURT DECISION-MAKING: NEW INSTITUTIONALIST APPROACHES 107 (Cornell W. Clayton & Howard Gillman, eds., University of Chicago Press 1999).
26. For an account of how law might be conceptualized in the context of this dialectical relationship between court judgments and public opinion, see Robert Post, *Theorizing Disagreement: Reconceiving the Relationship* between *Law and Politics*, 98 CALIFORNIA LAW REVIEW 1319 (2010).
27. Although Brandeis was widely rumored to be La Follette's first choice for a vice presidential running-mate, see *La Follette to Run for Presidency as Progressive*, NEW YORK TIMES (July 3, 1924), at A1, even Taft believed that Brandeis "would not go so far as La Follette with reference to the abolition of the power of the Court." WHT to Max Pam (September 12, 1924) (Taft papers).
28. OWH to John Henry Wigmore (May 17, 1906) (Holmes papers).
29. Brown v. Allen, 344 U.S. 443, 540 (1953) (Jackson, J., concurring).
30. OWH to John Henry Wigmore (May 17, 1906) (Holmes papers).

31. A.W.B. Simpson finds an analogous tension between "a concept of law rooted in reason, and one rooted in authority" in the genre of the legal treatise. A.W.B. Simpson, *The Rise and Fall of the Legal Treatise: Legal Principles and the Forms of Legal Literature*, 48 UNIVERSITY OF CHICAGO LAW REVIEW 632, 665 (1981). Simpson associates the latter view of law with "the spirit of positivism." *Id.* at 668. *See also* Charles W. Collier, *The Use and Abuse of Humanistic Theory in Law: Reexamining the Assumptions of Interdisciplinary Legal Scholarship*, 41 DUKE LAW JOURNAL 215–23 (1991) (distinguishing "institutional authority from intellectual authority").
32. *See* NONET & SELZNICK, *supra* note 16.
33. Because Holmes believed that the understanding of an "experienced Judge" could not be rivaled, he was not himself tempted to appeal to the realm of legal scholarship to supplement the persuasiveness of his reasons when authoring opinions or dissents. *See* Figures IV-27, IV-28, and IV-29.
34. Holmes, *supra* note 8, at 460.
35. Harlan F. Stone, *Dissenting Opinions Are Not Without Value*, 26 JOURNAL OF THE AMERICAN JUDICATURE SOCIETY 78, 78 (1942).
36. To which Stone added, "But that is sufficient justification for me." HFS to Felix Frankfurter (January 16, 1930) (Stone papers).
37. *Id.*
38. So, for example, the editors of the *American Law Review* argued in 1886 that "the practice of writing dissenting opinions" ought not to be prohibited by legislation because:

> It has always been recognized that judicial decisions which merely announce conclusions of law, without either referring to authority for such conclusions or offering reasons in support of them, carry little weight. If mere legislation is the office of the courts, they would carry the weight which an act of legislation carries. Experience, we take it, shows that judicial decisions which are neither founded on authority nor on sound reasoning are never allowed to remain unquestioned by the profession. Cases are known where such decisions, always unsatisfactory to the profession, have been constantly assailed and finally overthrown after the lapse of many years. It is the office of the judge who writes a judicial decision to give the reasons upon which the court proceeds. The proper administration of justice is not satisfied with anything else. If these are omitted, the judgment becomes a mere arbitrary exercise of power. If it is the office of the judicial courts to furnish the reasons which the court gives for its decision, it cannot be affirmed with any show of logic that it is not equally their office to furnish the reasons which a portion of the court may give for the opposing view.

Dissenting Opinions, 20 AMERICAN LAW REVIEW 428, 429 (1886).
39. On the tension between the judiciary and the new profession of legal academia, see JEROLD S. AUERBACH, UNEQUAL JUSTICE: LAWYERS AND SOCIAL CHANGE IN MODERN AMERICA 91–92 (New York: Oxford University Press 1976).
40. CHARLES EVANS HUGHES, SOME OBSERVATIONS ON LEGAL EDUCATION AND DEMOCRATIC PROGRESS DELIVERED ON THE OCCASION OF THE CELEBRATION OF THE CENTENNIAL OF THE HARVARD LAW SCHOOL 8, 11, 13, 14 (New York: Pandick Press 1917).
41. Benjamin N. Cardozo, *Introduction*, in SELECTED READINGS ON THE LAW OF CONTRACTS FROM AMERICAN AND ENGLISH LEGAL PERIODICALS vii, viii–ix (Association of American Law Schools, ed., New York: Macmillan Co. 1931).

42. Learned Hand, *Have the Bench and Bar Anything to Contribute to the Teaching of Law?*, 24 MICHIGAN LAW REVIEW 466, 468 (1926).
43. Charles E. Hughes, *Foreword*, 50 YALE LAW JOURNAL 737, 737 (1941). When Stone circulated the draft of his opinion in Raffel v. United States, 271 U.S. 494 (1926), Holmes remarked apropos of Stone's citation of a *Harvard Law Review* note: "If this is one of those editorial notes, I should not cite it." (Stone papers). Stone, however, refused to remove the citation. 271 U.S. at 499.
44. Hughes, *supra* note 43, at 737.
45. *Id.*
46. LDB to Felix Frankfurter (October 10, 1922), in BRANDEIS-FRANKFURTER CORRESPONDENCE, at 121. Law reviews, Brandeis continued, are "in the main, inaccessible to the bench and the bar. Now that the law journals have become an incident of the law schools of the Universities, the number of valuable contributions should increase rapidly. Would it not be desirable that the Law Schools should cooperate in publishing an Index covering all valuable articles, which have appeared during the last 35 years ... and arrange for supplements to be published annually thereafter? The fact that articles would be thus made accessible should tend to encourage production." *Id.* at 121–22.
47. *Brandeis-Frankfurter Conversations*, at 309 (July 20, 1922). Brandeis emphasized to Zechariah Chafee "the value of a Law School professorship, as a fulcrum in efforts to improve the law and through it, society." LDB to Zachariah Chafee (June 5, 1921), in 4 LETTERS OF LOUIS D. BRANDEIS, at 564.
48. Washington v. W.C. Dawson & Co., 264 U.S. 219, 236 n.18 (1924) (Brandeis, J., dissenting). Fifteen years after *W.C. Dawson*, Brandeis's appeal to the usefulness of law review literature would evolve in the hands of his protégé Frankfurter into a Court opinion that could overrule a precedent (Evans v. Gore, 253 U.S. 245 (1920)) on the basis of a frank avowal that "[t]he decision met wide and steadily growing disfavor from legal scholarship and professional opinion." O'Malley v. Woodrough, 307 U.S. 277, 281 (1939). Butler grumbled in dissent that as against "the deliberate judgments of this Court," Frankfurter could adduce only the "selected gainsaying writings of professors, – some are lawyers and some are not – but without specification of or reference to the reasons upon which their views rest. And in addition it cites notes published in law reviews, some signed and some not; presumably the latter were prepared by law students." *Id.* at 298 (Butler, J., dissenting).
49. HFS to Hessel E. Yntema (October 24, 1928) (Stone papers).
50. "It helps the cause of justice, and it helps the courts; and while there may be differing opinions as to the particular criticism and its soundness, this does not in the slightest degree detract from its usefulness." WHT to A.G. Gulliver (February 6, 1922) (Taft papers).
51. WHT to Horace D. Taft (January 7, 1929) (Taft papers). The oddly agonistic relationship between Taft and the legal academy is nicely captured by what happened when Roscoe Pound asked Taft to consent to be interviewed by Pound's student Olson for the purpose of legal research. Taft graciously accepted, and then wrote Pound this deadpan account of the interview:

> Mr. Olson presented your letter of introduction of December 24th. I am afraid I was not very helpful to him. I don't quite understand what his

The Authority of the Taft Court

> particular purpose was. You describe it and he describes it as the investigation of the psychology of judicial decisions. So far as he developed it to me, it was to read me a criticism of my opinions and to question their reasoning, and then to invite my dissent or answer to his criticisms. Of course I could not spend my time meeting criticisms of my opinions and arguing them out with a law student. Just what kind of a study in psychology he was engaged in, other than that of the use of his reasoning powers to assault the opinions of our Court, I was unable to see. Of course it is the right of every law student ... to read opinions and to approve or question their soundness, but I am sorry that I haven't the time to give to Mr. Olson the opportunity to practice his psychological research by defending each one of my opinions which he happens to differ with. I, therefore, asked him to excuse me from what I really did not have time for. Of course it is the privilege of every student and every American citizen to question the opinions of a Court, but it is hardly the duty – perhaps it is hardly proper – for the Judge who has written them, to supplement what he may have said in his opinions and to sustain the correctness of his conclusions by further discussion of them with young gentlemen pursuing their research.

WHT to Roscoe Pound (January 3, 1924) (Taft papers).
52. James M. Beck to WHT (October 24, 1929) (Taft papers). Beck observed, "As often, the College Professors attempt to reverse the Supreme Court." *Id.*
53. WHT to James M. Beck (October 25, 1929) (Taft papers). When Milton Handler, fresh from his clerkship with Stone, sent Taft a copy of Handler's article that had just appeared in the *Columbia Law Review*, he evinced full awareness of the strained relationship between legal academia and the Court:

> I suppose that the chief raison d'etre of an article is the sublimation of the ego of the writer, and how else can this be done but by a restrained criticism of Judicial opinion. Only by showing the Courts to be wrong can the author display his own unparalleled wisdom. I fear that in this paper I fall into this pattern of law writer. While somewhat critical of the work of the Court, I have tried to approach the problem in a truly impartial and scientific way and I hope that my study will be of some value in this field.

Milton Handler to WHT (November 19, 1928) (Taft papers). Taft replied graciously, thanking Handler for the article and adding that "[w]e are always glad to be advised by academic leaders." WHT to Milton Handler (November 23, 1928) (Taft papers).
54. WHT to Horace D. Taft (June 8, 1928) (Taft papers).
55. 277 U.S. 438, 471 (1928).
56. WHT to Horace D. Taft (June 8, 1928) (Taft papers). Four days later, Taft confided to his brother that "I shall continue to be worried by attacks from the academic lawyers who write college law journals but I suppose it is not a basis for impeachment." WHT to Horace D. Taft (June 12, 1928) (Taft papers). Brandeis, Taft wrote his son apropos of Myers v. United States, 272 U.S. 52 (1926), "can not avoid writing an opinion in a case in which he wishes to spread himself, as if he were writing an article for the Harvard Law Review. When that is not in his mind, he writes a very concise and a very satisfactory opinion, but his dissents are of a different character." WHT to Robert A. Taft (October 24, 1926) (Taft papers).
57. WHT to Horace D. Taft (December 1, 1929) (Taft papers).
58. It was a noteworthy occasion when every so often an article favorable to the majority appeared in the law journals. *See, e.g.,* WHT to WVD (January 12, 1929) (Taft

papers) ("I call your attention to the fact that once in a while even the Yale Law Journal thinks that the opinion of the majority of the Court should be sustained."). *See also* Joseph R. Long to WHT (December 10, 1922) (Taft papers) (enclosing Long's article praising Taft's opinion in Bailey v. Drexel Furniture Co., 259 U.S. 20 (1922)); WHT to Joseph R. Long (December 12, 1922) (Taft papers) ("I appreciate much your article."); Henry St. George Tucker to WHT (December 11, 1922) (Taft papers) (calling Taft's "attention" to the "very interesting" article by Long).

59. Thus when Taft began a campaign to persuade Yale to grant Willis Van Devanter an honorary degree, see *supra* Chapter 6, at 230 and notes 65–66, Taft was forced to explain Van Devanter's relative public obscurity by the fact that "[h]e has not what some of our Judges have by reason of their relations to Law Schools – a claque who are continually sounding their praises." WHT to William Phelps (May 30, 1927) (Taft papers).

60. Jerold S. Auerbach has written that "In the two decades preceding World War I a sense of public responsibility and an identification with political reform provided law teachers with their special identity." AUERBACH, *supra* note 39, at 81; *see also* Jerold S. Auerbach, *Enmity and Amity: Law Teachers and Practitioners, 1900–1922*, 5 PERSPECTIVES IN AMERICAN HISTORY 551 (1971) (reviewing the teaching of law as a profession). Taft was particularly outraged by mobilization within the law schools over the Sacco and Vanzetti case. He wrote an unsolicited letter to the president of Yale University complaining of the involvement of the law faculty in protesting the convictions:

> I don't know how much influence you can exercise with respect to the Yale Law School, but I am a good deal troubled in respect to something I have seen in the newspapers. The Harvard Law School is suffering from the exercise of influence upon it by Felix Frankfurter. He seems to be closely in touch with every Bolshevistic communist movement in this country. I know him very well. He is a man of ability and can be in certain directions quite useful, but for some reason or other he is against courts and recognized authority, a very bad tendency in a college law professor. I don't know anything about this criminal prosecution of two Italians. ... I have no objection to the criticism of judicial opinions or judicial judgments – that is necessary. Nor have I any objection to this by professors of law schools, because they are competent men and may often exercise a very useful influence upon judges to help the science of the law, but I think it quite unwise for a law school of Connecticut, far removed from the situation, to have its Dean and Professors join in a public meeting and protest against the conduct of litigation in another State and second an article by Frankfurter. I don't know that anything can be done about the further activities of Dean Hutchins in this matter, but I think it would be wise to talk to him on the subject and say that as the Dean of the Law School he should restrain himself and not rush in, as he evidently has, and put the Law School, of which he is the head, in such a movement which involves the weighing of facts as well as of law, and relates to a trial which took place when Hutchins must have been a boy. ... [M]y interest in Yale makes me feel that I am justified in suggesting to you that you restrain Hutchins.

WHT to James R. Angell (May 1, 1927) (Taft papers). *See also Yale Liberals Defend Sacco and Vanzetti*, NEW YORK TIMES (April 30, 1927), at 23; *cf.* Robert M. Hutchins, *Cross-Examination to Impeach*, 36 YALE LAW JOURNAL 384, 385–88 (1927). For Angell's cool reply, see James R. Angell to WHT (May 3, 1927) (Taft papers). The following week Taft complained to Elihu Root:

> I think our Law Schools might be about better business than attempting to decide how trials ought to be conducted in capital cases in old Massachusetts,

without other knowledge of the record than that derived from a magazine article by Prof. Felix Frankfurter, who has become an expert in attempting to save murderous anarchists from the gallows or the electric chair. I don't like to characterize any great profession, but I think the profession of law teacher, as well as the clerical profession, does not always exercise the best judgment in keeping out of fields in which they are apt to make egregious mistakes.

WHT to Elihu Root (May 12, 1927) (Taft papers). After Sacco's and Vanzetti's executions, Taft wrote an advisor to Massachusetts Governor Fuller: "It is remarkable how Frankfurter with his article was able to present to so large a body of readers a perverted view of the facts and then through the world wide conspiracy of communism spread it to many many countries. Our law schools lent themselves to the vicious propaganda. The utter lack of substance in it all is shown by the event. It was a bubble and was burst by the courage of the Governor and his advisors." WHT to Robert Grant (November 4, 1927) (Taft papers).

61. WHT to Horace D. Taft (December 8, 1929) (Taft papers). In 1930, Van Devanter's intimate friend, Federal District Judge John C. Pollock, wrote him: "I notice in a recent Law Review very high commendation of the legal opinions, more especially dissenting opinions, of a couple of gentlemen, you will readily realize to whom I refer. I cannot understand this and do not appreciate the viewpoint from which they are written. I apprehend you have seen the same. I begin to think every once in a while that as we grow older we grow out of touch with a lot of ideas that some people appreciate very highly, but which will not work out in practice." John C. Pollock to WVD (April 17, 1930) (Van Devanter papers).

62. WHT to Moses Strauss (February 19, 1929) (Taft papers). Taft brushed off Edward Corwin's criticisms of Taft's opinion in Bailey v. Drexel Furniture Co., 259 U.S. 20 (1922), characterizing them as the objections "of the class not of lawyers but of government philosophers who think that the Constitution ought to be moulded to suit their particular sociological views as they may vary from time to time." WHT to Horace D. Taft (September 7, 1922) (Taft papers). In other contexts, however, Taft fully recognized that, as he told the American Law Institute in February 1924, "The power over the profession is now exercised by the professors of law who carry on the education of the youth and who make them better lawyers than those who are active in the profession; and whose time is so much occupied in making the large arrangements of a professional character that their time is too valuable to occupy themselves with educating the judges." 2 PROCEEDINGS OF THE AMERICAN LAW INSTITUTE 93 (February 23, 1924).

63. 273 U.S. 70, 76 (1927).

64. *See, e.g.*, Edwin M. Borchard, The Declaratory Judgment, A Brief Submitted to the Committee on the Judiciary of the United States Senate Relating to S. 5304 To Authorize the Federal Courts of the United States to Render Declaratory Judgments, 65th CONG. 3rd SESS. (Committee Print 1919); Edwin M. Borchard, *The Declaratory Judgment – A Needed Procedural Reform*, 28 YALE LAW JOURNAL 1, 105 (1918); Edwin M. Borchard, *The Declaratory Judgment*, 25 NEW REPUBLIC 192 (1921).

65. Edwin M. Borchard to HFS (February 4, 1927) (Stone papers). *Grannis* was decided on January 3, 1927.

66. HFS to Edwin M. Borchard (February 7, 1927) (Stone papers). For Borchard's reply, see Edwin M. Borchard to HFS (February 9, 1927) (Stone papers). At the

time, Stone was writing the Court's opinion in Fidelity National Bank & Trust Co. v. Swope, 274 U.S. 123 (1927), in which the Court in effect upheld federal jurisdiction of a state declaratory judgment. Stone had been assigned *Swope* at the end of January when Taft, "[i]n the redistribution of cases to help out our dear friend Van, because of his near breakdown," had asked Stone to take over the case. WHT to HFS (January 26, 1927) (Stone papers). Taft added, "All the members of the Court voted to reverse the case except McReynolds, who was passed. Your forced familiarity with questions of this kind in the St. Louis case [Missouri v. Pub. Serv. Comm'n, 273 U.S. 126 (1927)], which you were not able to use in the opinion handed down recently, may prove to be of use to you in this case. I hope so." *Id. Swope* issued on April 11, 1927. *See* 274 U.S. at 123. Van Devanter judged it "a fine opinion, judicial through and through. Enriches straight from the beginning to the conclusion." (Stone papers). Taft also thought it "a good opinion." *Id.* On April 29, Walter Wheeler Cook wrote Stone to congratulate him on the *Swope* opinion, confessing that *Grannis* had "alarmed me greatly. I feared the court was getting into a position where it would find itself bound to hold a federal declaratory judgment statute unconstitutional as giving non-judicial power." Walter Wheeler Cook to HFS (April 29, 1927) (Stone papers). Stone replied to Cook that "I was not a little troubled when I came to write" *Swope* "about some of the things that had been said about what is a 'case' or 'controversy' or 'judicial power' within the meaning of the Constitution." HFS to Walter Wheeler Cook (May 2, 1927) (Stone papers).

67. *See* Edwin M. Borchard, *Declaratory Actions as "Cases" or "Controversies,"* 36 YALE LAW JOURNAL 845 (1927).

68. Edwin M. Borchard to WHT (April 15, 1927) (Taft papers). In full, the letter said,

> I venture to ask your consideration of this Comment, which deals with the decision of the Supreme Court in the case of Liberty Warehouse Co. v. Grannis.... In that case, the Court, speaking through Mr. Justice Sanford, held, or intimated that the declaratory judgment procedure, now adopted by statute in some twenty-one states, was unconstitutional, because it did not present a "case" or "controversy". This conclusion is not, I respectfully venture to think, justified by the facts, and I have, in the Comment referred to, expressed the opinion that the question was not adequately argued before the Court. I would not dare trouble you with my views on this matter, but for the fact that I believe that the opinion of the Court, which may or may not have been dictum, threatens with extinction, on insufficient grounds, what, in my opinion, is one of the most useful procedural reforms of recent years.... I trust you will be kind enough to give this matter your consideration, and perhaps take some occasion, if you find it consistent, to prevent the unfortunate result to which the Court's opinion in the Liberty Warehouse case may easily lead. I beg also to call your attention to the April (1927) Harvard Law Review (page 903), in which the editor appears to share the subscriber's view of the effect of the Court's decision in the Liberty Warehouse case.

Id. We have extant the letters that Borchard sent to Van Devanter, Taft, Sanford, and Sutherland. They are identical. Taft's copy is marked "No ans."

69. Edwin M. Borchard to HFS (April 15, 1927) (Stone papers).
70. HFS to WHT (April 18, 1927) (Taft papers). On Taft's daily memorandum of things to do for April 21, 1927, the fourth item on the list reads: "Take up Borchard's letter." (Taft papers).
71. Taft held very definite views of Borchard prior to this incident. In 1924, Nicholas Murray Butler had written Taft asking for recommendations for an international law

The Authority of the Taft Court

scholar to replace John Bassett Moore at Columbia. Taft replied in what may be one of his nastiest letters:

> There is a man who has had a good deal of experience in international matters, who is now the Law Librarian at Yale. His name is Edwin Borchard. He has gotten up a compendium on a phase of international law which I think has been well regarded. But I think he has reddish tendencies and I doubt if you would wish to take him over. He is Hebraic in look, and I have no doubt in fact. He is always for the Brandeis view of every constitutional question. I lodged a complaint with Swan against having him instill in the minds of the Yale Law School men that spirit of constitutional construction, for I believe that they have been using him on the subject of Federal Constitutional Law.

WHT to Nicholas Murray Butler (December 30, 1924) (Taft papers). Taft might have had in mind Borchard's stinging criticism of Adkins v. Children's Hospital, 261 U.S. 525 (1923). *See* E.M. Borchard, *The Supreme Court and the Minimum Wage*, 32 YALE LAW JOURNAL 829, 830 (1923).

72. WHT to HFS (April 24, 1927) (Taft papers). The following year the Court decided Willing v. Chicago Auditorium Ass'n, 277 U.S. 274 (1928), in which Brandeis, in his opinion for the Court, offhandedly remarked (citing *Grannis*) that a declaratory judgment "is beyond the power conferred upon the Federal judiciary." *Id.* at 289. Taft responded to Brandeis's draft opinion, "Borchard will moan but he can not by tears change our jurisdiction." (Brandeis papers). On *Willing*, see *supra* Chapter 8, at note 19.

Curiously enough, Taft had a second encounter with Borchard at the end of the 1926 term. In June 1927, Taft announced the opinion for the Court in an obscure case, Weedin v. Chin Bow, 274 U.S. 657 (1927), which concerned the citizenship status of children of American citizens who did not reside in the United States. The original version of Taft's published opinion, which was released on June 6, 1927, deliberately and specifically criticized a passage from Borchard's book, THE DIPLOMATIC PROTECTION OF CITIZENS ABROAD (New York: The Banks Law Publishing Co., 1915), charging that it relied on evidence that "does not bear out the conclusion to which it is cited." (Taft papers). Borchard instantly telegraphed Taft at his summer residence in Murray Bay, Canada, to explain that Taft's charge rested on an apparent confusion regarding the reference of various footnotes. *See* Telegram from Edwin M. Borchard to WHT (June 9, 1927) (Taft papers). He also complained that Taft's accusation, which was based on "an inadvertent mistake," "might by the profession be deemed to impugn my reliability." Edwin M. Borchard to WHT (June 9, 1927) (Taft papers). *See also* William Crosskey to WHT (June 9, 1927) (Taft papers). After consulting with his law clerk, William Crosskey, Taft removed the offending passages. *See* 274 U.S. at 673–74; WHT to Charles Cropley (July 5, 1927) (Taft papers); Charles Cropley to WHT (June 30, 1927) (Taft papers); Telegram from WHT to Charles Cropley (June 10, 1927) (Taft papers).

73. HFS to WHT (April 25, 1927) (Taft papers). Stone added, "My experience, however, in writing the opinion in the Swope case convinces me that we ought to approach this type of question when it comes up again with the greatest caution, and that we ought not to follow some of the things that have been said in earlier cases, although quite possibly we can follow what was actually decided." *Id.*

675

74. *Id.* Borchard clearly had no idea of the hornet's nest he had aroused. He wrote Stone again in 1928, affirming that "the law journals ... have agreed that Judge Sanford made a mistake" in *Grannis*, and complaining of further *dicta* damaging to a potential federal declaratory judgment statute in Liberty Warehouse Co. v. Burley Tobacco Growers' Co-Operative Marketing Ass'n, 276 U.S. 71 (1928). Edwin M. Borchard to HFS (March 1, 1928) (Stone papers). He asked Stone "to talk this matter over with the Chief Justice" and perhaps to arrange "a meeting with Judge Sanford or any of the other Judges who would aid in preventing a further disaster to the declaratory judgment." *Id.* In December, crediting Brandeis's public professions of respect for scholarly opinion but ignorant of Brandeis's personal opposition to declaratory judgments, see *supra* Chapter 8, at note 19, Borchard wrote Stone once again, enclosing Borchard's latest article responding to *Willing*. *See* Edwin M. Borchard, *The Supreme Court and the Declaratory Judgment*, 14 AMERICAN BAR ASSOCIATION JOURNAL 633 (1928). Borchard wrote:

> Justice Brandeis has, on numerous occasions, praised the function of the Law Journals in exercising a critical function upon the work of the Court. I trust he still adheres to that view. At all events, I endeavored to indicate in the article the utmost respect for the Court and its judges, but to suggest that the random remarks made concerning the declaratory judgment, being unnecessary in each of the three cases in which such remarks were uttered, were not necessarily as well considered as they might have been.

Edwin M. Borchard to HFS (December 21, 1928) (Stone papers). Borchard noted that he had not sent a copy of his article "to any member of the Court," and he asked Stone whether it would "hurt the cause of the declaratory judgment if I sent it to [Brandeis]. Or would you hand it to him if I sent it to you?" *Id.* Stone advised Borchard that "[b]y all means I would send a marked copy of your article to each member of the Court without any comment." HFS to Edwin M. Borchard (December 24, 1928) (Stone papers).

75. Taft would later say of Stone that "He has great difficulty in getting his opinions through, because he is quite disposed to be discursive and to write opinions as if he were writing an editorial or a comment for a legal law journal, covering as much as he can upon a general subject and thus expressing opinions that have not been thought out by the whole Court. He is a learned lawyer in many ways, but his judgments I do not altogether consider safe, and the ease with which he expresses himself and his interest in the whole branch of the law in which he is called upon to give an opinion on a single principle make the rest of the Court impatient and doubtful. I am afraid he is disposed to interject a general disquisition looking toward an embarrassing recurrence on his part to some other principle that has been questioned or denied by the Court when that principle was plainly before us." WHT to Charles P. Taft 2nd (May 12, 1929) (Taft papers).

76. 274 U.S. 112 (1927). The draft opinion is located in the Stone papers. It seems to have circulated on April 11, 1927.

77. *See* Young B. Smith, *Frolic and Detour*, 23 COLUMBIA LAW REVIEW 444, 716 (1923). As it happens, Stone wrote the front piece of the issue in which Smith's article appeared. *See* Harlan F. Stone, *Charles Thaddeus Terry*, 23 COLUMBIA LAW REVIEW 415 (1923).

78. Stone papers. For a subsequent and very public attack on the Court's consideration of "unknown, unrecognized and nonauthoritative text books, Law Review articles,

and other writings of propaganda artists and lobbyists" in the field of anti-trust law, see the remarks of Representative Wright Patman, 103 CONG. REC. 16159, 16160 (August 27, 1957).
79. Stone papers.
80. *Id.*
81. HFS to Young B. Smith (April 15, 1927) (Stone papers). Eventually Stone began to appreciate the depth of the Court's hostility. In 1928, he wrote his friend Hessel Yntema about the latter's project to organize academic inquiry in a way that would be useful to courts: "The problem of how to make use of your studies in the most effective way so that they will be of assistance to courts is not as easy as might first appear." HFS to Hessel E. Yntema (October 24, 1928) (Stone papers).

> Ordinarily, where a brief is filed amicus curiae, it is filed in behalf of someone who has a similar case and who will therefore be directly affected by the determination of the court. The fact that there are those who have a scientific interest in the law would seem to me to be equally good ground for getting their idea before the court, and for the court's welcoming any assistance which they will be able to give. As a matter of fact, I am bound to say that I think there are many judges who distrust all such assistance, and hesitate to use or cite it. This is based partly on the kind of self confidence which leads a certain type of mind to reject ideas that it has not evolved itself, or which do not fall within the range of its own experience, and partly on the fact that in recent years there have been some rather unpleasant examples of men who have written what purported to be scientifically inspired articles in law journals who were actually secretly serving the interests of clients. There are also judges who firmly believe that "academic" persons who have devoted their talents to research in the investigation of particular fields cannot possibly know as much about a subject as those who have had a lifelong judicial and professional experience. Of course, there are some courts which know better. The Court of Appeals, headed by Judge Cardozo, and possibly some other courts, have reached that happy stage, but that attitude is, I am convinced, not a general one among judges the country over, despite the fact that because of faulty presentation, pressure of work, etc., they have little opportunity to go into questions as thoroughly and as scientifically as can those engaged in research in the universities.

Id.
82. Wes Daniels, *"Far Beyond the Law Reports": Secondary Source Citations in United States Supreme Court Opinions, October Terms 1900, 1940, and 1978*, 76 LAW LIBRARY JOURNAL 1, 4 (1983). For a sampling of the very large literature studying this phenomenon, see, for example, Brian T. Detweiler, *May It Please the Court: A Longitudinal Study of Judicial Citation to Academic Legal Periodicals*, 39 LEGAL REFERENCES SERVICES QUARTERLY 87 (2020); Michael D. McClintock, *The Declining Use of Legal Scholarship by Courts: An Empirical Study*, 51 OKLAHOMA LAW REVIEW 659 (1998); Louis J. Sirico, Jr. & Jeffrey B. Margulies, *The Citing of Law Reviews by the Supreme Court: An Empirical Study*, 34 UCLA LAW REVIEW 131 (1986); Neil N. Bernstein, *The Supreme Court and Secondary Source Material: 1965 Term*, 57 GEORGETOWN LAW JOURNAL 55 (1968); Chester A. Newland, *Legal Periodicals and the United States Supreme Court*, 7 UNIVERSITY OF KANSAS LAW REVIEW 477 (1959); Douglas B. Maggs, *Concerning the Extent to Which the Law Review Contributes to the Development of the Law*, 3 SOUTHERN CALIFORNIA LAW REVIEW 181 (1929); *cf.* Lawrence M. Friedman *et al., State Supreme Courts: A Century of Style and Citation*, 33 STANFORD LAW REVIEW 773 (1981); Michael

I. Swygert & Jon W. Bruce, *The Historical Origins, Founding, and Early Development of Student-Edited Law Reviews*, 36 HASTINGS LAW JOURNAL 739 (1985); William H. Manz, *The Citation Practices of the New York Court of Appeals, 1850–1993*, 43 BUFFALO LAW REVIEW 121 (1995).

83. Michael McClintock argues that "The number of judicial citations of law reviews ... declined dramatically from 1975 to 1996." McClintock, *supra* note 82, at 684. The decrease in the Supreme Court was 58.6 percent. *Id.* at 685. Given this decline, the contrast with the Taft Court revealed by Figure IV-26 is all the more stark.

84. There were forty-one citations to law review articles in the 1,554 court opinions published in the terms between 1921 and 1928. By contrast, there were fifty-seven such citations in the ninety-six court opinions in the 1997 term. For the modern Court's use of legal scholarship, see Lee Petherbridge & David L. Schwartz, *An Empirical Assessment of the Supreme Court's Use of Legal Scholarship*, 106 NORTHWESTERN UNIVERSITY LAW REVIEW 995 (2012); Whit D. Pierce & Anne E. Reuben, *The Law Review Is Dead; Long Live the Law Review: A Close Look at the Declining Judicial Citation of Legal Scholarship*, 45 WAKE FOREST LAW REVIEW 1185 (2010). On the use of scholarship in federal appeals courts, see Robert J. Hume, *Strategic-Instrument Theory and the Use of Non-Authoritative Sources by Federal Judges: Explaining References to Law Review Articles*, 31 JUSTICE SYSTEM JOURNAL 291 (2010). On the use of scholarship in state courts, see Friedman *et al.*, *supra* note 82, at 811; and Manz, *supra* note 82, at 157.

85. *See, e.g.*, John W. Johnson, *Adaptive Jurisprudence: Some Dimensions of Early Twentieth-Century American Legal Culture*, 40 HISTORIAN 16, 24 (November 1977); Chester A. Newland, *Innovation in Judicial Technique: The Brandeis Opinion*, 42 SOUTHWESTERN SOCIAL SCIENCE QUARTERLY 22, 24–26 (1961).

86. *Cf.* JOHN W. JOHNSON, AMERICAN LEGAL CULTURE: 1908–1940, at 41 (Westport: Greenwood Press 1981) (observing that Brandeis referred to social scientific studies in his dissents, but not in his opinions).

87. Cardozo, *supra* note 41, at ix.

88. *Id.* at x. Cardozo continued, "Under the drive of this impulse, the law teacher and the law reviews are coming to their own." *Id.*

89. *See infra* Chapter 37, at 1172–73. The application of a balancing test always depends upon an evaluation of better or worse results.

90. *But see* Simpson, *supra* note 31, at 670 ("From Story's time onwards, the production of treatises was associated with organized, systematic legal education.... This does not mean that the typical treatise writer was a cloistered academic, as the law schools until Langdell's time employed practitioners as professors.").

91. Cardozo, *supra* note 41, at viii.

92. PAUL D. CARRINGTON, STEWARDS OF DEMOCRACY: LAW AS A PUBLIC PROFESSION 184 (Boulder: Westview Press 1999). Treatises and encyclopedias tended to perform the function that Harvard President Eliot imagined would be served by law professors; they would, he said, function "as expounders, systematizers, and historians" of the law. Quoted in ARTHUR E. SUTHERLAND, THE LAW AT HARVARD: A HISTORY OF IDEAS AND MEN, 1817–1967, at 184 (Cambridge: Harvard University Press 1967).

93. *See* JOHNSON, *supra* note 86, at 19, 55–58; Friedman *et al.*, *supra* note 82, at 811 ("[M]ost older treatises did no more than compile cases; they wrapped the confusion

The Authority of the Taft Court

of prior case law into a convenient package, usually in the form of black letter rules."); Simpson, *supra* note 31.
94. AUERBACH, *supra* note 39, at 76.
95. Roscoe Pound, *The Need of a Sociological Jurisprudence*, 19 GREEN BAG 611 (1907). See also *Law as a Social Instrument*, 58 NEW REPUBLIC 158 (1929).
96. *See* WILLIAM E. NELSON, THE LEGALIST REFORMATION: LAW, POLITICS, AND IDEOLOGY IN NEW YORK, 1920–1980, at 143–44 (Chapel Hill: University of North Carolina Press 2000); LAURA KALMAN, THE STRANGE CAREER OF LEGAL LIBERALISM 16 (New Haven: Yale University Press 1996).
97. Evan A. Evans, *The Dissenting Opinion – Its Use and Abuse*, 3 MISSOURI LAW REVIEW 120, 126–27 (1938).
98. Antonin Scalia, *The Dissenting Opinion*, 1994 JOURNAL OF SUPREME COURT HISTORY 33, 39.
99. Corley, Steigerwalt, & Ward, *supra* note 21, at 40.
100. Quoted in MARK V. TUSHNET, THE HUGHES COURT: FROM PROGRESSIVISM TO PLURALISM, 1930–1941, at 335 (Cambridge University Press 2021).
101. Corley, Steigerwalt, & Ward, *supra* note 21, at 36, 39.
102. William Howard Taft, *Chief Justice White* (May 20, 1921), in VIVIAN, at 581.
103. *See supra* Chapter 19, at 612–17.